Encyclopedia of the American Revolution

SECOND EDITION

Library of Military History

Editorial Board

Encyclopedia of the American Revolution

SECOND EDITION

Library of Military History

VOLUME 2
M–Z

Harold E. Selesky
EDITOR IN CHIEF

CHARLES SCRIBNER'S SONS
An imprint of Thomson Gale, a part of The Thomson Corporation

THOMSON
™
GALE

Detroit • New York • San Francisco • San Diego • New Haven, Conn. • Waterville, Maine • London • Munich

Encyclopedia of the American Revolution, Second Edition
Library of Military History
Harold E. Selesky
Editor in Chief

© 2006 Thomson Gale, a part of the Thomson Corporation.

Thomson and Star Logo are trademarks and Gale and and Charles Scribner's Sons are registered trademarks used herein under license.

For more information, contact
Thomson Gale
27500 Drake Rd.
Farmington Hills, MI 48331-3535
Or you can visit our Internet site at
http://www.gale.com

For permission to use material from this product, submit your request via Web at http://www.gale-edit.com/permissions, or you may download our Permissions Request form and submit your request by fax or mail to:

Permissions Department
Thomson Gale
27500 Drake Road
Farmington Hills, MI 48331-3535
Permissions Hotline:
248-699-8006 or 800-877-4253 ext. 8006
Fax: 248-699-8074 or 800-762-4058

LIBRARY OF CONGRESS CATALOGING-IN-PUBLICATION DATA

Encyclopedia of the American Revolution : library of military history
Harold E. Selesky, editor-in-chief. 2nd ed.
    p. cm.
   Includes bibliographical references and index.
  ISBN 0-684-31513-0 (hardcover set : alk. paper) ISBN 0-684-31471-1 (vol 1 : alk. paper) ISBN 0-684-31472-X (vol 2 : alk. paper)
  United States–History–Revolution, 1775-1783 Encyclopedias.
Selesky, Harold E.
  E208.E63 2006
  973.3–dc22

2006002323

This title is also available as an e-book and as a three volume set with Landmarks of the American Revolution.
E-book ISBN 0-684-31545-9
Three volume set ISBN 0-684-31470-3
Contact your Gale sales representative for ordering information.

Printed in the United States of America
10 9 8 7 6 5 4 3 2

M

MACHIAS, MAINE. 12 June 1775. On 2 June 1775 the British schooner *Margaretta* (four guns) entered the port of Machias, in the province of Maine, with two sloops (*Polly* and *Unity*) to get lumber for the British garrison in Boston. Determined to prevent the British from accomplishing their mission, local Patriots conceived a plan to capture the enemy officers while they were in church on 11 June. But Midshipman James Moore, commander of the *Margaretta*, and some of his officers escaped through the windows of the church and regained their ship. A hastily organized pursuit by about forty volunteers under Jeremiah O'Brien and Joseph Wheaton resulted in capture of the *Unity* on Sunday and of the *Margaretta* the next day (12 June). A considerable chase had ended with a brisk skirmish in which seven men were killed or wounded on each side. Midshipman Moore was among the dead. O'Brien became the first naval hero on the Patriot side, and the action is generally considered to be the first naval engagement of the war.

O'Brien was given command of the *Unity*, which was armed with guns from the captured schooner and renamed the *Machias Liberty*. A few weeks later he captured the British naval schooner *Diligent* and her tender off Machias without a shot, and, under his command, the two schooners became the first ships of the Massachusetts navy.

SEE ALSO *O'Brien, Jeremiah.*

BIBLIOGRAPHY

Clark, William Bell, ed. *Naval Documents of the American Revolution.* Vol. 1: *American Theatre, December 1, 1774–September 2, 1775, and European Theatre, December 6, 1774–August 9, 1775.* Washington, D.C.: Naval History Division, 1964.

Fowler, William M., Jr. *Rebels Under Sail: The American Navy in the Revolution.* New York: Scribners, 1976.

revised by Harold E. Selesky

MACLEAN, ALLAN. (1725–1798). British army officer. Born at Torloisk on the Isle of Mull, Scotland, MacLean was a Jacobite officer in the rising of 1745–1746 and afterward took service in the Scots brigade in the Dutch Republic. Wounded and captured with Francis MacLean at Bergen-op-Zoom, he was at once paroled and exchanged in 1748. In 1750 he took advantage of George II's amnesty to Scots rebels to return home. Now apparently reconciled to the Hanoverian regime, he became a lieutenant in the new Sixtieth Foot (Royal Americans) on 8 January 1756. He was wounded at Ticonderoga in 1758, promoted captain-lieutenant on 27 July, and on 16 January 1759 transferred to a New York independent company with the rank of captain. He was wounded again at Niagara later in the year and took part in the capture of Quebec. Returning to Scotland in 1761, he raised the 144th Regiment of Royal Highland Volunteers and served as major-commandant in America until it was disbanded in 1763. Now on half-pay, he was granted land on St. John (now Prince Edward) Island but did not live there, for he married in Westminster, London, in 1771. He was restored to full pay by promotion to lieutenant colonel by brevet on 25 May 1772.

On June 1775 MacLean was commissioned to raise a provincial regiment, the Royal Highland Emigrants, which he recruited mostly from veterans settled on

Prince Edward Island. His officers were nearly all MacLeans from Mull or Morvern. When the Americans invaded Canada in the autumn, he marched from Quebec to reinforce Governor Guy Carleton at Montreal, and later attempted unsuccessfully to relieve St. Johns. Learning of Benedict Arnold's appearance opposite Quebec, he made a forced march with about eighty men, arriving at Quebec on 13 November, six days ahead of Carleton. Appointed second in command, he repulsed the final American attack on 31 December with heavy losses. On 6 May 1776, when General John Burgoyne's reinforcements arrived, MacLean led a sortie that routed the few remaining besiegers. He then remained in Quebec to feed reinforcements through to Carleton as he completed the expulsion of the American forces. That summer MacLean visited Britain, in the vain hope that the government would honor a promise to make his regiment permanent. Returning to Canada in 1777, he was made military governor of Montreal and a local brigadier general. In late September he reinforced Fort Ticonderoga, and in October, after the Saratoga disaster, he fell back to a defensive position at St. Johns. He was at Quebec in the winter of 1778, where he organized amateur theatricals. In 1779 his regiment was at last made permanent as the Eighty-fourth Foot, but it was Henry Clinton, not MacLean, who became its colonel. In 1781 he was posted to Niagara and became colonel by brevet on 17 November 1782. He returned to Britain in 1783, retired the following year, and settled in London, where he died on 18 February 1797.

SEE ALSO *Arnold's March to Quebec; MacLean, Francis; Quebec (Canada Invasion); St. John's, Canada (5 September–2 November 1775); Ticonderoga, New York, American Capture of.*

revised by John Oliphant

MACLEAN, FRANCIS. (1718–1781). British officer. Commissioned as an ensign in the Cameronians in 1738 and promoted in 1742, Francis MacLean resigned in 1745 to join the Clan Maclean Battalion of the Jacobite army as a lieutenant. He became a fugitive after the battle of Culloden, in which insurgents challenged the rule of the British king. He joined the Dutch army, but resigned his Dutch commission in 1750, when he rejoined the British army and purchased a lieutenancy in the forty-second ("Black Watch") Regiment two years later. As a captain of this regiment he fought in Canada and the West Indies before taking part in the capture of Belle Isle, off Brittany, in 1761.

Having distinguished himself in Portugal during the years from 1762 to 1778, he was ordered back to England,

promoted to brigadier general, and sent to Canada as governor of Halifax. After routing the Patriots who mounted the Penobscot expedition, a naval assault that took place from July to August 1779, MacLean returned to Halifax, where he died on 4 May 1781.

SEE ALSO *Culloden Moor, Scotland; Penobscot Expedition, Maine.*

revised by Michael Bellesiles

MACLEAN'S CORPS. MacLean's Corps is another name for the Provincial Regiment, officially the Royal Highland Emigrants, raised in Canada in 1775 by Lieutenant Colonel Allan MacLean. They were recruited from among Highland veterans of the French and Indian War.

SEE ALSO *MacLean, Allan.*

revised by Harold E. Selesky

MAD ANTHONY. Nickname of Anthony Wayne.

SEE ALSO *Wayne, Anthony.*

Mark M. Boatner

MADISON, JAMES. (1751–1836). Continental congressman, fourth president of the United States. Virginia. Born on 5 March 1751 in King George County, Virginia, James Madison received his bachelor's degree from the College of New Jersey (later Princeton University) in 1771 and remained another year for further study. An early advocate of religious toleration, Madison also favored being prepared to defend Virginia's civil liberties by force of arms. He was elected to the Orange County committee of safety on 22 December 1774, but there is no proof that he wrote its enthusiastic response of 19 May 1775 to Patrick Henry's call for arming the militia. On 25 April 1776 he was chosen as a delegate to the fifth Virginia convention. Although the twenty-five-year-old Madison held a militia commission as colonel, he was "too slightly built (5'6" [tall], thin, with light blue eyes and dark brown hair) and too frail (subject to fits of a sort of epilepsy) to take the field" (*Revolutionary Virginia*, 1, p. 471). He served on the committee that framed the

state constitution and bill of rights and proposed an amendment declaring that "all men are equally entitled to the full and free exercise" of religion. A member of the first assembly under the new constitution, he was not reelected in 1777 because he refused to canvass or buy drinks for votes. In November 1777, however, the assembly elected him to the governor's council, and two years later it elected him to the Continental Congress.

Taking his seat on 20 March 1780, he served in Congress until November 1783, where he "acquired a continental reputation for his mastery of legislative business" and was "soon regarded as the most effective member of the Congress" (Lance Banning in ANB). He supported efforts by Robert Morris to reform the department of finance and advocated levying duties on foreign imports to raise a national revenue. In September 1783 he worked out an agreement by which Virginia agree to cede its claims to the territory north of the Ohio River (thus creating a national domain) and, by suggesting that five slaves be considered the equivalent of three free persons, he broke a deadlock about how to use population figures to calculate state contributions to the central government.

His most important contribution to the new nation was his work in framing the federal Constitution at the Philadelphia Convention in 1787. Madison wrote twenty-nine numbers of *The Federalist* urging ratification of the document, and then he drafted its first ten amendments (the Bill of Rights) and guided them through the House of Representatives, in which he sat as majority leader until 1797. He was Jefferson's secretary of state (1801–1809) and twice won the presidency, serving from 1809 to 1817. But the disgraceful performance of an unprepared and disunited country in the War of 1812 cost him popularity. He retired to his country home, Montpelier, after his presidency and spent the rest of his life as a country gentleman. He died at Montpelier on 28 June 1836.

Dolley Payne Todd, a widow, was introduced to Madison by Aaron Burr, and they were married in 1794. Almost twenty years younger than her husband, Dolley was friendly and tactful and had a remarkable memory. She was extremely popular and earned a reputation as an effective Washington hostess. Fleeing from the British invaders of Washington in August 1814, she saved many state papers and the Gilbert Stuart portrait of George Washington. After her husband's death she moved into a house on Lafayette Square, opposite the White House. She died on 12 July 1849 at Washington, D.C.

SEE ALSO *Populations of Great Britain and America.*

BIBLIOGRAPHY

Brant, Irving. *James Madison.* 6 vols. Indianapolis, Ind.: Bobbs-Merrill, 1941–1961.

Rakove, Jack N. *James Madison and the Creation of the American Republic.* 2nd Edition. New York: Longman/Pearson Education, 2002.

Van Schreeven, William J., comp., and Robert L. Scribner, ed. *Revolutionary Virginia: The Road to Independence—A Documentary Record.* Vol. 1: *Forming Thunderclouds and the First Convention, 1763–1774.* Charlottesville, Virginia: University Press of Virginia for the Virginia Independence Bicentennial Commission, 1973.

revised by Harold E. Selesky

MAHAM, HEZEKIAH.

(1739–1789). Militia officer. South Carolina. Born in St. Stephen's Parish, South Carolina, on 26 June 1739, Hezekiah Maham was active in Patriot politics and had been a member of the First South Carolina Provincial Congress before becoming a captain in Isaac Huger's First South Carolina Rifle Regiment in 1776. He took part in the unsuccessful defense of Savannah on 29 December 1778, and the action at Stono Ferry on 29 June 1779, before becoming a major of the State Dragoons. In 1780 he was promoted to lieutenant colonel, and the next year he became colonel of an independent dragoon regiment. The siege tower known by his name was first used in the capture of Fort Watson on April 1781. Maham took part in the actions at Quinby Bridge on 17 July 1781 and Fair Lawn on 27 November 1781, in addition to many smaller, independent operations. While home on sick leave, he was captured in August 1782 and paroled, seeing no further combat. He died in 1789.

SEE ALSO *Fair Lawn, South Carolina; Fort Watson, South Carolina (15–23 April 1781).*

revised by Michael Bellesiles

MAITLAND, JOHN.

(??–1779). British army officer. Eighth son of the earl of Lauderdale, he had been a lieutenant colonel of marines and member of Parliament for Haddington before appointment as lieutenant colonel of the First Battalion of a Highland regiment, the Seventy-first Foot, on 14 October 1778. He was with Archibald Campbell at the fall of Savannah on 29 December. In command of Prevost's rearguard when he retreated from Charleston, Maitland won the action at Stono Ferry (20 June 1779) before withdrawing to Port Royal Island (Beaufort). Although already ill with malaria, he then made an epic eighty-mile withdrawal by swamps and waterways, evading French blockaders and American troops to join Prevost at Savannah. He died a few days after the repulse of the Franco-American assault on 9 October 1779.

SEE ALSO *Charleston Raid of Prevost; Savannah, Georgia (29 December 1778); Stono Ferry, South Carolina.*

BIBLIOGRAPHY

Mackesy, Piers. *The War for America, 1775–1783.* London: Longman, 1964.

revised by John Oliphant

MALCOLM'S REGIMENT. Colonel William Malcolm commanded one of the sixteen "additional Continental Regiments."

SEE ALSO *Additional Continental Regiments.*

Mark M. Boatner

MALMÉDY, MARQUIS DE. Continental officer. He appears to have descended from an Irish family named Gray that settled in France. As a *sous lieutenant* of cavalry in the French army, Malmédy reached America in 1776 from Martinique and was breveted major in the Continental army on 19 September of that year. In December 1776 he was made chief engineer and director of defense works in the Rhode Island militia with the rank of brigadier general, largely on a recommendation of Charles Lee that included the warning, "You must excuse his heat of temper at times."

On 10 May 1777, two months after his services to Rhode Island were terminated by the arrival of Continental officers, he was given the Continental commission of colonel. Malmédy wrote to Washington complaining that this rank was beneath his merit and his former grade. In a blistering reply, Washington expressed his astonishment that the former lieutenant did not feel Congress had recognized his service in commissioning him a colonel. When Gates requested Malmédy's transfer to his forces, Washington replied that he was "glad" to approve the transfer.

Malmédy commanded a light infantry company on one flank of the American force at Stono Ferry, South Carolina, on 20 June 1779. After Gates's defeat at Camden, Malmédy was accused of spreading "poison" about Greene and calling for his dismissal. Before the Battle of Ninety Six, Greene sent him to the North Carolina legislature to obtain supplies and militia, a task with which he had difficulty. At Eutaw Springs, South Carolina, on 8 September 1781, Malmédy commanded the North Carolina militia, for which Greene commended his "great gallantry and good conduct" on the battlefield.

After refusing to carry dispatches to the governor of North Carolina, Malmédy appears to have been killed in a duel in November 1781. On 13 March 1782, Robert Morris directed the paymaster to pay $3,025 to his estate. Malmady, Malmedy, and Malmédy-Gray are variations of his name.

SEE ALSO *Eutaw Springs, South Carolina.*

BIBLIOGRAPHY

Bartlett, John Russell. *Records of the Colony of Rhode Island and Providence Plantations, in New England.* 10 vols. Providence: A. C. Greene, 1856-1865.

Bodinier, André. *Dictionnaire des officiers de l'armée royale qui ont combattu aux Etats-Unis pendant la guerre d'Indépendance 1776–1783.* Vincennes, France: Service historique de l'armée, 1982.

Greene, Nathanael. *The Papers of Nathanael Greene.* Edited by Richard K. Showman, et al. 11 vols. to date. Chapel Hill: University of North Carolina Press, 1976–.

Lee, Charles. *Papers of Charles Lee.* 4 vols. New-York Historical Society *Collections* 4–7 (1871–1874).

revised by Robert Rhodes Crout

MAMARONECK, NEW YORK. Raid of 22 October 1776. During the American withdrawal from Pell's Point and Harlem Heights to White Plains, New York, the village of Mamaroneck was abandoned by the Americans—unjustifiably, in General George Washington's view. The area was then occupied by Major Robert Rogers and his notorious "Queen's American Rangers," an aggressive band of Loyalists who had been attacking local militia companies and raiding supply depots. They formed a detached camp of about 500 men near the British right wing at New Rochelle. Colonel John Haslet was selected to lead his Delaware Regiment, reinforced by certain Virginia and Maryland companies to a total strength of 750, in a raid against Mamaroneck. With accurate information about Rogers's dispositions, Haslet started out near White Plains, marched some five miles, slipped undetected past the British flank, and silenced the single sentinel who covered the approach to Rogers's bivouac. During the day, however, Rogers had realized the possibilities of surprise along this route and had posted sixty men between the lone sentinel and his main camp. Haslet's advance guard stumbled on this unsuspected force, and a melee ensued. The enemy added to the confusion by echoing the cry, "Surrender, you Tory dogs! Surrender!" The Americans managed to capture thirty-six prisoners,

sixty muskets, sixty highly prized blankets, and a pair of colors, all of which they evacuated safely. Rogers's main camp forced the raiders to withdraw after an exchange of fire. American casualties were three killed and twelve wounded; there is no record of enemy losses. The incident boosted American morale.

SEE ALSO *Haslet, John; Rogers, Robert.*

BIBLIOGRAPHY

Freeman, Douglas Southall. *George Washington*, 7 vols. New York: Scribner's, 1948–1957.

Ward, Christopher. *The War of the Revolution*, 2 vols. New York: Macmillan, 1952.

revised by Barnet Schecter

MANCHAC POST (FORT BUTE).

Bayou Manchac or the Iberville River was the northern boundary of the Spanish Isle of Orleans and provided a water route from the Mississippi east into the Amite River and through Lakes Maurepas, Pontchartrain, and Borgne into the Gulf of Mexico. Pierre Le Moyne, Sieur d'Iberville, used this route when he returned in 1699 from his exploration up the Mississippi to the mouth of the Red River. Because the Treaty of Paris in 1763 left the Isle of Orleans in Spanish hands (ceded by France in 1762), this route was of vital importance as an outlet for British navigation from the upper Mississippi. At the mouth of the Manchac–Iberville stream, on the Mississippi, the British established Fort Bute or Manchac Post in 1763. From then until its capture by Governor Bernardo de Gálvez on 7 September 1779, it was an important military and trading post. The Battle of Fort Bute, as it is often called, was the opening salvo in Spain's war on Britain in North America. Even though a hurricane had destroyed much of Gálvez's fleet on 15 August, the governor quickly assembled a small army of regulars and Acadian and Spanish militia, and led them on a brutal eleven-day march through the bayou. The Spanish attack caught the garrison completely by surprise, as they were unaware that Spain and Britain were at war.

SEE ALSO *Gálvez, Bernardo de.*

revised by Michael Bellesiles

MANDAMUS COUNCILLORS. The

Massachusetts Government Act of 20 May 1774 (also called the Massachusetts Regulating Act), one of the Intolerable Acts, prescribed that effective 1 August the Massachusetts Council, the upper house of the legislature, would no longer be elected by a joint vote of the incoming members of the House of Representatives and the outgoing members of the Council (as provided for in the Charter of 1692). Rather, it would be appointed by the governor on a "royal writ of mandamus." The thirty-six men appointed by Governor Thomas Gage, only two of whom had been among the twenty-eight councillors elected previously, became marked men, their names being published by the radical press along with the "Addressers" and "Protesters." Only twenty-five of the thirty-six accepted the position, and nine of them soon resigned. Six of the remaining councillors lived in Boston, where they were protected, up to a point, by the British army. Of the final ten who lived elsewhere, all were driven into exile in Boston. After John Murray, a long-time representative from Rutland, had fled to Boston, a group of neighbors, men who had voted for him since 1751, told his son that his house would be destroyed if he did not resign. A mob of four thousand armed men forced Thomas Oliver to resign. Old Israel Williams of Hatfield tried to hide in his chimney when a mob came calling, but he was smoked out when the doors were closed and a fire started indoors. These episodes of intimidation and violence demonstrate the power of the resistance movement to force a renunciation of those traditional leaders who tried to remain loyal to Britain.

SEE ALSO *Addressers; Protesters.*

BIBLIOGRAPHY

Knollenberg, Bernard. *Growth of the American Revolution, 1766–1775.* Edited by Bernard W. Sheehan. Indianapolis, Ind.: Liberty Fund, 2002.

Matthews, Albert, ed. "Documents Relating to the Last Meetings of the Massachusetts Royal Council." *Publications of the Colonial Society of Massachusetts* 32 (1933–1937): 461–504.

revised by Harold E. Selesky

MANHATTAN ISLAND, NEW YORK. At the time of the Revolution this was also

called City Island, New York Island, and York Island. At its northern tip was strategically important Kings Bridge.

SEE ALSO *Kings Bridge, New York.*

Mark M. Boatner

MANLEY, JOHN. (1732?–1793). American

naval officer. Massachusetts. John Manley may have been born in Torquay, England, perhaps in 1732, and may have served in the British navy. It is known that Manley was living in Boston in the late 1750s and was the captain of a merchant ship. He was selected by General George Washington to command one of the vessels in the "navy" being organized in the fall of 1775 to operate against British supply vessels. As captain of the armed schooner, *Lee*, he left Plymouth on 4 November 1775, but his first three captures were all returned to their owners. Toward the end of the month he made the first important capture of the war, when he took the *Nancy* and its shipment of 2,000 muskets and other munitions in the entrance to Boston harbor, within sight of its escort. The next month he took several other prizes and was hailed as a naval hero. In January 1776 Washington named him commander of his "navy." Congress confirmed Manley as a captain in the new Continental navy on 17 April 1776. With his flag aboard the thirty-two-gun *Hancock*, he made several successful cruises. On 8 June he and the *Boston* captured the twenty-eight-gun frigate *Fox*, but on 7 July he and his prize were taken off Halifax by the forty-four-gun *Rainbow*, which was commanded by Sir George Collier. Even though the Americans out-gunned the British, the commander of the *Boston*, Captain Hector McNeill, who loathed Manley, refused to come to the *Hancock's* aid. After being confined on a prison ship in New York Harbor, Manley was exchanged in March 1778. A court-martial acquitted him of losing his ship, but McNeill was suspended from the navy.

With no suitable new command awaiting him, Manley went to sea as a privateer, and in the fall of 1778 made a successful cruise in the *Marlborough*. Early in 1779, as captain of the *Cumberland*, he was captured by the *Pomona* near Barbados. Escaping from prison, he was captured again while making his second cruise in the *Jason*, and spent two years in Old Mill Prison, England, before being exchanged. In September 1782 he took command of the *Hague*, one of two frigates remaining in the Continental navy. (The other was Commodore John Barry's *Alliance*.) Manley's last cruise, in the West Indies, was marked by a brilliant escape from a British ship of the line (seventy-four guns) and by his capture of the *Baille* in January 1783. This conferred upon him the distinction of closing the regular maritime operations of the United States in the Revolution: The man who took the first important prize of the war also took the last one captured by a Continental ship. He died in Boston on 12 February 1793.

SEE ALSO *Privateers and Privateering.*

BIBLIOGRAPHY

Smith, Philip Chadwick Foster. *Fired by Manley Zeal: A Naval Fiasco of the American Revolution.* Salem, Mass.: Peabody Museum, 1977.

revised by Michael Bellesiles

MANTELET. A movable shelter to protect men

attacking a fortified place. British engineer Moncrieff used them in the Charleston expedition of 1780.

SEE ALSO *Charleston Expedition of Clinton in 1780; Regular Approaches.*

MANUFACTURING IN AMERICA.

American industry had not developed sufficiently by the time of the Revolution to be able to supply the rebel armies with the means to resist increased imperial control, and few of the shortcomings in the supply of manufactured goods were remedied during the war. The limited American industrial base was overwhelmed by the sudden, sharp, and continuing spike in demand for clothing, weapons, shelter, munitions, and the whole host of other things required to sustain the war effort. Enlisting men into military service meant that manpower was being reallocated away from manufacturing, and this phenomenon, plus the often extreme dislocation caused by active military operations, ensured that Americans remained dependent on foreign, especially French, sources of supply until 1783.

Before the war, the British imperial government had discouraged the development of manufacturing in the colonies, preferring to use them as sources of raw materials and markets for finished goods. Because the cost of land in the colonies was relatively low and the cost of labor relatively high, those colonists who managed to accumulate risk capital generally invested it in acquiring land rather than in establishing manufactories. A notable exception was the shipbuilding industry: by 1760 a third of all British tonnage was American-built. In the ten years up to 1775, 25,000 tons a year were turned out, at costs that were 20 to 50 percent lower than in Europe, thanks largely to the widespread local availability of timber and naval stores.

The manufacture of iron goods provides an example of the handicaps under which American industry labored. Iron manufacturing actually expanded rapidly before the war, despite restrictions in 1750 and 1757 under the Navigation Acts, because the demand was so high. In 1775 the colonies produced 15 percent of the world's iron, but imperial legislation inhibited the development of the sorts of workshops needed to turn bar iron into finished products. Imported iron goods were cheaper than nearly anything that could be produced domestically, including such simple items as iron nails. Efforts were made at the outset of the war to expand the capacity to manufacture metal goods, and to produce war materiel. By late 1775, the foundries of Philadelphia were casting cannon of bronze and iron, but they ceased these operations after a few years. Salisbury Furnace, in northwest Connecticut, also started casting cannon in 1775, but it, too, had almost ceased to operate by 1778. Technical knowledge was undeveloped, and the homemade products were inferior and more expensive than cannon imported from France.

American gunsmiths were among the finest craftsmen of individual firearms in the world and although, for example, more than 4,000 stand of arms were made in Pennsylvania over the winter of 1775–1776, they did not develop the mass production techniques needed to meet the extraordinary demand for small arms during the war. The arsenal at Springfield, Massachusetts, established in 1778, was so poorly managed that, in 1780, the Board of War recommended it be abandoned. A new United States arsenal was established at Springfield only in 1794.

Gunpowder was the single most important manufactured commodity necessary to wage an armed struggle, and the American armies never had enough of it. Six powder mills in Pennsylvania managed to produce several thousand pounds of powder a week by 1776, but a general shortage of saltpeter and sulfur, plus a lack of technical knowledge, frustrated this and other local efforts. American gunpowder was considered to be inferior in quality, and more expensive, than gunpowder manufactured in, and imported from, Europe. The Continental Congress and individual states bent every effort to acquire gunpowder and other munitions from overseas suppliers, especially in France, and managed to import directly or via the West Indies sufficient quantities to sustain the war effort through 1775 and 1776. The clandestine activities of Pierre Caron de Beaumarchais and his front company of Hortalez et Cie began to have an impact on army supplies in 1777. Once France openly allied with the rebels in February 1778, a steady stream of clothing and munitions made its way to American ports, where it faced the further problems involved in transporting the material to the American armies. The relative abundance and low cost of French supplies further dampened American efforts to supply war materiel for themselves. For example, lead mines in Virginia were abandoned early in the war, in part because importing lead from France was cheaper.

Textiles were another area of critical shortage. Women made linen at home, but the colonies had little wool for winter clothing and blankets. Canvas was needed for tents and sails, but demand rose so rapidly that supplies could not keep up. Canvas already in use for awnings and sails was remanufactured to provide tents and idle ships were eyed for the cloth in their sails. Pre-war efforts to pressure the imperial government to reverse its policies by refusing to import British manufactures had given an impetus to weaving, but the industry had not developed sufficiently to supply clothes for soldiers whose constant activity created a continual need for resupply.

Non-importation had also given an impetus to shoemakers, and during the war the Americans tried to manage the problem of turning the hides of cattle slaughtered for the army into shoes. A commissary of hides was appointed in 1777 to organize and oversee this task, but the results were unsatisfactory. The pressure to produce more shoes, a soldier's most indispensable article of clothing, led to shortcuts in the tanning process and in sewing shoes. The result was uncomfortable footwear that lacked durability.

Manufacturing enterprises in colonial America tended to be concentrated in towns and cities, where markets attracted the largest numbers of artisans and skilled workers. Philadelphia, for example, was a center for the production of hats, shoes, stockings, earthenware, cordage, and soap. Market pressures also created areas of specialized manufacturing. Lancaster, Pennsylvania, was a center of woolen and linen weaving as well as gunsmithing. Lynn, Massachusetts, was known for its concentration of families that produced shoes. Other enterprises, especially the production of raw metals, were located in areas, mostly rural, where the required resources were grouped closely together. The Brown family of Providence, Rhode Island, for example, established an iron furnace at Hope, on the Pawtuxet River, where ore, wood for conversion to charcoal, limestone, and water power were all readily available.

SEE ALSO *Mercantilism; Muskets and Musketry; Naval Stores; Nonimportation; Supply of the Continental Army.*

BIBLIOGRAPHY

Bartenstein, Fred and Isabel. *New Jersey's Revolutionary War Powder Mill.* Morristown, N.J.: Morris County Historical Society, 1975.

Bining, Arthur C. *Pennsylvania Iron Manufacture in the Eighteenth Century.* Harrisburg, Penn.: Pennsylvania Historical Commission, 1938.

Bishop, James L. *A History of American Manufactures from 1608 to 1860.* 3 vols. 3d ed. Philadelphia, Penn.: Edward Young and Company, 1868.

Doerflinger, Thomas M. "Hibernia Furnace during the Revolution," *New Jersey History,* 90 (Summer 1972): 97–114.

Goldenberg, Joseph A. *Shipbuilding in Colonial America.* Charlottesville, Va.: University Press of Virginia for the Mariners Museum at Newport News, 1976.

McCusker, John J., and Russell R. Menard. *The Economy of British America, 1607–1789*. Chapel Hill, N.C.: University of North Carolina Press, 1985.

Miller, Robert L., and Harold L. Peterson. "Rappahannock Forge: Its History and Products," *Military Collector and Historian* 4 (December 1952): 81–84.

Mulholland, James. *A History of Metals in Colonial America*. University, Ala.: University of Alabama Press, 1981.

Perkins, Edwain J. *The Economy of Colonial America*. 2d ed. New York: Columbia University Press, 1988.

Risch, Erna. *Quartermaster Support of the Army: A History of the Corps, 1775–1939*. Washington, D.C.: Government Printing Office, 1962.

———. *Supplying Washington's Army*. Washington, D.C.: Center of Military History, 1981.

Rome, Adam W. *Connecticut's Cannon: Salisbury Furnace in American Revolution*. Hartford, Conn.: Connecticut American Revolution Bicentennial Commission, 1977.

Salay, David L. "The Production of Gunpowder in Pennsylvania During the American Revolution," *Pennsylvania Magazine of History and Biography* 99 (1975): 422–442.

Stephenson, Orlando W. "The Supply of Gunpowder in 1776," *American Historical Review* 30, no. 1 (1925): 271–281.

York, Neil L. "Clandestine Aid and the American Revolutionary War Effort: A Re-Examination," *Military Affairs* 43, no. 1 (1979): 26–30.

———. *Mechanical Metamorphosis: Technological Change in Revolutionary America*. Westport, Conn.: Greenwood Press, 1985.

revised by Harold E. Selesky

MARINE COMMITTEE.

Formally established by Congress on 14 December 1775 with thirteen members, one from each colony, the Marine Committee was the immediate successor of the Naval Committee as Congress's agent for directing naval affairs. Its most important accomplishment was probably its first: sponsorship of a Rhode Island proposal to create an actual navy, made up of thirteen purpose-built warships rather than a passel of converted merchantmen. Plagued by a constant turnover in membership, it struggled to build the land-based infrastructure of administration needed to support ships at sea. Unable to exercise effective control over its far-flung agents, especially the Navy Board of the Eastern Department at Boston, and enmeshed in an accounting nightmare of cost overruns and unclear expenditures, it failed on three successive occasions in the spring of 1779 to reach a quorum. It took the Congress the rest of the year to decide what to do, but finally in December the delegates decided to replace it with a Board of Admiralty, consisting of two delegates and three commissioners who were not members of Congress.

SEE ALSO *Naval Committee; Naval Operations, Strategic Overview.*

BIBLIOGRAPHY

Clark, William B., et al., eds. *Naval Documents of the American Revolution: December 1774–December 1777.* 10 vols. to date. Washington: Naval History Division, 1966–.

Fowler, William M., Jr. *Rebels under Sail: The American Navy during the Revolution.* New York: Charles Scribner's Sons, 1976.

Paullin, Charles O. *The Navy of the American Revolution: Its Administration, Its Policy, and Its Achievements.* Cleveland, Ohio: Burrows Brothers, 1906.

———. *Out-Letters of the Continental Marine Committee and Board of Admiralty, August 1776–September 1780.* 2 vols. New York: De Vinne Press, 1914.

revised by Harold E. Selesky

MARINES.

One theory as to the origin of "marines" as a distinct category of troops stems from the requirement in the early eighteenth century to protect British officers on shipboard from their "pressed" crews (men who had been, in essence, kidnapped and forced to serve on ships—a common recruitment method in use at the time). The marines, in this circumstance, were a species of seaborne military police. But there also was a requirement for crack troops who could constitute landing parties, boarding parties, and deliver musket fire from the rigging in close sea fights.

British marines made up a considerable portion of the Boston Garrison. Although they did not accompany the British column to Lexington and Concord on 19 April 1775, a marine officer, Major John Pitcairn, was second-in-command of this force and figured prominently in the day's historic events. Two battalions of British marines took part in the assault on Bunker Hill, where Pitcairn was mortally wounded. British and French marines figured in subsequent land operations in America and in practically all sea battles. When determining force strength, the rule of thumb was one marine assigned on board a ship for each gun.

The first American use of marines can be traced to the War of Jenkins's Ear (1739–1843, fought in retaliation for an act of Spanish torture against a British privateer). At that time, an American regiment of marines was raised in 1740. Commanded by Colonel William Gooch of Virginia and officially identified as the Sixty-First Foot, "Gooch's Marines" were raised in the colonies and fought creditably in the West Indies. American marines served on board privateers during the French and Indian War (1754–1763), and were sometimes known as "gentlemen sailors."

On 10 November 1775 the Second Continental Congress resolved that two battalions of American marines be raised. Established as a package deal offered by the Committee on Nova Scotia, the two battalions were designed to be used as an amphibious landing force, for a projected naval expedition against British facilities at Halifax. In December, officers assembled their marines as the Continental navy put together its first squadron. On 3 January 1776, the fleet sailed from Philadelphia. With hopes of gaining powder for Washington's beleaguered army before Boston, 230 marines and fifty seamen landed on the island of New Providence two months later. The island's two forts were captured and all military stores and ordnance on the island were removed.

The first Continental marine detachment on record, however, was the seventeen-man group under Lieutenant James Watson that served on board the sloop *Enterprise* from 3 May 1775. Although originally from Connecticut, on 10 June they came under control of the Continental Congress when the delegates voted themselves the control of all forces on Lake Champlain. This marine force later took part in the battle of Valcour Island, 11–13 October 1776.

Throughout the remainder of the war, marines continued to serve on board Continental ships, and in one instance, with the Continental army during the battles of Trenton and Princeton, both in New Jersey. The concept of an independent corps of marines quickly disappeared, but their "amphibious" nature did not. In October 1777, marines executed a landing off Billingsport, New Jersey, and evacuated the besieged American garrison. In January the following year, marines captured and briefly held the island of New Providence for a second time.

A company of marines under Captain James Willing left Fort Pitt on 10 January 1778 in the armed boat *Rattletrap* for an expedition to New Orleans, and on 3 February the company took part in the capture of two French trading vessels near Kaskaskia. Along the lower Mississippi, Willing's marines raided Loyalist settlements in an attempt to wrest control of the river. The company reached New Orleans, where Willing remained, but a portion returned to Kaskaskia, Illinois, under the command of Captain Robert George and enlisted in a new artillery company. This unit participated in George Rogers Clark's operations against the Indians. The remainder later took part in the abortive attempt to seize Mobile, in British controlled West Florida.

The major marine amphibious effort came in July 1779. A joint force made up of New England militia and state troops, along with the Continental navy force engaged in an expedition to seize a British fort that had been established at Penobscot Bay, Massachusetts (now a part of Maine). Although the intervention of a superior British squadron prevented the successful accomplishment of the assigned mission, the force of slightly more than 300 Continental and state marines performed admirably. They also took part in the unsuccessful defense of Charleston in 1780. On the high seas they were in practically every battle involving privateers and ships of the state navies, as well as those battles in which ships of the Continental navy were engaged. Marines served under John Paul Jones in his raids on Whitehaven, England, and St. Mary's Isle, Scotland, and were with him in the *Bonhomme Richard–Serapis* engagement on 23 September 1779.

James Fenimore Cooper has written:

> At no period of the naval history of the world, is it probable that Marines were more important than during the War of the Revolution. In many instances they preserved the vessels to the country, by suppressing the turbulence of ill-assorted crews [in accordance with what was mentioned at the beginning of this article as their original purpose], and the effect of their fire . . . has usually been singularly creditable to their steadiness and discipline.

The navy and marines ceased to exist in 1783 and were not revived until 1794, when American merchant ships were attacked by the corsairs of the Barbary Coast of Northern Africa. The need to protect American shipping led to the revival of the navy, and by the spring of 1798 there were marines on board the ships that had been completed to address this emergency. On 11 July 1798 the U.S. Marine Corps became an individual service within the American navy.

SEE ALSO *Clark, George Rogers; Fort Montagu, Bahamas; Kaskaskia, Illinois; Pitcairn, John; Princeton, New Jersey; Trenton, New Jersey; Valcour Island.*

BIBLIOGRAPHY

Millett, Alan Reed. *Semper Fidelis: The History of the United States Marine Corps.* New York: Macmillan, 1980.

Smith, Charles R. *Marines in the Revolution: A History of the Continental Marines in the American Revolution, 1775–1783.* Washington, D.C.: U.S. Government Printing Office, 1975.

revised by Charles R. Smith

MARION, FRANCIS.

(1732–1795). Southern partisan leader who came to be known as the "Swamp Fox." South Carolina. The grandson of Huguenots who came to South Carolina in 1690, Marion has been described as being "not larger than a New England lobster, and might easily enough have been put into a quart pot" (Bass, pp. 6, 11). He was a frail child with badly formed knees and ankles. When he was about six years old

Francis Marion. *Marion, a wily partisan leader from South Carolina, became known as the "Swamp Fox."* © BETTMANN/ CORBIS

his family moved from St. John's Parish (in modern Berkeley County, astride the Cooper River) to the vicinity of Georgetown. He was reared under modest circumstances and received a country school education. After surviving a shipwreck at the age of sixteen, he settled down to the life of a farmer on the family property.

In 1761 he was a lieutenant in the militia company of Captain William Moultrie that took part in the Cherokee Expedition led by Colonel James Grant. In his first experience under fire, Marion was selected to lead an attack to clear an Indian force from a critical defile, and despite sustaining twenty-one casualties in his party of thirty men, he accomplished the mission. His performance having been witnessed by important South Carolina men, he rose to a position of respect in his community. In 1773 he was able to buy Pond Bluff plantation on the Santee River, four miles below Eutaw Springs. In 1775 he was a delegate to the South Carolina Provincial Congress, and on 17 June was named a captain in Moultrie's Second South Carolina Regiment. He took part in the bloodless operations that drove the royal governor from South Carolina, and on 10 February 1776 he was at Charleston, ready to take part in the fortification of the harbor. On 22 February he was promoted to the rank of major (although some scholars date his promotion to 14 November 1775).

In the defense of Charleston, 28 June 1776, Major Marion commanded the heavy guns on the left side of Fort Sullivan (later Fort Moultrie), and tradition has it that he fired the last shot of the engagement. On 23 November (again, there is some disagreement of the date) he became a lieutenant colonel, and on 23 September 1778 he took command of the regiment. Owing to a new congressional policy of keeping regimental commanders in the grade of lieutenant colonel, (to simplify the matter of prisoner exchange, which was done on a grade-for-grade basis), his title was lieutenant colonel, commandant of the Second South Carolina Regiment. Military operations in the Southern theater had been limited up until this time, and monotony increased the problems of commanders. Marion, however, established high standards of discipline. At Savannah, on 9 October 1779, he led his regiment in a gallant but unsuccessful assault.

When General Benjamin Lincoln returned to Charleston, Marion commanded the three regiments left at Sheldon, South Carolina. On 19 March 1780 he resumed command of his own regiment at Charleston. When the city was surrendered on 12 May, he is said to have had a lucky break that saved him from capture. Soon after his arrival in the city, the austere little Huguenot attended a dinner party given by Moultrie's adjutant general, Captain Alexander McQueen. According to historian Benson J. Lossing, "the host, determined that all of his guests should drink his wine freely, locked the door to prevent their departure. Marion would not submit to this act of 'social tyranny,' and leaped from a second story window to the ground. His ankle was broken, and before communication toward the Santee was closed he was carried to his residence, in St. John's parish, on a litter." (p. 769)

With all organized resistance in the South soon destroyed, Marion and a few followers joined General Johann De Kalb at Coxe's Mill on Deep River in North Carolina. He was sent to Cole's Bridge, but rejoined the American force about 3 August as it moved into South Carolina under General Horatio Gates. He was received unenthusiastically by the regulars in that force. When the Williamsburg district militia petitioned Gates for a Continental officer, Gates chose Marion, who left the Continentals around 14–15 August. Thus Marion avoided being involved in disaster at Camden. After the action at Great Savannah on 20 August, in which he rescued 147 Continentals that had been captured at Camden, Marion then led his 52 men in an audacious ambush that scattered 250 militia under Major Ganey near Blue Savannah on 4 September. Marion then retreated into North Carolina and camped at White Marsh, but returned to South Carolina, routed the Tory outpost of Colonel Ball at Black Mingo Creek on 29 September, and broke up a Tory uprising at Tearcoat Swamp on 26 October 1780.

After the British disaster at Kings Mountain (7 October), Marion's operations were of such concern to General Charles Cornwallis that he gave General Benastre Tarleton permission to take most of his legion off in an attempt to eliminate this guerrilla menace. While Tarleton was gone, General Thomas Sumter's operations at Fishdam Ford (9 November) were so successful that Cornwallis sent an urgent order for Tarleton's return to the vicinity of Winnsboro. "Come, my boys! Let us go back, and we will find the Gamecock [as Sumter was known]," Tarleton is reported to have said after trailing Marion for seven hours through 26 miles of swamp. "But as for this damned old fox, the devil himself could not catch him!" (Rankin, p. 113) Unsuccessful in an attack on Georgetown on 15 November, Marion skirmished with a British column at Halfway Swamp on 12–13 December 1780, and then established a camp on Snow's Island. This "island" was a low ridge, five miles long and two miles wide, that was protected by the Peedee River on the east, Lynches River on the north, and Clark's Creek on the south and west. It is traditionally believed to have been the Swamp Fox's favorite base. Here he now organized "Marion's Brigade."

Nathanael Greene's southern campaigns were now under way, but after teaming up briefly with Lee's Legion for the raid against Georgetown on 24 January 1781, Marion was left to his own devices for another three months. In February 1781, Thomas Sumter started an expedition into Marion's district, and called on the Swamp Fox to join him. The two partisan leaders did not succeed in uniting, and as Sumter withdrew the British undertook a serious campaign to wipe out Marion's guerrillas.

Lieutenant Colonel John W. T. Watson was detached with a force of Tories "for the purpose of dispersing the plunderers that infested the eastern frontier." Since Watson was lieutenant colonel of the Third Foot Guards, some writers have assumed that he led this crack regiment, but Watson himself states that Rawdon (Sir Francis Rawdon-Hastings, a British commander) gave him a detachment of the Sixty-fourth Foot Brigade in addition to the Tories of Major John Harrison's Regiment. Marion checked Watson at Wiboo Swamp and blocked his drive toward Kingstree at Lower Bridge. Marion caught Watson as he crossed the Sampit River on the way to the British base at Georgetown. In the confrontation, Watson's horse and about twenty of his men were killed. "I have never seen such shooting before in my life," said Watson, but he complained that Marion "would not fight like a gentleman or a Christian." This battle successfully drove the British out of Marion's district.

While Marion was scoring this remarkable success, however, the enemy achieved one that was equally brilliant: Colonel Welbore Doyle found and destroyed Marion's base at Snow's Island. Hugh Horry led the pursuit of Doyle's New York Volunteers, and Marion followed with the rest of his command. After Horry had shot down nine and captured sixteen, and after two casualties were inflicted on the enemy rear guard at

Witherspoon's Ferry, Colonel Doyle destroyed his own baggage to speed his rush to Camden. It was not Marion's pursuit that prompted this sudden speed, but a message from Rawdon that Greene's army was again approaching Camden. Marion made contact with Henry Lee's Legion at Black River on 14 April, but only eighty partisans now remained with him. The rest had gone home. Nevertheless, Marion and Lee operated together during April and May 1781 to capture Fort Watson and Fort Motte, two critical outposts that protected British supply lines between Charleston and Camden.

Marion occupied Georgetown on 28 May, and then moved farther south to support the attacks on Augusta and Ninety Six. Lieutenant Colonel Alexander Stewart cleverly eluded Marion's attempt to block his move from Charleston to reinforce Rawdon at Orangeburg.

While Greene's main body was recuperating in the Santee Hills, Marion came under the orders of Sumter and took part in an unfortunate action at Quinby Bridge, 17 July. Marion had such sufficient doubts regarding Sumter's leadership that he had avoided service under "the Gamecock." These doubts were realized in this poorly managed and costly skirmish. Marion then raced off to win a skirmish at Parker's Ferry. The date of this skirmish is in question, and many sources give 13 August as the date. However, a letter from Marion to Nathanael Greene gives the date as 30 August. After the skirmish, Marion rejoined Greene to command the militia forces of North and South Carolina, including his own brigade, at Eutaw Springs on 8 September. It was due largely to Marion's personal influence on the field that Greene could tell Congress, "the militia gained much honor by their firmness," and could write Steuben, "such conduct would have graced the veterans of the Great King of Prussia."

Elected to the state senate, Marion was at Jacksonboro for the General Assembly, beginning on 8 January 1782, but his brigade was given the mission of protecting the area. On 10 January he wrote Colonel Peter Horry and asked him to assume command, but on 24 February Marion had to take leave from his urgent political duties and rush back to take over. There was jealousy between Horry and Colonel Hezekiah Maham, who commanded the brigade's dragoons, prompting these officers to find one pretext after another to turn their responsibilities over to subordinates. At this critical moment, Colonel Benjamin Thompson led a 700-man expedition from Charleston, crossed the Cooper River on 23 February, and scattered Marion's divided forces. He rallied the remnants and directed a counterattack, but poor execution on the part of some of his untrained horsemen led to another reverse near Wambaw Bridge, about forty miles northeast of Charleston. Marion withdrew to his old camp at Cantey's Plantation (near Murray's Ferry), much demoralized by this sorry performance. The next summer found Marion again assigned the mission of patrolling east of the Cooper River. At Fair Lawn, on 29 August 1782, he ambushed a force of 200 dragoons under Major Thomas Fraser, who had been sent from Charleston to surprise him. Captain Gavin Witherspoon's reconnaissance party led the enemy into a trap that cost Fraser twenty men. The British captured an ammunition wagon, however, and Marion was forced to retreat for lack of powder. He had fought his last action.

When the war ended, Marion was appointed commandant of Fort Johnson, a sinecure that brought £500 a year and compensated him somewhat for having lost virtually all his personal property during the Revolution. He was re-elected to the state senate in 1782 and 1784, and sat in the state's constitutional convention in 1790. Also in 1790 Marion left his post at Fort Johnson, and in 1791 he was elected to fill an unexpired term in the state senate. Meanwhile, in 1786, he married Mary Esther Videau, a wealthy spinster cousin about his own age. He died on 27 February 1795 at the age of about 63.

The "Marion Legend" has long obscured the history of his life, and the principal villain is Parson Weems, who also invented much of the "Washington Legend." Weems rewrote a manuscript on Marion's life that Peter Horry had drafted, taking some liberties with the details. After reading the Weems's book, Horry wrote him in despair: "Most certainly 'tis not my history, but your romance." William James, who joined Marion at the age of 15, wrote a simple biographical sketch of his idol, and William Gilmore Simms fashioned this into another fantasy. Historian Robert D. Bass gives this summary of the "Swamp Fox":

> He was neither a Robin Hood nor a Chevalier Bayard. He was a moody, introverted, semiliterate genius who rose from private to Brigadier General through an intuitive grasp of strategy and tactics, personal bravery, devotion to duty, and worship of liberty. . . . By nature Marion was gentle, kind, and humane. Yet his orders, orderly books, battle reports, and personal letters reveal another side of his character. He shot pickets, retaliated from ambush, failed to honor flags of truce, and knowingly violated international law. He could forgive the Tories, and yet he could court-martial his closest friend. (p. 4)

Unlike Thomas Sumter, Marion could subordinate himself to higher military authority and fit his partisan operations into the over-all strategy of of leaders like Nathanael Greene. While most famous as a guerrilla, he had the military standards of a regular soldier.

SEE ALSO *Black Mingo Creek, South Carolina; Camden Campaign; Cherokee Expedition of James Grant; Eutaw Springs, South Carolina; Southern Campaigns of Nathanael Greene.*

BIBLIOGRAPHY

Bass, Robert D. *Swamp Fox: The Life and Campaigns of General Francis Marion.* New York: Holt, 1959.

Clinton Papers. "Letter of John Watson Tadwell" (vol. 232, p. 21). Ann Arbor, Mich.: William L. Clements Library.

Conrad, Dennis M., Roger N. Parks, and Martha J. King. *The Papers of General Nathanael Greene.* Volume IX (11 July–2 December 1781). Chapel Hill and London: The University of North Carolina Press, 1997.

Lee, Henry. *Memoirs of the War in the Southern Department of the United States.* New York: University Publishing Company, 1869.

Lossing, Benson J. *The Pictorial Field Book of the Revolution.* 2 vols. New York: Harper and Brothers, 1851.

Rankin, Hugh F. *Francis Marion: The Swamp Fox.* New York: Thomas Y. Crowell Company, 1973.

revised by Steven D. Smith

MARION'S BRIGADE.

After being named brigadier general of the South Carolina militia in December 1780, Marion was given command of all regiments east of the Santee, Wateree, and Catawba Rivers. The brigade's composition changed frequently, but began with the cavalry under the command of Colonel Peter Horry and was comprised of troops under Major Lemuel Benson and Captains John Baxter, John Postell, Daniel Conyers, and James McCauley. Lieutenant Colonel Hugh Horry (Peter's brother) commanded the foot regiment, while Colonel Adam McDonald was on parole. Companies were headed by Major John James and Captains John James, James Postell, and James Witherspoon. Colonel Hugh Ervin was Marion's second in command. Serving as aides de camp were Captains John Milton, Lewis Ogier, and Thomas Elliott, the latter handling the semiliterate commander's correspondence. An estimated 2,500 men served at one time or another in the brigade.

SEE ALSO *Marion, Francis.*

BIBLIOGRAPHY

Rankin, Hugh F. *Francis Marion: The Swamp Fox.* New York: Thomas Y. Crowell Company, 1973.

revised by Steven D. Smith

MARJORIBANKS, JOHN. (1757–1781).

British officer, hero of Eutaw Springs. Commissioned as an ensign on 24 May 1749, John Marjoribanks became a lieutenant in the Scotch-Dutch Brigade on 21 October

1749. He was promoted to lieutenant in the Nineteenth Foot Brigade on 22 September 1757, and was wounded in the siege of Belle Isle (1761), after which he was promoted to captain of the 108th Foot Brigade. On 2 April 1762 he returned to the Nineteenth Foot as captain-lieutenant, was advanced to captain on 15 June 1763, to brevet-major on 29 August 1777, and to major on 17 November 1780. From December 1779 to June 1780 he commanded a light infantry company at Kilkenny, Ireland. Sent to reinforce General Henry Clinton in the South, Marjoribanks and his regiment arrived at Charleston on 4 June 1781, and marched with Lord Francis Rawdon-Hastings to the relief of Ninety Six. As commander of the flank battalion he was mortally wounded at Eutaw Springs on 8 September, and died 23 October 1781.

SEE ALSO *Eutaw Springs, South Carolina; Rawdon-Hastings, Francis.*

revised by Michael Bellesiles

MARKSMANSHIP.

Military marksmanship during the eighteenth century was tailored to the requirements of linear tactics. Measured against the norms that began to be developed at the end of the nineteenth century, marksmanship in line regiments during the Revolution ranged from very bad to almost nonexistent. Specialized units armed with rifled muskets were a partial exception, but even here the ratio of hits to shots fired was low by modern standards. Historian Christopher Ward calculated that at Lexington and Concord (19 April 1775), "only one American bullet out of 300 found its mark . . . [and] only one [militia]man out of 15 hit anybody" (p. 50). At Wetzell's Mills, North Carolina, on 6 March 1781, twenty-five expert riflemen, all of them veterans of the action at Kings Mountain, in South Carolina, fired from relatively close range at the gallant British Lieutenant Colonel James Webster as he led his troops on horseback across a ford they were covering. Eight or nine of these riflemen even succeeded in firing twice, and Webster was not hit once.

British regulars were not taught to aim, because in the case of linear tactics, the volume of fire was more important than its accuracy. Indeed, their Long Land Service musket (the Brown Bess) did not have a rear sight and had only the bayonet lug for a front sight. An American, captured at Fort Washington (16 November 1776), reported that not fewer than ten muskets were fired at his group within a range of forty to fifty yards, some at within twenty yards, and he was alive to give this critique: "I observed that they took no aim, and the moment of presenting and firing was the same" (Curtis, p. 19). Given

that the weight of the musket was concentrated in its barrel, firing by volleys was prone to shooting both over and under the nominal target. Soldiers might hold the barrel too high with their left hand at the start of a fire fight, thereby sending their projectile over the target, while fatigue later in the encounter might cause them to let the barrel droop, causing the projectile to hit the ground in front of the target.

It is also worth remembering that eighteenth-century firearms were based on a double-ignition principle. The striking of flint on steel produced the sparks that ignited the powder in the priming pan, which then communicated part of the explosion through the touch hole to the main charge in the barrel. Many things could go wrong to interrupt the sequence. Wet weather could so dampen gunpowder that only about one shot in four could even be fired. Flints had to be held tightly and at the right angle in the jaws of the lock, and their utility could deteriorate quickly. Whereas a good American flint could be used to fire sixty rounds without resharpening, a British flint was good for only six.

Legends abound about American marksmanship. Perhaps the tallest of the tall tales was reported on 1 October 1774 by John Andrews, a Boston resident, and is quoted by the historians Henry S. Commager and Richard B. Morris:

> It's common for the [British] soldiers to fire at a target fixed in the stream at the bottom of the common. A countryman stood by a few days ago, and laughed very heartily at the whole regiment's firing, and not one being able to hit it. The officer observed him, and asked why he laughed. . . . "I laugh to see how awkward they fire. Why, I'll be bount I hit it ten times running" (*Spirit of '76*, p. 30).

The British officer then challenged the boastful American to prove his ability, whereupon the American, who carefully loaded the musket offered by the officer, hit the target three consecutive times. Andrews' narrative continues:

> He took aim, and the ball went as exact in the middle as possible. The officers as well as soldiers stared, and thought the Devil was in the man. "Why," says the countryman, "I'll tell you naow. I have got a boy at home that will toss up an apple and shoot out all the seeds as it's coming down" (*Spirit of '76*, p. 30).

The rifle shot that mortally wounded Brigadier General Simon Fraser at the battle of Freeman's Farm (First Battle of Saratoga, 19 September 1777) apparently was one of a dozen shots fired from a range of perhaps a quarter of a mile. Daniel Morgan, commander of an ad hoc unit of riflemen, sent as many as twelve of the men he considered his best shots into the tree canopy, to gain them elevation and a clear field of fire. One of them—in the nineteenth century the credit was lodged with Timothy Murphy—managed to hit an average-size man riding a horse 440 yards away. It seems reasonable to conclude that this success was as much a matter of luck as of skill.

SEE ALSO *Lexington and Concord; Murphy, Timothy; Wetzell's Mills, North Carolina.*

BIBLIOGRAPHY

Commager, Henry S., and Richard B. Morris, eds. *The Spirit of '76: The Story of the American Revolution as Told by Participants.* Bicentennial Edition. New York: Harper and Row, 1976.

Curtis, Edward E. *The Organization of the British Army in the American Revolution.* New Haven, Conn.: Yale University Press, 1926.

Ward, Christopher. *The War of the Revolution.* 2 vols. Edited by John R. Alden. New York: Macmillan Company, 1952.

revised by Harold E. Selesky

MARQUE AND REPRISAL, LETTERS OF.

Papers authorizing the operations of privateers. The ship itself was often referred to as a letter of marque.

SEE ALSO *Privateers and Privateering.*

Mark M. Boatner

MARRINER, WILLIAM.

Whaleboat guerrilla. New Jersey. Natives of New Brunswick, he and Adam Hyler operated in small boats between Egg Harbor (near modern Atlantic City, New Jersey) and Staten Island to prey on British and Loyalist vessels. Captain Marriner was a prisoner on Long Island; after being exchanged he returned to capture his captor, a Major Sherbrook. He also captured the Loyalist Simon Cortelyou from his house on Long Island. Marriner was particularly busy in 1780, famously capturing two British ships on successive days in August.

SEE ALSO *Hyler, Adam.*

revised by Michael Bellesiles

MARSHALL, JOHN.

(1755–1835). Continental army officer, fourth chief justice of the U.S. Supreme Court. Virginia. Marshall first saw action as an officer in the Culpeper minutemen in the operations that drove Lord Dunmore, the royal governor, from Virginia at Great Bridge on 9 December 1775 and at Norfolk on 1 January 1776. On 30 July 1776 he became a first lieutenant in the Third Virginia Continental Regiment. He was promoted to captain lieutenant in the Fifteenth Virginia in December, with rank retroactive to 31 July 1776. On 20 November 1777 Marshall was appointed deputy judge advocate, and on 1 July 1778 he was promoted to captain. On 14 September 1778 he transferred to the Seventh Virginia, and on 12 February 1781 he retired from the army. He fought at Brandywine, Germantown, Monmouth, and Stony Point and also survived the winter at Valley Forge, where he said he served "with brave men from different states who were risking life and everything valuable in a common cause."

In the spring and summer of 1780 he attended a course of law lectures given at the College of William and Mary by Professor George Wythe, Jefferson's mentor, and on 28 August 1780 he was admitted to the Virginia bar. In 1783 he moved to Richmond from the frontier region where he had been reared and quickly became a successful lawyer. He was a member of the Virginia assembly (1782–1791 and 1795–1997), a delegate to the state convention that ratified the federal Constitution, and a member of the XYZ mission to France (1797–1798). He was a Federalist congressman from 1799 to 1800 and succeeded Timothy Pickering as secretary of state in May 1800. President John Adams nominated him to succeed Chief Justice Ellsworth of the U.S. Supreme Court, a position he accepted on 4 February 1801. During the next thirty-four years, the Court under his leadership became "the preeminent guardian and interpreter of the Constitution . . . and arbiter of conflicts arising from the clash of federal and state sovereignties" (Charles F. Hobson in ANB). His five-volume *Life of Washington* was published between 1804 and 1807.

BIBLIOGRAPHY

Faulkner, Robert K. *The Jurisprudence of John Marshall.* Princeton, New Jersey: Princeton University Press, 1968.

Hobson, Charles F. *The Great Chief Justice: John Marshall and the Rule of Law.* Lawrence: University Press of Kansas, 1996.

Marshall, John. *An Autobiographical Sketch by John Marshall.* Edited by John Stokes Adams. Ann Arbor: University of Michigan Press, 1937.

Stites, Francis N. *John Marshall: Defender of the Constitution.* Boston: Little, Brown, 1981.

revised by Harold E. Selesky

MARTHA'S VINEYARD RAID. 10–11

September 1778. After his Bedford–Fair Haven Raid in Massachusetts, on 6 September, Major General Charles Grey descended on the island of Martha's Vineyard to continue the British policy of harassing the New England coast. He landed at Holmes's Hole (Vineyard Haven), confiscated the militia's weapons, and wrecked its salt works. By destroying the vessels he found, Grey seriously hurt the island's whaling industry. His expedition also confiscated thousands of sheep and several hundred cattle to feed the garrison of New York.

SEE ALSO *Bedford–Fair Haven Raid, Massachusetts.*

revised by Robert K. Wright Jr.

MARTIN, JOHN. (1730?–1786). Soldier, poli-

tician. Born in Rhode Island, Martin moved to Georgia with his brother James in 1767. He served in a number of public offices, beginning in 1775 as a delegate from the town and district of Savannah to the first Provincial Congress and then on the Council of Safety. This was followed by election to public office for Chatham County as sheriff (1778–1779), justice of the peace (1781), and member of the assembly (1782). In the military he served as first lieutenant, then captain, of the Seventh Company of the Georgia Continental Battalion (1776); lieutenant colonel of the First Battalion, First Regiment (1777); town major of Savannah (1778); and lieutenant colonel, Chatham County (1781). In October 1781 he was appointed commissary in charge of military stores and elected governor in January 1782.

Continental General Nathanael Greene sent General Anthony Wayne and his forces into Georgia that month, and Martin saw to it that the rebel militia and civil government cooperated as fully as possible. Martin and Greene had met in the vicinity of the Congaree River in South Carolina, probably in 1781, and each left a favorable impression on the other. Martin did his best to get militia into the field and supplies to the troops, but this was difficult to achieve due to near-famine conditions. While offering attractive bounties for joining the militia, Martin gave precedence to the planting of crops. He also located food supplies in neighboring states for the commissary to distribute to needy civilians. As Wayne, along with supporting militia, closed in on the British in Savannah, Martin moved the seat of government out of the backcountry. The British evacuated Savannah in July 1782, and the state government was reestablished there for the first time since 1778.

Martin's administrative abilities and understanding of human nature enabled him to guide Georgia on its first steps toward rebuilding its shattered infrastructure. Violence did not end with the departure of the British, and Martin expressed his determination to end plundering. He used former raiders and the limited militia forces available to curb widespread outlaw activities and to locate badly needed slaves, horses, and cattle hidden by plundering gangs. Martin gained East Florida Governor Patrick Tonyn's cooperation in curtailing crossborder plundering activities. While he was unsuccessful in getting the General Assembly to adopt a lenient attitude toward Loyalists and the confiscation of their property, Martin correctly anticipated that it would eventually do so. The board of commissioners he established to manage confiscated property remained active for forty years.

Martin served as state treasurer in 1783–1784, and in early 1783 he was appointed a commissioner to meet with Creek and Cherokee Indians; he did not attend, however. Although little is known of his private life, he mentioned that his family was dependent upon food from the commissary during 1782, and he married Mary Deborah Spencer in December 1783. Martin died during January 1786 while traveling west for the recovery of his health.

BIBLIOGRAPHY

Ferguson, Clyde R. "Functions of the Partisan-Militia in the South during the American Revolution: An Interpretation." In *The Revolutionary War in the South: Power, Conflict, and Leadership.* Edited by W. Robert Higgins. Durham, N.C.: Duke University Press, 1979.

Klein, Rachel N. "Frontier Planters and the Revolution: The Southern Backcountry, 1775–1782." In *An Uncivil War: The Southern Backcountry during the American Revolution.* Edited by Ronald Hoffman, Thad W. Tate, and Peter J. Albert. Charlottesville: University Press of Virginia, 1985.

Leslie Hall

MARTIN, JOSIAH. (1737–1786). Royal

governor of North Carolina, British officer. Born in Dublin, Ireland, on 23 April 1737, Josiah Martin entered the army in 1757. He saw action on Martinique and Guadeloupe, and took part in the Canadian campaign, rising in rank to lieutenant colonel of the 22d Foot Regiment. In 1761 he married his cousin, Elizabeth Martin, of "Rockhall" on Long Island. In 1764 he joined the Sixty-eighth Regiment on Antigua, where he stayed until bad health forced him to sell his commission as lieutenant colonel in 1769. Aided by family connections, he was commissioned the royal governor of North Carolina in 1770, succeeding William Tryon. He took up his new office at New Bern on 12 August 1771.

Arriving shortly after Tryon had forcefully put down the Regulators, Martin faced a number of difficult obstacles. He was immediately embroiled in a losing battle on matters of taxation, the "foreign attachment issue" when the legislature insisted on the right of North Carolina creditors to seize the property of British debtors, and other local matters. Since he could not reconcile the demands of the assembly with his instructions from the Crown, Governor Martin saw the colony's juridical system collapse even before he was faced with the local Patriot movement that started in 1774. He had the unfortunate impression that he could muster sufficient Loyalist strength to hold his province, and in March 1775 he urged General Thomas Gage to send him arms and ammunition. As the Patriot militia gathered around him, Martin sent his family off to New York, and on 31 May 1775 he himself fled to the safety of Fort Johnston, on Cape Fear, in South Carolina. On 18 July he boarded the *H.M.S. Cruizer*, just a jump ahead of capture.

Martin's incorrect evaluation of the local situation, coupled with that of other royal governors-in-exile, led the British to send Henry Clinton's ill-fated expedition to Charleston in 1776 and helped bring about the abortive Loyalist uprising that was crushed at Moores Creek Bridge on 27 February 1776.

After watching the Charleston fiasco in June, Martin went to his wife's home on Long Island. In 1779 he returned to Charleston with Clinton and served creditably as a volunteer under General Charles Cornwallis in the Carolinas in 1780 and 1781, taking part in the battles of Camden and Guilford. Again bothered by ill health, he left Cornwallis at Wilmington in April 1781, and after a visit to Long Island he sailed to London. He drew his salary as governor until October 1783 and was compensated for the loss of his property in North Carolina. He died in London on 13 April 1786.

SEE ALSO *Regulators; Tryon, William.*

BIBLIOGRAPHY

Martin Papers. London: Manuscript Collections, British Museum.

Stumpf, Vernon O. *Josiah Martin: The Last Royal Governor of North Carolina.* Durham, N.C.: Carolina Academic Press, 1986.

revised by Michael Bellesiles

MARTIN'S STATION, KENTUCKY.

Because Kentucky was part of Virginia during the Revolution, it may be said that two places existed in the Old Dominion called Martin's Station. The more famous was on the Wilderness Road in the western tip of modern Virginia and within twenty miles of Cumberland Gap. The other Martin's Station, named for John Martin, was captured and destroyed by British and Indian forces in the Kentucky Raid of Bird in June 1780.

SEE ALSO *Kentucky Raid of Bird.*

revised by Michael Bellesiles

MARYLAND, MOBILIZATION IN.

Because of its proprietary government, the movement towards independence in Maryland involved opposition to the Calvert family's control of the colony as well as increasing discontent with parliamentary policies regarding imperial governance. By 1773 the last vestiges of proprietary support had disappeared in the General Assembly and control of Maryland's local and colonial government increasingly fell to extralegal county meetings, committees of observation, provincial conventions, and a council of safety. The mobilization for such "out-of-door" politics required the traditional gentry-led, antiproprietary leadership to negotiate an often treacherous path through the forests of reaction, moderation, and radicalism.

For example, the enforcement of the Continental Congress's Articles of Association required coercion of those loyal to the crown. Coercion sometimes required the use of force; often this force came from crowd mobilization by some of the most radical leaders. For instance, when one Annapolis merchant attempted to unload tea from the brigantine *Peggy Stewart* in October 1774, a mass meeting dominated by militiamen defied conservative advice and forced the merchant to burn not only the tea but the ship carrying it. The arson of the *Perry Stewart* was so radical that the historian Arthur M. Schlesinger Sr. commented that "Annapolis had out-Bostoned Boston" (*Colonial Merchants*, p. 392).

As in other colonies, the Maryland Convention reacted adversely to the Intolerable Acts, and in February 1775 it issued an "Association of Freemen of Maryland." This document required the signature of each citizen to support the colonial cause or be disarmed. Those not signing and posting a bond for good behavior were to be imprisoned. While many Loyalists voluntarily left the colony, others were forced to leave as local committees of observation became increasingly more radical.

By the next summer, the February association was no longer sufficient, and a second document, "Association of Freemen of Maryland, July 26, 1775," pledged military and financial support against British armed forces in American to back the common colonial quest "for the lives, liberties and properties of the subjects in the united colonies." While the proprietary governor, Robert Eden, tried valiantly to preserve a nominal "hold on the Helm of Government," he feared he would be unable to steer a course that would avoid "those Shoals, which all here must sooner or later . . . be shipwreck'd upon." He lost his symbolic control of the ship of state when the council of safety allowed him to escape in April 1776.

REVOLUTIONARY MILITIA

As Governor Eden became a mere figurehead, the real power devolved to the extralegal agencies. The Maryland Convention that met in December 1774 created a rudimentary military force when it resolved that "a well regulated militia, composed of the gentlemen, freeholders, and other freemen, is the natural strength and the only stable security of a free government." The convention then argued that the creation of a militia relieved the British government of the necessity of taxing colonials for the maintenance of "any standing army (ever dangerous to liberty) in this province." It then disbanded the largely moribund colonial militia system and created a new militia under its direction. The governor lost to the convention his power to appoint officers and to direct the deployment of the militia. Soon volunteer militia companies appeared throughout the province, each electing its own officers. But these companies needed funds to purchase arms and ammunition and local Patriots began demanding "voluntary contributions" from all citizens for their support, in effect, taxation without official sanction. This effort sparked considerable controversy between those supporting the resistance to the crown and those opposing it. With the outbreak of hostilities in Massachusetts in April 1775, the situation became grave, and greater organization was required.

Not only did the convention face the possibility of military opposition from the British, it also found the militia companies becoming an enforcement arm of the increasingly more radical county committees of observation. A third threat emerged when Governor Lord Dunmore of Virginia offered freedom to slaves and indentured servants who joined him in opposition to the revolutionary movement. This required the regularization of the military structure of the province to defend against a possible social upheaval. The July–August convention called again for every able-bodied freeman to enroll in the common militia and declared that every eight companies constituted a battalion. These units constituted a strategic reserve. The more active component was forty companies of minutemen with twenty-nine Western Shore companies organized into three battalions and with eleven independent companies on the Eastern Shore. The convention armed the minutemen companies with provincial weapons. For both the common militia and minuteman battalions, the convention assumed the right to commission the field grade command and staff officers rather than have them elected, as were company officers.

But legal structure and reality differed greatly. By the time of the December 1775–January 1776 meeting of the convention, it had become apparent that reorganization was necessary. This time the convention disbanded the minutemen units and created a force of regular Maryland troops consisting of a battalion and seven independent companies of infantry plus two batteries of artillery. The regular battalion contained eight infantry companies and one light infantry company and was stationed at Annapolis and Baltimore. The convention posted two of the regular companies on the southern Western Shore and the remaining five on the Eastern Shore. These regular troops numbered only two thousand under the command of Colonel William Smallwood, with all of the officers commissioned by the convention rather than by election. Its leadership included some of the most ardent advocates of American rights; Smallwood, his regimental lieutenant colonel, and four of his captains were also members of the convention. This unit became the basis of the famous Maryland Line, one of General George Washington's most famous Continental army fighting units. Its reputation for gallantry is the reason Maryland calls itself the "Old Line State."

The remaining common militia units became one of the most important and, at least early in the independence movement, most radical elements in the revolutionary era. The pressure to enforce the universality of militia service brought tensions between those with Loyalist, neutral, and religious objections to joining and those who felt it was necessary to present a united front against British tyranny. Revolutionary leaders learned to accept those with traditional religious pacifist orientations, such as the Quakers and German pietistic sects. Dealing with Anglicans, Methodists, and Baptists who objected to this particular war and often had Loyalist leanings proved a more difficult problem. Nonetheless, the revolutionaries gradually obligated most white adult males to military service and with it the semblance of treason to the British Crown.

The militia units became the enforcement arm of the revolutionary movement. They forced individuals to observe the importation and exportation policies of the Continental Congress; those who did not obey were subject to punishment or banishment. They enforced the ordinances of the revolutionary conventions and later of the state government. They maintained order throughout most of the state with the exception of the lower Eastern Shore. The militia became the police force of the new state government and legitimized it in the eyes of residents who had to obey state laws and officials. From its ranks, the state's Continental Line recruited replacements. Because Maryland was never occupied by British soldiers, the militiamen never had to counter regular soldiers. But because the state's Chesapeake coastline was constantly threatened by British and Loyalist raids, eventually most white adult males took up arms merely to protect themselves from raiders who made little distinction in their activities between the persons and property of Loyalists, neutrals, or Revolutionaries.

During 1775–1776 a few militia regiments called for far more dramatic social and political change than the more traditional antiproprietary leadership thought necessary. Perhaps the most dramatic representation of the radical position was that of the Anne Arundel militia resolves of July 1776, which urged the adoption of a new state constitution with universal white manhood suffrage, a plural executive, an annually elected legislature, elected county officers, real estate instead of poll taxes, and low fees for officials. These resolves also called for the election of all militia officers, including those of field grade and general ranks, and opposed the creation of standing armies. While these ideals were too radical for the long-established leadership to incorporate into the constitution of 1776, they demonstrated how the requirement to mobilize a militia system dramatized a desire for a more egalitarian social and political order. The historian Ronald Hoffman has argued that the members of the traditional elite "sacrificed principle for power" in order to overcome "the disequilibrating social forces unleashed by the revolutionary movement" and thereby preserved their leadership status from those they considered to be egalitarian demagogues (*Spirit of Dissension,* pp. 3, 222).

The greatest military crisis in the state's history came in 1777, when Admiral Richard Lord Howe brought into Chesapeake Bay 267 sail, including 26 men-of-war, and General Sir William Howe's army. Many militia units did not muster, while those that did often were without arms, gunpowder, or shot. There was more bravado than bravery among those assembled to defend Annapolis and Baltimore, but fortunately the admiral headed for the Head of Elk, where he disembarked his brother's army for its assault on the Continental army in Pennsylvania. For the next several months Royal Navy vessels and Loyalist privateers created considerable alarm but did little damage along the Chesapeake coast. More dangerous were Loyalist uprisings on the Delmarva Peninsula during late 1777 and the first half of 1778. With the British army ensconced in Philadelphia and Royal Navy ships in the Chesapeake, militia units failed to muster and Loyalists openly flaunted their political preferences. The most significant event was an insurrection in Queen Anne's County led by a romantic figure named Cheney "China" Clow in the spring of 1778. Brigadier General William Smallwood led the suppression effort that forced Clow and his followers into the Eastern Shore swamps, where they hid out but did little damage for several years.

For most of the war, ground operations of Loyalists were centered in the lower Eastern Shore and the Potomac River. In many respects the militia became more efficient as it devised means to react quickly upon learning of the approach of the enemy, to move threatened livestock and foodstuffs inland, to operate under the command of a county lieutenant who coordinated local defenses, and to incorporate returning Continental army veterans into leadership positions. For instance, Charles County's lieutenant was Colonel Francis Ware, a distinguished veteran of the Maryland Line's campaigns of 1775–1776, whose leadership contributed significantly to the defense of the Lower Potomac Valley. Success in these activities involved coordination of local militia regiments with state naval vessels.

NAVAL OPERATIONS

Because the people of Maryland and Virginia depended so much on the Chesapeake for their livelihoods and the bay presented an inviting avenue for British and Loyalist incursions along the vulnerable coastline, the colony's Patriot leadership provided naval as well as ground forces. In 1775 Maryland created its own navy by converting a merchant ship into the *Defence,* carrying eighteen six-pounder and two four-pounder cannon. Its mission was to escort merchant vessels past Lord Dunmore's outpost at Norfolk and to clear enemy raiders from the Chesapeake Bay. Commanded by James Nicholson, she drove off the British sixteen-gun sloop-of-war *Otter* on 9 March 1776. When Nicholson became a Continental navy captain, command of the *Defence* went to Captain George Cook, formerly of the Royal Navy, who took her on a successful Atlantic cruise until November. The vessel remained inactive until it served as a state-owned merchantman sailing to France in 1778–1779. Sold to a Baltimore merchant in 1779, the *Defence* concluded its wartime career carrying supplies to the French navy in the West Indies.

Besides James Nicholson, who became the Continental navy's senior officer, Maryland furnished a number of leading officers in the continental service; these included such distinguished commanders as Lambert Wicks and Joshua Barney. To man their vessels, hundreds of the state's sons served in the junior officer and enlisted ranks.

Far more damaging to the enemy than the state's Continental navy contributions were the efforts of her privateers. From Baltimore there sailed 250 privateers, and other ports provided more vessels that crippled British commercial shipping from the Irish Sea to the Caribbean. By 1778 over 559 captures were recorded by the state's daring seamen, who found themselves amply rewarded for the risks they took. Often these efforts were combined with the transportation of foodstuffs to the French West Indies. However, the profits to owners, officers, and crew were such that privateering adversely affected recruitment for the Continental army and Continental navy.

One of the most famous of these privateers was the brig *Sturdy Beggar,* owned by a group of Baltimore merchants, whose Caribbean exploits in 1776–1777 resulted in several notable captures, including a merchant vessel from Senegal containing gold dust, ivory, and over four hundred slaves that sold in Hispaniola for over twenty thousand pounds. Before she sank in a storm, *Sturdy Beggar* earned an infamous reputation among British merchantmen. The naval historian William James Morgan concluded, however, that "American privateers were a festering and annoying thorn in the British Lion's paw, but they were in no manner the decisive factor in the outcome of the war" (Morgan, "American Privateering," p. 86).

Besides these private enterprises, the state found itself involved in thwarting Royal Navy and Loyalist forays along the shores of the Chesapeake Bay. In June 1776 the council of safety let contracts for the construction of seven row galleys. While the exact dimensions of these vessels are unknown, they probably had a keel length of eighty-one feet but drew only eight feet of water. Problems procuring cordage, sailcloth, anchors, guns, and other items delayed the completion of five of these vessels in late 1777. As a result, they were unable to counter Vice Admiral Richard Lord Howe's incursion into the bay the summer of 1777. But for the next two years these vessels escorted merchant vessels and troop convoys, hindered smuggling, served as police boats, and transported war matériel. Usually armed with between two and four eighteen-pounders and ten to fourteen four-pounders, these small vessels combined with those of Virginia were able to keep the bay mostly under Patriot control until early 1780. At that time Maryland sold the galleys. Shortly thereafter, the British returned to the lower bay area and depredations along Maryland's bay shore resumed.

Throughout the war Loyalism flourished on the Eastern Shore, particularly in Dorchester, Worcester, and Somerset Counties. Whenever British warships appeared, small Loyalist craft joined them and conducted raids against Patriot leaders, magazines, tobacco warehouses, military supplies, naval and commercial vessels, and private property. One such raid came in 1779, when Commodore Sir George Collier conducted an expedition into the lower bay that brought with it the plundering of accompanying privateers. Operating out of the islands on Tangier Sound, armed Loyalist barges grew bolder after British army units occupied the James River and Norfolk area in 1780. They were navigated by knowledgeable local watermen. "Commodore" Joseph Wheland commanded four armed barges that raided in St. Mary's, Dorchester, and Somerset Counties. This plundering activity continued well into 1783, long after Lord Cornwallis's surrender at Yorktown.

To counter these activities, the Maryland leadership had to rebuild the state's naval forces. In the autumn of 1780 the General Assembly enacted the Bay Defence Act, and the state began gradually to build a series of barges for shoal water operations. This pace was too deliberate for those on the lower Eastern Shore, and privately built barges with crews of approximately twenty-five men soon began operating in local defensive operations. Small squadrons commanded by local commodores such as Zedekiah Walley and Thomas Grason appeared in 1781. Since the British navy operated in the bay at this time, Grason found it difficult to recruit men for his four-barge squadron, but he boldly undertook to counter a five-barge Loyalist force in the Tangier Islands on 10 May 1781 and lost his life and flagship in the process.

French naval dominance of the bay in the late summer and fall of 1781 curtailed Loyalist operations. During this time the state mobilized every possible water craft to transport the Continental and French armies from the north end of the bay to the encampment near Yorktown. The Yorktown victory did not end the Loyalist-Patriot struggle in the central Chesapeake Bay; instead, it seems to have intensified in 1782. A Virginia Loyalist named James Kidd, with seven barges and a galley, engaged Commodore Walley's Maryland squadron near Tangier Island. The subsequent Battle of the Barges or of Crager's Strait on 30 November 1782 was the bloodiest naval engagement of the Revolution in Maryland. The Loyalists drove off the Americans, killed Commodore Walley, and captured his flagship. The victory emboldened the Loyalists for months thereafter. The state's final naval activity of the war was a successful raid by army Captain John Lynn against a Loyalist base on Devil's Island (later Deal's Island) on 21 March 1783.

CONTINENTAL ARMY UNITS

The regular Maryland troops of the December 1775 convention became part of the Continental army in the summer of 1776 as the 1st and 2nd Maryland Regiments. They participated in the defense of New York City, New Jersey, and Philadelphia during the 1776–1777 campaigns. In 1777 the 3rd, 5th, and 7th Maryland Regiments joined the Continental army, and along with the 1st Regiment became part of the 1st Maryland Brigade. The 4th and 6th Maryland Regiments became part of the 2nd Maryland Brigade along with the 2nd Regiment. Collectively known as the Maryland Line, these brigades fought in the 1777 and 1778 campaigns in New Jersey and Pennsylvania and remained part of the main army until the spring of 1780, when they were reassigned to the Southern Department and served in the Carolinas for the remainder of the war. All the Maryland regiments were reorganized in 1779 to consist of nine companies. William Smallwood eventually became a major general in the Continental army and commanded the Marylanders for most of the war.

Recruitment remained a constant problem as losses to battle, disease, accident, and desertion depleted the ranks. For instance, in the winter of 1777–1778, the Maryland and Delaware brigades stayed in Wilmington, Delaware, where they recruited replacements. Losses in the Southern Campaign, especially after the Battle of Camden, forced General Nathanael Greene to refill the 1st and 2nd Regiments from a provisional brigade created from the remnants of the Maryland and Delaware Lines. He disbanded the 6th and 7th Regiments. The 3rd, 4th, and 5th Regiments returned as cadre units to Maryland and recruited slowly. Eventually, they returned to the Southern Department—the 5th in February 1781, the 3rd in August, and the 4th in September. The latter two participated in the Yorktown siege. Another recruitment effort came during the winter of 1781–1782 and included bounties that the state hoped would entice enlistments and which in fact secured 308 new men. The battle honors of these seven regiments are now perpetuated in the 175th Infantry of the Maryland National Guard.

LOYALIST UNITS

From 1775 to the end of the war, Maryland's mobilization efforts also included a number of Loyalist units, mostly from the Eastern Shore. During the British occupation of Philadelphia, General Howe commissioned James Chalmers lieutenant colonel of the Maryland Loyalist Battalion. It recruited over three hundred men for a unit that participated in the 1778 New Jersey campaign and spent most of the war in Pensacola, Florida. More that half its men were lost to disease, death, and desertion, and the Spanish captured its remnants at Pensacola in 1781. Only fifty survivors received grants in New Brunswick, Canada, after the war was over.

By far the largest number of Loyalists fought in irregular militia and naval units in the wetlands and islands of the Eastern Shore, where they cooperated with Loyalists from southern Delaware and Virginia's Eastern Shore to harass the Revolutionaries and to support British forces in the area. Attempts to eradicated them by both Continental army and Maryland militia forces never completely achieved their goal, and the Loyalists continued their hit-and-run tactics until 1783.

THE YORKTOWN CAMPAIGN

Continental army Brigadier General Mordecai Gist was in Baltimore when word was received that the Continental and French armies were coming to the Chesapeake. Gist immediately organized the owners and captains of vessels in the harbor to go to the Head of Elk to carry arriving units, ordnance, and supplies for movement to Yorktown. Soon more vessels sailed northward to engage in a massive transportation effort. Governor Thomas Sim Lee ordered a mobilization of militia units from across the Western Shore to march to Annapolis and Baltimore and assist in the effort. John Calhoun and Henry Hollingsworth, commissary generals of the Western and Eastern Shores respectively, worked under great stress to provide foodstuffs, supplies, and forage for the allied armies. After delivering the initial shipments to Yorktown, Maryland vessels returned to Georgetown, Annapolis, Baltimore, Head of Elk, and Eastern Shore ports for new cargoes for the allied forces. Gist found that the prospect of victory encouraged enlistments in the Maryland Line, which he took to Yorktown. George Washington later wrote that the supplies provided by the state were "so liberal, that they remove every apprehension of Want."

The war severely damaged Maryland's tobacco-centered economy, but it stimulated a variety of industrial activities, including the production of guns and gunpowder, iron, blankets and other textiles, shoes, saddles, and harnesses and the agricultural production of cereal grains and livestock. Rural Frederick County also found itself providing guards and food for the thousands of prisoners of war that were brought there following victories from Trenton to Yorktown. In Baltimore, water-powered enterprises dyed and carded wool; made linen, paper, and hardware; and ground flour. Baltimore shipyards build the continental cruisers *Hornet, Wasp,* and *Virginia,* plus a host of privateers. Like the rest of the fledgling Republic, the state found inflation eroding the financial situation of many of its citizens. The financial cost of the war created considerable stress in state politics from the late 1770s until the ratification of the Constitution in 1789.

SUMMARY

Because it was never invaded, Maryland's mobilization effort primarily consisted of providing a manpower base for important elements of the Continental army, the Continental navy, and privateer naval forces. Its militia served to keep Loyalism to a minimum except in the lower Eastern Shore, and its agricultural and industrial output made important contributions to the war effort. While its Loyalist battalion served the British army well, it was the partisan bands of Loyalists on the Eastern Shore that proved a pacification problem throughout the war.

SEE ALSO *Chase, Samuel; Eden, Robert; Gist, Mordecai; Paca, William; Smallwood, William; Stone, Thomas.*

BIBLIOGRAPHY

Alexander, Arthur J. "How Maryland Tried to Raise Her Continental Quota." *Maryland Historical Magazine* 42 (1947): 184–196.

Batt, Richard John. "The Maryland Continentals, 1780–1781." Ph.D. dissertation, Tulane University, 1974.

Clark, William Bell. *Lambert Wickes, Sea Raider and Diplomat: The Story of a Naval Captain of the Revolution.* New Haven, Conn.: Yale University Press, 1932.

Eller, Ernest McNeill, ed. *Chesapeake Bay in the American Revolution.* Centerville, Md.: Tidewater, 1981.

Herron, Richard D. "Chesapeake Bay Privateering during the American Revolution: The Patriots, the Loyalists, and the British." Master's thesis, East Carolina University, 1984.

Hoffman, Ronald. *A Spirit of Dissension: Economics, Politics, and the Revolution in Maryland.* Baltimore: Johns Hopkins University Press, 1973.

Krug, Andrew. "'Such a Banditty You Never See Collected!' Frederick Town and the American Revolution." *Maryland Historical Magazine* 95 (Spring 2000): 5–28.

Lee, Jean B. *The Price of Nationhood: The American Revolution in Charles County.* New York: Norton, 1994.

Mason, Keith. "A Region in Revolt: The Eastern Shore of Maryland, 1740–1790." Ph.D. dissertation, Johns Hopkins University, 1985.

Morgan, William James. "American Privateering in America's War for Independence, 1775–1783." *American Neptune* 36 (April 1976): 79–87.

New, M. Christopher. *Maryland Loyalists in the American Revolution.* Centerville, Md.: Tidewater, 1996.

Norton, Louis Arthur. *Joshua Barney: Hero of the Revolution and 1812.* Annapolis: Naval Institute Press, 2000.

Overfield, Richard Arthur. "The Loyalists of Maryland during the American Revolution." Ph.D. dissertation, University of Maryland, 1968.

Papenfuse, Edward C. "The Legislative Response to a Costly War: Fiscal Policy and Factional Politics in Maryland, 1777–1789. In *Sovereign States in an Age of Uncertainty.* Edited by Ronald Hoffman and Peter J. Albert. Charlottesville: University Press of Virginia for the United States Capitol Historical Society, 1981.

Papenfuse, Edward C., and Gregory A. Stiverson. "General Smallwood's Recruits: The Peacetime Career of the Revolutionary Private." *William and Mary Quarterly,* 3rd ser., 30 (1973): 117–132.

Rieman, Steuart. *A History of the Maryland Line in the Revolutionary War, 1775–1783.* Towson, Md.: Society of the Cincinnati of Maryland, 1969.

Schlesinger, Arthur M., Sr. *The Colonial Merchants and the American Revolution, 1763–1776.* New York: Facsimile Library, 1939.

Shy, John. *A People Numerous and Armed: Reflections on the Military Struggle for American Independence.* New York: Oxford University Press, 1976.

Skaggs, David Curtis. *Roots of Maryland Democracy, 1753–1776.* Westport, Conn.: Greenwood, 1973.

Steiner, Bernard C. "Maryland Privateers in the American Revolution." *Maryland Historical Magazine* 3 (June 1908): 99–103.

Tinder, Robert W. "Extraordinary Measures: Maryland and the Yorktown Campaign." *Maryland Historical Magazine* 95 (Summer 2000): 133–159.

Wright, Robert K., Jr. *The Continental Army.* Washington, D.C.: U.S. Army Center of Military History, 1983.

David Curtis Skaggs

MARYLAND LINE.

The Maryland Line, despite its significant combat performances from Long Island in 1776 through the southern campaigns of Horatio Gates and Nathanael Greene, is one of the least understood of the state lines in the Revolutionary War. It started on 1 January 1776 as full-time state troops authorized by the Maryland Convention—a single regiment plus seven independent infantry companies (there were also two artillery companies). The Continental rifle companies raised in 1775 were organized under the supervision of the Frederick County Committee of Safety, not the Convention. In the summer of 1776 the Congress created two Extra Continental Regiments—the Maryland and Virginia Rifle Regiment and the German Battalion—and Maryland furnished half of each of these. The riflemen, the German Battalion, and the artillery companies furnished by Maryland to the war effort were not formally a part of the Maryland Line. The state also agreed to send four volunteer militia battalions to the Flying Camp (a flying camp was a unit specifically intended to operate swiftly in response to a threat; it was the era's equivalent of today's "mobile strike force").

The Maryland Line in the Continental army appeared on 17 August 1776, when Congress assigned a quota of two infantry regiments to Maryland and the state troops changed their status without creating a second command and staff element for the independent companies. The expanded quota assigned for 1777 called for eight regiments. Careful groundwork by a visiting committee on 10 December 1776 assigned the officers who were in charge of raising the companies called for by the quota. The old regiment reenlisted as the First Maryland Regiment and the independent companies as the Second; the Third through Seventh Regiments were built around the rest of the veterans of the 1776 campaign. The cadre for the Third Regiment came from some of the regulars, but the others drew from the four flying camp battalions. Maryland refused to form an eighth regiment, arguing that its contributions to the two extra Continental Regiments counted as a whole additional regiment. This issue remained a bone of contention until 1781.

The Maryland Line served as a two-brigade division (with one outside regiment filling the hole left by the "missing" Eighth) and marched south to reinforce Charleston in 1780 with the Delaware Regiment. The division did not arrive before the city fell, but formed the heart of the replacement southern army of Major General Horatio Gates. On 15 July 1780 at Deep River, North Carolina, Major General Johann De Kalb issued division orders that temporarily reorganized the division for better combat efficiency into a single brigade of four full battalions, and sent the surplus officers home to recruit, planning to resume the official configuration when the replacements arrived. The First and Seventh Regiments formed the First Battalion, led by Lieutenant Colonel Peter Adams. The Second Maryland and the Delaware Regiment formed the Second Battalion, under Lieutenant Colonel Benjamin Ford. The Third and Fifth Regiments formed the Third Battalion, under Colonel John Gunby. The Fourth and Sixth Regiments formed the Fourth Battalion under Colonel Williams.

At Camden the brigade fought brilliantly, but suffered heavy losses. This led to a second provisional reorganization at Hillsboro, North Carolina, on 3 September 1780. The survivors now formed a single, full-strength regiment commanded by Colonel Otho Holland Williams and deploying as two four-company battalions plus a light company. Officially the Maryland Line dropped to five regiments on 1 January 1781, but in reality the two battalions were reconstituted as the First and Second Maryland Regiments, which fought under Major General Nathaniel Greene. When replacements arrived in February 1781, these troops were used to nominally reconstitute the Fifth Regiment. In practice they formed a company that served in combat as attachments to the First and Second Regiments. The Third and Fourth Regiments reorganized later in the year in Maryland, and served in the Yorktown campaign before heading south. In 1782 and 1783, as the British evacuated the south, Greene sent the Marylanders home in stages, with the last of the Line disbanding on 15 November 1783.

SEE ALSO *Gates, Horatio; Greene, Nathanael; Southern Campaigns of Nathanael Greene.*

BIBLIOGRAPHY

Alexander, Arthur J. "How Maryland Tried to Raise Her Continental Quota." *Maryland Historical Magazine* 37 (September 1942): 184–196.

Balch, Thomas, ed. *Papers Relating Chiefly to the Maryland Line During the Revolution.* Philadelphia: T. K. and P. G. Collins for The Seventy-Six Society, 1857.

Batt, Richard John. "The Maryland Continentals, 1780–1781." Ph.D. dissertation, Tulane University, 1974.

Papenfuse, Edward C., and Gregory A. Stiverson. "General Smallwood's Recruits: The Peacetime Career of the Revolutionary Private." *William and Mary Quarterly,* 3d series, 30 (January 1973): 117–132.

Steuart, Rieman. *A History of the Maryland Line in the Revolutionary War, 1775–1783.* Towson, Md.: Society of the Cincinnati of Maryland, 1969.

Tacyn, Mark Andrew. "'To the End': The First Maryland Regiment and the American Revolution." Ph.D. dissertation, University of Maryland, College Park, 1999.

Robert K. Wright Jr.

MASON, GEORGE. (1725–1792).

American statesman, constitutionalist. Virginia. Born in Stafford County, Virginia, in 1725, George Mason was the son of a wealthy planter. He became well known as the master of Gunston Hall, built on the Potomac River below Alexandria between 1755 and 1758, which was accounted one of the finest buildings in colonial Virginia. For several reasons, his important role in the years preceding the Revolution were played off stage: he valued his privacy, suffered from chronic ill health, his wife died early in 1773, and he had nine children. He sat in the House of Burgesses from 1758 to 1761, served as Treasure of Ohio County in 1752, and came to know every powerful man in the Chesapeake region over the ensuing twenty years.

In 1769 he drafted the nonimportation agreement introduced in the assembly by his friend and neighbor, George Washington. He did likewise with the Fairfax resolves of 18 July 1774. In July 1775 he succeeded Washington in the Virginia convention. He was immediately elected to the Committee of Safety that took over the powers vacated by John Murray Dunmore. As a member of the May 1776 convention, he framed the Virginia Bill of Rights and Constitution. This piece of writing had wide influence: Thomas Jefferson drew on it in drafting the first part of the Declaration of Independence; it was copied by many states; it was the basis for the first ten amendments to the U.S. Constitution; and it even had influence in the French Revolution. Mason's state constitution was also a remarkably successful pioneering effort. He was involved with the revision of state laws and with disestablishment. He was on the committee that authorized the Western operations of George Rogers Clark, and he received Clark's full report.

A believer in states' rights, Mason was one of three of the forty-two delegates to the Constitutional Convention of 1787 in Philadelphia who refused to sign the final draft. (The others were Gerry and Edmund Randolph.) His views were expressed in "Objections to This Constitution of Government," which was widely read and influenced the structure of other anti-federalist writings. He attended the Virginia ratifying convention, where he and Patrick Henry almost succeeded in defeating the Constitution. Mason never reconciled to the new form of government, even after the passage of the Bill of Rights. He died at Gunston Hall on 7 October 1792.

SEE ALSO *Murray, John.*

BIBLIOGRAPHY

Miller, Helen Hill. *George Mason, Gentleman Revolutionary.* Chapel Hill, N.C.: University of North Carolina Press, 1975.

Rutland, Robert A., ed. *The Papers of George Mason, 1725–1792.* 3 vols. Chapel Hill, N.C.: University of North Carolina Press, 1970.

revised by Michael Bellesiles

MASONRY IN AMERICA.

MASONRY IN AMERICA. Early in the seventeenth century, a society of London stone workers started admitting honorary members as "accepted masons" and initiating them into their secret signs and legendary history. By the early 1730s, lodges affiliated with the grand lodge of London had formed in the colonies. The Philadelphia lodge lasted only five years but was revived in 1749 by Benjamin Franklin. In Boston, the original lodge flourished and another was organized in 1756. They included such men as James Otis, Joseph Warren, and Paul Revere, part of a self-selected group based on shared values rather than on wealth or prestige. Men became Masons for a variety of reasons, "including status enhancement, social mobility, camaraderie, civic-mindedness, the satisfaction of mastering a ritual, or curiosity about the occult" (York). Their belief in the brotherhood of man happened to coincide with the spirit of the American Revolution. Many prominent Revolutionaries therefore happened to be Masons, and the secret nature of their meetings lent itself to radical politics. Washington was initiated in Fredericksburg, Virginia, in 1752, took the oath of office as president of the United States on his Masonic bible, and used a Masonic trowel to lay the cornerstone of the Capitol building.

The historian Neil L. York has stated: "It is doubtful whether Freemasons *qua* Freemasons played a significant role in the American Revolution, even as their members joined the Revolutionary movement or stayed loyal to Britain. Masonry as an institution did not figure in the eventual revolt; even so, the ideas and values of Masons may have played a role, along with other beliefs that historians have traditionally linked to the Revolutionary cause."

BIBLIOGRAPHY

York, Neil L. "Freemasons and the American Revolution." *The Historian* 55 (1993): 315–330.

revised by Harold E. Selesky

MASSACHUSETTS, MOBILIZATION IN.

MASSACHUSETTS, MOBILIZATION IN. When Britain forced France to concede its colonies in North America in 1763, Americans were jubilant and proud. While basking in victory, Britain determined to reduce its war debt and to rationalize its expanded colonial holdings. By 1775, Americans' political views had shifted diametrically from taking pride in the British empire to making war against Britain as a result of the headlong conflict between British policies and the colonial experience of political and economic autonomy.

POLITICIZATION

British decisions to limit settlement in the Ohio Valley (Proclamation Line, 1763) frustrated land-hungry colonists. The Sugar Act (1764) and the Stamp Tax (1765) struck at the pocketbooks of colonists across the board. The Sons of Liberty organized to promote street protests that prevented the Stamp Act from going into effect. Parliament repealed the Stamp Act in 1766, but simultaneously claimed its right to "make laws and statutes of sufficient force and validity to bind the colonies and people of America, in all cases whatsoever" (Declaratory Act). They followed up with a series of new taxes on imported goods (Townsend Revenue Act), and attitudes both in America and Britain hardened over who would control colonial policy. What seemed reasonable to Parliament was perceived by Americans as an assault on their traditional constitutional rights.

Massachusetts leaders like Samuel Adams and James Otis turned the new British policies into public debates. In response to British-imposed taxes, women joined men in boycotting British goods. Radical polemicists inundated Massachusetts with political broadsides and pamphlets that drew increasing numbers of ordinary citizens into imperial politics. However, many Americans were reluctant to side with radical critics of Britain. Some Massachusetts merchants with ties to London, office holders, royal appointees, and others with an affinity for Britain, felt that the economic and political interests of the colonies were best served by remaining within the empire. Others, like Massachusetts-born Governor Thomas Hutchinson and stamp distributor Andrew Oliver, considered the rebellious faction as "rabble" who threatened social stability.

British authorities responded to the harassment of royal officials by stationing troops in Boston in 1768, and tensions between Bostonians and British troops flared sporadically into violence (Boston Massacre, 1770). In 1772, Boston political radicals (Whigs) led by Samuel Adams formed the first Committee of Correspondence after a dispute over control of judges' salaries. Their litany of complaints addressed royal tax policies, tax collectors, the quartering of troops, judicial jurisdictions, the independence of colonial assemblies, restrictions of colonial manufactures, and a controversial British proposal for an American episcopate. New Englanders saw expansion of

The Site of the Boston Massacre. *A circle of cobblestones in front of Boston's Old State House marks the site of the Boston Massacre, a clash in March 1770 between colonists and British soldiers that left five Americans dead.* © **KEVIN FLEMING/CORBIS**

the Church of England as a direct attack on their congregations. The Committee of Correspondence framed its campaign as a defense of their traditional rights as Englishmen to stimulate popular political debate. Local committees quickly dominated local governance and put pressure on Loyalist sympathizers (Tories). Still, many Americans remained reluctant to disavow Loyalty to the crown, blaming Parliament or other political officials for the ills that had befallen the colonies.

When Parliament passed the Tea Act (1773) granting exclusive distribution to the failing East India Company, public protest ignited, culminating in the destruction at Boston harbor of British-owned tea (Boston Tea Party, 1773). Outraged British authorities determined to punish the people of Massachusetts and the port of Boston with the passage of the Intolerable (Coercive) Acts in 1774. Key provisions of the Intolerable Acts closed the port and suspended local government. Massachusetts activists were poised to respond. They met across the state in county conventions and vowed to defend their liberties and to prepare for armed resistance, if necessary.

In August 1774, royal Governor General Thomas Gage learned that county conventions were meeting to challenge his administration of British policy. Berkshire County was first, but nearly every county quickly followed, to discuss how to respond to what they saw as a royal *coup d'etat*. After the Worcester County convention in September 1774, 6,000 militiamen assembled on Worcester common to prevent royally appointed judges from opening the courts. Additionally, the Worcester convention voted a series of resolves that rounded out its "revolution" by taking control of the militia. All militia officers with royal appointments were ordered to publicly resign, and the towns were ordered to select new officers. General Gage wrote Lord Dartmouth (William Legge) in London that "the Flames of sedition had spread universally throughout the Country beyond Conception."

The county resolutions demonstrate a convergence of thought rather than simply a top-down inculcation of revolutionary discourse. Popular political activism conjoined with continuous missteps by the British imperial government to produce a cautious consensus among the people of Massachusetts, expressed as concern with "the dangerous and alarming situation of public affairs," and they determined to adopt a course that would "promote the true interest of his majesty, and the peace, welfare, and prosperity of the province." The Massachusetts Provincial Congress continued to meet, despite being banned, and ordered that tax collections be withheld from the royal collector, Harrison Gray. Having taken control of local government, the militia, and tax revenue, Massachusetts colonists decided to arm themselves.

In October 1774, the Provincial Congress drew up a shopping list for some £20,000 of arms, including 5,000 muskets and bayonets, five tons of lead musket-balls, some twenty field pieces, and thirty tons of shot. "Apprehensive of the most fatal consequences" resulting from Britain's warlike preparations, subversions of constitutional rights, and endangerment of "lives, liberties, and properties," the Congress resolved that there ought to be a provincial Committee of Safety responsible for monitoring threats and mustering the militia in defense of the province. New militia officers filled the spots vacated by discredited Loyalists.

Additionally, the Massachusetts Provincial Congress ordered the formation of armed companies comprising "fifty privates who shall equip and hold themselves in readiness, on the shortest notice from the said committee of safety, to march." These "minutemen" were to be rapid response teams, ready to defend against any British incursions into the countryside. While riding through Massachusetts, Ezra Stiles noted that "at every house Women & Children [were] making Cartridges, running Bullets, making Wallets, baking Biscuit, crying and bemoaning, and at the same time animating their Husbands and Sons to fight for their Liberties" (Stiles, 1901, p. 180).

The Bostonians in Distress. *This mezzotint, attributed to Philip Dawe and published in London in 1774, depicts the plight of Boston residents after the passage of the Intolerable Acts. Bostonians are shown in a cage suspended from the liberty tree, which is surrounded by British cannons, soldiers, and warships. The men feeding the encaged Bostonians represent colonists who sent supplies to the city during the crisis.* NATIONAL ARCHIVES AND RECORDS ADMINISTRATION

The Lexington Minuteman. *Erected in 1900 on Lexington Battle Green, this statue by sculptor Henry Hudson Kitson commemorates the militia who fought against British incursions into the countryside.* © **KEVIN FLEMING/CORBIS**

THE MILITIA TRADITION

Once a decision was reached to arm its citizens, Massachusetts set out to reinvigorate its militia, which, John Adams wrote, was one of the cornerstones of colonial society. In the seventeenth century the New England militia was a ubiquitous institution that obligated every free, white, adult male from sixteen to sixty, with few exceptions, to serve in defense of his local community. In the eighteenth century, local militias were not, for the most part, a significant fighting force, and they served primarily as a manpower pool for military service in the eighteenth-century British-French imperial wars.

According to the militia tradition, independent-minded colonial recruits enlisted for a fixed time with set pay rates, specified rations, and strict geographic limits. Expedition service was a voluntary contract, while local militia duty was a civic obligation. The French-Indian War (1756–1763) was an important training ground for the generation of American colonists who fought in the Revolution. American governments and merchants had gained experience in meeting the logistical demands of armies. Most importantly, the imperial expeditionary experience provided a traditional model for meeting emergencies and staffing long-term expeditionary forces.

THE REVOLUTION, EARLY STAGES

When tensions between the royal governor and the people of Massachusetts erupted in open hostilities at Lexington and Concord on 19 April 1775, thousands of Massachusetts militia surrounded the British garrison in Boston. Local militias immediately swept through their locales to neutralize potentially dangerous Loyalists. However, no sooner had the Americans caged up a powerful British army in Boston than the minutemen citizen-soldiers began to return to their farms and spring planting, leaving provincial commanders without enough troops to fortify their lines. The minute companies were only provisioned for fourteen days and were not prepared for a long siege. This first exodus of troops exemplifies a pattern of the ebb and flow of manpower into and out of the American armies that characterized mobilization throughout the eight-year war.

Massachusetts quickly called for an army of 30,000 to maintain the siege at Boston. Enlistments were to last for eight months, on the model of the earlier colonial expeditionary forces. Recruiting efforts were slow, not because of a lack of enthusiasm, but because of the prevailing belief in volunteerism, in limited contractual obligations, and in short-term service. Racial attitudes also slowed enlistment. In May 1775, the Committee of Safety in Massachusetts ordered that "no slaves be admitted into this army upon any consideration whatever," despite the presence of a number of African Americans already serving in militia companies.

In June 1775, the Continental Congress agreed to nationalize the military effort and take responsibility for the Massachusetts army, selecting Virginian Colonel George Washington as commander in chief. The army of 15,000 soldiers that Washington inherited upon his arrival in Massachusetts was an amateur enterprise by every measure except magnitude. The American army was short of everything but manpower, and its most critical shortage was of arms and ammunition. Enough Massachusetts citizen-soldiers had turned out to deter a major counteroffensive by the British. However, the first year of the war caught Americans in the contradiction of committing themselves more deeply to a full-scale war, while maintaining that they were only fighting for the restoration of their rights as Englishmen.

When the opening hostilities did not produce reconciliation with Britain, American leaders had to prepare for a long-term struggle. In the fall of 1775, Congress approved a plan for a "Continental Army" that would constitute a stable and truly national military. The decision was made to recruit men for one year of duty, a compromise between Washington's desire for professional troops and public resistance to a standing army. Year-round soldiering was not part of traditional colonial military experience, and long enlistments hindered recruiting. American mobilization survived the rotation of troops because local militia companies turned out to fill the gaps while regiments were being reformed.

The first year of the Revolution provided a stark contrast between citizen-soldiers and professional European troops, as raw American recruits had to learn military skills and regulations in the field. This accounts in part for the unpredictable performance of American troops, but over time, as soldiers rotated in and out of service, the pool of experienced manpower grew. General Washington celebrated the survival of the colonial army at the end of its first year: "To maintain a post within musket shot of the Enemy for six months together, without powder, and at the same time to disband one Army and recruit another within that distance of twenty odd British regiments is more than probably ever was attempted" (Fitzpatrick, vol. 4, 1970, p. 208).

In the second year of fighting, the war was transformed from a fight to preserve the traditional rights of Englishmen to a war for political independence from Britain, and Massachusetts mobilization developed the procedures it would employ for the rest of the war. Mobilization began with Continental Congress requisitions to the state for troops and materials. State officials divided the quotas for recruits according to county populations, and then spread the quota among the towns, where the ultimate responsibility fell for maintaining the stream of recruits. Town records show improvised and modified incentives for each call for troops, as wary Yankees negotiated the best possible contract for their military services. Towns tailored their contracts to the changing marketplace for manpower, offering the most for longer term Continental enlistments and less for short-term militia calls. The bounties were reduced for service in New England and increased for out-of-state postings.

RECRUITMENT, ENLISTMENT, AND THE DRAFT

When sufficient recruits were not forthcoming, Massachusetts employed drafts, but in the Revolution a draft had a different meaning than it does in modern America. The modern draft brings the full power of the federal government to bear directly upon individuals, whereas recruiting in the Revolution left it to the towns to best determine how to raise troops. There was considerable room for negotiation in the context of local government. Not everyone was expected to serve personally, but everyone had a civic obligation to help the town meet its quotas.

The first "draft" in Massachusetts took place on 11 July 1776, the last in March 1782. Towns divided the taxpayer list or the militia roll into "classes" or small groups of from eight or ten up to twenty individuals. Each "class" would then be responsible for producing one enlistee. Individuals in the class often pooled their resources to sweeten the official state or national bounties to entice a recruit. Failure to comply invited penalties that included fines, but in Massachusetts, social pressure was more important and effective than any coercive power, because the drafts were conducted by local officials dealing with their neighbors. In fact, social pressure was the only really effective leverage available, because fines were not easily collected. General Charles Lee once said that Americans would only fight if they wanted to; they could not be forcibly marched off to war.

The absence of coercive power to enforce conscription meant that the transitions of army personnel were unnerving to the officers who contended with a professional British opponent. Each year, after negotiations, Massachusetts men turned out to fill the ranks, but people generally felt that the military obligation ought to be widely shared among all of the able-bodied men. Despite a degree of uncertainty, the continued flow of recruits demonstrates that the recruiting processes, though decentralized and market-based, remained reasonably effective. Civil authorities in Massachusetts towns maintained sufficient credibility and popular support to sustain the flow of men and materials to the army. When recruiting was slow, the militia could be called to fill the shortfalls that typically occurred during the winter months, when regular enlistments expired and new recruits were forming replacement regiments.

In the second year of fighting, Washington pressed for longer enlistments to build a professional army capable of standing up to the British regulars. However, Americans were suspicious of establishing a professional army. They worried about the expense of a standing army, and popular republican rhetoric touted the superiority of the American citizen-soldier over European mercenaries. Despite these reservations, in late 1776 Congress called for a new establishment of eighty-eight battalions (regiments) to serve for three years or "during the war." The task remained to win over the sentiments of potential recruits. In the early months of 1777, the American army sent many junior officers like Lieutenant Henry Sewall to their home towns across Massachusetts to enroll recruits for the new three-year terms in the Continental army. In support of Congress, the Massachusetts General Court issued a resolve "demanding 1/7 part of the Militia to engage for 3 Years in the Continental Service." This call for troops was read in meeting houses across the state, but young men accustomed to the militia tradition of short term engagements were leery of the new call for multi-year tours of duty. To meet the new quotas, many towns ordered a draft. The minutes of a town meeting in Northampton in April 1777 illustrate the process:

> The Town then voted that the Officers of the several Companies of the Militia within this Town should be directed to ascertain the number of men that are still wanting in their respective companies and [divide] them in so many classes as there are men wanting . . . and enjoin it upon each of those Classes to procure one good effective man to engage in the Continental Service. (Holbrook, microfiche 138, nos. 24, 72)

Draftees would be paid the thirty pounds bounty by the town committee.

Even as Washington slowly built a national army, the Massachusetts militia continued to play a critical role. The British surrender at Saratoga in 1777 was arguably one of the war's most pivotal moments, and it was accomplished by an American army reinforced by a large number of militia from Massachusetts. In addition to vigorous militia recruiting, Massachusetts mobilization produced robust levels of recruits for the Continental lines and state regiments. Throughout a steady barrage of calls for recruits and materials in 1777, Massachusetts produced increasing numbers of troops serving for longer terms than before, and the cumulative effect of that upswing carried forward into subsequent years.

THE REVOLUTION, LATER YEARS

In 1778 and 1779 Massachusetts mobilization produced recruits in an uneven stream to the Continental Army, while simultaneously providing state militia to the Rhode Island campaign and the Penobscot Expedition. Meeting the quotas of 1778–1779 required almost continual recruiting in Massachusetts. Requisitions came at a rate of two, three, or four per month, and Massachusetts towns faced increasing difficulty meeting their quotas as the pool of men who had not already served grew ever smaller. Participation rates gradually diminished as the main British threats moved southward in 1779, and the main theaters of operation became more remote from Massachusetts.

The ongoing calls for troops were matched by continuous calls for shoes, blankets, beef, and all manner of things that are the lifeline of an army in the field. Massachusetts found it increasingly difficult to meet the calls for supplies as the wartime economy deteriorated. In Plymouth and Salem, the fishing and merchant vessels lay perishing at the wharves, according to observers, and the men went off to the army or aboard privateers, leaving the local economy and their families in dire straits. Nonetheless, Massachusetts towns repeatedly agreed to fulfill requisitions for the army and to subsidize soldiers' families at home.

During 1780s about half of the Massachusetts soldiers that had been mobilized were serving on active duty with the Continental Army in New York, the remainder in New England. They engaged in constant, small-scale fighting along the coast from New Jersey to Maine. In response to a Congressional request, Massachusetts called for 4,240 recruits to fill Continental vacancies in December 1780. This act authorized towns to classify their inhabitants and increased fines for shortages to £128 per man. The turn-out was slow, but steady. Even after the American victory at Yorktown, the British still had two large armies in the field, at New York and in the South, and troop requisitions continued. Massachusetts was called to provide 1,500 Continental recruits on 1 March 1782. Bounties were increased, but deflation exacerbated a difficult situation. Active-duty pay had become nearly worthless. Depreciation so reduced the value of the currency that the town of Beverly offered a recruiting bounty consisting of a hundred pounds of beef, coffee, and sugar, ten bushels of corn, and fifty pounds of cotton.

SOCIAL AND ECONOMIC FACTORS

In the final analysis, the decentralized character of patriot organization was less efficient than the imperial bureaucracy, but the effectiveness of the Massachusetts mobilization lay in the fact that decisions to support the war were ultimately made locally. Younger men took the brunt of service in later years, as families adjusted to the necessity of long term service. Recruits who lived in regions with the worst economic disruption, like Salem, turned to the Continental army to make a living. African Americans and Native Americans strengthened their claims to freedom and citizenship through military service.

Mobilization tapped young men seeking excitement, those with ambition, and others who were attracted by the incentives and promise of army pay during a period of economic disruption. Some rural debtors saw the war as a chance to redistribute power in a legal system that seemed to privilege merchants and bankers. But the strength of the Massachusetts mobilization derived from the sense of Massachusetts soldiers that they had "Something more at Stake than fighting for six Pence per Day." Many were stirred by the rhetoric of liberty, which warned that they must fight or become "hewers of wood and drawers of water to British lords and bishops." Washington never assembled a professional army in parity with that of the British empire, but he was successful, nonetheless, and his success was due, in part, to the fact that Massachusetts primarily mobilized the sons of the Yankee farmers, seamen, and merchants who served as citizens, not as hired mercenaries. In a sense, the successes and shortcomings of the mobilization in Massachusetts amounted to an ongoing popular referendum on the war itself.

The Massachusetts mobilization tapped recruits from across the social spectrum of their communities. A large proportion of them had strong social and economic ties to their communities, through marriage, kinship, and economic stakes in their towns. There were complaints of inferior quality troops, like those voiced by General "Mad Anthony" Wayne, who remonstrated that one-third of his troops were "Negroes, Indians, and Children," but empirical evidence indicates that most Massachusetts soldiers who mobilized were yeoman farmers or their sons. The patterns of enlistments among Massachusetts soldiers in Continental, state, and local militia suggest that the multi-tiered mobilization system of local militia, state regiments, and the Continental army was suited to Massachusetts. Soldiers served at different times in different units—local, state, or Continental—depending on circumstances in their own lives and in the fortunes of the war. Mobilization was most successful with limited-term enlistments, in the militia tradition, and with the wide distribution of the obligations of military service among the adult male population.

AFTER THE WAR

As the war wound down in 1783, the new United States set a precedent that would last until World War II, that is, as soon as the fighting was over, the army was dismantled. Besides the deep-rooted suspicion of standing armies, the economic demands of maintaining an army had become almost unbearable during the latter years of the war. As early as March 1780, Massachusetts General William Heath reported that the people in the western counties were overwrought by taxes and were calling conventions, reminiscent of those of 1774, to discuss how to attack the problem.

While the state's war debt and currency policies were the underlying causes of irritation, western Massachusetts farmers felt that the burden fell disproportionately upon them. The discontinuance of wartime paper money meant taxes and debts had to be paid in sterling currency while prices were falling for farm commodities. However, the problem was exacerbated by the fact that farmers had benefited from high commodity prices during the war and had taken on imprudent levels of debt. Battles between farmers and tax collectors became common, and servicing debts during a period of deflation was nearly impossible. The first explosion came in February 1782, when a Hampshire County convention determined to close the county court in order to end foreclosure proceedings. Samuel Adams went out to Hampshire in the summer of 1782 in an unsuccessful attempt to quiet the protests. More than sixty Hampshire County soldiers turned out in June 1782, not on alarm to meet the British, but to defend the new state government against irate citizens, pitting veterans against veterans who felt

the government was not considering their interests. The protesters were dispersed, but the underlying problems were not resolved. Within a few years, Continental Army veteran Captain Daniel Shays came out of the hills to lead a larger insurrection of disgruntled farmers. This event so unsettled the Massachusetts elite that they joined the call for a constitutional convention in 1787.

SEE ALSO *Bounties (Commercial); Continental Army Draft; Massachusetts Provincial Congress; Minutemen; Sons of Liberty.*

BIBLIOGRAPHY

Bailyn, Bernard. *The Ideological Origins of the American Revolution.* Enlarged edition. Cambridge, Mass. and London: Belknap Press, 1992.

Baller, Bill. "Kinship and Culture in the Mobilization of Colonial Massachusetts." *Historian* 57, no. 2 (1995): 291–302.

Brown, Richard D. *Revolutionary Politics in Massachusetts: The Boston Committee of Correspondence and the Towns, 1772–1774.* New York: Norton, 1976.

Carter, Clarence Edwin, ed. *The Correspondence of General Thomas Gage.* Hamden, Conn.: Archon Books, 1969.

Commonwealth of Massachusetts, *The Journals of the Provincial Congress of Massachusetts in 1774 and 1775, and of the Committee of Safety, with an Appendix.* William Lincoln, supervisor. Boston: Dutton and Wentworth, 1838.

Dexter, Franklin B. ed. *The Literary Diary of Ezra Stiles, D.D., LL.D.* 3 Vols. New York: C. Scribner's Sons, 1901.

Fitzpatrick, John C., ed. *The Writings of George Washington from the Original Manuscript Sources 1745–1799.* 39 vols. Prepared under the direction of the United States George Washington Bicentennial Commission and published by authority of Congress. Westport, Conn.: Greenwood Press, 1970.

French, Allen. *The First Year of the American Revolution.* Boston: Houghton Mifflin Company, 1934.

Holbrook, Jay Mack. *Massachusetts Vital Records: Northampton, 1654–1893.* Microfiche 138, #34, 72. Oxford, Mass.: Holbrook Research Institute, 1994.

Maier, Pauline. *American Scripture: Making the Declaration of Independence.* New York: Random House, 1997.

Norton, Mary Beth. *Liberty's Daughters: The Revolutionary Experience of American Women, 1750–1800.* Harper Collins Publishers, 1980.

Peckham, Howard H. *The Toll of Independence: Engagements and Battle Casualties of the American Revolution.* Chicago: University of Chicago Press, 1974.

Royster, Charles. *A Revolutionary People at War: The Continental Army and American Character, 1775–1783.* Chapel Hill, N.C.: University of North Carolina Press, 1979.

Shy, John. *A People Numerous and Armed: Reflections of the Military Struggle for American Independence,* Rev. edition. Ann Arbor, Mich.: University of Michigan Press, 1990.

Tagney, Ronald. *The World Turned Upside Down: Essex County During America's Turbulent Years, 1763–1790.* West Newbury, Mass.: Essex County History, 1989.

Taylor, Robert J. *Western Massachusetts in the Revolution.* Providence: Brown University Press, 1954.

Walter L. Sargent

Nicolson, Colin. *The "Infamas Govener" Francis Bernard and the Origins of the American Revolution.* Boston, Mass.: Northeastern University Press, 2001.

revised by Harold E. Selesky

MASSACHUSETTS CIRCULAR LETTER.

11 February 1768. To inform the other twelve colonies of the steps taken by the Massachusetts General Court to oppose the Townshend Revenue Act, this letter, drafted by James Otis and Samuel Adams, was approved on 11 February 1768 and sent to the speakers of the assemblies in the other British colonies in North America. It denounced the act as "taxation without representation," reasserted that Americans could never be represented in Parliament, attacked British moves to make colonial governors and judges independent of colonial assemblies, and invited proposals for concerted resistance.

Governor Francis Bernard dissolved the Massachusetts General Court on 4 March 1768 on the grounds that the circular letter was seditious. Before other colonial governors received a message from the earl of Hillsborough, (the new secretary of state for the American colonies), dated 21 April, asking them to prevent their assemblies from endorsing the letter, Virginia (14 April), New Jersey (6 May), and Connecticut (10 June) had already voted to support the Massachusetts position. After Hillsborough's letter arrived, eight more colonies joined in questioning the right of Parliament to levy taxes of any kind in the colonies. The New York assembly, the last to act, adopted in December a resolution urging the repeal of the Townshend Act.

Meanwhile, Adams, Otis, and Joseph Hawley led the majority in the Massachusetts House of Representatives that on 30 June 1768 voted ninety-two to seventeen against rescinding the letter. "The Massachusetts 92" became, like issue No. 45 of John Wilkes's *North Briton*, an emblem of resistance to tyrannical government. Governor Bernard dissolved the new General Court on 1 July. The seventeen "Rescinders" were publicly vilified and physically intimidated by the Sons of Liberty, and five lost their seats in the election of May 1769.

SEE ALSO *Adams, Samuel; Otis, James; Taxation without Representation Is Tyranny; Taxation, External and Internal; Wilkes, John.*

BIBLIOGRAPHY
Knollenberg, Bernhard. *Growth of the American Revolution, 1766–1775.* Edited by Bernard W. Sheehan. Indianapolis, Ind.: Liberty Fund, 2003.

MASSACHUSETTS LINE.

Massachusetts furnished more regiments to the Continental Army than any other state, and the story of its line is the most complex. Although the Provincial Congress was in the process of planning a "Constitutional Army" to keep watch over the royal forces in Boston in early 1775, the fighting at Lexington and Concord caught it by surprise. Minutemen and militia had already set up siege lines around the port by the time that the Committee of Safety began to take charge, on 21 April 1775. The Committee voted to enlist 8,000 of those men and organize them into regiments subject to approval when the Provincial Congress reassembled. Two months later, on 14 June, when the Continental Congress adopted the existing forces as the Continental army, the colony still was unable to give precise information on exactly what units existed and how many men they contained. As it turned out, they had created twenty-three infantry regiments and one of artillery. These carried the names of their colonels. Massachusetts also furnished Henry Knox's Artillery Regiment and the First Continental Artillery, neither of which were part of the Massachusetts Line.

On 1 January 1776 the reorganized and reenlisted infantrymen became Sixteen of the numbered Continental Regiments: 3d, 4th, 6th, 7th, 12th, 13th, 14th, 15th, 16th, 18th, 21st, 23d, 24th, 25th, 26th, and 27th. The 1777 quota established by the Continental Congress dropped to fifteen regiments, mostly by consolidating and reorganizing existing units. The old Twelfth and Fourteenth Regiments disbanded and four new units were formed, again drawing heavily on veterans. In marked contrast to the other states, the Massachusetts units did not take numbers until 1 August 1779, as the army attempted to sort out competing claims to seniority. The quota fell to ten regiments in 1781, to eight on 1 January 1783, and to four on 15 June of that year, when the men who had enlisted for the duration of the war were sent home on furlough. On 3 November 1783 the entire infantry contingent of the Continental Army dropped to the 500 Massachusetts men of Jackson's Continental Regiment in garrison at West Point. That unit went home on 20 June 1784.

Because Boston had been under British occupation when Massachusetts raised its forces in 1775 and 1776, its population had not been given the responsibility for forming any units. Individuals who had escaped from the city served, but only as individuals. When the 1777 reorganization took place, the absence of existing Boston units meant that it was again omitted. But since the city was now free and had made substantial progress in its recovery, General George Washington remedied the omission by allocating three additional Continental Regiments to Massachusetts officers, with the expectation that they would concentrate their recruiting efforts in Boston. Henley's, Henry Jackson's and Lee's had trouble reaching full strength, forming only five, seven, and six companies respectively. They formed a provisional group which joined the main army in 1777, leaving recruiters behind. Late in October the provisional formation broke up and its troops were assigned to Jackson's and Lee's units, while the men still in Boston became Henley's. On 9 April 1779 Washington amalgamated the three units under Jackson. On 24 July 1780 the state adopted Jackson's unit and it joined the line as the Sixteenth Massachusetts Regiment.

SEE ALSO *Knox's "Noble Train of Artillery"*; *Minutemen.*

BIBLIOGRAPHY

Billias, George Athan. *General John Glover and His Marblehead Mariners.* New York: Holt, Rinehart and Winston, 1960.

Egleston, Thomas. *The Life of John Paterson: Major-General in the Revolutionary Army.* 2d ed. New York: G. P. Putnam's Sons, 1898.

Gilbert, Benjamin. *Winding Down: The Revolutionary War Letters of Lieutenant Benjamin Gilbert of Massachusetts, 1780–1783.* Edited by John Shy. Ann Arbor, Mich.: University of Michigan Press, 1989.

Goold, Nathan. *History of Colonel Edmund Phinney's 31st Regiment of Foot Eight Months's Service Men.* Portland, Me.: Thurston Print, 1896.

———. *History of Colonel Edmund Phinney's 18th Continental Regiment Twelve Months' Service in 1776 with Complete Muster Rolls of the Companies.* Portland, Me.: Thurston Print, 1898.

———. *Colonel James Scamman's 30th Regiment of Foot 1775; Also Captain Johnson Moulton's Company.* Portland, Me.: Thurston Print, 1900.

Hall, Charles W., ed. *Regiments and Armories of Massachusetts; An Historical Narration of the Massachusetts Volunteer Militia, with Portraits and Biographies of Officers Past and Present.* 2 vols. Boston: W. W. Potter Co., 1899–1901.

Henshaw, William. *The Orderly Book of Colonel William Henshaw, of the American Army, April 20–September 26, 1775.* Boston: A. Williams, 1881. [Originally published in *Proceedings of the Massachusetts Historical Society* 15 (October 1876): 75–160.]

———. *The Orderly Books of Colonel William Henshaw, October 1, 1775, through October 3, 1776, reprinted from the Proceedings for April, 1947.* Worcester, Mass.: American Antiquarian Society, 1948.

Lincoln, Rufus. *The Papers of Captain Rufus Lincoln of Wareham, Mass.* Edited by James Minor Lincoln. N.P.: Privately printed, 1904.

Lovell, Albert A. *Worcester in the War of the Revolution: Embracing the Acts of the Town from 1765 to 1783 Inclusive.* Worcester, Mass.: Tyler & Seagrove, 1876.

Massachusetts Secretary of the Commonwealth. *Massachusetts Soldiers and Sailors of the Revolutionary War; A Compilation from the Archives.* 17 vols. Boston: Wright & Potter, 1896.

Sherman, Sylvia J., ed. *Dubros Times: Selected Depositions of Maine Revolutionary War Veterans.* Augusta, Me.: Maine State Archives, 1975.

Tagney, Ronald N. *The World Turned Upside Down: Essex County During America's Turbulent Years, 1763–1790.* West Newbury: Essex County History, 1987.

Vose, Joseph. *Journal of Lieutenant-Colonel Joseph Vose April–July 1776.* Edited by Henry Winchester Cunningham. Cambridge, Mass.: John Wilson and Son, 1905.

Robert K. Wright Jr.

MASSACHUSETTS PROVINCIAL CONGRESS.

1774. The Massachusetts Government Act of 20 May 1774 virtually annulled the Massachusetts Charter of 1692. It stripped the General Assembly (the lower house of the General Court) of its charter right to elect the Council (the upper house) and prescribed that, effective 1 August, members of the Council would be appointed by the king and hold office at his pleasure. In accordance with the king's orders, Major General Thomas Gage (the royal governor of Massachusetts as well as the British commander in chief in North America) moved the seat of the Massachusetts government to Salem, where on 17 June the Assembly met under protest against its removal from Boston. After locking the door to prevent Gage's order to dissolve the legislature from taking effect, the Assembly proposed that a congress of delegates from all the continental North American colonies be held at Philadelphia in early September 1774 to concert a collective response to these violations of self-government. The Assembly promptly elected five delegates to represent Massachusetts.

A few weeks later Gage appointed thirty-six members to the Governor's Council, the so-called mandamus councillors because they were appointed by a writ of mandamus. Eleven immediately declined to serve, and the others came under such public pressure that they were forced to take refuge in Boston. On 1 September, the same day he sent 250 soldiers to seize government gunpowder from the Cambridge powder house, Gage called for the Council and General Assembly to meet together in a General Court at Salem on 5 October. Dismayed by the enormous turnout of armed citizens who responded to his seizure of the powder, and unable in the subsequent days to find a means to quiet the province, Gage on 28 September withdrew the summons because he realized that his fugitive councillors would not be permitted to attend. Opponents of the Government Act chose to assume that Gage had no right to cancel his call for the Assembly to meet, so a majority of towns around the colony elected delegates to that body, who were seated at Salem on the announced date, 5 October. Gage made it a point not to appear, and after two days the delegates adjourned to Concord, where on 11 October they organized themselves into a provincial congress and elected John Hancock as president of this extralegal body. The Provincial Congress thereafter operated as the government of all Massachusetts outside British-controlled Boston.

SEE ALSO *Gage, Thomas; Mandamus Councillors.*

BIBLIOGRAPHY

Alden, John R. *General Gage in America: Being Principally a History of His Role in the American Revolution.* Baton Rouge: Louisiana State University Press, 1948.

Wroth, L. Kinvin, et al., eds. *Province in Rebellion: A Documentary History of the Founding of the Commonwealth of Massachusetts, 1774–1775.* Cambridge, Mass.: Harvard University Press, 1975.

revised by Harold E. Selesky

MASSACRES AND "MASSACRES."

SEE *Boston Massacre; Cherry Valley Massacre, New York; Gnadenhutten Massacre, Ohio; Haw River; Little Egg Harbor, New Jersey; Logan; Paoli, Pennsylvania; Paxton Boys; Tappan Massacre, New Jersey; Waxhaws, South Carolina; Wyoming Valley Massacre, Pennsylvania.*

MATHEW, EDWARD. (1729–1805). British general. He entered the Coldstream Guards (Second Foot Guards) as an ensign in 1746 and in 1775 rose to colonel and aide-de-camp to George III. He went to North America as a brigadier general in 1776 and led a brigade of guards at Kips Bay on Manhattan on 15 September. At the taking of Fort Washington he led the two light infantry battalions that secured a foothold for Cornwallis's troops below Laurel Hill. He was promoted major general in America in 1778 and on the general establishment in 1779. In May of that year he made a dramatically successful raid on the Virginia coast with Admiral George Collier. In 1780 he led a brigade during Knyphausen's Springfield raid and commanded the turning movement across Vauxhall Bridge on 23 June. He returned to Britain later in the year and became commander in chief in the West Indies in November. He rose to full general in 1797.

SEE ALSO *Collier, George; Fort Washington, New York; Kips Bay, New York; Springfield, New Jersey, Raid of Knyphausen.*

BIBLIOGRAPHY

Mackesy, Piers. *The War for America, 1775–1783.* London: Longman, 1964.

revised by John Oliphant

MATHEWS, GEORGE. (1739–1812). Continental officer, postwar governor of Georgia. Virginia and Georgia. Born in Augusta County, Virginia, George Mathews was the son of an Irish immigrant. He led a volunteer company against the Indians when he was twenty-two, and took part in the battle at Point Pleasant (in what is now West Virginia) on 10 October 1774. He became a lieutenant colonel of the Ninth Virginia Regiment on 4 March 1776, and was promoted to colonel on 10 February 1777. With this unit he fought at the Brandywine, and led the regiment in a deep penetration at Germantown, Pennsylvania, on 4 October 1777, where he and most of the Ninth Virginians were surrounded and captured. Mathews is said to have received nine bayonet wounds. After spending several months on a prison ship in New York Harbor, he was exchanged on 5 December 1781. On his release he joined Nathanael Greene's army in the south as a colonel in the Third Virginia Regiment led by Abraham Buford. He was breveted as a brigadier general on 30 September 1782.

By 1785 Mathews had moved his family to Georgia. He became a brigadier general of the militia, was elected governor in 1787, represented the state in Congress from 1789 to 1791, and again served as governor from 1793 to 1796. During the latter period he opposed the trans-Oconee adventures of Elijah Clarke and signed the notorious Yazoo Act, which authorized the sale of millions of acres of Georgia land to land speculating companies for ridiculously low prices. In 1798 President Adams nominated him as the first governor of the Mississippi Territory, but within a month his name was withdrawn because of dubious new land speculations and for suspected complicity in the Blount conspiracy, which sought to help British interests gain a foothold in Spanish-held territory in what is now Louisiana.

Mathews then became involved in highly questionable activities whose aim was to draw the then Spanish-held territories of east and west Florida into the United States. His technique was ahead of the times—he sought first to stir up an insurrection of the English-speaking element, then to support these insurrectionists with recruits from Georgia, and finally to bring in "volunteers" from U.S. regular army units. Although the local military commander put a stop to that last part of the plan, the "insurgents" nonetheless rose up and, on 17 March 1812, they declared their independence of Spain. With the insurgents and Georgia volunteers, Mathews took formal possession of Fernandina on 18 March in the name of the United States, and by June was within sight of St. Augustine. Secretary of State James Monroe finally stepped in to repudiate Mathews and bring his adventure to a halt. Mathews was on his way to defend himself before the federal government when he died at Augusta, Georgia, in 1812.

SEE ALSO *Dunmore's (or Cresap's) War; Germantown, Pennsylvania, Battle of; Southern Campaigns of Nathanael Greene.*

BIBLIOGRAPHY

Cusick, James G. *The Other War of 1812: The Patriot War and the American Invasion of Spanish East Florida.* Gainesville, Fla.: University Press of Florida, 2003.

Lamplugh, George R. *Politics on the Periphery: Factions and Parties in Georgia, 1783–1806.* Newark, N.J.: University of Delaware Press, 1986.

Magrath, C. Peter. *Yazoo: Law and Politics in the New Republic: Case of Fletcher v. Peck.* Providence, R.I.: Brown University Press, 1966.

revised by Leslie Hall

MATROSS.
A soldier who assists artillery gunners in loading, firing, sponging, and moving the guns.

Mark M. Boatner

MATSON'S FORD, PENNSYLVANIA.
11 December 1777. After Howe's sortie toward Whitemarsh from 5 to 8 December, Cornwallis was sent from Philadelphia with thirty-five hundred men and almost all the dragoons and mounted jägers to forage along the south bank of the Schuylkill. He left the night of 10–11 December—at 3 A.M., according to André. By coincidence, Washington started from Whitemarsh toward Valley Forge winter quarters on the 11th, and his leading elements clashed with the foragers at the Gulph, near Matson's Ford (modern West Conshohocken, Pennsylvania) just after crossing the Schuylkill. The

American vanguard withdrew, destroying its makeshift bridge of wagons and planks. The raiders returned to Philadelphia the evening of the 12th with two thousand sheep and cattle (Baurmeister, *Journals,* p. 139). Washington's army stayed on the north bank through the 13th, remained in the vicinity of the Gulph until the 19th, and then moved to Valley Forge.

SEE ALSO *Whitemarsh, Pennsylvania.*

BIBLIOGRAPHY

Baurmeister, Carl Leopold. *Revolution in America: Confidential Letters and Journals, 1776–1784.* New Brunswick, N.J.: Rutgers University Press, 1957.

Freeman, Douglass Southall. *George Washington.* 7 vols. New York: Scribner, 1948–1957.

Mark M. Boatner

MAWHOOD, CHARLES.
(?–1780). British officer. Cornet in the First Dragoons from 13 August 1752 and lieutenant from 8 November 1756, he became captain-lieutenant in the Fifteenth Light Dragoons on 20 March 1759, captain in the Eighteenth Light Dragoons on 6 December 1759, major in the Third Foot (Buffs) on 17 May 1763, and lieutenant of the Nineteenth Foot on 17 June 1767. On 26 October 1775 he became lieutenant colonel of the Seventeenth Foot, a unit that had been sent to America prior to August of that year (Fortescue, vol. 3, p. 173 n.). He led British forces at Princeton on 3 January 1777, Quinton's Bridge on 18 March 1778, and Hancock's Bridge on 21 March 1778. Having been appointed colonel of the Seventy-second Regiment (Manchester Volunteers) on 16 December 1777, he died on 29 August 1780, shortly after joining his regiment at Gibraltar.

SEE ALSO *Hancock's Bridge, New Jersey; Princeton, New Jersey; Quinton's Bridge, New Jersey.*

BIBLIOGRAPHY

Fortescue, Sir John W., ed. *A History of the British Army.* 13 vols. London: Macmillan, 1899–1930.

Mark M. Boatner

MAXWELL, WILLIAM.
(1733–1793). Continental general. Ireland-New Jersey. Coming to America with his Scots-Irish parents around 1747, Maxwell received a very ordinary education as a farm boy

in what became Warren County. At the age of twenty-five, during the French and Indian War, he became an ensign in Colonel John Johnston's New Jersey Regiment and subsequently a lieutenant in the New Jersey Regiment of Colonel Peter Schuyler. On 8 July 1758 he and his fellow New Jersey Blues were ensconced in the rear guard of General James Abercromby's expeditionary force in its futile, bloody assault on Fort Ticonderoga.

Leaving the army in 1760, Maxwell entered British military service as a civilian post commissary and was stationed at frontier forts of New York and the Great Lakes area, ranging from Schenectady to Detroit. From 1766 to 1773 Maxwell dispensed provisions for two companies of the Royal (Sixtieth) American Regiment at Fort Michimackinac. Maxwell managed to hold his own among the rough-hewn, carefree troops at Michimackinac. When most of the Sixtieth was transferred to the West Indies, Maxwell returned to New Jersey to work his parents' farm. He soon became a leader in the Revolutionary movement.

"Scotch Willie" was a tall, ruddy-faced, stalwart man who spoke with a Scottish brogue. He was a member of the New Jersey Provincial Congresses of May and October 1775 and in August of that year became chairman of the Sussex county committee of safety. On 8 November he was commissioned colonel and raised the Second New Jersey Regiment. In February 1776 he marched north with five full companies and joined the American force invading Canada just as it began its retreat. He had charge of the rear guard of American troops as it skirmished with the enemy. Maxwell commanded his regiment in the disaster at Trois Rivières on 8 June and was one of those who, the next month, opposed abandonment of Crown Point. He complained to Congress when Arthur St. Clair was promoted ahead of him on 9 August. On 23 October he was appointed brigadier general. He returned to his home state about the time that the British turned to chase Washington's army across the Delaware. Maxwell had the assignment of clearing boats from the Delaware River so that the British could not use them. In command of four new regiments of New Jersey Continentals, on 21 December, Maxwell was sent by Washington to take charge of the militia at Morristown. A few days later, after the American success at Trenton, Maxwell got Washington's appeal for a diversionary effort against the British flank to speed the enemy's withdrawal from New Jersey, but he was not able to accomplish anything worthwhile.

Maxwell became the first commander of the light infantry corps, which was initially formed to oppose the advance of the enemy on Philadelphia. His troops bravely engaged the British van on 3 September 1777 at Cooch's Bridge (Iron Hill). At the Battle of Brandywine on 11 September 1777, Maxwell's light infantry harassed lead units of the British army as he and his men conducted a retrograde movement back across the Brandywine.

A principal critic of Maxwell at this time was one of the light infantrymen, Major William Heth, a veteran of Morgan's Rifles, who wrote his former commander on 2 October that since the enemy's landing at Head of Elk, "Maxwell's Corps 'twas expected would do great things—we had opportunities—and any body but an old-woman, would have availd themselves of them—He is to be sure—a Damnd bitch of a General."

At the Battle of Germantown on 4 October 1777, the New Jersey Continentals suffered heavy casualties as they unsuccessfully stormed the Benjamin Chew house. After this battle Maxwell stood a court-martial, charged generally with misconduct and excessive drinking. On 4 November he was given what the historian Douglas Freeman has called "something of a Scotch verdict" (Freeman, vol. 4, p. 535). He was not exonerated, but the charges were not proved. During the winter at Valley Forge, Maxwell's brigade comprised the First, Second, Third, and Fourth New Jersey Regiments.

On 7 May 1778 Maxwell was ordered to Mount Holly, New Jersey, as Washington coped with the complex strategic problems preceding the Monmouth campaign. Maxwell figured prominently in the maneuvers that followed and in the Battle of Monmouth on 28 June. He testified at Lee's court-martial that the accused was so out of touch with the tactical situation in the initial phase of the battle that he did not know on which wing Maxwell's brigade was located.

In July 1778 Maxwell guarded the New Jersey coast opposite Staten Island, and he continued with this mission until the next year, when he led his brigade in Sullivan's expedition against the Iroquois. He returned to New Jersey and opposed General Wilhelm Knyphausen's Springfield raid on 7 and 23 June 1780. For reasons unknown, but certainly relating to a cabal of New Jersey officers from the Elizabethtown area, Maxwell was pressured into resigning from the army in July 1780; upon reflection he tried to withdraw his resignation, but Congress accepted it. Maxwell was elected to the New Jersey assembly for one term in 1783. He took over the ownership and management of his parents' farm (just south of Phillipsburg, New Jersey; the farmhouse is extant). Maxwell never married. He died suddenly while visiting the farm of his neighbor, Colonel Charles Stewart.

Maxwell was one of Washington's most reliable generals. Although regarded as a bit of a comical character, he performed brilliantly whenever he was given command responsibility in the field.

SEE ALSO *Lee Court Martial; Monmouth, New Jersey.*

BIBLIOGRAPHY

Freeman, Douglas Southall. *George Washington.* Vols. 4 and 5. New York: Scribner, 1951–1952.

Smith, Justin H. *Our Struggle for the Fourteenth Colony: Canada and the American Revolution.* 2 vols. New York: Putnam's Sons, 1907.

Smith, Samuel S. *The Battle of Brandywine.* Monmouth Beach, N.J.: Philip Freneau Press, 1976.

Ward, Harry M. *General William Maxwell and the New Jersey Continentals.* Westport, Conn.: Greenwood Press, 1997.

revised by Harry M. Ward

MAXWELL'S LIGHT INFANTRY.

Having detached Colonel Daniel Morgan and his Corps of Rangers to the Northern Army to help defeat the white and native American skirmishers supporting Burgoyne's invasion, Washington on 28 August 1777 ordered the creation of a new formation to take its place. He directed that each of his seven brigades detach 9 officers and 108 enlisted men to form an elite corps of light infantry, and two days later placed this 800-man force under the command of Brigadier General William Maxwell of New Jersey. Washington ordered Maxwell to skirmish in front of Sir William Howe's army as it advanced from Head of Elk, Maryland, toward Philadelphia. On 2 September Washington sent Colonel Charles Armand's four-company partisan corps to join the light infantry and ordered Maxwell to?

> Be prepared to give them [the British] as much trouble as you possibly can. You should keep small parties upon every road that you may be sure of the one they take, and always be careful to keep rather upon their left flank, because they cannot in that case cut you off from out main body (Washington, *Papers,* Vol. 11, pp. 127–128).

The light infantry men fought their first action at Cooch's Bridge, Pennsylvania, on 3 September 1777, but ran out of ammunition and, lacking bayonets, were forced to retreat by a British bayonet charge. They were part of Major General Benjamin Lincoln's division at the battle of Brandywine (11 September 1777), initially posted on the enemy side of Brandywine Creek, and then helped to defend Chadd's Ford. They covered the retreat of the main body of Washington's army, collecting stragglers and the wounded. The corps was disbanded on 25 September, and Maxwell resumed command of the New Jersey Brigade. Reconstituted by 28 September, although now with only 450 men, it was held in reserve during the battle of Germantown on 4 October 1777 and was permanently disbanded shortly thereafter. Maxwell was later acquitted by a court-martial of charges brought by a senior subordinate, Lieutenant Colonel William Heth of Virginia, that he had been drunk at Brandywine.

SEE ALSO Brandywine, Pennsylvania; Cooch's Bridge; Light Infantry; Maxwell, William.

BIBLIOGRAPHY
Ward, Harry M. *General William Maxwell and the New Jersey Continentals.* Westport, Conn.: Greenwood Press, 1997.

Washington, George. *The Papers of George Washington, Revolutionary War Series.* Vol. 11: August–September 1777. Edited by Philander D. Chase et al. Charlottesville: University Press of Virginia, 2001.

revised by Harold E. Selesky

McALLISTER, ARCHIBALD. (?–1781).

Continental officer. Maryland. A lieutenant in the Maryland battalion of the Flying Camp in July 1776, he became an ensign in the Second Maryland Continentals on 10 December, was promoted to second lieutenant of the First Maryland on 17 April 1777, and became first lieutenant on 27 May 1778. With Michael Rudolph, he was breveted captain on 24 September 1779 for their "military caution so happily combined with daring activity" at Paulus Hook, in the words of the congressional resolution. He died on 16 January 1781 (The name is also spelled McCallister).

SEE ALSO Flying Camp; Paulus Hook, New Jersey; Rudolph, Michael.

BIBLIOGRAPHY
Heitman, Francis B. *Historical Register of Officers of the Continental Army.* Revised edition. Washington, D.C.: Rare Book Shop Publishing. Co., 1914.

Mark M. Boatner

McARTHUR, ARCHIBALD.

British officer. Promoted to captain of the Fifty-fourth Foot on 1 September 1771 and to major of the Seventy-first Foot on 16 November 1777, he was captured at Cowpens on 17 January 1781. On 24 April 1781 he was made lieutenant of the Third Battalion of the Sixtieth (Royal Americans) (Ford, *British Officers*).

SEE ALSO Cowpens, South Carolina.

Mark M. Boatner

McCREA ATROCITY.

Daughter of a New Jersey Presbyterian minister, Jane McCrea (also known as Jenny) lived with a brother who had settled along the Hudson River about halfway between Saratoga and Fort Edward. She was engaged to Lieutenant David Jones, a Loyalist with Burgoyne's invading army. When her brother moved to Albany in early 1777, McCrea went to Fort Edward with the hope of meeting her fiancé when the invaders arrived. She was taken in as a guest by the elderly Mrs. McNeil, a cousin of British General Simon Fraser. On 27 July 1777 a band of Burgoyne's Indians reached abandoned Fort Edward, two days ahead of the main body of the British army. Taking the two women, they started back to Fort Ann, where the army had its headquarters at the time. They arrived with Mrs. McNeil and a scalp that was promptly identified by Jones as that of his fiancée, Jane McCrea. The most generally accepted version of her death is that she had been shot, scalped, and stripped of her clothing after her drunken captors had gotten into an altercation as to which should be her guard.

Burgoyne was put in a difficult position. If he disciplined the murderer he risked losing his Indian allies; but doing nothing would be condoning the murder. Burgoyne chose to pardon the murderer and deliver a lecture to his allies on the need to show restraint in warfare. The lecture did not go over well, and most of the Indians left Burgoyne's camp.

General Horatio Gates wrote Burgoyne personally, holding him responsible for the murder. Burgoyne wrote back in a lame attempt to defend his pardoning of the murderer as "more efficacious than an execution to prevent similar mischiefs."

The Patriots skillfully exploited this atrocity to whip up popular indignation against the invaders. Ironically, the murder of this Loyalist woman became a very effective recruiting tool for the United States. Washington wrote militia officers throughout New England urging them to turn out to save their own wives and daughters from a fate similar to McCrea's. The story spread with remarkable rapidity. Newspapers in every state published it as a dire warning of the fate that faced all American women if the British won. The first fruit of this propaganda campaign came at Bennington, where an unexpectedly large and effective body of militia turned out and annihilated a detachment from Burgoyne's army. Militiamen continued to gather, and they proved a major factor in the ultimate defeat of Burgoyne. The story of Jenny McCrea's murder, as improved by American propagandists, played a large part in mustering this mushroom army.

SEE ALSO *Propaganda in the American Revolution.*

BIBLIOGRAPHY

Namias, June. *White Captives: Gender and Ethnicity on the American Frontier.* Chapel Hill: University of North Carolina Press, 1993.

revised by Michael Bellesiles

McCULLOCH'S LEAP.

After bringing reinforcements to Wheeling on 1 September 1777, Major Samuel McCulloch (or McColloch) was separated from his men and pursued by Indians. He later claimed to have escaped by riding his horse down an almost vertical, 150-foot precipice to the bank of Wheeling Creek and across the stream to safety. How much of this descent was free fall and how much of it was a perilous slide is uncertain. Although Benson J. Lossing speaks of a "momentous leap," he calls the cliff "almost perpendicular" and says the horse and rider "reached the foot of the bluff" and then "dashed through the creek," making good his escape.

SEE ALSO *Wheeling, West Virginia.*

BIBLIOGRAPHY

Lossing, Benson J. *The Pictorial Fieldbook of the Revolution.* Vol. 2. New York: Harper and Brothers, 1851.

revised by Michael Bellesiles

McDONALD, DONALD.

A major in the British army at the outbreak of the Revolution, this elderly veteran of Culloden saw action at Bunker Hill before being appointed by General Gage to recruit Loyalists in North Carolina. Promoted to brigadier general of militia, he figured prominently in the Loyalist defeat at Moores Creek Bridge, 27 February 1776, was paroled and later exchanged in Philadelphia. Continuing to serve until the end of the Revolution, he died shortly thereafter in London. American accounts generally spell his name as given above, but he himself signed as MacDonald.

SEE ALSO *Moores Creek Bridge.*

revised by Michael Bellesiles

McDONALD, FLORA.

(1722–1790). Jacobite and Tory heroine. As a schoolgirl, Flora McDonald (her name is also often spelled MacDonald) helped Charles Edward Stuart (known in history as "Bonnie

Prince Charlie" and "the Young Pretender") escape to the Isle of Skye in June 1746, after the battle of Culloden. Captured, tried as a traitor to the British Crown, and imprisoned in the Tower of London, MacDonald was eventually released after the story of her exploit aroused national admiration. She even was presented in court, and when George II asked why she had helped an enemy of the kingdom she replied, "It was no more than I would have done for your majesty, had you been in like situation." This simple answer epitomized the "defense" that won her life and freedom.

Four years later, on 6 November 1750, Flora married Allan McDonald (a kinsman). In August 1774 she went with him and their children to join the colony of Highlanders that had settled in North Carolina. Here she did much to rally the Scots to the standard of Donald McDonald, who commanded Loyalist forces at the Battle of Moores Creek. Her husband, who had become a Tory brigadier general, was captured at Moores Creek Bridge on 27 February 1776 and sent to Halifax, Virginia. On his advice, Flora returned to Scotland in 1779, and he followed later. Two of their sons were lost with the French warship, the *Ville de Paris*, on 12 April 1782, when it commander, Francois Joseph Paul Grasse surrendered the ship. Flora is buried on the Isle of Skye.

SEE ALSO *Grasse, François Joseph Paul, Comte de; McDonald, Donald; Moores Creek Bridge.*

BIBLIOGRAPHY

Powell, William S., ed. *Dictionary of North Carolina Biography.* Chapel Hill, N.C.: University of North Carolina Press, 1878–1996.

revised by Robert M. Calhoon

McDOUGALL, ALEXANDER. (1732–

1786). Continental general. Scotland and New York. Born at Islay, of the Inner Hebrides Islands, in 1732, McDougall came to America with his family at the age of six, and they settled in New York City. McDougall commanded two privateers during the Seven Years' War (1756–1763), the *Barrington* and *Tiger*. Having accumulated sufficient capital, he set up a store in New York City, became a successful merchant, and undertook to educate himself. With the Stamp Act of 1765, he emerged as one of the most prominent radical leaders in New York.

In 1769 he wrote under the pseudonym "A Son of Liberty" the popular pamphlet, "To the Betrayed Inhabitants of the City and Colony of New-York." The New York assembly declared this document libelous and ordered McDougall's arrest on 8 February 1770. Refusing to give bail, he was thrown into prison and became famous

as "the John Wilkes of America." (Wilkes was a newspaper publisher in England who was famous for his attacks on the king and the Parliament.) Imprisoned for 162 days, McDougall was never convicted of a crime, and the government finally had to release him. Organizing the opposition to the Tea Act, he presided over the "meeting in the Fields" on 6 July 1774 that proclaimed the people's willingness to resist the Coercive Acts of Parliament. In addition, he served in the provincial congress of 1774–1775.

With the outbreak of the Revolution, McDougall became actively involved in the New York City militia, becoming its commanding colonel. Commissioned colonel of the First New York Regiment on 30 June 1776, he was appointed brigadier general on 9 August, just before the start of the New York campaign. He took part in the battles of White Plains (28 October 1776) and Germantown (4 October 1777), but rendered his most important service in the Hudson Highlands, where he was the commanding general during much of the war. Having been appointed a Continental major general on 20 October 1777, he succeeded Benedict Arnold as commander at West Point in 1780. He represented New York in the Continental Congress of 1781–1782, declined appointment as minister of marines in 1781, was court-martialed in 1782 for insubordination to William Heath and reprimanded, and twice headed delegations of officers to discuss pay problems with Congress, in 1780 and 1782.

McDougall retired from the Continental army on 3 November 1783, as served as state senator (1783–1786) and in Congress (1784–1785). The man who had roused rabbles in his youth grew conservative with age, becoming an ally of Alexander Hamilton and the first president of the Bank of New York. He died in New York City on 9 June 1786.

SEE ALSO *Continental Congress; Fields, Meeting in the.*

BIBLIOGRAPHY

Champagne, Roger J. *Alexander McDougall and the American Revolution in New York.* Schenectady, N.Y.: Union College Press, 1975.

McDougall Papers. New York: New-York Historical Society.

revised by Michael Bellesiles

McGOWN'S PASS, NEW YORK. Mc-

Gown's Pass (also spelled McGowan's Pass) is a defile located at the northeast corner of modern Central Park, where the Post Road ran between two steep hills before winding down a steep grade to Harlem Plains. This terrain feature was one of British General William Howe's objectives after landing at Kips Bay on 15 September 1776.

William Smallwood's First Maryland Regiment, much reduced by losses suffered at the battle of Long Island, was posted in front of the pass that day to stall the British advance. The Marylanders had orders to fall back to the pass and ambush the British there. Instead, the Marylanders inadvertently deflected the British toward a column of Americans escaping up the west side of Manhattan. The pass was held by Lord Hugh Percy when the main British force moved toward White Plains. Here the traitor William Demont entered the British lines, and it was from this position that Percy started his attack on Fort Washington, on 16 November 1776.

SEE ALSO *Demont, William; Kips Bay, New York; Long Island, New York, Battle of.*

revised by Barnet Schecter

McINTOSH, JOHN. (1755–1826). Continental officer. Georgia. A nephew of Lachlan McIntosh and born in McIntosh County, Georgia, John McIntosh was an officer of the Georgia Line in 1775 and on 7 January 1776 became a captain in the First Georgia Regiment. On 1 April 1778 he was promoted to lieutenant colonel and commandant of the Third Georgia Regiment. In his *Historical Register of the Continental Army* (1893), the military historian Francis B. Heitman identifies McIntosh by the nickname "Come and take it," a phrase included in his reply of 25 November 1778 to the demand of Colonel Lewis V. Fuser that McIntosh surrender Fort Morris (Georgia, near Sunbury) with the honors of war. He was not present at the British capture of Sunbury on 9 January 1779, but was taken prisoner at Briar Creek, 3 March 1779, and was exchanged in the fall of 1780 (possibly early September) for John Harris Cruger, who had been captured in June 1780. After returning from captivity, McIntosh served to the end of the war.

Moving to Florida after the war, McIntosh settled on St. Johns River. There he was suddenly arrested by Spanish troops and imprisoned at St. Augustine on suspicion of illegal activities against the government. He then was held for a year in Morro Castle, Havana. After his release, McIntosh is credited with further acts against the Spanish in Florida, including his participation in a successful attack on a fort near Jacksonville, on the shores of the St. John's River. Some historians also suggest that, during the last months of the War of 1812, he was a major general of militia at Mobile, Alabama, but this is not confirmed in Heitman's *Register*.

SEE ALSO *Fort Morris, Georgia; McIntosh, Lachlan.*

BIBLIOGRAPHY

Dederer, John Morgan. *Making Bricks Without Straw: Nathanael Greene's Southern Campaign and Mao Tse-Tung's Mobile War.* Manhattan, Kan.: Sunflower University Press, 1983.

Heitman, Francis B. *Historical Register of Officers of the Continental Army during the War of Revolution, April 1775 to December 1783.* Baltimore: Genealogical Pub. Co.: 1967.

Searcy, Martha Condray. *The Georgia–Florida Contest in the American Revolution, 1776–1778.* Tuscaloosa, Fla.: University of Alabama Press, 1985.

revised by Leslie Hall

McINTOSH, LACHLAN. (1725 or 1727–1806). Continental general. Scotland and Georgia. Born at Inverness, Scotland, Lachlan McIntosh came to Georgia with his parents in 1736, shortly after James Oglethorpe established that colony, and settled at the place later named Darien. Little is known of his life prior to 1775. One historian, Benson Lossing, suggests that his father was taken as a prisoner to St. Augustine when Lachlan was 13 years old. In 1748 Lachlan went to Charleston, South Carolina where he is said to have become a friend of Henry Laurens, a future signer of the Declaration of Independence. It is believed that McIntosh lived in Laurens's home, and and that he became a clerk in Laurens's counting house. Lossing further suggests that, when he returned home from Charleston, he became a surveyor and "was considered the handsomest man in Georgia."

In July 1775 McIntosh appeared in Savannah as a member of the Georgia Provincial Congress. On 7 January 1776 McIntosh became a colonel in a Georgia battalion that later was augmented and incorporated into the Continental army. On 16 September 1776 he was promoted to brigadier general. A pragmatist, McIntosh tried to defend Georgia from its many enemies with his few and ill-supplied troops. In March 1776 he organized the defense of Savannah from British naval vessels, with little support from citizens or civil authority. In August 1776 he raided northern East Florida, breaking up the Loyalist settlements north of St. Johns River, but had to pull back across the Altamaha River in October. Fort McIntosh, the southernmost rebel fort and named for him, surrendered to the British and was burned by them in February 1777. McIntosh's recommendation to Washington that a large force should defend Georgia went unheeded.

McIntosh also requested clarification regarding whether civil or Continental authority held control of the military. While the question went unanswered in the abstract, it was dramatically played out in Georgia.

Beginning in late 1776 and lasting throughout the war, the radical faction, which supported state control over the military, campaigned vigorously to discredit General McIntosh, in part by declaring that he and various family members were Tories. In late 1776 they accused his brother William of conniving with the enemy and forced him to resign his commission. Button Gwinnett, leader of the radical faction, became president of Georgia in March 1777, and arrested another McIntosh brother, George, on suspicion of treason. Neither McIntosh nor Gwinnett would relinquish authority during the subsequent military expedition to invade East Florida, which failed as a result. They fought a duel, and Gwinnett died of his wounds. The radical faction circulated a petition to have McIntosh removed from the state. Prior to any formal action by the assembly, McIntosh was ordered to report to General George Washington for reassignment.

In December 1777 McIntosh joined the army under Washington at Valley Forge and was placed in charge of the North Carolina Brigade. He then inspected military hospitals in Pennsylvania and New Jersey and in May 1778 was placed in command of the Western Department with headquarters at Fort Pitt (now Pittsburg). He established Fort McIntosh and Fort Laurens (both in Ohio), despite encountering factionalism and lack of cooperation. Back in Georgia by July 1779, McIntosh assumed command of both the Continental and militia forces in the state, and radicals launched a renewed effort to discredit him. His wife and children were trapped in Savannah as siege preparations began in September 1779 and his request that all women and children be allowed to leave the town was denied, first by the British and then by the French and rebels.

McIntosh led Benjamin Lincoln's march from Charleston to make contact with Admiral Charles Hector Theodat Estaing, urging the latter to attack promptly (which he did not do), and commanding the First and Fifth South Carolina Regiments, along with some Georgia militia, in the second echelon of the attack. During November 1779, George Walton requested tht the Continental Congress remove McIntosh from command. In February 1780 Congress did so, and McIntosh was informed while he was serving in the defense of Charleston. He became a prisoner of war on 12 May 1780, when Lincoln surrendered Charleston. Hewas released during the summer of 1781 and went to Philadelphia, where the Continental Congress cleared him of all charges in July.

McIntosh returned to Georgia in 1783, "incredibly poor," as he put it. In February 1783 the Georgia assembly declared Walton's 1779 accusations against him to be unjust. This did not inhibit Walton's appointment as Chief Justice of the state, however. McIntosh's son, Captain William McIntosh, publicly horsewhipped Walton after his first session in court. McIntosh was brevetted as a major general in 1784. He never recovered financially from the war and took little part in public life.

SEE ALSO *Fort Laurens, Ohio; Fort McIntosh, Georgia; Gwinnett, Button; Lincoln, Benjamin; McIntosh, John.*

BIBLIOGRAPHY

Carp, E. Wayne. *To Starve the Army at Pleasure: Continental Army Administration and American Political Culture, 1775–1783.* Chapel Hill, N.C.: University of North Carolina Press, 1984.

Jackson, Harvey H. *Lachlan McIntosh and the Politics of Revolutionary Georgia.* Athens, Ga.: University of Georgia Press, 1979.

Lossing, Benson J. *The Pictorial Field Book of the Revolution.* 2 vols. New York: Harper and Brothers, 1860.

Searcy, Martha Condray. *The Georgia-Florida Contest in the American Revolution, 1776–1778.* Tuscaloosa, Ala.: University of Alabama Press, 1985.

revised by Leslie Hall

McKEAN, THOMAS. (1734–1817). Signer.

Delaware and Pennsylvania. Born in Chester County, Pennsylvania, on 19 March 1734, Thomas McKean studied law with his cousin, David Finney, in Delaware, and set up a prosperous practice in Pennsylvania, Delaware, and New Jersey. Living mostly in Delaware until 1773, he served as deputy attorney-general in 1756, clerk of the assembly from 1757 to 1759, and in the assembly from 1762 to 1779. He was speaker of the assembly in both 1772 and 1779. In 1762 he helped Caesar Rodney revise the state assembly laws. Becoming increasingly outspoken against British rule, McKean was one of the more radical members of the Stamp Act Congress of 1765. As justice of the court of common pleas and quarter sessions, he ordered the use of unstamped paper. As speaker of the assembly he led the movement in December 1772 for a colonial congress.

McKean entered the first Continental Congress in 1774 as a delegate from Delaware. In the Second Continental Congress he advocated reconciliation with England until early 1776, then started working for independence, serving on the vital Secret Committee. Although still a member of the Delaware delegation, he was influential in swaying opinion in Pennsylvania toward independence. When his vote for the resolution for independence was tied with that of fellow delegate George Reed, McKean's initiative brought Caesar Rodney, the third Delaware representative, racing back to cast the decisive vote.

Exactly when he became a signer of the Declaration of Independence is uncertain. Returning to Delaware,

McKean led a battalion of Philadelphia Associators (a militia unit) to Perth Amboy to reinforce General George Washington's hard-pressed army on 2 August 1776. He then went to Dover, where he helped frame the first constitution of Delaware. Failing re-election to Congress—he did not sit during the period from December 1776 to January 1778—McKean became speaker of the Delaware Assembly. For two months of 1777 he was acting president of the state. During the period from 1777 to 1799 he also was chief justice of Pennsylvania, but he remained politically active in Delaware and was re-elected to Congress from that state.

On 10 July 1781 he was elected president of Congress, serving in Congress until 1783. In 1787 he sat in the Pennsylvania constitutional ratification convention, where he supported the Constitution. He drew many protests in Pennsylvania from those who felt he should not hold so many important and conflicting political jobs. In 1792 the Federalist foreign policy drove him to the other party, and in 1799 he was elected governor of Pennsylvania as a Jeffersonian. He served three tumultuous terms, being frequently accused of nepotism, constitutional violation, and other abuses of the office. McKean died in Philadelphia on 24 June 1817.

SEE ALSO *Associators.*

BIBLIOGRAPHY

McKean Papers. Philadelphia: Historical Society of Pennsylvania.

Rowe, G. S. *Thomas McKean: The Shaping of an American Republicanism.* Boulder, Colo.: Colorado Associated University Press, 1978.

revised by Michael Bellesiles

McKEE, ALEXANDER. (1735?–1799). Loyalist Indian agent.

Born on the western Pennsylvania frontier, Alexander McKee was the son of fur trader Thomas McKee and a Shawnee mother. He served with British forces during the French and Indian War (1754–1763), acting as a scout during General John Forbes's expedition to the forks of the Ohio River and taking part in James Grant's ill-fated attack against Fort Duquesne in September 1758.

Resigning from the military in 1759, McKee remained at Fort Pitt to act as George Croghan's assistant at the garrison's Indian trading post. In 1766, Sir William Johnson, superintendent of the British Indian Department, named McKee to the post of Indian commissary for Fort Pitt and charged him with the responsibility of regulating the fur trade with tribes throughout the Ohio Valley. In 1769, he married a Shawnee woman living in western Ohio. By the early 1770s his career had brought him land, wealth, and influence both among Native peoples and British officials.

After the beginning of the Revolution, McKee remained in Pittsburgh and discretely aided British interests within the region. Publicly, however, he disavowed his affiliation with the Crown in an attempt to protect his substantial economic assets in the Upper Ohio Valley and to provide a measure of personal protection in what was becoming an increasingly hostile environment. Threatened with arrest, assault, and death by area Patriots in March 1778, he joined Matthew Elliott, Simon Girty, and several others in fleeing Pittsburgh for British-held Detroit.

In June 1778, Henry Hamilton, the British lieutenant governor of Detroit, commissioned McKee as a captain in the British Indian Department. McKee spent the remainder of the conflict cementing the Crown's alliance with the region's Indian nations and participating in raids against Patriot settlements throughout the Ohio Valley. He accompanied Hamilton in an expedition against Vincennes in late 1778. In 1780 he led successful attacks against (Joseph) Martin's and (Isaac) Ruddell's Stations in Kentucky, and in 1781 participated in the defeat of Colonel William Crawford near Upper Sandusky. In 1782 he commanded an expedition against (William) Bryant's Station in Kentucky and defeated Kentucky irregulars at the Battle of Blue Licks. At the war's conclusion, he held a series of councils with the Ohio Country Indian nations, at which he convinced them to accept the terms of the 1783 Treaty of Paris.

Following the war, he remained active in the Indian Department. At the time of his death he held the position of deputy superintendent general and inspector for Indian affairs for Upper and Lower Canada.

SEE ALSO *Indians in the Colonial Wars and the American Revolution.*

BIBLIOGRAPHY

Allen, Robert S. *His Majesty's Indian Allies: British Indian Policy in the Defence of Canada, 1774–1815.* Toronto and Oxford: Dundurn Press, 1992.

Nelson, Larry L. *A Man of Distinction among Them: Alexander McKee and the Ohio Country Frontier, 1754–1799.* Kent, Ohio and London: Kent State University Press, 1999.

Larry L. Nelson

McKINLY, JOHN. (1721–1796). President of Delaware.

Ireland and Delaware. Born in Ireland on 24 February 1721, McKinly moved to Wilmington, Delaware, in the 1740s. He practiced medicine and was active in local civil and militia affairs. He served as sheriff (1757–1759) and was twelve times elected chief burgess of the borough of Wilmington, between 1759 and 1776. In October 1771 he was elected to the colonial assembly, two years later he became a member of the assembly's five-man standing Committee of Correspondence, and he had a part in the major events leading to his state's joining the Continental Association (28 November 1774). He served as chairman of the Committee of Vigilance, and was charged with the enforcement of that Committee's rulings.

In September 1775 he became president of the Delaware Council of Safety and brigadier general of the New Castle County militia. The following year he was elected speaker of the new House of Representatives. In February 1777 McKinly was chosen president and commander in chief of Delaware for a term of three years. When the British occupied Wilmington on the night of 12–13 September 1777, shortly after the battle of Brandywine (11 September), they took McKinly prisoner and evacuated him to Philadelphia after the capture of that city. When the British left Philadelphia, they took him to New York City, where he was paroled in August 1778. Having gone to Philadelphia to get agreement of the Continental Congress, he was exchanged for William Franklin, former Royal governor of New Jersey, and in September he was free to resume his medical practice in Wilmington. McKinly took no further part in public life, refusing his election to the Continental Congress in 1784. He died in Wilmington, Delaware, on 31 August 1796.

SEE ALSO *Brandywine, Pennsylvania.*

BIBLIOGRAPHY

McKinly Papers. Wilmington, Del.: Historical Society of Delaware.

revised by Michael Bellesiles

McLANE, ALLEN.

(1746–1829). Continental Army officer. Delaware. McLane was born in Philadelphia, the son of Allan McLeane, a leather breeches maker who had come to America in 1738 from Scotland. In 1767–1769 young Allen traveled to Europe and visited cousins in Scotland. By 1770 he had settled at Smyrna, Delaware. In July 1775 he changed his name to McLane "to avoid confusion with that renegade Scot serving the Hanoverian King," a reference to Allan MacLean, who had just reached Canada to recruit his Royal Highland Emigrants. His father died about this time, leaving Allan property worth more than fifteen thousand dollars.

After fighting as a volunteer at Great Bridge, Virginia, on 9 December 1775 and at Norfolk on 1 January 1776, McLane served with Washington's army in New York as lieutenant and adjutant of Caesar Rodney's militia regiment. At Long Island on 27 August 1776, he captured a British patrol. After fighting at White Plains on 28 October, he was with the rear guard in the retreat across New Jersey, took part in the attack on Trenton, and was promoted for gallantry at Princeton on 3 January 1777. He was promoted to captain in Colonel John Patton's Additional Continental Regiment in early 1777. After seeing action at Cooch's Bridge and the Brandywine on 3 and 11 September 1777, he was detached to raise in Delaware his own company of about one hundred men, to which task he dedicated his personal fortune.

After serving as advance guard for Washington's main column at Germantown on 4 October 1777, McLane on 7 November was given the mission of screening the army as it prepared to take up winter quarters at Valley Forge. On 3 December he warned Washington of a large-scale sortie from Philadelphia, intelligence that contributed to the Continental Army's successful defense of its concentration around White Marsh a few days later. McLane's company harassed enemy convoys and foraging parties so successfully during the winter that they earned the nickname of "market stoppers." During January and February 1778 his men gathered livestock in Delaware and the Eastern Shore of Maryland to supply Valley Forge and Smallwood's command at Wilmington. Rejoining the main army with 100 to 150 mounted men, he resumed his reconnaissance missions, reinforced on occasion by 50 Oneida Indian scouts. As the Mischianza was breaking up in Philadelphia, around dawn of 19 May, his company, supported by a company of dragoons, brought many a red-eyed redcoat running to repel an "attack" he simulated by galloping along the enemy's outpost line dropping iron pots full of gunpowder and scrap metal. The next night his scouts detected the movement to surprise Lafayette at Barren Hill, a piece of good outpost work that saved a large portion of the army from ambush. On 8 June he himself narrowly escaped an ambush. He may well have been the first American to reenter Philadelphia when the British evacuated the city ten days later. He apparently had an instinctive dislike for Benedict Arnold; soon after Arnold took command in Philadelphia, McLane went to Washington to expose Arnold's profiteering. For his pains he received a rebuke from Washington.

During the Monmouth Campaign of June–July 1778, McLane's company operated with Dickinson's militia, and he claimed to have lost only four men killed in taking more than three hundred stragglers. The company was attached to Henry Lee's new "Partisan Corps" on 13 July 1779. Under Lee's command he had an important role in the events leading up to Wayne's capture of Stony

Point on 16 July, and he figured prominently in Lee's raid on Paulus Hook on 19 August 1779. McLane envied Lee, however, and Washington solved the problem by sending McLane to reinforce Lincoln at Charleston. Fortunate in not reaching the city in time to be captured, he came under Steuben's command and was promoted to major.

Early in June 1781 he left Philadelphia carrying dispatches that urged de Grasse to come from the West Indies to support Washington and Rochambeau. On the return voyage he commanded the marine company on the privateer *Congress* (twenty-four guns) during its capture of the British sloop of war *Savage* (sixteen guns). During the Yorktown campaign he scouted New York City from Long Island to keep Washington informed on the essential point of whether the British were detaching strength to reinforce Cornwallis. He retired on 9 November 1782, a brevet major.

His personal fortune gone, McLane entered a mercantile venture with Robert Morris. In 1789 Washington named him the first federal marshal for Delaware and in 1797 made him collector for the port of Wilmington, a post he retained for the rest of his life. He commanded the defenses of Wilmington during the War of 1812, observed the British capture of Washington, and commented that with the three hundred men he had led at Paulus Hook he could have saved the capital.

SEE ALSO *Additional Continental Regiments; Barren Hill, Pennsylvania; Germantown, Pennsylvania, Battle of; Long Island, New York, Battle of; MacLean, Allan; Mischianza, Philadelphia; Paulus Hook, New Jersey; Stony Point, New York; Whitemarsh, Pennsylvania.*

BIBLIOGRAPHY

Cook, Fred J. *What Manner of Men: Forgotten Heroes of the American Revolution.* New York, Morrow, 1959

Garden, Alexander. *Anecdotes of the Revolutionary War in America.* 1822. Reprint, Spartanburg, S.C.: Reprint Co., 1972.

Munroe, John A. *Louis McLane: Federalist and Jacksonian.* New Brunswick, N.J.: Rutgers University Press, 1973.

revised by Harold E. Selesky

MECKLENBURG DECLARATION OF INDEPENDENCE.

On 31 May 1775 a committee met at Charlotte, Mecklenburg County, North Carolina, and drew up twenty resolutions for the North Carolina delegation to present to the Continental Congress. They stated—among other things—that all laws and commissions derived from royal or Parliamentary authority were suspended and that all legislative or executive power henceforth should come from the Provisional Congress of each colony under the Continental Congress. Although adopted, the resolutions never were presented to Congress. In 1819 the Raleigh *Register* printed what was claimed to be a document that the Charlotte committeemen had adopted on 20 May 1775, in which they declared themselves "a free and independent people" and which contained other phrases later made famous in the Declaration of Independence.

Before his death in 1826, Thomas Jefferson rejected the "Mecklenburg Declaration of Independence" as spurious. Nonetheless, for many years it was believed, primarily by people in North Carolina, that the Mecklenburg document had inspired the real Declaration of Independence. No written copy of the document was found until 1847, when a copy of a Charleston newspaper of 16 June 1775 was discovered to contain the full text of the twenty resolutions adopted 31 May 1775. The word "independence" was not mentioned. The explanation appears to be this: The records of the 31 May proceedings were destroyed by a fire in 1800; the version printed in 1819 was from memory—including that of the North Carolina iron manufacturer Joseph Graham, who had been fifteen years old at the time—and was embellished with phrases taken from the real Declaration of Independence. All evidence to the contrary has not prevented people from insisting on the veracity of the fraudulent document and posting it on web sites. These two documents, the real Resolves of 31 May and the contrived "Declaration" of 20 May, and their dates are often confused. For instance, the state of North Carolina still features the date of the fictional document on its seal and flag.

SEE ALSO *Graham, Joseph.*

BIBLIOGRAPHY

Hoyt, William Henry. *The Mecklenburg Declaration of Independence: A Study of Evidence Showing that the Alleged Early Declaration of Independence by Mecklenburg County, North Carolina, on May 20th, 1775, Is Spurious.* (1907). New York: Da Capo Press, 1972.

revised by Michael Bellesiles

MEDALS.

During the nine years of the War for Independence, Congress voted to award eight medals to officers of the Continental army in recognition of significant accomplishments on the battlefield. The first was given to George Washington to commemorate the taking of Boston in March 1776. The next went to Horatio Gates for the capture of Burgoyne's army at Saratoga in October 1777. Four were awarded in 1779 for victories that were not of the same significance as Boston or Saratoga. Brigadier General Anthony Wayne, Colonel Walter

Stewart, and Lieutenant Colonel François Teissedre de Fleury received medals for the capture of Stony Point on 16 July 1779, and Major Henry Lee received a medal for the raid on Paulus Hook on 19 August 1779. The last two congressional medals were awarded to Brigadier General Daniel Morgan and Colonel John Eager Howard for the victory at Cowpens on 17 January 1781, a success that provided a significant fillip to the morale of American troops in the South.

SEE ALSO *Howard, John Eager; Lee, Henry ("Light-Horse Harry"); Morgan, Daniel; Stewart, Walter; Teissedre de Fleury, François Louis; Wayne, Anthony.*

revised by Harold E. Selesky

MEDICAL PRACTICE DURING THE REVOLUTION.

On both sides in the American Revolution, many more soldiers died from disease than in combat, and many more died from wounds than were killed outright. The most feared killer in North America at this time was smallpox, which played a critical role in defeating the American invasion of Canada. As a result of that disaster Washington instituted a requirement in the winter of 1776–1777 requiring all new recruits to undergo inoculation for that disease before reporting to the army. This was one of the first instances, worldwide, of that now-common practice. Other diseases swept through eighteenth-century army camps, including diphtheria, dysentery, malaria, measles, and even scurvy. Surgery was primitive, and because microbes and sterilization were not yet understood, those who survived the shock and the bleeding risked lethal infections.

Armies at the time of the Revolution provided a surgeon and surgeon's mates at the regimental level and a more extensive medical staff charged with operating hospitals—both fixed ones at major bases and field hospitals that accompanied forces on military operations. The regimental personnel provided battlefield triage and critical care; the hospitals conducted long-term treatment with a staff of trained medical personnel (physicians, the lower-status surgeons, and apothecaries) supplemented by civilians employed as nurses, orderlies, cooks, and individuals performing any other appropriate support functions. Most combat medical care came after the shooting stopped. The regimental quartermaster would search for the wounded using the regiment's fifers and drummers as stretcher-bearers. Naval vessels of any size also carried a surgeon and sometimes an assistant; large squadrons, or more commonly their bases, would also have hospital ships, which were most often converted obsolete warships.

British military medical practices were quite conventional and operated with the disadvantage that all supplies and replacement personnel had to come three thousand miles from the British Isles. The Hesse-Cassel contingent of Germans also had its own medical staff that operated a hospital; the smaller German forces had much more modest provisions. All of the German regiments had a slightly different arrangement than those of the British or Americans. They would have a surgeon for the regiment but provided a surgeon's mate (*Feldscher*) for each company, although this individual had far less training than his Anglo-American counterparts.

Within the Continental Army treatment tended to be easier because inoculation centers and hospitals could be placed almost anywhere except on the immediate front lines. The army had a much more difficult time creating an effective and efficient medical administration. The colonies had excellent doctors, including some who had trained in London and Edinburgh. Although in many ways the American doctors were more skillful than the Royal Army's, they lacked infrastructure and a logistical system that could provide specialized medicines. The Continental Congress also had trouble finding a proper head for its medical program. The first choice was Benjamin Church of Massachusetts, who turned out to be a British spy. John Morgan succeeded Church; although a good doctor and administrator, he had an abrasive personality and made so many enemies that he had to be relieved. The third head, William Shippen Jr., was also relieved, a victim of professional back-stabbing. Both of those men were Philadelphians. Benjamin Rush, like his two predecessors a Philadelphian, became mixed up in political intrigue and also had to be jettisoned. On 17 January 1781 Congress appointed John Cochran of New Jersey, a veteran of the French and Indian War, and in him finally found a competent head who served until the end of the war. The head of the Continental Army medical department carried the title of director general.

SEE ALSO *Church, Benjamin; Cochran, John; Morgan, John; Rush, Benjamin; Shippen Family of Philadelphia.*

BIBLIOGRAPHY

Bell, Whitfield J., Jr. *John Morgan, Continental Doctor.* Philadelphia: University of Pennsylvania Press, 1965.

Blanco, Richard L. *Physician of the American Revolution: Jonathan Potts.* New York: Garland STPM Press, 1979.

Cash, Philip. *Medical Men at the Siege of Boston, April 1775–April 1776: Problems of the Massachusetts and Continental Armies.* Philadelphia: American Philosophical Society, 1973.

————. "The Canadian Military Campaign of 1775–1776: Medical Problems and Effects of Disease." *Journal of the American Medical Association* 236 (5 July 1976): 52–56.

Duncan, Louis C. *Medical Men in the American Revolution, 1775–1783.* Carlisle Barracks, Pa.: Medical Field Service School, 1931.

Fenn, Elizabeth A. *Pox Americana: The Great Smallpox Epidemic of 1775–1982.* New York: Hill and Wang, 2001.

Gibson, J. E. *Dr. Bodo Otto and the Medical Background of the American Revolution.* Springfield, Mass.: Charles C. Thomas, 1937.

Gillett, Mary C. *The Army Medical Department, 1775–1818.* Washington, D.C.: U.S. Government Printing Office, 1981.

Saffron, Morris H. *Surgeon to Washington: Dr. John Cochran, 1730–1807.* New York: Columbia University Press, 1977.

Tilton, James. *Economical Observations on Military Hospitals and the Prevention of Disease Incident to an Army.* Wilmington, Del.: Wilson, 1813.

Torres-Reyes, Ricardo. *Morristown National Historical Park: 1779–80 Encampment. A Study of Medical Services.* Washington, D.C.: U.S. Department of the Interior, 1971.

Van Swieten, Baron. *The Diseases Incident to the Armies with the Method of Cure.* Translated by John Raby. Philadelphia: Bell, 1776.

revised by Robert K. Wright Jr.

MEETING ENGAGEMENT.

The term "meeting engagement" is applied to a battle that takes place before either side can execute its planned attack or defense. Normally, both sides are still moving part of their forces toward the battlefield while other troops are already engaged in combat. Such encounters hold enormous potential for the side that can better understand what is happening on a fluid battlefield and can better direct forces to take advantage of often fleeting opportunities for success. The encounters at Princeton (3 January 1777) and at Monmouth (28 June 1778) are good examples of meeting engagements in Americas' War for Independence.

revised by Harold E. Selesky

MEIGS, RETURN JONATHAN.

(1740–1823). Continental officer. Connecticut. Son of a hatter named Return Meigs, Return Jonathan Meigs was born in Middletown, Connecticut, and became a merchant in his hometown. Elected lieutenant of his local militia company (in the Sixth Militia Regiment) in October 1772, he won promotion to captain in October 1774 and led the company to Boston, where it served for eight days after the Lexington alarm. Appointed major of the Second Connecticut Regiment on 1 May 1775, he served over the summer at the siege of Boston and in September volunteered as second-in-command of Lieutenant Colonel Roger Enos's battalion in Arnold's march to Quebec. Meigs continued with part of the battalion after Enos turned back. He was captured after scaling the walls of Quebec on 31 December 1775. Paroled in May 1776, he returned to Connecticut in July and was formally exchanged on 10 January 1777. On 22 February he became lieutenant colonel of Colonel Henry Sherburne's Additional Continental Regiment.

Meigs is famous for his brilliant Sag Harbor raid in New York on 23 May 1777, for which Congress voted him an "elegant sword." On 10 September he was appointed colonel of the Sixth Connecticut ("Leather Cap") Regiment, and during the summer and fall of 1777 he led it in the principal actions along the Hudson. He headed a composite regiment of Connecticut light infantry at Stony Point on 16 July 1779. Washington sent him a personal note of thanks for his part in stopping the Mutiny of the Connecticut Line on 25 May 1780, and his regiment was one of the first sent to reinforce the Hudson Highlands when Arnold's treason was discovered in September. He retired on 1 January 1781, when the Connecticut Line was consolidated and reduced.

Becoming interested in western lands, he secured an appointment as one of the Ohio Company's surveyors. In April 1788 he led a small party of settlers that founded the town of Marietta at the mouth of the Muskingum River on the Ohio. An important leader in early Ohio, in 1801 he was also appointed agent to the Cherokee. Known for trying to deal firmly but fairly with Native Americans, he endeavored to get the best deal he could for the tribes while promoting their acculturation and acceptance of white settlement. He died of pneumonia at the age of eighty-two in 1823. His son and namesake became governor of Ohio, U.S. senator, and postmaster general.

SEE ALSO *Arnold's March to Quebec; Mutiny of the Connecticut Line; Sag Harbor Raid, New York; Sherburne's Regiment; Stony Point, New York.*

BIBLIOGRAPHY

Johnston, Henry P. "Return Jonathan Meigs: Colonel of the Connecticut Line." *Magazine of American History* (1880).

Roberts, Kenneth, comp. *March to Quebec: Journals of the Members of Arnold's Expedition.* New York: Doubleday, Doran, 1938.

revised by Harold E. Selesky

MERCANTILISM.

Mercantilism is the name for a set of beliefs that developed in Europe in the sixteenth century about how the components of society could best be organized to promote the public good. Developed in policies, regulations, and laws through the eighteenth century, mercantilism was intended to support the nation-states of western Europe by channeling private economic behavior for the benefit of the state. A form of economic nationalism, it found expression in efforts by governments to regulate trade and commerce, maintain a favorable balance of trade, develop agriculture and manufacturing, keep up a strong merchant marine, establish colonies for the enrichment of the mother country, create monopolies in foreign trade, and accumulate gold and silver (on the premise that specie alone is wealth). There was no single set of policies advocated by all states, just a sense that the accumulation of wealth and prosperity was a zero-sum game in which ad hoc measures ought to be taken to keep one's own advantage from slipping away to a foreign competitor.

According to the tenets of mercantilism, colonies existed primarily to furnish the mother country with commodities (gold, silver, raw materials) and markets that could not be obtained at home or were too expensive to obtain from competitors. In various statutes, rulings, and proclamations over more than a century, from the first Navigation Act in 1651 to the set of regulations and taxes imposed after the French and Indian War, the imperial government in London tried to translate the broad precepts of mercantilism into effective policy. For most of that time, these policies were more or less benign, even beneficial, because they guaranteed markets for colonial goods, offered some protection against foreign competitors, and did not greatly conflict with what might be called the natural flow of commerce. But policies that might have been appropriate for infant colonial economies seemed much less so, to the colonists, as their economic activity grew in size, complexity, and ambition. Mercantilism, considered as a set of beliefs, did not cause the colonists to rebel. It would be more appropriate to say that a too-rigid adherence by successive imperial politicians to policies that seemed to privilege the British economy caused a growing number of colonists to rethink the value of their relationship with the mother country and to perceive in its actions much they came to regard as tyrannical.

SEE ALSO *Background and Origins of the Revolution.*

BIBLIOGRAPHY

Coleman, Donald C. "Mercantilism Revisited." *Historical Journal* 23 4 (1980): 187–204.

Heckscher, Eli F. *Mercantilism.* 2d ed. Edited by Ernst F. Soderlund. 2 vols. London: George Allen and Unwin, 1955.

McCusker, John J. *Mercantilism and the Economic History of the Early Modern Atlantic World.* Cambridge, U.K.: Cambridge University Press, 2001.

revised by Harold E. Selesky

MERCER, HUGH.

MERCER, HUGH. (1725?–1777). Continental general. Scotland, Pennsylvania, and Virginia. Born in Aberdeen, Scotland, perhaps in 1725, Hugh Mercer was educated as a doctor at the University of Aberdeen (1740–1744) and was in the surgeons' corps of Prince Charles Edward in 1745. After the battle of Culloden he emigrated to America, settling near what is now Mercersburg, Pennsylvania. He became a captain in the Pennsylvania Regiment during the Seven Years' War, and may have been present at Major General Edward Braddock's defeat by the Indians at the Monongahela River (near modern Pittsburgh). He took part in the expedition against the Indian settlement at Kittanning, Pennsylvania (September 1756) and was promoted to lieutenant colonel of the militia. Then, after General John Forbes's expedition to Fort Duquesne (1758), he was promoted to colonel of the Third Battalion on 23 April 1759, and was made commandant of Fort Pitt.

During these frontier operations, Mercer met George Washington, and it may have been at Washington's suggestion that Mercer moved to Fredericksburg, Virginia, where he opened an apothecary shop. On 12 September 1775 he was elected colonel of the minutemen in four counties. Having narrowly lost out to Patrick Henry for command of the First Virginia Regiment, the fifty-year-old doctor was commissioned colonel of the Third Virginia Regiment on 13 February 1776. Appointed brigadier general of the Continental army on 5 June, he was put in command of the flying camp, comprised of mobile militia forces. He led a column at Trenton, New Jersey, and is one of several officers credited in contemporary accounts with suggesting the strategy leading to the triumph at Princeton, New Jersey, on 3 January 1777. Mortally wounded in this action, he died on 11 January of that same year.

SEE ALSO *Flying Camp; Princeton, New Jersey; Trenton, New Jersey.*

BIBLIOGRAPHY

English, Frederick. *General Hugh Mercer: Forgotten Hero of the American Revolution.* New York: Vantage Press, 1975.

Waterman, Joseph M. *With Sword and Lancet: The Life of General Hugh Mercer.* Richmond, Va.: Garrett and Massie, 1941.

revised by Michael Bellesiles

MERLON.

MERLON. Part of a fortification wall, or of the battlements on top of the wall, between two embrasures (openings).

Mark M. Boatner

METHODISTS.

METHODISTS. The military conflict of the Revolutionary era dramatically reshaped the Methodist movement in America, from a small missionary wing of the Church of England to a rising evangelical power. But this transformation had little to do with the compatibility of Anglican John Wesley's version of Christianity with the American struggle for independence. Rather, the formation of what was to become the largest denomination in the United States on the eve of the Civil War emerged from the lessons that American Methodists drew from their wartime sufferings, and from their leaders' ability to seize opportunities.

THE PROBLEM OF LOYALISM

On the eve of Lexington and Concord in April 1775, the Methodists in America were comprised of a small band of traveling preachers, led by minister John Wesley's Scottish deputy, Thomas Rankin, and a little over 3,000 adherents. Although Methodist converts first immigrated to New York and Maryland in the early 1760s, Wesley's itinerants had arrived only in 1769, in the midst of the Patriot movement. Rankin was known to the American Whigs primarily as a critic of American slavery, and the Methodists' mission to recruit free people and slaves did not win them friends in the Patriot leadership. Congregationalists and Presbyterians, who still adhered to the Calvinist doctrine of predestination and among whom many favored the American cause, condemned the Methodists for teaching that individuals possessed free will to achieve, or conversely to fall away from, Christian rebirth. The ordained ministers of the Church of England considered Wesley's itinerants to be uneducated upstarts with too great an insistence on the equality of all believers. Whether or not the Methodists had a future in America depended on their English founder's willingness to send over more British preachers. Wesley, an old man and concerned with his legacy in Britain, had other priorities.

American resistance to Parliamentary measures was largely ignored by the rank-and-file itinerants, instructed by their leaders to avoid political conflicts. But as American resistance gathered steam in the mid-1770s, Wesley boldly attacked the Patriots in a series of royalist pamphlets. The first, titled *A Calm Address to Our American Colonies* and published in 1775, borrowed from a pamphlet by Samuel Johnson, asserted that the colonists were "descendants of men who either had no votes, or resigned them by emigration." It was further argued that the American Whigs had been duped by enemies of the monarchy—the former Puritans of New England—aiming to erect "their dear [Puritan] Commonwealth upon its ruins."

The outbreak of war with Britain placed Wesley's American followers in an inevitably difficult position.

Although a small cohort of the preachers were Americans—generally under the guidance of a maverick Irish itinerant, Robert Strawbridge—most were British and several were overtly Loyalist. Noteworthy among the latter was Thomas Webb, an aging veteran of the French and Indian War and popular preacher in New Jersey. Webb maintained a correspondence with William Legge, the second earl of Dartmouth, Secretary for the Colonies, and a Methodist patron in Britain. In this correspondence, Webb claimed to have provided the British command with intelligence on General George Washington's attack on Trenton on 26 December 1776. Webb's activities, which included gathering information on American military movements in Baltimore County, prompted at least one Maryland official to report that the Methodists used religious recruitment to mask their conspiracy against the American cause. Webb was ultimately arrested and sent into exile.

In 1777, several other Methodists, including British itinerant Martin Rodda in Maryland and American Tory Cheney Clow in Delaware, raised armed forces against the Americans. Other British preachers proselytized among the regulars in British-occupied New York. But most, including Thomas Rankin, returned to Britain. Of the more than sixty preachers recruited by the Wesleyans between 1773 and 1777, only twenty-eight, or fewer than half, were still traveling through the colonies in 1778. Of Wesley's formally licensed preachers, only one, Francis Asbury, remained in Patriot territory.

PATRIOT SENTIMENT AND THE MISSIONARY CAUSE

The Loyalist reputation of the Methodists was tempered by the number of adherents who supported the Patriots. Marylanders Samuel Owings Jr., Richard Dallam, and Jesse Hollingsworth served the Patriot military in varying capacities. Owings was a colonel in the Soldier's Delight Battalion of Militia in Baltimore County; Dallam served in the Harford County Rifles; and Hollingsworth was a privateer. In New Jersey, John Fitch, who later invented the steamboat, as well as James Sterling and Thomas Ware were all prominent Methodist Patriots. Fitch served time on a British prison ship in New York harbor. Undoubtedly, many more examples have escaped the historical record.

Many American Methodists, furthermore, struggled less about taking sides than about the proper role of Christian missionaries, especially since recruitment to the itinerancy was a relatively simple process that did not require ordination. Preacher John Littlejohn complained of being fatherless and friendless because he was not a Patriot volunteer, but he believed the American cause was blessed by God. Marylander Joseph Everett's conversion transformed him from a Whig and active militiaman into a pacifist itinerant, but he did

America's First Methodist Episcopal Church (c. 1768). *This church in New York, seen here in an engraving by Joseph B. Smith, was reputedly the first Methodist Episcopal Church in America.* © **MUSEUM OF THE CITY OF NEW YORK/CORBIS**

not become a Loyalist in the process. Preacher Jesse Lee refused to bear arms, but served as a wagon driver for the Continental army in North Carolina. Thomas Ware came to view warfare as a worldly distraction, but he was nonetheless a war veteran.

Beginning in 1776, American itinerants in New Jersey and Maryland nonetheless faced prosecution for non-adherence to militia drafts, and many were subject to mob violence. State loyalty oaths in Maryland, Delaware, and Pennsylvania restricted the preachers' mobility. For example, the Maryland Act for the Better Security of Government, passed in December 1777, required an oath or affirmation of allegiance to the state government, and barred non-compliers from many activities, including preaching. The itinerants objected to the form of the oath and many were indicted—twenty alone in October 1778—for preaching without having taken the oath. Several served jail sentences or paid substantial fines. A number of the American command, particularly General William Smallwood, repeated the charge that the itinerants were a threat to the common cause.

A TRANSFORMATION OF PERCEPTION

As the war continued into the late 1770s and early 1780s, courts in the upper Chesapeake Valley faced numerous cases involving religious pacifists drawn from among the Quakers, Mennonites, and Moravians, as well as the Methodists. This led to the practical need to ease up on prosecutions. Instead, hostility to the Methodist itinerants came from other quarters. Throughout the war, the preachers had persisted in recruiting African Americans, laborers, and women, single and married, into their movement, with or without the permission of their masters or husbands. This was perceived as a threat to the order and authority of households and plantations, which was feared by customary authorities everywhere, but especially in the South. Freeborn Garrettson and Philip Gatch, both of Maryland, left vivid descriptions of their trials in the face of mob violence during the war. Garrettson was persecuted, in part, for his strong opposition to slaveholding; and Gatch for converting one man's wife, for which he was treated to a tarring that blinded him in one eye.

Despite these inauspicious circumstances, the conflict with Britain would ultimately serve the American Methodists well. By 1782, the year the war ended, close to 12,000 Americans, especially in Delaware, Maryland, and Virginia, had joined the movement, four times as many as at the start of the war. Judging by later numbers, African Americans probably comprised from 10 to 15 percent of this followership, and made up a great proportion of audiences who attended Methodist preaching without creating formal societies.

This slow but impressive success would ultimately explode after 1800, for essentially two reasons. One was that the war had seriously undermined the Anglican presence in America, particularly in the Middle Atlantic and southern states, where the Methodists were most active. The Church of England was a rising power in the colonies, but nearly 40 percent of its American clergy were Loyalists and few Anglican churches were still functioning north of Delaware shortly after independence. The declining condition of the Church of England—once the proud ecclesiastical elite of the colonies—prompted Robert Strawbridge's followers to meet in Fluvanna, Virginia in 1777. During this meeting they formed themselves into an informal presbytery with powers to administer baptism and communion—the powers heretofore restricted to an ordained clergy. Francis Asbury strongly opposed this unorthodox move, but the Methodists soon moved into the Anglican vacuum. Wesley's postwar emissary, Thomas Coke, persuaded Asbury and the Americans to form the Methodist Episcopal Church in Baltimore in December 1784. In a sermon delivered on 27 December 1784 (and printed in Baltimore the following year), Coke proclaimed that the Revolution had struck off the "intolerable fetters" that tied the Methodists to the Anglicans and had "broken the antichristian union which before subsisted between Church and State." The Anglicans' decline meant the Methodists' rise.

The second more comprehensive reason for Methodist success was the nature of the audience attracted by their egalitarian message—women, African Americans, and other laboring-class men—many of whom were outsiders to the revolutionary leadership. They joined Methodist churches run largely by professionals—middling merchants, and assorted industrial capitalists in the cities, and farmer gentry in the countryside and on the western frontier. But the opportunities to rise in these churches and especially in the ministry were very great. There seemed to be few people unaffected by the Methodist message, and many were as drawn to it as the Patriots had been to republican virtue.

In time the Methodists would claim as close a tie to the founding conflict of the United States as any other denomination, and would lose the memory of their low reputation during the war. But without the solidarity that their wartime sufferings provided, and the conditions that the war itself created, the Methodists might have become one missionary agency among the many. t. Instead, in the eighty years following the Revolutionary war, they outpaced all other Protestant churches in popularity and geographical expanse and became a dominant force in American culture and society.

SEE ALSO *Religion and the American Revolution.*

BIBLIOGRAPHY

Andrews, Dee E. *The Methodists and Revolutionary America, 1760–1800: The Shaping of an Evangelical Culture.* Princeton, N.J.: Princeton University Press, 2000.

Hatch, Nathan O. *The Democratization of American Christianity.* New Haven, Conn.: Yale University Press, 1989.

Heyrman, Christine Leigh. *Southern Cross: The Beginnings of the Bible Belt.* New York: Alfred A. Knopf, 1997.

Lyerly, Cynthia Lynn. *Methodism and the Southern Mind, 1779–1810.* New York and Oxford: Oxford University Press, 1998.

Mathews, Donald G. "Evangelical America: The Methodist Ideology." In *Rethinking Methodist History: A Bicentennial Historical Consultation.* Edited by Russell E. Richey and Kenneth E. Rowe. Nashville, Tenn: Kingswood Books, 1985.

Richey, Russell E. *Early American Methodism.* Bloomington, Ind.: University of Indiana Press, 1991.

Rhoden, Nancy L. *Revolutionary Anglicanism: The Colonial Church of England Clergy during the American Revolution.* New York: New York University Press, 1999.

Wigger, John H. *Taking Heaven by Storm: Methodism and the Rise of Popular Christianity in America.* New York: Oxford University Press, 1998.

Dee E. Andrews

METUCHEN MEETING HOUSE, NEW JERSEY SEE *Short Hills, New Jersey.*

M'FINGAL. Published in 1782, *M'Fingal* is the eponymous name of the pseudo-Scottish poet in the mock epic poem by John Trumbull. Written in the satiric style of the seventeenth-century English versifier Samuel Butler, the author of *Hudibras,* this crude but effective epigrammatic form was a popular vehicle in America for political commentary at the time of the Revolution. Condemned in Britain, the poem was very popular in the United States in celebrating the struggle for independence.

SEE ALSO *Salem, Massachusetts; Trumbull, John (the poet).*

revised by Harold E. Selesky

MIDDLE BROOK, NEW JERSEY SEE
Bound Brook, New Jersey.

MIDDLE FORT, NEW YORK.
Middleburg, New York. With Upper and Lower Forts, Middle Fort was built to defend the Schoharie Valley.

SEE ALSO *Schoharie Valley, New York.*

Mark M. Boatner

MIDDLETON, ARTHUR. (1743–1787).
Signer. South Carolina. Born on the South Carolina estate of his wealthy father, Henry Middleton, in 1743, Arthur Middleton, like so many of his class in the South, was educated in England. After two years of travel in Europe he returned to South Carolina in 1763 and married the daughter of Walter Izard. In 1765 he was elected to the state House of Representatives, where he sat for many years. He was elected to the South Carolina Provincial Congress of 1775, and served on the Committee of Safety. He took his father's seat in the Continental Congress in 1776, signed the Declaration of Independence, and was a delegate again in 1777. In 1778 he declined the governorship. After taking an active part in the defense of Charleston, he became a prisoner on 12 May 1780 and was sent to St. Augustine. Exchanged in July 1781, he returned to Congress for two more years. With the war's end he refused another term in Congress. He returned to "Middleton Place," his estate on the Ashley River, near Charleston, inherited from his mother in 1771 and partially destroyed by the British in 1780. He died there 1 January 1787.

SEE ALSO *Middleton, Henry.*

revised by Michael Bellesiles

MIDDLETON, HENRY. (1717–1784).
Second president of the Continental Congress. South Carolina. Born in 1717 on his father's plantation near Charlestown, South Carolina, Henry Middleton would become one of the largest land- and slave-owners in the state. He was educated in England and elected to the state assembly shortly after his return, serving as speaker in 1747 and 1754. In 1755 he became commissioner of Indian affairs. He sat on the state council until he resigned in 1770 to become leader of the opposition. Sent to the first Continental Congress, he succeeded Peyton Randolph as president on 22 October 1774, and held this office until the re-election of Randolph on 10 May 1775. He also was president of the South Carolina Provincial Congress from 1775 to 1776. An advocate of reconciliation, he refused re-election to the Continental Congress in February 1776, when the radicals seemed to gain control. He was succeeded by his son, Arthur. Although a member of the Council of Safety after 16 November 1775, and active in state affairs until General Henry Clinton's invasion of the South in the spring of 1780. At that point, he came to feel that the Patriot cause was hopeless. After the fall of Charleston, he sought and received the protection of the British, but did not suffer property loss as a consequence. He died in Charleston, South Carolina, on 13 June 1784.

SEE ALSO *Middleton, Arthur.*

BIBLIOGRAPHY

Horne, Paul A. Jr. "Forgotten Leaders: South Carolina's Delegation to the Continental Congress, 1774–1789." Ph.D. dissertation, University of South Carolina, 1988.

revised by Michael Bellesiles

MIDDLETON FAMILY OF SOUTH CAROLINA.
The Middletons were among the dozen or so families that controlled South Carolina during the eighteenth century. As was the case throughout the colonies, the imperial crisis divided families. Henry Middleton (1717–1784) represented South Carolina in the Continental Congress (and served as its president from 22 October 1774 to 10 May 1775), but resigned in February 1776 because he disagreed with the drift toward independence. His eldest son, Arthur Middleton (1742–1787), was an early supporter of a total break with Britain, and, as a delegate to Congress from 26 February 1776, he voted for independence. Although Henry accepted British protection after the fall of Charleston, his estates were neither confiscated nor amerced, in part because of his son's prominence in the Patriot cause but also because he had lent the state over 100,000 pounds.

SEE ALSO *Middleton, Arthur; Middleton, Henry.*

BIBLIOGRAPHY

Edgar, Walter B., and N. Louise Bailey, eds. *Biographical Directory of the South Carolina House of Representatives.* Vol. 2: *The Commons House of Assembly, 1692–1775.* Columbia: University of South Carolina Press, 1977.

revised by Harold E. Selesky

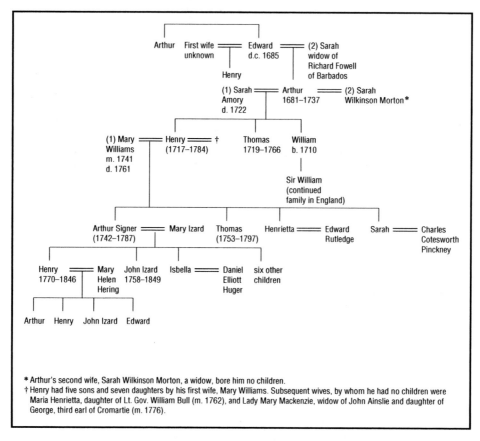

* Arthur's second wife, Sarah Wilkinson Morton, a widow, bore him no children.
† Henry had five sons and seven daughters by his first wife, Mary Williams. Subsequent wives, by whom he had no children were Maria Henrietta, daughter of Lt. Gov. William Bull (m. 1762), and Lady Mary Mackenzie, widow of John Ainslie and daughter of George, third earl of Cromartie (m. 1776).

Middleton Family of South Carolina. THE GALE GROUP

MIFFLIN, THOMAS. (1744–1800). Continental general, politician. Pennsylvania. Born in Philadelphia of Quaker parents on 10 January 1744, Mifflin graduated from the College of Philadelphia in 1760 and entered a business partnership with his brother before entering politics. He was in the Pennsylvania Provincial Assembly in 1772 and 1773, one of the most radical members of the Continental Congress in 1774, and an ardent Whig in the Pennsylvania House of Representatives until 1775. In the early stages of the war he was active in recruiting and training troops, which led his Quaker meeting to expel him. He was elected major of a volunteer company of troops. On 4 July he became one of General George Washington's aides-de-camp, and on 14 August he became quartermaster general. He was promoted to colonel on 22 December, brigadier general on 16 May 1776, and major general on 19 February 1777. Mifflin had been exceptionally valuable as a soldier-politician, famous for enhancing troop morale with his speeches. But his tenure as quartermaster general was marked by controversy and charges of corruption and inefficiency. He resigned that post in October 1777. Blamed for the sufferings during the Valley Forge Winter Quarters and closely linked with the Conway cabal that sought to dismiss George Washington, Mifflin resigned from the army in August 1778.

Despite its many suspicions regarding Mifflin's conduct, Congress appointed him as one of the commissioners charged with reorganizing the military in 1780. He was a delegate to Congress from 1782 to 1784. He was elected president of that body in 1783 and received Washington's resignation of his military commission (December 23, 1783). Continuing an active career in state and national politics, Mifflin attended the 1787 Constitutional Convention, supporting the federal Constitution. He presided over the Pennsylvania constitutional convention of 1790, served as governor of Pennsylvania from 1790 to 1799, and personally commanded the militia to put down the Whiskey insurrection of 1794. Mifflin remained remarkably inconsistent in his politics, inspiring profound anger from his many political opponents; yet he kept winning elections. He died at Lancaster, Pennsylvania, on 20 January 1800.

SEE ALSO *Supply of the Continental Army; Valley Forge Winter Quarters, Pennsylvania.*

BIBLIOGRAPHY

Rossman, Kenneth R. *Thomas Mifflin and the Politics of the American Revolution.* Chapel Hill, N.C.: University of North Carolina Press, 1952.

revised by Michael Bellesiles

MILE SQUARE, NEW YORK.

Later in Yonkers, this place got its name when a tract of land one mile square was sold in 1676. It was the scene of skirmishes after the British landing at Pell's Point and in their movement to White Plains in October 1776.

SEE ALSO *Pell's Point, New York; White Plains, New York.*

Mark M. Boatner

MILITARY JUSTICE.

Military justice during the Revolutionary War played an important role in making the military subordinate to civilian authority and in making soldiers out of ordinary citizens. For the soldiers, military law not only enforced discipline on the field of battle and in camp but also enforced the respect for rank necessary for military discipline. In developing the policies and practices of military justice, officers, soldiers, and policy makers drew on their experience of observing the British army, the experiences of organizing militia and colonial troops for imperial wars, and accepted civilian practices. They established a system of military justice that through courts-martial and corporal and capital punishment helped make the Continental army into an effective fighting force.

THE COLONIAL TRADITION

When the colonists came to North America, they brought a distrust of standing armies with them from Britain. A standing army is one that exists at all times, not just when there is war with an external enemy. Many British people thought that a standing army was a potential threat to liberty because when it was not engaged in fighting an enemy, it might be used by a monarch against the citizens. In British law, one of the important ways that a standing army was kept under civilian control was to require soldiers to surrender some civil rights when they enlisted. Soldiers were brought to trial very quickly; they could receive a capital sentence handed down with only a two-thirds majority rather than the unanimous verdict needed in civilian life; and most importantly, they lost the right to a jury trial. They became subject to courts-martial, where the presiding panel was both judge and jury. And, finally, soldiers could be sentenced to corporal punishments much more brutal than anything a civilian court was likely to hand down.

The colonists adapted these practices in organizing their local militias and the provincial troops that they raised to fight alongside the British in imperial wars. Militia regulations usually avoided corporal punishment since many militiamen were taxpayers and voters, so instead offenders were punished by fines. But in those colonies where slaves, indentured servants, or apprentices were allowed to serve, corporal punishment was used, as those men had no money.

For their provincial armies, colonial governments felt that service in faraway places for long periods of time and often involving large numbers of poor men meant that sentences had to be tougher. Most colonies used punishments that reflected their civilian practices and held to a maximum punishment of thirty-nine lashes. The thirty-nine- lash limit came from the biblical injunction in Deuteronomy, "Forty stripes he may give him, and not exceed," (Deut. 25:3) and in Paul's Second Letter to the Corinthians. In the latter Paul noted "Of the Jews five times received I forty stripes save one" (2 Cor. 11:24). Therefore, most civilian courts held to the thirty-nine-lash limit, occasionally going over it for multiple offenders. New England colonial assemblies followed this practice for their provincial armies, but some southern colonies, such as Virginia, allowed more severe punishments. In 1757, during the Seven Years' War, the British decided that all provincial troops would come under British military law when they were operating with the British army. From that date on, colonial troops came under a system many saw as barbaric.

The British Army used the lash freely, supplemented by a wide range of other punishments, such as running the gauntlet. There was no limit to lash sentences, which were commonly for more than seven hundred lashes and sometimes as high as fifteen hundred. For these sentences prisoners would be lashed in installments. Colonists were appalled, and even some British officers had come to question the usefulness of these sentences. Consequently, some colonial officers did what they could to prevent their men from being subject to British military justice.

By the time the Revolutionary War began in 1775, then, colonists had gained a great deal of experience with writing articles of war, the codes that laid out military regulations. Naturally, in the first weeks colonial assemblies quickly produced legislation that looked very much like the codes they had written for their provincial armies. Massachusetts passed its legislation first, setting up the usual courts-martial system but limiting the number of lashes to thirty-nine. In the preamble, the assembly indicated it was avoiding the "severe articles and rules (except in capital cases) and cruel punishments as are usually practised in standing armies," hoping instead that soldiers and officers would obey the rules for "their own honor and the public good." The Rhode Island, Connecticut, and New Hampshire assemblies quickly passed articles modeled on those of Massachusetts, and so did the Continental Congress when it organized the Continental Army in June 1775.

THE CONTINENTAL ARMY

The Continental Congress accepted that the way to subordinate the army to civilian authority was that its servicemen had to surrender some civil liberties. The first judge advocate general, William Tudor, a Boston lawyer and a friend and former clerk of John Adams, stated that "When a man assumes a Soldier, he lays aside the Citizen, & must be content to submit to a temporary relinquishment of some of his civil Rights" ("Remarks on the Rules"). It quickly became clear to some in Congress, to Washington and other military leaders, and to Tudor that the thirty-nine-lash limit was too lenient and that the army needed harsher punishments if it was to become a disciplined body.

The first changes to the Continental articles of war came in November 1775 when sedition, mutiny, giving information to the enemy, and desertion were made capital offenses. Massachusetts' objections to "cruel punishments" soon disappeared. In the summer of 1776, as the army faced a string of military setbacks, Congress set to work revising the articles and Tudor, on behalf of Washington and others, lobbied Congress for change. On 20 September 1776, Congress passed new articles of war. The legislation was modeled closely on the British articles of war but limited the number of lashes to one hundred.

For New England soldiers, the new legislation was a radical departure from previous military practice. For the first year of the war, courts-martial sentencing New England soldiers had rested heavily on fining, shaming punishments such as having to walk around camp wearing humiliating signs, and lash sentences well below the thirty-nine-lash limit. By the end of the year, once the new regulations had been distributed and officially read to the assembled troops, one-hundred-lash sentences became common and shaming punishments, although still occasionally used, became much less frequent.

A different kind of transition took place for the troops from South Carolina. The South Carolina assembly had decided to adopt the British articles to regulate its troops from the beginning of the conflict. Courts-martial had handed down sentences as high as eight hundred lashes, and although most of these had been partially remitted

and lesser sentences given, punishments were usually well above one hundred lashes. South Carolina was very different from New England, which was a collection of homogeneous societies where for the first year of the war at least, men of property served as ordinary soldiers. With a large slave population and a small wealthy planter class, South Carolina had some difficulty finding soldiers for its forces. Young planters competed for the officer corps but soldiers were poor farmers, laborers, and recent immigrants. The legislature saw these as men in need of a firm hand and so adopted harsh punishments. For these soldiers, when their regiments were transferred into the Continental army, the new Continental articles meant their conditions of service became less harsh as one hundred lashes quickly became their standard punishment, too.

The articles of September 1776 stood without alteration for the duration of the war. There was only one other serious attempt to try to change them. In 1781, after the mutiny of the Pennsylvania line, Washington asked Congress for the lash limit to be increased to five hundred. The lower limit, Washington felt, forced court-martial panels to hand down too many death sentences. Although a congressional committee recommended the change to the higher number, it was voted down in Congress. The one-hundred-lash limit stayed.

The fast acceptance of the 1776 articles and the regularizing of court-martial practices was part of a number of changes within the army. That fall, Congress reorganized the army and allowed for longer terms of enlistment that enabled soldiers to develop a greater sense of professionalism. Some states introduced drafts in 1777 that drew many poorer men into the army, men who accepted their subordinate status more readily. The skills of soldiers and officers improved, especially after the arrival of Baron Von Steuben in 1778 to help in training. A standardized and predictable system of military justice was a critical part of these changes.

MILITIA PUNISHMENTS

Men in the militia continued to be largely free from corporal punishments. In the September 1776 articles of war, Congress tried to make the militia subject to harsher punishments when it was "joined, or acting in conjunction with" the Continental Army. However, there was a provision that court-martial panels could only be made up of officers from the militia corps with which the offender served, so in practice, little changed. Courts-martial were few and sentences other than fines were rare. When a lash sentence was given, it was to someone who was an outsider to the community, such as a transient or a recently arrived immigrant who might be serving as a substitute.

THE DEATH PENALTY

The death penalty was widely used in the military, most commonly for desertion. It was also used for mutiny, aiding the enemy, or leaving the field of battle without authority, but these were rare cases compared to the number of sentences for desertion from camp or on the march. All executions were carried out in front of all troops in the area so they could be suitably awed by military authority and threatened by what their own fate would be if they transgressed. However, reprieves were common. Washington used the death penalty sparingly. His soldiers were mostly volunteers who served for short terms. His goal was to instill discipline but not to appear so brutal that punishment actually encouraged further desertions or that men declined to reenlist when their terms were up. At the most, no more than 30 percent of capital sentences were carried out and possibly much less.

A DISCIPLINED ARMY

Central to military justice was the hierarchy of army life. Only officers, who were by legal definition gentlemen, sat on court-martial panels, yet it was mostly soldiers who stood charged before them with crimes. Thus, the panel members were not peers of the accused. Only soldiers were ever subject to corporal punishment. When officers were convicted of crimes, their punishments ranged from a private reprimand to being cashiered, or dismissed, from the service. When corporal punishment was inflicted, it was carried out by other soldiers supervised by officers. An important part of military regulations was that soldiers had to show appropriate deference to officers, saluting them and otherwise being respectful to them. Courts-martial were critical in forcing soldiers into habits of respect.

Courts-martial were busiest and handed down their most severe sentences when the army was in a difficult position, for example, during the bad winter at Valley Forge or on the disastrous expedition to Florida in 1778, when too many unhappy soldiers were deserting. But more commonly, military justice was concerned with the discipline of camp life, and panels focused their attention on soldiers' drunkenness, sleeping on duty, and petty theft.

Colonists blended military traditions, civilian practices, and experience to create an effective fighting force. The system of military justice established during the Revolutionary War continued with only minor revisions until after World War II, when Congress passed the Uniform Code of Military Justice in 1950.

BIBLIOGRAPHY

Bowman, Allen. *The Morale of the American Revolutionary Army*. Washington, D.C.: American Council on Public Affairs, 1943.

Cox, Caroline. *A Proper Sense of Honor: Service and Sacrifice in George Washington's Army*. Chapel Hill: University of North Carolina Press, 2004.

Heller, Francis H. "Military Law in the Continental Army." *University of Kansas Law Review* 25 (1977): 353–360.

Tudor, William. "Remarks on the Rules and Articles for the Government of the Continental Troops" (c. August 1775). In *Papers of the Continental Congress*. Vol. 1, pt.1, item 41. National Archives Microfilm Publication M247, r48.

Winthrop, William. *Military Law and Precedents*. 2 vols. Boston: Little Brown, 1896.

Caroline Cox

MILITARY MANUALS. Scores of military manuals were used, and useful, during the Revolutionary War. Among the works popular with both armies were Humphrey Bland's *Treatise of Military Discipline* (8th ed., 1759), comte Lancelot Turpin de Crisse's *Essay on the Art of War* (1761), and Campbell Dalrymple's *Military Essay* (1761). The hodgepodge of American officers in particular sought direction. Hessian Captain Johann Ewald was impressed by the variety of publications found in American officers' captured knapsacks, writing in December 1777,

> when we examined the haversack of the enemy, which contained only two shirts, we also found the most excellent military books translated into their language. For example, Turpin, Jenny, Grandmaison, La Croix, Tielke's *Field Engineer*, and the *Instructions* of the great Frederick to his generals I have found more than one hundred times. Moreover, several of their officers had designed excellent small handbooks and distributed them. . . . I have exhorted our gentlemen many times to read and emulate these people, who only two years before were hunters, lawyers, physicians, clergymen, tradesmen, innkeepers, shoemakers, and tailors. (Edwald, p. 108)

The single most important American work was Major General Friedrich Wilhelm von Steuben's standardized manual of discipline, introduced in the spring of 1778 and published in 1779. Steuben's system did not appreciably simplify the largely ornamental manual of arms, but did introduce set marching rates and uniform tactical formations, for the first time allowing Continental regiments to work as a unified battlefield force.

British forces were fortunate in beginning the conflict with a uniform set of regulations, Edward Harvey's *Manual Exercise as Ordered by His Majesty in 1764*, a treatise that provided a single rule book on which all crown regiments based field organization, formations, and maneuvers. Another influential work was the never-published system of light infantry drill introduced by General Sir William Howe at the Salisbury, England, training camp in late summer 1774. Howe's drill was an expansion of General George Townshend's "Rules and Orders for the Discipline of the Light Infantry Companies in His Majesty's Army in Ireland" (1772). The lessons instilled at Salisbury had a profound effect on the conduct of the American war.

SEE ALSO *Steuben, Friedrich Wilhelm von.*

BIBLIOGRAPHY

Ewald, Johann. *Diary of the American War: A Hessian Journal.* Edited and translated by Joseph P. Tustin. New Haven and London: Yale University Press, 1979.

Houlding, J. A. *Fit for Service: The Training of the British Army, 1715–1795.* Oxford: Clarendon Press, 1981.

Peterkin, Ernest W. *The Exercise of Arms in the Continental Infantry.* Alexandria Bay, N.Y.: Museum Restoration Service, 1989.

Rilng, Joseph R. *The Art and Science of War in America: A Bibliography of American Military Imprints, 1690–1800.* Bloomfield, Ontario: Museum Restoration Service, 1990.

John U. Rees

MILITIA IN THE NORTH.

The opening shots of the Revolutionary War brought the local colonial militia into the spotlight, forcing the local militiamen into a combat role against the army of their king. However, even as these local civilians took up arms, they also shouldered other responsibilities that would prove critical to the overall success of the American rebels in this war against the British Empire. Militia soldiers were used not only to fight alongside the Continental soldiers and to serve as partisans in a guerrilla war throughout the northern states; they also served the local political needs of the rebel Whig leaders, spy on enemy activities, act as enforcers for political leaders, round up enemies of the state, and generally do whatever task had to be done when there was no one else available to do it. The militia proved to be versatile and adaptive in this revolutionary war fought throughout the northern states.

SOCIAL CONTROL

The months following Lexington and Concord saw the militia emerge quickly as a ready source of social control for the emerging rebel governments in the northern colonies. Even as Whig committees and conventions passed regulations to restrain and punish colonists who remained loyal to the British government, the politicians turned to the local militia forces to enforce them. Anyone speaking out against the Whig-controlled colonies became targets of Whig militia forces. Also targeted were those who provided information or supplies to the British forces stationed along the coast, notably in New York City and Boston. Local militia forces were well organized and prepared to fulfill this vital role in the opening months of the war, whereas the British authorities did not make full use of pro-British Loyalists, who were less numerous and more scattered throughout the northern colonies. Local committees, backed by the armed might of the Whig-controlled militia, were able to intimidate the Loyalists, forcing many to take oaths of allegiance to the newly forming Whig governments and imprisoning and exiling those who refused. This form of social and political control was directed by local and colonial authorities.

Loyalist leaders faced a serious danger posed by the local Whig militia. One of the most notorious Whig militiamen in the early war was Isaac Sears of New York. Contrary to General George Washington's orders, Sears attempted unsuccessfully to kidnap New York's royal governor, William Tryon, in August 1775. In November 1775 Sears entered New York City with about eighty volunteers, took the Loyalist James Rivington's press, and then disarmed some Loyalists in Westchester County. In New Jersey, militiamen held the royal governor, William Franklin, a prisoner in February 1776; later, in the summer of 1776, New Jersey militiamen arrested Franklin and sent him to prison in Connecticut, where he stayed until his release in 1778.

In general, Washington fully supported efforts to suppress the Loyalist population in the northern colonies. Militia forces were used to suppress Loyalist threats, especially around New York City, in the spring and summer of 1776. The arrival of the British forces in July and August 1776 increased the threat from internal anti-revolutionary resistance and thus led to increased use of Whig militia to maintain control of the Loyalist population in the area. New York established a secret committee to counter any Loyalists who tried to influence people to support the British or resist the new Whig government. Militia soldiers were responsible for seizing anyone accused of treason against the newly formed United States, and they tried to prevent all communication between British forces on the coast and Loyalists in the interior.

Throughout the middle states, in particular, militia forces were used to disarm suspect people because of a heightened fear that they might try to join the British forces in the area. Dealing with such threats often took precedence over filling recruitment needs for the Continental army. For example, in the summer of 1776 New Jersey's Provincial Convention excused the militia of Loyalist-infested Monmouth County from providing its quota to fulfill a request from the Continental Congress. Washington at times even supported militia activities against Loyalists with detachments of the Continental army. At other times, he released militiamen from the army to return to their home counties in order to suppress Loyalist activities.

The movement of suspected people was monitored by militia troops. Connecticut required people to have certified passes to travel throughout the state, and militia soldiers inspected these passes. This helped prevent Loyalists from forming larger forces and also helped prevent them from sending intelligence and supplies to the British forces stationed nearby.

At times, the local need to control dangerous people took precedence over the military needs of the army. In September 1776, as Washington fought desperately to hold Manhattan Island and prevent British landings along the coast, the New York Convention refused to call out all of the militia from the southern counties of the state because of the large number of Loyalists and slaves in the area. Connecticut also retained militia units for internal control and defense during the summer and autumn. Washington understood these local needs and accepted these actions. In fact, he would at times detach militia units to help suppress Loyalists. In October 1776 he sent a detachment of Massachusetts militia from Manhattan Island to help the New York Convention stop an anticipated Loyalist uprising along the Hudson River. As his army retreated across New Jersey in November 1776, Washington detached a regiment of New Jersey militia to go to Monmouth County to prevent a threatened Loyalist insurrection. Washington even allowed his scouts, both Continentals and militia, to plunder Loyalists and keep the plunder as a reward for their service, but by 1777 Washington had stopped this practice. He preferred to leave it up to the state governments to deal with Loyalists and their property.

The presence of the large British force in New York City heightened fears of Loyalist trouble, so the state government created the Committee for Detecting Conspiracies and authorized it to use militia forces as necessary to prevent hostile uprisings within the state. Other states had similar committees, which used militia troops to maintain a watch on suspected people within their states.

Ultimately, once the Whigs had established control of the state governments in 1776, the militia became the main policing force for these new governments. For the rest of the war, they used militia detachments to hunt down suspected Loyalists. Militiamen were especially active in performing this duty during the lulls in the active campaign seasons of the main armies. For example, in the spring of 1777 New York militia troops scoured the region known as the Highlands and the area between the

American and British lines for Loyalists, breaking up Loyalist bands and generally trying to intimidate those hostile to the United States. In fact, throughout the early war years in particular, the state governments had to carefully balance the needs of the war itself with the need to maintain internal control, including the suppression of Loyalist dangers. Fortunately for the war effort, the governments of the northern states proved very good at maintaining this balance, making militia forces available for the field even while retaining others at home in the state to keep the peace.

The internal threat from Loyalists had largely ended by 1778. States like New York and New Jersey had recurring problems near the British stronghold of New York City, but elsewhere throughout the northern states, the threat of Loyalist uprisings had mostly ended by then. Monmouth County, New Jersey, and the Neutral Ground in New York between the American and British armies remained the only places that faced any kind of threat from Loyalists. The threat in Monmouth, however, remained so intense that as late as November 1779, Washington sent a detachment of Continental soldiers into Monmouth to support the local militia in its endeavors to suppress the remaining Loyalist danger. As the militiamen went home, more Continentals were sent into the county to control the population. Thus, Washington understood the critical need to prevent any Loyalist uprising to gain any foothold within the states and had learned to use regular soldiers from the Continental Army when necessary to support the militia in this vital work.

The other area that remained a dangerous zone right until the end was Westchester County, New York, along with western Fairfield County, Connecticut, the site of the infamous Neutral Ground. As soon as the British army occupied New York City in September 1776, the area around it became a scene of constant raids, larceny, and brutality. Much of it was loosely connected to the armies and the campaigns, but the presence of numerous Loyalists made it imperative for the state government to suppress them. Loyalists raided, took livestock, and forced inhabitants to flee the area. Sometimes these raids were intended to help the British, but often they were made just for the sake of plunder and revenge. The New York government, headed by Governor George Clinton, maintained a constant presence of Whig militia in Westchester County until the end of the war. By 1781, as with Monmouth County, Washington began to increase the Continental presence to relieve the exhausted militia forces, which had stood guard for the previous five years.

Militiamen not only helped hunt dangerous persons, but also helped escort endangered people from areas about to be overrun by the enemy. This duty became especially important on eastern Long Island after the British landed and captured Brooklyn in late August 1776. Even as some militiamen skirmished with the British forces advancing eastward across Long Island, others helped move people, goods, and livestock across Long Island Sound to Connecticut.

The Highlands of New York, situated along the Hudson River north of New York City, also contained many lawless bands. The Committee for Detecting Conspiracies sent militiamen into the area to hunt down these robbers, but with little success. Only the end of the war, and with it the loss of the British market in New York City, brought an end to these outlaws' careers.

BALANCING THE MILITIA'S DUTIES

Another balancing act that the state and national leadership had to maintain in relation to the militia was the very real need for the militiamen to be available for farming. During the spring planting season and the late summer and autumn harvest season, these men were needed to produce the food necessary to feed not only the army, but also the civilian population. Washington and his generals learned early in the war that to call out the militia in the spring or late summer was usually an exercise in frustration, and if the militia was in the field when these key farming seasons arrived, the it tended to melt away quickly. By the latter years of the war, Washington often planned his militia requests by the season, and at critical times in the agricultural cycle he expected the militiamen to turn out only in a military emergency. State governments also understood the vital logistical significance of planting and harvesting and therefore allowed units, or at least parts of them, to go home when farming needs called. When Washington tried to coordinate as large a force as possible to meet with expected French forces later in the war, he would hold off calling out the militia until after spring planting, or if some militia were already mustered and it became clear the French were late or would not arrive, he would release them for the harvest.

In addition, Washington had to learn to respect the local needs that the state governments had for their militia. As he did when he released militia units to suppress Loyalist activity, he also had to learn to leave militia available for the other duties so critical within the states. He did, in fact, learn this after the 1776 campaign. In 1776, when he tried to draw out every available militiaman from the neighboring states, Washington found the state governments reluctant to part with all of their internal strength; he also found that the militia soldiers were reluctant to leave their homes undefended from enemy soldiers and internal dangers and that they also hated to leave their farms untended. Washington quickly became aware that the militia worked best when left for local duties, military and nonmilitary alike. Over the years, he and the other army generals learned to use the militia for reinforcements

sparingly, leaving them available for all of the local duties so vital to securing the states.

The militia of New Jersey provided another service to the army outside of the latter's campaigns. In January 1781 the Pennsylvania Continentals mutinied, and Washington feared that British leaders might try to induce the mutineers to join the British in New York City. Governor William Livingston of New Jersey immediately ordered General Philemon Dickinson, the commander of the eastern New Jersey militia, to station militia detachments along all of the roads between the Pennsylvanians' camp in Trenton and Staten Island. Thus, the militia not only guarded against any move by the mutineers toward the British but helped prevent the British from contacting the Pennsylvania troops. Fortunately for the Continental army, this mutiny ended calmly, but it was followed almost immediately by a mutiny of the New Jersey Continentals. When these new mutineers learned that a substantial force of New Jersey militia had already assembled nearby, they returned to their barracks. Thus, the New Jersey militia helped avert two major crises in the early months of 1781.

LATE WAR DUTIES

As the war drew toward a close in 1782–1783, the militia began to take on new roles, even as it continued to perform some of its traditional functions. Militiamen continued to guard areas such as the Neutral Ground, trying to stop plundering and raids by outlaws loyal to neither side. Efforts by the British commanders in New York City, Washington, and New York's Governor Clinton to stop the brutal raids of Whig and Loyalist forces against each other proved only partially successful. Occasional raids occurred throughout the summer of 1782 as partisan soldiers from both sides captured and plundered each other. As late as the early spring of 1783, Whig militia launched attacks on Loyalist bases, including the key one at Morrisania, New York.

Finally, in April 1783, orders for a cease-fire were issued from the British and American headquarters. As the war came to an end, the state militia began to make the transition to a peacetime role. In Connecticut, for example, militiamen remained on guard in southwestern Connecticut to protect equipment and defensive works, mainly from plundering by local inhabitants. Throughout the summer, militiamen guarded forts along the coast to prevent people living nearby from stealing supplies and hardware. Three men stood guard in New London as of September 1783, and their officers asked to be relieved because the locals not only kept stealing state property but also threatened to blow up the fort along with its men. Even after the British evacuated New York City in November 1783, militia officers were authorized by the Connecticut state legislature to enlist men to continue to stand guard, no longer against British or Loyalist threats, but against dangers posed by local inhabitants.

Meanwhile, in Westchester County, the New York state government found it could not immediately regain control of the dangerous and volatile situation caused by lawless bands. As the British and American armies contracted their lines, the Neutral Ground was unguarded by soldiers from either side, thus leaving the door open for an escalation of raids and plundering by the bands that infested the area. Governor Clinton wanted to reestablish civilian control as quickly as possible, and so naturally he turned to the militia of the area to help him achieve this important purpose. Washington, understanding the importance of a swift and peaceful transition from civil war to civilian government, sent a Continental detachment to support the New York militia in the area. Despite the best efforts by the British commander, General Sir Guy Carleton, Washington, and Governor Clinton, the outlaws in the area continued to raid. These plunderers clearly worked for neither side, but only for themselves. A clear example was Captain Isaac Honeywell and his group of fifty men, who refused to obey commands from Governor Clinton to stop all activities. Such activities by Honeywell's and a few other bands continued throughout the summer of 1783, even as New York militia moved into the area to hunt them down and protect local political authority.

Committees began to emerge, especially along the war-torn coastal areas, that used militiamen to hunt down and harass Loyalists in the area. As a result, an increased number of Loyalists asked General Carleton for permission to leave with the British army, which in turn delayed the British withdrawal from New York, which in a vicious cycle delayed efforts to reestablish civilian control of the affected areas.

A similar situation existed in Monmouth County, New Jersey, where local militia formed a Committee of Retaliation to control the Loyalist element in the county as the war drew to an end. The committee had control of the local sheriffs and courts and thus could treat inhabitants pretty much as it pleased. The committee's men plundered people accused of being Loyalists and made sure they never won any local election. Others were jailed only on the basis of a simple accusation. Former Brigadier General David Forman was one of the leaders of this committee. Complaints against it were numerous but largely ignored.

Such activities were at their worst in Westchester County. The New York government set up commissioners to deal with the area's Loyalists, who were allowed to leave with a minimal share of their possessions. These commissioners used local militia to force Loyalists who resisted into leaving. In the process, many pro-British Americans received brutal treatment and lost most if not all of their goods, and some were prevented from getting to their homes and families. Honeywell was one of the most notorious of these commissioners, brutalizing many Loyalists, some of whom simply fled to the British army in New York City. Governor Clinton sent in other militia to try to establish some control, and Washington even sent in some light infantry from the army to help. By late summer, Washington reported that some order had finally been established.

Finally, the British army completed its evacuation of New York City in November 1783, and when George Washington and George Clinton rode triumphantly into the city, they arrived with an escort of Westchester Light Dragoons. Thus, the militia of the state of New York provided the honor guard for the moment of victory.

Questions existed then and have persisted concerning the efficiency of the militia in its many combat roles during the war. However, there is little doubt that the local militia of the northern states proved very effective in its primary role of protecting the states from internal dangers posed by the pro-British Loyalists. Whig militia suppressed the Loyalists from the start, and British sympathizers never gained a real foothold within the states. As the war progressed, the need to suppress Loyalists declined, but right until the end of the war, and even into the postwar period, militiamen prevented Loyalists from ever posing any real threat to Whig control of the northern states. Another vital aspect of the success of the war in the North was the cooperation between Washington and the state governments. The commander in chief understood the very real needs of the state governments to maintain internal control, and not only did he release or avoid calling the militia when it was needed elsewhere, but he also proved increasingly willing to detach Continental forces to support the militia in its efforts to suppress dangers.

SEE ALSO *Clinton, George; Franklin, William; Hudson River and the Highlands; Neutral Ground of New York; Sears, Isaac; Tryon, William.*

BIBLIOGRAPHY

Buel, Richard, Jr. *Dear Liberty: Connecticut's Mobilization for the Revolutionary War.* Middletown, Conn.: Wesleyan University Press, 1980.

Chadwick, Bruce. *George Washington's War: The Forging of a Revolutionary Leader and the American Presidency.* Naperville, Ill.: Sourcebooks, 2004.

Freeman, Douglas Southall. *George Washington: A Biography.* 7 vols. New York: Scribner's Sons, 1948–1957.

Higginbotham, Don. *The War of American Independence: Military Attitudes, Policies, and Practice, 1763–1789.* New York: Macmillan, 1971.

Ketchum, Richard M. *Divided Loyalties: How the American Revolution Came to New York.* New York: Holt, 2002.

Kwasny, Mark V. *Washington's Partisan War, 1775–1783*. Kent, Ohio: Kent State University Press, 1996.

Tiedemann, Joseph S. "Patriots by Default: Queens County, New York, and the British Army, 1776–1783." *William and Mary Quarterly* 3rd series, 48 (1986): 35–63.

Ward, Christopher. *The War of the Revolution*. 2 vols. Edited by John R. Alden. New York: Macmillan, 1952.

Ward, Harry M. *Between the Lines: Banditti of the American Revolution*. Westport, Conn.: Praeger, 2002.

Mark V. Kwasny

SEE ALSO *Fontenoy, Battle of; Germain, George Sackville; Grey, Charles ("No-flint"); Percy, Hugh; Phillips, William; Riedesel, Baron Friedrich Adolphus; Seven Years' War.*

BIBLIOGRAPHY
Mackesy, Piers. *The Coward of Minden: The Affair of Lord George Sackville*. New York: St. Martin's Press, 1979.

revised by Harold E. Selesky

MILLSTONE, NEW JERSEY SEE *Somerset Courthouse*.

MINDEN, BATTLE OF. 1 August 1759.

Britain sent an expeditionary force to the continent in August 1758 as part of an Anglo-Hanoverian-Prussian army to defend George II's beloved electorate of Hanover against France. The decisive action took place a year later on the plain outside the Westphalian fortress of Minden, for which the battle was named. Six British infantry battalions, three of which had been part of the column at Fontenoy fourteen years earlier, advanced by mistake from the allied center toward the French lines. Although exposed on three sides, this force—reinforced by three Hanoverian battalions and supported by the superb allied field artillery—shattered more than fifty squadrons of French cavalry and thirty-one battalions of French infantry sent against it in a display of controlled fire discipline (rolling volleys by platoons) of which there were few peers in the eighteenth century. With a gaping hole torn in their center, the French retreated and never menaced Hanover again for the remainder of the war. Controversy swirled around the battle because the senior British officer present, George Sackville (later George Germain), was alleged to have disobeyed the orders of the army commander, Ferdinand, duke of Brunswick, to bring his right wing cavalry to the timely support of the advancing infantry. A cloud hung over Sackville for the rest of his life, including during his service as principal architect of the military response to the American rebellion. Many other veterans of the battle also played prominent roles in the war of American independence. Among those who distinguished themselves at Minden were William Phillips (commander of the artillery), Friedrich von Riedesel, Charles Grey, and Hugh Percy. The father of the marquis de Lafayette was killed leading the Touraine Regiment, which subsequently took part in the Yorktown Campaign.

MINISINK, NEW YORK. 19–22 July

1779. While the Patriots were slowly preparing for Sullivan's expedition against the Iroquois, the Mohawk chief Joseph Brant led a force of Indians and Loyalists down the Delaware from Oquaga. Leaving his main body at Grassy Brook on the east bank of the Delaware, he moved on with sixty Indians and twenty-seven Loyalists to surprise the village of Minisink on the night of 19–20 July.

This village was about twenty-five miles east of Grassy Brook and ten miles northwest of Goshen. Brant entered the sleeping village and had several fires started before the inhabitants awoke to their danger. Making no effort to man their "paltry stockade-fort," they took to the hills. The raiders were bent on booty and destruction, and therefore let most of the settlers escape. Brant reported that four scalps and three prisoners were taken. After looting and burning the fort, mill, and twelve houses and doing their best to damage the crops and drive off the livestock, the raiders retraced their route toward Grassy Brook.

Word of the raid reached Lieutenant Colonel (also Dr.) Benjamin Tusten in Goshen the next day. In answer to his call, 149 militia reported for duty at Minisink. Tusten argued against pursuing the renowned Brant, but the inexperienced militia was swayed by Major Samuel Meeker, who mounted his horse, drew forth his sword, and shouted: "Let the brave men follow me; the cowards may stay behind!" Their manhood challenged, most of the men moved forward, giving Tusten little choice but to join in. The small force followed Brant's trail for seventeen miles before camping for the night.

The next morning, 22 July, Colonel John Hathorn joined them with a few men of his Warwick regiment and, being senior to Tusten, he assumed command. They covered only a few miles before coming upon the recently occupied camp of the enemy. The number of still-smoking fires in the campsite indicated a larger force than the Patriot militia might prudently challenge. Again Tusten counseled caution but was ignored. Captain

Bezaleel Tyler led the advance party but was almost immediately shot by an unseen Indian, a clear indication that Brant knew he was being pursued. But Hathorn pressed forward, catching sight of Brant crossing the Delaware near the mouth of the Lackawaxen. Hathorn planned to ambush Brant, but the latter doubled back behind the Americans, ambushing them in turn.

After a few shots had been exchanged, Brant claimed, he walked forward to tell his enemy it was cut off and to offer quarter. His answer was a shot that hit his belt and that, but for this good luck, might well have been fatal. Early in the hard-fought contest, Brant executed a skillful maneuver that cut off one-third of the militia force. The rest were surrounded, with Brant holding the high ground, patiently firing the occasional shot at the militiamen as they wasted their ammunition in ineffective fire. Around dusk, when the defenders were low on ammunition, Brant noticed that a rebel who held one corner of the position had been taken out of action. His attack penetrated this weak spot, organized resistance collapsed, and a massacre started. Tusten was killed with 17 wounded that he had been tending. Several men were shot as they tried to swim the Delaware. Of the 170 militia, only 30 returned home, while Brant's smaller force suffered only a few casualties. The monument to this battle erected in Goshen lists the names of 45 of those killed in the battle. Hathorn was on hand to lay the monument's cornerstone in 1822.

Brant's raid may have been intended as a strategic diversion to draw rebel forces away from Clinton and Sullivan in order to delay preparations for Sullivan's expedition. Alternatively, Brant may have been seeking provisions in striking at Minisink. He had no intention of doing battle with the militia, which foolishly insisted on pursuing one of the best frontier fighters of the Revolution.

SEE ALSO *Brant, Joseph; Oquaga; Sullivan's Expedition against the Iroquois.*

BIBLIOGRAPHY

Kelsay, Isabel T. *Joseph Brant, 1743–1807: Man of Two Worlds.* Syracuse, N.Y.: Syracuse University Press, 1984.

revised by Michael Bellesiles

MINISINK, NEW YORK. c. 4 April 1780.

This place was revisited by Brant after his destruction of Harpersfield on 2 April.

SEE ALSO *Border Warfare in New York; Harpersfield, New York.*

Mark M. Boatner

MINUTEMEN.

The term *minutemen* denotes members of the militia who volunteered to be ready to turn out for active service at literally a moment's notice. While the need to spring instantly into arms existed from the earliest days of settlement, in Massachusetts at least, the term *minnit men* seems to have been used first in 1756, during the French and Indian War. In the months before the outbreak of hostilities with Britain, volunteer military organizations with this mandate sprang up in all the colonies, although not all of these units were institutionally distinct from the militia.

The term *minuteman* is most closely associated with the units that appeared in Massachusetts in the wake of the Powder Alarm of 1 September 1774. As a means of eliminating supporters of royal government from the existing militia organizations, the Worcester County Convention called on 6 September for the resignations of all officers in the three county regiments and for the town militia companies to elect new officers. The town companies were rearranged to form seven new regiments, and new field officers were elected and instructed to organize one-third of the men in each new regiment to be ready to assemble under arms on a minute's notice. On 21 September 1774, this rapid-response portion of the militia was specifically referred to as "minutemen." The Massachusetts Provincial Congress, meeting in October, found that the militia in other counties were adopting the same system, and on 26 October it directed that this reorganization be completed across the colony.

Over the next six months, the process of purging royal supporters and creating new minuteman companies was undertaken with a mixture of urgency and deliberateness. The transition had not been completed by mid-April 1775, but enough had been accomplished so that the opponents of royal government were in firm command of the dual system of militia and minutemen when the regulars marched out of Boston on the night of 18 April. The men who stood in Captain John Parker's company on Lexington green on the morning of 19 April 1775 were true minutemen, and minuteman companies from surrounding towns led the attack at Concord Bridge later in the day. While the minutemen fulfilled the function for which they had been created, the bulk of the Massachusetts citizen-soldiers who turned out on 19 April were enrolled in ordinary or "common" militia companies. Once in the field, there was little to distinguish minuteman from militiaman, although the parallel command structure did have to be sorted out during active combat. When the Provincial Congress a few days later authorized the creation of volunteer companies enlisted for eight months of service (to the end of December 1775), the separate structure of minuteman companies and regiments was allowed to lapse. Men who had served in the minuteman and militia companies on 19 April formed the backbone of the "eight-months' army," demonstrating once again their willingness to undertake the defense of their rights by force of arms.

On 18 July 1775, Congress recommended that other colonies organize units of minutemen for short terms of service, and Maryland, North Carolina, New Hampshire, and Connecticut are known to have complied. The creation of separate minuteman companies was generally replaced by designating a rotating portion of the existing militia companies as the first responders.

SEE ALSO *Lexington and Concord.*

BIBLIOGRAPHY

Castle, Norman, ed. *The Minutemen, 1775–1975.* Southborough, Mass.: Yankee Colour Corporation, 1975.

French, Allen. *The First Year of the American Revolution.* Boston: Houghton Mifflin, 1934.

———. "Minutemen." In *Dictionary of American History.* Edited by James Truslow Adams. 2d revised. edition. 5 vols. New York: Scribners, 1942.

Massachusetts, Secretary of the Commonwealth. *Massachusetts Soldiers and Sailors of the Revolutionary War: A Compilation from the Archives.* 17 vols. Boston: Wright and Potter Printing, State Printers, 1896–1908.

Wroth, L. Kinvin, et al., eds. *Province in Rebellion: A Documentary History of the Founding of the Commonwealth of Massachusetts, 1774–1775.* Cambridge, Mass.: Harvard University Press, 1975.

revised by Harold E. Selesky

MIRÓ, ESTEBAN RODRÍGUEZ.

(1744–1795). Spanish officer and governor. Born in Reus, Spain, in 1744, Miró served during the Seven Years' War in the Zamora Regiment, taking part in the invasion of Portugal in 1762. After the war he transferred to the Corona Regiment as a lieutenant, serving in Mexico into the early 1770s. After taking part in the unsuccessful attack on Algiers in 1775, he attended the Avila Military Academy. In 1778 he went to Louisiana as second in command of the Fixed Louisiana Infantry and was brevetted lieutenant colonel. When Spain declared war on Britain, Miró acted as aide-de-camp to Governor Bernardo de Gálvez in the campaigns that seized British garrisons in West Florida: Manchac and Baton Rouge in 1779, Mobile in 1780, and Pensacola in 1781. In the latter year Miró was promoted to colonel and made commander of his regiment the following year. In January 1782 he became acting governor of Louisiana and West Florida, being named governor in August 1785 and intendant in 1788. After the Revolution, Miró's primary responsibility was keeping the new American Republic out of Spanish territory. In addition to negotiating two treaties clarifying

their mutual boundaries, he subsidized Indian nations to resist U.S. attacks, supplying them with arms through British firms, and built a series of forts along the Mississippi. After closing the Mississippi River to the Americans in 1784, Miró had to contend with several invasion threats, most notably from Georgia in 1785. Lacking sufficient troops for the protection of Louisiana, he funded the wild schemes of Lieutenant Colonel James Wilkinson, the former Continental officer and adventurer, who came to New Orleans in 1787. Miró resigned on 30 December 1791 and returned to Spain. With the war against France in 1793, Miró returned to duty as a field marshal, dying while on the front on 4 June 1795.

SEE ALSO *Gálvez, Bernardo de; New Orleans; Wilkinson, James.*

BIBLIOGRAPHY

Burson, Caroline Maude. *The Stewardship of Don Esteban Miró, 1782–1792.* New Orleans, La.: American Printing, 1940.

Michael Bellesiles

MISCHIANZA, PHILADELPHIA.

18 May 1778. Also known as "Howe's Farewell Party," this extravaganza was organized and directed by Captain John André and Captain Oliver De Lancey to mark General William Howe's departure as commander in chief of the British army in America. The Mischianza, which is an Italian term for a medley or mixture of different forms of entertainment, featured a grand regatta of decorated barges, gun salutes, a mock tournament between the Knights of the Blended Roses and the Burning Mountain, a banquet, fireworks, and a concluding exhibition in which an allegorical Fame saluted Howe with the words, "Thy laurels shall never fade." Loyalist American girls graced the event, and soldiers participated as silk-clad pages. The hosts sent 750 invitations, and the affair lasted from 4 P.M. to 4 A.M. A London firm is said to have sold 12,000 pounds' worth of silk, laces, and other fine materials for use in the event. Not everyone in the city was impressed. In her diary, Elizabeth Drinker, an affluent Philadelphia Quaker, dismissed these displays of excess as just so many "scenes of Folly and Vanity." André wrote a long account of the party that was published in the *Annual Register for 1778* and can be found in *The Spirit of Seventy-Six,* edited by Henry Steele Commager and Richard B. Morris.

SEE ALSO *André, John; De Lancey, Oliver (1749–1822); Howe, William.*

BIBLIOGRAPHY

Commager, Henry Steele, and Richard B. Morris, eds. *The Spirit of 'Seventy-Six: The Story of the American Revolution as Told by Participants.* New York: Da Capo Press, 1995.

revised by Michael Bellesiles

MOBILE. 14 March 1780. Captured by the Spanish. Considered a satellite of Jamaica's defense, the unhealthful British post at Mobile was garrisoned by three hundred men. It was captured after a brief siege by Bernardo de Gálvez, the governor of Louisiana, with a small force supported by a single armed vessel. Pensacola was saved by the intervention of a British squadron but fell the next year.

SEE ALSO *Jamaica (West Indies); Pensacola, Florida.*

revised by Michael Bellesiles

MOHAWK VALLEY, NEW YORK.
A strategic avenue of approach into the American colonies from Canada and situated in Tryon County, it was the objective of St. Leger's offensive in 1777 and a cockpit of border warfare.

SEE ALSO *Border Warfare in New York; St. Leger's Expedition; Tryon County, New York.*

Mark M. Boatner

MOLLY PITCHER LEGEND. The term "Molly Pitcher" seems to have been applied generically to the women—soldiers' wives or other camp followers—who carried pitchers of water to thirsty soldiers on the battlefield. The name "Molly Pitcher" came to be applied in the nineteenth century to two women whose husbands served in the American army. Margaret Corbin helped man an artillery piece after her husband, a gunner, was killed at the Battle of Fort Washington (16 November 1776). The name is more often associated with Mary Hays McCauley, a stout, strong Irish woman from Carlisle, Pennsylvania, who helped man a cannon in Captain Francis Proctor's company of the Fourth Continental Artillery at the Battle of Monmouth (28 June 1778). In his memoirs, published in 1830, Joseph Plumb Martin recorded his eyewitness account of the woman we know as Molly Pitcher:

A woman whose husband belonged to the artillery and who was then attached to a piece in the engagement, attended with her husband at the piece the whole time. While in the act of reaching [for] a cartridge and having one of her feet as far before the other as she could step, a cannon shot from the enemy passed directly between her legs without doing any other damage than carrying away all the lower part of her petticoat. Looking at it with apparent unconcern, she observed that it was lucky it did not pass a little higher, for in that case it might have carried away something else, and continued her occupation.

Mary McCauley died in 1832.

SEE ALSO *Corbin, Margaret Cochran.*

BIBLIOGRAPHY

Martin, David G. *The Story of Molly Pitcher.* 2d ed. Hightstown, N.J.: Longstreet House, 2000.

————. *A Molly Pitcher Sourcebook.* Hightstown, N.J.: Longstreet House, 2003.

Martin, Joseph Plumb. *Private Yankee Doodle: Being a Narrative of Some of the Adventures, Dangers and Sufferings of a Revolutionary Soldier, Joseph Plumb Martin.* Edited by George F. Scheer. Boston, Mass.: Little, Brown, 1962.

Smith, Samuel S. *A Molly Pitcher Chronology.* Monmouth Beach, N.J.: Philip Freneau Press, 1972.

————. "The Search for Molly Pitcher." *Daughters of the American Revolution Magazine,* April 1975.

revised by Harold E. Selesky

MONCK'S CORNER, SOUTH CAROLINA. 14 April 1780. During the Charleston expedition of 1780, Clinton sent Lieutenant Colonel James Webster, with Tarleton's cavalry, to threaten the American line of communication east of the Cooper River. Tarleton moved with his legion and Ferguson's corps toward Monck's Corner on the evening of 13 April. A captured slave revealed complete information about Huger's dispositions and served as guide. About 3 A.M. the British made contact, routed the Continental cavalry posted in front of Biggin's Bridge, and then scattered the militia posted to the rear near Biggin's Church. Tarleton's troops temporarily captured Lieutenant Colonel William Washington, but he escaped in the darkness. Lieutenant Colonel Webster arrived on the 15th with two regiments to consolidate Tarleton's gains, and the rebel line of communications to Charleston was seriously hindered. Tarleton commented that his surprise was made easier by Huger's faulty tactical dispositions: not only had he failed to send out patrols to detect and delay an enemy's approach, but he had used mounted troops to screen the bridgehead instead of employing foot troops on this mission.

Huger's command consisted of militia (many of them without arms) and from three hundred to five hundred Continental cavalry. The latter comprised remnants of the regiments of Baylor, Bland, Horry, and Moylan, plus what was left of Pulaski's legion (under Major Vernier, who was mortally wounded).

American losses were fifteen killed and eighteen wounded. Including the wounded, sixty-three men were captured along with ninety-eight dragoon horses and forty-two wagons loaded with food, clothing, cavalry equipment, and ammunition. The defeat prevented the Patriot cavalry from actively opposing the British for several weeks. Tarleton reported one officer and two of his men wounded and five horses killed and wounded.

SEE ALSO *Charleston Expedition of Clinton in 1780; Vernier, Pierre-François.*

revised by Carl P. Borick

MONCK'S CORNER, SOUTH CAROLINA.
27 November 1781. A British logistical base lay a few miles east of the village of Monck's Corner at Fair Lawn Plantation on the Cooper River, guarded by a small redoubt. A British field hospital was located in the brick mansion. On 27 November Brigadier General Francis Marion raided the base with about six hundred men. The fifty defenders of the redoubt under Captain Murdock McLean refused to surrender, but the hospital was captured and the doctors and ambulatory wounded taken away as prisoners; the others were left behind on parole. Soon afterward the mansion caught fire and burned to the ground.

BIBLIOGRAPHY

Barbour, R. L. *South Carolina's Revolutionary War Battlefields: A Tour Guide.* Gretna, La.: Pelican Publishing, 2002.

revised by Robert K. Wright Jr.

MONCKTON, HENRY. (1740–1778).
British officer. Fourth son of John Monckton, the first Viscount Galway, and brother of Robert Monckton, he commanded the Forty-Fifth Foot, known as the Sherwood Foresters, from 25 July 1771. He led this unit as part of

Henry Clinton's right wing in the battle of Long Island. As commander of the Second Battalion of grenadiers, he was wounded and captured at Monmouth, 28 June 1778, dying from his wounds a few hours later.

SEE ALSO *Monckton, Robert; Monmouth, New Jersey.*

revised by Michael Bellesiles

MONCKTON, ROBERT. (1726–1782).
British army officer and colonial governor. Second son of the first viscount Galway and his wife, Lady Elizabeth Manners, who was the daughter of the second duke of Rutland, Monckton was educated at Westminster School from 1737. He entered the Third Foot Guards as an ensign in 1741. He fought in Germany and the Netherlands during the War of the Austrian Succession, including the battles of Dettingen (1743) and Fontenoy (1745). He became a captain in the Thirty-fourth Foot in 1744, major in 1747, and lieutenant colonel in the Forty-seventh Foot in 1751. In the latter year he was also elected to Parliament.

In 1752 he joined the Forty-seventh in Nova Scotia. He was commander of Fort Lawrence on the Bay of Fundy before becoming a member of the provincial council at Halifax in August 1753. A little later he pacified some rioting German settlers without bloodshed. On 21 August 1754 he became lieutenant governor of Annapolis Royal, and in Boston that winter he helped to plan the northern prong of the British offensive for 1755: a surprise attack on the French forts dominating the isthmus between the peninsula of Nova Scotia and the mainland. While Edward Braddock was defeated and William Shirley and William Johnson failed, Monckton at the head of 2,000 Massachusetts volunteers and 280 regulars, took Forts Beauséjour and Gaspereau with hardly a shot fired. The success emboldened Governor Charles Lawrence to demand an oath of allegiance from the French Acadians, who had passively or actively resisted British rule since 1713. Monckton had the still controversial duty of rounding up 1,100 of those who refused and deporting them for dispersal among the mainland colonies. In December he became lieutenant governor at Halifax and on 20 December 1757 colonel commandant of the Second Battalion of the Sixtieth Foot, the Royal Americans. Toward the end of 1758 he destroyed French settlements on the St. Johns River, and in 1759 he was James Wolfe's second in command during the Quebec campaign. Badly wounded in the battle on the Plains of Abraham, he became colonel of the Seventeenth Foot on 24 October. In 1760 he was sent to Philadelphia to command the troops in the south; in February 1761 he was promoted major general, and in March he became governor of New York. In 1762 he led the successful assault on Martinique before returning to New York in June. Twelve months later he sailed for England, where in 1770 he was promoted lieutenant general. In 1769 he lost heavily on East India Company stock, making him desperate for further military employment. In 1773 his application to be commander in chief in India was refused, but his sympathies obliged him to decline a consolation offer of the same post in America. He died in London on 21 May 1782.

SEE ALSO *Abraham, Plains of (Quebec); Austrian Succession, War of the; Braddock, Edward; Shirley, William; Wolfe, James.*

revised by John Oliphant

MONCRIEFF, JAMES. (1744–1793). British

military engineer and army officer. Born in Fife, Scotland, James Moncrieff trained at the Royal Military Academy, Woolwich, from 11 March 1759 to 28 January 1762, when he was appointed to the post of practitioner engineer with the rank of ensign. He served at the siege of Havana, where he joined the One-hundredth Foot and was wounded. When the One-hundredth was disbanded in 1763, Moncrieff transferred to the Royal Engineers, afterwards serving mainly in the West Indies and mainland North America. He was promoted sub-engineer and lieutenant on 4 December 1770 and to captain on 10 January 1776. He probably served in the New York campaign, and in 1777 built across the Raritan River a bridge that was sufficiently unusual for a model to be kept at Woolwich. He may have been briefly captured by American raiders on Long Island early in 1778, but at Brandywine he led the Fourth Foot Regiment across Chadd's Ford in the wake of the Seventy-first Regiment, Ferguson's Riflemen (named for their commander, Major Patrick Ferguson), and the Queen's Rangers. The following month Moncrieff was commended for his part in capturing an American warship, the *Delaware*.

It was, however, in the southern campaigns that Moncrieff became famous. He accompanied Andre Prevost's expedition to Savannah, Georgia, and participated in the abortive attack on Charleston, South Carolina, in May 1779. When Prevost fell back to Savannah, Moncrieff was with the rearguard that was left on James Island under John Maitland's command. On 20 June Moncrieff took part in the successful action at Stono Ferry, and personally captured an ammunition wagon, while in pursuit of the fleeing enemy. Arriving in Savannah, he energetically devised and built the defensive works that enabled Prevost to repulse an attack led by Benjamin Lincoln and Charles

Hector Theodat D'Estaing on 9 October. He was brevetted major on 27 December, and remained at Savannah until the arrival of Henry Clinton's Charleston expedition in February 1780. At the siege of Charleston, it was the steady approach of his works and batteries, built with the aid of huge mantelets (protective screens) shipped from New York, that compelled Lincoln to surrender on 12 May. Moncrieff remained in Charleston as chief engineer, now with particular responsibility for its defenses. Breveted lieutenant colonel on 7 September 1780, he settled into Charleston society and was elected president of the St. Andrew's Society in 1781.

Moncrieff's works were built by hundreds of African (slave) laborers. Moncrieff was keenly aware of the Crown's responsibility for their welfare, and even suggested forming a brigade of black soldiers. It may have been he who organized the evacuation of about 800 slaves when the British left the city on 14 December 1782. The Americans called this theft, and accused Moncrieff of profiteering by sending 200 of them to his own plantations in Florida.

After the war Moncrieff was chiefly employed in southern England, becoming quartermaster general on 14 July, but he had to wait until 18 November 1790 to be promoted colonel in the army. On 25 February 1793, Moncrieff's extraordinary expertise and achievements brought him the post of quartermaster general (and unofficial chief engineer) to the duke of York's expedition to the Austrian Netherlands. Moncrieff, a regimental lieutenant colonel Moncrieff distinguished himself at the successful sieges of Valenciennes and Mons, but was mortally wounded during a French sortie from Dunkirk on 6 September. He died the following day, and was buried with full honors at Ostend on 10 September 1793.

SEE ALSO *Maitland, John; Stono Ferry, South Carolina.*

BIBLIOGRAPHY
Mackesy, Piers. *The War for America 1775–1783.* London: Longman, 1964.
Pancake, John S. *This Destructive War: The British Campaign in the Carolinas 1780–1782.* Tuscaloosa: Alabama University Press, 1995.

revised by John Oliphant

MONEY OF THE EIGHTEENTH

CENTURY. A chronic shortage of specie existed in the British colonies before 1775. The colonies mined no precious metals and, because the cost of imports always exceeded the value of exports, most of the specie that flowed into the colonies flowed back out to Britain to pay for imported goods. Efforts to create a circulating

Continental Dollar. *This American coin, issued in 1776, was probably minted in New York City. Although its exact denomination is uncertain, its value is surmised to have been one dollar.* THE GRANGER COLLECTION, NEW YORK

currency were closely regulated by Britain, so the colonists were compelled to use readily available commodities like tobacco as substitutes and to maintain complicated accounts of book debts. Britain also discouraged colonial efforts to coin money, like the crude silver pieces minted in Massachusetts between 1652 and 1682, the best-known of which was the Pine Tree shilling, about the size of a modern quarter.

In the absence of locally minted coins, many different coins minted by the imperial powers circulated in the British colonies. The value of these coins was based on intrinsic value, fineness, and weight, the latter being affected by wear and sometimes by clipping or other forms of mutilation. Spanish coins, most of them minted in the New World, eventually predominated, especially the Spanish milled dollar or piece of eight, a silver coin about the size of a modern silver dollar.

Paper money was produced in the colonies for the first time in 1690, when Massachusetts printed twenty-shilling bills of credit to pay for the expedition against Canada. Britain monitored the paper bills of credit issued thereafter by the colonies, most closely in New England, an effort that generally kept the depreciation of the currency under reasonable control. It has been estimated that the money

supply in 1775 amounted to over twelve million dollars, about four million in paper currency and the rest, perhaps as much as ten million dollars, in specie.

After 1775 the high demand for all metals and the flood of new paper currency combined to drive specie out of circulation. The only coins minted during the war were the Continental dollars of 1776 (six thousand in pewter, many fewer in brass and silver) and a handful of Massachusetts and New Hampshire patterns; the new nation relied almost entirely on various forms of paper money as its circulating currency until 1780, when specie became more plentiful. Shortly after the Articles of Confederation took effect on 1 March 1781, Robert Morris, the superintendent of finance, began to make plans to establish a mint, an authority given to Congress by Article 9. However, by the time he had the plan in place in August 1783, the end of the war, the scarcity of silver bullion, and the need to economize on congressional expenses combined to scuttle the project. The first dollar coins were issued by the United States in 1794, modeled on the Spanish dollar.

Money accounts in the colonies were almost always kept in pounds, shillings, and pence: twelve pence to a shilling and twenty shillings (240 pence) to a pound.

Money reckoned in "pounds sterling," in values tied to specie by the British government, was always worth more than any of the local currencies, which were also denominated in pounds, shillings, and pence and whose value against sterling fluctuated widely across the colonies. In the late colonial period, a British pound sterling had a value of one pound 6 shillings 89 pence (320 pence) in Massachusetts, one pound 13 shillings 4 pence (400 pence) in Pennsylvania, and one pound 15 shillings 7 pence (427 pence) in New York. Maryland issued the first paper money denominated in dollars in 1767. When Congress authorized the emission of three million dollars on 22 June 1775, it made the paper money payable in Spanish milled dollars; a Spanish dollar was worth roughly 4 shillings 6 pence in sterling, 6 shillings in Massachusetts, 7 shillings 6 pence in Pennsylvania, and 8 shillings in New York. In his report to Congress (2 September 1776) on the value of the coins in circulation relative to the Spanish milled dollar, Thomas Jefferson was the first to use a decimal notation, and he continued to be an advocate of the system. On 6 July 1785, while Jefferson was in Paris as minister to France, Congress adopted his decimal system, with the dollar as the standard unit.

SEE ALSO *Continental Currency; Hard Money; Specie.*

BIBLIOGRAPHY

Jordan, Louis. *The Coins of Colonial and Early America.* Robert H. Gore, Jr., Numismatic Endowment, Department of Special Collections. University of Notre Dame, South Bend, Ind. Available online at http://www.coins.ed.edu.

————. *Colonial Currency.* Robert H. Gore, Jr., Numismatic Endowment, Department of Special Collections. University of Notre Dame, South Bend, Ind.. Available online at http://www.coins.ed.edu.

Michener, Ronald. "Backing Theories and the Currencies of Eighteenth-Century America: A Comment." *Journal of Economic History.* 48 (September 1988): 682–692.

Mossman, Philip. *Money of the American Colonies and Confederation Period: A Numismatic, Economic, and Historical Correlation.* New York: American Numismatic Society, 1993.

Newman, Eric P. *The Early Paper Money of America.* 4th ed. Iola, Wis.: Krause Publications, 1997.

————. and Richard Doty, eds. *Studies on Money in Early America.* New York: American Numismatic Society, 1976.

revised by Harold E. Selesky

MONMOUTH, NEW JERSEY.

The Battle of Monmouth, on 28 June 1778, was one of the most complex, least decisive, and ultimately most controversial actions fought by the Continental army during the Revolution. It implicated the reputation of George Washington, the army's commander in chief; it ended the military career of Washington's principal subordinate commander, Charles Lee; and in many respects it ended both the middle period of the war and major campaigning in the northern states. Understanding the dynamics of the battle is impossible without considering the state of the Revolution itself in the early summer of 1778.

THE BATTLE'S CONTEXT

The Valley Forge winter ended neither with a bang nor with a whimper, but rather with a frenetic flurry of activity as both sides adjusted to the fact that a war for independence had become entangled with—or even subsumed by—a world war between Great Britain and France. The announcement in early May 1778 of the February treaties of alliance and commerce between France and the United States provided the occasion for a demonstration at Valley Forge of the new drilling skills of the American army after six weeks of intensive training under the Prussian volunteer, Friedrich Steuben. Whether or not the army's capacity to march, whirl, and display on the camp's Grand Parade ground would reflect or predict its ability to perform better in harsh combat conditions than it had the previous year at Brandywine and Germantown was not known. Whether its next battle, at Monmouth seven weeks later, meaningfully tested that question, is a matter of debate among modern historians. The view expressed below is that it did not.

The entry of France into the war meant that Britain would reduce its levels of material involvement in the North American colonies, first in order to protect its even more vital economic interests in the West Indies sugar islands, which were sure to be a focus of naval activity, and second in order to guard against invasion across the English Channel. On the North American continent, military resources would be deployed more selectively. New York City would remain the British headquarters. Major detachments would be made to the Caribbean and to East and West Florida. The British army would intensify its search for a soft or vulnerable location where enthusiastic civilian support of the king would multiply the return on military investment. Pennsylvania had clearly not proved to be such a place during and after the 1777 campaign. In practice, British land campaigning would be pulled toward the one remaining area where this theory had not been tested: the southern plantation states. There, land troops could also cooperate more easily and supportively with British naval forces operating nearby, in and around the Caribbean Basin.

MARCHING THROUGH NEW JERSEY

The new British commander in chief, Henry Clinton, arrived in Philadelphia in early May to take command of

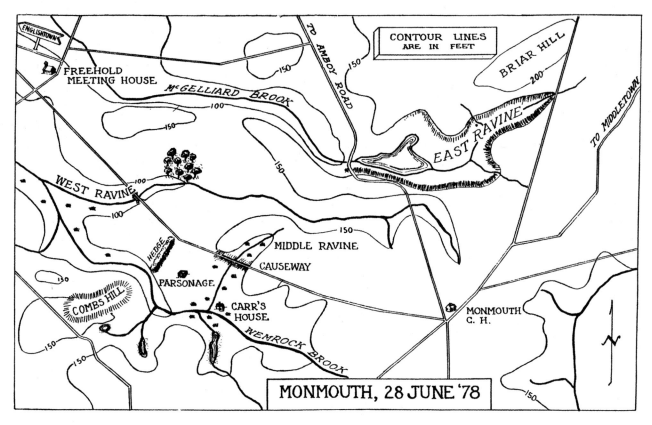

MONMOUTH, 28 JUNE '78

the army from William Howe. He had been directed by the War Office to detach troops to the southern theaters from that place. Operating within a reasonable window of command discretion, however, he decided that such a delicate operation could best be performed from New York rather than Philadelphia. He therefore began preparing the army for withdrawal from Pennsylvania. When the large and influential Delaware Valley Loyalist community, whose members had risked their fortunes for the crown, resisted being abandoned by the redcoats, Clinton knew that he would have to offer its members passage to New York. This would encumber Lord Howe's fleet and require the British army to march back overland to New York.

Washington and his commanders knew that Philadelphia would be evacuated soon. During the spring he canvassed his generals on a range of options, from attacking Philadelphia, to transferring the "seat of war" to New York, to letting the British initiate the campaign. The generals split on these alternatives and Washington himself chose to wait and see. By early June the decision made itself. The British accelerated their preparations to retreat to New York while the Americans concentrated on building up their forces, making logistical preparations

for the new campaign, and pressing Steuben's training program to the maximum possible extent.

Clinton began loading his ships and ferrying troops and equipment across the Delaware to New Jersey after 11 June. Washington's logistical officers responded by plotting out routes toward the Delaware above Trenton and from there toward the Hudson, and by stocking supply depots along those routes. On 16 June, Washington issued orders for the army's march toward three river crossing points between Coryell's Ferry and Easton. The news two days later that the British had evacuated Philadelphia triggered a race toward the north. The British force of about ten thousand men (many of the German troops were sent with the fleet) marched in two parallel columns north through New Jersey along the Delaware River toward Allentown, southeast of Trenton. They were encumbered by a large baggage train, which— with the columns themselves—stretched awkwardly for almost twelve miles. The weather was hot and the roads were badly worn. Washington's troops left Valley Forge, continuing to display their ability to march very quickly, something that they had done the previous summer and fall, long before Steuben began to train them. Lightly encumbered by baggage, they reached and crossed the

Delaware before Clinton's force reached the bend in that river below Trenton. When Washington reassembled his army in Hopewell, New Jersey, he decided that it might be appropriate to go on the offensive. A council of war on 24 June split on the matter. A majority of generals, led by Charles Lee, argued for at most a cautious engagement with rear elements of Clinton's force but for avoiding a general engagement. A smaller number, articulated by Nathanael Greene and Anthony Wayne, wanted more aggressive measures. Washington favored the latter position but held his counsel.

Clinton's scouts kept him aware of the shadowy presence of this Continental escort, and—feeling pressured by it—he abandoned plans to march straight across the waist of New Jersey to New Brunswick and Perth Amboy, and from there across Staten Island toward New York City. Instead, Clinton bent his march northeast toward Sandy Hook, in Monmouth County, from where the army would have to be ferried up the harbor to the tip of Manhattan Island. This course took the British army through an alternating landscape of farmland and barrens or wetlands, with the latter increasing as it approached the Atlantic coast. The roads became increasingly sandy. The army, now marching as a single column rather than two, spread over an even longer stretch of terrain. Soldiers in woolen uniforms began to feel the effects of an early summer heat wave.

The Americans were moving due east from Princeton through Cranbury, closing on the left rear flank of the British army. Clinton sent much of his baggage, and the units in which he had the least confidence—consisting of about four thousand troops—to the front of his column, under the command of the German general, Wilhelm Knyphausen. He commanded the main body of the army itself, numbering about six thousand men, from the center, and dispatched Lord Cornwallis to the rear of the column to guard against sniping attacks. He intended to have Knyphausen march rapidly toward Middletown and then to Sandy Hook. Cornwallis would move more leisurely, while Clinton himself would lag in the middle in order to be able to support Cornwallis if his tempting presence drew the Americans into a general engagement. Clinton's main responsibility was to get his army back into headquarters unharmed and quickly enough to make the strategic detachments ordered by the War Department. But he had no objection to an opportunity to bloody his adversary on the way there if Washington was willing to fight it out.

THE BATTLE SETTING

On 25 June, Washington decided to send forward a probing detachment of about fifteen hundred men to see if Cornwallis's rear guard might be roughed up. He offered

command of the detachment, as a matter of protocol, to General Lee, but Lee—having counseled against aggressive tactics and considering the projected probe to be at best a paltry maneuver—refused the assignment. Washington then gave his protégé, the Marquis de Lafayette, the command of the enterprise. As an evolving series of decisions increased the number of troops committed to the enterprise to twenty-five hundred, and then to four thousand men, Lee reconsidered the matter and claimed the right to command it as a prerogative of his rank as second-in-command of the army as a whole. Washington may have thought better about allowing a dissenter against offensive action to undertake the project, but he again deferred to Lee's entitlement as a matter of military custom. By late in the day on the 27th, the detachment had been increased again to about five thousand men.

On that day the British rested at a sandy crossroads village called Monmouth Court House, where the seat of the county government and its judicial bodies sat. The courthouse lay at the intersection of five roads that converged from all directions across central northeastern New Jersey. A small stream called Wemrock Brook, and its several branches, carved the countryside into a series of ravines—designated the West, Middle, and East Ravines—interspersed with piney woods and marshy lowlands. Washington did no more—indeed, he did considerably less—than he had done the day before the Battle of Brandywine nine months earlier, to survey the ground that might be fought over. If he had developed an overly complex tactical plan for the attack at Germantown, now he obviated that difficulty by developing no particular plan at all. Rather, he directed Lee and his subordinate officers, the Marquis de Lafayette, and Generals Anthony Wayne, William Maxwell, and Charles Scott, to push ahead of the main American force and to make contact the next day with rear units of Clinton's army. If they could precipitate a significant engagement without becoming overwhelmed, they should do that. Washington promised to be following nearby with the main body of the army, close enough to the action to reinforce Lee and his commanders whenever necessary.

EARLY AMERICAN RETREAT

In the middle of the night on 27 June, Clinton sent Knyphausen and his segment of the army forward toward Middletown with the baggage train. Clinton followed with the rest of the army toward daybreak on the 28th. Washington had almost immediate notice of the movement and he ordered Lee to engage the enemy as soon as possible. Some of Lee's skirmishers clashed briefly and inconclusively with Knyphausen's force beyond the sleeping village, but they broke off the chase. Lee then brought his main body of troops up and formed a line along the road between the courthouse and the East Ravine to the

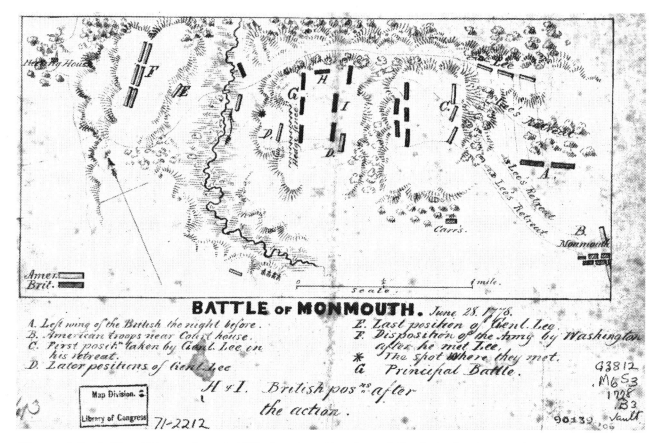

Monmouth Battle Plan. *This map, drawn in 1778, shows the position of troops before the Battle in Monmouth in New Jersey on 28 June 1778.* THE LIBRARY OF CONGRESS, GEOGRAPHY AND MAP DIVISION

northwest. Clinton waited until Knyphausen's troops and wagons were well under way and then ordered Cornwallis to turn around and march back to Monmouth to receive Lee's force. Lee's improvised arrangement of units was struggling to maintain its shape as more and more British troops arrived on the battlefield against it. His efforts to shift regiments from one location to another as the clash grew were counterproductive. It soon became clear that generals such as Lafayette and Wayne, who had advocated engaging the British in councils of war, were less than confident under the direction of Lee, who had not. The confusion communicated itself to ordinary soldiers as an invitation to panic, and groups of men began to withdraw in search of safer positions. Lee decided that he had little ability to protect his force as a whole, especially against mounted redcoats, who could maneuver easily in sand and swamps while exhausted American infantrymen were all but helpless there. Lee tried to retract his troops toward the second ravine, but the retreat quickly became a general one.

Washington, meanwhile, pursuant to his promise to Lee and the other commanders the previous evening, was hurrying his main body of troops toward Monmouth Court House to support what he hoped would become a decisively successful action. He expressed puzzlement when initial indications that the battle had been joined were followed by silence as the retreat began. Lee, Wayne, and Lafayette heroically struggled with some success to reform their units and to stop the withdrawal, but stragglers from the various divisions moved to the west. By ones and twos, and then by small groups, these individuals came into Washington's line of vision as he hurried toward the village. He incredulously and angrily queried several of these parties, not wanting to believe, and then not understanding, as evidence mounted of an action going badly wrong.

Washington finally encountered Lee himself near the West Ravine. He heatedly demanded an explanation of the situation from Lee, who took several minutes even to become coherent. Lee believed that he had creditably extracted his force from imminent disaster stemming from intelligence problems and insubordinate assistants, complicated by Clinton's unexpected willingness to commit a large part of his force to repel an attack on his rear guard. He professed incredulity that, instead of being congratulated, he was subjected to an impromptu cross-

736

examination. When Washington expressed angry dissatisfaction with Lee's explanations, perhaps inevitably, the latter reminded his commander that he had urged against instigating a general action. This rightly caused Washington to exclaim that orders were orders, whatever the recipient may have thought about their soundness, and, inevitably, to wonder why Lee had accepted the command of the detachment in the first place if he was opposed to its mission.

Both men then remembered that a battle was raging around them, and Washington, as was his custom, moved forward toward the fighting to try to restore order. At Brandywine the previous year, he had done the same thing, except that he had then worked toward the rear of the Birmingham Meeting clash. At Monmouth he headed forward toward the point of action. Before he moved out, Washington ordered Nathanael Greene, who was in the main section of the army that had arrived with Washington, to move his division to the right onto a hill to try to cover the battlefield. Greene took several artillery units with him and scrambled onto the elevation.

THE AMERICANS REGROUP

Washington then learned that Cornwallis, after allowing the Americans to retreat in front of him with relatively little pressure, had begun to advance, hoping to turn the withdrawal into a rout like the one at Germantown. The redcoats were less than fifteen minutes away, moving between the East and Middle Ravines. Washington assumed that the British would continue their march toward Middletown and Sandy Hook after repelling Lee's probe, rather than continue the action. The news that he was mistaken portended a long and difficult afternoon. His aides found an officer from the New Jersey line who was familiar with the ground in the area and who suggested that it could be defended. Washington ordered that the most stricken and heat-exhausted of the retreating troops should be taken into the woods in the immediate rear to be cooled, calmed, and refreshed. Of the remaining units in the forward group, Anthony Wayne's appeared to be the most intact. Washington sought to use it to anchor a holding action until he could bring the fresh troops that he had brought forward into play. He ordered several broken regiments to merge temporarily into a new one and placed them behind a hedgerow near the West Ravine. Wayne would nominally command the holding action. Washington and Charles Lee achieved a sort of impromptu battlefield détente when the commander in chief asked, and his subordinate agreed, that Lee assume command of the rear guard supporting Wayne's troops. Nathanael Greene's force—including some artillery—which had shifted to the American right, overlooked the scene from an elevation known as Comb's Hill. Henry Knox, the commander of the Continental artillery forces,

took the rest of his gunmen to an elevation on the left side of the American line, which also commanded the impending clash.

Before these positions could be consolidated the advancing redcoats, displaying the wall of bayonets that were famously presumed to terrorize less seasoned and less disciplined troops, reached the front and fell on the Americans. General Clinton also brought up mounted troops—another element in which the British had a clear technical superiority to the revolutionaries. These cavalry charged into the Continental line. The fighting became fierce in the late afternoon heat. The Americans at first seemed to buckle under the pressure but then regrouped and resisted furiously. Gradually and grudgingly, the Continentals yielded control of the West Ravine, but Lee's reserves absorbed some of the pressure and prevented the American line from breaking down. At this point the American artillery, advantageously positioned on the heights on both sides of the battlefront, emerged as a decisive element. Greene's units and Knox's force fired from close range into both sides of the British advance, and redcoat casualties mounted sharply. Clinton's heavy guns attempted to suppress the American fire, but they were firing from the plain onto small rises on either side and were unable to accomplish their objective. The general slope of the ground meant that the British were mostly fighting uphill, even when they moved forward.

Clinton made several more almost desperate efforts to throw enough strength at the American line to break it and thereby to secure the ground beyond the ravine, but in every case the advances were driven back with heavy casualties on both sides. After 5 P.M., with considerable daylight remaining barely a week past the summer solstice, there were indications that the British attack was ebbing. Washington was tempted to resume the role of the aggressor and to try to drive the British from the battlefield, but with the continuing heat, the need to attend to casualties, and a sense of the army's long-term interests, he declined to do so. Clinton withdrew his army to Monmouth Court House and camped overnight. As William Howe had done at Brandywine, Washington camped on the battlefield, claiming one of the main technical criteria of victory. He planned to resume the action in the morning, but the British rose early and marched toward Sandy Hook, from where they were ferried into New York City.

WHO WON?

While both sides claimed victory in the engagement, they implicitly did so on the basis of different assessments of what the battle had been about and what their objectives for it were. For the first time in a year and one-half—since Trenton and Princeton—the Americans could make a plausible claim to be called the victors in a significant armywide confrontation. Their casualties were somewhat

Molly Pitcher. *Mary Hays McCauley, better known as Molly Pitcher, carried pitchers of water to American troops and helped operate a cannon during the Battle of Monmouth in June 1778. Nineteenth-century engraving.* THE LIBRARY OF CONGRESS

fewer than those of the British (see below); they slept on the core part of the battlefield while the enemy pulled back and then withdrew altogether; and they measurably improved their confidence in terms of being able to hold their own in the face of enemy fire. Still, the battle itself was a hybrid or even a mongrelized event, and the British had a plausible case to make as well. General Clinton was trying to get his awkward train of men and equipment back to New York City, and he did so expeditiously, after fighting off a concerted rebel effort to disrupt his march. From the British perspective, a rebel insurgency had morphed into a more familiar Atlantic and even a global war against an enemy that they knew well how to fight. They were determined to embrace that reality, and Monmouth did nothing to prevent that end.

POST-ACTION CONTROVERSY

The outcome at Monmouth at first split and then solidified the American command structure. Although Washington and Charles Lee patched up their confront-ation and worked together on the battlefield to extract the army from danger, Lee could not contain his anger. He had expected to be praised for doing just that with the forward elements when he met Washington behind the Middle Ravine on June 28, and he was amazed to be criticized instead. Several days of brooding enlarged this hurt into the sense that he had actually delivered Clinton's and Cornwallis's rear guard into Washington's hands on advantageous terrain, and that he was thus significantly responsible for any success. Washington could brook neither of these claims, especially since they were delivered to him in several impetuous and curt letters, which implied that Lee hoped to defend his honor in an administrative proceeding. Washington was more than willing to give him that opportunity. On 30 June he had Lee formally arrested in preparation for a court-martial. He charged Lee with disobedience of his orders for failing to attack the enemy, of "misbehavior" for "making an unnecessary, disorderly, and shameful retreat," and finally with displaying disrespect to himself in the course of their post-battle correspondence.

To address these charges here would be to re-describe the battle and is not really necessary. Historians generally agree that Lee was innocent of the first two charges but unquestionably guilty of the third. The strategic and political needs of the Continental establishment itself, and of its military institutions, cannot be separated from an account of the post-action controversy. Washington had withstood what he and his partisans believed to have been a winter-long effort by his enemies—represented principally by General Thomas Conway—to undermine his position and supplant him from his command. He had made significant strides in shaping the army that he himself called "new" the previous summer into a credible long-term military instrument. The Revolution had been irrevocably transformed by the reality of French diplomatic recognition and material assistance and by the fact of the new international war.

How these circumstances would impact the battlefield was not clear, but the commander in chief's impregnable control of the army had to be reaffirmed. Washington's officer corps had overwhelmingly rallied around him at Valley Forge, despite some inevitable carping and complaint. The court-martial staff was drawn from that corps, and Lee's fate was sealed: he was convicted on all three of Washington's charges. Congress confirmed the result, although it modified some of the specific language of the decree and softened the penalty. Lee was suspended from his commission in late 1778 and—after continuing to protest bitterly his innocence—dismissed from the army two years later. He died in 1782 in obscurity and became a temporary scapegoat for the Revolution's travails. If not for the disgrace in 1780 of Benedict Arnold—who spent the week of Monmouth reestablishing Revolutionary control in Philadelphia as its temporary military governor—Lee might have become the great scapegoat of the war itself.

ASSESSING STEUBEN'S IMPACT

As it had after another engagement in central New Jersey eighteen months before—the Battle of Princeton—the Continental army veered northwest from Monmouth Court House in a relatively exuberant mood. If it had not earned an unequivocal victory, it had at least showed its mettle and resourcefulness. It is doubtful that Monmouth provides, as some scholars have claimed, the "proof of the forge," convincing evidence of the transformational character of the army's stoic virtue on the Schuylkill River and of Friedrich Steuben's professional training of its members. The battle was too idiosyncratic in its structure and cadence to constitute such a test. The Continentals showed much of the willingness to attack a stronger force that they had done at Germantown the year before. When that attack quickly unravelled—whether because of the ineptness of Lee or the impulsiveness of his immediate subordinates—the privates showed the same ability to regroup under hot fire that they had done at Brandywine. Once Washington reestablished a stable front line, they withstood repeated charges from some of Clinton's best units in a way that may well suggest general improvements over the preceding ten months. This probably reflects, however, the contributions of Continental artillery forces, which seized advantageous high ground on either side of the West Ravine, and whose members repeatedly fired devastating volleys into the flanks of the British attackers during the last hours of the battle. If so, it should be noted that these skillful, fractious individualists were less involved in Steuben's training exercises at Valley Forge than perhaps any other parts of the army.

After Monmouth, the army did little if any organizationwide campaigning in the North for the rest of the war. Washington marched his force to White Plains, New York, east of the Hudson River. After surveying its condition, he gradually distributed it along a broad crescent running from Fairfield, Connecticut, to Westchester County, New York, then stretching across the Hudson at the Highlands and finally curving south and east across the New York-New Jersey border to an anchor on the Atlantic near New Brunswick and Perth Amboy. The "lessons" of Valley Forge that Washington applied between 1778 and 1783 reflected the value of maintaining an alert but loose grip around an entrenched, urban enemy headquarters.

The patrolling and skirmishing that the army did in support of this modest but critical mission depended less on Steuben's manual of arms and close-order drill than on a pride in military professionalism and a commitment to the principles of civilian supremacy and republican liberty. The impromptu Continental march to Yorktown and the 1781 siege there, as well as the use of elements from the northern army in the chaotic southern campaigns of 1778–1781, may reinforce Monmouth's role in demonstrating the army's conventional combat prowess imbibed at Valley Forge. But if this is the case, that point remains to be demonstrated.

CASUALTIES

These are more highly disputed and indeterminable than for most Revolutionary war actions. The Americans suffered at least 106 men killed, 161 wounded, and 95 missing, some of whom undoubtedly died, probably of the heat, and were buried in the woods near the battlefield. The British admitted losses of 177 killed, 170 wounded, and 64 missing. Again, heat-related deaths were considerable on both sides and may not have been included in official totals.

SEE ALSO *Brandywine, Pennsylvania; Clinton, Henry; Germantown, Pennsylvania, Battle of; Greene, Nathanael; Howe, William; Knyphausen, Wilhelm;*

Lafayette, Marquis de; Lee Court Martial; Lee, Charles (1731–1782); Maxwell, William; Princeton, New Jersey; Scott, Charles; Steuben, Friedrich Wilhelm von; Wayne, Anthony.

BIBLIOGRAPHY

An Account of the Action from Brandywine to Monmouth: A Seminar on the Impact of the Revolutionary War on the Delaware Valley. Philadelphia: Council of American Revolutionary Sites, 1997.

Lengel, Edward G. *General George Washington, A Military Life.* New York: Random House, 2005.

Smith, Samuel Stelle. *The Battle of Monmouth.* Monmouth Beach, N.J.: Philip Freneau Press, 1964.

Stryker, William S. *The Battle of Monmouth.* 1927. Reprint, Port Washington, N.Y.: Kennikat Press, 1970.

revised by Wayne K. Bodle

MONROE, JAMES. (1758–1831).

Continental army officer and fifth president of the United States. Virginia. Born in Westmoreland County, Virginia, on 28 April 1758, Monroe was the son of a modestly prosperous family. He entered the College of William and Mary in 1774 but left on 28 September 1775 to enlist as a second lieutenant in Colonel Hugh Mercer's Third Virginia Regiment. He volunteered to accompany Thomas Knowlton and his rangers in attempting to encircle the British light infantry at Harlem Heights on 16 September 1776. Monroe also fought at White Plains (28 October) and at Trenton (26 December), where he helped to lead the vanguard and was seriously wounded. He was promoted to major on 20 November 1777 and named aide-de-camp to William Alexander (Lord Stirling). He fought at Brandywine, Germantown, and Monmouth before resigning on 20 November 1778.

In 1780 Monroe began studying law under Thomas Jefferson, then governor of Virginia, and stayed with him until 1783. He was elected to the House of Burgesses in 1782 and later sat in the Confederation Congress (1783–1786). In 1786 he married Elizabeth Kortwright, the daughter of a New York City merchant who was a Loyalist officer. He was a member of the state convention that ratified the Constitution and was a prominent anti-Federalist. He served as a U.S. Senator (1790–1794), minister to France (1794–1796), governor of Virginia (1799–1802 and 1811), negotiator for the Louisiana Purchase (1803), minister to Great Britain (1803–1807), secretary of state (1811–1817), secretary of war (1814–1815), and president (1817–1825). The most notable accomplishments during his two terms as president were in foreign affairs, including the acquisition of Florida and the promulgation of the Monroe Doctrine (2 December 1823).

SEE ALSO *Harlem Heights, New York; Trenton, New Jersey.*

BIBLIOGRAPHY

Ammon, Harry. *James Monroe: The Quest for National Identity.* New York: McGraw-Hill, 1971.

revised by Harold E. Selesky

MONTGOMERY, RICHARD. (1738–1775).

Continental general. Ireland and New York. Richard Montgomery was born in Swords, Ireland, on 2 December 1738. The son of an Irish member of Parliament, he became an ensign in the Seventeenth Foot in 1756. Going to Canada the next year (1757), he took part in the siege of Louisburg (1758), was promoted to lieutenant, and served under Jeffery Amherst in the successful operations against Ticonderoga, Crown Point, and Montreal. Meanwhile, he became regimental adjutant in 1760. In the West Indies he was at the capture of Martinique and Havana (1762), becoming a captain by the end of those actions. Returning to Great Britain, he became a friend of Edmund Burke and Charles James Fox, two prominent Whig politicians of the time, and was greatly influenced by their liberal views. Disgusted with the British patronage system and his failure to advance further in the army, he sold his commission on 6 April 1772 and emigrated to America, settling on a 67-acre farm he had bought at Kings Bridge, New York. Having married Janet Livingston, the daughter of Robert R. Livingston, Montgomery became quickly involved in American politics and was elected a delegate to New York's first provincial congress in May 1775. He accepted a commission as Continental brigadier general on 22 June 1775.

Leaving his young wife and their new home near Rhinebeck (her estate), Montgomery went north to become second in command to General Philip Schuyler in the invasion of Canada in 1775 and 1776. With Schuyler soon evacuated for illness, Montgomery showed real military ability in leading an offensive into Canada, despite the poor quality of troops and subordinate leaders at his disposal and the logistical problems he faced. After taking St. Johns on 5 September–2 November 1775, and Montreal shortly afterwards, he pushed on to make the unsuccessful attack on Quebec (31 December–1 January 1776). He was killed in the latter action, never knowing that Congress had made him a major general on 9 December 1775. In death, Montgomery became a hero and martyr to the cause of American independence.

SEE ALSO *Canada Invasion; Quebec (Canada Invasion); St. John's, Canada (5 September–2 November 1775).*

The Death of General Montgomery in the Attack on Quebec (1786). *John Trumbull's dramatic painting depicts Richard Montgomery's battlefield death in December 1775 during the American attack on Quebec.* LANDOV

BIBLIOGRAPHY

Shelton, Hal T. *General Richard Montgomery and the American Revolution.* New York: New York University Press, 1994.

revised by Michael Bellesiles

MONTMORENCI FALLS, CANADA.

31 July 1759. On the north shore of the St. Lawrence River below these falls, a few miles east of Quebec City, Major General James Wolfe tried to penetrate the French defenses. His lack of success prolonged the siege of Quebec and ultimately persuaded him to undertake the gamble of threatening Quebec from the bluffs west of the city, on the Plains of Abraham.

SEE ALSO *Colonial Wars; Plains of Abraham (13 September 1759).*

revised by Harold E. Selesky

MONTOUR FAMILY. Elizabeth Catherine "Madam" Montour was born at Trois-Rivières, Quebec, in 1667, the daughter of Pierre Couc dit Lafleur and his Algonquian wife, Marie Miteouamigoukoue. Her family was involved in the Indian trade, which is how she met Roland Montour, a Seneca, whom she married, spending the rest of her life among the Iroquois. Madam Montour, as she was widely known, was employed as an interpreter by New York's governor, Robert Hunter, and served in the same capacity for the Iroquois on many occasions. Her first husband was killed in the early 1720s, apparently while fighting the Catawba in South Carolina. In 1727 she married Carondowana, an Oneida chief. She died near the town named in her honor, Montoursville, Pennsylvania, in 1753.

Madam Montour's son, Andrew, also known as Sattelihu, was an accomplished linguist, serving as an interpreter at many conferences between colonial governments and Indians. He received a captain's commission from Virginia in 1754 and served as a guide for British and allied Indians during the Seven Years' War, being present at both Fort Necessity and Braddock's defeat.

Pennsylvania rewarded him with two land grants. He died in 1772.

Andrew Montour's son, John, also served as an interpreter for the British and the American colonists. During the Revolution he led a company of Delaware Indians allied to the rebels.

Madam Montour's niece, "French Margaret," married an Indian and had daughters named Catherine and Esther. The latter married a ruling chief and lived near Tioga. She may have taken part in the Wyoming Valley Massacre and was accused of murdering prisoners.

SEE ALSO *Wyoming Valley Massacre, Pennsylvania.*

revised by Michael Bellesiles

MONTREAL. 25 September 1775. Ethan Allen's abortive attack. When Richard Montgomery started his siege of St. Johns (now St-Jean, Quebec), he sent Ethan Allen ahead to recruit Canadians along the Richelieu River for the American army. John Brown went toward La Prairie with the same purpose while Canadians James Livingston and Jeremy Duggan also started assembling men around Chambly and Pointe Olivier. Allen discovered widespread opposition among the farmers to Governor Guy Carleton's efforts to mobilize the Canadian militia; he decided to try taking Montréal, which was virtually undefended owing to the governor's decision to concentrate his regulars at the border. Although the colony's fate seemed to be hanging in the balance, Allen could not find enough men willing to attack immediately. He turned back briefly to join forces with Brown and Duggan and developed a plan to capture the city. Allen would cross the St. Lawrence with his 110 men (30 Americans and 80 Canadians) at Longueuil below Montreal while Brown with 200 crossed upstream at La Prairie; the two forces would then attack simultaneously.

Allen and Duggan began crossing at 10 P.M. on 24 September, but he had to shuttle the men over in canoes. By dawn on the next day, Allen's band was in the village of Longue-Pointe, but Brown had not been able to get across. Allen was immediately detected, and the inhabitants of the city shut its gates, buying time for the surprised Carleton to organize his defenses. Encouraged by the support he was receiving from the population, Carleton sallied out with a polyglot force: 34 regulars from the Twenty-Sixth Foot, 20 staff members of the Indian Department, 80 English-speaking Canadians, 120 French-speaking Canadians, and a half-dozen Indians. At the approach of this force, most of Allen's Canadians melted away. The dozen or so left, plus the Americans, tried to set up a defense at Ruisseau-des-Soeurs but were quickly overwhelmed.

Carleton lost 3 killed and 2 wounded; Allen and 35 of his band were captured and 5 were killed.

This quixotic escapade had an impact far beyond the tiny numbers involved. It shored up British morale, encouraged the northern Indians, and kept most Canadians sitting on the fence. It also left Carleton free and gave Quebec City time to prepare its own defenses.

SEE ALSO *Allen, Ethan; Brown, John; Canada Invasion; St. John's, Canada (5 September–2 November 1775).*

BIBLIOGRAPHY

Lanctot, Gustave. *Canada and the American Revolution, 1774–1783.* Translated by Margaret M. Cameron. Cambridge, Mass.: Harvard University Press, 1967.

Stanley, George F. G. *Canada Invaded, 1775–1776.* Toronto: Hakkert, 1973.

revised by Robert K. Wright Jr.

MONTREAL. 13 November 1775. Occupied by Americans. The fall of St. Johns on 2 November left Montreal open to capture. Brigadier General Richard Montgomery sent an advance detachment of Americans and Canadians toward Sorel the next day, and they brushed aside light resistance; Montgomery followed with his main body two days later. The first of Montgomery's men crossed the St. Lawrence River and landed upstream from Montreal on 11 November. Governor Guy Carleton had only about a hundred troops and a few militia, so during the night of 12–13 November he spiked his cannon and embarked on a few small vessels; in the morning of 13 November the citizens opened the gates of the city to the Americans. The garrison's retreat was turned back twice by blocking positions set up at Sorel. Carleton escaped on 19 November by disguising himself as a Canadian and reached Quebec the next day on the armed scow *Fell.* Brigadier Richard Prescott and the bulk of the garrison surrendered on 20 November along with their collection of small vessels headed by the six-gun brig *Gaspée.*

SEE ALSO *Canada Invasion; Quebec (Canada Invasion); St. John's, Canada (5 September–2 November 1775).*

revised by Robert K. Wright Jr.

MONTRESOR, JAMES GABRIEL. (1702–1776). Military engineer in the colonial wars. Son of a naturalized Huguenot immigrant, Montresor entered the Royal Artillery in 1724 and over the next thirty years served as a surveyor and military engineer at Minorca and Gibraltar, where he became chief engineer in 1746. In 1754 he was appointed Braddock's chief engineer, but because of ill health did not arrive in Virginia until after the debacle at the Monongahela. Thereafter, he supervised the construction or repair of most of the forts on the New York frontier as director of engineers and lieutenant colonel after 4 January 1758 and served under Amherst in the 1759 campaign. Plagued by ill health, he was allowed to return on leave to England in the spring of 1760. John Montresor was a son of his first marriage.

SEE ALSO *Montresor, John.*

revised by Harold E. Selesky

MONTRESOR, JOHN. (1736–1799).

British military engineer. Born at Gibraltar, the son of James Gabriel Montresor, John Montresor went to America ahead of his father in 1754 and, appointed an additional engineer by Edward Braddock, was wounded at the Monongahela on (9 July 1755). He then served on the New York frontier and took part in the earl of Loudoun's so-called Cabbage Planting Expedition to Halifax, Nova Scotia, in 1757. He served under Jeffrey Amherst at the capture of Louisburg (1758), James Wolfe at the siege of Quebec (1759), and James Murray in the final conquest of Canada in 1760. During most of this time he specialized in scouting missions and dispatch carrying. In 1761 he explored the route up the Kennebec River in Maine that was later used by Benedict Arnold in his march to Quebec.

At the start of Pontiac's uprising, Lieutenant Montresor was sent from New York City with letters for the commander at Detroit. Delayed at Niagara for almost a month awaiting passage, he sailed on 26 August 1763 with provisions and a seventeen-man detachment of the Seventeenth Regiment commanded by Captain Edward Hope. Shipwrecked two days later, Montresor fortified the temporary camp and enabled the survivors and a one-hundred-man reinforcement that arrived on 2 September to beat off Indian attacks that lasted from dawn to dusk on 3 September. Finally reaching Detroit, he stayed there until 20 November 1763, when he left with Robert Rogers (the famous ranger) and a large detachment to return to Niagara. The next year he fortified the portage at the latter place and went with John Bradstreet to Detroit, where he improved the defenses.

He returned from England in 1766 as a captain lieutenant and barrackmaster. During the next few years he worked on fortifications or barracks at New York City, Boston, Philadelphia, and the Bahamas. Montresor surveyed the boundary line between New York and New Jersey in 1769, and in 1772 he bought what was later called Randall's Island in the East River and lived there with his wife and family.

Montresor saw considerable service during the first three years of the War of American Independence. He was present at Lexington and Concord (19 April 1775) and laid out a redoubt on Bunker Hill to cover the retreat of the British to Boston that General Thomas Gage ordered abandoned later that day. He fought in the Battle of Bunker Hill on 17 June to regain the position Gage had let slip away two months earlier. Montresor was appointed chief engineer in America on 10 December 1775 and promoted to captain on 10 January 1776. He blew up Castle William, at the mouth of Boston harbor, when the British evacuated in March. He served as an aide to William Howe at the Battle of Long Island (27 August 1776), directed the artillery at the Battle of Brandywine (11 September 1777), and was present at the Battle of Germantown (4 October 1777). He supervised the construction of the British defenses around Philadelphia in the fall of 1777 and directed the attack on the Delaware River forts. (He had begun the fort on Mud Island, renamed Fort Mifflin, in 1771.) He organized the Mischianza, an elaborate entertainment held on 18 May 1778 at Philadelphia to honor Howe on the eve of his return to Britain. He fought under Sir Henry Clinton, Howe's successor, at Monmouth (28 June 1778), but his ties to Howe seem to have incurred him the displeasure of Clinton, who praised James Moncrieff as "an engineer who understood his business" but did not mention John Montresor once in his memoirs. Montresor returned to England later that year and retired from the army. He died in debtor's prison at Maidstone on 26 June 1799

SEE ALSO *Arnold's March to Quebec; Bunker Hill, Massachusetts; Moncrieff, James; Montresor, James Gabriel; Montresor's Island, New York.*

BIBLIOGRAPHY

Skull, G. D., ed. *The Montresor Journals.* New York: New-York Historical Society, 1882.

revised by Harold E. Selesky

MONTRESOR'S ISLAND, NEW YORK.

Owned by John Montresor from 1772 until the British evacuation of New York in November 1783, Montresor's Island (now called Randall's Island) lies at the mouth of the Harlem River. It was occupied by the British on 10 September 1776. "From that well-chosen advance post," comments the historian Douglas Southall Freeman, "they could land either on the plains of Harlem, south of

Kings Bridge, or on the Morrisania estate, whence they could flank the position at Kings Bridge by a march of six or seven miles" (vol. IV, p. 187). Up until this time it had been used by the Americans as an isolation area for troops inoculated with smallpox. Learning from two deserters that the island was lightly held, General William Heath got General George Washington's authority to retake it. Lieutenant Colonel Michael Jackson of the Sixteenth Massachusetts Continental Infantry led 240 men in an attempt to surprise the outpost at dawn on 23 September (some sources give 24 September as the date of this action).

An American sentinel near the mouth of Harlem Creek had not been informed of this operation and fired at the friendly force as it passed on the way to Montresor's Island. Jackson landed about dawn with three field officers and men from the first boat. When the British guard attacked, the men in the other two boats pulled away instead of landing to join their leaders. In the withdrawal, about fourteen Americans were killed, wounded, or captured. Major Thomas Henly, General Heath's aide-de-camp, who had insisted on accompanying the attack, was killed as he re-entered the boat. Jackson was wounded by a musket ball in the leg. Freeman notes: "The delinquents in the other boats were arrested, and tried by court-martial, and one of the Captains cashiered" (vol. IV, pp. 73–76).

SEE ALSO *Heath, William; Jackson, Michael; Montresor, John.*

BIBLIOGRAPHY
Freeman, Douglas Southall. *George Washington,* 7 vols. New York: Scribner's, 1948–1957.

revised by Barnet Schecter

MOODY, JAMES. (1744–1809). Loyalist spy.

Born in Little Egg Harbor, New Jersey, on 31 December 1744, Moody settled as a farmer in Knowlton. He demonstrated no interest in politics until 1777, when he refused to swear allegiance to the state's revolutionary government. After being beaten by members of the local committee of safety, he was fired upon by the Knowlton militia near his house. All the shots missed, however, and Moody fled to the British lines, where he enlisted in the New Jersey Volunteers. He took part in numerous raids behind enemy lines to gather information, destroy arms depots, seize foodstuffs, capture Patriot officers and officials, and recruit Loyalists. Moody gained a reputation as being very good at these tasks and was credited with enlisting five hundred men to the Loyalist cause in 1777 alone. On 17 July 1780 he was returning to British lines at Bull's Ferry, New Jersey, when it came under a Patriot attack in

which he was captured. Imprisoned at West Point under inhumane conditions, he was transferred to Washington's camp for trial as a spy, making a bold escape on 21 September. Back in New York City, he was promoted to lieutenant. A trap was set for Moody in May 1781, and he was surprised by seventy militiamen. They opened fire and demonstrated their marksmanship when all of them missed. In his last raid that November, Moody attempted to steal congressional papers in Philadelphia but was betrayed. Moody escaped, but his brother was captured and executed.

In 1782 he went to London, where he wrote a popular account of his experiences. The crown awarded him an annual pension of £100, in addition to £1,608 to cover his losses. In 1785 Moody settled in Sissiboo, Nova Scotia, where he became a successful builder, local official, colonel of militia, and representative in the assembly from 1793 to 1806. He died in Sissiboo on 6 April 1809.

BIBLIOGRAPHY
Jones, E. Alfred. *The Loyalists of New Jersey: Their Memorials, Petitions, Claims, etc., from English Records.* Boston: Gregg Press, 1972.

Moody, James. *Lieutenant James Moody's Narrative of his Exertions and Sufferings.* 1783. New York: New York Times, 1968.

Michael Bellesiles

MOORE, ALFRED. (1755–1810). Continental officer, jurist. North Carolina. Born in New Hanover County, North Carolina, on 21 May 1755, Moore was the son of Judge Maurice Moore, with whom he studied law. He was licensed to practice in 1775, and on 1 September 1775 he became a captain in the First North Carolina Regiment, which was commanded by his uncle, James Moore. He took part in the Moores Creek Bridge campaign in February 1776 and the defense of Charleston in June. On 8 March 1777 he resigned his commission, but he continued to serve as a colonel of militia. In this capacity he was active in harassing the British based at Wilmington, Delaware, through much of 1781. The British plundered and burned his plantation in Brunswick County, North Carolina, in retribution. Moore joined the pursuit of General Charles Cornwallis's army into Virginia, and was present for the surrender at Yorktown in October 1781.

Elected attorney general of North Carolina on 3 May 1782, Moore served with distinction until 1791. He then went on to become a successful criminal lawyer. President John Adams appointed him an associate justice of the U.S. Supreme Court in December 1799. In 1804 he had to resign because of poor health. He died at his estate on 15 October 1810.

SEE ALSO *Moore, James; Moore, Maurice.*

revised by Michael Bellesiles

MOORE, JAMES. (1737–1777). Continental

general. North Carolina. Born in New Hanover County, North Carolina, in 1737, Moore served in the Seven Years' War as a captain. For a year he was commandant of Fort Johnston at the mouth of the Cape Fear River. In provincial politics he sat in the House of Commons from 1764 to 1771 and in 1773. He actively opposed enforcement of the Stamp Act in 1765 and became a Son of Liberty at that time. During the troubles with the Regulators (an ad hoc organization of private citizens who took law enforcement in their own hands) he sided with the eastern oligarchy and the established government. He served as an artillery colonel in Governor William Tryon's expedition of 1768 and in the battle of Alamance, in North Carolina, on 16 May 1771.

Moore played a prominent role in driving Governor Josiah Martin from the province, being the first to sign the circular letter calling for the first Revolutionary Provincial Congress, which was held in New Bern in August 1774. He represented his county (New Hanover) at the Third Provincial Congress, which met on 20 August 1775 at Hillsboro. On 1 September he was selected by this body to command the First North Carolina Continental Regiment. In this capacity he directed the campaign that ended with the important victory at Moores Creek Bridge on 27 February 1776.

Appointed brigadier general by Congress on 1 March 1776, he was made commander in chief of the Patriot forces in North Carolina. During the defense of Charleston that year, Moore had the relatively inactive role of observing a small British fleet in the Cape Fear River. On 29 November he was ordered to Charleston, where he remained until February 1777. On 5 February he was ordered north to join General George Washington. He died suddenly at Wilmington, North Carolina, where his command had been delayed by lack of money for supplies, on 15 April 1777.

SEE ALSO *Moores Creek Bridge; Regulators.*

BIBLIOGRAPHY
Rankin, Hugh F. *The North Carolina Continentals.* Chapel Hill, N.C.: University of North Carolina Press, 1971.

revised by Michael Bellesiles

MOORE, MAURICE. (1735–1777). North

Carolina jurist and Patriot. North Carolina. Born in New Hanover County, North Carolina, Maurice Moore was the brother of General James Moore, brother-in-law of General John Ashe, and father of Justice Alfred Moore. He became a prominent politician at a young age, entering the assembly in 1757, where he sat nearly every year until 1774. His support of the royal government led to his appointment to Governor William Tryon's council in 1760 (he served a year) and to an associate judgeship. His pamphlet attacking the Stamp Act on the grounds that there was no American representation in Parliament led to his suspension as judge, but he was reinstated in 1768 and served until the court ceased to function in 1772.

Although he initially sympathized with the Regulators, Moore served as a colonel in Tryon's expedition against them in 1768 and was a judge in the Regulator trials of 1768 and 1771 (after the battle of Alamance). Having become bitterly hated by the Regulators, he switched sides again, becoming their champion and calling for leniency. In the Revolutionary politics that led to war with Great Britain, Moore served on important committees of the Third Provincial Congress in 1775, but was considered to be too conservative to become a leader. His brother's victory over the Loyalists at Moores Creek Bridge destroyed all chances for the course he advocated: reconciliation on the basis of political conditions in 1763. Although elected to the Fifth Provincial Congress of November 1776, he did not attend. Equally suspected by both Patriots and Loyalists, Moore retired from politics and died early in 1777 at his home in Brunswick.

SEE ALSO *Moore, James.*

BIBLIOGRAPHY
Price, William S. Jr., ed. *Not a Conquered People: Two Carolinians View Parliamentary Taxation.* Raleigh, N.C.: North Carolina State University Graphics, 1975.

revised by Michael Bellesiles

MOORES CREEK BRIDGE. 27 February

1776. Reports of Lexington and Concord so fanned the flames of revolution in North Carolina that within a few months the royal governor, Josiah Martin, fled; the so-called Mecklenburg Declaration of Independence was adopted; a provincial congress was organized; and North Carolina raised two Continental regiments.

In spite of this revolutionary progress, North Carolina was deeply divided. In part, these divisions were the legacy of the recent Regulator conflict, but there was strong

Loyalist sentiment as well as numerous advocates of neutrality. Those supporting the crown included a variety of groups across the entire colony. Some had been Piedmont Regulators; others were Tidewater planters or Highland Scots along the Cape Fear River. They were united only by their opposition to the revolt, and in some cases, opposition was created by antipathy toward the rebellion's leadership. Quakers and German Pietists, wanting nothing to do with either side's politics, sought only to be left alone. Perhaps only 30 percent actively supported the Whig cause. The Provincial Congress had little or no success in winning over the lukewarm and disaffected, but the Loyalists were not united initially. Their inertia enabled North Carolina to assist Virginia and South Carolina and be ready when the Loyalists finally began active opposition.

TORY PLANS AND WHIG RESPONSE

General Henry Clinton's Charleston expedition in 1776 was prompted largely by Martin's assurance, supported by other refugee governors and planters, that the South could be retained if a military force were present to support the Loyalists. Dartmouth approved Clinton's strategic diversion; Lord Germain endorsed it despite the protests of Generals Edward Harvey and William Howe. When Martin learned that reinforcements to augment Clinton's expedition would leave Ireland on 1 December 1775, he made plans for a coordinated Loyalist uprising in North Carolina. Included in his plans were instructions to the Loyalists to have their troops at Brunswick Town on 15 February.

In the meantime, General Thomas Gage sent Lieutenant Colonel Donald McDonald and Captain Donald McLeod to North Carolina to recruit for the Royal Highland Emigrant Regiment. Arriving in Cross Creek (later Fayetteville), the two officers, Allen McDonald, and other Highland Scots raised the royal standard at Cross Creek on 5 February 1775, calling for armed supporters to assemble. Because of his reputation as a veteran of Culloden and the work of others, including the legendary Flora McDonald, one thousand Highland Scots had gathered by 18 February. Most were recent immigrants motivated not so much by loyalty to George III as by their dislike for the Lowlanders and Ulstermen so prominent in the rebel camp. Another five hundred men, including former Regulators, joined McDonald at Cross Creek.

In the absence of Colonel Robert Howe's Second North Carolina Regiment, Colonel James Moore's First North Carolina Continentals, about 650 men and five guns, formed the nucleus of the force that marched from Wilmington and camped about twelve miles south of Cross Creek at Rockfish Creek on 15 February. On the 18th Moore was joined by Colonel Alexander Lillington's 150 Wilmington minutemen, Colonel James Kenan's 200 Duplin County militia, and John Ashe's 100 Volunteer Independent Rangers.

About this time, McDonald sent Moore a copy of Governor Martin's proclamation and a letter calling on Whigs to join the royalist colors. After a delay in sending an express message to Colonel Richard Caswell, who was approaching from New Bern with eight hundred Partisan Rangers, Moore sent McDonald the Test Oath with the suggestion that bloodshed be avoided by the Loyalists joining the Whigs.

GATHERING AT MOORES CREEK

By this time McDonald knew the enemy was gathering around him. He decided to avoid a general engagement and march to the coast. His route was generally east across the Cape Fear and South Rivers, thence southeast toward Wilmington. Moore had to withdraw along the Cape Fear River and then intercept McDonald's march. When Caswell reported that he was between the Black River and Moores Creek, and that the Loyalists had crossed the former, Moore sent word to stop the Tories at Moores Creek Bridge, about eighteen miles above Wilmington. He asked Caswell to meet him there if possible, otherwise to follow the enemy toward that place.

Lillington and Ashe reached Moores Creek on the 25th. Caswell arrived the next day and threw up earthworks on the enemy (or west) side of the narrow but deep stream. He later abandoned the west camp and joined Lillington and Ashe on the east side, where a breastwork had been erected. After removing some of the bridge flooring, leaving a gap where the enemy could cross only on the log stringers, the one thousand Whigs deployed to cover the bridge. If subsequent Tory accounts are to be believed, the Whigs also greased the stringers. Through the chilly night of 26–27 February, they rested on their arms. Lillington seems to deserve most of the credit for the preparations at the bridge and for the subsequent action. Moore, at Elizabethtown blocking the route to Cape Fear, did not arrive until after the battle.

The Tories had been advancing for three days through rough, swampy terrain, and late on 26 February they camped six miles from the bridge. After scouts reported the enemy occupying a position on the west bank of Moores Creek (see above), the Loyalists resumed their advance at 1 A.M. McDonald had become ill on 26 February, and command passed to Donald McLeod, now promoted to lieutenant colonel of the North Carolina Loyalist militia. Captain John Campbell led the advance guard of eighty picked Scots armed only with claymores; fourteen hundred men made up the main body, and three hundred riflemen brought up the rear. A shortage of arms meant that only about five hundred men were equipped for combat.

THE FIGHTING

The Tories intended to surprise the Whigs camped on the west bank. On entering the camp, they found it abandoned. This led the Tories to believe that their crossing would be unchallenged. As they formed into a battle line before crossing the bridge, rifle shots were fired near the bridge. Campbell's advance guard, accompanied by a few others, including McLeod, immediately went out onto the bridge, shouting "King George and Broadswords!" Once across, they moved up the road at a rush. Whig infantry and two artillery pieces opened fire at a range of thirty yards from behind breastworks, and the Tory attack was shattered. McLeod and Campbell were killed with several of their men within a few paces of their objective. Others were hit on the bridge or simply fell into the deep stream and drowned.

The Whigs then counterattacked. Some rushed forward to replace planks on the bridge and pursue the panic-stricken Tories. A small detachment forded the creek, pushed through the swamp, and hit the enemy rear.

Moore had directed the Second and Fourth North Carolina Regiments, under Lieutenant Colonels Alexander Martin and James Thackston, to occupy Cross Creek, and their presence undoubtedly accounts for the numerous prisoners and weapons taken after the battle. General McDonald, several other officers, and 850 men were taken prisoner. The booty included £15,000 in specie, 13 wagons, 1,500 rifles, 350 muskets, and 150 swords and dirks. This haul came not only from prisoners but also from known and suspected Tories in the region. The prisoners were jailed and their property was subjected to looting and burning, forcing many Highlanders to flee the province.

About thirty Tories were killed or wounded in the brief action at the bridge. Moore estimated total enemy casualties in killed, wounded, or drowned as about fifty. Only two defenders were hit, and one, John Grady, died on 2 March.

COMMENT

While Moore, Lillington, and Caswell deserve praise, as do the North Carolina political leaders responsible for raising their armed forces, the king's representatives failed him at all levels of planning and execution. Governor Josiah Martin was overoptimistic about Loyalist support and premature in calling it out. The Charleston expedition, delayed by late arrival of the fleet, was doomed to failure because local support had been defeated. McLeod went forward without knowing what lay in front of them. The east bank breastworks were not only across the road, but paralleled it. McLeod appears to have run into a classic ambush and paid the price. At least nine bullets and some twenty-four shot

struck him down, evidence the Whigs were firing buck and ball, and at very short range.

The Halifax Resolves were adopted on 12 April 1776 by North Carolina's Provincial Congress, and exactly a month later, Sir Henry Clinton declared North Carolina in a state of rebellion. Lord Cornwallis landed from Clinton's fleet at Brunswick Town and ravaged the area. Colonel Robert Howe's plantation was virtually destroyed and Brunswick Town burned, but North Carolina was spared further British military operations for almost five more years. The delay bought by the Whig victory at Moores Creek Bridge gave the new North Carolina state government time to solidify its hold over the populace and build the infrastructure that would support the revolt.

SEE ALSO *Charleston Expedition of Clinton in 1776; Halifax Resolves; McDonald, Flora; Mecklenburg Declaration of Independence; Norfolk, Virginia; Reedy River, South Carolina; Regulators; Test Oath.*

BIBLIOGRAPHY

Johnston, Peter R. *Poorest of the Thirteen: North Carolina and the Southern Department in the American Revolution.* Haverford, Pa.: Infinity Publishing, 2001.

Rankin, Hugh F. *The Moores Creek Bridge Campaign, 1776.* Conshohocken, Pa.: Eastern National Park and Monument Association, 1986.

revised by Lawrence E. Babits

MORAVIAN SETTLEMENTS.

Count Nicolaus Ludwig Zinzendorf (1700–1760) helped revive the evangelical sect of Protestants called Moravians after giving a group of them refuge on his Saxon estate in 1722. He looked to the New World as a place where the Moravians could escape persecution and exercise their missionary zeal. Bishop Augustus Gottlieb Spangenberg (1704–1792) reached Georgia in 1735 with a few Swiss colonists, and thirty other Moravians later followed. In 1741 the Moravians established Nazareth and Bethlehem, Pennsylvania, as a communistic society. That year Count Zinzendorf arrived in America with hopes of uniting all German Protestants in Pennsylvania. Despite many Protestants' suspicious attitude toward his pacifist and generous theology, which included an opposition to slavery, Zinzendorf exerted an important influence on ecclesiastical affairs in the colonies. His daughter Benigna organized what would become the Moravian College in Bethlehem.

As Zinzendorf left, Spangenberg, the newly appointed bishop of the North American Moravians, returned. In 1749 he was removed from his office in disputes over church politics but, because of mismanagement by his successor, was reinstated in 1751. He led a party of Bethlehem Moravians south to find a new home, and in August 1753 they purchased 100,000 acres from Lord Granville in North Carolina, where they established what was known as the Wachovia: the towns of Betharaba (Dutch Fort), Bethania, Friedberg, Friedland, Hope, and Salem. The latter is now part of Winston-Salem. Spangenberg's new settlements were organized under a plan of family life, as opposed to communistic labor, and became the Moravian center of the South. The North Carolina Moravian towns were trade centers that served much of the South. They suffered from robberies by highwayman during the war.

As a result of immigration, the Moravian population of Pennsylvania swelled to 2,500 people by 1775. The Moravians were more active than any other religious body in conducting missionary work among the Indians, enjoying particular success among the Mahicans and Delawares, hundreds of whom converted to Christianity. Their converts were given special protection by the government of Pennsylvania, which promised their security from attacks by both white settlers and non-Christian Indians, though that status did not save them from attacks by frontier militia during the Seven Years' War and the American Revolution.

As pacifists, the Moravians generally attempted to avoid the American Revolution, though many served in non-combatant roles with the Patriot side. In December 1776 George Washington appropriated the Brothers' House (the residence for single men) in the Bethlehem community for use as a military hospital. By the time the hospital was moved from this site in April 1778, more than 1,000 Continental soldiers were treated, with many Moravians offering their services. The Moravians worked hard to protect Christian Indians from the war's violence, with mixed results. A few missionaries, most famously David Zeisberger, served as translators and even intelligence agents for the Patriots. Like the Quakers, the Moravians were persecuted for their pacifism. Finding greater security in isolation, the Moravians withdrew further into their communities at Bethlehem and Salem, as the Revolution put a halt to many of their missionary activities.

SEE ALSO *Gnadenhutten Massacre, Ohio; Zeisberger, David.*

revised by Michael Bellesiles

MORGAN, DANIEL. (1735?–1802). Continental general. New Jersey, Pennsylvania, and Virginia. Morgan's place and year of birth are uncertain. After quarreling with his father, a Welch immigrant, Morgan

Daniel Morgan. *The American Revolutionary general, in a portrait based on a nineteenth-century painting by Alonzo Chappel.* PICTURE COLLECTION, THE BRANCH LIBRARIES, THE NEW YORK PUBLIC LIBRARY, ASTOR, LENOX AND TILDEN FOUNDATIONS

moved to the Shenandoah Valley in 1753, working as a farm laborer and teamster. In 1755 he joined Edward Braddock's expedition as a teamster, where he was punished with a life-threatening 500 stripes for knocking down a British officer who had hit him with a sword. After Braddock's defeat, Morgan helped to evacuate the wounded and hauled supplies to frontier posts. In 1758 Morgan became an ensign. While carrying dispatches to Winchester he was struck by an Indian bullet that passed through his neck and his mouth. He lost all the teeth on one side of his face. In 1762 he took possession of a small grant near Winchester, Virginia, and moved in with Abigail Curry, whom he married ten years later. The next year he served as a lieutenant in Pontiac's War, and he took part in Dunmore's War (1774). In between, he prospered as a farmer and slave owner.

Commissioned a captain of one of the two Virginia rifle companies on 22 June 1775, he enlisted the prescribed 96 men in the next ten days, and led them the 600 miles to the Boston lines without losing a man.

Morgan's company volunteered to join Benedict Arnold in his march to Quebec, which occurred from September to November 1775. In the disastrous assault on Quebec, 31 December, Morgan took command from the wounded Arnold and drove on with magnificent élan until subordinates prevailed on him to make a decision that probably was fatal to the enterprise. A prisoner in Quebec until the next summer, he returned on parole and was included in a prisoner exchange in January 1777. Commissioned a colonel of the Eleventh Virginia Regiment by Congress, Morgan joined Washington's main army a few months later. After serving with distinction in the New Jersey operations of 1777, Morgan was selected by Washington to lead 500 riflemen personally selected by the commanding general. This unit was known as "the Corps of Rangers." Washington then ordered this corps, the only rifle unit in the American army, to join the campaign against General John Burgoyne.

Morgan and his riflemen played a decisive role in winning the two battles of Saratoga, which occurred on 19 September and 7 October 1777, decimating the British in both instances. Morgan immediately led his corps back to Washington's main army, arriving in time to skirmish several times with British troops in December 1777. While in winter quarters at Valley Forge, Morgan's Eleventh Virginia Regiment was brigaded with the Seventh Virginia Regiment under the command of Brigadier General William Woodford. Morgan was not engaged in the battle of Monmouth on 28 June 1778, but he did conduct a preliminary harrassment and a vigorous pursuit after that action.

Morgan took an extended furlough from the army on 18 July 1779, after Anthony Wayne rather than Morgan was chosen to command a new light infantry brigade. Congress ordered him in June 1780 to report to Horatio Gates in the southern theater of operations, but he declined to comply. He took this action in protest, since Congress apparently did not value his services highly enough to accompany its call with the restoration of his relative rank, much less make him a general. When Morgan learned of the disaster at Camden, however, he rejoined the army regardless of rank. On 2 October he was given command of a corps of light troops that had been organized by Gates. On 13 October Congress at last appointed him brigadier general, and when Nathanael Greene succeeded Gates he confirmed the assignment of Morgan as commander of the elite corps.

At Cowpens, South Carolina, on 17 January 1781, Morgan displayed tactical genius in feigning a rout before turning on Lieutenant Colonal Banastre "Butcher" Tarleton's legion and winning a battle that is considered a classic. Morgan then, and wisely, started running again. Soon after linking up with the main body under Greene,

Morgan, riddled with disease, took a leave of absence (10 February 1781).

Morgan was deaf, at first, to appeals to support the Marquis de Lafayette in halting British raids in Virginia, although he did arrive after the real danger was over. Back on the frontier, the old warrior's aches and pains—arthritis, rheumatism, and sciatica, according to different accounts—did not prevent an active life in diverse enterprises. As a major general, Morgan led the Virginia militia into Pennsylvania during the Whiskey Rebellion of 1794, encountering no opposition. He ran unsuccessfully for Congress as a Federalist in 1795, and was elected in 1797. Ill health forced Morgan's decision not to seek re-election. He retired to Winchester, the old teamster now a major landowner, and died there in 1802.

SEE ALSO *Arnold's March to Quebec; Cowpens, South Carolina; Riflemen.*

BIBLIOGRAPHY

Higginbotham, Don. *Daniel Morgan: Revolutionary Rifleman.* 1961.

revised by Michael Bellesiles

MORGAN, JOHN. (1735–1789).

Medical director of the Continental army. Pennsylvania. Born in Philadelphia, Pennsylvania, on 16 October 1735, Morgan graduated with the first class of the College of Philadelphia (now the University of Pennsylvania) in 1757. Almost immediately he enlisted as a lieutenant and surgeon for the provincial troops during the Seven Years' War. In 1760 he undertook a period of study abroad, during which he enjoyed a very successful education in London and Edinburgh. His studies culminated in his election to the Royal College of Physicians and to the Royal Society in 1765. He returned to Philadelphia that year, and played a key role in establishing a medical school at his alma mater, becoming its first professor. In doing so, he acted without consulting other Philadelphia physicians, and thus made a bitter enemy of William Shippen, Jr.

On 17 October 1775 the Continental Congress elected Morgan to be the director-general of hospitals and physician-in-chief of the American army. Joining the army at Cambridge and accompanying it later to New York, he worked skillfully to achieve an efficient organization of his service but, in so doing, made so many enemies that, on 9 October 1776, he was demoted, his directorship being reduced to only those hospitals east of the Hudson River. On 9 January 1777 he was removed even from this reduced authority without explanation and replaced by his old Philadelphia rival, Shippen. Embittered, Morgan published "A Vindication" in 1777, making the inevitable charges of Congressional meddling and the plotting of "a mean and invidious set of men" to remove him. Although he was cleared of any misconduct by Congress in 1779, he considered himself disgraced and withdrew from public life, except to bring charges of fraud against Shippen, who was court-martialed in 1781 and forced to resign. Morgan died in Philadelphia on 15 October 1789.

BIBLIOGRAPHY

Bill, Whitfield J., Jr. *John Morgan: Continental Doctor.* Philadelphia: University of Pennsylvania Press, 1965.

revised by Michael Bellesiles

MORNINGSIDE HEIGHTS (MANHATTAN), NEW YORK.

Modern name of Vandewater's Heights, which figured in the Battle of Harlem Heights on 16 September 1776.

SEE ALSO *Harlem Heights, New York.*

Mark M. Boatner

MORRIS, GOUVERNEUR. (1752–1816).

American statesman. New York. Born on 30 January 1752 in the manor house at Morrisania (now the Bronx), Gouverneur Morris was reared as a cultured provincial aristocrat and the son of a judge of the court of vice-admiralty. His mother, Sarah Gouverneur, was the daughter of the speaker of the New York Assembly.

Morris graduated from King's College (now Columbia) in 1768, studied under William Smith, later chief justice of New York, and was admitted to the bar at the age of 19, in 1771. He soon built up a successful practice in New York City. As a member of the landed aristocracy, he naturally had misgivings about revolution. Although his half-brothers, Lewis and Richard, were Patriots, his mother was a Loyalist and his half-brother, Staats Morris, was a general in the British army. Gouverneur Morris nevertheless adhered to the Patriot cause when it appeared that war was inevitable, despite expressing fears, in 1774, that this would bring "the domination of a riotous mob." In 1775 he was elected to the New York Provincial Congress, where he proposed a plan for a Continental paper currency that was adopted by the Continental Congress. Over the next two years he promoted a strong central government, with representatives selected from electoral districts rather than states.

With John Jay and Robert L. Livingston, he drafted the constitution under which New York was governed for the next 50 years. Responsible for the constitution's conservative franchise-property qualification, Morris surprised many contemporaries with his consistent and impassioned opposition to slavery. He strongly supported General Philip Schuyler and, with Jay, attempted to prevent Schuyler from being superseded by Horatio Gates. Elected to Congress in October 1777, the youthful Morris was interested primarily in financial, military, and diplomatic matters. He drafted many important documents, including the diplomatic instructions for Benjamin Franklin and, later, for the peace commissioners. One of his most dramatic actions came in the official response to the Britain's conciliatory Carlisle Commission of 1778. Morris called for the United States to be "an Assylum to mankind. America shall receive to her bosom and comfort and cheer the oppressed, the miserable, and the poor of every nation and of every clime." He visited Valley Forge early in 1778, and returned to Philadelphia committed to military reforms, and was a firm supporter of General George Washington.

Defeated for re-election to Congress because he refused to enlist congressional support for the claims of New York in the dispute over Vermont, Morris transferred his citizenship to Pennsylvania and set up his home and law practice in Philadelphia. Pursuing an early interest in currency and credit, he contributed a brilliant series of financial articles to the *Pennsylvania Packet* from February to April 1780, under the pen name "An American." This brought him an invitation to serve as assistant to Robert Morris (the "financier of the Revolution," no relation to Gouverneur) in 1781. He held this post until 1785, while Robert Morris performed his remarkable feat of keeping the United States solvent. Gouverneur Morris worked out a decimal system of coinage later perfected by Thomas Jefferson and Alexander Hamilton that spared America the miserable pounds, shillings, and pence of the mother country. That same year he put forth a proposal for a Bank of North America, which Congress chartered in December 1781 and funded with a large French loan.

By a narrow majority, the Pennsylvania Assembly chose Morris as one of its delegates to the Constitutional Convention of 1787. An opponent of democracy—"Give the votes to the people who have no property and they will sell them to the rich," he said—Morris worked at the Convention to craft a conservative constitution that would respect private property, except for ownership of slaves, and which would foster a strong central government. Morris was almost responsible for the collapse of the Convention when he demanded that they take a stand against the spread of slavery. He lost this battle to the supposed compromise of the three-fifths clause, but put aside his doubts in support of the finished document. Now only 35, Morris abandoned his political career and returned to Morrisania, which he had bought from his elder half-brother, but soon went to Europe (in 1789) as agent for Robert Morris and other business associates.

Early in 1792, Washington appointed Morris to the post of minister to France. Morris openly supported the monarchy and feared the consequences of the revolution, which did not endear him to most French. In 1794, in retaliation for the American dismissal of its envoy to the United States (Edmund Charles "Citizen" Genet), the French government requested that Washington recall Morris, which he did. Morris went from Paris to London and attempted to persuade Britain's prime minister, William Pitt, to invade France.

After another four years traveling through Europe, Morris returned to the United States in 1798. In April 1800 he had what he called in his diary "the misfortune" to be elected a Federalist senator to fill an unexpired term. With the Jeffersonians in control of the legislature, Morris was not re-elected and in 1802 again retired to Morrisania, spending the last thirteen years of his life there. In 1810 he joined with De Witt Clinton in proposing the construction of the Erie Canal, serving as chairman of the board of canal commissioners from 1810 to 1816. By 1814 he had lost all hope that the United States could survive, and proposed that New York and New England secede and form a separate country.

SEE ALSO *Burr, Aaron.*

BIBLIOGRAPHY
Adams, William Howard. *Gouverneur Morris: An Independent Life.* New Haven, Conn.: Yale University Press, 2003.

revised by Michael Bellesiles

MORRIS, LEWIS. (1726–1798). Signer, militia general. New York. Born at the family manor of Morrisania in Westchester County, New York, on 8 April 1726, Morris attended Yale College. He left Yale in 1746, before he finished his degree, and assisted his father in the management of the extensive family estates. On the death of his father in 1762, Lewis Morris became the third and last lord of the family manor. Now, for the first time, he showed an interest in politics. After a single term in the provincial assembly in 1769, and finding that few of his Westchester County constituents endorsed his anti-British sentiments, he succeeded in organizing that minority. Despite opposition from the powerful families of the area—the De Lanceys, Pells, and Philipses—he succeeded in having a meeting called on 28 March 1775 to select the county's deputies to the

provincial convention in New York City. Morris was named chairman of the eight-man delegation elected by his faction. At the convention Morris was elected a delegate to the Continental Congress, an honor he had enthusiastically sought.

Taking his seat on 15 May 1775, and remaining a delegate for two years, Morris served on committees to decide what posts should be defended in New York, to acquire military stores and munitions, and to deal with Indian affairs. On 7 June 1776 he was appointed brigadier general of the Westchester County militia, and was on leave of absence from Congress when the Declaration of Independence was approved. Later in 1776 he returned to Philadelphia and became a signer of that document. He took part in the New York campaign of 1776, when the forces of General William Howe chased George Washington and his troops right through the Morris family manor and the rest of Westchester. For the remainder of the war, Morris retained his militia rank but his services appear to have been valued by the state more in the civil domain. He was county judge in Westchester from 1777 to 1778, and served intermittently in the upper house of the state legislature between 1777 and 1790.

At the end of the war he retired as a major general of militia and restored Morrisania, which had been the scene of skirmishes on 5 August 1779, 22 January 1781, and 4 March 1782. Morris was at the Poughkeepsie ratification convention in 1788, where he supported the adoption of the federal Constitution that his half-brother, Gouverneur Morris, had helped to draft. He died at his estate on 22 January 1798.

SEE ALSO *Morris, Gouverneur.*

BIBLIOGRAPHY
Young, Alfred F. *The Democratic Republicans of New York: The Origins, 1763–1797.* Chapel Hill, N.C.: University of North Carolina Press, 1967.

revised by Michael Bellesiles

MORRIS, ROBERT. (1734–1806). Merchant and congressman, called the "Financier of the Revolution." Pennsylvania. Robert Morris was born in Liverpool, England, on 20 January 1735. At the age of thirteen he came to America with his father and went to work in the Philadelphia mercantile house of Charles Willing. By 1754 he had become a partner. Three years later, with Charles's son Thomas, he formed Willing and Morris, a firm that with its successors held a leading position in American trade for the next thirty-nine years. His first public political act was to sign the nonimportation

Robert Morris. *The "Financier of the American Revolution" and a signer of the Declaration of Independence, in a portrait (c. 1782) by Charles Willson Peale.* PENNSYLVANIA ACADEMY OF FINE ARTS, PHILADELPHIA, PA/BRIDGEMAN ART LIBRARY

agreement of 1765; thereafter, he served on many committees formed to resist increased imperial control. After the shooting started in April 1775, Morris became a leading figure in the Patriot cause. On 30 June 1775 the assembly named him to the Pennsylvania Council of Safety, where his commercial talents were immediately put to use; when Franklin was absent, Morris ran the council.

VITAL WORK IN CONGRESS

Elected to the Second Continental Congress in November 1775, he quickly became a member of several important congressional committees, including the Secret Committee of Trade, "Congress's war department," where he succeeded his partner, Willing. Among many other activities, he personally arranged for the procurement of vessels, munitions, and naval armament in November 1775 and drew up the instruction for Silas Deane in February 1776, all the while continuing to tend to the commercial affairs of Willing and Morris. In performing his valuable official services he remained a businessman, collecting his broker's commissions and

overlooking no opportunity to make a profit. While he made great profits, largely because of his ability, he also took huge risks in accomplishing the financial missions assigned by Congress and the Pennsylvania authorities, a fact that was understood and accepted by his colleagues. According to John Adams, in a letter to Horatio Gates on 27 April 1776:

> I think he has a masterly Understanding, an open Temper and an honest Heart: and if he does not always vote for What you and I should think proper, it is because he thinks that a large Body of People remains, who are not yet of his Mind. He has vast designs in the mercantile Way. And no doubt pursues mercantile Ends, which are always gain; but he is an excellent Member of our Body. (Taylor, *Adams Papers*, 4, p. 148)

Morris thought the movement toward independence in 1776 was premature. He abstained from voting on the Declaration of Independence in July, but when he saw it was the will of the majority, he signed the document in August 1776. When Congress fled to Baltimore in December 1776, Morris remained in Philadelphia to carry out the work of the Secret Committee and on 21 December was designated by Congress along with George Clymer and George Walton as its executive committee. As Washington prepared the desperate strategy that was to end with his brilliant riposte at Trenton and Princeton, it was Morris who furnished him the necessary backing of the civil authority of the country. Simultaneously looking after the commercial interests of his firm—which may have been an important reason why he did not flee to Baltimore—Morris bore a tremendous personal burden at this critical period of American history and carried it off without a stumble.

In March 1778 Morris signed the Articles of Confederation. From August to 1 November 1778, the expiration of his term, he was chairman of Congress's Committee on Finance. Ineligible for reelection under the terms of the new state constitution of Pennsylvania, Morris was immediately elected to the Pennsylvania assembly and took his seat on 6 November.

TAINTED BY SCANDAL

The burden of his dual public and private role had already begun to take its toll. During the winter of 1777–1778, the misconduct of Thomas Morris, a younger half-brother for whom Robert had secured appointment as commercial agent in France, precipitated a temporary misunderstanding between Morris and the American commissioners in Paris, Silas Deane and Benjamin Franklin. The controversy that followed the recall of Deane involved Morris after January 1779, when Thomas Paine attacked Morris and Deane in the press and Henry Laurens, then president of Congress, charged Willing and Morris with fraud in the management of the covert operations of Hortalez et Cie that sent vital military supplies across the Atlantic. An investigation exonerated both Hortalez et Cie and Willing and Morris, but public opinion—led by opponents who resented his success—began to turn against Morris. He was denied reelection to Congress in November 1779, although a year later he regained his seat in the Pennsylvania assembly, where he served until June 1781. In these years, he was acknowledged as the leading merchant in America and probably its wealthiest citizen.

SUPERINTENDENT OF FINANCE

Meanwhile, the financial underpinning of the Revolution had collapsed. On the nomination of Hamilton, Congress on 20 February 1781 named Morris superintendent of finance, a unique office established to salvage what appeared to be a near-total loss of confidence in the fiscal management of the Confederation government. Insisting first that Congress permit him to continue his personal business and that he be allowed to control the personnel of his department, Morris accepted the post on 14 May. He had always been opposed to the carefree and financially irresponsible procedures that had led to the collapse of the Continental currency, including the price controls and legal pressure designed to make people accept worthless paper money at par value. With the government nearly insolvent, Morris, according to the historian Clarence L. ver Steeg:

> believed that the public credit of the Confederation could be revived only by utilizing private credit. He took steps to achieve two goals: in the short term to provide the military with supplies to win the war; and, more important, in the long term to introduce a comprehensive national financial program to strengthen the Confederation politically. (Ver Steeg, ANB)

He persuaded Congress to charter the Bank of North America (and used its bank notes to pay urgent expenses, especially pay and supplies for the Continental army), pledged his own personal credit to the government (and issued "Morris's notes" to supplement the public credit), and extolled the virtues of funding the public debt by means of a permanent national revenue. The message he sent to Congress about funding on 29 July 1782 has been called "the most important single American state paper on public credit written prior to 1790," but the scheme failed when Rhode Island and Virginia rejected the impost that would have provided the revenue stream.

Relying on various economies in purchasing and administration, his own Morris's notes, some financial sleight of hand, and the loan of two hundred thousand dollars in specie from France, he financed the Yorktown campaign, which so foreclosed British military options to regain her colonies that it broke Britain's will to continue the fight. Morris endured a torrent of criticism, especially because he contracted for the public as many debts during his two years in office as there had been before his advent. Since the states still refused to accept their obligations and furnish the revenue needed for a viable currency, Congress remained impotent. In despair and disgust, Morris submitted his resignation on 24 January 1783, part of a plan to shock the states into action that included foreknowledge of the effort undertaken by Gouverneur Morris (no relation) and Alexander Hamilton to foment unrest in the Continental army as a pressure tactic. Washington quashed this so-called Newburgh conspiracy in March. But since nobody stepped forth to take Morris's job, in May he was prevailed upon to retain his office and eventually found the funds—with the help of a Dutch loan secured by John Adams—to pay and demobilize the army by the end of the year. Morris finally resigned his office in September 1784.

FINANCIAL DOWNFALL

Convinced of the need for a strong central government, he served in the Constitutional Convention in 1787 and actively supported the Federalists thereafter. He declined Washington's offer to be the first secretary of the treasury (he recommended Hamilton instead) but served in the Senate from 1789 through 1795. His financial downfall came because he overextended himself in land speculation. In February 1798 he was hauled off for over three and a half years in debtors' prison. Released on 26 August 1801 under terms of the Federal Bankruptcy Act of 1800, he lived his last five years in a small house in Philadelphia, supported by the annuity Gouverneur Morris had secured for his wife. He died on 8 May 1806.

SEE ALSO *Deane, Silas; Finances of the Revolution; Hortalez & Cie; Newburgh Addresses.*

BIBLIOGRAPHY

Ferguson, E. James. *The Power of the Purse: A History of American Public Finance, 1776–1790.* Chapel Hill, N.C.: University of North Carolina Press, 1961.

Ferguson, E. James et al., eds. *Papers of Robert Morris, 1781–1784.* 8 vols. Pittsburgh, Pa.: University of Pittsburgh Press, 1973–1995.

Taylor, Robert J., et al., eds. *Papers of John Adams.* Vol. 4, *February–August 1776.* Cambridge, Mass.: Harvard University Press, 1979.

Ver Steeg, Clarence L. *Robert Morris: Revolutionary Financier, with an Analysis of His Earlier Career.* Philadelphia: University of Pennsylvania Press, 1954.

Harold E. Selesky

MORRIS, ROBERT. (1745–1815). Jurist.

Natural son of Robert Hunter Morris and grandson of the first lord of the manor of Morrisania.

SEE ALSO *Morris, Robert Hunter.*

revised by Michael Bellesiles

MORRIS, ROBERT HUNTER. (1713?–1764).

Chief justice of New Jersey, governor of Pennsylvania. Born at the family manor in Westchester County, New York, perhaps in 1713, Robert Morris was the second son of the wealthy and powerful Lewis Morris, first lord of the manor of Morrisania. When Lewis Morris became governor of New Jersey in 1738 he made his son, Robert, chief justice of that state. In this capacity, Robert Morris belligerently supported his father's defense of the royal prerogative. In the 1740s he was the most active member of the East Jersey Board of Proprietors, which sought to throw settlers off their lands and led to a decade of controversy in New Jersey. Morris went to London in 1749 to make the case for using British troops to put down the riots. While in London he became close to the Penn family. In 1754 Thomas Penn, proprietor of Pennsylvania, appointed Morris deputy governor of that state. Morris immediately came into conflict with the Quaker-dominated legislature, which refused to allow a militia or to approve military funding. They also failed to pay Morris a salary, leading to his resignation in 1756. He returned to his job as chief justice in New Jersey, a position he had held even while in Britain and Pennsylvania for nearly seven years. He continued as chief justice until his death on 27 January 1764, after a wild night with a minister's wife. He never married, but had at least three children. One of these, Robert Morris (c. 1745–1815), inherited most of his large estate and was chief justice of the New Jersey Supreme Court from 1777 to 1779.

SEE ALSO *Morris, Gouverneur; Morris, Lewis.*

BIBLIOGRAPHY

McConville, Brendan. *These Daring Disturbers of the Public Peace: The Struggle for Property and Power in Early New Jersey.* Ithaca, NY: Cornell University Press, 1999.

Robert Hunter Morris Papers. Newark, N.J.: New Jersey Historical Society.

revised by Michael Bellesiles

MORRIS, ROGER. (1727–1794). British officer and Loyalist.

Born in Yorkshire, England, on 28 January 1727, Morris served at the Battles of Falkirk and Culloden and then in Flanders as a captain of the Forty-eighth Regiment. In 1755 he went to America as General Edward Braddock's aide-de-camp and was wounded in the disastrous expedition against Fort Duquesne on 9 July 1755. After purchasing the rank of major in the Thirty-fifth Regiment on 16 February 1758, Morris served at the siege of Louisbourg, the capture and defense of Quebec, the siege of Montreal, and as aide-de-camp to Generals Thomas Gage and Jeffrey Amherst. In May 1760 he was promoted to lieutenant colonel of the Forty-seventh Regiment. Having married Mary Philipse, one of the wealthiest women in America, in 1758, Morris sold his commission in 1764 and settled in New York City, becoming a member of the colony's royal council. With the outbreak of the Revolution, Morris went to England, returning in December 1777, when the British restored the council under Governor James Robertson. Morris again served on the council, was given the rank of colonel, and from January 1779 until the end of the war was inspector of refugee claims. The New York legislature confiscated Morris's property, worth an estimated quarter-million pounds in October 1777. Morris left New York City with the British army. Back in London, he petitioned the government for £68,384, which he claimed was the value of property lost in the Revolution; the government awarded him £12,205. He and his family settled in York, where he died on 13 September 1794.

Michael Bellesiles

MORRISANIA, NEW YORK. Actions at.

Located in what now is the South Bronx, Morrisania was the ancestral home of the Morris family. It first experienced the war by being on the British route of advance to White Plains during the New York Campaign. Thereafter it became a key point in the British defensive lines and a frequent camp location for Loyalist forces. The three most serious skirmishes there occurred on 5 August 1779, 22 January 1781, and 4 March 1782. Only the second of these is mentioned in most accounts of the war. In a bold raid that pushed more than three miles within the British lines, Lieutenant Colonel William Hull of Parsons's Connecticut Brigade attacked the quarters of the Third Battalion of De Lancey's Loyalist Brigade. He burned barracks and the ponton bridge over the Harlem River, destroyed a great store of forage, and at the price of twenty-five casualties withdrew with fifty-two prisoners, some horses, and some cattle. At daybreak on 23 January, Lieutenant Colonel James De Lancey and his Refugee

ENCYCLOPEDIA OF THE AMERICAN REVOLUTION

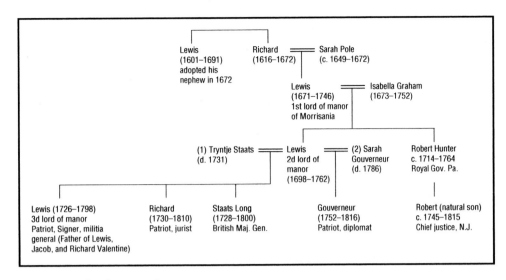

Morris Family of New York. THE GALE GROUP

troops contested the rebels' retreat as far as Williams's bridge, which was defended on the far side by Patriot troops. The Refugees then fell back.

In the maneuvers of July 1781 preceding the Yorktown Campaign, the duc de Lauzun proposed another attack on De Lancey's battalion, but when the element of surprise was compromised the plan was canceled.

SEE ALSO *Morris, Gouverneur; Morris, Lewis; Yorktown Campaign.*

BIBLIOGRAPHY

Crary, Catherine S. "Guerrilla Activities of James De Lancey's Cowboys in Westchester County: Conventional Warfare or Self-Interested Freebooting?" In *The Loyalist Americans: A Focus on Greater New York.* Edited by Robert A. East and Jacob Judd. Tarrytown, N.Y.: Sleepy Hollow Restorations, 1975.

Hufeland, Otto. *Westchester County during the American Revolution, 1775–1783.* Harrison, N.Y.: Harbor Hill Books, 1974.

revised by Robert K. Wright Jr.

MORRIS FAMILY OF NEW YORK.

The founder of the family in America was Richard Morris (1616–1672), a veteran of Cromwell's army, who became a merchant in Barbados and married the wealthy Sarah Pole. With his brother Lewis (1601–1691), he bought 500 acres in New York just north of the Harlem River, then known as Bronck's land (now the Bronx). Richard and Sarah Morris died there in 1672, only two years after the purchase, and their infant son, Lewis (1671–1746), was adopted by his uncle Lewis. Lewis Morris (1601–1691) built the Bronx estate to almost 2,000 acres and also acquired 3,500 acres in Monmouth County, New Jersey, all of which he passed on to his nephew and ward in 1691. In May 1697 the New York estate became the manor of Morrisania. Richard and Sarah's son Lewis (1671–1746) then became first lord of the manor, a title that passed to his son Lewis (1698–1762), the second lord, who passed it on to his son, Lewis Morris (1726–1798), the third (and last) lord of the manor and a Signer. Lewis the Signer's brother Staats Long (1728–1800) served in the British army, although not in America during the Revolution. Another brother, Richard (1730–1810), was chief justice of the supreme court of the state of New York. And his half-brother, Gouverneur Morris (1752–1816), was a delegate to the Continental Congress, a close associate of Robert Morris, the so-called "Financier of the Revolution" (who was no kin), one of the architects of the Constitution, and minister plenipotentiary to France. Lewis the second lord's brother, Robert Hunter Morris (c.1714–1764), was chief justice of New Jersey and governor of Pennsylvania, and his illegitimate son Robert (c.1745–1815) became chief justice of the state of New Jersey in 1777.

SEE ALSO *Morris, Gouverneur; Morris, Lewis; Morris, Robert (1734–1806); Morris, Robert Hunter; Morrisania, New York.*

BIBLIOGRAPHY

Howard, Ronald W. "Lewis Morris." *American National Biography Online* at www.anb.org.

Lefferts, Elizabeth Morris Waring. *Descendants of Lewis Morris of Morrisania.* New York: T. A. Wright, 1907.

Mintz, Max M. "Gouverneur Morris." *American National Biography Online* at www.anb.org.

———. *Gouverneur Morris and the American Revolution.* Norman: University of Oklahoma Press, 1970.

revised by Harold E. Selesky

MORRISTOWN WINTER QUARTERS, NEW JERSEY.

6 January–28 May 1777. After his operations at Trenton and Princeton, Washington established winter quarters at Morristown. Although he first considered this to be merely a temporary location, the merits of the place became more apparent as circumstances required him to prolong his stay. Several ranges of hills protected his army from the enemy, whose winter quarters were around New York City, thirty miles away. Morristown, though a small town of some fifty houses, was centrally located with respect to the British main outposts at Newark, Perth Amboy, and Brunswick (later New Brunswick), and it constituted a sort of flanking position from which Washington could threaten an enemy move up the Hudson or through New Jersey toward Philadelphia. Morristown was also in the center of an important agricultural region, which not only gave Washington access to important resources but also denied them to the enemy, and the place was close to the forges and furnaces of Hibernia, Mount Hope, Ringwood, and Charlottenburg.

While coping with the eternal problems of recruiting, reorganization, and logistics, Washington undertook a bold medical program of inoculating his troops and the neighborhood civilians against smallpox, which initially helped to spread the disease to those who had not been inoculated. Though his army shrank by a high rate of desertion to just over three thousand men, Washington kept up a vigorous patrol activity against the enemy in New Jersey. By the time General Howe bestirred himself and resumed operations in May 1777, Washington's army had been built up to over eight thousand effectives and was reasonably well supplied. Washington and his army returned to Morristown for the horrific winter of 1779–1780.

SEE ALSO *Philadelphia Campaign; Princeton, New Jersey; Trenton, New Jersey.*

revised by Michael Bellesiles

MORRISTOWN WINTER QUARTERS, NEW JERSEY.

1 December 1779–22 June 1780. As 1779 dragged to a close without major military operations in the North, and after Admiral Charles Estaing failed to appear off Sandy Hook with his powerful French force, Washington decided on 30 November that the main army would go into winter quarters just outside Morristown, New Jersey. The weather turned bitterly cold and most units were faced with a hard march to reach Morristown. Units started arriving the first week in December, and the last arrived at the end of that month. Four Massachusetts brigades were left in the Highlands; Poor's brigade and most of the cavalry units were sent to Danbury, Connecticut, with the mission of guarding the coastal towns on Long Island Sound; and the North Carolina brigade and Pawley's New York state troops were posted with Lee's dragoons around Suffern, New York.

The winter quarters of 1779–1780 became an ordeal of almost unbelievable suffering because of the record-breaking cold. As desertions rose and his army declined to around ten thousand men, Washington wrote the governors of all the states on 16 December, "The situation of the Army with respect to supplies is beyond description alarming"(Washington, Series 3c, Letterbox 3). With his men already on half rations, conditions were about to get worse. The commissariat again broke down and the troops at Morristown faced death from cold and starvation. At least the army had the experience of previous winter encampments to draw on, and the soldiers built an extensive "log-house city," consuming about six hundred acres of woodland. Soldier huts had a standard floor plan of about fourteen by fifteen feet and accommodated twelve men; they were about six and one-half feet high at the eaves, with wooden bunks, a fireplace at one end, and a door at the other. Construction was of notched logs, and chinks of clay sealed the walls. Windows apparently were not cut until spring. The huts were in rows of eight, three or four rows to a regiment. Officers' cabins were larger and less crowded. Parade grounds and company streets were laid out at regular intervals. Most of the men were able to move into huts before the end of December, but it was another six weeks before all the officers were accommodated.

Jockey Hollow was the name of the site about three miles southwest of Morristown where most of the army was camped—here were seven infantry brigades: Hand's New York, the First and Second Maryland, the First and Second Connecticut, and the First and Second Pennsylvania; The three Virginia brigades (Muhlenberg's, Scott's, and Woodford's), Stark's brigade; and the New Jersey brigade occupied separate camps within a mile of Jockey Hollow. Knox's artillery brigade and the gun park were about a mile west of Morristown. "On the Lines" were detachments at Princeton, Brunswick, Perth Amboy, Rahway, Westfield, Springfield, Paramus, and other outposts. These detachments, totaling from two hundred to two thousand at different times, were periodically relieved.

The severity of the winter limited military operations during the first months of 1780, but it also made possible the remarkable (although unsuccessful) Staten Island expedition of Alexander on 14–15 January. The action at Young's House in New York on 3 February was a British attempt to annihilate a unit "on the Lines." The British operations around Springfield, New Jersey, from 7 June to 23 June heralded the start of the 1780 campaign in the North.

SEE ALSO *Alexander, William; Estaing, Charles Hector Théodat, Comte d'; Hand, Edward; Morristown Winter Quarters, New Jersey (6 January–28 May, 1777); Poor, Enoch; Springfield, New Jersey, Raid of Knyphausen; Stark, John; Staten Island Expedition of Alexander; Young's House.*

BIBLIOGRAPHY
Smith, Samuel Stelle. *Winter at Morristown, 1779–1780: The Darkest Hour.* Monmouth Beach, N.J.: Freneau Press, 1979.
Washington, George. *George Washington Papers, Presidential Papers Microfilm.* Library of Congress: Washington, D.C., 1961, series 3c, letterbox 3.

revised by Michael Bellesiles

MORTAR.
So named because of its resemblance to pharmacist's mortar, a military mortar is a short gun used for firing projectiles at a high angle. It is most suitable for lobbing projectiles over walls of fortifications and over high ground that would mask the target from weapons having a flatter trajectory or for firing from and into heavy woods. There were gigantic siege mortars and diminutive coehorns or royals.

Mark M. Boatner

MORTON, JOHN.
(1725?–1777). Signer. Pennsylvania. Born in Tinicum, Pennsylvania, perhaps in 1725, Morton was elected to the Provincial Assembly in 1756, serving nearly every year until 1776, the last two as speaker. Meanwhile he had been justice of the peace for Chester (now Delaware) County, and served as judge on several courts. He attended the Stamp Act Congress in 1765 and was in the Continental Congress from 1774 to early in 1777. He played a critical role in organizing Pennsylvania's first militia in 1775. An advocate of independence, he joined with Benjamin Franklin and James Wilson to give the Pennsylvania delegation a majority of one in voting for the Declaration of Independence, and he was one of those who signed that document. He was chairman of the Committee of the Whole that adopted the Articles of Confederation, which were ratified after his death. After an extended illness, he died at his home in Tinicum, Pennsylvania, on 1 April 1777.

SEE ALSO *Declaration of Independence.*

BIBLIOGRAPHY
Springer, Ruth L. *John Morton in Contemporary Records.* Harrisburg, Penn.: Pennsylvania Historical Museum, 1967.

revised by Michael Bellesiles

MOTTIN DE LA BALME, AUGUSTIN.
(1736–1780). French volunteer. Though of noble ancestry, he was the son of a bourgeois father and a mother who was the daughter of a *conseiller du roi*. He entered the Scottish company of Gendarmerie in 1757 and became quartermaster with the rank of cavalry captain in 1765. Having been employed at the school of horsemanship, he wrote two books on the cavalry. Deane wrote to Congress recommending him in October 1776, but La Balme was unable to get out of France. He approached Franklin in December about an American command. Masquerading as a doctor, he embarked at Bordeaux with two other officers on 15 February 1777 carrying Franklin's introduction of 20 January 1777. It recommended him as an able cavalry officer who might be valuable in forming that branch of service.

On 26 May 1777 La Balme was commissioned lieutenant colonel of cavalry in the Continental army. Continuing to promote himself among the members of Congress, he presented copies of his two books to John Adams in June. On 8 July he was promoted to colonel and inspector general of cavalry, but he submitted his resignation to Congress on 3 October because Pulaski had been preferred to command the cavalry. La Balme proposed to Henry Laurens a Canadian project for exciting a "revolution," which Laurens referred to the Board of War. When it finally recommended an "irruption . . . into Canada," it was to be under the command of Lafayette; Congress approved the proposal on 22 January 1778. On 13 February 1778 Congress accepted his resignation with "no farther occasion for his services." Henry Laurens complained to his son John—perhaps tongue in cheek—that La Balme had not left him any books.

In 1778 La Balme received authority from Gates in 1778 to take part in the operations around Albany. He organized a bureau twenty-eight miles from Philadelphia and issued manifestos in French, English, and German calling for volunteers to join the cause of liberty.

On 13 May 1779 he left Boston with others to rally support in the frontier settlement of Machias. Arriving on the 19th, he established contact with Indians who traded at the village and was warmly received by the former subjects of the French king. Because of events described in connection with the Penobscot expedition, La Balme's timing was unfortunate. He organized a body of Indians and marched toward the British, but their force was crushed by superior numbers. La Balme was captured, but he escaped or was exchanged.

In reply to his 5 March 1780 request, Washington declined to give him a certificate of service. The commander in chief had earlier complained that La Balme never entered into his inspector duties. James Lovell on 17 April 1780 returned copies of La Balme's European letters of recommendation to him, adding his regrets that "America did not longer than seven months enjoy the benefits of your exertions as inspector general." On 27 June 1780 he was at Pittsburgh, and for the next three months he conducted recruiting operations in the direction of Vincennes, Cahokia, and Kaskaskia. With about one hundred French and American volunteers, he started on his own an advance through Kaskaskia toward Detroit. La Balme was killed on 5 November 1780 by Indians under the orders of Little Turtle. About forty of his men died in the massacre.

SEE ALSO *Canada Invasion (Planned); Deane, Silas; Franklin, Benjamin; Laurens, Henry; Penobscot Expedition, Maine; Pulaski, Casimir.*

BIBLIOGRAPHY

Bodinier, André. *Dictionnaire des officiers de l'armée royale qui ont combattu aux Etats-Unis pendant la guerre d'Indépendance, 1776–1783.* Vincennes, France: Service historique de l'armée, 1982.

Butterfield, Lyman H., et al., eds. *Adams Family Correspondence.* 6 vols. to date. Cambridge, Mass.: Harvard University Press, 1963–.

Deane, Silas. "The Deane Papers." New-York Historical Society *Collections* 19–23 (1886–1890).

Ford, Worthington C., et al., eds. *Journals of the Continental Congress, 1774–1789.* 34 vols. Washington, D.C.: U.S. Government Printing Office, 1904–1937.

Franklin, Benjamin. *Papers of Benjamin Franklin* Edited by Leonard W. Labaree, et al. 37 vols. to date. New Haven, Conn.: Yale University Press, 1959–.

Mottin de La Balme, Augustin. *Essais sur l'équitation; ou principes raisonnés sur l'art de monter et de dresser des chevaux.* Amsterdam: Jombert fils ainé, 1773.

———. *Elemens de tactique pour la cavalerie.* Paris: Jombert, 1776.

———. *Avis au public . . . to the Public . . . Offentliche bekanntmachung.* Philadelphia: Henri Miller, 1778.

———. Papers. Additional MSS 21, 844. British Library, London.

Smith, Paul H., et al., eds. *Letters of Delegates of the Continental Congress, 1774–1789.* 26 vols. Washington, D.C.: U.S. Government Printing Office, 1976–2000.

revised by Robert Rhodes Crout

MOULTRIE, JOHN.

(1729–1798). Loyalist lieutenant governor of East Florida. South Carolina-Florida. Born in Charleston, South Carolina, on 18 January 1729, Moultrie in 1749 became the first American to graduate from Edinburgh with a medical degree. His thesis was the first study of yellow fever in North America and became the standard work on the subject for a century. Returning to Charleston in 1749, he established a practice that he abandoned in 1753 upon marrying the wealthy Dorothy Morton, who died four years later. Entering the assembly in 1761, Moultrie held a number of offices, including posts in the militia. In 1760 he became a major in the Provincial Regiment, joining the following year in the Cherokee expedition of Grant, in which Moultrie was responsible for the garrison of Ninety Six. After he took the side of Lieutenant Colonel James Grant in his dispute with Colonel Thomas Middleton, Moultrie became a favorite of Grant.

When Grant established the government of East Florida in 1763, he named Moultrie to the council, where he served as president from 1765 to 1771. Moultrie took up fourteen thousand acres in land grants, built a mansion called Bella Vista near St. Augustine, and when he succeeded Grant as acting lieutenant governor in 1771 (Grant was invalided home and arranged for Moultrie's appointment to become permanent), he sold his South Carolina properties and moved his two hundred slaves to Florida. He immediately entered into a sharp political dispute with Chief Justice William Drayton, who promoted the creation of a legislature in Florida. Moultrie preferred executive rule, especially as he was the chief executive until the arrival of the new governor, Colonel Patrick Tonyn, on 1 March 1774. Moultrie sided with the British during the Revolution and helped organize the militia, of which he was colonel. In July 1784, when England handed Florida over to Spain, he sailed to England and three years later was awarded about forty-five hundred pounds for his war losses, slightly more than half of his claim. He settled in Shropshire, where he died on 19 March 1798. Three brothers, Alexander, Thomas, and William, were Patriot soldiers.

SEE ALSO *Cherokee Expedition of James Grant.*

BIBLIOGRAPHY

Mowat, Charles L. *East Florida as a British Province, 1763–1784.* Gainesville: University of Florida Press, 1964.

revised by Michael Bellesiles

BIBLIOGRAPHY

Moultrie, William. *Memoirs of the American Revolution.* 2 vols. New York: New York Times, 1968.

revised by Michael Bellesiles

MOULTRIE, WILLIAM. (1730–1805).

Continental general. South Carolina. Born in Charleston, South Carolina, on 23 November 1730, Moultrie was a member of the Commons House through most of the 1750s. Appointed captain in the militia on 16 September 1760, he took part in Lieutenant Colonel James Grant's expedition against the Cherokee in 1761. He remained active in the militia, rising to colonel in 1774, and served in the South Carolina Provincial Congresses of 1775–1776. On 17 June 1775 he became colonel of the Second South Carolina Regiment, leading a notorious raid in November against an encampment of escaped slaves on Sullivan's Island that resulted in the slaughter of fifty people. Against the Charleston expedition of Clinton in June 1776, he became a national hero in his defense of the palmetto and sand fort that was renamed in his honor. He was appointed a Continental brigadier general on 16 September 1777 but had no opportunity for significant field operations until after the British capture of Savannah on 29 December 1778. During Lincoln's operations in the southern theater, Moultrie was employed in a semi-independent role. He commanded the successful action at Beaufort, South Carolina, on 3 February 1779. When General Augustin Prevost pushed through his screening force and threatened Charleston on 11–12 May, Moultrie helped organize the defenses of the city. He was criticized for failing to act aggressively at Port Royal on 3 February 1779 and Stono Ferry on 20 June 1779, allowing the British to get away in each instance.

When Charleston fell to the British in May 1780, Moultrie became a prisoner of war, spending almost two years in the British prison at Haddrell's Point, South Carolina. He was freed as part of the exchange for General Burgoyne in February 1782, and on 15 October he became a Continental major general—the last officer appointed to that grade—but the fighting was over. In 1783 he sat in the South Carolina House of Representatives and the next year was lieutenant governor. He served two terms as governor (1785–1787 and 1792–1794). He was a federalist member of the state ratifying convention in 1788. He died at Northampton, South Carolina, on 27 September 1805.

S E E A L S O Beaufort, South Carolina; Charleston Expedition of Clinton in 1776; Charleston, South Carolina; Southern Theater, Military Operations in.

MOUNT PLEASANT, NEW YORK
S E E *Young's House.*

MOUNT PLEASANT, SOUTH CAROLINA S E E *Haddrel's Point.*

MOUNT WASHINGTON, NEW YORK. (Washington Heights). Site of Fort Washington, which was renamed Fort Knyphausen after its capture by the British on 8 November 1776.

S E E A L S O *Fort Washington, New York.*

Mark M. Boatner

MOYLAN, STEPHEN. (1737–1811). Continental officer. Ireland and Pennsylvania. Born in Cork in 1737, Moylan was the son of a prosperous Catholic merchant. Following in his father's trade, he too became a widely traveled merchant before settling in Philadelphia in 1768. On the recommendation of a friend, John Dickinson, he became muster-master general of the Continental army on 11 August 1775. He joined General George Washington at Cambridge, where his duties included the fitting-out of privateers. On 5 March 1776 he became secretary to Washington, and on 5 June Congress elected him quartermaster general, with the rank of colonel. He succeeded Thomas Mifflin in this new post.

Moylan was not successful as quartermaster general, although it must be pointed out that his difficulties were virtually insurmountable. Washington blamed him for failing to get more of the army's matérial away from Long Island and New York City during the American army's retreat in the summer of 1776. Moylan resigned as quartermaster general on 28 September 1776, and Mifflin was reappointed to the post. Moylan remained on Washington's staff as a volunteer, however, and served with distinction in the victory at Princeton on 3 January 1777. He responded to a request from Washington to raise a mounted regiment, which started as a Pennsylvania volunteer unit, the First Pennsylvania Cavalry Regiment. This later became the Fourth Continental Dragoons. Moylan was commissioned colonel of this unit on 5 January, an assignment he held for the rest of the war.

Casimir Pulaski's appointment as over-all cavalry commander on 21 September 1777 raised problems of cooperation that came to a head in the next month. Acquitted of court-martial charges pressed by Pulaski in October, Moylan spent the winter at Valley Forge and became temporary commander of the four mounted regiments when Pulaski resigned this post in March 1778. For the next three years he served on the Hudson River and in Connecticut, taking part in the battle of Monmouth on 28 June 1778. He also participated in Anthony Wayne's expedition to Bull's Ferry, New Jersey in July 1780 and the Southern campaign of 1780 and 1781. After Charles Cornwallis surrendered in the name of the British forces, Moylan's health forced him to return to Philadelphia. He was brevetted as a brigadier general on 3 November 1783, the date he left the army. After the war Moylan again became a merchant. Washington appointed him commissioner of loans in Philadelphia in 1793. He died in Philadelphia on 11 April, 1811.

SEE ALSO *Mifflin, Thomas; Monmouth, New Jersey; Princeton, New Jersey.*

BIBLIOGRAPHY

Griffin, Martin I. J. *Stephen Moylan: Muster-Master General, Secretary and Aide-de-Camp to Washington.* Philadelphia: printed for the author, 1909.

revised by Michael Bellesiles

MUHLENBERG, JOHN PETER GABRIEL. (1746–1807).

Lutheran clergyman, Continental general, politician. Pennsylvania and Virginia. Born 1 October 1746 in Trappe, Pennsylvania, Muhlenberg was sent by his father, a Lutheran missionary, to Halle, Germany, at the age of sixteen to be educated. It was hoped that he would become a minister. Instead, he was apprenticed to a grocer in Lübeck. After three years of misery, Muhlenberg ran away and in 1766 joined the 60th Foot ("Royal Americans"). As secretary to one of the regiment's officers, he traveled to Philadelphia and was discharged in 1767. He studied theology and became an assistant to his father.

In 1772 he moved to Woodstock, Virginia, to be pastor of the large colony of German immigrants in the Shenandoah Valley. That same year he went to England, and on 23 April 1772 was ordained by the bishop of London. Back in the Shenandoah Valley, he soon emerged as a leader of his community, being elected to the House of Burgesses in 1774. He became associated with the Patriot cause and was elected chair of the Dunmore County Committee of Correspondence and Safety. In March 1775 he became a member of the Virginia Convention, and on 12 January 1776 he accepted their appointment as a militia colonel charged with raising a regiment. He preached a famous final sermon back in Woodstock. "There is a time for all things," he said, taking his text from Ecclesiastes 3:1, "a time to preach and a time to pray; but there is also a time to fight, and that time has now come." At this point he supposedly threw aside his robes to reveal his militia uniform, ordered the drums to beat for recruits, and enlisted most of the adult males in his congregation into the Eighth Virginia, which was better known as the "German Regiment." Marching south, the regiment helped repel General Henry Clinton's Charleston expedition in 1776. Afterwards, they continued into Georgia, where disease eventually forced the unit to return to Virginia.

Muhlenberg was appointed brigadier general on 21 February 1777, and his brigade saw action as part of General Nathanael Greene's division at the battle of the Brandywine River, on 11 September 1777. At Germantown, on 4 October 1777, "the Parson-General," as he was known, led his brigade in a deep penetration of the enemy's line, and then fought his way back as superior enemy forces tried to cut him off.

After the winter at Valley Forge, Muhlenberg, William Woodford, and George Weedon, became engaged in the patriot pastime of fighting over primacy of rank. At Monmouth, on 28 June 1778, Muhlenberg commanded the second line of Greene's right wing, which was not engaged until the final phase of the battle. Later in 1778 Muhlenberg was assigned to Israel Putnam's division on the Hudson River, and he commanded the division during the winter while Putnam was absent. After winter quarters at Middlebrook, Muhlenberg commanded a 300-man reserve during Anthony Wayne's assault of Stony Point on 16 July 1779. In December he was sent by General George Washington to take command in Virginia, but it was March 1780 before he reached Richmond. During this delay, caused by snows of the exceptional winter, Friedrich Steuben was given chief command in Virginia, and Muhlenberg became his second. He was involved in the unsuccessful attempt to keep William Phillips and Benedict Arnold from destroying supplies in Petersburg on 25 April 1781. He and Weedon then worked to assemble Virginia militia units and continued to command troops on the south bank of the James River. In the final operations against General Charles Cornwallis, Muhlenberg commanded a brigade in the light infantry division led by the Marquis de Lafayette and again in the assault on Redoubt Number Ten during the Yorktown campaign.

Brevetted a major general on 30 September 1783, Muhlenberg retired on 3 November, settled his affairs at Woodstock, and moved to Philadelphia. Among the Pennsylvania Germans, he now was a hero second only to Washington, and a political career lay before him. In 1784 he was elected to the Supreme Executive Council of Pennsylvania, and during the period 1785–1788 he was vice president of the state under Benjamin Franklin. He was influential in the early adoption of the Constitution in the state, and both he and his brother, Frederick, were elected representatives to the first Congress. Defeated for re-election, he returned to Congress in 1793–1795 and 1799–1801. On 18 February 1801 he was elected senator, but resigned a month later to become supervisor of revenue in Philadelphia. From 1802 until his death five years later he was collector of customs in the city. He died at his home at Gray's Ferry, Pennsylvania, on 1 October 1807.

SEE ALSO *German Regiment; Yorktown Campaign.*

BIBLIOGRAPHY

Wallace, Paul A. W. *The Muhlenbergs of Pennsylvania.* Philadelphia: University of Pennsylvania Press, 1950.

revised by Michael Bellesiles

MURRAY, DAVID SEE *Stormont, David Murray, Seventh Viscount.*

MURPHY, TIMOTHY. (1751–1818). War hero. Pennsylvania. A legendary Continental rifleman, perhaps the most famous marksman of the Revolution, Murphy was born near the Delaware Water Gap in 1751. As a young man he settled in the Wyoming Valley of Pennsylvania. On 29 June 1775, he and his brother John were mustered into Captain John Lowdon's Northumberland County militia company.

Murphy served in the Boston siege, at Long Island, and in the New Jersey campaign. In the summer of 1777 he was one of 250 picked riflemen sent north under Morgan to oppose Burgoyne. Murphy is generally credited with shooting Sir Francis Clerke and General Simon Fraser in the Second Battle of Saratoga on 7 October 1777, although no contemporary account validates this claim. Many unverifiable legends circulate around Murphy, such as his ability to hit a target at three hundred yards and the claim that he used a double-barreled rifle that is not known to have existed during the Revolution.

Murphy was at Valley Forge. He did not take part in the Battle of Monmouth but the next day, on 29 June 1778, he, his constant companion David Elerson, and two other riflemen captured the elaborate coach of a British general. Moving north with three companies of Morgan's Riflemen to the Mohawk Valley, Murphy tracked down and killed the notorious Christopher

Service. He took part in the action at Unadilla in October 1778 in the pursuit of the raiders who had sacked Cherry Valley and also participated in Sullivan's expedition. When his enlistment with Morgan's Riflemen expired in late 1779, Murphy enrolled in Captain Jacob Hager's company of Peter Vrooman's Albany County militia (Fifteenth Regiment). Scouting with militia captain Alexander Harper in the Delaware County forest during the spring of 1780, he was captured by Indians and taken toward Oquago. During the night he and another captive freed each other's bonds and methodically knifed ten sleeping Indians before making their escape.

During the action at Schoharie Valley on 15–19 October 1780, Murphy famously fired on British officers attempting to surrender. Early in 1781 he reenlisted in the Continental army and served in the Pennsylvania Line under General Anthony Wayne and was present at Yorktown. After the war he returned to the Wyoming Valley and became active in local politics. He died in 1818.

SEE ALSO *Clerke, Sir Francis Carr; Fraser, Simon (1729–1777); Saratoga, Second Battle of; Schoharie Valley, New York.*

BIBLIOGRAPHY

O'Brien, Michael Joseph. *Timothy Murphy, Hero of the American Revolution.* New York: Eire Publishing, 1941.

revised by Michael Bellesiles

MURRAY, JOHN. Royal governor of Virginia. Son of the third earl of Dunmore, John Murray succeeded his father to become the fourth earl of Dunmore in 1756, and it is by this name that he is best known. He was an army officer from 1749 to 1760, when he resigned his commission. He was elected in 1761 as one of sixteen Scottish peers to sit in Parliament. He supported Lord North for the office of prime minister, and in 1770, when Lord North took that office, Dunmore was named governor of New York by Wills Hill, the earl of Hillsborough, who was the colonial secretary at the time.

Arriving in New York on 19 October 1770, Dunmore readily accepted and participated in the provincial aristocracy's thirst for land speculation. Eleven months later he was promoted to governor of Virginia, Britain's most important mainland colony, to succeed Governor Norborne Berkeley, baron de Botetourt, who had died on 15 October 1770. Dunmore arrived at Williamsburg in September 1771, and was initially popular with Virginia's land-hungry aristocrats, including George Washington. The House of Burgesses even named the new frontier counties of Dunmore and Fincastle (another of his titles) in his honor.

When the Shawnee, beset by land-hungry whites from Pennsylvania and Virginia, precipitated a conflict, Dunmore responded by raising the western militia and taking the field himself to subdue the tribe and lay claim to their lands. When Colonel Andrew Lewis defeated the Shawnee at Point Pleasant on 10 October 1774, Dunmore reached the zenith of his popularity in the colony, a fact which was reflected by his naming his eleventh child Virginia in January 1775.

Attention paid to frontier matters diverted Dunmore from a rising tide of opposition to imperial control in Virginia. The first discordant note was struck in 1773, when Dunmore dissolved the House of Burgesses after it proposed forming a committee of correspondence. He did the same thing the next year when the burgesses set a day of mourning over the Boston Port Bill. While he was away on the frontier in 1774, the first Virginia Convention embargoed British trade, began to make preparations for armed resistance, and sent delegates to the first Continental Congress. Dunmore thought the unrest was the work of a few troublemakers and took measures in the spring of 1775 that shattered his reputation with Virginians, making him arguably the most reviled of all the royal governors.

On 21 April Dunmore seized the gunpowder in the Williamsburg magazine, threatened to raise the slaves against those who protested this action, and broke completely with the House of Burgesses on 1 June 1775 over Lord North's peace proposal. He and his family fled to the safety of a British warship on 8 June. With a small fleet, he eventually gathered in the strongly Loyalist Norfolk area a force composed of sailors, marines, and a few companies of the Fourteenth Regiment of Foot. He also began to recruit the Queen's Own Royal Regiment and the Ethiopian Regiment, made up of runaway slaves. With this amphibious force, he raided the area around the tidewater through the fall, but the presence of runaway slaves as soldiers in his force was inflammatory to nearly every white Virginian. On 14 November 1775 he issued his Emancipation Proclamation which, by offering freedom to military-age male slaves who left their rebel masters to join him, destroyed his appeal with the rebel aristocrats.

Overconfidence led to Dunmore's defeat by Colonel William Woodford at Great Bridge, Virginia, on 9 December 1775, after which Dunmore withdrew to his ships. An attempt to retake part of the town on 1 January 1776 led to its destruction, for which Dunmore was blamed. Sir Henry Clinton made contact with Dunmore in February, but Clinton was on his way to Charlestown,

South Carolina, and left no reinforcements. By May 1776 Dunmore had to withdraw to Gwynn Island, from which he was driven in July. He raided up the Chesapeake River to the Potomac before sailing for New York with a force that included the 300 soldiers of the Ethiopian Regiment. He shortly returned to Britain. He again sat as a Scottish peer in Parliament before being named governor of the Bahamas from 1786 to 1796. He died at Ramsgate, Kent, on 25 February 1809.

SEE ALSO *Great Bridge, Virginia; Gwynn Island, Virginia; Hampton, Virginia.*

BIBLIOGRAPHY

Selby, John E. *Dunmore.* Edited by Edward M. Riley. Williamsburg, Va.: Virginia Independence Bicentennial Commission, 1977.

Thwaites, Reuben G. and Kellogg, Louise P., eds. *Documentary History of Dunmore's War, 1774.* Madison, Wis.: Wisconsin Historical Society, 1905.

revised by Harold E. Selesky

MURRAY HILL MYTH.

Historians have contended that after his landing at Kips Bay on 15 September 1776, Sir Henry Clinton could have moved promptly across the island of Manhattan, a mere three thousand yards, and captured a large portion of the American army. The story of Mary Murray first appeared in Dr. James Thacher's *A Military Journal during the American Revolutionary War* (2d ed., 1827) and seemed so plausible that other writers picked it up. After the landing the American militia fled in panic, isolating General Israel Putnam's thirty-five hundred Continentals. At this point Mrs. Murray, a Quaker and wife of the merchant Robert Murray, invited General William Howe and Governor William Tryon (and in some versions, General Clinton as well) in for some wine and cakes. Apparently the British army ground to a halt while their commanders enjoyed Mrs. Murray's Madeira and witty conversation, and Putnam's troops made good their escape. As Thacher wrote in his journal on 20 September 1776, "It has since become a common saying among our officers that Mrs. Murray saved this part of the American army."

Historians disagree about these events. Almost all early American scholars from Benson Lossing to George Bancroft to John Fiske accepted the story without question. Most contemporary popular histories of the Revolution also repeat the story as fact. More careful scholars, such as Samuel Willard Crompton, argue that the evidence leaves little doubt that Mary Murray entertained the British commanders at her house on Murray

Hill, but that these refreshments in no way stopped the British army from performing its duties. Putnam's escape has more to do with the American's evasive skills and with the realities of securing the ground after a successful landing. There is absolutely no evidence that Mary Murray, whose husband had Loyalist leanings, had any ulterior motive.

SEE ALSO *Kips Bay, New York.*

BIBLIOGRAPHY
Thacher, James. *A Military Journal during the American Revolutionary War, from 1775 to 1783.* 2d ed. Boston: Cottons and Barnard, 1827.

revised by Michael Bellesiles

MUSGRAVE, THOMAS. (1738–1812).
British officer. Born on 26 November 1738 at Hayton Castle, Cumberland, Musgrave entered the army in 1754 as an ensign in the Third ("Buffs") Regiment. After serving in the Sixty-fourth Regiment and being brevetted as a major in 1772, he joined the Fortieth Foot Regiment and came to America with this unit in 1776, gaining promotion to lieutenant colonel after the battle of Long Island on 28 August 1776. Commanding the Fortieth in the Philadelphia campaign, he distinguished himself in the defense of the Chew House at Germantown on 4 October 1777. The next year he accompanied General James Grant's expedition to St. Lucia as quartermaster general. Invalided home, he was made a colonel and aide-de-camp to the King in 1782. In this same year he returned to America as a brigadier general to serve as the last British commandant of New York City. He then went to India, was promoted to major general in 1790, to lieutenant general in 1797, and to full general in 1802. He died at his London home on 31 December 1812.

SEE ALSO *Germantown, Pennsylvania, Battle of.*

revised by Michael Bellesiles

MUSGROVE'S MILL, SOUTH CAROLINA.
18 August 1780. In the skirmishing that preceded the Battle of Kings Mountain, Lieutenant Colonels Elijah Clarke, Isaac Shelby, and James Williams combined their two hundred volunteers from Georgia, the Watauga settlements, and South Carolina, respectively, sharing the command between them. They attempted a surprise attack against the Loyalists at the rear of Major Patrick Ferguson's main force. They launched their assault at Musgrove's Mill on the Enoree River. But the surprise failed and Ferguson turned on them. The rebels took up a defensive position and repulsed an attack in which they claimed to have killed sixty-three Loyalists, wounded ninety, and captured seventy, with a loss of only four rebels killed and eight wounded. If these figures are accurate, they make this one of the most one-sided battles of the Revolution.

SEE ALSO *Kings Mountain, South Carolina.*

revised by Michael Bellesiles

MUSIC, MILITARY.
Military music was essential to the Revolutionary armies, contributing greatly to discipline and order both in camp and on the battlefield. Specialized drum and fife signals called musicians or officers to assemble and detachments to gather wood or informed the men when it was time to receive rations. Music provided a cadence to regulate the marching rate, and transmitted or supplemented officers' commands in battle.

MUSICALLY REGULATED ACTIVITIES
George Washington early on recognized the value of well-trained musicians, as indicated in his 4 June 1777 general orders: "The music of the army being in general very bad; it is expected, that the drum and fife Majors exert themselves to improve it. . . . Nothing is more agreeable, and ornamental, than good music; every officer, for the credit of his corps, should take care to provide it." He then outlined the musically regulated daily routine. "The *revellie* to be beaten at day-break—the *troop* at 8 o'clock in the morning, and *retreat* at sunset." Two days later he ordered, "The morning gun at day-break to be a signal for the *revellie;* and the evening gun at sun-set a signal for the *retreat.*" To these calls can be added the end of day "tap-too," when "all lights must be put out at 9 o'Clock in the evening, and every man to his tent."

The routine was altered for an army on the move, General Washington giving details on 16 August 1777:

1. When the army is to march, the General (and not the Revellie) is to beat in the morning.

2. At the beating of the General, the officers and soldiers are to dress and prepare themselves for the march, packing up and loading their baggage.

3. At the beating of the troop, they are to strike all their tents and put them in the wagons.

The Spirit of '76 (1875) by Archibald Willard. *During battles of the American Revolution, musicians playing fifes and drums helped transmit messages from commanders. The music also helped bolster soldiers' morale.* LANDOV

4. At least a quarter of an hour before the time appointed for marching, the rummers are to beat a march, upon which the troops are to march out and form at the head of their encampment.... Precisely at the hour appointed for marching, the drummers beat the march a second time, at that part of the line from which the march is to be made ... upon which the troops face or wheel ... and instantly begin the march.

Further orders, tinged with criticism, were issued for the march through Philadelphia later the same month:

The drums and fifes of each brigade are to be collected in the center of it; and a tune for the quick step played, but with such moderation, that the men may step to it with ease; and without *dancing* along, or totally disregarding the music, as too often has been the case.

Whatever the musical quality, the daily schedule often changed to fit situational needs.

Several works have discussed battlefield drum signals, most notably Raoul Camus's *Military Music of the American Revolution* (1976), but there is much yet to be learned on their practical use. William Windham's *Plan of*

Discipline for the Use of the Norfolk Militia (1768) provided twenty drum commands for everything from "Fix bayonets, marching" to "Form Battalion!" Other manuals followed suit. In actuality, battle and maneuver signals varied. During Major General John Sullivan's expedition against the Iroquois in 1779, orders for 4 August stipulated signals for marching in files, advancing by sections and platoons, closing columns, and displaying into line. By comparison, Major General Friedrich Wilhelm de Steuben's *Regulations* (1779) gives only three different signals for marching forces: the "Front to halt," "the Front to advance quicker," and "to march slower." In 1780 British Captain John Peebles of the Forty-second Regiment noted the "General Rules for Manouvring the Batt[alio]n. by the Commanding Officer," appended to which are "Signals by Drum":

1. *Preparative* to begin firing by Companies, which is to go on as fast as each is loaded till the first part of the General when not a shot more is ever to be fired.

2. *Grenad[ie]rs March* to advance in Line.

3. *Point of War* to Charge.

4. *To Arms* to form the Batt[alio]n. (whether advancing or Retreating in Column) upon the leading division.

5. *Double flam* to halt Upon the word forward, in forming, the Divisions to run up in Order.

HORNS

Another instrument, the bugle horn (also called the French, hunting, or German post-horn) was commonly used by light and mounted troops. Horns were especially associated with the British light infantry. Massachusetts Lieutenant Joseph Hodgekins wrote of the Battle of Harlem Heights (16 September 1776), "The Enemy Halted Back of an hill and Blood [blowed] a french Horn which whas for a Reinforcement." Xavier della Gatta's painting, *The Battle of Germantown* (1782), shows a horn-blowing musician at the head of two files of British light infantry, and the song "A Soldier" (1778) begins with the lines:

Hark! hark! the bugle's lofty sound
Which makes the woods and rocks around
Repeat the martial strain,
Proclaims the light-arm'd British troops.

It is uncertain when American light troops first used horns, but during the Monmouth campaign in June 1778, New York Lieutenant Bernardus Swartwout noted,

• [25 June] The Horn blowed (a substitute for a drum in the [light] Infantry corps) we marched about four miles ...

• [26 June] At the sound of the horn we marched eight miles and halted.

Bands of music, playing orchestral instruments, were also present with some units, serving a largely ornamental purpose. Most British regiments had their own bands at one time or another, several surrendering at Saratoga and Yorktown. Only a few Continental units followed suit, most notably the Third and Fourth Artillery, Second Virginia, and Webb's Additional Regiments.

Proficient field musicians (drummers, fifers, and for light troops and cavalry, buglers) were hard to find. That was because they were expected to learn many tunes, from popular melodies like "Roslyn Castle" to practical beats such as "Water Call" or "Roast Beef."

UNIFORMS

Recognizing musicians' special duties, efforts were made to provide them with regimental coats with reversed colors based on European practice. In May 1777 the Continental clothier general informed Colonel Elias Dayton of the Third New Jersey that "there is 395 Blue coats faced red on the road from Boston . . . which I design to furnish your regmt. . . . I have also . . . sent you 12 Red Coats fac'd with blue of the clothing taken from the enemy for your drums & fifes." This variation was not always possible, as some units wore un-dyed linen hunting shirts, while in the autumn of 1778 Washington's army was issued French-made coats of blue or brown with red facings, with no distinction for musicians.

MUSICIANS' AGE AND EXPERIENCES

Because of their responsibilities, musicians were relatively mature, in the Continental army on average 18.5 years (the average age for drummers was 19 years, for fifers 17). Youthful musicians were sometimes kept out of harm's way. Drummer James Holmes of the Eleventh Pennsylvania Regiment, 13 years old when he joined in 1778, stated "he was not in Any engagements not being permitted by his Captain, [and] on account of his Youth was generally ordered to the rear." Younger and smaller musicians were more likely to play the fife, with some fifers changing to the drum as they matured. In 1782 Congress decided to take new musicians from the ranks, causing some difficulty, as a Tenth Massachusetts officer testified, "we want three Drummers and two Fifers but at present can find but one Fifer and two Drummers who have natural Geniuses for music . . . they are men of small stature and I believe will answer the purpose."

Musicians sometimes experienced duty-related hardships. Revolutionary fifer Samuel Dewees also served in the Fries Rebellion of 1799. Sent to recruit troops in Northampton, Pennsylvania, he stayed "two or three days . . . I had played the fife so much at this place, I began to spit blood. . . . By the aid of the Doctor's medicine and the kind nursing treatment . . . I was restored to health again in a few days and able to play the fife as usual." Fifer Swain Parsel of the Third New Jersey Regiment had a similar experience. He "enlisted in the beginning of [1776] . . . as a fifer for one year." Reenlisting in the same regiment, "the practice of fifing being injurious to his health, he entered the ranks as a private soldier."

MEMENTOS OF SERVICE

Prospective pensioner John McElroy of the Eleventh Pennsylvania had a unique story to tell, stating in his pension deposition, "As to my occupation I have none being nearly blind by reason of my eyes being nearly destroyed by the accidental bursting of cartridges in the year 1779 at Sunbury Pennsylvania." Despite his injury McElroy was appointed fife major in 1780. John McElroy and Aaron Thompson of the Third New Jersey both retained mementos of their military service well after the war. The former wrote in 1820 that "I have my old Fife and knapsack yet," while a friend of Thompson noted after his death that he "had heard him [Thompson], often say so, and mention, the fact of his, having mutilated his fife in order to prevent its being stolen and that he might preserve it, as a relic, of his services in that Struggle."

BIBLIOGRAPHY

Camus, Raoul F. *Military Music of the American Revolution.* Chapel Hill, N.C.: University of North Carolina Press, 1976.

Dewees, Samuel. *A History of the Life and Services of Captain Samuel Dewees.* Compiled by John Smith Hanna. Baltimore: R. Neilson, 1844. Available online at http://www.dillonmusic. com/historic_fifes/sammy_the_fifer.htm.

Fitzpatrick, John C., ed. *The Writings of George Washington from the Original Manuscript Sources 1745–1799.* 39 vols. Washington, D.C.: Government Printing Office, 1931–1944.

Katcher, Philip R. N. *Encyclopedia of British, Provincial, and German Army Units 1775–1783.* Harrisburg, Pa.: Stackpole Books, 1973.

Rees, John U. "'The Musicians Belonging to the Whole Army': An Abbreviated Study of the Ages of Musicians in the Continental Army." *Brigade Dispatch* 24, no. 4 (Autumn 1993): 2–8; and 25, no. 1 (Winter 1994): 2–12.

———. "'The Great Neglect in Provideing Cloathing': Uniform Colors and Clothing in the New Jersey Brigade during the Monmouth Campaign of 1778." *Military Collector & Historian* 46, no. 4 (Winter 1994): 165; and 47, no.1 (Spring 1995): 18.

———. "'Bugle Horns,' 'Conk Shells,' and 'Signals by Drum': Miscellaneous Notes on Instruments and Their Use during the American War for Independence." *Brigade Dispatch* 26, no. 4 (Winter 1996): 13–15.

Steuben, Friedrich Wilhelm de. *Regulations for the Order and Discipline of the Troops of the United States Part I.* Philadelphia, Pa.: Styner and Cist, 1779.

Strachan, Hew. *British Military Uniforms, 1768–96: The Dress of the British Army from Official Sources.* London: Arms and Armour Press, 1975.

John U. Rees

MUSKETS AND MUSKETRY.

The principal infantry projectile weapon of the eighteenth century was the muzzle-loading flintlock musket. Using a complex double-ignition system, this smoothbore firearm threw a lead ball weighing about an ounce and up to three-quarters of an inch in diameter with an accuracy and rate of fire that suited the linear tactics used by western European armies and their colonial descendants in this period. Personal firearms had been introduced on a mass scale in the sixteenth century and incorporated into the linear tactical formations that were then dominated by thrusting and cutting weapons. As incremental improvements in the technology of firing the weapon were developed (the manner of igniting the gunpowder went from using a slow-burning match to striking flint on steel), firearms gradually replaced pikes and pole arms. The most common firearm, and the prototype of most other military firearms of the period, was the British army's famous Long Land Service musket, colloquially known as the Brown Bess.

Authors writing after the development of rifled military firearms have denigrated the musket for its inaccuracy at ranges much above fifty yards. By modern standards, it certainly was an imprecise weapon. But it is also true that the smoothbore musket was deeply intertwined with the history and technology of infantry combat of the period, as well as with social attitudes about who should fight and how they should be organized to succeed in battle. Rather than viewing the smoothbore musket as the ineffective precursor of subsequent improvements, it should be recognized as the most effective infantry combat weapon of its day, both influencing and being influenced by contemporary infantry tactics, an integral part of how societies and their leaders went about achieving the ultimate goal of prevailing on the battlefield.

DEPLOYMENT AND DISCIPLINE

The smoothbore musket was designed to be fired on command in massed volleys by soldiers standing upright shoulder to shoulder in lines several ranks deep. Volley fire could be based on groups as small as a platoon (say, at full strength, perhaps twenty-five men) or as large as a battalion, in numbers approaching a thousand men. Recognizing that bringing the maximum number of muskets to bear was the best way to impose one's will on the enemy, beginning in the seventeenth-century commanders gradually thinned down their lines from the eight or ten men deep appropriate for combat with pikes and pole arms to three ranks. The first rank of musketeers, with bayonets fixed, would kneel before firing and might remain in that position without reloading, partly because it was difficult to reload a muzzle-loading musket while on one knee and partly to offer with their bayonets protection for their colleagues against a charge by cavalry or infantry. At the same time, the men in the second and third lines would stand and fire, the third line firing in the gaps—next to the shoulders—of the men in the second line. In a well-organized, full-strength battalion, commanders might reserve another line of "file closers," drawn up at a short distance behind the third line, men who would step up when soldiers on the firing line fell wounded or killed. The British army was generally better trained than its European competitors in firing volleys by platoons, a more flexible tactic that gave fire all along the face of a battalion while ensuring that a portion of the soldiers were always loaded and ready to fire against any unexpected approach by the enemy.

At a range of fifty yards, volleys fired by soldiers arrayed in line would lay down a pattern of fire—more like that from a shotgun than from a precision firearm—that could have a devastating impact on a group of enemy soldiers similarly arranged. The key to success in battle was creating a larger volume of continuous fire than your enemy could produce. If a projectile struck a soldier, its low muzzle velocity meant that it would splay and produce an exit wound far larger than its point of entry. Firing as fast as one could reload in the general direction of the enemy line produced a hail of bullets that could unnerve a foe, almost regardless of how many projectiles actually struck home. No soldier would consciously want to take the chance of being hit; only the most rigorous inculcation of discipline could allow a soldier to suspend rational thought, as it were, and to keep reloading and firing in the hope that, if enough of his colleagues did the same thing, they might overmatch the enemy's musketry and simultaneously be safe against a bayonet charge from opponents who were, after all, only fifty yards away, perhaps obscured behind the cloud of gun smoke that hid them from observation.

ACCURACY OF FIRE

Accuracy, in the sense of aiming at a particular individual soldier on the opposite side and actually hitting your target, was not a significant part of the system of linear tactics. George Hanger remembered that:

> A soldier's musket, if not exceedingly ill-bored (as many of them are), will strike the figure of a man

at eighty yards; it may even at 100; but a soldier must be very unfortunate indeed who shall be wounded by a common musket at 150 yards, provided his antagonist aims at him.... I do maintain ... that no man was ever killed at 200 yards, by a common soldier's musket, by the person who aimed at him. (Peterson, p. 163)

Greater accuracy at longer ranges was, of course, possible. Gunsmiths had long understood that cutting slightly twisting grooves along the interior length of a gun barrel would impart spin to a projectile that had been wedged tightly enough on top of the powder charge that it deformed slightly when the powder exploded, thus enabling it to grip the lands (as the grooves were called) and go spinning down the barrel. The projectile had enough velocity to be effective at a range of up to three hundred yards. Riflemen were superior to musketeers on certain special missions but were no match in a linear battle because of their slow rate of fire and because their rifles lacked bayonets. Their marksmanship was less astounding than claimed at the time or than is popularly assumed.

RATE OF FIRE

The primary aim of military discipline was to produce soldiers who could endure the enormous physical and psychological strain that was part of fighting in a line, while simultaneously performing properly and efficiently the dozen or so motions necessary to reload their muskets. Constant practice was essential in giving the soldier the confidence and experience to fire and reload faster than an opponent who was going through the same motions trying to kill or incapacitate him. An average soldier might be able to fire two rounds a minute, while a nimble and well-trained man might be able to get off as many as four or five shots, meaning that he took only twelve to fifteen seconds to reload. (It was alleged, by Prussians no doubt, that Frederick II's troops could fire six rounds per minute, a remarkable figure that accomplished its objective if it induced nervous Austrians, Russians, and Frenchmen to glance about for a line of retreat even before coming within range of the rapid-fire Prussians.) In battle, speed in reloading was, according to the historian Harold L. Peterson, "everything. Speed for the defending force to pour as many bullets into the attacking force as possible; speed for the attacking force to close with its adversary before it had been too severely decimated to have sufficient strength to carry the position" with the bayonet (*Arms and Armor*, pp. 160, 162).

High rates of fire were possible only because the musket was designed to have enough windage (the gap between the spherical projectile and the inside of the barrel) so that the bullet essentially fell into place at the bottom of the barrel. Ramrods (thin, wooden, dowel-like sticks) were carried by every musketeer and used to tamp the bullet tightly against the powder charge in the barrel, thereby creating a tighter seal that maximized the propulsive force exerted on the bullet. The first volley in any battle always tended to be the most effective because soldiers would take time before going into action to load and carefully ram the first round in place, time they would not have to seal the second and subsequent rounds. If tactical circumstances required the soldier to fix his foot-long bayonet on the end of the muzzle of his firearm (held in place by a lug that doubled as the only aiming device the weapon possessed), then reloading would become a more complex process. It was said that one of the marks of a battalion that had been in a stiff firefight was the scraped and bloody knuckles of soldiers forced to reload with bayonets fixed.

IMPEDIMENTS TO EFFECTIVE USE

A rate of fire of even two rounds a minute was bound to decline quickly in battle. Black powder, the only available propellant, combusted incompletely and left a residue that clogged the touch hole (the vent whereby the explosion of the priming powder in the pan, ignited by the striking of flint on steel, communicated itself to the main charge in the barrel). The flints themselves were held precariously in a set of steel jaws called a cock or a hammer; the soldier had to tighten a small screw to clamp the flint in the proper position, with enough of an edge exposed so that it would produce a shower of sparks when the soldier pulled the trigger that released the spring which snapped it down against the steel (also called the frizzen or the battery). Flints were fragile and susceptible to cracking and flaking. They would have to be replaced if broken, or reset if misaligned; we can only begin to imagine how difficult that process must have been in the heat of battle.

Even when the charge was properly loaded in the gun barrel and the flint was held firm and ready in the jaws of the hammer, a whole host of things could still go wrong that would prevent the soldier from using his weapon effectively. Black powder is hygroscopic, so even the smallest amount of moisture would destroy its explosive potential; a rainstorm in the middle of a battle would turn the contest into a bayonet fight. Moreover, its constituent ingredients separate and settle out over time and with motion, a characteristic seen more often when gunpowder was stored or transported in large wooden barrels. If, while loading, the soldier placed too little powder in the priming pan, failed to close the steel tightly over the pan, or did not examine and, if necessary, clean the touch hole, the initial explosion of powder would not ignite the main charge, a phenomenon known as "flash in the pan." The soldier would be left with a live charge in the barrel and a number of equally bad choices about how to fix the problem. A fumble-fingered soldier might not successfully extract the ramrod in time with his colleagues and, in order to maintain volley fire, be compelled to present arms and fire away his ramrod. The hammer normally rested in the ready position, where a notch on its sear exerted minimal tension on the spring while the musket was being loaded. Before firing, the soldier had to pull the hammer back to the point where a second sear engaged and exerted the maximum tension on the leaf spring so that when released by the trigger, it would snap forward with maximum force against the steel, a position called "full cock." At any point once the musket was loaded, the hammer might jump free from the ready position and strike the steel with enough force so that the weapon fired; this sequence of accidents became known as "going off at half-cock."

It is also worth remembering that fatigue played a role in reducing the effectiveness of the men who wielded the smoothbore musket. On a hot summer day in western Europe, soldiers dressed in wool coats would quickly begin to slow down and wear out as they constantly loaded and fired their weapons. If the air were still, they would soon be breathing an unhealthy amount of gun smoke. Even if water were available, there might be no time for the soldier to slake his thirst or rinse from his mouth the taste and grit of the gunpowder he ingested in the process of ripping open cartridges with his teeth. Finally, the musket was so barrel-heavy that fatigue might cause the soldier to lower the barrel to the point where his bullets struck the ground in front of his line rather than flying in a slow arc to impact on the enemy line.

TACTICS FOR VICTORY

The pinnacle of smoothbore-musket-based linear tactics was to coordinate an advance on the enemy so as to maximize the impact of one's musketry. With muskets loaded and bayonets fixed, the attackers moved forward, keeping their alignment, knowing that until within one hundred yards they were relatively safe from enemy musketry. Their officers tried to exert leadership and impose discipline so that they could induce the men to hold their fire. The object was to receive the enemy's first volley, absorb the losses, and continue advancing to a point so close to the enemy's line that one's own first volley produced many casualties, enough to make the enemy break and run. The British army brought to North America a reputation for battlefield success earned by the repeated application of these tactics, most notably against the French. When, for example, British and French commanders at the Battle of Fontenoy on 11 May 1745 invited each other to fire first, they were shrewdly trying to gain an advantage, not being naively gallant. French discipline broke first, and the British survivors methodically annihilated their opponent with coolly delivered volley fire.

The symbiosis between smoothbore musketry and linear tactics produced battles in western Europe that were complex ballets of coordinated motion. Every man on the field had a specific part in the dance, from the soldier with the courage to stand in line and the training to reload until disabled by bullets or fatigue, up the chain of command to officers who had to judge the right moment to maneuver the appropriate units over suitable ground to engage an enemy with the best chance of winning the fight. Even though most of the men in the ranks were illiterate, unhealthy, and destined for a cruel fate, they were not unthinking cogs in some aristocratic machine. Battle was a far cry from being a clash of faceless automatons marching soullessly toward the cauldron of fire created by an inept tactical system.

AMERICAN MUSKETRY

At the start of the hostilities with Britain, many influential American leaders, including George Washington, wanted to create a "continental army" based on European-style smoothbore muskets and linear tactics. Their desire was in large part the product of political and ideological calculations. They wanted to prove to their oppressors that they were a civilized people fighting for its rights and therefore worthy of respect, not a bunch of dirty, savage rebels taking potshots at their betters from behind trees because they were afraid to stand and fight. They recognized, too, that a European-style army was their best chance of winning a clear-cut victory that might shorten the war, reduce the enormous costs involved, and minimize the disruption and strain war would inevitably impose on American society.

But Americans could never create an exact duplicate of the British army. It took long enlistments and intensive training to make men proficient in linear tactics, and Americans were generally disinclined to undertake either. Instead, they created a hybrid version of war making, a version that combined elements of linear tactics with the experience they had gained over the course of a century and a half confronting Native Americans and European competitors. In general, they tried to avoid open-field, stand-up fights against British regulars early in the war because they understood they were unprepared to fight in that fashion. They largely succeeded in dodging that sort of combat, in part because the British army's vision of war making based on linear tactics did not offer it any easy ways of forcing a reluctant opponent to fight. As hostilities continued, American units gradually gained experience and began to venture into more stand-up fights, as at Saratoga in September and October 1777. At Valley Forge over the winter of 1777–1778, Friedrich Steuben began the process of regularizing, standardizing, and installing a stripped-down system of linear tactics for the Continental army. The improved performance of Washington's army at the Battle of Monmouth Courthouse on 28 June 1778 demonstrated that American regular units were approaching a large-scale parity with the British army in America.

The colonists had no capacity to manufacture large numbers of new muskets in 1775. They began the war with a hodgepodge of firearms, mostly leftovers from shipments Britain had sent to arm provincial soldiers during the colonial wars, some still in government storage, but most in the hands of the men who had taken them to war. Privately owned guns from a variety of sources were a significant component of the firearms used before 1777. Many were remanufactured from parts salvaged from worn out or discarded muskets, including—in New England and New York—the recycling of weapons acquired in war and trade from Canada. Captured British arms were also part of the mix, whether sequestered from local royal sources (as in the raid on Fort William and Mary at Portsmouth, New Hampshire, on 14–15 December 1777) or captured by privateers from supply ships intended for British garrisons. The supply of firearms did not always meet the demand, and the pace of operations and the carelessness of American soldiers imposed a further drain on the number of serviceable muskets. Both the states and the Continental Congress immediately saw the need to acquire more firearms and did what they could to encourage local manufacture. Early in the war, committees of safety let contracts to local gunsmiths to produce muskets of a standard size and caliber; in the age before manufactured parts were interchangeable, all muskets were still the products of skilled craftsmen. There were centers of production across the colonies, including Harvard, Massachusetts, Goshen, Connecticut, Trenton, New Jersey, and Philadelphia, where the committee of safety led by Benjamin Franklin contracted for muskets from local gunsmiths in July 1775. That same month, Virginia established its own state arms manufactory at Fredericksburg. Congress later established its own Continental firearms factory at Lancaster, Pennsylvania, along with a shop that produced gunlocks in Trenton.

Despite herculean efforts to ramp up domestic manufacture, the demand for firearms could not have been met without supplies purchased from overseas. Individual states sent agents to Europe to purchase muskets, gunpowder, flints, and lead; the fruits of their efforts were smuggled into the colonies, mostly through the Dutch West Indies island of St. Eustatius. Congress itself sent Silas Deane of Connecticut to France in March 1776 with instructions to solicit clothing and arms for twenty-five thousand men. In May, France decided to supply military material to the colonies under the guise of the fictitious trading company Hortalez & Cie, run by Pierre-Augustin Caron de Beaumarchais. Eventually, over 100,000 high-quality French military muskets were sent to the Americans, firearms that provided a critical boost in the fighting power of the rebel armies. For example, thirty-seven thousand stand arrived at Portsmouth, New Hampshire, in the spring of 1777, many of which armed the troops that stopped Burgoyne's army at Saratoga. The victory at Saratoga, in turn, was crucial in prompting France to enter into a treaty of alliance with the United States 6 February 1778, after which French supplies could flow openly across the Atlantic. The French muskets, of .69 caliber, were largely a combination of the 1766 model and upgrades of earlier models undertaken between 1768 and 1773. They were produced at the three royal arms manufactories of St. Etienne, Maubeuge, and Charleville, the last named becoming the common designation for all French muskets. The French model 1766 was chosen as the design for the first muskets produced in the United States after the war, the model 1795.

SEE ALSO *Bayonets and Bayonet Attacks; Brown Bess; Fontenoy, Battle of; French Covert Aid; Hanger, George; Line; Marksmanship; Riflemen; Steuben, Friedrich Wilhelm von.*

BIBLIOGRAPHY

Curtis, Edward E. *The Organization of the British Army in the American Revolution.* New Haven, Conn.: Yale University Press, 1926.

Darling, Anthony D. *Red Coat and Brown Bess.* Ottawa, Canada: Museum Restoration Service, 1970.

Duffy, Christopher. *The Military Experience in the Age of Reason.* New York: Atheneum, 1988.

Houlding, J. A. *Fit for Service: The Training of the British Army, 1715–1795.* Oxford: Clarendon Press, 1981.

Neumann, George C. *Battle Weapons of the American Revolution.* Texarkana, Tex.: Surlock, 1998.

Peterson, Harold L. *Arms and Armor in Colonial America, 1526–1783.* Harrisburg, Pa.: Stackpole, 1956.

———. *The Book of the Continental Soldier.* Harrisburg, Pa.: Stackpole, 1968.

Risch, Erna. *Quartermaster Support of the Army: A History of the Corps, 1775–1939.* Washington, D.C.: U.S. Government Printing Office, 1962.

———. *Supplying Washington's Army.* Washington, D.C.: Center of Military History, 1981.

revised by Harold E. Selesky

MUTINY ACT OF 1765 SEE *Quartering Acts.*

MUTINY OF GORNELL. April 1782.

Inadequate supplies and other administrative grievances, combined with a lack of military activity, produced considerable discontent in Major General Nathanael Greene's southern army in October 1781. When these same conditions reappeared in the spring of 1782, the Pennsylvania battalions that had marched south under Brigadier General Anthony Wayne after Yorktown became the most agitated, still feeling lingering resentment from their previous mutiny. Before this trouble could spread to the Maryland troops, Greene determined to crack down, especially as he suspected British agents to be at work. Greene arrested the ringleader, a Sergeant Gornell, and tried him in a court-martial. On 23 April he was executed, ending the disturbance. The historian Carl Van Doren has identified him as George Goznall of the Second Pennsylvania Regiment.

SEE ALSO *Southern Campaigns of Nathanael Greene.*

revised by Robert K. Wright Jr.

MUTINY OF GRIFFIN. October 1781.
Continental private Timothy Griffin of South Carolina got drunk and insulted an officer. He was shot for mutinous conduct.

SEE ALSO *Southern Campaigns of Nathanael Greene.*

revised by Michael Bellesiles

MUTINY OF HICKEY. June 1776. On 15
June 1776, when General George Washington was in New York City and Governor William Tryon was a refugee aboard a British ship in the harbor, Thomas Hickey and another Continental soldier were brought before the Provincial Congress on the charge of passing counterfeit currency. Both men were members of Washington's Life Guard, a special military unit. In jail, Hickey bragged openly about being part of a conspiracy to turn against the Americans as soon as the British army arrived. Another prisoner, who had conversed with both Hickey and the solder who had been arrested with him, informed the authorities. The plot allegedly involved blowing up American powder magazines, setting fire to New York City, spiking the cannons, destroying the Kings Bridge, and assassinating Washington. The extent of the conspiracy was so magnified and propagandized, however, that the facts were never known for certain.

It seems to have been established at Hickey's trial that Governor Tryon had been sending money to Gilbert Forbes, a gunsmith on Broadway, to recruit men for the king. The money was passed by Mayor David Mathews of New York, who had authority to visit Tryon and who claimed he did not know the purpose of the money. There was no proof that Tryon was counterfeiting money on shipboard, or that he had offered land bounties to stimulate recruiting. Nor could it be proved that as many as 700 men had signed up for the plot, much less that the plans included the assassination of Washington and other leaders.

John Jay headed the committee that investigated the affair for the New York authorities. Only Hickey was tried, but 13 others, including Forbes and Mathews, were imprisoned in Connecticut. They all escaped or were sent back to New York before they could be given a hearing. Hickey was convicted of mutiny and sedition by a court-martial on 26 June 1776, and two days later was hanged on the Common in the presence of 20,000 spectators. It was the first military execution of the American Revolution. The main result of the affair was to further blacken the name of "Loyalist."

SEE ALSO *Jay, John; Tryon, William.*

BIBLIOGRAPHY
Van Doren, Carl. *Secret History of the American Revolution: An Account of the Conspiracies of Benedict Arnold and Numerous Others, Drawn from the Secret Service Papers of the British Headquarters in North America Now for the First Time Examined and Made Public.* New York: Viking Press, 1941.

revised by Barnet Schecter

MUTINY OF THE CONNECTICUT LINE. 25 May 1780. While in quarters at Basking Ridge, New Jersey, near Morristown, the Eighth Connecticut Regiment turned out about dusk on 25 May to protest a lack of food. There were no ringleaders in this spontaneous event, which spread to the Third, Fourth, and Sixth Connecticut Regiments as well. Colonel Walter Stewart of Pennsylvania mediated a settlement and the troops returned to their huts, although Colonel R. J. Meigs, acting brigade commander, had been accidentally bayoneted in the side. The historian Carl Van Doren has said, "The whole affair was soon over and afterwards disregarded" (*Mutiny,* pp. 22–23).

BIBLIOGRAPHY
Van Doren, Carl. *Mutiny: The Story of a Crisis in the Continental Army.* New York: Viking, 1943.

revised by Robert K. Wright Jr.

MUTINY OF THE FIRST NEW YORK REGIMENT. June 1780. Thirty-one
men of the First New York Regiment deserted from Fort

Schuyler (Stanwix) in early June 1780. Lieutenant Abraham Hardenbergh led a party of Oneidas in pursuit to prevent the deserters from joining the British. The fugitives were caught while in the process of crossing a river, and thirteen were shot. According to Carl Van Doren, "This is perhaps the only time in the history of the American Army when an officer used Indians to kill white soldiers" (*Mutiny in January*, p. 20).

BIBLIOGRAPHY

Van Doren, Carl. *Mutiny in January: The Story of a Crisis in the Continental Army Now for the First Time Fully Told from Many Hitherto Unknown or Neglected Sources Both American and British.* New York: Viking, 1943.

revised by Robert K. Wright Jr.

MUTINY OF THE MASSACHUSETTS LINE.

1 January 1780. William Heath wrote in his memoirs: "Early in the morning about 100 soldiers belonging to the Massachusetts regiments [of the West Point garrison] . . . marched off with intent to go home: they were pursued and brought back: some of them were punished; the greater part of them pardoned." Once back in quarters the individual cases were reviewed, and some of the men received their discharges. As would be the case again a year later, the cause of the problem was a difference of opinion on the meaning of the phrase—regarding length of service—"three years or the duration."

BIBLIOGRAPHY

Heath, William. *Heath's Memoirs of the American War.* Reprinted from the original edition of 1798 with introduction and notes by Rufus Rockwell Wilson. New York, 1904.

revised by Robert K. Wright Jr.

MUTINY OF THE NEW JERSEY LINE.

20–27 January 1781. The two regiments of the reorganized New Jersey Brigade were in winter quarters at Pompton, New Jersey, with a small detachment at Suffern, New York, when the Mutiny of the Pennsylvania Line started on 1 January. Brigadier General Anthony Wayne ordered part of the brigade south, and they eventually camped at Chatham under the command of Elias Dayton. The portion of the brigade remaining at Pompton was commanded by Colonel Israel Shreve. Having the same complaints as the Pennsylvania regulars, men of the Jersey Brigade followed developments of the Pennsylvania mutiny with avid attention. Even after New Jersey granted its men some of the benefits won by the Pennsylvania troops, a mutiny broke out on 20 January at Pompton. In many ways it seemed a small-scale repetition of the recently concluded performance. Several hundred men left their camp at Pompton and headed for Chatham. Shreve trailed them, just as Wayne had followed the Pennsylvanians. Dayton managed to disperse much of his detachment before the Pompton mutineers arrived on 21 January, so only a few recruits were acquired at Chatham. After two disorderly days the Pompton group agreed to follow Shreve back to camp, and the men were promised pardon if they subsequently behaved.

Washington, meanwhile, learned of the new disorder the evening of 21 January and ordered Major General William Heath in the Highlands to make five or six hundred good troops available to stamp it out. He placed Major General Robert Howe in command of the operation and told him to enforce unconditional submission. After a hard march through deep snow the troops from around West Point reached Ringwood, New Jersey, on 25 January. Here they were joined by other reliable units and by three guns. Washington arrived at midnight the next night and Howe led his command forward an hour later.

The troops at Pompton, eight miles away, became disorderly again soon after their return from Chatham. They obeyed some officers but not others. Sergeants George Grant, Jonathan Nichols, and John Minthorn had been the nominal leaders of the original uprising (although they apparently were forced by their men into assuming leadership); Sergeants David Gilmore (or Gilmour) and John Tuttle were the most conspicuous agitators of the later disorders.

With some well-founded doubts about whether his Massachusetts, Connecticut, and New Hampshire troops would do their duty, Howe surrounded the Pompton encampment before daylight on 27 January. With the three cannon in plain view of the huts, Howe sent in word for the mutineers to assemble without arms. After some hesitation they complied.

Officers of the New Jersey Brigade submitted the names of the worst offenders and from these candidates selected one from each regiment (including a veteran of the Third New Jersey, which had been disbanded on 1 January in the reorganization). Grant, Gilmore, and Tuttle were named, tried on the spot, and sentenced to be shot immediately. The latter two were executed by a firing party formed by twelve other mutineers who had been named as prominent offenders. Grant was reprieved at the last minute; Van Doren comments that "it is tempting to guess that he may have been privately told by Shreve not to worry over the trial and sentence" (*Mutiny in January*, p. 223). A journal kept by a contemporary, Dr. Thacher, who saw the trials and executions, gives no indication that he suspected Grant's case was rigged.

SEE ALSO *Mutiny of the Pennsylvania Line; Shreve, Israel.*

BIBLIOGRAPHY

Lender, Mark. "The Enlisted Line: The Continental Soldiers of New Jersey." Ph.D. dissertation, Rutgers University, 1975.

Van Doren, Carl. *Mutiny: The Story of a Crisis in the Continental Army.* New York: Viking, 1943.

White, Donald. *A Village at War: Chatham, New Jersey, and the American Revolution.* Rutherford, N.J.: Fairleigh Dickinson University Press, 1979.

revised by Robert K. Wright Jr.

MUTINY OF THE PENNSYLVANIA LINE.

1–10 January 1781. Inactivity during winter quarters, plus accumulated grievances about food, clothing, quarters, pay, bounties, and terms of enlistment, finally led the Pennsylvania Continentals to mutiny on 1 January 1781. Many of these troops had enlisted "for three years or during the war"; they contended that the phrase "whichever comes first" was implied and that their contracts were now fulfilled. Almost nothing is known for certain about how this mutiny was organized—the mutineers kept no written records and none of them wrote of the event afterward. The names of only two leaders are known for sure: William Bowzar, secretary of the twelve-man Board of Sergeants that represented the mutineers, and Daniel Connell, who signed the Board's final communication. A man named Williams—probably John Williams—was president of the Board of Sergeants, but does not appear to have been the real leader or organizer of the revolt.

THE MUTINY BEGINS

The ten disaffected infantry regiments and the artillery regiment of General Anthony Wayne's Pennsylvania Line were encamped near Morristown, New Jersey, where they occupied huts built during the previous winter at Jockey Hollow (also known as Mount Kemble). The total strength in officers and men was about 2,500. The mutiny started about 10 P.M. the evening of 1 January, when soldiers emerged from their huts under arms and with field equipment, captured the guns and ammunition, and assembled to march away. Initially, fewer than half the men participated, and probably not more than 1,500 eventually joined the march. During a confused hour before they left camp, the mutineers resisted the efforts and the eloquence of Wayne and about 100 officers to stop

them. They did this with a remarkable lack of violence, offering with the simple argument that the officers could do nothing to settle their grievances—they intended to present these directly to Congress in Philadelphia.

Lieutenant Francis White and Captain Samuel Tolbert were shot (not fatally) while trying to keep their men from moving to the assembly area. Captain Adam Bettin was mortally wounded by a soldier who was chasing Lieutenant Colonel William Butler (of the Fourth Pennsylvania Regiment) and who mistook Bettin for Butler. One man was killed accidentally by a fellow mutineer who, unknown to the other, had replaced the regular guard on the captured magazine. These are the only identified casualties, although it is hard to believe that there were not others.

When Wayne rode onto the scene with several field officers he was unable to restore order, but according to one participant, Lieutenant Enos Reeves, the men stated "it was not their intention to hurt or disturb an officer of the Line, two or three individuals excepted." The majority of the troops were reluctant to join the mutiny. The Second Pennsylvania Regiment of Colonel Walter Stewart was forced at bayonet point to go along. Captain Thomas Campbell turned out part of the Fourth Pennsylvania Regiment and attempted to recapture the artillery, but his men would not carry through with the attack. The Fifth (Colonel Francis Johnston) and Ninth (Colonel Richard Butler) Regiments occupied huts some distance from the others, and joined only after being threatened with the cannon. Other men hid as mutineers ran from hut to hut gathering supporters. At 11 P.M. the column marched away to camp at Vealtown (Bernardsville), New Jersey, four miles distant, to await stragglers before resuming their advance toward Philadelphia the next morning.

Wayne had long feared a mutiny, and had urged higher authority to do something about the legitimate grievances of his troops, but he was surprised by the events that had just taken place. Powerless to stop the marchers, and not a bit sure they did not intend to go over to the enemy—or that the British would not strike at this critical time—Wayne prepared to follow his men and try to restore order. He was accompanied by Colonels Walter Stewart and Richard Butler. Before the dawn of 2 January, however, Wayne wrote out "what he called an order but what was a request and a promise":

> Agreeably [sic] to the proposition of a very large proportion of the worthy soldiery last evening, General Wayne hereby desires the noncommissioned officers and privates to appoint one man from each regiment, to represent their grievances to the General, who on the sacred honor of a gentleman and a soldier does hereby solemnly promise to exert every power to obtain immediate

redress of those grievances; and he further plights that honor that no man shall receive the least injury on account of the part they have taken on the occasion.

The mutineers entered Princeton in the late afternoon or evening of 3 January, took control of this village of some 70 houses, and prepared to wait there until Congress responded to the appeals they had sent forward to Philadelphia. The Board of Sergeants established themselves in the ruins of Nassau Hall and the men pitched tents south of the College. The sergeants had sent back a delegation to confer with Wayne, who was following at a safe distance, but they would not halt their advance on Princeton to let him address the troops. The sergeants had also furnished Wayne with a personal guard, and when the general and his colonels took up quarters in a tavern near Nassau Hall on 3 January they had some doubts as to whether this guard was a mark of respect or indicated that they were hostages.

PRELIMINARIES AT PRINCETON

During Thursday, 4 January, Wayne and the colonels negotiated with the Board, and later in the day Wayne sent word to the state authorities—the Council of Pennsylvania—that somebody should come and consult with the mutineers. Congress and the Pennsylvania Council, both sitting in what is now Independence Hall, had learned on 3 January of the alarming developments at Morristown. That afternoon Congress appointed a committee to deal with the Pennsylvania Council on the mutiny. When the Council received Wayne's letter on Friday, it met with the committee of Congress and decided to send Joseph Reed, President of the Pennsylvania Council and therefore of the state, and General James Potter, a militia officer and Council member. The three original members of the Congressional committee—General John Sullivan, the Reverend John Witherspoon, and John Mathews—were now augmented by Samuel John Atlee and Theodorick Bland. Reed and Potter left Philadelphia late Friday afternoon with an escort of twenty light horsemen from the famous city troop, and entered Trenton by noon the next day (6 January). Sullivan's committee (less Mathews, who stayed in Philadelphia) reached Trenton after dark on 6 January and stayed there during the negotiations. Captain Samuel Morris, with the rest of his Philadelphia Light Horse, accompanied them.

Meanwhile, the Board of Sergeants had had a number of visitors in Princeton on 4 January. Major General Arthur St. Clair, senior officer of the Pennsylvania Line; the Marquis de Lafayette; and Lieutenant Colonel John Laurens were in Philadelphia on 3 January when the newly created Congressional committee decided that some officers should go see what could be done about the mutiny.

These three were received by the Board of Sergeants and talked to Wayne, but the Board then told them to leave—the sergeants preferred to continue their negotiations through Wayne, Butler, and Stewart. On this same day, Colonel Thomas Craig approached with eighty armed officers from Morristown and sent word to Wayne of his coming. The officers were not allowed to enter Princeton, and they sat out the subsequent negotiations at Pennington, nine miles away. Some members of the New Jersey legislature also showed up on 4 January from Trenton, but they were not allowed to enter Princeton.

General George Washington, the commander in chief, got his first news of the mutiny about noon on 3 January. Located at New Windsor with the main portion of the army, he was too far away to exert much influence on subsequent events, and as it turned out, Wayne on his own initiative was following almost precisely the course Washington advocated. Washington's letter of 3 January, received by Wayne on 7 January, recommended that Wayne stay with his troubled men, that he not attempt force, and that he try to have the mutineers move south of the Delaware River. Washington disagreed with Wayne's proposal that Congress leave Philadelphia in order to avoid the mutineers, but this point turned out to be academic once Congress decided to stay. Washington had made preparations to ride south, but changed his mind at 7 A.M. on 4 January when he realized he could not arrive in time and that he had the more important task of keeping the mutiny from spreading through the rest of the army. The sympathy of the troops was with the mutineers, particularly since the latter had shown such good discipline in pressing their demands and displayed no disposition to deal with the enemy. Nonetheless, civil and military authorities went ahead with plans to surround Princeton with militia and regulars.

British headquarters in New York City had learned of the mutiny before Washington, and Sir Henry Clinton promptly sought a means of exploiting the situation. He alerted troops for a possible march into New Jersey and started looking for emissaries to offer the mutineers pardon, payment of the money owed them by Congress, and the privilege of declining military service if they would come over to the British.

REED REPRESENTS THE CONGRESS

Many agencies were concerned with the mutiny, but Joseph Reed promptly assumed the key role. Although General Potter stayed by Reed's side, Potter contributed nothing but an occasional signature. The Congressional committee (Sullivan, Witherspoon, and Mathews) may be regarded as a rubber stamp that waited in Trenton to approve Reed's solution. Washington was virtually out of the picture. St. Clair sat at Morristown, in command of the troops who had not joined the mutiny, and muttered about using force. So, probably, did the eighty officers who had left the government's bed and board to live at their own expense at Pennington.

Reed did not go straight to Princeton where, for all he knew, Wayne and the colonels were prisoners and his own safety would be uncertain; he undertook a line of action designed to remind the anonymous sergeants of his personal dignity and their lack of status. Reed started a correspondence with Wayne, but wrote with the expectation that these letters would be read by the sergeants. When he received a letter from Sergeant Bowzar assuring him safe conduct—for several days the Board was not convinced that President Reed had really been sent to deal with them—Reed played dumb and, in a letter to Wayne wrote: "I have received a letter from Mr. Bowzar, who signs as secretary but does not say to whom." Reed very well knew "to whom" Bowzar was secretary, but he wanted to avoid even tacit recognition of the Board and to stress that Wayne was still their lawful commander.

Reed and Potter had ridden on to Maidenhead (now Lawrenceville, four miles south-west of Princeton) on Saturday evening and they now proposed that Wayne meet them there. After the sergeants were made to understand that Reed's reluctance to enter Princeton was due to their inhospitality toward St. Clair, Wayne sent word he would meet Reed at Maidenhead Sunday morning. Reed returned to Trenton, where the Committee (which arrived that evening) gave him final guidance.

A significant development took place during the night. Clinton's emissaries—John Mason and a guide named James Ogden—got into Princeton and presented the enemy's proposals to Sergeant Williams. The latter promptly slapped them under guard and delivered them to Wayne at 4 A.M. Reed was riding to Maidenhead Sunday morning when he met the prisoners being escorted to Trenton. Any suspicion that the mutineers were flirting with the enemy was now dispelled. Taking the prisoners with him, Reed rode on to Maidenhead, met Wayne, and accepted the latter's recommendation that they proceed to Princeton. Meanwhile, just as Wayne, Reed, and their parties were leaving Maidenhead, a message came from the Board of Sergeants asking that the captive emissaries be returned to their custody. Apparently the mutineers had figured, on second thought, that they would be in a better bargaining position if they held these two men.

The mutineers were formed along the post road to honor Reed's arrival at about 3 P.M. In this unreal situation Reed took the salutes of sergeants, who stood before their men in the positions normally occupied by officers, and he returned the salutes ("though much against my inclination"). The artillery was drawn up to fire a salute, but Reed or Wayne managed to stop this rendering of honors, on the ground that it might alarm the countryside.

NEGOTIATIONS BEGIN

The first order of business in Princeton on that Sunday afternoon was what to do with Mason and Ogden. Van Doren writes that "Reed and the officers were plainly much afraid that the British would land and the mutineers either join them, or refuse to fight, or try to drive some bargain before they fought" (p. 127). Most of the sergeants favored Wayne's proposal that the men be promptly executed as spies, but Williams, who was a British deserter, and another sergeant of the same antecedence blocked this solution. Williams had the novel idea of sending the men back to Clinton "with a taunting message." Reed objected to this pointless suggestion and proposed a compromise that was adopted: the sergeants would hold the prisoners subject to Reed's call, and their disposition would be decided later. Meanwhile there was fresh intelligence of an enemy move from Staten Island into New Jersey, and there was now no time to waste in settling the mutiny.

A good deal of preliminary work had already been done between Wayne and the sergeants. The Committee of Congress had instructed Reed to honor Wayne's promise of total amnesty, and they agreed that the men should not be considered traitors unless they were considering deserting to the enemy or refused to compromise on terms for settling the mutiny. It had also been decided in Trenton that men who had enlisted for three years or for the war should be discharged if they had served three years and had not re-enlisted. Men who had voluntarily enlisted or re-enlisted for the war were not, however, to be released.

At the Sunday night conference in Princeton, the sergeants advanced a single proposal that embodied the wishes of the men who had the longest service and who represented the strongest of several factions in their camp. This proposal was:

> That all and every such men as was enlisted in the years 1776 and 1777 and received the bounty of twenty dollars, shall be without any delay discharged and all the arrears of pay and clothing to be paid unto them immediately when discharged; with respect to the depreciation of pay the State to give them sufficient certificates and security for such sums as they shall become due.

Reed could not agree to this proposal, because it would permit the release of men specifically precluded by the guidance he had received from the Committee of Congress. Although this proposal was undoubtedly phrased to release some men not honestly entitled to discharge, the sergeants proceeded to open the eyes of the President of Pennsylvania—and, to a lesser extent, those of their commanding officer of the Line—to certain sharp and dishonest practices that military officers had employed in enlisting them. In short, according to Van Doren, "the enlistment papers did not tell all the truth of what had happened" (p. 128).

The sergeants showed much difference of opinion among themselves. They were incapable of drafting a new set of compromise proposals, they had doubts about getting the men to accept such proposals if drafted, and Sergeant Williams was not the man to unify their demands. In order to have some basis for working out a solution. Reed undertook to write up a document which, Van Doren reports, "promised as much as he thought he could perform and as little as he thought the men would accept." (p. 130) After some minor alterations by Wayne, Reed's proposals were generally as follows: no man would be held beyond the time for which he freely and voluntarily enlisted; a commission would decide on disputed terms of enlistment; if enlistment papers were not promptly produced by official custodians, the soldier's oath on the matter would be accepted; and back pay, adjustment for depreciation, and clothing shortages would be taken care of as soon as possible.

RESOLUTION OF THE MUTINY

On Monday, 8 January, the mutineers announced their general acceptance of Reed's proposals, and on the next morning they marched to Trenton for final negotiations. That evening, the Board of Sergeants had a long conference with the Committee of Congress. On the morning of 10 January Reed informed the sergeants that, since they had accepted his proposals and these would now go into effect, he would like the spies surrendered as evidence of the mutineers' willingness to abide by their agreement. The Board countered with a demand that the mutineers remain together under arms until final arrangements were completed. Reed refused to accept this condition and asked for a final answer within two hours. Within the time limit the Board agreed to give up the prisoners and to turn in their weapons. This communication came "Signed by the Board in the absence of the President, [by] Daniel Connell, Member." Van Doren comments that Williams and Bowzar may actually have been absent, or they may have been unwilling to sign this paper. John Mason and James Ogden, Clinton's emissaries, were convicted on 10 January of spying and were hanged the next morning. Mason was a hard character with a long record as a criminal Loyalist. Ogden is known in history only as Mason's guide.

Putting the settlement into effect involved resolving a number of knotty problems and took several weeks. On 29 January, however, Wayne wrote Washington that the task was completed. About 1,250 infantrymen and 67 artillerymen were discharged; nearly 1,150 remained. Enlistment papers had been gathered quickly and most of them clearly committed the men for the duration of the war, but the commissioners discharged men of the first five infantry regiments and most of the artillery by 21 January without waiting for the papers, and many men got away on false

oaths. There was talk of bringing action against these perjured soldiers, but the State decided against this because it was finding it impossible to raise the money to fulfill its own part of the bargain. A high percentage of the discharged men subsequently re-enlisted, and all the Pennsylvania Line—mutineers and others—were furloughed until 15 March, with instructions to rendezvous at various places in accordance with a reorganization plan that originally had been scheduled for 1 January. This plan, which went into effect on 17 January, eliminated the Seventh through Eleventh Pennsylvania Regiments and deployed the others as follows: the First and Second were placed under Daniel Brodhead and Walter Stewart at Philadelphia; the Third, under Thomas Craig, at Reading; the Fourth, under William Butler, at Carlisle; the Fifth, under Richard Butler, at York; and the Sixth, under Richard Humpton, at Lancaster. Only recruiting sergeants and musicians were not given furloughs.

Other soldiers with the same grievances as the Pennsylvania Line had followed these developments with keen interest. The mutiny of the New Jersey Line, which took place between 20 and 25 January, was the most significant result. Wayne was preparing to lead the Second, Fifth, and Sixth Pennsylvania Regiments to join Lafayette when a small-scale mutiny flared up in York, Pennsylvania. As a result of this action, six men were convicted and four of them executed on 22 May.

SEE ALSO *Mutiny of Gornell; Mutiny of the New Jersey Line; Pennsylvania, Mobilization in; Reed, Joseph; St. Clair, Arthur; Sullivan, John; Wayne, Anthony; Witherspoon, John.*

BIBLIOGRAPHY

Van Doren, Carl. *Mutiny in January: the Story of a Crisis in the Continental Army, Now for the First Time Fully Told from Many Hitherto Unknown or Neglected Sources, both American and British.* New York: Viking Press, 1943.

revised by Robert K. Wright Jr.

MUTINY ON PROSPECT HILL.

10 September 1775. Cambridge, Massachusetts. Riflemen from Pennsylvania and Virginia served effectively at the siege of Boston, but their ill discipline in camp was a constant cause of concern to those responsible for military law and order. The worst incident, on Sunday, 10 September, reached the dangerous depths of mutiny. Such behavior had to be suppressed before other riflemen decided they, too, could disobey army regulations. When the adjutant of Colonel William Thompson's Pennsylvania Rifle Battalion, Lieutenant David Ziegler, confined a

sergeant for "neglect of duty and murmuring," members of the sergeant's company threatened to release him (*Pennsylvania Archives,* second series, 10, p. 8). As Ziegler reported his action to the colonel and lieutenant colonel, the men made good on their threat. The officers seized the malefactor and sent him to the main guard in Cambridge. Some men of Captain James Ross's notably ill-disciplined company from Lancaster County swore to release him and, joined by men of other companies, a group of thirty-two riflemen headed for the jail with loaded weapons. The guard detail was strengthened to five hundred men, and several Rhode Island regiments were turned out under arms for what could have been the biggest brawl of the Boston siege. The mutineers had gone about half a mile when they were confronted on Prospect Hill by General Washington, along with Charles Lee and Nathanael Greene. Washington ordered the mutineers to ground their arms, which they did "immediately" (*ibid.,* 10, p. 9). Another Pennsylvania rifle company (Captain George Nagel's men from Berks County) surrounded the subdued riflemen and marched them back to camp, backed up by two New England regiments.

In a court-martial on 12 September, of which Colonel John Nixon of Massachusetts was president, thirty-three men were convicted of disobedient and mutinous behavior. Since a draconian sentence ran the risk of reigniting and spreading the mutiny, the court was content with fining each mutineer twenty shillings. The ringleader, John Leaman, got the additional punishment of six days' imprisonment. The riflemen did not threaten to spring him, but they continued to be a disciplinary problem throughout the siege.

SEE ALSO *Riflemen.*

BIBLIOGRAPHY

Abbot, W. W., et al., eds. *The Papers of George Washington, Revolutionary War Series.* Vol. 1, *June–September 1775.* Charlottesville, Va.: University Press of Virginia, 1985.

Pennsylvania Archives. Second series. Vol. 10. Reprinted under direction of the Secretary of the Commonwealth. Edited by John B. Linn and William H. Egle. Harrisburg, Pa.: C.M. Busch, State Printer, 1896–.

Trussell, John B. B. Jr. *The Pennsylvania Line: Regimental Organization and Operations, 1776–1783.* Harrisburg, Pa.: Pennsylvania Historical and Museum Commission, 1977.

revised by Harold E. Selesky

MYTHS AND MISCONCEPTIONS.

The historical record does not always supply sufficient evidence from which to build unassailable conclusions about what happened in the past. Even when the evidence is abundant, different people may, in good faith, interpret it in different ways. Because all historical scholarship is a form of argument in which the interpreter emphasizes certain facts and points of view to build a case for his or her particular conclusions, it is easy to see how the history of so complex an event as the American Revolution offers a fertile field for nearly endless revision.

In the decades since the end of the war, historians have combed through the evidence and examined again and again what we think we know about people and events, and in the process they have corrected many misconceptions and altered many interpretations. Sometimes a closer look was all that was needed. Examples abound. The noble titles "Lord Stirling" (William Alexander), "Baron von" Steuben, and "Baron de" Kalb were all bestowed by those individuals on themselves. Early commentators elevated the resolves adopted by a committee at Charlotte, North Carolina, in May 1775 into a "Mecklenburg [County] Declaration of Independence." Americans celebrate the 4th of July as Independence Day, even though the Declaration of Independence was adopted, not signed, on the 4th.

Other misconceptions arise out of undocumented assertions that we, after all, cannot say definitively are not true. It just sounds better if Ethan Allen demanded the surrender of Fort Ticonderoga with the ringing phrase "in the name of the Great Jehovah and the Continental Congress," or if John Parker declared on Lexington green that "if they [the British] want war, let it begin here!" Some stories are so appealing that we want them to be true, like the heroism of Molly Pitcher, the devotion of Betsy Ross, or the intrigue of the silver bullets of Ticonderoga. Other stories fit our preconceptions, like Washington's alleged temper tantrums at Kips Bay and Monmouth or the idea that he almost won at Germantown. Many misconceptions arise from the opinions some contemporaries used to smear the reputations of particular individuals. Both Walter Butler and Simon Girty were accused of atrocities at places where they were not present. William Howe was allegedly a libertine whose indiscretions caused him to lose the war (the Murray Hill Myth). Benedict Arnold was clearly a black-hearted traitor (the Arnold Legend). His treason, for Americans the most discordant note in the entire symphony of the founding of the Republic, has led to questions about whether Arnold or Gates deserves credit for the victory over Burgoyne at the Second Battle of Saratoga and over the role played by Peggy Shippen Arnold in her husband's defection.

It is worthwhile to distinguish misconceptions from myths. Myths may or may not have a firmer grounding in the evidence than misconceptions, but they almost always gain a wider currency because they reflect or support some idea that is fundamental to how a society views, understands, and even defines itself. Perhaps the best example of this phenomenon in the Revolution is the myth of the militia. Americans wanted to believe that they were virtuous men fighting in the righteous cause of resisting British tyranny. Rather than relying on an odious standing army like their oppressors, Americans were free men who turned out to protect their rights. No matter that they might lack formal military training, Americans believed that, as citizen-soldiers, they had had the determination and ingenuity to win through to victory, a point of view that minimized the crucial contributions made by both the Continental army and their French allies.

The nineteenth century saw the apogee of this attitude. On 4 July 1837 the people of Concord dedicated a memorial obelisk on the site where their ancestors had stood against the British on 19 April 1775. Ralph Waldo Emerson solemnized the occasion with his "Concord Hymn," in words that entered our language and still fill Americans with pride and awe:

> By the rude bridge that arched the flood,
> Their flag to April's breeze unfurled,
> Here once the embattled farmers stood
> And fired the shot heard round the world.

Thirty-eight years later, on the centennial of the fight at Concord Bridge, the townspeople unveiled the great visual symbol of how Americans remembered their Revolution. The bronze statue, the *Minuteman,* was the first landmark in the distinguished career of the then twenty-five-year-old sculptor Daniel Chester French. (His final contribution to the American pantheon would be the statue of Abraham Lincoln sitting as the centerpiece of the Lincoln Memorial.). The *Minuteman* immediately took its place alongside the Liberty Bell among the icons of the Revolution. Dressed in civilian clothes, the handsome young farmer stands forthrightly in his field, one hand on his plow, the other clutching the musket he is about to use to defend his land and his liberty. So powerful was the moment captured by French that the *Minuteman* came in the twentieth century to embody all the virtues of American citizen-soldiers in the fights against fascism and communism. So powerful, too, was the legacy of French's evocation that historians have been working to place it in its proper context ever since.

SEE ALSO *Militia in the North; Propaganda in the American Revolution; Riflemen.*

revised by Harold E. Selesky

N

NANCY CAPTURE. 28 November 1775. On 8 September H.M. Frigate *Phoenix* departed England escorting a convoy of victuallers and two ordnance transports to Boston. The convoy was scattered by storms as it made its way across the Atlantic, and the frigate reached Boston on 9 November to report that one of the transports, the brigantine Nancy, was missing. Acting on information possibly sent by Arthur Lee, Washington alerted his small squadron of cruisers to be on the watch. One of those vessels, the 74-ton schooner *Lee* (formerly the *Two Brothers*) had recently been fitted out with six small cannon in Marblehead by John Glover and on 28 October she was officially commissioned under the command of Captain John Manley with a crew made up of seamen detached from Washington's infantry regiments. At dusk on 28 November Manley captured the much larger (250-ton) but unarmed *Nancy.*

This was the first important prize taken by the Americans, and Washington sent reinforcements to Cape Ann to secure her. She yielded 2,000 muskets, 100,000 flints, 30,000 round shot, 30 tons of musket shot, and a 13-inch brass mortar weighing over 2,700 pounds. The latter entered into American service and was dubbed *"Congress"* in a joyous mock christening ceremony. The materiel taken from the *Nancy* provided significant logistical support for the ordnance-starved Continental Army.

While this event is not mentioned in many general accounts of the Revolution, Major General William Howe immediately wrote to the Ministry to warn them that the capture gave the Americans the ability to set Boston on fire if they chose to exercise it. (Naval Documents, 2:1251–1252.) Although not technically a navy victory, this capture was the highlight of the Americans' first efforts at sea and gave an important impetus to the establishment of the Continental Navy. More importantly, the loss shocked the British government and brought a major change in policy requiring the Admiralty to provide escorts for all Ordnance Department shipments, and for all ordnance vessels hereafter to be armed and capable of self-defense.

revised by Robert K. Wright Jr.

NANTASKET POINT, MASSACHU-SETTS SEE *Great Brewster Island, Massachusetts.*

NANTASKET ROAD, MASSACHU-SETTS. 17 and 19 May 1776. When the British evacuated Boston, they left behind a small naval force in Nantasket Road (the point where vessels entering Boston Harbor from the open sea would assemble to await favorable tides) to protect transports and merchantmen known to be coming from Europe from interception by Washington's squadron or privateers. On 17 May, Captain James Mugford, in the sixty-ton schooner *Franklin* (sixty), captured the three-hundred-ton ordnance ship *Hope,* which was bringing a cargo that included one thousand carbines and fifteen hundred barrels of gunpowder from Ireland in sight of British warships. Two days later, while cruising in company with the tiny privateer *Lady Washington* (seven men), Mugford ran aground near

779

Point Shirley. Eager for revenge, the British sent about two hundred men in a dozen or so small boats to attack her after darkness fell. After a half-hour fight in which the only American casualty was Mugford, who was killed, the battered British withdrew. Americans estimated that the enemy suffered forty or fifty killed or wounded. The British would lose several troop transports before the Americans constructed a heavy battery that chased the Royal Navy off.

revised by Robert K. Wright Jr.

NASH, ABNER. (1740–1786).

War governor of North Carolina. North Carolina and Virginia. Born in Amelia County, Virginia, around 1740, Abner Nash became an attorney and served in the Virginia legislature from 1761 to 1762. He then moved to Halifax, North Carolina, with his brother Francis Nash in 1762. Elected to the North Carolina Assembly in 1764, 1765, and from 1770 to 1771, Nash married the widow of Governor Arthur Dobbs. He sued the estate of the governor for his wife's property in a case that eventually set the assembly against the royal governor and accelerated the controversy with the Crown. Following the death of his wife in 1771, Nash moved to New Bern, serving in Tryon's forces as a major of militia at the battle at Alamance on 16 May 1771. The following year he became a leader of the Patriot cause, helping to drive Governor Martin out of North Carolina. He served in the Provincial Congress and on the provincial council from 1774 to 1776.

After helping to write North Carolina's constitution, Nash was elected the first speaker of the House of Commons in 1777, moving up to the state senate in 1779, where he was again elected speaker. In the spring of 1780, as his state became a theater of active military operations, Nash was elected governor. While he was energetic, he chafed under the constitutional weaknesses of his office and then objected to what he considered to be unconstitutional acts by the Assembly in appointing Richard Caswell as commander of the militia, in establishing a board of war and, subsequently, in creating a council extraordinary with powers that undermined his own. The Loyalist uprising of 1781 led to the temporary dissolution of the state's government, as well as to the burning of Nash's home during Major James Craig's raid on New Bern in August 1781. Declining a second term, Nash returned to the House of Commons in 1782, 1784, and 1785. He declined election to Congress in 1778, but accepted in 1782, 1783, and 1785. However, he did not attend a single session in these last two years. Elected again in 1786, Nash decided to attend Congress, but died in New York City on 2 December 1786.

SEE ALSO *Alamance, Battle of the; Nash, Francis.*

revised by Michael Bellesiles

NASH, FRANCIS. (1742–1777).

Continental general. Virginia and North Carolina. Born in Amelia County, Virginia, 1742, Nash moved to Halifax, North Carolina, with his brother Abner Nash in 1762, where he became a merchant and attorney. In 1763 he became clerk of the court of pleas and quarter sessions. He was representative from Orange County to the House of Commons in 1764, 1765, and 1771, and for Hillsboro from 1773 to 1775. He became a target of the Regulators, ad hoc groups in North and South Carolina who resisted what they saw as the biased legal system of the coastal elite. The Regulators charged Nash with taking excessive fees for his services.

Nash served in William Tryon's forces as a captain of militia at the battle at Alamance on 16 May 1771. As the Revolution approached, he identified himself with the Patriots. He was elected to the second and third provincial congresses of North Carolina in April and August 1775, and on 1 September was named lieutenant colonel of the First North Carolina Continentals. He was promoted to colonel on 10 April 1776, became brigadier general on 5 February 1777, was ordered to raise troops in western North Carolina, and joined General George Washington for the Philadelphia campaign. He commanded a brigade in Nathanael Greene's division at the battle of the Brandywine on 11 September, but did not reach Plowed Hill in time to see action. At Germantown on 4 October 1777, his thigh was broken by a cannon ball as he led his North Carolina brigade into action from the reserve. He died on 7 October, 1777.

SEE ALSO *Germantown, Pennsylvania, Battle of; Nash, Abner; Regulators.*

BIBLIOGRAPHY
Rankin, Hugh F. *The North Carolina Continentals.* Chapel Hill, N.C.: University of North Carolina Press, 1971.

revised by Michael Bellesiles

NASSAU, BAHAMAS.

3–4 March 1776. In the first major operation of the Continental Navy, Commodore Esek Hopkins sailed from Delaware Bay on 18 February 1776. Acting on intelligence that the British had a large amount of materiel stored on the island of New Providence in the Bahamas, but no troops to protect them,

Congress sent the squadron to seize them. The Americans assembled at nearby Abacco, transferring all their marines to the sloop *Providence* and two captured local fishing sloops. Early in the afternoon of 3 March, Captain Samuel Nicholas, senior marine officer, led 250 men ashore and quickly captured Fort Montagu after token resistance. During the night Governor Montfort Browne removed most of the gunpowder stored in Fort Nassau, the other defensive work, and moved it to the Royal Navy's schooner *St. John* and a merchant sloop, and sent them off to St. Augustine. On 4 March the Americans moved on to secure Fort Nassau and the rest of the stores. Over the next two weeks the squadron loaded sixteen mortars, fifty-two cannon, and a large amount of ammunition. It sailed for home on 16 March with Governor Browne and two other prisoners.

SEE ALSO *Bahamas.*

BIBLIOGRAPHY

Fowler, William M., Jr. *Rebels under Sail: The American Navy during the Revolution.* New York: Scribners, 1976.

revised by Robert K. Wright Jr.

NASSAU RAID OF RATHBUN. 27–30

January 1778. Marines and seamen from Captain John Peck Rathbun's twelve-gun sloop *Providence* rowed ashore and landed on New Providence Island in the Bahamas at midnight on 27 January. Under the command of Marine Captain John Trevett, they marched overland and seized Fort Nassau in the dark. Reinforced by liberated prisoners of war, Trevett proceeded to capture five anchored vessels before the sloop could overcome adverse winds and enter the harbor. The Americans then dismantled Fort Montagu. Rathbun loaded sixteen hundred pounds of captured gunpowder, spiked the guns of the forts, and departed late on 30 January. This raid is considered to mark the first time that the Stars and Stripes flew over a foreign fortification.

SEE ALSO *Bahamas; Rathbun, John Peck.*

BIBLIOGRAPHY

Rider, Hope S. *Valour Fore and Aft: Being the Adventures of the Continental Sloop Providence, 1775–1779.* Annapolis, Md.: Naval Institute Press, 1977.

revised by Robert K. Wright Jr.

NAVAL COMMITTEE. On Friday, 13

October 1775, the Continental Congress resolved, "after some debate," that two ships, one a "swift sailing vessel, to carry ten carriage guns, and a proportionable number of swivels, with eighty men," the other of fourteen carriage guns, "be fitted, with all possible dispatch . . . to cruize eastward, for intercepting such transports as may be laden with warlike stores and other supplies for our enemies, and for other purposes as the Congress shall direct" (Clark, pp. 441–442). It then appointed three of its members as a committee to procure the two vessels: Silas Deane of Connecticut, John Langdon of New Hampshire, and Christopher Gadsden of South Carolina. On 30 October, Congress resolved to procure two additional, larger vessels, one of twenty guns and another of thirty-six guns, "to be employed for the protection and defence of the United Colonies" (Clark p. 647). It added four new members to the committee: John Adams of Massachusetts (who had been a constant advocate of creating a Continental navy), Stephen Hopkins of Rhode Island, Joseph Hewes of North Carolina, and Richard Henry Lee of Virginia. During the day the committee members attended sessions of Congress and, every evening at six o'clock, met in a rented room in the Tun Tavern on the Philadelphia waterfront "in order," as Adams wrote, "to dispatch this business with all possible celerity" (Butterfield, p. 345). They accomplished an amazing amount of work in a matter of weeks—what Adams later called "the pleasantest part of my labours for the four years I spent in Congress" (Butterfield, p. 202). On 14 December, Congress established a standing Marine Committee, which took over, and expanded on, the functions of the Naval Committee.

SEE ALSO *Marine Committee; Naval Operations, Strategic Overview.*

BIBLIOGRAPHY

Butterfield, Lyman H., et al., eds. *The Adams Papers, Series I, Diaries: Diary and Autobiography of John Adams.* 4 vols. Cambridge, Mass.: Harvard University Press for the Massachusetts Historical Society, 1961.

Clark, William B., ed. *Naval Documents of the American Revolution.* Vol. 2: *American Theatre: September 3, 1775–October 31, 1775; European Theatre: August 11, 1775–October 31, 1775; American Theatre: November 1, 1775–December 7, 1775.* Washington, D.C.: Naval History Division, 1966.

Paullin, Charles O. *The Navy of the American Revolution: Its Administration, Its Policy, and Its Achievements.* Cleveland: Burrows Brothers Company, 1906.

revised by Harold E. Selesky

NAVAL OPERATIONS, BRITISH.

In the eighteenth century the Royal Navy was Britain's principal instrument of foreign policy. It was a powerful, complex, and ponderous institution. More than two centuries of war had dramatically increased its technological sophistication, on the one hand, and had burdened it with dogmatic tradition, on the other. The Royal Navy's warships made their sixteenth-century ancestors look like ornate toys. But the tactical and strategic thinking that governed those ships' behavior had stagnated for several generations.

The great event of naval history was the sea battle, and the professional bible of the British admiral was a document called the Fighting Instructions, which told him how to bring about such an event. The opposing fleets would form themselves into long, straight "lines of battle" and spend a grisly afternoon slamming cannonballs into each other, giving one side decisive victory and turning some admiral into a national hero. That, at least, was how the navy, the government, and the public perceived British naval history. The truth was considerably different.

In 1775 Britain had spent thirty-one of the preceding ninety years at war with France. During that period the fleet action on the classical model—two parallel lines of battle exchanging broadsides with decisive results—had never taken place. When rival fleets did encounter each other, things seldom went according to the Fighting Instructions. Either the French would withdraw to leeward, a land mass would intrude at an awkward point, or the British formation would fall apart. The blame usually would be attributed to either French cowardice or some British admiral's ineptitude. Few in the British naval establishment considered the possibility that their concepts of strategy and tactics might be flawed. Still fewer bothered to consider how an eighteenth-century navy could suppress a revolution.

The administration of the Royal Navy was presided over by the lords of the Admiralty, headed by John, fourth earl of Sandwich. When word reached the Admiralty office (in late May 1775, five weeks after the fact) that the Revolutionary War had started, they had to confront an unusual problem: how best to employ the world's largest navy against an enemy that had no navy at all. The two obvious answers were, first, for the navy to collaborate with the army in amphibious operations, and second, to set up a naval blockade of the rebellious colonies. The Admiralty instructed its senior officer in North America, Vice Admiral Samuel Graves, to carry out those two tasks.

Both sorts of operation turned out to be more complex than expected. Graves never had enough ships at his disposal to hinder colonial trade significantly. He did launch one amphibious raid, on the village of Falmouth in northern Massachusetts (later Maine), on 18 October 1775, but the incident turned into a public relations disaster without accomplishing anything of military consequence.

THE HOWES

In 1776 Vice Admiral Richard Lord Howe and his brother, General William Howe, took over the British command in North America. With the largest combined military and naval force Britain had ever sent overseas at their disposal, they were expected to end the Revolution by means of brute force. General Howe was to capture New York City, and Admiral Howe was to clamp a blockade on all the ports of the colonies and destroy the rebels' economic capacity.

Historians have been unable to figure out why the Howe brothers failed. One scholar, Ira Gruber, has suggested that the Howes' fascination with diplomacy led to their downfall. They had insisted on being named commissioners of the peace, with authority to negotiate a treaty on almost any terms (except American independence). According to Gruber, the Howes were so determined to resolve the conflict peaceably that they sacrificed several military opportunities to win it. The admiral, for instance, ordered his warships to seize only those merchant ships that could be identified with certainty as carrying cargoes to support the rebel military effort. Peaceable merchantmen that were carrying merchandise to loyal businessmen were not to be molested, and the colonial fishing fleet was allowed to carry on business as usual.

The scarcity of Howe papers makes it impossible to prove or disprove Gruber's theory, but in any case the British blockade never achieved the government's objectives. Howe constantly begged his superiors to send him more ships. Like every other naval officer in every war, he never got as many ships as he thought he needed. Even if it had been carried out with the vigor Sandwich wanted, though, the blockade probably would have been too porous to undermine the rebel war effort.

In the campaign of 1777, the Royal Navy got another key assignment: transporting a large segment of the army from New York to some point within striking range of the colonies' largest city, Philadelphia. The initial plan was to approach it via Delaware Bay, but the rebels had established an elaborate series of defenses and obstructions in its mouth. The Howes therefore decided to take their fleet to Philadelphia by way of Chesapeake Bay.

The voyage up the Chesapeake was skillfully executed but, even by eighteenth-century standards, depressingly slow. By the time the army landed at the northern end of the bay it was late August. General Howe made relatively quick work of taking Philadelphia, but in the meantime, some two hundred miles to the north, the British army that General John Burgoyne's army had brought down from Canada was expiring. On 17 October 1777 Burgoyne surrendered at Saratoga.

FRANCE ENTERS THE WAR

When France declared war on Britain on 13 March 1778, the fundamental nature of the conflict changed. For its first three years it had been a relatively small-scale fight between a rebellious element of a colonial society and an imperial government. Henceforth it would have to be perceived as the latest in the series of dynastic struggles that had dominated Europe for generations. North America had become one theater in a world war.

It would be, to a large extent, a naval war, and the various offices along Whitehall initially tried to fight it by adopting the same strategy that had won the last one. Tradition and experience suggested that the naval effort should be centered on Europe, with naval squadrons blockading the French fleets in their Atlantic and Mediterranean bases. Smaller British forces could be sent off to conduct limited offensives against the French possessions in the East and West Indies and to foil any enemy thrust that might develop.

Four days after the French declaration of war, the Admiralty sent Lord Howe a secret dispatch: "We judge it necessary . . . to acquaint your Lordship that the object of the War being now changed, and the Contest in America being a secondary consideration, the principal object must be the distressing [of] France and defending His Majesty's own possessions against Hostile Attempts." The British war effort in North America was to become strictly defensive. The bulk of the Royal Navy would return to the role in which it was most comfortable: fighting the French (and, eventually, the Spanish as well) in European waters.

EARLY BRITISH-FRENCH SKIRMISHING

On 23 July 1778 a British fleet encountered a French fleet off the island of Ushant, near the mouth of the English Channel. The ensuing battle, like most such affairs, was indecisive; its chief consequence was a feud between two British admirals, Augustus Keppel and Sir Hugh Palliser.

Another British force, commanded by Admiral Sir Charles Hardy, spent the following summer glowering sullenly at a combined French and Spanish squadron under the comte d'Orvilliers. Hardy, suffering from advanced age, ill health, and a remarkable lack of energy, made little effort to bring his enemy to action, and d'Orvilliers eventually decided to return to port. No Franco-Spanish invasion ever materialized.

In the western hemisphere both the British and the French had to operate in two distinct but interrelated theaters: North America and the West Indies. For the rest of the war the navies played an intricate game of chess on two overlapping boards, with the lucrative sugar islands as the stakes. It was a strange, complicated war, with armies fighting repeatedly over the same real estate and navies transporting the armies, escorting and pursuing convoys, and occasionally fighting battles that ended before either admiral could claim victory. All participants had to pay heed to one inescapable fact of nature: between August and November of each year the war must take an intermission. No sane naval officer tried to navigate in the Caribbean during the hurricane season.

The first move was made by a French admiral, the comte d'Estaing. In July 1778 d'Estaing brought twelve ships-of-the-line to New York. Lord Howe, though outnumbered and outgunned, defended the harbor so skillfully that d'Estaing retreated. He then proceeded to Narragansett Bay and made a half-hearted attempt to seize control of Rhode Island. Howe followed him, and the two fleets were on the verge of fighting a battle in Long Island Sound when a storm came up and separated them. D'Estaing then withdrew to Boston.

The Admiralty had dispatched a squadron under Vice Admiral John Byron in pursuit of d'Estaing. After one of the most difficult crossings on record, Byron arrived at New York in September 1778. Lord Howe, disgusted and enervated by the turn the war in North America had taken, resigned his command and sailed for England. A few weeks later D'Estaing, having repaired the storm damage his ships had suffered, decided, in accordance with his orders, to take his fleet to the West Indies. Byron followed.

SHIFT TO THE SOUTH

The command of the Royal Navy's forces in North America thereupon fell onto the shoulders of the unimpressive Vice Admiral James Gambier. He happened to be on hand when, during the winter of 1778–1779, the British military effort began to shift in the direction it would take for the remainder of the war. The government was concerned about the safety of the southern colonies. If, as expected, Spain were to enter the war, its bases in the Caribbean and at New Orleans would be excellent staging areas for an attack on Georgia or the Carolinas.

On 29 December 1778 a naval squadron under Commodore Hyde Parker the Younger landed a force of Hessians, Loyalists, and Scottish Highlanders on the coast of Georgia. The army commander, Lieutenant Colonel Archibald Campbell, promptly took the city of Savannah and made himself master of Georgia, thereby returning one of the thirteen colonies to British rule.

To command in the "secondary" theater of North America, the Admiralty next selected Vice Admiral Marriot Arbuthnot, an officer of limited experience, ill health, and advanced age. His tenure in command was characterized by frequent accusations of ineptitude and his colossal feud with his army counterpart, General Sir Henry Clinton. Arbuthnot seems to have found Clinton an irritating and uncooperative colleague;

Clinton concluded that Arbuthnot was incompetent and either out of his mind or hopelessly senile.

The two did manage to collaborate effectively in one of the most important British victories of the war: the capture of Charleston, South Carolina. By this time the Royal Navy had worked out most of the problems involved in landing an army on a hostile shore. The siege of Charleston took more than four months, but the city's surrender, on 12 May 1780, gave the British a major base of operations in the southern colonies.

TERNAY AND DES TOUCHES

In the meantime another squadron of French ships-of-the-line, commanded by the chevalier de Ternay, was sailing for North America. When intelligence of that development reached London, the Admiralty placed six ships-of-the-line under the command of Rear Admiral Thomas Graves. As Byron had chased d'Estaing, Graves was to chase Ternay.

Ternay was hardly a dynamic officer, but his arrival in North America had far-reaching consequences. His seven French ships-of-the-line anchored in the harbor of Newport, Rhode Island—which the British had evacuated—on 10 July 1780, landed six thousand troops under the comte de Rochambeau.

Arbuthnot, with the newly arrived Graves as his second in command, spent eight months sailing back and forth in Long Island Sound, keeping Ternay's ships under blockade. Ternay himself died of an undiagnosed fever shortly before Christmas. His successor was Commodore Souchet des Touches, a younger man of considerable ability. On 8 March 1781 des Touches took his squadron to sea, carrying a detachment of Rochambeau's army. The French objective was Chesapeake Bay, where des Touches intended to land the troops and attack a British force under the newly recruited Brigadier General Benedict Arnold.

Arbuthnot caught up with des Touches off the mouth of the Chesapeake on 16 March 1781. The ensuing Battle of Cape Henry was typical of its species: a murky affair of dirty weather, misinterpreted signal flags, and missed opportunities. Des Touches was a skilled officer who did not want to fight—the most difficult sort of adversary to defeat. At the end of the day Arbuthnot was in possession of the battlefield, but the French fleet sailed back toward Rhode Island with minimal damage.

THE WEST INDIES

The powerful British battle fleet stationed in the West Indies was known as the Leeward Islands Squadron. From 1779 onward it was commanded by Britain's foremost naval hero of the day, Admiral Sir George Rodney. On 3 February 1781, having been informed that the States

General of Holland had entered the war on the American side, Rodney seized the Dutch island of St. Eustatius. The capture of that tiny but wealthy island set into motion a series of naval events that led directly to American independence.

The two officers in charge of British naval affairs at the most crucial juncture of the naval war were thrust into the historical limelight by accident. On 4 July 1781 Admiral Arbuthnot sailed for England, turning the North American Squadron over to Thomas Graves. On 1 August, Rodney, having spent the past six months snapping up and condemning merchant ships that had sailed into his arms at St. Eustatius, also departed for home—largely because, with the St. Eustatius prize money due to land in his bank account, his financial affairs demanded his attention. Rodney took three ships-of-the-line with him and sent another to Jamaica for repairs. He left the remainder of the Leeward Islands Squadron under the command of Rear Admiral Sir Samuel Hood.

The French naval force in the Caribbean consisted of twenty-four ships-of-the-line commanded by the comte de Grasse. Rodney's departure coincided with the beginning of the hurricane season. Calculating that de Grasse might take some of his ships to North America, Rodney ordered Hood to look for them.

CHESAPEAKE BAY

Hood, not a man to loiter while his enemy was on the move, made his way up the American coast as rapidly as he could. He paused briefly at the mouth of Chesapeake Bay, where seven thousand troops under Charles Lord Cornwallis were establishing a post at the mouth of the York River. Seeing no sign of de Grasse, Hood continued on to New York. Arriving there on 28 August, he introduced himself to Graves and told him that a French fleet was operating somewhere off the coast.

Hood was junior to Graves, so when the two combined their forces, the latter was in command. Their nineteen ships-of-the-line sailed from New York on 31 August and headed south, intending to find de Grasse and fight a battle with him. The British arrived off the Chesapeake Capes on 5 September 1781 to find that de Grasse's entire fleet was anchored just inside the bay.

The Battle of the Chesapeake was one of the most important naval actions in history. Tactically, it was remarkable only in that the British tactical system worked even less efficiently than usual. The opposing fleets arranged themselves into more-or-less parallel lines of battle, intent on deciding the outcome with their great guns. The ships in the British van grappled with their French opposite numbers in accordance with the Fighting Instructions, but the rear division, under Hood's command, failed to become engaged. Afterward,

Graves claimed Hood had ignored a signal ordering his division into action; Hood claimed Graves had flown an incomprehensible combination of signal flags.

The outcome of the battle was tactically indecisive but strategically crucial. Several ships on both sides were damaged; one British ship had to be scuttled. The fleets remained in sight of each other for four days, drifting gradually away from the Chesapeake as their crews worked to repair the damage.

On the morning of 10 September the French vanished. Graves sent frigates to look for them and discovered that de Grasse had anchored his fleet in a powerful position blocking entrance to the bay. Having fought a traditional battle to a draw and seeing no likelihood of winning another one, Graves took his fleet back to New York.

While Graves, Hood, and de Grasse were fighting the Battle of the Chesapeake, the Franco-American army under George Washington and the comte de Rochambeau was marching headlong to the southward. Its target was Cornwallis's little army, which had dug in around the village of Yorktown.

Graves and General Clinton worked up an elaborate plan to break the siege of Yorktown. On 19 October 1781 the biggest British naval force ever seen in North American waters sailed from New York. Embarked on board the warships were more than seven thousand troops. Clinton and Graves intended to force their way through de Grasse's fleet, land the troops at Yorktown, and relieve Cornwallis. It was a desperate scheme but, if nothing else, the War of American Independence would end with an epic sea and land action.

The great battle, however, never took place. On the same day the fleet sailed from New York, Cornwallis surrendered.

BATTLE OF THE SAINTES

On the morning of 12 April 1782, near a West Indies archipelago called the Saintes, Rodney caught up with de Grasse. The two commanders arranged their fleets in the standard lines of battle. A stroke of luck, however, kept the Battle of the Saintes from becoming one more in the list of indecisive eighteenth-century sea fights. A gap appeared in the French line, and several of Rodney's ships went through it to assault a section of the French formation from both sides simultaneously. By sunset, five French ships-of-the-line had surrendered.

FAILED STRATEGIES AND TACTICS

Rodney's victory gave British diplomats a powerful card to play during the peace negotiations, ensuring that Britain would keep its possessions in the West Indies. The Saintes also obscured, temporarily, the fact that the Royal Navy had lost one of the great naval wars of the eighteenth century. Some of the reasons had to do with ineptitude and bad luck. Others were rooted deep in the British military and naval establishment.

Neither the earl of Sandwich, Lord George Germain, nor anyone else in the British government ever produced a coherent scheme for fighting the naval war. In its early stages the Revolution presented problems that the most original naval thinking probably would have been unable to solve. But from 1778 onward, the Royal Navy was fighting the war it had been built to fight, and it found that conflict just as difficult to win.

The administration's decision to treat the American theater as secondary seemed a shrewd and dynamic move. The government failed to realize, however, that such decisions could not be taken unilaterally. The French made North America a center of their military effort because that was the only theater where their alliance with the United States could benefit them. The British let the French take the naval initiative in North America and failed, until the fact had been brought to their attention in the most brutal manner imaginable, to realize that giving up that initiative might mean losing the colonies.

The Admiralty relied on what may be called the "detachment theory," assuming that if the two belligerents had about the same number of ships-of-the-line in the same hemisphere, things would eventually work out in Britain's favor. Such thinking ignored the realities of naval warfare. Fleets moved fast and communications were slow. After the enemy had been handed the opportunity to take the offensive, the only effective way to frustrate him was to defend every place at which he might strike, and that was impossible. To chase him in the hope of catching him before he struck anywhere was to invite disaster. The Battle of the Chesapeake was the product of personality clashes, coincidences, and remarkable international cooperation between the Americans and the French. But it would not have taken a great strategic brain to figure out that something of the sort was bound to happen eventually.

Eight years of fighting failed to persuade the government to establish a clearly defined, understandable chain of command. Sir George Rodney's assertion that one general and one admiral should command in America and the West Indies fell on deaf ears. Furthermore, no one seems to have suggested that either the admiral or the general in North America be directed to take orders from the other. Asking two individuals whose professional reputations were in constant jeopardy to collaborate harmoniously under outdated orders that came from three thousand miles away was asking the near impossible.

The British land and naval commanders suffered from a misconception of how this particular war worked. William Howe and Henry Clinton tried to win it by occupying geographic objectives, thereby avoiding the decisive battlefield encounter with Washington's army that probably offered the best chance of British victory. In Europe that strategy might have made sense, but neither the generals, the admirals, nor their superiors in London realized a basic truth about the War of American Independence: there was no geographic objective that the rebels could not afford to lose. During the course of the war the British army, with the Royal Navy's assistance, took, and held for some prolonged period, every major city in the colonies. Yet the war continued—and the longer it continued, the harder it was for the British to win.

While the generals were looking for ways to occupy real estate without fighting battles, the admirals were searching for the opportunity to fight sea battles. A century after the Revolution, Alfred Thayer Mahan, the most influential of naval philosophers, articulated the theory that the sea battle was the centerpiece of naval warfare. The British admirals of the eighteenth century, though they never voiced such a doctrine as coherently as Mahan did, probably had some notion that destroying the French fleet would let them get on with the business of suppressing the Revolution. But in the war's early stages the Royal Navy's command of the sea had been uncontested, and Britain had found the commodity almost useless. Little if any evidence suggests that a British victory in a naval battle with the French would have prevented, or even significantly delayed, American independence.

In any case, British doctrine almost guaranteed that no such victory would take place. The Royal Navy, like most of its European counterparts, operated on the basis of tactical theories based on the uniquely simple strategic realities of the Anglo-Dutch Wars. The War of American Independence established that those theories would not work in any other context. The concept of the line of battle was predicated on the assumption that the opposing admirals would have identical strategic objectives and would try to fight a battle as a means of achieving them. In the wars between Britain and France that situation rarely, if ever, existed. The basic naval tactic of European navies, the line of battle, was successful in making defeat unlikely. Richard Howe, Marriot Arbuthnot, and Thomas Graves merely committed the standard sin of their generation in failing to realize that the line of battle also made victory almost impossible.

Asking a navy to suppress a revolution was like asking a whale to catch a bird: the excess of force was ludicrous but the inevitable outcome was frustration. The War of American Independence subjected the Royal Navy's human and material resources to demands that they simply could not meet. The navy was asked to meet French and Spanish invasion threats, defend Gibraltar and India, maintain supply lines between England and the West Indies, protect British commerce from privateers and cruisers—and simultaneously help the army fight a war

in North America. Until the last moment the war hung in the balance, for the rebel military effort had problems of its own. Whether the British could have won the war is debatable. But it is reasonable to suspect that a final British victory would have occurred not because of the Royal Navy but in spite of it.

SEE ALSO *Arbuthnot, Marriot; Byron, John; Chesapeake Capes; Estaing, Charles Hector Théodat, Comte d'; Falmouth, Massachusetts; Gambier, Baron James; Grasse, François Joseph Paul, Comte de; Graves, Samuel; Hood, Samuel; Howe, Richard; Parker, Sir Hyde, Jr.; Rodney, George Bridges; Sandwich, John Montagu, fourth earl of; Ternay, Charles Louis d'Arsac, chevalier de; Yorktown Campaign.*

BIBLIOGRAPHY

Allen, Gardner W. *Naval History of the American Revolution.* 2 vols. New York: Houghton Mifflin, 1913.

Billias, George N., ed. *George Washington's Opponents: British Generals and Admirals in the American Revolution.* New York: Morrow, 1969.

Creswell, John. *British Admirals of the Eighteenth Century: Tactics in Battle.* London: George Allen and Unwin, 1972.

Gardiner, Robert. *Navies and the American Revolution, 1775–1783.* London: Chatham, 1996.

Gruber, Ira. *The Howe Brothers and the American Revolution.* New York: Knopf, 1964.

James, William M. *The British Navy in Adversity: A Study of the War of American Independence.* Boston: Little Brown, 1913.

Mackesy, Piers. *The War for America, 1775–1783.* Cambridge, Mass.: Harvard University Press, 1964.

Mahan, Alfred Thayer. *Major Operations of the Navies in the War of American Independence.* Boston: Little Brown, 1913.

Patterson, Temple. *The Other Armada: The Franco-Spanish Attempt to Invade Britain in 1779.* Manchester, U.K.: Manchester University Press, 1960.

Rodger, N. A. M. *The Insatiable Earl: A Life of John Montagu, 4th Earl of Sandwich.* New York: Norton, 1994.

Spinney, David. *Rodney.* London: George Allen and Unwin, 1969.

Stout, Neil R. *The Royal Navy in North America, 1760–1775.* Annapolis, Md.: Naval Institute Press, 1973.

Syrett, David. *The Royal Navy in American Waters, 1775–1783.* London: Gower, 1989.

———. *The Royal Navy in European Waters during the American Revolutionary War.* Columbia: University of South Carolina Press, 1998.

Tilley, John A. *The British Navy and the American Revolution.* Columbia: University of South Carolina Press, 1987.

Tracy, Nicholas. *Navies, Deterrence, and American Independence: Britain and Sea Power in the 1760s and 1770s.* Vancouver, Canada: University of British Columbia Press, 1988.

John A. Tilley

NAVAL OPERATIONS, FRENCH.

One of the prime factors in the defeat of Great Britain, and thus of the establishment of the United States of America as an independent nation, was the remarkable military role played by the French navy during the conflict. Traditionally the underdog since the 1690s when pitted against Britain's Royal Navy, France's navy defied the British against the odds and was often successful between 1778 and 1783.

REVITALIZING THE FLEET

This transformation of the French navy from a relatively moribund force in 1760 to a vigorous and aggressive entity by 1778 was not achieved overnight. It was a process that had started in the final years of the Seven Years' War (1756–1763), during which the French fleet had been rendered incapable of seriously challenging the British enemy. The loss of substantial naval power, leading to the loss of overseas territories and trade as well as a metropolitan coastline open to naval raids, provoked a strong reaction in France for the navy's rehabilitation. The whole country rallied to the idea, and even before the Seven Years' War had ended, money was being raised by public subscriptions to build ships-of-the-line, mostly of seventy-four guns. This is how such ships as the seventy-four-gun *Le Marseillais,* the seventy-four-gun *Bourgogne,* and the ninety-gun *Ville de Paris* were financed; they were named after the donating cities or provinces. The new vessels, especially the seventy-four-gun ships, were remarkably fast and sturdy, with well-designed gun decks allowing a maximum of firepower. The gunners were relentlessly trained and became very proficient.

During this era, the duc de Choiseul came to power as prime minister, holding the portfolios of the ministries of war, foreign affairs, and the navy. The energetic Choiseul was given wide authority in these desperate times, and he used them fully. Naval budgets rose sharply, while incompetent officers were retired in favor of younger men with fresh ideas. The education of officer-cadets and officers was considerably expanded, and examinations for proficiency were introduced. The organization of officers was transformed by a series of orders in 1765 that checked the powers of the administrative officers "of the quill pen" in favor of the fighting officers "of the sword," who now had the last word when it came to resources and supplies for combat vessels. Engineers had also become something of a power in the officers' structure, and they were now told to design the best ships possible for the fighting fleet officers. Transformations came to naval bases as well. Brest now became the primary base with thirty ships-of-the-line, while the main bases of Toulon and Rochefort got twelve each. Lorient was added in 1770. Secondary bases at Bayonne, Marseille, and Bordeaux were activated. In 1768, a base in Corsica was added to counter the British at Minorca. Overseas, naval bases at Martinique, Haiti, and Mauritius formed part of the French navy's network.

Choiseul lost power in 1770, and for a few years the navy was in something of a limbo, but this situation was temporary. The appointment of Antoine de Sartine as minister in 1774 brought a new round of reforms and fostered the fleet's capacity and fighting spirit. Now technically equal to or better than anything afloat, its main and largely unsolvable problem was a shortage of sailors to man what was becoming a truly large fleet. The impact of this shortage included a reduction in the number of training cruises the squadrons could undertake.

THE WAR STARTS

The outbreak of the American Revolution in 1775 quickly raised tensions between France and Britain, with many Frenchmen itching to avenge the humiliations of the Seven Years' War. The fleet was obviously going to be at the forefront of an eventual conflict, and preparations were accordingly made. The naval budget shot up from 47 million French pounds in 1776 to 125 million two years later. This time, France was putting in substantial money to match its ambitions. The American victory at Saratoga in October 1777 had a great impact in France, and it was now a question of when the break with Britain would come, particularly after the Treaty of Alliance between France and the United States was made in February 1778.

As it turned out, the break came off the coast of Brittany in a naval engagement on 17 June 1778 between the French frigate *La Belle-Poule* and the British frigate *Arethusa,* detached from Admiral Keppel's squadron and sent to keep an eye on Brest. After a ferocious fight, both damaged ships went back to their bases and claimed victory, but the real victory went to the French. The *Belle-Poule* had not been struck, and it became a symbolic embodiment of the fleet's new fighting spirit. Thousands lined the walls of Brest, cheering her wildly as she proudly entered the harbor. Before long, all of France was cheering her. After this first action of the new war against Britain, King Louis XVI on 10 July ordered his fleet to give chase to the British. It was a declaration of war.

In July 1778 the French navy had fifty-two ships-of-the-line in commission against the British Royal Navy's sixty-six. At the time, some thirty French ships were deployed on France's Atlantic coast, five in the Mediterranean, twelve en route to America, and two in the Indian Ocean. The British had thirty-one ships in Britain, nineteen in America (including five in the West Indies), two in the Indian Ocean, one off St. Helena, and only one in the Mediterranean. France also had some thirty frigates. The French navy then had about 75,000 sailors led by some 1,300 officers while the Royal Navy had about 85,000 officers and men. Two years later, the French navy stood at seventy-nine ships-of-the-line, eighty-six frigates, and one hundred and seventy-four lesser vessels. A tremendous effort had raised the budget to 155 million, but the Royal Navy had grown as well, to ninety five ships-of-the-line. The French were therefore numerically weaker, but the British had to detach many ships overseas, including along the North American coast. It was not quite an even match, but if France deployed its squadrons wisely, it stood a chance of some success.

Leadership was the unknown factor in the French navy. Would the new admirals be able to hold their own against Britain's renowned flag officers? Certainly, ministers such as Choiseul and de Sartine spared no effort to find talent and intelligence, wherever it was. Too often in the past, the French flag officers had been seen as too cautious and conservative, so that tactical initiative sometimes escaped their grasp. A new generation of "fighting" officers was required to counter the more conservative elements in the fleet. One way to do this was to seek brilliant officers in the army and entice them into the navy. Louis-Antoine de Bougainville and the count d'Estaing had been brought in this way by Choiseul. There were also talented officers commissioned within the navy who despaired of the ambient conservatism in tactical theory and whose innovative spirit had to be channeled. An example was Pierre André de Suffren. His aggressive stance previously had largely benefited the Order of Malta's navy; now, however, he was given a decent command in his own French navy. Also, not all of the older able officers were excluded from senior commands. The comte d'Orvilliers was sixty-eight years old in 1778; the comte de Guichen was sixty-six. They were shrewd masters of maneuvers, and their experience was valued.

EARLY FRENCH SUCCESSES

D'Orvilliers led the Brest fleet of twenty-seven ships that met, on 27 July 1778, Admiral Keppel's thirty Royal Navy ships off the Île de Ouessant (Ushant) off Brittany. The action was inconclusive, and both sides claimed victory, but the French had more grounds to be pleased. The British squadron had certainly not vanquished the French; rather, it had met an opponent that had badly damaged many of its ships thanks to remarkably good shooting. D'Orvilliers had not destroyed the British but had kept his position. This was very bad news for the British, whose control of the French coast now vanished and who now had to protect the English Channel at all cost.

Meanwhile, Admiral Estaing had sailed with twelve ships-of-the-line for North America. His squadron's arrival in August 1778 at Newport, Rhode Island, brought a palpable sign to the Americans that they now had a

powerful ally. After some inconclusive engagements with elements of Admiral William Howe's fleet, Estaing sailed for the West Indies. There, the aggressive governor general of Martinique, the marquis de Bouillé, had already captured Dominica from the British. During the following years, this daring and brilliant officer, who would later be all but forgotten, masterminded the conquest of most of the British Leeward and Windward Islands, often personally taking part in the assaults. De Bouillé was an ideal officer for working with a fleet commander, as he understood combined operations perfectly. It seems, however, that Estaing was less proficient in this area, and in November things were rather bungled at St. Lucia, to Bouillé's considerable disappointment.

The naval campaigns of 1779 got off to a brilliant start for the French in the West Indies, with Bouillé's and Estaing's assault on Grenada on July 3 and the repulse of Admiral Byron's relieving British squadron three days later. The island of St. Vincent had already fallen in late June. Estaing then sailed for Haiti, picked up troops there, and landed them for a joint operation with the Americans against Savannah, Georgia, in October. The siege failed, however, and Estaing, who was badly wounded in the attempt, finally sailed for Europe. Elsewhere, a small squadron under the comte de Vaudreuil had captured the British forts on the coast of Senegal.

THE SPANISH AGENDA

Meanwhile, Spain had declared war on Britain on 16 June 1779. This brought the world's third largest navy into the conflict, which gave the allies on paper a comfortable superiority of some ninety ships-of-the-line over the Royal Navy. However, the Spanish navy's strategic objectives were historically quite different than those of the French or the British. Spain's fleet was far more concerned with protection, notably for the safety of the treasure convoys from America, than with fast movements and elaborate maneuvers. Spanish ships were therefore built as floating fortresses and were thus slower than other vessels of their class. As a result, Spanish navy officers tended to be cautious and did not have a truly aggressive stance or doctrine. The courts of France and Spain had hatched a plan for a combined Hispano-French fleet of sixty-six ships-of-the-line to take control of the English Channel and land a French army in England. Overall command was given to Spanish Admiral de Cordoba with French Admiral d'Orvilliers as second-in-command. The British Isles certainly feared an invasion that summer, but nothing went according to plan for the allies. Besides operational difficulties, bad weather set in. And the reinforced Royal Navy home fleet was not about to be swept away from the Channel. The invasion plan was finally abandoned and the joint fleet went back into Brest in late September.

Sir G. B. Rodney's Action on the 12th of April 1782. *On 12 April 1782, Admiral Rodney's ships intercepted the fleet of comte de Grasse near the Windward Islands. Rodney's victory in the ensuing battle, pictured here in a 1799 engraving by R. Pollard after a painting by Nicholas Pocock, was seen as a triumph, but it was not in fact a major setback to the French.* PICTURE COLLECTION, THE BRANCH LIBRARIES, THE NEW YORK PUBLIC LIBRARY, ASTOR, LENOX AND TILDEN FOUNDATIONS

BATTLES OF 1780–1783

In February 1780 Admiral Guichen sailed for the West Indies; in April and May, his twenty-two ships fought inconclusive engagements with Admiral Rodney's twenty-one ships. On 12 July, Admiral de Ternay with seven ships arrived at Newport and landed General Rochambeau with a French army of five thousand men to assist the Americans. The French squadron stayed on the New England coast to counter British naval movements. In Europe, de Cordoba and d'Orvilliers captured a British convoy of some sixty supply ships intended for America on 9 August. In October the portfolio of minister of the navy passed from de Sartines to the marquis de Castries. He also proved to be a most able administrator.

In March 1781 a small squadron of five ships under Admiral Suffren sailed for the Indian Ocean. On 16 April he attacked and damaged a Royal Navy squadron of six ships moored at La Praya in the Cape Verde Island, thus preventing an attack on the Dutch Cape Colony. (The Netherlands had declared war on Britain the previous year.) There were great plans for joint operations with the Spanish in the Mediterranean for 1781. Minorca and Gibraltar, the latter under siege since 1779, were still British. De Guichen's twenty-four ships joined de Cordoba's twenty-two ships and landed Spanish and

French troops on Minorca in August. The island finally capitulated in early February 1782, eliminating the British presence in the western Mediterranean. Only Gibraltar would remain British as the Spanish repeatedly failed to thwart the Royal Navy's supply convoys. America was not neglected, and the comte de Grasse now assumed command of the West Indies fleet. On 2 June he landed troops that captured Tobago. In July he sailed from Martinique and, after a stop in Haiti to embark three thousand troops, arrived in Chesapeake Bay in late August. There, the French squadron that had sailed down from New England reinforced his fleet. On 5 September, Admiral Graves arrived in the area with nineteen ships and was quite surprised to find a large French squadron of twenty-four ships there. In the ensuing Battle of the Virginia Capes, de Grasse drove Graves off, and the fate of the British army in Yorktown, besieged by Washington and Rochambeau's troops, was sealed. The place surrendered on 19 October.

The year 1782 started with a French assault on St. Kitts, which capitulated on 13 February, leading to the surrender of Nevis and Montserrat. In Versailles and Madrid, a joint attack on Jamaica was planned. The Spanish fleet at Havana would join de Grasse's squadron at Haiti and there embark some seven thousand French and Spanish troops to invade the British island. The

British naval forces simply had to prevent the junction and, on 12 April, Admiral Rodney's ships intercepted de Grasse's fleet off the Saints archipelago in the Windward Islands. In the ensuing battle, four French ships and Admiral de Grasse were captured and the expedition to Jamaica cancelled as a result. Rodney's victory, hailed as a triumph by countless British historians, was not a major setback to the French. Since de Grasse was not a popular commander, some did not regret his loss, and most of his fleet actually made its junction with Admiral Salcedo's fifteen Spanish ships-of-the-line. By the end of the year, more French ships had arrived in the West Indies to replace the losses.

During the last year of the war, the most notable actions occurred in the Indian Ocean. There, Suffren fought a series of engagements that revealed his great innovative talent in naval tactics. Had his battle orders been fully obeyed by his conservative captains, it is likely that the British would have been beaten. By June 1783, he nevertheless had pushed back Admiral Hughes's squadron and landed a French army in southern India to assist Indian princes against the British. The arrival of a frigate from Europe bearing news of the peace treaty stopped the hostilities and probably saved the British from defeat.

As it was, Suffren came back to France in triumph, rightly acknowledged as the country's best admiral. The war had been won, American independence had been secured, and France's navy had regained the nation's place as a redoubtable world power.

SEE ALSO *Bougainville, Louis Antoine de; Chesapeake Capes; Choiseul, Etienne François, Comte de Stainville; Estaing, Charles Hector Théodat, Comte d'; French Alliance; Grasse, François Joseph Paul, Comte de; Rochambeau, (fils) Donatien Marie Joseph de Vimeur; Rochambeau, Jean Baptiste Donatien de Vimeur, comte de; Rodney, George Bridges; Spanish Participation in the American Revolution; St. Kitts, Captured by the French; Suffren de Saint Tropez, Pierre André de; Ternay, Charles Louis d'Arsac, chevalier de; Yorktown Campaign; Yorktown, Siege of.*

BIBLIOGRAPHY

Carr, J. A. "Virginia Capes: The Unknown Battle." *National Defense*, April 1983, 32–35.

Dull, Jonathan. *The French Navy and American Independence.* Princeton, N.J.: Princeton University Press, 1975.

Guérin, Léon. *Les marins illustres de la France.* Paris: Belin-Leprieur, 1846.

Jouan, René. *Histoire de la Marine française.* Paris: Payot, 1950.

Lacour-Gayet, G. *La marine militaire de la France sous le règne de Louis XVI.* Paris: Honoré Champion, 1905.

Taillemite, Étienne, "La marine et ses chefs durant la guerre de l'Indépendance américaine." In *Revue historique des armées* no. 4, 1983.

Varende, Jean de la. *Suffren et ses ennemis.* Paris: Flammarion, 1948.

René Chartrand

NAVAL OPERATIONS, STRATEGIC OVERVIEW.

In theory, Britain's Royal Navy should have been the key to crushing the American Revolution. It was the most powerful navy in the history of the world; the American colonies were so disposed along the coast and so divided by estuaries and navigable rivers as to make all regions accessible to sea power; and the rebelling colonies lacked the resources necessary for constructing a navy capable of contending with that of the mother county. Yet the Royal Navy did not win the war, and even before 1778, when France sent ships to support the colonies, the British failed to exploit an advantage that should have been decisive. As a result, the naval battles of the Revolution were secondary in strategic importance to the land operations, which British strategists expected to produce a quick victory early in the war. Meanwhile, privateering was exploited by the colonists, to their great advantage.

In 1775 Britain's Royal Navy had 131 ships of the line and 139 craft of other classes. By 1783 this total of 270 had been swelled to 468, of which about 100—mainly frigates and lighter vessels—were committed in America. In quality, however, the British navy was in an incredibly bad state. Many of the ships had been reduced by neglect to virtual wrecks, many of its officers and men were substandard, and debts incurred while fighting the French and Indian War had led to cuts in government spending, which left the Royal Navy the without a supply of seasoned timber for ship construction.

Those ships which the navy could send to North American waters in 1775 and 1776 were employed mostly in rendering assistance to Royal governors and supporting army operations, rather than in blockading the American coast. During the summer of 1776, Royal Navy vessels were involved in evacuating army troops from Boston and supporting expeditions against Quebec, New York City, and the Carolinas. The next year they supported the campaign against Philadelphia. This left colonial ports open to receive assistance from other European nations (particularly France) and to export commodities to pay for munitions and interest on loans. That the Royal navy could have blockaded the American coast to economically strangle the rebellion is demonstrated the success of its blockade of the coast between Cape Cod and Delaware Bay during the winter of 1776–1777, a time when it was not needed to support the army.

"WASHINGTON'S NAVY"

An action off Machias, in Maine, in May 1775, has been called the first naval engagement of the war, although this is stretching the point somewhat. A few months later, during the Boston Siege, General George Washington organized a flotilla of six schooners and a brigantine to prey on enemy supply ships. He had the double purpose of depriving the enemy of cargoes and of getting critically needed supplies for his own forces.

On 2 September 1775 he commissioned the *Hannah*, which has been called America's first war vessel. (The *Machias Liberty*, rechristened after the action of May 1775, could probably be called the first war vessel in the service of an American state.) Washington's little navy took thirty-five prizes, with cargoes valued at over $600,000, before it was absorbed into the Continental navy. Captain John Manley made the most important capture when he took the *Nancy*, on about 27 August 1775.

THE CONTINENTAL NAVY

"What think you of an American Fleet?" asked John Adams in a letter of 19 Oct. 1775 to James Warren. "I don't mean 100 ships of the Line," he went on to say, but suggested instead that the colonists should be able to create a small force that could do something. The idea was popular with the New England delegates and opposed by others, but by the end of the month Congress had authorized four armed vessels and, on 30 October, it appointed John Adams and six others to constitute a Naval Committee. On 10 November the Marines were born, and on 23 November Congress considered John Adams's draft of "rules for the government of the American navy," based on those of the British. On 25 November Congress passed the resolutions that established the American navy.

Naval affairs were controlled thereafter by various bodies designated by Congress. Until December 1779 a Marine Committee of thirteen members, one from each colony, was responsible. The Board of Admiralty was then established. to comprise three private citizens and two members of Congress. After 1781 the administration was handled by Robert Morris, Director of Finance, as an addition to his normal duties. Subordinate boards in Boston and Philadelphia were also established.

Esek Hopkins was appointed commander in chief of this fleet of eight vessels purchased and assembled at Philadelphia by the end of the year. The largest were the merchant vessels *Alfred* and *Columbus*, which had been converted into frigates of 24 and 20 guns. Others were the brigs *Andrea Doria* and *Cabot* with fourteen six-pound guns apiece, and the *Providence* (twelve guns), *Hornet* (ten guns), and the *Wasp* and *Fly*, each with eight guns. The captains, in order of seniority, were Dudley Saltonstall, Abraham Whipple, Nicholas Biddle, and John B. Hopkins. Heading the list of lieutenants was John Paul Jones.

Ice-bound in the Delaware for several weeks after all other preparations were completed, the American navy put to sea on 17 February 1776. Congress had given Esek Hopkins orders to clear the Chesapeake Bay of Lord Dunmore's fleet, drive the British from the Carolina coasts, and then run the Royal Navy away from Rhode Island—obviously an overly ambitious set of orders for a force of only eight ships mounting 110 guns. At the time, the British had seventy-eight ships with over 2,000 guns in American waters. But Hopkins took advantage of a discretionary clause in his orders that authorized him to use his judgment in adopting whatever other course of action appeared to be more promising.

Hopkins sailed directly to the Bahamas, where he captured Nassau on 3–4 March. Returning to the American coast, he took a British armed schooner and a brig before the unfortunate encounter occurred between his flagship, the *Alfred*, and the British vessel, the *Glasgow*, which occurred on 6 April. The American ships put into New London and then went to Providence, Rhode Island. As a result of the 6 April action, Esek Hopkins was through as commander in chief of the Continental navy. A court-martial convicted Captain John Hazard of cowardice, and John Paul Jones succeeded him as commander of Hazard's ship, the *Providence*. Although he was placed behind seventeen other captains on the seniority list established by Congress in October 1776, Jones promptly established himself as the top American naval commander. During the last six months of 1776 he captured or destroyed five transports, two ships, six schooners, seven brigantines, a sloop, and a sixteen-gun privateer. Most valuable of these prizes was the armed transport *Mellish*, which carried a cargo of winter uniforms and other supplies intended for Quebec, on 12 November 1776. Further naval operations occurring during the first two years of the war occurred on Lake Champlain, including the action at Valcour Island in October 1776.

Naval supremacy was the cornerstone of British strategy in America during the years 1776–1777. It enabled them to evacuate Boston in March 1776, and to mass a large army on Staten Island for the New York campaign after dispatching Henry Clinton's expedition to Charleston. This superiority made the Hudson River a line of operations, while confronting Washington with the problems of defending against an amphibious attack toward Philadelphia and such southern ports as Charleston, South Carolina, and Savannah, Georgia.

OPERATIONS IN EUROPEAN WATERS

The Franco-American alliance, negotiated in February 1778 was scheduled to take effect should war break out between France and Britain, which it did in June of that year. This event significantly altered the strategic situation by shifting the balance of naval forces in the war. In 1778 France had seventy-nine ships of the line in service compared to the Royal navy's seventy-three. This gap widened further after Spain, which had forty-nine ships of the line, entered the war as an ally of France (although not of the United States) on 21 June 1779. With the widening of the war, operations could be anticipated on a worldwide basis, much like those of the Seven Years' War, which had recently concluded.

Prior to this time, naval operations had been limited almost exclusively to American waters, although a few American warships had appeared in the Atlantic off Europe. Continental ships were tasked with conveying American diplomats to Europe, and, during the first of such voyage, Captain Lambert Wickes took as prizes two British merchantmen while delivering Benjamin Franklin to France (26 October–4 December 1776). After landing Franklin at Auray, Wickes cruised the English Channel. taking five more prizes. Joined by ships commanded by Captains Henry Johnson and Samuel Nicholson, Wickes, aboard the *Reprisal*, circumnavigated Ireland clockwise and, in the Irish Sea, took captive eight merchantmen and destroyed another ten. Six months later Gustavus Conyngham, in command of the lugger *Surprise* (owned in part by the American government), carried two British ships into Dunkirk. He returned to sea with a commission in the Continental navy and, in a two-month cruise, took additional prizes before shifting shifted his base of operations to Spain. He then crossed the Atlantic to the Caribbean in 1778. Meanwhile, John Paul Jones had arrived in France in command of the *Ranger*.

Open war between Britain and France was precipitated by the clash off Ushant, an island off Brittany, on 27 July 1778. French Admiral Louis Guillouet, comte d'Orvilliers, put to sea on 8 July with plans to intercept homebound British convoys. British Admiral Augustus Viscount Keppel weighed anchor the next day with orders to protect the convoys. The fleets sighted one another on 23 July and, after extended maneuvering, passed on opposite tacks and exchanged broadsides before the French eluded the British and returned to port. For the next year France sent fleets to America while working to lure Spain into active involvement in the war.

When Britain rejected Spain's 3 April 1779 ultimatum that it cede Gibraltar in return for Spanish neutrality in the war, Spain began conducting joint naval operations with the French in May, and, a month later, formally entered the war. Mustering a superior number of warships in the eastern Atlantic, the French and Spanish laid siege to Gibraltar from 21 June 1779 to 6 February 1783, and planned a joint invasion of the Isle of Wight. The invasion was so ill-managed that it disintegrated before a single

soldier reached English soil. The Royal Navy was able to slip enough supply vessels through the Franco-Spanish blockade of Gibraltar to keep its defenders provisioned. On 16 January 1780, Admiral George B. Rodney, in command of a convoy en route to Gibraltar, defeated a squadron under the command of Spanish Admiral Juan Langara, sinking one ship, driving two to destruction on shoals, and capturing four before resupplying Gibraltar. After capturing Minorca in the Mediterranean (5 February 1782), the allies launched an assault on Gibraltar on 13–14 September 1782, but were rebuffed. The British garrison held out until it was reinforced and resupplied by a fleet commanded by Admiral Richard Howe.

During 1780 Britain's naval position eroded further when Russia formed the League of Armed Neutrality, and war broke out with the Netherlands on 20 December 1780. The following spring, Admiral Pierre André de Suffren, in command of a French fleet en route to reinforce the Dutch colony at the Cape of Good Hope, sailed into Porto Praya in the Cape Verde Islands. There, on 16 April 1781, he found a British squadron commanded by Commodore George Johnston at anchor, and, disregarding Portuguese neutrality, attacked and crippled the British expedition which was also bound for the Cape.

The British naval position remained precarious in American waters during 1781, but it improved in Europe during the summer. On 5 August 1781, Admiral Sir Hyde Parker defeated a Dutch squadron commanded by Admiral Johann A. Zoutman in the battle of Dogger Bank, off the Northumberland coast. Four months later Admiral Richard Kempenfelt defeated a French squadron commanded by Admiral Luc Urbain Bouëxic, comte de Guichen, at the second battle of Ushant (12 December 1781), capturing fifteen of the twenty merchantmen de Guichen was attempting to convoy to the West Indies. From that point forward, British leaders could feel confident of their position in European waters and direct the majority of their naval resources to American waters, where they regained control of the Caribbean in the battle of the Saints, 9–12 April 1782.

FRENCH FLEET IN AMERICAN WATERS

French naval operations were no more conclusive off North America until 1781. Even before a formal declaration of war between England, France dispatched Admiral Charles, comte d'Estaing and a large French fleet to America with orders to support Continental army operations. The result was a heart-breaking series of failures. After taking eighty-seven days to cross the Atlantic, d'Estaing arrived too late to bottle up the British fleet in the Chesapeake, was too timid to attack Admiral Richard Howe's fleet at New York, 11–22 July, failed at Newport on 29 July–31 August, and abandoned a proposed attack on Newfoundland, before sailing for the West Indies in

November. There he did some damage to the British, but failed to gain any real advantage. In September and October 1779, he returned to North America, but refused to remain off Savannah long enough to force the surrender of the British garrison that had captured the city on 29 December 1778. In 1780 France shifted its primary naval attention to the West Indies. Without a French fleet on the American coast, Henry Clinton was free to launch his expedition against Charleston, which resulted in the scuttling of the *Queen of France* and the capture of the *Ranger, Providence, and Boston,* all of which were taken into the Royal Navy.

Alarmed by the French capture of St. Vincent and Grenada in June and July, Britain dispatched a fleet to the Caribbean under the command of Admiral Sir George Rodney in late 1779. His fleet duelled indecisively with that of comte de Guichen in 1780 and 1781 and sought to counter the capture of Mobile and Pensacola by Spanish forces led by Benardo de Gálvez. Though inconclusive in the Caribbean, naval operations set the stage for the decisive American victory in the war, when the French fleet of Admiral François Joseph, comte de Grasse, sailed north from the West Indies to participate in the Yorktown campaign of 1781.

OPERATIONS IN THE INDIAN OCEAN

After attacking the British at Praya, Suffren continued on to Ile de France in the Indian Ocean, arriving in October 1781. On 7 December he weighed anchor for India and captured the HMS *Hannibal* (18 Jan 1782), which was also en route to India. When Commodore Thomas, comte d'Orves died, Suffren succeeded him as commander of all eighteen French warships in the Indian Ocean.

Learning of the Dutch entry into the war, Admiral Sir Edward Hughes seized the Dutch port of Trincomalee to prevent its use by the French fleet (5–11 January 1782). Determined to seize a base for his fleet that was nearer to India than Ile de France, Suffren sought battle with Hughes, who had eleven warships. Over the next eighteen months, Suffren and Hughes fought a series of engagements, off Sadras (17 February), Provedien (12 April), Negapatam (6 July), and Trincomalee (3 September). No ships were lost by either side, but Suffren kept the British on the defensive. This allowed Suffren to land troops and support France's ally, Hyder Ali, who had captured the British-held Cuddalore (4 April 1782). Suffren also was able to seize the anchorage at Trincomalee on 30 August 1782. Its position in India threatened, Britain sent reinforcements to Hughes, including five ships of the line, bringing his forces to eighteen by the spring of 1783. Suffren received three additional ships of the line by March. The fleets

fought another inconclusive battle off Cuddalore on 23 April 1783 before news arrived of the war's end.

AMERICAN NAVAL BATTLES

While Britain and France focused on European waters during 1779, on the West Indies between 1780 and 1782, and the Indian Ocean during 1782 and 1783, the five remaining Continental navy vessels, *Trumbull, Deane, Alliance, Confederacy,* and *Saratoga,* were able to get to sea. Captain James Nicholson took command of the *Trumbull* in September 1779, and fit the frigate out for sea over the winter. In the spring he cruised the American coast from Boston to New York to drive off British privateers. On 2 June 1780, he engaged the British ship, the *Watt,* in a battle that was second in severity only to that between the *Bonhomme Richard* and *Serapis* of the previous fall. The following summer, Nicholson was forced to strike his colors in the engagement with the *Iris* on 8 August 1781.

During the same period the *Deane, Confederacy, and Saratoga* cruised the Caribbean before taking on military stores and escorting a convoy carrying additional stores for the Continental army. On 18 March 1781 the *Saratoga* sank when caught in a sudden gale three days out of Cape Français, Hispaniola. A month later two British warships captured the *Confederacy* off the Virginia Capes. Only the *Deane* reached port safely, arriving in Boston. In late 1782 the *Deane* sailed to the West Indies, were it eluded capture by at least four British warships which thought that they had cornered John Manley and the *Deane* off Martinique in January 1783.

Among Continental Navy vessels, only the *Alliance* and *Deane* enjoyed significant success during the closing years of the war. When Silas Deane's loyalty came under suspicion, the *Deane* was renamed the *Hague,* set sail for the West Indies under the command John Manley, and captured the *Baille* in January 1783. More illustrious was the career of the *Alliance.* On 29 May 1781, it forced the British brigs *Trepassy* and *Atalanta* to strike their colors. It also fought the war's final naval engagement (excepting some privateering exploits) when, under the command of John Barry, it fought the *Sybille* off the coast of Florida in March 1783.

Meanwhile, state navy vessels scored their two greatest oceanic victories. A frigate from the Massachusetts navy won a memorable victory in the *Protector–Duff* engagement of 9 June 1780. Two years later the Pennsylvania navy sloop-of-war, *Hyder Ally,* captured the British brig *General Monk* after a fierce half hour battle off Delaware Bay on 8 April 1782.

In summary, the raid on Nassau on March 1776, was virtually the only planned major operation of the Continental navy. A total of fifty-three ships served in

John Paul Jones Engages the **Serapis.** *American naval officer John Paul Jones became a great hero when on 23 September 1779, he commanded the* Bonhomme Richard *in a daring battle at sea against the British* Serapis. © BETTMANN/CORBIS

the Continental fleet. Of the 13 original frigates, only four were at sea by 1777, and only two (Barry's *Alliance* and Manley's *Hague*) were in action in 1783. Lack of resources kept the rebels from getting to sea anything larger than a frigate, and privateering proved to be a more formidable enemy than the British navy.

Whereas the Continental and state navies did not commission more than a hundred ships during the war, the British increased their navy from 270 to 468 ships, 174 of which carried sixty or more guns. The American frigates nevertheless sank or captured almost 200 British vessels. Privateers cost the British another 600 ships. The Royal Navy performed miserably under a succession of incompetent admirals and an inept ministry. In 1783, however, the British navy rebounded from adversity, and its successes in the West Indies, European waters, and India enabled Britain to stiffen its terms of peace with America and to convince France and Spain that the war should end.

SEE ALSO Alfred-Glasgow *Encounter; Armed Neutrality;* Bonhomme Richard–Serapis *Engagement; Hopkins, Esek; Howe, Richard; Jones, John Paul; Machias, Maine; Manley, John; Marines; Nassau; Naval Committee; Rodney, George Bridges;* Trumbull–Iris *Engagement;* Trumbull–Watt *Engagement; Virginia, Military Operations in; West Indies in the Revolution; Wickes, Lambert.*

BIBLIOGRAPHY

Bradford, James C., ed. *Command Under Sail: Makers of the American Naval Tradition, 1775–1850.* Annapolis, Md.: Naval Institute Press, 1985.

Clark, William B. *George Washington's Navy; Being an Account of His Excellency's Fleet in New England Waters.* Baton Rouge, La.: Louisiana State University Press, 1960.

————. *The First Saratoga; Being the Saga of John Young and his Sloop-of-War.* Baton Rouge, La.: Louisiana State University Press, 1953.

Cogliano, Francis D. *American Maritime Prisoners in the Revolutionary War: The Captivity of William Russell.* Annapolis, Md.: Naval Institute Press, 2001.

Dull, Jonathan. *The French Navy and American Independence: A Study in Arms and Diplomacy, 1774–1783.* Princeton, N.J.: Princeton University Press, 1975.

Dupuy, R. Ernest, Gay Hammerman, and Grace P. Hayes. *The American Revolution: A Global War.* New York: David McKay, 1977.

Eller, Ernest McNeill, ed. *Chesapeake Bay in the American Revolution.* Centreville, Md.: Tidewater Publishers, 1981.

Fowler, William M., Jr. *Rebels Under Sail: The American Navy during the Revolution.* New York: Scribner's, 1976.

Jackson, John W. *The Pennsylvania Navy, 1775–1781: The Defense of the* Delaware. New Brunswick, N.J.: Rutgers University Press, 1974.

Lewis, James A. *Neptune's Militia: The Frigate* South Carolina *during the American Revolution.* Kent, Ohio: Kent State University Press, 1999.

McCusker, John J. *Alfred: The First Continental Flagship.* Washington, D.C.: Smithsonian Institution Press, 1973.

McGuffie, T. H. *The Siege of Gibraltar, 1779–1783.* London: B. T. Batsford, 1965.

Miller, Nathan. *Sea of Glory: The Continental Navy Fights for Independence, 1775-1783.* New York: D. McKay and Company, 1974.

Morgan, William James. *Captains to the Northward: The New England Captains in the Continental Navy.* Barre, Vt.: Barre Press, 1959.

Rider, Hope S. *Valour Fore & Aft: Being the Adventures of the Continental Ship* Providence, *1775–1779, Formerly Flagship* Katy *of Rhode Island's Navy.* Annapolis, Md.: Naval Institute Press, 1977.

Rodger, N. A. M. *The Insatiable Earl: A Life of John Montagu, 4th Earl of Sandwich.* New York: W. W. Norton, 1993.

Smith, Myron J., Jr. *Navies in the American Revolution: A Bibliography.* Metuchen, N.J.: Scarecrow Press, 1973.

Syrett, David. *The Royal Navy in European Waters during the American Revolutionary War, 1775–1783.* Columbia, S.C.: University of South Carolina Press, 1998.

Tilly, John A. *The British Navy and the American Revolution.* Columbia, S.C.: University of South Carolina Press, 1987.

Tuchman, Barbara W. *The First Salute: A Naval View of the Revolution.* New York: Knopf, 1988.

James C. Bradford

NAVAL STORES.

The term "naval stores" refers to various items, materials, and substances that were essential to building, maintaining, and operating the wooden sailing ships that made up the navies and merchant fleets of the world from ancient times. Many products were derived from pine trees in the southern colonies, including resin, tar, pitch, and turpentine, and were valued for their ability to help ships withstand salt water. The term also included other items, like the masts and spars made from the tall white pines growing in the interior of New England and cordage made of hemp; it sometimes included certain types of insect-resistant timbers from which durable hulls could be constructed. At the turn of the twenty-first century, much of the world's supply of pine-based naval stores comes from the American Southeast, but before the establishment of Britain's North American colonies, western Europe's principal source for these substances, and for the tall, straight pine trees needed for a ship's masts, was the Baltic region. Naval stores were so important to Britain's naval and maritime strength that in 1704 they were designated enumerated commodities that the colonies could send only to the mother country.

SEE ALSO *Enumerated Articles.*

revised by Harold E. Selesky

NELSON, HORATIO.

(1758–1805). British admiral and naval hero. Nelson first went to sea in 1770 in a ship commanded by his uncle, and passed for lieutenant on 9 April 1777. In the West Indies in 1778 he was taken up by Peter Parker, who took him into his flagship, gave him the brig *Badger* in 1778, and in 1779 appointed him to a post ship, the frigate *Hinchinbrook*. His first experiences of action came in the expedition to Nicaragua, where disease nearly killed him. In 1783 he unsuccessfully attacked the French garrison of Turk's Island in the Bahamas.

SEE ALSO *Bahamas.*

revised by John Oliphant

NELSON, THOMAS.

(1739–1789). Patriot, Signer, militia general, governor of Virginia. Born in Yorktown, Virginia, on 26 December 1738, Nelson was the son of the wealthy merchant, planter, and council member known as "President (William) Nelson." Thomas Nelson was educated in England, spending three years at Cambridge. Returning to Yorktown in 1761, he immediately found a place in the House of Burgesses and as a colonel of militia with the assistance of his father. In 1764 he took his place on the King's Council. On his father's death in 1772, Nelson inherited 20,000 acres and 400 slaves, although his style of living kept him perpetually in debt. Remaining in the Burgesses through this period, Nelson became steadily more political. By 1774 he was calling for a boycott of all British goods and led a local tea party. When state regiments were organized in July 1775, Nelson became a colonel in the Second Virginia Regiment. He resigned this commission later in the year when he was elected to fill the vacant seat of George Washington in the Continental Congress. The new Virginia delegate played a leading role in getting his state to support independence, and he signed the Declaration of Independence. In May 1777 a sudden and serious illness forced his resignation from Congress. In 1779 he was re-elected, but after a few months he again had to resign because of asthma.

Nelson was appointed brigadier general and commander of Virginia's state forces in August 1777. When Congress called for volunteer units, he raised a cavalry troop largely at his own expense. He led them to Philadelphia, but they were disbanded when Congress decided they could not be supported financially. In 1779 the British started a series of devastating raids in Virginia, and Nelson took the leading part in organizing militia resistance. On 12 June 1781 he was elected governor to succeed the militarily inept Thomas Jefferson, and he was given emergency powers by the frightened refugees of the raid on Charlottesville.

During the six months of his governorship, Nelson was virtually a military dictator. He struggled to raise the men and supplies needed to support the Marquis de Lafayette's 1781 expedition to secure Virginia, and when Washington and the comte de Rochambeau (Jean Baptiste Donatien de Vimeur) marched south, the governor-general was in the field to join them for the kill, even directing artillery fire against his own house to support the military effort. In November 1781 he resigned his commission, again because of illness aggravated by asthma.

Nelson had signed off on huge loans during the Revolution in order to arm and equip Virginia's forces. The legislature refused to reimburse Nelson for any of the extensive debts he had accrued in the state's service. Nelson devoted the rest of his life attempting to pay off his creditors. He died at his plantation in Hanover County, Virginia, on 4 January 1789.

SEE ALSO *Yorktown Campaign.*

BIBLIOGRAPHY

Evans, Emory G. *Thomas Nelson of Yorktown: Revolutionary Virginian.* Charlottesville, Va.: University Press of Virginia, 1975.

revised by Michael Bellesiles

NELSON, WILLIAM, JR. (1756?–1813).

Continental officer. Virginia. Of the Nelson family, he graduated from William and Mary in 1776 and returned as professor of law from 1803 until his death ten years later. He was a militia private in 1775 and on 29 February 1776 became a major in the Seventh Virginia Continentals. He was promoted to lieutenant colonel on 7 Oct. 1776. He resigned his commission on 25 October 1777. He and his brother Robert were captured by Tarleton in June 1781 during the Charlottesville raid but were immediately released on parole. He admitted that he preferred reading to either the practice of law or overseeing his plantations and investments, and excelled only at reading.

SEE ALSO *Charlottesville Raid, Virginia; Nelson Family of Virginia.*

revised by Michael Bellesiles

NELSON FAMILY OF VIRGINIA.

"Scotch Tom" Nelson (1677–1745) came to Virginia from Penrith, a town on the English side of the Scottish border that then was part of Scotland. Around 1700 he settled at Yorktown, Virginia, and became a wealthy merchant, slave trader, and landholder. His son Thomas (c. 1716–1782) was defeated by Patrick Henry in the first election for governor under the new constitution of Virginia (29 June 1776). Known as "Secretary Nelson," being secretary of the governor's council for thirty years, his elder brother was "President" William Nelson (1711–1772), who was in the Virginia Council from 1744 until his death, president of that body for many years, and ex officio acting governor from the death of Botetourt to the arrival of Dunmore (October 1770–August 1771). Between them, these two brothers dominated the government of pre-Revolutionary Virginia. William's eldest son, Thomas Nelson Jr., was a signer of the Declaration of Independence. Two others, Robert and William Nelson Jr. also achieved some eminence.

SEE ALSO *Nelson, Thomas; Nelson, William, Jr.*

revised by Michael Bellesiles

NEUTRAL GROUND OF NEW YORK. 1776–1783.

The term applies, narrowly, to the territory east of the Hudson River between the British positions around New York City (on Manhattan Island at Kings Bridge, where the Boston Post Road crossed the Harlem River) north to the American positions in the southern part of the Highlands of the Hudson. Extending roughly thirty miles north and south, it included most of The Bronx and Westchester County. A broader definition extends the term to include the entire wedge of land beginning at the northern end of Manhattan Island and fanning out north up the Hudson River and northeast along Long Island Sound toward Connecticut.

There was nothing "neutral" about the Neutral Ground. The term meant that neither side had the capacity to control what happened in this region. Each side could deploy sufficient forces to obtain a temporary superiority, but both were too close to the main forces of the enemy to linger for too long in the Neutral Ground. The modern equivalent would be the no-man's-land between the established positions of two rival armies. Civilians found it extremely difficult to live in the area, since parties from both sides continually raided and ravaged their farms and possessions.

Conditions similar to those existing in the Neutral Ground also afflicted New Jersey from the Amboys and New Brunswick north through the Hackensack Valley into southern Orange County, New York, on the west side of the Hudson River, but the term "neutral ground" did not normally include this region.

revised by Harold E. Selesky

NEUVILLE. Two French brothers incorrectly identified in American works as the chevalier de la Neuville and Noirmont de la Neuville should properly be identified by the family name of Penot Lombart. They are most properly identified as Louis Pierre Penot Lombart, chevalier de La Neuville, and Rene-Hippolyte Penot Lombart de Noirmont de la Neuville.

SEE ALSO *Penot Lombart de Noirmont, Rene-Hippolyte; Penot Lombart, Louis-Pierre.*

revised by Michael Bellesiles

NEVILLE, JOHN. (1731–1803). Continental officer. Virginia. Born in Prince William County, Virginia, in 1731, Neville took part in Braddock's expedition to capture Fort Duquesne in 1755, during the French and Indian Wars (1689–1763). He then settled near Winchester, where he became sheriff. He later bought large tracts of land near Pittsburgh and became joint holder of an additional 1,000 acres as a reward for his military service. In August 1775 the Virginia Committee of Safety ordered him to occupy Fort Pitt, and he was commandant of that frontier post for the next year. Commissioned as a lieutenant colonel of the Twelfth

Virginians on 12 November 1776, Neville fought with General George Washington's army at Trenton, Princeton, and Germantown. On 11 December 1777 he became a colonel of the Eighth Virginians and led them in the Monmouth campaign. Transferred to the Fourth Virginians on 14 September 1778, he was brevetted as a brigadier general on 30 September 1783.

Neville's land became part of Pennsylvania after the war. He was appointed to the position of U.S. Inspector of Excise (in addition to the other offices he held), and became the primary target of the Whiskey Rebellion of 1794. Crowd actions halted his tax collecting, burned his house, and drove him into temporary exile, but he returned with the federal force that put down the rebellion. He died at his estate on Montour's Island, near Pittsburgh, on 29 July, 1803.

SEE ALSO *Monmouth, New Jersey.*

BIBLIOGRAPHY
Slaughter, Thomas P. *The Whiskey Rebellion: Frontier Epilogue to the American Revolution.* New York: Oxford University Press, 1986.

revised by Michael Bellesiles

NEVILLE, PRESLEY. (1756–1818). Continental officer. Son of John Neville, Presley Neville was born in Pittsburgh and graduated from the College of Philadelphia in 1775. On 9 November 1776 he became a lieutenant in the Twelfth Virginia Regiment (of which his father was lieutenant colonel), and transferred to the Eighth Virginia Regiment on 14 September 1778. In that same year he served as aide-de-camp to the Marquis de Lafayette with the temporary grade of manor. On 21 October 1778 he became brevet lieutenant colonel. On 10 May 1779 he was given the regular rank of captain, and on 12 May 1780 he was captured at Charleston. He was included in a prisoner exchange a year later. After this he became brigade inspector and was elected to the state assembly. He married a daughter of Daniel Morgan, and from 1792 until his death in 1818 he was a merchant in Pittsburgh.

SEE ALSO *Neville, John.*

revised by Michael Bellesiles

NEW BERN, NORTH CAROLINA. August 1781. On 1 August, Major James Craig led 250 British regulars and 80 Loyalists north from Wilmington on a punitive expedition. Reinforced en route by another three hundred Loyalists, he destroyed rebel plantations along his seventy-five-mile march to New Bern; entered that town on 19 August; destroyed property; and returned to Wilmington, meanwhile burning additional Whig plantations. Craig also liberated several scores of slaves along the way.

SEE ALSO *Wilmington, North Carolina.*

revised by Michael Bellesiles

NEW BRUNSWICK, NEW JERSEY.

The town was generally known as Brunswick during the Revolution, although both names were used. The original settlement was called Inian's [sic] Ferry and was home to the Lenape people. General William Howe's troops seized the city in their sweep through New Jersey in December 1776, creating panic in Philadelphia.

revised by Michael Bellesiles

NEWBURGH ADDRESSES. 10 and 12

March 1783. Angered that their pay was several months in arrears and that Congress consistently opposed pensions for members of the Continental army, a number of officers began planning what verged on a coup. They were spurred on by some members of Congress and also by Robert Morris, the superintendent of finance, who hoped to use the crisis to increase national power, and especially to levy taxes. Early in January 1783 a delegation of officers sent Congress a memorial listing officer grievances. Major General Alexander McDougall headed the committee of senior officers that formulated this document and took it to Philadelphia. The prime organizer of the movement, however, was Colonel Walter Stewart, who argued that the officers should act in concert to insist that Congress promptly pay all that had been promised them. It is not clear how far the officers were willing to go to win their demands, but there were rumors of marching on Philadelphia and seizing power.

Washington supported the monetary claims of his officers and often called on Congress to make good on its promises. Washington was aware of the increasing discontent among his officers but suspected nothing ominous until 10 March, when he was handed a written call for a meeting of general and field officers the next day and was also given a copy of the fiery and rhetorical appeal subsequently known as the first Newburgh address. The anonymous document proposed that the officers inform Congress that unless their demands were met, they would refuse to disband when the war ended, and that if the war

should continue, they would "retire to some unsettled country" and leave Congress without an army. In General Orders of 11 March, Washington denounced the "irregular invitation" and the "disorderly proceedings" and directed that representatives of all regiments meet on 15 March to decide how "to attain the just and important object in view." A second anonymous address appeared on 12 March, expressing the crafty view that the language of Washington's General Orders made him party to the complaints. Deeply worried, the commander in chief reported developments to Congress. He realized that he would also have to step forward at the meeting of the 15th and do all within his power to keep his officers from going further with their movement.

What followed was one of the most dramatic moments of the Revolution. Visibly agitated, Washington appeared before a tense group of officers on 15 March and read them a statement he had prepared, probably with the help of Jonathan Trumbull Jr. Commenting that the anonymous addresses showed a good literary style, he criticized them for the implication that the civil authorities were guilty of "premeditated injustice." He denounced the alternatives proposed in the first address and entreated his officers to not take "any measures which, viewed in the calm light of reason, will lessen the dignity and sully the glory you have hitherto maintained." He warned that the Revolution itself was at stake, with the threat of civil war looming before them. Climaxing his appeal with a call for them to once more show their greater patriotism in the face of adversity, Washington assured them that by trusting in the American people to do right, "you will, by the dignity of your conduct, afford occasion for Posterity to say, when speaking of the glorious example you have exhibited to Mankind, 'had this day been wanting, the World have never seen the last state of perfection to which human nature is capable of attaining'" (Fitzpatrick, ed., 26, pp. 226–227).

Not quite sure that he had convinced his officers that Congress meant well toward them, Washington took from his pocket a letter from Virginia delegate Joseph Jones, who had written of the financial problems with which Congress had to cope before it could meet the just claims of the officers. After stumbling over the closely written letter, Washington stopped to get out his glasses "and begged the indulgence of his audience while he put them on, observing at the same time that he had grown grey in their service and now found himself growing blind" (Smith, 2, p. 1770). The assembled officers were deeply moved by these simple and sincere remarks, and by the time Washington left the meeting a few minutes later, the conspiracy was dead. Against mild opposition from Timothy Pickering, the meeting voted Washington its thanks and, without dissent, expressed its confidence in the justice of Congress and repudiated the anonymous addresses issued in the officers' names.

Washington never knew the entire history of these addresses, which were the work of General Horatio Gates's aide-de-camp, Major John Armstrong Jr. They were copied by Gates's friend, Captain Christopher Richmond, and distributed by Major William Barber. Armstrong and others considered reviving the movement in April 1783, but they abandoned their plans when Armstrong came to believe they had been revealed to Washington.

In his handling of this incident, Washington demonstrated firm leadership and set the stage for the peaceful demobilization of the Continental Army. Congress remained weak and unable to pay its soldiers as it had promised.

S E E   A L S O *Armstrong, John Jr.; McDougall, Alexander; Morris, Robert (1734–1806); Pickering, Timothy; Stewart, Walter; Trumbull, Jonathan, Jr.; Washington, George.*

BIBLIOGRAPHY

Fitzpatrick, John C., ed. *The Writings of George Washington.* 39 vols. Washington, D.C.: U.S. Government Printing Office, 1931–1944.

Kohn, Richard H. *Eagle and Sword: The Federalists and the Creation of the Military Establishment in America, 1783–1802.* New York: Free Press, 1975.

Smith, Page. *A New Age Now Begins: A People's History of the American Revolution.* 2 vols. New York: McGraw-Hill, 1976.

revised by Michael Bellesiles

NEWCASTLE, THOMAS PELHAM HOLLES, DUKE OF.

(1793–1768). British statesman. A privy councillor from 1717, in 1724 Newcastle became one of Robert Walpole's secretaries of state. From the start he understood the need for a European ally, preferably the Hapsburg monarchy, in order to offset a move by France, possibly in alliance with Spain, against an isolated Britain. In 1754–1756, when he was prime minister, he failed to anticipate Maria Theresa's move toward France and found himself committed to Prussia instead. The initial disasters of the Seven Years' War drove him from office in 1756. However, once William Pitt recognized the necessity of Newcastle's "continental" policy, Newcastle returned as nominal prime minister in 1757. Later, especially after Pitt's resignation in 1761, Newcastle shared Lord Bute's alarm at the spiraling national debt; but, to avoid future diplomatic isolation, he opposed the government's desertion of Prussia. Obliged to resign in May 1762, he found his influence gravely weakened, and he was unable to work with Pitt in opposition. Apart from a few months

as lord privy seal in 1765, his days in office were over. Perhaps his last significant act was to support both repeal of the Stamp Act and the Declaratory Act, and to persuade George III that Rockingham's conciliation policy was correct.

Historians used to portray Newcastle as a comically inept politician who owed his prominence entirely to his great wealth and parliamentary interest. However, toward the end of the twentieth century a more balanced picture emerged: Newcastle may have lacked the judgment and confidence of a prime minister, but he had diligence, skill with people, a good grasp of detail, and energetic (if not always coherent) oratory. Above all, he consistently worked to avoid the very isolation that proved so calamitous during the War of American Independence.

S E E   A L S O *Chatham, William Pitt, First Earl of; Declaratory Act; Rockingham, Charles Watson-Wentworth, Second Marquess of; Stamp Act; Walpole, Horatio (or Horace).*

BIBLIOGRAPHY

Black, Jeremy. *A System of Ambition? British Foreign Policy, 1660–1793.* London and New York: Longman, 1991.

Kelch, Ray A. *Newcastle: A Duke without Money: Thomas Pelham-Holles, 1693–1768.* London: Routledge and Kegan Paul, 1974.

Middleton, Richard. *The Bells of Victory: The Pitt-Newcastle Ministry and the Conduct of the Seven Years' War, 1757–1762.* Cambridge, U.K., and New York: Cambridge University Press, 1985.

Langford, Paul. *The Eighteenth Century: 1688–1815.* London: A. and C. Black, 1976.

———. *A Polite and Commercial People: England 1727–1783.* Oxford: Clarendon Press, and New York: Oxford University Press, 1989.

Speck, W. A. *Stability and Strife: England, 1714–1760.* Cambridge, Mass.: Harvard University Press, 1977.

revised by John Oliphant

NEW HAMPSHIRE, MOBILIZATION IN.

After much careful research in the 1930s, the New Hampshire historian Richard Francis Upton concluded that mobilization there seems to have begun spontaneously in the winter of 1774–1775. As early as 28 May 1773 the New Hampshire legislative assembly had established a Standing Committee of Correspondence in response to the circular letter sent from the Virginia Committee of Correspondence. New Hampshire's Royal Governor John Wentworth promptly adjourned the assembly. It met again on 7 April 1774 and formed another Committee of Correspondence on 28 May.

Wentworth again adjourned it until 8 June, at which time he dissolved the assembly, not calling for it to reconvene until 4 May 1775. In keeping with suggestions from other states, New Hampshire's legislative leaders called an extralegal meeting of the assembly for 21 July 1774 to elect delegates to a general congress scheduled to convene in Philadelphia on 1 September 1774. This New Hampshire Assembly, the first of New Hampshire's five Provincial Congresses, selected Nathaniel Folsom and John Sullivan, a Durham lawyer, to attend the general congress but adjourned without establishing any military organization outside of the existing militia. Counties had held their own political organization but likewise had avoided any formal military development.

New Hampshire citizens had been affected by the Stamp Act, the Intolerable Acts, and the attempts to tax tea, but until 1775 few thought in terms of military retaliation against the mother country. Early in December 1774 the New Hampshire Committee of Correspondence sent around a written appeal to each town urging participation in the Continental Association, an effort led by the Continental Congress to limit trade with Britain. There is no record that any town rejected the association.

In Philadelphia, in the fall of 1774, the Continental Congress met but established no military. As the royal government tightened its control, several New Hampshire leaders worried about the potential need for arms and ammunition. To secure munitions, a force put together by John Langdon and John Sullivan slipped into British Fort William and Mary in Portsmouth Harbor on the night of 14 December 1774 and took gunpowder from the seven troopers that guarded it. Upon news of the battles at Lexington and Concord in neighboring Massachusetts, New Hampshire began its mobilization efforts in earnest. New Hampshire's Fourth Provincial Congress, meeting on 17 May 1775, with 133 delegates attending, ignored the royal government at Portsmouth and established a tax to raise funds, created a post office to enhance communication, and voted to raise a force of two thousand men ages fifteen to fifty, to be organized into three regiments, for six months' service. The mobilization was achieved in three weeks' time—a notable feat for a small province with a population estimated at 100,000, larger only than Georgia, Delaware, and Rhode Island.

Yet armed forces were already part of New Hampshire's heritage. Militia units stood in nearly every town. Under colonial law each male inhabitant between the ages of sixteen and sixty was required to maintain arms and ammunition, and each town had to provide its militia with gunpowder, lead, and flints. The frontiers to the north and west had required continuous observation. Calls to the General Court (the legislature) for men, arms, and gunpowder had come continuously from those

regions as settlements and towns encroached on territory that had been traditionally home to the Abenakis and other Indian tribes. In addition, having seen New Hampshire thrive under the lengthy administration of Governor Benning Wentworth (from 1741 to 1767), and having a generally good relationship with his nephew and successor, Governor John Wentworth, many residents had taken part in the Louisbourg campaigns of the 1740s and 1750s, and many, including John Stark and Robert Rogers, had played significant roles in helping the British control French aggression during the French and Indian War in the 1750s.

The two thousand New Hampshire men mobilized for the war effort included those who had already gone individually or in small groups to aid Massachusetts following Lexington and Concord. These men were designated as part of the First New Hampshire Regiment to be under the command of Colonel John Stark of Dunbarton. The Third Provincial Congress on 21 April 1775 appointed Colonel Nathaniel Folsom of Exeter to the rank of brigadier general with the charge to coordinate and command those troops. In late June, as part of its mobilization for a possibly extended conflict, the Fourth Provincial Congress made Folsom a major general. The Second and Third New Hampshire Regiments were created on 24 May 1775 and placed under the command of Colonel Enoch Poor of Exeter and Colonel James Reed of Fitzwilliam. Both Poor and Reed, having earned military respect through command of their local militia, were in positions to inspire men to join the ranks.

While these developments were taking place in Exeter, John Sullivan, serving as a delegate to the Continental Congress in Philadelphia, was exhibiting great personal presence and passionate opposition to Parliament. Sullivan had displayed military skill in 1774 while commanding militia forces as well as in the raid on Fort William and Mary, and was well-respected at home. In Congress, Sullivan vociferously opposed what he considered to be Parliament's oppression, calling the Quebec Act Britain's most dangerous. On 22 June 1775 Congress appointed him a brigadier general under George Washington, and on 27 June he joined Washington at Cambridge.

When the new rebel army, under the overall command of General Artemas Ward, encountered its first major contest, on 17 June, at Bunker Hill and Breed's Hill, New Hampshire regiments played a vital role. Although Colonel James Reed was ill, his troops displayed the knowledge and extensive training that Reed had given them. Under the command of John Stark, and in unison with Stark's First Regiment, Reed's men manned their places along the famous "rail fence" and valiantly defended their positions by remaining steady and firing low.

The Committee of Safety, chaired by Meshech Weare, loomed large in New Hampshire's war efforts.

Established by the Provincial Congress on 26 May 1775, the Committee's charge was to fill the gap left by the absence of a chief executive and thus to execute policy efficiently, secretly, and speedily. The Committee entertained questions, correspondence, petitions, and visitors. During the war it heard arguments, made thousands of recommendations and executive decisions, oversaw security measures, solved disputes, directed military activity, and regulated trade. The Committee's most important power, according to Upton, was the authority it held over a network of local committees of safety.

In addition to the three infantry regiments authorized and formed in 1775, the state sanctioned Bedel's Regiment of Rangers, authorized on 26 May 1775 to be commanded by Captain Timothy Bedell of Grafton County; Long's Regiment, authorized in May 1776 and formed by Pierce Long at New Castle; and Whitcomb's Rangers, authorized 15 October 1776 and attached as an element of the Northern Department. Bedel had begun to form his regiment in January 1776 near Plymouth, to take part in the Canada Expedition then in progress. Men signing on were to get a bounty of forty shillings plus one month's pay as authorized by the Continental Congress. Officers were to receive two months pay plus bounty. Bedel's unit was disbanded on 1 January 1777 in Coos County, Long's in July 1777 in New York, and Whitcomb's on 1 January 1781 at Coos County. One goal that neither the Committee of Safety nor the General Court could meet was the formation of an artillery regiment. There simply were not enough artillery volunteers or supplies. In fact, following the evacuation of the British from Boston in March 1776, the New Hampshire Committee of Safety dispatched Captain Titus Salter of Portsmouth to regain the artillery that had been lent to the Continental Army. He was to return with the cannon, balls, supplies, and an engineer to operate the artillery. Salter reported in April that he had seen four cannon belonging to New Hampshire, with balls and supplies, but that he could not find any engineer who would return with him.

All three of New Hampshire's regular infantry regiments went through several organizational alterations between the Northern Department and the Main Army of George Washington. The original Third Regiment, formed under Reed, was disbanded on 1 January 1781 at Continental Village, New York. The Second Regiment, originally under Poor, was consolidated with the New Hampshire Regiment (the original First Regiment) on 22 June 1783, and the original First Regiment was disbanded as the New Hampshire Regiment on 1 January 1784.

As the war progressed, victories, assignments to meet specific needs, and individual characteristics of officers all helped spur on generally slow recruitment. A sufficient number of men agreed to join the expedition to Canada in late fall of 1776, but others felt the need to return to their farms and families. By the end of 1776 they were ready to return home, and most did so. Following the victories at Trenton and Princeton, recruitment again generally filled quotas imposed by the state on the towns. When it became generally known that the British planned to send General John Burgoyne's army from Canada over Lake Champlain to Albany and then to merge with its army in New York City to cut off New England, in the summer of 1777, New Hampshire men stepped forward. This was to bring the conflict to New Hampshire's backyard. John Stark, though upset at being passed over by the Continental Congress for a generalship, as a state general was able to raise an entire regiment inside of several weeks, owing largely to his personal power of persuasion. Stark's men slowed Burgoyne's advance at Bennington and finally brought him to captivity at Saratoga.

In 1778 men went to serve in Rhode Island with the mission of protecting New England from invasion. Similarly, in 1779, when John Sullivan led off his expedition from Easton, Pennsylvania, young New Hampshire recruits, were present, including Colonel Enoch Poor's Second New Hampshire Regiment. The brusque Sullivan and the trusted Poor led them to victory over the Six Nations in western Pennsylvania and New York.

Mobilization meant guarding the coasts, the port, and commercial traffic to the state. The Continental Congress authorized the building of thirteen navy ships, one of which the Naval Committee assigned to New Hampshire. John Langdon, who owned a shipyard in Portsmouth, contracted to build New Hampshire's ship. So efficient was the project that the *Raleigh* resulted as the first of the thirteen to be built and put into service. (Today the building of the ship is the central symbol on New Hampshire's state flag.) Congress authorized two more ships during the war to be built in New Hampshire—the *Ranger,* which sailed under John Paul Jones, and the *America.*

The war proved a burden for many and was not borne cheerfully. Those who sent husbands or sons suffered from loss of their presence on the farm or in the shop. Numerous petitions to the legislature, for two decades after the war, asked for disability relief or reimbursement of expenses for a wide variety of wounds, losses, and general expenses. During the war and into the 1780s, everyone felt the effects of devalued currency, leading to a clamor for issuance of state paper money. Individuals pelted the legislature with demands for unpaid wages, compensation for lost time and production on farms, reimbursements for medical costs, pensions due but never received, and satisfaction of claims for disabilities from wounds and lost limbs. As late as June 1792, Thomas How, a farmer in Barrington, was seeking wages and bounty payment due for service in the Second

Regiment during 1777. His petition, one of many, refers to having returned from the "horrors of war" only to be forgotten and overlooked.

Mobilization delayed the adoption of a new state constitution. The January 1776 Plan, hailed today as the first American written constitution, was intended to be very temporary. Not until 1779 did policy makers put a proposal before the people, who then voted it down. The people then rejected another in 1781, and another in 1782, before adopting one in October of 1783 that took effect with the opening of the legislative session on 2 June 1784. Among other articles, it established a state senate of twelve popularly elected members, thus creating a true bicameral legislature. The constitution retained the Executive Council, still very active in 2005, as a form of restraint on the executive and the legislative branches.

New Hampshire was the ninth (thus the operative) state to ratify the proposed Federal Constitution on 21 June 1788. As a United States senator, John Langdon held the Bible on which Washington took his oath of office as President of the United States.

SEE ALSO *Fort William and Mary, New Hampshire; Langdon, John; New Hampshire Line; Poor, Enoch; Quebec Act; Reed, James; Stark, John; Sullivan, John; Ward, Artemas.*

BIBLIOGRAPHY

Bouton, Nathaniel, ed. "Records of the New Hampshire Committee of Safety." *Collections of the New Hampshire Historical Society* 7 (1863): 1–339.

Bouton, Nathaniel, et al., eds. *Documents and Records Relating to New Hampshire.* 40 vols. Concord and Manchester: State of New Hampshire, 1867–1940.

Daniell, Jere R. *Experiment in Republicanism: New Hampshire Politics and the American Revolution, 1741–1794.* Cambridge, Mass.: Harvard University Press, 1970.

Potter, Chandler E. *The Military History of the State of New Hampshire, 1623–1861.* 1866. Reprint, Baltimore: Genealogical Publishing, 1972.

Upton, Richard Francis. *Revolutionary New Hampshire.* 1936. Reprint, New York: Kennikat, 1970.

Wright, Robert K., Jr. *The Continental Army.* Washington, D.C.: Center for Military History, U.S. Army, 1983.

Frank C. Mevers

infantry regiments, using most of the volunteers at Boston for the first and completing the two others by new recruiting. The colonels of the regiments were John Stark (for the First New Hampshire Regiment), Enoch Poor (for the Second), and James Reed (for the Third). Nathaniel Folsom was the brigadier general. In 1776 they reenlisted respectively as the Fifth, Eighth, and Second Continental Regiments, respectively, reverting to their old state numerical designations in 1777. The Third Regiment disbanded on 1 January 1781. On 1 March 1783 the First became the New Hampshire Regiment, while the Second was reduced to the New Hampshire Battalion. Those two units were merged on 22 June 1783 as a five-company battalion and disbanded on 1 January 1784 at New Windsor, New York. In addition to the formal New Hampshire Line, the state also furnished three other infantry units to the Continental army. These were employed primarily on the northern frontier: Bedel's Regiment (which operated as rangers) in 1775–1776; Long's Regiment (1776–1777); and Whitcomb's Rangers (1776–1780).

SEE ALSO *Lexington and Concord.*

BIBLIOGRAPHY

Dearborn, Henry. *Revolutionary War Journals of Henry Dearborn 1775–1783.* Edited by Lloyd A. Brown and Howard H. Peckham. Chicago: Caxton Club, 1939.

Kidder, Frederick. *History of the First New Hampshire Regiment in the War of the Revolution.* Albany, N.Y.: Joel Munsell, 1868.

Potter, Chandler Eastman. *Military History of New Hampshire, from Its Settlement, in 1623, to the Year 1861.* 2 vols. Concord, N.H.: Adjutant General's Office, 1866–1868.

Resch, John. *Suffering Soldiers: Revolutionary War Veterans, Moral Sentiment, and Political Culture in the Early Republic.* Amherst, Mass.: University of Massachusetts Press, 1999.

Robert K. Wright Jr.

NEW HAVEN, CONNECTICUT.
5–6 July 1779. Plundered during Connecticut coast raid.

SEE ALSO *Connecticut Coast Raid.*

Mark M. Boatner

NEW HAMPSHIRE LINE.
New Hampshire mobilized volunteers to participate in the siege of Boston as soon as news arrived of the fighting at Lexington and Concord, but did not take formal action until the Provincial Congress met on 17 May 1775. Three days later it voted to form 2,000 men into a brigade of three

NEW JERSEY, MOBILIZATION IN.
In war, as in real estate, location can be everything. During the war for American Independence, location determined that New Jersey would be one of the most active—if not *the* most active—theaters of operations. Situated between the chief British garrison in New York and the de facto

rebel capital in Philadelphia, New Jersey became the contested middle ground. Between 1775 and 1783, the state witnessed some 600 large and small (mostly small) actions, including naval engagements fought on the state's rivers or off its long coastline. Military affairs became part of the state's routine. Morristown (often called the "military capital of the Revolution") emerged as a critical base area, and the main contingent of the Continental army spent more time in New Jersey than in any other the state, including the winters of 1777 (Morristown), 1778–1779 (Middlebrook), and 1779–1780 (Morristown again, the bitterest winter of the war). For soldiers and civilians alike, conflict, or the threat of conflict, was a virtual constant in most parts of the state.

Yet New Jersey was not originally a hotbed of revolutionary sentiment. In fact, through the early 1770s, most residents were generally content to remain within the empire. New Jersey was a small colony of no more than 120,000 people, and it lacked urban centers or significant commercial communities to feel the sting of British mercantilist policies. Without claims to western lands, New Jersey also remained calm in the face of the Proclamation of 1763, which curtailed settlement beyond the established colonial frontier. Nor did the colony have a redcoat garrison, the source of so much friction in Massachusetts and New York. Indeed, New Jersey had gotten along rather well with the British regulars quartered there during the French and Indian War—army payrolls and contracts were boons to the local economy. Even the Stamp Act crisis found the colonial legislature reticent to mount a protest. Although local political officials ultimately agreed to participate, they initially declined to send delegates to the Stamp Act Congress. A large Quaker population shrank from conflict with Britain; and in any case, with much of the colony's economic prosperity dependent on its larger neighbors, New York and Pennsylvania, New Jersey Patriots would have been largely powerless had the two more influential colonies not acted first.

Opponents of the British government gained traction, however, as protests broadened in the other colonies. There was considerable anger in New Jersey over British opposition to the colony's effort to issue its own currency, a measure dear to New Jersey's largely agricultural populace; and local Patriots did join the inter-colonial protests against the Tea Act. As in the other colonies, an informal Whig political infrastructure gradually supplanted or took over established local and provincial governments, and by 1775 the Whigs effectively controlled New Jersey. Still, sentiment for outright independence remained muted. While a small number of New Jersey volunteers marched north to join the rebel army besieging Boston, Patriots did not oust the royal governor, William Franklin, until June 1776. The definitive break with the empire came only in

July, when a new state constitution finally declared New Jersey independent.

It remained for New Jersey to defend its newly proclaimed independence. Until the contest ended in 1783, the state struggled to mobilize its human and material resources and to coordinate its war effort with the other rebellious states and the Continental Congress. It was never easy, as manpower was always in short supply and New Jersey lacked any significant manufacturing or financial base. But efforts to maintain the fight were sustained, and sometimes imaginative, even if results were uneven.

MILITARY STRUCTURE

New Jersey troops served in three legally distinct military organizations: the militia, which served rotating tours of duty of short duration, and which could be called out at any time in emergency situations; "state troops," raised for long-term duty within the state; and New Jersey's Continental regiments. In addition to these formal organizations, however, Jerseymen also bore arms in ad hoc, irregular outfits, in an active privateer fleet, and in Continental battalions raised under direct Congressional authority. Over the course of the war, many men saw action in several of these guises.

The formal militia structure emerged from what was left of the colonial militia (purged of Tory personnel) and units raised on private or local authority, mostly during the spring of 1775. The first militia law (June 1775) called for the enrollment of all men between the ages of 16 and 50 into companies of about eighty men each. They were to elect their company officers, who in turn elected regimental officers. Companies were based on townships, and it was not uncommon to find ten or fewer family names comprising the bulk of a militia company. Companies reported to county-based regiments. Many subsequent laws attempted to improve militia effectiveness through experiments with "minute" companies, unit boundary changes, and brigade organizations. Throughout the war, however, most militia operations were local, and regional commanders had a great deal of autonomy. Regimental efforts were of limited scale and duration, and the brigades were never effective.

Whatever its organizational limitations, the New Jersey militia became a potent force. True, it performed poorly during the early stages of the British invasion of 1776, famously evoking Commander-in-Chief George Washington's wrath. But it quickly rebounded and played a major role in the revival of Whig military fortunes in late 1776 and early 1777. While there was never the level of militia participation that Patriot leaders desired, enough men came out to keep the local troops functional. Over the course of the war, the militia made any British moves into the New Jersey interior dangerous; and the militias proved invaluable in suppressing the Tories, guarding regional crops and supplies, providing local security and intelligence, and, buttressed by Continentals, fighting in occasional large-scale actions (such as Monmouth in 1778 and Springfield in 1780). Certainly the British came to dread the incessant harassment by local rebels that occurred during operations in New Jersey; and in the end, the lack of any tight, statewide legal or command structure made little difference in militia effectiveness.

From time to time, New Jersey also raised "state troops." There were units recruited for longer-term duty than the militia—generally six or nine months—during periods of particular need or when the state was unable to persuade Continental commanders to post regulars in New Jersey. These troops took on in-state assignments, usually the guarding of sensitive coastal locations or along the northwestern frontier, and in positions across from British-occupied New York. Three artillery companies (of sixty-four men each) were raised over 1776 and 1777, while a more ambitious effort tried to field 2700 infantry between November 1776 and April 1777. Subsequent legislation kept various bodies of state troops in the field through the end of 1782, by which time every county had at least one company assigned to it. In effect, these troops were state regulars, and many of them saw considerable action in conjunction with Continental and militia forces.

However, most New Jersey troops who served as regulars did so in the Continental line. In the autumn of 1775, Congress asked New Jersey to raise two battalions, with a third requested in April 1776. These men were to serve for a year, and with enthusiasm for the cause high, the state enlisted approximately 2,000 men relatively quickly. Some companies, recruited by their company commanders and other junior officers, were filled within days. Despite supply shortages, they deployed to the northern theater of operations, where two of the regiments suffered cruelly in the debacle of the Canadian invasion. The last of these Continentals returned home by February 1777, and a core of the veterans reenlisted. However, many others, discouraged by hard service in 1776—including major losses to disease—had had enough and were lost to the Patriot effort.

New Jersey recruited a "Second Establishment" beginning in late 1776 (although enlistments did not begin in earnest until early 1777). This time, Congress asked the state for four regiments, for a total of 2,720 men of all ranks. These soldiers would be enlisted for three years or the duration (in other words, "for the war"). Of the requested number, however, the state could raise only 1,586, and only three of the regiments maintained reasonable strength levels. With the ranks thin, Congress reduced the New Jersey quota to three regiments in 1779, with an official roster of 1,566 officers and men. But the actual tally for the New Jersey Brigade (for most of the war, the regiments served as a brigade under Brigadier General William Maxwell) rarely exceeded 1,200 men. Indeed, in 1781, Congress allowed the consolidation of the New Jersey Brigade into two regiments, the total strength of which generally remained below 700 men. Jerseymen also served in regiments raised directly under Congressional authority (the "sixteen additional regiments" and artillery and other units outside of the New Jersey Brigade). But throughout the war, New Jersey Patriots complained that the manpower quotas requested of their state were simply more than the small state could field.

RECRUITING

There was some validity to such complaints, as the realities of recruiting and maintaining troop strength actually were daunting. New Jersey's human resources were too limited to maintain a large militia, the state troops, government functions, the farming economy, and Continental battalions. Of the state's 120,000 residents, probably fewer than 25,000 were men of military age. But of these, some 6,000 were Quakers and thus lost to the recruiting pool; and a conservative estimate indicates that another 3,200 were lost to the Tories, including about 1,900 Jerseymen who served as Loyalist regulars (the balance were variously organized "refugees" raiding their home state out of New York, "Pine Robbers" in southern New Jersey, or other local irregulars). The privateer fleet drained additional manpower, and the state granted exemptions to teachers, elected officials, iron workers, express riders, and various government employees. In all, at least 10,000 men were not available for any sort of military duty. The remaining manpower (probably around 14,000 individuals, not much more) had to be shared with agriculture. New Jersey's rich farms were not only vital to the state economy, but also a critical source of military food and forage (and thus hotly contested by the rival armies). Heavy calls on the state militia could be economically disruptive, and thus highly unpopular.

Thus, even as New Jersey complained about the number of men it was to levy, there still was general agreement that the use of regular troops seemed the most efficient use of the state's limited human resources. Washington, of course, as well as many other Patriots, preferred regular Continentals for practical military reasons. Regulars were enlisted for a minimum of three years, better trained and disciplined, and lacked qualms about long-term operations in distant theaters. But (no doubt to spur Continental enlistments) Washington and other senior commanders also pointed out that a stable force of regulars would reduce the necessity for many militia call-ups. New Jersey's governor, William Livingston, agreed, arguing for the "superiority" of a policy that recruited men the economy needed least as regulars—implying the poor and rootless— and leaving "the more industrious farmer" to his husbandry.

This is essentially what New Jersey tried to do as it recruited the Second Establishment. Significantly, recruiting operations changed. Formerly, officers recruited their own units. There was thus no central recruiting service to forward new men to the Continental battalions. But by late 1776, most officers could not be spared off the lines for recruiting purposes. Although Washington sent officers on this duty whenever he could, Congress asked the states to put recruiting on a firmer institutional footing. In October 1777, the New Jersey legislature designated the counties as recruiting districts, and assigned two civilian recruiting officers (although some of them may have been militia officers) to each. The law also allowed extra recruiters for locales where recruiting seemed especially promising. The effects of this system were uncertain. Continental officers still recruited Jerseymen personally when they could; and by 1780, each New Jersey battalion also assigned an officer to full-time recruiting duty in the state. The recruiting districts probably helped, but they neither replaced personal recruiting by unit commanders nor ended manpower shortages.

The fiscal aspects of recruiting were important as well. Perhaps the most expensive (and best publicized) aspects of recruiting were bounty monies. A Congressional bounty of January 1777, allowing each soldier $20, a clothing allotment, and a hundred acres after the war (for men who served for the duration), proved too little to attract enough men. Consequently, states, and even towns, offered supplemental enticements. New Jersey towns never issued bounties, but by 1778 the state was offering recruits $40, a blanket, clothing, and—if they enlisted by October 1778—a regimental coat and more clothes. In 1779, this increased to $250 above the Continental bounty. At this juncture, Washington and Congress feared dissension between veterans and new recruits enlisted under the more lucrative state bounties. The states, however, still went their own ways, and in 1780 New Jersey even increased its bounty to $1,000, with subsequent increases to adjust for inflation. Recruiting personnel also received bounties. In 1779, New Jersey gave recruiters $20 a man, a sum increased in 1780 to $200. In 1781, payments were made in specie, also to compensate for inflation. Although not mentioned in the laws, noncommissioned personnel also received bounties for signing up recruits. In addition, the state provided funds to support recruits until they reached their units, and even paid $16 per man to the muster master who swore them into the army.

Obviously, any funding shortage imperiled recruiting. Whenever it could, New Jersey turned to Congress to pay recruiting bills; but this aid was never sufficient or punctual, and the state often had to use its own resources.

In 1778 and 1781 the legislature enacted loans to cover recruiting costs. Some New Jersey Patriots became so distressed with the high costs of raising men, and so incensed with Congress for failing to reimburse the state, that they threatened to halt recruiting operations. It was an empty threat, but indicative of the strain that recruiting placed on the state.

ALTERNATIVES TO REGULAR RECRUITMENT

Even with the inducements of bounties, however, it became clear that voluntary enlistments would never fill the New Jersey Brigade. The alternative was conscription, and the idea was not new. During the French and Indian War, Quaker opposition had prevented New Jersey from drafting militiamen for long-term duty. Yet other states had; and as early as 1776, Washington had suggested that New Jersey implement a draft to meet its Continental manpower quotas. Initially, the state balked, but in April 1778, faced with a dire recruiting shortfall, the legislature acted.

The new law divided the militia regiments into "classes" of eighteen men. Upon a full regimental muster, commissioners were to explain the recruiting laws and bounties, and then allow each class ten days to present a volunteer or substitute to serve nine months in the New Jersey Brigade. If, after ten days, a class did not present a recruit, one of the men in the class would be drafted by lot, and he then had five days to report for duty, find a substitute, or pay a $300 fine. Over April and May, the militia sent hundreds of draftees and substitutes to the army in consequence of this law, and New Jersey raised more Continentals in 1778 than in any other year. This success, however, was countered by popular distaste for the draft, and the law was allowed to lapse. A draft for six months of duty, passed in 1780, was less successful; after this, New Jersey simply lived with troop shortages and a small New Jersey Brigade for the rest of the conflict.

It is worth noting that not all recruiting activity took place within the formal recruiting structure, or within established regulations. In January, 1777, Washington issued recruiting regulations calling for freemen between seventeen and fifty years old, excluding enemy deserters and Tories. New Jersey, however, was never so particular. The state immediately decided it could not rely solely on "freeman volunteers," and in April 1777, it acted on a Congressional suggestion to exempt any two militiamen from duty if they found a Continental substitute. The legislature also asked persons otherwise exempted to hire substitutes and made provisions for enlisting indentured servants. Nor did New Jersey demand only "freemen." Any "able . . . bodied and effective volunteers" were sufficient. The use of servants and other substitutes demonstrated less a commitment to a yeoman soldiery ideal than to filling the ranks with anyone available.

In fact, with scant manpower among New Jersey Patriots, the state turned a blind eye to virtually all of Washington's recruiting prohibitions. Enemy deserters appeared frequently in New Jersey ranks, especially as the war dragged on and recruiting became harder. Tories served as Continentals as well. Men accused of Loyalism frequently received a choice of punishment, including hanging, or enlisting in the New Jersey line. In one dramatic incident, the state Council of Safety condemned seventy-five Tories at Morristown and hanged two as an example to the others—who promptly joined the Continental Army. Petty criminals often received similar treatment. There is no complete documentation of the number of Tories and felons compelled into the New Jersey ranks, but available records attest to over two hundred, hardly an insignificant number given the manpower needs of the day.

Yet the mobilization effort was more successful than recruiting difficulties and the thin rosters of the New Jersey Continentals indicated. Accurate numbers are unavailable, but by the end of the conflict, something under 4,000 Jerseymen had served in Continental ranks, while another 10,000 (more or less) saw duty with the militia, state troops, or in supply or other capacities with some military organization. No doubt some men were counted more than once in these tallies (such as those militiamen who also served a tour in the New Jersey Brigade as draftees). In addition, there is evidence that men from neighboring states and even some foreigners served in New Jersey ranks. Even so, given the limited manpower pool—recalling here the losses to Quaker pacifism, loyalism, official exemptions, and other causes—the state did quite well in exploiting its human resources; in fact, it came close to using every available man.

MANPOWER: WHO SERVED?

The social profile of the New Jersey regulars reflected a recruiting effort that, as Governor Livingston put it, tried to leave farmers to their fields and put the least prosperous into the rank and file. A majority of the troops were young: more than 54 percent were twenty-two years old or younger, while over 73 percent were no more than twenty-seven. Most also came from the lowest socioeconomic strata. Of the soldiers carried on state tax rolls, fully 90 percent came from the poorest two-thirds of the population, while 61 percent came from the poorest third of taxpayers. Probably some 60 percent of the regulars owned nothing of consequence at all. In a state where 30 percent of the populace owned at least 100 acres of land, only 9 percent of the Continentals could say the same. Many of these men were poor by virtue of youth—they simply were too young to have established themselves, or to have inherited property, before enlisting. But there is no doubt that New Jersey regulars tended toward the lowest rungs of the state's economic ladder. For many of these men, the bounties of 100 acres must have seemed quite appealing.

In marked contrast to the enlisted men, New Jersey officers were well-to-do. Eighty-four percent came from the wealthiest third of society, and almost 32 percent from the upper tenth. The officer corps also held proportionately more of the largest farms than either the enlisted ranks or the general population. Indeed, just over 31 percent of the officers used slave labor on their farms. While there were some poorer officers, few (if any) advanced beyond captain. The New Jersey officers, then, represented the state's traditional social elite; and in the eighteenth century, it was normal for military elites to derive from social elites.

None of this is to argue that the enlisted New Jersey Continentals were essentially a coerced force. Far from it: they served for a variety of reasons, some with a genuine enthusiasm for the cause. Most rendered faithful service, often under appalling conditions, in a war they could have avoided. But most also left little enough behind them when they enlisted, and with only shallow roots in society, the Continental Army offered (at least at this stage of their lives) more than the civilian world.

WAR MATERIEL

New Jersey also mobilized its material resources, although beyond agriculture these were quite limited. Significantly, there was no pre-war armaments industry at all. The militia and the first Continental regiments had to rely on privately-owned weapons and munitions, supplemented by purchases from out of state. In 1776, the state initially could arm only two of its Continental regiments. Weapons shortages delayed the march of the third considerably. But maintaining even such arms as New Jersey could find was difficult, because the state lacked enough skilled gunsmiths and blacksmiths. The most prominent gunsmith was Ebenezer Cowell, whose shop in Trenton manufactured gunlocks under a contract with the Continental Congress. But the invasion of 1776 drove him out of Trenton, and he transferred is operations to Pennsylvania for the rest of the war. The events of 1776 also displaced other Patriot blacksmiths and gunsmiths, which seriously disrupted local production of war materiel. Some blacksmiths were able to produce limited numbers of bayonets, ram rods, and other accoutrements, and a trickle of gun repairs continued. Yet the number of guns and parts produced were small, and New Jersey troops were largely dependent on imported arms throughout the war.

Gunpowder was a problem as well. New Jersey had essential deposits of sulfur and saltpeter, and Patriot authorities provided incentives for production of these commodities. But the state had no powder mill. Responding to a Congressional plea, the New Jersey Provincial Congress loaned Colonel Jacob Ford Jr. the funds to construct a mill in Morristown. Ford was in production by August 1776, and the powder mill operated through at least 1779 (the records are obscure thereafter). Production was sometimes impressive—up to 750 pounds of powder per week—but the Morristown mill was the only one established in New Jersey. Consequently, the state's over-all contribution to patriot gunpowder supplies was never great. Nevertheless, at a time when American munitions manufacturing was in its infancy, and when munitions were in demand, for a vital period Morristown remained a steady source of crucial powder supply.

The only major industrial success was in iron. The state was rich in ore, and small-scale production had begun in the late colonial period. By 1775, New Jersey had seventeen furnaces producing pig iron and twenty-two forges capable of producing wrought iron—from which blacksmiths could produce tools, blades, and other implements. The furnaces also could turn out shot and, as war production geared up, cannon. During the conflict, the British destroyed or otherwise halted production at some of these facilities. In 1778, for example, royal troops wrecked important iron works at Bordentown and Mount Holly, which never went back into service. But twelve of the furnaces and seventeen forges remained safely in Patriot hands. The most productive works lay north of Morristown at Hibernia, Mount Hope, and other locations in Morris and Bergen Counties.

Iron production also faced problems. Interruptions in mining could disrupt the furnaces, and skilled labor was always at a premium. Ironmasters used anyone helpful as workers. Hessian and British deserters, and some prisoners, worked at furnaces and forges, and the state agreed to exempt skilled ironworkers from militia duty in order to assist production. Inflation and other fiscal challenges also threatened operations, but iron production managed to expand over the course of the war. In 1777 alone, the Hibernia furnace produced some 120 tons of shot for the army, and was successfully casting and boring cannons. New Jersey production—or American production generally—never made the Patriot military self-sufficient in iron weapons or munitions, but in this area, at least, a domestic industry made dramatic strides.

THE IMPACT OF MOBILIZATION AND WAR

New Jersey began to mobilize in the spring of 1775 and remained on a war footing for eight years. The duration of the war, coupled with the virtually constant military presence in the state, left a varied legacy. There was considerable physical damage. Some towns, such as Connecticut Farms and Springfield, suffered major battle damage, pillaging, and wanton destruction. Churches and public buildings along the various British lines of march suffered as well, with Presbyterian churches singled out for particular British wrath. Private homes also were targets, and hundreds of farms lost fences, livestock, and crops to pillaging or hungry soldiers in both armies. Bergen and Middlesex Counties were especially hard hit during 1776, and foraging in 1777 led to damage and theft on farms across central New Jersey. Well over 600 farms, buildings, or other private properties were plundered, damaged, or destroyed in Middlesex County alone. Despite pleas for help, there was little the financially-strapped state—New Jersey government debts totaled some $750,000—could do for these communities and individuals. Indeed, the state felt it had to raise taxes to meet its obligations, and New Jersey property owners faced some of the stiffest tax bills that any generation in the state would see down to the Civil War.

There was considerable social dislocation as well. Thousands of Tories had been driven into exile, and their estates often were seized and sold off by the state. The vast majority never returned to New Jersey. Major real estate interests, notably the East Jersey Board of Proprietors, ended the war with their business affairs in disarray. Renters had not made payments, business records were scattered or lost, and some prominent proprietors had fled with the British. Moreover, demobilization had sent most troops home only with promissory notes, and most of these men found few immediate prospects in the civilian economy. Hundreds of war widows and orphans had little access to public support, which was small enough anyway, and had only meager private resources to sustain them.

Somewhat perversely, however, agriculture prospered in the final two years of the struggle. Without any major battles, the occasional skirmishes did not prevent a flourishing if illegal trade between New Jersey farmers and the British garrison in New York City. This commerce brought welcome consumer goods as well as specie into the state, relieving some of the hardships of the war years. But a major economic downturn followed the departure of the British in 1873, and farmers, like almost everyone else, were hard pressed to pay taxes and to make ends meet. Even the iron industry suffered before resuming normal production by 1787. Merchants, hoping to develop international trade out of New Jersey ports, lacked capital and trading connections, and retreated largely into local or coastal commerce.

The distress was general across New Jersey, but the state showed considerable ingenuity in dealing with the situation. A series of fiscal measures, including paper money issued against landed security, gave the state a stable currency and allowed debtors to pay their bills with public securities. While refusing further financial support to the Congress, New Jersey did assume payment of the interest on Continental debts held by its citizens, and it implemented a special tax to pay arrears due New Jersey soldiers and military suppliers. By 1787, the state's fiscal house was generally in order, most war-related damage had been repaired, and the post-war economic slump was passing. Given New Jersey's location as a chief military theater, the impact of the war could have been much worse, and the state's problems in the so-called "critical period" were more political (especially in its relations with the larger states and the Confederation) than economic or social.

SEE ALSO *Continental Army, Draft; Livingston, William; Middle Brook, New Jersey; Monmouth, New Jersey.*

BIBLIOGRAPHY

Bill, Alfred Hoyt. *New Jersey and the Revolutionary War*. Princeton, N.J.: D. Van Nostrand, 1964.

————. *The New Jersey Soldier*. Trenton, N.J.: New Jersey Historical Commission, 1976.

————. "The Social Structure of the New Jersey Brigade: The Continental Line as an American Standing Army." In *The Military in America: From the Colonial era to the Present*. Edited by Peter Karsten. New York: The Free Press, 1980.

————. "The Cockpit Reconsidered: Revolutionary New Jersey as a Military Theater." In *New Jersey in the American Revolution*, edited by Barbara J. Mitnick. New Brunswick, N.J.: Rivergate Books, Rutgers University Press, 2005.

Lundin, Leonard. *Cockpit of the Revolution: The War for Independence in New Jersey*. Princeton, N.J.: Princeton University Press, 1940.

McCormick, Richard P. *New Jersey from Colony to State, 1609–1789*. Newark, N.J.: New Jersey Historical Society, 1981.

Munn, David G., compiler. *Battles and Skirmishes of the American Revolution in New Jersey*. Trenton, N.J.: Department of Environmental Protect, Bureau of Geology and Topography, 1976.

Salay, David L. "The Production of War Material in New Jersey during the Revolution." In *New Jersey in the American Revolution, III*. Edited by William C. Wright. Trenton, N.J.: New Jersey Historical Commission, 1976.

Mark Edward Lender

NEW JERSEY BRIGADE.

Early in the war, training and unit cohesiveness was difficult for many Continental brigades, there being no comprehensive program in place for a uniform system of tactical formations and field maneuver. This matter, therefore, was left to individual division or brigade commanders. Added to this was the matter of brigade subunits' detached service and the absorption of troops from disbanded units. Despite recruiting shortfalls and desertion, some continuity was achieved at the company and regimental level, with a core of veteran soldiers remaining, many of whom served side by side with the same comrades and officers for the entire war. This leavening of old soldiers was important. In New Jersey, for example, the brigade's composite regiments were augmented by short-term drafts and volunteers in 1778 and 1780, or as companies swelled with soldiers from the disbanded Jersey regiments from 1779 onwards. The advent of Major General Wilhelm Friedrich von Steuben's uniform system of maneuver in 1778 (published in spring 1779) further alleviated the problem of attaining and maintaining cohesive tactical units.

The New Jersey Brigade, originally comprising the First through Fourth Regiments, first served as such beginning in May 1777, and until 1780 was commanded by Brigadier General William Maxwell. Following the 1776 campaign, when three regiments served their single-year enlistment in Canada and New York, four New Jersey regiments were authorized in 1777, all the men signing on for three years or the war's duration. Two others, Forman's and Spencer's Additional Regiments, recruited all or a portion of their men in New Jersey, the latter's unofficial title being the Fifth, later the Fourth, New Jersey. In 1779 Forman's regiment was absorbed by Spencer's, that unit serving with the Jersey Brigade beginning in 1779 until its men were dispersed among the two remaining Jersey regiments in January 1781. As the conflict went on, the numbered Jersey regiments were reduced: in 1779 to three regiments; in 1781 to two; and in the war's final year, one regiment and one battalion.

The brigade served together at the Battles of Short Hills, Brandywine, Germantown, Monmouth, Connecticut Farms, Springfield, and Yorktown and in Major John Sullivan's expedition in 1779 against the Iroquois. The First and Third Regiments fought at Staten Island in August 1777, while the New Jersey Light Companies served with the Marquis de Lafayette's Light Division in 1780 and went with Lafayette to Virginia in the spring and summer of 1781.

BIBLIOGRAPHY

Rees, John U. "'I Expect to be Stationed in Jersey Sometime . . .': An Account of the Services of the Second New Jersey Regiment: December 1777 to June 1778." Unpublished MSS. David Library of the American Revolution, Washington Crossing, Pa.

————. "'One of the Best in the Army': An Overview of the 2nd New Jersey Regiment and General William Maxwell's Jersey Brigade." *Continental Soldier* 11, 2 (Spring 1998): 45–53. Also available online at http://revwar75.com/library/rees/njbrigade.htm

John U. Rees

NEW JERSEY CAMPAIGN.

November 1776–January 1777. After the Battle of White Plains on 28 October 1776, Washington set up three principal concentrations of forces to enable him to block British efforts in case Sir William Howe tried to move east, north, or southwest. Washington would keep one large part of the army (7,000) in New Jersey, using Fort Lee as his base; Major General Charles Lee would keep a similar force (7,000 of the best troops) in Westchester County to block an advance into New England; and Major General William Heath would use the smallest of the pieces (4,000) to protect the Hudson Highlands forts and lines of communications between Washington and Lee. A small force remained on the northern tip of Manhattan, but it was to be withdrawn to New Jersey.

The balance of that plan collapsed when Howe suddenly shifted his troops and captured Fort Washington, New York, on 16 November 1776 and Fort Lee, New Jersey, on the 18th. Washington was forced to retreat to Newark, opening a gap between his troops and the other contingents. As the British maintained pursuit and forced him to keep falling back, the chances of being able to use the coordinated action upon which the original disposition depended gradually evaporated.

As early as 10 November, after the Battle of White Plains and before loss of the Hudson River forts, Washington had written Lee: "If the enemy should remove the whole, or the greatest part of their force, to the west side of Hudson river, I have no doubt of your following with all possible dispatch, leaving the militia and invalids to cover the frontiers of Connecticut in case of need." On 20 November, Washington suggested that Lee cross the river and there await further orders. The next day Washington reiterated that Lee should make this move, unless "some new event should occur, or some more cogent reason present itself." Lee's inaction has led to speculations that he was deliberately jeopardizing the American cause by allowing the British to defeat the forces under Washington's personal command so that Congress would make him commander in chief, but there is no proof to support this charge. Lee had not received a specific order, and he still thought that his force would be more effective east of the Hudson. Instead of going himself, he tried to order Heath to send two thousand of his garrison to Washington, arguing that Heath was closer and could get reinforcements to Washington sooner. Heath, however, had direct orders from Washington not to weaken his defenses of the strategic river crossings under any circumstances, and so he refused Lee.

Howe did not move against Heath and clear the lower Hudson because the onset of winter would limit naval support and make it too hard to retain any gains; the notion of cooperating with British forces from Canada had not been part of anyone's plans for the year. He also saw no value in trying to invade New England because the region was too strongly behind the Revolution; the plan for the year had called for isolating it and slowly wearing down the will to resist by bringing the other colonies back into the fold. Nor did Howe see any realistic chance to move against Philadelphia with his entire force, knowing that he still had to consolidate his hold on New York and its environs and that it was too late in the year to risk the long overland movement that would be involved. Instead, he began preparations to go into winter quarters.

The Royal Navy did not consider New York to be a suitable port in cold weather, an opinion that modern Americans find extremely hard to understand. Admiral Richard Howe and his captains felt that Newport, Rhode Island, was a far better winter anchorage, and William Howe agreed to get it for them. General Henry Clinton left New York with six thousand troops on 1 December and sailed through Long Island Sound, landing and securing Newport on the 7th without any casualties.

WASHINGTON RETREATS

As part of his plan to establish winter quarters, Howe wanted to gain space and access to forage by placing part of the British forces in New Jersey. He sent Cornwallis from Fort Lee with instructions to push Washington beyond Brunswick; Cornwallis boasted that he would catch Washington as a hunter bags a fox. Washington started his withdrawal on 21 November to avoid being trapped east of the Passaic River and reached Newark on the 22nd. There he paused and regrouped by sending the sick to safety at Morristown and detaching other troops to stamp out the first hints of a Loyalist uprising near Monmouth; other officers were sent to assemble all the boats on the Delaware River. Meanwhile, Congress searched the Philadelphia area for additional forces to send to his aid, mobilizing three battalions of the city's Associator infantry under Colonel Lambert Cadwalader and Captain Samuel Morris's City Troop of light horse and giving orders to Captain Thomas Forrest's company of full-time state artillery to go with them. Washington withdrew from Newark on the 28th in two columns, keeping ahead of the British vanguard. The Americans followed two different routes to Brunswick, and from there they crossed the Raritan River just ahead of the jägers leading Cornwallis's advance. The pursuit had failed to catch Washington, and now Cornwallis's exhausted men had to stop and rest.

On 1 December the enlistments of the Flying Camp's militia regiments officially expired and most of the remaining members headed home, further reducing Washington's effectives. That same day the British began pushing across the Raritan but were held at bay by an aggressive rear guard that included Captain Alexander

Hamilton's company of New York artillery. On the 2nd, Washington reached Princeton and directed Brigadier General William Alexander (Lord Stirling) to remain with his and Brigadier General Adam Stephen's brigades (fourteen hundred men from Virginia and Delaware). Their mission was to buy time for the rest of the army to cross over the Delaware River to safety on the Pennsylvania side. While men and supplies ferried across using the boats assembled earlier, Washington started reinforcing Stirling's group. On the 6th, however, Howe joined Cornwallis at Brunswick with several more brigades of British and Hesse-Cassel regulars and then advanced to Princeton the next day. Stirling did not engage, but fell slowly back as ordered, and by the end of the afternoon of the 7th, most of the men had safely crossed using Beatty's ferry and the Trenton ferry. The rear guard crossed early on the 8th, just as the leading British patrols entered Trenton. Cornwallis wasted a day unsuccessfully searching for boats to use in getting his troops across.

For his part, Washington deployed his men along a twenty-five-mile front and began moving supplies forward from Philadelphia to refit the exhausted regiments. The right was opposite Burlington, New Jersey, and the center rested near the Pennsylvania side of McKonkey's Ferry (the New Jersey end later became Taylorsville). Having missed his fox, Cornwallis got permission to stop at the Delaware, and he began to establish winter garrisons in New Jersey. On 13 December, the day Lee was captured at Basking Ridge, Howe announced that the year's campaign had ended. The preceding day Congress had resolved to move from Philadelphia to Baltimore. Howe believed the campaign had come to an end. While older authors (depending heavily on allegations made by disgruntled Loyalists after the war) have accused Howe of being lazy or of "pulling his punches" in order to try to find a way to end the war through negotiations, the simple fact is that he had accomplished as much as the weak British logistical system would allow. He and Clinton had favored contracting the occupied zone to a line between Brunswick and Newark, but Cornwallis persuaded him to hold a greater area. Howe established forward garrisons at Bordentown, Pennington, and Trenton, with a larger base twenty-five miles to the rear at Brunswick. The rationale for this expanded area was that every square mile held encouraged Loyalist support and deprived Washington of recruits; the British felt there were only minimal risks to the more extended lines of communications.

WASHINGTON STRIKES BACK

Washington was not as badly off as American mythology depicts. The retreat through New Jersey had been executed with precision, exploiting the superior land mobility of the American forces to carefully stay out of range of the British. Detachments assembled in the hills to the west of the British supply lines during the withdrawal, creating a potential for future attacks on rear areas. Washington's defensive positions along the bend of the Delaware River provided access to the logistical support of the depots in Philadelphia. And during the month of December, reinforcements began arriving. Militia detachments came from New Jersey; Colonel John Cadwalader came up with one thousand Philadelphia Associators; several new Continental regiments came up from recruiting areas, including the German Battalion that Congress released from garrison duty in Philadelphia; and veteran troops from other commands in the north worked their way around the British. On the 20th, Sullivan (who took command when Lee was captured) joined with two thousand of the men originally left on the east side of the Hudson, and Brigadier General Benedict Arnold was a day's march behind with seven more regiments from the Lake Champlain front. Also on the 20th, Brigadier General Alexander McDougall reached Morristown with three regiments of Continentals from Heath's forces to reinforce seven hundred New Jersey militia. Washington sent Brigadier General William Maxwell, a native of the area, to take command and begin harassing British supply trains. And Thomas Paine's first number of *The Crisis* was beginning to have a major impact on military and civilian morale.

By Christmas, Washington had some seven thousand officers and men under his immediate command capable of offensive action. More militia, stiffened by another brigade of Continentals, guarded positions further downstream but still close enough to cooperate. Washington also knew that the enlistments of many of the Continentals would expire on 31 December, and his officers began making passionate appeals for them to volunteer to stay another six weeks until the new recruits could arrive. But Washington wanted to use the veterans before year's end while he knew they would be available, and so he issued orders for a blow against the scattered British garrisons. On Christmas night his main force crossed the ice-choked Delaware and defeated the Hessians at Trenton, New Jersey, on 26 December 1776.

When the last of the Americans returned to the Pennsylvania side of the Delaware at daylight on 27 December, Washington watched the British reaction. The Bordentown garrison (another Hesse-Cassel brigade) immediately fell back to Princeton, policing up the Trenton survivors on the way. Cadwalader crossed back over to the east bank at midday and began probing towards Burlington to develop better intelligence. He reached Burlington that night and started receiving additional militia coming up from Philadelphia. As intelligence started to flow, Washington began to contemplate another offensive blow—this time a spoiling attack.

Battle of Princeton (1786). *This painting by William Mercer is a dramatic illustration of the battle between troops led by Washington and Cornwallis in Princeton, New Jersey, on 3 January 1777.* © **ATWATER KENT MUSEUM OF PHILADELPHIA/BRIDGEMAN ART LIBRARY**

THE PRINCETON CAMPAIGN BEGINS

On 30 December, Washington—having regrouped, received new supplies, and moved the prisoners to the rear—started back across the Delaware. The Americans reoccupied Trenton and sent patrols forward. The next evening copies of the congressional resolutions that granted Washington dictatorial powers reached Trenton. Although his numbers had been somewhat reduced by expired enlistments and detachments left in Pennsylvania, Washington still had over six thousand men available, thanks to the two thousand militia reinforcements. He also knew that the British had moved more troops into New Jersey and had them on the way to Princeton. When those forces arrived he would be outnumbered by several thousand. So he ordered Cadwalader and Mifflin to join him with their militia forces. He also sent a covering force to delay the expected enemy approach from Princeton.

This covering force was made up of the riflemen from Colonel Edward Hand's First Continental Regiment, Colonel Nicholas Haussegger's German Battalion, and Colonel Charles Scott with the Fourth, Fifth, and Sixth Virginia Regiments, reinforced by the six cannon of

Forrest's artillery company. On 1 January they were in position along Five Mile Run (later Little Shabbakunk Creek), and on the next day, while Cadwalader's units were still arriving at Trenton, the British appeared on the road from Princeton. Brigadier General Matthias de Roche-Fermoy, the American commander, inexplicably left the advanced position for Trenton, but Hand took over and conducted the delaying action with great skill. Five times the Americans caught the approaching column and forced the enemy to deploy, taking advantage of every creek and defile. Sometimes it was only fire from pickets, other times it was a more substantial blocking party, as at Five Mile Run and Big Shabbakunk Creek. Each time Cornwallis's men had to deploy for a coordinated attack, wasting valuable daylight. Hand then dropped back in good order and with few casualties. Half a mile north of Trenton at Stockton Hollow, the Americans made another stand, this time from woods behind a ravine. Once again the British had to deploy from column into line in the slush of open fields, where they were particularly vulnerable to Hand's riflemen and Forrest's guns, and to bring up artillery. The covering force, supported by other troops, then continued its delaying action through the town at about 4 P.M. and finally reached the main line Washington had set up south of Assunpink Creek. At about sunset, Cornwallis's larger force faced some sixty-eight hundred men in a very strong defensive position, and in the twilight—around 4:45–5:00 P.M.—he launched a series of probing attacks on the various fords. The Americans held firm and shattered a series of attempts by Hessian grenadiers and British infantry to storm the bridge. Washington had achieved his vitally important purpose of delaying a coordinated attack on his main position during daylight, and in this Second Battle of Trenton probably inflicted 365 casualties at relatively small cost. The American units conducted themselves well, and Washington's defensive battle was brilliantly managed.

However, the Americans were in a bad spot: they were outnumbered; vulnerable to being enveloped or pounded by artillery on 3 January; and lacked the boats to fall back across the Delaware. Thanks to the Americans' domination of the reconnaissance–counter-reconnaissance contest, Washington knew that another course of action was open. It was risky and unorthodox, but it caught Cornwallis flat-footed. Patrols had determined that the back roads were open and that Princeton and Brunswick in the British rear were vulnerable. Leaving his campfires burning, Washington slipped out of his positions during the night to execute the brilliant strategic envelopment that led to the Battle of Princeton on 3 January.

The American army then went into winter quarters at Morristown, New Jersey. On 4–6 January, other American contingents attacked patrols near Springfield, and the confused British evacuated Elizabethtown.

SIGNIFICANCE

In a whirlwind campaign that Frederick the Great at the time called a masterpiece and that the historian Howard H. Peckham has called "The Nine Days' Wonder," Washington had driven Howe from all his posts in New Jersey except Amboy and Brunswick. Although five thousand British remained in each of the latter places, they presented no strategic threat. American morale bounded upwards; New Jersey Loyalists who had revealed themselves had to flee. The time and space bought by a cadre of veteran Continentals and their supporting militia enabled the new, larger Continental army of 1777 to recruit and come forward.

Howe's failures in this campaign resulted from an understandable overconfidence based on the earlier success in taking New York. He might have shown more caution had he considered the strong fights put up by various Continental formations on Long Island, Harlem Heights, and Pell's Point, but that is more apparent in hindsight than it was in December 1776. Conventional

thinking by the winter garrison commander, especially Colonel Rall, gave Washington his opening, and the Virginian took full advantage of it. Cornwallis, an aggressive commander, reacted as he often would during this war by trying to force a decisive action on a more mobile opponent, ignoring critical logistics. During the spring the "forage war" in New Jersey would gradually convince Howe that an overland move against Philadelphia in 1777 simply was not feasible.

SEE ALSO *Associators; Basking Ridge, New Jersey; Fort Lee, New Jersey; Fort Washington, New York; Morristown Winter Quarters, New Jersey (6 January–28 May, 1777); Princeton, New Jersey; Trenton, New Jersey; Washington's "Dictatorial Powers"; White Plains, New York.*

BIBLIOGRAPHY

Bill, Alfred H. *The Campaign of Princeton, 1776–1777.* Princeton, N.J.: Princeton University Press, 1948.

Dwyer, William H. *The Day Is Ours! November 1776–January 1777: An Inside View of the Battles of Trenton and Princeton.* New York: Viking, 1983.

Fischer, David Hackett. *Washington's Crossing.* New York: Oxford University Press, 2004.

Ketchum, Richard M. *The Winter Soldiers.* New York: Doubleday, 1973.

Lefkowitz, Arthur S. *The Long Retreat: The Calamitous American Defense of New Jersey, 1776.* New Brunswick, N.J.: Rutgers University Press, 1998.

Smith, Samuel S. *The Battle of Trenton.* Monmouth Beach, N.J.: Philip Freneau Press, 1965.

————. *The Battle of Princeton.* Monmouth Beach, N.J.: Philip Freneau Press, 1967.

Stryker, William S. *The Battles of Trenton and Princeton.* Boston: Houghton, Mifflin, 1898.

revised by Robert K. Wright Jr.

NEW JERSEY LINE.

New Jersey was one of the states which raised its line in response to a request from the Continental Congress. On 9 October 1775 the Congress asked for two regiments, which the New Jersey Provincial Congress agreed to organize on the 26th of that month. These were the First New Jersey Regiment, raised in East Jersey (the northeastern part of the colony), and the Second, raised in West Jersey. On 8 January 1776 Congress directed the Second Regiment to move as soon as possible to support the invasion of Canada, and two days later approved raising a third regiment. During February the First Regiment started deploying to New York City, and the Third followed as soon as it was formed. Both later moved up to the Northern

Department. In 1777 the Congress increased the state's quota to four regiments by reenlisting the three existing ones and forming one more. Declining manpower led to the disbanding of the Fourth New Jersey Regiment on 7 February 1779, incorporating its members into the remaining three to bring them up to strength. In 1781 the quota again dropped, calling for two regiments that were formed using the same process. Finally, on 1 March 1783, the First Regiment became the New Jersey Regiment, and the Second Regiment shrank to become the four-company New Jersey Battalion. Both units were furloughed on 6 June of that year and were formally disbanded on 15 November 1783. One other infantry regiment was recruited primarily in New Jersey in 1777. This was Spencer's Additional Continental Regiment, which was often called the Fifth New Jersey Regiment, particularly after absorbing New Jersey men from Forman's and Malcolm's Additional Regiments in 1779), but it was never part of the New Jersey Line. The state also furnished several artillery companies and a company of light dragoons to the Continental army.

SEE ALSO *Spencer's Regiment.*

BIBLIOGRAPHY

Gerlach, Larry R., ed. *New Jersey in the American Revolution, 1763–1783: A Documentary History.* Trenton, N.J.: New Jersey Historical Commission, 1975.

Gilman, Charles Malcom B. *The Story of the Jersey Blues.* Red Bank, N.J.: Arlington Laboratory for Clinical and Historical Research, 1962.

Leiby, Adrian C. *The Revolutionary War in the Hackensack Valley: The Jersey Dutch and the Neutral Ground.* New Brunswick, N.J.: Rutgers University Press, 1962.

Lender, Mark Edward. *The New Jersey Soldier.* Trenton: New Jersey Historical Commission, 1975.

Stryker, William S. *General Maxwell's Brigade of the New Jersey Continental Line in the Expedition Against the Indians, in the Year 1779.* Trenton, N.J.: W. S. Sharp Printing Co., 1885.

———, comp. *Official Register of the Officers and Men of New Jersey in the Revolutionary War, Compiled under Orders of His Excellency Theodore F. Randolph, Governor, by William S. Stryker, Adjutant General.* 1872; Repr. Baltimore, Md.: Genealogical Publishing Co., 1967.

Robert K. Wright Jr.

NEW JERSEY VOLUNTEERS.

Cortlandt Skinner, the last royal attorney general of New Jersey, was commissioned a brigadier general of Provincial forces on 4 September 1776, authorized to raise a brigade of six battalions from among the numerous New Jersey Loyalists already organized and organizing to fight the rebels.

Although none of the battalions reached its authorized strength of five hundred men each, the New Jersey Volunteers was the largest single Provincial unit raised during the war.

The First and Second Battalions were part of the force that chased Washington as he retreated from Fort Lee, New Jersey, in December 1776, and were successful in raising recruits, especially in Monmouth County. Headquartered at New Brunswick, New Jersey, after Washington's victories at Trenton (26 December 1776) and Princeton (3 January 1777), they retired to Staten Island when William Howe withdrew his forces from New Jersey in June 1777 as a prelude to the Philadelphia campaign. The Second Battalion was converted to artillery on 30 April 1777, accompanied Howe to Philadelphia, fought at Monmouth (28 June 1778), was reconverted to infantry in November 1779, sent into garrison at Lloyd's Neck and Sandy Hook, and disbanded in June 1781.

The five other battalions continued to mount forays into New Jersey from their base on Staten Island, and although initially surprised by rebel Major General John Sullivan's counterraid on 22 August 1777, they managed to defeat the raiders, the Fourth Battalion distinguishing itself in action against the New Jersey Continentals. The number of battalions was reduced to four on 25 April 1778, when the Fifth merged with the First and the Sixth merged with the Third. In late November 1778, the Third Battalion was sent south as part of Lieutenant Colonel Archibald Campbell's expedition to capture Savannah, Georgia (29 December 1778), beginning a long association with the First Battalion of Delancey's Brigade. It extended through the defense of Savannah against Franco-American attack (9 October 1779) and the defense of Ninety Six, South Carolina (May–June 1781), against Nathanael Greene, culminating at the hard-fought battle of Eutaw Springs (8 September 1781), where the Third Battalion suffered 40 percent of its strength killed, wounded, and missing. (It returned to New York in January 1783, after the evacuation of Charleston). The battalions also contributed drafts to two temporary units raised from among the Provincial regiments for service in the south: Major Patrick Ferguson's corps, American Volunteers, that was captured at Kings Mountain (7 October 1780), and the Provincial Light Infantry Battalion that operated in the South from December 1780 until its last battle, at Eutaw Springs.

Back north, a detachment of the Fourth Battalion helped defend Paulus Hook against Henry Lee on 19 August 1779, and the First and Fourth Battalions participated in Baron von Knyphausen's raid on Springfield, New Jersey, during June 1780. The Fourth (renumbered the Third after the disbanding of the Second Battalion) was part of Benedict Arnold's force that raided New London, Connecticut, on 6 September 1781. The two battalions were together at Newtown, Long Island, by the summer of 1782 and—joined by the Third (by then the Second) Battalion from Charleston—sailed on 3 September 1783 from New York for New Brunswick, where they were disbanded on 10 October.

Cortland Skinner rarely led his brigade on active operations. Most of his time was spent coordinating the gathering of intelligence in New Jersey from his base on Staten Island.

SEE ALSO *Eutaw Springs, South Carolina; Georgia, Mobilization in; New London Raid, Connecticut; Paulus Hook, New Jersey; Savannah, Georgia (29 December 1778); Savannah, Georgia (9 October 1779); Skinner, Cortlandt; Springfield, New Jersey, Raid of Knyphausen.*

BIBLIOGRAPHY

Cole, Nan, and Todd Braisted. "The On-Line Institute for Advanced Loyalist Studies." Available online at http://www.royalprovincial.com.

revised by Harold E. Selesky

NEW LONDON RAID, CONNECTICUT.

6 September 1781. As a diversion to draw strength from the allied army marching south for the Yorktown Campaign, Benedict Arnold proposed another amphibious raid on the Connecticut coast. New London became the target because it was the state's most active port, held important stores, and was in easy striking distance (135 miles). In addition, Arnold knew it well because he had been born and raised nearby. The town was on the west bank of the Thames River and about three miles from its mouth. A mile below New London and on the same side of the river was a small work called Fort Trumbull; oriented for protection of the harbor and virtually defenseless from the land side, it was occupied by twenty-four state troops under Captain Adam Shapley. Across the river was Fort Griswold (on Groton Heights), a more substantial square fortification with stone walls, fraised ditch, and outworks. Lieutenant Colonel William Ledyard commanded here with a 140-man garrison drawn from the local militia.

Arnold intended a night attack, but the adverse wind held him offshore until 9 A.M. on 6 September. He landed at 10 A.M. on the west bank with the Thirty-eighth Foot, two Loyalist regiments (the Loyal Americans and the American Legion), a detachment of jägers, and some guns. Major Edmund Eyre landed on the other side of the river with the Fortieth and Fifty-fourth Foot, the Third Battalion of New Jersey Volunteers, a jäger detachment, and artillery.

Captain Millett was detached from Arnold's column with four companies of the Thirty-eighth (subsequently joined by Captain Frink's Loyalist company) to take Fort Trumbull. Captain Shapley delivered one volley of grape and musketry, spiked his eight guns, and crossed to reinforce Ledyard at Fort Griswold. Arnold pushed on to New London, sweeping aside minor resistance at "Fort Nonsense" and a couple of points along the road. In New London local Loyalists helped carry out the destruction of public buildings and storehouses, but damage spread to private property as well. After the war an investigation estimated the value at almost a half-million dollars, including a significant number of dwellings that had not been legitimate military targets. About a dozen ships were destroyed, but fifteen escaped up the river. Patriot propagandists accused Arnold of viewing the scene with the satisfaction of a Nero, but he claimed his men made every effort to put out the fires that started accidentally.

Fort Griswold, meanwhile, put up fierce resistance for forty minutes and threw back several attacks. Eyre fell mortally wounded in the first assault, and Major Montgomery was killed as he mounted the parapet. As the British finally overran the fort, Ledyard attempted to surrender, but was stabbed with his own sword and then bayoneted to death.

Governor Trumbull reported American losses at Fort Griswold as 70 to 80 killed, all but 3 of them after the surrender. Arnold reported that he found 85 dead and 60 wounded, most of them mortally, in the fort. He also stated that he took 70 prisoners, not including seriously wounded who were left behind on parole. Total American losses (including those on the west bank) were about 240. Arnold admitted his own casualties as 48 men killed and 145 wounded, which testifies to the stubborn defense of Fort Griswold.

This was the last large action in the North during the Revolution. It contributed nothing to the British war effort, and it further blackened Arnold's name—although the evidence does not support propagandists' allegations that he deliberately carried out an atrocity.

SEE ALSO *Fraise; Propaganda in the American Revolution.*

BIBLIOGRAPHY

The Battle of Groton Heights: A Collection of Narratives, Official Reports, Records, etc., of the Storming of Fort Griswold. Introduction and notes by William W. Harris. Revised and enlarged by Charles Allyn. 1882. Mystic, Conn.: Seaport Autographs, 1999.

Powell, Walter L. *Murder or Mayhem? Benedict Arnold's New London, Connecticut Raid, 1781.* Gettysburg, Penn.: Thomas Publications, 2000.

revised by Robert K. Wright Jr.

NEW ORLEANS. A source of Spanish military aid. When the British naval blockade cut off normal routes of American supply from Europe, the colonists turned to Spanish New Orleans as well as the Dutch and French West Indies. Although the Spanish were careful to avoid war with Great Britain, they had much to gain by furnishing supplies to the rebels, not the least of which was the weakening of their British competitor. Oliver Pollock was invaluable as the intermediary between American agents and the Spanish authorities starting in 1776, and the rebels were able to purchase weapons, ammunition, blankets, and such critical medical supplies as quinine. These supplies were moved up the Mississippi under the Spanish flag, which got them safely past British posts above New Orleans. Under the governorship of Bernardo de Gálvez, who succeeded Luis de Unzaga in 1777, the support became even more significant. Spanish supplies sent by Gálvez made George Rogers Clark's campaign in the Northwest possible. French entry into the war opened the Atlantic routes of supply in 1778, and the Spanish alliance in 1779 eliminated the need for secrecy in the river trade, which by then had diminished in importance.

SEE ALSO *Pollock, Oliver.*

revised by Michael Bellesiles

NEWPORT, RHODE ISLAND. September 1777. An amphibious operation from Tiverton, Massachusetts, against the British position on the island of Rhode Island was cancelled at the last minute when Major General Joseph Spencer learned that his plan had been compromised.

SEE ALSO *Spencer, Joseph.*

revised by Harold E. Selesky

NEWPORT, RHODE ISLAND. 29 July–31 August 1778. Franco-American failure. In December 1776 General Sir Henry Clinton was sent from New York to occupy Newport, which the Royal Navy considered a superior winter anchorage to New York. By the summer of 1778 the British had already survived two American efforts to oust them and had developed a significant network of defensive fortifications. In June 1778 the 3,000-man garrison under Major General Robert Pigot included four Hesse-Cassel regiments, three British regiments, and one Loyalist regiment, along with a detachment of artillery. On 15 July, following

the evacuation of Philadelphia, a reinforcement convoy landed an additional 2,000 men, including one British regiment, two Anspach-Bayreuth regiments, and another Loyalist regiment. Meanwhile the Americans had begun massing an assault force at Providence under Major General John Sullivan. These troops included about a thousand Continentals and a variety of militia and state troops that had been maintaining a loose cordon. When it became apparent that the task force of Admiral Charles comte d'Estaing could not participate in an attack on New York because of British ships stationed inside Sandy Hook, Congress proposed an attack on Pigot at Newport.

In preparation for a combined operation that held such promise Washington called on the New England states to mobilize 5,000 New England men. He also sent Sullivan the veteran Continental brigades of James Varnum and John Glover and two additional major generals with special backgrounds: the Frenchman the Marquis de Lafayette and Nathanael Greene, a Rhode Island native. Although it took a long time to assemble the militia and volunteers, they eventually gave Sullivan an army of about 10,000 by early August. In accordance with Washington's instructions to provide stiffening to the volunteers, he mixed the militia and Continental units to organize two divisions, one under Greene and the other under Lafayette. D'Estaing had an impressive fleet and several thousand troops serving as ships' garrisons that he could put ashore for land operations.

The French fleet reached Rhode Island (Point Judith) on 29 July and established contact with the American army. Despite the tone of exaggerated compliment to Sullivan in d'Estaing's early communications, there was friction between the two allied leaders from the start. And unlike the situation with Lieutenant General comte de Rochambeau's later expedition, the two forces this time had no appreciation for each other and no common tactical doctrine. D'Estaing had expected everything to be ready when he appeared and was not impressed by Sullivan's preparations: "We found that the troops were still at home," d'Estaing wrote in his report of 5 November (quoted in Dearden, *Rhode Island Campaign*, p. 48). He mistook Varnum's and Glover's Continental brigades for militia and complained that the Americans did not have water and provisions ready for his ships when they arrived.

While Sullivan collected the boats needed to move the troops from the mainland the French started isolating the British. On 30 July two frigates and a brigantine moved into the East Passage, and the Royal Navy's crews had to destroy the sloop of war *Kingsfisher* and the galleys *Alarm* and *Spitfire* to prevent their capture. On 5 August three ships of the line in the West Passage moved around the northern tip of Conanicut Island and caught another portion of the British garrison's squadron by surprise, forcing the crews to destroy the frigates *Cerberus, Juno,*

Orpheus, and *Lark* and the galley *Pigot.* Other vessels were scuttled over a period of days to form underwater obstructions blocking approaches to the Newport harbor. The grounded sailors now took up positions manning defensive batteries in the British lines.

Despite misgivings, d'Estaing agreed to Sullivan's concept of operations. On 8 August his ships would enter the Middle Passage, running past the British defenses. The next night (9–10 August) Sullivan's troops would cross from Tiverton to the northeast tip of Rhode Island and prepare to attack south. Early on 10 August the French were to land as many men as possible on the west side of the island, opposite the Americans, and bombard the enemy fortifications from the water; the combined ground forces would then assault. The French moved up the Middle Passage according to plan on 8 August, forcing the British to scuttle their last two warships, the frigate *Flora* and the sloop *Falcon,* and destroy the last of the transports.

Then the trouble started. Shortly after dark Pigot withdrew his units on the north end of the island and concentrated all 6,700 men at the main defensive lines. In the morning of 9 August Sullivan wrote to d'Estaing confirming the plan to carry out the invasion as planned on 10 August. But at 8 A.M. Sullivan confirmed reports from British deserters and realized that Pigot had fallen back, so he immediately crossed over to occupy the northern works before the enemy could return. When d'Estaing learned of the landing, only an hour after he had received the earlier message, many of the French officers were offended by what they interpreted to be a breach of military etiquette—the Americans landing ahead of the French, and without prior notification. In spite of this, d'Estaing began preparing to land his own troops when about noon a large fleet was detected offshore.

At 3 P.M. a scouting frigate confirmed that the ships were those of Howe's fleet from New York. Admiral d'Estaing now had to make a decision: continue on with the invasion as planned, or stand out to sea with his warships to deal with the new problem. Given the size advantage of his force, he could easily have duplicated Howe's earlier feat at Sandy Hook and denied the British any chance to come to Pigot's aid.

NAVAL ACTION OFF NEWPORT, 10–12 AUGUST 1778

Since the standoff at Sandy Hook, Admiral Lord Richard Howe had received two additional ships of the line (one from the squadron under Admiral John Byron sent out from England to offset d'Estaing) and two fifty-gun ships. Howe was bothered by adverse winds, but finally sailed from Sandy Hook on 6 August with a squadron of seven ships of the line, five fifties (which could be pressed into fighting in the line), seven frigates, two bomb ketches, three smaller warships, and four galleys; the Twenty-third Foot (Royal Welch Fusiliers) embarked to augment his marines. On 9 August, while Howe anchored off Point Judith, the southerly wind held the French in position, but during the night it shifted to the north. About 8:00 A.M. on 10 August, d'Estaing stood out to sea to give battle with a squadron of eleven ships of the line, one fifty, and four frigates. When Howe detected this movement he detached one of his frigates to escort the smaller craft back to New York and took the main body (including the fireships) out to sea. Knowing that he was outnumbered, and more importantly that he was outgunned (both in numbers and in size) by the larger French ships, he retreated to the south.

For the rest of that day and the next Howe maneuvered, trying to gain the weather gauge, which was the only condition under which he could even think about engaging in line of battle That night the weather deteriorated, and heavy seas and gale-force winds scattered both fleets and inflicted considerable damage before blowing out on 13 August. Howe was left with one fifty, four frigates, and an armed ship still sailing in company; the rest were limping back to Sandy Hook for repairs. However, as the day ended two of the other British fifties—*Renown* and *Preston*—fell in with two of the large but badly damaged French ships of the line. The eighty-gun flagship *Languedoc* had lost all of her masts in the storm and was virtually defenseless; the seventy-four-gun *Marseillois* had only one of her masts left, drastically reducing her maneuverability. The British pounded both vessels until darkness fell but were driven off by other French ships the next morning when they sought to resume the battle. Three days later, on 19 August, another fifty, the *Isis,* fought for an hour and a half with the seventy-four-gun *César* twenty leagues from Sandy Hook before the two battered antagonists separated. Howe finally rejoined the rest of his squadron at New York on 18 August, while d'Estaing returned to Rhode Island on 20 August to take stock of his condition. On the night of 21–22 August, knowing that Byron could arrive at any time and shift the balance of power, d'Estaing sailed off to carry out repairs at Boston.

THE AMERICANS CARRY ON

The land forces continued their contest while the fleets were gone. The handful of French frigates left in harbor gave the Allies total control of the coastal waters, so Sullivan continued bringing his troops across to the island and, after the storm cleared, on 15 August pushed south to camp two miles from the outer line of Pigot's fortifications. These works stretched 1,372 yards across the island and were held by 1,900 men. They posed a formidable challenge, so Sullivan started the approach trenches for a formal siege. He concentrated on the eastern side of the line, apparently leaving the other side for the French as in the original plan.

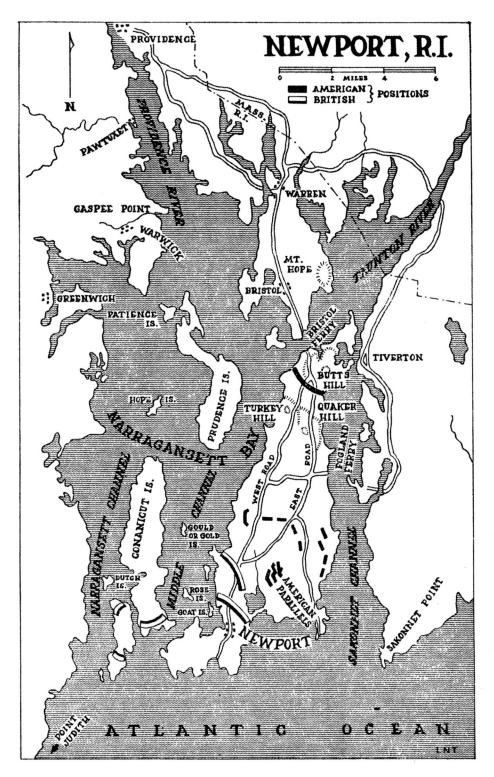

The steady massing of forces left Pigot increasingly worried. Despite the strong natural advantages of the terrain he held, he knew that control of the sea would leave him vulnerable to flank or rear attacks and subject to being starved into surrender. D'Estaing's reappearance on 20 August further eroded British morale. The pendulum quickly swung the other way when the French departed for Boston. The volunteers and militia started melting away while infuriated American officers made heated comments that would poison diplomatic relations. Sullivan kept his positions for several days in the hopes that something positive might happen but quietly started moving supplies and heavy equipment back to the mainland. Information from Washington alerted Sullivan that Howe and Clinton were assembling a strong relief force in New York, and when three British frigates arrived he correctly concluded that the task force would soon follow. At 8:00 P.M. on 28 August Sullivan started slowly withdrawing his remaining 5,000–6,000 men.

BATTLE OF RHODE ISLAND, 29 AUGUST

The Americans halted at 3 A.M. in the vicinity of Butts Hill, where there were some covering earthworks. They were twelve miles north of Newport. Glover's brigade held the left (east) end of the line; Colonel Christopher Greene commanded a brigade in the center with Brigadier General Ezekiel Cornell's brigade on his right; on the west end was Varnum's brigade. Detachments protected both coasts back to Bristol Ferry, while a skirmish line stood in front. Pigot detected the withdrawal at first light and decided to harass the Americans. About 6:30 he sent forward three columns, with covering parties, but retained over half of his strength in the fortifications as a precaution. Major General Richard Prescott moved in the center with the Thirty-eighth and Fifty-fourth Foot; Brigadier Francis Smith went up the east road with the Twenty-second and Forty-third Foot plus the flank companies of the Thirty-eighth and Fifty-fourth. Major General Friedrich Wilhelm von Lossburg took the west road with the two Anspach-Bayreuth regiments led by Captain Wihelm von der Malsburg's and Captain August Christian Noltenius's Hesse-Cassel chasseur companies. A half-hour later the chasseurs collided with Lieutenant Colonel John Laurens's skirmish force and the battle began. Moments later Smith on the other side of the island, who had not put out flankers or an advance guard, walked into a trap set by Colonel Henry Beekman Livingston's covering force.

The firing made it clear to Pigot that Smith was in a significant fight, and he started feeding in reinforcements. He ordered Prescott to send him the Fifty-Fourth while Pigot sent up the Loyalists of the Prince of Wales's Volunteers. He also pushed up the Hesse-Cassel Huyn Regiment and Fanning's Kings American Regiment to Lossburg. The covering parties fell back to the main American line, fighting all the way, and the British formed a line of battle on Turkey and Quaker Hills.

Before all of the supporting forces had come up, Smith launched an attack on the east that Glover stopped cold. The British supporting artillery then entered the fight about 9 A.M. and action settled back down to sporadic skirmishing. Four British ships moved up into position off the western shore and at 10 A.M. opened fire on the American right. With this support Pigot shifted his main effort to envelop Sullivan's right. Lossburg's troops charged the First Rhode Island Regiment holding the key redoubt but were driven back twice. Meanwhile some heavy American guns chased the ships back to a position off the British flank. Between 2 and 3 P.M. Lossburg made a third try and after some initial success was pushed back by Nathanael Greene's counterattack. When the American force on that wing of increased about 1,500 men, Greene moved forward towards Turkey Hill. At this point Sullivan called Greene off rather than risk a defeat. Both sides kept up sporadic fire until dark.

Pigot sent back to Newport for additional artillery, and Sullivan made a show of preparing to receive his attack, but neither commander wanted to bring on a decisive battle. During the night of 30–31 August, however, the Americans successfully executed the difficult operation of evacuating the island. Most of the troops crossed to Tiverton. A smaller number of troops crossed to Bristol, where the heavy baggage and stores had been sent earlier. Clinton reached Newport the morning of 1 September with 5,000 troops, bringing the campaign to an end. Sullivan's army discharged the bulk of the militia, and the Continentals moved to Providence. On the way back to New York, Clinton detached Major General Charles Grey for operations in Massachusetts (the Bedford–Fair Haven Raid, 6 September, and Martha's Vineyard raid, 10–11 September 1778).

NUMBERS AND LOSSES

American losses were 30 killed, 137 wounded, and 44 missing on 29 August. Pigot reported his casualties officially as 38 killed, 210 wounded, and 44 missing—most of the casualties among the German units. One Anspacher thought the true total was closer to 400.

SIGNIFICANCE

From a military standpoint neither side gained any significant advantage from the attack on Newport. Howe survived until Byron's arrival restored British control of the seas. Pigot (unlike Cornwallis in 1781) hung on until relief arrived, but the British had seen how tenuous their hold was, and within a year would voluntarily evacuate the outpost. The need to mount a rescue operation delayed Clinton from complying with the Ministry's orders to transfer forces to the Caribbean and initiate a "southern strategy," but did not cause any fatal harm.

Perhaps the worst damage came in the rift that opened between the Americans and the French. Popular anger erupted in Boston while d'Estaing was repairing his ships. On 5 September the young chevalier de Saint Sauveur was mortally wounded when he tried to stop a Boston mob from pilfering a bakery established by the fleet in the town. Three or four French sailors were killed at Charlestown in another riot. Finally the Massachusetts House of Delegates resolved to erect a monument over Saint Sauveur's grave. Preceded by the failure outside New York, 11–22 July 1778, and followed by the fiasco at Savannah, 9 October 1779, d'Estaing's performance at Newport did not bode well. But on 10 July 1780 a new French expedition, commanded by a much more diplomatic general, Rochambeau, landed in Newport and restored harmony, making the Yorktown campaign possible.

SEE ALSO *Bedford–Fair Haven Raid, Massachusetts; Estaing, Charles Hector Théodat, Comte d'; Martha's Vineyard Raid; New York Campaign; Savannah, Georgia (9 October 1779); Weather Gauge.*

BIBLIOGRAPHY

Amory, Thomas C. "The Siege of Newport, August, 1778." *Rhode Island Historical Magazine* 5 (October 1884): 106–135.

Crawford, Michael J. "The Joint Allied Operation at Rhode Island, 1778." In *New Interpretations in Naval History: Selected Papers from the Ninth Naval History Symposium Held at the United States Naval Academy, 18-20 October 1989.* Edited by William R. Roberts and Jack Sweetman. Annapolis, Md.: Naval Institute Press, 1991.

Dearden, Paul F. *The Rhode Island Campaign of 1778: Inauspicious Dawn of Alliance.* Providence: Rhode Island Bicentennial Foundation, 1980.

Rider, Sidney S., ed. *The Centennial Celebration of the Battle of Rhode Island, at Portsmouth, R.I., August 29, 1778.* Providence: Sidney S. Rider, 1878.

Syrett, David. *The Royal Navy in American Waters, 1775–1783.* Aldershot, U.K.: Scholar Press, 1989.

revised by Robert K. Wright Jr.

NEWTOWN, NEW YORK. 29 August
1779. In a move known as Sullivan's Expedition, Major General John Sullivan left Tioga on 26 August with 4,000 troops and advanced slowly up the left (east) bank of the Chemung River. Major John Butler, a Loyalist who had been watching Sullivan's buildup from Genesee, moved to join his son Walter fourteen miles from Tioga. Together they then pushed on with 250 Loyalists and 15 men of the British Eighth Foot and reinforced the 800 Indians and Loyalists under Joseph Brant near the destroyed village of Chemung. Against John Butler's judgment—the Indians insisted on making a stand—these forces prepared an elaborate ambush near Newtown, about six miles southeast of modern Elmira. A camouflaged log breastwork along a ridge parallel to the river had its left side anchored by a steep hill and right protected by a defile. The plan was not particularly original: throw Sullivan's column into confusion by surprise fire from the flank and then charge both ends. Brant and Captain John McDonnell (a Loyalist who had been with Brant at Cherry Valley) commanded the Indians and some Loyalists on the right, which was the least vulnerable sector. The left, under Walter Butler, and the center, under John Butler, contained mostly Loyalists and the sprinkling of regulars.

About 11 A.M. the advance guard of Sullivan's column approached the location. Alert members from the Rifle Corps spotted the trap. This warning let Sullivan halt the column and organize an attack. Major James Parr with his three companies of riflemen were attached to Enoch Poor's Brigade, and Poor was directed to envelop the enemy left. James Clinton's Division was to follow in support. The light howitzers and field pieces were to provide enfilade fire support.

In a well-managed maneuver through difficult terrain and against sporadic musket fire, Poor led his column onto the steep hill the Butlers had expected to protect their flank. The New Englanders charged with the bayonet, and the artillery opened up about the same time. According to John Butler, "the shells bursting beyond us made the Indians imagine the enemy had got their artillery around us and so startled and confused them that great part of them ran off."

Brant held a larger Indian force together, however, and put up a stiff fight against the much larger number of Continental veterans. Colonel John Reid's Second New Hampshire Regiment, on the right of Poor's Brigade, was hit on three sides by a savage counterattack but got prompt support from the Third New Hampshire Regiment and two of Clinton's New York regiments. Meanwhile, the brigades of Hand and Maxwell worked their way along the river and got on the enemy's right flank. The defenders, now at risk of annihilation, managed to break contact and retreat safely to Nanticoke, five miles away. Some of Sullivan's troops pursued less than half that distance.

NUMBERS AND LOSSES

The American losses were only 3 killed and 33 wounded. Sullivan reported to Congress that the total loss on the campaign only amounted to 40. Butler admitted the loss of 5 killed or captured and 3 wounded, and while these are probably well under the true numbers, they could not have been too great.

SIGNIFICANCE

Newtown is an example of the flexibility of the tactical system implemented by Washington and Steuben since the majority of the infantrymen engaged here were not from the frontier. The enemy certainly had made blunders (that is, electing to fight at Newtown and failing to withdraw as soon as it became apparent that the ambuscade had failed) and Sullivan did hold a four-to-one superiority, but critics have charged that Sullivan failed because he did not pursue aggressively. This charge is faulty—he correctly chose to remain focused on the primary objectives of the campaign and followed Washington's instructions to avoid needless risk.

SEE ALSO *Sullivan's Expedition against the Iroquois.*

BIBLIOGRAPHY

Fischer, Joseph R. *A Well-Executed Failure: The Sullivan Campaign against the Iroquois, July–September 1779*. Columbia: University of South Carolina Press, 1997.

Journals of the Military Expedition of Major General John Sullivan Against the Six Nations. Edited by Frederick Cook. 1887. Freeport, N.Y.: Books for Libraries Press, 1972.

revised by Robert K. Wright Jr.

Laurens reached the fleet to establish liaison between d'Estaing and Washington. Laurens informed d'Estaing of the near impossibility of crossing the bar into New York Harbor for an attack on the British.

After days at anchor off the treacherous coast while the best available pilots were consulted, d'Estaing was told they could take his ships in only if a strong northeast wind coincided with a spring tide. Ignorant of the deeper draft of the French ships, Sir Henry Clinton considered abandoning New York before the expected attack. But on 20 July the French admiral decided to leave New York and follow Washington's suggestion of a combined French and American operation against the British at Newport, Rhode Island.

Many military historians have been critical of d'Estaing for failing to chance crossing the bar into New York Harbor, insisting that a bolder commander might have won the Revolution by trapping the British in New York. Others agree with d'Estaing in thinking that such an effort would have been foolhardy and have led to the destruction of the French fleet.

The French Alliance was off to a bad start. Until Rochambeau arrived in America, it would deteriorate further.

SEE ALSO *French Alliance; Laurens, John; Monmouth, New Jersey.*

revised by Michael Bellesiles

NEW YORK. 11–22 July 1778. D'Estaing at the bar.

On 8 July the comte d'Estaing reached the Delaware Capes after taking eighty-seven days to cross the Atlantic from Toulon. Three days earlier the British fleet had completed ferrying Clinton's army from the vicinity of Sandy Hook at the heights of Navesink, where they had marched after evacuating Philadelphia. Although the slow passage of the French fleet across the Atlantic had saved the British fleet from being trapped in the Delaware, Admiral Richard Howe's problem now was to protect his fleet in New York Harbor against a superior force. D'Estaing's problem, on the other hand, was to get ships drawing twenty-seven feet across a bar where there were no more than twenty-one feet of water at low tide.

D'Estaing wasted no time off the Delaware when he saw there was no enemy fleet to engage and no promise of making contact with Washington. He had many sick aboard and was low on water and provisions, so on 9 July he sailed north to New York, reaching Sandy Hook on the 11th after capturing a number of British supply vessels. At Sandy Hook the American pilot who had come aboard off the Delaware reneged on his promise to take the fleet inside the Hook. It was not until 16 July that John

NEW YORK, MOBILIZATION IN.

New York was one of the major theaters of the War of Independence, and it endured hard conflict longer than any other state. Perhaps its people suffered worst of all from war's destruction. The war struck New Yorkers like none in their past, and no New Yorker escaped it. How it came to them and how they joined in it began a redefinition of what it meant to be a New Yorker, of how New York's people dealt with each other, and even of the boundaries within which they lived.

There is no adequate account of how New Yorkers came to join the Continental Army and the revolutionary militia. We know little about how their previous lives fed into military service and have only fragmentary information about how they mustered for service, what they did on duty, and how they met their needs for food, shelter, and weapons. This entry summarizes what we do know.

Conflict had played an important role in shaping colonial New York. The Dutch founders had waged war against the Indians of the Hudson Valley. The Five Haudenosaunee Nations (the French called them the Iroquois) had fought the French and other Indians, in good part to control the trade in beaver pelts; these wars continued after the English conquered Nieuw Amsterdam and Beverwyck in 1664 and renamed them New York and Albany. By the end of the seventeenth century, the Iroquois were exhausted. In the "Grand Settlement" of 1702 they promised neutrality to the French and, to placate their English allies, deeded over a hunting ground they did not possess, sprawling across the Niagara Peninsula to Detroit and perhaps beyond. Even after the outbreak of the final Anglo-French war for empire in 1755, the Iroquois tried to play off the Europeans; but with the defeat of the French the Iroquois were no longer able to balance the European powers. Although some Senecas joined in Pontiac's Rebellion in 1763 to drive the British back, most Iroquois understood that warfare on their own against the Europeans was futile.

Although the line of settlement was pushed in, until 1761 farmers and artisans prospered—and merchants got rich—by supplying the foodstuffs and goods that fed and equipped the British soldiers and sailors who flowed through New York City to the war fronts north and west of Albany. Seventy-five New York City privateers preyed on French shipping, and some of their captains and owners also got rich. But the end of wartime procurement brought economic depression. Profits sank and jobs became scarce. City people suffered, whereas mixed-crop farmers in the Hudson and Mohawk Valleys could alter what they planted and survive.

Peace allowed settlement to spread into the territory between Lake Champlain and the Connecticut River, but new opportunities raised new issues. Although the Privy Council awarded title to the region to New York in 1764—it was also claimed by New Hampshire and Massachusetts—it could not prevent Connecticut migrants from entering the region. In the Hudson Valley, New Englanders pushing westward joined with long-term tenants to protest against economic conditions on estates in the valley, and in some cases the estates' very existence. In 1766 tenants from Westchester County north to Albany rose in protest. The royal governor had to dispatch British troops, accompanied by light artillery, from New York City to quell the insurrection.

All of these issues—Indian-white relations, postwar economic woes, uncertain land boundaries, a quasi-feudal land system, and the irritating presence of British troops—shaped the ways New Yorkers confronted the imperial crisis between 1765 and 1775. In New York City the combination of British troops and economic doldrums proved volatile. Two garrison companies had been stationed in the city since the conquest in 1664, but after 1763 the garrison rose to several regiments. Off-duty soldiers chopped down the Liberty Poles raised by radical New Yorkers and brawled with civilians in taverns. Even worse, they competed with local residents for scarce jobs.

In January 1770 the rage spilled out into fights on the city's streets, but no shots were fired; a similar situation in Boston led two months later to the Boston Massacre. Like the residents of Boston, many ordinary people in New York City disliked the "lobsterbacks" and were just as ready to organize to protest their presence, although many of their leaders tagged behind.

Massachusetts was ready to resist when the imperial government punished Boston for the "destruction of the tea" at the Boston Tea Party. New Yorkers were slower, but they did follow. During 1774 and early 1775 committees of correspondence (the "Fifty-One") and inspection (the "Sixty") formed in New York City to exchange information and to enforce the Continental Association. The First Continental Congress wanted committees of inspection everywhere, but they appeared only in a few places in New York: at Rye in Westchester County in August 1774; at Albany over the winter; at Kingston in December; and at New Windsor in Ulster County not until March 1775. The committee of Palatine District, in the upper Mohawk Valley, met in secret for fear of the power of Sir William Johnson's family. These committees made no bid to overthrow colonial and royal institutions, as did their Massachusetts counterparts in the late summer and autumn of 1774.

Governor William Tryon remained popular (though New Yorkers loathed Lieutenant Governor Cadwallader Colden, who stood in while Tryon journeyed to England). The provincial assembly made laws, the mayors and city councils in New York and Albany continued to pass ordinances, and the courts stayed open. A few zealots, such as the radical leaders Isaac Sears and Alexander McDougall, wanted to go farther, but they knew they could not. McDougall was "sure . . . that we shall be the last of the provinces to the northward of Georgia, that will appeal to the sword." James Duane, his reluctant fellow patriot, agreed in principle: "It seems to be agreed here that every pacific and persuasive Expedient ought to be tried before a Recourse to Arms can be justified." New Yorkers were not ready for war, and despite the hot temper of some in the city, most of the province's people had no desire for confrontation. Many Americans outside the province scorned New York's apparent timidity.

Yet observant people could see that New Yorkers were not timid. They remembered the ferocious, destructive protests that had nullified the Stamp Act in 1765–1766 and the subsequent brawls with the garrison soldiers. In New York City a "committee of mechanics" took shape and bought its own meeting place. Outside the city, branches of the Sons of Liberty sprang up. During the crisis of 1773–1774 over East India Company tea, the zealous McDougall horrified the cautious William Smith Jr. by suggesting that "we prevent the landing [of the tea] and kill the Gov[erno]r. and the council." It was dark humor, but like all joking it

New Yorkers Defend a Liberty Pole. *In New York City, the combination of British troops and economic doldrums proved volatile. Off-duty soldiers brawled with civilians in taverns and chopped down Liberty Poles raised by radical New Yorkers.* © BETTMANN/ CORBIS

had a kernel of truth. While New Englanders were preparing for war, New Yorkers were donating goods and labor to support them. New Yorkers even destroyed a small tea cargo themselves in April 1774 when the ship *London* tried to bring some in secretly.

New Yorkers as a whole were not in a state of readiness to resist British authority in 1775. The closest they came was in New York City, but even there the likes of Duane did not want to make preparations. The likes of McDougall did not yet dare. Reluctant or bold, they understood that New York did not have and could not yet have anything like the province wide organization and the growing consciousness that Boston's leaders had fostered since well before the tea crisis. They understood that their province was far more heterogeneous, far more complex than the Yankee colonies. No amount of preparation could have mobilized New York's diverse people at the same time, at least in the same direction. But McDougall had predicted in 1774 to William Cooper of Massachusetts that "the attack of the Troops on your People" might make his fellows "fly to arms." The news from Lexington proved him right.

This was the moment that New York City radical leaders and Sons of Liberty like Isaac Sears and Alexander McDougall had been waiting for; it was the moment that cooler heads like James Duane and John Jay anticipated without relish; and it was also the moment that William Smith, who wanted desperately to remain neutral, and outright loyalists like King's College president Myles Cooper had foreseen with dread. When the news of the fighting in Massachusetts reached New York City on 23 April 1775, Sears seized the initiative. Organizing other Sons of Liberty and the "negroes, boys, sailors, and pickpockets," as well as many hard-working laborers and artisans, he led a march on the city armory, broke in, and handed out its contents. Another crowd stopped a sloop from sailing for Boston with provisions for the British troops there. Events cascaded. On 6 June, Marinus Willett, who would become a colonel in the Continental Army, led a group that seized the firearms of British soldiers who were being taken on shipboard to prevent them from deserting. As late as July it seemed to one observer that "all authority, power, and government . . . is in the hands of the lower class of people."

But crowd action was not enough. New York City replaced its 60-member committee of observation and inspection with a 100-member committee of safety. Albany's half-secret committee published a call for meetings in every town in Albany county, "to take the sense of the citizens." The result was the creation of a 153-member committee of "safety, protection, and correspondence," empowered to "transact all such measures . . . as may tend to the welfare of the American cause." Committees took shape in the other counties as well. Building on a short-lived Provincial Convention, elections for the new committees also chose delegates to the first of four Provincial Congresses. Congresses and committees alike began to drain power from the old institutions. On 3 May 1775 Albany's new committee of safety organized a "strict and strong watch, well armed and under proper discipline," and called on townsmen to form militia companies. Five days later New York City's Committee of One Hundred ordered that all known opponents of the movement be stripped of their firearms. It too was organizing militia companies, urging them to start training and secure munitions and supplies. But British troops remained in the city, and the sixty-four-gun ship *Asia* lay at anchor off lower Manhattan. Not wanting a confrontation, or the damage that would result if the *Asia* fired on the town, radical leaders agreed that the British army and the navy should continue to receive supplies. As a precaution, the Provincial Congress resolved that the militia be "in constant readiness" to repel any attempt to take over and restore the old government's full power.

New York was passing through a situation of "dual power," as two sets of institutions, one dying and the other emerging, and their incumbents vied for control. Such a situation is at the very heart of a political revolution. At the end of 1775, when Governor Tryon dissolved the assembly and called an election for its successor, the first congress also dissolved and called an election of its own. Tryon's goal was to stop the revolutionary movement. The congress's goal was to "awe a corrupt Assembly . . . from interfering with political subjects." The new assembly that Tryon hoped for never met. When the new provincial congress did assemble, there was no "official" institution to compete with it. In 1775 New York, like the other provinces, followed Massachusetts in preparing seriously for armed conflict, each at its own pace but in the same direction. Although the outbreak of fighting had provoked a sharp, if short-lived, burst of anger among New Yorkers, even loyalists-to-be, New Yorkers mobilized for conflict not as a united people but rather with the prospect of deep division.

Governor Tryon returned to New York from England on 25 June, the same day Washington passed through the city on his way to take command in Boston. Tryon wisely stayed on shipboard to avoid the celebrations for Washington, and both men received warm welcomes. Nonetheless, British authority was eroding. For his own safety Tryon retreated to the *Asia* and then to the merchant vessel *Duchess of Gordon*. In a nighttime operation on 22 August, with the approval of the Provincial Congress, the Sons of Liberty began removing cannon that had been stored for shipment at the Battery. The *Asia* did fire, including one full broadside at 3 A.M. The gunners aimed only at the storage site of the cannon and, despite the terrifying noise, the city suffered little damage. The next day the tenuous truce returned, but the balance of power had shifted a bit: the rebels now controlled twenty-one pieces of heavy artillery.

At the same time, the Provincial Congress was organizing four regiments to meet New York's quota of Continental Army troops. Each regiment was raised in a particular part of the colony, with the officers, who raised soldiers to earn their rank, reflecting the prevailing political sentiments of their region. The First Regiment was raised in New York City and County, with a strong cadre of officers with military experience in the final French and Indian war or in the city's elite militia battalions. The Second Regiment came from northern New York, from the city of Albany north through Albany and Charlotte Counties toward Canada, Tryon County (the Mohawk Valley), and Cumberland County (the Hampshire Grants, later the State of Vermont); it had a strong Dutch influence. The Third Regiment was raised mainly in the Hudson Valley between Albany and New York City, on the west side in Ulster and Orange Counties and on the east side in Dutchess County; a company from Suffolk County on Long Island completed the regiment. The Fourth Regiment came from the counties around New York City: southern Dutchess, Westchester, King's (Brooklyn), Queen's, and Richmond (Staten Island).

Enlistment records and the pension applications of elderly veterans that are preserved in the National Archives give us a glimpse of the men who joined and how they served in the war. The median age of 286 noncommissioned officers and men in the Third Regiment, for example, was 23 years (the average was 25 years). In height, they averaged over 5 feet, 8 1/2 inches tall; 70 percent had a fair complexion, sixteen were pockmarked, and one had a harelip. Three-quarters were born in the colonies (54 percent in New York itself); Irish were the majority of the foreign-born. Half described themselves as laborers, less than 10 percent were farmers, and the rest were artisans of some sort, mostly weavers and shoemakers.

We know more about New Yorkers' scramble for officer commissions. The Continental Congress recognized New York's importance by allocating it several general officer appointments. The senior appointee was Major

General Philip Schuyler, a grandee landlord from Albany County, but the English-born and professionally trained Brigadier General Richard Montgomery was probably the most talented officer; he died in the assault on Quebec on 31 December 1775. In subsequent years, the former radical leader Alexander McDougall and the Ulster County brothers George and James Clinton received Continental commissions. James Clinton led one wing of the American army that ravaged Iroquois country in 1779 and opened the way for the ruthless destruction of Iroquois power after the war. Most of the generals associated with New York campaigns—including Washington; Arthur St. Clair at Ticonderoga; John Stark at Bennington; Horatio Gates, Benedict Arnold, and Benjamin Lincoln at Saratoga; John Sullivan on the 1779 Iroquois campaign; and Anthony Wayne in the Hudson Highlands—were not New York–born.

The unpretentious George Clinton, who held both militia and Continental commissions as a brigadier general, became the first commander of the state militia at the age of thirty-six. He proved more popular than Schuyler with New York's soldiers, and their votes gave him the state governorship in 1777. County and local notables scrambled for lesser rank, in both the Continental Army and the militia. After the war, scarcely a legislator or judge could not call himself general, colonel, major, or at least captain. Most militia officers provided important, if unremarkable, service. A few gained wider renown. Nicholas Herkimer was perhaps the most famous militia general. A local notable in the Mohawk Valley, he won election to the new state legislature. He won enduring military fame by helping to turn back St. Leger's expedition in 1777. Although British troops, their Loyalist allies, and pro-British Iroquois trapped his force of Tryon County militiamen in a ravine at Oriskany on 6 August and inflicted heavy casualties, including mortally wounding Herkimer himself, the expedition itself was crippled.

For militiamen, the first stage in commitment was to sign a voluntary "military association," or else face the contempt of neighbors. But not everybody joined in. Even in the heated atmosphere of the spring of 1775, the prosperous, mostly Dutch people of Richmond, King's, and Queen's Counties wanted nothing to do with the revolutionary movement. Efforts to organize committees and militia units among them came to virtually nothing. Continental general Charles Lee moved troops into Queen's County in January 1776, disarmed its open Loyalists, and arrested eighteen leaders. Still, its people would not support the patriots: 462 of them signed Lee's oath that they would not actively aid the British, and 340 more swore that they had surrendered all their firearms, but with no promises about future conduct. After the British arrived in August, more than 1,300 men signed a congratulatory address to the conquerors. Such men

joined royalist militia units, raiding across Long Island Sound into Westchester County and Connecticut. But as with the patriot militia, we know far too little about them.

Serious "disaffection" appeared upstate as well. One in eight of the potential militiamen in Orange County refused the military association, more than half of them from just one town, Haverstraw. About the same proportion refused in Ulster, the next county to the north on the west bank of the Hudson. In Westchester, Dutchess, and Albany Counties, thousands refused and were stripped of their firearms. A clandestine meeting late in 1776 on the Helderberg Escarpment west of Albany shows such men, mostly tenant farmers from the Manor of Rensselaerswyck, making up their minds. Thanks to a spy from the revolutionary committee, we know that one of them, a recent Scottish immigrant named John Commons, put the question. Supporters of Congress should leave, he said; the king's friends should stay. But Commons did not "know who was right." Until the end of the war patriot militiamen and the "Commissioners for Detecting and Defeating Conspiracies" worked hard to keep these "disaffected" under control.

The most enduring and most fiercely fought problems erupted in the upper Mohawk Valley, where white settlement melded into Indian country. There was no simple demarcation. The Mohawks were fragmented and surrounded by whites, with whom they often worshipped, prayed, and intermarried. Farther west, white land grants and settlements pressed in on the Oneidas. The situation of the Onondagas, Cayugas, and Senecas seemed safer, but whites were firmly emplaced at Oswego and Niagara. At war's outbreak the Haudenosaunee "great league" still held the Iroquois together, but on religious terms that allowed them to maintain peace among themselves, not as a political unit that would let them act together in wartime. Their other pan-tribal institution was the "Covenant Chain," in which the Six Nations were the central links binding other Indians, separate British colonies, and the distant crown. But the crown's hold on the colonies was shaking. Would the chain still reach to London? Would it stop in Albany, where New York leaders were reviving their earlier primacy in Iroquois affairs? Or would it end now at Congress, in Philadelphia?

The white Mohawk Valley was fragmented too. Until his death late in 1774, Sir William Johnson was a great lord in all but formal title of nobility. He treated the largely Scottish Catholic tenant laborers on his enormous estate well, supplying needs and forgiving debts. He controlled assembly elections and decided who would be sheriff or judge. He had good relations with most of the Iroquois, particularly the Mohawks and the Senecas. These relations did not extend to many of the Oneidas, who did not think Johnson would help them protect their land. Knowing they needed a white ally, they looked to

Mrs. Schuyler Burning her Wheat Fields on the Approach of the British. *This engraving, based on an 1852 painting by Emanuel Leutze, depicts a legend in which the wife of American General Philip Schuyler set fire to their wheat fields near Saratoga, New York, to deny sustenance to British troops.* HULTON ARCHIVE/GETTY IMAGES

Samuel Kirkland, a pro-American, New England-born Presbyterian minister who had promised never to acquire an acre of their land. Yet the baronet did not own the whole valley. German and English settlers were moving in, resentful of his power, envious of his great landholdings, and casting covetous eyes on Indian land.

Johnson's heirs intended to keep the power and influence the baronet had acquired. Perhaps they did not learn about the secret committee that formed in 1774; but after Lexington there was no hiding. In June 1775 the committee called an open-air militia election. Sir John Johnson chanced to be passing and broke into the meeting, flailing his horsewhip at the candidate for captain. Another contretemps the next month saw five hundred of his armed tenants face down an equal number of insurgents at his own house, Johnson Hall. Leaders from Albany arranged a truce, but it did not last. Western New York and the Six Nations country were embarking on years of bitter warfare that would devastate the Indian and white communities alike. At the war's end the destruction of Iroquois power and grabbing of Iroquois property would surge, regardless

of what side the Indians chose, as New York assumed its modern shape. But this was not a race war. There were Indians and whites on both sides: Mohawks and Oneidas, Scots and Germans, tenants and freeholders chose for their own reasons.

Where they could, African Americans chose sides for their own reasons too, particularly after British commander Sir Henry Clinton promised freedom to slaves of rebels who would join him. Slavery was beginning to crumble; black men enlisted, fought, and won freedom on both sides. Still, white New Yorkers were among the slowest of all northerners to wake up to the great contradiction between the Revolution's claim that all men are created equal and the harsh reality that white men imposed on black people. At the war's end Patriots would try to reclaim slaves who had rallied to Sir Henry. The British refused in as many cases as they could.

Women in New York also had choices to make. They felt the same patriotic desires and pressures for action that led women elsewhere into open politics. Some ended their marriages rather than accept their husbands' political

The Burning of New York City. *British soldiers attack suspected arsonists as New York City burns on the night of 19 September 1776, during the British occupation. The scene is depicted here in a late-eighteenth-century French engraving.* HULTON ARCHIVE/GETTY IMAGES

decisions. In 1778 and 1779 Hudson Valley women joined crowds that sought to set prices on necessary goods, sometimes with soldiers' protection. Cross-dressing soldier Deborah Sampson saw combat as "Robert Shurtleff" on New York ground. Throughout revolutionary America, women learned that bearing the burden of supporting the war on the home front on their own, with their men sometimes far away, transformed them.

In the Green Mountains, Yankee migrants turned "revolutionary outlaws" nullified New York authority by the early 1770s, closing courts, breaking jails, horsewhipping officials, and driving out New York settlers. Lexington and Concord brought a brief reconciliation. Ethan Allen, leader of the Green Mountain Boys, joined Benedict Arnold to seize decrepit Fort Ticonderoga and its valuable artillery. Condemned to death by name in a New York statute of 1774, Allen appeared before the Provincial Congress and accepted its commission as colonel. Late in 1776 his followers realized that they could grasp their own independence, if they were bold. To New York they became "revolted subjects" living in the "pretended state" of Vermont. But New York needed them. When his army bogged down in the upper Hudson Valley north of Albany in the late summer of 1777, General John Burgoyne sent a

raiding party of German troops toward Bennington. Green Mountain Boys and New Hampshire militia met the raid; some pretended to be Loyalists and led the Germans into a bloody trap. The expedition's failure helped to guarantee that Burgoyne's army would not reach Albany, where it intended to link up with other British troops coming down the Mohawk Valley and up the Hudson.

Burgoyne's southward advance from Montreal toward Albany was the second (of two) great military tests of mobilized New York. The first had been Washington's futile defense of New York City and successful retreat from it a year earlier, in 1776. Both the battle for New York and the battles around Saratoga were national efforts, with the Continental Army at the center. The American commander at Saratoga was British-born Horatio Gates, who lived in Virginia. Gates had replaced New York's Schuyler both because Schuyler had endorsed his subordinate's decision to abandon Fort Ticonderoga rather than try to block Burgoyne and because ordinary troops disliked him. Schuyler did, however, initiate a scorched-earth strategy along Burgoyne's route south from Lake Champlain, which succeeded in its goal of delaying the British, isolating them from their supplies, and weakening them to the point that Gates could defeat them.

New Yorkers by themselves could not have raised sufficient troops for either campaign. Regiments from other states made up the bulk of the American forces at both New York City in 1776 and Saratoga in 1777. Continental soldiers from the fishing ports of Massachusetts ferried much of Washington's army from Long Island to safety on Manhattan Island in August 1776. Beginning in the late summer of 1777, New Englanders were foremost among the militia who swelled Gates's army to the point that it vastly outnumbered the invaders. Despite a wave of panic as Burgoyne advanced south, New Yorkers did turn out at Saratoga in large numbers, where their presence tipped the scales even though they engaged in little fighting. When 1,800 Albany County militiamen joined the American force it helped to convince the British that their cause was hopeless. So stripped was the Hudson Valley during the Saratoga crisis that there was no resistance to a small British expedition that burned and ravaged as far north as Kingston, in a vain effort to support Burgoyne.

New Yorkers of all sorts remained mobilized for five years after Saratoga. Continentals and patriot militiamen faced down Loyalists and raiders both in the Iroquois borderlands and in Westchester County around New York City. Even after Cornwallis surrendered at Yorktown in October 1781, the rump of the Continental Army remained camped at Newburgh, expecting a final battle for New York City itself that never came. Like the story of how New Yorkers entered the Revolutionary War, the story of how they endured the war and, eventually, left it behind remains to be explored more fully.

SEE ALSO *Allen, Ethan; Arnold, Benedict; Bennington Raid; Boston Massacre; Boston Tea Party; Clinton, George; Clinton, James; Duane, James; Gates, Horatio; Herkimer, Nicholas; Iroquois League; Jay, John; Johnson, Sir John; Johnson, Sir William; Lincoln, Benjamin; McDougall, Alexander; Montgomery, Richard; Oriskany, New York; Pontiac's War; Sampson, Deborah; Saratoga, First Battle of; Saratoga, Second Battle of; Schuyler, Philip John; Sears, Isaac; Smith, William (II); Sons of Liberty; St. Clair, Arthur; St. Leger's Expedition; Stark, John; Sullivan, John; Sullivan's Expedition against the Iroquois; Ticonderoga, New York, American Capture of; Tryon, William; Wayne, Anthony; Willett, Marinus.*

BIBLIOGRAPHY

Bellesiles, Michael A. *Revolutionary Outlaws: Ethan Allen and the Struggle for Independence on the Early American Frontier.* Charlottesville: University Press of Virginia, 1993.

Carp, Benjamin L. "Fire of Liberty: Firefighters, Urban Voluntary Culture, and the Revolutionary Movement." *William and Mary Quarterly*, third series, 58 (2001): 781–818.

Countryman, Edward. *A People in Revolution: The American Revolution and Political Society in New York, 1760–1790.* Baltimore: Johns Hopkins University Press, 1981.

Gross, Robert A. *The Minutemen and Their World.* New York: Hill and Wang, 1976.

Ketchum, Richard M. *Divided Loyalties: How the American Revolution Came to New York.* New York: Holt, 2002.

———. *Saratoga.* New York: Holt, 1997.

Schechter, Barnet. *The Battle for New York.* New York: Walker, 2002.

Tiedemann, Joseph S. *Reluctant Revolutionaries: New York City and the Road to Independence, 1763–1776.* Ithaca, N.Y.: Cornell University Press, 1997.

Wonderley, Anthony. "1777: The Revolutionary War Comes to Oneida Country." *Mohawk Valley History* 1 (2004): 15–48.

Edward Countryman

NEW YORK ASSEMBLY SUSPENDED.

1767–1769. On 13 December 1765, Major General Thomas Gage, the British commander in chief in North America, asked Governor Henry Moore to request the New York assembly to make provisions for complying with the Quartering Act. The assembly refused full compliance in January 1766, contending that because more regular troops were stationed at New York City (Gage's headquarters) than in any other colony, New York was being unfairly burdened by the act. On 13 June 1766, Moore again informed the assembly that provisions should be made for quartering more regular troops expected to arrive at New York City. On the 19th the assembly again refused full compliance, pleading insufficient financial resources. A period of mounting tension led to a clash between soldiers and citizens on 11 August. When the assembly refused for a third time to support the Quartering Act (15 December), the governor prorogued it (19 December). On 15 June 1767 the king gave his assent to Charles Townshend's act suspending the legislative powers of the New York assembly, effective from 1 October until such time as it complied with the Quartering Act. About the same time, the assembly finally voted some funds for troop support, and the governor used this as a basis for not carrying out the suspension. Although the assembly was never suspended, the willingness of the imperial government to take this drastic step showed the colonists the extent to which the mother country was ready to browbeat them into submission.

When the Board of Trade reviewed the matter in May 1768, it ruled that the acts of the New York assembly after 1 October 1767 were invalid. After a new assembly was dissolved for failure to cooperate, a third one, elected in January 1769, made the required provisions for quartering in December 1769 when it voted an appropriation of two thousand pounds. The radicals considered this compliance a betrayal by the assembly, and the ensuing friction between soldiers and citizens culminated in the "battle" of Golden Hill on 19 January 1770.

SEE ALSO *Gage, Thomas; Golden Hill, Battle of; Quartering Acts; Townshend, Charles.*

BIBLIOGRAPHY

Douglas, David C., gen. ed. *English Historical Documents.* Vol. 9, *American Colonial Documents to 1776.* Edited by Merrill Jensen. New York: Oxford University Press, 1955.

Shy, John. *Toward Lexington: The Role of the British Army in the Coming of the American Revolution.* Princeton, N.J.: Princeton University Press, 1965.

Thomas, Peter D. G. *British Politics and the Stamp Act Crisis: The First Phase of the American Revolution, 1763–1767.* Oxford: Oxford University Press, 1975.

———. *Tea Party to Independence: The Third Phase of the American Revolution, 1773–1776.* Oxford: Oxford University Press, 1991.

revised by Harold E. Selesky

NEW YORK CAMPAIGN.
In a letter of 6 January 1776, John Adams directed George Washington's attention to New York, to the "vast Importance of that City, Province, and the [Hudson] River which is in it." New York, Adams wrote, was "the Nexus of the Northern and Southern Colonies, as a kind of Key to the whole Continent . . . a Passage to Canada, to the Great Lakes, and to all the Indian Nations. No Effort to Secure it ought to be omitted." Besieged in Boston—a peninsula with a very narrow neck—the British were keenly aware of New York City's strategic advantages. Located at the center of the Atlantic seaboard and at the mouth of a deep, navigable river penetrating some three hundred miles northward towards Fort Ticonderoga, New York, was the portal to the Lake Champlain-Lake George-Hudson River axis, a water highway used to transport invading armies to and from Canada during the French and Indian War.

Stung by their defeats at Lexington, Concord, and Bunker Hill, the British by August 1775 had devised a new grand strategy. By having one army seize New York City and march northward to rendezvous at Albany with a second force coming down from Canada, the British intended to divide the colonies along the line of the Hudson River. The American struggle for independence was expected to collapse if New England could be isolated

from other cockpits of the rebellion in the mid-Atlantic and southern provinces. The British were forced to retreat from Boston to Halifax when the Americans placed artillery on Dorchester Heights. Departing on 17 March 1776, they planned to regroup and follow the advice of Lord George Germain, soon to become secretary of state for the American colonies, to deliver a "decisive blow" at New York.

AMERICAN DEFENSES

Washington, who remained in Boston with the army in case the British retreat was merely a feint, had dispatched his second in command, Major General Charles Lee, to recruit volunteers in Connecticut and begin the work of fortifying New York City. Arriving on 4 February, Lee concluded that the city, covering less than a square mile at the southern tip of Manhattan, would ultimately be captured by the British because their powerful navy would dominate the surrounding waterways. Nonetheless, with forts and trenches in and around the city and barricades at every street corner, Lee hoped to inflict heavy losses on the invaders by drawing them into protracted urban warfare.

Lee's plan also focused on sealing off both ends of the East River with sunken obstructions and shore batteries and controlling Brooklyn Heights, which would secure Manhattan's entire east side while enabling the Americans to command the city with their artillery, as they had done from Dorchester Heights outside Boston. However, Lee's plan failed to capitalize on two choke points: the channel at Sandy Hook, which was the only entrance to the Lower Bay from the Atlantic, and the Narrows between Staten Island and western Long Island leading to the Upper Bay. A combination of shore batteries and artillery mounted on floating platforms might have taken a heavy toll on the British fleet passing single file through these straits, but these recommendations from at least one New York resident and from Congress were never implemented.

Nonetheless, John Adams and other members of the Continental Congress were so pleased with the work Lee had begun that he was sent to perform similar service in Charleston, South Carolina. This faith in Lee's abilities stemmed in part from the congressmen's own lack of military experience. Moreover, they ultimately concurred with Lee's assessment of the situation: they could not hope to mount a successful defense of the New York archipelago against the world's greatest naval power, but they calculated that the second largest city in America (after Philadelphia) should not be handed over without a fight. To do so would depress American morale, pushing tenuous supporters of the Revolution and neutrals into the Loyalist camp.

AMERICAN DISPOSITIONS

When Lee departed on 7 March, Brigadier General William Alexander, known as Lord Stirling because of his claim to a Scottish peerage, assumed command in New York and supervised the construction of the forts. Ten days later, when the British evacuated Boston, Washington was convinced they were headed for New York and began sending his best units down to the city. New York was "a post of infinite importance both to them and us," Washington wrote, "and much depends on priority of possession." The brigades of Thompson, Heath, Sullivan, Greene, and Spencer traveled over muddy roads and by boat from Connecticut, reaching New York by early April, followed by Major General Israel Putnam, who imposed martial law in the city and commanded the army until Washington arrived on 13 April.

Washington reorganized the army into four brigades under Heath, Spencer, Stirling, and Greene, assigning the first three to complete the defenses on Manhattan and sending Greene to Long Island. With nineteen thousand troops present and fit for duty, Washington spread them out in a thin defensive line broken by two rivers and stretching from the New Jersey shore in the west and eastward through northern Manhattan, New York City, Governors Island, and onto Long Island.

In addition to the many miles of shoreline where the British might land to capture New York City, the threat of an invasion from Canada also diluted Washington's forces. Following orders from Congress, Washington in May dispatched ten regiments under Thompson and Sullivan to reinforce the American invasion of Canada, led by Major General John Thomas, whose forces continued to besiege Quebec. Congress hoped to secure the northern border with a fourteenth colony in Canada; Britain's two-pronged strategy meant that Washington had to fight for both ends of the Champlain-Hudson corridor at once.

LORD HOWE'S PEACE INITIATIVE

On the other hand, the American expedition in Canada forced the British commander in chief, Major General William Howe, to divert troops from Halifax to the St. Lawrence River, which delayed his departure for New York until June 1776. During the last week of June, Howe and his fleet of 130 ships—the largest ever seen in North America—sailed past Sandy Hook and arrived in the Lower Bay. On 2 July, the day Congress voted for independence, Howe's forces sailed unopposed through the Narrows and landed on Staten Island.

On 12 July, with a strong wind blowing from the south, the British sent two ships, the *Phoenix* and *Rose*, up the Hudson to test the American defenses. American shore batteries blazed away but did little more than damage the rigging on the warships. The American

guns were not powerful enough, the river was too wide at its mouth, and with the wind at their backs the British vessels were too swift. The British captains celebrated by breaking out the claret and punch while they proceeded up the river as far as Tarrytown, thirty miles north of New York City. For the Americans, it was a distressing start to the New York campaign. The British had demonstrated that they could enter the Hudson both to control the river and to arm the Loyalists along its banks, while interrupting American communications and supply lines leading down from Albany to New York City. The British also stood a good chance of destroying several American frigates then under construction further upriver.

That same evening, Vice Admiral Richard Lord Howe, the general's brother and co-commander in chief, arrived from England after an arduous Atlantic crossing and protracted negotiations in London with George Germain, the American secretary who finally conferred the title of peace commissioner on both brothers. Having lost their older brother, George, who was killed in 1758 while leading Massachusetts troops in the French and Indian War, Richard and William Howe were deeply grateful for the creation of a monument to him in Westminster Abbey funded by the Massachusetts government, and they considered Americans their friends and countrymen. The Howe brothers hoped an overwhelming show of force in New York would bring the Americans to the negotiating table and end the rebellion without further bloodshed.

General William Howe greeted his brother and informed him of the Declaration of Independence; the Americans had dug in and were prepared to fight. Nonetheless, on the following day, 13 July, Admiral Richard Howe proceeded with his peace initiative. He issued a proclamation offering to pardon any colonists who would return to the fold and help reestablish the royal governments in America. Admiral Howe also dispatched letters to this effect to each of the colonial governors, leaving them unsealed so that couriers would report their contents to the Continental Congress. Thus began the Howe brothers' attempt to wield the olive branch in one hand and the sword in the other, a strategy that would punctuate the New York campaign over the next several months and significantly shape its outcome.

Without acknowledging Washington's rank as the commander in chief of a national army, on 13 July, Admiral Howe addressed a letter to him proposing a face-to-face meeting. When a British naval officer attempted to deliver the letter the following day under a flag of truce, Washington's aides rejected the overture, insisting that he be addressed in writing by his proper title. On the third attempt, the messenger verbally requested a meeting between "His Excellency General

Washington" and the adjutant general of the British army, and it was duly arranged for 20 July.

Washington received Admiral Howe's envoy at his headquarters but spurned the idea that Americans should seek pardons from the British and retreat from the defense of their natural rights. Knowing that the British did not recognize the legitimacy of the Continental Congress, he nonetheless directed Admiral Howe to that body as the proper authority for conducting negotiations. In the meantime, Howe's letters to the governors had reached Congress as he had expected, and the members decided to publish them immediately in order to expose what they viewed as a hollow peace offer and to dispel any impression among Americans that Congress was intransigent.

BRITISH DELAYS AND BUILDUP

Thwarted in his diplomatic initiative, Admiral Howe was ready to try force, but General Howe, despite the passage of three weeks since the arrival of the British fleet in New York, insisted on delaying the campaign further. Displaying the caution that would mark his conduct throughout the battle for New York, Howe decided to wait for reinforcements and for camp equipment, including kettles and canteens his troops would need in the summer heat.

On 1 August, Major General Henry Clinton and his subordinate, Major General Lord Charles Cornwallis, returned to New York with three thousand troops aboard the battered British fleet. The fleet had not overcome the fortifications designed by Charles Lee and so had failed to capture Charleston at the end of June. General Howe had been eager to put some distance between himself and Clinton, his second in command, after they quarreled over tactics at Bunker Hill a year earlier. Clinton's return after failing in his first independent command did not improve their relationship.

On Staten Island, the British built wooden landing craft with hinged bows to facilitate amphibious operations with troops, horses, and artillery. On 12 August a convoy of more than one hundred ships arrived after a three-and-one-half-half-month passage from Europe on stormy seas. Escorted by ships of the line, the eight-five transports carried one thousand British Guards and a contingent of seventy-eight hundred Hessians, the first such auxiliaries to arrive in America. The British also organized a regiment of some eight hundred fugitive black slaves from various states, including Virginia, where a proclamation by Lord Dunmore, the royal governor, had promised freedom to able-bodied indentured servants and slaves willing to desert their "Rebel" owners and fight for the king.

By mid-August the British invasion force had reached full strength, with some twenty-four-thousand ground troops and ten thousand sailors to man the rigging and guns of thirty warships along with four hundred supply ships and transports. Rivaling the population of Philadelphia, this was the largest expeditionary force in British history before the twentieth century. It was also the greatest concentration of forces the British would have in America at any time during the Revolution. The New York campaign presented the British with their best opportunity to win the war quickly and decisively.

BRITISH STRATEGIC OPTIONS

Such a bold stroke was imperative, because the task of subduing and occupying the American colonies would be too great even for the Howe brothers' mighty army and fleet. Admiral Howe had only seventy-three warships in the North American squadron with which to support the army's operations in Quebec, Halifax, New York, and St. Augustine while blockading all of American trade from Nova Scotia to Florida. General Howe faced an analogous problem on land, where his force was totally inadequate to occupy the vast expanses of the North American continent. Germain believed this problem would be overcome when British military victories emboldened American Loyalists—the vast, silent majority, in his view—to defy the Continental Congress and local Revolutionary leaders and to help reestablish royal governments throughout the colonies.

General Howe had publicly declared that the entire British army was not large enough to occupy America, and he concluded that the best way to avoid a long and costly war was to capture Washington's army or destroy it in a single decisive battle. However, on the eve of launching the New York campaign in mid-August, he suddenly switched to a plan that would drive them out of the area, enabling the British to use New York as a base of operations. Howe's new strategy would lead to multiple campaigns and rely on a gradual collapse of the rebellion with a minimum of casualties on both sides.

Howe had been chosen to put down the American rebellion because of his success during the French and Indian War using the unconventional tactics demanded by the varied and densely wooded terrain of the New World. However, with the sudden shift of strategy in New York, he reverted to traditional principles of military science, which emphasized the capture of key territory: high ground, water routes, and cities. The loss of New York was expected to confront the Americans with the hopelessness of their cause and prompt them to surrender before massive casualties could engender lasting bitterness.

Much of the Howe brothers' personal correspondence has been destroyed by fire, and beyond their official pronouncements, their precise motives remain unclear. Nonetheless, William Howe's reversal in mid-August suggests that his brother Richard and his peace initiative had exerted a strong influence on him during the preceding month. General Howe's new, more cautious approach also appears to have been a defensive reaction to British losses at Bunker Hill, the defeat of the Charleston expedition by American shore batteries, and his overestimate of Washington's forces in New York, which he placed at thirty-five thousand. Also, Howe was intent on protecting his troops, who would soon be adept at fighting in the terrain of the colonies—and difficult to replace.

Clinton argued for a landing at the northern tip of Manhattan to cut the Americans off on two islands—Manhattan and Long Island—but General Howe rejected the proposal. The disagreement echoed the situation at Bunker Hill, where Howe had disregarded Clinton's advice to land behind the Americans and trap them by seizing the neck of the Charlestown peninsula. In New York, Howe decided instead to land on Long Island in order to capture Brooklyn Heights and to keep the Americans from dominating the city with their artillery, much as they had done from Dorchester Heights outside Boston.

This plan would keep Howe's forces more concentrated and less vulnerable than if they were spread out in northern Manhattan, Staten Island, and Long Island. Moreover, the farmland of Long Island promised to feed the British army, making it less dependent on shipments of food from England, which might be delayed or destroyed in the three-thousand-mile Atlantic crossing. Finally, Howe, like Germain, expected Loyalists to turn out in large numbers on Long Island to welcome and support the British invasion.

COMPLETION OF AMERICAN DEFENSES

While the British spent the summer building up their invasion force, Washington's troops completed and extended Charles Lee's plan for the American fortifications. In June, Washington had decided to fortify the northern end of Manhattan in order to control the Kings Bridge and the Freebridge, the island's only links to the mainland. Washington would need them both for supplies coming in and as escape routes should the army be forced to retreat. The main citadel, soon named Fort Washington, was enormous, but it was crudely constructed and inadequate to withstand a siege. Fort Constitution, later called Fort Lee, was built directly across the Hudson from Fort Washington in order to aim guns from both shores at a line of obstructions in the river. Fort Independence was added in lower Westchester County to support Fort Washington and protect the Kings Bridge from the north.

On Long Island, Major General Nathanael Greene had put his four thousand troops to work on a new chain of forts, redoubts, and connecting trenches a mile and one-

half long across the neck of the peninsula to protect the Brooklyn Heights forts from the rear. Three more forts were built inside this principal line. The soldiers' habit of relieving themselves in the ditches around the forts caused fecal contamination of the water supply, which spread typhoid fever and typhus in the American ranks. Disease significantly impacted Washington's fighting strength, incapacitating one-quarter of his troops. General Greene was stricken with a high fever on 15 August, leaving Washington without the trusted commander most familiar with the critical Brooklyn Heights fortifications—and with the surrounding terrain.

Major General John Sullivan was appointed to fill Greene's command, and Sullivan made the most important addition to Charles Lee's scheme of defense: he decided to take advantage of the natural barrier provided by Gowanus Heights, a densely wooded ridge running parallel to the chain of redoubts and two miles to the south. To attack the American fortifications at the base of the peninsula, the British would have to go through one of the four passes where roads crossed the ridge through its natural depressions. Sullivan had fortified the three westernmost passes and planned to station eight hundred men at each one, where they could attack the advancing British forces and then drop back to Brooklyn Heights. However, the Jamaica Pass, four miles from the Brooklyn Heights fortifications on the American left wing, was left virtually unguarded.

INVASION OF LONG ISLAND

Misinformed by spies on Staten Island, Washington on 21 August anticipated a three-pronged attack—on Long Island, the Kings Bridge, and the New Jersey shore—and his troops were spread out in a precarious line straddling the Hudson and East Rivers. If British ships took control of either one, the American army would be divided into several parts that could easily be trapped. Such was the dilemma of defending the New York archipelago: Washington could only put his troops on alert for a possible night attack and await the results. The aggressive plan of cutting off and capturing the Americans resembled Clinton's approach, not General Howe's, and the attack on 21 August never came. Instead, the skies opened and barraged Washington's troops with rain, thunder, and lightning in massive doses, striking terror into the American camps and causing more that a dozen deaths along with other casualties.

On 22 August the British invaded Long Island, landing fifteen thousand troops at Gravesend Bay. Washington received erroneous reports that only eight thousand British troops had landed and still expected another twelve thousand to land at Kings Bridge. However, on 25 August, after the landing of almost five thousand Hessian troops, Washington was convinced that the main attack would be

The Battle of Long Island. *The passage of British troops from Staten Island to Gravesend Bay on 22 August 1776 is depicted in this nineteenth-century wood engraving.* THE GRANGER COLLECTION, NEW YORK

on Long Island, and he brought over additional reinforcements. With some nine thousand troops, the Americans were still outnumbered more than two to one by the twenty thousand British and Hessian soldiers on Long Island. Together, the number of participants from both sides made the ensuing engagement—the Battle of Long Island—the largest battle of the American Revolution.

BATTLE OF LONG ISLAND

On 26 August, the eve of the battle, Oliver De Lancey, a Loyalist adviser to General Howe, convinced him that a daring plan devised by Clinton to outflank the Americans at the Jamaica Pass was feasible with the help of local guides. That night the British marched a large column of troops around the American left wing and through the pass. They arrived behind the American positions on Gowanus Heights on the following morning, 27 August, and fired two cannon, signaling to the British forces arrayed in front of the ridge to press their attacks. The Americans sensed the trap and fled from the ridge to the fortifications on Brooklyn Heights. Some eight hundred Americans were captured, but a sacrificial rearguard action by Lord Stirling and the First Maryland Regiment on the right wing enabled hundreds of others to escape across Gowanus Creek.

AMERICAN EVACUATION TO MANHATTAN

The Battle of Long Island was not the massive slaughter that has often been described, but it was, nonetheless, a traumatic defeat for the Americans, who were penned in behind their line of defense with their backs to the East River. However, a strong wind blowing from the northeast kept the British fleet from sailing up the river to cut off their retreat, and General Howe opted to begin siege operations instead of storming the American lines, believing he could accomplish his purpose that way with fewer casualties. This gave Washington time to carry out a thorough evacuation of his men and matériel across the East River on the night of 29 August, leaving the British stunned and empty-handed.

Washington had reviewed the American disposition of troops on the eve of the Battle of Long Island and bore ultimate responsibility for the failure to secure the Jamaica Pass. More important in the long run was Howe's failure to follow up his victory on 27 August, which led to speculation that his friendly feelings for the Americans were shaping his strategy and tactics. Indeed, a two-week lull in the fighting that followed the American evacuation also reinforced the impression that the Howe brothers were reluctant to crush the rebels.

BATTLE FOR MANHATTAN

On 11 September, Admiral Howe hosted a peace conference on Staten Island attended by Benjamin Franklin, John Adams, and Edward Rutledge. Howe emphasized his gratitude for the monument to his brother George and a desire to reunite the colonies with the mother country. Having issued the Declaration of Independence, and mindful of displaying their steadfastness to their French and Dutch allies, the Americans refused to negotiate, and the conference ended abruptly.

Washington, who had secured the permission of Congress to abandon New York City to the British, began evacuating his forces up to a naturally strong defensive position on the plateau of Harlem Heights in northern Manhattan. At the same time, he dispatched Nathan Hale to spy on the British and determine when and where they would invade Manhattan. Washington also deployed the first combat submarine, the *Turtle*, which nearly succeeded in blowing up Admiral Howe's flagship, the *Eagle*. While the retreat was still in progress, hostilities resumed on 15 September with the British invasion of Manhattan at Kips Bay and the capture of New York City. American militiamen fled the British bombardment at Kips Bay despite Washington's personal efforts to rally them.

On a hill overlooking the landing area, General Howe and his top aides spent two hours taking tea at the home of Robert and Mary Murray while they waited for the troops to disembark and while thirty-five-hundred American troops escaped up the west side of the island. The incident gave rise to a morale-boosting myth in the American army that Mary Murray and her two daughters had deliberately charmed and delayed the British high command in order to save the American troops, who would otherwise have been trapped on the southern end of Manhattan. Howe's cautious approach of waiting for the invasion force to reach full strength before setting out across the width of Manhattan further fueled discontent among junior officers over the commander in chief's failure to pursue the Americans vigorously.

On 16 September, Washington sent an elite corps of rangers under Lieutenant Colonel Thomas Knowlton to reconnoiter Bloomingdale Heights, the plateau to the south of the American position, in order to determine British dispositions and plans. The rangers clashed with British forces, sparking the Battle of Harlem Heights, a small but significant morale-building victory for the Americans, who saw the British turn and flee for the first time. The British suffered a far more serious setback on 20–21 September, when a fire in New York destroyed a thousand buildings, one-quarter of the city. Convinced that American incendiaries had started the fire, the British became highly protective of their base of operations in New York, a habit that greatly influenced their strategic planning for the rest of the war. The British captured Nathan Hale and hanged him as a spy on 22 September.

INVASION OF WESTCHESTER COUNTY

Having failed in their first two attempts to trap the Americans—in Brooklyn and in lower Manhattan—the British launched a third amphibious landing, this time in Westchester County, in order to get behind Washington's position on Harlem Heights and cut him off from the mainland while severing his supply lines to Connecticut. On 12 October they sailed up through Hell Gate and landed on Throg's Neck, an island at high tide, where the Americans had pulled up the planks on the footbridges across the creek, enabling twenty-five riflemen behind a woodpile to fend off four thousand British troops.

Having lost several days, the British re-embarked and made a second landing at Pelham Bay, where Colonel John Glover and his regiment ambushed them from behind the stone walls lining the roads. The Battle of Pelham Bay was strategically important, because it delayed the British for a day while Washington's vulnerable army of thirteen thousand retreating troops made its way from Harlem Heights to White Plains. Washington entrenched his forces in the hills around the town. In the Battle of White Plains on 28 October, the British captured Chatterton's Hill on the American right wing, but at a high cost in casualties. Washington retreated into the hills north of White Plains, and Howe once again failed to

follow up swiftly. When Howe was ready to attack, a rainstorm lasting twenty hours cancelled his offensive.

FALL OF FORT WASHINGTON

On 2 November, Howe gave up the chase and headed south to capture Fort Washington in northern Manhattan. Fort Washington was now an American outpost behind British lines and had to be wiped out to consolidate Howe's grip on New York City and its environs. Fort Washington, along with Fort Lee, directly across the Hudson, was supposed to keep the British out of the river but had proved ineffective. Greene had told Washington the fort could be defended and if necessary evacuated across the river to New Jersey. Washington was dubious about the value of the fort but deferred to Greene as the commander on the spot. On 16 November, Howe issued an ultimatum for the surrender of the fort, and Colonel Robert McGaw, the garrison commander, refused. The British closed in on four fronts, securing the fort, a huge cache of supplies, some twenty-eight hundred American prisoners, and the entire northern end of Manhattan. This brought American losses in the New York campaign—killed, wounded, and captured—to forty-four hundred. The Americans captured in the campaign were among the estimated eleven thousand who perished during the war on British prison ships in Brooklyn's Wallabout Bay.

SIGNIFICANCE

The fall of Fort Washington, often erroneously labeled the worst American defeat of the war, ended the New York campaign and—along with the Battle of Long Island and the flight of the militia at Kips Bay—cast a pall on its memory. (In fact, the worst single loss of the war was Clinton's capture of Charleston, South Carolina, in 1780, when he seized the neck of the peninsula on which the city was built and took fifty-five hundred American prisoners.) Had the Howe brothers followed Clinton's very similar advice with regard to New York City, the American cause might have been crushed in 1776. Instead, Washington and his French allies adopted the tactics the British had failed to use in the New York campaign to trap them on the Yorktown peninsula in 1781, ushering in their final defeat two years later.

In New York, Washington's ability to execute timely retreats and prevent such a scenario from unfolding in favor of the British exposed General Howe's sluggish movements, cast doubt on his determination to defeat the Americans, and began to destroy his reputation. With the exception of the catastrophe at Fort Washington, the New York campaign was viewed by some contemporaries as a victory in disguise. Washington was in flight across New Jersey with a greatly diminished army at the end of

November 1776, but the core of a fighting force had escaped to carry on the Revolution. The British had captured a city they considered strategically vital, but maintaining control of New York during the next seven years would in large part cost them the war: reluctant to spare troops and ships from the defense of their principal base, the British failed to rescue Burgoyne at Saratoga in 1777 and Cornwallis at Yorktown in 1781—the two critical turning points of the American Revolution.

During the military occupation of the city from 1776 to 1783, the British also lost the battle for the hearts and minds of their Loyalist supporters. In the absence of civil courts, British soldiers and officials committed abuses and crimes against civilians with impunity. Corruption and profiteering within the army were rampant, while the city, crowded with Tory refugees, suffered from hyperinflation and acute shortages of shelter, food, and fuel. Efforts to reform the military regime and restore civil law came too late for the British to regain the moral high ground. On 25 November 1783, the British evacuated New York and, in a peaceful transfer, Washington triumphantly marched into the city he had lost in the campaign of 1776.

SEE ALSO *Harlem Heights, New York; Kips Bay, New York; Long Island, New York, Battle of; Staten Island Peace Conference; White Plains, New York.*

BIBLIOGRAPHY

Alden, John R. *Charles Lee: Traitor or Patriot?* Baton Rouge: Louisiana State University Press, 1951.

Bliven, Bruce, Jr. *Battle for Manhattan.* Baltimore: Penguin/Pelican, 1964.

Chase, Philander, ed. *The Papers of George Washington. Revolutionary Series.* Charlottesville: University of Virginia Press, 1988.

Clinton, Henry. *The American Rebellion.* Edited by William B. Willcox. New Haven, Conn.: Yale University Press, 1954.

Fitzpatrick, John, ed. *The Writings of George Washington.* 39 vols. Washington, D.C.: U.S. Government Printing Office, 1931.

Fleming, Thomas. *1776: Year of Illusions.* Edison, N.J.: Castle Books, 1996.

Gallagher, John. *The Battle of Brooklyn, 1776.* New York: Sarpedon, 1995.

Gruber, Ira D. *The Howe Brothers and the American Revolution.* New York: Atheneum, 1972.

Johnston, Henry P. *The Campaign of 1776 around New York and Brooklyn.* 1878. Reprint, Cranberry, N.J.: Scholar's Bookshelf, 2005.

Manders, Eric. *The Battle of Long Island.* Monmouth, N.J.: Philip Freneau Press, 1978.

Martin, Joseph Plumb. *A Narrative of a Revolutionary Soldier.* 1830. Reprint, New York Penguin/Signet Classics, 2001.

McCullough, David. *1776.* New York: Simon and Schuster, 2005.

Schecter, Barnet. *The Battle for New York: The City at the Heart of the American Revolution.* New York: Penguin, 2003.

Willcox, William B. *Portrait of a General: Sir Henry Clinton in the War of Independence.* New York: Knopf, 1964.

Barnet Schecter

NEW YORK CITY FIRE.

20–21 September 1776. Shortly after midnight on 21 September a fire broke out in a wooden house near Whitehall Slip and spread rapidly north with the help of a stiff breeze. A shift of wind at about 2 A.M. confined the fire to an area between Broadway and the Hudson River, but 493 houses were destroyed before British troops and residents of the city could put out the flames. The British accused the Americans of setting the fire, but the charge was never supported by anything more than circumstantial evidence. More than 200 suspects were questioned and released, but no one was ever convicted. The fire caused the British army a great deal of trouble, because they had counted on billeting troops in the city. During the seven years of British occupation, from 1776 to 1783, New York—having lost a quarter of its buildings in the fire—endured an acute housing shortage as Loyalist refugees flocked to the city. Despite the temptation to burn New York and deprive the enemy of winter quarters, Congress had prohibited the destruction of the city on the assumption that the Americans would eventually win it back. General George Washington commented that "Providence, or some good honest fellow, has done more for us than we were disposed to do for ourselves."

SEE ALSO *New York.*

BIBLIOGRAPHY

Commager, Henry Steele, and Richard B. Morris, eds. *The Spirit of Seventy-Six: The Story of the American Revolution as told by Participants,* 2 vols. New York: Harper & Row, 1967.

revised by Barnet Schecter

NEW YORK LINE.

New York was the first of the colonies outside of New England to face the idea of raising full-time troops, fearing exposure to British attacks from the sea or Canada. The Continental Congress recommended that it raise defensive garrisons on 25 May 1775. Six days later the Provincial Congress in New York City accepted the concept, although it did not decide on the composition of that force until 30 June. Meanwhile, on 14 June 1775 when it created the Continental Army, the Philadelphia body adopted the New York forces about to be raised as part of the national force. That summer the

New York Line came into being with four regiments. In the first year of the war these units held New York City, began fortifying the Hudson Highlands, and deployed to Lake Champlain and Canada.

When enlistments expired, the New Yorkers went through a bit of a tangled reorganization. One unit, Nicholson's Regiment, was created in Canada from veterans of all four of the 1775 regiments who had agreed to remain on duty during the siege of Quebec. The First, Third, and Fourth New York Regiments of 1775 regrouped and became (respectively) the First, Second, and Third New York Regiments of 1776. The 1775 Second Regiment, which was the unit raised in the northern end of the state, reenlisted under its former colonel, Goose Van Schaick, and returned to Canada as Van Schaick's Regiment, while a new Fourth Regiment was recruited in the same geographical area. In June 1776 other veterans, especially from that part of the 1775 Third New York which had gone into Canada, regrouped in the north as Dubois's Regiment. Thus the state provided a total of seven infantry regiments during the year.

In 1777, Congress reduced New York's quota to five regiments, partially reflecting the loss of New York City and Long Island to the British. The old First New York, which was the city's regiment, was disbanded, as was Nicholson's statewide formation. The two Albany-area regiments, Van Schaick's and the Fourth, merged and reenlisted as the new First New York Regiment. The 1776 Second and Third New York Regiments became, respectively, the 1777 Fourth and Second Regiments, while Dubois's Regiment became the new Third. Finally, a new Fifth New York Regiment was recruited, although with a heavy veteran cadre drawn primarily from the downstate counties. On 1 January 1781 the quota dropped further, to just two regiments. This was achieved by consolidating the First and Third Regiments of 1777 to form a new First New York Regiment, and the combining the Second, Fourth, and Fifth Regiments of 1777 to form the new Second New York. Both of these units served until the end of the war.

New York also contributed several other Continental Army elements which did not form part of the Line: Warner's Extra Continental Regiment (the Green Mountain Boys—Vermont was still a part of New York); most of Malcolm's Additional Continental Regiment; and the majority of the Second Continental Artillery Regiment were all recruited from New York.

SEE ALSO *Green Mountain Boys.*

BIBLIOGRAPHY

Clinton, George. *Public Papers of George Clinton, First Governor of New York.* Edited by Hugh Hastings, 10 vols. Albany, N.Y.: State printers, 1899–1914.

Egly, Theodore W., Jr. *History of the First New York Regiment 1775–1783.* Hampton, N.H.: Peter E. Randall, 1981.

Fernow, Berthold, ed. *New York in the Revolution.* Albany, N.Y.: Weed, Parsons and Co., 1887.

Gardner, Asa Bird. "The New York Continental Line of the Army of the Revolution." *Magazine of American History* 7 (December 1887): 401–419.

Lauber, Almon W., ed. *Orderly Books of The Fourth New York Regiment, 1778–1780; The Second New York Regiment, 1780–1783 by Samuel Tallmadge and Others with Diaries of Samuel Tallmadge, 1780–1782 and John Barr, 1779–1782.* Albany, N.Y.: University of the State of New York, 1932.

Lobdell, L. S., ed. "The Four New York Regiments." *Magazine of American History* 26 (August 1891): 147–150.

New York (State) Secretary's Office. *Calendar of Historical Manuscripts, Relating to the War of the Revolution, in the Office of the Secretary of State, Albany, New York.* 2 vols. Albany, N.Y.: Weed, Parsons, and Co., 1863–1868.

Roberts, James A., comp. *New York in the Revolution as Colony and State.* 2d ed. Albany, N.Y.: New York State, 1898.

Van Cortlandt, Philip. *Philip Van Cortlandt's Revolutionary War Correspondence and Memoirs.* Edited by Jacob Judd. Tarrytown, N.Y.: Sleepy Hollow Restorations, 1976.

Willett, William M. *A Narrative of the Military Actions of Colonel Marinus Willett, Taken Chiefly from his own Manuscript.* New York: G. & C. & H. Carvill, 1831.

Robert K. Wright Jr.

NEW YORK VOLUNTEERS.

Major General Thomas Gage, the British commander in North America, began the process of raising this unit when he sent two lieutenants from Boston to New York City on 18 July 1775 with orders:

> "to receive on board your [transport] ship such men as may be inclined to serve His Majesty, and you are particularly to attend to the arrival of ships from Scotland, and to procure as many men out of them as you possibly can, and . . . not to suffer any of those emigrants to join the rebels on shore."

The Volunteers were formally established at Halifax, Nova Scotia, in January and February 1776, and two companies joined William Howe's expedition against New York City in July. They fought at Long Island, White Plains, and Fort Washington and then became part of the garrison of New York City, joining other British and Provincial light forces in skirmishing against the Americans. With other elements of the New York garrison, they took part in Sir Henry Clinton's capture of Fort Montgomery, New York, on 6 October 1777. Sent south in late November 1778 under Lieutenant Colonel George Turnbull as part of Lieutenant Colonel Archibald Campbell's expedition against Savannah, Georgia, the

Volunteers stayed to help defend the city from the Franco-American counterattack in September–October 1779. On the American Establishment as the Third American Regiment from 2 May 1779, the Volunteers joined Clinton's expedition against Charleston, South Carolina, in May 1780. They remained in the South and fought at Hobkirk's Hill, outside Camden, on 25 April 1781, and again at Eutaw Springs on 8 September. Back in New York by August 1782, they were evacuated to Canada the next year and disbanded.

SEE ALSO *Turnbull, George.*

BIBLIOGRAPHY

Cole, Nan, and Todd Braisted. "The On-Line Institute for Advanced Loyalist Studies." Available online at http://www.royalprovincial.com.

Katcher, Philip R. N. *Encyclopedia of British, Provincial, and German Army Units, 1775–1783.* Harrisburg, Pa.: Stackpole Books, 1973.

Mills, T. F. "Land Forces of Britain, the Empire, and Commonwealth: The New York Volunteers (3rd American Regiment)." Available online at http://regiments.org.

Smith, Paul H. "The American Loyalists: Notes on Their Organization and Numerical Strength." *William and Mary Quarterly,* third series, 25 (1968): 259–277.

revised by Harold E. Selesky

NICARAGUA.

The operations of Britain in Central America were part of its war against Spain. They initially began as retaliatory actions against the Spanish with the relatively modest enterprise of taking the port of Omoa in Honduras. The success of the assault, which included the capture of large amounts of bullion, emboldened more ambitious plans that were attempted in 1780. The object was no less than to divide the Spanish Empire in the Americas and to open commercial routes with the Pacific by an expedition along the San Juan River through Lake Nicaragua to Granada and León. It was envisaged that, by creating of chain of posts across Central America, a single force might divide the northern and southern dominions of Spanish America. The plan also anticipated the possibility of fermenting insurrections among the Indians and other inhabitants against Spain, taking advantage of the presence of British settlers on the Mosquito Shore and the Moskito Indians.

The plan was primarily conceived by the governor of Jamaica, Major General John Dalling. On 3 February 1780 a force of four hundred regulars under Captain Polson sailed from Jamaica. They were accompanied by H.M.S. *Hinchinbrook*, commanded by Captain Horatio Nelson, the future victor of Trafalgar. The expedition stalled for three weeks at Cape Gracias à Dios before departing for the mouth of the San Juan on April 1. In fact, the river proved a major obstacle. Its navigation caused delays that deprived the expedition of the vital element of surprise and that exposed the troops to onset of the season of torrential rainfall before they had taken possession of the river. It proved dangerously shallow and unnavigable in some sections.

The enterprise proved a fiasco. It succeeded in the capture, after a six-day siege, of Fort San Juan on 29 April but failed to reach Lake Nicaragua and was called off by the middle of May. Colonel Stephen Kemble, who had assumed the command, withdrew to the sea, leaving a small garrison at the fort, which was subsequently evacuated and partly demolished on 4 January 1781. The original plan was conceived in ignorance of the realities of the region's geography, while the expectations of support among Native people and settlers were too optimistic. The primary reason for failure was disease among the troops. Dr. Benjamin Moseley, who participated in the expedition, calculated that of about 1,800 people involved, not more than 380 ever returned. Six of the nine officers lost their lives. Only 10 of the 200 crew members survived in the *Hinchinbroke*. Nelson and Lieutenant Edward Marcus Despard had to position the guns themselves owing to sickness among the troops at Fort San Juan. They alone received credit for their valor in what was otherwise regarded as a debacle.

The British government had committed additional resources for the campaign at a time when it denied extra troops to Sir Henry Clinton in New York. It is another example of the extent to which British interests outside North America deflected resources from the war for America after 1778. The Spanish, after repulsing the attack, fortified the mouth of the river to the lake and began their own offensive, in which they successfully removed the British from the Mosquito Shore.

SEE ALSO *Despard, Edward Marcus.*

BIBLIOGRAPHY

Conner, Clifford D. *Colonel Despard: The Life and Times of an Anglo-Irish Rebel.* Conshohocken, Pa.: Combined Publishing, 2000.

Pocock, Tom. *The Young Nelson in the Americas.* London: Collins, 1980.

revised by Andrew O'Shaughnessy

NICHOLAS, SAMUEL.

(1744–1790). Senior Continental marine officer. A native of Philadelphia, Samuel Nicholas was appointed captain of marines on 28 November 1775, and his commission was confirmed prior to that of any other officer of the Continental naval service. It remains uncertain whether he achieved his appointment because of his vocation or through a recommendation by one or more of his many prominent Philadelphia acquaintances. He led the storming of Fort Montagu, New Providence, Bahamas, on 3–4 March 1776, and on 25 June was promoted to major. He commanded the Marine battalion of 150 men that reinforced General George Washington's army at Trenton and Princeton, New Jersey, on 2–3 January 1777. From 1777 to 1780 he executed orders for the Marine Committee and the Board of Admiralty as a major of marines and as a muster master. He died in 1790 in Philadelphia.

SEE ALSO *Marines.*

revised by Charles R. Smith

NICOLA, LEWIS.

(1717?–1807). Continental officer. Ireland and Pennsylvania. Probably born in Ireland, perhaps in 1717, Nicola joined the British army as ensign in 1740, rising to the rank of major. He resigned his commission in 1766 to emigrate to America. Settling in Philadelphia, he established the *American Magazine* in 1769 and became active in the American Philosophical Society.

Early in 1776, Nicola became the barrack master of Philadelphia, and from December 1776 until February 1782 he was town major in command of the volunteer "home guards." In June 1777 Congress put him in command of the Invalid Regiment of Continental soldiers seriously wounded yet still capable of service, and among the useful duties he found for these incapacitated veterans was the instruction of recruits. Meanwhile he had been active as a recruiting officer, compiled and published *A Treatise of Military Exercise* (1776), and translated and published the Chevalier de Clairac's *L'Ingénieur de Campagne: or Field Engineer* (1776) and General De Grandmaison's *A Treatise, on the Military Service, of Light Horse and Light Infantry* (1777).

For about two years, starting in the summer of 1781, Nicola was with the main encampment of the army around Newburgh. In May 1782 he wrote to General George Washington, proposing that a monarchy be established with the commander-in-chief as king. Though others probably supported Nicola's proposal, Washington ignored it and it received no further attention. Congress did not know about Nicola's proposal that they be put out of business and innocently included Nicola among the twenty-six officers brevetted as brigadier generals in their resolution of 30 September 1783. He held various offices

in Philadelphia until 1798, when he moved to Alexandria, Virginia., where he died on 9 August 1807.

SEE ALSO *Invalid.*

revised by Michael Bellesiles

NINETY SIX, SOUTH CAROLINA.

Before the Revolution, the settlement called Ninety Six was a stockaded village on the "Charleston Path" into Cherokee territory and a critical junction in South Carolina's trade with Native Americans. Its name came from the erroneous belief that it was 96 miles from Fort Prince George, but the straight-line distance actually was less than 65 miles. It was the center of conflict between Tories and Patriots of the region in 1775 (see next article). When the British reoccupied the South in 1780 they established an important post at Ninety Six: in addition to being healthy and already fortified to a degree, its location maintained contact with the Indians and formed a base to rally local Loyalists. Unfortunately for the British, it also threatened the "Over Mountain" white settlements in what is now Tennessee. One reason why Cornwallis reacted so promptly to Morgan's movements before the battle of Cowpens was because he thought Morgan's objective was Ninety Six. The most important action at Ninety Six, was Greene's siege of 22 May–19 June 1781 (see below).

revised by Robert K. Wright Jr.

NINETY SIX, SOUTH CAROLINA.

19 November 1775. As tension mounted between Patriots and Loyalists, the South Carolina Council of Safety sent William H. Drayton, a member of the Provincial Congress, and the Reverend William Tennent inland during the month of August 1775 to organize Patriot forces. The Loyalist leaders Thomas Fletchall, Moses Kirkland, Robert and Patrick Cunningham, and Thomas Brown reacted by taking the field with a body of armed supporters. In September, one thousand Patriot militia under Drayton were confronted near Ninety Six by a larger force under Fletchall. Drayton persuaded the Loyalists to disperse, but they were later encouraged by his inability to rally militia and took the field again. On 3 November, Patrick Cunningham seized a group of wagons carrying a large shipment of gunpowder and lead that was intended as a gift from the Council of Safety to the Cherokee. On 19 November about six hundred Patriots under Major Andrew Williamson were driven into Ninety Six by eighteen

hundred Loyalists. For two days these frontiersmen exchanged heavy gunfire, the Loyalists losing four killed and twenty wounded, while the Patriots lost one dead and a dozen wounded. Facing a stalemate, the two sides agreed to a truce under which they would go their separate ways.

SEE ALSO *Reedy River, South Carolina.*

revised by Michael Bellesiles

NINETY SIX, SOUTH CAROLINA.

22 May–19 June 1781. Being the most important interior post after Camden, South Carolina, Ninety Six became Nathanael Greene's objective after the British abandoned Camden. Francis Lord Rawdon ordered Ninety Six evacuated, but his message was intercepted. At the time of Greene's approach, this strategic post had been considerably strengthened by Lieutenant Henry Haldane, a British army engineer. A stockade surrounded the village. On the east end was the Star Fort, a strong, star-shaped redoubt encircled by a ditch and abatis. Connected by a covered way to the west end of the village was an outpost called Fort Holmes, which consisted of a stockade to protect parties going for water from a little stream. The tactical weakness of the position came from the lack of a more protected source of water. At the time Lieutenant Colonel John Harris Cruger commanded a garrison of some 550 Loyalists at Ninety Six. Provincial units were the Second Battalion of James De Lancey's Brigade (New York; 150 men) and part of Skinner's New Jersey Volunteers (200 men), backed up by 200 South Carolina militia. The northern troops were veterans who had started their operations on Long Island and who had been seasoned not only by the partisan warfare of the South but also by service with British regulars at Savannah, Charleston, and around Camden; they were dedicated Loyalists who believed that loss of their fort would devastate the region's Tories. Provisions were adequate, but their artillery was limited to three three-pounders.

The Southern Department army under Greene reached Ninety Six on 22 May in a driving rain. Henry Lee's Partisan Corps was off supporting Andrew Pickens's militia in the siege of Augusta (22 May–5 June), Thomas Sumter was still fighting his own war and not paying attention to Greene, and Francis Marion was occupied dogging Rawdon's heels from Camden to the vicinity of Charleston (at Monck's Corner) and then patrolling the lower Santee (after taking Georgetown, South Carolina on 29 May). Greene had about one thousand regulars at Ninety Six and hoped to be reinforced as the detachments completed their missions. However, he had to start operations against a strong position with the forces immediately available. His most reliable troops were his two weak infantry brigades—the more experienced Maryland and Delaware veterans and the reconstituted Virginians—backed up by a small North Carolina militia contingent. Lacking heavy artillery—which were too difficult to bring along the wretched road network—Greene had no choice but to undertake formal siege operations by regular approaches.

GREENE'S ERRORS

After a hasty reconnaissance by his engineer, Thaddeus Kosciuszko, Greene—who was inexperienced in this type of operation—committed two errors right off the bat that would hobble the American siege. First, he directed his main effort against the strongest point of Cruger's defenses, the Star Redoubt, instead of against his water supply. Second, he started his works too close to the enemy's lines.

Cruger had seen Greene's scouts appear on 21 May and the main army arrive the next day to make camp at four points around his post. The morning of the 22d a rebel trench was seen a mere seventy yards away from the abatis that surrounded the Star. At 11 A.M. Cruger had completed construction of a gun platform on which his men had been working for several days. Covered by a surprise artillery fire from this platform and by small arms fire as well, Lieutenant John Roney sallied forth to wipe out the rebel work party. He was followed by militia and black laborers who filled in the trench and withdrew with the enemy's tools before Greene could react. It was a brilliant little coup, although Roney was mortally wounded.

The night of 23–24 May, Greene started his trenches a second time, at the respectable distance of four hundred yards. The defenders sent out raiding parties at night to interrupt this work, but by 3 June the second parallel of the formal siege's three-step approach was completed and the rebels were at about the point where Roney had scored his victory, some sixty yards from the Star Fort. Using the Fort Motte experience, Greene had also erected a Maham Tower. Cruger reacted by adding three feet of sandbags to the Star Fort but was unable to set the tower on fire with artillery hot shot. Greene now went through the formality of summoning the garrison to surrender, which Cruger refused, although he had already run out of fresh food and estimated that he only had a month's worth of supplies left. On the positive side, his losses to date had been insignificant and, unknown to the garrison, a powerful force of three fresh regiments from Ireland had just landed in Charleston to reinforce Rawdon.

As Greene's artillery raked the Star and the village from the completed portion of the approaches, work on the third and last leg of Kosciuszko's parallels went on night and day. Cruger ordered trenches dug for the protection of the refugees. When the attackers tried to set fire to the buildings with fire arrows, Cruger had the shingle roofs stripped off. When enemy artillery made the gun platform in the Star untenable during daylight, the defenders used them only at night.

AMERICAN REINFORCEMENTS

On 8 June Henry "Light-Horse Harry" Lee arrived from the successful capture of Augusta with major reinforcements in the form of his Second Partisan Corps. The defenders had momentarily hoped this troop movement was Rawdon coming to their rescue, knowing neither that he had only set out from Charleston the day before nor that his relief column had to take a roundabout route to avoid being ambushed. Now, as part of Lee's force marched within artillery range of the fort with its prisoners from Fort Cornwallis at Augusta, Georgia, the Ninety Six garrison assumed that Greene was conducting psychological warfare. They particularly objected to the thought that the rebels were using prisoners to shield themselves from retaliatory fire. Henry Lee presented a different picture, saying that the officer commanding this detachment took the wrong road and was "very severely reprimanded by Lieutenant Colonel Lee, for the danger to which his inadvertence had exposed the corps."

Lee's reinforcements allowed Greene to begin additional siege operations from the north, correcting the flaws in his original attack plan by finally applying pressure against Fort Holmes with a view to cutting off the enemy's water supply. Although Lee said in his *Memoirs* that Kosciuszko's "blunders lost us Ninety Six" and comments on his failure to attack the water supply, Lee does not claim credit for proposing that his troops be assigned this mission; the historian Christopher Ward, on the other hand, has said in *The War of the Revolution* that Lee "immediately suggested" the plan, and others have echoed this opinion. (Most likely, the belief that Lee made the proposal is a logical assumption that just happens to be wrong, since false modesty was not one of Lee's character defects.)

Cruger continued to maintain an active defense, sending out frequent patrols under the cover of darkness to check on American activities and to try slowing down the siege by damaging the artillery and trenches. On the night of 9–10 June the defenders sent two raiding parties. One overran a four-gun battery but lacked the specialized equipment needed to spike the tubes and put them out of action; on the other hand, this party discovered the mouth of the mine that had been started north of the Star. The other group of raiders attacked the covering party in Lee's sector.

GREENE'S DECISIONS

On 11 June, Greene got a message from Sumter saying that British reinforcements had reached Charleston and were marching to the relief of Ninety Six. He responded in two ways. First, he ordered Pickens and William Washington, with all his cavalry, to join Sumter and Marion in blocking this movement. Then he redoubled his efforts to reduce the little fortress. At 11 A.M. on the 12th, covered by "a dark, violent storm . . . from the west, without rain," a sergeant and nine privates of the Legion infantry crawled toward Fort Holmes in an attempt to set fire to the stockade; they were discovered in the act of starting the fire and the sergeant and five men were killed (Lee, op. cit., 373). But by the 17th the Americans were finally able to cut the garrison off from normal access to its water supply.

Cruger's hopes rebounded that same day, however, when the first messenger from Rawdon finally made it through the besiegers' lines. He reported that the relief column was on the march. Sumter had assumed that Rawdon would march by way of Fort Granby, and by trying to block that route he took himself out of position so that Rawdon slipped past the trap.

Greene now had three alternatives: give up the entire operation and retreat; move against Rawdon; or storm the fort before Rawdon could arrive, even though the parallels had not yet been completed. With only half the number of regular infantry as Rawdon, Greene adopted the third alternative. According to Lee, Greene probably would have retreated, but:

> his soldiers, with one voice, entreated to be led against the fort. The American army having witnessed the unconquerable spirit which actuated their general . . . recollected, with pain and remorse, that by the misbehavior of one regiment at the battle of Guilford, and of another at Hobkirk's Hill, their beloved general had been deprived of his merited laurels; and they supplicated their officers to entreat their commander to give them now an opportunity of obliterating their former disgrace. This generous ardor could not be resisted by Greene.

THE ASSAULT

A coordinated attack by Lee and Lieutenant Colonel Richard Campbell was to be made against Fort Holmes and the Star Redoubt, covered by an artillery barrage and snipers in the Maham Tower. The advance team, known in the era as the Forlorn Hope, was commanded by Captain Michael Rudolph on Lee's front and by Lieutenants Isaac Duval and Samuel Seldon on Campbell's. Another team, equipped with iron hooks on long poles to pull down the sandbags and fascines to bridge the ditch, followed the Forlorn Hope at the Star. Assault forces moved into position in the trenches at 11 A.M. on the 18th. A signal cannon fired at noon began the assault.

Rudolph fought his way into Fort Holmes, which was now lightly held; the rest of Lee's infantry and Kirkwood's company followed. Lee then awaited the outcome of Campbell's attack and prepared to attack across the stream. The assault groups of Duval and Seldon moved forward as planned. Axmen cut gaps through the abatis at two points; others used the fascines to fill in the ditch, and the men with the hooks began pulling down sandbags. Campbell's main body waited for the gaps to open while the remaining Virginia and Maryland Continentals fired by platoons from their trenches.

Cruger had chosen to mass his three small guns in an attempt to make them decisive, and he personally directed their fire. He first engaged Lee but then shifted the guns against Campbell with greater effect. The Star was defended by Major Green and 150 New York Loyalists. Seeing that passive measures would lead inevitably to defeat, he gambled and launched most of his men in a counterattack. Two thirty-man groups under Captains Thomas French and Peter Campbell exited from a sally port behind the Star, circled in opposite directions to the front, and attack the rebels who were in defilade in the ditch. American supporting fire prevented the defenders from engaging troops in the ditch by sweeping away anyone who exposed himself in an effort to lean over. This aggressive solution succeeded in defeating the Forlorn Hope in desperate hand-to-hand combat after both Duval and Seldon were disabled by wounds. At that point Campbell's attack failed and the men retreated. Forty-five minutes after it had begun, the assault was over.

Greene had been beaten again; although his men performed as well as any commander could ask, he, Kosciuszko, and Sumter had made too many mistakes against an enemy that was energetic and well-led. Lee's forces withdrew from Fort Holmes after dark, and Greene lifted the siege on the 19th. That day he fell back ten miles to put the Saluda River between his men and Rawdon. The cavalry rejoined him there, and the Americans then retreated in the direction of Charlotte, North Carolina, to begin refitting and preparing for their next mission. Rawdon reached Ninety Six the morning of the 21st, having marched almost two hundred miles under a blazing sun through desolated country with two thousand troops. After a dramatic welcome by Cruger and his garrison, Rawdon pursued Greene, but when he reached the Enoree River (about thirty miles northeast of Ninety Six), he received intelligence that convinced him he was too far behind and so returned to Ninety Six. In spite of Cruger's heroics, the strategic situation rendered Ninety Six untenable. Rawdon had no choice but to abandon the post and fall back toward Charleston, harassed by the American cavalry and militia. Marching back and forth caused particular suffering for his three new regiments (3d, 19th, and 30th Foot), which had just completed the arduous voyage from Ireland and had not yet acclimated themselves.

LOSSES

During the 28-day siege, the rebels lost 185 killed and wounded, according to Lee. Ward has said they lost 147: 57 killed, 70 wounded, and 20 missing. Cruger lost 27 killed and 58 wounded. Only one officer was killed on each side, Roney and George Armstrong (First Maryland).

SIGNIFICANCE

The siege of Ninety Six marked the last gasp of the crown's southern strategy. Local Loyalist support had not been sufficient to exert a hold on the interior portions of Georgia or the Carolinas, and the ministry never had enough regular troops to commit to hold all of the ports and inland settlements. Greene's policy of preserving his main Southern Department force of Continentals and maneuvering it in a manner that tied up Rawdon's regulars, while at the same time using Lee and Washington to "stiffen" the southern partisans, succeeded. Although he never won a decisive battlefield victory, his subordinates systematically eliminated all of the outlying posts. The siege would also be Rawdon's last engagement before he started back to Britain (and was captured at sea).

SEE ALSO *Augusta, Georgia (22 May–5 June 1781); Cruger, John Harris; De Lancey, James; Kosciuszko, Thaddeus Andrzej Bonawentura; Lee, Henry ("Light-Horse Harry"); Marion, Francis; Monck's Corner, South Carolina; Pickens, Andrew; Rawdon-Hastings, Francis; Southern Campaigns of Nathanael Greene; Sumter, Thomas; Washington, William.*

BIBLIOGRAPHY

Bass, Robert D. *Ninety-Six: The Struggle for the South Carolina Backcountry.* Lexington, S.C.: Sandlapper Store, 1978.

Cann, Marvin L. "War in the Backcountry: The Siege of Ninety Six, May 22–June 19, 1781." *South Carolina Historical Magazine* 72 (January 1971): 1–14.

Lee, Henry. *Memoirs of the War in the Southern Department of the United States.* 1827. Revised edition. New York: University Publishing, 1869.

Ward, Christopher. *War of the Revolution.* New York: Macmillan, 1852.

revised by Robert K. Wright Jr.

NIXON, JOHN. (1727–1815). Continental general. Massachusetts. Son of a man who also spelled his name Nickson, he was born at Framingham, Massachusetts, on 1 March 1727. At age eighteen he enlisted in Sir William

Pepperrell's Regiment and took part in the attack on Louisburg, Canada, in 1745. He was a lieutenant in the first contingent (7 March 1755) raised in Massachusetts at the start of the final French and Indian War, became a captain six months later (8 September) in Colonel Timothy Ruggles's Regiment, and fought at the battle of Lake George. He spent the winter on the frontier, and the next year was again a captain under Ruggles. After moving over the Framingham town line to Sudbury in 1758, he served as a captain in three more expeditions (1759, 1761, and 1762).

On 19 April 1775 he marched as captain of the minuteman company from Sudbury to the South Bridge at Concord, and there joined in harrying the British back to Boston. Five days later, he was appointed a colonel in the Massachusetts eight-months' army. He led his men across Charlestown Neck to support the redoubt and breastworks at Bunker Hill on 17 June and was seriously wounded in action. He took part in the siege of Boston and the defense of New York City, becoming colonel of the Fourth Continental Regiment on 1 January 1776 and brigadier general on 9 August 1776. His brigade of three Rhode Island and two Massachusetts regiments was assigned to Major General Nathanael Greene's division. It did not take part in the battle of Long Island, but a detachment was heavily engaged at Harlem Heights on 16 September and again at White Plains on 28 October. Nixon's brigade remained in the Hudson Highlands at the start of the New Jersey campaign, but moved south with the column led by Major General Charles Lee. During the Trenton campaign the brigade was down the Delaware River with the forces led by John Cadwalader and saw no action.

Appointed to command the First Massachusetts Brigade (Third, Fifth, Sixth, and Seventh Regiments) at the start of the 1777 campaign, Nixon and his men were ordered to reinforce the Northern army against the invasion of Burgoyne's army, reaching Fort Edward on 13 July. Major General Philip Schuyler, commander of the Northern Department, was anxious for reinforcement and complained that Nixon had taken four days to cover 46 miles with his brigade of only 575 rank and file fit for duty. Major General Horatio Gates, who replaced Schuyler on 4 August, placed Nixon's brigade on the extreme right of the defensive line atop Bemis Heights, overlooking the Hudson River, and it held this position during the two battles of Saratoga. The brigade led the tardy pursuit, however, and was halted at the Fishkill on 11 October after drawing fire from what Gates suddenly learned was not the enemy's rear guard but his main force. Nixon suffered permanent impairment to an eye and an ear during the fighting when a cannon ball passed close to his head. After escorting the Saratoga prisoners to Cambridge, Nixon spent several months on sick leave, married the widow of a comrade killed at Harlem Heights (Micajah Gleason), sat on the court-martial of

Philip Schuyler (October 1778), and on 12 September 1780 resigned because of ill health.

He took no part in public life after the war. About seven years before his death he moved from Sudbury to Middlebury, Vermont, where he died on 24 March 1815.

SEE ALSO *Boston Siege; Bunker Hill, Massachusetts; Harlem Heights, New York; Saratoga, First Battle of; Saratoga, Second Battle of.*

BIBLIOGRAPHY

Merriam, John M. "The Military Record of Brigadier General John Nixon of Massachusetts." *Proceedings of the American Antiquarian Society*, New Series, vol. 36 (April 1926): 38–70.

revised by Harold E. Selesky

NIXON, JOHN.

(1733–1808). Patriot merchant, financier. Pennsylvania. Born in Philadelphia in 1733, Nixon (not to be confused with General John Nixon) inherited his father's shipping business and wharf in Philadelphia when he was about sixteen years old. He was soon a leading figure in the city's public affairs, becoming a lieutenant of the Dock Ward Company in 1756, signing the nonimportation agreement in 1765, helped organize the "Silk Stockings" volunteer militia (Third Battalion of Associators) of which he was lieutenant colonel, and in late 1775, acted as president of the provincial Committee of Safety when Benjamin Franklin and Robert Morris were absent. In 1776 he had a particularly active year; after commanding the defense of Fort Island in the Delaware in May, he took command of the Philadelphia city guard, served on the Continental Navy Board, gave the first public reading of the Declaration of Independence in Philadelphia on 8 July, marched a short time later with his battalion to the defense of Amboy, and then took the field in the Trenton and Princeton campaign, succeeding John Cadwalader as colonel.

In 1779 he was an auditor of public accounts and was involved in settling and adjusting the depreciated Continental currency. The next spring he helped organize the Bank of Pennsylvania to supply the army, contributed five thousand pounds, and was appointed one of its two directors. In 1784 he became a director of the Bank of North America; in 1792 he became its second president and held this post until his death. Meanwhile, he was a city alderman from 1789 to 1796. His son, Henry, married a daughter of Robert Morris and was the bank's fourth president. Nixon died in Philadelphia on 31 December 1808.

revised by Michael Bellesiles

NOAILLES, LOUIS MARIE. (1756–1804).

French officer. Born in Paris on 17 April 1756, the vicomte de Noailles was the son of Marshal Philippe duc de Mouchy. Becoming a captain at the age of seventeen, Noailles sought to go to America with his brother-in-law, the marquis de Lafayette, but was discouraged by his family. Instead he was appointed aide to the quartermaster in 1778 and made second in command of the Hussards regiment in 1779. Gaining a reputation for his cool head at the siege of Grenada in July 1779, Noailles took part in the unsuccessful attempt to capture Savannah, where he again distinguished himself. Awarded the chevalier de Saint-Louis on 20 January 1780, Noailles joined Rochambeau's army in Rhode Island in July 1780. Active in the Battle of Yorktown in October 1781, he was given the honor of serving as the official French representative at Cornwallis's surrender. Returning to France with Lafayette, Noailles was made commandant of the King's Dragoons on 27 January 1782. In the early phase of the French Revolution, Noailles was a prominent liberal, serving in the Estates-General, where he and Lafayette led the contingent of aristocrats who joined with the other orders in creating the National Assembly on 25 June 1789 and proposing an end to all privileges of the nobility on 4 August. In 1791 he was elected president of the Constituent Assembly. Noailles fled France for England in 1792 as the Revolution spun out of control, moving on the following year to Philadelphia, where he became a successful businessman. In 1802 he went to the West Indies, again taking command of French troops. He was wounded in a sea battle and died in Havana on 7 January 1804.

BIBLIOGRAPHY

Balch, Thomas W. *The French in America during the War of Independence of the United States, 1777–1783.* 2 vols. Philadelphia: Porter and Coates, 1891–1895.

Michael Bellesiles

"NO-FLINT." Nickname of Charles Grey.

SEE ALSO *Grey, Charles ("No-flint").*

NO-MAN'S LAND AROUND NEW YORK CITY.

Westchester County, New York, had the misfortune to be situated between the American and British lines for seven years, from 1776 to 1783. During that time detachments from both armies, as well as local militia for both sides and outlaws and plunderers for neither side, ravaged the countryside and the population. A county that started the war as a prosperous farming area with perhaps twenty-two thousand people would end the war with a mostly depleted populace, farms ruined, and years of rebuilding ahead of it. This Neutral Zone, as it was often called during the war, proved to be one of the deadliest and most dangerous locations in the American Revolution, caught in the crosshairs of the two contending armies.

The trouble for this doomed region actually began in November 1775, when a Whig supporter of the rebellion, Isaac Sears, decided to take matters into his own hands and led a band of eighty supporters into New York City and destroyed James Rivington's pro-British printing press. Sears and his men then left the city and headed toward Connecticut, stopping along the way in Westchester County to disarm several Loyalists. Other Loyalists throughout the New York City area began to band together to protect themselves from similar treatment.

THE BRITISH ARMY ARRIVES

The real problems started after the British army arrived in August 1776 and took control of New York City in a series of battles between August and October 1776. The British maintained a garrison in the county from that point until the end of the war, evacuating in November 1783. During that time the British lines usually extended about ten miles north of Manhattan Island, up to Phillipsburgh on the Hudson River to the north and eastward to Eastchester on Long Island Sound. The American lines were centered on Peekskill and the southern part of the Highlands, a rough and mountainous region that extended on both sides of the Hudson River about twenty-five miles north of Manhattan Island. The land in between these lines became the Neutral Zone, a battleground for every type of military formation, from scouting parties and foragers from the regular armies to militia and to lawless elements intent on plundering for their own profit. Many men fled the area, especially Loyalist males, who feared harassment, imprisonment, or even death at the hands of the Whig militia and outlaws roaming the area. Many of these Loyalist men would make their way to New York City and ultimately join bands of Loyalists that raided back into the Neutral Zone.

Soon after the British occupied Staten Island, Manhattan Island, and Long Island, the Whig-controlled New York state convention ordered all livestock and grain in the area between the armies to be confiscated to keep it out of the hands of the enemy. New York militia forces swarmed through the region, taking everything they could find. This process became an annual event, as parties from both sides tried desperately to control the vital food supplies of the area. Since the British were often low on food in New York City, they were especially desirous of obtaining as many supplies as they could from the territory north of their lines.

COWBOYS AND SKINNERS

Into this vacuum emerged the Cowboys, a mostly pro-British unit made up of Loyalist militiamen and some soldiers detached or deserted from the British army itself. William Tryon, the former royal governor of New York, initially raised the unit. The Cowboys specialized in rustling cattle from farms in the area and from herds being driven from New England through the area south toward the American forces in New Jersey and Pennsylvania. The Cowboys' numbers varied from a few dozen to a few hundred over the years. By 1780 they were commanded by the notorious Loyalist, James De Lancey. They raided throughout Westchester County, often preying on the easiest targets, such as lone farmers, plundering them and then moving on. They were not interested in fighting, just stealing. At times, the Cowboys would act in conjunction with units detached from the British army in order to gather forage and other supplies to be taken back to the army for its use. In addition, the Cowboys often sold their plunder to the British army, making a good profit for themselves.

Another Loyalist unit that raided the area was the Loyalist Westchester Refugees, created by the British command in 1777. These partisans were considered more of a combat unit, sent out to fight the growing partisan war against Whig militia forces and Continental army detachments operating in the area, as well as collecting plunder when possible. The Westchester Refugees numbered about five hundred men by the end of the war, usually about half of them mounted when going into action.

The main rebel unit that emerged in this Neutral Zone was the Skinners. This force consisted of local militiamen and other raiders unattached to any particular military unit. The Skinners were less careful about whom they plundered than were the Cowboys, as they stole from anyone on either side of the war. The Westchester militia was not called to serve outside of the county because of the chaotic and dangerous situation that existed there, so the local militiamen were free to focus their energies on plundering the area and hunting the Cowboys. Occasionally, detachments from nearby Continental units assisted the Skinners on their raids. The Skinners had a brutal reputation, perhaps worse than the Cowboys, and there were reports of Skinners using torture to get local inhabitants to reveal the whereabouts of their valuables. At times, the Skinners would even sell stolen goods to the Cowboys to buy goods from within the British lines in New York City. Skinners also were known to steal cattle from within the American lines, claiming they thought they were taking the cattle from the Cowboys.

One unexpected benefit that came from this incessant warfare between the Cowboys and the Skinners was the capture of Major John André, the agent who was in contact with Benedict Arnold during his treasonous activity in 1780. A party of local militia, out hunting Cowboys, ran into André, questioned him, refused an offer of money from him, and sent him to General George Washington, who was at West Point at that time. This action helped prevent the fall of the fort at West Point to the British, which Arnold and André were trying to coordinate.

Washington's Continental army became directly involved in the hunt for the Cowboys and the effort to stop the plundering in 1778, when he used the newly created Light Infantry Corps to guard the Neutral Zone. This unit consisted of regular infantry and dragoons as well as Westchester militia forces. The fighting in the area escalated that autumn when the Light Infantry corps skirmished with Hessian Jägers and Lieutenant Colonel John Simcoe's Queen's Rangers. In 1781 Washington ordered a mixed force of militia and Continentals to attack De Lancey's base at Morrisania. They burned the barracks, killed and captured over seventy Loyalists, and lost only twenty-five men. However, nearby British soldiers garrisoning a fort joined the surviving Loyalists and then pursued the American force on its withdrawal. Such larger-scale operations might slow down the raids for a while but never stopped them. Well into 1783, the Cowboys and Skinners pursued their careers of plunder and theft.

THE ARMIES BATTLE

Another aspect of the war in this Neutral Zone was the constant skirmishing between the two main armies stationed in the area. Westchester County became a battleground, twelve months a year for almost six years, as both armies contended for critical forage and supplies as well as trying to keep the other side as far away as possible. This no-man's-land was a very dangerous place to be, stuck right between the lines of what usually amounted to the two largest forces for both sides during the war.

At its least perilous, this Neutral Zone was the crossroads through which the contending forces traveled to get at each other. This started in January 1777, when New York militia forces assembled at North Castle and marched against the British fortifications near Manhattan Island. Then, starting in the winter of 1777, Washington initiated a deliberate policy of harassing all enemy movement outside of the British lines, and this led to constant skirmishing between units of the main armies and associated militia forces. The Neutral Zone became a key battlefield of this struggle over the next years. The American goals were to collect the forage of the area, deny it to the enemy, and force the British to fight constantly and thus take losses. The local Westchester militia, aided at times by militia from southwestern Connecticut, had the primary responsibility for protecting the region. Continental troops usually garrisoned the forts in the Highlands north of the area and occasionally moved into the no-man's-land to lend a hand. In addition, as noted earlier, in a few instances Washington ordered larger army units, such as the Light Infantry Corps, into the region. Winter and spring were the most deadly times for the skirmishing in the area. During the summer and autumn, the armies tended to focus on the larger campaigns, and this left the region mostly to the continued contest between forces such as the Cowboys and Skinners.

The maneuvers in the area tended to target either opposing supply concentrations or local fortifications. In the spring of 1777 the British moved up the Hudson River and attacked the American supply magazine at Peekskill, while in August 1777, Americans moved against the British post at Kings Bridge at the northern end of Manhattan Island. In September–October 1777, British General Sir Henry Clinton moved in force against the American forts in the Highlands. Though the Neutral Zone was not a prime target of these kinds of maneuvers, soldiers from both sides regularly traversed the area. Clinton's operation of 1777 included subsidiary raids into Westchester County to divert American militia forces. As the Americans withdrew northward, Connecticut militia tried to fill the void, but with only partial success. British foragers collected supplies, while Loyalists under Tryon moved toward the Connecticut border. Connecticut militia forces were able to repel this advance. As the British withdrew back toward New York City in late October, General Israel Putnam pursued them through this Neutral Zone, while Continental and militia forces from Connecticut pushed southwestward to support Putnam. In November, Putnam threatened the British posts near Manhattan Island but withdrew without seriously attacking.

In 1778 George Clinton, the governor of New York, ordered long-term militia units to stand guard in Westchester County to protect the forage of the area and to prevent communication between the Loyalists and the British army. A regiment of Continental soldiers remained at White Plains to support the local militia. One regiment of Westchester militia, commanded by Lieutenant Colonel Morris Graham, took post very near the British garrison at Fort Independence, just outside New York City. From this advanced post, Graham was able to scout on enemy movements and engage any enemy parties when they first emerged from the British lines. Meanwhile, Connecticut militia continued to guard southwestern Connecticut and help support the Westchester militia as well.

By this point, Washington had learned the need to support the militia in the Neutral Zone, and in the spring of 1778 he ordered a cavalry regiment to station itself along the Hudson to be available. He also advised commanders in the area to keep the infantry, both regular and militia, back

nearer fortifications, while sending out only light infantry and cavalry to engage the enemy. Washington, as always, also urged offensive operations against nearby British outposts, but General Horatio Gates, who commanded in the region, declined, considering such moves too risky.

Later that summer, after the British had evacuated Philadelphia and the two main armies had returned to their positions in and around New York City, Washington took further measures to deal with the growing problems in Westchester County. This is when he decided to place a newly created Continental unit there. First, a party of two thousand regulars and militia scoured the area for forage at his behest; then he sent in the Light Infantry Corps, commanded by General Charles Scott. Consisting of Continental infantry, a New York state militia regiment, and the army's dragoons, this corps maintained a forward defense to block British incursions and protect the inhabitants from plundering. Washington withdrew this corps in September, but he kept Continental detachments in the area to support the local militia and to relieve it from its constant duty. Later that autumn, Scott's Light Infantry Corps returned to the area to collect forage once again and to prevent British raids.

Governor Clinton also tried to support the local militia of the Neutral Zone. He ordered militia rangers and other militia detachments into the area from neighboring locations to ease the burden of the local militia and to help hunt down plunderers such as the Cowboys.

In September 1778 the British launched large-scale raids into New Jersey and up the Hudson River, and in the Neutral Zone, Scott's Corps fell back slowly, fighting and skirmishing with the advancing enemy forces. The British commander, Sir Henry Clinton, used this advance to collect supplies and to lure Washington into a large-scale battle. Clinton succeeded at his first goal but failed to gain his desired battle. As always, the people of Westchester County found themselves caught between the movements of the opposing armies.

On the other hand, because of the heightened fears for the area, Washington maintained a strong Continental presence in the county through the winter of 1778–1779. This lent increased protection for the inhabitants and allowed the local militia to gain some needed rest. But still the raids and plundering continued. British raiding parties, consisting of from one to four thousand soldiers, marched through the area in November and December, gathering everything they could find. In addition, these parties in December tried but failed to strike the Continental army's baggage train.

Increasingly, the British need for supplies drove their policy in the Neutral Zone. The month of January 1779 was a time of crisis for the British as supply levels hit critically low levels in New York City. Loyalists, Cowboys, and many others looking to make money tried to get supplies from Westchester County to the city to sell for hard British gold, and Continental patrols and local militia tried to intercept them. Despite the strenuous efforts to stop such trade, the British were able to acquire enough supplies to last until a supply fleet arrived in late January.

Again, in May–June 1779 British forces advanced northward through the county to attack American positions at Stony Point and Verplank's Point. As the British lingered in the area, Washington detached Continental units to join with the local militia to harass the British advance forces and to threaten their rear by marching through the Neutral Zone behind the British force. Finally, the British withdrew toward the city, but they took the field again in July, marching northeastward toward Connecticut in conjunction with increased amphibious raids along Long Island Sound. The British marched through Westchester County from Phillipsburgh on the Hudson to Mamaroneck on the Sound, right through the heart of the Neutral Zone. Then they marched to Bedford, burned it, and finally withdrew back to Kings Bridge. Finally, by late July 1779, these latest maneuvers came to an end, and a relative calm descended on the Neutral Zone once again. Raids and counterraids continued through the autumn months.

LATE WAR RAIDS

This pattern persisted for the next two years as large-scale operations were few in Westchester County, but foraging, raids, and skirmishes were constant, towns were burned, and people fled. Early in the winter of 1779–1780 saw raids by Connecticut militia against a Loyalist base near the Cowboy base at Morrisania in January and a clash in February between British, German, and Loyalist forces on one side and Continentals stationed just north of the British lines on the other. Fortunately, these raids were actually fewer in number during this winter than previously because a large portion of the British army was with Sir Henry Clinton in South Carolina, and General Wilhelm Knyphausen, commanding in New York City, feared to send out too many men.

Throughout the campaigning season, Westchester County was pretty well protected by the proximity of larger units from the Continental army, but by September, Washington had begun to withdraw the army, and by December 1780 the army was going into winter quarters, leaving Westchester County once again open to the increased depredations of Loyalists, Cowboys, and Skinners. More and more inhabitants fled and more and more towns became deserted. The Neutral Zone was becoming a literal no-man's-land as few men were still living in the area. The militia detachments and Loyalist raiders were often the only men there. By the end of 1780, North Castle and Bedford were both mostly destroyed and empty. The British were scouring the area with abandon,

gathering supplies from as far away as the Connecticut border. About two thousand Continentals were sent to Bedford, but they were of little help in stopping the depredations through the early months of 1781, as even southwestern Connecticut towns were increasingly abandoned.

In fact, the devastation was so bad in Westchester County by the summer of 1781 that when the French army marched through on its way to join Washington outside New York City, many French officers were shocked at what they saw. The arrival of the French in New York in July 1781 led to larger-scale fighting in the part of Westchester County near the British lines. As French and American forces linked, they advanced through the area towards Kings Bridge and Morrisania. British units emerged from their lines, and over the next two days confused fighting raged throughout the area. In the end, both armies disengaged and withdrew, ending the possibility of a full-scale battle. The Cowboy base at Morrisania survived, much to the misfortune of the people still living in the Neutral Zone.

After this, the usual patterns of raids and revenge plagued the no-man's-land through the rest of 1781 and into 1782. Winter skirmishing and depredations, including attacks on North Castle and Morrisania, all occurred once again, with no real change in the situation other than more death, destruction, and misery for the few people still living in the area. The major victory of the Continental and French armies at Yorktown did not immediately end the brutal contest in the Neutral Zone. Loyalists, local militia, and detachments of Continental soldiers continued to skirmish right through the spring of 1782.

Finally, in May 1782 the British commanders in New York City ordered all such raids by British and Loyalist parties to stop, and slowly the hostilities in Westchester County eased but did not totally end. Increasingly, the raids were now made by outlaws and plunderers out for themselves rather than organized units fighting for one side or the other. However, as late as March 1783, local militia attacked the Loyalist base at Morrisania one last time.

By April 1783 both sides had ordered an end to all fighting, but until the state government could reestablish civilian control, people took advantage of the chaos and continued to plunder and steal from local inhabitants. New York militia and even Continental detachments were sent into the area to aid civilian authority in establishing control, but renegade bands continued to scour the area. This violence continued right up until the final evacuation of the British army from New York City in November 1783. At that point, the relentless partisan war, constant raids, and plundering and looting finally came to an end in this divided and war-torn no-man's-land.

SEE ALSO *Arnold's Treason; Cowboys and Skinners; De Lancey, James; Guerrilla War in the North; Hudson*

River and the Highlands; Loyalists in the American Revolution; Militia in the North; Queen's Royal Rangers; Scott, Charles; Sears, Isaac; Tryon, William.

BIBLIOGRAPHY

Barnes, Ian. *The Historical Atlas of the American Revolution.* New York: Routledge, 2000.

Buel, Richard, Jr. *Dear Liberty: Connecticut's Mobilization for the Revolutionary War.* Middletown, Conn.: Wesleyan University Press, 1980.

Freeman, Douglas Southall. *George Washington: A Biography.* 7 vols. New York: Scribner's Sons, 1948–1957.

Higginbotham, Don. *The War of American Independence: Military Attitudes, Policies, and Practice, 1763–1789.* New York: Macmillan, 1971.

Kwasny, Mark V. *Washington's Partisan War, 1775–1783.* Kent, Ohio: Kent State University Press, 1996.

Nelson, Paul David. "William Tryon Confronts the American Revolution, 1771–1780." *The Historian: A Journal of History* 53 (1991): 267–284.

Peckham, Howard H. *The Toll of Independence: Engagements and Battle Casualties of the American Revolution.* Chicago: University of Chicago Press, 1974.

Ranlet, Philip. *The New York Loyalists.* Knoxville: University of Tennessee Press, 1986.

Ward, Christopher. *The War of the Revolution.* 2 vols. Edited by John R. Alden. New York: Macmillan, 1952.

Ward, Harry M. *General William Maxwell and the New Jersey Continentals.* Westport, Conn.: Greenwood Press, 1997.

———. *Between the Lines: Banditti of the American Revolution.* Westport, Conn.: Praeger, 2002.

Weigley, Russell F., John R. Galvin, and Allen R. Millett. *Three George Rogers Clark Lectures.* Washington, D.C.: University Press of America, 1991.

Mark V. Kwasny

NONIMPORTATION.

Nonimportation was a form of economic sanction by which the colonies sought on several occasions to pressure Parliament to repeal acts they found offensive or illegal. The idea that the colonies should unite in boycotting the importation of British goods was first proposed at a Boston town meeting on 24 May 1764 that had been called to denounce provisions in the Sugar Act. The potential effectiveness of a peaceful economic protest appealed to activists elsewhere, and by the end of the year merchants in other colonies, notably New York, had agreed, or been pressured, to accept nonimportation. The Stamp Act of 1765 gave added urgency to the program, but repeal of the act, news of which arrived at New York City on 26 April 1766, led to abandonment of nonimportation.

The Townshend Revenue Act of 1767 revived the idea of nonimportation, and by the end of 1769 only merchants in New Hampshire had not joined the local Associations that sprang up to enforce nonimportation. The agreements were effective enough so that the value of British imports was reduced by almost 40 percent between 1768 and 1769. When the Townshend duties were limited to tea in April 1770, the appearance of some success and an unwillingness to endure further economic pain led merchants and others to abandon nonimportation, despite efforts by Boston activists to keep the movement alive. The collapse of nonimportation started at Albany, Providence, and Newport in May 1770 and spread to New York City in July; by the end of the year Philadelphia (12 September), Boston (12 October), and Charleston, South Carolina (13 December), had withdrawn from the nonimportation associations. Virginia, which had organized the first Association, finally abandoned the idea in July 1771.

The effectiveness of nonimportation always depended on collective action and cumulative effect. Merchants who originally advocated nonimportation might later take the initiative in ending it when it went on too long and brought them to the verge of economic ruin. Nonimportation depended on vigilant and widespread enforcement by local extralegal groups that were willing to use threats and intimidation to secure compliance, and some merchants were horrified that this tactic was passing from their control into the hands of the activists and the mob. Nonimportation sputtered out in 1771 because the pain was too great, the provocation too small, the impact on imperial policy too unclear, and the prospect of social instability too great. The collapse of nonimportation was a severe setback for the activists, who lamented that "the Spirit of Patriotism seems expiring in America in general" (Miller, p. 315).

Nonimportation was revived a final time in September 1774. At that time the first Continental Congress recommended it as appropriate action to protest the Intolerable Acts.

SEE ALSO *Association; Continental Congress; Grenville Acts; Stamp Act; Sugar Act; Townshend Acts.*

BIBLIOGRAPHY

Miller, John C. *Origins of the American Revolution.* Boston: Little, Brown, 1943.

revised by Harold E. Selesky

NOOKS HILL, MASSACHUSETTS

SEE *Dorchester Heights, Massachuesetts.*

NORFOLK, VIRGINIA. 1 January 1776.

Burned by Lord Dunmore. After defeating Dunmore's forces at Great Bridge on 9 December 1775, Colonel William Woodford entered Norfolk on the 13th. Colonel Robert Howe arrived the next day with a North Carolina regiment and took command. Dunmore had taken refuge on British ships in the harbor where he and his Loyalist recruits suffered from cramped accommodations and lack of provisions. When Colonel Howe refused to stop snipers on shore from firing at the shipping and refused to supply provisions, Dunmore announced the morning of 31 December that he was going to bombard the town. At 4 A.M. of the New Year he put his threat into effect. Captain Edward Bellew's squadron of one frigate and two sloops, backed up by tenders and Dunmore's provincial flotilla, shot into the town for twenty-five hours and landing parties set fire to warehouses near the waterfront. Wind helped spread the flames through the prosperous town of six thousand inhabitants. A few men were wounded on each side, along with a few noncombatants. Lieutenant Colonel Edward Stevens was conspicuous in fighting off the landing parties.

The historian Lynn Montross had correctly identified the long-term significance of the action in saying that "as Virginia's largest town went up in flames the loyalist cause perished with it" (*Reluctant Rebels,* p. 134). The portion of the town that had not been destroyed was razed to prevent its use by the enemy when Colonel Howe ordered the last troops withdrawn on 8 February. Dunmore then landed and built barracks with a view to maintaining a beachhead, but Howe's troops, from their camps at Kemp's Landing, Great Bridge, and Suffolk, made it impossible for the enemy to get provisions from the countryside. With his miserable collection of refugees and Loyalist militia, Dunmore returned to his ships and on 26 May left to establish a new base on Gwynn Island.

SEE ALSO *Gwynn Island, Virginia; Howe, Robert; Murray, John; Woodford, William.*

BIBLIOGRAPHY

Montross, Lynn. *The Reluctant Rebels: The Story of the Continental Congress, 1774–1789.* New York: Harper, 1950.

revised by Robert K. Wright Jr.

NORTH, SIR FREDERICK. (1732–1792).

British politician and prime minister. He was born on 13 April 1732 in Albermarle Street, off Piccadilly in London. The eldest son of Frederick North, Lord Guilford, and his first wife, Lady Lucy Montagu, he came of a line of courtiers, politicians, and crown servants stretching back to the reign of Henry VIII. Through his mother he was related to Lord Halifax and young William, second earl of Dartmouth, later became his stepbrother and close friend. Because Guilford was tutor in the household of Frederick, prince of Wales, North was closely connected to the Leicester House interest and knew George III from birth. This connection, alongside his upright character, was to serve North well in later days.

Educated at Eton (the first of his family to go there) and Trinity College, Oxford, young North displayed a curious mixture of conscientious scholarship, sobriety, deep-rooted conservatism, popularity, wit, a generous sense of humor, and a constitutional inability seriously to challenge authority. Because his father refused to make him a generous allowance and died only two years before his son, North was far from wealthy by the standards of his class and needed to achieve and keep office in order to make ends meet. All these characteristics had a bearing upon his long tenure as first minister.

North came down from Oxford in 1751 and, after taking the Grand Tour with Dartmouth, entered Parliament for his father's pocket borough of Banbury in Oxfordshire, a seat he was to hold until his father's death almost forty years later. Thus, although known by the courtesy title of "Lord North," he spent almost the whole of his political life in the House of Commons.

While George II lived, North was confined to opposition by his links with Leicester House, but he nevertheless built up a reputation for honesty, ability, and an almost unrivaled grasp of financial issues. In 1767 he become Grafton's chancellor of the Exchequer and in 1770 the first lord of the Treasury and head of the ministry. Coming to office after a string of unstable and short-lived administrations, his great gift was the ability to keep a parliamentary majority together. Here his popularity, moral character, and dislike of radical change were great strengths. But the real key was to placate the independent country squires on the cross-benches by keeping the land tax down. Given the size of the national debt left over from the Seven Years' War, the need to keep up a significant army in America, and the failure to raise revenue from the relatively undertaxed colonists, this was a nearly impossible task. Economies were essential. That meant keeping the smallest possible armed forces, which in turn led North to take an overly sanguine view of both the Bourbon menace and the situation in America. On these grounds he must take some responsibility for the ultimate loss of the colonies. On the other hand, he kept his ministry together for twelve years, a considerable achievement.

THE TEA ACT

An understanding of North's Tea Act requires a global rather than a transatlantic perspective. Dangerously isolated in Europe since 1763, Britain had good reason to fear a French war of revenge, perhaps in alliance with Spain. Rumors that the French were preparing to intervene in India, rapidly succeeded by the Falkland Islands crisis, led North to reform and tighten government control over the ailing East India Company by the Regulating Act of 1773. The *quid pro quo* was to be government financial support and permission for the company to market its tea directly to the colonies. The Tea Act of 1773 thus really had its roots in Britain's dangerous strategic isolation. The hope that the tea concession would ruin American smugglers, so forcing the colonies to accept the tea duty and tacitly acknowledge Parliament's right to tax, certainly existed. But it was never the primary purpose of a law intended to mitigate serious financial, naval, and military weaknesses.

AN INADEQUATE AMERICAN POLICY

In these circumstances, there was a certain amount of wish fulfillment in North's appreciation of the situation in the colonies. The ministry consistently underestimated both the extent of American resistance and the level of force necessary to suppress it. The coercive legislation that followed the Boston Tea Party rested on the notion that the trouble was principally confined to a violent New England (principally Massachusetts) minority. Even after war broke out in 1775 the government at first preferred a largely paper blockade to sending adequate military reinforcements with a view to reconquest. At the same time, North had to watch his European enemies in home waters, in the Americas, and in the East; yet he still would not allow Sandwich properly to prepare the fleet. The situation became critical when France openly entered the conflict in 1778 and desperate when the Spanish fleet was thrown into the balance in 1779. Such a crisis needed a war minister of genius, able to take the right strategic decisions and impose a coherent policy upon his colleagues.

Unfortunately, North—for all his more attractive virtues—was no Pitt. He failed to resolve the ruinous differences between Germain and Sandwich, and even after Germain's departure, he allowed the situation to drift. North, from 1779 without faith in the war, would have resigned but for George III's insistence that he stay. Consequently, the war in America was carried on with inadequate numbers and insufficient naval support until the debacle of Yorktown.

AFTER HIS MINISTRY'S FALL

After Yorktown, even North found it impossible to stay in office, and only the king's desire made him hang on until March 1782, when he resigned. However, he was far from finished. In February 1783 he joined with Fox to bring down Shelburne's ministry over the preliminary peace terms. On 2 April, despite his loathing for Fox, the king was forced to accept Portland as nominal first minister with North and Fox as secretaries of state.

It was, however, a short-lived and limited triumph. Alliance with Fox the opportunist seriously compromised North's reputation for integrity, and the king was anxious to get rid of his new ministers at the first opportunity. In the end, North and Fox had to accept the very terms they had just censured in order to avoid charges of warmongering and intransigence. Ironically, North was finally laid low by the old problem of India, when the defeat of Fox's India Bill of 1783 in the Lords allowed the king to immediately sack his ministers. North never held high office again. He succeeded his father as Lord Guilford in 1790 and died two years later in 1792.

SEE ALSO *Fox, Charles James; Tea Act.*

BIBLIOGRAPHY
Thomas, P. D. G. *Lord North.* London: Allen Lane, 1976.
Smith, C . D. *the Early Career of Lord North the Prime Minister.* London: Athlone Press, 1979.
Whitley, Peter. *Lord North: The Prime Minister Who Lost America.* London, Hambledon, 1996.

revised by John Oliphant

NORTH CAROLINA, MOBILIZATION IN.

Of all the rebellious mainland colonies at the approach of conflict with Britain, North Carolina was arguably the least commercial, the most internally fractured, and the most diffusely settled. Each of these attributes contributed to North Carolina's difficulties mobilizing resources during the eight-year struggle, and so each merits some explanation at the outset.

Commercially speaking, North Carolina's extensive network of barrier islands severely hampered the development of good port facilities and discouraged shipping. The main exception was the lower Cape Fear River, and especially the hubs at Wilmington and Brunswick, from which North Carolinians exported rice and pine-based naval stores. North Carolina in the late 1760s and early 1770s was also racked by a serious internal rebellion, known as the Regulator movement, led primarily by farmers of the Piedmont region (between the coastal plain and the Blue Ridge mountains) against the authority of the royal governor and the colonial Assembly. Drawn out over several years, this crisis proved a major distraction from other political issues and ended only through a climactic battlefield confrontation between the militia and the assembled Regulators. The rebellion highlighted a serious split between the eastern and western portions of the colony, which in turn reflected North Carolina's history of settlement. Where the east had primarily been settled by English immigrants coming from overseas or from eastern Virginia, the western counties were filled with Scots-Irish, Germans, and some Englishmen who had come down the Great Wagon Road from the valley of Pennsylvania and Virginia. This settlement pattern limited familial connections between east and west, and although this did not cause the Regulator rebellion, it certainly did not help in easing the tensions the rebellion created. Furthermore, this pattern of settlement left wide expanses of the colony only sparsely settled, a factor that would prove significant in the recruiting and supplying of armies during the war.

IMPERIAL TENSION

North Carolina's history and its economic and demographic condition also shaped its approach to the imperial tensions developing with the mother country. North Carolinians reacted to the Stamp Act along lines very similar to most of the other colonies. While the first colonial riot took place in Boston on 14 August 1765, North Carolina remained quiet into the fall. The approach of the 1 November 1765 date for the enactment of the law and word of resistance in New England and elsewhere spurred North Carolinians to riot, especially in the main coastal towns of Wilmington and Brunswick. North Carolina's protestors borrowed from two traditions to structure their actions. One was the familiar crowd-based, festive burnings of symbolic effigies, at times expanding into an obstructionist riot. Significant to the later development of armed resistance, however, North Carolinians also responded militarily, calling out the armed militia to prevent the landing of the stamps and marching in soldierly fashion (possibly armed) to the governor's house to demand the resignation of the comptroller. Festive and military-style protests often overlapped, but the striking willingness to resort to the potent symbolism of armed resistance held ramifications for the future.

The repeal of the Stamp Act muted imperial tensions in North Carolina for years to come. The Townshend Act of 1767 caused fewer problems in the relatively less commercial colony, although the Assembly did prepare to adopt resolutions condemning the act. The governor then dissolved the Assembly, leading many of the legislators to meet extralegally and create a nonimportation association. Nonimportation never gained much purchase in North Carolina, and in part the crisis was overshadowed by the now burgeoning Regulator movement. The Assembly finally locked horns with the governor in 1773 when they could not agree on a bill to keep the county and superior courts in session. Without an agreement, the courts lapsed, affecting virtually everyone in the colony. Most easterners blamed the royal governor (now Josiah

Martin), whereas many western residents, still embittered from the suppression of the Regulator movement, blamed the Assembly. When the Assembly convened again in December 1773 its members virtually refused to do business, passing only one act. At the urging of Virginia, however, the Assembly did create a Committee of Correspondence, composed of prominent easterners, to coordinate resistance efforts with those of other colonies.

The Committee kept abreast of developments in other colonies and guided the colony's response to Parliament's punitive laws passed to punish Boston for the Boston Tea Party (the so-called Intolerable Acts). North Carolina followed Virginia's lead in protesting the acts, and then called the first of five extralegal Provincial Congresses to determine their response. The Congress in turn created local Committees of Correspondence and Committees of Safety, designed to spread information and to enforce the resolutions of the Congress. Thus by the spring of 1775 a skeleton of an alternative government existed, particularly but not exclusively in the eastern port towns. It would take a major catalyst, however, for resistance to ignite and become general.

THE DECISION FOR WAR: LEXINGTON AND CONCORD, SLAVES, AND INDIANS

It seems clear, at least in North Carolina, that the catalyst for the crucial transition from resistance, to armed resistance, to revolution was initially the British march on Concord, and then the apparent threats to mobilize slaves and Indians against the colonists. The rhetoric in reaction to the Intolerable Acts had been heated and defiant, but the reaction to Lexington and Concord, and specifically to the reports of atrocities and unprovoked killings—however exaggerated—was explosive. Whig adherents rallied supporters with the oldest and most legitimate recruiting cry: self-defense. To "repel force by force" had always been acceptable. Blood had been shed, and that simple fact changed the game enormously.

Whigs in Craven and New Bern Counties immediately propagated an Association oath that promised resistance while still professing loyalty to the king. But other Whigs in North Carolina went much further. In the Piedmont county of Mecklenburg, word of the march on Concord led the committee there, led by Thomas Polk and affirmed by the mustered militia, to issue a much more radical document. The so-called Mecklenburg Declaration of Independence, published on 16 June 1775, denied the authority of Parliament and even that of the king. These political responses to apparent British atrocities then fed into other colonial fears.

For eastern North Carolinians a major worry was that Governor Martin would incite a slave rebellion. Such a fear was all too vivid in the eastern counties, with their large population of slaves: in 1767 in the lower Cape Fear region the black population was 62 percent of the total. Accusing the British of seeking to inspire a slave rebellion was standard practice in the days immediately after Lexington, and in June the Whigs accused Governor Martin of planning to arm the slaves and of offering them freedom if they would fight for the king. On 15 July 1775 the Safety Committee of Pitt County reported that a slave in Beaufort County had confessed a projected insurrection. Forty slaves were quickly arrested, jailed, and interrogated. Other county committees quickly joined the chorus of connecting suspected slave conspiracies to the active encouragement of British officials. Finally, Governor Lord Dunmore of Virginia seemingly justified North Carolinians' suspicions of royal governors when he announced in November 1775 that he would arm the Indians and free those slaves who joined his force.

Whereas fears of slave rebellion agitated easterners, fears of a Cherokee invasion rallied the westerners. Whig publicists regularly served up the probable use of Indians against the colonies as proof of the essential corruption of Britain. The Cherokees did in fact launch raids in North and South Carolina in the early summer of 1776. As David Ramsay wrote immediately after the war, in his *History of the Revolution in South-Carolina*, those attacks "increased the unanimity of the inhabitants.... Several who called themselves Tories in 1775 became active Whigs in 1776, and cheerfully took arms in the first instance against Indians, and in the second against Great-Britain" (vol. 1, p. 160).

The development of imperial tensions in the 1760s and 1770s, followed by the striking reports of violence in Massachusetts and the apparent impending use of slaves and Indians, combined to strengthen the will to resist. These factors provided a powerful element of legitimacy to the resistance movement and pushed many fence sitters off the fence. Having mobilized the will to resist, it was still necessary to seize the reins of power, organize and equip that will, lend it shape, and prepare it to fight a war. Fortunately, the long development of colonial institutions and the drawn-out evolution of tensions with Britain had already created the necessary bureaucratic infrastructure and skills.

SEIZING CONTROL

Increasingly confident of popular support, the county committees and the Provincial Congress moved to seize control of government. Over the course of the summer of 1775, county after county established Revolutionary committees, who first identified their enemies and the waverers by requiring the Association oath, and then assumed a judicial role in enforcing their own edicts and those of the Continental Congress. Intimidation played a major role in this process, as armed militiamen served the

committees as enforcers; in perhaps the most telling moment of all, in June 1775, John Ashe, who had recently resigned his colonelcy in the New Hanover militia regiment, marched into Wilmington leading several hundred militiamen and demanded that the merchants of the town subscribe to the Association oath. When asked his authority for making such a demand, Ashe merely pointed to the assembled troops.

Such a basis for government invited a certain level of anarchy, and in some cases the local committees, or individuals acting on their own initiative, pushed the limits of revolutionary propriety. Royal government also evaporated in July as Governor Martin took refuge aboard ship, from which he prorogued the Assembly and later refused to call it into session at all. Recognizing these problems, the Whig leadership in late summer called for a new Provincial Congress to take up the duties of a central government. The Congress momentarily adopted a moderate stance toward independence, but did create the political, economic, and military mechanisms that independence would require. Politically they established a provincial executive council of thirteen men to oversee district committees of safety, who in turn supervised the county and town committees. The council, and through them the committees, were given the operational control of the province's military and the right to draw on the provincial treasury. Congress proceeded to create both.

ESTABLISHING AN ARMY

In September 1775, as part of its other measures creating an alternative government, the Provincial Congress formally organized a military, creating two regiments of Continental troops and outlining a new framework for the state militia. The new militia law differed only slightly from its colonial antecedents, the most important differences being administrative. First, the new law divided the province into six districts, allowing for a brigadier general to organize and command the forces of each district. Each district would nominally comprise a brigade formed of the county-based regiments. Second, the local companies were divided into five classes or divisions. One consisted of the old and infirm; the other four served to spread the burden of service. When the militia were called up, in theory only one class, or division, from each company would be susceptible to service and then usually for only three months. The law also specified that musters be held monthly rather than at the more occasional intervals of the colonial era. Finally, the Congress created a separate organization known as the minutemen. The minutemen proved to be a short-lived institution, largely collapsing by the end of 1776.

In the course of forming its military North Carolina made a distinct effort to found them on European principles of discipline. North Carolina even requested copies of

Thomas Simes's *Military Guide* from the Continental Congress, and duly received twelve dozen copies in August 1776, along with twenty-four copies of Simes's *New System of Military Discipline.* Unfortunately, the Congress was unwilling, and probably unable, to impose a strong centralized control over the militia. The Congress expressly left it to the individual companies to establish rules to cover misbehavior and disobedience.

The military also needed equipment, and the Congress sought to cover that problem by establishing a Committee of Secrecy to encourage the production of war materiel. To finance the new troops and pay for supplies, the Congress assumed the power to tax, creating a two-shilling poll tax that would begin in 1777, and on its strength issuing £125,000 in bills of credit.

THE CHALLENGES OF 1775 AND 1776

These basic structures of government and military organization would continue, with some modification and much expansion, throughout the war. But first they had to survive the major challenges of 1775 and 1776. In late 1775 North Carolina dispatched troops against threats to Norfolk and to the South Carolina backcountry even as it continued to struggle to pin down the loyalties of its own inhabitants and arrange for a stream of arms and supplies—a stream that would rarely ever exceed a trickle. At the same time Governor Martin convinced the British government that the Loyalists in the area awaited only a contingent of British regulars to spark a full-scale counter-revolution. Persuaded that such help was imminent, on 10 January 1776, Martin called on the Loyalists to rise. Some fourteen hundred, mostly recently arrived Highland Scots, did so, leading to a much larger mobilization of Whig forces, who decisively defeated the Loyalists at Moores Creek Bridge on 27 February.

In the end the victory at Moores Creek Bridge squashed any further effort by the British to reassert control over North Carolina until 1780. But in March and April of 1776 that was not yet apparent, and the decision for independence had not yet been made. The Fourth Provincial Congress convened in April and vastly expanded North Carolina's commitment to war at the same time as it put the province on a firm path to independence. The Congress increased North Carolina's Continental regiments from two to six (there would eventually be ten); called up eastern militiamen in response to a British fleet assembled at the mouth of the Cape Fear under Sir Peter Parker; issued £500,000 more in bills of credit; appointed county collectors of arms; and proposed measures to encourage the production of saltpeter, gunpowder, salt, iron, and weapons. On 12 April the Congress passed the Halifax Resolves, making North Carolina the first colony to urge the Continental Congress to proclaim independence.

There remained yet one further challenge to the Whigs in 1776, and it served to confirm for many their disgust with British rule: beginning with intermittent attacks in April, by July the Cherokees were moving against the western settlements on a large scale. Brigadier General Griffith Rutherford mustered the western militia, and in conjunction with Virginia and South Carolina forces, marched into and devastated the Cherokee towns in August and September.

THE DEMANDS OF A DISTANT WAR, 1777–1779

Although the war moved away from the South after the defeat of Parker's attempt on Charleston, South Carolina, in June 1778 (some fourteen hundred North Carolina troops participated in the defense), the demands on the resources of the state continued. Calls for men were nearly constant. Although it is impossible to accurately quantify the number of North Carolinians who actually served in the ranks of the Continentals and the militia over the course of the whole war, the sum of calls for troops announced in these years of relative quiet in the South give some sense of the squeeze on North Carolina's manpower. From 1777 to 1779 there were seven separate major calls for men totaling 11,348. All of these were for expeditionary forces and thus did not include numerous local militia musters for routine enforcement or in response to several local Tory risings. These numbers also do not include those who were already serving in North Carolina's Continental regiments in Washington's army to the north. Nowhere near 11,348 men actually responded to those requests, in part because that number was roughly 15 percent of the white male population of North Carolina; but it is indicative of the recruiting pressure on the state.

The constant demand for men was not always met with enthusiasm, and the actual process for selecting recruits varied widely. The legislature usually assigned a quota to each county, set a bounty for volunteers, and provided a lower bounty for those drafted to make up the quota. Theoretically, this system accommodated the division of the militia into the four classes specified in the militia law passed at the beginning of the war (the fifth division of the infirm and elderly had been eliminated). A draft supposedly would come from one of the four "classes," and that class would not be susceptible to another draft until the other three had had their turn. The class system was used, but not necessarily as strictly as intended. In practice at the county level a call for troops led to a muster, where the militia officers called for volunteers. When insufficient numbers came forward the officers would arrange some kind of draft. Those arrangements varied and aroused numerous protests.

There are differing accounts of how men were selected for the draft. In some units names were "drawn," whereas other units, according to the law passed in April 1778, "elected" those who were to be drafted. Other, probably illegal, methods further inspired resistance to the draft. In an old and widespread tradition, drafted men could also hire substitutes (or persuade relatives to substitute).

The new Whig government had also embarked on an increasingly severe program of confiscating Loyalist property and requiring and actually enforcing the taking of the loyalty oath. These two measures, in combination with the unpopular demands for troops, generated resistance. In turn, the North Carolina government relied on the militia to enforce these measures, in what came to be called "scouring for Tories." Drafting, oath-taking, confiscating, and scouring all contributed to keeping a large portion of the countryside at a slow boil, in some cases creating "Tories" where none had been before. But if the Tories (and some wishful neutrals) were outraged, the Whigs were scared. Real and reported Tory conspiracies, violent draft resistance, Indian scares, and projected British landings all contributed to an environment of fear. Loyalist and neutral resistance and Whig fear mutually reinforced each other. Reports, for example, of a band of draft resisters would lead to a call for militia to hold them in check. To raise that militia, a draft might be required, and the militia would need to be supplied from local sources. Some of those militia units, once in the field, found it all too easy to commit acts of violence that further alienated the waverers.

The Provincial Congress had designed a supply system to avoid alienating the countryside, and through 1779 the system more or less worked. The state had a quartermaster-general who oversaw the quartermasters of each militia district. The law specified that no goods could be taken without a press warrant signed by two justices of the peace of that county. Furthermore, two "indifferent" people had to appraise the items pressed, and the owner would either be paid in North Carolina currency or be given a certificate. The system was far from perfect, and the ad hoc measures taken in 1776 to increase gunpowder or iron production had had only minimal effects. Furthermore, North Carolina's soldiers were rarely well-dressed; in 1778 the legislature conceded that they could not handle the load and delegated to the counties the task of supplying basic clothing. It was in 1779, however, that all the state and Continental currencies began to devalue at a terrific rate, and when the British invaded the state in 1780–1781, the system virtually collapsed.

NADIR AND TRIUMPH, 1780–1782

The problems of mobilization dramatically escalated as the British turned to a southern strategy and then successfully captured Charleston, South Carolina, in May 1780. More than two thousand North Carolina troops, militia and Continental, were captured at Charleston, and the state struggled to replace them. To make matters worse in North Carolina, in January 1781 a separate British expedition descended on Wilmington by sea and established a garrison there. Mobilization of the will to fight became crucial. Where initially despair had set in after the disaster at Charleston and then at Camden, British actions quickly supplied the necessary anger; and where official means of raising troops faltered, volunteer organizations often filled the gap.

We can never know all the reasons why men rallied as volunteers to the Whig cause in 1780 and 1781. It is clear that the official raising of militia troops continued, and militia brigades continued to take their place in the ranks of the American army re-formed after Camden by Continental Army General Nathanael Greene. Indeed, in the face of crisis, North Carolina virtually abandoned recruiting for its Continental regiments, focusing instead on the militia. There were now, however, additional units of volunteers, more or less formally acknowledged by the state. Some of the men in these units were motivated by the hope of plundering their neighbors; some were surely motivated by the cause itself; but many served in fear of British atrocity or in hopes of revenge. Whatever the case, the volunteers had a profound impact on the war, both in increasing the level of fratricidal violence between themselves and Loyalists, and in providing all of the manpower for the crucial victory at Kings Mountain, South Carolina.

Meanwhile the collapse of the American currencies and the locust-like eating habits of armies criss-crossing a sparsely settled backcountry caused the already tenuous supply system to disintegrate. Backcountry residents, especially along the much contested border with South Carolina, found themselves plagued by provisioning agents from both sides. In 1780 the state government had concluded that running the war with a legislative committee was inefficient and replaced it with the Board of War (composed of five commissioners elected by the legislature). In 1781 the Board was replaced by the Council Extraordinary (composed of three men advising the governor). In March 1781 this Council, in response to the logistical crisis, enacted a tax in kind for all those areas not already denuded by the competing armies. Under this plan each household would give up one-fifth of its bacon and salted meat for the army, but even this expedient suffered from a lack of transport to move supplies to the army.

In yet another move born of desperation, captured Loyalists were frequently forced to enlist in Continental or militia service to expiate their sins. For example, most of the nearly six hundred prisoners taken at Kings Mountain were paroled on the condition that they enlist for a three-month tour in the militia. This was not an isolated incident, and in fact such enlistments became virtually state policy in the last year of the war.

Even after General Cornwallis's army moved on to Virginia and ultimate defeat at Yorktown, North Carolina continued to contend with several active and successful Loyalist units, as well as with the British garrison in Wilmington (evacuated in November 1781)—all while attempting to support Greene's reconquest of South Carolina.

MAKING PEACE

Finally, in May 1782, David Fanning, the last major Loyalist guerrilla leader, fled the state for South Carolina. With his departure the internal war in the state quickly tapered off, and the rebel government could turn to the problems of peace. A year later the state finally declared an amnesty covering most Tories, although specifically excluding certain groups; it appears that North Carolina for the most part peacefully reintegrated the former Loyalists into a peacetime society, although not without economic cost. One telling statistic is that 57 percent of the surviving officers of Fanning's notorious guerrilla band were still living in the United States, the majority in North Carolina. Their fates speak well for reintegration. On the other hand, the state government felt compelled to protect Whig fighters who were occasionally brought to trial for their crimes in the years after the war. No comprehensive survey exists, but there were several notable cases of men tried for illegitimate violence in the 1780s to whom the legislature granted protection from prosecution.

CONCLUSION

The complexities and difficulties faced by the North Carolina revolutionary government in mobilizing men and materials to fight such a long war can hardly be fathomed. Relative to their available resources, the state did a remarkable job. The key to mobilizing men and materiel, however, rested in the mobilization of will. The will to fight was born in a sense of betrayal at the outset of the war, but sustaining it proved another matter. At times will almost faltered, but a complex combination of fear, desire for revenge, a commitment to independence, and a belief that the new state government would bring order kept men in the ranks. The flow of materiel, on the other hand, depended largely on the desperate perseverance of a few state leaders.

SEE ALSO *African Americans in the Revolution; Ashe, John; Charleston Siege of 1780; Fanning, David; Indians in the Colonial Wars and the American Revolution; Intolerable (or Coercive) Acts; Kings Mountain, South Carolina; Lexington and Concord; Mecklenburg Declaration of Independence; Moores Creek Bridge; Nonimportation; Regulators; Rutherford, Griffith; Stamp Act; Townshend Acts.*

BIBLIOGRAPHY

Crow, Jeffrey J. "Liberty Men and Loyalists: Disorder and Disaffection in the North Carolina Backcountry." In *An Uncivil War: The Southern Backcountry during the American Revolution.* Edited by Ronald Hoffman, Thad W. Tate, and Peter J. Albert. Charlottesville: University Press of Virginia, 1985.

DeMond, Robert O. *The Loyalists in North Carolina during the Revolution.* Durham, N.C.: Duke University Press, 1940.

Ekirch, A. Roger. "Whig Authority and Public Order in Backcountry North Carolina, 1776–1783." In *An Uncivil War: The Southern Backcountry during the American Revolution.* Edited by Ronald Hoffman, Thad W. Tate, and Peter J. Albert. Charlottesville: University Press of Virginia, 1985.

Fanning, David. *The Narrative of Col. David Fanning.* Edited by Lindley S. Butler. Davidson, N.C.: Briarpatch Press, 1981.

Ganyard, Robert L. *The Emergence of North Carolina's Revolutionary State Government.* Raleigh: North Carolina Department of Cultural Resources, 1978.

Kay, Marvin L. Michael, and Lorin Lee Cary. *Slavery in North Carolina, 1748–1775.* Chapel Hill: University of North Carolina Press, 1995.

Lee, Wayne E. *Crowds and Soldiers in Revolutionary North Carolina: The Culture of Violence in Riot and War.* Gainesville: University Press of Florida, 2001.

Ramsay, David. *The History of the Revolution of South-Carolina, from a British Province to an Independent State.* Trenton, N.J.: Printed by Isaac Collins, 1785.

Rankin, Hugh F. *The North Carolina Continentals.* Chapel Hill: University of North Carolina Press, 1971.

Russell, Phillips. *North Carolina in the Revolutionary War.* Charlotte, N.C: Heritage Printers, 1965.

Wheeler, Earl Milton. "Development and Organization of the North Carolina Militia." *North Carolina Historical Review* 41 (July 1964): 307–323.

Wayne E. Lee

NORTH CAROLINA LINE.

North Carolina created its first two full-time regiments on 1 September 1775 and they passed to the Continental Army on 28 November 1775, when the Congress accepted them. Four more regiments were added during 1776, and in the expansion of 1777 the total number of regiments rose to nine, all of which were sent north to serve with Commander in Chief George Washington. One of the Additional Continental Regiments (Sheppard's) was known familiarly as the Tenth North Carolina Regiment and also served in Pennsylvania, but technically it was not considered to be part of the state line. The Seventh through Ninth North Carolina Regiments and Sheppard's unit were disbanded at Valley Forge on 1 June 1778, and the men were redistributed in an effort to maintain troop strength. The remaining regiments moved back to North Carolina, and in November 1779 all of the enlisted men from the Fourth through Sixth North Carolina Regiments transferred to replace the troops of the First and Third, which had been captured at Charleston. On 1 January 1781 the state's quota of regiments dropped to three, but only the First and Second Regiments were able to fill their ranks and return to combat status that summer. The last of the Line went home on furlough in early April 1783 and then were formally disbanded on 15 November 1783. North Carolina also raised three separate troops of light dragoons and a separate artillery company for the Continental army in 1776 and 1777, but these units were not part of the state line.

SEE ALSO *Charleston, South Carolina.*

BIBLIOGRAPHY

Davis, Charles L. *A Brief History of the North Carolina Troops on the Continental Establishment in the War of the Revolution.* Philadelphia: N.p., 1896.

Hay, Gertrude Sloan, ed. *Roster of Soldiers from North Carolina in the American Revolution with an Appendix Containing a Collection of Miscellaneous Records.* Durham: North Carolina Daughters of the American Revolution, 1932.

Rankin, Hugh F. *The North Carolina Continentals.* Chapel Hill, N.C.: University of North Carolina Press, 1971.

Robert K. Wright Jr.

NORTH'S PLAN FOR RECONCILIATION. 1775.

With the grudging consent of George III, Lord North presented a plan for reconciliation, often called the "olive branch," that was received by the House of Lords on 20 February 1775, endorsed by the House of Commons on 27 February, and rejected by the Continental Congress on 31 July 1775. The plan prescribed that the British would deal with individual colonies and thereby avoided tacit recognition of the Continental Congress. By its terms, Parliament had royal approval to "forbear to any further duty, tax or assessment," though it could still lay regulatory ("external") taxes on any American colony whose own assembly passed "internal" taxes to support the civil government and judiciary and to provide for the common defense. Though North hoped to deal with individual colonies, their legislatures also rejected the proposal. "This was merely a repetition of the gesture that Grenville had made in advance of the stamp act, and it was still as vague and undefined, still as unacceptable, as it had been then," the historian Edmund Morgan has commented. (*Birth*, p. 69).

BIBLIOGRAPHY

Morgan, Edmund. *The Birth of the Republic, 1763–1789.* Chicago: University of Chicago Press, 1966.

revised by Michael Bellesiles

NORTHUMBERLAND, DUKE OF.

Hugh Percy inherited the title of duke of Northumberland on the death of his father, the first duke, in 1786. He was known as Lord or Earl Percy between 1766 and 1786.

SEE ALSO *Percy, Hugh.*

revised by Harold E. Selesky

NORWALK, CONNECTICUT. 11 July 1779.

Plundered and destroyed during Connecticut coast raid.

SEE ALSO *Connecticut Coast Raid.*

Mark M. Boatner

NS SEE *Calendars, Old and New Style.*

O

O'BRIEN, JEREMIAH. (1744–1818). American naval officer. Maine. Born in Kittery, Maine, which was then in the province of Massachusetts, in 1744, O'Brien and his family moved to Machias, Maine, in 1765. He became the first naval hero of the Revolution in the action off Machias in May 1775. Commanding a small fleet of the Massachusetts navy, he took a few prizes before his ships were put out of commission in the fall of 1776. As a privateer he was captain of the *Resolution* in 1777 and captured the British-owned *Scarborough*. His *Hannibal* was captured in 1780, and he was imprisoned by the British, first in the *Jersey* prison ship at New York, and then in Mill Prison, England. After suffering considerable hardship, he escaped. Free again, he commanded the *Hibernia* and then the *Tiger*. For the last seven years of his life he was collector of customs at Machias, where he died on 5 September 1818.

SEE ALSO *Machias, Maine.*

BIBLIOGRAPHY
Sherman, Andrew. *Life of Captain Jeremiah O'Brien.* Morristown, N.J.: G. W. Sherman, 1902).

revised by Michael Bellesiles

ODELL, JONATHAN. (1737–1818). Loyalist secret agent, satirist. New Jersey. Descended from William Odell, who settled in Concord, Massachusetts, around 1639 and a grandson of the Reverend Jonathan Dickinson, the first president of Princeton, Jonathan graduated from the latter college in 1759, was educated as a doctor, and became a surgeon in the British army. After serving in the West Indies he left the army, studied in England for the Anglican ministry, and in January 1767 was ordained. In July 1767 he became a missionary in Burlington, New Jersey, under the Society for the Propagation of the Gospel. In addition, he took up the practice of medicine in 1771. While studying in England he had shown a talent for poetry, and in the early stages of the Revolution he so antagonized the Patriots with his Loyalist verses that on 20 July 1776 New Jersey's Provincial Congress ordered that he be placed on parole, whereby his movements were limited to within a short distance of Burlington. On 18 December he escaped to the British.

Becoming a secret agent, he joined Joseph Stansbury in handling the correspondence between Arnold and André during Arnold's treason. He published essays and verses in Rivington's *Gazette* in New York City and other newspapers that lampooned patriots of New Jersey. His political verses have been described as among the most effective of the time. The versatile Odell was chaplain of a regiment of Pennsylvania Tories, a translator of French and Spanish political documents, and assistant secretary to the board of directors of the Associated Loyalists. On 1 July 1783 he became assistant secretary to Guy Carleton, who then was the British commander in chief in America. Odell went to England with Carleton after the war, taking his wife and three children, but in 1784 he returned to the Loyalist settlement in New Brunswick, Canada. Throughout his years in New Jersey and New York, he had been closely associated with New Jersey's royal governor, William Franklin, who was the godfather of his only son. The latter, William Franklin Odell (1774–1844), is confused with the Tory leader, William Odell.

Jonathan Odell's poetry mirrored Loyalist consciousness. Writing as "Yoric" in 1776 and 1777, Odell shamelessly puffed William Howe's military reputation and boosted Loyalist morale during the occupation of Philadelphia, masking his impatience with Howe's restrained use of military force because he needed the general's patronage to work as pro-British poet and essayist. By the time Odell wrote his longest and most serious Loyalist poem in 1780, *The American Times,* he had become "America's first anti-war poet," condemning British taxation of the colonies as "the kindler of the flame," "unjust," "unwise," "impolitic and open to abuse."

Odell's furtive, energetic activity in the New York garrison town must be viewed through the lens of his poetic sensibility. As a biographer and literary student of his poetry has observed, "the violent, paranoid, harshly judgmental political culture" of the New York city loyalist community profoundly "disturbed" Odell. His "poetry political intelligence [was] of a very high order: the aesthetic ordering of disorder" (Edelberg, "Jonathan Odell and Philip Freneau," p. 118).

SEE ALSO *Arnold's Treason; Odell, William; Stansbury, Joseph.*

BIBLIOGRAPHY

Calhoon, Robert M., Timothy M. Barnes, and George A. Rawlyk, eds. *Loyalists and Community in North America.* Westport, Conn.: Greenwood, 1994.

Edelberg, Cynthia Dubin. *Jonathan Odell, Loyalist Poet of the American Revolution.* Durham, N.C.: Duke University Press, 1987.

————. "Jonathan Odell and Philip Freneau" in *Loyalists and Community in North America.* Edited by Robert M. Calhoon, Timothy M. Barnes, and George A. Rawlyk. Westport, Conn: Greenwood Press, 1994.

Sargent, Winthrop, ed. *The Loyal Verses of Joseph Stansbury and Doctor Jonathan Odell relating to the American Revolution.* Albany, N.Y.: J. Munsell, 1860.

revised by Robert M. Calhoon

ODELL, WILLIAM.

Loyalist officer who raised and commanded the Loyal American Rangers. He became notorious among Patriot prisoners of war for his methods of recruitment, which mixed threats with offers of good food and other luxuries if the prisoners would join his Rangers. A major in 1780, Odell was promoted to lieutenant colonel in 1783 and stationed in Jamaica after the war.

SEE ALSO *Loyal American Rangers.*

revised by Michael Bellesiles

OGDEN, AARON.

(1756–1839). Continental officer, governor of New Jersey, steamboat pioneer. New Jersey. Brother of Matthias Ogden, Aaron Ogden was born in Elizabethtown, New Jersey, on 3 December 1756. He graduated from Princeton in 1773 in the same class as Harry ("Light Horse") Lee and a year behind Aaron Burr, who was a childhood companion. After teaching school for three years he became paymaster of a militia regiment on 8 December 1775. His first military exploit was to assist in the capture of the Blue Mountain Valley in January 1776. On 26 November 1776 he was commissioned as a first lieutenant in the First New Jersey Continental Regiment, his brother's unit. He became regimental paymaster on 1 February 1777, fought at the Brandywine, was made brigade major of William Maxwell's light infantry brigade on 7 March 1778. In the Monmouth campaign he served in the advance element under General Charles Lee. During this campaign he also served as assistant aide-de-camp to General William Alexander, having been promoted to captain of the First New Jersey Regiment on 2 February 1779.

During the next year, Ogden was Maxwell's aide-de-camp during John Sullivan's expedition against the Iroquois, and in 1780 he took part in the delaying action of Maxwell's brigade against Wilhelm Knyphausen's raid against Springfield, Connecticut. When Maxwell resigned, Ogden joined the light infantry corps of the Marquis de Lafayette. In the fruitless exchange of correspondence between Sir Henry Clinton and Commander in Chief George Washington that preceded John André's execution as a spy for his role in Benedict Arnold's treason, Captain Ogden served as a courier between British and American headquarters. His part in the dubious matter of proposing the exchange of André for Benedict Arnold seems to have been nothing more than the delivery of the letter written in a disguised hand by Alexander Hamilton. Ogden was wounded during the Yorktown campaign, during the storming of Redoubt Ten on 14 October 1781.

After the war he studied law with his brother Robert and became one of the leading lawyers in New Jersey. When war with France threatened the new nation, he became lieutenant colonel of the Eleventh United States Infantry on 8 January 1799 and deputy quartermaster general of the army, being discharged on 15 June 1800. In 1812 he was elected governor of New Jersey on a peace ticket but defeated the next year. President James Madison nominated him to the rank of major general in 1813, apparently with the intention of giving him a command in Canada, but Ogden declined in order to retain command of the state militia.

During the War of 1812 Ogden turned from the law to participate in a steamboat venture that was his undoing. Having built the *Sea Horse* in 1811, he proposed to operate a line between Elizabethtown Point (New Jersey) and New York City, but in 1813 the monopoly of James Fulton and Robert R. Livingston was upheld, and his boat was barred from New York waters. He then got into a long, expensive monopoly fight with another line, that of Thomas Gibbons. Ogden won his case in the New York courts, but lost the Supreme Court appeal in *Gibbons v. Ogden,* 1824. In 1829 Congress created the post of customs collector at Jersey City for Ogden. Despite this assistance, the impoverished Ogden was soon imprisoned for debt, but the New York legislature—apparently at the instigation of Burr—released him by passing a quick bill prohibiting the imprisonment of Revolutionary War veterans for debt. He died in Jersey City, New Jersey, on 19 April 1839.

SEE ALSO *Ogden, Matthias; Springfield, New Jersey, Raid of Knyphausen.*

BIBLIOGRAPHY

Ogden, Aaron. *Autobiography of Colonel Aaron Ogden, of Elizabethtown.* Paterson, N.J.: Press Printing, 1893.

revised by Michael Bellesiles

OGDEN, MATTHIAS. (1754–1791). Continental officer. New Jersey.

John Ogden emigrated from Hampshire, England, to Long Island about 1640. In 1664 he established himself at Elizabethtown, New Jersey. His descendants were prominent in the province. Robert (1716–1787), father of Matthias, was a member of the king's council, speaker of the legislature in 1763, delegate to the Stamp Act Congress (New York City, 1765), and chairman of the Elizabethtown committee of safety in 1776.

Matthias and Aaron Burr left the college at Princeton after the Battle of Bunker Hill, joined the Boston army, and as unattached volunteers accompanied Arnold's march to Quebec. Ogden made the first attempt to present Arnold's surrender summons at Quebec and "retreated in quick time" after an eighteen-pound shot hit the ground near him. He was wounded in the attack on the city that started 31 December 1775. Having served as brigadier major in this expedition, he became lieutenant colonel of the First New Jersey Continentals on 7 March 1776 and assumed command of the regiment on 1 January 1777. As part of General Lord Stirling's division his regiment performed well in slowing the British advance on "the plowed hill" in the Battle of the Brandywine on 11 September 1777. During the Valley Forge winter quarters, he was in the brigade of William Maxwell. In the Battle of Monmouth of 28 June 1778, he took part in the initial action under Charles Lee. At the latter's court-martial, Lieutenant Colonel Richard Harrison testified that in attempting to find out why Lee was retreating, he came on Ogden's regiment, which was near the rear of the column. "He appeared to be exceedingly exasperated," Harrison testified, "and said, 'By God! they are flying from a shadow.'" He was captured at Elizabethtown on 5 October 1780 and exchanged in April 1781. He fought at Yorktown in September–October of 1781.

Colonel Ogden proposed a plan for the capture of Prince William Henry, the future William IV, when the sixteen-year-old prince was in New York City. According to General William Heath, the rebels learned on 30 September 1781 that the prince had arrived five days earlier with Admiral Digby and was lodged in the mansion of Gerardus Beekman in Hanover Square. Washington approved Ogden's plan of leading forty officers and men into the city on a rainy night to land near the mansion and kidnap Digby and William. The plan was compromised, however, and had to be abandoned.

On 21 April 1783 Ogden was granted leave to visit Europe and did not return to the army. Louis XVI honored him with *le droit du tabouret,* (the right of the stool) which permitted him to sit in the royal presence. He returned to the United States with news of the Treaty of Paris. Congress breveted him brigadier general on 30 September 1783.

After the war Ogden had many business interests, including land speculation, the minting of coins, and the practice of law. He died of yellow fever in 1791.

SEE ALSO *Brandywine, Pennsylvania; Digby, Robert; Maxwell, William.*

BIBLIOGRAPHY

Ogden, Matthias. "Journal of Major Matthias Ogden, 1775." Edited by A. Van Doren Honeyman. In *Proceedings of the New Jersey Historical Society,* new series, 13 (1928): 17–30.

Thayer, Theodore. *As We Were: The Story of Old Elizabethtown.* Elizabeth, N.J.: Grassman Publishing, 1964.

Trudgen, Gary A. "Matthias Ogden, New Jersey State Coiner." *The Colonial Newsletter* 28 (June 1988): 1032–1051.

revised by Harry M. Ward

OGHKWAGA. Variant of Oquaga.

SEE ALSO *Oquaga.*

O'HARA, CHARLES. (1740?–1802). General
of the British Coldstream Guards. Charles O'Hara was the
illegitimate son of James O'Hara, who was the second
Lord Trawley and colonel of the Coldstream Guards.
Charles O'Hara was educated at Westminster School,
appointed cornet of the Third Dragoons on 23 December
1752, and on 14 January 1756 entered his father's regiment with the grade of "lieutenant and captain." After
service in Germany and Portugal, O'Hara was appointed
commandant of the Africa Corps at Goree, Senegal, on
25 July 1766 with the rank of lieutenant colonel. The
Africa Corps was a unit composed of military offenders
who were pardoned in exchange for life service in Africa.
Maintaining his seniority in the Coldstream, he was
named captain and lieutenant colonel of that regiment
in 1769, and was made brevet colonel in 1777.

Highly critical of the British policy toward America,
O'Hara favored a ruthless approach that would bring the
war to civilians. He arrived in New York City in October
1780, and went from there with his Guards Brigade to join
General Charles Cornwallis's southern operations. He
spearheaded the latter's frustrating pursuit of American
general Nathanael Greene across North Carolina to the
Dan River, leading the gallant attack at Cowan's Ford on
1 February 1781.

Commanding the Second Battalion of Guards at
Guilford on 15 March 1781, O'Hara rallied his troops
after receiving one dangerous wound and led them forward
again to deliver the final blow that broke the resistance of
Greene's army. During that attack he was wounded a
second time. Moving to Virginia with Cornwallis,
O'Hara represented the British in the Yorktown surrender,
and dined that night with General George Washington.
When he was exchanged on 9 February 1782 he returned to
England as a newly appointed major general, and received
the highest praise from Cornwallis.

After serving in Jamaica and as the commanding
officer at Gibraltar from 1787 to 1789, O'Hara was
appointed lieutenant governor of Gibraltar in 1792, and
promoted to lieutenant general in the following year. He
was captured on 23 November 1793 at Fort Mulgrove,
Toulon (France), in the operations that brought an
obscure French officer named Napoleon to the attention
of his military superiors. Imprisoned in Luxembourg, he
was exchanged for Rochambeau in August 1795, named
governor of Gibraltar, and promoted to full general in
1798. He proved himself an efficient commander of that
stronghold during this critical time. After much suffering
from his wounds he died at Gibraltar on 21 February 1802.

SEE ALSO *Cornwallis, Charles; Cowans Ford, North
Carolina; Yorktown Campaign.*

revised by Michael Bellesiles

OHIO COMPANY OF ASSOCIATES.
1787. Under the leadership of Rufus Putnam and
Benjamin Tupper, two Continental army brigadier generals from Massachusetts, former officers and soldiers
formed an association for the settlement of western
lands. On 1 March 1786 their delegates met in Boston
to organize a company for the purchase of land around
what is now Marietta, Ohio. After former Major General
Samuel Holden Parsons had proved unsatisfactory in the
role, the Reverend Manasseh Cutler became the company's representative before Congress and, jointly with
a group of New York speculators led by William Duer,
he eventually made arrangements to purchase 1,781,760
acres of western land. The terms were $500,000 down and
the same amount when the survey was completed, but
both sums could be paid in government securities worth
about twelve cents on the dollar. The Scioto Company of
Duer was authorized to buy nearly 500,000 acres.

The Ohio Associates were unable to complete their
payments, but Congress granted them title to 750,000
acres, granted 100,000 acres free to actual settlers, and
authorized that 214,285 acres be bought with army warrants. Rufus Putnam led the group that established
Adelphia, Ohio, on 7 April 1788.

SEE ALSO *Duer, William; Parsons, Samuel Holden;
Putnam, Rufus; Tupper, Benjamin.*

revised by Harold E. Selesky

OHIO COMPANY OF VIRGINIA.
1747–1773. A group of prominent land speculators in
Virginia organized this company in 1747 to promote
settlement and trade with the Indians in the Ohio
Valley. The imperial government in London viewed the
company as a useful means to promote British territorial
claims in the area. In March 1749 the Privy Council
directed Governor William Gooch to grant to the company 500,000 acres in the upper Ohio Valley, which he
did on 12 April 1749. After explorations by Christopher
Gist in 1750 and 1751, the company established a string
of storehouses on the route across the Appalachians to
the Ohio country, culminating in February 1754, when
construction began on Fort Prince George at the Forks
of the Ohio (later Pittsburgh, Pennsylvania).

The new governor of Virginia, Robert Dinwiddie,
a strong supporter of the company, had already commissioned George Washington to lead a force to support the
new fort at the Forks when a French counter-expedition
captured the place on 17 April. The clash on 28 May
between Washington's force and a French force from
France's new Fort Duquesne at the Forks led to the

French and Indian War; because the frontier remained a battleground, the clash also resulted in a temporary cessation in the company's plans to send settlers into the Ohio valley. Victory in the war ousted the French from Canada, and the Treaty of Paris (10 February 1763) extinguished all French claims to the Ohio region. But the British Crown's Proclamation of 1763 (7 October) recognized Native American claims to ownership of much of the Ohio Valley, including the land granted to the company. The Ohio Company was unsuccessful in persuading the crown to recognize its grant, and in 1773 the crown re-granted the company's land to the Walpole (or Grand Ohio) Company. George Mason became a member of the Ohio Company in 1752 and served as its treasurer until its rights were transferred in 1773.

SEE ALSO *Colonial Wars; Mason, George; Washington, George.*

BIBLIOGRAPHY

Abbot, W. W., et al., eds. *The Papers of George Washington, Colonial Series.* Vol. 1, *1748–August 1755.* Charlottesville: University Press of Virginia, 1983.

Abernathy, Thomas P. *Western Lands and the American Revolution.* Charlottesville: University of Virginia Institute for Research in the Social Sciences, 1937.

revised by Harold E. Selesky

OLIVE BRANCH PETITION. 5 July
1775. After the first armed clashes of the Revolution (Lexington and Concord, Bunker Hill), the Patriots made one more attempt to settle their grievances with Great Britain by means short of war. Written by John Dickinson, adopted on 5 July by the delegates in the Continental Congress (who, however, signed as individuals and not as members of the Congress), and carried to London by Richard Penn (a staunch Loyalist and descendant of William Penn), the petition reiterated the grievances of the colonists but professed their attachment to the king, expressed the desire for a restoration of harmony, and begged the king to prevent further hostile action until a reconciliation could be worked out. Penn reached London on 14 August 1775. On 9 November 1775 the Continental Congress learned that George III had refused to see Penn or receive his petition.

Mark M. Boatner

OMOA SEE *Honduras.*

"ON COMMAND." "On Command" in
eighteenth-century military parlance meant "on detached service."

ONONDAGA CASTLE, NEW YORK.
19–25 April 1779. As a preliminary response to British raids on the Mohawk Valley, which would lead to John Sullivan's expedition, Colonel Gose Van Schaick led a 550-man force from his First New York Regiment and Colonel Peter Gansevoort's Third New York Regiment on a 180-mile sweep against the Onondaga villages between Fort Stanwix and Oswego. Without losing a man, he inflicted heavy damage, including destroying the primary village, known as the Onondaga Castle. On 10 May the Continental Congress thanked the participants in a special resolve.

SEE ALSO *Gansevoort, Peter; Sullivan's Expedition against the Iroquois; Van Schaick, Gose.*

BIBLIOGRAPHY

Roberts, Robert B. *New York's Forts in the Revolution.* Rutherford, N.J.: Fairleigh Dickinson University Press, 1980.

revised by Robert K. Wright Jr.

"ON THE LINES". Outposted towns or other
locations were referred to as being "on the lines" when the bulk of the army was in winter quarters or otherwise disposed in garrison.

Mark M. Boatner

OQUAGA (ONOQUAGA), NEW
YORK. Iroquois village on the east branch of the Susquehanna River about twenty miles southwest of Unadilla (near Windsor). In 1765 it had about 750 inhabitants, most of them Oneidas. It was Joseph Brant's headquarters during St. Leger's Expedition and in much of the subsequent border warfare in New York. Its name is Mohawk for "place of wild grapes," and the *Handbook of American Indians* gives over fifty spelling variations ranging from Anaquago through Oghkwaga to Skawaghkee. The village was destroyed in October 1778 by troops under Colonel William Butler and Colonel Philip Van Cortlandt.

SEE ALSO *Border Warfare in New York; St. Leger's Expedition; Unadilla, New York.*

BIBLIOGRAPHY

Calloway, Colin G. *The American Revolution in Indian Country: Crisis and Diversity in Native American Communities.* Cambridge, U.K.: Cambridge University Press, 1995.

Hodge, Frederick Webb, ed. *Handbook of American Indians, North of Mexico.* 2 vols. Washington, 1907–10. Reprinted, New York, 1960.

revised by Michael Bellesiles

ORANGEBURG, SOUTH CAROLINA.

11 May 1781. Refusing to join General Nathanael Greene for the campaign leading to the Battle of Hobkirk's Hill, General Thomas Sumter led his partisans first against Fort Granby but, finding it too strongly defended, decided to take Orangeburg on the North Edisto River, fifty miles south. Lieutenant Colonel Francis Rawdon had ordered this post abandoned, but the message was not received. After Sumter invested it, the garrison of fifteen British regulars and some thirty Loyalists surrendered without a fight. There were no casualties on either side.

SEE ALSO *Hobkirk's Hill (Camden), South Carolina; Southern Campaigns of Nathanael Greene.*

revised by Michael Bellesiles

ORANGE RANGERS SEE *Coffin, John.*

ORANGETOWN, NEW YORK. Another name for Tappan.

ORISKANY, NEW YORK. 6 August 1777.

St. Leger's expedition was a few days' march from Fort Schuyler (Stanwix). During the march a friendly Oneida reported its advance on 30 July to Brigadier General Nicholas Herkimer, commander of the Tryon County, New York, militia brigade. Despite the settlers' considerable concern for the safety of their families, Herkimer managed to assemble about eight hundred men. On 4 August they left Fort Dayton escorting a supply convoy of forty ox carts to Stanwix. They camped the next night about ten miles short of Stanwix at Deerfield, and Herkimer sent runners ahead to inform Colonel Peter Gansevoort and ask him to make a sortie from the fort as they approached.

In the morning of 6 August, the cautious Herkimer wanted to wait for Gansevoort's cannon signal indicating the beginning of the sortie before starting forward. However, his regimental commanders—Ebenezer Cox, Jacob Klock, Frederick Visscher, and Peter Bellinger—insisted on an immediate advance. Against his better judgment Herkimer authorized the move, leaving most of the carts behind under guard and eliminating advance and flank guards in the hope of improving the column's speed. The legend that the colonels shamed him into this decision by questioning his courage and loyalty seems to be based on the claim of nineteenth-century historian Benson J. Lossing and not on contemporary accounts.

St. Leger learned of Herkimer's approach on the evening of the 5th. During the night the British commander detached Joseph Brant with a mixed party variously estimated at from four hundred to seven hundred men to ambush them. Brant selected a place later known as Battle Brook, six miles from the fort, where a ravine two-hundred-yards wide could be crossed only on a corduroy causeway and where the surrounding woods provided concealment. Brant assigned his Loyalists—part of John Johnson's Royal Regiment of New York (Royal Greens) and a small contingent of rangers recently raised by John Butler—to form the blocking force, and he put the larger contingent of Indians (mostly Mohawk and Seneca) in positions from which to attack the flanks and rear.

Herkimer's sixty Oneida scouts somehow failed to detect signs of the ambush, and when the twenty-man vanguard stopped to drink from the stream, the half-mile-long column plunged blindly ahead. The front was on the west bank, climbing up the ridge; the fifteen carts were on the bridge; and Visscher's regiment (about two hundred strong) as rear guard had not yet started across when the shooting began. Either Brandt's men got trigger-happy, the most probable explanation, or some alert militiamen saw something, but in any case the result was that the trap snapped shut prematurely.

Although some of Visscher's men apparently panicked, the rest reacted with a courage and tactical instinct seldom shown by veterans. Instead of bunching on the road, they counterattacked and fought their way out of the kill zone. The Indians' inability to follow up the initial surprise and close in for the kill let the militia take up defensive positions on higher ground. The wounded Herkimer had the saddle taken from his dead horse and placed on the ground among his men. He then sat on it to direct the fight; although presenting a conspicuous target, he is said to have calmly smoked his pipe and refused all urging to take cover. The Americans formed first in small groups, which made them vulnerable from all directions, but then they tied together into a single perimeter.

The action started at 10 A.M.; after three-quarters of an hour, the vicious fighting stopped temporarily when heavy rain silenced all firearms for an hour. During this enforced armistice Herkimer ordered another change in tactics. Individual defenders had been strung along his perimeter, and the Indians would wait until a man fired and then rush in to dispatch him with a tomahawk before he could reload. So the militia started operating in mutually supporting pairs: while one reloaded, the other held his fire to pick off any enemy who charged.

When Major Stephen Watts arrived with a reinforcement of Royal Greens, Butler had them turn their coats inside out and approach the beleaguered Americans in the guise of a friendly sortie from Fort Stanwix. A sharp-eyed Palatine recognized a neighbor just in time, and a terrific hand-to-hand fight ensued. At about 1 P.M., an hour into the post-rainstorm, second phase of the battle, John Butler heard firing from Fort Stanwix and correctly guessed that the Americans were making a sortie. By this time the Indians were ready to quit, and the sortie's threat to their camps gave urgency to their desire to break contact. As their allies retreated, the remaining Loyalists also withdrew.

NUMBERS AND LOSSES

Because the participants were all irregulars, accurate statistics are not possible. American historians such as Benson Lossing tend to inflate the militia's losses. While officer casualties were heavy—Herkimer died of his wounds; one of the four colonels died and another was captured—the assertion that 160 men were killed is surely inflated. It is more probable that the number reflects total casualties, including the walking wounded. Estimates of Brant's losses are also higher in historians' accounts than they probably were on the battlefield. Probably from 70 to 100 Indians were killed or wounded, and the Loyalists' casualties must be added to that total.

SIGNIFICANCE

It is hard to make a case that this battle affected the outcome of the 1777 campaign, or even that it altered the outcome of the siege of the fort. But it was very important for the local history of the Mohawk Valley, poisoning relations between former neighbors. And the superb fight put up by relatively untrained militia in an ambush that would have tested veteran troops became an important morale factor.

SEE ALSO *Brant, Joseph; Butler, John; Fort Schuyler, New York; Herkimer, Nicholas; Johnson, Sir John; St. Leger's Expedition.*

BIBLIOGRAPHY

Foote, Allan D. *Liberty March: The Battle of Oriskany.* Utica, N.Y.: North Country Books, 1998.

Nickerson, Hoffman. *The Turning Point of the Revolution or Burgoyne in America.* Boston: Houghton Mifflin, 1928.

Swiggett, Howard. *War out of Niagara: Walter Butler and the Tory Rangers.* New York: Columbia University Press, 1933.

revised by Robert K. Wright Jr.

OS SEE *Calendars, Old and New Style.*

OSBORNE'S (JAMES RIVER), VIRGINIA.

27 April 1781. Osborne's on the James River served as the main facility for the small Virginia state navy, which by 1781 lay in mothballs under the guard of a small caretaker detachment. Major General William Phillips marched from Petersburg the morning of the 27th with the main British force and proceeded to Chesterfield Court House to keep the Americans at bay. Learning of the weak defenses, he detached Benedict Arnold with a strike force built around John Simcoe's Queen's Rangers, the Hessian jägers, and the Seventy-sixth and Eightieth Foot to destroy them. Arnold skillfully employed four light British field-pieces to drive the supporting militia from the opposite bank, and one of them silenced the *Tempest*, the only vessel capable of action, when a lucky shot severed its cable. The caretaker crews attempted to set the vessels on fire, but quick action by Simcoe's men secured them. Arnold captured five vessels and more than two thousand hogsheads of tobacco. A number of other craft and the shore installations were destroyed.

SEE ALSO *Arnold, Benedict; Petersburg, Virginia; Phillips, William; Simcoe, John Graves; Virginia, Military Operations in.*

BIBLIOGRAPHY

Simcoe, John Graves. *A Journal of the Operations of the Queen's Rangers.* New York: New York Times, 1968.

revised by Robert K. Wright Jr.

OSWALD, ELEAZER. (1755–1795).

Continental artillery officer, journalist. England and Connecticut. Born in Falmouth, England, in 1755, Oswald became sympathetic to the American cause and emigrated to New York City in about 1770. He apprenticed himself to the publisher of the *New-York Journal*, John Holt, whose daughter he married. He served as a private during the "Lexington Alarm" (19 April 1775) and volunteered to join Benedict Arnold's forces in their march to Quebec, He became Arnold's secretary and commanded the forlorn hope at Quebec, where he was wounded and captured on 31 December 1775. Exchanged on 10 January 1777, he was commissioned lieutenant colonel in John Lamb's Second Continental Artillery, and became famous as an artillerist. He particularly distinguished himself at Compo Hill during the Danbury raid of April 1777. After the battle of Monmouth on 28 June 1778, he was praised in official orders for his performance. As a result of his failure to be credited with the seniority he felt he deserved, Oswald resigned from the army in 1779.

Oswald then joined William Goddard in publishing the *Maryland Journal*, in which he printed General Charles Lee's criticisms of General George Washington. This article led to a popular demonstration against Oswald, and he was forced to publish an apology. In April 1782 he started publishing the violently partisan *Independent Gazetteer* in Philadelphia. Between 1782 and 1787 he also took over Holt's old New York City paper and published it as the *Independent Gazette, or New York Journal Revived*. He attacked the policies of Alexander Hamilton and challenged him to a duel, but friends adjusted the matter before the confrontation could take place. In 1792 Oswald left his publishing interests in the hands of his wife, Elizabeth, and went to England and then to France. There he was commissioned as a colonel of the artillery and regimental commander in the Republican army, seeing action at Gemape (France). Sent on a secret mission in connection with a contemplated French invasion of Ireland, he reached that country and submitted his report. Receiving no further instructions from his superiors at Vergennes, he returned to the United States. Shortly after reaching New York City, Oswald died of yellow fever, on 30 September 1795.

SEE ALSO *Compo Hill; Danbury Raid, Connecticut.*

BIBLIOGRAPHY

Wheeler, Joseph Towne. *The Maryland Press 1777–1790.* Baltimore, Md.: Maryland Historical Society, 1938.

revised by Michael Bellesiles

OSWALD, RICHARD. (1705–1784). British

diplomat. Scotland. Married to Mary Ramsay, whom Robert Burns celebrated in one of his poems, he was related to the famous Continental artillery officer, Eleazer Oswald. Richard spent many years in America, first as a factor for his cousins' Glasgow firm and then for his own London company that specialized in the sugar, tobacco, and slave trades. During the Revolution he worked behind the scenes to try to persuade the government toward a policy of conciliation. In 1781 he put up fifty thousand pounds to bail his old friend Henry Laurens out of the Tower. In March 1782 Lord Rockingham selected Oswald, an ally of the earl of Shelburne, for the peace negotiations in Paris. Initially frustrated by the other members of the commission who represented Shelburne's opponents within the government, Oswald became the sole responsible British representative during the final peace negotiations following Lord Rockingham's death in July and replacement as chief minister by Shelburne. Oswald, like Shelburne and most British merchants, was most concerned to maintain profitable trade relations with the United States and worked to craft a final peace treaty that would protect British economic interests. Though the terms of the treaty led to the removal of both Shelburne and Oswald, the terms Oswald negotiated remained the final treaty agreed to in Paris in September 1783. Oswald died in London the following November.

SEE ALSO *Oswald, Eleazer; Peace Negotiations.*

revised by Michael Bellesiles

OTIS, JAMES. (1725–1783). Patriot politician,

publicist, and orator. Massachusetts. Otis, born in West Barnstable, Massachusetts on 2 February 1725, graduated in 1743 from Harvard, which he hated. He then studied law under Jeremiah Gridley, a prominent Boston attorney, after which he established his own practice in Boston in 1750. In 1755 Otis married the weathy Ruth Cunningham. Within a few years, Otis was considered one of the leading lawyers in the province. He was an expert in common, civil, and admiralty law, in addition to being a scholar whose *Rudiments of Latin Prosody* (1760) became a Harvard text. In 1761 he resigned his lucrative office as king's advocate general of the vice admiralty court at Boston rather than argue for the Writs of Assistance, unlimited search warrants that allowed the authorities to search anywhere they pleased. Instead, Otis took the side of the Boston merchants in opposing the writs, which the royal customs collectors were seeking in order to find evidence of the violation of the Sugar Act of 1733.

James Otis. *The American patriot, statesman, and all-around agitator in a nineteenth-century engraving by Oliver Pelton.* THE LIBRARY OF CONGRESS

In his famous speech against the writs, delivered on 24 February 1761, Otis gave one of the earliest statements of the doctrine that a law that violates "Natural Law" is void. He decried the writs as an exercise of arbitrary power and, as such, contrary to the British constitution. No formal record of his argument exists, but young John Adams took notes and, 60 years later, recalled: "Otis was a flame of fire! . . . He hurried away everything before him. American independence was then and there born" (Adams, vol. 10, p. 247). Otis lost the case to Chief Justice Thomas Hutchinson, who argued that the Massachusetts Superior Court had the same power as British courts, which had been granted the authority to issue such writs by Parliament. In 1766 the British vacated Hutchinson's ruling on the grounds that this act of Parliament did not apply to Massachusetts. Otis's arguments against the writs of assistance did not circulate widely, but exerted great intellectual influence among the emerging patriot leadership.

Some scholars have questioned Otis's motivation in opposing British authority, finding personal causes in his resignation from his post as advocate general in 1760. It is known that Otis blamed Governor Francis Bernard and then-Lieutenant Governor Thomas Hutchinson for

violating an agreement to elevate the senior James Otis to the Superior Court. Much to the shock of the two James Otises, Hutchinson was himself made chief justice (13 November 1760), even though he continued to serve as lieutenant governor of Massachusetts. The younger Otis denied that his opposition to arbitrary government was motivated by a desire to avenge frustrated family ambitions.

In May 1761, two months after his famous speech against the writs, Otis became one of Boston's four representatives to the provincial legislature. His father was re-elected as speaker of the House, and the two Otises formed a popular bloc of Boston and rural interests to oppose the crown officials. In 1762 Otis wrote his first pamphlet, "A Vindication of the Conduct of the House of Representatives," in which he put forth the proposition that the legislature had complete power of the purse; the executive could spend no funds without their approval. In 1764 he wrote "The Rights of the British Colonies Asserted and Proved," putting forth the increasingly popular idea that there could be no taxation without representation, and the following year published "A Vindication of the British Colonies," mocking the British principle of virtual representation.

Yet even as Otis put forth a series of radical political positions, he cautioned moderation in resistance. Otis was made head of the Massachusetts Committee of Correspondence in 1764, and the next year he made a proposal that resulted in the Stamp Act Congress. He considered the Virginia resolves of Patrick Henry treasonable, and on 26 November 1765 wrote that he preferred "dutiful and loyal Addresses to his Majesty and his Parliament, who alone under God can extricate the Colonies from the painful Scenes of Tumult, Confusion, & Distress." At the Stamp Act Congress he argued for petitions rather than resistance. Even when British troops landed at Boston in 1768, Otis persisted in his insistence that no action beyond petitioning and letter writing was appropriate.

Though he stood still while political affairs accelerated away from him, Otis continued to play a key role in Massachusetts through 1770. Elected to the General Court in the spring of 1766, he formed a triumvirate with Samuel Adams and Joseph Hawley that led the legislative attack against the embattled Governor Francis Bernard and his deputy, Hutchinson. Otis presided over the town meeting that revived the nonimportation movement (28 October 1767), and, with Samuel Adams produced the Massachusetts circular letter, leading the majority that voted not to rescind it. Throughout these activities, which caused British authorities to threaten Adams and Otis with trial for treason, Otis viewed the idea of independence with abhorrence and repeatedly opposed what he saw as mob violence. Although his confederates worried about the violence of Otis's tongue, it was he who time and again stopped them from actions that would have provoked a crisis. He organized and moderated the town meeting of 12–13 September 1768 that quashed Samuel Adams's calls for armed resistance against the British regulars coming to establish the Boston Garrison.

Otis fell from leadership under unusual circumstances. On the evening of 5 September 1769 he charged into the British Coffee House and loudly demanded an apology from some officials who had accused him of provoking disloyalty. In a brawl that followed, John Robinson laid Otis's head open with a sword. The blow, aggravated by heavy drinking, drove Otis over the brink of madness, and although his reason returned from time to time he was finished as a public figure. He sued Robinson, was awarded damages of £2,000, and then refused any restitution beyond his legal and medical costs. In 1771 he seemed so completely restored that he returned to the general court, but in December he was declared legally insane. With a borrowed musket he rushed into the Battle of Bunker Hill, 17 June 1775, and emerged unscathed. Early in 1778 he was able, during one of his periodic lucid intervals, to argue a case in Boston, but he found the physical exertion too much and the darkness descended. Although he sometimes became violent and had to be tied down, during most of his final years he was harmless. The end came dramatically to this man who could have been the protagonist of a classical tragedy. Otis had always predicted that he would be killed by lightning, and on 23 May 1783 he was struck by lightening while standing on a friend's doorstep.

SEE ALSO *Adams, John; Adams, Samuel; Boston Garrison; Massachusetts Circular Letter.*

BIBLIOGRAPHY

Adams, John. *Works of John Adams, Second President of the United States.* Boston: Little, Brown and Co., 1851–1865.

Mullet, Charls F., ed. "Political Writings of James Otis." In *University of Missouri Studies,* vol. 4 (1929).

Waters, John J., Jr. *The Otis Family in Provincial and Revolutionary Massachusetts.* Chapel Hill, N.C.: University of North Carolina Press, 1968.

revised by Michael Bellesiles

OTTO, BODO.

OTTO, BODO. (1711–1787). Continental army surgeon. Pennsylvania. Born in Hanover, Germany, in 1711, Bodo Otto studied medicine for several years before setting up his practice in Luneberg in 1736. In 1755 he emigrated to Philadelphia, moving in 1773 to Reading, Pennsylvania, where he achieved great influence among the German population. At the start of the Revolution he was a leader in the Patriot cause. He held several elected offices before being appointed senior surgeon of the Middle Division in 1776, seeing action at Long Island that summer. On 17 February 1777 the Continental Congress ordered Otto to establish a smallpox hospital at Trenton, New Jersey, where he remained until September. He was then assigned to a hospital at Bethlehem, Pennsylvania, where he served until the spring of 1778. He next took charge of the hospitals at Yellow Springs, near Valley Forge, where he remained for the duration of the war. During this period he held a commission as colonel in the New Jersey militia. When the medical department was reorganized, Otto was one of fifteen physicians selected for the hospital department. He was given the title of Hospital Physician and Surgeon on 6 October 1780. He retired from the army on 1 February 1782 and reopened his Philadelphia office, but soon moved to Baltimore, Maryland. In 1784 he moved to Reading, Pennsylvania, where he died on 12 June 1787. Three of his sons assisted him during his Revolutionary War service.

SEE ALSO *Medical Practice during the Revolution.*

BIBLIOGRAPHY

Gibson, James Edgar. *Dr. Bodo Otto and the Medical Background of the American Revolution.* Springfield, Ill.: Thomas, 1937.

revised by Michael Bellesiles

"OUT LIERS." Patriots, particularly in the Carolinas, who left their families at home and hid out to avoid taking the oath of allegiance to the King. The term also was applied to patriots or Tories escaping the vengeance of their political enemies.

Mark M. Boatner

OVER MOUNTAIN MEN.

OVER MOUNTAIN MEN. Although this term is loosely applied to other groups of American colonists beyond the Blue Ridge Mountains, it is more accurately restricted to those living in what later became Tennessee. Also known as back water men—"apparently," according to Sydney George Fisher, "because they lived beyond the sources of the eastern rivers, and on the waters which flowed into the Mississippi"—their principal settlements were along the Watauga, Nolachucky (later

Nolichucky), and Holston Rivers (*Struggle for American Independence,* vol. 2, p. 350 n.). Principal leaders were John Sevier and Isaac Shelby. Although they are often referred to as "mountain men," Fisher points out that "very few people lived in the mountains at the time of the Revolution, and the Back Water men were merely North Carolinians, mostly of Scotch-Irish stock, who had crossed the mountains to enjoy the level and fertile lands of Tennessee, in the same way that the Virginians who followed Boone crossed the mountains into Kentucky" (ibid., vol. 2, p. 351 n.). Another misconception is that the Battle of Kings Mountain was won by the over mountain men; although their leaders, Shelby and Sevier, deserve credit for this *levée en masse,* their manpower contribution was only 480 out of the 1,800 or so who eventually arrived on the eve of the battle.

Aside from their part in the skirmishes leading up to this battle and in the battle itself, the over mountain men did little fighting. Sevier and Shelby showed up with some men after the Battle of Eutaw Springs (8 September 1781),

but they faded back into the mountains when Greene asked them to reinforce Marion during the subsequent operations leading up to the advance on Dorchester, South Carolina, on 1 December 1781 (Ward, *War of the Revolution,,* p. 838). William Campbell's Virginia mountain riflemen, who figured prominently at Kings Mountain and appeared in the final phases of Lafayette's maneuvering against Cornwallis in the Virginia military operations, were not over mountain men in the strict sense of the term.

SEE ALSO *Kings Mountain, South Carolina; Virginia, Military Operations in.*

BIBLIOGRAPHY

Fisher, Sydney George. *The Struggle for American Independence.* 2 vols. Philadelphia and London: Lippincott, 1908.

Ward, Christopher. *The War of the Revolution.* Edited by John R. Alden. 2 vols. New York: Macmillan, 1952.

Mark M. Boatner

P

PACA, WILLIAM. (1740–1799).

Signer, governor of Maryland, jurist. Maryland. Born near Abingdon, Maryland, on 31 October 1740, Paca graduated from Philadelphia College in 1759, entered the Middle Temple in 1760, and was admitted to the bar in Annapolis the following year. In 1765 he and Samuel Chase organized the Anne Arundel County Sons of Liberty in opposition to the Stamp Act. He was in the Maryland legislature from 1771 to 1774, when he became a member of the Committee of Correspondence and a delegate to the first Continental Congress. After his state removed restrictions from its delegates in June 1776, Paca voted for independence and became a signer of the Declaration of Independence. He remained a delegate to the Continental Congress though 1777, helped frame the Maryland constitution in August 1776, and served as state senator from 1777 to 1779. In 1778 he became chief judge of the Maryland General Court. Two years later, Congress made him chief justice of the court of appeals in admiralty and prize cases. In November 1782 he was elected governor. Twice reelected, he served until 26 November 1785. During this period he took a particular interest in veterans' affairs. He finally voted for the Constitution as submitted to the Maryland Convention of 1788, although he was far from satisfied with the document and had proposed 28 amendments. Washington appointed Paca as a federal district judge in 1789, and he held this post until his death on 13 October 1799.

SEE ALSO *Sons of Liberty.*

BIBLIOGRAPHY

Stiverson, Gregory A., and Phebe R. Jacobsen. *William Paca, A Biography.* Baltimore, Md.: Maryland Historical Society, 1976.

revised by Michael Bellesiles

PAINE, ROBERT TREAT. (1731–1814).

Signer, jurist. Massachusetts. Born in Boston, Massachusetts, on 11 March 1731, Robert Treat Paine graduated from Harvard in 1749, served as chaplain on the Crown Point Expedition of 1755, and signed on as a whaler for a long sea voyage to Carolina, Europe, and Greenland. Admitted to the bar in 1757, he practiced first in Boston, but in 1761 moved his office to Taunton. His identification with the Patriot movement led to his selection as associate prosecuting attorney in the trial resulting from the Boston "Massacre," and his prosecution of British Captain Thomas Preston, although unsuccessful, gave him widespread publicity as an advocate of colonial rights. He represented Taunton in the Provincial Assembly during the periods 1773–1775 and 1777–1778. He was delegate to the first Continental Congress, and served in the Second Congress until the end of 1776. Initially opposed to independence, Paine signed both the Olive Branch petition (a final attempt to avoid war with Britain) and the Declaration of Independence. He also had been chairman of the committee to provide gunpowder for the Patriot forces, and after leaving the Congress he continued to experiment with its manufacture. Again elected to Congress in 1777, Paine declined to assume his office, remaining in Massachusetts to serve as speaker in the assembly. Later that year he became the first attorney general of the state. In 1787 he prosecuted those charged in Shays's Rebellion, a clash between local farmers and merchants which had occurred in the previous year. Paine declined a Massachusetts supreme court appointment in 1783 on financial grounds, but finally accepted the position in 1790. After 14 years in this post he was forced by increasing deafness to retire from the bench. He died in Boston on 11 June 1814.

SEE ALSO *Olive Branch Petition; Shays's Rebellion.*

BIBLIOGRAPHY

Hanson, Edward W. "'A Sense of Honor and Duty': Robert Treat Paine (1731–1814) of Massachusetts and the New Nation." Ph.D. dissertation. Boston College, 1992.

Riley, Stephen T., and Edward W. Hanson, eds. *The Papers of Robert Treat Paine,* 2 vols. to date. Boston: Massachusetts Historical Society, 1992–.

revised by Michael Bellesiles

PAINE, THOMAS. (1737–1809).

British author and revolutionary. Thomas Paine was born at Thetford, an inland Norfolk town, on 29 January 1737, the son of a Quaker stay maker and tenant farmer. He was later confirmed in the Church of England, his mother's faith, although his father forbade him to learn Latin and Greek when he entered the local grammar school at seven. He showed some ability at mathematics and literature and absorbed the seagoing stories of one of the masters, before leaving at eleven to be apprenticed to his father. Early in the Seven Years' War, when he was about twenty, he joined the privateer *King of Prussia* for one or possibly more voyages. At around this time he also worked for a London stay maker, thus combining the prim with the semi-piratical. In the spring of 1758 he was employed by a Dover stay maker, and in 1759 he set up on his own account in Sandwich. Here he seems to have become a Methodist lay preacher, at a time when Methodism was an evangelical movement within the Church of England. He married Mary Lambert in September and, when his business began to fail, moved with her to Margate where in 1760 she died in childbirth. In 1762, after training in Thetford, he entered the excise service only to be dismissed two years later for malpractice. He had to return to stay making until he was reinstated in 1766. While waiting for a posting he taught in two London schools, and in February 1768 he accepted an excise job in Lewes, Sussex. There, though a poor public speaker, he was prominent in the town debating society and wrote some poems and other literary pieces. He lodged at first in the High Street with the family of the innkeeper Samuel Ollive, with whom he set up a tobacco mill to supplement his excise pay. After Ollive died in 1769, he started a shop with Ollive's widow and in 1771 married her daughter, Elizabeth.

Up to this time he appears to have been some sort of Whig, but he began to move in a radical direction by

Thomas Paine. *The political writer and philosopher Thomas Paine in a portrait (c.1806) by John Wesley Jarvis.* © BETTMANN/ CORBIS

writing his first political pamphlet, *The Case of the Officers of Excise,* which argued for higher salaries. Toward the end of 1772 he travelled up to London with a petition signed by three thousand excise men, and although his lobbying was ignored by both ministers and Parliament, he associated with Oliver Goldsmith, moved in scientific circles, and probably met Benjamin Franklin. He returned to Lewes in April 1773 to find his businesses in ruins. Twelve months later he was sacked by the excise board for neglect of duty and forced to sell the tobacco mill. In May he and Elizabeth parted, and in June their separation became formal. In October, with a letter of introduction from Franklin in his pocket, he took ship for America.

Soon after his arrival in Philadelphia on 30 November 1774, he met Franklin's son-in-law, Richard Bache, and went into partnership with the bookseller Robert Aitkin to found the *Pennsylvania Magazine.* One of Paine's contributions, an argument against slavery, led to a meeting with the physician Benjamin Rush, who in the autumn of 1775 encouraged Paine to write a pamphlet in favor of independence.

Common Sense, "written by an Englishman," appeared in Philadelphia on 10 January 1776, price two shillings. It was unique in that it was written for an audience wider than the educated elite and in that it articulated radical notions already abroad but until then never so directly or plainly expressed. Paine argued that society, in its natural origins, was free and without government. As vice crept in laws, governments became a necessary evil at best, repressive tyrannies at worst. The earliest, most nearly natural, and least repressive form of government was republican, whereas monarchy was a later invention that enslaved the people. Paine claimed that in "the early ages of the world, according to the Scripture chronology there were no kings; the consequence of which was there were no wars"; this was breathtakingly specious and misleading, but Paine, of course, was dealing in effects, not facts. Having established that monarchical Europe was corrupt and war-ridden, he went on to argue that even the British constitution was no more than a mongrel blend of republican freedoms with monarchical and aristocratic remnants. It was now America's divinely appointed destiny, her duty to the world, to break free of this old world corruption and establish a pure free republic. "O receive the fugitive, and prepare in time an asylum for mankind!"

While hardly original, and assailable on many counts, this brilliant piece of propaganda reduced argument for independence to a formula anyone could understand. Appearing on the very day of news of the king's rejection of American petitions, it turned disappointment into outright hostility to monarchy, especially among artisans whose notion of a republic was quite different from that of grandees like Washington. Pirate editions appeared within three weeks, (120,000) copies of Paine's version alone were sold within three months, and total sales may have reached 500,000 in America and abroad. There were immediate counter-blasts from those who (like James Chalmers) opposed independence and those who (like John Adams) disliked Paine's kind of republic: a united republic with a single legislature elected on the widest possible franchise. As "The Forester," Paine found himself composing replies to these criticisms and becoming drawn into both local provincial politics and the politics of the Continental Congress. He may even have helped to draw up Jefferson's Declaration of Independence, passed by Congress on 4 July 1776.

A few days later, having committed himself to the war of words, Paine now tried to join in the shooting war with a company of Philadelphia volunteers marching to join the "flying camp," Washington's mobile strategic reserve, forming at Amboy, near New York. William Howe, of course, did not attack until late August, so Paine became a headquarters secretary. Even after Howe struck, like so many unfit flying camp soldiers Paine saw little or nothing

of the front line. He became aide-de-camp to Nathanael Greene at Fort Lee, where most of the garrison was from flying camp units, and wrote propaganda reports, playing down major defeats, playing up minor successes, and explaining away Washington's blunders. He escaped across the Delaware in 1776 and returned to Philadelphia to find revolutionary morale in collapse. He immediately began writing a series of propaganda essays, starting with *The American Crisis*, brilliantly designed to stiffen rebel resolve in adversity. More practically, he became secretary first to a mission to the Susquehanna Indians and, beginning in March 1777, to the congressional committee on foreign affairs. In September, with Washington defeated at Brandywine and Howe's army at the gates of Philadelphia, Paine fled from the city and soon after became the Pennsylvania observer with Washington's army.

With France's entry into the war early in 1778, and with Congress's return to Philadelphia in June, Paine began to believe that victory was assured. In October he revived *American Crisis* number 6, shortly followed by number 7, to attack the Carlisle mission's peace proposals. His secretarial duties with the foreign affairs committee, while not demanding, and probably intended merely to provide him with a living, gave him an inflated idea of his political importance, which led him to accuse Silas Deane of profiteering in collusion with French interests. The dispute seriously embarrassed the French government, and in January 1799 Congress forced him to resign. Short of income, Paine took a job in a merchant's office before entering a bitter dispute over America's Newfoundland fishing rights, which he defended. In November he returned to respectability with appointment as clerk to the Pennsylvania assembly. In May 1780, driven by his belief that rich and poor had a common stake in victory, he made a first move toward establishing the Bank of North America to raise funds for the war. In 1781 he was dissuaded from going home to stir up revolution in Britain and took part in a successful mission to France instead. Later in the year he once again combined conviction with pecuniary need by writing for Congress a series of tracts demanding more powerful federal government. He was probably getting money from the French as well, so *Crisis* number 11 decried the notion that America could possibly make peace separately from her Bourbon allies.

In 1784 he was rewarded with a confiscated Loyalist estate and grants from the federal and Pennsylvania governments. He divided his time between a property in Bordertown, New Jersey, and New York City, writing in support of the independence of the Bank of North America, dabbling in scientific experiments, and developing plans for an iron bridge across the Schuylkill River. When the cost of the bridge turned out to be beyond American resources, he took his models to Europe in the spring of 1787, eventually persuading a Rotherham firm to put a scaled-down version across the Thames. The bridge, erected in May 1790, was a failure by the autumn, but Paine was already launched on a new journalistic project—the defense of the French Revolution.

He answered Edmund Burke's *Reflections on the Revolution in France* (November 1790) with *The Rights of Man* (21 February 1791), a muddled scissors-and-paste job that nevertheless became immensely popular. In April 1791 he returned to France, where he joined the Girondins (also called the Brissotins after their leader, Brissot de Warville) as a republican publicist. Returning to Britain in February 1792, he brought out a much more coherent second part of the *Rights of Man*, which credited the American Revolution with sparking the revolt against European despotisms and suggested a union between a republican Britain and France. Already rewarded with French citizenship, Paine prudently retired to Paris in September, where he became a member of the Convention, was briefly imprisoned under the Jacobins, and wrote *The Age of Reason*, an attack on organized religion. In 1796 he bitterly attacked Washington, who he thought had abandoned France. He returned to America in 1802 and died there on 8 June 1809.

Paine was a man of humble origins in an age when aristocratic connections mattered, who failed in both business and the service of the state. Combined with a modest education, a talented pen, and a gift for polemic, it is hardly surprising that he turned a prolific, radical pamphleteer. Against that accomplishment must be set his alcoholism, laziness, inordinate vanity, and carelessness with money. Neither a systematic philosopher nor a careful historian, he never let facts get in the way of his grand polemic. Nevertheless, his capacity to articulate and popularize radical ideas turned him into perhaps the greatest propagandist of the age of revolution.

SEE ALSO *Brandywine, Pennsylvania; Burke, Edmund; Deane, Silas; Franklin, Benjamin; Howe, William; Propaganda in the American Revolution; Rush, Benjamin; Washington, George.*

BIBLIOGRAPHY

Conway, M. D. *The Life of Thomas Paine.* Vol. 1. London: Routledge/Thoemmes, 1996.

Philp, Mark. *Paine.* Oxford: Oxford University Press, 1989.

revised by John Oliphant

PALATINE, NEW YORK (19 OCTOBER 1780) SEE *Fort Keyser, New York.*

PAOLI, PENNSYLVANIA.

21 September 1777. When Washington withdrew across Parker's Ford on 19 September, he left Brigadier General Anthony Wayne's Pennsylvania Division (perhaps fifteen hundred men and four guns) on the west side of the Schuylkill to observe Howe and to strike his rear should he attempt to force a passage across the river. But Wayne was strictly ordered to avoid being caught by the British main body. On the 20th, Wayne camped along a wooded ridge 1.75 miles southwest of the General Paoli Tavern and about 4.5 miles from Howe's position in the South Valley Hills.

Howe decided to strike at this force while it was isolated and sent Major General Charles "No Flint" Grey with almost two thousand men to make a night attack. Grey marched at 10 P.M. on the 20th with the Second Battalion of Light Infantry, supported by the Forty-second ("Black Watch") and the Forty-fourth Foot. He was followed an hour later by the Fortieth and Fifty-fifth Foot under Lieutenant Colonel Thomas Musgrave. Since accidental discharges of muskets were the most common way to betray night attacks, Grey directed that the British regulars were to remove the flints from their weapons and rely entirely on the bayonet, thereby earning his nickname. Musgrave's column did not directly figure in the resulting battle, as his task was to cut the Lancaster Road and prevent Wayne from retreating.

Grey's main body, with a dozen dragoons attached, probably amounted to from twelve hundred to fifteen hundred men. The light infantry led, with the Forty-fourth following and the Highlanders at the end of the column. Expertly guided by several local Loyalists, Grey made a fast and skilful approach. Mounted videttes and American sentries detected the movement and fired sporadically, while the British guides became confused just as they reached the outskirts of Wayne's bivouac. As they made contact, the light company of the Fifty-second Foot led the British advance. The attack hit about one in the morning, striking the Seventh Pennsylvania Regiment, which bore the brunt of the blow. Its resistance, with support, bought time for the rest of the division to disengage and for all of the artillery to get to safety. British pursuit continued for several miles.

NUMBERS AND LOSSES

Estimates of Wayne's losses ran as high as 500 (Howe's claim), but modern investigations have identified 163 individuals by name and conclude that the probable total count was at least 53 killed and another 200 wounded or captured. The British lost no more than 20 killed and 40 wounded, although Howe reported less. Civilian accounts of the "mangled dead" gave rise to the perception of a "Paoli Massacre."

SIGNIFICANCE

This engagement had very little impact on the Philadelphia campaign, although American propagandists succeeded in whipping up anti-British sentiment with exaggerated accusations that Grey's men had refused quarter and massacred defenseless patriots who tried to surrender. Wayne was acquitted by a court-martial "with the highest honors" of charges that he had failed to heed "timely notice" of the attack.

SEE ALSO *Philadelphia Campaign.*

BIBLIOGRAPHY

Gilbert, Stephen. "An Analysis of the Xavier della Gatta Paintings of the Battles of Paoli and Germantown." *Military Collector and Historian* 45 (Fall 1994): 98–108, and 47 (Winter 1995): 146–162.

McGuire, Thomas. *The Battle of Paoli.* Mechanicsburg, Pa.: Stackpole Books, 2000.

revised by Robert K. Wright Jr.

PARALLELS SEE *Regular Approaches.*

PARIS, TREATY OF. 10 February 1763. The Treaty of Paris ended the French and Indian War in North America and the Seven Years' War in Europe. France ceded to Britain all claims to Canada, Acadia, Cape Breton Island, and the islands in the St. Lawrence, in effect all her territories east of the Mississippi River, retaining only the islands of St. Pierre and Miquelon in the Gulf of St. Lawrence and fishing rights off Newfoundland. To compensate Spain for her losses as France's ally, France had previously ceded to Spain by the secret Treaty of San Ildefonso on 3 November 1762 the Isle of Orleans (New Orleans) and all her territory west of the Mississippi. The Treaty of Paris thus completed the removal of French power from North America and left only Britain and Spain as imperial powers on the continent. Of the West Indies islands captured during the war, Martinique and Guadeloupe were restored to France; St. Vincent, Dominica, and Tobago were restored to Britain. Britain restored Cuba to Spain in return for the Floridas. Spain acknowledged Britain's rights to maintain

log-cutting settlements in Central America. France agreed to evacuate her position in Hanover and to restore Minorca to the British. The status quo in India was restored.

The Treaty of Paris ratified Britain's preeminent position in Europe and North America, but while Britons rejoiced in the success of their armies and navies, those very victories, by so thoroughly upsetting the balance of power, left their leaders to deal with a world in which her foes would be eager for revenge. France was temporarily shattered, exhausted, and humiliated, but she had not been, nor could have been, permanently crippled. Britain now had also to deal with other complications, especially regarding how to govern the newly enlarged empire. Some Englishmen recognized the emerging problem of imperial governance and even argued that, instead of Canada, Britain should have retained the sugar-rich island of Guadeloupe.

revised by Harold E. Selesky

PARIS, TREATY OF. SEE *Peace Treaty of 3 September 1783.*

PARKER, SIR HYDE. (1714–1782/3). British admiral. Hyde Parker served in merchant ships before entering the navy at the advanced age of twenty-four. A post-captain from 1748, he was in the East Indies from 1760 to 1764, and was next employed in the Channel in 1776–1777. On 26 January 1778 he was promoted rear admiral and appointed John Byron's second in command of the squadron that chased d'Estaing to North America and the West Indies. From August 1779 Parker was in temporary command in the Leeward Islands, and in March 1780 he prevented an attack on St. Lucia by Comte de Guichen's numerically superior fleet. When George Rodney arrived, Parker stayed on as his second in command and led the van in the indecisive action off Martinique on 17 April. Because Rodney had not properly explained his intentions, Parker had not engaged as he wanted; although not blamed directly, Parker was sent home with the trade convoy in July. On 26 September 1780 he was promoted vice admiral, and on 5 August 1781 he failed to destroy a Dutch force of similar size in an action off the Dogger Bank. Blaming the Admiralty, Parker resigned, telling the king that he should employ younger commanders and better ships. In 1782 the Rockingham ministry appointed him commander in chief in the East Indies, and on 10 July he succeeded to his brother's baronetcy. He sailed in October, but sometime after leaving Rio on 12 December his ship was lost at sea. Its fate has never been established.

SEE ALSO *Byron, John; Dutch Participation in the American Revolution; Estaing, Charles Hector Théodat, Comte d'; Guichen, Luc Urbain de Bouexic, Comte de; Rodney, George Bridges.*

revised by John Oliphant

PARKER, SIR HYDE, JR. (1739–1807).

British admiral. Second son of vice admiral Sir Hyde Parker, baronet (1714–1782), Parker served for some time in his father's ships, rising to the post of captain on 5 July 1763. From 1763 he served in West Indian and North American waters. At New York on 12–18 July 1776 he led the raid to Tappan Sea aboard the *Phoenix* (40 guns), and on 27 August his ship helped to cover General William Howe's landing on Long Island. In October he was again in action in the North River. He convoyed troops to Savannah at the end of 1778. In 1779 the *Phoenix* returned to Britain, where her captain was knighted for his services at New York Escorting an outward-bound Jamaica convoy, the *Phoenix* was wrecked in a hurricane off Cuba on 4 October 1780. Parker got most of his crew ashore with rescued provisions and guns, constructed defence works, and held off enemy forces until they were rescued. He was with his father's squadron in the Dogger Bank action on 5 August 1781 and, aboard the *Goliath*, he took part in the relief of Gibraltar in 1782. Promoted to rear admiral in February 1793, he served with Samuel Lord Hood at Toulon and Corsica. A vice admiral from 1794, in 1796 he promptly pursued a Spanish squadron across the Atlantic after it had escaped from Cadiz, and from 1796 to 1800 he was in command at Jamaica. At Copenhagen in 1801, his famously ill-judged signal to Admiral Horatio, Lord Nelson to withdraw, and his subsequent failure to advance into the Baltic Sea, ruined his reputation. He was not employed again. However, the hesitation and slowness of 1801, and the inevitable comparison with Nelson, should not be allowed to obscure his considerable achievements.

SEE ALSO *Long Island, New York (August 1777); Tappan Sea.*

revised by John Oliphant

PARKER, JOHN. (1729–1775).

Hero of the battle of Lexington. Massachusetts. A native of Lexington, Massachusetts, John Parker served in the French and Indian War, fighting at Louisburg and Quebec and probably serving as one of Robert Roger's rangers for a time. When the Revolution started he was a farmer and mechanic, and held various town offices. As captain of the local company of minutemen, he figured prominently in the battle of Lexington, 19 April 1775. It is unlikely that he said the famous words carved on the stone at Lexington: "Stand your ground. Don't fire unless fired upon. But if they mean to have a war, let it begin here." This is, however, what he should have said. Parker assembled as many militia as possible after the action on the green, then marched toward Concord to harass the British on their retreat to Boston. He then led a small force to Cambridge, but was too ill to take part in subsequent actions. He died on 17 September 1775.

SEE ALSO *Lexington and Concord.*

BIBLIOGRAPHY

Fleming, Thomas. *The First Stroke: Lexington, Concord, and the Beginning of the American Revolution.* Washington, D.C.: U.S. Government Printing Office, 1978.

revised by Michael Bellesiles

PARKER, SIR PETER. (1721–1811).

British admiral. A post-captain from 1747, in October 1775 Parker was appointed commodore with orders to escort Charles Cornwallis's transports to America. Unable to sail until February 1776, and delayed by storms en route, the convoy did not join Henry Clinton until May. Parker and Clinton then cooperated to attack the fort on Sullivan's Island in Charleston Harbor on 28 June 1776. Although the troops were unable to reach the fort, the naval bombardment was frustrated only when three of Parker's ships ran aground. Parker then joined William Howe at New York and supported the landings on Long Island. He escorted Clinton's expedition to Rhode Island and remained there well into 1777. Promoted rear admiral on 20 May 1777, he was later appointed to command the Jamaica station, where in 1778 he became Horatio Nelson's chief patron. Promoted vice admiral on 29 March 1779, Parker supported Dalling's expeditions to Honduras and Nicaragua (1779–1780). Concerned for the safety of Jamaica, he resisted demands to send naval support to save Mobile and Pensacola and was slow to release ships to reinforce the North American squadron under Thomas Graves and Samuel Hood in 1781. Parker was awarded a baronetcy on 13 January 1783 and in due course rose to admiral of the fleet. He died in London on 21 December 1811.

SEE ALSO *Jamaica (West Indies); Long Island, New York, Battle of; Sullivan's Island.*

revised by John Oliphant

PARKERS FERRY, SOUTH CAROLINA.

13 August 1781. Colonel William Harden commanded a body of rebel troops near this place, some thirty miles west northwest of Charleston, when British Major Thomas Fraser was sent with 200 dragoons to support an uprising of some 450 Loyalists. Harden called for help, and General Nathanael Greene called on General Francis Marion to respond as he thought fit. Leaving his base in the Santee Hills, Marion led two hundred picked men on a remarkable march of about one hundred miles, moving only at night and undetected by the enemy. He reached Harden on 13 August and immediately set up an ambuscade on the causeway leading to Parkers Ferry. He then sent a party of his fastest horsemen to lure Fraser into the trap. Fraser took the bait and charged in to take a surprise fire of buckshot at fifty yards range. Courageously, Fraser rallied his men, launched another attack in the face of a second volley, and was hit by a third when his horsemen again came parallel to the hidden partisans. Marion estimated that his forces had killed or wounded one hundred of the enemy without losing a single man. Because Marion's ammunition was almost exhausted, he could not exploit this success by pursuing the enemy and so returned to his base. After covering a total of four hundred miles, he rejoined Greene in time for the major engagement at Eutaw Springs.

revised by Michael Bellesiles

PARLEY.

As early as the sixteenth century, this term was used to mean an informal conference between military opponents to treat or discuss terms. A parley usually was requested to discuss surrender, but it also was called to arrange a truce to care for wounded men lying between the lines. It often was a means of gaining time. A parley with the Indians was known in America as a powow.

SEE ALSO *Chamade.*

revised by Mark M. Boatner

PAROLE.

Derived from the French *parole d'honneur* (word of honor), a parole is a pledge or oath under which a prisoner of war is released with the understanding that he will not again bear arms until exchanged. Sometimes the parole included geographical restrictions. The victor often is happy to parole prisoners because this relieves him of the administrative burden of caring for them; also, sometimes he does not have the transportation or guards to evacuate prisoners, particularly the wounded. Another sense of "parole," as defined in Thomas Wilhelm's *Military Dictionary* (rev. ed, 1881), is a "watch-word differing from the countersign in that it is only communicated to officers of the guard, while the countersign is given to all members."

revised by Mark M. Boatner

PARSONS, SAMUEL HOLDEN.

(1737–1789). Continental general. Connecticut. Born on 14 May 1737 at Lyme, Connecticut, Parsons was the son of a clergyman whose support for George Whitefield made him so unpopular with his congregation that he moved to Newburyport, Massachusetts, in 1746. The son graduated from Harvard College in 1756 and returned to Lyme, where his mother, Phebe Griswold, had important family connections. He studied law under his uncle, Matthew Griswold (later deputy governor and governor of Connecticut), was admitted to the bar in 1759, and settled in Lyme where he became a prominent figure in Patriot politics. He was repeatedly elected to the General Assembly after 1762 (he served eighteen consecutive terms) and was appointed king's attorney for New London County in 1773, the same year he became a member of the assembly's committee of correspondence. He moved to New London in 1774.

An early advocate of independence, he was one of the first to suggest holding an intercolonial congress. As lieutenant colonel of the Third Militia Regiment from October 1774, he led a company to Boston on news of the Lexington alarm (19 April 1775). He figured prominently in the plan to capture Fort Ticonderoga (accomplished on 10 May) and was named colonel of the Sixth Connecticut Regiment on 1 May 1775. He remained on duty at New London until 17 June, when the governor's council ordered his regiment to Boston where, stationed at Roxbury, it took part in the Boston siege until the end of its enlistment on 10 December. From his old regiment, Parsons recruited the Tenth Continental Regiment for 1776 and was ordered to New York City in April. Promoted to brigadier general on 9 August 1776, Parsons was heavily engaged in the fighting on the American right (William Alexander's wing) at the Battle of Long Island on 27 August and distinguished himself by holding his position until almost completely surrounded. His letters of 29 August and 8 October 1776 to John Adams provide some of the best descriptions of the battlefield; the historian Douglas Freeman has called his 8 October 1776 letter "a model of lucid and simple explanation" (vol. 4, p. 158). At Kips Bay on 15 September, his brigade of Connecticut Continentals proved it could run as well as militia, but he himself joined Washington in trying to stop the rout. After the Battle of Harlem Heights, he was posted in the Highlands until December 1776, when he was detached to reinforce Washington's troops in New Jersey.

Parsons spent the rest of the war recruiting in Connecticut, commanding troops in the Hudson Highlands, and orchestrating the defense of the Connecticut shore against British raiders. From his recruiting post at New Haven, he was unable to oppose William Tryon's Danbury raid in late April 1777. In late September he warned Israel Putnam that three thousand British reinforcements had reached New York City, but he could do little in response when these troops were employed in Clinton's expedition up the Hudson in October. He spent the winter of 1778–1779 in charge of construction at West Point. In July 1779 he finally managed to deploy 150 Continental recruits to attack British raiders at Norwalk, but he could not help other towns along Long Island Sound that were attacked at the same time. In December 1779 he succeeded Israel Putnam as commander of the Connecticut division, always stationed in or near the Highlands, and on 23 October 1780 he was promoted to major general. He devoted most of his energy to keeping the Connecticut Line in good order, a difficult job amid privation and inaction. He organized occasional raids into the Neutral Ground, the most successful of which was Lieutenant Colonel William Hull's attack on Morrisania on 22–23 January 1781, for which he received the thanks of Congress.

As early as December 1777, Parsons had been alarmed by the depreciation of Continental currency, which was wiping out the small fortune he had invested in government securities when he entered the army. A year later he was increasingly impatient to be released from military service, but Congress would not approve his resignation because his efforts were too valuable. During this time he dealt with the double agent William Heron on espionage matters, and Heron thought the discontented general might be won over to the British cause, but according to the historian Carl Van Doren, Parsons "never showed himself disloyal or treacherous" (p. 400).

Retiring from the army on 22 July 1782, Parsons practiced law in Middletown, Connecticut, and was elected several times to the legislature. He was quick to see the advantages of getting government land in exchange for his pay certificates and undertook to get an appointment that would enable him to evaluate western lands.

This opportunity came when Congress named him an Indian commissioner on 22 September 1785. He then became a promoter of the Ohio Company and on 8 March 1787 was chosen one of its three directors. In October he was named the first judge of the Northwest Territory and in April 1788 moved to Adelphia (later Marietta, Ohio). At the age of fifty-one he embarked on the life of a frontiersman and undertook to recoup his fortune. He drowned on 17 November 1789 when his canoe capsized in the rapids of the Big Beaver River while he was returning from a visit to the Western Reserve, where he also had an interest.

SEE ALSO *Clinton's Expedition; Kip's Bay, New York; Long Island, New York, Battle of; Morrisania, New York; Ticonderoga, New York, American Capture of.*

BIBLIOGRAPHY

Buel, Richard V., Jr. *Dear Liberty: Connecticut's Mobilization for the Revolutionary War.* Middletown, Conn.: Wesleyan University Press, 1980.

Freeman, Douglas Southall. *George Washington.* 7 vols. New York: Scribner, 1948–1957.

Hall, Charles S. *Life and Letters of Samuel Holden Parsons.* Binghamton, N.Y. : Otseningo Publishing, 1905.

Sibley's Harvard Graduates. Vol. 14. Boston, Mass.: Harvard University Press, 1968.

Van Doren, Carl. *Secret History of the American Revolution.* New York: Viking, 1941.

revised by Harold E. Selesky

PARSON'S CAUSE.

1763. When droughts in the 1750s brought on several crop failures and shot up the price of tobacco, the Virginia House of Burgesses in 1755 and 1758 passed the Two Penny Acts, which made it temporarily legal to pay debts formerly callable in tobacco at the rate of two pence a pound. This price was considerably below the soaring free market price of tobacco, which reached four and a half pence a pound in Virginia currency. The Anglican clergy in Virginia was collectively entitled to an annual salary of 17,280 pounds of tobacco a year, and some clergymen clamored to collect the windfall increase in the value of their maintenance. They took their case to the colony's Privy Council, which on 29 August 1759 exercised its right by disallowing the act of 1758 on the grounds that it did not have the required clause suspending its operation until approved by the king, thereby enabling the clergy to sue for the anticipated value of their salary.

The Reverend James Maury presented such a suit in the Hanover County court in 1763, and the judges had to declare the act null and void. But when a jury was called to determine how much the "parson" would collect, young Patrick Henry's brilliant defense resulted in Maury's being awarded only one penny. The effort of the Anglican clergy to profit from the economic distress inflicted by natural causes, as well as the unwillingness of the imperial government to allow a colony to deal in a timely way with an unforeseen natural disaster, began to sour many Virginians on the imperial connection. The case also marked the beginning of Henry's political career.

SEE ALSO *Henry, Patrick.*

BIBLIOGRAPHY

Knollenberg, Bernhard *Origin of the American Revolution, 1759–1766.* Edited by Bernard W. Sheehan. Indianapolis, Ind.: Liberty Fund, 2002.

revised by Harold E. Selesky

PATERSON, JAMES.

British general. Appointed adjutant general in America on 11 July 1776, he held this office until he was sent home with dispatches after the Battle of Monmouth on 28 June 1778. With the local rank of brigadier general, he commanded three infantry battalions and a jäger detachment in the capture of Stony Point on 1 June 1779. Taking part in the Charleston expedition of Clinton in 1780, Paterson initially was put in command of a force that was to make a diversion toward Augusta, Georgia, but subsequently was called back to support the siege of Charleston. He returned with Clinton to New York City in June 1780. In the spring of 1781 he commanded the defenses of Staten Island and in October of that year was preparing to take part in the expedition to relieve the siege of Yorktown when news was received of Cornwallis's surrender.

SEE ALSO *Charleston Expedition of Clinton in 1780; Stony Point, New York.*

revised by Michael Bellesiles

PATERSON, JOHN.

(1744–1808). Continental general. Connecticut-Massachusetts. Born at Farmington in late 1743 or early 1744, John Paterson was the son of John Paterson, who served in six campaigns of the French and Indian War and who died at Havana on 5 September 1762, just before his son graduated from Yale College. The son taught school for several years while studying the law and then began to practice. In 1774 he moved to Lenox, Massachusetts, and quickly became prominent in the Revolutionary politics of Berkshire County. He was elected to the General Court in May 1774, was a member of the county convention in July 1774 that supported Boston's boycott of British imports, and in 1774 and 1775 sat in the Provincial Congress, which appointed him colonel of his local minuteman regiment. An impressive-looking man, over six feet tall and vigorous until late in life, he had long shown a taste for military life. When news of Lexington and Concord reached Lenox, he marched within eighteen hours (on 22 April) for Boston with his regiment fully armed and almost completely in uniform. On 27 May 1775 he was commissioned colonel of a provincial regiment created around six of the former minuteman companies. The regiment was posted near Prospect Hill, where it built and garrisoned Fort No. 3, and served through the siege of Boston. It was held in reserve during the Battle of Bunker Hill. On 9 November 1775 it was involved in driving off an enemy foraging raid on Lechmere Point.

Paterson continued in service as colonel of the Fifteenth Continental Regiment from 1 January 1776. In March 1776 he accompanied the army to New York City and was then sent with Brigadier General William Thompson to Canada. Major Henry Sherburne led one hundred men of the regiment to relieve a American force under attack at The Cedars and was nearly wiped out in an ambush on 20 May. Paterson and the rest of the regiment retreated south up Lake Champlain with Benedict Arnold's column. After working on the defenses of Mount Independence, opposite Ticonderoga, from July until November 1776, he moved south to join Washington's army on the Delaware and took part in the Battles of Trenton and Princeton.

He was promoted to brigadier general on 21 February 1777 and returned to the Northern Department with his brigade, serving with Matthias de Fermoy's and Enoch Poor's brigades under Arthur St. Clair in the operations that ended with the evacuation of Ticonderoga from 2 to 5 July. His Third Massachusetts Brigade (10th, 11th, 12th, and 14th Massachusetts Regiments) helped to hold the lines on Bemis Heights, not seeing combat at Freeman's Farm (19 September 1777). At Bemis Heights (7 October) the brigade joined Benedict Arnold in the attack on the Balcarres redoubt, where Paterson's horse was shot out from under him by a cannonball. The brigade wintered at Valley Forge in 1777–1778 and participated in the Monmouth Campaign in June and July 1778, without seeing any action. Paterson spent the rest of the war in the Hudson Highlands, watching the Massachusetts Line deteriorate through inaction. He sat on the court-martial that condemned John André to be hung as a spy in September 1780. He helped to found the Society of the Cincinnati, was breveted major general on 30 September 1783, and retired from the army on 3 November.

Paterson resumed his law practice at Lenox after the war and held many public offices. In early 1786 he helped Rufus Putnam and Benjamin Tupper organize the Ohio Company and later that year displayed compassion and moderation in helping to end Shays's Rebellion as commander of the Berkshire militia. In 1790 Paterson became a proprietor of the Boston Purchase (ten townships in Broome and Tioga Counties in New York, north of the Susquehanna River and west of the Chenango River), and in 1791 he moved to Lisle (later Whitney's Point) with his family. He served in the New York legislature (1792–1793), the state constitutional convention of 1801, and in the U.S. House of Representatives (1803–1805). In 1798 he was appointed to the bench and was judge of the two counties. He died on 19 July 1808 at Lisle.

SEE ALSO *Cedars, The; Lechmere Point, Massachusetts; Ticonderoga, New York, British Capture of.*

BIBLIOGRAPHY

Egleston, Thomas. *The Life of John Paterson: Major General in the Revolutionary Army.* New York: Putnam's Sons, 1894.

revised by Harold E. Selesky

PATTISON, JAMES. (1724–1805). British

general. An artillery officer, he was promoted to colonel on 25 April 1777 and reached New York on 24 September 1777 with the "local rank" of brigadier general. Clinton promoted him to major general on 19 February 1779. After assisting General James Paterson in the operations against Stony Point and Verplancks Point on 1 June 1779, he won the praise of Clinton for his work in organizing a local militia for the defense of New York City. Although Pattison served as commandant of New York City during most if not all of his time in America, he also commanded a brigade in the field operations during June 1779. On 4 September 1780 he sailed from New York to England with the fleet that took Governor Tryon home.

SEE ALSO *Paterson, James.*

BIBLIOGRAPHY

Baurmeister, Carl Leopold. *Revolution in America: Confidential Letters and Journals, 1776–1784.* New Brunswick, N.J.: Rutgers University Press, 1957.

Clinton, Sir Henry. *The American Rebellion: Sir Henry Clinton's Narrative of His Campaigns, 1775–1782.* Edited by William B. Willcox. New Haven, Conn.: Yale University Press, 1954.

Mark M. Boatner

PATTON'S REGIMENT. Colonel John

Patton commanded one of the sixteen "additional Continental regiments."

SEE ALSO *Additional Continental Regiments.*

Mark M. Boatner

PAULDING, JOHN. (1758–1818). A captor

of John André. New York. Paulding claimed to have served the Patriot cause throughout the Revolution, being taken prisoner by the British three times and escaping heroically in each instance. However, there is no evidence for his claims and many contemporaries and scholars have charged that he was a highwayman rather than a patriot soldier. What is known is that Paulding, Isaac Van Wart, and David Williams volunteered for the militia in 1780, shortly after New York passed a law allowing those who seized Loyalists or enemy agents to keep any property they found on the prisoner. This motivation accounted for André's capture, as the three men rifled his pockets looking for valuables. Congress rewarded Paulding, Van Wart, and Williams with a silver medal and a $200 pension; in addition a county in Ohio was named for each of the three men. Paulding's seventh child, Hiram Paulding (1797–1878), later became a naval hero.

SEE ALSO *Arnold's Treason.*

revised by Michael Bellesiles

PAULUS HOOK, NEW JERSEY. 19

August 1779. Henry Lee's Raid. Soon after Brigadier General Anthony Wayne's brilliant coup at Stony Point on 16 July, reconnaissance elements pushed south into Bergen County, New Jersey, to look for new opportunities. One of these was Captain Allan McLane's company. Raised in Delaware, it had just been assigned to Major Henry Lee's Corps of Partisan Light Dragoons as its fourth troop, serving on foot in a light infantry configuration. Under Washington's instructions McLane started from a position at Schraalenburgh and, without ever spending two nights in the same location, he systematically swept Bergen County over a span of ten days. He also used men from the immediate area, posing as farmers selling their produce, to enter the British strongpoint at Paulus Hook. Although Washington's primary focus at this point was strengthening the fortress complex at West Point, the critical strategic pivot for the second half of the war, he still wanted to maintain morale and whittle down the British by conducting set-piece attacks on isolated outposts. McLane's information provided such an opportunity.

BRITISH DEFENSE WORKS

Paulus (or Powles) Hook (in modern Jersey City, near Washington and Grand Streets) was a low point of sand protruding into the Hudson that formed the western end of a ferry. Americans had started fortifying it in the 1776 campaign, and the works had been greatly expanded by the British, who used it as a bridgehead for foraging operations in Bergen County. The most commonly cited British map, in the Clinton Papers in at Ann Arbor, Michigan, does not show the actual defenses at the time of the American attack in 1778. The Hesse-Cassel topographical engineers made a detailed inspection of the site right after the attack, and this better depiction is in the Portuguese army archives in Lisbon. It confirms that the British had dug a ditch to separate the higher ground at the tip of the peninsula from a wide salt marsh and then flooded it to serve as a moat.

A causeway led from the ferry landing across about five hundred yards of marsh before reaching dry ground; a creek fordable in only two places ran through the marsh. In addition to a double row of abatis, a palisade wall made from logs inside the ditch provided security for the enclosure, which contained a number of buildings. A large blockhouse protected the gate and the drawbridge over the moat, while two smaller ones supported the palisade. Several breastworks at various points on the perimeter furnished further security.

Inside the enclosure on low elevations were two redoubts, each surrounded by its own ditch and abatis. One, which mounted six cannon, was a circle about 150 feet across. The other was slightly larger, shaped like an oval and 150 feet wide and 250 feet long; it mounted four guns. Major William Sutherland of the Royal Garrison Battalion commanded the post. His troops consisted of a detachment of his own unit, which was formed from invalids who had been transferred from line units, the Loyalists of Lieutenant Colonel Abraham Van Buskirk's Fourth Battalion of the New Jersey Volunteers (Cortlandt Skinner's), some men from the Royal Artillery, a handful of men from the Sixty-fourth Foot, Captain Francis Dundas's light infantry company from the Guards Brigade, and forty Hessians from the Erb Prinz Regiment under Captain Henrich Sebastian von Schallern. At the time of the attack this force probably amounted to between 200 and 220 men, as a large number of Van Buskirk's men were absent on a foraging expedition and Dundas and von Schallern's men had only arrived the night before the attack to take their place.

THE AMERICAN ATTACK FORCE

While historians have engaged in controversy over who planned the attack, the reality of military operations is that no plan has a single author. In this case, Washington provided the overall guidance; the attack on Stony Point provided a tactical model; McLane provided the detailed intelligence; and Lee had the command. The specifics probably evolved in discussions between McLane and Lee. A general supervision came from Major General William Alexander (Lord Stirling), whose division had geographical responsibility for Bergen County, and Washington insisted that he give a final blessing to the plan to ensure that it was feasible and to furnish the majority of the troops and the party that would cover the task force as it withdrew. To carry out the operation, Lee had his own unit and three hundred of Stirling's men. Lee formed them into three columns plus a reserve. The left (east) column formed the main effort under Lee himself, with McLane's and part of John Rudolph's troop serving dismounted and one hundred men from the First Virginia Brigade; Lieutenant James Armstrong led its "forlorn hope" (vanguard) from Rudolph's troop. The right (west) column had one hundred men from the Second Virginia Brigade with Lieutenant Mark Vanduval leading its "forlorn hope." The center column had one hundred men from the First Maryland Brigade under Captain Levin Handy plus Forsyth's and the rest of Rudolph's troop, who were dismounted; Lieutenant Philip Reid had this "forlorn hope." Lee left his mounted element under Captain Henry Peyton as part of the covering party along with some Virginia infantry under Captain Nathan Reid.

THE ATTACK

On Wednesday, 18 August, Lee set out from Paramus at 10:30 in the morning, using wagons to convey the impression that he was only on a foraging expedition. His unit and the Marylanders linked up with the Virginia detachment at New Bridge, and at about 4:30 in the afternoon they started a twenty-mile march towards their assault positions, planning to make the attack about 3 A.M. in order to take advantage of darkness. Guides got them lost, and a variety of delays caused by the "friction of war" caused them to reach the edge of the marsh an hour late; they were worried about first light, which could come at any time. Rudolph went forward on a reconnaissance and returned with the news that the operation was still feasible, an important point as Washington had given orders that prohibited the attack if it did not achieve surprise. From here the center column had the mission of proceeding down the causeway, breaking through the gate, and securing the blockhouse at that location. The other two columns went along the river edge and struck the fort from the corners, secured their respective blockhouses, and then pushed into the center to attack the oval redoubt. As at Stony Point, the muskets were not loaded and the men were told not to make any noise, even cheering, to buy time for the

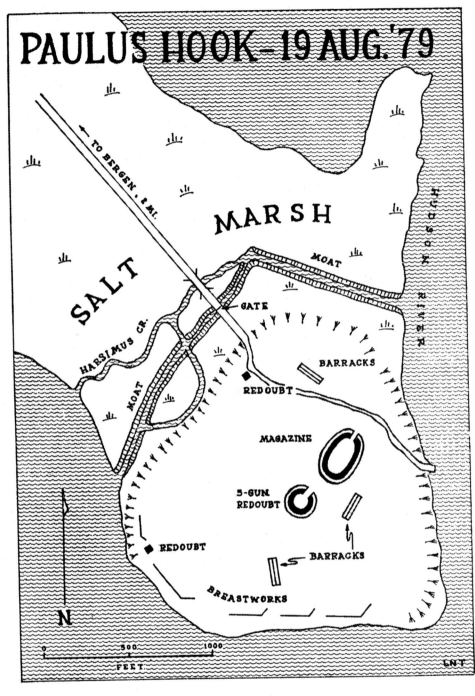

PAULUS HOOK—19 AUG. '79

THE GALE GROUP

prisoners and supplies to be collected and the task force to withdraw with minimal risk of detection.

The columns reached the edge of the moat unde-tected, and the "forlorn hopes" waded across. Just as they were emerging, the first sentry detected the Americans and fired a warning shot, but to no avail. The columns quickly broke in before the sleepy defenders could react. All of the

blockhouses fell as planned, and the oval redoubt followed swiftly. Only small pockets put up any resistance; the rest of the British and Loyalists surrendered almost immedi-ately. But von Schallern's Hessians had been more alert at the circular redoubt and could not be talked into laying down their arms. Knowing that nothing was to be gained by trying to assault it, Lee quickly gathered up the

ENCYCLOPEDIA OF THE AMERICAN REVOLUTION

prisoners and headed back to the mainland. He had neither the time nor the equipment to spike the cannon that fell into American hands, nor did he catch Major Sutherland, who had made it into the German strong point.

Lee's fears that firing would alert the British in New York City, a mile and a half away on the east side of the Hudson, were well-founded. They heard the shooting, but since Sutherland never fired the signal to indicate that he was under attack, Major General James Pattison assumed that it was only Van Buskirk's party skirmishing with militia. Not until a messenger came over from Sutherland did he learn the truth. At that point he quickly sent Lieutenant Colonel Cosmo Gordon of the Guards Brigade across with the rest of the flank companies of the brigade, some artillerymen, and one hundred more Germans.

WITHDRAWAL

Lee's withdrawal followed the plan, although he was now running well behind schedule. He headed for Douwe's Ferry, where Peyton's men were supposed to be waiting with boats to cross the Hackensack River. After putting that obstacle between his force and any pursuit, he intended to take the Polifly Road back to New Bridge. But when the attack party had not appeared an hour after schedule, Peyton assumed that the attack had been called off and headed back to Newark with the boats. Fortunately, McLane had excellent knowledge of the various roads as the result of his original reconnaissance, and Lee quickly changed the withdrawal route to the more dangerous Bergen Road. The rear guard trying to cover the main body got lucky when Captain Thomas Catlett arrived with fifty fresh men (Virginians who had missed the original attack) who had dry ammunition. There was a chance encounter with some of Van Buskirk's foragers near Liberty Pole Tavern (at modern Englewood), but it never developed into anything significant, and Gordon's light infantry never caught up. Lee arrived safely at New Bridge at around 1 P.M.

The next day, 20 August, a furious General Clinton convened a court-martial to try Sutherland on charges of general misconduct. He was acquitted but shortly thereafter was transferred to Bermuda.

NUMBERS AND LOSSES

Lee lost only two men killed and three wounded, which was very light, given that he had more than four hundred men in the action. The low numbers came from the tactics of the surprise attack and the cover of the darkness that prevented any type of a coherent defense. British official reports claimed that they had lost only 9 killed, 2 wounded, and 113 missing, but as usual these figures carefully omitted the Germans and the Loyalists. A more reasonable estimate is 173 killed, wounded or captured; only about 50 of the men in Paulus Hook escaped.

SIGNIFICANCE

The action amounted to nothing more than a mosquito bite from a military point of view, but it had an important impact on the morale of the Americans and British, with the latter considering the poor showing of the garrison as a mark of dishonor. The Germans all took enormous pride in von Schallern's performance. The Continental Congress voted Lee a gold medal like those given for Stony Point, which prompted a lingering war of memoirs with some of the officers from the attached infantry involving perceived slights and squabbles about who deserved credit for what.

SEE ALSO *Forlorn Hope; Lee, Henry ("Light-Horse Harry"); MacLean, Allan.*

BIBLIOGRAPHY

Dornfest, Walter T. "British, Hessian, and Provincial Troops at Paulus Hook, 18th–19th August, 1779." *Journal of the Society for Army Historical Research* 45 (1967): 177–183.

Koke, Richard J. "The Britons Who Fought at Stony Point: Uniforms of the American Revolution." *New-York Historical Society Quarterly* 44 (1960): 443–471.

Lee, Henry. *Memoirs of the War in the Southern Department of the United States.* Revised edition. New York: University Publishing, 1869.

Richardson, William H., and Walter P. Gardner. *Washington and "The Enterprise against Powles Hook": A New Study of the Surprise and Capture of the Fort Thursday, August 19, 1779.* Jersey City: New Jersey Title Guarantee and Trust, 1938.

revised by Robert K. Wright Jr.

PAXTON BOYS. 1763–1765. As a result of Indian depredations that began during the French and Indian War and culminated in Pontiac's uprising, many Scots-Irish and German settlers on the Pennsylvania frontier came to believe that they had license to exterminate all Native Americans. They also nursed a grudge against the Quaker-dominated government of the colony, which they thought should have done more to protect their homes and families. On 14 December 1763, some fifty-seven rangers from Paxton and Donegal in Lancaster County, led by Lazarus Stewart, senselessly massacred six Christian Indians living at Conestoga Manor, eight miles west of Lancaster. Two weeks later, another gang rode into Lancaster and, pushing aside token resistance from the sheriff, broke into the workhouse where they slaughtered the remaining fourteen Conestoga Indians who had taken shelter there. Five of the twenty Indians were women and eight were children. Governor John Penn ordered the culprits brought to trial, but sympathetic justices and juries made this impossible. The "Boys" then undertook a political campaign to win better representation for the settlers in the legislature and backed it up with the very real threat of violence. In early February 1764, some 600 of them marched under arms towards Philadelphia, intending, it seems, to kill 140 Indians who had taken refuge in the city's military barracks. When 250 of them reached Germantown, they were confronted by over 500 armed citizen-volunteers and 250 regular troops, with artillery at the ready. The crisis abated when the "Boys" accepted promises of amnesty for their previous actions from government spokesmen (including Benjamin Franklin), along with the promise of a chance to present their grievances to the governor and legislature. "Their major grievances—paucity of frontier defenses, underrepresentation, and Quaker favoritism to Indians—received scant attention from the legislature," according to the historian Alden T. Vaughn. ("Frontier Banditti," p. 85).

Thereafter, the Pennsylvania frontier degenerated into a morass of violence and murder, where white men were effectively free to kill Indians at will and where no Indian could expect to receive any sort of legal protection or justice. In May 1765 at Sideling Hill, a group of frontier banditti with blackened faces, called by some the "Black Boys," even went so far as to hijack a convoy of gifts and trade goods being sent to Fort Pitt and faced down the regular troops sent to recover the wagons. From London, Franklin was aghast: "The outrages committed by the frontier people are really amazing," he said (ibid., p. 87). By then, the name "Paxton Boys" had become an umbrella term for all frontiersmen who were willing to use violence to achieve their ends. As can readily be imagined, Native Americans on the Pennsylvania frontier had no sympathy for the rebel fight against the British imperial government after 1775.

Lazarus Stewart, disgusted with the proprietary government and threatened with prosecution, moved with his followers to the Wyoming Valley in 1769 and was granted a township by the Connecticut authorities. He was killed in the Wyoming Valley massacre of 3–4 July 1778.

SEE ALSO *Pontiac's War.*

BIBLIOGRAPHY

Dunbar, John R., ed. *The Paxton Papers.* The Hague: M. Nijhoff, 1957.

Hindle, Brooke. "The March of the Paxton Boys." *William and Mary Quarterly,* 3d series, 3 (1946): 461–486.

Martin, James K. "The Return of the Paxton Boys and the Historical State of the Pennsylvania Frontier, 1764–1774." *Pennsylvania History* 38 (1971): 117–133.

Vaughan, Alden T. "Frontier Banditti and the Indians: The Paxton Boys' Legacy." In *Roots of American Racism: Essays on the Colonial Experience.* Edited by Alden T. Vaughn. New York: Oxford University Press, 1995.

revised by Harold E. Selesky

PAY, BOUNTIES, AND RATIONS.

Raising armies and making war were the costliest activities that societies in the eighteenth century could undertake. Governments of every description invariably tried to keep their expenses as low as possible, even to the extent of placing cost-cutting ahead of fielding effective forces. Feeding, clothing, equipping, and transporting troops were the biggest ongoing expenses, but the costs of procuring and paying soldiers were also substantial. A society's willingness to pay bounties to procure the services of some of its members, the rates of pay society's leaders thought were appropriate for different war-related activities, and even the fact that the amount of rations varied according to rank all provide insight into how a society thought about making war, over and above the actual amounts involved. Pay, bounties, and rations are related and are therefore considered together.

PAY

Everyone understood that soldiers had to be paid for their service. Historically, rates of pay were low in both the British and American armies. In the British army, soldiers were recruited from the bottom of the social hierarchy and so were believed by most of the elite to be worth only the lowest possible amount of pay. During the Revolution, the pay of a British private amounted, nominally, to eight shillings a day, from which were deducted the costs of food, clothing, repair of equipment, and various fees. The net amount paid in specie to the private often hovered around zero, a reality that did nothing to promote recruiting in an age when the standard of living was rising.

In the colonies, low pay reflected both the lack of financial resources and the fact that military service still retained some aspects of the early days of settlement, when men had to serve if their community was to survive. There were variations in the rates of pay among the colonies—higher in the northern colonies, lower in the South—reflecting each colony's historical experience, most recently in the French and Indian War.

Massachusetts set the pace for rates of pay at the start of the war. A private in the militia who turned out for the Lexington alarm or who enlisted in the eight-months' army received two pounds per calendar month. The Continental Congress on 14 June gave privates in the new rifle companies from Pennsylvania and Virginia $6.67 per calendar month, an amount roughly equivalent to the Massachusetts pay. A captain in the 1775 army received three times as much per month as a private (twenty dollars), while a colonel received two-and-a-half times as much as a captain (fifty dollars). (Captains in the artillery got more, $26.67 per month.) Delegates from the southern colonies objected that the pay of officers was too low and that of privates too high, and perhaps too that most of the pay was going to New Englanders. They forced a three-member congressional committee sent to Cambridge in October 1775 to ask Washington what he thought the rates of pay ought to be for the new 1776 army. A conference of Washington, the committee, and seven senior leaders from Massachusetts, Connecticut, and Rhode Island "unanimously agreed" that the pay of the privates "cannot be reduced, and agreed by a majority that raising the pay of the officers would be inconvenient and improper" (Chase, ed., *Papers*, vol. 1, p. 191). Explaining its opposition to reducing pay, the conference stated, "It [appeared] on a full discussion and consideration of all circumstances that any attempt to reduce the present pay would probably prevent the soldiers [from] re-enlisting." Congress accepted the recommendations about privates but on 4 November raised the pay of an infantry captain to $26.67 per month, the existing artillery captain's rate. A British captain drew about twice as much as an American captain, but a more significant difference was that he could buy almost anything he needed at moderate rates.

Continental pay rates remained at these levels for over two and one-half years, even as the currency began to inflate. Congress next revised pay rates on 27 May 1778, when it raised the pay for an infantry colonel to $75 dollars per month and an infantry captain to $40 per month but amazingly left a private's pay at $6.67 per month. (Privates in the artillery, cavalry, and military police received $8.33 per month.) There the rates remained for the rest of the war. Inequities in the pay scales between the Continental army and the militia, constant arrears in pay, and rampant inflation plagued American commanders, including Washington, and created serious morale problems. When Congress proved unable to pay even these sums, the long-suffering Continentals mutinied. When, after Yorktown, the regiments were first consolidated and then disbanded, Continental soldiers left the service with little more than Congress's promise to pay their wages in the future. Many soldiers sold those chits to brokers in return for some immediate funds to get home or to a place they thought offered a better economic opportunity.

BOUNTIES

The colonies frequently used enlistment bounties during the wars against the French, especially during the French and Indian War, and continued the practice when they undertook to raise troops to oppose the British. Bounties were offered for a man's enlistment, but also if he came equipped with a gun and a blanket, a useful way of accumulating civilian items for war service in the absence of a well-developed supply network. Because bounties fostered voluntary enlistment, they also allowed leaders to avoid straining their authority by trying to draft men for military service.

Congress took up the issue of bounties when it came time to enlist a new army for 1776. Influenced by delegates from the southern colonies, it initially refused to offer any bounty but agreed to an advance payment of forty shillings, equal to one month's pay. According to John Adams (in a letter of 25 November 1775 to a fellow New Englander), the southerners' opposition to bounties, and higher wages, was a cultural phenomenon: "These gentlemen are accustomed, habituated to higher notions of themselves and the distinctions between them and the common people, than we are."

Congress tried to hold the line against rising expenses but grudgingly came to realize that money was the key to raising and keeping an army. On 19 January 1776 it advised the states to offer a bounty of $6.33 (one month's pay) to all men who would enlist with a good firearm, a bayonet, and other accoutrements and to offer $4 to those who enlisted without these items. On 26 June the delegates resolved to offer ten dollars to all men who would enlist for three years. A few weeks later they extended this offer to all regulars who would continue their service in the Continental army for three years after expiration of their current tour. On 16 September, when it voted to raise an army of eighty-eight battalions for 1777, Congress increased the bounty to twenty dollars plus one hundred acres to all enlisted men who would agree to serve "during the war." Two days later it extended this offer to all "who are enlisted or shall enlist for during the war" in the Continental army. Any of these veteran enlistees who had already received a Continental bounty of ten dollars for a former enlistment would, however, receive only ten dollars more under the new offer. On 8 October, Congress agreed to give a twenty-dollar suit of clothes each year (or the same amount in cash if the man's captain would certify that he had procured such a suit himself) to all men enlisted for the duration. Officers were authorized recruiting expenses at the rate of $1.33 per new man.

Washington, a taxpayer as well as the commander in chief, disliked bounties but soon realized that the system was a necessary evil. Writing to John Hancock, president of Congress, from the "Heights of Harlem" on 25 September 1776 as his army was about to be kicked out of New York, Washington offered some of his most candid comments on the character of the American army:

> With respect to the men, nothing but a good bounty can obtain them upon a permanent establishment, and for no shorter time than the

continuance of the war, ought they to be engaged, as facts incontestibly prove, that the difficulty and cost of inlistments increase with time. When the army was first raised at Cambridge, I am perswaded the men might have been got without a bounty for the war; after this, they began to see that the contest was not likely to end so speedily as was immagined, and to feel their consequence by remarking that to get the militia in, in the course of the last year, many towns were induced to give them a bounty.... [I]f the present opportunity is slip'd, I am perswaded that twelve months more will increase our difficulties four fold. I shall therefore take the freedom of giving it as my opinion that a good bounty be immediately offered, aided by the proffer of at least 100 or 150 acres of land and a suit of cloaths and blanket to each non-com[missione]d officer and soldier, as I have good authority for saying, that however high the mens pay may appear, it is barely sufficient in the present scarcity and dearness of all kinds of goods, to keep them in cloaths, much less afford support to their families. (Chase, ed., *Papers*, vol. 6, pp. 395–396)

The states, also faced with the problem of raising men, undertook to compete for recruits by increasing their bounties. Early in 1777 some of the New England states agreed to offer $33.33 in addition to the $20 set by Congress. When Massachusetts then doubled this ante, offering $86.67, other states fell in line and some went higher. These offers curtailed reenlistments in the Continental regiments, and they also led men to desert the Continental army in order to enlist fraudulently in state regiments for the larger bounty. Bounty jumpers would enlist, collect their bounty, desert, reenlist, and collect another.

The bounty battle continued to rage throughout the war as the conflict wore on and the currency rapidly lost value. On 23 January 1779, Congress authorized Washington to grant up to two hundred dollars to each able-bodied man who would enlist or reenlist for the war. On 9 March, the delegates resolved to pay this bounty out of the Continental treasury to men recruited by the states or, if the state was giving this amount or more, to credit the state with two hundred dollars for each man enlisted against its quota. On 29 March, Congress recommended that Virginia and North Carolina raise as many regular battalions as possible and give the recruits the two-hundred-dollar bounty for a single year's service in Virginia, the Carolinas, or Georgia.

Again the states outbid the central government. New Jersey added $250 to the congressional bounty of $200, land, and clothing. On 3 May 1779, Virginia offered $750, a suit of clothes each year, and 100 acres of land to men who signed up for the duration; the state deducted and

retained from this bounty the cash and clothing offered by Congress. In 1780 New Jersey increased its bounty to one thousand dollars more than all Continental offers. Much of this increase was due to depreciation of Continental currency, which hit the officers particularly hard, and on 21 October 1780, Congress finally adopted Washington's urgent recommendation that—in order to keep good officers in service until the end of the war—they be granted half pay for life.

As the war dragged on, the bounty offers became very creative. To meet their quotas of recruits, many states by 1780 had organized their citizens into "classes" in each locality, distributing the wealthy and the poor into groups that were then responsible for finding one soldier. In Salem, Massachusetts, in June 1780, one class offered an eighteen-year-old man a series of inducements to serve in the Continental army: a few dollars in specie; several hundred dollars in the rapidly inflating paper currency; and half a dozen head of three-year-old cattle when he completed his enlistment, thereby paying for service now with animals that the class did not then possess and which the young man might not live to collect.

RATIONS

Integrated with the system of pay and bounties was the matter of rations. Whereas a private soldier was entitled to a single ration (three meals a day), officers were authorized extra rations in an effort to provide them the wherewithal to set a table befitting their rank. For example, the scale prescribed by Congress on 22 April 1782 was five rations for a major general, four for a brigadier general, two for a lieutenant colonel commandant, one and a half for a major or captain, and one for a subaltern.

The Continental Congress prescribed the army's ration on 12 September 1775. As finalized on 4 November, the ration was to:

> consist of the following kind and quantity of provisions: 1 pound of beef, or 1/2 pound of pork or 1 pound of salt fish, per day; 1 pound of bread or flour, per day; 3 pints of peas or beans per week, or vegetables equivalent, at one dollar per bushel for peas or beans; 1 pint of milk, per man per day, or at the rate of 1–72 of a dollar; 1 half pint of rice, or one pint of Indian meal, per man per week; 1 quart of spruce beer or cider per man per day, or nine gallons of molasses, per company of 100 men per week; 3 pounds of candles to 100 men per week, for guards; 24 pounds of [soft] soap, or 8 pounds of hard soap, for 100 men per week.

The ration, heavy on salted meat and carbohydrates, was roughly equivalent to what civilians were eating and was only occasionally supplemented with fresh provisions. Foodstuffs, of course, had to be chosen with an eye to what could be procured locally and transported with the army. Keeping food edible and water potable were the primary considerations; there was no awareness of whether or not the diet was nutritious or whether it provided soldiers with the caloric intake required to maintain their level of activity. Alcohol, in the form or spruce beer, hard cider, rum, and even whiskey (the latter two were authorized but seldom issued because of expense), was important because it reduced reliance on water that might be contaminated, or when mixed together with water, as in grog (water cut with rum), rendered water at least semi-potable.

Congress or the commander in chief might authorize a particular type and quantity of foodstuff, but as was the case with pay, it was not always possible to provide the prescribed amount. As long as the army was stationary in the Boston area, Quartermaster General Jonathan Trumbull Jr. could draw on the relatively abundant resources of the rich Connecticut River valley and actually issued the troops more than the prescribed ration. Active operations always increased the difficulty of providing food to the troops, and nearly every campaign of the war saw soldiers enduring some form of privation. Poorly preserved meat, grains infested with insects, and even otherwise inedible plant matter like unripe fruits and vegetables were better than no food, although they could cause gastrointestinal distress that sometimes, as at the Battle of Camden (16 August 1780), could have tactical significance.

Insufficient logistics, especially in winter, inflicted enormous suffering on American troops. Benedict Arnold's men were reduced to boiling shoe leather to survive their march to Quebec in the fall of 1775, and the winter encampments of Washington's army at Morristown and Valley Forge became notorious examples of the privations soldiers could endure when necessary. Competition with the French expeditionary force that arrived at Newport, Rhode Island, in July 1780 put further strain on the procurement system, especially since the French paid in specie while the Americans offered only nearly worthless paper money. The dislocations caused by wartime operations, the lack of credit, British naval superiority, and competing demands for labor all reduced the food supply, as did crop diseases, most notably the Hessian fly that attacked the wheat crop.

The British ration varied in accordance with what was locally available, but in a representative contract of 1778–1779, it provided each soldier with one pound of flour per day, either one pound of beef or slightly more than nine ounces of pork per day, three pints of peas per week, one-half pound of oatmeal per week, and either six ounces of butter or eight ounces of cheese per week. The British relied in part on preserved food that was shipped across the Atlantic from England and Ireland, and although stocks on hand occasionally dipped to worrisome levels, they generally did a good job in feeding their armies. They were also adept at fashioning local procurement networks for their garrisons at New York City, Philadelphia, Newport, and Charleston. Indeed, without a brisk and clandestine trade with American suppliers, they would have been hard put to sustain those enclaves.

Although quartermasters in both armies issued firewood and cooking utensils when possible, soldiers prepared their meals individually or formed small groups in which men took turns cooking. Since flour and beef were the only items usually issued, food preparation was an all-too-simple task. According to the historian Erna Risch, "an unrelieved diet of half-cooked meat and hard bread was responsible for much of the sickness that reduced the strength of the Army when it frequently was most needed" (p. 10).

SEE ALSO *Quartermasters of the Continental Army.*

BIBLIOGRAPHY

Bowler, R. Arthur. *Logistics and the Failure of the British Army in America, 1775–1783.* Princeton, N.J.: Princeton University Press, 1975.

Buel, Richard V., Jr. *In Irons: Britain's Naval Supremacy and the American Revolutionary Economy.* New Haven, Conn.: Yale University Press, 1998.

Chase, Philander D., ed. *The Papers of George Washington, Revolutionary Series.* Vol. 6, *August–October 1776.* Charlottesville, Va.: University Press of Virginia, 1994.

Curtis, Edward E. *The Organization of the British Army in the American Revolution.* New Haven, Conn.: Yale University Press, 1926.

Hatch, Louis C. *The Administration of the American Revolutionary Army.* New York: Longmans, Green, 1904.

Risch, Erna. *Quartermaster Support of the Army: A History of the Corps, 1775–1939.* Washington, D.C.: Government Printing Office, 1962.

———. *Supplying Washington's Army.* Washington, D.C.: Center of Military History, 1981.

Shy, John W. "Logistical Crisis and the American Revolution: A Hypothesis." *Feeding Mars: Logistics in Western Warfare from the Middle Ages to the Present.* Edited by John A. Lynn. Boulder, Colo.: Westview Press, 1993.

Smith, Paul H. et, al., eds. *Letters of Delegates to Congress, 1774–1789.* Vol. 2, September–December 1775. Washington, D.C.: Library of Congress, 1977.

revised by Harold E. Selesky

PEACE COMMISSION OF CARLISLE.

1778. Stunned by Britain's defeat at Saratoga and fearing that its former colonies would enter into an alliance with France, Lord North reversed direction in early 1778 and proposed to Parliament that

Britain send a peace commission with powers to negotiate with Congress and promise to suspend all acts affecting America passed since 1763. Parliament approved the "Royal Instructions to the Peace Commission" on 16 March 1778. To head the commission, North selected Frederick Howard, fifth Earl of Carlisle, a young man not yet thirty but very wealthy and a gambling friend of opposition leader Charles James Fox (which was expected to please the Americans). In addition to the Howe brothers, already in America, North also appointed William Eden, a close friend of Carlisle since Eton and member of the Board of Trade, Captain George Johnstone of the Royal Navy, a former governor of West Florida who had fought a duel with George Sackville Germain in December 1770. The commission's secretary was Adam Ferguson, renowned professor of moral philosophy at Edinburgh, whose work had influenced many American leaders. Carlisle and his colleagues left Portsmouth on the sixty-four-gun *Trident* on 16 April. Also on board was Lord Cornwallis, on his way to become Henry Clinton's second in command. They reached Philadelphia on 6 June.

Carlisle immediately encountered almost insurmountable obstacles: Congress had resolved on 22 April that any man or group that came to terms with the commission was an enemy of the United States; furthermore, Clinton was preparing to evacuate Philadelphia. When Carlisle requested a conference, Congress replied on 17 June that the only negotiable points were British withdrawal and recognition of independence. Before leaving Philadelphia, Johnstone attempted to bribe Congressmen Joseph Reed, Robert Morris, and Francis Dana; this led to his resignation on 26 August. Funds for covert activities had been given to the commission, and Sir John Temple and John Berkenhout followed Carlisle from England to join him in New York City as secret agents early in August. The last week of August, Berkenhout left New York City with a pass from Clinton, managed to pick up a pass from U.S. General William Maxwell at Elizabeth, New Jersey, and proceeded to Philadelphia. Introducing himself to Richard Henry Lee as a friend of Arthur Lee—he had known the latter in London—the agent pretended interest in settling in America. But a suspicious Maxwell warned Richard Lee, and Berkenhout was questioned by the Council of Pennsylvania on 3 September, jailed, paroled on 14 September, and on 19 September was back in New York City, his mission having only further prejudiced Congress against dealing with the commission.

As early as 21 July, Carlisle admitted to his wife that his mission was a complete failure and indicated that the government had no idea what the situation was in America. Congress itself circulated Parliament's act of conciliation and the peace commission's proposals. At spontaneous demonstrations the public denounced and burned these documents, indicating to Carlisle that the "common people hate us in their hearts." In October Lafayette challenged Carlisle to a duel on the grounds that he was personally responsible for the commission's attacks on France in letters to Congress; on 11 October Carlisle informed the offended Frenchman that he was answerable only to his country for his "public conduct and language," and Lafayette ended in looking somewhat ridiculous. On 3 October Carlisle and Eden made a fruitless appeal directly to the people, offering a general pardon for past disloyalty and full pardons to all military or civil officers who asked for it within the next forty days. They met only mockery.

Conceding failure, the commissioners left on 20 December 1778, Carlisle issuing a parting proclamation warning the Americans that by the French treaty they would become tributaries of France, leaving Britain no choice but to "destroy" the colonies. This statement, like so many other actions of the British government, undermined the Loyalists while strengthening the conviction among common Americans that independence was the wisest course of action.

SEE ALSO *Germain, George Sackville.*

BIBLIOGRAPHY

Berkenhout, John. "Dr. Berkenhout's Journal, 1778." *Pennsylvania Magazine of History and Biography* 65 (1941): 79–92.

Brown, Weldon A. *Empire or Independence: A Study in the Failure of Reconciliation, 1774–1783.* Baton Rouge: Louisiana State University Press, 1941.

Idzerda, Stanley J. *Lafayette in the Age of the American Revolution: Selected Letters and Papers, 1776–1790.* Vol. 2. Ithaca, N.Y.: Cornell University Press, 1979.

Van Doren, Carl. *Secret History of the American Revolution: An Account of the Conspiracies of Benedict Arnold and Numerous Others Drawn from the Secret Service Papers of the British Headquarters in North America.* New York: Viking, 1941.

revised by Michael Bellesiles

PEACE COMMISSION OF THE HOWES.

1776–1778. Early suggestions by British politicians to send commissioners to settle the dispute with the American colonies had been rejected by George III as an indication of weakness. In March 1776 the government gave overall command for the war against the colonies to Admiral Lord Richard Howe, who favored a policy of conciliation and insisted that he and his brother, General William Howe, retain the right to negotiate a peace with the rebels. Though Admiral Howe's final instructions of 6 May 1776 authorized the two brothers, as special commissioners, to do little more than offer pardons, the Howes were assured that they could negotiate once they had crushed the rebellion. In reality, their mission was in many ways critically handicapped from the start as there was no way that either the King or Lord North was willing to weaken Parliamentary supremacy or British sovereignty by entering into some substantive compromise with the American rebels. Further complicating their task was the requirement that the Howes win approval from the government for any concessions they might grant the Americans, necessitating the usual long delay of trans-Atlantic communication. They also had little hope of persuading the rebels of entering into such hazy negotiations.

On 7 June 1776, soon after reaching Massachusetts with a large naval force and reinforcements for his brother, Lord Howe issued a declaration announcing his role as commissioner and stating his authority to grant pardons but not mentioning the rest of what Sir William later characterized as "our very limited commission and instructions." On 14 July, the Howes issued a joint declaration and sent a copy under a flag of truce addressed to "George Washington, Esq. etc. etc." Colonels Reed and Knox, on instructions from General Washington, informed the British emissary that they knew of no such person in the American army as the gentleman to whom the envelope was addressed. When Lieutenant Colonel James Paterson, General Howe's adjutant general, finally got to Washington with a lame explanation about the "etc. etc." and informed the rebel commander of the Howes' authority and desire for negotiations, Washington replied that he had no authority as the military commander to work out any accommodation, but commented that the Howes appeared to offer nothing but pardon, which the Americans did not need nor desire.

The next overture came after the British victories on Long Island, which led to the peace conference on Staten Island on 11 September 1776, which in turn led nowhere. When these meetings proved pointless, the Howes issued a proclamation appealing directly to the people on 19 September; there is no evidence that anyone paid attention to this offer of pardon.

On 30 November, when rebel military fortunes were at a particularly low ebb, the Howes offered absolute pardon to all those who would subscribe to a declaration of allegiance within sixty days. For a few days it appeared that this offer, in combination with the British advance, would bring all of New Jersey into submission, but several things combined to sour this effort. First, the misconduct of British troops alienated the people of New Jersey. Second, Washington issued a proclamation stating that anybody who received a pardon had the choice of surrendering it and swearing allegiance to the American cause or moving immediately within the British lines. Third, Washington's winter campaign of 1776–1777 gave new

heart to those backing independence. Furthermore, Germain took exception to this wholesale offer of pardons, and although he gave his formal approval to the idea, he warned the Howes in a letter of 18 May 1777 not to be too softhearted. By this time, however, the Howes had about given up hope of a peaceful solution to the war. During the winter of 1776–1777 they attempted, through Charles Lee, who was their prisoner in New York City, to have Congress send two or three members to visit him, but Congress flatly refused. The Howes made no further significant efforts toward a political settlement, though they were both appointed to the peace commission of Carlisle, which reached America early in 1778. They played almost no part in this commission's activities. In summary, the Howes's hopes for a negotiated settlement to the war that kept the colonies within the empire went against both the actual policies of their government, which was intent on defeating the rebellion, and the realities of American independence.

SEE ALSO *Lee, Charles (1731–1782); New Jersey Campaign; Peace Conference on Staten Island.*

BIBLIOGRAPHY

Brown, Gerald S. *The American Secretary: The Colonial Policy of Lord George Germain.* Ann Arbor: University of Michigan Press, 1963.

Fisher, David Hackett. *Washington's Crossing.* New York: Oxford University Press, 2004.

Greene, Jack P. "The Plunge of Lemmings: A Consideration of Recent Writings on British Politics and the American Revolution." *South Atlantic Quarterly* 67 (1968): 141–175.

Gruber, Ira D. *The Howe Brothers and the American Revolution.* New York: Atheneum, 1972.

revised by Michael Bellesiles

PEACE CONFERENCE ON STATEN ISLAND.

11 September 1776. General John Sullivan, who was captured in the Battle of Long Island on 27 August 1776, got the impression from discussions with Admiral Lord Richard Howe that the Howe brothers had greater powers under their peace commissions than the Americans realized. After a congenial dinner together, Lord Howe persuaded Sullivan to visit Congress with a proposal that they begin talks toward a possible negotiated settlement. Howe deliberately left all the particulars vague. Sullivan arrived in Philadelphia to make his report to Congress, which was less than enthusiastic. After some heated debate, Congress resolved on 5 September to send a committee to find out whether Lord Howe could treat with representatives of Congress and, if so, what proposals

he had for negotiations. Congress hoped thereby to both delay the attack on New York City and give a public indication of its desire for peace. Although Lord Howe was disappointed to learn upon Sullivan's return, on 9 September, that the committee was coming not to treat but merely to secure information, he and his brother decided to go ahead with the conference in hopes that negotiations might follow.

On 7 September, Benjamin Franklin, John Adams, and Edward Rutledge were elected for this mission, and on the 11th they met with Lord Howe on Staten Island, opposite Amboy. General William Howe excused himself because of military duties. Richard Howe was extremely gracious, but Adams was convinced that he knew nothing of the real causes of the Revolution and Franklin mildly mocked the admiral. The Americans confirmed their previous understanding that the Howes had no real power and that anything to which they agreed would have to be referred back to London. Although Lord Howe painted the rosiest possible picture of what he hoped to do for the Americans, he was honest, telling the representatives of Congress that he could not actually enter into a treaty with Congress and that all he could offer were assurances that George III and Parliament "were very favorably inclined toward redressing the grievances and reforming the administration of the American colonies" (Smith, p. 758). Adams politely informed Howe that they would only negotiate further in the name of the Congress and that a "complete revolution" had occurred in America from which there was no turning back. This left no basis for further discussion, and after expressions of personal good will, the three went back to Philadelphia and reported to Congress on the 17th. Howe reported himself disillusioned, finding the Americans dogmatic and their leaders "men of low or of suspicious Character" (*ibid.,* 1, p. 758). Adams, Franklin, and Rutledge, for their part, thought Howe out of touch with reality and lacking sufficient authority to warrant further discussions.

BIBLIOGRAPHY

Smith, Page. *A New Age Now Begins: A People's History of the American Revolution.* New York: McGraw-Hill, 1976.

revised by Michael Bellesiles

PEACE NEGOTIATIONS. 1780–1784.

Military operations in America virtually ceased when Cornwallis surrendered on 19 October 1781. The British proclaimed a cessation of hostilities on 4 February 1783, and Congress issued a similar proclamation on 11 April 1783. What follows is a chronology of steps leading to the uneasy peace.

On 15 February 1779 a committee of Congress completed a report on minimum peace demands. They were independence, specific boundaries, British withdrawal from all U.S. territory, fishing rights in the waters off Newfoundland and Nova Scotia, and free navigation of the Mississippi River. This report was submitted to Congress on 23 February. Only the last two points were controversial, and on 14 August, Congress accepted all points but the one having to do with fishing, though the final instructions concerning peace negotiations were not completed until the end of September. On 27 September 1779, Congress selected John Adams to negotiate peace with England and also to draw up a commercial treaty and John Jay as minister to Spain with instructions to confer on the peace treaty with the leaders of that country. Each man, however, found that his mission was premature.

On 11 June 1781 Congress, largely in response to the demands of the French minister to the United States, the chevalier de la Luzerne, that Adams be recalled, decided to have the peace with Britain negotiated by a committee rather than by Adams alone. Jay was named to this committee on the 13th; Franklin, Henry Laurens, and Jefferson were appointed on the 14th. The next day Congress limited essential peace demands to independence and sovereignty, giving the committee discretion on all other points, including borders. Furthermore, in deference to the nation without whose help victory would have been impossible, Congress instructed the commissioners to act only with the knowledge and approval of the French ministry and to be "ultimately governed by the advice of the French Court or Minister" (Commager and Morris, p. 1251). Jefferson never left America, and Laurens was captured at sea by the British (3 September 1780).

On 12 April 1782, Richard Oswald reached Paris as representative of the Rockingham ministry and started talks with Franklin, the only American commissioner on the scene. Before leaving for France, Oswald—an old friend of Laurens—paid Laurens's bail and helped him get to the Netherlands to meet with Adams. Adams was at The Hague to secure Dutch recognition of the United States (which came on 19 April), arrange a loan, and bring about a treaty of amity and commerce (obtained in October 1782). Laurens returned to London and did not reach Paris until November 1782.

On 19 September the new Shelburne ministry authorized Oswald to treat with the commissioners of the "13 United States." This tacit recognition of independence started formal negotiations between Oswald, Franklin, and Jay. On 5 October, Jay gave Oswald the draft of a preliminary treaty. Henry Strachey joined Oswald on 28 October and by about 1 November, Jay and Adams (who reached Paris on 26 October) prevailed on Franklin to exclude France from preliminary treaty negotiations in violation of their congressional instructions. On 5 November a new set of articles was agreed to by the U.S. and British commissioners. With a few last-minute modifications, agreed to on 30 November, these articles became the final Peace Treaty of 3 September 1783. Vergennes, meanwhile, voiced his objections to the unilateral action of the commission but was impressed by the favorable results it had achieved. Franklin's tactful reply to the French minister on 17 December 1782 and the latter's desire for a speedy settlement prevented serious discord; so much so that Franklin was able to squeeze another huge loan out of the French government.

The treaty won for the United States almost everything Congress had originally desired, from Britain's recognition of American independence and a promise to withdraw all their troops to rights of navigation on the Mississippi and some fishing rights. Most astounding, however, were the new borders of the United States, which extended well beyond the original thirteen colonies to include the entire Northwest territory. Just about the only thing Britain received in return were American promises to honor pre-war debts and to recompense Loyalists for their losses. But the British also got what they were desperate for, namely, peace, as America's allies followed its lead in coming to terms with the British. In addition, as Jonathan Dull has written of the treaty, "The terms represented a considerable triumph for the American commissioners, but their victory was partly illusory," as so many details remained unstated and would haunt U.S. relations with Britain for the next half century (*Diplomatic History*, p. 150) Equally disruptive of relations between these two nations was the conviction on the part of most British leaders that the United States could not possibly last as an independent republic.

On 20 January 1783, Great Britain signed preliminary articles with France and Spain. Peace preliminaries then were complete and hostilities were officially ended. On 4 February the British Parliament proclaimed the cessation of hostilities. Though furious over the generosity of the treaty with the United States, Parliament voted 207 to 190 on 21 February to both approve and denounce the treaty. Shelburne resigned as prime minister, and Parliament eventually saw no alternative but to accede to the treaty in order to end a long and devastating war. Congress received the text of the provisional treaty on 13 March and on 11 April proclaimed hostilities ended. After considerable criticism of the commissioners for not consulting France, Congress ratified the provisional treaty on 15 April. On 3 September the treaty was signed in Paris, on 14 January 1784 it was ratified by Congress, and on 12 May ratifications were exchanged to complete the peace negotiations. Both Spain and Great Britain found reasons for not honoring all the terms of the treaty.

SEE ALSO *Jay's Treaty; Peace Treaty of 3 September 1783; Spanish Participation in the American Revolution.*

BIBLIOGRAPHY

Commager, Henry Steele, and Richard B. Morris, eds. *The Spirit of 'Seventy-Six: The Story of the American Revolution As Told by Participants.* New York: Harper and Row, 1967.

Dull, Jonathan R. *A Diplomatic History of the American Revolution.* New Haven, Conn.: Yale University Press, 1985.

Hoffman, Ronald, and Peter J. Albert, eds. *Peace and the Peacemakers: The Treaty of 1783.* Charlottesville: University Press of Virginia, 1986.

Morris, Richard B. *The Peacemakers: The Great Powers and American Independence.* New York: Harper and Row, 1965.

revised by Michael Bellesiles

PEACE OF PARIS SEE *Paris, Treaty of (10 February 1763).*

PEACE TREATY OF 3 SEPTEMBER 1783.

After the peace negotiations that started in 1781, the treaty was signed in Paris on 3 September. The nine articles may be summarized as follows: (1) U.S. independence was recognized by Great Britain; (2) the U.S. boundaries were established as the St. Croix River between Maine and Nova Scotia, the St. Lawrence–Atlantic watershed, the forty-fifth parallel, a line through the Great Lakes westward to the Mississippi and down that river to the thirty-first parallel, eastward along that parallel, and the Apalachicola and St. Mary's Rivers to the Atlantic; (3) the United States obtained the "right" to fish off Newfoundland and Nova Scotia and the "liberty" to cure their fish on unsettled beaches of Labrador, the Magdalen Islands, and Nova Scotia; (4) creditors of each country were to be paid by citizens of the other; (5) Congress would "earnestly recommend" that states fully restore the rights and property of Loyalists; (6) no future action would be taken against any person for his or her actions during the war just ended; (7) hostilities were to end and all British forces were to be evacuated "with all convenient speed"; (8) navigation of the Mississippi "from its source to the ocean shall forever remain free" to U.S. and British citizens; and (9) conquests made by either country from the other before the arrival of the peace terms would be restored.

The treaty was ratified by Congress on 14 January 1784, and on 12 May ratifications were exchanged to complete the action. Jay's Treaty of 1794 and Pinckney's

Treaty of 1795 ended many U.S. difficulties with, respectively, Britain and Spain that arose from the treaty.

SEE ALSO *Jay's Treaty; Peace Negotiations; Spanish Participation in the American Revolution.*

BIBLIOGRAPHY
Dull, Jonathan R. *A Diplomatic History of the American Revolution.* New Haven, Conn.: Yale University Press, 1985.

revised by Michael Bellesiles

PEALE, CHARLES WILLSON. (1741–1827).

Portrait painter, naturalist, Patriot. Maryland. Born on 15 April 1741 in Queen Anne's County, Maryland, Charles Willson Peale was son of a forger who had been shipped to America in 1735 as a punishment for his crimes. Charles Peale became a saddler, but his success as an amateur portrait painter encouraged him to seek instruction in art, and in 1767 he was accepted as a student of Benjamin West, in London. Three years later he returned to Maryland and soon was established as a portrait painter in the middle provinces. Early in 1776 he moved to Philadelphia, Pennsylvania, where many prominent Patriots subsequently sat for him.

Peale enlisted in the Philadelphia militia in 1776 and was elected lieutenant. After taking part in the Trenton–Princeton campaign, he was promoted to captain of the Fourth Pennsylvania Regiment of Foot. Until the British evacuation of Philadelphia, Captain Peale served with the army, and while in uniform he painted many miniatures of American officers. He also held a number of public offices, being chairman of the Constitutional Society and a representative in the Pennsylvania General Assembly from 1779 to 1781. Identified with the radical democrats, Peale lost his wealthier clients, forcing him to abandon politics entirely in 1787.

During the post-war depression he started engraving mezzotints of his portraits. At this time he also developed an interest in natural history after recovering and making drawings of two skeletons of mammoths. His art gallery became a repository of natural curiosities, and evolved into the Philadelphia Museum. The Pennsylvania Academy of the Fine Arts owed its establishment in 1805 largely to Peale's efforts. Peale is best known for his many pictures of Washington. An estimated 60 such pictures were created between 1776 and 1795, and seven of these were done from life. Peale died in Philadelphia on 22 February 1827.

BIBLIOGRAPHY
Miller, Lillian B., et al., eds., *Selected Papers of Charles Willson Peale and His Family.* 5 vols. New Haven, Conn.: Yale University Press, 1983–2000.
Sellers, Charles C. *Charles Willson Peale.* New York: Scribner's, 1969.

revised by Michael Bellesiles

PEEKSKILL RAID, NEW YORK. 23

March 1777. Peekskill served as an important riverside depot for American forces in the Hudson Highlands during the winter of 1776–1777. To disrupt the fortification efforts and the assembly of newly raised Continental regiments, William Howe dispatched a small raiding force upriver on 22 March. Lieutenant Colonel John Bird, with five hundred men and four light guns, provided the land contingent; the frigate *Brune,* three galleys, four transports, and eight flatboats made up the naval component. After feinting to draw the American defenders off, Bird's men landed at Lunt's Cove about 1 P.M. on the 23rd; Brigadier General Alexander McDougall's small garrison burned some of the stores and withdrew. One American was killed; Bird had no casualties. Lieutenant Colonel Marinus Willett led a Patriot force from Fort Constitution against the raiders on the 24th and captured a cloak that would become part of the Fort Stanwix flag later in the year. This action confirmed Washington's belief in the importance of the forts and passes of the Hudson; it encouraged the British to undertake the Danbury raid on 23–28 April.

SEE ALSO *Danbury Raid, Connecticut; Howe, William; McDougall, Alexander.*

BIBLIOGRAPHY
Hufeland, Otto. *Westchester County during the American Revolution, 1775–1783.* New York: Knickerbocker Press, 1926.

revised by Robert K. Wright Jr.

PELL'S POINT, NEW YORK.

18 October 1776. Frustrated in his attack on Throg's Neck, New York, British General William Howe shifted his line of operations to Pell's Point, three miles to the north. Meanwhile, General George Washington had started withdrawing northward from Harlem Heights, having scouted Howe's latest attempt to encircle him and decided that the American positions were untenable.

In the Pell's Point area was a small brigade commanded by Colonel John Glover. It consisted of about 750 men from four Massachusetts regiments: his own Marbleheaders, Joseph Read's, William Shepard's, and Laommi Baldwin's. They were supported by three guns.

From his position near Eastchester (about a mile from Pell's Point), Glover looked out over Eastchester Bay early on 18 October and saw that British ships had come in during the night. He ordered a captain and forty men forward as a delaying force. Meanwhile, he deployed the rest of his brigade behind the stone walls on both sides of the road the British would have to take from the shore to the interior of Westchester County, thus creating an ambush. Read's regiment was on the left, Shepard's on the right, and Baldwin's still further back on the left; Glover's regiment was in reserve to the rear.

The American delaying force exchanged fire with the British advance party and fell back in good order. Read's regiment, which was the first to come within range (the other two being echeloned to his right rear) let the British get within 100 feet before rising from behind a stone wall to deliver a fire that drove the enemy back. It was an hour and a half before the British main body organized an attack, which was supported by seven guns. Read's men fired seven volleys before withdrawing behind Shepard's regiment. The latter poured forth seventeen volleys, forcing the British to make several attacks before they could advance. Glover then ordered a withdrawal to a new position, which the enemy did not attack. The two forces exchanged artillery fire until after dark, when Glover withdrew another three miles and pitched camp.

American losses were eight killed and thirteen wounded. Among the latter was Shepard. Howe reported three killed and twenty wounded, but his figures may not have included the Hessians, who comprised most of the attacking force. However, the adjutant general of the Hessian forces, Carl Leopold Baurmeister, also passed over the action without any mention of German casualties. While the number of Hessian casualties remains in doubt, historians agree on the strategic importance of the battle: Glover delayed the British for an entire day, and helped Washington reach the safety of White Plains before Howe could intercept the American retreat.

On 21 October the British occupied New Rochelle, New York, without resistance. On that same day, Washington's forces were hurrying to White Plains, New York, which they expected to be Howe's next objective. John Haslet raided the detached Tory camp of Robert Rogers at Mamaroneck, New York, on 22 October of that year.

SEE ALSO *Harlem Heights, New York; Long Island, New York, Battle of; Throg's Neck, New York.*

BIBLIOGRAPHY

Abbatt, William. *The Battle of Pell's Point.* New York: W. Abbatt, 1901.

Billias, George. "Pelham Bay: A Forgotten Battle." *New-York Historical Society Quarterly* (Jan. 1958): 20–38.

revised by Barnet Schecter

PENN, JOHN.

PENN, JOHN. (1740–1788). Signer. Virginia and North Carolina. Born in Caroline County, Virginia, 6 May 1740, John Penn studied law with his kinsman Edmund Pendleton, passing the bar in 1761. He moved to Williamsboro, North Carolina, in 1774, where he became a local political leader. He was elected to the Continental Congress in 1775, serving until 1780, becoming famous for rarely speaking in public yet having an active social life. Initially favoring reconciliation, Penn became an advocate in 1776 of both independence and foreign alliances, and signed the Declaration of Independence. During the foreign affairs controversy involving Silas Deane and Richard Henry Lee, Penn became such a violent defender of Robert Morris against the accusations of Henry Laurens (a Deane supporter) that, in January 1779, Laurens challenged Penn to a duel. As he assisted his elderly opponent across the street from the boarding house they shared, Penn realized the absurdity of the situation and suggested that they call it off. Laurens agreed.

Returning to his state, Penn became a member of the North Carolina board of war in 1780. General Charles Cornwallis was moving north, the state authorities were clashing with the Continental officers that were being sent to defend the South, and Penn waged an administrative battle against all three. His post was abolished when Thomas Burke became governor of North Carolina in 1781. In July he returned to the private practice of law. He died on 14 September 1788.

SEE ALSO *Deane, Silas.*

BIBLIOGRAPHY

Morgan, David T., and William J. Schmidt. *North Carolinians in the Continental Congress.* Winston-Salem, N.C.: J. F. Blair, 1976.

The John Penn Papers. Duke University Library, Durham, N.C.

revised by Michael Bellesiles

PENNSYLVANIA, MOBILIZATION IN.

PENNSYLVANIA, MOBILIZATION IN. In 1680, founder William Penn established Pennsylvania to serve as a Quaker colony and as an experiment in diversity. He succeeded beyond his fondest dreams and most dreaded nightmares—by the late eighteenth century, Pennsylvania had become one of the most varied polities in the Atlantic world.

A COMPLEX COLONY

Although technically under the umbrella of a single colonial and, later, state government, Revolutionary-era Pennsylvania consisted of four distinct regions, each with its own political, economic, ethnic, and geographic characteristics. Each of these regions experienced the upheavals of imperial and internal conflict differently from the others. Furthermore, Pennsylvanians jealously guarded local control over their affairs, and often conceived politics on local, colonial-state, and national scales. Thus, although connected by shared governmental structures and engaged in the same imperial and national struggles, Pennsylvanians mobilized for and fought several connected but unique American Revolutions.

From east to west, Pennsylvania was home to a major Atlantic port city, a few counties of primarily English Quaker stock that held disproportionate political power in the colonial legislature, a large and very agriculturally productive central area settled mostly by Germans and Scots-Irish, and rugged western country hotly contested among two groups of settlers and several Indian groups. Boasting a population of over 20,000 people in 1770, Philadelphia had grown to become the largest city in the British colonies, and indeed one of the largest in the British empire, and it was the colony's economic, cultural, and political capital. The city's artisans and laborers produced a myriad of goods, while its merchants bought grains, beef, flour, and other local surplus commodities and distributed them throughout the Atlantic world in exchange for goods that they distributed throughout the colony.

Bucks and Chester Counties, adjacent to Philadelphia, generally provided goods as well as political sympathy for Philadelphia. Together with Philadelphia, these two counties held enough seats in the colonial legislature to dictate colonial policy, and both areas proved at best to be ambivalent about the Revolutionary cause. Central Pennsylvania boasted perhaps the finest farmland in the Atlantic world—it was called by many "the best poor man's country." Its residents provided most of Pennsylvania's men, materials, and passion in support of the rebel side. Finally, the Juniata and Wyoming Valleys became the site of some of the Revolution's most brutal fighting. In the Juniata Valley, the violence largely occurred between whites and Indians. In Wyoming Valley, rival groups of white settlers battled over land claims rather than over ideology or imperial authority.

ROOTS OF RESISTANCE

In contrast to the colony's diversity and internal conflict, most Pennsylvanians hesitated to engage in resistance against British imperial policies. In this they reflected the attitudes of their middle-colony neighbors more than those of their New England or Virginia cousins. During the late 1760s and early 1770s, with the exception of the Stamp Act that was universally opposed in all the continental colonies, few Pennsylvanians strongly objected too, much less protested, changes in imperial policy. For decades two elite, Philadelphia-based political factions had dominated Pennsylvania politics: a proprietary party that supported the Penn family and was composed primarily of Anglicans and Presbyterians, and an assembly party that favored converting Pennsylvania to a crown colony and was composed primarily of Quakers and their allies. While quick to oppose each other's policies, both factions were cautious when it came to resisting royal authority.

The first rumblings of discontent came from Philadelphia. This is not surprising, given that the city was more closely connected through commerce and politics to the empire and to other colonists than were the other Pennsylvania communities. Thus it was only natural that the people of the city were the first to sense and react to changes in the political winds. Even here, however, resistance to the Stamp Act that sparked such vehement demonstrations in New York, Boston, and elsewhere in the spring of 1765 resulted in comparatively muted protests. Neither of the two elite political factions favored strong action. Not until March 1769 did Philadelphia merchants finally and reluctantly join the non-importation agreements that other colonial merchants had immediately initiated to protest the Townsend Duties that had been passed nearly two years before, and the Quaker City men only did so after much prodding from a popular coalition of laborers and artisans. That radical coalition managed to get several of its members elected to the city council from 1770 on, and would lead the colony-wide resistance to British rule.

Although resistance to British authority built slowly in Pennsylvania, events moved swiftly from 1774 forward. Despite the local protests of Philadelphia's popular coalition and a colonies-wide call for delegates to attend the first Continental Congress, Governor John Penn decided upon a course of inaction by not allowing the colonial legislature to meet. He thereby effectively prevented the colony's elected representatives from selecting delegates to the Convention, which nonetheless would be held in Philadelphia. Accordingly, the city radicals and their moderate allies began the process of creating a network of Committees of Correspondence that served as the backbone of resistance to British authority and the skeletal beginnings of Pennsylvania's Revolutionary government. These Committees nominated delegates to the Continental Congress, which soon returned the favor by authorizing Committees of Associators (whose members were often the same as those who staffed the Committees) to enforce Continental Congress edicts and, after 1775, to raise militias.

Throughout Pennsylvania, these Committees took it upon themselves to supplant legal authorities and to harass those that opposed them or even tried to remain above the fray. They were especially effective in central Pennsylvania, which soon surpassed Philadelphia in terms of support for the rebellion. Nonetheless, unlike in most other colonies, the colonial assembly still steadfastly clung to its vision of an America that remained underneath the protection and authority of Britain, neither recognizing the Committees nor voting for independence—despite meeting in the same building as the Continental Congress while it debated the issue of independence during the spring of 1776.

The Committees of Correspondence finally called for a Provincial Assembly to write a new constitution in June 1776. In some ways, Pennsylvania's resulting founding document was the most democratic of all the new state constitutions, in that it established a unicameral legislature, legislators served one-year terms, the executive branch had almost no power, and nearly all white men could potentially be eligible to vote. However, that last and most crucial measure—the extension of the franchise—was only offered to those willing to swear allegiance to the new government. In requiring this, the new constitution created both a political and religious litmus test for citizenship. Those who did not support the new government or its policies, or those whose religions did not allow swearing (a provision clearly directed at Quakers, who could not take oaths), were not only out of power but beyond civil protection. The Quaker colony was dead, and the Commonwealth of Pennsylvania took its place.

REVOLUTIONARY GOALS

Pennsylvanians fought the Revolution within Pennsylvania on two parallel tracks. In most of the new state, Revolutionaries had seized the upper hand by the summer of 1776. Thus, on a state scale, the goals at first were clear. The Revolutionaries fought to secure their own sovereignty—that is, to establish and maintain Pennsylvania as a republican member of the new United States. The Loyalists, on the other hand, fought to restore the authority of their sovereign, King George III. In more practical terms, for Revolutionaries at the beginning of the War this meant pursuing a defensive strategy of defending the new state's territory and waters from the depredations of British regulars, auxiliaries, and their Indian allies, while for Loyalists it entailed encouraging British troops and their allies to re-establish control. The main exceptions to that rule would be Philadelphia for a brief time, which the British occupied from September, 1777 to June, 1778; parts of the

Wyoming Valley controlled by nominal Loyalists; and areas of western Pennsylvania—especially the Juniata Valley—that constituted a no-man's-land for much of the war.

Viewed from the local level, however, Pennsylvanians fought for a variety of ends. In Philadelphia, radical workers and tradesmen aimed to keep and institutionalize the power they had gained through the Committees of Correspondence. Not only did they want a more egalitarian government, but they also hoped to use it to enforce an economy in which local needs and fair prices for necessary goods superceded transatlantic commerce and profiteering. Many were also sympathetic to the state's largest concentration of enslaved African Americans, who saw the Revolution as their opportunity for freedom. Other tradesmen, including a large portion of the merchant community, sided with moderate Revolutionaries, who hoped that the Revolution would bring relief from imperial trade restrictions without replacing those measures with American ones or upending the colonial social, political, and economic order. Philadelphia remained home to a large Loyalist population, although as many as 3,000 fled when the British occupying forces evacuated in the summer of 1778.

While many states were home to "disaffected"—that is, people who tried to avoid choosing sides, generally out of fear—Pennsylvania was unusual in that a significant slice of Philadelphia's population and an even larger proportion of the people in nearby Bucks and Chester Counties refused to fight at all: the pacifist principles of the Quakers prohibited taking up arms under any circumstances, and indeed, during the course of the war, Quaker meetings in Pennsylvania shunned members who joined the fight on either side. Members of some pacifist German religious settlements, such as the Moravians and the Mennonites, did the same. In addition, Bucks and Chester Counties also hosted many disaffected and only a small but active community of Revolutionaries.

Most central Pennsylvanians strongly supported the Revolutionary effort. Much of the German population there fought in the Revolution to demonstrate their equality to their English-speaking neighbors. Having suffered under-representation in the colonial Pennsylvania legislature, central Pennsylvanian Revolutionaries also saw the war as a chance to level the political playing field with eastern Pennsylvanians. At the same time, many men in local Committees of Associators exploited their positions in order to establish local politics along new lines and to settle local scores, nearly always in the name of weeding out perceived traitors but often with the purpose of humiliating or fleecing unpopular neighbors.

Wyoming Valley residents welcomed the Revolution merely by taking on new labels. Both the colonial Pennsylvania and Connecticut governments claimed the

Paoli Tavern *(1777) by Saverio Xavier della Gatta.* *On 21 September 1777, British forces led by General Charles Grey staged a nighttime attack on General Anthony Wayne's brigade near Paoli Tavern in Pennsylvania. The encamped Americans were taken by surprise and dozens were killed. The attack became known as the "Paoli Massacre."* PAOLI TAVERN, 1777 (OIL ON CANVAS) BY GATTA, SAVIERO (FL.1777-1820) VALLEY FORGE HISTORICAL SOCIETY, VALLEY FORGE, PA/BRIDGEMAN ART LIBRARY

land, so the white settlers who upheld Pennsylvania claims (called "Pennamites") and those supporting Connecticut authority (called "Yankees") had already been skirmishing since 1769. The two groups quickly took sides in the Revolutionary conflict. The now-Loyal Pennamites and the Revolutionary Yankees remained much less concerned about who governed in Pennsylvania (or, for that matter, in Connecticut) than they were about gaining clear title to their lands.

Finally, in the Juniata Valley, most whites did not hesitate to take arms on the Revolutionary side. For decades, they had complained that the eastern-tilted, Quaker-heavy legislature had neither the interest nor the stomach to drive Indians off lands that the Juniata settlers coveted, or even to retaliate for what settlers argued were Indian atrocities (notwithstanding that white settlers committed more than their share). Like those in the central part of the state, they were heartened by the combination of increased legislative representation and the effectual banishment of Quakers from government. At the same time, Indian groups such as the Iroquois, Delawares, and Ohios had little love for Pennsylvania settlers and could easily see that the British would be more likely to protect their interests than would

the new Pennsylvania government. Accordingly, the Native Americans of the region either took the British side almost immediately or were to drawn into the fight against the Revolutionaries as the violence mounted.

JOINING THE FIGHT

Just as much of the fighting in Pennsylvania hinged on local relationships and ambitions, Pennsylvania's efforts at mobilization and supply were often prompted by national or state officials, but took place mostly at the local level, especially in terms of recruitment. Pennsylvanians not only fought in Continental units (which were collectively known as the "Pennsylvania Line"), but also as members of the state militias, as sailors in the Pennsylvania navy, and as irregulars on both sides of the conflict. In the first year or two of the campaign, many Pennsylvanians were eager to serve. That eagerness would not last.

Unique among the colonies, Pennsylvania had little militia tradition to call on: because of the long-standing pacifist influence of the Quakers in the colonial legislature, the colony had never established a permanent militia, although it had briefly raised troops at a couple of junctures

892

during the Seven Years' War (1756–1763). Revolutionary Pennsylvanians first organized fighting forces in May 1775, after they learned of the battles of Lexington and Concord. Local Committees of Associators, already active in enforcing boycotts of British goods and essentially in control of local affairs in much of the state, formed militias to send to Massachusetts. In many areas, for the first two years of the war these local, voluntary, loosely-organized units often did more to establish what they considered a proper Revolutionary order at home than they contributed to combat, especially because some of their more militarily inclined members joined up with Continental forces. In the Wyoming Valley, little additional organization was necessary. After all, these men had already been engaged in skirmishes for six years before war broke out in Massachusetts.

In the Juniata Valley and other western areas, the colonial government had done all it could to restrain frontier violence, so settlers needed little prompting from outside to begin hostilities with Indians, regardless of whether those Indians were friendly or hostile. For their part, motivated by their desire to protect their land and to revenge their losses, and prompted by British promises of security and arms, the Iroquois retaliated against the settlers, as did Ohios. Eventually, the Delaware also joined the fight on the British side. Although they tended to act in small raiding parties, on occasion the Native American groups could raise large forces and work in concert with Loyalists to overwhelm their settler opponents.

Pennsylvanians mobilized to fight both on land and on water. In July 1775 the Pennsylvania Committee of Safety established the Pennsylvania navy. The navy was charged with defending the Delaware River, which offered access to the Atlantic for the state's eastern counties and for Philadelphia. As with the Associators, service was voluntary and the response was impressive. Within a year more than 700 men had enlisted and they had already built a 27-craft fleet, including galleys, fire rafts, and floating batteries. They would construct yet another 21 smaller boats by the end of 1776.

Pennsylvania's contribution to the Continental army was swift, significant, and sustained. In June 1775 the Continental Congress more formally requested that Pennsylvania raise six companies of riflemen. Enthusiasm was so strong that enough men volunteered to fill out nine companies of what became the Pennsylvania Battalion of Riflemen. Later that year Pennsylvania formed a number of new units to contribute to the Continental cause: one artillery company and one infantry battalion in October, four more infantry battalions in December, and yet another infantry battalion in early January 1776. By the spring of 1776, it became clear to Pennsylvania legislators that they could not depend upon the Continental army to protect the state, so in March the state government authorized the

formation of a rifle regiment to consist of 1,000 men and a musketry regiment to consist of 500 men. Nonetheless, in response to George Washington's desperate request for reinforcements on Long Island, these units, too, were transferred from state to Continental command. They would eventually be incorporated into the Continental army. Within the next year, the state raised another eight regiments to join the Continentals, including a cavalry regiment, a regiment dedicated to supply and ordnance repair, and one of German-speaking soldiers primarily recruited from the central part of the state.

Of course, the war effort on all sides involved much more than combat. In Bucks and Chester Counties, although most farmers were at best reluctant to join the either side, they did not hesitate to sell flour, meat, and butter to either side. Indeed, they preferred to supply the British, because the British paid more regularly and with more reliable money. More eager to support the Revolutionary side, farmers in the productive and relatively peaceful central part of the state may have supplied more grain to the Continental army than farmers in any other part of the country. And when men went off to fight, women served in their stead by keeping the farms operating until their husbands returned, if they did return. Women also contributed by weaving homespun to replace British textile imports after they were cut off. Established in 1780, the Ladies Association of Philadelphia raised money that it hoped to use to buy ammunition for the Continentals. Washington, disturbed by the propriety of having women supplying war materiel, gently replied that he would prefer shirts and blankets, which, given the ragged condition of soldiers' clothing, probably was a more significant contribution to the troops than bullets would have been.

A LONG WAR

By 1777 Pennsylvanians had realized that the war would be a drawn-out affair, and, as in most of the states, early enthusiasm had given way to a combination of grim determination and fatalistic resignation. Recognizing that the volunteer Associators possessed neither the will or the numbers to defend the state, in March 1777 the Commonwealth of Pennsylvania officially established a militia system. Even though it did provide some manpower, like the state government whose banner it flew it seemed designed for widescale participation but minimal effectiveness. All white men between 18 and 53 and able to bear arms were to enroll in neighborhood training companies, each of which was divided into eight classes. Upon necessity, the state could call up classes from various counties—but only for two-month stints, after which they would be replaced by the next class in line until the state exhausted the eight-class rotation and began the cycle again. Furthermore, would-be soldiers found it easy to avoid duty, either by hiring substitutes or paying fines. Men's increased readiness to pay their way out of service served as a significant revenue enhancer for militia operations. Still, the few men unwilling or unable to avoid militia duty complained bitterly and with reason about the state's inability to pay them on a regular basis, if at all.

The Pennsylvania Line suffered the physical, emotional, and even financial ravages of war. Combat took some—for example, two entire companies wiped out during the disastrous Continental foray into Canada in late 1775—more died from disease. Soldiers grumbled that while they continued to serve, civilians seemed increasingly disengaged from the cause. After the initial rush to sign up, enthusiasm had dwindled to the point at which Congress, with no other good options, decided to extend their enlistments, first from two years to three, and then, in 1780, for as long as the war would last. To add insult to injury, although fewer and fewer men volunteered to reinforce their depleted ranks, new recruits got bonuses larger than the men who had served for years. Fed up, in Morristown on 1 January 1781, every unit in the Pennsylvania line stationed at Morristown mutinied. Most of the men were discharged, significantly depleting Pennsylvania's contribution to Continental forces.

Exhaustion set in among the civilian population, as well. Philadelphians weary of the British occupation became even more impatient with inflated grain prices, while Pennsylvanians in nearly all parts of the state became increasingly frustrated with the depreciation of Pennsylvania and Continental currency that threatened to cripple the economy. The presence of British troops in Philadelphia and Continental ones at Valley Forge had led to the depletion of firewood and livestock in the eastern part of the state. In Pennsylvania's western reaches, the scattered violence of the early parts of the war became increasingly widespread, vicious, and brutal by the late 1770s, with whites and Indians striking at each others' homes, fields, and children with little discrimination. Nonetheless, unrest continued there until 1783. In the Wyoming Valley, the combatants prolonged the fight even more. There, hostilities lasted until 1784, although many families grew increasingly fatigued by the strain and stress of more than a decade of raids and reprisals.

EVALUATING EFFORTS

As the war came to a close, Pennsylvanians could begin to assess what they had lost and gained through the use of violence. By the early 1780s, the Philadelphia radicals began to lose their grip on city politics, as did their radical counterparts in the state legislature. In the late 1780s, Pennsylvania's more moderate men successfully passed new city and state government structures that tempered the city and state's radical leanings. The test oath was abolished but, even so, Quakers never regained the

political prominence they had held before the Revolution. As a prime example of this shift, the new 1790s state government kept its predecessor's militia system, which it would not revise until 1842. Central and western Pennsylvanians continued to enjoy more proportional representation than they had under the colonial structure, and white settlers thus had some confidence that the state would help them keep the gains they had won against their Indian foes, who retreated further westward and entered into fierce competition with the Indian groups already in the Great Lakes area.

Nonetheless, not all the groups that appeared to be on the winning side ended up better off. Ironically, the Loyalist Pennamites won in the Continental Congress what they could not gain by force in the Wyoming Valley: the national government honored the Pennsylvania claims, thus spurning the Yankee settlers who had supported its cause. Men who had served in the militia and Continental army waited years for their pay, and many ended up selling off their government IOUs for far less than face value in in the tough economy of the 1780s. Soldiers who had been paid in land certificates either had to sell them off or move far away, and the national government did not offer the soldiers any land in Pennsylvania. During the 1780s and early 1790s, farmers in the central part of the state engaged in a series of court and road closings in response to the state government's conservative turn in economic policy. In 1794 many of those same farmers joined the Whiskey Rebellion to protest federal taxes that, to them, resembled the British taxes that had angered them two decades earlier. Washington, now president, led federal troops to put down the revolt. The Revolutionary War was now over in Pennsylvania.

SEE ALSO *Mutiny of the Pennsylvania Line.*

BIBLIOGRAPHY

Bodle, Wayne K. *The Valley Forge Winter: Citizens and Soldiers in War.* University Park, Penn.: The Pennsylvania State University Press, 2002.

Bouton, Terry. "A Road Closed: Rural Insurgency in Post-Independence Pennsylvania." *Journal of American History* 87 (December 2000): 855–887.

Brunhouse, Robert L. *The Counter-Revolution in Pennsylvania, 1776–1790.* New York: Octagon Books, 1971.

Fox, Francis S. *Sweet Land of Liberty: The Ordeal of the American Revolution in Northampton County, Pennsylvania.* University Park, Penn.: The Pennsylvania State University Press, 2001.

Frantz, John B., and William Pencak, eds. *Beyond Philadelphia: The American Revolution in the Pennsylvania Hinterland.* University Park, Penn.: The Pennsylvania State University Press, 1998.

Illick, Joseph E. *Colonial Pennsylvania: A History.* New York: Charles Scribner's Sons, 1976.

Jackson, John W. *The Pennsylvania Navy, 1775–1781: The Defense of the Delaware.* New Brunswick, N.J.: Rutgers University Press, 1974.

Knouff, Gregory T. *The Soldiers' Revolution: Pennsylvanians in Arms and the Forging of Early American Identity.* University Park, Penn.: The Pennsylvania State University Press, 2004.

Moyer, Paul. "Wild Yankees: Settlement, Conflict, and Localism along Pennsylvania's Northeast Frontier, 1760–1820." Ph.D. diss., College of William and Mary, 1999.

Osterhout, Anne M. *A State Divided: Opposition in Pennsylvania to the American Revolution.* New York: Greenwood Press, 1987.

Ryerson, Richard Alan. *The Revolution is Now Begun: The Radical Committees of Philadelphia, 1765–1776.* Philadelphia: University of Pennsylvania Press, 1978.

Slaughter, Thomas P. *The Whiskey Rebellion: Frontier Epilogue to the American Revolution.* New York: Oxford University Press, 1986.

Trussell, John B. *The Pennsylvania Line: Regimental Organization and Operations, 1775–1782.* 2nd ed. Harrisburg, Penn.: Pennsylvania Historical and Museum Commission, 1993.

Andrew M. Schocket

PENOBSCOT EXPEDITION, MAINE.

May–August 1779. In February 1779 General Henry Clinton in New York informed Brigadier Francis McLean in Halifax that the king wished to have a fort and settlement established on the Penobscot River and that he, Clinton, had decided to conduct the operation from Halifax rather than New York. After carrying on further discussions and allowing time for making preparations, Clinton on 13 April ordered McLean to proceed. The task force left Halifax on 30 May with 440 men from the Seventy-fourth Foot and 200 from McLean's own Eighty-second Foot, a slightly larger garrison than Clinton had contemplated. McLean explained that he intended to use the extra men as an amphibious raiding party once the fort was completed. A frigate and four sloops of war escorted the transports, which arrived at Magebeguiduce (near modern Castine, Maine) on the Penobscot River on 12 June and landed four days later. Actual construction of the four-bastioned square fort began only at the start of July. On the 21st of that month, when McLean learned that an American force had left Boston, only two of the bastions had low walls; the ditch was not finished; and the only guns mounted were four twelve-pounders in a detached battery guarding the anchorage, which held three sloops of war.

As soon as they learned of the invasion of their "Downeast" territory, Massachusetts organized an expedition to eliminate the threat. Generals Solomon Lovell and Peleg Wadsworth commanded the one thousand militia and state troops that were quickly assembled at Boston. Continental navy Captain Dudley Saltonstall led the two-thousand-man naval element composed of three ships of the Continental navy (the thirty-two-gun frigate Warren served as his flagship), three brigs from the Massachusetts state navy, one New Hampshire state navy vessel, a dozen hired privateers, and about twenty transports. The task force sailed from Boston on 19 July and arrived in Penobscot Bay on the 25th. After some inconsequential skirmishing, the Americans finally started landing on 28 July, the same day that a British rescue force from New York City dropped down to Sandy Hook.

The Americans remained unaware of their danger, and Lovell proceeded in a deliberate manner. Saltonstall had urged a more aggressive course, but the authority for land operations lay with Lovell. Siege batteries opened fire on the 30th. Commodore Sir George Collier arrived on 11 August from Sandy Hook with ten vessels, including the sixty-four-gun ship of the line *Raisonable,* five frigates, a sloop of war, and sixteen hundred troops. They found the American squadron drawn up at the mouth of the river and promptly bottled up the inferior force. Much to Collier's surprise, the Americans promptly fled upstream. The British pursued but were only able to capture one ship; the American crews destroyed the rest of their squadron to prevent its capture. On the land side, the American force abandoned its positions during the night of 13–14 August and joined the ships' crews in an arduous retreat through the wilderness. The British maintained a strong post at Penobscot for the rest of the war.

Recriminations abounded and several American officers were court-martialed for misconduct. Paul Revere, who commanded the artillery, was acquitted. Lovell and Wadsworth were praised by the Massachusetts authorities. The state authorities blamed Saltonstall, and on 7 October 1779, Congress dismissed him from the service.

NUMBERS AND LOSSES

The Americans lost 474 men, several cannon, and all of the ships on the expedition. British casualties were 18 men killed; 2 officers and 38 enlisted men wounded (5 of whom died soon after); and 11 men missing.

SIGNIFICANCE

The affair had little impact outside of Maine and aside from the dissension caused in the American ranks. British possession of the area did not survive the peace treaty.

BIBLIOGRAPHY

Buker, George E. *The Penobscot Expedition: Commodore Saltonstall and the Massachusetts Conspiracy of 1779.* Annapolis, Md.: Naval Institute Press, 2002.

Cayford, John E. *The Penobscot Expedition: Being an Account of the Largest American Naval Engagement of the Revolutionary War.* Orrington, Maine.: C&H, 1976.

Kevitt, Chester B., comp. *General Solomon Lovell and the Penobscot Expedition, 1779.* Weymouth, Mass.: Weymouth Historical Commission, 1976.

Leamon, James S. *Revolution Downeast: The War for American Independence in Maine.* Amherst: University of Massachusetts Press, 1993.

revised by Robert K. Wright Jr.

PENOT LOMBART, LOUIS-PIERRE.

Chevalier de La Neuville (1744–1800). French volunteer. On 25 February 1750, La Neuville became a lieutenant in the Paris militia, and in 1759 he was promoted to captain of the same unit. In 1759 he was made captain and in 1766 became *aide-major* in the regiment of recruits of the colonies. In 1774 he was appointed major of the Provincial Regiment of Laon. He was bestowed the title of chevalier in the Order of Saint Louis in 1776. On 5 March 1777 the court granted him leave of absence for the alleged purpose of tending to business in Saint Domingue but actually to enable him (and his brother) to fight the British in North America. He wrote Franklin on 16 March 1777 that he was prepared to go to America whether as a colonel or volunteer.

Arriving in America with glowing letters of recommendation and accompanied by his younger brother, René Hippolyte, La Neuville was appointed colonel with rank as of 21 March 1777. On 14 May he was named inspector general of the Northern Army (under Gates) with the promise that he would be promoted at the end of three months in accordance with his merit. A year later he was still waiting for advancement. In May 1778 he was recommended to Congress for promotion to brigadier general, and on 28 June General Parsons signed a eulogistic recommendation regarding his service, but Congress postponed action on 29 July. Congress finally breveted him brigadier general on 14 October 1778, with date of rank of 14 August, and on 4 December accepted his request for retirement. On 11 January 1779 he sailed with Lafayette for France, carrying a glowing commendation from Gates. On 24 June 1780 he received a commission in the French army as a lieutenant colonel. Two years later he asked for permission to return to America, but Ségur refused the necessary authority. In early 1783 he was placed in command of a battalion of colonial auxiliaries at Cadiz preparing to accompany the proposed expedition to the West Indies, but the peace intervened. Lafayette appears to have written a recommendation in his file in 1787 stating that "M. de La Neuville has always shown much intelligence and zeal. He conducted himself perfectly in America" (Lasseray, *Les Français,* vol. 2, p. 356). He was in New York in 1790 on business when his uncle, Lieutenant General Merlet, sought on his behalf the rank of adjutant general. He returned to France that year. La Neuville retired effective 20 March 1791 and died during the Napoleonic era.

BIBLIOGRAPHY

Bodinier, André. *Dictionnaire des officiers de l'armée royale qui ont combattu aux Etats-Unis pendant la guerre d'Indépendance, 1776–1783.* Vincennes, France: Service historique de l'armée, 1982.

Contenson, Ludovic de. *La Société des Cincinnati de France et la Guerre d'Amérique.* Paris: Editions Auguste Picard, 1934.

Ford, Worthington C. et al., eds. *Journals of the Continental Congress, 1774–1789.* 34 vols. Washington, D.C.: U.S. Government Printing Office, 1904–1937.

Franklin, Benjamin. *Papers of Benjamin Franklin.* Edited by Leonard W. Labaree et al. 37 vols. to date. New Haven, Conn.: Yale University Press, 1959–.

Lafayette, Gilbert du Motier de. *Lafayette in the Age of the American Revolution: Selected Letters and Documents, 1776–1790.* Edited by Stanley J. Idzerda et al. 5 vols. to date. Ithaca, N.Y.: Cornell University Press, 1977–.

Lasseray, André. *Les Français sous les treize étoiles (1775–1783).* 2 vols. Mâcon, France: Imprimerie Protat Frères, 1935.

revised by Robert Rhodes Crout

PENOT LOMBART DE NOIRMONT, RENÉ HIPPOLYTE.

(1750–1792). French volunteer. A *sous lieutenant* attached to the dragoons on 1768, he became lieutenant in the Royal Comtois infantry five years later. In February 1777 he received a leave of absence to accompany his older brother, Louis- Pierre, to America. On 13 December 1777 he entered the American army as a volunteer, and from that date to 28 April 1778 was Thomas Conway's aide-de-camp. On 14 May 1778 he became assistant inspector general of infantry in the Northern Army, where his brother had been serving as inspector general for the preceding year. He was promoted to major on 29 July with date of rank of 13 December 1777. Next assigned as aide de camp to Lafayette, he held this position until the latter returned to France in January 1779. Noirmont was ordered by Congress on 1 April 1779 to join Lincoln in the Southern Department. In the operations around Savannah, he served as a lieutenant of infantry. Lafayette having noted in his 27 October and 22 December 1778 recommendations to Congress that Noirmont had commanded many French officers then serving as lieutenant colonels, Congress finally breveted him lieutenant colonel on 18 November 1779 in recognition of his services and granted him leave to return to France.

On 1 January 1781 Noirmont was ordered to the West Indies and assigned to the chasseur company of the Second Battalion, Royal Comtois. He returned to France in 1784 and in 1788 was made a chevalier in the Order of Saint Louis. He became lieutenant colonel in his reorganized infantry regiment in July 1791 and served there until he was discharged. Three weeks later, on 30 November, he became captain in the Garde Constitutionnelle. He was at the Tuileries palace when the monarchy fell on 10 August 1792, was arrested, and on 2 or 3 September 1792 he died in the general massacre of prisoners.

SEE ALSO *Conway, Thomas.*

BIBLIOGRAPHY

Bodinier, André. *Dictionnaire des officiers de l'armée royale qui ont combattu aux Etats-Unis pendant la guerre d'Indépendance, 1776–1783.* Vincennes, France: Service historique de l'armée, 1982.

Ford, Worthington C. et al., eds. *Journals of the Continental Congress, 1774–1789.* 34 vols. Washington, D.C.: U.S. Government Printing Office, 1904–1937.

Lafayette, Gilbert du Motier de. *Lafayette in the Age of the American Revolution: Selected Letters and Documents, 1776–1790.* Edited by Stanley J. Idzerda et al. 5 vols. to date. Ithaca, N.Y.: Cornell University Press, 1977–.

revised by Robert Rhodes Crout

PENSACOLA, FLORIDA. 9 May 1781.

Captured by the Spanish. The unhealthful British outpost and seat of the British government of West Florida was threatened by Louisiana Governor Bernardo de Gálvez in March 1780, when Mobile was captured. Pensacola's strong defenses convinced Gálvez that he needed a larger force for the attack, and he went to Havana to organize the expedition. However, a hurricane scattered his fleet in October, and it was not until the following February that he was able to sail for Florida. Meanwhile, Governor Sir John Dalling of Jamaica, who was responsible for Pensacola, wanted to reinforce that base with a regiment of American Loyalists but was unable to get the necessary naval escort.

The British garrison at Pensacola was commanded by General John Campbell and counted nine hundred regulars, primarily of the Sixteenth Foot and Sixtieth Regiments, the latter composed largely of Germans, and two battalions of provincial infantry from Maryland and Pennsylvania. The fortifications bristled with cannon. When the Spanish naval commanders saw these cannon

in early March, they refused to enter the bay. Not so easily intimidated, Gálvez took command of the brig *Galveztown* and led his colonial troops aboard a flotilla of smaller craft to land near the British fort. Shamed, the rest of the Spanish navy followed, landing several thousand troops. A rather leisurely siege ensued. It was not until the end of April that the Spanish began firing in earnest upon the British positions. On 8 May one of their shells landed on the fort's principal magazine, setting off an explosion that killed or wounded nearly one hundred of Campbell's men and demolished one of redoubts in the process. The Spanish attacked and were being beaten off by the British the first time. But the Spanish then seized part of the fort's walls and set up cannon with which they could fire down into the garrison. Campbell capitulated the next day. West Florida was now in Spanish hands. Gálvez was rewarded with promotion to lieutenant general and ennobled by Carlos III.

SEE ALSO *Jamaica (West Indies); Mobile.*

revised by Michael Bellesiles

PENSIONS AND PENSIONERS.

Between 1775 and 1906 state and federal governments awarded pensions to about 55,000 Revolutionary War veterans and 23,000 of their widows at a cost of nearly $70 million, an amount greater than was spent winning independence. These entitlements resulted from the adoption of colonial precedents, a fundamental change in the political culture and status of veterans, and a new social policy that departed from the Founders' principles.

THE REVOLUTION: INVALID AND HALF-PAY PENSIONS

At the beginning of the Revolution, states continued practices inherited from English and colonial militia laws by providing pensions for injured soldiers. The amount of the invalid pension was rated to the degree of the soldier's disability, which was measured by the capacity of the veteran to work rather than by the type of injury. Invalid pensions were dispersed by local officials and would increase or decrease with changes in the veteran's ability to be self-supporting. Benefits varied according to local law and custom. States also provided pensions for widows and orphans of soldiers who died in service. This aid more closely resembled poor relief than an entitlement. Generally, recipients had to be destitute before being eligible for assistance. Support ended when the widow remarried. As in prior wars, pensions for invalids and widows were intended to assist the recruitment and retention of soldiers, although they were not part of the formal agreements for enlistment. Revolutionary governments continued to distinguish between wages obligated by contract and benefits granted in cases of disability or death. Wages were enforceable under law. Pensions, on the other hand, were discretionary and thus could be changed or withdrawn.

Federal pension laws began when the struggle for independence required Americans to form a national army instead of relying on local militias and state troops. In 1776 the Continental Congress passed the first national pension law, which applied only to invalids who served in Washington's army. The law provided half-pay for life for any soldier or officer who lost a limb in battle or who was disabled so as to be unable to work. The law also granted partial benefits to men who were disabled but still capable of some labor. Adopting the British practice of an invalid corps, these invalid men could be called on to do light military duty. Although the law was federal, administration and payment were left to the states. In 1778 the law providing for Continental soldiers expanded to cover any soldier who fought in the militia. In 1785 Congress tried to standardize benefits by recommending that states grant half-pay to totally disabled officers, $5.00 a month to noncommissioned officers and soldiers who were unable to work, and partial benefits to all invalids rated by the degree of their disability. Whereas the 1776 law treated all invalids equally, the 1785 resolutions marked a significant change in the principle of invalid benefits by distinguishing between officers and men.

In 1790, after adoption of the Constitution, the federal government assumed payment of invalid pensions from the states. In 1792 the federal government took over the administration of the invalid pension program for veterans of the Continental Army. By 1800 the program enrolled about 1,500 men and cost less than $100,000 a year. In 1806 Congress consolidated all invalid programs by extending benefits to all Revolutionary War soldiers. Furthermore, Congress provided benefits to any veteran who had become disabled after the war owing to causes directly related to their service. Under this law the War Department required court-certified medical proof of the disability and evidence linking it to military service. In 1808 the federal government assumed all payments for invalid pensions, thereby ending remaining state programs. In 1816 benefits were increased to privates and officers below the rank of captain. Even so, the program remained small, with 2,200 recipients at an annual cost of about $200,000.

Departing from English practices, revolutionary leaders opposed lifetime service pensions to officers because they were antithetical to republican ideals. These leaders believed such pensions subverted civic virtue by creating a privileged class of "placemen and pensioners." In 1776 Washington rejected half-pay pensions for officers, but in 1777 he advocated them to slow the resignation of officers. He argued that the officers must be tied to service by self-interest as well as devotion to liberty. Thus arose a contentious issue that was not resolved until 1828. Its history is a reflection of the conflict between revolutionary ideals and expedient measures needed to sustain the army.

In 1778 Congress approved a compromise measure that provided half-pay to officers for seven years and one year's pay, or $80, to noncommissioned officers and men who served until the end of the war. In 1780 officers, with Washington's support, succeeded in getting a reluctant Congress to award them half-pay pension for life if they served throughout the war. Officers viewed the pension as part of their wages and as compensation for their sacrifices. Opponents of the pensions, by contrast, viewed the measure as a stopgap to retain officers. But more important, they deplored what they saw as the creation of a privileged class sustained by public taxes. The pensions, in their view, were more suited to a corrupt monarchy than to a new republic, in which citizen-soldiers should return to the ranks of civilian life without preferment. The newly formed Society of Cincinnati, whose membership was limited to officers and their male heirs, added a taint of aristocracy to the disparity between lifetime pensions for officers and the one-time payment of $80 to the rank and file who also served until the end of the war. The uproar of insurrection in 1783 coming from officers encamped in Newburgh, New York, further discredited the claim for half-pay. In early 1783, with the end of the war in sight, Congress reneged on its promise to award half-pay pensions for life. The country was bankrupt and could not pay them. Nevertheless, Congress compromised by awarding officers certificates worth five years' full pay and bearing 6 percent interest until redeemed. All others still received one year's pay. Upon leaving the army in 1783 most officers, desperate for cash, sold their commutation certificates at a fraction of their value. A bitter seed had been planted among these veterans.

In 1790, under Hamilton's plan of assuming debts incurred during the Revolution, the federal government redeemed the certificates at face value, a windfall for speculators and the few officers who held them. Rather than concluding the matter, these payments led to nearly forty years of lobbying and petitions by officers to secure half-pay pensions. Officers claimed that they had been cheated twice—once by their government, which had reneged on its promise in 1783, and again by speculators, who exploited men who had given years of service to their country. In 1809, 1810, and 1819, and from 1825 to 1827, officers submitted claims to Congress stating that they had a legal right to the pensions. Congress rejected these claims on the grounds that its obligations toward these veterans had been met with the 1783 commutation certificates.

The half-pay controversy ended in 1828, when Congress granted full-pay pensions for life to any soldier—not only officers—who had served until the end of the war. This solution upheld the objection made in 1783 that half-pay pensions for officers only was a practice associated with aristocratic societies. The law also sustained the principle that pensions were a gratuity, not a property right protected by contract as the officers claimed. This resolution of the half-pay controversy was less a testimony to the persistence of officers, however, than it was to a fundamental change in American political culture, social policy, and the status of veterans in American society. The passage of the Revolutionary War Pension Act in 1818 codified this shift and established a new precedent for veterans' benefits that eventually benefited those nagging officers.

VETERANS AS ICONS

Following the war and through the first decade of the nineteenth century, Fourth of July celebrants reserved their accolades for the war's leaders while still paying paid tribute to the "Spartan mothers" and the citizen-soldiers represented by militia. The contributions of the Continental Army, on the other hand, were diminished because of lingering anti-army sentiment. In light of the Newburgh conspiracy and demands for half-pay pensions, many viewed professional troops as vice-ridden and their officers as presumptuous and self-serving.

Between 1804 and 1816 the cultural status of rank-and-file veterans of the Continental Army was transformed. To a new generation, veterans emerged as icons of the spirit of '76, a combination of militant patriotism and self-sacrifice for revolutionary ideals. They were idealized as models of American character whose example would unite the nation and inspire future generations to achieve even greater patriotic deeds. The generation that came of age following the Revolution sought to memorialize veterans and show their gratitude toward them, especially as their numbers declined. Thinking of how future generations would view them, younger Americans were aware that neglecting the soldiers of the Revolution would dishonor the nation.

The esteemed status that veterans came to enjoy was partly a product of early nineteenth-century revisionist histories of the Revolution, which focused on the valor of the Continental Army. These histories recounted how the army overcame privations made vivid by images of bloody feet and hunger at Valley Forge. They portrayed the army as composed of citizen-soldiers, unlike England's army of social dregs and misfits, and as an exception to the rule that professional soldiers were a threat to liberty. The Newburgh conspiracy was recast from near treason to an expression of anguish by soldiers who had endured years of suffering as a result of the public's hostility toward them and its failure to pay and provide for them. The troops' restraint

and loyalty under these conditions were celebrated as evidence of their virtue, whereas during the Revolution their demands for pensions were viewed as confirmation of their corruption. By removing the stain of treason and highlighting the courage of Continental veterans, revisionist histories provided younger Americans a view of the Revolution that accentuated the role of ordinary soldiers in securing Independence and as models of the spirit of '76.

Political conflict over defense policies during Thomas Jefferson's administration and military failures in the War of 1812 also elevated the status of Revolutionary War veterans. Republicans and Federalists used veterans as political symbols in their rhetorical clashes over foreign and defense policies. They celebrated veterans to portray themselves as defenders of the Revolution and protectors of American security. Republicans also used veterans to reinforce their image as the party of the people, as they had in 1808 by honoring the thousands of revolutionary soldiers who died on English prison ships in New York City.

The war with England (1812–1815) tested the nation's patriotism and military. Instead of a renewal of the spirit of '76, however, Americans experienced defeat, failure to fill ranks, and deep sectional divisions. Americans looked for lessons from the Revolution to explain their failures and for guidance to build a stronger and more united nation. Nationalists, informed by revisionist histories of the Revolution, made military valor a central theme in uniting the country and defining the character of Americans. Revolutionary War veterans became the symbols of renewed nationalism. Comparing America to ancient Greece and Rome, nationalists called for the preservation of battlefields and encampments such as Valley Forge, for monuments to fallen heroes including a national military cemetery, and for artists and writers to memorialize Revolutionary War veterans.

Sentimentalism and nostalgia reinforced nationalism. Orators and writers invoked the image of suffering soldiers in an effort to shape the public's attitude toward veterans. Romantic stories of their suffering while in service to the nation and in their old age conveyed the soldiers' heroism and sacrifice, establishing them as models of American character. At the same time, this emphasis on veterans' suffering highlighted the nation's ingratitude toward the soldiers who had won independence. Society's failure to aid these aged veterans tarnished America's reputation and set a poor example for future generations.

Veterans contributed to view that they deserved and needed assistance. Old soldiers applying for disability pensions, rather than making medical claims, portrayed themselves as becoming infirm and poor as a result of hardships while in service. They distinguished themselves from paupers, who had brought on their own miseries as a result of vice, by casting their poverty and infirmities as the price paid for the nation's independence. Rather than evidence of shame and personal failure, their infirmities and poverty became symbols of courage and devotion to the revolutionary spirit.

REVOLUTIONARY WAR PENSION ACT OF 1818

In December 1817 President James Monroe called on the nation to honor and assist the nation's Revolutionary War veterans by awarding life-time pensions to all men who had served in the war and who needed assistance. With the federal treasury overflowing, he urged Congress to act quickly for the few thousand thought to be still alive. Monroe viewed the pensions as a debt of gratitude to these veterans and as a means to unite the nation by renewing its revolutionary heritage. Considering that in 1816 Congress had given itself a substantial raise and increased benefits to disabled veterans, withholding pensions for Revolutionary War veterans would appear crass and heartless.

The public and House of Representatives responded enthusiastically to Monroe's request. The House passed a bill that provided pensions to all veterans of the Revolution in the amount of $8 for men and $20 for officers, the same rates paid under the 1816 Invalid Pension Act to totally disabled men and captains. Although the bill restricted eligibility to men "who were in reduced circumstances," the wording was intentionally vague so as not to exclude any veteran except for a few wealthy individuals. The Senate, however, fought over veterans' pensions.

The original draft of the Senate version of the bill restricted the pension to Continental soldiers who served for three years or the duration of the war. This version resembled the claim for half-pay pensions submitted by officers and set off a bitter conflict in the Senate. Opponents argued that service pensions were unconstitutional because granting them exceeded Congress's enumerated powers; that such pensions were antithetical to the principles of the Revolution because they singled out a class of men for preferment; and that restricting benefits to Continental soldiers distorted the true history of the Revolutionary War by ignoring the contributions of militia and the sacrifices of civilians. Opponents and supporters alike attacked the indigence qualification as demeaning and inconsistent with the nation's wish to honor veterans. After the bill survived a vote to kill it, senators from the New England and middle Atlantic states united to expand eligibility to Continental soldiers who served at least nine months. In the House, even supporters of the original comprehensive bill voted to pass the Senate's restricted version. As one congressmen remarked, half a loaf was better than none. With signing of the law in March 1818 the precedent was established to extend benefits to all other veterans.

The 1818 Pension Act awarded $240 a year to officers and $96 to rank and file who served at least nine months in the Continental Army and who were "in reduced circumstance and need of assistance from their country." The implementation of the law was a cause for public celebration, especially during Fourth of July parades when veterans mustered to submit their applications for pensions before courts. Rather than the few thousand pensioners expected to apply, by December 1818 the War Department received nearly 25,000 applications, overwhelming the pension office. The cost had increased from an estimated $300,000 to $2,000,000, with a further increase predicted to reach $5,000,000. In addition, the pension program was rocked by scandal involving fraud and corruption. In 1820 Congress amended the law by suspending all recipients and requiring them to reapply with proof of their poverty in the form of an inventory of all of their possessions except for clothing and bedding. The number of recipients was reduced by a few thousand and the scandal subsided. Although the pension office established a means test, it applied it liberally by awarding pensions to veterans who deeded their property to kin or caregivers in return for housing and support. Legally, these veterans were poor but not destitute. Through successful administration, the pension program became entrenched, and veterans regained their image as worthy recipients. In 1823 Congress extended benefits to Continental veterans who had disposed of their property to pass the means test. With this amendment nearly every veteran who met the service qualification was eligible for the pension.

America's first entitlement program eventually benefited just over 20,000 veterans and some 47,000 of their dependents. By enacting service pensions the Monroe administration departed fundamentally from the principles that had guided the Founders. The act established the precedent for the use of entitlement programs not only for veterans but for others groups to address a wide variety of social issues.

PENSION ACTS OF 1832 AND 1836

The expansion of benefits to Continental Army veterans established a pattern that was repeated in the Pension Acts of 1832 and 1836. Facing a budget surplus, in 1829 President Andrew Jackson proposed that service pensions be awarded to veterans of the Revolution not yet covered under existing law. Echoing the arguments for and against the precedent-setting act in 1818, Congress debated the extension of benefits. The pension proposal also became part of the sectional conflict in the Senate over the tariff, with opponents alleging that the purpose of the bill was to support the continuation of high tariffs that produced income for the federal government. Veterans' affairs continued to be enmeshed with larger political issues. Nevertheless, Congress approved a bill granting full pay for life to any veteran who had completed a total of two years of service, whether in the Continental Army, militia, or state regiments. As with prior laws, officers were to receive up to $20 a month. The bill also granted partial pensions rated by the months of service to any soldier who served a total of six to twenty-four months at any time during the war. Unlike the 1818 and especially the 1820 laws, the 1832 law did not require an oath of poverty or a means test. In essence, the 1832 law implemented the intent of the first bill introduced to Congress in 1818 that proposed service pensions to all veterans.

Once again, Congress had grossly underestimated the number of recipients and the cost of the program. Instead of the projected 9,000 to 10,000 recipients and $450,000 in cost, nearly 28,000 veterans received the pension at an annual cost of $1.8 million. Fraud and corruption marred the program, leading some to observe that there would be more pensioners than there were soldiers in the Revolution. Congress responded by making the Pension Office a separate branch of the War Department. In 1834 Commissioner James L. Edwards, who had headed the branch since 1818, reported that about 43,000 veterans were then on the pension rolls under the various acts of Congress and that $2,325,000 had been paid that year, a figure that represented about 20 percent of the federal expenditures that year.

CONCLUSION

The pension laws greatly benefited veterans and their families. Unlike poor relief, which varied by need and could end with improved circumstances, the pensions provided a stable, guaranteed annual income. Pensions were welcomed locally because men who received them would not become paupers in need of other forms of public assistance. On the social level, pensioners reliant on their children for support regained at least some of their independence, to the mutual benefit of both generations. Veterans used their pensions to support their dependents and in some cases to reunite families divided by poverty. Besides the financial and family benefits, service pensions elevated veterans' status by honoring them as patriots who deserved the nation's gratitude. Subsequent veterans' benefits were built on this cultural and political heritage.

With even more federal revenue to spend, in 1836 Congress awarded pensions for widows of any soldier who would have been eligible for a pension under the Pension Act of 1832. The law restricted eligibility to wives who became widows when their husbands died while serving in the Revolution. In subsequent years, eligibility expanded to include nearly every veteran's widow. In 1906, 130 years after declaring independence, the pension program for Revolutionary War soldiers ended with the final payment to a veteran's widow.

SEE ALSO *Cincinnati, Society of the; Congress; Continental Army, Social History; Continental Congress.*

BIBLIOGRAPHY

Bailyn, Bernard. *The Origins of American Politics.* New York: Random House, 1968.

Cray, Robert E., Jr. "Commemorating the Prison Ship Dead: Revolutionary Memory and the Politics of Sepulture in the Early Republic, 1776–1808." *William and Mary Quarterly* 5 (July 1999): 565–590.

Glasson, William H. *Federal Military Pensions in the United States.* New York: Oxford University Press, 1918.

Jensen, Laura. *Patriots, Settlers, and the Origins of American Social Policy.* Cambridge, U.K., and New York: Cambridge University Press, 2003.

Purcell, Sarah J. *Sealed with Blood: War, Sacrifice, and Memory in Revolutionary America.* Philadelphia: University of Pennsylvania Press, 2002.

Resch, John. *Suffering Soldiers: Revolutionary War Veterans, Moral Sentiment and Political Culture in the Early Republic.* Amherst: University of Massachusetts Press, 1999.

Travers, Len. *Celebrating the Fourth: Independence Day and the Rites of Nationalism in the Early Republic.* Amherst: University of Massachusetts Press, 1997.

Waldstreicher, David. *In the Midst of Perpetual Fetes: The Making of American Nationalism, 1776–1820.* Chapel Hill: University of North Carolina Press, 1997.

John Resch

PEPPERRELL, SIR WILLIAM. (1696–1759). Colonial merchant and military officer, first American-born baronet. Born at Kittery, Maine, on 27 June 1696, William Pepperrell was the son of one of the most prosperous merchants in New England. He received a limited formal education and joined his father as a partner in the senior Pepperrell's mercantile firm. He was elected to the General Court in 1726, appointed colonel of all the militia in Maine the same year, elected to the governor's council in 1727, and appointed chief justice of the York county court in 1730. By the time his father died in 1734, Pepperrell was one of the wealthiest and most prominent residents of Massachusetts, and certainly the most influential man in Maine.

Pepperrell's greatest fame derived from his command of the New England expedition that captured the French fortress of Louisburg on Cape Breton Island in 1745. Governor William Shirley of Massachusetts was the principal architect of the expedition, and he gave Pepperrell command of the provincial forces because of his prominence, popularity, mercantile connections, and experience as militia colonel in Maine. The New England colonies raised and transported a forty-three-hundred-man force to Cape Breton Island, and in their most notable feat of arms before the Revolution, managed to force Louisburg to capitulate on 17 June 1745. While good luck, strong backs, and French mistakes contributed greatly to this outcome, Pepperrell was responsible for keeping the army together and, critically, for maintaining good relations with Commodore Sir Peter Warren, the commander of the Royal Navy squadron that convoyed the New England transports and blockaded Louisburg. For his success in this operation, Pepperrell was commissioned a colonel in the British army on 1 September 1745 and allowed to raise his own colonial regiment as part of the garrison of the conquered town, the governorship of which he shared with Warren until late in the spring of 1746. In November 1746 he was created a baronet, the first native-born American to be so honored. (The regiment was disbanded when Louisburg was returned to the French in 1748 at the Treaty of Aix-la-Chapelle.)

Promoted to major general on 27 February 1755, he commanded on the eastern frontier in Maine during the unfortunate military events elsewhere that year. For about six months between the death of Lieutenant Governor Spencer Phips and the arrival of Governor Thomas Pownall in August 1757, Pepperrell was de facto governor of Massachusetts by virtue of being president of the governor's council. After raising troops for the defense of Massachusetts, he was commissioned lieutenant general in the British army on 20 February 1759 but was prevented by failing health from taking part in subsequent operations of the French and Indian War. He died on 6 July 1759 at Kittery.

Pepperrell's only son died unmarried, but his grandson, William Pepperrell Sparhawk, inherited the bulk of his estate after accepting the stipulation of the will that he change his name to Pepperrell. In 1774 his grandson also was created baronet. A Loyalist, he fled to England shortly thereafter and lost his entire estate by confiscation.

SEE ALSO *Colonial Wars; Shirley, William.*

BIBLIOGRAPHY

Fairchild, Byron. *Messrs. William Pepperrell: Merchants at Piscataqua.* Ithaca, N.Y.: Cornell University Press, 1954.

revised by Harold E. Selesky

PERCY, HUGH. (1742–1817). British army officer and politician. Hugh Percy was born in London on 14 August 1742. He was the eldest son of Sir Hugh Smithson, who in 1750 changed his name to Percy when he inherited the dukedom of Northumberland from his father-in-law. He was educated at Eton (1753–1758) before being gazetted as an ensign in the Twenty-fourth Foot on 1 May 1759. It is possible that he fought at Minden, Germany, during the Seven Years' War, He exchanged into the Eighty-fifth Regiment of Foot as captain only weeks after his seventeenth birthday. Percy was at St. John's College, Cambridge, in 1760, but his university studies barely interrupted his accelerated military career. In 1762 he became lieutenant colonel in both the Eleventh Foot and the Grenadier Guards. In 1763 he was elected to Parliament, where he supported the Grenville legislation, which included the Stamp Act. In 1764 he married the third daughter and in 1766 he voted against repealing the Stamp Act. A supporter of the ministry of William Pitt (the elder), Earl of Chjatham, he was made colonel of the Fifth Regiment in 1768, and from 1770 he opposed Lord North, Pitt's rival and successor to the post of prime minister. In 1774 Percy left with his regiment for America.

On 19 April 1775 Percy took 1,400 infantry and two six-pound cannon out of Boston to rescue Colonel Francis Smith's force as it marched back from Concord under fire. At Lexington he coolly deployed his troops to cover Smith's men while they reformed, and then made a fighting retreat to Boston. Now a local hero, Percy was given a local promotion to major general (effective only in America) in July, and the rank was officially recognized throughout the army in September of that year. He became a full general in America on 26 March 1776. He led a division at Long Island (Brooklyn) on 27 August and at the storming of Fort Washington on 16 November. In December he went with Sir Henry Clinton's expedition to capture Newport, Rhode Island, where he remained after Clinton's departure in January 1777 and became surprisingly popular there. However, he fell out with William Howe, who repeatedly interfered with Percy's command and criticized his decisions. Percy may, as might be expected with a young man owing his rapid rise a powerful family, have thought Howe insufficiently deferential to his social rank. He sailed for home on 5 May 1777, officially to inherit his mother's barony, but in fact to escape further disagreements with his commander in chief. Though promoted to lieutenant general in August, and to general in 1793, he saw no further active service.

In 1779 Percy divorced his wife and remarried. He inherited his father's title, estates, and parliamentary influence in 1786, and for a short time he supported the prime ministerial policies of William Pitt, the younger. Howe apart, most people found Percy modest and courteous. His generosity matched his exceptional wealth—he paid homeward fares and gratuities to the widows of his men who were killed in America—and was famous as a considerate landlord. He died in London on 10 July 1817.

SEE ALSO *Clinton, Henry; Howe, William; Lexington and Concord.*

BIBLIOGRAPHY

Bowler, R. A. *Logistics and the Failure of the British Army in North America 1775–1783.* Princeton, N.J.: Princeton University Press, 1975.

Gruber, Ira D. *The Howe Brothers and the American Revolution.* Chapel Hill, N.C.: University of North Carolina Press, 1974.

Mackesy, Piers. *The War for America 1775–1783.* London: Longman, 1964.

revised by John Oliphant

PERTH AMBOY, NEW JERSEY SEE *Amboy, New Jersey*

PETERSBURG, VIRGINIA.

25 April 1781. The combined forces of Benedict Arnold and William Phillips landed at City Point on 24 April and advanced the next day toward Petersburg, where Muhlenberg guarded important military supplies and tobacco with some one thousand militia. About noon the British, advancing along the road on the south bank of the Appomattox River, came in sight of the rebel position near Blandford, a village about a mile east of Petersburg. Phillips, an artilleryman by training, demonstrated a very high degree of skill in this action. He knew that he enjoyed a wide advantage in both numbers and quality of men, but also that he could not replace losses anywhere near as easily as the Americans. Therefore, Phillips refused to pay the price of a frontal attack and opted to maneuver Muhlenberg out of position. Jägers hit the flank of the American outpost line and drove them back on the main battle position. John Simcoe's Rangers and the light infantry fixed and enveloped the Americans, who put up a spirited defense for a while. But when the British finally got four of their own guns into position on the American right and the turning movement was detected by the defenders, Muhlenberg started an orderly withdrawal. By the time Phillips cautiously advanced to the high ground near Blandford Church, Muhlenberg had made it across the Appomattox and destroyed the bridge.

In this creditable little action, each side probably suffered sixty or seventy casualties. Phillips burned four thousand hogsheads of tobacco and several small vessels, but he did not destroy the buildings. The main body went on to destroy barracks and stores at Chesterfield Court

House on 27 April, while Arnold led a column to surprise and destroy a rebel force at Osborne's on the same day.

SEE ALSO *Arnold, Benedict; Muhlenberg, John Peter Gabriel; Osborne's (James River), Virginia; Phillips, William; Simcoe, John Graves; Virginia, Military Operations in.*

BIBLIOGRAPHY

Simcoe, John Graves. *A Journal of the Operations of the Queen's Rangers.* New York: New York Times, 1968.

revised by Robert K. Wright Jr.

PHILADELPHIA.

Located about one hundred miles up the Delaware from the Atlantic, Philadelphia was established in 1682 by William Penn as a Quaker colony. Its name means "City of Brotherly Love." The site was first occupied by the Delaware or Leni Lenape people, and the Swedes established a settlement there not later than 1643. Often considered the first truly American city in layout because of its grid pattern, it had parallel streets that were numbered and cross streets that were named after trees. As early as 1751, the city had illuminated its streets and organized a body of paid constables to replace the traditional nightwatch. In 1768, when London and Paris still contended with medieval filth, Philadelphia contracted for garbage collection and street cleaning. After a lusty growth in the decade preceding the Revolution, by 1775 Philadelphia's population of an estimated thirty-eight thousand was third in the British realm behind only London and Edinburgh. London had 750,000 people, followed by Edinburgh with just over 40,000. Philadelphia was the center of manufacturing in America. The first Continental Congress met at Philadelphia in 1774, and Congress sat there during most of the war.

When the British occupied this capital on 26 September 1777, nearly six hundred houses were unoccupied, over two hundred shops were closed, and fewer than fifty-five hundred males of military age (from eighteen to sixty years) were in town. Most of the latter were Quakers and Loyalists. Most scholars agree that the British occupation of Philadelphia served no real strategic purpose. Congress moved to York, carrying on its business there, and Philadelphia proved a poor base for the British. The American public saw more evidence of British decadence as stories of their wild parties and luxurious living leaked out. As Benson Bobrick has written, "the apparent moral contrast betweeen the self-indulgent Howe in Philadelphia and the spartan Washington at Valley Forge—Vice and Virtue—could not have been more pronounced" (*Angel in* the *Whirlwind,* p. 311). On 18 June 1778 the British army evacuated the city. Within hours, General Benedict Arnold led American forces back into their capital, which he commanded as military governor until March 1779.

SEE ALSO *Manufacturing in America; Monmouth, New Jersey.*

BIBLIOGRAPHY

Bobrick, Benson. *Angel in the Whirlwind: The Triumph of the American Revolution.* New York: Simon and Schuster, 1997.

Taaffe, Stephen R. *The Philadelphia Campaign, 1777–1778.* Lawrence: University Press of Kansas, 2003.

revised by Michael Bellesiles

PHILADELPHIA CAMPAIGN.

During the last week of 1776 and the first week of 1777, a disintegrating American army closing out a disappointing campaign won two small but sharp engagements with regular British and Hessian mercenary forces at Trenton and Princeton, in New Jersey. These unexpected setbacks cost the British their hard-earned ascendancy in New Jersey, as well as the widespread assumption that the Revolution would soon end favorably to them in military terms. The British commander in chief, William Howe, withdrew his troops to winter quarters in New York City, leaving a small garrisoning force to secure an enclave in eastern New Jersey near Perth Amboy. Howe's American counterpart, George Washington, briefly considered attacking that remnant of British strength, but instead he prudently led his rapidly dwindling force to winter camps in the hills around Morristown, New Jersey.

The Trenton-Princeton campaign was of incalculable morale and psychological advantage to American revolutionaries, and it was politically critical to the rebel governments; but it did nothing to preserve the existence of what Washington soon remembered as his "old" army. Indeed, his object in placing that force in the Morris County hills was less to protect it than to conceal its dissolution from the enemy and from Americans as well. Some scholars have argued that one dividend of the year-ending triumphs was the retention of a core group of about one thousand veterans of 1776 who agreed to remain in arms indefinitely, as a skeleton force around which Washington could build his "new" army. Surviving strength records for the Continental Army are nowhere more fragmentary than for the first three months of 1777, however, and this claim is very doubtful. From Morristown in February, March, and April, Washington presided over the almost complete departure of his veteran troops, as his terse hints to civilian

leaders and military peers suggest, while waiting for their long-promised replacements to materialize.

The sobering, but gratifying, end of the 1776 campaign persuaded an ideologically and fiscally reluctant Continental Congress to heed Washington's pleas to authorize the formation of a large "standing" army of soldiers enlisted for at least three years or the duration of the war. While recruiting officers scoured the hills of New England, ports in the Middle Atlantic states, and the southern backcountry, for men willing to accept these terms, Washington could do little except fret and try to keep the formal shell of his army alive. He borrowed militia forces from the Middle Atlantic states and deployed them with the dwindling remnants of his old force, maneuvering in and out of the New Jersey hills, both to beleaguer the enemy's Raritan River enclave and to deceive his foes about his temporary weakness. Washington expressed recurrent surprise that Howe and his aides did not see through this charade, and the contempt he came to feel toward his adversaries for their carelessness in this regard may explain some aspects of his behavior during the 1777 campaign.

William Howe, meanwhile, rightly considered Washington too strongly situated to attack, whatever his strength in troops, and instead contemplated how to launch a new campaign in the spring. The overall British campaign plan had evolved since the late fall of 1776 in personal discussions in London by Howe's subordinate, General John Burgoyne—who had returned to London to promote his ideas—and in correspondence between Howe and the British secretary of state for the American colonies, George Sackville Germain. That plan involved an invasion, led by Burgoyne, down the Lake Champlain–Hudson River corridor from Canada to New York City to isolate the militant head of the rebellion in New England from what Britain hoped was the more moderate rest of the continent. Howe's specific role in supporting this operation was left at best ambiguous in these discussions. Howe wanted try to end the rebellion in the Middle Atlantic states by carrying the fight to Pennsylvania. He was encouraged in this notion by Pennsylvania Loyalists, especially by that colony's former Assembly Speaker Joseph Galloway, who claimed that Pennsylvanians were eager to return to their king's side with protection from his army. Howe believed that he could achieve this and still return to New York, if necessary, to support Burgoyne's campaign.

Washington understood that he would soon engage Howe's forces, whether in the lower Hudson Valley or elsewhere in the Middle States, and he desperately tried to organize and if possible train the new recruits who began reaching his camps near Morristown in early May. Scholars have debated the social and economic character of the "new" army and its successors later in the war. A broad but disputed consensus suggests that the American regular army after 1776 was drawn from poorer and socially less secure groups than the broad cross-section of the populace who responded eagerly to the 1775 mobilization. This social transition had important implications for the army's military temperament and for its relationship to the larger society. Washington himself, viewing the new musters, speculated that recruiting agents were now meeting their goals from among "a Lower Class of People." Whatever their origins, the belated opening of the 1777 campaign allowed Washington to give at least some conditioning exercise to the recruits, even if more formal training was impossible. In June Howe moved large numbers of troops into New Jersey. By threatening to cross the flat lowlands toward the Delaware River, he hoped to lure Washington down from the Morris hills for the decisive engagement he craved. Washington might have willingly met his adversary in the hills, but he refused to fight on Howe's chosen ground. In early July, Howe withdrew his forces to Staten Island, where he loaded about fourteen thousand of them on the oceangoing transports of his brother, Adm. Richard Howe. The fleet put to sea on 23 July, leaving about seven thousand redcoats in New York City under the command of Howe's subordinate, General Henry Clinton.

Intelligence reports about the destination of the British force varied wildly and changed frequently. Washington knew that Howe might sail north to belabor the New England coast, trapping that region between Atlantic and interior invaders. He also might head south to secure a port like Charleston, or to harass the Chesapeake and Carolina coasts as their vital staple crops of tobacco and rice neared harvest. Or, Howe might lure the Continental Army off guard and return to New York to support Burgoyne's invasion of the Hudson. Delegates to the Continental Congress understandably credited threats to their own constituents most heavily, and that weak and regionally factionalized body exerted contradictory pressures on the army's leadership.

The Howe fleet was sighted in the mouth of the Delaware Bay on 29 July, supporting the view of many that the British in fact intended to rout the American civilian government and capture Philadelphia. Washington, who had marched his men back and forth across central New Jersey for two weeks, entered Pennsylvania the next day. The sudden disappearance of the fleet into the Atlantic upset these calculations, and strategic or political debates immediately resumed. Washington camped his force of ten thousand men in Bucks County, Pennsylvania, to await events, but he was prepared to march north or south as needed. Finally, on 23 August, reliable intelligence showed that the Howes were sailing up the Chesapeake Bay. General Howe still intended to campaign for Pennsylvania, if by a different route than he had initially imagined.

Howe's army began landing at the head of the Elk River in Maryland on 25 August. The men were considerably weakened by five weeks on shipboard, and the horses and other animals on which they depended for mobility were in even worse shape. It took several days for British commanders to prepare for overland campaigning. Howe's critics have complained that he used weeks of the summer campaign season bringing his army only fifty miles closer to Philadelphia than it had been in New Jersey. But until that time, the friendliness of Quaker Pennsylvanians was only an untested promise from Joseph Galloway. The disinclination for rebellion—identified at the time as "disaffection"—by inhabitants of Maryland's eastern shore and the lower counties of Delaware was well-known. Additionally, by opening the campaign near the narrow neck of the Delmarva Peninsula, Howe could threaten Washington's southern supply lines even as Burgoyne might succeed at severing the northern ones.

When it was clear that Howe would invade Pennsylvania from the south, Washington marched his army through Philadelphia, fretting about whether its members made a sufficiently "military" appearance to sustain morale among civilians and especially delegates to Congress. He brought the army to Wilmington, Delaware. Then, when the British left Head of Elk, he backtracked into Chester County, Pennsylvania, skirmishing and trying to stay between the redcoats and both Philadelphia on the one hand and, on the other, the vital American supply depots and forges in the upper Schuylkill Valley near Reading. By 10 September the Americans had formed behind Brandywine Creek, near the small village of Chads Ford. Howe's efforts the next day to force passage of that place provoked the first pitched battle of the 1777 campaign.

That engagement began in the morning with artillery fire and maneuvering in the British lines south of the Brandywine. Washington feared a direct assault across that stream, which was running low in the late summer heat, and he concentrated his forces there, detaching units to cover other fords several miles north and south of that point. Howe, who the previous year at Long Island had observed American difficulty responding to flanking attacks, left the Hessian general, Wilhelm von Knyphausen, with five thousand troops to maneuver and display noisily at Chads Ford. With his subordinate, Charles Lord Cornwallis, Howe marched nine thousand men northwest along the Brandywine to obscure fords across the two branches into which the creek divided. Washington either ignored or failed to receive warnings from soldiers and local farmers about this maneuver. Soldiers were presumed not to know the local territory well, while its inhabitants were mostly Quakers whose political reliability the army doubted. Joseph Galloway's boast that Pennsylvanians would eagerly deliver their province back to their king was about to be tested in the field.

Washington's Headquarters at Brandywine. *Shortly before the Battle of Brandywine in September 1777, General Washington moved his headquarters to this farmhouse near Chadds Ford.* © **RICHARD CUMMINS/CORBIS**

In the late afternoon of a hot day, Howe and Cornwallis's troops fell on the army's right flank, commanded by General John Sullivan of New Hampshire. Their assault was somewhat halting, which allowed Sullivan to prepare for the blow, but the attack unraveled the American line. Washington, once he was convinced that the attack was in earnest, rushed two divisions from the center of his lines, and eventually a third, into the breach. Fighting desperately for several hours, the Americans stabilized the situation sufficiently to organize an orderly retreat. The Battle of Brandywine resulted in an unequivocal victory for the British side, but the inexperienced Americans emerged from it with a sense that they could survive on the field with their enemy. Washington had casualties of about three hundred killed, as many wounded, and perhaps three hundred prisoners of war. Howe lost ninety men killed and about five times that many wounded. The British rested on the battlefield for a day while the Americans limped away toward Philadelphia.

When Congress received formal notice of the day's result (the cacophony of battle itself was audible in Philadelphia, and confused oral reports filtered into the city that night), it made plans to relocate the seat of government if necessary. The weak and embattled state government arrested and exiled to Virginia a group of mostly Quaker men of doubtful political loyalty. The documentary records of the Independence and war efforts were dispersed. The soon-to-be-named Liberty Bell was sent to the Lehigh Valley for safekeeping. Civilians of "disaffected" sentiment began to taunt their "patriot" neighbors and to prepare for occupation.

On September 16 advance elements of both armies stumbled into each other in Chester County and another decisive battle seemed likely. A fierce rainstorm, however, washed out the encounter. The Americans retreated to the upper Schuylkill Valley in search of dry munitions. Howe led his army to an obscure iron-making settlement on the Schuylkill River called Valley Forge. They burned the industrial facilities there and crossed the river into Philadelphia County. Congress adjourned on 18 September and went to Lancaster. When the state government arrived a few days later and claimed that town, the dispirited rump of Continental delegates trooped off to York, a relatively new frontier settlement west of the Susquehanna River, to await events.

On the night of 20 September, a detachment of about fifteen hundred American troops that Washington had sent under Pennsylvania general Anthony Wayne to shadow the British was attacked in their camp at Paoli by a much larger force of redcoats. The rebels were savaged, mostly receiving bayonet wounds, and the event was spun into the Paoli "Massacre," an important propaganda issue for the Patriot side. For the second year in a row it looked like the military part of the Revolution was disintegrating. Howe adroitly maneuvered his forces in the middle Schuylkill Valley to threaten both Philadelphia and the Reading storage depots. Washington chose to protect the latter, and on 26 September Philadelphia was lost. Thousands of prorevolutionary civilians fled west with the political bodies, but thousands more remained behind. The demeanor of even the evacuees was more determined—and far less visibly panicked—than had been the case in 1776 immediately before the Trenton surprise. This little-noted fact would soon have important military consequences.

Howe at first brought only 5,000 troops into the city proper, which extended between the Delaware and Schuylkill Rivers, and ran from modern Vine Street to South Street in the north and south. He had witnessed civil-military tensions in Boston and New York before 1777, and he needed time to prepare the town for occupation. He left nine thousand troops camped in and around Germantown, a small crafts and manufacturing village currently inside the municipal limits of Philadelphia but then a half-day's march to the northwest. In addition to political sensitivities, Howe needed to open the Delaware River and make contact with his brother's fleet. Richard Howe had left the army in the Elk River and sailed around the Delmarva Peninsula in late August to return to the Delaware Bay. Below Philadelphia, rebel authorities had blockaded the river by building fortifications on either bank and placing floating obstructions hazardous to vessels in the shipping lanes. On the New Jersey side of the river lay Fort Mercer. On an island in the channel near the mouth of the Schuylkill River, where Philadelphia's airport is today, the Americans built a facility called Mud Fort, or Fort Mifflin. Admiral Howe anchored his fleet just below this bottleneck and began cautious operations, assisted by his brother's troops, to reopen the river.

The British army, and especially the largely Loyalist or neutralist residual civilian population of Philadelphia, were dependent on the stores and provisions in the fleet's holds. William Howe's commissary general reported that the army had lived off the land during the late summer, reaching Philadelphia with slightly more provisions than it had taken from Head of Elk. Those supplies began to dwindle rapidly now. If the British could not feed civilians, they would risk the political consequences of their alienation. Suspecting that Howe's tactical attention was divided between the river and the land sides of his defensive lines, and impressed by his own army's resilience after Brandywine, Washington began planning an assault on Germantown. During the last week of September, the Continental Army moved cautiously down the northern side of the Schuylkill River. Morale at headquarters was boosted on 28 September when preliminary news arrived from the north of American general Horatio Gates's success in stopping Burgoyne's invading army in the first Battle of Freeman's Farm, near Saratoga, New York.

On 3 October Washington divided his army into four columns, one of which was largely made up of Pennsylvania militia troops. These forces marched along four parallel roads toward Germantown. Washington planned for the columns to reach the British lines simultaneously at dawn and to fall on the surprised redcoats in successive waves. The plan was too complicated for the brave but inexperienced American soldiers and officers to execute. The day began well. The American columns marched under cover of an early autumn fog, and they were successful in surprising the British sentries. The two middle columns converged on the Germantown Road running through the village and drove the enemy back. The militia column, marching along the Schuylkill River, however, became lost in the fog and never found its way up from the ravine and into the battle. The leftmost column arrived too late and fell in on the rear and flank of the third column. Those forces soon engaged each other in a "friendly fire" episode. General Howe, awakened at his billet near Philadelphia, raced north with reinforcements and rallied his troops. American units fired too freely and began to exhaust their ammunition. Gun smoke added to the fog as a disorienting force, and Continental soldiers began to panic and withdraw from the field. The retreat became general as officers were unable to calm their men. Washington's unfortunate effort to seize the large stone house of colonial Pennsylvania's former chief justice, Benjamin Chew—into which British soldiers had retreated—consumed too much of his attention and contributed to the momentum shift. Once the Americans were in full retreat they continued so for more than twenty miles, coming to an exhausted halt far into the wilds of upper Philadelphia County.

The British thus had their second successive indisputable victory over the Americans. The rebels suffered casualties of about 150 killed, 500 wounded, and over 400 captured, while Howe's total losses in all categories were about 550. The British held the field at the day's end. Continental officers, however, saw more evidence at Germantown to reinforce their impressions from Brandywine that the performance gap between their troops and the enemy was not that great. Their correspondence emphasized their misfortune in snatching defeat from the jaws of victory, and their firm expectation of soon having "another brush" with Howe's troops, from which many of them confidently expected to emerge victorious. The specific accuracy of this view is less important than the fact of its existence, and its implications for the army's willingness to endure. Until the Howe brothers succeeded in opening the Delaware River, many rebels doubted that the British would be able to consolidate their successes in Pennsylvania. And the enemy remained subject to news of reverses in other sectors. This recurred on 15 October, when Washington learned that Horatio Gates had followed up on his initial success against Burgoyne and defeated the British in a second battle near Saratoga. That defeat led to Burgoyne's effective surrender, and at least to the temporary removal of the northern British army from the field.

As these mixed events occurred on American battlefields, developments in parts of the military establishment ordinarily less visible than armies themselves converged to change the direction of the Philadelphia campaign. The complex logistical organizations that Congress had created in 1775 to supply and transport the army began to unravel during the early fall of 1777. Congress reformed the commissary department in the spring, replacing New England officers with merchants from the Middle Atlantic states thought better suited to the new "seat of war." The idea worked on paper but it failed disastrously in the field. The army discovered this only when food and supplies mysteriously failed to arrive in its camps in sufficient amounts in mid-October. By early November neither the ambitious dreams of the junior and middle-grade officers nor the far more cautious hopes of their headquarters-level superiors were realistic. Washington had to bring the army to rest at Whitemarsh, north of Germantown, to have any hope of feeding it, and he began to develop a more subtle plan to neutralize the British strategic and political advantages resulting from their capture of Philadelphia.

After November 1 the focus of the campaign—to the extent that it still had one—lay in the increasingly violent struggle for control of the Delaware River below Philadelphia. The Continental Army, as such, had only a modest formal role to play in that struggle. Washington brought it to the camp at Whitemarsh so that the struggling commissary functionaries would have a reliable stationary target to which to direct whatever food and supplies they obtained. The actual management of the river war fell to the commanders of the two forts, to the state militia forces in both Pennsylvania and New Jersey who supported their operations, and to a crazy-quilt collection of Continental and Pennsylvania "navy" forces who operated on the river in small row galley vessels with initiative and bravery but relatively little heed to centralized command.

From Whitemarsh, Washington developed an impromptu secondary "front" in support of the river battle, which spread around the entire perimeter of occupied Philadelphia. To relieve the ecological strain on his weak commissary, he detached small parties of troops to patrol in the countryside. These forces were especially useful in contesting British efforts to run overland night convoys to bring their own supplies from ships at anchor below the forts to Philadelphia. The extent to which the British—at the end of a 3,000-mile supply line from England and Ireland—faced material shortages before and during the winter of 1777–1778 has not been appreciated because of the folkloric concentration on the epic of the Valley Forge winter. Until the Delaware was opened—and the river was known to be vulnerable to icing over during the eighteenth century—it could not be presumed that they would be able to hold Philadelphia.

Whether by design or otherwise, detachments from camp also served to relieve strain on the morale of Continental soldiers, and to give them at least the illusion that they were doing what they had joined the army to do—engage in active military operations. The mood of the camp in mid-November began the cyclical oscillations between dejection, exhilaration, and grim determination that would characterize the army's experience at Valley Forge the next winter. The army itself became more diverse as a result of the relocation to Pennsylvania of troops from the northern army that had defeated general Burgoyne. As soon as he was confident that Burgoyne's Convention Army would remain in captivity, Washington ordered his commanders in the central Hudson Valley to send him large numbers of troops as he attempted to close the campaign season with a triumph. Thousands of these soldiers reached Whitemarsh in November. They arrived at a scene of stasis, frustration, and some real deprivation. The northern troops were mostly Yankees or New Yorkers, and they mixed uneasily with the Middle Atlantic and southern troops who dominated the "main" army. The New Englanders could boast of their success—indeed, they quickly elevated the term "burgoyne" to the status of a generic verb—and they understandably wondered aloud what their new comrades had accomplished that autumn.

Washington kept as many of his troops as possible on rotating detached duty in the countryside. Many of the New Englanders were sent to New Jersey, where they supported the efforts of local units to defend Fort Mercer. There, on 22 October, a British overland assault led by Hessian mercenaries was repulsed with heavy loss to the enemy. Other Continentals patrolled roads in the three Pennsylvania counties outside the city—Bucks, Philadelphia, and especially Chester—where they developed a taste for partisan skirmishing that would prove useful the next winter when the army struggled to pacify the occupied countryside. Regrettably, some of them also developed talents and a taste for abusing civilian "peasants," plundering the goods of supposedly "disaffected" Pennsylvanians, and similar activities that presented Washington with a constant menu of delicate public relations work with civilians. Soldiers, especially recruits from land-poor environments in northern New England and the southern backcountry, had never seen countryside as rich and prosperous as that in southeastern Pennsylvania's "best poor man's country." Their arrival there coincided exactly with the army's plunge into material misery. They were less apt to attribute their new travails to bureaucratic shortcomings than to the moral deficiencies of Pennsylvania's mixed population. The terms "Quaker" or "quaking" became handy substitutes for unfamiliar sociocultural groups.

The battle for control of the Delaware came to a crescendo during the first two weeks of November, and, perhaps inevitably—given the extent of the logistical immobility of so many Continental troops—the British finally prevailed. William Howe's forces slowly established battle platforms on the marshy ground behind Mud Island, where Fort Mifflin lay, while his brother's warships carefully maneuvered upriver toward the *chevaux de frise* which obstructed the channels. Placing the fort in nearly point-blank range, the British began bombarding it day and night, slowly reducing its crude structures and earthworks to a pulpy mass of earth and debris. The defenders heroically endured this bombardment and fought back as well as they could for as long as they could. Continental and state "navy" forces flitted about on the river in small row galleys and other vessels and did what they could to endanger Lord Howe's sailors and their expensive warships. In the end, access and artillery power prevailed. On 16 November, Fort Mifflin surrendered. The Americans continued to hold its companion facility, Fort Mercer, on the New Jersey side, but without the Pennsylvania installation it could not provide coverage of the wide river. Washington detached generals to consider the wisdom of holding Fort Mercer, but they could not report favorably on the plan, and that site was abandoned on 20 November.

The loss of the forts ensured that the British would be able to remain in Philadelphia. But what had they won? Admiral Howe completed the work of clearing the obstructions from the river channels and was able to bring his transports to the city's docks by early December. His brother was already receiving criticism in London and in army circles for becoming bogged down in Pennsylvania while Burgoyne's invasion was swallowed up. Discouraged, Howe offered the king his resignation in October. The battle for the river was an enormously noisy affair, and reports from civilians indicate that the roar of artillery fire and the explosion of several British ships that ran aground could be heard dozens of miles inland. This reminds us that the campaign for Pennsylvania was not fought on an empty or abstract topography, but rather that it involved the reactions and ultimately the allegiances of the members of a complex, plural, modern society. Pennsylvania never produced the caricatured Quaker and other eager subjects of the king, waiting patiently for their liberation from republican radicals, that Joseph Galloway had described to General Howe. Rather, it was the diverse and dynamic community that individuals from the generation of William Penn to that of Benjamin Franklin had struggled to understand and govern.

The same civilian diaries and letters that tell us about the noise of war also document the ability of civilians to learn about and for the most part successfully adapt to the confusion and danger of war. Pacifists and profiteers, and ordinary citizens in between those extremes, closely watched the occupation of their world, adapted to military ways, adopted military vocabularies, and otherwise taught themselves to survive. Benjamin Franklin, in Paris hoping to negotiate a treaty of alliance with France, may or may not have proclaimed that "Philadelphia has taken general Howe." But in the long run, and even in the medium, the social order of the Delaware Valley rose up, enveloped, and in a manner triumphed over the best intentions of its invaders.

SEE ALSO *Brandywine, Pennsylvania; Burgoyne, John; Burgoyne's Offensive; Clinton, Henry; Cornwallis, Charles; Fort Mercer, New Jersey; Fort Mifflin, Pennsylvania; Franklin, Benjamin; Galloway, Joseph; Gates, Horatio; Germain, George Sackville; Germantown, Pennsylvania, Battle of; Howe, Richard; Howe, William; Knyphausen, Wilhelm; Liberty Bell; Morristown Winter Quarters, New Jersey (6 January– 28 May, 1777); Paoli, Pennsylvania; Princeton, New Jersey; Quakers; Saratoga, First Battle of; Saratoga, Second Battle of; Sullivan, John; Trenton, New Jersey; Valley Forge Winter Quarters, Pennsylvania; Valley Forge, Pennsylvania; Wayne, Anthony; Whitemarsh, Pennsylvania.*

BIBLIOGRAPHY

Bodle, Wayne. *The Valley Forge Winter: Civilians and Soldiers in War.* University Park: Pennsylvania State University Press, 2002.

Jackson, John W. *The Pennsylvania Navy, 1775–1781: The Defense of the Delaware.* New Brunswick, N.J.: Rutgers University Press, 1974.

———. *With the British Army in Philadelphia, 1777–1778.* San Rafael, Cal.: Presidio Press, 1979.

Lengel, Edward G. *General George Washington: A Military Life.* New York: Random House, 2005.

Reed, John F. *Campaign to Valley Forge: July 1, 1777–December 19, 1777.* Philadelphia: University of Pennsylvania Press, 1965.

Taafe, Stephen. *The Philadelphia Campaign, 1777–1778.* Lawrence: University Press of Kansas, 2003.

revised by Wayne K. Bodle

PHILLIPS, WILLIAM. (c.1731–1781). British army officer. Phillips entered the Royal Military Academy, Woolwich, on 1 August 1740 and rose with a rapidity that suggests powerful patronage. Early in 1747 he became a "lieutenant fireworker"; from 1750 to 1756 he was quartermaster to the Royal Regiment of Artillery; and from 1 April 1756 he was a first lieutenant and aide-de-camp to Sir John Ligonier, lieutenant general of the ordnance. During the Seven Years' War he served in Germany, where he founded the Royal Artillery's first band. In 1758 he was given a brigade of artillery, and at Minden (1759) he led it through a wood to engage the French guns. At Warburg (30 July 1760) he brought his guns up at a gallop to support Lord Granby's cavalry brigade, an unprecedented feat that impressed friend and foe alike. He was made a lieutenant colonel in the army on 15 August. From 1763 to 1775 he served in the Mediterranean and Woolwich and became lieutenant governor of Windsor Castle; during this time he also had two affairs and six children. Through his friendship with Sir Henry Clinton, he held a parliamentary seat from 1774 to 1780.

Phillips served under John Burgoyne and Guy Carleton in Canada in 1776, and from July to December was commandant at St. Johns, where he supervised the building of Carleton's Lake Champlain flotilla. In 1777 he took charge of the preparatory and supply arrangements for Burgoyne's expedition, being promoted major of artillery in April. His diligence prompted Burgoyne to give him command of mixed formations in the field, and on 5–6 July it was his energetic siting of four guns on Mount Defiance, dominating Ticonderoga and the bridge that was the Americans' only means of retreat, that forced the rebels to abandon the fort. At Stillwater, New York, in the Battle of Saratoga, he led the British left (including Baron Riedesel's Germans) and on 19 September personally led the Fourth Foot into battle in an attack that saved the day. After Burgoyne's surrender at Saratoga on 17 October 1777, Phillips became a prisoner of war, taking command of the Convention Army upon Burgoyne's departure in April 1778. His captors so disliked his persistent protests about treatment of his men that, when in June he vociferously denounced the shooting of an officer by a sentry, they briefly locked him up. During the appalling winter march to Virginia (November 1778–1779), Phillips borrowed money to keep his men fed. In August he and Riedesel were paroled, an agreement honored by Congress only after Phillips protested to Washington. Reaching New York in November 1779, he was adviser to his friend Sir Henry Clinton and in July 1780 was promoted lieutenant colonel in the artillery. In October he and Riedesel were formally exchanged in October, and thus free to serve once more.

Clinton sent him with two thousand men to the Chesapeake, where he was to join and take over from Arnold, secure the James and Elizabeth Rivers, and support Charles Cornwallis's operations. On 25 April he defeated a body of militia near Petersburg, Virginia; two days later his artillery destroyed a small American flotilla at Osborne's landing, on the James River; and on 30 April he directed a successful raid against rebel stores at Manchester. The next day at Osborne's landing he went down with typhoid fever and died at Petersburg on the 13 May 1781.

SEE ALSO *Burgoyne's Offensive; Champlain Squadrons; Convention Army; Osborne's (James River), Virginia; Petersburg, Virginia; Riedesel, Baron Friedrich Adolphus; Saratoga Surrender.*

BIBLIOGRAPHY
Davis, Robert P. *Where a Man Can Go: Major General William Phillips, British Royal Artillery, 1731–1781.* Westport, Conn.: Greenwood Press, 1999.

revised by John Oliphant

PHIPP'S FARM. 9 November 1775. Alternate name for Lechmere Point.

SEE ALSO *Lechmere Point, Massachusetts.*

PICKENS, ANDREW. (1739–1817). Militia general. South Carolina. Born near Paxton, Pennsylvania, on 19 September 1739, Andrew Pickens moved south with his parents and other Scotch-Irish families through the Shenandoah Valley, where they lived for a while. They ultimately settled on an 800-acre holding on Waxhaw Creek, South Carolina. Two years after taking part in James Grant's expedition against the Cherokee in 1761, Pickens and his brother sold their inheritance and obtained lands on Long Cane Creek in South Carolina. At the outbreak of the Revolution he was a farmer and justice of the peace. As a captain of militia, he took part in the conflict at Ninety Six on 19 November 1775. His services in the war against the Loyalists over the next two years brought him promotion to colonel, and he contributed greatly to the Patriot victory at the battle of Kettle Creek, Georgia, on 14 February 1779.

After the surrender of Charleston in May 1780 and the subsequent conquest of the southern states by the British, Pickens surrendered a fort in the Ninety-Six district and, with 300 of his men, went home on parole. When Captain James Dunlap's Loyalists plundered his plantation, Pickens gave notice that his parole was no longer valid and took the field again. With Francis

Marion and Thomas Sumter he was one of the most prominent partisan leaders in the subsequent guerrilla warfare of the region.

For his part in the victory at Cowpens, South Carolina, on 17 January 1781, he was given a sword by Congress and a commission as brigadier general from his state. In April of that year he raised a regiment of "state regulars" who were to be paid according to Sumter's Law, which permitted soldiers to take their pay in plunder gained from Loyalists. With these forces, Pickens had an active part in the capture of Augusta, Georgia, and the unsuccessful siege of Ninety-Six, May–June 1781. He and his troops also took part in the last pitched battle in the south, at Eutaw Springs, on 8 September 1781, where he was wounded. He contributed to the final operations in the South by carrying out punitive expeditions against the Cherokee in 1782.

Elected to represent the Ninety-Six district in the Jacksonboro Assembly in 1783, Pickens served in the state legislature until 1788, returning in 1796–1799, and 1812–1813. He was also elected to the state senate, in which he served from 1790 to 1791, and to Congress, from 1793 to 1795. In 1794 he became major general of the South Carolina militia, and for many years was engaged in dealing with the Indians on boundary matters. Pickens favored a peace policy, helping to negotiate the Hopewell and Coleraine Treaties (1786 and 1796, respectively). He died at his Tamassee, South Carolina, plantation on 11 August 1817.

SEE ALSO *Kettle Creek, Georgia; Pickens's Punitive Expeditions.*

BIBLIOGRAPHY

Andrew Pickens Collection. San Marino, Calif.: Henry E. Huntington Library.

Andrew Pickens Papers. Columbia, S.C.: South Caroliniana Library.

Waring, Alice Noble. *The Fighting Elder: Andrew Pickens, 1739–1817.* Columbia: University of South Carolina Press, 1962.

revised by Michael Bellesiles

PICKENS'S PUNITIVE EXPEDITIONS.

Andrew Pickens first fought against the Cherokees in 1761. As a major of militia he led the forces that destroyed their settlements in the western Carolinas in the summer of 1776, winning a key victory at Tugaloo River on 10 August 1776. In 1779 the Cherokees again allied with the British in hopes of retaining their lands after the war ended. Starting in late August, General Pickens led a campaign of less than three weeks in which he killed forty Cherokees, burned thirteen towns, and took many

prisoners while sustaining a loss of only two wounded. In his *Memoirs* (1827), Harry Lee commented on 'Pickens's effective use of mounted troops, against which the Indians proved to be surprisingly vulnerable. In 1782 Pickens and Colonel Elijah Clarke again moved against the Cherokees, first in March and April, then in September and October. These two swift campaigns forced the Cherokees to surrender all their lands south of the Savannah River and east of the Chattahoochie to the state of Georgia.

SEE ALSO *Georgia Expedition of Wayne.*

revised by Michael Bellesiles

PICKERING, TIMOTHY. (1745–1829).

Continental officer, adjutant general, quartermaster general. Massachusetts. Born on 17 July 1745 into a family that had been prominent in Salem since 1637, he graduated from Harvard College in 1763. He was employed in Salem in the office of the Essex County register of deeds until the eve of the war, as register from October 1774. Meanwhile, he studied law and in 1768 was admitted to the bar. He also studied military history and tactics beginning in 1766, when Governor Francis Bernard appointed him a lieutenant in the Essex County militia. His neighbors elected him to the town's committee of correspondence, and in February 1775 the Massachusetts Provincial Congress appointed him colonel of the First Regiment of the Essex County militia. His *Easy Plan of Discipline for a Militia,* published in 1775, was adopted by Massachusetts the next year and was widely used in the American army until replaced by the famous manual of Steuben after 1778.

Not initially an advocate of armed resistance to British authority, he "delayed rather than lead his regiment" in the Lexington Alarm of 19 April 1775 (ANB). He took no part in the siege of Boston or the 1776 campaign. Recognizing that no reconciliation was possible, early in 1777 Pickering led a volunteer unit to reinforce Washington's army at Morristown. Because Horatio Gates wanted to resign as adjutant general, Washington prevailed upon Pickering to replace him. Despite his lack of military experience, Pickering performed his exacting and tedious duties with competence, and he even showed a good grasp of tactics. He saw the dangers of Washington's plan for the Battle of Germantown (4 October 1777) and even urged the commander in chief to bypass the strong point at the Chew House.

When Congress organized a new Board of War (made up of persons outside Congress) during the Conway Cabal episode, it pulled Pickering out of Washington's headquarters to be a member. He was elected to the board on 7 November 1777, but since nobody qualified to take over as adjutant general was immediately available, he did not leave this post until 13 January 1778. Washington named Pickering to succeed Nathanael Greene as quartermaster general on 5 August 1780. Pickering wrote back on the 11th that since the appointment was altogether unexpected, it would be some time before he could wind up his affairs in Philadelphia. When Pickering had not arrived by 15 September, Washington sent him orders to report. Holding this vital post until 25 July 1785, he showed "indefatigable industry and iron determination" (DAB). A splenetic conservative—a curmudgeon devoid of illusions—on 6 March 1778 he wrote: "If we should fail at last, the Americans can blame only their own negligence, avarice, and want of almost every public virtue."

After going into business in Philadelphia he moved to the Wyoming Valley in early 1787 and was involved in the dispute between Pennsylvania authorities and the Connecticut settlers. He became "land poor," and to improve his finances he decided to seek a post in the new federal government. In the fall of 1790 President Washington appointed him to negotiate with the Senecas to prevent them from going to war against the United States. In what his modern biographer calls the "high point" of his public career, Pickering "proved patient, understanding, and sympathetic in his several negotiations with the Seneca, Oneida and other tribes. He made every effort to protect Native American peoples from exploitation by greedy land speculators" (ANB). Washington rewarded him with the job of postmaster general on 12 August 1791 and promoted him to secretary of war on 2 January 1795, replacing Henry Knox. He was secretary of state from August 1795 until 10 May 1800 but was dismissed after intriguing with Alexander Hamilton and other Federalists against President John Adams. He went back to Wyoming, but his Federalist friends arranged for the purchase of his lands and his return to Massachusetts, where they hoped he might come to the aid of the party. He was a senator from Massachusetts from 1803 to 1811 and became a formidable debater. Pickering's years in the Senate were marred by his leadership of an abortive scheme in 1803–1804 to take New York, New Jersey, and the five New England states out of the union to form a northern confederacy. Denied reelection to the Senate, he was elected to the House and served from 1813 to 1817. He died at Salem on 29 January 1829.

SEE ALSO *Conway Cabal.*

BIBLIOGRAPHY

Clarfield, Gerard H. *Timothy Pickering and the American Republic.* Pittsburgh, Pa.: University of Pittsburgh Press, 1980.

Pickering, Octavius. *The Life of Timothy Pickering.* 4 vols. Boston: Little, Brown, 1867–1873.

revised by Harold E. Selesky

PIECEMEAL.

PIECEMEAL. "Piecemeal" is the military term for committing portions of a command into action as they become available on the battlefield. It is good tactics provided it is possible to build up a preponderant force (superior combat power) faster than the enemy, and it is common in a "meeting engagement."

SEE ALSO *Meeting Engagement.*

revised by Mark M. Boatner

PIGOT, SIR ROBERT.

PIGOT, SIR ROBERT. (1720–1796). British general. A small, strongly built man, Pigot served in the War of the Austrian Succession, and in Minorca and Scotland from 1749 to 1752. Lieutenant colonel of the Thirty-eighth Foot from 1764, he went to America in 1774. In 1775 Pigot was with Lord Percy's column sent to rescue the force falling back from Concord. At Bunker Hill, as a local brigadier general, he led the left wing with great courage and distinction, being promoted colonel of the Thirty-eighth on 11 December 1776. He commanded William Howe's Second Brigade at Long Island (27 August 1776). In May 1777 he inherited his brother's baronetcy; he became commander of the Rhode Island garrison on 15 July and was promoted major general on 29 August. In August 1778 he held Newport against John Sullivan's army and comte d'Estaing's fleet, and on 29 August he tried unsuccessfully to dislodge Sullivan from Butts Hill. He gave up the command in October and sailed for home in 1779. He was made lieutenant general on 20 November 1782.

SEE ALSO *Long Island, New York, Battle of; Newport, Rhode Island (September 1777).*

revised by John Oliphant

PINCKNEY, CHARLES.

PINCKNEY, CHARLES. (1757–1824). Militia officer, governor of South Carolina, statesman, diplomat. South Carolina. Born on 26 October 1757 in Charleston, South Carolina, Pinckney studied law with his father just before the Revolution. Elected to the South Carolina House of Representatives in 1779, he was a militia lieutenant at Savannah, Georgia, in October 1779 and became a prisoner of war when Charleston surrendered on 12 May 1780. Refusing to follow his father's example of pledging allegiance to the British Crown, Pinckney remained a prisoner until June 1781. He served in Congress from 1 November 1784 until 21 February 1787. Pinckney attended the Constitutional Convention of 1788, where he made numerous proposals that became part of the finished document and successfully insisted that the Constitution defend slavery.

After working hard to achieve ratification of the Constitution in South Carolina, he was governor of that state from January 1789 to December 1792. His alienation from the Federalists may have started when his cousin, Thomas Pinckney, was given the post of minister to Great Britain—a position that he wanted for himself. He denounced John Jay's treaty in 1795, defeated his brother-in-law, Henry Laurens, Jr., to win a third term as governor in 1796, and in 1798 was elected to the U.S. Senate with the same back-country Republican support that enabled him to beat Laurens. He led Republican senators against the administration, and later managed Thomas Jefferson's presidential campaign in South Carolina, which led to his estrangement from his strongly Federalist cousins, Charles Cotesworth Pinckney and Thomas Pinckney. His effective support of Jefferson, who became president in 1801, won him an appointment that year as minister to Spain.

Returning to Charleston in January 1806, Pickney served a fourth terms as governor. Elected to Congress in 1814, Pinckney fought for Missouri's admission as a slave state in 1820, insisting that Congress could never touch that institution. At the end of this term, Pinckney retired to Charleston, South Carolina, where he died on 29 October 1824.

SEE ALSO *Pinckney, Charles Cotesworth; Pinckney, Thomas.*

BIBLIOGRAPHY

Matthews, Marty D. *Forgotten Founder: The Life and Times of Charles Pinckney.* Columbia, S.C.: University of South Carolina Press, 2004.

Pinckney Family Papers. Washington, D.C.: Library of Congress.

revised by Michael Bellesiles

PINCKNEY, CHARLES COTESWORTH. (1746–1825).

Brevet brigadier general in the Continental army, statesman, diplomat. South Carolina. Charles Cotesworth Pinckney was born on 14 February 1745 in Charleston, South Carolina. When his father became the agent representing South Carolina's interests in England in 1753, young Charles and his brother, Thomas, went to live London with their parents. After graduating from Oxford, 1764, Pinckney went on to further his training as a barrister at the Middle Temple, and was admitted to the bar in 1769. Pinckney then returned to South Carolina and was immediately elected to the legislature, where he sided with the Patriot cause. Already very wealthy, in 1773 he married Sarah Middleton, the daughter of the extremely rich Henry Middleton, who was prominent in South Carolina politics.

At the outbreak of the Revolution, Pinckney moved rapidly to prepare South Carolina for war. On 22 April 1775 he led a group in seizing British munitions. As a member of the Committee on Intelligence, he worked to enlist support from the backcountry and to plan the defense of Charleston, even while he chaired the committee that drafted the conservative constitution adopted by South Carolina in March 1776. Pinckney became senior captain of the First Regiment of South Carolina troops on 17 June 1775. Promoted almost immediately, he served under William Moultrie in the defense of Fort Sullivan (later renamed Fort Moultrie) on 28 June. Promoted to colonel on 16 September 1776, he took leave from his regiment and served as General George Washington's aide-de-camp at Brandywine and Germantown in the fall of 1777. He then led his regiment in an abortive expedition against Florida in 1778.

Meanwhile, Pinckney continued to advance his political career. He became president of the South Carolina senate in January 1779. He was involved in the military alarms and excursions occasioned by Augustin Prevost's appearance at Charleston on 11 and 12 May 1779. During the Charleston operations that occurred during the following year, Pinckney commanded Fort Moultrie. There was little action at this location, but Pinckney's insistence on the defense of the city led to Benjamin Lincoln's disastrous surrender on 12 May 1780. Pinckney spent the rest of the war on parole in Philadelphia, being included in an official prisoner exchange in February 1782. Rejoining the army, he served until 3 November 1783, on which date he was brevetted as a brigadier general.

In 1782 Pinckney was elected to the South Carolina legislature, and after the war he resumed his law practice and re-entered public life. Although a zealous Anglican and conservative Federalist, he strongly advocated disestablishment and opposed the imposition of any religious test for political office. After taking a prominent part in the Federal Convention (1787), the state convention that ratified the Constitution (1788), and the state constitutional convention of 1790, he set some sort of a record in declining presidential appointments. In 1791 he declined command of the army, leaving Arthur St. Clair to take the post. Both Pinckney and his brother-in-law, Edward Rutledge, turned down President Washington's urgent request that one of them become an associate justice on the Supreme Court. In addition, he twice refused the post of Secretary of War, and in August 1795 he declined to become Secretary of State.

Finally accepting an offer from Washington, he went to Paris in December 1796 as James Monroe's successor in the post of Minister to France. The revolutionary government in power there refused to accept Pinckney's credentials, however, and he subsequently was threatened with arrest. In February 1797 he stormed off to Holland, but in October of that same year he was back in Paris on a special diplomatic mission that resulted in the attempt by three French representatives to extort bribes from Pinckney in order to secure treaty negotiations. Dubbed the "XYZ Affair" (because the French officials were designated by these letters in American diplomatic dispatches), the extortion attempt failed due to Pinckney's integrity. In fact, when "X" made his proposal to Pinckney and pressed for an answer, Pinckney replied, "It is No! No! Not a sixpence!" The affair led many in America to call for war against France, and in preparation for that possibility Pinckney was commissioned as a major general on 19 July 1798. In this capacity he commanded the forces and installations in Virginia and Kentucky, and in the territories to the south. He served until 15 June 1800, after which he ran for the office of vice president as the Federalist nominee. He was that party's (unsuccessful) presidential candidate in 1804 and 1808, as well. He died in Charleston, South Carolina, on 16 August 1825.

SEE ALSO *Charleston Expedition of Clinton in 1780; Pinckney, Thomas.*

BIBLIOGRAPHY

Pinckney Family Papers. Washington, D.C.: Library of Congress.

Zahniser, Marvin R. *Charles Cotesworth Pinckney: Founding Father.* Chapel Hill: University of North Carolina Press, 1967.

revised by Michael Bellesiles

PINCKNEY, THOMAS. (1750–1828).

Continental officer, South Carolina governor, diplomat. South Carolina. Born in Charleston, South Carolina, on 23 October 1750, Pinckney shared a European education with his elder brother, Charles Cotesworth Pinckney, graduating from Oxford in 1768 before studying law at the Middle Temple and being admitted to the bar in 1774. He returned to Charleston the same year and set up his legal practice. Early the next year he became a lieutenant of rangers and—like his brother—captain in the First South Carolina Regiment (17 June 1775). He performed highly successful service as a recruiting and training officer before

assuming the duties of a military engineer at Fort Johnson at Charleston Harbor. After having an orchestra seat while his brother and Colonel Moultrie defended Fort Sullivan, Thomas was assigned to defend that post in August 1776. Except for a few months' absence recruiting in Maryland, Virginia, and North Carolina, he stayed two years at what was now called Fort Moultrie. On 17 May 1778 he was promoted to major, again helped organize and train new troops, and then took part in the unsuccessful expedition against Florida. As aide-de-camp to Lincoln he was at Stono Ferry, and as aide de camp to d'Estaing participated in the attack on Savannah on 9 October 1779.

Pinckney served in the legislature of 1778 and kept up his law practice while also serving in the army. In May 1779 the British burned his plantation and liberated his slaves. In 1780 he took part in the defense of Charleston, but he was sent from the city before the final stages of the siege to hurry forward reinforcements and escaped capture. After making his way to Washington's headquarters, he returned to the South, became aide-de-camp to Gates on 3 August 1780, was seriously wounded at Camden on 16 August, and was taken prisoner. Paroled to Philadelphia with his brother, Charles Cotesworth Pinckney, who had been captured at Charleston, Thomas Pinckney was exchanged in December 1780. In September 1781 he was recruiting in Virginia, where he met Lafayette and served under the latter's command through the siege of Yorktown; they became good friends. Pinckney also was a partisan of Gates, and on his return to South Carolina at the end of the war published a defense of him.

Pinckney became a successful Charleston lawyer after the war and served as governor from 1787 to 1789. In 1791 Washington made him minister to Great Britain. Though not very successful as ambassador to that nation, and offended by John Jay's appointment to negotiate a treaty with Britain, Pinckney enjoyed a triumph in his negotiations with Spain. With a combination of bold persistence (which had not worked in London) and unfailing tact, his efforts resulted in Pinckney's Treaty of 27 October 1795. Back in London, Thomas worked unsuccessfully to win Lafayette's release from an Austrian prison. Pinckney returned to South Carolina in September 1796, having been nominated by the Federalists for vice president. But Hamilton's conniving to have him elected president in order to defeat John Adams resulted in Pinckney's getting neither post. (His brother Charles Cotesworth lost out in a similar manner in the 1800 election, while their cousin Charles was building his own political career in the Jeffersonian camp.) He served in Congress from 1797 to 1801, when he retired from politics. He was appointed major general on 27 March 1812, but as commander of the region from North Carolina to the Mississippi he saw no active service during the War of 1812. He succeeded Andrew Jackson after the Creek War

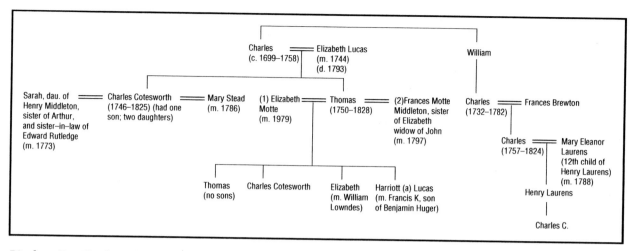

Pinckney Family of South Carolina. THE GALE GROUP

and negotiated the peace treaty. He died in Charleston on 2 November 1828.

SEE ALSO *Estaing, Charles Hector Théodat, Comte d'; Lafayette, Marquis de; Pinckney, Charles Cotesworth; Savannah, Georgia (9 October 1779); Southern Theater, Military Operations in; Spanish Participation in the American Revolution.*

BIBLIOGRAPHY

Leigh, Frances. *A Founding Family: The Pinckneys of South Carolina.* New York: Harcourt Brace Jovanovich, 1978.

Pinckney Family Papers. Library of Congress. Washington, D.C.

Rogers, Charles C. *Charleston in the Age of the Pinckneys.* Norman: University of Oklahoma Press, 1969.

revised by Michael Bellesiles

PINCKNEY FAMILY OF SOUTH CAROLINA.

During the colonial period, members of a few dozen families, including the Pinckneys, Rutledges, and Middletons, controlled South Carolina's Commons House of Assembly and dominated the Council (the upper house) until 1765, when they began to lose some power to British-born placeholders. The families intermarried to the point where they created a vast cousinage; the Pinckneys, for example, strengthened their ties by marrying into the Laurens and Middleton families. The first Charles Pinckney (1699?–1758) was chief justice of South Carolina (1752–1753) and the colony's agent in England (1753–1758). His nephew, the second Charles (1732–1782), father of the third Charles, was a wealthy lawyer and planter who was first president of the first South Carolina Provincial Congress (January–June 1775). He fled

Charleston in April 1780 but voluntarily returned in June and gave his parole. Two years later, his estate was amerced 12 percent; it would have been confiscated had not the rest of the family, including his son Charles and nephew Charles Cotesworth, been prominent Patriots.

SEE ALSO *Middleton Family of South Carolina; Pinckney, Charles; Pinckney, Charles Cotesworth; Pinckney, Thomas; Rutledge, Edward Ned.*

BIBLIOGRAPHY

Edgar, Walter B., and N. Louise Bailey, eds. *Biographical Directory of the South Carolina House of Representatives.* Vol. 2: *The Commons House of Assembly, 1692–1775.* Columbia: University of South Carolina Press, 1977.

revised by Harold E. Selesky

PISCATAWAY, NEW JERSEY.

10 May 1777. Major General Adam Stephen played a major role in the skirmishing between American patrols and British foraging expeditions in northern New Jersey during the early months of 1777. This role fell to him in large measure because his Virginia regiments had not been affected by the expiration of enlistments as the majority of units in the main army had been. British forces occupied positions stretching from Brunswick to Amboy. Acting on his own authority, Stephen decided to make a surprise attack on Piscataway, about midway between the extremes of the British line; the garrison consisted of the Highlanders of the Forty-second Foot (Black Watch) supported by six companies of light infantry. Stephen formed an 800-man strike force from detachments of the regiments in his division, but the British detected its approach and augmented the normal picket with another

300 men. The raiders collided with that outpost and a fight ensued which lasted about an hour and one-half until additional British troops arrived and forced Stephen's men to withdraw. Stephen reported that he had lost 3 killed and 24 wounded; he felt that the British had lost about 70 dead and another 120 wounded. British accounts claimed that they had lost one man wounded and estimated American casualties at 11 killed, 17 wounded, 33 captured, and an additional 73 missing. The truth is probably in between, as several Hessian accounts put the American casualties around 50 or 60 and the British put them closer to 30. Stephen filed his official report two days later, and Washington immediately rebuked him for exaggeration, citing contradictory reports he had received from other officers. While the skirmish itself had no military significance, it severely strained the "always uneasy relations" between the two generals (Ward, pp. 168–172).

SEE ALSO *Stephen, Adam.*

BIBLIOGRAPHY
Ward, Harry M. *Major General Adam Stephen and the Cause of American Liberty.* Charlottesville: University Press of Virginia, 1989.

revised by Robert K. Wright Jr.

PITCAIRN, JOHN. (1722–1775). British officer. Born at Dysart, Scotland, the son of a minister, he was commissioned a lieutenant in the Royal Marines in 1746. He was promoted to captain on 8 June 1756 and to major on 19 April 1771. He commanded a battalion of four hundred marines sent to garrison Boston in November 1774. He had a reputation for piety as well as for being a tough but fair disciplinarian who was well liked by his men, living with them in barracks "to keep them from their pernicious rum" (ANB). General Thomas Gage appointed him to settle disputes between soldiers and civilians, in which role he earned the respect of the people of Boston.

Gage named him as second in command of the expedition to Lexington and Concord on 19 April 1775. He led the advanced party of six light infantry companies onto Lexington Green in the early morning of the 19th, deployed his men when he saw Captain John Parker's minutemen in formation alongside the road to Concord, and lost control of the situation for several fateful minutes. When a shot rang out (or perhaps the sound was just the fizzle of powder exploding in pan of a flintlock), the light infantrymen fired into the minutemen, and although Pitcairn did his utmost to stop this unauthorized fire, eight Americans died. Pitcairn, a major of marines, was that day in command of

soldiers from six different infantry regiments. Neither Pitcairn nor the soldiers had trained or worked together before, and perhaps this unfamiliarity and lack of cohesion led the soldiers to disobey the major's positive order not to fire into the American ranks. The British marched on to Concord, but on the return to Boston they were almost engulfed by American militiamen firing from behind cover every step of the way. Pitcairn's horse, wounded at Lexington, finally threw him and ran into the American lines with a brace of his pistols on its saddle.

At the battle of Bunker Hill on 17 June 1775, Pitcairn commanded the marine battalion that was part of Robert Pigot's left wing demonstrating in front of the Breed's Hill redoubt. In the final assault, he led his men forward with the cry of, "Now for the glory of the marines." In one of the final volleys from the redoubt, his chest was crushed by a bullet said to have been fired by an African American, Peter Salem, an encounter that John Trumbull featured in the background of his painting, *The Death of General Warren at the Battle of Bunker's Hill.* Pitcairn was carried to a boat by his son, a marine lieutenant, but despite the efforts of Dr. Thomas Kast to stop the flow of blood, he died at Boston either later that day or early the next morning. He left eleven children. Ezra Stiles, Congregational minister at Newport and later president of Yale College, provided an appropriate epitaph when he wrote in his "Literary Diary" on 21 August 1775 that Pitcairn was "a good man in a bad cause."

SEE ALSO *Lexington and Concord.*

revised by Harold E. Selesky

PITCAIRN'S PISTOLS. Major John Pitcairn of the Royal Marines led the advanced guard of the British raid on Lexington and Concord, Massachusetts, on 19 April 1775. His horse threw him during the action at Fiske Hill near Concord and bolted into the American lines, where the two silver-mounted Scottish pistols that he carried on his horse furniture were captured by an American militiaman. The pistols were acquired by Major General Israel Putnam, who carried them during the war. They are now in the Lexington Historical Society.

SEE ALSO *Pitcairn, John.*

BIBLIOGRAPHY
Fischer, David H. *Paul Revere's Ride.* New York: Oxford University Press, 1994.

revised by Harold E. Selesky

PITCHER, MOLLY SEE *Molly Pitcher Legend.*

PITT, WILLIAM (THE ELDER) SEE *Chatham, William Pitt, First Earl of.*

PITTSBURGH. Previously Fort Pitt. Located west of the Alleghenies at the point where the Allegheny and Monongahela Rivers join to form the Ohio, the Forks of the Ohio—as the place was first known—was of key strategic importance as soon as white men started pushing into the Ohio Valley. In 1731 a few Frenchmen tried to establish a settlement but were soon driven off by the Shawnees. In 1748 the colonies of Pennsylvania and Virginia, both of which claimed the area, started trading activities that brought them into conflict with the French and led to the last of the colonial wars. In April 1754 a French force began construction of Fort Duquesne and subsequently defeated expeditions under Washington and Braddock to drive it out. The Forbes expedition forced the French to destroy Fort Duquesne, and Bouquet occupied the site on 25 November 1758 on behalf of the British, beginning reconstruction of the fortification under its new name of Fort Pitt.

In October 1772 General Gage ordered Fort Pitt abandoned, and it was partially dismantled. In January 1774 Dr. John Connolly occupied the place with an armed body of Virginia men to defy the Pennsylvania claim to the disputed region. But Connolly turned his attention to the local Indians, launching attacks that led to Dunmore's War in 1774. With the start of the Revolution, Virginia maintained Fort Pitt, using it as the headquarters for its western militia operations. But in 1777 increased attack from British, Indians, and Loyalists led Congress to claim control of the fort, appointing General Edward Hand its commander. During the rest of the Revolution, Pittsburgh was American army headquarters for western operations. Fort Pitt and West Point were the only military fortifications maintained by the U.S. Army after the Revolution.

SEE ALSO *Colonial Wars; Connolly, John; Dunmore's (or Cresap's) War; Forbes's Expedition to Fort Duquesne; Western Operations.*

revised by Michael Bellesiles

PLAINS OF ABRAHAM. 13 September 1759. On the night of 12–13 September 1759, forty-five hundred British troops led by Major General James Wolfe landed in a cove on the north side of the St. Lawrence above Quebec City and managed to climb the bluff to a thousand-yard-wide, relatively level area about a mile from the western walls of the city. Wolfe's reckless plan put the bulk of the army that had invested Quebec since 28 June in an untenable position; it could not be resupplied, French light forces were closing on its rear; and the impregnable walls of the city were to its front. Wolfe was saved from disaster and ignominy by the even more foolish response of the French commander, the marquis de Montcalm, who unaccountably decided to accept Wolfe's offer of battle. The French fought valiantly, some approaching to as close as forty yards from the British line, which stood stock-still, reserving its fire until the French were close enough. When the British opened fire with rolling platoon volleys and in some cases with volleys by entire regiments, the French line shattered and the men fled to safety behind the walls of Quebec. Both Wolfe and Montcalm were mortally wounded. Wolfe's senior unwounded subordinate, Brigadier General George Townshend, called off the pursuit and set about besieging the city from the west. The French were so rattled that they capitulated without resistance on 18 September 1759.

SEE ALSO *Colonial Wars; Wolfe, James.*

BIBLIOGRAPHY

Anderson, Fred. *Crucible of War: The Seven Years' War and the Fate of Empire in British North America, 1754–1766.* New York: Knopf, 2000.

revised by Harold E. Selesky

PLAINS OF ABRAHAM. 28 April 1760. Brigadier General James Murray, who commanded the British garrison of Quebec City over the winter of 1759–1760, sought to stop a French force advancing from Montreal, under the chevalier de Levis, first at the village of Ste. Foy, six miles from Quebec (from which an alternate name of the ensuing battle is derived). Murray pulled back, however, to the Plains of Abraham about a mile from the city, roughly the same site on which James Wolfe had defeated the marquis de Montcalm on 13 September 1759. The Second Battle of Quebec was much more sanguinary than the first, and it resulted in a British defeat that left Murray penned up in Quebec. The British kept control of Quebec, and with it the base from which to launch the conquest of the remainder of New France, only because the first ship to make its way up the still ice-choked St. Lawrence that spring, on 12 May, was a British vessel, HMS *Vanguard.*

BIBLIOGRAPHY

Anderson, Fred. *Crucible of War: The Seven Years' War and the Fate of Empire in British North America, 1754–1766*. New York: Knopf, 2000.

Harold E. Selesky

PLAINS OF ABRAHAM. 15 November

1775. After completing his famous march from Boston across Maine to Quebec city, Benedict Arnold crossed the St. Lawrence with seven hundred men, climbed the bluffs west of Quebec City, and established himself roughly on the same piece of relatively flat ground where the British under James Wolfe had defeated the French under the marquis de Montcalm sixteen years earlier (13 September 1759). His attempt to bluff the Quebec garrison into surrender was unsuccessful.

SEE ALSO *Arnold, Benedict; Arnold's March to Quebec; Canada Invasion.*

revised by Harold E. Selesky

PLAINS OF ABRAHAM. 6 May 1776.

At the end of a long winter in which Quebec City was loosely besieged by American forces, Major General Guy Carleton sallied forth from the city with 900 men and 4 guns. Carleton's forces routed the remaining 250 disease-ridden American soldiers under Major General John Thomas.

SEE ALSO *Canada Invasion; Carleton, Guy; Thomas, John.*

revised by Harold E. Selesky

POINT. Modern technical term for a patrol or recon-

naissance party that precedes an advance guard or follows a rear guard.

Mark M. Boatner

POINT OF FORK, VIRGINIA. 5 June

1781. With the worn-out men of the Queen's Rangers and the remnants of the Seventy-first Foot, John Simcoe moved from Cornwallis's camp on the North Anna to raid Friedrich von Steuben's main supply depot at Point of Fork. This place was where the Fluvanna and Rivanna joined to form the James River, about forty-five miles above Richmond. Steuben was located there with about four hundred of his Continental recruits. Learning of Simcoe's roundabout approach only at the last minute, the Americans were caught trying to evacuate the supplies across the Fluvanna. Simcoe skillfully entered Point of Fork with his one hundred cavalry, three hundred infantry, and one light three-pounder shortly before nightfall. Unable to pursue because he lacked boats, Simcoe knew that he had one major advantage over Steuben. Because the Americans lacked cavalry, they could not perform adequate reconnaissance. Simcoe deployed his troops along the river and lighted campfires to exaggerate his strength and make it appear that he was the advance of the entire British army. Deceived, Steuben abandoned the stores and marched his troops to safety during the night. The next morning Simcoe sent men across in canoes to destroy the supplies.

SEE ALSO *Cornwallis, Charles; Simcoe, John Graves; Steuben, Friedrich Wilhelm von; Virginia, Military Operations in.*

BIBLIOGRAPHY

Simcoe, John Graves. *A Journal of the Operations of the Queen's Rangers*. New York: New York Times, 1968.

Ward, Christopher. *The War of the Revolution*. 2 vols. New York: Macmillan, 1952.

Robert K. Wright Jr.

POLLOCK, OLIVER. (1737?–1823). Patriot

supply agent. Ireland, Pennsylvania, New Orleans. Born at Donagheady, Ireland, perhaps in 1737, Pollock emigrated with his father and brother in 1760, settling in Carlisle, Pennsylvania. Becoming a West Indies trader, he moved to Havana in 1762 and then New Orleans in 1768, where his Catholicism aided positive relations with the Spanish authorities. When Captain George Gibson arrived on his mission to acquire munitions for Virginia in 1776, Pollock got the covert assistance of the Spanish government in sending Gibson back to Fort Pitt with almost ten thousand pounds of powder. Despite efforts of the British to stop him, Pollock furnished vital supplies for the western operations of George Rogers Clark. His friendship with Louisiana governor Bernardo de Gálvez proved of enormous value to the Americans, as did Pollack's personal generosity. By the end of 1777 he had sent seventy thousand dollars worth of supplies on his own credit, and when this was exhausted in July 1779, he mortgaged personal property to raise one hundred thousand dollars and borrow another two hundred thousand. Having become commercial agent for Congress early in 1778, he procured goods from Spanish creditors for Washington's army. In 1779 he accompanied Gálvez in the capture of Manchac, Baton Rouge, and Natchez.

Although his postwar commercial ventures were highly successful, Congress and Virginia were slow in reimbursing him, and he spent eighteen months in custody for failure to satisfy his creditors. U.S. and state authorities eventually paid many of his claims, albeit thirty years after the Revolution ended. Pollock did not hold a grudge, serving from 1783 to 1785 as U.S. commercial representative in Havana and moving back to Carlisle in the 1790s. In 1805 he moved to Baltimore, where he headed up a successful business in the Caribbean trade. He died in Pinckneyville, Mississippi, on 17 December 1823.

SEE ALSO *Clark, George Rogers; Gibson, George; Western Operations.*

BIBLIOGRAPHY

Cummins, Light T. "Oliver Pollock and George Rogers Clark's Service of Supply: A Case Study in Financial Disaster." In *Selected Papers from the 1985 and 1986 George Rogers Clark Trans-Appalachian Conferences.* 1988.

James, James A. *Oliver Pollock: The Life and Times of an Unknown Patriot.* New York: Appleton-Century, 1937.

revised by Michael Bellesiles

POMEROY, SETH. (1706–1777). Continental general. Massachusetts. Born on 20 May 1706, he was a member of a family long prominent in Northampton. Seth took up the family trade of gunsmithing and became a solid and prosperous local citizen. He was commissioned a militia ensign in 1743 and a captain the next year. In 1745 the Massachusetts assembly appointed him major of the Fourth Regiment in the Louisburg expedition, and he performed valuable service in repairing captured French cannon for use against the defenders. He spent the next three years as major of the troops defending the frontier in western Massachusetts. At the start of the French and Indian War, he was appointed lieutenant colonel of Colonel Ephraim Williams's regiment of provincial troops from western Massachusetts that was raised for William Johnson's attack on Crown Point. After Williams was killed in the Bloody Morning Scout, he led the regiment in the heaviest fighting of the Battle of Lake George in New York on 8 September

1755 and, according to legend, captured Baron Dieskau, the French commander.

Not interested in local politics but considered by his neighbors to be a firm supporter of American rights, in 1774 he sat on the Northampton committee of safety and represented the town in the Massachusetts Provincial Congress, which appointed him a brigadier general of militia in October 1774. With Artemas Ward and Jedidiah Preble, he was responsible for preparing the militia for the day that resistance to increased imperial control led to war. His principal service was in helping to raise and train soldiers in western Massachusetts in 1775 and 1776. The sixty-nine-year-old veteran rode from Northampton to Cambridge in a single day to participate in the Battle of Bunker Hill on 17 June 1775. Carrying the musket he himself had made and had used at Louisburg thirty years earlier, he rode to Charlestown Neck on a borrowed horse, turned it over to a sentry so as not to expose it to enemy fire, and walked to the rail fence, where his presence helped to steady the younger men. In the action that followed, Pomeroy fought as a volunteer, had the stock of his musket shattered by an enemy ball, and "still facing the enemy," withdrew with the forces of Thomas Knowlton and John Stark at the end of the day (Ward, 1, p. 95).

The Provincial Congress named him a major general of militia on 20 June 1775, and the Continental Congress appointed him its first-ranking brigadier general on 22 June 1775, but he declined the latter appointment on 19 July and was superseded by John Thomas. On 19 February 1777, he died of pleurisy at Peekskill while on his way to join Washington's army in New Jersey. Few personal details are known about the man whom legend describes as a tall, lean, and intrepid soldier.

SEE ALSO *Thomas, John.*

BIBLIOGRAPHY

De Forest, Louis Effingham, ed. *The Journals and Papers of Seth Pomeroy.* New York: Society of Colonial Wars in the State of New York, 1926.

Ward, Christopher. *The War of the Revolution.* 2 vols. Edited by John Richard Alden. New York: Macmillan, 1952.

revised by Harold E. Selesky

PONTCHARTRAIN. A French fort at Detroit and a lake in Louisiana, they were named for the minister of the navy of Louis XIV.

Mark M. Boatner

PONTIAC'S WAR. 1763–1766. The surrender
of Canada to General Jeffrey Amherst (8 September 1760) gave the British title to the French posts in the territory known as the Old Northwest. Major Robert Rogers led a party to take possession of Detroit on 29 November 1760, and other scattered forts were subsequently garrisoned by small detachments of regulars, most of them from the Sixtieth ("Royal American") Regiment. In addition to these forts, thousands of Native Americans now fell under British claims to jurisdiction.

DETERIORATING BRITISH–NATIVE AMERICAN RELATIONS

Unlike the French, the British demonstrated a notable lack of sensitivity to their new subjects. Most importantly, the British government did nothing to halt the migration of their white subjects onto Indian lands in the Ohio River Valley. The Ottawa war leader Pontiac (c. 1720–1769) found many Indian nations receptive to his charge that the English intended to conquer their territories, as evidenced by the large number of British forts in these areas. Further exacerbating the situation, Amherst put a halt to the traditional annual distribution of gifts (clothing, arms and ammunition, food, and iron goods) to the Indians.

Captain Donald Campbell, commandant at Detroit, and Indian Superintendent Sir William Johnson initially managed to keep the peace, but Pontiac found a valuable ally in a visionary called the Delaware Prophet, who preached that the Indians should seek regeneration by eliminating the corrupting influence of the white man and his accompanying vices. Combining the Prophet's millennial teachings with the very real threat of English encroachments on their hereditary lands, Pontiac succeeded by early 1763 in forging a broad coalition of Indian nations that included the Ojibwa, Huron, Potawatomi, Seneca, and his own Ottawa.

From his base in three towns near Detroit, Pontiac launched the initial attack against the 120-man garrison at Fort Detroit, now commanded by Major Henry Gladwin. Gladwin correctly anticipated an assault, frustrating several attempts by Pontiac to take the fort by stealth in early May 1973. On 9 May the Ottawa attacked isolated settlers outside Fort Detroit and laid siege to the garrison. Within a few weeks other war parties took every fort west of Niagara except Detroit and Pitt. Sandusky (Ohio) fell on 16 May, followed by Fort St. Joseph on 25 May, Fort Miami on 27 May; Fort Ouiatenon on 1 June, and Fort Michilimackinac on the next day. Seeing British defenses collapsing, the commander of Fort Edward Augustus abandoned his post in mid June. Between 16 and 20 May, Forts Venango, Le Boeuf, and Presque Isle (Erie) also fell, with only the garrison at Le Boeuf successfully escaping to Fort Pitt.

The garrisons of most of these posts were slaughtered. Forts Ligonier and Bedford, along the Forbes Road east of Fort Pitt, repelled Indian attacks in June. The largest and most well coordinated Indian victory came at Devil's Hole near Niagara on 14 September, when a force of 300 Seneca ambushed a convoy of twenty-five wagons bound for Detroit, killing all but two of the thirty-one soldiers in its escort. The sounds of battle drew eighty regulars from Fort Niagara into a second ambush, which left fifty-one dead. By the time the rest of the fort's garrison arrived, the Seneca had departed with all the supplies, and the British had suffered their greatest defeat of the war.

The year 1763 is commonly taken as the start of the Revolutionary era, and many scholars hold that the weakness of Amherst's response to Pontiac's uprising may have misled many colonists into believing that there was little reality behind the boasts of British military might. Amherst saw matters very differently. He expected the colonists to play an active role in resisting this war on their frontier. But the settlers whose presence in the west had precipitated this conflict fled to the safety of the east, leaving Amherst with only a few absurdly weak garrisons—Fort Ligonier, for instance, was held by just twelve soldiers. Further limiting Amherst's options was the refusal of most of the colonies to offer any assistance. Then Amherst made the mistake of turning first for help to Pennsylvania, a province which did not have a militia. With time, Amherst was able to find just enough troops to battle Pontiac to a draw. British success hinged on their holding on to Forts Detroit and Pitt. Lacking artillery, Pontiac's only hope for capturing these outposts lay in breaking their lines of supply and starving their garrisons.

SIEGE OF DETROIT

Lieutenant Abraham Cuyler of the Queen's Rangers had left Niagara on 13 May with ninety-six men and 139 barrels of provisions in ten bateaux, bound for Detroit. Unaware that hostilities had broken out, he landed at Point Pelee, about twenty-five miles from Detroit, after dark on 28 May, being immediately attacked by Pontiac's forces. Cuyler escaped back to Niagara with only forty of his men. Cuyler returned on 30 June aboard the sloop *Michigan* with a reinforcement of fifty-five men and a quantity of supplies. Amherst sent his aide-de-camp, Captain James Dalyell, from headquarters in New York City via Albany and Niagara to collect reinforcements for Gladwin's garrison. Robert Rogers and twenty-one New York militia joined him at Albany, and he reached Niagara on 6 July with 200 men from the Fifty-fifth and Sixtieth Regiments. Picking up forty men of the eightieth Regiment at Niagara, Dalyell loaded his force in twenty-two bateaux and made the hazardous voyage to Detroit, arriving on 29 July with 260 men.

Against his better judgment, Gladwin acceded to the ambitious young aide's insistent demand that he be permitted to lead a sortie. Pontiac expected such action, and was waiting in ambush at the point where a narrow timber bridge crossed a creek two miles from the fort. At 2:30 on the morning of 31 July, 247 officers and men moved out from the fort. By 8 o'clock the survivors got back, owing largely to the rearguard action of Rogers and the sound leadership of Captain James Grant. Dalyell and 19 of his men were killed, and another thirty-seven were wounded at what became known as Bloody Run.

Pontiac's situation had been impossible from the start. Without supplies and matériel for siege operations, Pontiac was unable to properly besiege Detroit, which kept open its line of communications by water to Niagara. By September, Pontiac's allies began to melt away, frustrated by the stalemate which left them hungrier than the troops inside the fort. On 29 October Pontiac received official word from the French commander at Fort de Chatres of the Peace of Paris, in which France officially handed over the northwest to the British. On 31 October 1763 Pontiac wrote Gladwin a note of farewell and left the area with his remaining followers.

FORT PITT HOLDS OUT

Fort Pitt was commanded by the Swiss Captain Simeon Ecuyer, who bears the dubious distinction of carrying out General Amherst's grotesque suggestion that he employ biological warfare against the Indians. To indicate that his position was well supplied, Ecuyer provided the besieging Indians not only with food and alcohol, but also with blankets contaminated with small pox. With a garrison of 250 regulars and militia, sixteen cannon, and a well-fortified position, Ecuyer was not alarmed about the security of his post. By the end of June Colonel Henry Bouquet, who called Indians "vermin," had assembled a relief column of 460 regulars at Carlisle—214 men of the Forty-second ("Black Watch"), 133 of the Seventy-seventh Highlanders, a battalion of the Sixtieth ("Royal Americans"), and a party of rangers. His departure was delayed until 18 July because of difficulty finding wagoners willing to ride into the middle of a war zone.

By 2 August Bouquet had reached Fort Ligonier, having been forced to drop off regulars along the way to protect the panic-stricken settlers. He then pushed forward without his wagons but with 340 horses loaded with flour toward the fort from which no news had been heard for over a month. A parley with Delaware and Shawnee chiefs was held on 26 July, for which Ecuyer refused to leave Fort Pitt. The Indians launched an attack on the following day, but then abruptly lifted their siege on 1 August. Ecuyer, who had been wounded by an arrow, knew that they were going to attack Bouquet.

At 1 P.M. on 5 August 1763, Bouquet's advance guard was suddenly attacked at Edge Hill, twenty-six miles east of Fort Pitt, in what is known as the battle of Bushy Run. The regulars, who had already marched seventeen miles that day, attacked with bayonets to relieve the advance guard, but the Delaware, Shawnee, Mingo, and Wyandot worked their way around Bouquet and kept up a galling fire until dark (around 8 P.M.). Bouquet formed his forces onto a little hill behind stacked bags of flour for the night. Several officers and about 60 men had already been killed or wounded, the troops were tired from the long march and the seven-hour battle, and they suffered severely from lack of water.

The Indians renewed their attack at first light, but since victory was almost inevitable they confined their efforts to sniping. The regulars held their position, but time was against them. At 10 A.M. the British began to weaken from sheer exhaustion, the Indians saw men withdrawing from a portion of the perimeter, and they rushed toward this gap. Bouquet had resorted to a desperate stratagem, having pulled two companies from the west side of the line and sent them around to a point from which they could counterattack the south flank of the expected penetration. The Indians met this surprise fire bravely, but retreated when the regulars charged with bayonets. Then the Indians were again surprised, as Bouquet had advanced two more companies to the area of the expected Indian retreat, and their bayonet charge shattered the Indian forces, who fled in disorder.

Bushy Run proved a bloody battle, as Bouquet lost fifty killed and sixty wounded, with Indian losses estimated at sixty killed, including the able Delaware war chief, Wolf. With a fourth of his force killed or wounded, Bouquet limped into Fort Pitt on 10 August, unable to press the attack against the demoralized Indians, but having nonetheless won a significant victory.

LATER EXPEDITIONS AGAINST PONTIAC

Before he was recalled to England, Amherst had planned two expeditions against Pontiac's coalition: one from Niagara to Detroit and then south from Lake Erie against the Delaware and Shawnee in what now is central Ohio; the other to penetrate into this same area from Pittsburgh. Amherst's successor, General Thomas Gage, carried out these plans. The first of these operations, John Bradstreet's expedition of 1764, was badly mismanaged, but the other, Bouquet's expedition of 1764, was a complete success. Pontiac finally submitted to Sir William Johnson at Oswego on 24 July 1766, and was thereafter loyal to the British. On 20 April 1769 he was assassinated by a Peoria in Cahokia, Illinois.

As Ian Steele summarized, it produced "an unprecedented balance of power." The war "had become a stalemate, and the peace was an accommodation" (Steele, p. 246). The Indians had learned that they could not take the major British outposts, and that their lack of materials crippled any sustained military effort. The British, for their part, felt that allowing unhindered access to the northwest by their colonists at this time was not worth the high cost of defeating the Indians. They therefore returned to the practice of giving annual gifts to the those Indian nations that remained on friendly terms and promised to uphold the Proclamation of 1763, which sought to halt this westward migration. Although the war ended as a major success for the Native Americans, it was a victory that stood only until the creation of the United States, ten years later.

SEE ALSO *Biological Warfare; Bushy Run, Pennsylvania; Indians in the Colonial Wars and in the American Revolution; Proclamation of 1763.*

BIBLIOGRAPHY

Dowd, Gregory Evans. *A Spirited Resistance: The North American Indian Struggle for Unity, 1745–1815.* Baltimore, Md.: Johns Hopkins University Press, 1992.

Steele, Ian K. *Warpaths: Invasions of North America.* New York: Oxford University Press, 1994.

Michael Bellesiles

POOR, ENOCH.

POOR, ENOCH. (1736–1780). Continental general. Massachusetts and New Hampshire. Great-grandson of an English immigrant who settled at Newbury, Massachusetts, he was reared on the family farm in North Andover, Massachusetts, had little education, and was apprenticed to a cabinetmaker. In 1755 he took part in Colonel John Winslow's expedition to Acadia. Around 1760 he moved to Exeter, New Hampshire, where he established himself as a merchant and shipbuilder. After holding various public offices and being elected to sit in two of New Hampshire's provincial congresses, on 24 May 1775 he was named colonel of the Second New Hampshire Regiment. His regiment's first mission was to build fire rafts to protect Exeter and to work on coastal defenses. Poor then led his force to the Boston lines, moved to New York City in the spring of 1776, and was later sent to strengthen the forces withdrawing up Lake Champlain. In the council of war on 5 July 1776, he argued against the abandonment of Crown Point and organized a protest by twenty-one field grade officers (including John Stark and William Maxwell) to Washington when Schuyler wisely decided the place was untenable. He was president of the court-martial that acquitted Moses Hazen and ordered the arrest of Benedict Arnold. In December 1776 he went south to join Washington's army for operations at Trenton and

Princeton, and on 21 February 1777 he was promoted to brigadier general. Although his record had been as good as many others promoted to general officer rank, he owed his advancement partly to a factional dispute brought about through Colonel John Stark's abrupt departure from command due to what he thought was Congress's inept process of promotion.

After the perplexing British movements that preceded the Philadelphia campaign, his brigade and Varnum's were detached to Peekskill. Poor subsequently took part in the operations at Ticonderoga on 5 July 1777. His brigade of eight hundred men moved forward on the American right to open the Second Battle of Saratoga on 7 October 1777, and the men performed well. He then rejoined Washington for winter quarters at Valley Forge and had a prominent part in the action at Barren Hill on 20 May 1778. As part of Charles Lee's command, he marched with the first troops to leave Valley Forge for the Monmouth campaign, and he led one of the final movements of the battle of 28 June.

During the winter of 1779–1780, his brigade was posted at Danbury, Connecticut. Ordered to join Sullivan's expedition against the Iroquois, his troops figured prominently in the Battle at Newtown, New York, on 29 August 1779, which was the only major action of the campaign. In 1780 his brigade was incorporated into Lafayette's Light Infantry Division. He died 8 September 1780 at Paramus, New Jersey, of typhus (then called putrid fever).

SEE ALSO *Barren Hill, Pennsylvania; Monmouth, New Jersey; Newtown, New York.*

BIBLIOGRAPHY

Fischer, Joseph R. *A Well-Executed Failure: The Sullivan Campaign against the Iroquois, July–September 1779.* Columbia: University of South Carolina Press, 1997.

Potter, Chandler E. *The Military History of the State of New-Hampshire, 1623–1861.* 1868. Reprint, Baltimore: Genealogical Publishing, 1972.

Thompson, Dorothea M. "Enoch Poor." In *New Hampshire: Years of Revolution.* Edited by Peter E. Randall. Portsmouth, N.H.: Profiles Publishing, 1976.

Upton, Richard Francis. *Revolutionary New Hampshire.* 1936. Reprint, New York: Octagon Books, 1971.

revised by Frank C. Mevers

POPULATIONS OF GREAT BRITAIN AND AMERICA.

POPULATIONS OF GREAT BRITAIN AND AMERICA. In 1775 the British had an estimated 8,000,000 people; 2,350,000 of these could be considered the military manpower of the nation. However, the standard calculation for the eighteenth century is that one-tenth of the total population constituted

Population of the United States

State	1775		(est.)	1790		
	White	Black	Total	White	Black	Total
Conneticutt	198,076	5,279	203,355	232,374	5,572	237,946
Delaware	39,550	2,157	41,707	46,310	12,786	59,096
Georgia	14,981	12,484	27,465	52,886	29.662	82,548
Kentucky				61,133	12,544	73,677
Maine*	45,625	471	46,096	96.002	538	96,540
Maryland	134,844	65,856	200,700	208,649	111,079	319,728
Massachusetts	276,125	4,595	280,720	373,324	5,463	378,787
New Hampshire	80,644	656	81,300	141,097	788	141,885
New Jersey	125,781	9,032	134,813	169,954	14,185	184,139
New York	163,560	22,656	186,216	314,142	25,978	340,120
North Carolina	149,930	81,780	231,710	288,204	105,547	393,751
Pennsylvani	275,397	6,769	282,166	424,099	10,274	434,373
Rhode Island	56,366	3,796	60,162	64,470	4,355	68,825
South Carolina	57,652	88,334	145,986	140,178	108,895	249,073
Tennessee	940	235	1,175	31,913	3,778	35,691
Vermont	17,331	53	17,384	85,154	271	85,425
Virginia	304,807	220,435	525,242	391,524	300,213	691,737
TOTAL	1,941,609	524,588	2,466,197	3,172,006	757,208	3,929,214

*Part of Massachusetts until 1821.

SOURCES: Bureau of the Census, *Historical Statistics of the United States: Colonial Times to 1970* (CD-ROM; New York: Cambridge University Press, 1997) 2: 1168–71; United States Census Office, *Return of the Whole Number of Persons within the Several Districts of the United States* (Philadelphia: Childs and Swaine, 1791); R.C. Simmons, *The American Colonies: From Settlement to Independence* (New York, 1976), 175–77; Michael A. Bellesiles, Revolutionary Outlaws: *Ethan Allen and the Struggle for Independence on the Early American Frontier* (Charlottesville: University Press of Virginia, 1993) 280-83.

THE GALE GROUP

the potential arms-bearing population. Realistically, then, Britain had some 800,000 young men who were eligible for military service. Complaining of his difficulties in mobilizing an army for the Revolutionary War, Lord Shelburne commented that whereas 300,000 Englishmen entered the armies in the Seven Years' War, only 30,000 men, including German troops, could be raised to put down the American rebellion.

Since the first census was not until 1790, it is difficult to be certain about the population of the American colonies. The standard current estimate is that approximately 2,500,000 people lived in the thirteen colonies in 1775 (excluding Indians), of whom 460,000 were slaves. (Estimates for 1775 are based on censuses taken in some of the colonies during the Revolutionary period and projections derived from the degree of population growth discernable in these years, roughly 3.5 percent per year between 1760 and 1790.) Excluding the slaves, whom Congress initially did not allow to serve in the Continental army, the colonies could expect to draw upon some 200,000 men.

It is impossible to know what percentage of the population supported independence or how many remained loyal to the crown. Political allegiances could shift over time for any number of reasons, such as slaves being offered their freedom for joining the British. There were also dramatically different levels of commitment to politics. It seems most probable that the majority of Americans remained neutral throughout the Revolution. Given the size of the contending military forces, it appears obvious that most Americans gave only lip service to one side or the other. It is even difficult to determine the number of Loyalists who went into exile after the war, with estimates running from 85,000 to 200,000.

Approximate populations of major American cities in 1776 were: Philadelphia, 38,000; New York City, 25,000; Boston, 16,000; Charleston, 12,000; and Newport, 11,000. Although London's population of 750,000 dwarfed Philadelphia's, the Quaker City outranked Bristol and Dublin as the third largest city of the British empire—Edinburgh was second, having some 40,000 people.

The Native American population remains subject to speculation. Estimates of the number living east of the Mississippi River run between twenty-five thousand and one hundred thousand.

BIBLIOGRAPHY

Greene, Evarts B., and Virginia D. Harrington. *American Population before the Federal Census of 1790.* 1932. Reprint, Baltimore: Genealogical Publishing, 1993.

Simmons, Richard C. *The American Colonies: From Settlement to Independence.* New York: D. McKay, 1976.

U.S. Bureau of the Census. *Historical Statistics of the United States: Colonial Times to 1970.* New York: Cambridge University Press, 1997. CD-ROM.

revised by Michael Bellesiles

PORT ROYAL ISLAND, SOUTH CAROLINA, SEE *Beaufort South Carolina.*

PORT'S FERRY, PEE DEE RIVER, SOUTH CAROLINA.

Benjamin Port's ferry was an important river crossing and Francis Marion campsite near Snow's Island. Marion built a redoubt on the east bank in September 1780. Colonel Henry Lee also camped there in January 1781. The crossing is about three miles below the modern U.S. Highway 378 bridge.

SEE ALSO *Marion, Francis.*

BIBLIOGRAPHY

Rankin, Hugh F. *Francis Marion: The Swamp Fox.* New York: Thomas Y. Crowell Company, 1973.

revised by Steven D. Smith

POUNDRIDGE, NEW YORK.

2 July 1779. As part of the intense skirmishing for control of the Neutral Ground, after dark on 1 July, Sir Henry Clinton sent Banastre Tarleton with two hundred men toward this place, twenty miles northeast of White Plains. Tarleton's command included seventy regulars from the Seventeenth Light Dragoons, detachments of John Simcoe's Queen's Rangers and his own British Legion, and a detail of mounted jägers. His target was being used as a base for Westchester County militia, stiffened by part of Colonel Elisha Sheldon's Second Continental Light Dragoons. When his guide briefly took a wrong road, Sheldon's videttes spotted the British. Tarleton launched a charge that pushed Sheldon back two miles from the village before reaction forces began pouring in and he had to withdraw, completing a sixty-four-mile round trip in twenty-three hours. The raiders burned several buildings, including the church, to retaliate for snipers, and carried away a flag that had been found with some officers'

baggage. Although he claimed to have inflicted twenty-six or twenty-seven casualties, the Americans actually lost ten wounded and eight missing in action; Tarleton admitted having one man killed and one wounded. He gloated over the raid, but like most such actions in the area, it was inconclusive.

SEE ALSO *Clinton, Henry; Simcoe, John Graves; Tarleton, Banastre.*

revised by Robert K. Wright Jr.

POWDER ALARM (CAMBRIDGE, MASSACHUSETTS).

1 September 1774. As defiance of imperial regulation in Boston became more ominous, Major General Thomas Gage, British commander in chief in North America, decided on a risky move. Through the summer of 1774, agents and supporters of royal government had given him detailed information about the cannon, powder, and other military stores the radicals were collecting and hiding in Cambridge. On 27 August the town of Medford removed from the provincial powder house on Quarry Hill in Charlestown the last of the gunpowder belonging to the towns. All that remained were the 250 half-barrels of powder that belonged to the province and were thus legally under the control of Gage. Believing that keeping the gunpowder out of the hands of the radicals outweighed the risk of inflaming his opponents, he ordered the powder removed to Castle William in Boston Harbor. Before 5 A.M. on the morning of 1 September 1774, about 250 regulars embarked in thirteen longboats from Royal Navy ships in the harbor and were rowed up the Mystic River to the Ten Hills area of Charlestown, where they debarked and marched overland about a mile to the powder house. A detachment continued on to Cambridge, where the soldiers borrowed horses from a tavern keeper and confiscated two small field guns recently procured by the town militia. Both British forces accomplished their mission efficiently and without violence. By noon the munitions had arrived safely at Castle William.

The countryside was inflamed by reports that the redcoats had sallied forth in large numbers. As the news spread (by midnight it was known forty miles away in Shrewsbury), rumors embellished it: the citizens of Cambridge had resisted, the troops had fired, and six Patriots were dead. The Boston garrison was marching out in force! By the morning of 2 September, four thousand armed men had crowded into Cambridge, and more were coming. Word reached Israel Putnam at Pomfret, Connecticut, on 3 September that British ships had bombarded Boston and that as many as thirty thousand militia were moving toward Cambridge. The first Continental

Congress, meeting at Philadelphia, learned of the "dreadful catastrophe" on 6 September (Smith, p. 49). According to John Adams, Congress "received by an express an intimation of the bombardment of Boston, a confused account, but an alarming one indeed" (Smith, p. 27). The effect was electric, and helped at a significant moment to strengthen the resolve of those delegates who refused to submit to an imperial government willing to use armed force in this manner. Two days later, after Adams had learned that "no blood had been spilled," he wrote to his wife that "every gentleman seems to regard the bombardment of Boston as the bombardment of the capital of his own province. Our deliberations are grave and serious indeed" (Smith, p. 49).

The excitement died down as the rumors were proved to be false, but the episode had been an impressive demonstration of how ready the radicals were to touch off the powder keg. On 5 September Gage ordered the erection of defensive works on Boston Neck, an understandable military precaution but one that again alarmed the countryside and gave the radicals more evidence of imperial tyranny with which to bolster their calls for resistance. The delegates to the Continental Congress began to worry less about their differences and more about the task ahead.

SEE ALSO *Adams, John; Continental Congress; Gage, Thomas.*

BIBLIOGRAPHY

Alden, John Richard. *General Gage in America, being Principally a History of His Role in the American Revolution.* Baton Rouge: Louisiana State University Press, 1948.

French, Allen. *General Gage's Informers.* Ann Arbor, Mich.: University of Michigan Press, 1932.

Richmond, Robert P. *Powder Alarm, 1774.* Princeton, N.J.: Auerbach Publishers, 1971.

Smith, Paul H., et al., eds. *Letters of Delegates to Congress, 1774–1789.* Vol. 1: *August 1774–August 1775.* Washington, D.C.: Library of Congress, 1976.

revised by Harold E. Selesky

POWLES HOOK, NEW JERSEY SEE *Paulus Hook, New Jersey.*

POWNALL, THOMAS. (1722–1805).

Colonial governor. Born on 4 September 1722 and educated at Lincoln and Trinity College (Cambridge), after 1743 Thomas Pownall entered the office of the Board of Trade, where his brother was secretary. He accompanied Sir Danvers Osborn to New York as the new governor's secretary and remained after Osborn committed suicide in October 1753. In May 1755 he was appointed lieutenant governor of New Jersey and began a lifelong friendship with Benjamin Franklin. Attending the Albany Conference as an observer, he presented a memorandum on the importance of the Great Lakes to British control of the continent. He returned to England early in 1756, where he presented a paper stressing the need for unity of command in America and urging the need to gain control of Lake Ontario. Pownall accompanied Lord Loudoun, the new commander in chief, to America as his secretary, but he returned to London in October 1756 to present Loudoun's case against William Shirley. William Pitt was so impressed by the ambitious, knowledgeable student of colonial affairs that he appointed Pownall to succeed Shirley as governor of Massachusetts.

The thirty-five-year-old governor reached Boston on 3 August 1757. Reacting promptly to a desperate call from Major General Daniel Webb for reinforcements in the Hudson River-Lake Champlain corridor, he called out the militia without waiting to get the assembly's approval, but the troops were too late to prevent the surrender of Fort William Henry on 9 August. For the three years of his administration, he promoted the participation of Massachusetts in the French and Indian War, but he alienated the friends of Shirley, antagonized such crown supporters as Thomas Hutchinson, and clashed with Loudoun over the war powers claimed by the military. His only military exploit was as leader of the expedition to build a fort on the Penobscot River in Maine in May 1759.

The Board of Trade ordered him to South Carolina as governor in November 1759, but he resigned without assuming office. In the summer of 1761 he became commissary general to the Anglo-Hanoverian army on the Rhine, a post he held until the end of the Seven Years' War in 1763. In 1764, he published his famous *Administration of the Colonies,* in which he argued for greater centralization of colonial administration. It ran to five editions, the last in 1777.

In 1767 he was elected to Parliament and supported North's measures against the colonies. He opposed Burke's bill for conciliation but introduced a peace bill on 24 May 1780 when he realized that the war was lost. In the summer of 1781 he declined to run again for Parliament and spent the rest of his life in travel and writing. He died at Bath, England, on 25 February 1805.

SEE ALSO *Chatham, William Pitt, First Earl of; Fort William Henry (Fort George), New York; Unity of Command.*

BIBLIOGRAPHY

Schutz, John A. *Thomas Pownall, British Defender of American Liberty: A Study of Anglo-American Relations in the Eighteenth Century.* Glendale, Calif.: A. H. Clark, 1951.

revised by Harold E. Selesky

POWOW. Derived from Indian words for a priest, wizard, or magician, the term "powow" (or "powwow") came to mean "the noisy festivities preceding a council, expedition, or hunt; or a council or parley" (*Handbook of American Indians North of Mexico*, "Powow").

SEE ALSO *Parley.*

BIBLIOGRAPHY

Hodge, Frederick Webb, ed. *Handbook of American Indians North of Mexico.* 2 vols. New York: Greenwood Press, 1969.

revised by Harold E. Selesky

PRESBYTERIANS. While most Christian groups in America supported the War for Independence, Presbyterians were distinctive with respect to the extent and intensity of their enthusiasm for revolution. The denomination contained comparatively few Loyalists, the great exception being Scottish merchants, British officials, and Scottish Highlanders resident in the colonies, who tended to maintain their allegiance to the crown throughout the war. The denomination also contained few neutrals, especially after the war got under way, and fewer pacifists. Rather, the great majority of Presbyterians were Patriots, who in terms of the depth of support for and breadth of participation in the war had no rivals among the other major denominations, with the possible exception of the New England Congregationalists. Historians have frequently commented on the Presbyterian penchant for patriotism and, like Leonard Trinterud, author of *The Forming of an American Tradition* (1949), have wondered whether there wasn't "something inherent in Presbyterianism that made the cause of colonial independence congenial to it" (pp. 251–252).

SOURCES OF PRESBYTERIAN PATRIOTISM

American Presbyterian patriotism flowed from three initially separate streams of Reformed Protestant dissenting thought and behavior, each of which was intrinsic to the denomination's rise to religious and political prominence in the colonies. First, colonial Presbyterianism was founded on principles of English Puritan religious dissent,

revived by second and third generations of New Englanders embroiled in ecclesiastical conflict with the leaders of the Congregational way. Proclaiming the freedom to leave New England and to create their own churches, the dissenters formed in the Middle Atlantic region the first Presbyterian communities in America.

A second stream of dissent was Scotch-Irish Presbyterianism. Over 100,000 Presbyterians migrated from Northern Ireland to the colonies in the period from 1717 to 1776, populating principally the mid-Atlantic colonies of New York, New Jersey, and Pennsylvania, and adding greatly to the strength of Presbyterianism there. Having faced and resisted English religious and political persecution for many decades, the Ulsterites added to the church strong traditions of dissent that easily overlapped with and, in turn, deepened those inherited from British and early New England Puritans.

A third stream was the Great Awakening, an intercolonial religious revival sparked by the transatlantic evangelical ministry of George Whitefield, an English divine. Evangelizing the mid-Atlantic and southern frontiers during the 1740s and 1750s, Presbyterian revivalists helped convert frontier settlers, often of Scotch-Irish extraction, to New Light ideals of personal piety and individual conscience that rejected inherited authority and doctrinal traditions. In the period after the Great Awakening, the New Light converged with the other two dissenting streams of the denomination.

Puritan evangelism, religious revivalism, and Scots-Irish immigration together turned Presbyterianism into the second largest and the fastest growing denomination in America (as recently as 1700 it had been among the smallest). In the midst of this dramatic surge in membership, colonial Presbyterians succeeded in building a unified national Church, one based on a network of synods, presbyteries, and sessions, and on an American identity separate from the Ulster and Scotch Presbyterian churches. This identity contained radical political as well as religious elements. New principles of political dissent, introduced to Americans through the writings of English liberals such as John Locke, intermingled with traditions of Puritan, Scots-Irish, and New Light dissent. Initially, early modern English political science was considered a godless set of ideas, highly antagonist to Christian doctrine and theology. But during the Anglo-French wars of the 1740s and 1750s, Presbyterian ministers, among others, were found mixing political with religious dissent in diatribes denouncing "papalist" and "monarchist" French threats to American freedoms. When the crisis with England erupted, Presbyterians, redirecting their diatribes against their own mother country, lost much of their earlier reluctance to combine liberalism and Christian dissent, however increasingly volatile the compound. Presbyterians became widely know as uniquely patriotic, as is indicated by the many contemporary comments on the war as a "Presbyterian War."

PRESBYTERIANS IN REVOLUTION AND WAR

The war years led Presbyterians to fully embrace republican ideals and to complete the process of synthesizing them with Christian theology. The Presbyterians were not alone in effecting this merger, however. Other American denominations, especially the Congregationalists, helped to create a truly unique blend of republican and Christian convictions, the likes of which the world had never seen. Although Presbyterians never adopted a formal position on the conflict, it came close to doing so in May 1775 when, in response to Lexington and Concord, the synod of New York and Philadelphia issued a pastoral letter to the membership seeking to explain the nature of the crisis. This and other documents, including war sermons delivered by Presbyterian ministers and radical statements issued by the local laity, reveal a generally unified liberal-Presbyterian rationale for war and revolution.

Presbyterians saw themselves, first and foremost, as Christians, which meant that they were conscience-bound to support the Christian gospel of peace. As Christians they had consistently prayed for reconciliation with Britain throughout the crisis. They also had hesitated to criticize the king and his Parliament, and had sought to restrain the passions of the masses. But Britain had refused reconciliation, and had begun to commit atrocities against the colonists. By 1775 Presbyterians believed their backs were against the wall, and by 1776 they were convinced they had no recourse but to go to war against the mother country.

To Presbyterians this was thus a just war, a point that both Christian and liberal dissenting ideals could be used to defend. Christians, who professed to be lovers of peace, nevertheless had a duty to resist tyranny, even if the tyrant were a Christian king. In the face of tyranny, non-resistance or even passive resistance were not viable options. Once convinced of the the tyranny of the king, Presbyterians had a God-given responsibility to resist, even if that meant loss of limb or life. As an American battle flag proclaimed, "RESISTANCE TO TYRANTS IS OBEDIENCE TO GOD."

Presbyterians freely inserted liberal ideals into war sermons to strengthen the "just war" defense, borrowing freely from the ideas of Locke, among others. Political power had bounds and limits that rulers could not breech without threatening the natural rights and liberties of the people set by the laws of God and of reason. Britain had exceeded these bounds and, therefore, the people had the right to resist and to establish a new government, more attentive to their needs and happiness. Abraham Ketteltas, a Pennsylvania Presbyterian minister, put succinctly the multiple Christian and liberal justifications for war: "The cause of this American Continent, against the measures of a cruel, bloody, and vindictive ministry, is the cause of God. We are contending for the rights of mankind."

In addition to a "just war" defense, liberal and Christian ideals were brought together to prepare Presbyterians for the urgent yet fearful task of waging war against the world's mightiest military power. Such times called for civic virtue, the sacrifice of self for country, as well as Christian courage and fortitude. The New Light movement's stress on religious conversion was used to assuage rising Presbyterian anxieties regarding the war. Within the New Light movement, the main argument was that conversion, by giving believers assurance of salvation, provided the perfect antidote to fear of death, and thus the perfect source of Christian courage. Presbyterians also stressed the centrality of conversion to the achievement of success on the field of battle: "There is no soldier so undaunted as the pious man, no army so formidable as those who are superior to the fear of death" (quoted in Trinterud, p. 247).

Furthermore, Presbyterians argued that Christian piety and liberal ideals had to be mutually reinforcing if the republican revolution were to succeed. The Continental Congress could not achieve the democratic goals of the revolution unless it had the respect and support of all the people. Presbyterians could ensure political solidarity by working to unite Christians behind the new republic. By exercising Christian charity towards all religious denominations in America, Presbyterians could lay the groundwork for Christian, and hence republican, union.

Finally, Presbyterians saw religious and civil liberty as formerly antagonistic, but now necessary allies in the revolutionary struggle. There was "no example in history," the Synod of May 1775 observed, "in which civil liberty was destroyed, and the rights of conscience preserved entire" (Trinterud, p. 248). As John Witherspoon, president of the Presbyterian College of New Jersey, put it, "our civil and religious liberties, and consequently in a great measure the temporal and eternal happiness of us and our posterity, depended on the issue" of the war.

Historians have argued that the Christian use of republican language may have been determinative in drawing believers into the war and revolution. Certainly, Presbyterians helped lead the ideological campaign against Britain, and contributed a disproportionate number of people to the conflict. A particularly striking instance of this comes from the records of the College of New Jersey, now Princeton University. The college contributed so many leaders to the war and revolution that it became known as a "seminar of sedition" or "the Cradle of Liberty." Of 279 students who matriculated between 1746 and 1768 and were still alive in 1775, 94 saw some kind of service in the military, while only 8 became Loyalists. In addition, of the 178 students who studied under President Witherspoon in the period 1769–1775, 105 became important state or national officials, while a mere two became Royalists. By comparison, as many as 50 percent and 22 percent of King's College and Yale College students, respectively, whose political allegiance is known, were Loyalists.

IMPACT OF REVOLUTION ON PRESBYTERIANISM

Because of the political and religious changes wrought by war and revolution, Presbyterians saw a new ecclesiastical world arising once the smoke of battle had cleared. More than anything else, the disestablishment of the Anglican Church and the promotion of religious equality presented the Presbyterian Church with new challenges. Faced with rising competition for adherents from new denominations, especially the Methodists and the Baptists, Presbyterians responded by rejecting the idea of a state church and pushing the idea of the liberal arts school as the chief instrument of Presbyterian proselytism. In tune with the great ideological synthesis of 1776, they argued that a Liberal education would strengthen the church as well as the new republic, for knowledge of the world was a prerequisite for virtuous citizenship.

In the process of rushing to establish academies and colleges in the post-Revolution period, Presbyterians created what amounted to an educational empire. Because of their unique stress on higher education, Presbyterians acquired a distinctive denominational identity, which could be used for evangelical purposes in a world now marked by religious competition. Gone were the days of working for Christian union; Presbyterianism during the nineteenth century became a denomination devoted more to spreading distinctive modes of piety than to elaborating principles of American patriotism.

BIBLIOGRAPHY

Griffin, Patrick. *The People with no Name: Ireland's Ulster Scots, America's Scots Irish, and the Creation of a British Atlantic World 1689–1764.* Princeton, N.J.: Princeton University Press, 2001.

Miller, Howard. *The Revolutionary College: American Presbyterian Higher Education 1707–1837.* New York: New York University Press, 1976.

Mulder, Philip N. *A Controversial Spirit: Evangelical Awakenings in the South.* New York: Oxford University Press, 2002.

Neimeyer, Charles Patrick. *America Goes to War: A Social History of the Continental Army.* New York: New York University Press, 1996.

Noll, Mark. *America's God: From Jonathan Edwards to Abraham Lincoln.* New York: Oxford University Press, 2002.

Sandoz, Ellis, ed. *Political Sermons of the Founding Era: 1730–1805.* Indianapolis, Ind.: Liberty Press, 1991.

Tiedemann, Joseph S. "Presbyterianism and the American Revolution in the Middle Colonies." *Church History* 74, 2 (June 2005): 306–344.

Trinterud, Leonard. *The Forming of An American Tradition: A Re-examination of Colonial Presbyterianism.* Philadelphia: The Westminster Press, 1949.

Gerald F. Moran

PRESCOTT, OLIVER. (1731–1804).

Physician and militia general. Massachusetts. Born on 27 April 1731, the son of Benjamin and Abigail Oliver Prescott and younger brother of William Prescott, he was graduated from Harvard College in 1750 and built a successful medical practice in Groton, his birthplace. He was chairman of the town committee that protested the Stamp Act in 1765 and clerk of the town's committee of correspondence in 1774. He served in the militia before the Revolution, became brigadier general of the Middlesex County militia when the war started, and was promoted to second major general of the state militia in 1778. During the Boston siege, he was charged with setting up checkpoints to stop communication between the British garrison and pro-British sympathizers in the countryside. He held a number of important civil posts, helping to enforce the Association of 1774, serving on the Massachusetts supreme executive council from 1777 to 1780, sitting as judge of probate for Middlesex County from 1779 until his death, and playing a vital role in establishing Groton Academy. During Shays's Rebellion, he was active in recruiting and the dispatch of intelligence to the state authorities. Over six feet tall, inclined to being overweight, deaf in his later years, courtly in manner, he was a kindly and popular man. He died at Groton on 17 November 1804.

SEE ALSO *Boston Siege; Prescott, William.*

BIBLIOGRAPHY

Cash, Philip. *Medical Men at the Siege of Boston.* Philadelphia: American Philosophical Society, 1973.

Shipton, Clifford K. *Sibley's Harvard Graduates.* Vol. 12. Cambridge, Mass.: Harvard University Press, 1962.

revised by Harold E. Selesky

PRESCOTT, RICHARD. (1725–1788).

British general. Born in England in 1725, Prescott became a major in the Thirty-third Foot on 20 December 1756 and a lieutenant colonel of the Fiftieth Foot in May 1762, serving in Germany during the Seven Years' War. In 1773 he was brevetted colonel of the Seventh Foot and ordered to Canada, where his notorious abuse of the captured

Ethan Allen was followed by his own capture on 17 November 1775 when he failed in an attempt to escape from Montreal to Quebec. Holding the local rank of brigadier general, Prescott was exchanged for General John Sullivan in September 1776. In November 1776 Prescott became colonel of his regiment and the next month he was third in command of the British expedition that occupied Newport. Remaining there as commander of the garrison, he made himself an object of American hatred. On the night of 9–10 July 1777 he was taken prisoner by Major William Barton (1748–1831) and forty men in a daring raid. Despite his humiliating capture, Prescott was promoted to major general on 29 August 1777 while still a POW. Exchanged on 6 May 1778 for General Charles Lee, Prescott briefly resumed his command in Newport before being superseded by General Robert Pigot. He commanded a brigade in the Battle of Rhode Island on 29 August. About a year later he succeeded Pigot and in October 1779 complied with the orders of Clinton to destroy the works and evacuate his garrison of slightly more than four thousand effectives to New York. On 26 November 1782, he was promoted to lieutenant general. He died in England in October 1788.

SEE ALSO *Allen, Ethan; Newport, Rhode Island (29 July–31 August 1778).*

revised by Michael Bellesiles

PRESCOTT, ROBERT. (1727–1815).

British general. Born in Lancashire in 1727 (N.S.), Prescott was gazetted captain of the Fifteenth Foot in 1755 and saw action with them at Rochefort in 1757 and at Amherst's capture of Louisburg in 1758. The next year he was aide-de-camp to Amherst before joining the command of James Wolfe. In March 1761 he became major of the Ninety-fifth Foot and took part in Robert Monckton's expedition against Martinique. In November 1762 he advanced to the grade of lieutenant colonel. On 8 September 1775 he became lieutenant colonel of the Twenty-eighth Regiment and took part in the New York campaign (Long Island, Westchester County, and the capture of Fort Washington). He took part in the Philadelphia campaign and saw action at the Brandywine in 1777. The next year he was named first brigadier in James Grant's expedition against St. Lucia. On 6 July 1779 he was promoted to colonel and on 19 October 1781 he became a major general. Advanced to lieutenant general on 12 October 1793, he received orders to take command at Barbados. The next February he sailed for Martinique, landed unopposed, and on 22 March received the surrender of the island. In

1796 he succeeded Carleton as governor of Canada, and on 1 January 1798 he was promoted to full general. He was recalled in 1799, when Sir Robert Milnes became governor, and settled in Sussex, where he died on 21 December 1815 at Rose Green.

revised by Michael Bellesiles

PRESCOTT, SAMUEL. (1751–1777).

Physician. Massachusetts. Son of Dr. Abel and Abigail Brigham Prescott, he studied medicine with his father and began practicing with him in their home town of Concord, Massachusetts. An opponent of British policies, he stumbled upon the action for which he is best remembered early on the morning of 19 April 1775. Riding home to Concord from a meeting in Lexington, he met Paul Revere and William Dawes, who were carrying news that the British were on the move to confiscate provincial military stores at Concord. The trio rode on together. When they were approached by British officers on horseback, Dawes escaped, but Revere and Prescott were stopped. Both riders evaded their captors, although Revere was captured again momentarily. Prescott, thoroughly familiar with the countryside, made his escape and rode on to warn the minutemen at Lincoln and Concord, thereby enabling the activists to hide the munitions that were essential for armed resistance at Lexington and Concord, Massachusetts on 19 April 1775. Prescott served as a surgeon at Ticonderoga in 1776. About a year later he was captured on board a privateer and died while imprisoned at Halifax.

SEE ALSO *Lexington and Concord; Revere, Paul.*

revised by Harold E. Selesky

PRESCOTT, WILLIAM. (1726–1795).

Continental officer. Massachusetts. Born at Groton, Massachusetts, on 20 February 1726, the elder brother of Oliver Prescott, William Prescott served as a lieutenant in the expedition that took Louisburg in 1745. He settled in Pepperell, Massachusetts, became a prosperous farmer and militia captain (1756), and married Abigail Hale in 1757. Colonel of a regiment of Middlesex County minutemen, he arrived too late to see action at Concord on 19 April 1775, but he marched on to Cambridge, where he later became a member of the council of war and colonel of a provincial regiment.

On the night of 16–17 June 1775, he led his regiment and an assortment of others onto the Charlestown peninsula to fortify Breed's Hill. Over six feet tall, well-built, and possessing strong, clean-cut features, he had a way of inspiring respect and obedience as a military leader. The historian Christopher M. Ward has observed, "His customary movements were unhurried, and his coolness and self-possession in moments of danger were notable" (Ward, p. 76). As dawn broke on 17 June, he walked the parapet of the redoubt as his men dug furiously at his feet to finish their fortification before the British attacked it. A story based on later recollection captured the moment, even if it may be apocryphal:

> It is said that [Thomas] Gage, studying him [Prescott] from Boston as Prescott stood on the parapet, handed his [spy]glass to Abijah Willard, the councillor, and asked if he knew him. Willard named him: his own brother-in law. "Will he fight?" asked Gage. Willard replied, "I cannot answer for his men, but Prescott will fight you to the gates of hell." (French, p. 219)

He led his men in the defense of the redoubt, the most prominent portion of the field, against a series of British attacks. They retired only when their ammunition was exhausted and the British were about to envelop their position. Prescott's inspired leadership, along with equal efforts by Thomas Knowlton and John Stark, prevented the collapse of the American defenses and ensured that the British would gain no quick military victory that might have shattered the rebellion. He served for the remainder of the Boston siege and was appointed colonel of the Seventh Continental Regiment for 1776. He took part in the evacuation of Long Island and the action at Kips Bay. The elderly warrior, who was further handicapped physically by an injury sustained in farm work, retired to his home at the end of the campaign. In September 1777 he served as a volunteer in the militia sent to help stop Burgoyne's invasion from the north. Bunker Hill had showcased his talents, but an opportunity never again presented itself for him to repeat the performance. He died at Pepperell on 13 October 1795.

SEE ALSO *Bunker Hill, Massachusetts; Prescott, Oliver.*

BIBLIOGRAPHY

French, Allen. *The First Year of the American Revolution.* Boston: Houghton Mifflin, 1954.

Ward, Christopher. *The War of the Revolution.* 2 vols. New York: Macmillan, 1952.

revised by Harold E. Selesky

PREUDHOMME DE BORRE, PHILIPPE HUBERT, CHEVALIER DE.

(1717–1790 or 1791). Continental general. France. Entering the French army as a volunteer on the rolls of the Regiment of Champagne in 1740, he became *sous lieutenant* in 1741, lieutenant in 1742, and captain of a cavalry regiment (in Brittany, later Burgundy) in 1744. During the War of the Austrian Succession (1740–1748), he took part in several campaigns. In June 1745 he received four saber strokes on the head and one on the wrist; one hand was disabled permanently. He was deactivated in 1749. Promoted to lieutenant colonel, he organized a regiment from Liège (his birthplace) and was made a chevalier in the Order of Saint Louis in 1757. When his unit was reorganized in 1762, Borre was reassigned in grade to the Metz garrison and again deactivated later that year.

With a commission of brigadier general and official authority to go to America, Borre sailed from Le Havre on 14 December 1776 with Coudray and a large French contingent aboard the *Amphitrite,* but Coudray forced him off the ship. Borre changed to the *Mercure* and reached Portsmouth, New Hampshire, on 17 March. Reporting to Washington on 17 May, he was given a commission as brigadier general with date of rank from 1 December 1776. On 21 May he took command at Princeton of a brigade composed of Baron d'Arendt's German battalion and the Second, Fourth, and Sixth Maryland Continental Regiments and served in New Jersey during the summer of 1777. Borre drew Washington's ire when he took matters into his own hands and hanged a Tory civilian. In a blistering letter of 3 August, Washington ordered him not to take such initiative: "The temper of the Americans . . . will not countenance proceedings of this nature," the commander in chief wrote. Borre then tried and removed Major Thomas Mullens for insubordination, which Washington eventually supported. Borre commanded a brigade in the Staten Island raid of Sullivan on 22 August and at Brandywine on 11 September 1777. When Washington called for a court of inquiry on his behavior at Brandywine, Congress recalled him from the army on 13 September. The next day he offered his resignation, which was accepted. Borre later complained to Congress not only that he had been condemned without a hearing but that he deserved promotion to major general; Congress, however, rejected his request on 4 October. Richard Henry Lee was of the opinion that Congress's treatment of Borre was unfair.

Sailing from Charleston on 20 January 1779, the chevalier carried dispatches to d'Estaing at Cap Français in Saint Domingue. He reembarked on the *Andromaque* on 15 May, witnessed the fight in which this ship sank the British privateer *Tartar,* and reached Brest on 5 July. He received the rank of brigadier general in the French army on 1 March 1780. As early as 5 April, action was initiated to retire him for physical disability.

BIBLIOGRAPHY

Bodinier, André. *Dictionnaire des officiers de l'armée royale qui ont combattu aux Etats-Unis pendant la guerre d'Indépendance, 1776–1783.* Vincennes, France: Service historique de l'armée, 1982.

Ford, Worthington C. et al., eds. *Journals of the Continental Congress, 1774–1789.* 34 vols. Washington, D.C.: U.S. Government Printing Office, 1904–1937.

Rice, Howard C., Jr., and Anne S. K. Brown, eds. and trans. *The American Campaigns of Rochambeau's Army: 1780, 1781, 1782, 1783.* 2 vols. Princeton. N.J.: Princeton University Press, 1972.

Smith, Paul H. et al., eds. *Letters of Delegates of the Continental Congress, 1774–1789.* 26 vols. Washington, D.C.: U.S. Government Printing Office, 1976–2000.

Washington, George. *Writings of George Washington.* Edited by John C. Fitzpatrick. 39 vols. Washington, D.C.: U.S. Government Printing Office, 1931–1944.

revised by Robert Rhodes Crout

PRÉVOST, AUGUSTIN. (1723–1786).

British general. A French-speaking Protestant born in Geneva, Prévost served as a major in the Sixtieth Foot (Royal Americans) on 9 January 1756 and was dangerously wounded while serving under James Wolfe in the Quebec campaign of 1759. On 20 March 1761 he was promoted lieutenant colonel. In 1765 he married Nanette (Ann), daughter of Chevalier George Grand, an Amsterdam banker. Three sons and two daughters survived their father; the eldest, Sir George Prevost (born in New Jersey on 19 May 1767), became governor-in-chief of British North America in 1811 and oversaw the defense of his provinces from 1812 to 1814.

At the beginning of the War of American Independence, Prévost was the British military commander in East Florida. He left St. Augustine on 23 December 1778 with orders to cooperate with Archibald Campbell (who took Savannah from the rebels on 29 December) and take overall command of the British forces in the South. He captured Sunbury, Georgia, after a three-day siege on 9 January 1779, joined forces with Campbell, and on 19 February was promoted major general. While Campbell marched to Augusta, Prévost confronted the combined armies of Benjamin Lincoln and Robert Howe across the Savannah River. An amphibious operation against the rebel coast at Beaufort was beaten off; but on 3 March he annihilated John Ashe's force at Briar Creek, where Prévost's younger brother Marc led the enveloping column. When Lincoln thrust at Augusta, Prévost responded with a lunge at Charleston before withdrawing toward

Savannah. Supported by the talented military engineer James Moncrieff, he skillfully held the city against the combined Franco-American attack in October 1779. This victory consolidated the British hold on Georgia, attracted considerable Loyalist support, and damaged Americans' faith in the French alliance. Afterward Prévost returned to Britain, where he died in 1786.

SEE ALSO *Briar Creek, Georgia; Moncrieff, James; Savannah, Georgia (29 December 1778); Sunbury, Georgia (9 January 1779).*

BIBLIOGRAPHY

Mackesy, Piers. *The War for America, 1775–1783.* London: Longman, 1964.

Van Doren, Carl. *Secret History of the American Revolution: An Account of the Conspiracies of Benedict Arnold and Numerous Others.* New York: Viking, 1941.

revised by John Oliphant

PRIME MINISTERS OF BRITAIN.

"Prime minister" was the popular term used in Britain to designate the leader of the group or faction wielding the powers of government. According to the theory of balanced (or mixed) government, the king ruled the nation through his ministers who sat in Parliament, especially in the House of Commons, because it was that house alone that could originate the all-important measures having to do with money and taxes. The king had a great deal of leeway to select a prime minister and government, and generally sought someone whose policies he could endorse and whose personality he found compatible. Once satisfied he had found the right person, the king would ask him to form a government to manage the affairs of state, that is, to prepare a slate of men who would fill the offices of state because of their talents, their political connections, or a combination of both. The prime minister usually filled one of the senior offices of state, as there was no position called "prime minister" until the twentieth century.

The first statesman in British history who properly deserved to be called prime minister was Robert Walpole, first earl of Orford, who held sway between 1721 and 1742 during the reigns of George I and George II. Walpole was succeeded by the elderly Spencer Compton, the earl of Wilmington, who died on 2 July 1743. Wilmington was followed by Henry Pelham, a skilled parliamentary manager, who died on 6 March 1754. On Pelham's death, George II called on Pelham's brother, Thomas Pelham-Holles, the duke of Newcastle, whose strength was the management of patronage, to form a government. Newcastle, however, proved to be a poor manager of the war that broke out in North America in 1754 and extended to Europe in 1756. After installing a caretaker ministry led by William Cavendish, the fourth duke of Devonshire (October 1756 to April 1757), the king was forced to ask William Pitt the elder, later the earl of Chatham, to join in a coalition with Newcastle from 1757 to 1761. Pitt was a charismatic speaker in the House of Commons and a talented organizer of strategies and armies, but he was anathema to the king because of a lifetime spent opposing subsidy treaties for Hanover. When Pitt and Newcastle fell from power, the new king, George III, appointed his close friend and mentor, John Stuart, the third earl of Bute, as his principal minister, but the Scotsman was forced to resign on 8 April 1763 because he lacked support in Parliament. Rather than reappoint Newcastle and Pitt, the king turned to George Grenville, supposedly Bute's puppet but a force in the House of Commons in his own right. Best remembered for his advocacy of plans to tax and better control the American colonies, Grenville was dismissed on 10 July 1765 because the king found him "insolent in attitude and tedious in behaviour" (Beckett and Thomas).

The king next turned to Charles Watson-Wentworth, the second marquess of Rockingham, a younger member of the Newcastle-Pitt faction. An inexperienced administrator and poor parliamentary manager, he was more moderate than the king on American regulation and was dismissed on 30 July 1766. With nowhere else to turn, the king asked Chatham (Pitt) to form another ministry. But Chatham was physically frail, now a member of the House of Lords, and made haughty by his wartime success. Progressively retiring from business, he resigned in October 1768. Augustus Henry FitzRoy, the third duke of Grafton, who had been effective head of Chatham's ministry for over a year, became the next prime minister, but parliamentary politics and the deteriorating American situation led to his resignation on 30 January 1770. Frederick, Lord North, a true Commons man, had already agreed to become first lord of the Treasury (28 January).

For the next twelve years, with the king's firm friendship and support, North led the government with great skill as the American crisis turned into the American rebellion. Worn out by bad news from America and constant sniping from parliamentary opponents of the American war, he decided to resign on 20 March 1782, although his policies were still firmly supported by George III, who accused North of desertion when he resigned. Rockingham returned as prime minister, without the full confidence of the king; he died on 1 July 1782, before he could see the culmination of the negotiations he had set in train to end the war. William Petty, the second earl of Shelburne, continued many of Rockingham's initiatives, including peace with the United States (preliminaries were signed on 30 November), but he was personally unpopular

and unskilled in Parliament. He resigned on 22 February 1783 but stayed on until a coalition ministry under William Cavendish-Bentinck, the third duke of Portland, took office on 2 April 1783. The king had already come to detest the coalition by the time Charles James Fox introduced the India bill on 18 November. Seeing the bill as an attack on the prerogatives of the monarchy, the king took the unconstitutional step of comporting privately with Chatham's son, William Pitt the Younger, the rising star in Parliament, to take over the government. The coalition collapsed in December 1783, after the peace treaty ending the War of American Independence had been signed, and Pitt assumed office, inaugurating a period of relative calm that would be broken only by the next great war, against Revolutionary France.

The history of the prime ministership in this period highlights the reality that British politics was governed by the twin needs to manage Parliament, where intensely local and personal political relationships regularly overrode considerations of imperial policy, and to work with George III, Farmer George, the quintessential Englishman who could and did play an active role in shaping politics according to his notions of the place of the monarch in mixed government. A system of governance that had grown out of the interplay of forces in an island kingdom had yet to develop the means to govern an empire.

SEE ALSO *Bute, John Stuart, Third Earl of; Chatham, William Pitt, First Earl of; George III; Grafton, Augustus Henry Fitzroy; Grenville, George; Newcastle, Thomas Pelham Holes, Duke of; North, Sir Frederick; Rockingham, Charles Watson-Wentworth, Second Marquess of; Walpole, Sir Robert.*

revised by Harold E. Selesky

PRINCE OF WALES AMERICAN VOLUNTEERS.

Montfort Browne, governor of the Island of New Providence in the Bahamas from 1774 to 1780, was captured in the raid on Nassau on 3–4 March 1776. He and Major Cortlandt Skinner were exchanged in September 1776 for rebel Major General William Alexander (Lord Stirling). Early in 1777 Browne began raising a Provincial regiment on Long Island, largely from among Loyalist refugees from Connecticut. Mustered on 21 April, three days later it joined Major General William Tryon's force in the raid on Danbury, Connecticut. In August 1777 it numbered 450 men and was stationed at Kings Bridge, New York. On 24 May 1778 it embarked for Newport, Rhode Island, landing on 11 June, and fought in the battle of

Quaker Hill (Newport) on 28 August. After being evacuated from Rhode Island in October 1779, it served on Long Island until 25 March 1780, when it embarked with Lord Rawdon for the South. A detachment was virtually annihilated at Hanging Rock, South Carolina, on 6 August 1780; another detachment suffered heavy losses when attacked by Francis Marion at Great Savannah on 20 August. More losses were incurred when Major Andrew Maxwell surrendered Fort Granby to Henry Lee on 15 May 1781. The remainder of the regiment evacuated from Charleston in December 1782 and returned to New York. It was part of the Long Island garrison until 12 September 1783, when it embarked for New Brunswick, where it was disbanded on 10 October.

SEE ALSO *Browne, Montfort; Fort Granby, South Carolina; Great Savannah; Hanging Rock, South Carolina; Nassau Raid of Rathbun; Newport, Rhode Island (29 July–31 August 1778); Skinner, Cortlandt.*

BIBLIOGRAPHY

Baurmeister, Carl Leopold. *Revolution in America . . . Confidential Letters and Journals, 1776–1784.* Edited by Bernhard A. Uhlendorf. New Brunswick, N.J.: Rutgers University Press, 1957.

Cole, Nan, and Todd Braisted. "The On-Line Institute for Advanced Loyalist Studies." Available online at http://www.royalprovincial.com.

Katcher, Philip R. N. *Encyclopedia of British, Provincial, and German Army Units, 1775–1783.* Harrisburg, Pa.: Stackpole Books, 1973.

Mills, T. F. "Land Forces of Britain, the Empire, and Commonwealth: The Prince of Wales's American Volunteers." Available online at http://regiments.org.

Smith, Paul H. "The American Loyalists: Notes on Their Organization and Numerical Strength" *William and Mary Quarterly,* third series, 25 (1968): 259–277.

revised by Harold E. Selesky

PRINCETON, NEW JERSEY.

3 January 1777. Although his covering forces under Colonel Edward Hand delayed General Charles Cornwallis's approach to Trenton on 2 January so that the British did not reach the main American battle position along Assunpink Creek until dark, Washington knew that he could not stand up against the superior British forces upon the resumption of their attack the next day. Cornwallis was so sure of victory that he sought to avoid needless casualties and opted to wait until daylight rather than try to continue advancing in the dark.

Washington probably selected the position along Assunpink Creek with the thought of maneuvering in the direction of Princeton before he could be trapped. Washington convened a council of war in the evening of 2 January and, as was his custom, encouraged every member freely to speak his mind. Several offered an alternative to standing and fighting or risking a difficult night retreat. Brigadier General Arthur St. Clair had been on the extreme American right flank during the action that day and his patrols had uncovered a roundabout route to the north via Quaker Bridge. He suggested using that way to bypass Cornwallis; the Americans could then push six more miles and reach Princeton, where roads would allow them to go on to Brunswick. Adjutant General Joseph Reed, who had grown up in the area, confirmed the accuracy of the patrols' report and said that his own patrols with the Philadelphia Light Horse had found no evidence that the British were watching the route. At that point Brigadier General Hugh Mercer suggested that the move would appear to the public to be an advance, not a retreat, which would have a very important political impact. By the time the meeting broke up, virtually every member had supported this option, and Washington started making detailed plans to hit Princeton at dawn. As another piece of good fortune, the temperature dropped twenty degrees in a few hours, freezing muddy roads and making a rapid march possible.

MOVING TOWARD PRINCETON

Washington left a few hundred men to keep campfires burning as a deception, and the British interpreted the movements they saw as American preparations for another night attack like the one delivered on 26 December. At 1 A.M. on the 3rd, the last of the baggage and heavy guns headed south to Burlington under Brigadier General Adam Stephen, and Washington's main body started moving. Every precaution was taken to ensure secrecy. Only the generals knew where the expedition was headed, orders were given in whispers, and wheels of gun carriages were wrapped with rags to muffle their sound. It was a difficult feat for the veterans and the inexperienced militia, a few of whom panicked near South Trenton when they mistook another unit for Hessians. The column moved southeast for a bit to get clear of the lines and then swung east and finally turned north at Sandtown, a route that also had the added advantage of avoiding Brigadier Alexander Leslie's twelve hundred men in Maidenhead. At about first light (6:50 A.M.) it began to cross Stony Brook and deploy for the final advance. Major General John Sullivan took three brigades to the right in order to swing around and hit Princeton from the east. The main body under Washington and Major General Nathanael Greene formed the left wing and headed roughly north along a sunken road with Mercer's brigade in the lead. The scheme of maneuver was to have Sullivan drive the British to Worth's Mill,

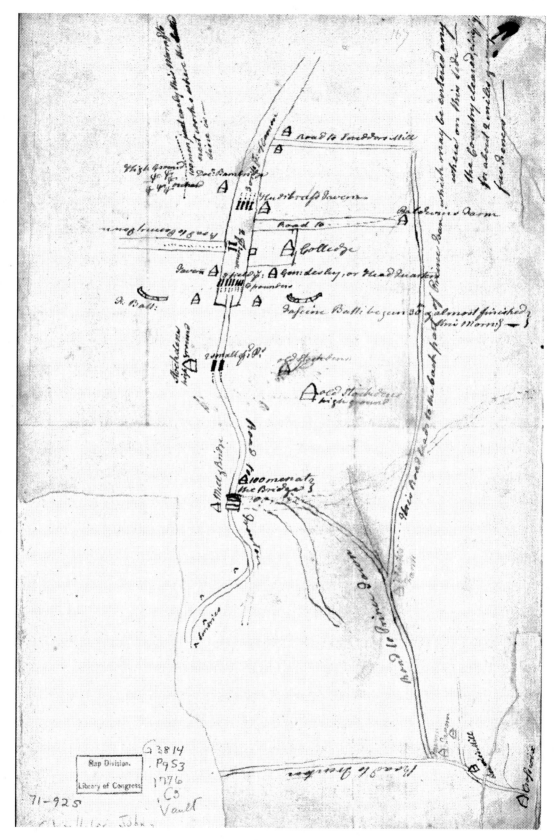

Plan of Princeton. *This American reconnaissance map, prepared in December 1776, shows the position of "Gen Lesley, or headquarters," near Princeton, New Jersey.* **THE LIBRARY OF CONGRESS, GEOGRAPHY AND MAP DIVISION**

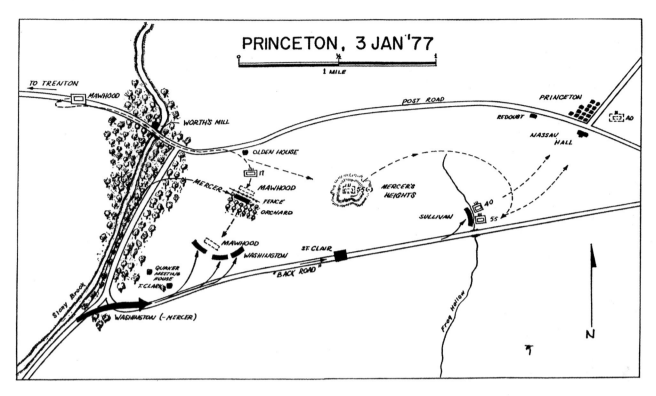

where part of Greene's force would be in a blocking position along Stony Brook, while the rest pushed on into town. Once again the Americans had missed their dawn attack because it had taken about five hours to travel nine miles, but they had done so without being detected.

Princeton was occupied by about twelve hundred British from Lieutenant Colonel Charles Mawhood's Fourth Brigade, which had orders to move up to join Cornwallis on the 3rd. About 5 A.M., unaware of Washington's approach, Mawhood set out with two of his regiments (the Seventeenth and Fifty-fifth Foot), some artillery pieces, a cumbersome supply convoy, and part of the Sixteenth Light Dragoons. He intended to join Leslie at Maidenhead and then move on to Trenton. The other regiment, the Fortieth Foot, stayed in Princeton to guard supplies. Shortly after sunrise (7:22), Mawhood had already crossed Stony Brook Bridge with the Seventeenth and part of the Fifty-fifth when his flankers detected Sullivan's column a mile away. Mawhood formed up to consider falling back to defend Princeton or pushing on to Maidenhead. But because he thought the Americans were trying to escape from a defeat at Trenton, he set out to attack them instead.

THE BATTLE

Because of the sunken road Mawhood did not see Greene's force, nor did Greene see him. Washington was on higher ground, however, and sent a messenger to tell Greene to change the plan and advance on the British as soon as he got clear of the ravine. As Mercer came into the open, he and Mawhood both headed for the high ground on William Clark's farm, and particularly for his orchard. Fifty dismounted British dragoons got there first, but Mercer's larger vanguard soon started gaining the upper hand. Both sides fed in more troops as fast as they came up, and they began exchanging volleys at a range of from forty to fifty yards. Mercer's men were getting the better of the fight, thanks to the presence of a number of companies armed with rifles, but after about five minutes, Mawhood launched a bayonet charge. Unable to counter because the rifles had no bayonets, the Americans crumbled. Mercer himself went down as did Colonel John Haslett, who was next in command, and a number of other key officers.

Colonel John Cadwalader's brigade of Philadelphia Associators, including Captain Joseph Moulder's artillery company, arrived at this time, and the British halted. Cadwalader attacked but was driven back in some confusion. That short pause, however, let other Americans (particularly Colonel Daniel Hitchcock's New England Continentals) build up a new line supported by eight guns firing from a hilltop. Washington himself came up and helped to rally Mercer's and Cadwalader's men. Then the Americans advanced using platoon volleys and at a range of thirty yards broke Mawhood's line. The remnants

The Death of General Mercer at the Battle of Princeton, January 3, 1777. *John Trumbull's painting depicts General Hugh Mercer's death in battle after Lieutenant Colonel Charles Mawhood's brigade launched a withering bayonet charge.* © FRANCIS G. MAYER/CORBIS

of the Seventeenth Foot headed towards Maidenhead, having entered the battle with about 250 men and endured around 100 killed or wounded and another 35 captured. The Fifty-fifth and the supply convoy fell back on Princeton. Meanwhile, the Fortieth Foot had heard the gunfire and formed up on the college grounds; it then moved up to the outskirts of the village.

Sullivan's right wing now entered the fight with Colonel Paul Dudley Sargent's brigade in the lead. They smashed into the line that the Fortieth was attempting to defend (at modern Frog Hollow) before it had been organized, driving the British back through town. Part of the Fortieth occupied Nassau Hall, the college building. Captain Alexander Hamilton unlimbered his guns and fired a round into the building; the 194 men inside promptly surrendered. The remaining 200 or so British troops retreated all the way to Brunswick, losing about 50 more prisoners along the way.

Cornwallis had started moving from Trenton as soon as he saw that the Americans were gone. As soon as Princeton had been secured, Washington sent Major John Kelly with a substantial militia force back to destroy the bridge over Stony Brook. This delayed Cornwallis's movement, and

the last Americans left town as the first enemy troops entered from the south. Although Washington wanted to continue his raid to Brunswick, his tired troops were not equal to the task. So rather than risk losing all that he had gained, he headed for safety in the high ground around Morristown and went into winter quarters on the 6th.

NUMBERS AND LOSSES

In the forty-five-minute battle near Princeton, the Americans lost around 35 killed and the same number wounded out of a total force of around 5,000—most of whom did not engage closely. Howe's notoriously shady official casualty reports admitted 28 killed, 58 wounded, and 187 missing. A more accurate accounting would be around 450 total losses, with 222 killed and wounded out of the 450 or so who bore the brunt of the fighting.

SIGNIFICANCE

The battle at Princeton effectively ended the British effort to occupy New Jersey outside of the strip near New York, where they could be supported and supplied by sea. It is significant primarily in the context of the greater campaign, and more for the political impact than the actual military damage inflicted. Unlike Trenton, which Howe and the ministry could blame on faults of the Germans, this time British regulars had been chewed up.

SEE ALSO *Hand, Edward; New Jersey Campaign.*

BIBLIOGRAPHY
Fischer, David Hackett. *Washington's Crossing.* New York: Oxford University Press, 2004.
Stryker, William S. *Battles of Trenton and Princeton.* Boston: Houghton Mifflin, 1898.

revised by Robert K. Wright Jr.

PRISONS AND PRISON SHIPS.

The lot of the Revolutionary War prisoner was hard, not solely because of deliberate policy, but also as neither the British nor the Americans were prepared in 1775 to take care of those they caught. Normal jail facilities soon were filled with political prisoners, both Whigs and Loyalists. Then came the large hauls: some four thousand rebels taken around New York City in 1776; nearly one thousand Germans at Trenton in 1776 and 1777; approximately five thousand British, Germans, and Canadians marched off from Saratoga as the Convention Army in 1777; over five thousand Americans surrendered in May 1780 at Charleston; and perhaps eight thousand British taken captive at Yorktown in October 1781. Naval prisoners continued to be taken throughout this period—fishermen, privateers, officers and men of the regular navies, and such special diplomatic prizes as Henry Laurens.

While the written record abounds with stories of hardships, atrocities, and escapes, precise facts and accurate figures about prisoners during the Revolution are difficult to arrive at and have only recently been explored by historians. We do not know how many were taken, although there is some reason to believe that the numbers for each side were about even at around twenty thousand each. Except for the notorious Simsbury mines in Connecticut, the Americans lacked—even more than the British—the means of securing prisoners. Most prisoners of war held by the Patriots were interned in the interiors of states, especially Pennsylvania, Virginia, and Maryland, where conditions were more healthful than that experienced by the prisoners of the British. Captured British and Germans tended to drift away from American camps after relatively short confinements; the Germans, in particular, were allowed and even encouraged to "escape" in the knowledge that they tended to end up as American farmhands rather than return to their British masters.

EXCHANGE OF OFFICERS

At the start of the war the two sides had no idea how to treat their prisoners. The British especially were at a loss. Many agreed with Lord Germain who thought that since those captured were rebels, they should be hanged. Many more saw the wisdom of the generals in the field, who appreciated that if they started hanging American prisoners, the Americans would reciprocate. The issue became an international one with the capture of Ethan Allen at Montreal in September 1775. The British authorities in Canada hated Allen, not just for the humiliating capture of Fort Ticonderoga, but also because of his efforts to arouse the Caughnawagas and other people of Canada against British rule. General Richard Prescott wanted to shoot him on the spot. But instead he was thrown in chains and sent to England, until allies there filed a writ of habeas corpus demanding that he either have charges brought against him, be declared a prisoner of war, or be freed. Baffled, the government decided to send Allen and most other prisoners back to America. Efforts to effect Allen's exchange for an officer of an equal rank, the traditional European method of handling officers, brought Washington into a long correspondence with the Howe brothers. The latter refused to address the former as a general, and Washington would not talk with the brothers unless they recognized his rank. When Washington heard of Allen's harsh treatment, he threatened to treat British officers the same way. Problems in connection with the exchange of prisoners prolonged the misery of captives and ran up the death rate. Finally, each side decided simply to ignore the details and proceed in traditional manner, exchanging officers and using a system of parole under which those captured agreed not to fight until they were exchanged.

RANK-AND-FILE SOLDIERS

However, the private soldier was treated with gruesome brutality, as Allen described in his popular *Narrative* of 1779. Most American military prisoners were packed into improvised jails and prison ships to suffer and die in large numbers. Elias Boudinot was the American commissary general of prisoners during 1777 and 1778, when policies concerning the prisoners of war (POWs) were put into place; his British counterpart was the corrupt Joshua Loring, whose wife, Elizabeth Lloyd, was the famous mistress of General Howe. Other British commissaries of prisoners were men named David Sproat and James [?] Lennox.

Britain's New York prisons. Infamous British prisons in New York City were Van Cortlandt's Sugar House (northwest corner of Trinity churchyard), Rhinelander's (corner of William and Duane Streets), the Liberty Street Sugar House (Nos. 34 and 36 Liberty Street), and the Provost Jail. The latter had been constructed in the Fields in 1758

Mill Prison. *Some American seamen captured at sea by the British during the American Revolution were held at Mill Prison in Plymouth, England. At the end of the war, there were more than one thousand seamen in captivity in Britain, primarily in Forton and Mill prisons.*
PLAN OF MILL PRISON (W/C AND INK ON PAPER) BY AMERICAN SCHOOL, 19TH CENTURY; PEABODY ESSEX MUSEUM, SALEM, MA/ BRIDGEMAN ART LIBRARY

and was known as the New Jail. It was administered by the notorious William Cunningham. The Provost and Liberty jails, in that order, were the most dreaded by patriots. Other places in New York City were used as prisons: some of the Dissenter churches, the hospital, King's College (Columbia), and one or more other sugar houses.

British prison ships. The prison ships were probably more horrible than the land jails. Originally used for naval captives, they subsequently were filled with soldiers. The British started using them not only to solve their problems of space in New York City—particularly after the fire of September 1776—but because they promised to be more secure and more healthful than conventional jails. Both assumptions proved wrong: any prisoner who could swim could escape from a ship more easily than from a land jail; improper administration of the prison ships—overcrowding, poor sanitation, inadequate food—turned them into death traps. Though again figures are only rough estimates, some seven thousand to ten thousand Americans died on these ships during the Revolution, the latter figure

supported by the discovery in 1803 of thousands of skeletons around the shores of Wallabout Bay.

Most notorious was the *Jersey,* a sixty-four-gun ship that had been dismantled in 1776 as unfit for service and that held one thousand or more prisoners. Other ships in Wallabout Bay were the *Hunter* and the *Stromboli.* The hospital ship *Scorpion* was moored off Paulus Hook; one of its guests was Philip Freneau, who wrote a dramatic poem about the horrors and hopelessness of life aboard a prison ship. At least thirteen different ships were used around New York City during the war. Others, of course, were used elsewhere. The *Sandwich*—although not a prison ship—was used to take political prisoners to St. Augustine from Charleston.

Other British prisoners. Other Americans were jailed at Halifax, and those taken on the high seas or in European waters saw the inside of such famous English prisons as Dartmoor, Old Mill Prison at Plymouth, Forton Prison at Portsmouth, and the Tower of London. Continental army prisoners taken at Charleston on 12 May 1780 were imprisoned for thirteen months at nearby Haddrel's

938

Point, where they suffered great hardships. Some elected to join the British army or to serve in units formed to fight in the West Indies. But the majority turned down freedom at the cost of serving the British. "The integrity of these suffering prisoners is hardly credible," Allen wrote. "Many hundreds, I am confident, submitted to death, rather than enlist in British service." Allen used his tale of the British mistreatment of POWs to persuade the public that Americans had no kinship with their enemy. Allen and many others reported on the privation that drove men to eat rats and insects, wood and stone; in one notorious instance, a prisoner ate his own fingers. It is certainly the case that stories of the horrific prisons in which Americans were placed fed patriotic feelings.

Seamen, and even fishermen, taken by the British were given the choice of joining the Royal Navy or spending the war in British jails. At the end of the war there were more than one thousand seamen in captivity in Britain, primarily in Forton and Mill prisons. Their treatment, being more routine, did not descend to the appalling levels of the prison ships.

IMPRISONING LOYALISTS

While the British were uncertain how to treat the American rebels, the latter also could not agree on their policy toward Loyalists. Some wanted to treat them as POWs and inter them with British and German prisoners; local Patriot leaders tended to take the view that they were criminals or traitors and should be dealt with accordingly. The Patriot government of New York imprisoned many Loyalists under the Kingston Court House, where the Provincial Congress held its sessions. The overcrowding and filth reached such a level that they disrupted the Congress's sessions. After many representatives complained, the Loyalists were moved to prison ships in the Hudson. In other states, some officials made arrangements with Loyalists taken in combat, confining them to their homes, while others hanged them on the spot. Americans, however, had very little experience incarcerating large numbers of people; most colonial towns did not have a jail. As a consequence, Loyalists often found it easy to escape, even from the brutal Simsbury mines. It seems that far fewer prisoners died in American hands than in British, but that may have as much to do with the lack of opportunity as with standards of humanity.

SEE ALSO *Boudinot, Elias; Convention Army; Cunningham, William; Exchange of Prisoners; Laurens, Henry.*

BIBLIOGRAPHY

Bellesiles, Michael A. *Revolutionary Outlaws: Ethan Allen and the Struggle for Independence on the Early American Frontier.* Charlottesville: University Press of Virginia, 1993.

Bowman, Larry G. *Captive Americans: Prisoners during the American Revolution.* Athens: Ohio University Press, 1976.

Cohen, Sheldon S. *Yankee Sailors in British Gaols: Prisoners of War at Forton and Mill, 1777–1783.* Newark, Del.: University of Delaware Press, 1995.

Metzger, Charles H. *The Prisoner in the American Revolution.* Chicago: Loyola University Press, 1971.

Sampson, Richard. *Escape in America : The British Convention Prisoners, 1777–1783.* Chippenham, U.K.: Picton, 1995.

revised by Michael Bellesiles

PRIVATEERS AND PRIVATEERING.

The term "privateer" refers to a privately owned and armed vessel that operates under the terms of a letter of marque, a document that allows the vessel to attack the enemies of its sovereign nation without the danger of being branded a pirate. The term itself, which can be traced to 1664, apparently is an abbreviation of "private man of war." Before that date, however, privateers were simply referred to as letters of marque, named after the document that legally separated their actions from piracy.

PRE-REVOLUTIONARY PRIVATEERING

Commerce raiding under the auspices of national sanction began as early as the thirteenth century in Europe. The crown traditionally issued letters of marque and reprisal to merchants during times of war. These documents were fundamentally based on the concept of reprisal. For instance, in 1242, when French vessels attacked the English coastline, Henry III issued letters of marque to the English merchants who had lost vessels to the attackers. Possession of a letter of marque legally separated a privateer from a pirate, which made the difference between life and death if captured. Whereas privateers sailed in the name of their mother country and within the constraints of a formal legal system, pirates illegally seized vessels without any recognition of nationality or sovereignty. Privateer prizes were adjudicated in admiralty courts, and the proceeds from the prizes were divided among crew and owners, with a portion given to the monarch. Based on such principles, the system remained essentially the same until the middle of the seventeenth century, when territorial expansion became increasingly important in the minds of most European politicians.

Throughout the seventeenth and eighteenth centuries, American colonists actively participated in Britain's commerce-raiding operations. Americans sanctioned, commanded, and served on privateers during every major intercolonial conflict of the period. During the colonial era, privateering reached an apogee along the North American Atlantic coast. Privateering's popularity soared throughout the British Empire. From the docks of London to the wharves of Charleston, wealthy merchants invested in privateering ventures. The profitability of privateering provided capital to many colonial economies. Colonial newspapers devoted entire pages to royal proclamations encouraging privateering, as well as advertisements on behalf of privateer owners. They reported the capture of prizes and the subsequent auctions of the cargoes.

During war years, seamen flocked to privateers in the hope of escaping service onboard Royal Navy vessels. Because it contributed to a state's sea power without putting large financial stress upon the national treasury, privateering offered a popular means of warfare during an age dominated by mercantilist ideas. Consequently, American society had become well accustomed to the privateering enterprise by the beginning of the American Revolution.

LEGAL JUSTIFICATION FOR PRIVATEERING

At the beginning of the Revolution, the rebelling colonies were faced with a series of dilemmas. How would they defeat or even challenge the mighty Royal navy? Would America's ports be laid waste by cannon shot and their commerce destroyed by blockades? There was no American navy, and the idea of building one seemed utterly foreign to most members of the Continental Congress. Although the colonies had united for mutual protection, most were primarily concerned with their own defenses on a local scale.

Faced with such daunting problems, the colonies and the Continental Congress had three options. The first involved building a national navy, something that Congress began on 14 December 1775, despite a complete lack of funds, equipment, and men. Most Americans, however, understood that confronting British naval power head-on was all but impossible. The second option concerned coastal defense through navies funded and outfitted by individual colonies. Nearly every colony chose this method of defense in late 1775 and early 1776. Nevertheless, relying on each state to finance a navy also proved to be impossible. Consequently, the colonies turned to privateering. In November 1775, Massachusetts began issuing letters of marque and reprisal, soon to be followed by several of the other colonies.

Privateering clearly provided Americans the best possible method of fighting the British at sea. On March 23, 1776, Congress resolved that: "The inhabitants of these colonies be permitted to fit out armed vessels to cruize on the enemies of these United Colonies," and that "all ships and other vessels . . . belonging to any inhabitant or inhabitants of Great Britain, taken on the high seas, or between

high and low water mark, by any armed vessel, fitted out by any private person or persons, and to whom commissions shall be granted, and being libeled and prosecuted . . . shall be deemed and adjudged to be lawful prize." Prizes were to be adjudicated in official state admiralty courts established upon the recommendations of Congress in 1775. Although suggested by Congress, these were not federal courts. The state courts, presided over by a judge and his marshal, both of whom were appointed by the state assemblies, included jury trials, payment in proportion of the vessel as salvage in the case of recapture, and a form of appeals. Congress established a federal appellate court, the first true federal court, and provided that appellants would pay triple costs if the state admiralty court's judgment was affirmed.

In legalizing privateering and recommending the establishment of admiralty courts, Congress realized the necessity of producing letters of marque for those individuals fitting out armed vessels. The commission, which closely resembled a British letter of marque, had blanks to be filled in by the state committees of safety or governors identifying the vessel, the master and owners, and the number of guns and crew. Obtaining a commission required posting a bond insuring compliance with congressional rules and regulations. Congress drafted the bond forms and issued them to naval officers in various ports and to the state governors.

NUMBER, NATURE, AND EFFECT OF PRIVATEERS

The total number of American privateers that operated from 1775 to 1783 is impossible to fully determine. Nevertheless, an intelligent estimate can be made that nearly 3,000 American private men-of-war set sail, of which some 2,768 have been identified to date by historian Joshua Howard. Earlier estimates were based solely on the Congressional records and those of a few New England states, However, these estimated excluded the activities of southern privateers, and so do not accurately reflect the true number. The majority of the privateers appear to been more accurately described as trading vessels than as war ships. The average American privateer carried only four guns and a crew of fifteen men, making it quite unlikely that most would have been strong enough to capture an enemy merchant vessel. This supports the conclusion that American privateers operated for the country's economic survival as much as for taking prizes. However, such vessels as the *Grand Turk*, carrying 28 guns and a 140-man crew and the 26-gun brig *Sturdy Beggar* with a crew of 105, indicate that some vessels were specifically intended for fighting.

The actual effect American privateers had on the outcome of the war has been hotly debated. Many historians have rightfully claimed that privateers took available seamen away from the Continental navy. Others have pointed out that the Continental navy never formed a viable threat to the Royal navy, and that privateering was indeed the fledgling nation's best option. Lloyd's of London records nearly 3,000 British vessels as having been captured. A good proportion of these were evidently retaken, however the number is most likely not completely accurate. Several privateers, such as the *John Hancock*, *General Stark*, and *Rattlesnake* performed several successful voyages, capturing numerous British prizes. Although British shipping continued to rise during the war, American privateers played an important role in dampening the morale of the British public, as well as providing much needed goods to the Patriot cause. Whether for patriotism or profits, or a combination of the two, America's privateersmen played an important and quite often neglected role in winning the country's independence from Britain.

BIBLIOGRAPHY

Bourguignon, Henry J. *The First Federsl Court: The Federal Appellate Prize Court of the American Revolution, 1775–1787.* Philadelphia: The American Philosophical Society, 1977.

Continental Congress. "Congressional Resolves on Privateering., March 23, 1776." In *Journals of the Continental Congress 1774–1789*, vol. IV. Washington, D.C.: Government Printing Office, 1904–1937.

Kendall, Charles Wye. *Private Men-of-War.* London: Philip Allen & Co., 1931.

Kert, Faye. *Prize and Prejudice: Privateering and Naval Prize in Atlantic Canada in the war of 1812.* St. John's, Nfld.: International Maritime Economic History Association, 1997.

Lewis, Archibald, and Timothy Runyan. *European Naval and Maritime History, 300–1500.* Bloomington, Ind.: University of Indiana Press, 1985.

Starkey, David. *British Privateering Enterprise in the Eighteenth Century.* Exeter, U.K.: University of Exeter Press, 1990.

revised by Joshua Howard

PRIZES AND PRIZE MONEY.

Although associated primarily with operations at sea, prize money also was awarded to officers and men who captured enemy property on land. The value of the capture was computed and prize money was awarded in accordance with a scale based on rank. Few disputes were as bitter and long lasting as those over prize money, with different ships, officers, and entire military services fighting over who deserved what share of captured property. For instance, after the British took Charleston in May 1780, the navy entered its claim to all of the goods seized, seeking to cut the army out of any share of the prize money. Sir Henry Clinton appealed to the Privy Council for a fair consideration of the army's claim but never received satisfaction.

In addition to every form of moveable property being subject to claims of ownership by the soldiers or sailors who captured them, slaves were considered prizes of war. Some Patriots were troubled by this standard. When a company of the Green Mountain Regiment captured a British officer in 1775, the company's men were informed that they were now considered the owner of his slave and her child. They voted unanimously that slavery violated the cause for which they fought and issued the woman a document proclaiming her freedom. Other Continental soldiers were not so scrupulous in their adherence to the ideals of liberty.

As for naval prizes and prize money, under maritime law the private property of an enemy power captured at sea under certain legal circumstances was a prize, and the proceeds of its sale were normally adjudicated by a prize court. On the English side, a healthy proportion, usually one-third, of all captured goods went to the king. Prize money usually went in its entirety to privateersmen, but if the prize were taken by a warship, then only half of the prize's value, prorated in accordance with the normal pay scale, went to the officers and men, with the rest going into state or congressional coffers. A prize master and crew took the captured ship into a home port or that of an allied power for condemnation in accordance with prize law. If the capture were illegal, that is, inside neutral waters and by a ship not bearing letters of marque and reprisal, the prize court would release the ship and award damages. Sailors were well aware that privateers did far better in the winning of prizes than ships of the Continental navy, and they therefore generally preferred service in the former over the latter. Later estimates of the amount awarded in prizes supports the judgment of the seamen. Eighteen million dollars worth of prizes were taken by six hundred American privateers whose crews averaged one hundred men, compared to two hundred prizes claimed by the Continental navy worth some six million dollars.

BIBLIOGRAPHY

Clark, William Bell. *Ben Franklin's Privateers: A Naval Epic of the American Revolution.* Baton Rouge: Louisiana State University Press, 1956.

Winslow, Richard E., III. Winslow III, "Wealth and Honour." In *Portsmouth During the Gold Age of Privateering, 1775-1815.* Portsmouth, N.H.: Peter Randall, 1988.

revised by Michael Bellesiles

PROCLAMATION OF 1763.

7 October 1763. To reduce Indian unrest stemming from land frauds and westward expansion, the imperial government and

several colonies had taken largely ineffective steps before 1763 to limit the migration of white settlers into lands claimed or controlled by Native Americans. The end of the French and Indian War opened the gates for a flood of settlers into western lands, putting further pressure on tribes trying to resist the creeping tide of white settlement. Moreover, the expulsion of the French from Canada eliminated the possibility that the tribes might strike a balance between competing European powers and thus negotiate a better deal for themselves.

Aware of the problem, Lord Shelburne, the president of the Board of Trade, drafted a plan that was put in final form by his successor, the earl of Hillsborough, and rushed to King George III for his signature on 7 October 1763. The Proclamation of 1763 was intended to provide a comprehensive solution to a wide range of issues raised by the expansion of the empire. Territories recently won from France were organized into four distinct and separate governments: the provinces of Quebec, East Florida, West Florida, and Grenada, the latter actually comprising the island of Grenada, the Grenadines, Dominica, St. Vincent, and Tobago, all in the West Indies. The boundary of Georgia was extended south from the Altamaha River to the St. Mary's River, the northern boundary of East Florida. The new province of Quebec (encompassing only the eastern portion of the former New France, from the St. Lawrence valley northwards) was put under English law, a provision that alarmed the overwhelmingly Roman Catholic, formerly French, inhabitants. The colonies reacted most strongly to the provision of the proclamation that established, for an indefinite period, a line along the watershed of the Allegheny Mountains as the western limit of British settlement and, in a modification of Shelburne's draft, ordered the withdrawal of colonists already west of this line, which meant those in the upper Ohio Valley. A vast territory west of Quebec and the Alleghenies was reserved for the indigenous Native Americans, who were nominally placed under the government of the British army, which was to garrison forts in the region to keep the peace and especially to regulate trade with the natives. The act specifically mentioned colonial land frauds and other offenses against the Indians and went into great detail about how these were to be prevented in the future.

The colonists strongly opposed the proclamation, which withdrew lands promised to veterans of the French and Indian War, restricted trade with the Indians, and curtailed the claims of the so-called Three-Sided colonies. Land speculators and frontiersmen objected to the restrictions on western migration. Canadians resented the imposition of English law, fearing it would be anti-Catholic and would call into question legal precedents established under the French regime. The colonists also recognized that the proclamation confined them to the seaboard, where they could be more easily controlled by the mother country; eliminated the chance for debtors to avoid prosecution by escaping over the Alleghenies; and curtailed the economic opportunities that seemed to shimmer just over the crest of the mountains.

SEE ALSO *Pontiac's War; Three-Sided States.*

BIBLIOGRAPHY

Douglas, David C. *English Historical Documents.* Vol. 9: *American Colonial Documents to 1776.* Edited by Merrill Jensen. New York: Oxford University Press, 1955.

Knollenberg, Bernhard. *Growth of the American Revolution, 1766–1775.* Edited by Bernard W. Sheehan. Indianapolis, Ind.: Liberty Fund, 2002.

Thomas, Peter D. G. *British Politics and the Stamp Act Crisis: The First Phase of the American Revolution, 1763–1767.* Oxford: Oxford University Press, 1975.

revised by Harold E. Selesky

PROPAGANDA IN THE AMERICAN REVOLUTION.

Americans realized early in their dispute with the mother country that they needed to tell their side of the story quickly and effectively in order to persuade people at home and abroad of the probity and justice of their cause. Their efforts to mould public opinion were often highly successful. Paul Revere's engraving of the Boston Massacre of 5 March 1770 made the case for activists in the other colonies that a garrison of regular soldiers was deadly for innocent, unoffending civilians. The murder of Jane McCrea showed that no one was safe from British-incited "savages." Americans condemned the successful British surprise attacks at Paoli, Pennsylvania, Tappan, New Jersey, and Wyoming, Pennsylvania, as "massacres." Contemporaries so besmirched the reputations of David Fanning, Banastre Tarleton, Joseph Brant, and Walter Butler that historians have been grappling to separate truth from fiction ever since.

SEE ALSO *Taxation without Representation Is Tyranny.*

revised by Harold E. Selesky

PROSPECT HILL.

This is an obvious name to give to any hill from which there is a good view. One was located near Cambridge, Massachusetts, and another was the place to which the American outposts withdrew in the preliminary maneuvers leading to the Battle of Long Island.

SEE ALSO *Long Island, New York, Battle of; Mutiny on Prospect Hill.*

Mark M. Boatner

PROTECTOR–ADMIRAL DUFF ENGAGEMENT.

9 June 1780. Massachusetts constructed the twenty-six-gun frigate *Protector* for her state navy in 1779, probably following the design of the Continental Navy's *Boston*. On 9 June 1780, during her first cruise, she ran into the thirty-two-gun privateer *Admiral Duff* from Liverpool, a converted East Indiaman. The engagement off the banks of Newfoundland was unusually fierce and ended only when the *Admiral Duff* sank with only fifty-five survivors. Captain John Foster Williams's frigate was also badly damaged, and was almost captured by the Royal Navy's *Thames* (thirty-two guns) in a running fight on her way back to Massachusetts.

BIBLIOGRAPHY

Millar, John F. *American Ships of the Colonial and Revolutionary Periods.* New York: Norton, 1978.

revised by Robert K. Wright Jr.

PROTESTERS.

This name was applied by Boston radicals to merchants in Massachusetts who refused to support the Solemn League and Covenant, a circular letter in which the Boston Committee of Correspondence asked every adult "to suspend all commercial intercourse" with Britain from 31 August 1774 until the Boston Port Act was repealed.

SEE ALSO *Solemn League and Covenant.*

revised by Harold E. Selesky

PROVINCIAL MILITARY ORGANIZATIONS.

American colonists who continued to be loyal to King George III organized military units to fight the rebels almost immediately after the start of hostilities in the spring of 1775. The Loyalist military response took forms that varied from what amounted to like-minded groups of thugs that banded together to support themselves with violence directed usually against the rebels to fully fledged military units with excellent discipline, superb tactical skills, and all the esprit de corps that uniforms, accoutrements, and distinctive emblems could reflect and reinforce. The military value of Loyalist units was a function of how and when they were raised, and by whom. The men in most of these formations were as capable of performing valuable military service—such as standing in battle, skirmishing in support of regular troops, ambushing rebel units, and raiding rebel settlements—as any American soldiers raised and led under similar circumstances. The men on both sides of the imperial civil war who trailed off into activity of no appreciable military value were nothing more than bandits and outlaws, and they had little if any positive impact on achieving the political outcomes each side was trying to obtain.

The majority of Loyalist units formed in America were authorized by the British commanders in chief in America or Canada and were thus entitled to be called "Provincials," an extension of the name applied by the British to colonial regiments raised during the French and Indian War. These Provincials were raised for a fixed term of service (usually two years or the duration of the war), were paid, clothed, armed, fed, and housed by the British government, were subject to the same discipline, and were liable for service anywhere in North America. They were not legally part of the regular establishment, having been created for temporary service in a particular theater. On 2 May 1779, however, three Provincial regiments were placed on a hybrid American Establishment that offered them higher status and certain tangible benefits like access to better clothing and half pay for officers upon disbanding. The first three units—the Queen's Rangers (or Queen's American Rangers), the Volunteers of Ireland, and the New York Volunteers—were designated the First through Third American Regiments, and they were followed on 7 March 1781 by two more American regiments, the King's American Regiment (Fourth) and the cavalry of the British Legion (Fifth). On Christmas Day 1782, four of the American Regiments (all but the Third) were elevated to the British Establishment, a mark of royal favor that allowed their officers the chance to find a place in the permanent military forces of the crown. All of the Provincial regiments were disbanded at the end of the war.

Major General William Tryon, the former royal governor of North Carolina and New York, was the commander in chief of the Provincial forces in America, headquartered at New York City. Oliver De Lancey of New York (formerly commanding De Lancey's Brigade) was the senior brigadier general. The other brigadier generals were Cortlandt Skinner of New Jersey (New Jersey Volunteers); Montford Browne, governor of the Island of New Providence in the Bahamas (Prince of Wales's

American Regiment); and in 1780, Benedict Arnold, the rebel defector. Alexander Innes served as inspector general, and Edward Winslow as muster-master general.

Any calculations concerning the Loyalist military effort—the history and number of Loyalist military units, the overall strength of those units, and the impact of armed Loyalism on the outcome of the War for American Independence—are complicated by a lack of records and problems in defining whom to count as a Loyalist. There seem to have been over 150 named Loyalist units during eight years of war, ranging from companies with a few tens of men to multiple-battalion regiments of well over one thousand soldiers. Somewhere between seventy and one hundred units seem to have had a significant military presence, at least to the extent of continuing to seek recruits and achieving an extended military presence. Perhaps three dozen units took the field with a maximum known strength of at least several hundred men; these are the units that can claim to have contributed materially to the British war effort.

The peak of Loyalist fighting strength—nearly ten thousand officers and men on the rolls of Sir Henry Clinton's command, headquartered at New York City— was recorded on 15 December 1780, but that figure does not include the units operating under Major General Frederick Haldimand's command from Canada or several units still in the process of organizing. According to Paul H. Smith, approximately twenty-one thousand men "saw service in the provincial corps during the War for Independence," but Nan Cole and Todd Braisted contend that "All told, perhaps 50,000 served at one time or another, on the land and on the sea," a difference that seems to rest on Smith's reliance on muster roll data and Cole's and Braisted's desire to be inclusive ("American Loyalists," p. 266; Cole and Braisted, "On-Line.")

SEE ALSO *Associated Loyalists; British Legion; Butler's Rangers; Guides and Pioneers; King's American Regiment of Foot; Loyal Americans; Loyalists in the American Revolution; New Jersey Volunteers; New York Volunteers; Queen's Rangers; Queen's Royal Rangers; Regular Establishment; Royal Highland Emigrants; Volunteers of Ireland.*

BIBLIOGRAPHY

Cole, Nan, and Todd Braisted. "The On-Line Institute for Advanced Loyalist Studies." Available online at http://www.royalprovincial.com.

Smith, Paul H. *Loyalists and Redcoats: A Study in British Revolutionary Policy.* Chapel Hill: University of North Carolina Press, 1964.

———. "The American Loyalists: Notes on Their Organization and Numerical Strength." *William and Mary Quarterly,* third series, 25 (1968): 259–277.

Ward, Harry M. *Between the Lines: Banditti of the American Revolution.* Westport, Conn.: Praeger, 2002.

revised by Harold E. Selesky

PROVOST JAIL SEE *Prisons and Prison Ships.*

PRUSSIA AND THE AMERICAN REVOLUTION.

On 6 April 1776, the Continental Congress resolved to open trade to all nations except Great Britain. While this international trade plan was developing, the fundamental question was whether the foreign governments involved might also be enlisted to protect or even legitimize that trade. Because of the structure of the Prussian state, its king, Frederick the Great, set foreign policy. His relationship with Britain had been strained before the disturbances in North America developed. During the Seven Years' War (1756–1763), Britain's alliance with Prussia had been abandoned by the policies of Britain's prime minister, John Stuart, the third Earl of Bute, in favor of reaching a settlement with Britain and Prussia's mutual enemy, France. Frederick felt himself betrayed. A decade later (at the time of the first Polish partition), Frederick was further embittered by the British attempt to prevent him from acquiring Danzig.

As the American crisis intensified, Frederick became a close observer of developments. Frederick was interested in seeing Britain humbled while trying to keep Prussia out of direct involvement. When his adviser, Count Joachim Karl von Maltzan, suggested open commercial relations with the Americans, Frederick replied on 3 June 1776 that the American situation was still too problematical and that, without a navy, Prussia would be unable to protect the trade. Therefore, Frederick was determined to maintain a strict neutrality. In November 1776, Silas Deane sent William Carmichael to Berlin to make proposals for direct trade. Frederick again declined, preferring that all such trade be conducted through French ports. On 14 February 1777, Deane, Benjamin Franklin, and Arthur Lee sent Frederick copies of the Declaration of Independence and the Articles of Confederation to indicate American resolve. This time Frederick instructed his foreign minister, Gebhardt Wilhelm von der Schulenberg, not to completely refuse— he hoped not to offend the colonies but to keep them in a friendly disposition. When the commissioners (a group including Deane, Franklin, and Lee) proposed sending a formal representative to his court, Frederick declined, but before his reply could be received, Arthur Lee arrived in

Berlin. The Prussians were willing to tolerate Lee's presence, provided that he act in a private capacity. This he was willing to do until the Elliot Affair.

On 26 June, during the absence of Lee from his residence, the British minister to Prussia, Hugh Elliot, sent one of his servants to take Lee's papers and have them copied. Elliot's private secretary, Robert Liston, carried the copies to London and sent the servant out of Prussia. Elliot, sensing an impending diplomatic furor over the theft of the papers, immediately acknowledged personal responsibility for the act. Frederick, hoping to avoid a diplomatic crisis, suspended all further investigations into the matter. Lee left Berlin amid the failed negotiations. During Lee's absence, his secretary, Stephen Sayre, attempted to continue negotiations with Prussia with a proposal that Prussia take the island of Dominica in exchange for sending Prussian officers to serve in the American army. This aroused little interest from Frederick. Further relations between Prussia and the Americans would be conducted by correspondence alone.

When Lee wrote again to propose the opening of Prussian ports to American vessels, Frederick instructed Schulenberg to "[p]ut him off with compliments." Frederick now acted to refuse the British permission to cross his lands with their mercenaries from Bayreuth, Anspach, and Cassel. Yet Frederick's actions were not so much a support of the American cause as concern about potential mutinies among these mercenaries. When Arthur Lee wrote to inform Schulenberg about American successes in the battle of Saratoga, Frederick directed his minister to reply that he was waiting on France to recognize American independence. This time the Prussians made a counter proposal: If the Americans wanted munitions, they were free to purchase them through the firm of Splittgerber. Arthur Lee purchased 800 guns, only to discover later that they were useless.

Through 1778, Frederick continued to resist William Lee's proposals for formal relations. On 2 January 1778, Schulenburg wrote to Lee that Prussian ports would be open to "all nations who come there to trade in goods not forbidden," but Prussia would not protect those vessels nor permit prizes into its ports. What especially interested Frederick was the Silesian linen trade, which had largely been a pre-war American market through Britain. It constituted one-third of Prussian exports. Yet Frederick did not recognize American independence until after Britain had. Only in June 1783 did the Prussian minister to France, Baron Bernhard Wilhelm von der Goltz, propose to Franklin a formal commercial agreement between the two countries. A commercial treaty would not be signed until 10 September 1785.

Had Frederick been friendlier to Britain, France might have hesitated to tie itself to the American cause, and more German states might have provided mercenaries to the British. Frederick seems to have been oblivious to any ideological significance from the American Revolution. As he had informed Prince Henry in 1777, "[w]ithout shocking anyone, we are profiting quietly from the opportunity offered to us."

SEE ALSO *Deane, Silas; Franklin, Benjamin; German Auxiliaries; Lee, Arthur.*

BIBLIOGRAPHY

Brown, Marvin L. Jr. "American Independence through Prussian Eyes: A Neutral View of the Negotiations of 1782–1783." *The Historian,* 18 (1955–1956): 189–201.

————, trans, ed. *American Independence through Prussian Eyes, A Neutral View of the Peace negotiations of 1782–1783: Selections from the Prussian Diplomatic Correspondence.* Durham, N.C.: Duke University Press, 1959.

Clem, Harold J. "Frederick the Great and the American Revolution." Ph.D. diss., Harvard University, 1945.

Dippel, Horst. "Prussia's English Policy after the Seven Years' War." *Central European History* 4 (1971): 195–214.

————. *Germany and the American Revolution.* Translated by Bernard A. Uhlendorf. Chapel Hill, N.C.: University of North Carolina Press, 1977.

Frederick the Great. *Politische Correspondenz Friedrich's des Grossen.* Edited by Gustav Berthold Volz, et al. 47 vols. Berlin: A. Duncker, 1879–.

Gunther, Hans K. "Frederick the Great, the Bavarian War of Succession, and the American War of Independence." *Duquesne Review* 16 (1971): 59–74.

Haworth, Paul Leland. "Frederick the Great and the American Revolution." *American Historical Review.* 9 (1904): 460–478.

Holzinger, Walter. "Stephen Sayre and Frederick the Great: A Proposal for a Prussian Protectorate for Dominica (1777)." *William and Mary Quarterly* 3d series, 37 (1980): 302–311.

Toborg, Alfred. "Frederick II of Prussia and His Relations with Great Britain during the American Revolution." Ph.D. diss., Columbia University, 1966.

revised by Robert Rhodes Crout

PULASKI, CASIMIR. (1748–1779).
Continental Army cavalry leader. Poland. A well-educated nobleman, Pulaski entered military service in 1767 and the next year fought with his family against the Russians, but he was forced to flee to Turkey after the first partition of Poland in 1773. By late 1775 he was in Paris, without money or prospects. He was introduced to Benjamin Franklin and Silas Deane and expressed an interest in joining the American struggle for independence. With a letter of introduction from Franklin and with funds advanced by Deane, Pulaski reached Boston in July 1777 and met with Washington a month later, during which meeting they spoke about his cavalry experience in Poland.

He served as a volunteer aide-de-camp to Washington at the Battle of the Brandywine, on 11 September, and performed so well in reconnoitering enemy positions and rallying dispirited American troops that Washington thought he might be the man to command the four regiments of dragoons authorized by Congress. Washington proposed his appointment to Congress in a letter dated 27 August. Congress created the post of "Commander of the Horse" on 15 September and appointed Pulaski to the position with the rank of brigadier general.

Like many of the other foreign officers in the Continental Army, Pulaski had already created considerable animosity by demanding a rank subordinate only to that of Washington and Lafayette. Unable to speak much English and unwilling to take orders from Washington (but reporting directly to Congress), he quickly became embroiled in controversy. He took little part in the Battle of Germantown on 4 October 1777 but thereafter performed outpost duty at Trenton and Flemington while the army was in winter quarters at Valley Forge and acted with Wayne on foraging expeditions. The two men did not get along, Wayne believing that Pulaski disparaged the fighting abilities of American soldiers and Pulaski resenting the fact that American officers disliked taking orders from a foreigner. During this time, he preferred court-martial charges against Stephen Moylan, one of his regimental commanders, for "disobedience to the orders of General Pulaski, a cowardly and ungentlemanly action in striking Mr. Zielinski, a gentleman and officer in the Polish service, when disarmed ... and giving irritating language to General Pulaski" (Freeman, vol. 4, p. 537 n.). Moylan was acquitted but became Pulaski's ardent enemy.

In March 1778 Pulaski resigned his post as chief of cavalry and to add to his grievances, Moylan was temporarily elevated to fill it. Congress granted Pulaski's request to raise an independent body of mounted troops and approved his proposal to include prisoners and deserters if Washington had no objection. Despite Washington's disapproval of his recruiting scheme, Pulaski started gathering prisoners over the summer from his headquarters at Baltimore. On 17 September he appeared before Congress to complain that he was being given no opportunity for action. Less than a fortnight later he got his chance. Ordered to Little Egg Harbor, New Jersey, to guard stores, his poorly disciplined and carelessly deployed legion was surprised by Ferguson on 4–5 October 1778. When the Cherry Valley Massacre in New York on 11 November brought cries for the protection of frontier settlements, his legion was posted on the Delaware River at Minisink. From there he wrote Congress plaintively on 26 November that he could find "nothing but bears to fight."

With the British capture of Savannah, Georgia, on 29 December 1778 and the desperate need for American cavalry in the South, on 2 February 1779 Pulaski was ordered to march to Charleston, South Carolina. He arrived in time to help defend the town against Prevost's raid, but when he crossed the Cooper from his post at Haddrell's Point on 11 May in an attempt to ambush a detachment of the enemy, he was badly beaten. Now under Lincoln's command, he wrote Congress on 19 August to complain of the "ill treatment" he had encountered in the American army, although he expressed hopes that he might still have a chance to prove his devotion to the American cause. He led the advance of Lincoln's army that besieged Savannah in late September and established communication with the French fleet. Mortally wounded in a gallant but foolhardy cavalry charge on 9 October 1779, he died aboard the U.S. brig *Wasp*, probably on the 11th, after a surgeon had been unable to extract a grapeshot from his upper right thigh. He was buried at sea.

It has been said that "his American career was ... a chronicle of disaster and embittered disappointment." However, the commentator continues, "his gallant death served to ennoble even his mistakes in the eyes of posterity" (Frank Monaghan in *DAB* 15, pp. 259–260).

SEE ALSO *Little Egg Harbor, New Jersey; Minisink, New York (19–22 July, 1779); Savannah, Georgia (29 December 1778).*

BIBLIOGRAPHY
Freeman, Douglas Southall. *George Washington.* 7 vols. New York: Scribner, 1948–1957.

revised by Harold E. Selesky

PUNISHMENTS.

Punishment in the military forces of the eighteenth century was intended to maintain the order and subordination necessary for proper and effective operation in the face of the enemy, with the ultimate goal of defeating the enemy before he defeated you. While the pain and suffering inflicted on soldiers and sailors were incredibly severe by modern standards, most of those who labored under military discipline accepted the need for the physical punishment of bad behavior, as long as it could be seen to be applied equally to similar infractions. Soldiers and sailors who brought the bad habits of civilian life into military service could be expect to be flogged for offenses like theft, gambling, and drunkenness, and to receive no sympathy from their peers who would otherwise have been their victims. The special circumstances of military and naval service also introduced a set of offenses that had no parallel in civilian life (like sleeping on guard duty, disrespect of officers, desertion, and mutiny) or that sometimes had a different standard of punishment than might apply to a similar crime in civilian life.

Flogging on the bare back with a nine-strand whip, called a cat-o'-nine-tails, was the most common punishment, performed by a drummer or drummers under the supervision of the regimental surgeon. It was intended both to punish current bad behavior and deter future misbehavior, impressing the miscreant with the seriousness of his offense but not killing him. Although flogging could maim a man for life, soldiers and sailors were too scarce a commodity to be regularly subjected to savage punishment and thereby rendered unable to perform the services for which they had been recruited in the first place. The system of military discipline gave officers considerable leeway when sitting on courts martial in judgment of men who were, in European armies at least, considered to be their social inferiors. While there was the occasional sadist in the officer corps, and many officers could be inattentive to the welfare of their men and their regiment, good officers tried to apply punishment fairly, with the goal of maintaining order among groups of unruly, mostly unmarried men, and of ensuring that in battle they responded swiftly and predictably to their officers' commands. Still, the scale and intensity of corporal punishment in European armies and navies seem cruel and capricious to the modern reader. A court-martial might award three hundred lashes for a misdemeanor infraction, or it might condemn a man it had to punish but thought it might rehabilitate to a thousand lashes. This latter punishment was administered in increments, but nonetheless approached a death sentence.

Colonial Americans generally found corporal punishment, as applied in the British army, to be excessive and distasteful, perhaps more because it ratified and emphasized the social gulf between officers and men than because of the severity itself. Americans derided the "Bloody Backs" (British enlisted men) for accepting this sort of degradation and, at the start of the Revolution, believed that they did not need to be beaten to be good soldiers. Their first articles of war (in Massachusetts and adopted by the Continental Congress) set a limit of thirty-nine lashes even for the most serious non-capital infractions. This limitation caused problems because it deprived General George Washington and his officers of a graduated scale of punishment. Congress gradually adopted a more flexible system, assigning a higher number of lashes for more serious crimes, thus disabusing Americans of the notion that discipline could be maintained by their innate virtuous behavior rather than by physical sanctions.

Some enlightened contemporaries questioned not the need for discipline, but differed as to the best means of maintaining it. Reflecting in his journal on soldiers who were marauding in the neighborhood of their winter quarters, Dr. James Thacher noted on 1 January 1780 that:

> General Washington . . . is determined that discipline and subordination in camp shall be rigidly

enforced and maintained. The whole army has been sufficiently warned, and cautioned against robbing the inhabitants, . . . and no soldier is subjected to punishment without a fair trial.

While Thatcher understood that corporal punishment "may be made sufficiently severe as a commutation for the punishment of death in ordinary cases," he remarked that it "has become a subject of animadversion and both the policy and propriety of the measure have been called into question." He went on to note:

> [I]t is objected that corporeal punishment is disreputable to an army; it will never reclaim the unprincipled villain, and it has a tendency to repress the spirit of ambition and enterprise in the young soldier; and the individual thus ignominiously treated, can never, in case of promotion for meritorious services, be received with complacency as a companion for other officers. . . . it remains to be decided, which is the most eligible for the purpose of maintaining that subordination so indispensable in all armies.

Much time would elapse before less draconian solutions won general acceptance. Flogging was not abolished in the U.S. Army until 1861, and other corporal punishments, like "riding the wooden horse," survived through the Civil War. The extent to which military justice was balanced between punishment and correction is seen in the way Washington occasionally used his power to commute a death sentence to make a point with his troops. Soldiers would be drawn up in formation on three sides of a square, assembled to witness the execution of serious criminals—deserters, murderers, mutineers—who were sitting or standing along the fourth side, when word would arrive that the commander in chief had pardoned one or more of the malefactors, perhaps because they were young soldiers led astray by their more culpable elders. One or more executions of those deemed to be hardened criminals would proceed, with the commuted—but flogged—survivors serving as living reminders that discipline would be enforced.

SEE ALSO *Bloody Backs; Corporal Punishment.*

BIBLIOGRAPHY

Frey, Sylvia R. "Courts and Cats: British Military Justice in the Eighteenth Century," *Military Affairs*, vol. 43. no. 1 (February 1979): 5–11.

———. *The British Soldier in America: A Social History of Military Life in the Revolutionary Period.* Austin, Tex.: University of Texas Press, 1981.

Gilbert, Arthur N. "The Changing Face of British Military Justice, 1757–1783," *Military Affairs*, vol. 49, no. 2 (April 1985): 80–84.

Neagles, James C. *Summer Soldiers: A Survey and Index of Revolutionary War Courts-Martial.* Salt Lake City, Utah: Ancestry Incorporated, 1986.

Thacher, James. *A Military Journal During the American Revolutionary War, from 1775 to 1783.* 2d Ed. Boston, Mass.: Cottons and Bernard, 1827.

revised by Harold E. Selesky

PURSUIT PROBLEMS.

The term "pursuit" means, in a tactical context, harrying a foe defeated on the battlefield in order to increase the enemy's disorganization and casualties. It is a way of using relentless speed and fresh troops to capitalize on battlefield success and inflict an even greater defeat on the enemy. Pursuit is difficult to accomplish because it requires a commander to look beyond the battlefield, anticipate the outcome, and collect forces in the right places to exploit what are sometimes fleeting opportunities. Eighteenth-century armies that were infantry heavy and used cavalry largely as battlefield shock troops were poorly configured for pursuit. Since most terrain in eastern North America was unsuitable for cavalry, European competitors during the colonial wars rarely expended the time and the almost prohibitive expense to get horse soldiers to the battlefield. The British had experimented with incorporating light cavalry, the most useful force for pursuing a broken foe, into the overall scheme of linear tactics. However, the only British victory in America that culminated in an effective pursuit was Camden, South Carolina, on 16 August 1780.

S E E A L S O *Camden Campaign.*

revised by Harold E. Selesky

PUTNAM, ISRAEL.

(1718–1790). Continental general. Connecticut. Born at Salem Village (later Danvers), Massachusetts, on 7 January 1718, "Old Put" was already an American hero when the Revolution started. Because he showed no interest in schooling, Putnam received only scant formal education. He moved to Pomfret, Connecticut, around 1740 and became a prosperous farmer. Although only about five feet six inches tall, he was powerfully built, square-jawed, and had a love for outdoor activity. One of the earliest legends associated with him is that in the winter of 1742–1743 he killed a large wolf in her den.

FRENCH AND INDIAN WAR

At the start of the French and Indian War in June 1755, this thirty-seven-year-old farmer left his wife and six children to enlist as a private in the Connecticut provincials. He displayed notable leadership and coolness under fire at the

Israel Putnam. *A Continental general who had fought in the French and Indian War, "Old Put" was already an American hero when the Revolution started.* © BETTMANN/CORBIS

Battle of Lake George (8 September) and shortly thereafter volunteered to join Robert Rogers's rangers. He proved adept at the hard and dangerous work of scouting and reconnaissance and was soon captain of an ad hoc Connecticut ranger company. He spent most of the next eight years in the field, much of the time leading rangers and scouts. Promoted to major in 1758, he was captured after a botched ambush in late July 1758 and was about to be burned at the stake by French-allied Native American warriors when he was rescued by a French officer. He spent four months as a prisoner in Canada, was exchanged, and was then promoted to lieutenant colonel, serving in that rank for the rest of the war (1759–1762, 1764).

In 1760 he marched with Jeffrey Amherst from Oswego to Montreal. Two years later he was among the few survivors of a shipwreck off Cuba in the disease-ridden expedition that captured Havana, and in 1764 he commanded Connecticut's five companies in John Bradstreet's march to Detroit during Pontiac's War. Connecticut's most famous soldier returned to his farm in Pomfret, married a second time (3 June 1767), and set up a tavern in the house his new wife had inherited from her first husband. He left home for an extended period only once more, from 1772 to 1774, when he and the former senior officer of Connecticut provincials, Major General Phineas Lyman, went up the

Mississippi as far as Natchez to examine land granted to Connecticut veterans of the Havana expedition and to see what possibilities existed for land speculation.

PATRIOT LEADER

At home in Pomfret, Putnam became a prominent member of the Sons of Liberty. He opposed the Stamp Act and led the mob of former soldiers that forced the colony's stamp distributor to resign. When the imperial government closed the port of Boston, he drove a herd of 125 sheep there to relieve the hunger of the townspeople (15 August 1774). He responded with his customary audacity when rumors arrived on 3 September that General Thomas Gage had seized provincial gunpowder at Charlestown, Massachusetts. Although he held no rank in the militia, he initiated the call that prompted perhaps a thousand armed Connecticut men to march toward Boston on the Powder Alarm. When the news that actual fighting had broken out at Lexington reached Pomfret on 19 April 1775, Putnam was plowing on his farm, and according to legend, he was said to have left the plow in the furrow, unhitched one of the horses, left word for the militia to follow, and ridden one hundred miles in eighteen hours to Cambridge.

In late April 1775, the General Assembly appointed him second brigadier general (after Major General David Wooster and First Brigadier General Joseph Spencer) and then colonel of the Third Connecticut Regiment (1 May), in which ranks he served during the first few weeks of the Boston siege. With typical aggressiveness, on 13 May he led two thousand men through the deserted streets of Charlestown "to show themselves to the regulars," but this reckless action did not draw a response (French, p. 187). A skirmish with British raiders removing cattle from Noodle's Island in Boston Harbor on 25 May so impressed Congress, sitting in Philadelphia, that it appointed him a Continental major general, fourth in seniority to Washington himself, an egregious violation of the Connecticut pecking order that enraged Wooster and Spencer. Although he had actual command only over the two Connecticut regiments then at Cambridge, he urged his Massachusetts colleagues to act aggressively in response to William Howe's plan to break the Boston siege. In the council of war that preceded the Battle of Breed's Hill (17 June 1775), he is alleged to have said that "Americans are not at all afraid of their heads, though very much afraid of their legs; if you cover these, they will fight forever" (Frothingham, p. 116). During the battle itself, he labored hard to send reinforcements to Colonel William Prescott and is alleged to have given the order (conventional wisdom in the age of smoothbore musketry and also attributed to, among others, Prescott himself), "Don't fire until you see the whites of their eyes." His display of confidence, vigor, and aggressiveness helped to sustain American morale and was the pinnacle of his career. After Washington arrived at Cambridge on 3 July, Putnam commanded the American center.

SUBSEQUENT CAMPAIGNS

At the start of the New York Campaign, Putnam was in overall command at New York City for a short period before Washington arrived. On 24 August 1776 he superseded John Sullivan in command of the forces that were later defeated in the Battle of Long Island on 27 August 1776. During the remainder of the New York Campaign and Washington's withdrawal to the Delaware, Putnam played no significant part. He was put in command of Philadelphia toward the end of the year, and when the British consolidated their position in northern New Jersey after Washington's victories at Trenton and Princeton, Putnam commanded the American wing posted at Princeton from January to mid-May 1777.

By this time, it was apparent to Washington that the old hero lacked the qualities of a field commander. In May 1777 he was made commander of the Hudson Highlands. He failed to prevent Sir Henry Clinton from capturing Forts Clinton and Montgomery on 6 October and from burning the town of Kingston on the 16th. Although a court of inquiry cleared Putnam of any misconduct or negligence in the temporary loss of the forts, Washington granted his request for a leave of absence to attend to family business and replaced him with Alexander McDougall on 16 March 1778.

During the winter of 1778–1779, Putnam commanded the forces quartered around Redding, Connecticut. On 26 February 1779 he is alleged to have escaped from Loyalist raiders near Stamford, Connecticut, by riding his horse in a headlong gallop down a flight of rocky steps, an improbable display of horsemanship by a sixty-one-year-old man but not out of character with either the man himself or the legend. In May he was in command of American forces on the west side of the Hudson until a paralytic stroke in December 1779 forced his retirement. He died at Brooklyn, Connecticut, on 29 May 1790 after an illness of two days. He was a cousin of Rufus Putnam and a granduncle of the founder of the G. P. Putnam's Sons publishing house.

ASSESSMENT

Putnam's greatest strength as a soldier was his ability to inspire raw American soldiers with confidence in their martial skill; his contributions during the early stages of the Boston siege were especially important. A courageous, energetic, and optimistic officer on the battlefield—"as colonel of a fighting regiment, he would have been admirably placed," the historian Christopher Ward has stated— he lacked the patience, insight, and administrative acumen to succeed as a general (vol. 1, p. 76). Putnam's enduring appeal rests on the image of him as a "self-made man, unlettered but wise, brave yet compassionate" (Bruce C. Daniels in ANB), the very embodiment of the ideal American citizen, a "rough-hewn Cincinnatus" who ranked "second only to Washington in the pantheon of revolutionary heroes" (Paul D. Nelseon in ODNB). Timothy Dwight, who served with him in the Highlands and was later president of Yale College, composed this epitaph: "Ever attentive to the lives and happiness of his men, he dared to lead where any dared to follow."

SEE ALSO *Clinton's Expedition; Long Island, New York, Battle of; New York Campaign.*

BIBLIOGRAPHY

French, Allen. *The First Year of the American Revolution.* Boston: Houghton Mifflin, 1934.

Frothingham, Richard. *History of the Siege of Boston.* 6th ed. Boston: Little, Brown, 1903.

Humphreys, David. *An Essay on the Life of the Honorable Major General Israel Putnam.* Hartford, Conn.: Hudson and Goodwin, 1788.

Livingston, William F. *Israel Putnam: Pioneer, Ranger, and Major-General, 1718–1780.* New York: G. P. Putnam's Sons, 1901.

Niven, John. *Connecticut's Hero: Israel Putnam.* Hartford: American Revolution Bicentennial Commission of Connecticut, 1977.

Tarbox, Increase N. *Life of Israel Putnam ("Old Put"), Major-general in the Continental Army.* Boston: Lockwood, Brooks, 1876.

Ward, Christopher. *War of the Revolution.* 2 vols. New York: Macmillan, 1952.

revised by Harold E. Selesky

PUTNAM, RUFUS. (1738–1824). Continental general and engineer. Massachusetts. Putnam was born at Sutton, Massachusetts. His father died when he was seven; after his mother remarried, the boy was reared by relatives. In 1754 he was apprenticed to a millwright in Brookfield. Three years later he enlisted as a private in the Massachusetts provincial service during the French and Indian War. He was a sergeant by 1759 and an ensign in 1760. Six feet tall and noted for his strength and activity, he had "a peculiar oblique expression" caused by a childhood eye injury (DAB). He lacked formal schooling, but his efforts at self-education supplemented his practical training, which he put to good use in the construction of defensive works around Lake Champlain. Back in Brookfield after the war, he farmed, built mills, and—having taught himself geometry—was supporting himself as a surveyor when the war broke out. In 1773 he helped survey lands granted to veterans along the Mississippi River.

He had just passed his thirty-seventh birthday when he became lieutenant colonel of Colonel David Brewer's Massachusetts Regiment on 19 May 1775. He became involved in military engineering during the Boston siege and made the valuable suggestion that timber frames (chandeliers) be used to solve the problem of erecting fortifications on frozen ground, a technique that contributed to the American success at Dorchester Heights on 4–5 March 1776. Meanwhile, he was commissioned lieutenant colonel of the Twenty-second Continental Infantry (Connecticut) on 1 January 1776. After he had worked on the defenses of New York City, Congress promoted him to colonel on 5 August and named him acting chief engineer. Putman resigned this appointment when Congress would not establish a corps of engineers, but in November 1776 he accepted a commission as colonel of the Fifth Massachusetts Regiment for 1777. He served at Saratoga under Horatio Gates, in John Nixon's First Massachusetts Brigade, but saw no important action. He served in the Hudson Highlands for much of the rest of the war, working on the defenses of West Point and its supporting posts. On 7 January 1783 he was appointed brigadier general. Putnam was prominent in presenting officer grievances to the state and Confederation authorities, and in June he chaired the board of officers that framed the Newburgh petition asking Congress for some definite provision to be made to give veterans land bounties in the Ohio territory, something Congress refused to do. On 3 November 1783 he retired from the army. "As a soldier he was brave and resourceful, but he was neither a great strategist nor an eminent military engineer" (DAB). He was limited by his lack of education, particularly in mathematics.

Between the summer of 1784 and the fall of 1785, Putnam surveyed lands in Maine (then a part of Massachusetts) and administered their sale as the state's superintendent of Surveys of Eastern Lands. In early 1786 he and Benjamin Tupper took the lead in organizing the Ohio Company of Associates, a joint-stock venture that attracted many veterans who were interested in moving west. Congress sold 1.5 million acres on the north bank of the Ohio River to the company in 1787. Putnam reached Adelphia (later Marietta, Ohio) on 7 April 1788 as superintendent of the company. President Washington appointed him a judge for the Northwest Territory in March 1790. As a brigadier general in the regular army (4 May 1792), he took part in negotiating Indian treaties and participated in the operations of Anthony Wayne. He became the first surveyor general of federal lands in Ohio, holding this post from 1 October 1796 until 1803. He died at Marietta on 4 May 1824.

SEE ALSO *Dorchester Heights, Massachusetts; Ohio Company of Associates; Wayne, Anthony.*

BIBLIOGRAPHY

Putnam, Rufus. *The Memoirs of Rufus Putnam.* Edited by Rowena Buell. New York: Houghton Mifflin, 1903.

revised by Harold E. Selesky

PUTRID FEVER. SEE *TYPHUS.*

Q

QUAKER GUN SEE *Rugeley's Mills.*

QUAKERS.

For the approximately sixty thousand members of the Society of Friends—known as Friends or Quakers—the American Revolution was a trying time. During a military conflict in which Americans were forced to choose sides, most Friends throughout British North America followed their spiritual convictions and rejected violence. Quaker pacifism arose from their belief that all individuals possessed an "Inner Light" and were thus spiritual equals before God who must be treated with kindness and respect. As a result, Quakers refused to take sides in the Revolutionary War, nor did they offer support to the military efforts of either American or British forces. At the same time, their spiritual beliefs led them to aid all those who suffered because of the war. Though Quaker charity work often garnered praise during and after the war, their refusal to choose sides after 1775 led to regular harassment, financial hardships, and deep suspicion, particularly among AmericanPatriots, the most ardent of whom viewed Friends as closet Loyalists.

A MILITANT PACIFIST STANCE

It had not always been so. When the imperial conflict between Great Britain and the colonies erupted in the mid-1760s, Quakers supported the Patriot cause and agreed that the colonies had a right to protest (peacefully) British incursions upon their liberties, particularly the imposition of taxes by the British Parliament without the consent of provincial assemblies. As the crisis deepened,

however, leading Friends worried that the coercive and extralegal nature of the Patriot response, particularly the enforcement of nonimportation agreements and the growing danger of crowd violence, threatened to violate the Quaker peace testimony. As a result, in January 1775 the Philadelphia Yearly Meeting, which played a leading role in establishing the rules (or discipline) of Quaker conduct, issued an epistle addressed to American Friends which declared that participation in the resistance movement constituted a violation of the sect's religious principles. After violence erupted in 1775, Quakers adopted a more resolute stand in favor of absolute neutrality. In January 1776 the Philadelphia Yearly Meeting issued an epistle addressed to the public at large designed to explain the sect's neutrality and avert a final break with Great Britain. Unfortunately, this public statement, which compared the "peace and plenty" Americans enjoyed under British rule with the "calamities and afflictions" that plagued public life in 1776, was interpreted by Patriots such as Thomas Paine, in a postscript to the second edition of *Common Sense,* as a sign of Friends' Tory sympathies. Quakers fell into further disrepute in August 1777, when Congress published a fabricated letter from the nonexistent "Spanktown Yearly Meeting" addressed to British military leaders that described in detail the size and location of George Washington's forces in Pennsylvania. Despite the Society's rebuttals, the widely publicized letter further stirred anti-Quaker sentiment.

A month later, this hostile environment and the British army's advance on Philadelphia prompted Congress to order the arrest of over forty suspected Loyalists, including many of Philadelphia's leading Quakers. Offered their freedom in exchange for pledging loyalty to Pennsylvania, eighteen Quakers could not in good conscience take the oath and remained incarcerated without charge. Ultimately, they were transported to Winchester, Virginia, where they were held for over seven months. Despite relatively tolerable conditions, two of the "Virginia exiles" died during the incarceration, while all faced the emotional trauma and economic disruption that resulted from enforced separation from their families, friends, and business concerns. Most galling to the exiles, however, was that they were held without charge or trial. For Quakers, the denial of habeas corpus seemed to belie the cause for which Patriots were fighting. Ultimately, many Patriots raised the same concerns, though it was mid-April 1778 before Congress and Pennsylvania ordered the exiles returned to the state and released. This episode was the most notorious example of repression faced by the Quakers, revealing that by 1777 many Patriots viewed Friends and Loyalists as one and the same.

In the meantime, the Philadelphia Yearly Meeting decided to clarify the sect's discipline to ensure that Quakers throughout America responded to threats in a unified fashion. Friends, the meeting decided in epistles issued in September and December 1776, were not allowed to hold positions in the new state governments, serve in the military in any capacity, or pay any war taxes or military fines. Failure to follow these injunctions, the Philadelphia Meeting added, would result in disownment from the sect. By mid-1777, all the yearly meetings in America had embraced these measures, ensuring that Friends throughout the new nation embraced a militant pacifist stance.

HARDSHIPS

Though conditions differed in each state, Quaker pacifists faced real hardships during the war. First, most of the various Patriot governments tried to force Friends to serve in the military, particularly during times of man-power shortages. Young Quaker men who refused service were frequently threatened, publicly ridiculed, or jailed and, less frequently, beaten or forcibly marched to the front. Quakers meticulously documented these abuses in newly-created executive committees, or "Meetings for Sufferings," believing that their trials represented an opportunity to spread their spiritual truths. Some Quakers, however, were unable to abide by the strict pacifism of the sect, particularly because so many shared the goals—political and civil liberty—if not the tactics of the Patriots. In all, some one thousand Friends were disowned for serving in the military over the course of the war, and in 1781 a small group of Philadelphia Friends who actively supported the Revolutionary cause established the Free Quakers, which survived as a separate meeting into the early nineteenth century. Still, despite the hardships involved, the vast majority of Friends remained faithful to the peace testimony and refused to serve in the military.

If demands for military service were the most visible problem faced by Quaker pacifists, a more widespread difficulty was the fines imposed by states for nonservice or refusing to hire substitutes. Seeking to avoid complicity in war making in any way, Friends refused to hire substitutes or pay fines for nonservice. The states responded by distraining, or seizing, Quaker property and jailing those who owned little of value. Ultimately, the loss of property was the biggest problem Quakers faced during the war, with estimated losses amounting to over 100,000 pounds. As in the case of military service, some Friends found themselves unable to uphold this aspect of the peace testimony; over the course of the war, local meetings dealt with over 450 individuals who paid fines or hired substitutes; ultimately, the meetings disowned 250. Still, it is striking how rare such violations were.

A third problem facing Friends during the war was the taking of loyalty oaths. Friends had long rejected oath taking, but during the Revolution oaths became still more problematic, because Quakers believed that by swearing loyalty to the new governments, they would be sanctioning the violence that created them. For this decision, Quakers suffered a variety of punishments. A Pennsylvania law of 1778, for example, denied nonjuror Friends access to the courts; required that they pay double (and later treble) taxes; and closed the medical, legal, and educational professions to them. Still, only 187 Friends were disowned for taking loyalty oaths.

The payment of taxes presented larger problems for Quakers. Though the sect agreed that Friends should refuse to pay specific war taxes, they divided over whether members should pay general taxes that were used for both peaceful and military purposes. The Philadelphia and Virginia Yearly Meetings called on members to avoid paying all taxes to the new American governments during wartime, but other meetings were less adamant, and ultimately no meeting made the payment of general taxes a disownable offense. Still, if calls for broad tax resistance failed to generate widespread support, the American Revolution marked the first time Friends as a body refused to pay war taxes. For their stand, Quakers suffered the distraint of property, in the process paying far more to the state governments than had they paid the taxes. Quakers also divided on whether they could use Continental currency, created to fund the war, in good conscience. A minority of steadfast Friends condemned the use of paper money, but ultimately the yearly meetings left this issue up the conscience of individuals, because widespread support for such radical measures did not exist.

AID TO THE SUFFERING

If Quaker spiritual values prompted Friends to embrace neutrality, they also pointed in another direction: providing aid to those who suffered because of war. Thus, despite their economic woes, the Society generously provided aid to Quakers and non-Quakers alike who faced hardship as a result of the fighting. For Friends, charitable contributions of this kind became an ideal way to display their spiritual principles while simultaneously enabling them to contribute to the new civil society taking shape in America. Early in the war, Friends sent aid to beleaguered families in New England and Norfolk, and the British occupations of New York in 1776 and Philadelphia in 1777–1778 prompted similar outpourings of relief. When the war turned south in 1778, Quakers raised funds for war-ravaged civilians in Georgia, the Carolinas, and Virginia. Friends also provided medical aid to wounded soldiers and helped to bury the dead of both armies when fighting took place in their vicinity.

The American Revolution was a time of suffering for Quakers. Paradoxically, however, the depredations of war also enabled the sect to forge a new sense of unity and strengthen its internal discipline. Perhaps more important, the war enabled Quakers to establish a novel public role for themselves in the new nation. During the war, Friends viewed both their willingness to suffer for their beliefs and their relief efforts as testimony to their higher spiritual values. After the war, they continued to adopt unpopular positions—opposition to slavery, defending the interests of Indians, and continued pacifism—as part of an ongoing battle to improve the nation by spreading virtue. In effect, Quakers became the conscience of the nation.

SEE ALSO *Religion and the American Revolution.*

BIBLIOGRAPHY

Brock, Peter. *Pioneers of the Peaceable Kingdom.* Princeton, N.J.: Princeton University Press, 1968.

Gilpin, Thomas. *Exiles in Virginia: With Observations on the Conduct of the Society of Friends during the Revolutionary War.* Philadelphia: n.p., 1848.

James, Sydney V. "The Impact of the American Revolution on Quakers' Ideas about Their Sect." *William and Mary Quarterly,* third series, 19 (July 1962): 360–382.

Mekeel, Arthur J. *The Relation of the Quakers to the American Revolution.* Washington, D.C.: University Press of America, 1979.

Oaks, Robert F. "Philadelphians in Exile: The Problem of Loyalty during the American Revolution." *Pennsylvania Magazine of History and Biography* 96 (1972): 298–325.

Tiedemann, Joseph S. "Queens County, New York, Quakers in the American Revolution: Loyalists or Neutrals?" *Historical Magazine of the Protestant Episcopal Church* 52 (1983): 215–227.

A. Glenn Crothers

QUARTER.

As a noun the word means the promise not to kill an enemy soldier if he surrenders; a soldier may offer quarter to an enemy who appears to be losing the fight, or the latter may "cry quarter"—ask for quarter. After the Battle of the Waxhaws in North Carolina on 29 May 1780, in which Patriots were said to have been killed after demanding quarter, the expression "Tarleton's Quarter" arose to mean "no quarter."

As a verb, "to quarter" means to put soldiers into "quarters" (billets, barracks, or other form of lodging).

SEE ALSO *Quartering Acts; Waxhaws, South Carolina.*

Mark M. Boatner

QUARTERING ACTS.

15 May 1765 and 2 June 1774. The Mutiny Act of 1765 was passed to improve discipline of the British army throughout the world, and it included a provision for quartering troops in private houses. Alarmed by the latter provision, Americans adopted the evasion of refusing to recognize any clause of the act that did not refer specifically to overseas British possessions. A supplementary act, generally known as the Quartering Act, was therefore passed—at the request of Major General Thomas Gage, commander in chief in North America—that required colonial authorities to furnish barracks and supplies to British troops in America. This Quartering Act was to take effect on 24 March 1765 and to be in force for two years; it eliminated the provision for billeting troops in private houses. Colonial assemblies not only were reluctant to vote money for such a purpose, but they also realized that compliance with this act would be evidence that they acknowledged the right of Parliament to tax them without their consent. They therefore were careful not to meet fully the requirements for supplies or else they furnished them as a gift. In 1766 a second act authorized the use of public houses and unoccupied houses for billets. On 2 June 1774 the act was applied to all the colonies and extended to include occupied dwellings.

SEE ALSO *New York Assembly Suspended.*

BIBLIOGRAPHY

Douglas, David C., gen. ed. *English Historical Documents.* Vol. 9: *American Colonial Documents to 1776,* edited by Merrill Jensen. New York: Oxford University Press, 1955.

Shy, John. *Toward Lexington: The Role of the British Army in the Coming of the American Revolution.* Princeton, N.J.: Princeton University Press, 1965.

Thomas, Peter D. G. *British Politics and the Stamp Act Crisis: The First Phase of the American Revolution, 1763–1767.* Oxford: Oxford University Press, 1975.

―――. *Tea Party to Independence: The Third Phase of the American Revolution, 1773–1776.* Oxford: Oxford University Press, 1991.

revised by Harold E. Selesky

QUARTERMASTERS OF THE CONTINENTAL ARMY SEE *Supply of the Continental Army.*

QUEBEC (CANADA INVASION).

31 December 1775–1 January 1776. Lacking siege artillery, faced with expiring enlistments, and unable to bluff the defenders into surrender, General Richard Montgomery determined that his only chance of capturing the fortified city of Quebec was by assault. But with only one thousand men against seventeen hundred assorted defenders, Montgomery would have to surprise the enemy. The operation would have to be undertaken at night and under cover of a snowstorm to permit getting close enough for the assault to have some hope for success. The western walls, facing the Plains of Abraham, being too strong to attack, the final plan called for feints in this area while Arnold and Montgomery converged on the lower town from opposite sides. The latter forces were to link up at Mountain Street, force Prescott Gate, and push their way into the upper town. British General Guy Carleton had, unfortunately for the Americans, seen that the attack would probably be directed against the lower town, and he had organized his defenses accordingly. The Sault-au-matelot, a narrow, winding street that Arnold's column would have to follow to reach the heart of the lower town from the north, was well defended. Astride the route that Montgomery would have to follow to enter the lower town from the other direction, the defenders had erected a blockhouse with a battery, called Pot-Ash, two hundred yards behind it, from which they could deliver cannon and musket fire along the narrow road before them.

On 29 and 30 December 1775, the weather was fair, but signs of bad weather became apparent on the 31st. The sky clouded over during the afternoon, the wind rose, and whiffs of fine snow appeared. Soon after dark a fierce snowstorm was in progress. The rebel forces assembled at 2 A.M. and two hours later were moving out. The feints fizzled out quickly without deceiving Carleton in the least; Colonel James Livingston's small force of Canadians approached St. John's Gate but then broke and ran; and one hundred Massachusetts men under Captain Jacob Brown (brother of John Brown) delivered a sustained fire against the Cape Diamond bastion, but without any significant effect.

MONTGOMERY'S COLUMN

From his position on the Plains of Abraham, Montgomery led three hundred men of the First New York through the howling blizzard, down a mile of narrow, twisting, snow-choked trail to Wolfe's Cove. From this point they struggled along the river's edge with their cumbersome scaling ladders. The Canadian guards in the blockhouse fled when they saw the rebels approaching. As Montgomery led the advance guard of some twenty men up to the battery, the defenders fired their cannon at near point-blank range, instantly killing Montgomery; Captain John Macpherson, his aide-de-camp; Captain Jacob Cheeseman; and two others. Only Aaron Burr, Edward Antil, and one or two men escaped unhurt. The unheroic Colonel Donald Campbell took command and led the New Yorkers to the rear, leaving Arnold unsupported.

ARNOLD'S COLUMN

Arnold led the vanguard of twenty-five men parallel to the northern wall of Quebec and within fifty yards of its defenders, through the suburb of St. Roque, and toward the Sault-au-matelot's northern end. Captain John Lamb followed with a six-pounder on a sled and forty artillerymen. In single file came the rest of Arnold's command: Virginia riflemen under Captain Dan Morgan and Pennsylvania riflemen under Lieutenant Archibald Steele and Captain William Hendricks. With the exception of Captain Henry Dearborn's company, which was late assembling, the New Englanders, with some forty Canadians and Indians, brought up the rear for a total strength of about six hundred men.

Arnold passed a two-gun battery undetected and was beyond the Palace Gate when the enemy opened fire from the wall. The Americans sustained several casualties as they pushed on another few hundred yards and came up against the first barrier outside the lower town. Lamb's cannon was supposed to be used to batter this down, but it had overturned and been abandoned. Although the weather had rendered most of their muskets useless, the rebels pressed ahead with their attack. Arnold was taken out of action by a leg wound, but Morgan assumed command and carried the first barrier, cutting off and capturing about fifty of its defenders. Morgan was blasted from the top of the first scaling ladder and knocked back into the snow, uninjured, but with his face pocked with grains of burned powder. He roared back to his feet, up the ladder, and over the barrier at the head of his men. The advance guard charged into the Sault-au-matelot to the next barrier, some three hundred yards away. Captain Humphreys led the attack against the next barricade but was killed as his men were driven back by bayonets, Carleton having been able to move defenders from elsewhere in the city to this position. With the British firing on the attackers from the houses above, Morgan ordered his troops to seek cover in nearby buildings. Before the Americans could effect their retreat, Carleton sent a force of two hundred men with two cannon to block their escape. Dearborn's company was surprised just outside the gate and overwhelmed. Arnold and many of his men managed to get away by fleeing across frozen St. Charles Bay; the remaining attackers, 426 men including Morgan, surrendered around 9 A.M.

Carleton lost five killed and thirteen wounded; the Americans suffered sixty casualties. The loss of Montgomery was a particularly hard blow for the rebels, since he was a general of exceptional promise.

CRITIQUE

Montgomery's attack was audacious and foolhardy, an act of desperation. A coordinated attack in a snowstorm is always a risky enterprise, especially with largely untrained troops. Montgomery refused to consider retreating back to winter bases, feeling that he had a unique opportunity to expel the British from Canada. Hampered by the short enlistments of his soldiers and faced with enormous provisioning difficulties, he hoped that a bold stroke would overwhelm the enemy. Unfortunately for the Americans, Carleton proved a well organized and intelligent opponent.

SEE ALSO *Brown, John; Burr, Aaron; Canada Invasion; Carleton, Guy; Dearborn, Henry; Lamb, John; Montgomery, Richard; Morgan, Daniel.*

BIBLIOGRAPHY

Shelton, Hal T. *General Richard Montgomery and the American Revolution: From Redcoat to Rebel.* New York: New York University Press, 1994.

revised by Michael Bellesiles

QUEBEC. 6 May 1776. A sortie by General Guy Carleton routed General John Thomas's force of American besiegers. The Americans fled, beginning the collapse of their northern army. Carleton did not pursue them, waiting for the arrival of his reinforcements under the command of General John Burgoyne.

SEE ALSO *Canada Invasion.*

revised by Michael Bellesiles

QUEBEC (STADACONA). Site of an Iroquois village named Stadacona (also called Kanata, the Iroquoian word for village, from which Canada gets its name) when first visited by Jacques Cartier in 1535, the town of Quebec was founded (and named) by Champlain in 1608. When captured by the British in 1629, the village—which served primarily as a trade and missionary center—had only two permanently settled families. Returned to France in 1632, Quebec was unsuccessfully besieged by Sir William Phips in 1690, and a large British expedition under Sir Hovenden Walker was shipwrecked in the Gulf of St. Lawrence in 1711 as it advanced on Quebec. The church Notre Dame des Victoires, begun in 1688 and finished in 1723, commemorates these British failures. The British under General James Wolfe captured Quebec in 1759 and the city passed into British hands, becoming the capital of Canada in 1763. Some 1,500 houses had been built in the Upper and Lower Town by 1775. (Construction of the citadel, located atop the 333-foot Cape Diamond, was not begun until 1823, but the place was well fortified.)

SEE ALSO *Colonial Wars; Quebec Act.*

revised by Michael Bellesiles

QUEBEC ACT. 20 May 1774. Although projected before the destruction of the tea in Boston Harbor that provoked the imperial government to crack down on Massachusetts, the Quebec Act alarmed the colonies as much as did the so-called Intolerable Acts. By extending Canada's boundaries to the Ohio River, it removed from control of the established colonies some of the western territories claimed by Connecticut, Massachusetts, and Virginia. By granting the French Canadians full enjoyment of their religion, it in effect established the Roman Catholic Church in Canada. By recognizing the mechanisms of land tenure that had been used under the French regime, it calmed Canadian nerves about the security of their property. By making the members of the royal council that governed the colony serve at the whim of the king, it strengthened the hand of the royal governor in dealing with the colony's legislature. All of these provisions were rooted in sound governmental reform for a conquered colony that had been under what amounted to military government since 1763. But in the context of the imperial crisis, each provision exacerbated an existing cause of controversy between the established colonies and the mother country. For most Canadians, the reestablishment of familiar customs and traditions made them less resentful of British rule, but because the act also favored

the traditional sources of power in Canadian society, Canadians were not actively loyal to Britain so much as neutral when the American rebels invaded in the summer of 1775.

SEE ALSO *Canada in the Revolution; Intolerable (or Coercive) Acts.*

BIBLIOGRAPHY

Knollenberg, Bernhard. *Growth of the American Revolution, 1766–1775.* Edited by Bernard W. Sheehan. Indianapolis, Ind.: Liberty Fund, 2002.

revised by Harold E. Selesky

QUEEN ANNE'S WAR. 1702–1713. British colonists called military operations in North America during the War of the Spanish Succession (1701–1714) "Queen Anne's War," after Queen Anne.

SEE ALSO *Colonial Wars; Spanish Succession, War of the.*

revised by Harold E. Selesky

QUEEN'S ROYAL RANGERS. This name was applied to a proposed Provincial regiment that was to be formed by Dr. John Connolly on the Pennsylvania and Virginia frontiers in the autumn of 1775.

SEE ALSO *Connolly, John.*

revised by Harold E. Selesky

QUINBY BRIDGE, SOUTH CAROLINA. 17 July 1781. While General Nathanael Greene's army was resting in the Santee Hills, General Thomas Sumter got authority to employ the forces of Lieutenant Colonel Henry Lee and General Francis Marion with his own to attack the outpost at Monck's Corner. The latter position was commanded by Lieutenant John Coates, who had his unseasoned Nineteenth Regiment and some mounted South Carolina rangers led by Major Thomas Fraser. When Sumter attempted a turning movement on 14 July, Coates withdrew to a strong defensive position around Biggin Church. On the afternoon of the 15th, as the Patriots settled into a camp expecting to do battle the next day, Coates launched a

bold attack. Caught off guard—and without proper pickets—Sumter's forces were on the verge of collapse when Lieutenant Colonel Edward Lacey led a counterattack that drove Fraser's Loyalists back to their positions around the church. Sumter again prepared for a difficult assault on Coates's force. But at about 3 A.M. on the morning of the 17th, he set fire to the church and withdrew another eighteen miles down the Cooper River toward Charleston, stopping at Quinby Bridge and placing his troops along the creek. To frustrate a cavalry pursuit he had loosened the flooring of the bridge but was waiting for his rear guard and baggage to cross before removing the planks. Unknown to Coates, Lee had captured his rear guard and the dragoons charged across the bridge, surprising the British and driving off all but Coates and a few men who stood by him. But the planks in the bridge had been loosened by the horses rushing across, creating an impassable gap that prevented anyone else from crossing. The British infantry rallied to their hard-pressed commander, forcing Lee's dragoons to retreat into the adjacent woods.

Marion arrived to reconnoiter with Lee and they decided the enemy position was now too strong to attack, especially as Coates had an artillery piece and they did not. But when Sumter came on the scene with his infantry at about 5 P.M., he overruled them. The British had formed a hollow square with a howitzer covering their front and their flanks protected by outbuildings and the rail fences of Captain Thomas Shubrick's plantation. Sumter formed Marion's infantry on the left, Colonel Thomas Taylor's veteran militia regiment and his own troops in the center, and Colonel Peter Horry's cavalry on the right flank. Taylor charged across an open field and took position along a fence, but the British counterattacked and drove Taylor's militia back. Marion's infantry moved over to reoccupy the fence line but had to withdraw after sustaining fifty casualties and almost exhausting its ammunition supply. Sumter's men, meanwhile, had been firing from the protection of buildings, and he had failed to bring forward his artillery. Furious at this useless sacrifice and at Sumter's failure to support the attack properly, Taylor walked up to his commander and informed him he would no longer serve under him. Marion and Lee, disgusted by Sumter's mismanagement of the approach march and by the abortive attack (in which Lee had not participated), retreated fifteen miles with their dead and wounded. The next morning they both left Sumter. Meanwhile, British reinforcements, numbering about seven hundred men, were on the way to join Coates, and Sumter's position was no longer tenable. The British suffered forty-four casualties, the Americans sixty.

revised by Michael Bellesiles

QUINTON'S BRIDGE, NEW JERSEY.

18 March 1778. Colonel Charles Mawhood embarked on transports on 12 March 1778 and dropped down the Delaware River to forage. His command consisted of British regulars, primarily from the Thirty-Seventh Foot and Forty-Sixth Foot, and Loyalists from the Queen's Rangers (Major John Graves Simcoe) and a detachment from the New Jersey Volunteers (Brigadier Cortlandt Skinner). He put Simcoe ashore at 3 A.M. on 17 March about six miles from Salem, New Jersey, with orders to seize horses and mount his sixty hussars. Simcoe was then to proceed overland to Salem while Mawhood landed directly there with the task force's infantry. Mawhood planned on the next day to sweep four miles southward through the peninsula formed by Salem and Aloes (or Alloway) Creeks. Mawhood expected to find American militia at three bridges that crossed Aloes Creek: Hancock's, nearest to the Delaware River; Quinton's in the middle; and Thompson's farthest upstream. Mobilized men from Cumberland and Salem Counties actually held Hancock's and Quinton's, with Colonel Asher Holmes in command at Quinton's. Mawhood planned to put screening parties to watch the two bridges while the bulk of his force carried out the foraging. But he also sent a force to Thompson's to move downstream on the Salem side of the creek to try to surprise the defenders of Quinton's, who would have seen only the screening party.

Mawhood accompanied Simcoe to Thompson's on 18 March and proceeded down the road paralleling the creek until he got within two hundred yards of the bridge. Messengers established contact with the screening party (seventy men from the Seventeenth Foot) and learned that the Americans were behind some breastworks on the steep opposite bank but that they had not occupied Wetherby's Tavern on the near bank. Captain Francis Stephenson moved through an orchard and occupied the tavern with his light infantry company of the Queen's Rangers without being detected; two other companies took cover behind a fence under the command of Captain John Saunders. The rest of the task force remained in some woods behind Saunders's position. Once everyone was in place, Mawhood had the detachment of the Seventeenth make a show of calling in their sentries and retreating down the road toward Salem. Holmes's men were taken in by the deception, and about two hundred of them replaced the planks on the bridge and crossed over in two groups to follow the retreating party.

A mounted officer went ahead of the first militia group and was passing the fence when one of the rangers started to laugh. He wheeled and started to gallop back to warn the militiamen but was quickly shot off his horse and captured. Saunders's men charged forward while Stephenson's poured out of the house. Cut off, the lead militia force retreated downstream through open fields, pursued by the mounted hussars and Mawhood's main body. Simcoe moved up to the bridge with the detachment of the Seventeenth and the Queen's Rangers' companies of grenadiers and Highlanders. The Americans fell back from the heights; Mawhood decided not to risk crossing and instead led the force back to Salem. One American was killed and the officer (who turned out to be a French volunteer) and several others were captured. Mawhood had one man mortally wounded. Simcoe believed that a large number of Americans were drowned trying to cross the creek, but there is no confirmation of this. Mawhood next attacked Hancock's Bridge on 21 March.

SEE ALSO *Hancock's Bridge, New Jersey; Mawhood, Charles; Simcoe, John Graves.*

BIBLIOGRAPHY

Simcoe, John Graves. *A Journal of the Operations of the Queen's Rangers.* 1787. New York: New York Times, 1968.

revised by Robert K. Wright Jr.

R

RAID. In the strict strategic or tactical sense, a raid differs from other offensive operations in that the attacker does not intend to hold the objective once he has taken it. Raids can be on a small (tactical) scale, to capture prisoners, knock out gun positions, or disrupt an enemy attack before it starts (a "spoiling attack"). Examples are the operations against Great Brewster Island, Massachusetts, during the Boston siege, and Abercromby's sortie during the Yorktown siege. Strategic raids were those to Lexington and Concord, Bennington, and Paulus Hook. The attack on Stony Point on 16 July 1779 was not planned as a raid, but Washington subsequently decided that the captured position could not be held, so it turned out to be a raid after all.

SEE ALSO *Bennington Raid; Great Brewster Island, Massachusetts; Lexington and Concord; Paulus Hook, New Jersey; Stony Point, New York.*

Mark M. Boatner

RAKE. To fire down the length of a vessel's deck. This is the sailor's equivalent of the soldier's enfilade.

SEE ALSO *Enfilade.*

Mark M. Boatner

RALL, JOHANN GOTTLIEB. (1720?–1776). Hessian colonel at Trenton. Born in Hesse-Kassel, probably in 1720, he was a veteran of the Seven Years' War and was proud of having subsequently fought the Turks in the army of Russian general Alexis Orloff. Rall made the journey to America with his regiment when they were hired from the elector of Hesse-Kassel in 1776 by the British. He led his regiment with vigor and distinction at White Plains and Fort Washington. Ignorant of English and contemptuous of the poorly trained American soldiers, Rall was given command of the isolated yet critical outpost at Trenton. He was mortally wounded in Washington's attack on Trenton on 26 December 1776, dying later that day.

SEE ALSO *Fort Washington, New York; Trenton, New Jersey; White Plains, New York.*

BIBLIOGRAPHY

Fischer, David Hackett. *Washington's Crossing.* Oxford and New York: Oxford University Press, 2004.

revised by Michael Bellesiles

RAMSAY, DAVID. (1749–1815). Historian, physician, politician. Pennsylvania-South Carolina. Born in Lancaster County, Pennsylvania, on 2 April 1749, Ramsay graduated from Princeton in 1765, studied medicine with Benjamin Rush, and obtained his degree from the College of Pennsylvania in 1772. In 1773 he opened his practice in Charleston. Although successful as a doctor, he soon became absorbed in local politics and represented Charleston in the legislature from 1776 to the end of the war, also serving on the governor's council. He served as a physician with the South Carolina troops at the sieges of Savannah in 1779 and Charleston in 1780. After the fall of the latter city, the British exiled Ramsay and thirty-two other eminent Charlestonians to St. Augustine. The following year these exiles were released and sent to Philadelphia. Ramsay was a delegate to the Continental Congress in 1782–1783 and 1785–1786. While John Hancock dallied over accepting the office of president of Congress, the delegates in New York City created the post of "Chairman of Congress" and elected Ramsay to fill it. He held this title until Nathaniel Gorham was elected president of Congress on 6 June 1786. As a delegate he supported moves to strengthen the central government. From 1784 to 1790 he was again in the South Carolina House of Representatives, and from 1791 to 1797 he sat in the state senate, serving as president of that body the entire time. A delegate to the South Carolina ratifying convention, Ramsay was a firm supporter of the Constitution. A moderate Federalist and representative of the Tidewater class, he opposed the issue of paper money, the easing of the obligations of debtors, and the importation of slaves. When he ran for the U.S. House in 1788 and the Senate in 1794, his support for his brother-in-law John Laurens's plan to enlist black troops during the Revolution came back to haunt him, and he was defeated as a suspected opponent of slavery.

Although able, honest, and influential in public affairs, he was inept in matters of personal finance and by 1798 had bankrupted himself by unwise and disorderly speculation and investment. As a doctor he subscribed to the unfortunate "system" of his friend Rush, but nevertheless he made important contributions to medical knowledge.

Despite his distinction as a doctor and political leader, Ramsay is best remembered as an historian. With a facile pen and a copious memory, he turned out a number of works. His several histories of the Revolutionary period, most particularly the *History of the American Revolution* (2 vols., 1789), set the national narrative of the war for the next several generations and went part way towards Ramsay's goal of crafting a national identity. But as he correctly predicted, slavery would undermine that goal. Ramsay died 8 May 1815, two days after being shot in the back by a maniac against whose sanity he had testified.

SEE ALSO *Hancock, John; Rush, Benjamin.*

BIBLIOGRAPHY

Brunhouse, Robert L. "David Ramsay, 1749–1815: Selections From His Writings." *Transactions* 55 (1965).

Cohen, Lester H. Foreword to *The History of the American Revolution* by David Ramsay. Edited by Lester H. Cohen. Indianapolis, Ind.: Liberty Classics, 1990.

Shaffer, Arthur H. "Between Two Worlds: David Ramsay and the Politics of Slavery." *Journal of Southern History* 50 (1984): 175–196.

———. *To Be an American: David Ramsay and the Making of the American Consciousness.* Columbia: University of South Carolina Press, 1991.

revised by Michael Bellesiles

RAMSAY, NATHANIEL. (1741–1817).

Congressional officer, politician. Maryland. The elder brother of David Ramsay, Nathaniel Ramsay was born in Lancaster County, Pennsylvania, on 1 May 1741. Graduating from Princeton in 1767 (two years later than the brother, who was eight years his junior), he studied law and settled in Cecil County, Maryland. In 1775 he was a delegate to the Maryland Convention and to the Continental Congress. On 14 January 1776 he was chosen captain in Smallwood's Maryland regiment. The next July that unit became part of the Continental army and distinguished itself at Long Island in August 1776. On 10 December 1776, Ramsay was commissioned its lieutenant colonel when the regiment was redesignated the Third Maryland, "Smallwood's Regiment." Ramsay is particularly famous for his role in checking the retreat of the American army at Monmouth on 28 June 1778, giving Washington time to rally his army. Ramsay was wounded, left for dead, and captured. On parole until his exchange on 14 December 1780, he retired from the army on 1 January 1781.

Returning to Congress where his brother David also was serving, from 1785 to 1787, he became U.S. marshal for the district of Maryland in 1790. Four years later he became naval officer of the Baltimore district, a position he held until his death on 23 October 1817.

SEE ALSO *Ramsay, David.*

BIBLIOGRAPHY

Stryker, William S. *The Battle of Monmouth.* Port Washington, N.Y.: Kennikat Press, 1970.

revised by Michael Bellesiles

RAMSEUR'S MILL, NORTH CAROLINA.

20 June 1780. Also known as Ramsour's, Ramsauer's, and Ramsay's Mill. The surrender of Charleston on 12 May 1780 and the establishment of British posts at Camden, Cheraw, and Ninety Six made it

apparent that the Revolutionary War was about to move into North Carolina. During the four preceding years there had been only one military engagement in the state, the Battle of Moores Creek Bridge, on 27 February 1776, and that humiliating Loyalist defeat had left the Patriots more or less in control of the state. But in the summer of 1780 the North Carolina Loyalists believed the time had come to rise up and even some scores. Although General Charles Cornwallis expressed the desire that the Loyalists delay their military activities until the wheat crop was harvested, thereby avoiding another premature uprising and also assuring provisions for his invading army, the North Carolina Loyalists did not wait. Colonel John Moore, returning to Ramseur's Mill in June after serving under Cornwallis in South Carolina, called a meeting of the area's leading Loyalists on 10 June at his father's house. Before the forty men left the meeting, at which Moore revealed Cornwallis's plan for pushing northward into the state, they learned that Major Joseph McDowell was approaching with a company of rebel militia. The Loyalists made an unsuccessful attempt to surprise McDowell. Moore then issued instructions for Loyalists to assemble at Ramseur's Mill. By 20 June he had thirteen hundred men, although one-quarter were unarmed.

The Patriots, meanwhile, had responded to General Griffith Rutherford's call for militia. While eight hundred gathered near Charlotte, Colonel Francis Locke assembled another four hundred at Mountain Creek, near Moore's camp, and on 19 June moved out to surprise the Loyalists. His column was led by three small groups of mounted men; the rest of his force, most of whom had never served in combat, followed in a double file.

Moore's men were camped on a hill about three hundred yards from the mill and half a mile north of the village later known as Lincolnton. At the approach of the rebel horsemen, a twelve-man outpost fired and fled six hundred yards to the Loyalist camp, which they threw into confusion. But the Loyalists had a clear field of fire facing downhill, and they easily repulsed the horsemen when the latter tried to charge up the hill. The unarmed Loyalists fled, but the others formed together and marched on the approaching militia. Neither side had much in the way of organization or command, and the battle consisted mostly of small groups clustering together, moving and firing at will. The Loyalists retreated back up the hill, followed by most of the rebels, some of whom worked their way around to the other side of the hill. Neither side had bayonets; lack of uniforms or insignia made it difficult to tell friend from foe, and many a skull was cracked by a "friendly" musket butt. Loyalist Captain Daniel Warlick rallied his men time and again to counterattack, but William Shays, seeing this, worked his way stealthily forward until he was in position to drop Warlick with a bullet. The Loyalist resistance faltered but rallied behind a creek at the base of the hill.

Locke could re-form only 110 of his original 400 men on the hill for the expected counterattack, and he sent an urgent message to Rutherford to hurry forward with the column from Charlotte. But the Loyalists had had enough. Moore joined Cornwallis at Camden with only thirty men.

Not more than 275 of Locke's 400 were actually engaged, but over 150 were killed and wounded; Loyalist losses were about the same, and they had approximately 700 engaged. Both forces dissolved after the battle; even the victorious Patriots simply drifted home afterward, and Locke was unable to organize any sort of pursuit.

Moore's abortive action was a disaster for the British cause, and Cornwallis threatened to court-martial him for violating instructions. When Cornwallis finally did get into North Carolina, most Loyalists were afraid to support him, and the British lost more by desertion than they gained in recruits.

SEE ALSO *Moores Creek Bridge.*

revised by Michael Bellesiles

RANDOLPH, EDMUND JENINGS.

(1753–1813). Statesman, U.S. attorney general and secretary of state. Virginia. Born on 10 August 1753 in Williamsburg, Virginia, Randolph attended William and Mary College and studied law with his father. When the war started, his parents left immediately for England. Randolph did not share their politics and joined the Continental army at Cambridge, becoming Washington's aide-de-camp on 15 August 1775. With the sudden death of his uncle, Peyton Randolph, on 22 October 1775, Edmund Randolph left the army and returned to Williamsburg. The next year he sat in the Virginia Convention, serving on the committee that drafted the state's constitution and Declaration of Rights. He became the state's first attorney general the same year. Holding this office until 1786, Randolph went to the Continental Congress in 1779. He soon resigned, but returned to Congress for most of 1781, where he befriended James Madison. On 7 November 1786 he defeated Richard Henry Lee and Theodorick Bland to become governor, and he led his state's delegation to the Federal Convention in 1787. He joined George Mason in refusing to sign the completed Constitution, believing that it was not sufficiently republican, but he suddenly reversed his position at the start of Virginia's ratifying convention in 1788, arguing strenuously that if Virginia did not ratify the Constitution, the United States would cease to exist. Shortly after the Convention ratified the Constitution, Randolph resigned as governor to enter the state legislature and take part in revising the Virginia legal code.

Washington appointed Randolph the nation's first attorney general in 1789. Later, Randolph succeeded Jefferson as secretary of state, holding that post in 1794–1795. After serving creditably through the storms of "Citizen" Genet's and Gouverneur Morris's recalls and the negotiations that led to Jay's Treaty, Randolph resigned on 19 August 1795. He had been charged by French minister Fauchet, Genet's successor, with improper conduct in negotiating the treaty; the charges, contained in a letter from Fauchet to his government that had been intercepted and revealed by the British, were subsequently found to be false. Returning to law practice, he served as senior defense counsel in the treason trial of Aaron Burr. He died at one of his plantations near Millwood, Virginia, on 12 September 1813.

SEE ALSO *Randolph, Peyton.*

BIBLIOGRAPHY

Reardon, John J. *Edmund Randolph: A Biography.* New York: Macmillan, 1974.

revised by Michael Bellesiles

RANDOLPH, PEYTON. (1721–1775).
Crown official, first president of the Continental Congress. Virginia. Born in Williamsburg, Virginia, in 1721, Randolph was the son of the wealthy and powerful Sir John Randolph. He went from William and Mary College, from which he did not graduate, to the Middle Temple in 1739 and was admitted to the bar in 1744. Returning the same year to Williamsburg as the colony's attorney general, he served in the House of Burgesses from 1748 until the termination of that assembly in 1775. When Randolph took the burgess's side in the pistole controversy of 1751–1754, he was dismissed as attorney general. In 1755 he organized a company of one hundred lawyers and other gentlemen who, at their own expense, moved out to support the survivors of Braddock's defeat. A major speculator in western lands, Randolph saw opportunity in the American conflict with the British Crown, overcoming his fear of the radical tendencies of some of his allies to become a leader of the Patriot cause. Randolph was elected speaker of the Burgesses in 1766, holding that office until he adjourned its last session in May 1775. Chairing the first three Virginia Conventions in 1774 and 1775, he topped the list of delegates to the first Continental Congress and became the first president of that body, serving from 5 September to 21 October 1774. In bad health, Randolph was succeeded by Henry Middleton on 22 October 1774 but was reelected to Congress on 10 May 1775. Two weeks later he had to

give up this post, and five months later he died suddenly of apoplexy in Philadelphia on 22 October 1775. Randolph exemplified the manner in which even conservative political leaders were attracted to the rebellion against British rule. Many Virginians looked to him to keep the insurgency in check and guide it away from radicalism.

BIBLIOGRAPHY

Randolph Family Papers. Virginia Historical Society. Richmond, Va.

Reardon, John J. *Peyton Randolph, 1721–1775.* Durham, N.C.: Carolina Academic Press, 1982.

revised by Michael Bellesiles

RANDOLPH FAMILY OF VIRGINIA.
The first William Randolph (c.1651–1711), an English gentleman, came to Virginia from Warwickshire around 1673 and in 1684 bought lands on the south bank of the James River that had been known from earliest colonial times as Turkey Island. By 1705 he owned ten thousand acres in Henrico County alone, and he willed a plantation to each of his seven sons. Meanwhile he had held a number of official appointments, including that of King's Attorney (an office subsequently held by his son John and the latter's two sons) and in 1699 he had been appointed lieutenant colonel of militia. Sometime prior to 1681 he married into the Isham family of "Bermuda Hundred," and the descendants of Colonel William and Mary Isham Randolph included not only those who retained the family name but also Thomas Jefferson, John Marshall, Henry "Light-Horse Harry" Lee, and the latter's son, Robert E. Lee. Colonel Randolph was among the founders (in 1693) of the College of William and Mary. Six of his seven sons attended the college, as did Jefferson and Marshall.

SEE ALSO *Randolph, Edmund Jenings; Randolph, Peyton.*

revised by Harold E. Selesky

RANK AND FILE.
In both the American and British armies, the term "rank and file" meant the enlisted men present in the line of battle with weapons in their hands ready to fight, including corporals and privates but not sergeants and drummers. In tactical terms, "rank" referred to the men standing more or less shoulder to shoulder facing forward next to each other and forming the front of a unit. In the linear formations used until the middle of the nineteenth century, a unit could be drawn up with a depth of several ranks. Every effort was devoted

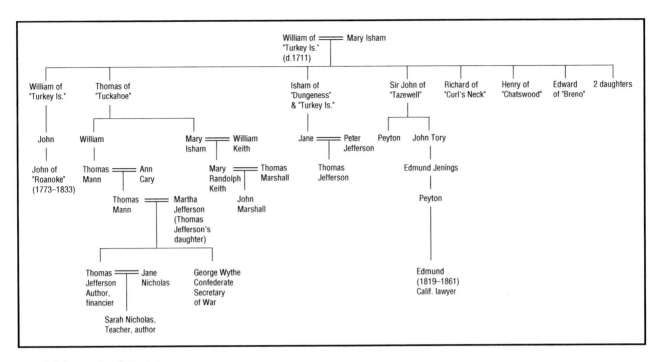

Randolph Family of Virginia. THE GALE GROUP

to maximizing the firepower that could be brought to bear on the ground directly ahead of the unit. In a three-rank formation, for example, the front rank would kneel (either ready to fire or presenting bayonets to hold off cavalry), the second rank would stand and fire in the gaps of the first rank, and the third rank would stand and fire in the gaps of the second rank, over the heads of the men in the first rank. Gradually from the last decades of the seventeenth century, the number of ranks was reduced, as commanders experimented with gaining breadth of formation at the expense of depth, until by the time of the War for American Independence, regiments in formal battle order in North America were typically arrayed in a depth of two ranks, the rear rank firing in the gaps of the front rank. "File" referred to the group of soldiers standing more or less directly behind each other, from the front rank to the rear rank of the formation.

revised by Harold E. Selesky

RANKIN, WILLIAM. Loyalist leader.
Pennsylvania. Until the Declaration of Independence, this influential landowner, judge, member of the assembly, and colonel of militia in York, Pennsylvania, had been a Whig. He then secretly switched sides, continuing to command a regiment of militia while looking for an opportunity to serve the crown. When ordered in 1776 to capture certain Loyalists of York County and destroy their estates, he contrived instead to assist them while giving the appearance of obeying his instructions. In 1778 he started organizing the Loyalists of Lancaster and York Counties, and eventually those of adjacent regions of Maryland and Delaware as well, until he claimed that six thousand would answer his call for an uprising, almost certainly a wishful exaggeration. Rankin established an intelligence network, maintaining contact with General Henry Clinton through his brother-in-law, Andrew Fürstner, and dealing with John André through Christopher Sower. When General John Sullivan's expedition of 1779 against the Iroquois was being planned, Rankin and other Loyalist leaders tried unsuccessfully to have one of their supporters put in command of the Pennsylvania militia that was to accompany the regulars. "If this can be obtained, of which they have the fairest prospects," Sower informed Clinton, "Colonel [John] Butler will have little to fear." Sower also told Clinton that if he would direct that Butler make a raid on Carlisle, where the principal rebel supply depot was located, Rankin and his supporters could not only assist in this operation but could also arm themselves for future action.

After André's death, Rankin and his associates in Pennsylvania, Delaware, and Maryland sent an address to the king through John Graves Simcoe—who had been André's friend and in whom they apparently had more confidence than Clinton—proposing that Simcoe lead an operation into the Chesapeake Bay area to rally the local Loyalists. Simcoe forwarded this communication to Clinton on 2 November 1780, and the British commander in chief ordered Arnold and Simcoe to conduct a raid in Virginia in December 1780 that Clinton supposed might partly satisfy the hopes of Rankin's supporters. But the Pennsylvania Loyalists did not rise.

Rankin was imprisoned in March 1781 but escaped to New York City within a month. Again he urged operations to the south, and on 30 April 1781, Clinton wrote Phillips in Virginia: "I do not now send Colonel Rankin to you (as I at first proposed), but I enclose his proposals. You will see by them that he is not much of an officer. But he appears to be a plain sensible man worth attending to, and Simcoe can explain a thousand things respecting him and his association which I cannot in a letter." Rankin made one brief visit to Virginia, where Cornwallis had arrived to take command, and finding no support from Cornwallis for a campaign into Pennsylvania, he returned to New York. Three years of planning an uprising had come to nothing. When the British evacuated New York in November 1783, Rankin went to England, where he lived on a pension of £120 a year and was awarded £2,320 to cover the loss of property confiscated by Pennsylvania.

SEE ALSO *Arnold, Benedict; Butler, John; Sower, Christopher.*

BIBLIOGRAPHY

Van Doren, Carl. *Secret History of the American Revolution.* New York: Viking, 1941.

revised by Michael Bellesiles

RASTEL, PHILIPPE FRANÇOIS, SIEUR DE ROCHEBLAVE. (c.1735–

1802). A French soldier who came to Quebec during the Seven Years' War, serving primarily in the Ohio region, including at Kaskaskia. After the war he transferred his allegiance to the Spanish, commanding the troops in the Illinois country. In 1773 he fell out with the Spanish governor and became commandant of Kaskaskia for the British. He was captured there at Fort Gage by George Rogers Clark on the evening of 4 July 1778. Sent to prison in Virginia, he was paroled and returned to New York City about a year later. After the war he settled in Montreal, serving as a member of the assembly from 1792 until his death in 1802.

SEE ALSO *Western Operations.*

revised by Michael Bellesiles

RATHBUN, JOHN PECK. (1746–1823).

Continental naval officer. Rhode Island. Having gone to sea as a boy, this virtually unknown officer (whose name is also spelled Rathburne and Rathbourne) served almost continuously on the *Providence* (twelve guns), first under John Hazard and then under John Paul Jones, taking command in May 1777. In a raid on the Bahamas he captured Nassau with his fifty-man crew, held it three days, liberated thirty American prisoners, and without the loss of a man withdrew with two captured schooners, a sixteen-gun ship, a brig, and a considerable quantity of war matériel. A year later he assumed command of the *Queen of France* (twenty-eight guns). In mid-July 1779 he was with Abraham Whipple when three American ships made one of the richest captures of the war.

Rathbun was captured with Whipple's small fleet at Charleston on 12 May 1780. Paroled, he returned to Boston and on 4 August 1781 got command of the brig *Wexford*, a twenty-gun privateer. Little more is known of Rathbun.

SEE ALSO *Whipple, Abraham.*

revised by Michael Bellesiles

RAVELIN. An outwork of two faces, pointed toward the enemy, open to the rear like a flèche or redan but placed outside the ditch of a fortification to cover the portion of the wall between two bastions (the curtain).

SEE ALSO *Flèche; Redan.*

Mark M. Boatner

RAWDON-HASTINGS, FRANCIS.

(1754–1826). British officer, later the first Marquess of Hastings and the second Earl of Moira. He was a distinguished soldier in the War for America, serving seven years with only one short furlough, and was still in his twenties when he went home, in 1781. Of noble ancestry, he was the son of John, Baron Rawdon, later the first Earl of Moira, and Lady Elizabeth Hastings, daughter of the ninth Earl of Huntingdon. In America, he was known by the courtesy title of Lord Rawdon. A tall, stately, grave man, he loved the profession of arms and exuded a soldierly air. He was educated at Harrow, and on 7 August 1771 entered the army as an ensign in the Fifteenth Regiment. On 23 October he also entered University College, Oxford, where he studied for two years. In 1773, he toured the continent in the company of his uncle, Lord Huntingdon.

He was promoted to the rank of lieutenant in the Fifth Regiment on 20 October 1773, and on 7 May 1774 he accompanied his regiment to Boston, Massachusetts.

EDUCATION AS A SOLDIER

Lord Rawdon reached Boston in July, when tensions between the colonies and Britain were escalating. General Thomas Gage commanded there. He joined the grenadier company of the Fifth Regiment, commanded by Captain George Harris, to replace a wounded lieutenant. In the battle of Bunker Hill on 17 June, he came under fire for the first time. Although he survived without a scratch, he received a bullet through his hat. When Captain Harris was wounded, Rawdon took command of the grenadiers and performed gallantly under fire. General John Burgoyne declared that Rawdon made his military reputation for life on that day. He was promoted captain in the Sixty-third Regiment on 12 July, and during the following winter performed in amateur theatricals. On 13 January he was appointed aide-de-camp to General Henry Clinton, and also deputy adjutant general. He served with Clinton during operations against North Carolina in May 1776, and in June observed abortive assaults by Clinton and Rear Admiral Sir Peter Parker on Charleston.

Rawdon returned with Clinton to New York in July 1776, arriving just in time to join General William Howe, the new British commander in chief, in opening his campaign. He was with Clinton at the battles of Long Island on 27 August, Kips Bay on 15 September, and White Plains on 28 October. During this time Clinton and his staff, Rawdon included, achieved a reputation for military excellence among British officers. In early December he joined Clinton in successful operations against Rhode Island, after which the two officers went home to Britain for the winter. Returning to New York on 5 July 1777, they remained there when Howe sailed southward with the main army to attack Philadelphia. Rawdon was with Clinton during successful attacks on America's highlands forts in early October, and on 7 October was dispatched to Howe's headquarters in Philadelphia with the news. After a few weeks' stay there, he returned to New York, where he spent the winter of 1777–1778. On 1 May 1778 he accompanied Clinton to Philadelphia, when Clinton assumed command of British armies in America.

With Clinton's encouragement, Lord Rawdon began raising a provincial regiment of Loyalists on 25 May. Recruiting this corps, the Volunteers of Ireland, from Irish deserters from the American army, Rawdon assumed most of the expenses involved. He was appointed its commander with the provincial rank of colonel. The Volunteers of Ireland proved to be one of the most effective provincial corps in British service. On 15 June Rawdon also was promoted permanent lieutenant colonel and appointed adjutant general. In the battle of Monmouth on 28 June, during the British retreat across New Jersey, Rawdon formed the British line of battle for Clinton, and performed other services. In July, after reaching New York City, he served temporarily on board the flagship of Admiral Lord Richard Howe. He accompanied Clinton and General Charles Grey a month later, when they went to the relief of the British garrison at Rhode Island.

During the next few months, Rawdon and Clinton gradually became estranged. On one occasion Clinton even publicly chastised Rawdon for supposed gaucheries in protocol. On 3 September 1779 Rawdon angrily resigned as adjutant general. He was left behind on 26 December when Clinton embarked with 7,600 men for his second expedition to Charleston. But in March 1780, Rawdon was ordered southward with a reinforcement of 2,500 soldiers. He joined Lord Charles Cornwallis's forces, and on 25 April assisted in capturing rebel works on Lempriere's and Haddrell's Points.

After Charleston's surrender on 12 May Rawdon was given command of a British garrison of 2,500 men at Camden. There he battled partisans, and in August he maneuvered against an American army led by Horatio Gates as it approached Camden. On 14 August, General Charles Cornwallis, who assumed command in the South after Clinton returned to New York, took charge of Rawdon's forces. Two days later, in the battle of Camden, Rawdon commanded the British left wing, acquitting himself well against Gates's regulars. He accompanied Cornwallis's army as it advanced to Charlotte in October, and as it fell back to Winnsboro after Patrick Ferguson was defeated at Kings Mountain on 7 October. Because Cornwallis was ill with a fever during the withdrawal, Rawdon was given temporary command. In the winter of 1780–1781 he commanded once more at Camden.

THE MATURE OFFICER

On 1 January 1781 Cornwallis invaded North Carolina, leaving Rawdon in command of the 8,000 British troops in South Carolina and Georgia. Promoted brigadier general in America at this time, Rawdon did not receive his commission before he departed America in August 1781. In South Carolina during the next few months, Rawdon came into his own as a soldier, demonstrating outstanding generalship against his able opponent, Nathanael Greene. After Cornwallis and Greene fought the battle of Guilford Courthouse on 15 March 1781, Cornwallis remained in North Carolina while Greene marched against Rawdon at Camden. Rawdon was gradually isolated there as Greene, Thomas Sumter, Francis Marion, and Henry Lee attacked his supply lines to Charleston. On 25 April, Rawdon and Greene fought the battle of Hobkirk's Hill, just north of Camden. Although Rawdon defeated Greene in a brilliantly conducted battle, he was compelled to abandon Camden on 10 May.

Retreating to Monck's Corner, thirty miles above Charleston, Rawdon gradually abandoned or lost most of his posts in South Carolina and Georgia. He contracted his defensive lines to protect Charleston and Savannah, and awaited expected reinforcements from Ireland. In late May he learned that Greene had besieged Ninety Six, and that its garrison of 550 New York Loyalists refused to surrender. On 3 June he received the reinforcements, 1,800 troops from Ireland, and marched to the relief of Ninety Six. Arriving on 21 June, he learned that Greene had retired northward the day before. On 3 July he abandoned Ninety Six and marched to Orangeburg. His health having been destroyed by a virulent fever, he turned over his command to Colonel Alexander Stewart on 20 July, and sailed for England on 21 August. His ship was seized by a French privateer, and he spent the next four months in captivity before his release was secuerd. In 1782 he successfully defended himself in Parliament against charges that he had acted with excessive cruelty in executing an American prisoner, Isaac Hayne, without trial. He was appointed lieutenant colonel of the 105th Regiment (formerly the Volunteers of Ireland) on 21 March 1782. On 20 November he was promoted permanent colonel and appointed aide-de-camp to the king.

LATER CAREER

Upon his return to England, Rawdon began a thirty-two year career as a politician by being elected to the Irish House of Commons. After his elevation to a barony on 5 March 1783, he became a member of the British House of Lords. At first a supporter of the Whigs, he later represented the interests of the Prince of Wales. He was master general of the ordnance in the Grenville ministry from 1806 to 1807, and attempted without success to form his own ministry in 1812. He succeeded as Earl of Moira on 20 June 1793, and on 12 October was promoted major general. In 1794 he served with distinction in the Duke of York's army in Flanders, battling the French. He was promoted lieutenant general on 1 January 1798, and general on 25 September 1803. He commanded in Scotland from February 1803 to February 1805. He was appointed colonel of the Twenty-seventh Regiment on 21 May 1804, and made constable of the Tower on 1 March 1806. He married Flora, Countess of Loudoun in 1804; they had six children. He was invested with the Order of the Garter on 12 June 1812.

Rawdon (now Lord Moira) was exceedingly extravagant with money. During his lifetime he squandered a huge estate and ran up debts of almost £1,000,000 in early nineteenth-century currency. By 1812 he was compelled to seek employment as governor-general of India. During his service in India, from 1813 to 1823, he prosecuted two successful wars: the Nepal War, 1814–1816, and the Third Maratha War, 1817–1819. In February 1817 he was created Marquess of Hastings, and twice received unanimous votes of thanks from Parliament. He implemented reforms in education, the press, and the judiciary. Additionally, he increased the annual profits of the East India Company. Coming under suspicion of giving special favors to his friends, although not guilty, he was removed from office. In 1824 he was given a sinecure, the governorship of Malta, and there ended his career of public service.

During his long and active life, Rawdon's first love was the military, and he developed into a sound strategist, tactician, and leader of men. In both America and India, he manifested the highest levels of military ability, organizing and directing armies to triumphs on the battlefield. He deserves his high reputation as a soldier.

BIBLIOGRAPHY

McCrady, Edward. *The History of South Carolina in the Revolution, 1780–1783*. Vol. 2. New York: Macmillan, 1902.

Nelson, Paul David. *Francis Rawdon-Hastings, Marquess of Hastings: Soldier, Peer of The Realm, Governor-General of India*. Madison, N.J.: Fairleigh Dickinson University Press, 2005.

Pancake, John S. *This Destructive War: The British Campaign in the Carolinas, 1780–1782*. University: University of Alabama Press, 1985.

Tarleton, Banastre. *A History of the Campaigns of 1780 and 1781, in the Southern Provinces of North America*. London: T. Cadell, 1787.

Ward, Christopher. *The War of the Revolution*. Edited by John R. Alden. Vol. 2. New York: Macmillan, 1952.

Wickwire, Franklin, and Mary Wickwire. *Cornwallis: The American Adventure*. Boston: Houghton Mifflin Company, 1970.

revised by Paul David Nelson

RAWLINGS'S REGIMENT.

Colonel Moses Rawlings commanded one of the sixteen "additional Continental regiments."

SEE ALSO *Additional Continental Regiments.*

Mark M. Boatner

READ, CHARLES.

(1715–1780). American deserter. New Jersey. Born in Philadelphia on 1 February 1715, Read succeeded his father as collector of the port of Burlington, New Jersey. He became a lawyer in 1753 and served several terms as mayor of Burlington. In the early 1760s he was appointed a judge on the New Jersey supreme court, holding that position and the collector's post until the start of the Revolution, when he resigned to serve as a colonel of militia. In 1776 he attended the convention that framed New Jersey's constitution and on 18 July was made colonel of a battalion of the flying camp. For reasons unknown, Read went over to the British in December 1776. He died in North Carolina in 1780.

revised by Michael Bellesiles

READ, GEORGE. (1733–1798). Lawyer, Signer, acting president of Delaware. Born in Cecil County, Maryland, on 18 September 1733, Read studied law in Philadelphia; was admitted to the bar in 1753; and settled in New Castle, Delaware. In 1763 he was elected attorney general of Delaware, holding this post for the next decade. Read's politics matched those of his close friend, John Dickinson. He was active in resisting British authority, being a leader of his province's committees of correspondence. In the Continental Congress from 1774 until September 1777, he opposed independence but became a Signer and enthusiastic supporter of the Declaration of Independence once it was adopted. He played a prominent part in shaping the state constitution and in 1776 became vice president of Delaware. When President John McKinly was captured by the British at Wilmington in September 1777, Read left Philadelphia to take over his duties and performed them until being relieved, at his own request, on 31 March 1778. He is credited with getting the maximum possible support of the war effort out of a lukewarm people and an inexperienced, incompletely organized legislature.

Continuing as a member of the Delaware Council, he played a prominent part in postwar politics. As an upholder of the rights of small states at the Constitutional Convention of 1787, and sharing the ideas of Hamilton for the strongest possible central government, he nevertheless accepted the Convention's compromises and is credited for his state's being the first to ratify the Constitution. Elected to the first U.S. Senate in 1788, Read supported the Washington administration on the assumption of state debts, the national bank, and the excise law. On 18 September 1793, Read resigned from the Senate to become chief justice of Delaware, a post he held until his death on 21 September 1798.

BIBLIOGRAPHY
Read, William T. *Life and Correspondence of George Read: Signer of the Declaration of Independence*. Philadelphia: Lippincott, 1870.

revised by Michael Bellesiles

READ, JAMES. (1743–1822). Militia officer, naval commissioner. Delaware. One of the Read brothers, James Read first served with the Pennsylvania militia, seeing combat at Trenton, Princeton, Brandywine, and Germantown and rising to the rank of major. On 4 November 1778 he was appointed one of three naval commissioners for the middle states, and on 11 January 1781 he was invested with sole power to conduct the navy board.

SEE ALSO *Read Brothers of Delaware.*

revised by Frank C. Mevers

READ, THOMAS. (1740?–1788). American naval officer. Delaware. The third of the Read brothers, he was master of vessels in the West Indies and Atlantic trade prior to being commissioned captain of the Pennsylvania navy on 23 October 1775. Commodore of thirteen rowing galleys initially, he took command of the newly purchased *Montgomery* in March 1776 and was stationed at Fort Island to guard the *chevaux de frise* (chains for blocking passage). On 5 June he became eighth-ranking captain in the Continental navy and was assigned to command the frigate *George Washington*. This vessel not being completed when the British pushed Washington back to the Delaware, Read marched on 5 December with a naval battery to join the army and took part in the defense of Assumpink Creek, near Trenton, the afternoon of 2 January 1777. When the British captured Philadelphia, Read and his superior, John Barry, dismantled and scuttled their ships, the *Washington* and *Effingham*, just below Bordentown in December 1777, and on 7 May 1778 they were destroyed by the British. Read saw little sea duty during the remainder of the war. In April 1778 he was in Baltimore fitting out the fast brigantine *Baltimore*, apparently making a single voyage in that ship. In February 1779 he was ordered to take station in the Chesapeake. Later in the year he was put in command of the frigate *Bourbon* being built in Connecticut, but the vessel was never completed. In 1780 he took out the privateer *Patty of Philadelphia*, and he was at sea in 1782. As captain of the frigate *Alliance*, purchased by his friend Robert Morris, Read made a remarkably fast trip to China by a new route east of the Dutch Indies. He left Philadelphia on 7 June 1787, reached Canton on 22 December, and was back at Philadelphia on 17 September 1788 with a tea cargo valued at $500,000. He died five weeks later.

SEE ALSO *Princeton, New Jersey; Read Brothers of Delaware.*

BIBLIOGRAPHY

Clark, William B. et al., eds. *Naval Documents of the American Revolution.* Washington, D.C.: Naval Historical Center, 1964–.

revised by Michael Bellesiles

READ BROTHERS OF DELAWARE.

Their father, John (1688–1756), a descendant of Sir Thomas Read of Berkshire, emigrated from Dublin, Ireland, in the early eighteenth century and became a large landholder in Maryland and Delaware. With six associates he established Charlestown at the head of Chesapeake Bay as a trade rival to Baltimore. Soon after 1734 he moved to nearby New Castle, Delaware. He and Mary Howell had three distinguished sons, George (b. 1733), Thomas (b. 1740?), and James (b. 1743). Another son, William, was in business in Havana. The Read brothers were closely associated with Robert Morris during and after the Revolution.

revised by Michael Bellesiles

RECRUITING IN GREAT BRITAIN.

At the time of the American Revolution, the strength of the British army was augmented in various ways. The most important, because it produced the majority of recruits, was the voluntary enlistment of individuals. The War Office issued to an existing regiment a set of "beating orders," whereupon the regiment would send out recruiting parties, usually an officer, several noncommissioned officers, and a drummer, who beat his drum to attract a crowd that the officer would then harangue in hopes of persuading eligible men "to take the king's shilling," as enlistment was colloquially known. A recruit had to be a Protestant, free from rupture and fits, "in no way troubled by lameness ... but have the perfect use of his limbs," and not be a runaway apprentice or a militia man (Houlding, p. 117n). In times of high manpower demand, substantial bounties and a reduced time of service (during the war, rather than for life) might be offered. In peacetime, coercion was used to force into military service some of those who had run afoul of the law, but its principal use was to enable justices of the peace and constables to compel the unemployed (the "idle and disorderly") into the ranks (ibid., p. 118). Wartime shortages frequently led to the enactment of a Press Act (as in 1778–1779), the principal purpose of which was "never simply to take up the rogues, vagabonds, and others socially undesirable but

rather *pour encourager les autres*—to drive others to volunteer for fear of being pressed" (ibid., p. 118). (Volunteers had the choice of which regiment they would join, at least initially, while draftees had none.)

The process of recruiting individuals led to a slow growth in the number of men under arms. Military service was not popular most of the time, even less so when the opponents were colonial Americans. Soldier pay was low (eight pence a day for a private), discipline could be brutal, living conditions could be miserable, and life aboard a transport bound for overseas service could be extremely taxing. Ireland, normally a good recruiting area, was enjoying a rare prosperity and thus was a source of fewer recruits than in prior years. Individual recruiting, however, did have the advantage of introducing individuals into an existing structure and tradition of training and discipline. George III insisted that the army be recruited this way at the start of the War for American Independence, both to preserve the old corps and to safeguard the value of the commissions of officers in those regiments against an influx of officers from newly raised corps.

The alternative to individual recruitment was a throwback to the days when colonels owned the regiments they raised and acted as a subcontractor by, in effect, renting their regiment to the army. The crown would contract with a distinguished officer or prominent civilian to raise a regiment as an entirety, giving him beating orders and bounty money for each recruit, and the right to sub-subcontract to company officers who were confirmed in their rank only when they had recruited a specified number of soldiers. This process, called "raising for rank," was employed only once early in the war, to create the hard-fighting Seventy-first Regiment of Foot (Fraser's Highlanders), but it became more common after 1778, when the need for complete regiments outweighed the king's scruples. Burgoyne's surrender and the entry of France into the war spurred voluntary mobilization in Britain; thirty-one regiments of foot were formed between 1778 and 1781, many of them in Scotland and most for domestic service.

The quickest way of augmenting the British army also had traditional roots: hiring complete regiments of well-trained professional soldiers from various German principalities. Only by hiring German auxiliaries was Britain able to send Major General William Howe's enormous expeditionary force against New York City in 1776. This heavy reliance on German troops diminished after 1778, when France entered the war. By 1781, only 9 percent of British army expenditures was used to hire Germans, compared with 24 percent in 1760, at the height of the Seven Years' War. According to Stephen Conway, "The Germans had become proportionately less important because more Britons and Irishmen than ever before went into uniform, and significant numbers of these

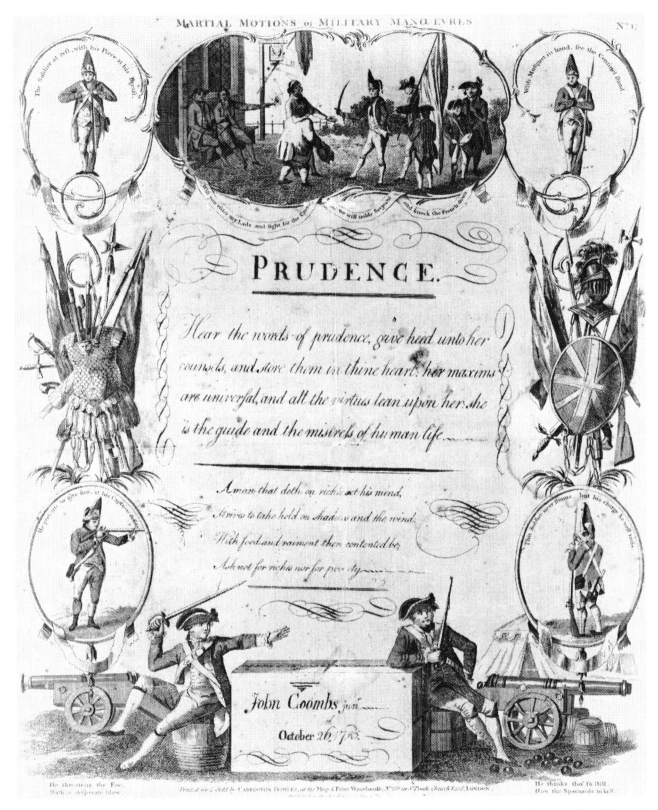

British Recruiting Poster. *This poster, published in 1781, depicts British soldiers and armaments, along with scenes of swordplay and soldiers interacting with civilians. It is signed at the bottom with the name of a soldier and his enlistment date.* **THE LIBRARY OF CONGRESS**

British and Irish soldiers, sailors, marines, militiamen, and volunteers came from social and occupational backgrounds not normally associated with eighteenth-century military or naval service" (p. 13).

British regiments serving in America also recruited locally among Loyalists and even accepted American deserters into their ranks. Approximately 250 of these deserters were evacuated from Yorktown on the *Bonetta* before Cornwallis's surrender.

SEE ALSO *German Auxiliaries.*

BIBLIOGRAPHY

Conway, Stephen. *The British Isles and the War of American Independence.* Oxford: Oxford University Press, 2000.

Curtis, Edward E. *The Organization of the British Army in the American Revolution.* New Haven, Conn.: Yale University Press, 1926.

Darling, Anthony D. *Red Coat and Brown Bess.* Ottawa: Museum Restoration Service, 1970.

Houlding, J. A. *Fit for Service: The Training of the British Army, 1715–1795.* Oxford: Oxford University Press, 1981.

Katcher, Philip R. N. *Encyclopedia of British, Provincial, and German Army Units, 1775–1783.* Harrisburg, Pa.: Stackpole Books, 1973.

revised by Harold E. Selesky

REDAN.

REDAN. A field work of two sides, pointing toward the enemy and open to the rear. It is virtually the same thing as a flèche or ravelin.

SEE ALSO *Flèche; Ravelin.*

Mark M. Boatner

RED BANK, NEW JERSEY

RED BANK, NEW JERSEY SEE *Fort Mercer, New Jersey.*

REDOUBT.

REDOUBT. A relatively small, independent outwork, completely enclosed. Fortresses are surrounded by redoubts covering the main avenues of enemy approach.

Mark M. Boatner

REED, JAMES.

REED, JAMES. (1723–1807). Continental general. Massachusetts-New Hampshire. His great-grandfather and grandfather emigrated (together) from England in 1635 and settled a few years later in Woburn, Massachusetts, where James was born in 1723. An elementary education enabled him to become a tailor. By 1748 he was a tavern keeper in Lunenburg and a selectman. As a captain during the French and Indian War, he took part in the expedition to Crown Point in 1755, Abercromby's mismanaged operations of 1758 (including Ticonderoga), and the final campaigns under Amherst. About 1765 he moved to Fitzwilliam, New Hampshire, where he kept a tavern, served in the militia, and was a large landowner. At the outbreak of the Revolutionary War he raised a unit and on 28 April 1775 was commissioned colonel of the Third New Hampshire Regiment His regiment marched to Boston and was posted near Charlestown Neck on 14 June. On 17 June his troops marched to battle under John Stark's command. It was this body of New Hampshire troops that General Howe observed moving from the true Bunker Hill to reinforce the redoubt on Breed's Hill and that caused him to delay his attack until more British troops landed. It was with Thomas Knowlton, along the "rail fence," that Reed's troops displayed the military discipline that Reed had instilled in them. In the military reorganization of January 1776, Reed's regiment became the Second Continental Infantry. After Bunker Hill, Reed was ordered to the Northern Department to reinforce the army that had retreated from Canada. There he suffered a sudden illness, probably smallpox, that left him blind and partially deaf. In August 1776 he accepted a commission as a brigadier general in the expectation that he would recover, but in September 1776 his impairment led him to resign. Despite his disability he lived another thirty years and remarried after the death of his first wife in 1791. He died in Fitchburg, Massachusetts, in 1807. His son, Sylvanus (d. 1798), was commissioned an ensign in January 1776 and served as an adjutant to General John Sullivan during the operations at Newport in 1778.

BIBLIOGRAPHY

Randall, Peter E. "James Reed." In *New Hampshire: Years of Revolution.* Edited by Peter E. Randall. Portsmouth, N.H.: Profiles Publishing, 1976.

revised by Frank C. Mevers

REED, JOSEPH.

REED, JOSEPH. (1741–1785). Patriot statesman and soldier. New Jersey and Pennsylvania. Born in Trenton, New Jersey, on 27 August 1741, Joseph Reed was the son of a wealthy merchant. He graduated from the College of New Jersey (now Princeton) in 1757, continuing to study law over the next three years with Richard

Stockton, a future signer of the Declaration of Independence. Reed also earned a master's degree, then went to study English law at the Middle Temple in London. Reed returned to Trenton in 1765 to find that his father had gone bankrupt and his studies were at an end.

After practicing law in Trenton and developing an extensive business that brought him into contact with important leaders in other colonies, Reed established his law practice in Philadelphia in 1770. In November 1774 he became a member of the committee of correspondence, and in the following year he was president of the Second Provincial Congress. Cosmopolitan, intellectual, and of a courteous nature, he reluctantly abandoned the cause of conciliation with Britain, but was often accused of lacking enthusiasm for the Patriot cause and of being too cautious in military affairs.

At the outbreak of hostilities the 34-year-old Reed was appointed lieutenant colonel of the militia, and on 19 June he agreed to join General George Washington as a temporary staff officer. With the rank of lieutenant colonel in the Continental army, he served as Washington's military secretary from 4 July 1775–16 May 1776. During this period he took an extended leave to serve in the Continental Congress. In March 1776 Washington was able to offer him the post of adjutant general, but Reed accepted only after considerable urging. His appointment, which carried the rank of colonel and gave him the equivalent of £700 a year, was dated 5 June 1776. The income apparently was an important consideration in his acceptance.

The shift of military operations from Boston to New York presented difficult problems that made Washington particularly anxious to regain the services of Reed, whose character, exceptional intelligence, legal experience, and skill as a writer the commander in chief valued highly. Reed played an important role in the military and political features of the New York campaign. He advocated that New York City be abandoned and destroyed to keep the British from using it for a base. He also advocated that Fort Washington be abandoned. When subsequent events bore out his judgment on Fort Washington, Reed wrote to Charles Lee criticizing Washington's direction of the campaign, an exchange which Washington stumbled upon but was able to overlook.

Reed was a key figure in the Trenton-Princeton operations, furnishing valuable information for the surprise attack on Trenton and the succeeding campaign. On the night of 28–29 December 1776, Reed hid in a house in Bordentown and received reports of Donop's movements that led him to recommend that Washington further advance into New Jersey. On the 29th he reported to Washington on the situation he found in Trenton, and this reinforced Washington's decision to cross back over the Delaware that day. With a dozen light horsemen, Reed pushed on to the outposts of Princeton on 2 January, and sent back the report that British reserves were moving toward that place.

Reed resigned from the army on 22 January 1777. Named brigadier general but denied command of the cavalry he had expected, Reed declined the appointment but served as an unpaid, volunteer aide-de-camp for Washington at Brandywine, Germantown, and Monmouth. He also declined the position of chief justice under the new constitution of Pennsylvania, accepting the advice of friends that he should not be associated with this radical government, but he accepted election to Congress, and in 1778 sat on many important committees.

In 1778 Reed prevented scandal by reporting directly to Congress on efforts by Lord Carlisle's peace commission to bribe him to support reconciliation with Britain. Through much of that year he proved his loyalty by prosecuting a series of treason trials, including several against Quakers who opposed the war on religious grounds. From December 1778 until 1781 he was president of the Supreme Executive Council of Pennsylvania. In this capacity he led the state's attack on Benedict Arnold and had the key role in settling the mutiny of the Pennsylvania Line in January 1781.

After losing an election to the assembly in 1781, Reed resumed his law practice. The following year he failed in his bid to become Chief Justice of Pennsylvania. Despite this rebuff, he successfully defended Pennsylvania before a special court empanelled by Congress to resolve the dispute with Connecticut over their competing claims to the Wyoming Valley. Also in 1782, Reed and General John Cadwalader of the Pennsylvania militia launched a nasty public feud after the latter accused Reed of lacking support for American independence and accused him of a weak military performance. While most contemporaries sided with Reed, who devoted a great deal of energy to the patriot cause, historians continue to debate his loyalty. Reed visited England in 1784 and was elected to Congress on his return. But his declining health prevented him from serving and Reed died the next year, at the age of 44.

SEE ALSO *Arnold, Benedict; Peace Commission of Carlisle; Peace Commission of the Howes.*

BIBLIOGRAPHY

Reed, William B. *Life and Correspondence of Joseph Reed.* 2 vols. Philadelphia: Lindsay and Blakiston, 1847.

Reed Papers. New York: New York Historical Society.

Roche, John F. *Joseph Reed: A Moderate in the American Revolution.* New York: Columbia University Press, 1957.

*revised by **Michael Bellesiles***

REEDY RIVER, SOUTH CAROLINA.

22 December 1775. After the truce that resulted from the actions at Ninety Six on 19 November, the Council of Safety sent a force of South Carolina militia and newly raised regulars under Colonel Richard Richardson and Lieutenant Colonel William Thomson into the region between the Broad and Saluda Rivers to break up Loyalists assembling there. They were reinforced by 700 North Carolina militia under Colonels Thomas Polk and Griffith Rutherford and 220 Continental regulars under Colonel Alexander Martin. By December the Patriot army totaled more than four thousand men, the largest force yet seen in the South. Loyalist resistance collapsed in the face of this strength, and Richardson captured leaders, including Thomas Fletchall, who was discovered hiding in a hollow tree. The only Loyalist unit that refused to disband, commanded by Patrick Cunningham, retreated to Cherokee territory. Richardson sent Thomson with his rangers to hunt them down. On the morning of 22 December, Thomson came upon their camp in the cane-brake next to the Reedy River. Loyalist pickets saw the Patriots before they were finished surrounding the camp and opened fire. No rangers were injured, and they took 130 prisoners while inflicting six casualties on the Loyalists. But Cunningham escaped with a handful of followers and joined the Cherokees further south. An error in dating has occasionally led some to believe that Reedy River and the Cane Brake were two separate battles.

SEE ALSO *Ninety Six, South Carolina (19 November 1775).*

revised by Michael Bellesiles

REGIMENT.

The British regiment, after which the regiments of the Continental army were modeled, was both an administrative organization and the principal tactical formation of the period. For almost all purposes, the terms "regiment" and "battalion" were synonymous, since most regiments had only one active-service battalion. The nominal head of a British regiment was its colonel, but the unit was normally led in battle by its second-ranking officer, the lieutenant colonel. The normal British regiment was composed of ten companies, eight of which were called "battalion," "line," or "hat" companies, after their tricorne hats. Two companies were called "flank" companies because, when the battalion was arrayed in line of battle, the grenadiers formed on the right of the battalion and the light infantry on the left.

British regiments were generally known by the names of their colonels until 1752, when they were numbered in order of seniority by the date when they were first created.

Many regiments had additional titles, most of which were honorifics granted by the king for some sort of outstanding service. Thus, the Fourth Regiment was the "King's Own" and the Eighth the "King's." Other titles combined a geographic location with royal favor: the Forty-second Regiment was the Royal Highland Regiment and the Sixtieth was the Royal American Regiment. Still others combined location, favor, and a reference to a former function: the Twenty-first Regiment was the Royal North British Fusiliers, and the Twenty-third was the Royal Welch Fusiliers, a fusil being a short flintlock firearm originally carried by regiments detailed to guard the artillery train, where the burning embers of the matchlocks carried by the other regiments might ignite open casks of gunpowder. Finally, several regiments newly raised in the Scottish Highlands combined the names of their colonels or the location of their muster with the term "Highlanders." For example, the British regiment that fought in more battles in the American war than any other was the Seventy-first Regiment, Fraser Highlanders.

Americans generally followed the British military models they had used effectively throughout the colonial wars, now with the additional desire of giving their armed forces credibility and respectability. At the start of the war, each colony raised its own regiments, generally with eight companies per regiment, but with regimental strengths that varied across the colonies because companies' strengths were different. Regiments from Massachusetts, New Hampshire, and Rhode Island, for example, were supposed to number 590 enlisted men at one time, while those from Connecticut varied from 1,000 to 600. In November 1775, Congress attempted to create a true "Continental army" for 1776 by merging the individual contingents of the four New England colonies, plus one Pennsylvania rifle regiment (essentially Washington's main army around Boston), into one numerical sequence of twenty-seven regiments. It prescribed that each regiment should have eight companies whose strength was set at 91 officers and men each, or a total of 728 men in a regiment. In the army of eighty-eight regiments raised for three years of service from 1 January 1777, most infantry regiments reverted to state designations. Those that did not initially carry a state number, like the sixteen Additional Continental Regiments, were raised by the states as part of their quotas, and those that became viable units eventually received state numbers. Congress continued the eight-company structure for the 1777 regiments and added a ninth company (light infantry) in 1779. In the American army, the colonel would be expected to lead the regiment himself. In 1781 Congress abolished the rank of colonel and created in its place the rank of lieutenant colonel commandant for regimental commanders. Since prisoners were exchanged on the basis of actual rank, the

Continental army needed more lieutenant colonels to swap for British regimental commanders.

The prescribed table of organization, called the "establishment," was in most cases no more than a pious hope. American regiments almost never operated in the field with the numbers required by the table. British regiments, too, were almost always understrength, although to a lesser extent because their recruiting system was better. For example, the average strength of the regiments under Washington at the Battle of Long Island on 27 August 1776 was about 350 officers, noncommissioned officers, and privates fit for duty. As the 1777 three-years army gave way to the 1780 reorganization, the tables of organization were revised to fit reality. Inspector General Friedrich Steuben reported that a minimum of 324 men in 9 companies (36 men per company) was required in each regiment for service in the field.

Because American militia units were organized on a geographical basis, militia regiments followed no standard table of organization and could vary wildly in size, especially when every able-bodied man turned out to resist a British incursion. At Lexington and Concord on 19 April 1775, for example, the mix of militia and minuteman regiments averaged 292 men per regiment.

SEE ALSO *Additional Continental Regiments; Battalion; Exchange of Prisoners; Flank Companies; Light Infantry; Rank and File; Regular Establishment.*

BIBLIOGRAPHY

Curtis, Edward E. *The Organization of the British Army in the American Revolution.* New Haven, Conn.: Yale University Press, 1926.

Darling, Anthony D. *Red Coat and Brown Bess.* Ottawa: Museum Restoration Service, 1970.

Houlding, J. A. *Fit for Service: The Training of the British Army, 1715–1795.* Oxford: Oxford University Press, 1981.

Katcher, Philip R. N. *Encyclopedia of British, Provincial, and German Army Units, 1775–1783.* Harrisburg, Pa.: Stackpole Books, 1973.

Wright, Robert K., Jr. *The Continental Army.* Washington, D.C.: United States Army Center of Military History, 1983.

revised by Harold E. Selesky

REGULAR APPROACHES.

One meaning of "approaches" is "entrenchments, etc., by which the besiegers draw closer to the besieged" (*Oxford Universal Dictionary*). When one reads that the attacker "undertook regular approaches," it means that he declined to attempt capturing a place by immediate assault (which often is less costly in the end) and elected the time-consuming and laborious process of formal siege operations. The basic technique was to dig a first "parallel" just outside the defender's artillery range; to run forward a zigzag trench, or sap; and then to dig a second parallel. This process is continued, with successive parallels enabling the besieger to move forward his work parties and artillery until the enemy surrenders or until a final assault can be made against his weakened fortifications.

SEE ALSO *Charleston Siege of 1780; Pensacola, Florida; Sap; Savannah, Georgia (9 October 1779); St. Leger's Expedition.*

BIBLIOGRAPHY

Onions, C. T., ed. *Oxford Universal Dictionary on Historical Principles.* 3rd ed. Oxford: Oxford University Press, 1955.

Mark M. Boatner

REGULAR ESTABLISHMENT.

The term "establishment" refers to several aspects of the organizational structure of the British army. At the highest level, the "regular establishment" was the entire standing British army, divided between the handful of household regiments of the king and the much larger number of regiments of the line. Together, they formed a permanent force that was administered by the king and the Parliament in accordance with laws and regulations that governed the pay, conditions of service, promotion, and retirement of its personnel; it was the equivalent of the modern U.S. regular army. The regular army was divided between two establishments, the British and the Irish, that varied in size and composition over time according to different combinations of need, cost, and tradition.

Strategic and operational requirements dictated which regiments served in different theaters, not which establishment they happened to be on. After the Peace of Paris in 1763, 17,500 men were stationed in Britain, 12,000 in Ireland, 10,000 in America, and over 4,000 at Minorca and Gibraltar. These allocations, plus 1,800 artillerymen, made a total of roughly 45,000 men to garrison an unprecedented worldwide empire. A dozen years later, on the verge of a war to suppress the rebellion in the American colonies, the number and distribution of troops were roughly the same. By the end of 1781, when large-scale active operations ceased, the British army numbered some 110,000 men, 57,000 of whom were serving in North America.

The expansion of the army in wartime was a common feature of the way Britain made war, as was the corresponding reduction in size and number of regiments when the war was over. In this way, the army can be said to have had both a wartime and a peacetime establishment.

During the War of American Independence, the British government created a hybrid form of establishment that reflected the wartime expansion of the number of men under British arms and in British pay. Effective 2 May 1779, the five most proficient and hardest fighting of the units raised among American Loyalists were placed on a new Provincial (or American) Establishment. The boost to the morale of Loyalist soldiers far outweighed the military value of this designation, although being placed on an establishment did mean that the officers were legally entitled to half pay for life when their regiment was disbanded. Four of the five were placed on the British Establishment on Christmas Day 1782; all were disbanded by the end of 1783.

Finally, "establishment" also refers to the authorized size of the army's constituent regiments. After the middle of the eighteenth century, a regiment was commonly composed of ten companies, eight of which were called, variously, battalion, line, or hat companies. The remaining two companies were elite formations, called flank companies from their standard position on the flanks of the regiment when it was drawn up in linear formation. Each wore specialized headgear, the grenadiers wearing tall, cone-shaped caps that did not interfere with the arm motion involved in throwing a grenade, the light infantry a cut-down version of the standard line company tricorne hat, as befitted a company intended to skirmish ahead of the battalion line. The numerical size of the regiment varied with the authorized size of its companies, which varied in this period from thirty-eight to fifty-six men per company.

SEE ALSO *Flank Companies; Provincial Military Organizations; Regiment.*

BIBLIOGRAPHY

Curtis, Edward E. *The British Army in the American Revolution.* New Haven, Conn.: Yale University Press, 1926.

Fortescue, John. *A History of the British Army.* Vol. 3. 2nd ed. London: Macmillan, 1911.

Houlding, J. A. *Fit for Service: The Training of the British Army, 1715–1795.* Oxford: Oxford University Press, 1981.

Mills, T. F. "Land Forces of Britain, the Empire, and Commonwealth: 'Regiments and Corps of the British Army, 1761 and 1781 Supplement.'" Available online at http://regiments.org.

Reid, Stuart. *King George's Army, 1740–1793.* Vol. 1. London: Reed International Books, 1995.

revised by Harold E. Selesky

REGULATORS.

After the final French and Indian war, regulator movements arose in the piedmont upcountry of the Carolinas which had, according to the Oxford English Dictionary, "the professed object of supplying the want of the regular administration of justice." In North Carolina, piedmont farmers who believed they were being exploited by tidewater elites began to organize politically in 1766 to seek legal redress of their grievances. They wanted, among other things, more equitable representation in the provincial assembly for the rapidly growing piedmont counties, and an end to corruption and the embezzlement of public funds by easterners acting in the name of the Crown. According to Marjoleine Kars the backcountry settlers "repeatedly petitioned the governor and the assembly, tried to set up meetings with local officials, and brought suits against officials. When such legal measures had little effect, they resorted to extralegal action: they refused to pay taxes, repossessed property seized for public sale to satisfy debts and taxes, and disrupted court proceedings" (Kars, p. 2). Their campaign of insurgency and intimidation culminated at Hillsborough in September 1770, when a group of regulators disrupted the superior court session and destroyed the house of Edmund Fanning, one of the most rapacious crown officials.

Governor William Tryon acted quickly to quell what he viewed as a spreading insurrection. With the support of the tidewater elite and the non-regulator faction of the piedmont elite, the assembly on 15 January 1771 passed a Riot Act that gave Tryon sweeping powers to raise the militia and hunt down regulators who refused to surrender. Tryon's army of 1,100 militiamen, overwhelmingly from the tidewater counties, arrived in the piedmont in early May 1771, and on the 16th met and defeated the disorganized regulators at the battle of the Alamance. Tryon's force marched through the peidmont for nearly a month after the battle, waging a campaign of intimidation and terror, seizing supplies, and destroying crops, orchards, and rail fences.

Tyron had one insurgent leader executed on the battlefield, six more hanged on 19 June at Hillsborough, and compelled nearly 6,500 backcountry settlers to swear allegiance to the government as the price of reconciliation. According to Kars, this amounted to three quarters of the free white male population in the backcountry (Kars, p. 240). Many former regulators later migrated to the trans-Allegheny region, one group settling on the Watauga river in what is now Tennessee. Tryon arrived back in New Bern in late June, and on the 30th sailed away to his new appointment as governor of New York, taking along his good friend Edmund Fanning as his personal secretary.

The new royal governor, Josiah Martin, arrived on 11 August, and immediately adopted a conciliatory policy toward the regulators. His conciliation came too late to win the regulators over to the royal cause, but the disaffected in the piedmont were also only lukewarm adherents to the anti-imperial cause. Neither Tryon nor the tidewater elites had ever championed solutions to the problems of the piedmont farmers, and they were therefore reluctant to join the elites of eastern North Carolina when they led the colony into rebellion against imperial control in the spring of 1775.

The regulator movement in South Carolina (1767–1769) stemmed from a desire on the part of members of the nascent upcountry planter class to suppress lawlessness and restore order on the frontier following the Cherokee Expedition of 1763. In South Carolina's case, the people of both the tidewater and piedmont regions supported this vigilante movement, which faded as it accomplished its goals over the next few years. Owing largely to the prudence of Lieutenant Governor William Bull, the interior settlements were quiet from 1769 until the Revolution.

S E E A L S O *Alamance, Battle of the; Fanning, Edmund; Over Mountain Men; Tryon, William.*

BIBLIOGRAPHY

Brown, Richard Maxwell. *The South Carolina Regulators.* Cambridge, Mass.: Belknap Press of Harvard University Press, 1963.

Crow, Jeffrey J. "Liberty Men and Loyalists: Disorder and Disaffection in the North Carolina Backcountry." In *An Uncivil War: The Southern Backcountry During the American Revolution.* Edited by Ronald Hoffman, Thad W. Tate, and Peter J. Albert. Charlottesville, Va.: University Press of Virginia for the United Edited by States Capitol Historical Society, 1985.

Kars, Marjoleine. *Breaking Loose Together: The Regulator Rebellion in Pre-Revolutionary North Carolina.* Chapel Hill, N.C.: University of North Carolina Press, 2002.

Klein, Rachel N. *Unification of a Slave State: The Rise of the Planter Class in the South Carolina Backcountry, 1760–1808.* Chapel Hill, N.C.: University of North Carolina Press, 1990.

Lee, Wayne E. *Crowds and Soldiers in Revolutionary North Carolina: The Culture of Violence in Riot and War.* Gainesville, Florida: University Press of Florida, 2001.

revised by Harold E. Selesky

RELIGION AND THE AMERICAN REVOLUTION.

Historians of the military conflict of the Revolutionary era have paid scant attention to religion. While political and social historians argue that religious belief and affiliation were critical ingredients in the coming of independence and the forming of the new republic, major works on the Revolutionary War include few references to churches, creeds, clergy, denominations, religious movements, and even chaplains. At the same time, the war itself—the armies and navies, commanders, soldiers, spies, prisoners of war, campaigns, and civil violence—make barely an appearance in political and social

histories. What accounts for this lack of connection between scholars' approaches to the war?

One simple answer is that ministers generally don't take up arms—though the Revolution provides numerous exceptions—and churches don't prosecute wars. But such assumptions of the separation of clerical and military spheres are themselves artifacts of the enlightened era in which the Revolutionary War took place. A more compelling explanation is that the relationship between religion and the war is far from unambiguous. For while religious ideology and affiliation served as an important, if not the main, inspiration for large numbers of Americans to become involved in, to oppose, or to ignore the war effort, and while the conflict produced a marked change in the direction of American religious culture, the military architects of the new American nation had no particular religious "policy" in mind, and many fighting men appeared to have been indifferent to the religious consequence of the war. The war was over the birth of a new nation, rather than a new nation-with-church, as had been the case in the past.

This was not surprising, since the prosecutors of the war on both sides needed to recruit Americans from every background; and for many Americans, the ecclesiastical tyranny of tax-supported religious establishments was another form of oppression they were fighting against. Anti-Catholicism and opposition to an Anglican bishopric in the colonies were long-standing manifestations of this resistance. At the same time, Loyalists, many of them Anglicans, bemoaned attacks upon "liberal" Christianity by those they considered to be religious fanatics and heirs to the Puritan Revolution. The "peace churches," in the meanwhile, aimed to keep government out of their lives entirely.

Ultimately, a people not only numerous and armed, to use historian John Shy's phrase, but also religious and armed would produce two religious outcomes in their fight with Britain: a more "liberal" form of church and state relations in the United States than existed either in the colonies or the mother country, and a national culture based on a unitary "civil religion" rather than one denominational identity. But the many religious conflicts that characterized the war suggest that these results were not entirely expected.

"PASSIONATE PROTESTANTISM" VERSUS "PAPIST TYRANNY"

Pro-war polemicists, political activists, and Patriot clergy possessed what one historian, Robert Middlekauff, has described as "the moral dispositions of a passionate Protestantism" (p. 48). From the Commonwealth writers of the seventeenth and early eighteenth centuries, they had inherited the political values of popular sovereignty, social contract theory, and the protection of life, liberty and property; and the religious virtues of frugality, hard work, and biblical faith. In the heated opening years of the conflict, it would not take much to persuade many Americans that the British had betrayed those shared ideals.

The British Parliament obliged by passing the Quebec Act, the religious Rubicon of the Revolution Legislated in the Spring of 1774 under the guidance of William Legge, Lord Dartmouth, the head cabinet officer for the colonies, the act provided toleration (along with some tax support) for Roman Catholicism and extended the boundaries of Quebec south to the Ohio River and west to the Mississippi River. In a stroke, the act effectively barred migration of Americans into the northwest, placing the region instead into the hands of Catholic settlers and a Catholic bishop—the very powers that British Americans had been fighting since the start of the Anglo-French Wars in 1689.

The reconstitution of Quebec and its religious implications formed the larger continental context of the war. It accounted for the misguided invasion of Canada by American forces in 1775 and Americans' persistent efforts to win victory on the frontier. Although Lord Dartmouth was a "low church" Anglican who favored a faith based on daily piety and evangelical conversion rather than the power of church officialdom, the statute persuaded large numbers of Americans that the British government aimed to institute a papal-style regency in North America. Many believed that, in this way, a corrupt British government would enslave Americans and enrich itself off the spoils of the continent. How did so many Americans and British come to such differing perspectives on the action of the British ministry?

CIVIL AND RELIGIOUS LIBERTY

The combatants on both sides of the Revolution shared the political heritage of civil and religious liberty from Puritan and Enlightenment sources, but Whigs and Patriots especially emphasized that relationship. Altogether, New England Congregationalists and Presbyterians, Scotch-Irish Presbyterians, many Baptists, and many low church Anglicans in the South—all in one way or another heirs of the Puritans or Puritan values—probably encompassed nearly half (fifty percent) of the church-attending population in America. The great majority sympathized with or overtly supported the Patriot cause. Speaking interchangeably in the language of Old Testament prophets and the discourse of enlightened, rational religion, their ministers exhorted Americans to love liberty, imitate virtue, reverence their pious but bold ancestors, and resist passive obedience to British political and clerical authorities. Their listeners were not always aware of these multiple sources. Captain Levi Preston, a participant at Lexington and Concord, had never heard of the great Commonwealth writers James Harrington, Algernon Sidney, or John Locke; instead he knew his Bible, church catechism, and almanacs, and sang the psalms and hymns of Isaac Watts. Yet his explanation

for fighting in the first skirmish of the war was clearly Commonwealth-inspired: "[W]hat we meant in going for those Redcoats was this: we always had governed ourselves and we always meant to. They didn't mean we should."

At the same time, Americans' understanding of religious liberty would undergo a significant transformation in the crucible of the war, from a condition "tolerated" by government to a one existing by natural right. Consequently, New England Baptists led by Isaac Backus and John Leland supported independence in the expectation that it would not only rid Americans of British control but also produce the disestablishment of the Congregational Church in Massachusetts, Connecticut, and New Hampshire, and the Anglican Church in the lower counties of New York and the southern states. In Virginia, they were joined by Presbyterians, who described church establishments as a form of religious bondage no worse than civil bondage and petitioned the Virginia state legislature to eliminate tax support for the Church of England.

The demand for freedom of conscience—the other element of religious freedom—also inspired figures like the commander of the Green Mountain Boys, Ethan Allen, to reject traditional Christianity entirely, in favor of Deism. The Franco-American Alliance in 1778, bringing thousands of French troops onto American soil, likely also exposed American soldiers to advanced forms of freethinking and anticlericalism, although the evidence is sketchy. At the least, the alliance dramatically modified the "No King, No Popery" rhetoric of many leading Patriots, and prompted General Washington to outlaw anti-Catholic Guy Fawkes Day celebrations in the Continental Army. This rejection of anti-Catholic antipathy and the new commitment to freedom of conscience for American Catholics was surely one of the more remarkable reversals of the war.

POPULAR MILLENNIALISM

Many historians have argued that the Patriots' powerful convictions regarding the justice of their cause, their ability to attract a wide and popular following, and their endurance through eight years of violent conflict can only be understood as a byproduct of biblical millennialism—a far more powerful form of theological worldview than Enlightenment-influenced forms of theology. American millennialists indeed believed that Great Britain was the new Anti-Christ, Americans were the chosen people, and North America would be the scene of Christ's Second Coming. But Americans were also attracted to a "secular millennialism" that combined biblical predictions of America's destiny with rationalist attacks on established authority in the manner of Thomas Paine's enormously influential *Common Sense*. The pamphlet's millennial-style passages are well known. "We have it in our power to begin the world over again, . . ." Paine wrote, adding: "The birth-day of a new-

Prayer in Congress. *This illustration by H. B. Hall after T. H. Matteson offers an image of the delegates to the Continental Congress in prayer in September 1774 in Philadelphia.* LANDOV

world is at hand." In Paine's view this new world would be far from a theocracy, grounded not on ecclesiastical authority, but on the principles of a democratic republic and equal rights. Secular millennialism like Paine's marked the beginnings of an American "civil religion," although it would be some years before Americans recognized its ingredients as a commonly shared national faith.

HIGH CHURCH LOYALISTS

The Whigs and more radical Patriots did not have a monopoly on religious culture, and one of the ironies of the Revolutionary conflict is how often Loyalists and pacifists saw the pro-independence party as the one which was oppressing Americans' religious and civil liberties. If there was a significantly "liberal" religious group outside the early Unitarian-leaning Congregationalists of Boston, it was the "high church" Anglicans, whose attachment to the enlightened ideals of reasonable Christianity was unmatched. Concentrated in the North, the high

church Anglicans epitomized the Anglicizing preferences of many wealthy Americans. They favored the advancement of gentility, British culture and literature, missionary outreach to the "heathens" throughout the empire, elegant ecclesiastical architecture, and other features of the Anglican "Renaissance" of the eighteenth century. They also supported the establishment of an episcopacy in America in order to expedite the ordination of ministers, a position opposed by most southern, "low church" Anglicans and increasingly excoriated by other Protestants. Joining them in enlightened religious practice were the moderate Scottish Presbyterians (as opposed to the strenuously Calvinist Scotch-Irish Presbyterians), Scottish Anglicans like William Smith, Provost of the College of Philadelphia, and Scottish highlander immigrants concentrated in North Carolina. But altogether these groups likely represented less than ten percent of the churchgoing population on the eve of the war.

Anglican Samuel Seabury (later to be anointed as the first Protestant Episcopal Bishop in America) accurately defined the Revolution as a civil war, and forcefully argued that the Continental Congress itself was tyrannical, especially in its arbitrary armed resistance against the British authorities. Seabury insisted that the Patriots were bringing about the very conditions that they claimed to oppose and would soon be forced to support a permanent British military establishment. British officers, Hessian observers, and Loyalists alike believed the Patriots were carrying on the Puritan fight against king and episcopacy from the 1640s into the 1770s. An American Loyalist surgeon communicating with the British command described the men encamped around Boston in 1775 as heirs to Oliver Cromwell's army. A British major expressed the point more succinctly: "It is your G-d damned Religion of this Country that ruins the Country; Damn your Religion" (Royster, p. 19). The American rebellion, the British believed—lumping together Congregationalists and their fellow former Puritans—was a "Presbyterian war." In the view of many of their clergy, the Patriot attack on enlightened religion and English culture was proof of the conflict's perversity.

QUAKERS AND GERMAN PACIFISTS

The certainty of High church Anglicans of their own liberty-loving rectitude was undercut by their persistent opposition to republican government and by their conservative social mores. This was not the case for the many religious pacifists in the states, including some Baptists, the "Peace Germans" (Amish, Brethren, Dunkards, Mennonites, and Moravians), and experimental groups like the Shakers and Universal Friends. Most important among these was the Religious Society of Friends, or Quakers, at one time (with Congregationalists and Anglicans) one of the three largest denominations in the colonies. Altogether, the peace churches probably comprised more than fifteen percent of the American population, and they were concentrated in key strategic areas, including the Hudson River Valley, New Jersey, Pennsylvania, and Delaware. They were distinguished by a pietist theology focusing on conformity to Christian simplicity and spiritual mysticism; by long experience of government harassment; by democratic church polities; and by unparalleled advocacy of gender equality. Although largely unexamined by historians, this last attribute, including the degree to which pietist women bore the burden of persecution equally with pietist men, may have been a central reason for the groups' long-standing abstention from the bearing of arms.

The Quakers' "peace testimony" was forged in the previous century of conflict between Puritans and Anglicans. The Quakers blocked the formation of a Pennsylvania militia before the French and Indian War drove them from power, and the Philadelphia Yearly Meeting likewise opposed the general militia law at the start of the Revolutionary war. The Patriot leadership alternatively viewed the Friends as a "mischievous" threat and likely Tories or as uncooperative nuisances. But a significant minority of Quakers (more than 750) in the new states, nicknamed "Fighting Quakers," believed that the Quaker doctrine of the inner light—and the millennial destiny of America—necessitated support for the enlightened American cause. Key Patriot Quakers were Thomas Paine (a lapsed English Friend), Betsy Ross (disowned, along with other important Patriot radicals, by the Philadelphia Friends), and Continental Army General Nathanael Greene, the indispensable man of the southern campaigns.

The German sects were universally pacifist, but the Baptists were divided between those who were confident in the future of religious freedom in America and those less convinced of this outcome: the former became Patriots, the latter—much smaller in number—became noncombatants. These groups were joined as well by John Wesley's "connexion" of unordained Methodist preachers, only recently arrived from Britain and comprised of increasing numbers of Americans. For all of these groups, the greatest tests of their faith came with state laws requiring loyalty oaths and militia service. Non-associators (that is, those who did not comply with the laws) were to be barred from public preaching or teaching, fined, or jailed. As a result, the war produced the first religious arguments in favor of resistance to the draft (for militia duty). And, once state authorities realized that their efforts to punish non-associators were counter-productive, the conflict also produced the first informal but state-sponsored recognition of conscientious-objector status based on religion.

CLERGY AND CHURCH FABRIC

The voice of clergymen in promoting and opposing American independence, the fate of their congregations and church buildings, and the experience of army chaplains illustrate further the ways in collective groups of religious believers shaped the course of the war and experienced its consequences. American clergy were compelling figures on both sides of the military conflict. Called the "black regiment" after their clerical garb, American Patriot clergy in particular included liberal Congregationalists like Jonathan Mayhew and Charles Chauncey in Boston; moderate Congregationalists like Samuel Cooper in the same city; revivalist Ezra Stiles, president of Yale College in Connecticut; moderate Scottish Presbyterian John Witherspoon, president of the College of New Jersey; Jacob Duche at Christ Church in Philadelphia (before the cause of independence forced him into the Loyalist camp); and many Scotch-Irish Presbyterians in New York, New Jersey, and the southern states, and on the western frontier. In Virginia, "Fighting Parson" John Peter Gabriel Muhlenberg, for just one example, left his Lutheran congregation in the Shenandoah Valley to join the Virginia militia and was ultimately commissioned as a brigadier general in the Continental army. The British correctly blamed American ministers for whipping up the *rage militaire* in the first year of the war, and the Continental Congress and state legislature relied on them to communicate with the larger American public to the end of the conflict.

Such partisanship had its price. The British never intruded far enough into New England to wreak havoc on dispersed congregations, burn church buildings, or silence the meetinghouse bells that called out the minutemen time and again. But to the south of New England the Patriot clergy faced significant threats to life and limb, and their churches were frequently desecrated or destroyed. In New York, New Jersey, and North Carolina, the British regularly burned Patriot meetinghouses or turned their copious spaces into horse stables and military hospitals. The main focus of both the British and Loyalist militias were the meetinghouses of Scotch-Irish Presbyterians, the largest non-English group in rebellion. Judging by the speed with which one Presbyterian pastor in western North Carolina responded to the threat of British incursion—stopping mid-sermon to form a company, which he then led against the invading forces—the British had reason to fear the popular strength of this particular denomination.

On the other side, high church Anglican clergy complained of their treatment at the hands of the Sons of Liberty, Committees of Observation, Committees of Safety, and less respectable groups. In New York they faced arrest and jailing, conscription for militia duty, and then fines for non-attendance. Their homes and offices were broken into by Patriot crowds and militia. The low church clergy of Virginia and the rest of the South were protected by their powerful vestries: more than half supported the American cause and a good number of their ministers joined the armed forces. But most of the northern Anglican clergy emigrated to Canada or returned to Britain, leaving their churches abandoned and shuttered. On the eve of 19 April 1775, one such sanctuary, the Old North (Christ) Church in Boston, provided the literal and figurative scaffolding for the start of the war.

The Quakers, "Peace" Germans, and other pacifists, although not providing any fighting parsons, were still affected by the military conflict. In 1777, the Supreme Executive Council of Pennsylvania accused the Philadelphia Quaker leadership of Toryism, and sent fifteen prominent Quakers to a prison camp in Virginia. Non-associator Methodist preachers were fined and jailed on a regular basis and were frequent objects of abuse by Patriot mobs. Their British-born leader, Francis Asbury, went into seclusion in loyalist Delaware.

CHAPLAINS IN THE CAMPS

The other significant service provided by clergy on both sides was as army chaplains. Military chaplains were first recruited for service in May 1775, by the new Massachusetts state government. With Washington's encouragement, the Continental Congress quickly established the office of the regimental chaplaincy in the Continental Army. In 1777 Congress elevated the office into a brigade chaplaincy. The chaplain received a colonel's pay as an incentive for enlistment and facilitate the expansion of the work of a relatively small numbers of ministers over greater numbers of troops. Washington delayed the establishment of this new office in order to prevent a reduction in the ministers' effectiveness. The brigade chaplain was expected to be an experienced clergyman with an established public reputation for piety, virtue, and learning. His duties included administering two Sunday services weekly and attending the sick and dying. Many also sought the advice of commanders in providing the appropriate martial content to their sermons.

The British army, of course, also included military chaplains, with many of the same duties as the Americans. But in both cases, although receiving commissioned rank and providing indispensable spiritual and medical assistance to fighting men, the work of regimental and brigade chaplains was of a different order of difficulty from their civilian work. British regimental chaplains frequently paid substitutes to take their places. These men, and those connected with them, faced genuine danger, even when not engaged in conflict. One example of this is found in the tragic killing of Presbyterian chaplain James Caldwell's wife in their New Jersey home by a British officer, who apparently singled out the minister's family for punishment. Caldwell's later murder by a disgruntled American soldier, makes clear that the threat came not only from the enemy.

Chaplains also came face to face with the real spiritual state of enlisted men. The British chaplains were specifically instructed to monitor the soldiers' behavior, from cursing and profanity to gambling and resorting to prostitutes. British commanders spoke glowingly of the piety of the Hessians who, in contrast to often indifferent British troops, broke into hymn-singing spontaneously and regularly, including before combat. As the *rage militaire* of the start of the war subsided, the regiments of the Continental army were filled with poor farmers, laboring men, and former slaves—more typical of British enlisted men than were the minutemen at the start of the war. The recollections of wartime participation by many of these soldiers contain almost no religious content. In a notable exception, black veteran Jehu Grant implied that religious education, might have deterred his enlistment since, had he "been taught to read or understand the precepts of the Gospel, 'Servants obey your masters,'" he might not have

Prayer at Valley Forge. *This nineteenth-century engraving by John McRae after a painting by H. Brueckner imagines General Washington in prayer during the difficult winter at Valley Forge.* **THE LIBRARY OF CONGRESS**

joined the military. Instead, his inspiration came from popular songs of liberty that "saluted my ear, thrilled through my heart" (Dann, p. 28).

One Baptist chaplain, Ebenezer David, was dismayed by the irreligious attitudes of the enlisted men in Rhode Island. But David was witnessing a new world, in which religious provincialism was fading fast. He worked with John Murray, a Universalist, who preached salvation for all believers—heretical doctrine to most Calvinists like David. He became fascinated with better ways of practicing medicine, a new professional outlet. He was surely familiar with some of the 200 black men who comprised the First Rhode Island Regiment, a new population of fighting men. Before he died of a fever at Valley Forge in the Winter of 1778, David was freely using soldiers' slang like "pilcocke" to refer to doctors and "camp geniuses" to describe camp followers, and he may have thought of himself as a "pulpit drum." Perhaps he came to better understand the earthy point of view of enlisted men like Joseph Plumb Martin. Recollecting his long service with the Continental army, Martin mordantly paraphrased

Tom Paine: "I often found that those times not only tried men's souls, but their bodies too; I know they did mine, and that effectually."

CONTESTED TERRAIN

Ultimately, for both American and British military commands, perhaps the biggest challenge in dealing with the religious implications of the war was determining who was reliably on which side. Historian Kevin Phillips has demonstrated how consistently regionally or ethnically defined denominational identity led to political allegiance in the war (*The Cousins' Wars*), as described above. But Phillips also confirms the importance of the divided or neutral (as opposed to pacifist) denominations. Various sources suggest that as many as twenty-five percent of church-attending Americans fit this description: including Huguenots, "Church Germans" (Lutherans and German Reformed), Dutch Reformed, Methodist laypeople (as opposed to their frequently pacifist ministers), Roman Catholics (English, Irish, and Canadian), and Jews. Added to these were as many as one-third of all

Anglicans, if the affiliations of Anglican ministers is taken as an indicator of their parishioners' views. British and American contenders alike were eager to have these populations on their side, making the regions south of New England not only militarily but also culturally contested terrain.

Phillips also correctly argues that the allegiance of blacks and Indians was of utmost importance in winning the war. Although conclusions are inevitably tentative with these far less well documented populations, the choices made by slaves, free blacks, and frontier tribes were likely to be as strongly influenced by denominational allegiance or religious conviction as were the choices made by whites in the conflict. So Lemuel Haynes, a Connecticut Congregationalist and later the first ordained African American minister of any denomination, joined the Continental Army immediately upon his emancipation. Phillis Wheatley, an evangelical Christian, was the first African American published author, and among her many poems was a paean to General Washington. James Forten, Philadelphia sailmaker and Anglican, was also an early abolitionist: he joined the liberty-loving Patriots.

How many of the black men in the First Rhode Island Regiment were native Baptists, inclined to the Patriots' side, cannot be known; but southerners must have regretted their unwillingness to accustom their slaves to the advantages of low church Anglicanism and fidelity to Whig mores when thousands escaped and fled behind British lines during "Lord Dunmore's War" in 1775. As many as 20,000 slaves in South Carolina alone were estimated to have joined the British. Many were betrayed by the British command and re-enslaved in the West Indies or impressed as "military slaves" into British regiments. Others were more fortunate—black Loyalist men and women alike escaped to new lives in Nova Scotia, where they joined Methodist and Baptist churches, membership so frequently denied them by slavemasters.

Similarly, victory in the West depended on the constancy of hundreds of potential Indian allies and French Catholic settlers. The Mohawks, including Chief Joseph Brant, an Anglican convert, allied with the British. So did the Cherokees and Creeks, working through Superintendent John Stuart, a moderate Scot and Loyalist. But the Stockbridge Indians, educated at the Presbyterian Mission in that Massachusetts town, were on the American side, and Superintendent Sir William Johnson feared the effect that Calvinist missionaries might have among the Iroquois. American commander George Rogers Clark promised political and religious freedom to French settlers and Indian tribes in Ohio Country, smoothing the way for American acquisition in the Treaty of Paris in 1783. Pietist Indians, on the other hand, like the ninety-six Moravians Indians, men, women and children massacred by American soldiers in northern Pennsylvania near the end of the war, were caught in the middle.

Here the story of religion and the Revolutionary war comes full circle. The depradations and displacements experienced by so many Indians during the conflict led to the revival of a quiescent nativism among northwestern and southwestern tribes. Aiming to rebuild Indian unity and to drive the whites back to the Appalachians, the new nativism was advanced by Chief Tecumseh and his brother, Shawnee Prophet, in the very same territory that had been assigned to Quebec in 1774. The Revolutionary war continued here in altered form for another thirty years.

CONCLUSIONS

Religious culture had an impact on the character, course, and consequences of the war. Without the anti-papal propaganda, the wedding of religious and political liberty, and the millennial expectations that formed the great triad of religious inspiration throughout the war, it is difficult to imagine the conflict lasting long beyond the arrival of the Howe brothers (George, Richard, and William) in 1776. Without the British conviction that the rebellion was a recurrence of Puritan treason against an anointed king, the British army's hatred of New England and violence against Congregationalist and Presbyterian churches would be inexplicable. And without the long historical experience of brutal religious warfare and persecution in their own histories, not least of all against women in these faiths, the rejection of the virile world of military service by German sects and Society of Friends might seem less worthy than they were.

The war also prompted a series of dramatic reversals in what might otherwise have been the natural progression toward Anglican cultural and institutional dominance, living in unquiet but tolerable coexistence with Calvinist adherents on the one hand and pietist pacifists on the other. Instead it produced the collapse of Anglican authority; New Englanders' abandonment of both anti-Catholicism and strict Calvinism; the rising popularity, even during the war, of emerging pietist—rather than scrupulously Calvinist—evangelical movements like the Methodists and Baptists, not least of all among African Americans. And finally, the war contributed to the initiation of new forms of tribal religious unity among Indians.

Most critically for the nation state, freedom of conscience and freedom from church establishments, though far from fully institutionalized, were increasingly espoused as aspects of American civil religion. So was the millennial-style conviction, expressed by General Washington in his *Circular to the States* in June 1783, that the future happiness of millions depended upon the favorable outcome of the great experiment in republican government, now that the war was won. Americans have come to adhere to this understanding of the special character of the Revolution, but for many combatants and noncombatants recovering from the political and religious enmities of the war, such a consensus was yet to be built.

SEE ALSO *Associators; Methodists; Presbyterians; Quakers; Roman Catholics; Stuart, John.*

BIBLIOGRAPHY

Albanese, Catherine L. *Sons of the Fathers: The Civil Religion of the American Revolution.* Philadelphia: Temple University Press, 1976.

Andrews, Dee E. *The Methodists and Revolutionary America, 1760–1800: The Shaping of an Evangelical Culture.* Princeton, N.J.: Princeton University Press, 2000.

Black, Jeannette D., and William Greene Roelker, eds. *A Rhode Island Chaplain in the Revolution: Letters of Ebenezer David to Nicholas Brown, 1775–1778.* Port Washington, N.Y. and London: Kennikat Press, 1972.

Bloch, Ruth H. *Visionary Republic: Millennial Themes in American Thought, 1756–1800.* Cambridge, U.K.: Cambridge University Press, 1985.

Cogliano, Francis D. *No King, No Popery: Anti-Catholicism in Revolutionary New England.* Westport, Conn. and London: Greenwood Press, 1995.

Dann, John C., ed. *The Revolution Remembered: Eyewitness Accounts of the War for Independence.* Chicago and London: University of Chicago Press, 1980.

Dowd, Gregory Evans. *A Spirited Resistance: The North American Indian Struggle For Unity, 1745–1815.* Baltimore and London: Johns Hopkins University Press, 1992.

Fischer, David Hackett. *Paul Revere's Ride.* New York and Oxford: Oxford University Press, 1994.

Frey, Sylvia R. *Water from the Rock: Black Resistance in a Revolutionary Age.* Princeton, N.J.: Princeton University Press, 1991.

Hutson, James H., ed. *Religion and the New Republic: Faith in the Founding of America.* Oxford: Rowman and Littlefield, 2000.

Kashatus, William C., III. *Conflict of Conviction: A Reappraisal of Quaker Involvement in the American Revolution.* Lanham, New York, and London: University Press of America, 1990.

Lambert, Frank. *The Founding Fathers and the Place of Religion in America.* Princeton, N.J., and Oxford: Princeton University Press, 2003.

Marietta, Jack D. *The Reformation of American Quakerism, 1748–1783.* Philadelphia. University of Pennsylvania Press, 1984.

Martin, James Kirby, ed. *Ordinary Courage: The Revolutionary War Adventures of Joseph Plumb Martin.* St. James, N.Y.: Brandywine Press, 1993.

Metzger, Charles H. *Catholics and the American Revolution: A Study in Religious Climate.* Chicago: Loyola University Press, 1962.

Middlekauff, Robert. *The Glorious Cause: The American Revolution, 1763–1789.* New York and Oxford: Oxford University Press, 1982.

Paine, Thomas. *Common Sense.* Edited by Isaac Kramnick. 1776. London and New York: Penguin Books, 1986.

Phillips, Kevin. *The Cousins' Wars: Religion, Politics, and the Triumph of Anglo-America.* New York: Basic Books, 1999.

Rhoden, Nancy L. *Revolutionary Anglicanism: The Colonial Church of England Clergy During the American Revolution.* New York: New York University Press, 1999.

Royster, Charles. *A Revolutionary People at War: The Continental Army and American Character, 1775–1781.* Chapel Hill: University of North Carolina Press, 1979.

Shy, John. *A People Numerous and Armed: Reflections on the Military Struggle for American Independence.* 1976. Rev. ed. Ann Arbor, Mich.: University of Michigan Press, 1990.

Dee E. Andrews

RESOURCES OF AMERICA AND GREAT BRITAIN COMPARED.

By every measure of military potential, the resources available to the British government vastly exceeded what the American colonists could muster. The population of the British Isles in 1775 was perhaps 12 million people, roughly five times the 2.5 million people in the colonies; the British advantage was even greater if the half-million slaves are subtracted from the colonial total. Britain maintained a standing army of perhaps 36,000 men, some 13,000 soldiers less than its authorized strength, along with 16,000 sailors who manned the Royal Navy's 270 ships. In nearly every category, too, Britain had the capacity to build up its military power faster than the colonies. The key factor here was not merely Britain's vastly greater wealth, but the existence of proven financial markets and mechanisms that would allow the government to borrow at reasonable interest rates. Britain could mobilize liquid capital to pay for more ships, more soldiers (recruited at home or hired on the Continent), and more military material (manufactured at home or purchased on the Continent) than could the colonies. By the end of the war in 1783, over 200,000 of George III's subjects from the British Isles were under arms (100,000 in the army and 107,000 in the navy), to which should be added nearly 30,000 German auxiliaries and at least 21,000 American loyalists. The Royal Navy numbered 468 ships in 1783, despite having lost 200 vessels to various causes during the war. Despite some shortfalls, British merchant shipping was able to transport soldiers and matériel across the Atlantic with reasonable efficiency, a necessary requirement for a war waged so far from sources of replacement and supply.

Still, given the staggering logistical and command problems in fighting a transatlantic war, the margin for error was sometimes very thin: only one British supply ship passed safely from Britain to Boston between August and November 1775. Faced with a colonial rebellion of unprecedented size and scope and with traditional enemies, especially France, waiting for an opportunity to exact revenge, Britain's leaders had to make the right decisions rapidly and use military force to maximum effect to achieve a political solution to the conflict, the only real way of returning the colonies to their prior political allegiance. The entry of France into the war as a partner of the American rebels in February 1778 turned a rebellion into a world war and forced the British to raise, equip, and field unprecedented numbers of armed forces.

AMERICAN RESOURCES

The contrast with the armed forces available to the colonial governments at the start of the conflict was so extreme as to be laughable. The colonies maintained no soldiers under arms in peacetime and relied for their defense (or for rebellion) on a militia that theoretically included all able-bodied men from eighteen years of age upwards to fifty, fifty-five, and even sixty years old, varying by colony. The most experienced soldiers in the colonies were the veterans of the French and Indian War, an invaluable resource for training and command purposes, but too few in number and, by 1775, too old to fill the ranks. The colonies maintained no standing navies, but here again would have to rely on veterans of the largely private war vessels (privateers) that had filled the seas in previous conflicts.

A questionnaire from Lord Dartmouth to all colonial governors in 1773 revealed the sorry state of military preparedness on the eve of the war. Virginia and New Jersey reported "not one fort now." All New Hampshire reported was a "quite ruinous" stone castle at Portsmouth, and Pennsylvania reported only a half-finished fort in the Delaware River to ward off pirates. Boston's Castle William was in ill repair, and there were only a few batteries to protect the other Massachusetts ports. Georgia had four forts. New York had a fort and batteries at the mouth of the Hudson River and forts at Albany and Schenectady, but none was properly equipped with cannon or adequately supplied.

One must assume that American military potential was not negligible, at least in the minds of the men who wanted to fight; presumably, enough colonists were convinced that they could successfully resist the British and defend their political freedoms by force of arms, or else they would not have begun an armed resistance in the first place. But American potential was largely latent, and it would take time to ramp it up to a point where enough potential had been transformed into actual, operational capability for success to be possible. Since manufacturing in the colonies was inadequate to support sustained combat, most military supplies would have to be purchased abroad (largely on credit) and shipped across the Atlantic. Because building an armaments industry in America was

out of the question, access to European sources of all sorts of military supplies was crucial.

Americans had the advantage of fighting on their own ground, where they were familiar with the types of terrain and climate that might limit the effectiveness of European-trained regulars. Few Americans, however, had training or experience as military engineers and artillerymen, and even fewer had any experience in army organization, administration, and training. (Washington, who had observed how Edward Braddock in 1755 and John Forbes in 1758 handled an expeditionary force, probably had more experience in these areas than any other American.) While many officers had tactical experience in the colonial wars and would provide essential leadership for the young soldiers in the army, the slow development of expertise above the regimental level was a nearly fatal shortcoming. Although urban dwellers might have limited experience with firearms, the fact that outside the cities the economy of the colonies was agricultural meant that many people owned and had some experience using guns. Settlers along the frontier in the interior had more experience hunting for game with Pennsylvania rifles, and many had participated in recent campaigns against Native American tribes. Despite the widespread ownership of firearms, owning a gun was a far cry from knowing how to use it in a military situation. Learning how to do that would inevitably take time.

LOYALISTS

The presence of Loyalists (in significant numbers in parts of New York, Pennsylvania, and the South) was not usually a handicap to the American war effort, since the rebels achieved and maintained political superiority in most areas. The actual or expected presence of British forces, on the other hand, could cause a recrudescence of Loyalist activity and led to major problems in the South. The British, however, suffered from a disinclination to mobilize Loyalist support early in the war and tended to base strategy on the assumption that Loyalists were present in large numbers and could be counted on for support in regions where the king's troops had not yet tried to operate. Once France entered the war in February 1778, British strategy relegated the suppression of the rebellion to second place behind survival against the rejuvenated forces of an ancient enemy. Reliance on residual Loyalist sentiment in the South was the only option open to the British, and it became their "southern strategy" in and after 1778.

LEADERSHIP

Leadership is the vital ingredient that transforms military potential into success in war. British military leaders were generally competent professional soldiers, no more or less prone to infighting than their American counterparts. British political leaders might be seen in retrospect as behaving in ways that lacked imagination and scope, but faced with a transatlantic military problem of unprecedented complexity, they generally acted with intelligence and dispatch in ways for which their experience had prepared them. Unfortunately for the survival of the first British Empire, the same lack of vision and statesmanship that had led them to lose the political allegiance of the American colonists also crippled the development of the indispensable political component that was needed to suppress the rebellion.

American military leadership was beset by intercolonial and sectional difficulties at the beginning of the war, not a surprising situation in what was essentially a military alliance of thirteen separate sovereignties. Men of talent worked unremittingly—none more so than Washington—to meet the challenge of organizing effective military forces from the most unpromising of parts. Much of American military activity continued throughout the war to have an ad hoc quality; significant mistakes in judgment were made by many senior officers, including Washington. But none of the mistakes proved to be fatal, and in large part because Washington inspired others with his commitment never to give up the fight, the American military had achieved by 1777 the most it could hope to achieve: by not losing, it ensured that the British would not win. Washington may have been the finest manipulator of military force ever to arise from the American nation, but even he could not win the war with American resources alone. When French aid arrived in sufficient quantity and with excellent leadership, Washington was astute enough to maximize its benefits to achieve a victory at Yorktown that proved to be the makeweight in shifting British political will toward ending active hostilities.

American political leadership also reflected the fact that the colonies were partners, not part of a single sovereignty. More political infighting occurred in Congress's management of the war than in the army, and Congress was less of a nation-building factor than was the Continental army. Congress did not squarely face the problem of how to pay for the war and so contributed significantly to the single greatest danger threatening the new nation: the collapse of the economy. But here, too, ad hoc solutions were found, and at the time of greatest danger, Robert Morris managed to use his financial expertise to cobble together an economic bandage that, with the help of many other financiers, agents, ambassadors, and people of good will, kept the nation afloat just long enough so that a peace treaty could be secured. In the end, American political will sustained the military effort to secure independence better than British political will sustained the military effort to suppress the rebellion. But only by a hair's breadth.

SEE ALSO Colonial Wars; Loyalists in the American Revolution; Manufacturing in America; Militia in the North; Populations of Great Britain and America; Recruiting in Great Britain; Riflemen.

BIBLIOGRAPHY

Conway, Stephen. *The British Isles and the War of American Independence.* Oxford: Oxford University Press, 2000.

Lengel, Edward G. *General George Washington: A Military Life.* New York: Random House, 2005.

Mackesy, Piers. *The War for America, 1775–1783.* Cambridge, Mass.: Harvard University Press, 1964.

revised by Harold E. Selesky

REVERE, PAUL.

(1735–1818). Patriot, artisan, and courier. Massachusetts. Known to every American schoolchild for his midnight ride, immortalized in the poem by Henry Wadsworth Longfellow (1861), Paul Revere was a relatively unknown figure until the appearance of that work. Yet Revere deserves an important place in American history, not particularly for his dramatic ride to warn the patriots of the British advance on Lexington and Concord, 19 April 1775, but for his activities as a leader among Boston's artisans, mariners, and shopkeepers, as an effective political cartoonist, and for several other important rides before and after he became the official courier for the Massachusetts Provincial Congress. He was also one of the period's finest silversmiths and pioneered significant developments in metallurgy and founding.

Revere was the third of thirteen children born to Apollos Rivoire, a Huguenot who came to Boston from Bordeaux, France, at the age of thirteen to apprentice to the silversmith John Coney. He Anglicized his name to make it easier to pronounce. His mother was Deborah Hitchbourn, whose family owned the Boston wharf of that name. Paul learned his father's trade, and served as a second lieutenant of artillery in the Crown Point expedition of 1756. There being an abundance of silversmiths in Boston, Revere branched out into copperplate engraving (portraits, a songbook, political cartoons, seals, bookplates, and coats-of-arms), and manufacturing dental devices. A strong opponent of British imperial policies, he was an influential leader in the artisan community of Boston, where his prominence brought him into close contact with John Hancock, Samuel Adams, and Dr. Joseph Warren. His engraving of the Boston Massacre of 3 March 1770 is a masterwork of visual propaganda, designed to tell the story of Boston's outraged and injured innocence to the rest of the colonies. He helped organized the Boston Tea Party on 16 December 1773 and likely participated as one of the "Indians."

Paul Revere. *Although best known for his dramatic ride in April 1775, Paul Revere, shown here in a 1768 portrait by John Singleton Copley, was one of the period's finest silversmiths.*
© BETTMANN/CORBIS

Revere began his career as a trusted courier after the Tea Party, when he made the long ride, in mid-winter, to inform New York City's Sons of Liberty of the event. The next spring he rode to New York City and Philadelphia with word of the Boston Port Bill and with an appeal for help. He carried the Suffolk Resolves (September 1774) to Philadelphia. When the radicals learned that General Gage had ordered the seizure of valuable military supplies at Fort William and Mary, Revere galloped to Durham, New Hampshire to warn John Sullivan, and then rode on to alert the radicals of Portsmouth. Two days before making his most famous ride he rode to warn the radicals to move their military stores from Concord.

Although he wanted a military commission, Revere was kept busy printing currency for the Massachusetts Provincial Congress, at Watertown where he set up shop during the siege of Boston, and learning how to make gunpowder at Canton, Massachusetts. On 29 March 1776 he became a member of the Boston committee of correspondence. On 10 April 1776, he was appointed major in a state regiment raised to fortify and defend Boston, and a month later he was appointed major in the state train of artillery, with the same mission. He was promoted to lieutenant colonel in the state train on 27 November 1776, and was given command of Castle William at the mouth of Boston Harbor. In early

September 1777, he escorted Brunswick prisoners, captured at Bennington, from Worcester to Boston, and on the 27th was ordered to join in the expedition against Newport, Rhode Island, which proved abortive. On 1 March 1778 his command of Castle William was extended to include defensive works on Governor's Island and Long Island, and he remained in command of the state train when it was reduced to three companies in early 1779.

Opportunity for field service came finally when he was ordered on 8 July 1779 "to hold himself and one hundred of the matrosses [artillerymen] under his command, including proper officers, in readiness at one hours notice to embark for the defence of this state, and attack the enemy at Penobscot" [the Majorbagaduce peninsula (the spelling varies), now Castine, in Penobscot Bay, Maine]. The Penobscot Expedition, July–August 1779, was a fiasco, and in the epidemic of recrimination that ensued, Revere was accused by Captain Thomas Carnes, who commanded the marines aboard the *Putnam*, of disobedience, unsoldierly conduct, and cowardice. Brigadier General Peleg Wadsworth, second-in-command of the expedition, also criticized his performance. On 6 September 1779 Revere was relieved of command at Castle Island and placed under house arrest. Historian Jayne E. Triber notes that a court of inquiry held in mid-September "neither condemned nor acquitted him," and that a second inquiry, on 16 November 1779, found him culpable for "disputing the orders of Brigadier General Wadsworth" and of leaving Penobscot River "without particular orders from his superior officer" (p. 138). After many delays a formal court-martial convened in February 1782 and found that he had refused "to deliver a certain boat to the order of General Wadsworth when upon the retreat up Penobscot River from Major Bagwaduce: but the Court taking into consideration the suddenness of the refusal, and more especially that the same boat was in fact employed by Lieutenant Colonel Paul Revere to effect the purpose ordered by the General . . ., are of the opinion that . . . Revere be acquitted of this charge." On the charge of leaving Penobscot River without orders, "the Court considers that the whole army was in great confusion and so scattered and dispersed, that no regular orders were or could be given, are of the opinion, that Lieutenant Colonel Paul Revere, be acquitted with equal honor as the other officers in the same expedition."

Revere, meanwhile, had been expanding his business as a silversmith. He also continued to be active in civic affairs, especially in working for ratification of the federal Constitution in January 1788. With his reputation as an innovative silversmith already established, he turned to the casting of bells and cannon at the foundry he opened in Boston's North End in November 1788. It later supplied the bolts, spikes, pumps, and copper accessories for the USS *Constitution* ("Old Ironsides"), the frigate built at the

Charlestown Navy Yard in 1797–1798. In January 1801 he embarked on his most significant industrial venture, the manufacture of sheet copper in a mill built on the site of the Revolutionary War powder mill at Canton, Massachusetts. The business prospered, and it produced rolled copper for the dome of the Massachusetts State House, a new copper bottom for the Constitution in 1803, and in 1808–1809 boilers for a steam boat built by Robert Fulton. By his first wife, Sarah Orne, whom he married 17 August 1757, he had eight children. By his second, Rachel Walker, whom he married 10 October 1773, he had eight more. He died at the age of 83 at Boston.

SEE ALSO *Fort William and Mary, New Hampshire; Lexington and Concord; Penobscot Expedition, Maine.*

BIBLIOGRAPHY
Fischer, David H. *Paul Revere's Ride.* New York: Oxford University Press, 1994.
Forbes, Esther. *Paul Revere and the World He Lived In.* Boston: Houghton Mifflin, 1988.
Triber, Jayne E. *A True Republican: The Life of Paul Revere.* Amherst: University of Massachusetts Press, 1998.

revised by Harold E. Selesky

RHODE ISLAND, BATTLE OF SEE

Newport, Rhode Island (29 July–31 August 1778).

RHODE ISLAND LINE.

On 25 April 1775 the Rhode Island Assembly created an "Army of Observation" under Brigadier General Nathanael Greene to assist in the siege of Boston. This force was made up of three infantry regiments and an artillery company. Colonels James Varnum, Daniel Hitchcock, and Thomas Church commanded the three regiments. In 1776 the first two regiments reenlisted as the Ninth and Eleventh Continental Regiments, and in 1777 they became the First and Second Rhode Island Regiments. Church's regiment disbanded on 31 December 1775. The First and Second Rhode Island Regiments merged as the Rhode Island Regiment on 1 January 1781, reorganized as the smaller Rhode Island Battalion on 1 March 1783, and disbanded its last two companies on Christmas Day, 1783. During the winter of 1775–1776, Rhode Island formed two new regiments in the state troops. This were led by Colonel William Richmond and Colonel Henry Babcock (later Colonel Christopher Lippitt). These regiments were later transferred them to the Continental Army—they disbanded during the 1776–1777 winter. The artillery company technically was not part of the state's line.

The two regiments suffered heavy losses during the defense of the Delaware River in the fall of 1777, and at Valley Forge the First Regiment transferred all of its rank and file to fill up the Second, and sent the officers and sergeants home to recruit additional troops. The legislature supported that effort by passing legislation to allow slaves to voluntarily enlist for the duration of the war. Slaves were purchased by the state, which granted them their freedom when they were discharged from military service. The First Regiment has sometimes been misidentified being African American, but in reality it was really a regiment of "men of colour" and included Native Americans and men of mixed ancestry. All of the officers and sergeants were white. The experiment in segregated troops ended on 1 January 1781, when the First and Second Regiments merged into a single, fully-integrated unit.

SEE ALSO *African Americans in the Revolution.*

BIBLIOGRAPHY
Angell, Israel. *Diary of Colonel Israel Angell Commanding the Second Rhode Island Continental Regiment during the American Revolution 1778–1781.* Edited by Edward Field. Providence, R.I.: Preston and Rounds, 1899.
Cowell, Benjamin. *Spirit of '76 in Rhode Island, or Sketches of the Efforts of the Government and People in the War of the Revolution.* Boston: A. J. Wright, 1850.
David, Ebenezer. *A Rhode Island Chaplain in the Revolution: Letters of Ebenezer David to Nicholas Brown 1775–1778.* Edited by Jeanette D. Black and William Greene Roelker. Providence: Rhode Island Society of the Cincinnati, 1949.
Gardiner, Asa B. *The Rhode Island Line in the Continental Army and Its Society of Cincinnati.* Providence, R.I.: Providence Press, 1878.
Rider, Sidney S. *Historical Inquiry Concerning the Attempt to Raise a Regiment of Slaves by Rhode Island During the War of the Revolution.* Providence, R.I.: S. S. Rider, 1880.
Walker, Anthony. *So Few The Brave: Rhode Island Continentals 1775–1783.* Newport, R.I.: Seafield Press, 1981.

Robert K. Wright Jr.

RICHMOND, VIRGINIA.

5–7 January 1781. Although it had a population of only eighteen hundred, half of them slaves, Richmond on the James River offered a secure place for supplies. Because it was also less vulnerable to a sudden amphibious attack than Williamsburg, it became the new capital of Virginia in May 1779. When Brigadier General Benedict Arnold's expedition landed eight hundred troops at Westover, thirty miles downriver, on 4 January, Governor Thomas Jefferson could only mobilize between two hundred and three hundred men to defend the town. The Americans moved most of the military supplies to safety before Arnold arrived on the 5th. The defenders withdrew without firing a shot and the British did not conduct a serious pursuit. Lieutenant Colonel John Graves Simcoe then led his Queen's Rangers and the flank companies of the Eightieth Foot to destroy the nearby Westham Foundry. After burning warehouses and a number of other buildings, Arnold withdrew on the 6th and arrived back at Westover on the 7th, losing nine men to desertion or straggling.

SEE ALSO *Arnold, Benedict; Jefferson, Thomas; Simcoe, John Graves; Virginia, Military Operations in.*

BIBLIOGRAPHY

Simcoe, John Graves. *A Journal of the Operations of the Queen's Rangers.* Exeter, U.K.: Printed for the author, 1787.

revised by Robert K. Wright Jr.

RIDGEFIELD, CONNECTICUT.

27 April 1777. As the British raiding force under Major General William Tryon retired from Danbury, Connecticut, militiamen gathered along its route back to the coast. Generals Benedict Arnold, David Wooster, and Gold Selleck Silliman managed to organize a blocking force at Ridgefield, about fifteen miles south of Danbury and made a gallant attempt to trap the raiders.

SEE ALSO *Danbury Raid, Connecticut; Silliman, Gold Selleck; Tryon, William; Wooster, David.?*

Harold E. Selesky

RIEDESEL, BARON FRIEDRICH ADOLPHUS. (1738–1800).

German general. Born in Lauterbach, Hesse, on June 3, 1738, Riedesel was attending the law school at Marburg when he was commissioned as an ensign in the Hessian battalion on duty in the city. At the age of 18 he went to England with a German regiment in the service of King George II. In the following year he returned to the Continent to serve in the Seven Years' War. He became aide-de-camp to Duke Ferdinand of Brunswick, distinguishing himself in the duke's campaigns, particularly at the Battle of Minden.

Feeling that he was not advancing rapidly enough in the Hessian army, he entered the service of the Duke of Brunswick, where he could capitalize on his friendship with Ferdinand. By 1761 he commanded two Brunswick regiments.

As a 37-year-old colonel of carabineers, Riedesel was commanding the garrison at Wolfenbuttel in January 1776 when the Duke of Brunswick contracted with King George III to furnish a body of 3,936 infantrymen and 336 dismounted dragoons for service in America. Riedesel, promoted to major general, was named commander of the first contingent of 2,282 troops, and on 4 April he sailed from Dover for America. On 1 June 1776 the convoy reached Quebec, bringing the reinforcements that Sir Guy Carleton needed to restore British control of Canada. After spending a year in Canada, where he was joined by his wife and three daughters, Riedesel took part in General John Burgoyne's offensive, which was an attempt to isolate New England from the rest of the colonies. He particularly distinguished himself at Hubbardton on 7 July 1777, strongly objected to the disastrous raid on Bennington Raid, and showed particularly vigorous leadership in the first battle of Saratoga. When Burgoyne was forced to surrender on 17 October 1777, Riedesel and General William Phillips were eventually exchanged for General Benjamin Lincoln on 13 October 1780.

After being given the local rank of lieutenant general and named commander on Long Island, Riedesel was ordered back to Canada in the summer of 1781. He went with a plan proposed by Sir Henry Clinton to Sir Frederick Haldimand for an offensive from the north. However, he did not submit this proposal until 25 September 1781, so it is obvious that Clinton could not expect this assistance to arrive until the campaign of 1782. By that time, the war was effectively over.

In mid-August 1783 the Riedesel family sailed from Quebec, reached England a month later, and were cordially received by the royal family. After a stay in London, they returned to Brunswick. Of the 4,000 troops who had followed Riedesel to Canada, only 2,800 returned. On 8 October 1783 he led these soldiers in a grand review for the new Duke of Brunswick. It was Riedesel's good fortune to be received as a hero, unlike another old Hessian, General Leopold von Heister, whom General William Howe blamed for the defeat at Trenton and had recalled in 1777, never to see further military duty. In contrast, the disaster at Saratoga was so great that the British hierarchy carefully avoided blaming anyone for the surrender and praised Riedesel for his bravery and fortitude. In 1787 Riedesel was promoted to lieutenant general and sent as commander of the Brunswick troops to support the Stadtholder (analogous to governor) of the southern provinces of Holland. After six years on this assignment he retired, only to be recalled to become commandant of the city of Brunswick, an office he held until he died on 6 January 1800. After his death, his wife, Friederike C. L. von Riedesel (1746–1808), published what has been called one of the most memorable memoirs to emerge from the American Revolution. It first appeared in Berlin in 1800.

SEE ALSO *Bennington Raid; Burgoyne's Offensive; Hubbardton, Vermont; Saratoga, First Battle of.*

BIBLIOGRAPHY

Riedesel, Friederike C. L. von. *Baroness von Riedesel and the American Revolution: Journal and Correspondence of a Tour of Duty, 1776–1783*. Translated by Marvin L. Brown, Jr. Chapel Hill: University of North Carolina Press, 1965.

Tharp, Louise H. *The Baroness and the General*. Boston: Little Brown, 1962.

revised by Michael Bellesiles

RIFLEMEN. A rifle differed from a musket in that a rifle (also called a rifled musket) had grooves cut in a spiral configuration down the length of its barrel that, when the weapon was discharged, imparted spin to the projectile. This spin was enough to stabilize the projectile's flight and give it both a longer range and greater accuracy. The barrels of muskets, by contrast, were smooth (hence the term "smooth-bore") and, when the weapon was fired, imparted no spin to the projectile. Where a musket might have some accuracy out to about sixty yards (although they were not intended for aimed fire), rifles could reach two to three hundred yards with some hope that the projectile would hit the target at which it was aimed.

The rifle's advantage in accuracy and range was well known in Europe from the sixteenth century. Hunters and early gunsmiths had found that wrapping the marble-shaped projectile in a greased patch of cloth or leather enabled it better to grip the rifling, and had the added advantage of loosening incompletely combusted gunpowder from the barrels' interior with each round. By the time of the Revolution, all armies placed a few such weapons in the hands of specialized marksmen. But the rifle's great drawback, which greatly limited its use as a military weapon, was the time, effort, and precision required to reload it. Moreover, because of the difficulties of reloading, the rifle could not be fitted with a socket bayonet. The musket, again in contrast, was much less of a precision weapon. It could take rough handling by a raw recruit who could learn by rote the physical motions he needed to load and fire the weapon in a way that maximized its capacity for high volumes of unaimed volley fire.

German immigrants brought the skills of rifle construction to America beginning about 1720, and by 1760 gunsmiths in the backcountry of Pennsylvania, Maryland, Virginia, and the Carolinas had evolved a unique American firearm. Typically, the American long rifle, as its name indicates, had a long barrel (forty inches or more, to allow for more complete combustion of the powder charge and a steadier aim), a smaller bore (to reduce the weight of the weapon and the projectiles, although at the cost of reduced stopping power), and a higher ratio of powder to projectile (to increase the distance the round would travel). In the hands of a well-practiced shooter who knew the characteristics of his particular weapon, the long rifle was a formidable firearm, and made the men who carried it into battle formidable light infantry troops. Exaggerated stories of prowess in marksmanship and reloading made them seem even more formidable. It was reported that, to the amazement of British regulars, an American frontiersman not only could deliver a reasonably high rate of fire (perhaps two, even three, rounds per minute) but also could reload on the run.

The Continental Congress had such a high opinion of the long rifle that its first important military decision (14 June 1775) was to authorize the raising of "six companies of expert riflemen" in Pennsylvania, along with two each in Maryland and Virginia. The response in Pennsylvania was so great that Congress raised this state's authorization to eight companies (22 June); they were subsequently organized as Colonel William Thompson's Pennsylvania Rifle Battalion. Men in the Valley of Virginia were just as enthusiastic. Daniel Morgan, a veteran of both the final French and Indian war and Dunmore's War, raised a company of 96 men in Frederick county, 40 percent more than his authorized strength, and marched 600 miles to Cambridge, Massachusetts, in 21 days (15 July– 6 August)—an average of 28½ miles a day—without losing a man from fatigue or illness. This feat allegedly moved Washington to tears. Although Morgan got the most publicity (most of the achievements of riflemen with the main army are associated with him), other rifle company commanders, like Michael Cresap and Hugh Stephenson, demonstrated comparable leadership skills.

The rifled gun was unknown in New England at this time, and the riflemen were as much of a curiosity around Boston as they would have been around London. John Adams, for example, wrote to his wife (17 June 1775) about "a peculiar kind of musket, called a rifle." The frontiersmen dazzled the Boston army with their marksmanship, but they soon became a disciplinary problem because of their rowdy, frontier ways. In the most serious incident, the so-called mutiny on Prospect Hill on 10 September 1775, some Pennsylvania "shirtmen" (as riflemen were called because of the hunting shirts they wore) tried to liberate a sergeant from confinement for neglect of duty and precipitated a confrontation with Washington, Charles Lee, Nathanael Greene, and an armed regiment of Rhode Islanders.

Several rifle-armed units served with the main army at New York City in 1776, including the First Continental Regiment (formerly Thompson's Pennsylvania Rifle Battalion), Colonel Samuel Miles's Pennsylvania State Rifle Regiment, and Colonel Hugh Stephenson's Maryland and Virginia Rifle Regiment; the first two saw hard fighting on Long Island, and Stephenson's was captured at Fort Washington, where Stephenson himself was killed. Service around New York highlighted the disadvantages of the rifle on a battlefield dominated by linear tactics. The man with the smoothbore musket—capable of putting out a higher volume of fire, accurate enough for the tactics of the day, and armed with a bayonet—was the man who won or lost battles. When Maryland offered to send a rifle company to Philadelphia for the Continental Army in October 1776, the secretary of the Board of War indicated his gratitude. However, the secretary wrote that "if muskets were given them instead of rifles the service would be more benefitted, as there is a superabundance of riflemen in the Army. Were it in the power of Congress to supply musketts they would speedily reduce the number of rifles and replace them with the former, as they are more easily kept in order, can be fired oftener and have the advantage of Bayonetts."

The virtues of riflemen, when given tasks appropriate to their abilities, were on display in the 1777 campaign. Daniel Morgan returned to active duty in early June, when Washington ordered him to assemble a Corps of Rangers from among Virginia, Maryland, and Pennsylvania riflemen who had already enlisted in the army. (Bored by inaction at the siege of Boston, he volunteered for Benedict Arnold's march to Quebec, was captured at Quebec City on 31 December 1775, and was exchanged in January 1777.) Before it was disbanded at the end of 1778, Morgan's corps of riflemen would become the most famous rifle-armed unit in the Continental Army. For two months, the riflemen screened the main army against British maneuvers in northern New Jersey, and then were sent to the Northern Army in mid-August to help counter the white and Indian skirmishers supporting Burgoyne's invasion. According to Washington, Morgan's men were all "well acquainted with the use of rifles, and with that mode of fighting which is necessary to make them a good counterpoise to the Indians." They had great success in turning the tables, intimidating enemy skirmishers in the Hudson and Mohawk Valleys and preventing Burgoyne from understanding the size and location of the American forces arrayed against him. On both occasions when Burgoyne tried to break through the American barrier on Bemis Heights (19 September and 7 October), Horatio Gates sent Morgan out into the

rolling, wooded terrain to blunt the British advance. The key to the American success was the fact that Gates paired the riflemen with a composite battalion of light infantrymen, led by Major Henry Dearborn and armed with bayonet-bearing, smooth-bore muskets. Whenever British troops launched a bayonet charge across a clearing in a desperate attempt to rid themselves of the galling, longer-range fire of the riflemen, they were met on the other side by Dearborn's bayonets. The two American units worked together to create a lethal battlefield puzzle that the British at Saratoga did not solve.

When the Americans failed to coordinate the rifle with the bayonet, there were many talented British and Hessian leaders of light infantry who would make them pay dearly. Lieutenant Colonel John Graves Simcoe, who, as commander of the Queen's Rangers, faced American skirmishers in many encounters in New Jersey and Virginia, thought that American riflemen "were by no means the most formidable of the rebel troops; their not being armed with bayonets permitted their opponents to take liberties with them" (Peterson, pp. 200–201). Major George Hanger, who commanded both Hessian jägers and the cavalry of Banastre Tarleton's British Legion, wrote:

> Riflemen as riflemen only, are a very feeble foe and not to be trusted alone any distance from camp; and at the outposts they must ever be supported by regulars, or they will constantly be beaten in, and compelled to retire. . . . When Morgan's riflemen came down to Pennsylvania from Canada [on 18 November 1777], flushed with success gained over Burgoyne's army, they marched to attack our light infantry, under Colonel [Robert] Abercrombie. The moment they appeared before him he ordered his troops to charge them with the bayonet; not one man out of four, had time to fire, and those that did had no time given them to load again; the light infantry not only dispersed them instantly but drove them for miles over the country. They never attacked, or even looked at, our light infantry again, without a regular force to support them. (Peterson, *Arms and Armor*, pp. 201 and 202, quoting Hanger, *To All Sportsmen and Particularly to Farmers, and Gamekeepers* [London, 1814], pp. 199 and 200).

Presumably the action Hanger described took place at Whitemarsh on 5–8 December, or at Matson's Ford on 11 December 1777. By that time, Morgan's riflemen may not have been at their best after months of hard campaigning; when Nathanael Greene had attempted to reinforce Fort Mercer, one of the Delaware River forts, in early November, only 170 riflemen had shoes stout enough so that they could accompany him. Washington himself understood the need for bayonets. When the riflemen went north to stop Burgoyne in 1777, Washington replaced them with a corps of bayonet-armed light infantry. He embodied a corps of light infantry for the campaigning season in each of the four succeeding years.

The war in the south in 1780 and 1781 also provided evidence of the value of rifles. Both Morgan at Cowpens (17 January 1781) and Greene at Guilford Courthouse (15 March 1781) deployed rifle-armed militiamen where they would not have to stand unsupported against British bayonets. The earlier action at Kings Mountain, South Carolina (7 October 1780), demonstrated a different lesson, that rifle-armed frontiersmen could beat a smaller number of bayonet-armed Loyalists on steep and heavily wooded terrain utterly unsuited to any version of linear tactics. It is ironical that this victory was won over Major Patrick Ferguson, Britain's foremost exponent of the rifle. Ferguson had invented an advanced breech-loading rifle, a hundred examples of which were issued to a corps of picked marksmen during the Brandywine campaign. These weapons, which were withdrawn from service when Ferguson was wounded and the corps disbanded, supplemented the thousand Pattern 1776 muzzle-loading rifles, with twenty-eight-inch barrels, issued in 1777 to light infantry companies and a few Loyalist units to counter the American long rifle. An estimated four thousand short-barreled rifles were available to the jägers who came to America as part of the German mercenary contingents; some were personal weapons, others were standard military models.

SEE ALSO *Abercromby, Sir Robert; Bayonets and Bayonet Attacks; Cowpens, South Carolina; Cresap, Michael; Ewald, Johann von; Ferguson, Patrick; Guilford Courthouse, North Carolina; Hanger, George; Kings Mountain, South Carolina; Light Infantry; Matson's Ford, Pennsylvania; Morgan, Daniel; Muskets and Musketry; Mutiny on Prospect Hill; Simcoe, John Graves; Thompson, William; Thompson's Pennsylvania Rifle Battalion; Whitemarsh, Pennsylvania.*

BIBLIOGRAPHY

Higginbotham, Don. *Daniel Morgan: Revolutionary Rifleman.* Chapel Hill: University of North Carolina Press, 1961.

Neumann, George C. *Battle Weapons of the American Revolution.* Texarkana, Tex.: Surlock Publishing Company, 1998.

Peterson, Harold L. *Arms and Armor in Colonial America, 1526–1783.* Harrisburg, Pa.: Stackpole, 1956.

Smith, Paul H. et al., eds. *Letters of Delegates to Congress, 1774–1789.* Vol. 1: *August 1774–August 1775.* Washington, D.C.: Library of Congress, 1976.

Washington, George. *The Papers of George Washington, Revolutionary War Series.* Vol. 10: *June–August 1777.* Edited by Philander D. Chase et al. Charlottesville: University Press of Virginia, 2000.

revised by Harold E. Selesky

RITZEMA, RUDOLPHUS. (1738?–1803).

Continental officer, turncoat. Rudolphus Ritzema graduated from King's College (later Columbia) in 1758. On 30 June 1775 he became a lieutenant colonel of the First New York Regiment. Taking part in the invasion of Canada under General Richard Montgomery's command, Ritzema was promoted to colonel of the regiment on 28 November 1775 and assumed command of the Third New York Regiment on 28 March 1776. He was praised for his performance during the battle at White Plains on 28 October 1776. Having been superceded by his rival Colonel Philip Van Cortlandt and convinced that the patriots were on the verge of defeat, Ritzema deserted to the British in November 1776. He held the rank of lieutenant colonel, but little more is known about Ritzema's life after his defection. He died in 1795.

SEE ALSO *Canada Invasion.*

BIBLIOGRAPHY

Ritzema, Rudolphus. "Journal of Colonel Rudolphus Ritzema of the First New York Regiment, August 8, 1775 to March 30, 1776." *Magazine of American History* 1 (1877): 98–107.

revised by Michael Bellesiles

RIVINGTON, JAMES. (1724–1802).

Bookseller, journalist, printer. Born in London on 17 August 1724, Rivington was the son of the publisher Charles Rivington. He and his brother John (1720–1792) continued their father's publishing business until March 1756 and then went into partnership with the firm of James Fletcher Jr. After a smashing success with Smollett's *History of England* and other works, Rivington indulged in a period of high living, gambling, and neglect of business that ended his publishing career in England. Declaring bankruptcy in 1760, he went to America and opened bookstores in New York City, Philadelphia, and Boston. About 1765 he concentrated his book business in New York City, but the next year he moved to Annapolis, remaining until his Maryland Lottery, a land scheme, led to bankruptcy. Again he recovered quickly from business failure, this time by marrying a wealthy widow, Elizabeth Van Horne, in 1769. He returned to publishing books, enjoying a modest success.

On 18 March 1773 he published a preliminary, free issue of what was to be *Rivington's New-York Gazeteer.* Unlike other American newspapers, this one proposed to appeal to all interests, to be nonpartisan, and to give good coverage to international news. Well edited and excellent in typography and layout, it was a success. Within little more than a year its circulation had reached thirty-six hundred copies, an impressive figure for the time.

But freedom of the press did not fit the views of the Sons of Liberty. They did not want both sides of the controversy with Britain to be printed, especially as Rivington's Loyalist views became more apparent. Several Whig meetings condemned Rivington's policy and, although he signed their Association after being arrested, his plant was attacked and destroyed on 27 November 1775 by a crowd led by Isaac Sears, who ordered the type carried away to be made into bullets. The Provincial Congress and then the Continental Congress investigated the loyalty of Rivington, who attempted to make peace with the Patriots. Giving up on this effort, he and his family sailed for England in January 1776. Appointed King's Printer in New York City, he returned to start publication on 4 October 1777 of a strictly Loyalist paper. *Rivington's New York Loyal Gazette* changed its title on 13 December 1777 to the *Royal Gazette*. During the period from May 1778 to July 1783, Rivington set up a mutual arrangement with other New York papers whereby they jointly produced what was virtually a daily newspaper for the first time in America.

When the British left New York in 1783, Rivington stayed behind. He removed the royal arms from his paper and changed its name to *Rivington's New York Gazette and Universal Advertiser* but could only keep the unpopular paper in circulation until 31 December 1783. He tried to stay in business as a bookseller and stationer but ended up in debtor's prison from 1797 to 1801, dying poor in New York on 4 July 1802. There has been some question as to why Rivington was allowed to stay in New York after the British evacuated. An old story held that Washington ordered that Rivington be protected because the publisher had spied for the Americans during the British occupation, but there is no solid evidence supporting this interpretation. More likely the victorious Patriots simply did not see him as much of a threat.

revised by Michael Bellesiles

ROBERTSON, JAMES. (1717–1788).

British officer and governor. Born in Newbigging, Scotland, on 29 June 1717, Robertson enlisted in the army as a private, earning promotion to sergeant before receiving a commission in the marines in 1739. He served in the wars against France and in Scotland against the Jacobite rising of 1745. Shortly thereafter he was able to purchase the rank of captain in the earl of Loudoun's regiment, seeing service in Ireland before going to America as a major in 1756. Robertson served as deputy quartermaster general during the Seven Years' War, seeing action at Louisburg, Ticonderoga, and Crown Point;

became a lieutenant colonel in 1760; and supervised Britain's acquisition of the Floridas at the war's end. His testimony in 1765 before Parliament is credited with spurring the passage of the Quartering Act.

Robertson, who lived in New York City during the Seven Years' War, was promoted to brigadier general at the start of the Revolution, advising General William Howe in the campaign that led to the successful occupation of that city in 1776. Promoted to major general, he was named military commandant of the city. Believing that most Americans were loyal to the crown, Robertson urged the restoration of civil government in occupied territories to win public support. In 1779 the royal government of New York was reestablished, with Robertson, now a lieutenant general, as governor. During his term as governor, he had to contend not just with Patriot raids and a flood of Loyalist refugees, but also with the politics of the officer corps and the opposition of many Loyalists to his policy of conciliation. He was also charged with incompetence, womanizing, senility, corruption, and smuggling; the charge of senility probably being inaccurate. Most significantly, General Sir Henry Clinton refused to end martial law, thereby alienating most of the inhabitants of New York City and Long Island. Out of office with the war's end, Robertson, now a wealthy man, moved to London, where he died on 4 March 1788.

BIBLIOGRAPHY

Klein, Milton M., and Ronald W. Howard, eds. *The Twilight of British Rule in Revolutionary America: The New York Letter Book of General James Robertson, 1780–1783.* Cooperstown: New York State Historical Association, 1983.

Michael Bellesiles

ROBINSON, BEVERLEY. (1721–1792).

(later changed to Beverly). Tory leader. Virginia-New York. Born in Middlesex County, Virginia, on 11 January 1723 to a prominent family—his father, John, was president of the Virginia council and acting governor at his death in 1749—Robinson raised a company in 1746 for a proposed expedition against Canada that never materialized. He led his troops to New York, where he stayed, becoming a business partner of Oliver De Lancey and marrying the wealthy Susanna Philipse in 1748. Robinson held a wide variety of offices, from judge to colonel of the Dutchess County militia to New York's commissary and paymaster during the Seven Years' War. He built a stately home called "Beverly" on the Hudson River, two miles south of West Point. One of his many visitors was George Washington, who stopped in to borrow money from Robinson in 1756. As one of the owners of the Highland

Patent, lands seized from the Wappinger Indians while they were off fighting for the British during the Seven Years' War, Robinson was a target of the riots by the local white settlers against this land grab. In 1765 Robinson had to flee to the safety of New York City until the government put down this uprising the following year.

By the time the Revolution started, he had increased his wife's fortune to include tens of thousands of acres—annual rents alone amounted to £1,250—and had become one of the state's wealthiest landowners. Initially, Robinson hoped to remain neutral during the Revolution. But on 20 February 1777, after John Jay told him he would have to choose one side or the other, Robinson refused to take the oath of allegiance. Leaving his fine house, which subsequently was used variously as American headquarters for the Highlands district and as a hospital, Robinson took refuge with the British in New York City. Here he raised, mostly among his tenants, the Loyal American Regiment, of which he was made colonel. Later he was named colonel and director of the Loyal Guides and Pioneers as well. He led his troops with distinction on several occasions, particularly in the storming of Fort Montgomery on 6 October 1777, during Clinton's expedition to the Highlands.

His main contribution, however, was in the secret service. General Henry Clinton used Robinson in an attempt to recruit leading Americans to the British. Robinson's efforts failed with General Israel Putnam (whose headquarters was in Robinson's house) and Colonel Ethan Allen but had more success with General Benedict Arnold. Robinson made the arrangements for a meeting between André and Arnold and served as Clinton's emissary to Washington in the effort to save André's life. In early 1780 the New York legislature banished Robinson and confiscated his property. In August 1782 he left New York for England. Appointed to the first council of New Brunswick, Robinson never took his seat, staying in England to pursue his claim for compensation of eighty thousand pounds; he eventually received seventeen thousand pounds for the loss of his estate. He settled in Thornbury, near Bath, where he died on 9 April 1792. Four of his sons fought with the British during the Revolution; one became a lieutenant general, another commissary general; both were knighted. The other two sons settled in New Brunswick.

SEE ALSO *Arnold's Treason; Clinton's Expedition.*

BIBLIOGRAPHY

Countryman, Edward. *A People in Revolution: The American Revolution and Political Society in New York, 1760–1790.* Baltimore: Johns Hopkins University Press, 1981.

revised by Michael Bellesiles

ROCHAMBEAU (FILS), DONATIEN MARIE JOSEPH DE VIMEUR, VICOMTE DE.

(1755–1813). French officer, son of the comte de Rochambeau. Entering the service in the Auvergne Regiment in 1767, he was attached to the artillery regiment of Besançon in 1769. In January 1779 he was named *mestre de camp en second* of the Bourbonnais Regiment. The next year he accompanied his father to America as assistant adjutant general. On 28 October 1780 he returned to France with dispatches, and in May 1781 he was back in America. Remaining with his father until the end of hostilities, he was promoted to colonel commanding the Saintonge Regiment on 11 November 1782 and in 1783 was promoted to command of the Royal Auvergne Regiment and made a chevalier in the Order of Saint Louis. In 1791 he became a *maréchal de camp* and lieutenant general on 9 July 1792.

In August 1792 he was appointed governor general of the Leeward Islands. After pacifying Saint Domingue and forcing his royalist predecessor, the comte de Behagues, to abandon Martinique, he surrendered on 22 March 1794 to a British force. Later he was reappointed as governor general of Saint Domingue but was recalled and imprisoned by the Directory. He returned to Saint Domingue under the command of Leclerc and succeeded him on 1 January 1803, but he surrendered to the British on 28 November 1803. He was then imprisoned in Jamaica and England until his exchange in 1811. As a division commander in the corps of Lauriston in 1813, he participated in the Battles of Lutzen and Bautzen and died at Leipzig. In that final campaign, Napoleon made him an officer in the Legion of Honor.

BIBLIOGRAPHY

Bodinier, André. *Dictionnaire des officiers de l'armée royale qui ont combattu aux Etats-Unis pendant la guerre d'Indépendance, 1776–1783.* Vincennes, France: Service historique de l'armée, 1982.

Contenson, Ludovic de. *La Société des Cincinnati de France et la Guerre d'Amérique.* Paris: Editions Auguste Picard, 1934.

Monti, Laura V., comp. *A Calendar of Rochambeau Papers at the University of Florida Libraries.* Gainesville: University of Florida Libraries, 1972.

Rochambeau, Donatien Marie Joseph de Vimeur, Vicomte de. "The War in America, An Unpublished Journal (1780–1783)." In *Rochambeau, Father and Son: A Life of the Maréchal de Rochambeau.* By Jean-Edmond Weelen. Translated by Lawrence Lee. New York: Holt, 1936.

Whitridge, Arnold. *Rochambeau.* New York: Macmillan, 1965.

revised by Robert Rhodes Crout

ROCHAMBEAU, JEAN-BAPTISTE DONATIEN DE VIMEUR, COMTE

DE. (1725–1807). Commander of the French army in America. Born at Vendôme of an old and honorable family, he was being trained for the church (the traditional career for a third son) when his older brother died. At the outbreak of the War of the Austrian Succession (1740–1948), he was commissioned in the cavalry regiment of Saint-Simon. In 1743 he took command of a cavalry troop (company), having served in Bohemia, Bavaria, and on the Rhine. In 1747 Rochambeau was promoted to colonel of the infantry Regiment de la Marche, and the next year he was appointed aide-de-camp to the duke of Orleans. He sustained a serious thigh wound at the battle of Laufeldt; took part in the siege of Maestricht (1748); became governor of Vendôme (1749); distinguished himself in the capture of Port Mahon, Minorca, from the British in 1756; and was promoted to brigadier general. He fought in Germany, where he distinguished himself at Crefeld, took command of the Auvergne Regiment in 1759, and saved the French army from a surprise attack at Clostercamp in October 1760. Wounded several times in the latter action, Rochambeau was commended for personal bravery and fine tactics and promoted to the rank of *maréchal de camp*. Early in 1761 he was named inspector general of infantry. In 1771 he was awarded the Great Cross of the Order of Saint Louis and in 1776 became governor of Villefranche-en-Roussillon, which provided him a steady, substantial revenue.

In 1780 Rochambeau was given command of the expeditionary force sent to America to start a new and decisive phase of the French alliance. Possessing the necessary virtues for such a command, Rochambeau was a consummate professional. Promoted to lieutenant general for this assignment, he took command of some seventy-six hundred soldiers assembled at Brest. He sailed on 1 May 1780 with the fifty-five hundred for whom there were transport accommodations, and with the escort of Admiral Ternay's fleet, he arrived off Newport on 11 July.

Rochambeau faced a difficult task. His instructions required his troops to act as auxiliaries to the Americans, yielding them the place of honor, and he was to maintain good relations with the them. If the British triumphed, he was to withdraw his force to Saint Domingue. Up until his arrival in America, the French alliance had been a frustrating disappointment to the Patriots, owing largely to the failures of Rochambeau's predecessor, Estaing. The British fleet promptly bottled up Ternay. Rochambeau was, because of his instructions, hesitant to commit to battle without clear superiority.

Since Washington did not understand French and Rochambeau did not understand English, Washington sought to use Lafayette as a mediator between the two.

Comte de Rochambeau. *The commander of the French army in America, in a nineteenth-century painting by Charles-Philippe Larivière.* **CHATEAU DE VERSAILLES, FRANCE, GIRAUDON/ BRIDGEMAN ART LIBRARY**

Yet when Lafayette tried to advise the old veteran on the unique nature of American combat, Rochambeau took offense, particularly as he was unclear which part of the advice was Washington's and which Lafayette's. The two disagreed over the feasibility of an assault on New York City and Long Island. With irritation and delicacy, Rochambeau wrote the impatient youth that in resisting his appeals, "Allow an old father to reply to you as a cherished son whom he loves and esteems immensely." Yet Rochambeau was not so delicate with La Luzerne; he complained about Lafayette's letters, written "surely at the instigation of some hotheaded persons." Complicating Rochambeau's problems was the inability of the French war and naval departments to send the full expeditionary force across the Atlantic in the spring of 1780; this was aggravated by lack of Spanish participation.

In Newport the French forces, systematically isolated from the local population, exercised cordial relations with the Americans. During their stay, they put a significant quantity of specie into the American economy, an amount that has been estimated at four million dollars. At a meeting with Washington at Hartford, Rochambeau made it clear that the French would not participate in any campaign during 1780. Inactivity began to create morale problems among Rochambeau's officers. Rochambeau's son, the vicomte de Rochambeau, reached Boston early in May 1781 with Admiral Barras and the bad news that the second division of French forces would not come; the good news, however, was that admiral Grasse was headed for the West Indies and would be available in "July or August." When Rochambeau and Washington met at Wethersfield, Connecticut, on 21–23 May 1781, Rochambeau was free to make only vague references to Grasse's availability. The combined French-American operation near New York was stalled in August until news arrived on 14 August of Grasse's movement toward North America.

Events led ultimately to Cornwallis's isolation on the Yorktown peninsula; Grasse's arrival in the Chesapeake, which closed off any British evacuation; and the superiority of land and naval forces that would result in the Yorktown siege. According to Captain Ludwig von Closen, Rochambeau had already participated in fourteen sieges. The standard principles had been laid out by the military engineer Sébastien Vauban a hundred years earlier. Rochambeau and Washington made plans with Grasse in a meeting on 17 September and the admiral agreed to remain in the Chesapeake to the end of October. The siege commenced on 9 October and ended on 17 October. As Rochambeau would later recall, when Cornwallis's representative at the surrender ceremony tried to hand him his sword, "I pointed to General Washington ... and told him that the French army being only an auxiliary on this continent, it devolved on the American General to tender him his orders."

In the aftermath of Yorktown, Rochambeau began planning the campaign of 1782, but without the naval force that would be necessary to act. By mid-1782, Rochambeau received word that the French fleet in the West Indies would return to Boston in August, and Rochambeau left Williamsburg on 1 July. At Philadelphia, Washington sought to interest him in a Canadian campaign, but Rochambeau ruled that it was beyond his instructions. Most of the French force left Boston on 24 November. Rochambeau sailed from Anne Arundel County, Maryland, on 8 January 1783, pursued by a British frigate across the Atlantic to Nantes, which he reached on 20 February. Louis XVI recognized his achievement with official commendation and royal favors that included the Blue Ribbon of the Order of the Holy Spirit, the highest honor the king could confer. Early in 1784 he was made commander of the northern district of France at Calais, where he remained for four years. Rochambeau took part in the second Assembly of Notables. Given command of the important Alsace

district in 1789, he was forced by ill health to retire in December of that year. In September 1790 he was put in command of the army of the North, and in December 1791 he became a marshal of France. During the Terror he was arrested and escaped the guillotine only because Robespierre's death brought a halt to the Terror. Rochambeau was released on 27 October 1794 after a six-months' detention. He lived out his life quietly on his estate near Vendôme.

SEE ALSO *Barras de Saint-Laurent, Jacques-Melchior, Comte de; Estaing, Charles Hector Théodat, Comte d'; French Alliance; Grasse, François Joseph Paul, Comte de; La Luzerne, Chevalier Anne-César de; Lafayette, Marquis de; Spanish Participation in the American Revolution; Ternay, Charles Louis d'Arsac, Chevalier de; Yorktown Campaign; Yorktown, Siege of.*

BIBLIOGRAPHY

Bodinier, André. *Dictionnaire des officiers de l'armée royale qui ont combattu aux Etats-Unis pendant la guerre d'Indépendance, 1776–1783.* Vincennes, France: Service historique de l'armée, 1982.

Closen, Ludwig von. *The Revolutionary Journal of Baron Ludwig von Closen.* Edited and translated by Evelyn M. Acomb. Chapel Hill: University of North Carolina Press, 1958.

Contenson, Ludovic de. *La Société des Cincinnati de France et la Guerre d'Amérique.* Paris: Editions Auguste Picard, 1934.

Kennett, Lee. *The French Forces in America, 1780–1783.* Westport, Conn.: Greenwood, 1977.

Lafayette, Gilbert du Motier de. *Lafayette in the Age of the American Revolution: Selected Letters and Papers.* Edited by Stanley J. Idzerda. 5 vols. to date. Ithaca: Cornell University Press, 1977–.

Rice, Howard C., Jr., and Anne S. K. Brown, eds. *The American Campaigns of Rochambeau's Army: 1780, 1781, 1782, 1783.* 2 vols. Princeton, N.J.: Princeton University Press, 1972.

Rochambeau, Jean Baptiste Donatien de Vimeur, comte de. *Memoirs of the Marshall Count de Rochambeau.* Translated by M. W. E. Wright. New York: New York Times, 1971.

Whitridge, Arnold. *Rochambeau.* New York: Macmillan, 1965.

revised by Robert Rhodes Crout

ROCHE, FERMOY SEE *Fermoy, Matthias Alexis de Roche.*

ROCHEBLAVE, CHEVALIER DE
SEE *See Rastel, Philippe Francois sieur de Rocheblave.*

ROCKINGHAM, CHARLES WATSON-WENTWORTH, SECOND MARQUESS OF.

(1730–1782). British prime minister. Born in Yorkshire on 13 May 1730, Wentworth entered Eton in 1738 and from 1746 to 1750 (when he succeeded his father as marquess of Rockingham) studied under tutors in Geneva and in Italy. He served as prime minister from 1765 to 1766. His profound belief in parliamentary supremacy and instinct for compromise led him to drive through the Declaratory Act alongside the repeal of the Stamp Act. As the leader of a faction in Parliament who opposed Lord North's American policy, he condemned the Boston Tea Party and supported the Coercive (or Intolerable) Acts and the Quebec Act of 1774; nevertheless he demanded the repeal of Charles Townshend's tea duty. An indolent politician prone to blame failure on court conspiracies, his leadership of the Rockingham Whigs was due primarily to his immense wealth and charm. During the war he defended Vice-Admiral Augustus Keppel in his court-martial (1778), attacked the earl of Sandwich's management of the navy, and organized the defense of Hull against American naval officer John Paul Jones. Not until 1780 did he reluctantly conclude that American independence was inevitable. When Lord North fell in 1782, Rockingham became prime minister again; but his cabinet was split between the views of Charles Fox and William Shelburne over the timing of a grant of independence. Rockingham died on 1 July before the dispute could be resolved.

SEE ALSO *Declaratory Act; Fox, Charles James; Intolerable (or Coercive) Acts; North, Sir Frederick; Quebec Act; Shelburne, William Petty Fitzmaurice, earl of; Stamp Act; Townshend Acts.*

BIBLIOGRAPHY

O'Gorman, Frank. *The Rise of Party in England: The Rockingham Whigs, 1760–82.* London: Allen and Unwin, 1975.

revised by John Oliphant

ROCKY MOUNT, SOUTH CAROLINA.

1 August 1780. Following the destruction of Loyalist Captain Christian Huck's detachment at Williamson's Plantation on 12 July 1780, more Whigs joined Thomas Sumter's Patriot force. With Continental troops approaching, Sumter felt he could operate more boldly against British lines of communications between Charleston and Camden and other interior posts. After notifying Major General Johann De Kalb about the possibilities, Sumter moved against Rocky Mount with about 600 men on 30 July, while Major William R. Davie threatened Hanging Rock, to the north. At that time, these two posts were garrisoned only by Loyalist provincial troops, because British regulars had been drawn closer to Camden.

Sumter's troops included South Carolina militia under the leadership of Colonels William Hill and Andrew Neale. In addition, he had the North Carolina militia of Colonel John Irwin. At Rocky Mount, Lieutenant Colonel George Turnbull held a strong, naturally defensible position with 150 New York Volunteers and 150 South Carolina Loyalist militia. Two fortified houses and a strong building with loopholes had been built on the knoll and were surrounded by an abatis (a defensive construction made of felled trees pointing outward toward the enemy). Sumter arrived at Rocky Mount early on 1 August and, rather than immediately attacking, called on Turnbull to surrender. Already alerted, the Tories told Sumter to "come and take it."

The post was assaulted repeatedly, although without the benefit of artillery, and the abatis was finally penetrated. During the initial action six men were lost, including Colonel Neale, from the Patriot side. Once through the outer defense, the attackers found the buildings well defended by heavy musket fire. Sumter sent men to burn the houses, even rolling a wagon filled with combustibles against one. Once the fire took hold, the defenders tried to surrender. A sudden rainstorm put out the fire and the Tories resumed fighting. Frustrated, Sumter withdrew to his camp near Land's Ford on the Catawba.

The engagement lasted almost eight hours, but was largely carried out through long-range skirmishing because few wished to overly expose themselves to injury. By the end of the battle, both sides had lost approximately a dozen killed and wounded. After a brief respite, Sumter went on to attack Hanging Rock, North Carolina, on 6 August 1780.

SEE ALSO *Camden Campaign; Hanging Rock, South Carolina.*

BIBLIOGRAPHY

Robinson, Blackwell P. *The Revolutionary War Sketches of William R. Davie.* Raleigh: North Carolina Department of Cultural Resources, Division of Archives and History, 1976.

Tarleton, Banastre. *A History of the Campaigns of 1780 and 1781 in the Southern Provinces of North America.* London, 1787. Reprint. Spartanburg, S.C.: Reprint Company, 1967.

revised by Lawrence E. Babits

RODNEY, CAESAR. (1728–1784). Signer.

Delaware. Born in Kent County, Delaware, on 7 October 1728, Caesar Rodney was high sheriff there from 1755 to 1758. He also served the county as justice of the peace and as and county judge. In 1756 he was named militia captain and held other important public offices. He was elected to the colonial legislature nearly every year from 1758 to 1776, serving as speaker in 1769 and from 1773 to 1776. He was an active delegate to the 1765 Stamp Act Congress in New York City. An early supporter of colonial rights, he was chairman of the Delaware Committee of Safety and was sent to the Continental Congress in 1774 and 1775. He was named a colonel in the Delaware militia in May 1775 and was promoted to brigadier general in the following September. During 1776 he sat in the Continental Congress and was influential in suppressing the Loyalists in Delaware. His hasty return to Congress on 2 July 1776 enabled the Delaware delegation to vote two-to-one for Richard Henry Lee's resolution for independence and for the adoption of the Declaration of Independence. A conservative backlash in Delaware excluded Rodney from the state's constitutional convention, the new legislature, and the next Continental Congress.

Rodney turned his attention to military affairs, and was active on the councils of safety and inspection. He helped collect supplies, recruited for General George Washington's army, and in raised militia companies. General William Alexander made him post commandant at Trenton, New Jersey, for a few weeks, and he then served at Morristown, New Jersey, but with Washington's permission returned home in February 1777. During the British advance into his state he commanded the militia, and in September 1777 he was named state major general. In March 1778 he was elected President of Delaware. He held this post until November 1781. Chosen for Congress that year and in 1783, he did not take his seat due to ill health. In 1784 he became speaker of the state senate, which met at his home to save him from having to travel. He died at home on 26 June 1784 from cancer of the face, a condition from which he had suffered for about ten years.

SEE ALSO *Declaration of Independence.*

BIBLIOGRAPHY

Ryden, George H., ed. *Letters to and from Caesar Rodney, 1756–1784.* Philadelphia: University of Pennsylvania Press, 1933.

revised by Michael Bellesiles

RODNEY, GEORGE BRIDGES. (c. 1718–1792). First baron Rodney, British admiral and politician. George Rodney was baptized on 14 February 1718 at

George Bridges Rodney. The British admiral, in an engraving based on a 1761 painting by Joshua Reynolds. THE LIBRARY OF CONGRESS

St. Giles-in-the-Fields, Middlesex, on the edge of London. His soldier father lost heavily in the South Sea Bubble and George became dependent upon wealthier relatives, an experience which may partly explain his later eye for prize money. Educated at Harrow School he joined HMS *Sutherland* as a "volunteer per order," a young prospective officer, on 7 July 1732. He became a lieutenant in 1740 and a post captain on 31 March 1743. Rodney distinguished himself in Hawke's "general chase" action off Ushant on 14 October 1747 and was commodore and governor of Newfoundland (1749–1752), after which he turned to politics and the gaming tables. During the Seven Years' War he conveyed Amherst to the siege of Louisburg (1758) and, promoted to rear admiral, bombarded and blockaded a French invasion flotilla at Le Havre. Appointed to the Leeward Islands station, he cooperated with Monckton in the conquest in 1759 of Martinique, St. Lucia, Grenada, and St. Vincent. When ordered to support the attack on Havana he kept back some ships to cover Jamaica, a foretaste of his way with orders he thought inappropriate or unwise. Fortunately for him, the expedition was an outstanding success. In 1763 he was made a baronet and, two years later, governor of Greenwich Hospital.

Rodney now fell into serious financial trouble, and not entirely because of his addiction to gambling. He had been a member of Parliament from 1752 to 1754 and again from 1761, but up to 1768 his election expenses had been defrayed by patrons. However, he had to find thirty thousand pounds for the election in 1768 out of his own pocket which, combined with a foolish agreement with a loan shark, ruined him. The Falkland Islands crisis of 1771 brought him command of the Jamaica squadron, but he was not allowed to keep the Greenwich governorship and its income. He returned home in 1774 to find his pay frozen over some unauthorized dockyard expenditure. When Parliament was dissolved Rodney, having lost his immunity from arrest, obtained leave of absence and fled to France.

When war with France broke out in 1778, Rodney was eager for command but dared not leave that country until the duc de Biron generously lent him one thousand louis to cover his debts. In May 1778 he returned to London, where his arrears of pay were released to him and he repaid his English creditors. Finally, in December 1779 he was appointed commander in chief in the Leeward Islands, with orders to relieve Gibraltar on the way.

NEW TACTICS

On 7 January 1780 he captured most of a large Spanish convoy off Cape St. Vincent and nine days later virtually destroyed a smaller Spanish squadron in the famous Moonlight Battle. Rodney then took his own convoy safely into Gibraltar and sailed to the West Indies with four ships of the line to add to the seventeen under Hyde Parker and Joshua Rowley. On 7 April Rodney led this combined fleet against the comte de Guichen off Martinique, aiming to concentrate on either the enemy's van or rear. Unfortunately, he had not fully explained his tactics to his officers, many of whom stuck to the formal line of battle and rendered the engagement inconclusive. Rodney learned the lesson and drilled the fleet in his new tactics. In encounters on 15 and 19 May the fleet responded better, only to be thwarted by the wind and Guichen's refusal to engage closely. Nevertheless, Rodney had become a leader in the growing revolution in naval tactics. Unwilling to encourage individual initiative or scrap the official fighting instructions, he had nevertheless adapted the general chase technique to concentrate on parts of an enemy line and, where possible, to break it.

POOR RELATIONS WITH SUBORDINATES

As the hurricane season approached, Rodney's penchant for arrogant and tactless handling of subordinates came to the fore. It was customary for squadrons to leave the West Indies at this time of the year and Rodney, fearing that all or part of the French fleet might go to North America,

sailed for New York This move, while it violated the letter of his orders, followed Admiralty expectations that the American stations would support each other. Unfortunately, Rodney tactlessly asserted his technical seniority over Vice Admiral Arbuthnot, interfered with his dispositions, appointed his own followers into Arbuthnot's ships, and claimed the commander in chief's share of prize money. On his return to the West Indies in November, Rodney alienated Peter Parker by demanding a monopoly of the overstretched Jamaica dockyards to repair his storm-damaged ships. Finally, on 7 January 1781 Rodney's erstwhile protégé, rear admiral Sir Samuel Hood, arrived to be second in command. Hood was as opinionated and touchy as Rodney and ever ready to criticise his superiors. His first opportunity came on 3 February, when Rodney and general John Vaughan took from the Dutch that emporium of contraband, St. Eustatius. Rodney immediately claimed the booty, much of it belonging to British merchants, as prize and shipped it for home in a special convoy. Hood accused Rodney of neglecting his strategic priorities in order to cover this convoy against any French sorties from Martinique. Thus were laid the seeds of the calamitous failure of cooperation of 1781.

In April, De Grasse brought twenty more ships of the line to the West Indies. Although warned, Rodney did not attempt to intercept him with his whole fleet. Hood, with a detachment, engaged De Grasse indecisively on 29 April and the two fleets did not fight again, apart from a single indecisive encounter off Tobago on 5 June. During this time and later, Rodney failed to keep close track of De Grasse's movements and to keep in touch with Arbuthnot. When the hurricane season came round again, Rodney had intelligence that De Grasse would sail northwards; but he neither gave Arbuthnot's successor, Thomas Graves, adequate information nor sent to him timely and adequate reinforcements. Instead, complaining of ill health and fretting about the lost St. Eustatius convoy, which had been intercepted by the French in European waters, he sailed for home on 1 August. He left Hood in command with instructions to send to Graves help which turned out to be too little and too late.

DEFEAT OF DE GRASSE

At home he retired to Bath and proceeded, as the news of Graves's failure and Cornwallis's surrender filtered through, to compose his own version of events. His famous Bath letter of 19 October, he for example, gave a very misleading view of the intelligence he was supposed to have sent to Graves. The government still thought highly enough of Rodney to send him back to the Caribbean with reinforcements to counter a new French offensive. On 19 February he rejoined Hood at St. Lucia to find St. Eustatius,

Demerara, St. Kitts, and Montserrat already lost. With Jamaica known to be De Grasse's next target, Rodney deployed his fleet to stop De Grasse at Martinique joining the rest of the invasion force at Haiti, moves which Hood characteristically denounced as disastrous. He was quite wrong.

On 9 April 1782 Rodney intercepted De Grasse near the islets called the Saints between Guadeloupe and Dominica. For three days Rodney struggled to close with the French as they worked their way to windward. On 12 April he succeeded, forming line of battle and engaging the French center soon after 8 A.M. The wind now veered four points, creating openings in the French line. Rodney at once ordered his ships through the gaps, breaking the French line into fragments. All afternoon Rodney pursued the disorganized survivors and by evening his ships had already taken six ships of the line, a frigate, and a sloop. When De Grasse's flagship, the 110-gun *Ville de Paris*, struck, Rodney finally called off the chase. In theory, as Hood was all too quick to point out, a chase through the night might have destroyed the French fleet entirely. Rodney, however, had to take account of the damage to his own ships and the dangers of collisions in the dark; his decision was probably wise.

The victory re-established British supremacy in the Caribbean, preserved Jamaica, and strengthened Britain's hand in the Paris peace negotiations. In May, Charles James Fox moved a vote of thanks in the House of Commons, thus embarrassing the new Rockingham administration, which had already sent Pigot to replace Rodney. The government responded by giving Rodney a barony, encouraging the Commons to vote him two thousand pounds per annum, and winding up a committee of inquiry into the St. Eustatius affair. In theory, Rodney should have returned home in September to find himself a wealthy national hero.

It was not to be. His failure to pursue the French into the night was publicly attacked by Hood, who claimed that Rodney was too preoccupied with securing the French flagship to see the bigger picture. Others suggested that the idea of breaking the French line came from Rodney's flag captain, Charles Douglas. Finally, while the Commons inquiry had folded, the merchants with claims against Rodney's St. Eustatius seizures continued to pursue him in the courts. Eventually their claims amounted to more than the total value of the lost convoy, and Rodney spent the last ten years of his life struggling to meet them.

ASSESSMENT

George Rodney was an inspired but flawed leader. There is no doubting his arrogance and tactlessness, his failure to cooperate properly with Graves during the Yorktown crisis, and his near-obsession with prize money. He was unreceptive to the new tactical ideas of Howe, Kempenfelt, and Graves, but his own tactical ideas, which reached triumphant maturity at the Saints, were far ahead of their time. The matter of who actually suggested breaking the line on 12 April 1781 is immaterial, for Rodney's ideas and training lay behind it, and it was Rodney's instantaneous decision that carried it into execution. Those who criticize Rodney for not being Nelson forget that without the Saints, there might have been no Trafalgar.

SEE ALSO *Grasse, François Joseph Paul, Comte de; Hood, Samuel.*

BIBLIOGRAPHY

Breen, Kenneth. "Divided Command in the West Indies and North America, 1780–81." In *The British Navy and the Use of Naval Power in the Eighteenth Century.* Edited by Jeremy Black and Philip Woodfine. Leicester, U.K.: Leicester University Press, 1988.

Syrett, David. *The Royal Navy in American Waters, 1775–1783.* Aldershot, U.K.: Scholar Press, 1989.

revised by John Oliphant

RODNEY, THOMAS. (1744–1811).

Continental Congressman. Delaware. Born in Sussex County, Delaware, on 4 June, 1744, Rodney was named justice of the peace in 1770 and reappointed in 1774. In the following year he became a member of the state assembly, the Council of Safety, the Committee of Observations, and a captain in the state militia. During General George Washington's retreat across New Jersey in 1776, Rodney and his company joined General John Cadwalader at Bristol, Pennsylvania, on Christmas Day. They fought in the second battle of Trenton and at Princeton. In 1777, when the British invaded Delaware, Rodney joined his brother, Caesar, as adjutant. He was the Delaware Judge of the Admiralty from 1778 to 1785, and from 1781 to 1788 was sent to the Continental Congress five times. In 1786 and 1787 he was also in the state assembly, and served as speaker of that body in 1787. In 1803 he was named U.S. judge for the Missouri territory. The town of Rodney, Mississippi,, where he owned a great deal of land, was named for him. He died there on 2 January 1811.

SEE ALSO *Rodney, Caesar.*

BIBLIOGRAPHY

Rodney, Thomas. *Diary of Captain Thomas Rodney, 1776–1777.* New York: Da Capo Press, 1974.

revised by Michael Bellesiles

ROGERS, ROBERT. (1731–1795). Ranger
hero of colonial wars, Loyalist. New Hampshire. Born in Methuen, Massachusetts, on 7 November 1731, Rogers entered the New Hampshire Regiment in 1755 to escape prosecution for counterfeiting. After showing skill as a leader of raids and scouting expeditions, in March 1756 he became captain of an independent ranger company, and in 1758 Abercromby made him the major of nine such companies to be used for reconnaissance; they became known collectively as "Rogers's Rangers." After serving with Loudoun at Halifax (1757), with Abercromby at Ticonderoga (1758), and with Amherst at Crown Point (1759)—during which campaign he destroyed the St. Francis Indians in an audacious raid—he took part in the final operations against Montreal in 1760 and then went west to receive the surrender of Detroit and down the Scioto River to Sonioto (Shawneetown) on the Ohio. Lieutenants in Rogers's Rangers were John Stark, Israel Putnam, and James Dalyell (killed at Detroit in Pontiac's Rebellion).

In 1761 Rogers led an independent company in the Cherokee expedition of James Grant. During Pontiac's Rebellion he commanded an independent New York company and took part in the relief and defense of Detroit. In 1765 he fled to England to avoid prosecution for his debts and illegal trading with the Indians. In England he published two accounts of his military service, *Journals* (1769) and *A Concise Account of North America* (1770), along with a play, *Ponteach: or the Savages of America* (1776), often accounted one of the first American dramas.

Rogers returned to America in 1766 as commander of Fort Michilimackinac. After repeated violations of his instructions, he was charged by Gage in 1768 with embezzlement of public property and with treasonable dealings with the French but was acquitted at a court-martial for lack of evidence. Returning to England in 1769, he was unable to get another appointment and was jailed for his debts until bailed out by his brother James. In 1775 he returned to America, perhaps as a spy for the British.

In 1776 Washington ordered Rogers imprisoned on suspicion of espionage. Escaping to the British, he was commissioned to raise the Queen's American Rangers. Defeated at White Plains, he was removed from his command and replaced by James.

In 1780 Rogers returned to England. He died in a cheap London boardinghouse on 18 May 1795.

SEE ALSO *Cherokee Expedition of James Grant; Pontiac's War; Putnam, Israel; Stark, John.*

BIBLIOGRAPHY
Cuneo, John R. *Robert Rogers of the Rangers.* New York: Oxford University Press, 1959.

revised by Michael Bellesiles

ROMAN CATHOLICS. Roman Catholicism
was a small but diverse religious community in 1776. Numbering about twenty-five thousand members (just one percent of the American population), it was confined principally to the states of Pennsylvania and Maryland, where there had evolved distinctive versions of the faith that produced different but equally fervent responses to war and revolution.

AMERICAN CATHOLICS' RELIGIOUS CULTURE

Maryland Catholicism was English, rural, and hierarchical, composed of a gentry class with extensive holdings in tobacco plantations and slaves; a middling group of small planters and farmers engaged in subsistence and commercial agriculture; and African slaves, three thousand of whom belonged to the church. Ministering to Maryland Catholics were seven Jesuit priests, who operated farms that served both as mission stations for an itinerant clergy and as informal parish churches.

Pennsylvania Catholicism, on the other hand, had a sizable urban, ethnic contingent. St. Joseph's Church, founded in Philadelphia in 1734 as the first urban Catholic Church in America, contained a rich ethnic mix of forty Irish, English, and Germans. By 1776 the church had grown to twelve hundred and included French as well as English, Irish, and Germans. Most of the parishioners were laborers, servants, and sailors, but the church came to include a group of English and Irish merchants whose rise to economic power reflected Philadelphia's growth as a seaport. Pennsylvania Catholicism had a lesser rural component, which was in part developed by Jesuit missionaries from St. Joseph's and in part by migrants and their Jesuit pastors from Maryland and Germany.

Catholics faced complex problems when the onset of Revolution made a choice of loyalties both mandatory and urgent. But from whom could they seek counsel on the crisis? Turning to the hierarchy for leadership was a possibility, but suppression of the Jesuits in 1773 had thrown the American clergy, Jesuits all, into a state of disarray. Suppression forced Jesuits to become secular priests, subject no longer to the direct authority of the Jesuit missionary superior but to the bishop of London. In addition, the Declaration of Independence and war severed formal ties between American Catholics and the London hierarchy, leaving leadership of the church in the hands of the Reverend John Lewis, pastor of Bohemia Manor, Maryland. But because he had received his appointment from the bishop of London, not a few American priests refused to submit to his authority. Individual pastors called upon Catholics to take the oath of loyalty to the Revolution and defended the morality of the war against England, but most priests were loath to enter the fray, believing that they should have "little to do with civil broils and troubled waters" (Henley, p. 179).

In the absence of clerical leadership, responsibility for steering the Church through the "troubled waters" of war and revolution was assumed by Catholic laymen belonging primarily to two elite groups. These were the Maryland gentry and the Philadelphia mercantile community.

THE REVOLUTION IN MARYLAND

The atmosphere in America in 1776 was hardly conducive to Catholic cooperation with the Patriots. Penal laws proscribing the civil or religious rights—or both—of Catholics existed in all the colonies, including Maryland. In addition, revolutionary ideology had heightened anti-Catholicism as Patriots blamed the crisis on the British royal court's flirtations with "popery." The Quebec Act of 1774, which extended religious toleration to the Catholics of Canada, raised American anti-papalism to a fever pitch. "GEORGE III REX. AND THE LIBERTIES OF AMERICA. NO POPERY," proclaimed a rebel banner. If American Catholics had good reasons for hesitating to join the "glorious cause" against England, they had equally strong reasons for choosing neither loyalty or neutrality. Siding with England raised the same objections as adopting patriotism, for England was as anti-Catholic as America. On the other hand, neutrality would subject Catholics to even more harassment than they had suffered under the penal laws.

Faced with difficult choices, many American Catholics were persuaded into choosing patriotism over neutrality or loyalty by laymen who had risen quickly to the defense of American liberty. To be sure, more than a few Catholics became Tories, but not in Maryland, where Loyalists were rare.

Charles Carroll of Carrollton, a Maryland planter and one of the wealthiest men in America, was the pre-eminent lay leader of the Catholic radical movement in America. Carroll chose to enter the political fray against England as early as 1773, when he published a pamphlet defending the principle of no taxation without representation against the conservative Maryland pamphleteer, Daniel Dulany. The pamphlet gained him notoriety in non-Catholic as well as Catholic circles, elevating him to a position of national leadership in the movement toward independence. He served as an adviser to the Continental Congress; made a trip to Canada in 1775 to secure that country's support for the Revolution; was elected a delegate to the Maryland Convention in 1776 that formed the new state constitution; and was the first to sign the Declaration of Independence as a newly elected delegate to Congress. For the remainder of the war he represented Maryland either in Congress or in the state's senate.

Carroll's radicalism must have come as a shock to Americans accustomed to associating Catholicism in religion with absolutism in politics. But his Jesuit teachers, who were active in the European Enlightenment, had taught him well the philosophy of republicanism, including natural rights theory and the legitimacy of revolution against tyrants. So when the crisis with England hit, Carroll immediately recognized in the rapidly evolving revolutionary ideology ideas that were congenial with his own. Carroll's great contribution to American Catholicism, at the moment of its inception, was to demonstrate, both in word and in deed, the compatibility between Catholic liberalism and the ideals of the new Republic.

THE REVOLUTION IN PENNSYLVANIA

In Pennsylvania, the local Catholic merchant community of Philadelphia provided the leadership for Catholics choosing to participate in the radical movement. Unlike Maryland's Catholics, they distinguished themselves less in civil than in military affairs, serving principally in the Continental army and not in provincial militias, as was mainly the case with Catholic combatants in Maryland. This was due in part to their proximity to Congress, which sat in Philadelphia for much of the war, and in part to their commercial and financial expertise, which were in great demand. In addition, Philadelphia's sizable community of laborers, a class from which the bulk of the Continental army's enlistees was recruited, provided a natural constituency for Catholic merchants inclined to express their patriotism by raising a troop of soldiers.

Stephen Moylan was Philadelphia's answer to Charles Carroll. A member of a prominent Catholic family and a wealthy wholesale merchant, Moylan was "the outstanding American Catholic solider in the Revolution" (Metzger, p. 218). He threw himself into the war as early as 1775, when in the wake of Lexington and Concord he financed a contingent of Catholic volunteers, drawn in part from the Friendly Sons of St. Patrick, a fraternal society that had recently elected him president. He then led it to Boston to join Washington's new army. Moylan went on to serve the Continental army in other important military capacities. Then, in January 1777, he became commander of the Fourth Continental Dragoons, a position he held to 1783, when he became a brigadier general.

Other Catholic merchants, drawing upon similar sources of wealth and commercial expertise, also moved into important congressional military and fiscal offices during the war. Two of Stephen Moylan's brothers played major roles in the fiscal affairs of thearmy, one as a commercial agent of the United States in France, the other as clothier general of the Continental forces. Thomas Fitz Simmons and George Meade, his brother-in-law, were partners in Meade and Company, an import and export firm that traded mainly with the West Indies. Throughout the war, the firm of Meade and Company engaged in a number of licit and illicit commercial activities, including privateering, for the purpose of provisioning American armies and French naval forces in desperate need of military supplies. Many of the privateers recruited for service by the two men came from the Catholic community of St. Mary's, which saw at least fourteen of its parishioners serve as privateers for Fitz Simmons and Meade. Such examples offer a mere glimpse into a complex community of Philadelphia's Catholic merchants and traders who made an impact on the Revolution.

In contrast to this record of patriotic leadership is the evidence regarding Catholic Toryism, which seemed to have been confined largely to Philadelphia and its environs. Catholic Loyalists made a brief but conspicuous appearance in Philadelphia between September 1777 and June 1778, when the town was under British occupation. Upon capturing Philadelphia, the British organized "three regiments of provincials," including one "wholly made up of Roman Catholics" (*ibid.*, pp. 244–245). But the force disbanded soon after the British abandoned Philadelphia in June 1778 and returned to New York, a city in which Catholics were a rarity. As historians have found, Philadelphia's Catholic Tories were not confined to any one class or ethnic group, but cut across all segments of the society.

IMPACT OF THE REVOLUTION

Despite their differences, American Catholics generally supported the Revolution, and as a result reaped the benefits of its success. Most revolutionary governments, including Maryland and Pennsylvania, abolished all penal laws against Catholics and implemented ideals of religious toleration, freedom, and equality. The impact on Catholics was immediate. Liberated from civil and religious restraints, American Catholics were free to form a new American church according to the principles of the religion and the Revolution. Leading Catholics in the radical transformation of the Church was the Reverend John Carroll, cousin of Charles of Carrollton, and—like Charles—educated in republicanism at various Jesuit schools in Europe. Returning to Maryland in 1774, he led an inconspicuous life as a missionary priest until 1784, when he was appointed superior of American missions. Committed primarily to the revival of Catholic devotion to the sacraments, Carroll took full advantage of the new toleration towards Catholics, convening the first American diocesan synod in 1791, in an effort to revitalize Catholic lay piety. Carroll was also guided by a vision of a national church with an independent system of governance, an objective achieved through the formation of institutions that also served as instruments of Catholic revival, the most significant of which was the system

of Catholic colleges founded soon after Carroll became the first American bishop in 1789. These included St. John's College (1789), Georgetown University (1791), St. Mary's Sulpician Seminary (1791), and Baltimore College (1803). Having demonstrated their worth as American Patriots, American Catholics suffered significantly less discrimination from Protestants until the arrival of the Irish in the nineteenth century.

SEE ALSO *Carroll, Charles; Moylan, Stephen.*

BIBLIOGRAPHY

Carey, Patrick W. *Catholics in America: A History.* Westport, Conn.: Praeger, 2004.

Cogliano, Francis D. *No King, No Popery: Anti-Catholicism in Revolutionary New England.* Westport, Conn.: Greenwood Press, 1995.

Dolan, Jay P. *The American Catholic Experience: A History from Colonial Times to the Present.* Garden City, N.Y.: Doubleday, 1985.

———. *In Search of an American Catholicism: A History of Religion and Culture in Tension.* New York: Oxford University Press, 2002.

Ellis, John Tracy. *Catholics in Colonial America.* Baltimore: Helicon Press, 1965.

Hanley, Thomas O'Brien. *The American Revolution and Religion: Maryland 1770–1800.* Washington, D.C.: Catholic University of America Press, 1971.

Hennesey, James. *American Catholics: A History of the Roman Catholic Community in the United States.* New York: Oxford University Press, 1981.

Metzger, Charles H. *Catholics and the American Revolution: A Study in Religious Climate.* Chicago: Loyola University Press, 1962.

Gerald F. Moran

ROSENTHAL, GUSTAV HEINRICH WETTER VON. (1753–1829). Born on 1 January 1753, Rosenthal (Rozental in Russian) was a nobleman of the Russian Empire. He came from a Baltic German family of the *Estländische Ritterschaft* (Noble Corporation of Estland), which owned estates throughout what is now Estonia. After studying law at the University of Göttingen, the baron went to St. Petersburg. There he fatally wounded his opponent in a duel and fled Russia for England. Learning of the events in the colonies and seeking refuge from his strict father, he sailed to America in 1775. After briefly studying medicine, he joined the Continental Army as Lieutenant "John Rose," becoming the only Russian subject and Baltic German to fight for the American patriots; throughout his stay in America, he would conceal his origins. On 12 June 1777 he was

made surgeon of William Irvine's Seventh Pennsylvania Regiment and was at Valley Forge. Found not competent as a doctor, Rose was transferred to the army's General Hospital at Yellow Springs as a surgeon's mate under the name of Gustavus Henderson, before returning to the Seventh Pennsylvania as a lieutenant in the brigade staff. He subsequently served in the Continental navy as a surgeon but was captured on the privateer *Revenge* (commanded by Gustavus Conygham) on 27 April 1779 and imprisoned.

Exchanged, Rose joined the Fourth Pennsylvania at Carlisle on 1 April 1781, became Irvine's aide-de-camp on 8 July 1781, was promoted to the rank of major, and headed to the western frontier with Irvine when the general was ordered on 8 March 1782 to take command at Fort Pitt. In part because of his refined manners, Rose became a great favorite of Irvine (who praised him in a letter to Washington) and his family. Based on his popularity with the local militia, Irvine appointed "Major Rose" as the aide-de-camp to Colonel William Crawford during his expedition to Sandusky. (In his private journal Rosenthal was highly critical of Crawford's leadership.) In the chaos after their defeat at the Battle of Sandusky in early June 1782, Rose and Colonel David Williamson led the successful retreat of the routed American volunteers back to Fort Pitt. For his bravery and combat command skills throughout the expedition, Rose was widely commended by his fellow officers. Transferred to the Third Pennsylvania on 1 January 1783, Rose successfully saw to it that Irvine's troops received their final payment. After his honorable discharge in June 1783, Rose was chosen by his fellow Pennsylvania Line officers to lobby on their behalf at the Pennsylvania Legislature during the negotiations on land grants along the Susquehanna and Allegheny.

Having been pardoned in Russia, Rosenthal left America in April 1784 bound for Estland. Rosenthal divulged his story to Irvine as his ship waited to sail from Philadelphia. Back in Estland, he married and became a major in the Russian army. Rosenthal served as the "captain of the nobility" of Estland from 1803 to 1806, during which time the province became a center of liberal agrarian reform. Although the U.S. government granted Rosenthal bounty land in Ohio, and Pennsylvania gave him two tracts in the northwest part of the state, he never returned to America. He died in Reval on 26 June 1829.

SEE ALSO *Crawford, William; Irvine, William.*

BIBLIOGRAPHY

Anderson, James H. "Colonel William Crawford." *Ohio Archaeological and Historical Society Publications* 6, no. 1 (1898): 1–34.

Rose, John (Baron Gustavus de Rosenthal). "Journal of a Volunteer Expedition to Sandusky, from May 24 to June 13, 1782." *Pennsylvania Magazine of History and Biography* 18, nos. 2–3 (July and October, 1894): 130–157 and 293–328.

William Irvine Papers (including Irvine-Rosenthal correspondence from 1780 to 1811). Manuscript collection, Historical Society of Pennsylvania.

revised by Philip Curtis Skaggs

ROSS, BETSY SEE *Flag, American.*

ROSS, GEORGE. (1730–1779). Signer, jurist. Delaware and Pennsylvania. Born at New Castle, Delaware, on 10 May 1730, George Ross became a lawyer in 1750 and established a successful practice at Lancaster, Pennsylvania. He was elected to the Provincial Assembly in 1768, and served in that body until 1775. He was also elected to the provincial conference at Philadelphia and, subsequently, to the first Continental Congress in 1774. A member of the Pennylvania Committee of Safety in 1775, he wrote rules of conduct for the state's military forces. He also served briefly as a colonel of the Pennsylvania Associators (an organization created by Benjamin Franklin, devoted to the defense of the Patriot cause) and attended the Second Continental Congress. An advocate of peaceful relations with the Indians, he helped negotiate the Fort Pitt treaty in 1776. That same year he was vice president of the Pennsylvania constitutional convention, although he opposed the final product as too democratic. He was re-elected to the Continental Congress on 20 July 1776 and signed the Declaration of Independence on 2 August. In 1778 Ross returned to the Pennsylvania Assembly, where he was elected vice president.

As judge of the Pennsylvania admiralty court, to which he was appointed in March 1779, Ross heard the significant *Olmsted et al. v. Rittenhouse's Executors* case. The British sloop *Active* had left Jamaica in August 1778 and sailed for New York. Four American crewmen, including Gideon Olmsted of Connecticut, took over the ship the night of 6 September. Two days later the *Active* was seized by the Pennsylvania brigantine *Convention* and the privateer *Gerard.* The captains of these ships claimed a share of the prize, which Olmsted contested. Although Ross sympathized with Olmsted, he confirmed the jury's verdict awarding the Connecticut captors one-fourth of the prize money. On 15 December a committee of Congress annulled the verdict and gave the entire prize to Olmsted and his three companions. Ross refused to acknowledge Congress's action, starting a controversy that raged between Congress and Pennsylvania until the U.S. Supreme Court upheld Congress in 1809. On 14 July 1779 Ross died suddenly of gout at his home in Lancaster.

SEE ALSO *Active Case.*

revised by Michael Bellesiles

ROYAL. A small mortar. A royal sail and mast were above the topgallant sail and mast.

Mark M. Boatner

ROYAL AMERICAN REGIMENT.

The Royal American Regiment entered the British Establishment on Christmas Day 1755 as the Sixty-second Regiment of Foot, an unusual four-battalion unit to be raised principally in Britain's North American colonies for service there. Renumbered the Sixtieth Regiment of Foot on 27 December 1757, Robert Rogers led two hundred men of the First Battalion west to receive the surrender of French posts in 1760.

Men of the Royal American Regiment were garrisoning the lonely western posts in 1763 when Pontiac's War broke out. They were part of the relief expedition under Colonel Henry Bouquet that defeated the Indians at Bushy Run on 5–6 August 1763 and joined Bouquet again for his expedition in 1764. The Third and Fourth Battalions then were disbanded, and the First and Second were sent to the West Indies.

When the American war started, the Third and Fourth Battalions were re-formed in Europe with Hanoverians and British soldiers and sent to Florida. Three companies from these battalions fought at Briar Creek, Georgia, on 3 March 1779, and they held one of the gun batteries and with the marines sallied forth from the Spring Hill Redoubt to clinch the British victory at Savannah on 9 October 1779. Thereafter, they helped to defend British possessions on the Gulf coast. Eight companies were surrendered with the garrison of Pensacola on 9 May 1781. The Third and Fourth Battalions were disbanded in 1783, and reconstituted in 1787.

The First and Second Battalions remained in the West Indies during the Revolution. At St. Vincent, the sickly garrison of four hundred Royal Americans surrendered to the comte d'Estaing on 16 June 1779. Men of the regiment were also stationed at Antigua and took part in the operations in Nicaragua in 1780.

Remnants of all four battalions were sent to St. Augustine, Florida, in November 1782, and from thence to New York, where the men were drafted into other regiments and the officers sent home to recruit new battalions for the Sixtieth

SEE ALSO *Bouquet, Henry; Bouquet's Expedition of 1764; Briar Creek, Georgia; Bushy Run, Pennsylvania; Monckton, Robert; Nicaragua; Pensacola, Florida; Pontiac's War; Rogers, Robert; Savannah, Georgia (9 October 1779).*

BIBLIOGRAPHY
Butler, Lewis. *The Annals of the King's Royal Rifle Corps.* Vol. 1: *The Royal Americans.* London: John Murray, 1913.

revised by Harold E. Selesky

ROYAL GOVERNMENT IN AMERICA.

The English settlement of North America was undertaken by groups of private individuals; the colonies were only gradually brought under the control of royal government. By 1763, nine of the thirteen colonies that would rebel in 1775 had royal governors. Pennsylvania and Maryland remained in the hands of their proprietors, and Connecticut and Rhode Island continued to elect their own governors under their seventeenth-century charters. Massachusetts was anomalous, with a royally appointed governor operating under a revised charter of 1692, until its privileges were wiped out by the Massachusetts Government Act of 1774, one of the so-called Intolerable (or Coercive) Acts.

Every colony had an elected assembly. The eight royal colonies had a governor and council (the upper house of the legislature) appointed by the crown and an assembly (lower house) chosen by a larger and more broadly based white male electorate than anywhere in Britain. The governor, as executive head of the legislature and the king's chief representative, was expected to execute the instructions he received from London, usually from the Board of Trade. The colonial assemblies waged a century-long struggle to limit his authority. After 1680 the assemblies had authority to initiate all colonial laws. The governor either vetoed the laws or sent them to the Privy Council, which had authority to accept or cancel (disallow) them. The assemblies also gained the all-important right to make financial appropriations and supervise actual expenditures; thereby, they got the whip hand on the governor and the provincial judges by controlling their salaries. The imperial government tried to make the assemblies establish fixed annual salaries, but the assemblies fought off all of the crown's efforts to establish a fixed civil list in the colonies, which would have given the governor a powerful patronage weapon. The assemblies were particularly successful in gaining ground against the governor during wartime, when they could bargain harder for additional power against a governor whose top priority was to have money available to pay for pressing military needs.

Sometimes the imperial government helped its governors, as when it succeeded after 1761 in establishing the governor's right to appoint judges "during the pleasure of the Crown," whereas the assemblies had fought to permit them to retain office "during good behavior." (Resentment over this point is reflected in the Declaration of Independence.) But London could also undercut its representative. After 1763 the secretary of state for the American colonies began appointing an increasing number of imperial officials, including the naval officer responsible for enforcing the Navigation Acts, an innovation that further reduced the patronage the governor controlled.

Royal governors acted as mediators between the demands of the imperial government in London and the needs and desires of the colonial oligarchs. Many royal governors were intelligent, clever politicians who understood that ingratiating themselves with the local leaders was the best way to persuade them to adhere to imperial controls. When there was a congruence of interest between London and the colony, the job of being a royal governor could be relatively pleasant. More often, however, the royal governor was obliged by his superiors to impose rules and regulations that local leaders resented or resisted. When that happened, a royal governor would need all the talents and powers he could muster to chivvy, cajole, and if necessary, coerce the colony into compliance. Successful royal government required the governors—indeed all imperial officials—to be honest, disinterested, and savvy politicians. Unfortunately for the prestige and, ultimately, the survival of royal government in America, the job of royal governor could also be extremely lucrative, and it attracted too many men who were venial, grasping, and contemptuous of the Americans they were supposed to govern effectively.

The only colonial governor who wholeheartedly supported the Revolution and remained in office was Jonathan Trumbull of Connecticut. Joseph Wanton Sr. of Rhode Island was deemed by the assembly to be a lukewarm supporter of resistance and was replaced by Nicholas Cooke. Thomas Hutchinson of Massachusetts had already given way to a military government led by Major General Thomas Gage; the former governor died in exile in London. William Tryon, who served as royal governor in North Carolina and New York, returned to his former life as an army officer, became the senior general officer of the Provincial (Loyalist) troops, and commanded several significant raids to suppress the rebels. William Franklin, the illegitimate son of Benjamin Franklin, was the last royal governor of New Jersey, and he too was prominent in trying to organize Loyalists to fight the rebels. Governors Josiah Martin, who succeeded Tryon in North Carolina, Sir William Campbell of South Carolina, Sir James Wright

of Georgia, and John Murray, fourth earl of Dunmore, of Virginia were all forced early in the war to flee for their own safety. Their overly optimistic reports of potential Loyalist support in the South led the British to send Major General Henry Clinton on an ill-fated expedition against Charleston, South Carolina, in the summer of 1776.

SEE ALSO *Campbell, William; Charleston Expedition of Clinton in 1776; Disallowance; Franklin, William; Hutchinson, Thomas; Intolerable (or Coercive) Acts; Martin, Josiah; Murray, John; Townshend Acts; Trade, The Board of; Trumbull, Jonathan, Sr.; Tryon, William; Wright, Sir James, Governor.*

BIBLIOGRAPHY

Andrews, Charles M. *The Colonial Background of the American Revolution.* New Haven, Conn.: Yale University Press, 1924.

———. *The Colonial Period of American History.* 4 vols. New Haven, Conn.: Yale University Press, 1934–1938.

Bailyn, Bernard. *The Origins of American Politics.* New York: Knopf, 1968.

Beer, George L. *British Colonial Policy, 1754–1765.* New York: Macmillan Company, 1907.

Labaree, Leonard W. *Royal Government in America: A Study of the British Colonial System before 1763.* New Haven, Conn.: Yale University Press, 1930.

Gipson, Lawrence H. *The British Empire before the American Revolution.* 15 vols. New York: Alfred A. Knopf, 1967–1970.

Greene, Evarts Boutell. *The Provincial Governor in the English Colonies of North America.* New York: Longmans, Green, 1898.

Greene, Jack P. *The Quest for Power: The Lower Houses of Assembly in the Southern Royal Colonies, 1689–1776.* Chapel Hill: University of North Carolina Press, 1963.

Marshall, Peter J., ed. *The Oxford History of the British Empire.* Vol. 2: *The Eighteenth Century.* New York: Oxford University Press, 1998.

Osgood, Herbert L. *The American Colonies in the Eighteenth Century.* 4 vols. New York: Columbia University Press, 1924.

revised by Harold E. Selesky

ROYAL GREENS.

The King's Royal Regiment of New York was also known as the Royal Greens, from the color of their uniforms.

revised by Harold E. Selesky

ROYAL HIGHLAND EMIGRANTS.

This Provincial regiment was the result of Allan McLane's efforts to enlist veteran Highland soldiers who had settled in Canada and the American colonies after the end of the French and Indian War. The first officers were commissioned in June 1775, and they spread out over northeastern British North America to recruit veterans as well as recently arrived emigrants from the Highlands. Two battalions were eventually raised, the First under Lieutenant Colonel MacLean at Quebec and the Second at Halifax, Nova Scotia, under Lieutenant Colonel John Small. Although the First Battalion was initially outfitted in green coats, the standard color of the Provincial service, both eventually received red coats with blue facings, bonnets, and kilts, uniforms modeled on that of the Forty-second Regiment of Foot (Royal Highland Regiment). The First Battalion remained in Canada throughout the war, rendering its most important service in helping to defeat the American attack on Quebec City in December 1775–January 1776. A detachment was sent to the relief of Fort Cumberland in 1776; other detachments participated in raids on the American frontier. The Second Battalion sent detachments far and wide in British North America, from Newfoundland to Jamaica, serving most notably in the South after April 1781. Placed on the British Establishment in December 1778–January 1779 as the Eighty-fourth Regiment of Foot (Royal Highland Emigrants), the Second Battalion was disbanded in Nova Scotia in 1783 and the First Battalion in Upper Canada in 1784.

SEE ALSO *MacLean, Allan.*

BIBLIOGRAPHY

Cole, Nan, and Todd Braisted. "The On-Line Institute for Advanced Loyalist Studies." Available online at http://www.royalprovincial.com.

Katcher, Philip R. N. *Encyclopedia of British, Provincial, and German Army Units, 1775–1783.* Harrisburg, Pa.: Stackpole Books, 1973.

Mills, T. F. "Land Forces of Britain, the Empire, and Commonwealth: 84th Regiment of Foot (Royal Highland Emigrants)." Available online at http://regiments.org.

Smith, Paul H. "The American Loyalists: Notes on Their Organization and Numerical Strength," *William and Mary Quarterly,* third series, 25 (1968): 259–277.

revised by Harold E. Selesky

RUDDLE'S STATION, KENTUCKY
SEE *Kentucky Raid of Bird.*

RUDOLPH, JOHN. (?–1782). Continental officer. Maryland. Joining Lee's legion as a lieutenant of light dragoons on 20 April 1778, he was promoted to

captain on 1 October 1778 and to major in 1781, dying on 8 December 1782. Brother of Michael Rudolph.

SEE ALSO *Rudolph, Michael.*

BIBLIOGRAPHY

Heitman, Francis B. *Historical Register of Officers of the Continental Army.* Rev. ed. Washington, D.C.: Rare Book Shop Pub. Co., 1914.

Mark M. Boatner

RUDOLPH, MICHAEL. (1754?–1794).
Continental officer of Lee's Legion. Maryland. Born in Maryland, perhas in 1754, Michael Rudolph and his brother, John, joined General Henry Lee's Legion in April 1778. Michael began with the rank of sergeant major, and on 1 April 1779 was made regimental quartermaster. Three months later he was promoted to lieutenant, and in a resolution of the Continental Congress on 24 September 1779 he and Archibald McAllister were brevetted as captains for their heroism in leading their forces in the successful surprise attack against the British position at Paulus Hook, New Jersey, on 19 August of that year. On 1 November 1779 he was confirmed in the rank of captain. In the Southern campaigns of General Nathanael Greene, Captain Rudolph performed gallantly and effectively with the infantry of Lee's Legion, being mentioned particularly in connection with the actions at Guilford, North Carolina, and Ninety Six and Eutaw Springs, both in South Carolina.

Serving to the end of the war, Rudolph settled at Savannah, Georgia, as a farmer and collector of taxes. He was commissioned a captain of the First U.S. Infantry on 3 June 1790 and as a major of light dragoons on 5 March 1792. On 22 February 1793 he was named adjutant and given the post of Inspector of the Army. Resigning on 17 July of that year he entered the West Indies trade. Two years later he vanished at sea.

SEE ALSO *Lee's Legion; McAllister, Archibald; Paulus Hook, New Jersey.*

revised by Michael Bellesiles

RUGELEY, COLONEL HENRY.
Loyalist officer. A leader of Loyalist forces in South Carolina, Rugeley held the rank of colonel in 1780. His home, Clermont or Rugeley's Mills, located twelve miles north of Camden on the road between that strategic place and Charlotte, North Carolina, figured prominently in

the war. Rugeley maintained friendships with several members of the Patriot elite during the Revolution, on one occasion in 1780 giving Governor John Rutledge, who was staying at Clermont, advance warning of a raid by Tarleton, allowing the governor to escape. His unit performed well in holding the center of the line in the fierce battle of Hanging Rock on 6 August 1780. Rugeley's military career came to a humiliating end in the action known as Rugeley's Mills when on 4 December 1780 he surrendered his entire command to William Washington's smaller force of dragoons. At the end of the Revolution, Rugeley settled in Jamaica.

SEE ALSO *Rugeley's Mills.*

revised by Michael Bellesiles

RUGELEY'S MILLS (CLERMONT), SOUTH CAROLINA.

4 December 1780. As part of General Daniel Morgan's newly organized light corps, Lieutenant Colonel William Washington rode with his dragoons to investigate a report that Colonel Henry Rugeley had gathered a body of Loyalist militia at his farm just north of Camden. Washington found the enemy in a fortified log barn surrounded by a ditch and abatis. Unable to make any impression with small arms and lacking artillery, he tried the Quaker gun trick—making a fake cannon out of a pine log, moving it into view, and summoning the Loyalists to surrender or be blown to bits. The ruse worked. Out came Colonel Rugeley, a major, and just over a hundred privates. They were marched back to the American camp, and the military career of Rugeley was ended.

SEE ALSO *Rugeley, Colonel Henry.*

revised by Michael Bellesiles

RUGGLES, TIMOTHY.

(1711–1795). Loyalist. Born in Rochester, Massachusetts, on 20 October 1711, Ruggles graduated from Harvard in 1732, setting up his legal practice in Plymouth the following year. Ruggles served numerous terms in the assembly from Plymouth, Sandwich, and Hardwick and was the assembly speaker in 1762. A militia colonel at the start of the Seven Years' War, he raised a regiment for Sir William Johnson's unsuccessful expedition against Crown Point in 1755 and then again in the failed effort to relieve Fort William Henry in 1757. Promoted to brigadier general in 1758, he commanded the right wing of the army during General James Abercromby's doomed attack on Fort Ticonderoga. In 1760 he finally took part in a successful military action, leading American troops in the Montreal campaign. Named to the Worcester County court of common pleas in 1757, he became its chief justice in 1762.

In the political conflicts leading up the Revolution, Ruggles consistently sided with the royal governors of Massachusetts, Francis Bernard and Thomas Hutchinson. Elected to the Stamp Act Congress of 1765, over whose deliberations he presided, he refused to sign its petition to the king and walked out, earning a reprimand from the Massachusetts assembly. In 1768 Ruggles was the only member of the assembly to vote against the nonimportation agreement and was one of the notorious seventeen representatives who voted to rescind the assembly's Circular Letter. By 1771 Ruggles's hometown of Hardwick was so deeply polarized that it was unable to decide on delegates to the assembly and sent no one. That polarization reached into his family, as his brother Benjamin adamantly supported the Patriot cause and threatened his brother with death if he continued to support the crown. Three of Ruggles's sons were Loyalists, but his wife and four daughters stood with the Patriots. In 1774, while Ruggles was away serving on the Mandamus Council, his house was plundered, the crowd apparently led by Benjamin Ruggles. Timothy Ruggles responded by raising a company of Loyalists to protect each others' property, and he told General Thomas Gage that he was prepared to raise a regiment of Loyalists. Gage's refusal infuriated Ruggles, who sat out the siege of Boston and was evacuated to Halifax when the British abandoned the city in March 1776. Joining General William Howe's army, Ruggles was given command of the Staten Island garrison, but Howe also rebuffed his offers to recruit a regiment. He spent the rest of the war trying to convince the British, who tended to hold the Loyalists in contempt, to allow him to raise and lead Loyalist troops until he left New York City in 1783 for Nova Scotia. The government rewarded his services with a large pension and five thousand pounds to cover his loses during the war. (Ruggles claimed twenty thousand pounds in losses.) He died in Wilmot, Nova Scotia, on 4 August 1795.

BIBLIOGRAPHY

Ruggles, Henry Stoddard. *General Timothy Ruggles, 1711–1795.* Wakefield, Mass.: privately printed, 1897.

Michael Bellesiles

RUMFORD, COUNT

SEE *Thompson, Benjamin Count Rumford.*

RUSH, BENJAMIN. (1746–1813). Physician, Signer. Pennsylvania.

Six years after graduating from Princeton, he entered the University of Edinburgh to complete his medical studies. In June 1768 he received his medical degree and went to London for intern training. At Edinburgh and London he showed a lively interest in what would later be called social science. Young Dr. Rush returned to Philadelphia in 1769 and soon was appointed professor of chemistry at the College of Philadelphia, the first such chair established in America. He also built up a successful medical practice and found time to associate with such Patriot leaders as Thomas Paine, John Adams, and Thomas Jefferson. In London he had been on friendly terms with Benjamin Franklin. In June 1776 he took a leading part in the movement toward independence, and the next month he became a delegate to the Continental Congress. He signed the Declaration of Independence on 2 August 1776.

Rush had volunteered in 1775 for service in the army, and he may have been an army surgeon in 1775–1776. On 11 April 1777 he became surgeon general of the Middle Department. His military career was brief. Not finding the administration of the medical service to his liking, he charged Dr. William Shippen with inefficiency, but a congressional investigation upheld Shippen. Dr. Rush then concluded that Washington's handling of military matters was unsatisfactory. After helping start what became known as the Conway Cabal, Rush wrote Patrick Henry anonymously from Yorktown on 12 January 1778 to recommend that Washington be replaced by Gates or Conway. Governor Henry forwarded the letter to Washington; the latter recognized Rush's excellent penmanship and confronted him with this evidence of personal disloyalty. Rush resigned on 30 April 1778.

Returning to his practice, Rush became a surgeon at the Pennsylvania Hospital, a position he held until his death. He specialized in care for mentally ill patients and became known as the "father of American psychiatry." He established the first free dispensary in America (1786), became president of the country's first antislavery society, demanded penal reforms, advocated the abolition of capital punishment, and supported free public education. He was responsible for the establishment of Dickinson College (1783). In the political arena he urged acceptance of the federal Constitution and was rewarded by President Adams with the post of treasurer of the U.S. Mint (1797–1813). In the field of medicine he developed a revolutionary "system" that, in simplest terms, was built around the hypothesis that all diseases resulted from too much or too little nervous stimulation and that all could be treated the same way: by drastic bleeding draining up to four-fifths of the patient's blood) and purging. This approach was soon condemned as idiotic, and it is fortunate that Rush lacked either the time or the inclination to test his hypothesis.

Rush is credited with pioneering in a number of medical fields, including experimental physiology, dental decay, and veterinary training. His medical essays earned literary distinction.

SEE ALSO *Conway Cabal.*

BIBLIOGRAPHY

Binger, Carl. *Revolutionary Doctor: Benjamin Rush, 1746–1813.* New York: Norton, 1966.

D'Elia, Donald J. *Benjamin Rush, Philosopher of the American Revolution.* Philadelphia: American Philosophical Society, 1974.

Hawke, David F. *Benjamin Rush, Revolutionary Gadfly.* Indianapolis: Bobbs-Merrill, 1971.

revised by Harry M. Ward

RUSSELL, WILLIAM, SR. (?–1793).

Continental officer. Virginia. Moving from Culpeper County to the Virginia frontier about ten years before the Revolution, he became colonel of the Thirteenth Virginia on 19 December 1776 and transferred to the Fifth Virginia on 14 September 1778. He was taken prisoner at Charleston on 12 May 1780, was exchanged six months later, and served until 3 November 1783. On the latter date he was breveted brigadier general. Father of William Russell Jr.

SEE ALSO *Russell, William, Jr.*

BIBLIOGRAPHY

Heitman, Francis B. *Historical Register of Officers of the Continental Army.* Rev. ed. Washington, D.C.: Rare Book Shop Pub. Co., 1914.

Mark M. Boatner

RUSSELL, WILLIAM, JR. (1758–1825).

Militia officer. Virginia. Born in Culpeper County, Virginia, in 1758, Russell claimed that at age fifteen he was on an expedition with Daniel Boone. During the Revolution he served as a militia lieutenant and was at Kings Mountain, South Carolina, in October 1780. As a militia captain he fought against the Cherokee and then took part in negotiating a peace treaty. Serving under William Campbell, Russell saw action at Wetzell's Mills and Guilford, North Carolina, in March 1781. Moving to Kentucky after the war, he took part in several campaigns against the Indians, leading the Kentucky volunteers in the final operations of General Anthony Wayne. Active in the movement for Kentucky statehood, he was elected annually to the legislature from 1792 until 1808, when President Madison appointed him colonel of the Seventh U.S. Infantry. Succeeding General William Henry Harrison as commander of the Indiana–Illinois–Missouri frontier in 1811, he led the 1812 expedition against the Peoria Indians. He died in Fayette County, Kentucky, on 3 July, 1825.

SEE ALSO *Campbell, William.*

revised by Michael Bellesiles

RUSSIA MERCHANT. This 243-ton British transport, carrying two hundred artillery personnel, foundered with valuable supplies needed for Clinton's Charleston expedition of 1780. All personnel were apparently saved, but the ship sank with four thousand muskets shipped for the use of Georgia Tories, which deprived the British of many armed irregulars. The loss also made Clinton more dependent upon his naval commander, Arbuthnot, from whom he had to borrow guns, shot, and powder. Some of the artillerymen from the ship reached the Charleston lines on 6 April 1780 from the Bermudas.

SEE ALSO *Charleston Expedition of Clinton in 1780.*

BIBLIOGRAPHY
Clinton, Sir Henry. *The American Rebellion: Sir Henry Clinton's Narrative of His Campaigns, 1775–1782.* Edited by William B. Willcox. New Haven, Conn.: Yale University Press, 1954.

Uhlendorf, Bernhard A., ed. and trans. *The Siege of Charleston, with an Account of the Province of South Carolina.* Ann Arbor: University of Michigan Press, 1938.

Mark M. Boatner

RUTHERFORD, GRIFFITH. (1731?–1805). Southern Patriot. North Carolina. Born in Ireland, perhaps in 1731, Rutherford settled in western North Carolina. He became a captain of militia in 1760, served in the North Carolina assembly from 1766 to 1775, was a sheriff from 1767 to 1769, and managed the difficult task of appeasing both sides in the Regulator crisis of 1769–1771. In 1775 he sat in the Provincial Congress, which made him colonel of the Rowan County militia, a militia that he led against backcountry Loyalists. On 22 June 1776

he was made brigadier general of state troops. In the Cherokee War of 1776, he led twenty-four hundred troops, combining with South Carolina militia to burn thirty-six Cherokee towns, which was hailed as a great victory. He took part in the unsuccessful efforts to keep the British from overrunning Georgia in the winter of 1778–1779, leading eight hundred men to reinforce Lincoln; his command was posted at Mathew's Bluff, South Carolina, when the Patriots were defeated, five miles away, at Briar Creek on 3 March 1779. Returning to North Carolina, he called out the militia to inflict a decisive defeat on the Loyalists at Ramseur's Mill on 20 June 1780, although he himself did not arrive in time to take part in the battle. He commanded a brigade at Camden on 16 August 1780, was wounded there, and was captured by Tarleton in the pursuit that followed the battle.

Held prisoner first at Charleston and then at St. Augustine, Rutherford was exchanged on 22 June 1781; he then returned to the field. He took command of Wilmington after its evacuation on 18 November 1781. He served off and on in the North Carolina senate from 1777 to 1786, being identified with the radicals, who favored a powerful legislature with equal representation for the western counties. He also advocated against former Loyalists, whom he called "imps of hell."

An opponent of the Constitution of 1787, Rutherford attended the first North Carolina ratifying convention in 1788, which rejected the Constitution. A major speculator in western lands, he moved into what became the state of Tennessee in 1792, and after September 1794, when it became a separate territory, was president of the legislative council. He died in Sumner County, Tennessee, on 10 August 1805.

SEE ALSO *Briar Creek, Georgia; Cherokee War of 1776; Ramseur's Mill, North Carolina; Regulators.*

revised by Michael Bellesiles

RUTLEDGE, EDWARD. (1749–1800). Member of Continental Congress and U.S. House of Representative, Signer, governor of South Carolina. Born in Christ Church Parish, South Carolina on 23 November 1749, Rutledge studied law with his elder brother, John Rutledge, entered the Middle Temple in 1767, and was admitted to the English bar in 1772. He returned to Charleston in January 1773 and a few months later represented the printer Thomas Powell in a case which established that the South Carolina Council could not order someone sent to jail. Rutledge served in the first and second South Carolina Provincial Congresses. Elected with brother John to the first and

Second Continental Congresses, the youthful Edward was characterized acidly by John Adams as "a perfect Bob-o-Lincoln—a swallow, a sparrow, . . . jejune, inane and puerile." Adams held the other Rutledge in equal contempt. Taking over leadership of the delegation after the departure of his brother and Gadsden, in 1776 Edward delayed action on the resolution for independence almost a month before finally influencing his delegation to vote for it on 2 July. Although he felt that confederation should have preceded independence, he was afraid of a strong central government. In all this he represented the views of the planter oligarchy of his state.

After accompanying John Adams and Benjamin Franklin to the Peace Conference on Staten Island on 11 Sept. 1776, in November 1776 Rutledge returned to South Carolina, where he was a member of the assembly until 1780 as well as a captain of artillery. After taking part in the action at Beaufort (Port Royal) on 3 February 1779, he became a prisoner when Charleston surrendered on 12 May 1780. Imprisoned at St. Augustine from September 1780 to July 1781, he lived in Philadelphia until most of the South had been liberated by Greene. He returned in time to sit in the Jacksonboro assembly that his brother convened in January 1782.

After the war he prospered in private and public life. He retained his aristocratic outlook while representing Charleston in the House of Representatives from 1782 to 1796 and in the state conventions of 1788 and 1790. He was an influential Federalist, elected to the state senate in 1796 and as governor in 1798. He died in Charleston on 23 January 1800.

SEE ALSO *Peace Conference on Staten Island.*

BIBLIOGRAPHY

Haw, James. *John and Edward Rutledge of South Carolina.* Athens: University of Georgia Press, 1997.

Rutledge, Edward. Papers. South Caroliniana Library, Columbia, South Carolina.

revised by Michael Bellesiles

RUTLEDGE, JOHN. (1739–1800).

Member of the Continental Congress, governor of South Carolina. Born in Charleston, South Carolina, in 1739, Rutledge studied law in Charleston before entering the Middle Temple in 1754, being admitted to the English bar in 1760. Returning to South Carolina, he built a thriving law practice, became a wealthy planter owning some thirty thousand acres and hundreds of slaves, served in the Commons House (1761–1775), attended the Stamp Act Congress in 1765, was a delegate to the Continental Congress (1774–1775), helped draft South Carolina's conservative state constitution of 1776, and became president of the South Carolina General Assembly (1776–1778). Objecting to the new constitution of 1778 as too democratic, Rutledge quit the assembly in March. In the desperate situation presented by the British invasion of the South, Rutledge was elected governor in January 1779, being the first Patriot to hold that post. (His predecessor, Rawlins Lowndes, had been the last to use the title of president of South Carolina.) When General Prevost menaced Charleston on 11–12 May 1779, the new governor favored the proposal by his council that the state should promise the British to remain neutral if Prevost would withdraw. The honor of South Carolina was saved by opposition to this deal from Gadsden, John Laurens, and Moultrie, and Lincoln arrived by forced marches, leading to Prevost's retreat from the state.

When Clinton closed in on Charleston in March 1780, the assembly adjourned after giving Rutledge virtual dictatorial powers. A month before Charleston's surrender, Rutledge slipped out of the doomed city to rally state resources in the interior. Tarleton was trying to capture him when the warning of Colonel Henry Rugeley saved the governor. Rutledge withdrew across the North Carolina border and joined the army of Gates in its move toward Camden. After that disastrous battle, he commissioned Thomas Sumter, Francis Marion, and other militia officers to conduct partisan operations and went to Philadelphia to urge that American regulars be sent to liberate the South.

Returning to his state in August 1781, he tackled the tremendous economic, legal, and military problems left in the wake of Greene's successful campaign. On 20 November he called for election of members of a legislature to meet at Jacksonboro on 8 January 1782, where he oversaw the confiscation of Loyalist estates. His term as governor ended on 29 January, and he returned to the legislature, serving also as a delegate to Congress in 1781–1783. In 1784 he was appointed senior judge on the state chancery court. Rutledge played a prominent role at the Constitutional Convention of 1787, ensuring that slavery was protected by the new frame of government, and was appointed to the first U.S. Supreme Court by Washington. Objecting to the need to ride the circuit of the southern district, Rutledge quit the court in February 1791 to accept appointment as chief justice of the South Carolina Court of Common Pleas. In response to Rutledge's request in June 1795 to succeed John Jay as Supreme Court chief justice, Washington immediately nominated him. At the same time, however, Jay's Treaty was published, and Rutledge killed his chances of Senate confirmation by leading a bitter attack on the treaty. Since the death of his wife, Elizabeth Grimké, in 1792,

Rutledge had showed signs of mental instability. About the time the Senate rejected his nomination in December 1795, he was forced by his derangement to withdraw from public life. He died in Charleston on 18 July 1800.

SEE ALSO *Rugeley, Colonel Henry.*

BIBLIOGRAPHY

Haw, James. *John and Edward Rutledge of South Carolina.* Athens: University of Georgia Press, 1997.

revised by Michael Bellesiles

S

SACKVILLE, GEORGE. (1716–1785).

Later Germain. Soldier and secretary of state for the colonies (1775–1782). Born in London on 26 June 1716, he was known from 1720 as Lord George Sackville and then Lord George Germain from 1770; subsequently, he became Viscount Sackville in February 1782. His father, Lionel Sackville, seventh earl and (from 1720) first duke of Dorset, made lavish use of his patronage and influence to start George on careers in the army and in politics. This influence was not inconsiderable—George I was George Sackville's godfather and George II his father's friend—and like many younger sons of the period, Sackville came to understand very well the need to court great men. His weakness was a tendency to overplay his hand, which, combined with a tendency to deviousness and arrogance, could alienate patrons and allies as easily as his ability and charm could win them.

PRE-REVOLUTIONARY CAREER

He was educated at Westminster School and at Trinity College, Dublin, which was then more academically rigorous than either Oxford or Cambridge. At the age of eighteen, he graduated with a master of arts degree and was at once bought a commission in the Seventh Horse, a regiment on the Irish establishment. In 1736 he accompanied his father, lord lieutenant of Ireland, on a diplomatic mission to Paris. Returning to Dublin in 1737 as aide to the new lord lieutenant, he was promoted to captain in his regiment and appointed to the Privy Council of Ireland. In 1741 he became lieutenant colonel in the Twenty-eighth Foot and also became a member of Parliament for the first time.

By then Britain was officially at war with Spain and, following the Prussian attack on the Hapsburg Empire, unofficially with France. Sackville went to war for the first time with the allied Pragmatic Army, which was intended to keep the enemy out of Hanover (George II's other realm) and the Austrian Netherlands. He is supposed to have distinguished himself near Dettingen on the river Main (in 1743, and on 11 May 1745 he was severely wounded in the chest at Fontenoy. He recovered in time to serve against the Jacobites and, as colonel of the Twentieth Foot, was prominent in the pursuit of the fugitives after Culloden. He was briefly governor of Dover Castle, and his father's influence ensured that he was chosen as member of Parliament for Dover before returning to the Pragmatic Army. In November 1749 he took over command of the Twelfth Dragoons before moving in 1750 to his old regiment, the Seventh Horse. By 1750 he was demonstrating considerable promise in Parliament, and during his father's second term in Ireland (1751–1756) was his principal secretary and secretary at war. Although his combative manner as secretary at war earned widespread disapproval, Germain, promoted to major general in 1755, continued to be a significant military and political figure during the first part of the Seven Years' War.

After taking part in the abortive raid on St. Malo in September 1758, he became second in command of the British contribution to Prince Ferdinand of Brunswick's allied army in Hanover. Soon afterwards, on his superior's death, he succeeded to command of the British contingent. His rise ended when, as commander of the British cavalry at Minden, he refused to obey repeated orders to charge the retreating French army. Sackville argued that

1013

the duke of Brunswick's commands were unclear and impracticable. Others, however, said he was motivated by personal pique and even cowardice. Although he was dismissed from his command, the affair might have come to nothing had not Sackville insisted upon a court-martial to clear his name. Sure of acquittal, he paraded such disdain for the court that on 5 April 1760 he was convicted of disobedience and declared unfit to serve the king in any military capacity. The king at once expelled him from the Privy Council, and he was effectively shut out of office of any kind for fifteen years. Only in the autumn of 1775 did North bring him in as secretary of state for the colonies.

NEW YORK CAMPAIGN

It thus fell to Sackville, now Lord George Germain, to direct the war in America. It may have been a mistake to place army officers under a man who had been so spectacularly disgraced for military misconduct, and still more one who did not get on with Carleton and Howe. But Germain had his virtues. Far from being the lazy bungler of legend, he was an efficient administrator and a perceptive strategist. Even before he took office he was arguing cogently in favor of a descent upon New York, which would make an ideal base from which to cut off New England and begin the recovery of the other provinces. Its capacious harbor would provide a safe haven for warships, transports, and supply vessels while the Hudson Valley would provide a waterway to the interior. The experience of Bunker Hill suggested that any frontal attack on a prepared position, even when manned by inexperienced militia, would be unacceptably costly, and that any breakout from Boston would probably involve a succession of suck attacks. However, an American army driven from New York City would have no strong place to make a stand short of the Delaware or the upper Hudson. Moreover, the middle colonies, where the Loyalists were believed to be stronger than in New England, would throw their weight into the balance once the British Army arrived to rescue them from the rebels. This analysis, though based upon imperfect knowledge, was intelligent and essentially sound. Pursued vigorously, it would have given the British at least a chance of securing victory before France could effectively intervene.

Where Germain, like other ministers, failed was in underestimating the scale of the revolt and therefore the scale of force needed to put it down. New England, and Boston in particular, had long been thought to be the heart of the rebellion. Curiously, this went with an underestimate of Loyalist strength in the middle colonies and an exaggeration in respect of the South. In 1776 the result was an unnecessary dissipation of force, which allowed Washington to survive his defeats and prevented Howe from giving adequate protection to the Tories of New

York and New Jersey. Germain failed to learn the lesson for the campaign of 1777: the Saratoga debacle came about partly because he did not order Howe directly to support. Burgoyne. Yet he was neither lazy nor negligent nor uncommonly lacking in perception: no one in Britain dreamed that Burgoyne would need to be rescued.

A BOLD APPROACH

Germain's political weakness was that he could not carry his colleagues with him without North's support, and North, better at conciliation than decision, was no Pitt. Germain was left to wrangle with Sandwich, who wanted to keep the bulk of the fleet in home waters in anticipation of a Bourbon invasion. There were strong arguments on both sides, but the effect of the dispute was to leave British land forces in America without adequate logistical or naval support. The results were crippling. In 1776 Howe's reinforcements and essential equipment arrived far too late in the season. In 1777 a lack of transports and escorts delayed the attack on Philadelphia as decisively as Howe's excessive caution, and afterwards the naval forces available were unable to quickly open the Delaware.

The moment France entered the war in 1778, the British army in America was in danger. The appearance of a powerful squadron off New York or the Delaware, combined with a land blockade, would cut off essential supplies and rapidly lead to capitulation. The Royal navy could not simultaneously keep a protective force in North American waters, cover the Channel, and meet its commitments elsewhere. Yet Germain remained an advocate of boldness in America. His decision to abandon Philadelphia was justifiable on two grounds. First, Philadelphia was now a strategic liability, with its only supply route via the Delaware constantly under threat. As it was, a French fleet appeared off the Delaware, forcing the troops to escape overland. Second, garrisoning the city and guarding the river tied up forces that could have been better used in offensive operations elsewhere—for example, to exploit the supposed Loyalist strength in the southern colonies and for an attack on French sugar islands. Third, the naval peril would remain the same, whether British strategy was offensive or defensive, and an aggressive policy promised at least a chance of victory. The plan's great weakness, as Sir Henry Clinton never tired of pointing out, was that it further dispersed the available troops and given early and vigorous Franco-American cooperation, should have led rapidly to defeat.

GERMAIN'S PLAN ALMOST SUCCEEDS

Yet, thanks partly to French mistakes, it came very close to success. Savannah was taken and held, Charleston and most of South Carolina fell, and American attempts at reconquest were routed. North Carolina was invaded. By 1781 Washington himself thought that the British might win the war. In the end, Germain's strategy was ruined by Cornwallis's overland march into Virginia (which Germain himself approved), which cut him off from the seaborne support so crucial to British successes. This critical error was followed by the ill fortune of an unprecedented coordination of French and American sea and land forces and capitulation at Yorktown. Even then the significance of Yorktown, where fewer than four thousand troops were lost, was political rather than military. Coming on top of reverses elsewhere, it turned the majority in Parliament against the war and raised demands for a change of ministry.

Germain still wanted to fight on. After all, Clinton's main army was intact and the British still held New York, Charleston, and Savannah. From these bases, amphibious operations could be launched to mobilize Loyalist support around the lower Delaware. It was a workable plan and consistent with his policy since 1778. But now he was completely isolated, even within the cabinet, and by the year's end he was asking the king's leave to resign. He finally left office on 10 February 1782, some weeks before the fall of the North administration.

Germain was neither a minister of genius nor an engaging personality. He could not obtain the consistent support of North and Sandwich, he made serious strategic errors, and he underestimated the popularity and determination of the rebels. Yet he was far from alone in these failings. In addition, he was intelligent, able, and conscientious. While his offensive strategy from 1778 carried with it enormous risks, it also brought the British within sight of victory.

SEE ALSO *North, Sir Frederick; Sandwich, John Montagu, fourth earl of.*

BIBLIOGRAPHY

Brown, Gerald S. *The American Secretary: The Colonial Policy of Lord George Germain, 1775–1778.* Ann Arbor: University of Michigan Press, 1963.

Mackesy, Piers. *The War for America.* London: Longman, 1964.

revised by John Oliphant

SAG HARBOR RAID, NEW YORK.

23–24 May 1777. In retaliation for Tryon's Danbury raid, Colonel R. J. Meigs planned an attack on a British foraging party that had gone from New York City to Sag Harbor, near the eastern end of Long Island. The British force comprised 12 vessels, an armed schooner of 12 guns that carried 40 men, and a 70-man company of the Second Battalion of James De Lancey's brigade. Leaving Guilford, Connecticut, with 170 men of Sherburne's Additional Continental Regiment in 13 whaleboats and escorted by two armed sloops, Meigs moved across Long Island Sound under cover of darkness, landed on Long Island, and surprised the Loyalists before dawn. After killing six, capturing the rest, burning all the vessels except the schooner, and destroying the stores, Meigs withdrew without the loss of a man. He was back at Guilford by noon, having covered almost 100 miles in 18 hours. Congress commended the raiders on 25 July.

SEE ALSO *Meigs, Return Jonathan.*

BIBLIOGRAPHY

Ward, Christopher. *The War of the Revolution.* 2 vols. New York: Macmillan, 1952.

revised by Robert K. Wright Jr.

ST. CLAIR, ARTHUR. (1737–1818).

Continental general. Scotland–Massachusetts–Pennsylvania. Born in Thurso, Scotland, on 23 March 1737, St. Clair gave up his medical education to buy an ensign's commission in the Sixtieth Foot (Royal Americans) on 13 May 1757. He took part in Amherst's capture of Louisburg and Wolfe's attack on Quebec, was promoted to lieutenant on 17 April 1759, resigned on 16 April 1762, and settled in Boston. After his Massachusetts wife inherited fourteen thousand pounds, he moved to the Pennsylvania frontier, where he used this money and his own military service claims to buy some four thousand acres in the Ligonier Valley. This made him the largest resident landowner "beyond the mountains," and he soon attained considerable influence. He was involved in the ugly land disputes between Pennsylvania and Virginia, but the latter province had gained the upper hand and St. Clair, an advocate of Pennsylvania's rights, accomplished little.

The Revolution made that dispute moot. In July 1775 he became colonel of a militia regiment, and in the fall he played a minor role in negotiations with Indians at Fort Pitt. On 3 January 1776 he became colonel of the Second Pennsylvania Battalion, led it north, and took part in the disaster at Trois Rivières in Canada on 8 June. On 9 August he was appointed brigadier general and in November he joined Washington's army. Authorized by the commander in chief to raise the New Jersey militia, he was at Trenton and Princeton. On 19 February 1777 he was promoted to major general and returned to the

Northern Department to succeed Gates as commander on Lake Champlain.

His abandonment of Ticonderoga on 2–5 July 1777 climaxed his career as a field commander. St. Clair used sound military judgment in not risking his command in the defense of this untenable position and showed rare moral courage in ordering the withdrawal. Furthermore, his plans for this difficult operation were excellent, though ruined by incompetent subordinates. A court-martial in 1778 cleared him, but in their search for a scapegoat, many people suspected St. Clair of disloyalty. His foreign birth made this suspicion plausible, and when Arnold's treason in 1780 brought rumors that another high-ranking American officer was involved in dealings with the enemy, St. Clair's name was again mentioned.

The discredited general served Washington as a volunteer aide-de-camp at Brandywine, assisted Sullivan in mounting his expedition against the Indians, was a commissioner to arrange a cartel with the British at Amboy on 9 March 1780, served on the board that investigated André's conduct, and commanded West Point in October 1780. He had a minor part in settling the mutiny of the Pennsylvania Line, helped raise troops for the Yorktown campaign, and joined Washington a few days before Cornwallis surrendered. Soon thereafter he led two thousand regulars south to reinforce Greene, joining him near Charleston on 4 January 1782. On 3 November 1783 he retired from the Continental army.

St. Clair was in Congress from 2 November 1785 to 28 November 1787, and ended as president of that body. He became the first governor of the Northwest Territory, serving in1789–1802. On 4 March 1791 he was named major general and commander of the U.S. Army. Badly defeated by the Miami Indians under Little Turtle on 4 November, he was refused a court of inquiry and on 5 March 1792 resigned his military commission. A congressional investigation cleared him of responsibility for the disaster. Jefferson removed him as governor in 1802 because St. Clair opposed statehood for Ohio. Unable to gain remuneration from Congress for his many financial losses, St. Clair retired to a simple log cabin in Chestnut Ridge, Pennsylvania, where he died in a carriage accident on 31 August 1818.

SEE ALSO *Champe, John; Ticonderoga, New York, British Capture of; Trenton, New Jersey; Trois Rivières.*

BIBLIOGRAPHY

Cayton, Andrew R. L. *Frontier Republic: Ideology and Politics in the Ohio Country, 1780–1825.* Kent, Ohio: Kent State University Press, 1986.

Smith, William Henry, ed. *The St. Clair Papers: The Life and Public Services of Arthur St. Clair.* 2 vols. Cincinnati: R. Clarke, 1882.

Wilson, Frazer Ells. *Arthur St. Clair, Rugged Ruler of the Old Northwest: An Epic of the American Frontier.* Richmond, Va.: Garrett and Massie, 1944.

revised by Michael Bellesiles

ST. EUSTATIUS.

Taken by the Dutch in 1632, this island of about nine square miles in size, located eight miles northwest of St. Kitts, became one of the leading centers of West Indies trade in the eighteenth century. It came to be called the "Golden Rock" as Dutch merchants took advantage of its neutral status to make money selling to all sides during wartime. At the beginning of the Revolution it was a center of contraband trade between Europe and America, with even British merchants being involved. On 16 November 1776, Governor Johannes de Graaf ordered Fort Oranje to fire what is regarded as the first official salute of the American flag as the Continental navy ship *Andrew Doria* entered the harbor. De Graaf was recalled as a result of British diplomatic pressure, but although guilty of encouraging trade with the rebels, he was exonerated and sent back to his post. When Admiral George Rodney learned that Britain had declared war on the Netherlands, he moved almost immediately against the Dutch island. He and General John Vaughan took the Dutch, who were still unaware of the declaration of war, by surprise, capturing St. Eustatius on 3 February 1781. However, because Rodney was busy plundering St. Eustatius, he failed to intercept De Grasse's fleet on its way to the Chesapeake, where it helped trap Cornwallis's army. The French captured first Rodney's prize fleet and then St. Eustatius on 26 November 1781.

SEE ALSO *Rodney, George Bridges.*

BIBLIOGRAPHY

O'Shaughnessy, Andrew Jackson. *An Empire Divided: The American Revolution and the British Caribbean.* Philadelphia: University of Pennsylvania Press, 2000.

revised by Michael Bellesiles

ST. FRANCIS INDIANS SEE *Abenaki.*

ST. JOHN (ACADIA).

Quebec. This town, later the largest city in New Brunswick, Canada, is likely to be confused with St. Johns on the Richelieu River, later called St. Jean, in Quebec Province, Canada. The St. John in New Brunswick was a center of Loyalist settlement after the Revolution. St. John's (written with an apostrophe) is in Newfoundland.

revised by Michael Bellesiles

ST. JOHN'S, CANADA.

ST. JOHN'S, CANADA. (now called St-Jean), 14–18 May 1775. As part of the operation against Ticonderoga on 10 May, the Americans had sent a detachment to capture Skenesboro. On the afternoon of 14 May, this party reported to Benedict Arnold with a captured schooner, and Arnold immediately headed for St. John's with fifty of his men in the vessel now called *Liberty*. Ethan Allen followed in bateaux with about sixty men. Early on 17 May Arnold surprised the fifteen-man British garrison; captured the fifty-five-ton sloop *George* (no guns mounted), which in American hands would become the *Enterprise*; destroyed five bateaux; evacuated the prisoners, some stores, and the prizes; and headed back for Ticonderoga. About fifteen miles away he encountered Allen, who—despite Arnold's advice—decided to occupy and hold St. John's. Allen landed just before dark and made dispositions to ambush the British relief column advancing from Chambly, twelve miles away. But then he wisely reconsidered and withdrew his undisciplined, tired, and hungry men. Just before dawn the pursuit caught Allen's rear guard. Arnold had no casualties, and Allen lost three prisoners.

USAGE NOTE. This place is variously identified in the primary sources as Saint John, Saint John's, or St. Johns. The original French settlers called it St. Jean-Iberville. The correct modern usage is St-Jean. In 1775 it consisted of a fort and a small settlement nearby, both with the same name. See next article for strategic importance of this place and the sources.

SEE ALSO *Ticonderoga, New York, American Capture of.*

revised by Robert K. Wright Jr.

ST. JOHN'S, CANADA.

ST. JOHN'S, CANADA. 5 September– 2 November 1775. Twenty miles southeast of Montreal and near the head of navigation from Lake Champlain down the Richelieu River to the St. Lawrence, St. John's occupied a critical position along a historic invasion route. Military works established there by the Marquis de Montcalm in 1758 were enlarged and strengthened by Guy Carleton, governor of Quebec and commander of British forces in Canada, after the fall of Ticonderoga. Carleton considered it to be critical to the defense of Canada. In addition to the fortifications and barracks complex, St. John's also had a small shipyard and a modest civilian settlement. When the Americans approached on 5 September, Major Charles Preston was in command with about two hundred regulars from the Twenty-sixth Foot and small Indian contingent.

On 17 August, General Philip Schuyler left Brigadier General Richard Montgomery in temporary command on Lake Champlain and went to Albany for a meeting. While Schuyler was gone, Montgomery learned that the British were rushing to complete two small vessels under construction at St. John's and realized that naval control of Lake Champlain could be lost. The crisis did not allow him to get Schuyler's approval to cross the border. On 28 August he set out for Ile aux Noix, a swampy island in the Richelieu, twenty miles south of St. John's; here he intended to set up defenses that could prevent the vessels from entering the lake.

Montgomery's command comprised about 1,200 men and a few cannon. They moved north in a small fleet of two sailing vessels (the sloop *Enterprise* and schooner *Liberty*), and an assortment of bateaux and canoes. Troops involved were most of Waterbury's Fifth Connecticut Regiment and half of the First New York Regiment under Lieutenant Colonel Rudolphus Ritzema. The latter included Captain Gershom Mott's infantrymen, who had been temporarily converted to an artillery section.

Schuyler caught up with his aggressive subordinate the morning of 4 September, approved his action, and by night the invaders were at Ile aux Noix. Although the expected Canadian allies did not appear to reinforce them, neither did the majority of the French-speaking militia turn out for Carleton. Schuyler stripped his men of baggage and pushed toward St. John's. On 6 September they landed a mile and a half away and were advancing through the swamps to attack when a flank patrol ran into an Indian ambush. The resulting skirmish in dense underbrush ended when the Indians withdrew, but the Americans lost sixteen men and did not pursue. That night a man who was apparently sympathetic to the American cause visited Schuyler's entrenched camp and convinced him that St. John's was too strongly held for him to capture, so the next day he fell back to Ile aux Noix.

Additional Connecticut and New York troops arrived, swelling Schuyler's strength to about 1,700 men (more than twice the entire strength of British regulars in Canada). Although his health was failing, Schuyler sent out aggressive combat patrols to gather better intelligence and prepared for a second attack. Montgomery and Ritzema landed at the previous camp site after dark on 10 September. Montgomery remained with a party at the site while Ritzema and 500 New Yorkers started forward with the mission of investing St. John's from the north. Within fifteen minutes the advance turned into a fiasco. In the darkness of the heavy woods, the skittish

New Yorkers thought they were ambushed and stampeded back to the boats. Montgomery rallied them and tried again. The second movement ground to a halt when Preston's cannon fired a few rounds and the vanguard had a small skirmish. About 3 A.M. the Americans withdrew to the beachhead. A third try the next morning ended when the men were panicked by a report that the *Royal Savage*, one of the new ships, was near their boats and ready to go into action, and Montgomery had to return to his base.

Back on Ile aux Noix, Montgomery assumed command on 16 September when Schuyler was invalided to the rear. Despite a sick list of 600, and all the makings of a mutiny among his demoralized, ill-disciplined troops, Montgomery was able to resume the offensive. He had received additional reinforcements: 170 Green Mountain Boys under Seth Warner, 100 New Hampshire Rangers under Timothy Bedel, and an Independent Company of Volunteers that included some Dartmouth students. Others were on the way.

THE BRITISH DEFENSE

Rather than pull in his outposts and concentrate his meager forces around Montreal and Quebec, General Carleton adopted a "forward strategy": he reinforced St. John's to a total of 500 regulars from the Seventh ("Royal Fusiliers") and Twenty-sixth Foot. Another 90 officers and men of the Seventh Foot were posted at nearby Chambly. Preston was further reinforced by 225 men scraped together from all the sources at Carleton's disposal: an ensign and 12 sailors from the Gaspée, 100 Canadian militia, and 70 of Allan MacLean's newly recruited Royal Highland Emigrants.

On 17 September Montgomery finally made it to St. John's and began siege operations. The Americans contended with illness, cold weather, swampy ground, and a shortage of supplies as they struggled to construct their lines and batteries. Although an effective artillery fire could be delivered into the British camp, the raw Americans lacked the training and discipline to take the place by assault.

Schuyler at Ticonderoga kept pushing food forward, which boosted morale considerably. With the surrender of Chambly on 18 October, the Americans obtained supplies that permitted successful conclusion of the siege. The arrival of Captain John Lamb's artillery company (along with more Connecticut infantry) soon after enabled the attackers to utilize that materiel effectively. Carleton's attempt to rescue Preston was stopped at Longueuil on 30 October, when American forces kept the British from crossing the St. Lawrence; another detachment kept MacLean from crossing farther up the river. After having delayed the American invasion almost two months, and with only three days' supplies left, Preston surrendered St. John's on 2 November 1775. Among the prisoners was Lieutenant John André. During the actual forty-six-day siege, few men were killed on either side.

SIGNIFICANCE

Although Carleton lost most of his regular troops at Chambly and St. John's, the time spent eliminating them bought him time to organize resistance at Quebec. Forcing the Americans to fight a winter campaign is generally considered to have saved Canada for the British.

SEE ALSO *André, John; Canada Invasion; Chambly, Canada; Green Mountain Boys; Longueuil, Canada.*

BIBLIOGRAPHY

Huot, Lucien. *Siege of the Fort of St. Johns in 1775.* St. Johns, 1889.

Naval Documents of the American Revolution. Edited by William B. Clark. Vol. 2. Washington, D.C.: U.S. Government Printing Office, 1964–1996.

revised by Robert K. Wright Jr.

ST. KITTS, CAPTURED BY THE FRENCH.

11 January–12 February 1782. The fall of St. Kitts represented the nadir of the Revolutionary War for the British. The rumor of the loss, together with that of Minorca, circulated in England in the last weeks of the government of Lord North and encouraged opposition claims that the ministry was not only losing the former colonies of North America but also destroying the rest of the British Empire.

After the Battle of Yorktown, French Admiral De Grasse ignored the requests of George Washington to remain in America and sailed for the Caribbean on 4 November 1781, arriving in Martinique on 26 November. After two failed attempts to attack Barbados in December, he landed unopposed in St. Kitts on 11 January 1782 with eight thousand troops commanded by the governor of Martinique, the marquis de Bouillé, who immediately captured the capital city of Basseterre. They forced the twelve thousand British military regulars and militia to retreat to a defensive position nine miles away in the formidable fortifications at Brimstone Hill, against which the French began siege operations.

On 24 January, almost two weeks after the start of the siege, Admiral Hood arrived with a relief expedition of twenty-two ships from Barbados against the superior fleet of twenty-nine ships under De Grasse. In a brilliant maneuver, Hood managed to lure the French fleet from its moorings and to displace it with his own fleet, but apart from an exchange of messages on the first day, he was unable to communicate with the besieged garrison despite landing troops under General Robert Prescott, who engaged in an intense action that left both sides claiming victory. On 12 February, after almost five weeks of resistance, the sick and exhausted garrison on Brimstone Hill, depleted of ammunition and provisions, with only five hundred men left in defense, finally submitted to the French, giving them full possession of St. Kitts and the neighboring island of Nevis. On 20 February, Montserrat also capitulated to the French.

Hood blamed the loss of St. Kitts upon the treachery of the colonists, who he claimed had failed to remove ammunition near the fortifications that were used by the French, who had lost their own cannon at sea. In fact, the fault was due more to the negligence of the local army commanders and to their long-running dispute with the governor of the island. The defense of Brimstone Hill contributed to the delay of De Grasse's plan to combine with the Spanish fleet in an attack on Jamaica. It also allowed Admiral Sir George Rodney crucial time to arrive with reinforcements from England to link with Hood, which paved the way for the British victory over the French at the Battle of the Saintes.

SEE ALSO *Naval Operations, British; Naval Operations, French; West Indies in the Revolution.*

BIBLIOGRAPHY

O'Shaughnessy, Andrew Jackson. *An Empire Divided: The American Revolution and the British Caribbean.* Philadelphia: University of Pennsylvania Press, 2000.

Watts, Arthur P., ed. *Nevis and St. Christopher, 1782–1784: Unpublished Documents.* Paris: Les Presses Universitaires de France, 1925.

revised by Andrew Jackson O'Shaughnessy

ST. LEGER, BARRY.

(1737–1789). British officer. St. Leger entered the army as an ensign of the Twenty-eighth Foot on 27 April 1756, becoming known during the Seven Years' War as a good leader in frontier warfare. His experience in this war included service under Abercromby in 1757, the siege of Louisburg in 1758, and the capture of Quebec by Wolfe in 1759. In July 1760 he became brigadier major, in which capacity he participated in the campaign that captured Montreal. On 16 August 1762 he was promoted to major of the Ninety-fifth Foot.

As a lieutenant colonel he led St. Leger's expedition (June–8 September 1777), the operation for which he is generally remembered. During the remainder of the Revolution he commanded a body of rangers in operations based out of Montreal, being promoted to colonel in 1780. In 1781 he led two unsuccessful expeditions, one aimed at capturing Philip Schuyler and another to meet commissioners from Vermont at Ticonderoga to bring that region back under crown control. He served in Canada until 1785, when his name disappeared from the Army List.

SEE ALSO *St. Leger's Expedition.*

revised by Michael Bellesiles

ST. LEGER'S EXPEDITION.

June–September 1777. General John Burgoyne's "Thoughts for Conducting the War on the Side of Canada" received approval from the British government and formed the basis for his operations in 1777. A part of that plan involved a small secondary attack from Canada advancing through western New York by way of the grain-producing Mohawk Valley. Burgoyne envisioned this column joining his own main force at Albany. Although this plan had some military value as a diversion, the significant advantages were political. If, as expected, the column rolled over patriot opposition, it would encourage both the Loyalists and the Indian tribes to actively support Burgoyne.

Energetic Lieutenant Colonel Barry St. Leger of the Thirty-fourth Foot left Montreal on 23 June 1777, reached Oswego on 25 July, and started his offensive the next day. (At this time Burgoyne was almost to the Hudson.) St. Leger's column, about 2,000 strong, consisted of an unusually mixed force. Half were Indians, and a third were Loyalist and Canadian auxiliaries. Only 340 could be called regulars, small detachments of British Eighth and Thirty-fourth Foot and part of the Hesse-Hanau Jäger Corps. The latter, a mix of true jägers and light infantry (chasseurs), comprised the advance elements of a brand-new unit that rushed into action as soon as they arrived from Europe and were probably still trying to recover from their voyage. The best Loyalist troops came from Sir John Johnson's Royal Regiment of New York, also known as the Royal Greens; the others, led by John Butler, were of value in working alongside the Indians but not in heavy fighting. The Canadian militia acted only as a labor and transportation element. Artillery support comprised forty men with two six-pounders, two three-pounders, and four small mortars. Larger guns capable of knocking down fortifications could not make it through the wilderness, and transportation concerns drastically limited artillery ammunition.

St. Leger advanced at the creditable rate of ten miles a day through a wilderness worse than the one Burgoyne faced. St. Leger's vanguard reached Fort Stanwix on 2 August, followed on the next day by the main body. Just before the British approached from the west, a hundred Massachusetts Continentals from James Wesson's Regiment escorting a supply convoy entered the fort from the east, swelling the garrison to about eight hundred. Burgoyne based his "Thoughts" on outdated intelligence that seriously underestimated both the probable opposing force and the condition of the old works. St. Leger had enough men to invest the fort but not to storm it. He staged a review in sight of the garrison, trying to bluff them into surrendering. When that failed he went through the motions of a formal siege, hoping for some type of lucky break.

THE AMERICAN DEFENSES

Strategic Fort Stanwix had been erected at the Oneida Carrying Place (modern Rome, New York) during the French and Indian War. Americans reoccupied it and had seriously started refurbishing it in 1776, renaming it Fort Schuyler (the new name has largely been ignored by historians). Colonel Peter Gansevoort's Third New York Regiment took over as the garrison in April 1777. The regiment had a strong cadre of experienced veterans and an exceptionally capable second in command, Lieutenant Colonel Marinus Willett. When the siege began, the garrison had the Third New York, about half of Wesson's, and some artillerymen. Terrain favored the defense, and the fort constituted a formidable obstacle for anything short of heavy artillery. The large rectangular earthwork with bastions at the corners had seventeen-foot-high walls and was surrounded by a fourteen-foot-high stockade and a forty-foot-wide dry ditch. St. Leger threw a loose cordon of Indians around the fort but put the bulk of his men into three main camps that formed a triangle about a mile on each side. Regulars occupied the largest camp, more than a quarter of a mile northeast of the fort on slightly higher ground. Most of the Loyalists and Indians occupied the Lower Landing on the west bank of the Mohawk and half a mile from the fort. The rest of the Loyalists set up the smallest camp on Wood Creek, also half a mile from the fort.

Indian marksmen and jägers sniped at the fort on 4 and 5 August while large work parties tried to clear Wood Creek and cut sixteen miles of supply track through the woods. St. Leger kept about 250 regulars in camp as a reaction force. In the evening of 5 August, a message from Molly Brant gave word that an American relief column was ten miles away. Although his forces were already dispersed, the British commander accepted the danger of splitting them further.

The Battle at Oriskany, 6 August, ended in a tactical draw, but St. Leger's troops did turn back Nicholas Herkimer's relief column, leading the invaders to believe that they had won a victory. In the long run, however, it led to St. Leger's failure. The Indians had borne the brunt of the battle and suffered heavier losses than usual. Then they returned to find that their camp had been smashed during their absence by a sortie. Messengers sent ahead of Herkimer's relief column informed Gansevoort of Herkimer's coming and asked him to make a diversion to cover the final approach march. After waiting for the end of the same shower that caused the lull at Oriskany, Willett led 250 men with one field piece out the sallyport. He easily scattered the few enemies in his way, methodically ransacked the camps, and returned to the fort before St. Leger could intervene, all without the loss of a single man.

ARNOLD RELIEVES STANWIX

When news of Oriskany reached General Philip Schuyler at Stillwater, Burgoyne was only twenty-four miles away at Fort Edward with about seven thousand men. Schuyler knew that his policy of obstructing the roads and streams ensured that Burgoyne could not cover the distance at a sufficient pace to prevent the Americans from detaching enough troops to raise the siege. But he did have significant political problems. A faction in Congress already sought to strip his command because of the loss of Ticonderoga. Now New Englanders, including some of his own officers, raised the charge that in order to protect his fellow New Yorkers Schuyler would draw off the troops protecting the New England frontier. Schuyler accepted the risk to his reputation and started organizing the relief of Fort Stanwix. Although the column would normally have needed only a brigadier general as commander, Major General Benedict Arnold exercised his seniority to claim the post.

On the evening of the Oriskany ambush of Herkimer's relief troops, St. Leger started trying to persuade Gansevoort to surrender because the relief force had been thrown back. He sent him a letter from two American prisoners, Colonel Peter Bellinger and Major John Frey, recommending that the garrison give up. Whether or not they wrote it under duress is a point of debate among historians. Either way, real negotiations began the next day when St. Leger called for a cease-fire and the Americans allowed three officers, including John Butler, suitably blindfolded, to enter and meet with the senior officers of the garrison. The British informed Gansevoort of the terms: the Indians had reluctantly agreed to spare American lives and personal property if the garrison would surrender; otherwise, St. Leger would probably be powerless to prevent the savages from massacring the inhabitants of the valley. This summons was a deliberate attempt to conjure up memories of the Fort William Henry Massacre during the French and Indian War. The reference had exactly the opposite effect, infuriating the American officers.

Gansevoort agreed to St. Leger's proposal for a three-day armistice. Willett and an experienced frontiersman from the Third New York (Lieutenant Levi Stockwell) slipped away at 10 P.M. on 10 August, worked their way through the lines via a cedar swamp, and reached the American outpost at Fort Dayton where he learned from Colonel Wesson that Schuyler had in fact already ordered a relief column. Willett met Arnold at Albany and accompanied the column back to Fort Dayton, reaching it on 21 August. The remnants of the Tryon County militia brigade (smashed at Oriskany) mobilized a hundred men to support the Continentals, and on 23 August Arnold started on the final leg of the journey to Stanwix. After covering ten miles, he received a message from Gansevoort reporting that St. Leger was retreating.

HON YOST'S RUSE

Lieutenant Colonel John Brooks, who later became governor of Massachusetts, may have suggested the stratagem that Arnold readily approved: The Americans held an individual named Hon Yost Schuyler, who had been sentenced to death for participating in a Loyalist plot. This man, apparently retarded, had lived among the Iroquois and exercised influence on them because of his mental condition. Arnold offered to reprieve him (while holding a brother as hostage) if Hon Yost went ahead of the column and told St. Leger's Indians exaggerated stories of the relief column's strength. The stratagem worked.

Arnold reached Fort Stanwix the evening of 23 August. A detachment shadowed St. Leger back to Lake Oneida, and scouts watched the last enemy boats pull out of range. Arnold left reinforcements with Gansevoort and led the main part of his column, about twelve hundred men, back to Albany. They rejoined the northern army during the first week of September as it moved to the battlefield near Saratoga.

Although historians generally accept the story of Hon Yost's trick, it was probably not decisive in St. Leger's decision to fall back. He had no hope of overpowering the fort, only of playing for time until the Americans gave up. When Gansevoort did not crumble, the game was over. The entire operation had little military impact on either the campaign or the outcome of the war, but it had enormous significance for the Mohawk Valley: it polarized the inhabitants (Indians as well as the white settlers) and set the stage for years of bitter frontier warfare, in a sense starting the process of breaking the unity and power of the Iroquois Confederacy.

SEE ALSO *Brant, Molly; Burgoyne's Offensive; Fort Stanwix, New York; Oriskany, New York; Schuyler, Hon Yost; Tryon County, New York.*

BIBLIOGRAPHY

Luzader, John, Louis Torres, and Orville Carroll. *Fort Stanwix.* National Park Service. Washington, D.C.: U.S. Government Printing Office, 1976.

Nickerson, Hoffman. *The Turning Point of the Revolution, or, Burgoyne in America.* 1928. Port Washington, N.Y.: Kennikat Press, 1967.

Scott, John A. *Fort Stanwix (Fort Schuyler) and Oriskany.* Rome, N.Y.: Rome Sentinel Company, 1927.

Stone, William Leete. *The Campaign of Lieutenant General John Burgoyne, and the Expedition of Lieutenant Colonel Barry St. Leger.* New York: Da Capo Press, 1970.

Venable, Robert. "Tryon County." Ph.D. dissertation, Vanderbilt University, 1967.

Willett, William M. *A Narrative of the Military Actions of Colonel Marinus Willett.* 1831. New York: New York Times, 1969.

revised by Robert K. Wright Jr.

ST. LOUIS, MISSOURI. 25 May 1780.

A British expedition sent out by Lieutenant Governor Patrick Sinclair from Michilimackinac was repulsed by Captain Don Fernando de Leyba, Spanish commandant of San Luis de Ylinueses (modern St. Louis, Missouri). Sinclair had hoped to gain significant control over the Indian trade on the Upper Mississippi River by pushing the Spanish and Americans out of the Illinois region. The raiders amounted to as many as 1,000 Indians and a handful of British under the leadership of Emanuel Hesse, but they were not prepared to encounter resistance. Leyba's 29 regulars and about 280 French-speaking militia refused to be intimidated, and Hesse withdrew in part because he feared being hit in the rear by Americans from Cahokia. A companion British force from Detroit had greater success in June in capturing Riddle's and Martin's Stations in Kentucky. A retaliatory Spanish counteroffensive took Fort Saint Joseph on 12 February 1781.

SEE ALSO *Fort Saint Joseph, Michigan.*

BIBLIOGRAPHY

Kinnaird, Lawrence. "The Western Fringe of Revolution." *Western Historical Quarterly* 7 (July 1976): 253–270.

McDermott, John F. "The Battle of St. Louis, 25 May 1780." *Missouri Historical Society Bulletin* 36 (April 1980): 131–151.

revised by Robert K. Wright Jr.

ST. LUC DE LA CORNE, PIERRE (OR LOUIS).

French Canadian soldier. Known by many variations of this name, St. Luc was a Quebecois who played a key role in French and Indian military operations during the Seven Years' War. Present for the siege and slaughter at Fort William Henry in 1757, he was wounded at the Rapids, Lake Ontario, in 1759 while serving as a commander of French colonial troops. He was again wounded when General James Wolfe took Quebec that same year.

When Canada passed into British hands, St. Luc started a long and effective career in organizing and leading Indian auxiliaries, though it is unclear if he was always loyal to the British. There is some evidence that during Pontiac's War (1763–1766) St. Luc attempted to persuade the Indians along the St. Lawrence to join in the uprising against the British. At the start of the Revolution St. Luc worked to unite the Iroquois Confederation with Abenakis and Caughnawagas against the colonists, with mixed success. During the siege of Saint Johns by General Robert Montgomery from September through November 1775, St. Luc sent over some Caughnawagas to propose an "accommodation." Montgomery distrusted St. Luc, whom he called "cunning as the devil," but he sent "a New Englander (John Brown) to negotiate with him," Montgomery finding New Englanders to be equally cunning. The conference between the "devil" and the "New Englander" came to nothing, however.

St. Luc and General Sir Guy Carleton were repulsed at Longueuil on 30 Oct. 1775 when they attempted to relieve the installation at Saint Johns. Charles Michel de Langlade and St. Luc led the Indians during General John Burgoyne's offensive. St. Luc is said to have advised the British commander not to punish the Native American charged with killing and scalping a young woman named Jane McCrea, an event that galvanized support for the American cause against the British. In the raid on Bennington, Vermont, the Indians were led by St. Luc and the Canadians by his son-in-law, Charles de Lanaudière.

SEE ALSO *Abenaki; Bennington Raid; Brown, John; Caughnawaga; McCrea Atrocity.*

revised by Michael Bellesiles

ST. LUCIA, CAPTURED BY THE BRITISH.

12–28 December 1778. Following the declaration of war by France in 1778, Britain briefly subordinated military activities in North America for objectives in the Caribbean. Although almost paralyzed by divisions about how best to respond to the new threat, the cabinet agreed upon a plan for the conquest of St. Lucia on 14 March. With its view of Martinique's Fort Royal Harbor, it was strategically important to the British as the main gateway to French Martinique, the base of the French navy in the Americas. It possessed a fine harbor at Gros Islet Bay that was more spacious than the narrow anchorage at English Harbour in Antigua.

The plans were carried out in the utmost secrecy. Lord George Germain directed Sir Henry Clinton to send five thousand troops and most the ships of the line in America to participate in the conquest of St. Lucia. Rear Admiral Barrington, commanding the naval squadron in the Leeward Islands, was ordered to wait at Barbados to be joined by an expeditionary force, with the result that he was unable to sail to the defense of Dominica, which fell to the French on 7 September. The arrival of the troop convoys was long delayed owing to Clinton's need to evacuate Philadelphia and the delay of naval reinforcements from England, commanded by Byron, due to bad weather. The expedition under Major General James Grant did not leave New York until 4 November. It was fortunate not to have suffered capture by the French, since it sailed on a parallel course with the fleet of Admiral D'Estaing, who simultaneously left Boston for Martinique.

Grant, together with Admiral William Hotham commanding the troop transports, arrived in Barbados on 10 December. They landed at St. Lucia on 12 December and, with the arrival of the remaining troops, conquered the island on the 14th, only hours before the arrival of Admiral D'Estaing with a superior fleet and 9,000 troops from Martinique. Finding the British in possession of the island, D'Estaing was unable to dislodge Barrington's squadron at Cul de Sac. On the16th he landed his troops and attempted to storm the British lines at La Vigie in order to open the harbor to his fleet. His two attempts were successfully repulsed, with—after three hours of intense action—1,300 wounded and 400 dead, compared to 158 British wounded and 13 killed. After almost ten days of inaction, D'Estaing embarked his troops and on the 29th finally quit the island for Martinique.

The St. Lucia campaign seriously compromised the British war for America. The British withdrew from Philadelphia primarily to free five thousand troops for the conquest, despite the warning of Sir Henry Clinton that the loss of the troops, together with redeployments to Florida and Canada, might force him to abandon his headquarters in New York for Halifax. By forcing the abandonment of Philadelphia, the campaign also undermined the negotiating strength of the Carlisle Peace Commission.

SEE ALSO *Naval Operations, British; Naval Operations, French; West Indies in the Revolution.*

BIBLIOGRAPHY

O'Shaughnessy, Andrew Jackson. *An Empire Divided. The American Revolution and the British Caribbean.* Philadelphia: University of Pennsylvania Press, 2000.

Robson, Eric. *The American Revolution in Its Political and Military Aspects, 1763–1783.* New York: Norton, 1966.

revised by Andrew Jackson O'Shaughnessy

SAINT-SIMON, CLAUDE HENRI DE ROUVROY, COMTE DE. (1760–1825).

French officer, social philosopher. He entered the French army in 1775 as a second lieutenant, was promoted to captain in the cavalry of the Touraine Regiment on 3 June 1779, and transferred to the infantry of that regiment on 14 November 1779. His regiment sailed from Brest for Saint Domingue in the autumn of 1779. He participated in attacks on Barbados during April and May 1780 and was transferred later to the Spanish service in the Caribbean. He received permission from Governor Lillancourt of Saint-Domingue to join Grasse's 1781 force sailing for America. At the siege of Yorktown he commanded the regimental gunners. He left Virginia with Grasse's force on 4 November. His siegecraft skills led to another victory in the capture of Brimstone Hill, Saint Kitts, in February 1782. On 12 April 1782 he was captured in the action off Saints Passage and taken to Jamaica. In 1782 he was made a *mestre de camp en second* in the Aquitaine Regiment on 1 January 1784 and colonel attached to the cavalry in 1788. In 1790 he was made a chevalier in the Order of Saint Louis.

He played no important part in the French Revolution but was imprisoned during the Terror. To finance his project of reorganizing society he had made a small fortune in land speculation during the French Revolution, but he lost it and spent most of his remaining years in poverty. Shortly before his death he published his *New Christianity* (1825), a seminal work in French socialism. He summed up the importance of his American experience to his later life this way: "It was in America, while fighting in the cause of industrial liberty, that I conceived the first desire to see this plant from another world come to flower in my own country."

SEE ALSO *West Indies in the Revolution.*

BIBLIOGRAPHY

Larabee, Harold A. "Henri de Saint-Simon at Yorktown: A French Prophet of Modern Industrialism in America." *Franco-American Review* 2 (1937): 96–109.

Leroy, Maxime. *La Vie véritable du comte Henri de Saint-Simon (1760–1825).* Paris: B. Grasset, 1925.

Manuel, Frank. *The New World of Henri Saint-Simon.* Cambridge, Mass.: Harvard University Press, 1956.

revised by Robert Rhodes Crout

SAINT-SIMON MONTBLÉRU, CLAUDE-ANNE DE ROUVRAY, MARQUIS DE. (1743–1819).

French general. Often confused with his brother, Claude de Rouvroy, baron de Saint-Simon (1752–1811), and his cousin, Claude-Henri de Rouvray, comte de Saint-Simon (1760–1825), he was commander of the French troops that reached Yorktown with Admiral Grasse. The 3,470 man division served under Lafayette.

SEE ALSO *Yorktown Campaign; Yorktown, Siege of.*

BIBLIOGRAPHY

Contenson, Ludovic de. "La Capitulation d'Yorktown et le Comte de Grasse." *Revue d'Histoire Diplomatique* 42 (1928): 378–399, and "Deux Documents sur la Guerre d'Amérique," and ibid. 44 (1930): 20–24.

Lafayette, Gilbert du Motier de. *Lafayette in the Age of the American Revolution: Selected Letters and Documents, 1776–1790.* Edited by Stanley J. Idzerda et al. 5 vols. to date. Ithaca, N.Y.: Cornell University Press, 1977–.

Larabee, Harold A. "A Neglected French Collaborator in the Victory of Yorktown: Claude-Anne, Marquis de Saint-Simon (1740–1819)." Société des Américainistes de Paris, *Journal,* new series, 35 (1925): 46–63.

Rice, Howard C., Jr., and Anne S. K. Brown, eds. and trans. *The American Campaigns of Rochambeau's Army: 1780, 1781, 1782, 1780.* 2 vols. Princeton, N.J.: Princeton University Press, 1972.

revised by Robert Rhodes Crout

SALEM, MASSACHUSETTS.

26 February 1775. On orders from Major General Thomas Gage, the British commander in chief in North America, Colonel Alexander Leslie sailed with his Sixty-fourth Regiment of Foot from Castle William (in Boston Harbor) at midnight on 25 February 1775 to destroy an ordnance depot reported to be at Salem. The raiders dropped anchor about twelve hours later in Marblehead Bay, and at about 2 P.M. they started the five-mile march to Salem. Major John Pedrick, an American whom Leslie knew and believed to be loyal, managed to pass through the 240-man column of redcoats on horseback and race ahead to alert the citizens of Salem, who were attending church. Colonel Timothy Pickering, the local militia commander, sent forty minutemen to Captain Robert Foster's forge near the North River Bridge to remove nineteen brass cannon that were there to be fitted with carriages. When the regulars arrived, the cannon had been removed, the draw of the bridge leading to the forge had been opened, and a large crowd had joined the militia on the opposite bank.

Some redcoats barely failed to capture the last available boat in the area, but Joseph Wicher smashed in its bottom and then, in a grandstand gesture, bared his breast—literally—to the enemy. A British soldier obliged him with a bayonet thrust that inflicted a slight but bloody wound. When the British threatened to fire, the Loyalist minister Thomas Barnard and Captain John Felt countered with a face-saving offer to let them cross unmolested if they would then withdraw peacefully. Leslie accepted, marched his troops some 30 rods (165 yards) to the agreed limiting point, faced about, and headed back to Marblehead. Despite its comic-opera nature, this affair came close to setting off the "shot heard round the world"; a company of Danvers militia arrived just as the British were leaving, and other armed citizens were gathering. Salem can claim the distinction of seeing the first shedding of American blood; it also generated a Barbara Fritchie–type heroine in Sarah Tarrant, who after taunting the redcoats from an open window and being threatened by one of them, is alleged to have said, "Fire if you have the courage, but I doubt it" (Commager and Morris, eds., p. 65). Leslie is said to have retreated to the tune of *The World Turned Upside Down*.

SEE ALSO *Leslie, Alexander; World Turned Upside Down*.

BIBLIOGRAPHY

Barnes, Eric W. "All the King's Horses . . . and All the King's Men." *American Heritage*, October 1960, 56–59, 86–87.

Commager, Henry S., and Richard B. Morris, eds. *The Spirit of 'Seventy-Six: The Story of the American Revolution As Told by Participants*. Bicentennial ed. New York: Harper and Row, 1975.

revised by Harold E. Selesky

SALEM, OHIO TERRITORY SEE *Gnadenhutten Massacre, Ohio*.

SALLY PORT.
A sally or sortie is a going forth, particularly by besieged against besiegers. A sally port is an opening in a fortification to permit this operation.

Mark M. Boatner

SALOMON, HAYM.
(c. 1740–1785). Patriot financier. Born to Jewish parents in Poland around 1740, Salomon had settled in New York City by 1775. After serving briefly as a sutler provisioning the American forces around Lake Champlain, he returned to New York City just before the British captured the it and decided to stay on under the occupation. Briefly imprisoned in the provost's jail on suspicion of being an American agent, he was released under the supervision of General Leopold Heister, commander of the German troops in the city. Heister employed Salomon, who spoke German and several other languages, in his commissary department. Salomon took advantage of the situation to improve his own economic standing even while endangering himself by encouraging German troops to defect to the Patriot side and providing money to American and French prisoners. Discovered in August 1778, he fled the city just ahead of arrest by the British and made for Philadelphia. Congress ignored his petition for help and Salomon, though destitute, set himself up as a financier, where his language skills proved useful as he became the primary dealer in foreign bills of exchange. In June 1781 Robert Morris, the superintendent of finance for the United States, turned to Salomon to handle Congress's foreign transactions, most particularly the sale of U.S. notes. As the economy of the nation worsened, Salomon played an ever-more-critical role in buttressing the nation's finances. In July 1782 he became Congress's official broker and was widely respected for his honesty and generosity. He died in Philadelphia on 6 January 1785, leaving his family mostly worthless U.S. securities.

BIBLIOGRAPHY

Haym, Salomon. Haym Salomon Collection. American Jewish Historical Society, Waltham, Mass.

Schwartz, Laurens R. *Jews and the American Revolution: Haym Salomon and Others*. Jefferson, N.C.: McFarland, 1987.

Michael Bellesiles

SALT.
Salt was vital to the American economy, because it was needed to preserve meat and fish. While salt-making was one of the earliest industries attempted in the colonies, the commodity was not produced in sufficient quantity and had to be imported. Turks Island in the West Indies was the principal source, and the Royal navy was able to cut off this supply to all but smugglers and privateers during the War for American Independence. (Naval vessels could carried salt as ballast and would trade it for fresh provisions whenever possible.)

The great Onondaga salt deposits in New York were known in the seventeenth century, but they were not worked until after the war, nor were the large deposits of rock salt that later supplied the country. When the shortage became critical, the Americans set up salt factories along the coast, from Cape Cod to Georgia, to produce salt by evaporating sea water. Bounties were offered and state works were established, and even

Benjamin Franklin turned his talents to drawing up instructions for salt production. During the war era, non-combatants went to considerable lengths to procure the commodity. On 29 August 1777 John Adams wrote to his wife from Philadelphia that "all the old women and young children are gone down to the Jersey shore to make salt. Salt water is boiling all around the coast." Nonetheless, the shortage was never alleviated. Profiteers did a thriving business, and mobs rioted for salt. Salt works themselves were prime objectives for British sea-borne raiders, and many were destroyed by the coastal storms for which the North Atlantic seaboard is noted.

BIBLIOGRAPHY

Lossing, Benson J. *The Pictorial Field Book of the Revolution.* 2 vols. New York: Harper and Brothers, 1851.

Smith, Paul H. et al., eds. *Letters of Delegates to Congress, 1774–1789.* Vol. 7: *1 May–18 September 1777.* Washington, D.C.: Library of Congress, 1981.

revised by Harold E. Selesky

SALTONSTALL, DUDLEY. (1738–1796).

Continental naval officer. Connecticut. Born at New London, Connecticut, on 8 September 1738, Saltonstall was a merchant captain in the West Indies trade and a privateer during the Seven Years' War. At the start of the Revolution he commanded the fort at New London but sought his own ship in the new U.S. Navy. Through the intercession of his brother-in-law, Silas Deane, who was a member of Congress's naval committee, Saltonstall was given command of Esek Hopkins's flagship, the *Alfred,* on 27 November 1775. Taking part in the first of the war's naval operations, he was exonerated after several courts-martial and a congressional investigation of wrongdoing in the Alfred–Glasgow encounter of 6 April 1776. The next year he was named to command the new frigate *Trumbull.* Although this vessel did not get to sea for two years because it could not get over the shallows of the harbor where it was built, Saltonstall did command a ship by the same name and captured two British transports off Virginia. He succeeded the more capable John B. Hopkins as captain of the *Warren* (thirty-two guns) and commanded the fleet in the Penobscot expedition disaster. After a court-martial in Boston, he was dismissed from the navy on 27 December 1779. He later was successful as a privateer and after the war returned to the merchant service. He died of yellow fever in Haiti in 1796.

SEE ALSO *Alfred-Glasgow Encounter; Naval Operations, Strategic Overview; Penobscot Expedition, Maine.*

BIBLIOGRAPHY

Buker, George E. *The Penobscot Expedition: Commodore Saltonstall and the Massachusetts Conspiracy of 1779.* Annapolis, Md.: Naval Institute Press, 2002.

revised by Michael Bellesiles

SALUTARY NEGLECT.

In the generation of British politicians that arose after the end of the War of the Spanish Succession (1701–1714), management of domestic politics, especially in Parliament, was more important than the close supervision of overseas colonies. Accommodation of interests and the promotion of trade were valued more highly than strict enforcement of the Navigation Acts or confrontation over new policy initiatives, so much so that the years after the rise of Robert Walpole as the king's chief minister in 1721, to about the middle of the eighteenth century, were called a period of "salutary neglect." To be sure, when serious conflicts of interest arose, the concerns of North American colonists were subordinated. In the Hat Act of 1732, English hatters won from Parliament a prohibition against the production of hats in the colonies. In the Molasses Act of 1733, British West Indian sugar planters influenced Parliament to levy a higher duty on sugar from the French islands as the price of allowing North Americans to continue importing a non-British-produced commodity. Nonetheless, local elites in the colonies were able to prosper, consolidate their positions, and become self-aware in a time when the burden of empire was comparatively light. By mid-century, when this period began to come to an end after the Treaty of Aix-la-Chapelle, colonial elites had come to view "salutary neglect" as the correct state of affairs between the mother country and the North American colonies. Many colonists believed they participated in the crisis of the final French and Indian war as junior partners rather than subordinates, and thus were stunned when, after 1763, the imperial government began to enforce regulations and generate new ways of mulcting the colonial economies.

BIBLIOGRAPHY

Henretta, James A. *"Salutary Neglect:" Colonial Administration under the Duke of Newcastle.* Princeton, New Jersey: Princeton University Press, 1972.

revised by Harold E. Selesky

SAMPSON, DEBORAH. (1760–1827).

Continental heroine. Massachusetts. Born in Plympton, Massachusetts, on 17 December 1760, Sampson was reared by relatives and friends until she was ten years old and was an indentured servant the next eight years. By the time she was twenty, she had educated herself to the degree of qualifying as a part-time teacher. Early in 1782 she masqueraded as a man and enlisted in the Massachusetts militia as Timothy Thayer, but she was exposed while drinking in a tavern. In May 1782 she enlisted as Robert Shurtlieff in Captain George Webb's company of the Fourth Massachusetts Regiment. Sampson marched to West Point with her outfit on 23 May. She gave a good account of herself in skirmishes with Loyalists at Tappan Zee and Tarrytown, New York. She was wounded in the latter encounter and carried to the aid station with a serious musket wound in the thigh. Knowing that she again faced exposure, she removed the musket ball herself. After another skirmish at Fort Edward, she was transferred to Philadelphia, where she came down with a fever. She was treated by Dr. Barnabas Binney, who discovered her secret but concealed it. After joining the Eleventh Massachusetts Regiment for a surveying expedition in western Pennsylvania, Sampson returned to West Point. Robert Shurtlieff was honorably discharged on 23 October 1783.

Sampson married Benjamin Gannett, a farmer of Sharon, Massachusetts, in 1784. The couple had three children. Sampson did not conceal her service record. In 1797 she related her experiences to Herman Mann, who published *The Female Review: or, Memoirs of an American Young Lady* (1797). In 1802 she began giving lectures in New England and New York. As perhaps the first female lecturer in the country, she delivered a set speech about her experiences and normally concluded by appearing in military costume to do the manual of arms. After Massachusetts awarded her a bonus, Congress in 1805 gave her a pension of four dollars a month as an invalided soldier, and in 1818 this was doubled. She died in Sharon on 29 April 1827.

BIBLIOGRAPHY

Young, Alfred F. *Masquerade: The Life and Times of Deborah Sampson, Continental Soldier.* New York: Knopf, 2004.

revised by Michael Bellesiles

SANDERS (OR SAUNDERS) CREEK, SOUTH CAROLINA SEE *Camden Campaign.*

SANDUSKY, OHIO. 4–5 June 1782. Site of Crawford's defeat.

SEE ALSO *Crawford's Defeat.*

SANDWICH, JOHN MONTAGU, FOURTH EARL OF. (1718–1792).

First lord of the Admiralty. Sandwich was once denounced by Whiggish historians as lazy, corrupt, and largely responsible for the unprepared state of the Royal Navy for war in 1778. More recent research has shown that Sandwich was, in fact (for his time), a hardworking and conscientious administrator, who repeatedly warned his colleagues of the danger of falling behind Bourbon preparations, and did his best to mitigate the effects of parsimony. His preference for a concentration in home waters had much to recommend it. If he can be taken to task, it is for his ruinous clash with Germain over strategy; his ill-concealed ambition and his cleverness, which made him an object of suspicion; and his failure to argue clearly his case.

Born on 13 November 1718, he was first educated at Eton, where he received a thorough classical education. In 1729 he succeeded to the earldom on the death of his father. Leaving Eton in 1735, he spent two years at Trinity College, Cambridge, before embarking upon a tour of the Ottoman Empire, including Constantinople, Greece, and Egypt. In Florence during 1737 he met Dorothy Fane, the younger daughter of an Irish peer, and on his return from the East they married on 3 March 1741.

Entering politics, Sandwich became the duke of Bedford's deputy at the Admiralty, where he worked closely with Admiral George Lord Anson on the development of the Western Squadron strategy. In 1748, still collaborating with Anson, he became first lord of the Admiralty and launched an investigation into the state of the dockyards, only to lose office in 1751 as part of an assault on his patron, Bedford. He did not regain office until 1763, when he again briefly became first lord before being moved to the secretaryship of state for the Northern Department and becoming responsible for the prosecution of John Wilkes. Sandwich lost office when Grenville ministry fell in July 1765, but he became first lord for the third time under North in 1771.

Once again he threw himself into dockyard reform, energetically resisted North's plans for economy, and restored the navy's stocks of seasoned timber within three years. He expanded building capacity by contracting some work to private yards. Long before war with France broke out in 1778, Sandwich repeatedly warned the ministry to fully mobilize the fleet in anticipation of a Bourbon threat—warnings that were ignored until too late.

Sandwich's demands for a concentration in home waters were opposed by Germain, who had the direction of the war in America. Sandwich failed to prevent the detachment of Byron in hot pursuit of the Toulon fleet in April 1778, a move which arguably saved New York but so weakened Keppel that he was unable to win a decisive victory off Ushant in July. It turned out to be the last chance to do so before Spain intervened in 1779. Even then, Sandwich had the worst of the strategic argument and repeated detachments were made to American waters, with the result that a Franco-Spanish fleet briefly dominated the Channel and posed a real danger of invasion. On the other hand, Sandwich generally managed to keep these detachments relatively weak, and there was little coordination between them, a strategic failing for which he must shoulder some responsibility and which in 1781 led to the Yorktown catastrophe.

But in other spheres Sandwich was brilliantly successful. By 1782 the Royal Navy had achieved parity with the combined Bourbon fleets, and the British ships had the advantage of copper bottoms. Sandwich lost office forever when North fell in 1782, but he had laid the foundations of the naval recovery that allowed Britain to survive as a Great Power. He died in London on 30 April 1792 and was buried at Barnwell, Northamptonshire, on 8 May.

He may or may not have invented the sandwich, but if he did it was probably connected with his work habits rather than with gambling. There is no evidence to sustain the suspicions of corruption and quite a lot to the contrary. His exceptional ability and ambition made him many enemies, as did his refusal to promote except on merit. As an administrator, however, he had the respect of his admirals. Though unimpressive as a wartime strategist, he held fast to the fundamental principle of concentration in home waters—the key to British naval success in a hostile Europe.

SEE ALSO *North, Sir Frederick.*

BIBLIOGRAPHY

Martelli, George. *Jemmy Twitcher: A Life of the fourth Earl of Sandwich, 1718–1792.* London: Cape, 1962.

Rodger, N. A. M. *The Insatiable Earl: a life of John Montagu, fourth Earl of Sandwich 1718–1792.* London: Harper-Collins, 1993.

Tilley, John A. *The British Navy and the American Revolution.* Columbia: University of South Carolina Press, 1987.

revised by John Oliphant

SAN ILDEFONSO, TREATY OF SEE *Paris, Treaty of, 10 February 1763.*

SAP. Underground gallery dug to get beneath fortifications, usually for the purpose of blowing a mine. It is also a trench pushed toward the enemy by digging at the saphead (head of the sap) while using the trench for defilade. If the earth is thrown to one side for additional protection, it is known as a full or single sap; if dirt is thrown to form parapets on both sides, it becomes a double sap. A flying sap is one constructed under fire by using two gabions for cover and pushing them forward, side by side, as the work progresses. A sap roller is a gabion rolled forward to protect the sappers as they work. A sapper is a military engineer trained not only for this type of siege work but also for other varieties of field fortification.

SEE ALSO *Gabion.*

Mark M. Boatner

SARATOGA, FIRST BATTLE OF. 19

September 1777. John Burgoyne's offensive entered its final phase on 13 September when he crossed to the west side of the Hudson River. The slow movement southward resulted partly from inadequate transportation, but also from a collapse of intelligence. The losses suffered at Bennington and the constant attrition of sniping and disease had stripped away most of the Loyalists, Canadians, and Indians who had been his sources of information. In fact, he only realized that Horatio Gates's main force was nearby when he heard the reveille drums of the American camp on 16 September. He halted and only moved another three miles on the 17th. At that point he deployed along a front extending about a mile and a half west from Sword's House. The 18th produced no further intelligence, and he developed plans to carry out a reconnaissance in force to assess the situation.

The Americans had observed Burgoyne's every move, and their patrols harassed his advance. Gates's army now numbered at least seven thousand, with more militia arriving every day. They had been digging in on the commanding ground of Bemis Heights since 12 September. Knowing that time was on his side because Burgoyne had cut his own lines of communication, the American commander chose to exploit the tactical advantage of defending a fortified position.

BURGOYNE'S PLAN

The reconnaissance in force would be executed by three task forces. Brigadier Simon Fraser, with about twenty-two hundred men, would make a wide sweep on the right to the vicinity of the clearing known as Freeman's Farm. His command consisted of his own Twenty-fourth

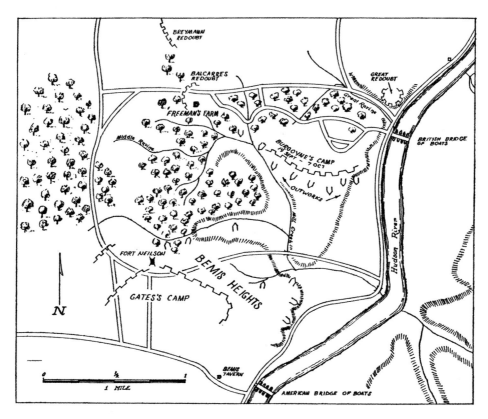

BATTLE OF SARATOGA. THE GALE GROUP

Foot; Major John Ackland's light infantry battalion; Major Alexander, earl Balcarres's battalion of grenadiers; Lieutenant Colonel Heinrich Breymann's battalions of Brunswick grenadiers; and the remaining Canadians, Indians, and Loyalists. The center column of about eleven hundred men from the Twentieth, Twenty-first, and Sixty-second Foot under Brigadier James Hamilton was to move south and then turn west to make contact with Fraser. Burgoyne accompanied Hamilton, and the reserve (Ninth Foot) followed closely behind. The left (east) column, eleven hundred Germans commanded by General Friedrich Riedesel and accompanied by General William Phillips and the artillery, took the river road. Hoffman Nickerson is on target with his comment: "What was next to be done—if the Americans did not come out and attack one or more of the advancing columns—we do not know" (p. 305). Since Burgoyne's troops were moving in broken, wooded terrain without the means of coordinating the three columns, the plan invited defeat in detail.

The 19th dawned cold and foggy but turned bright and clear by 11 A.M. A signal gun then set the columns in motion; an American patrol on the east bank of the Hudson quickly reported this to Gates. At about 12:30 the advance guard of the center column occupied the cabin of Freeman's Farm, and Burgoyne halted for word of

Fraser's location. Riedesel, slowed by the need to repair bridges, was on the river road due east of Freeman's Farm and about a mile and a half away.

Gates waited passively until Benedict Arnold's arguments finally persuaded him to send Daniel Morgan's riflemen and Dearborn's light infantry out from his left (east) to make contact. Arnold's division, on this flank, was alerted to support them.

THE ACTION BEGINS

About 1 P.M., Morgan encountered the pickets of the center column. Accurate fire picked off every British officer and many of the men and drove the survivors back to Hamilton's line. The riflemen pursued too aggressively and were in turn driven off by the British. In the heavy brush Morgan at first thought that his corps had been destroyed, but the scattered soldiers reassembled at the sound of his turkey call.

The skirmish briefly unnerved the some of Hamilton's men, but order returned quickly and Burgoyne decided he could no longer sit idle while waiting for word from Fraser. Again a signal gun told the other two forces to move. The center column moved out into the clearing of Freeman's Farm with the Twentieth on the left,

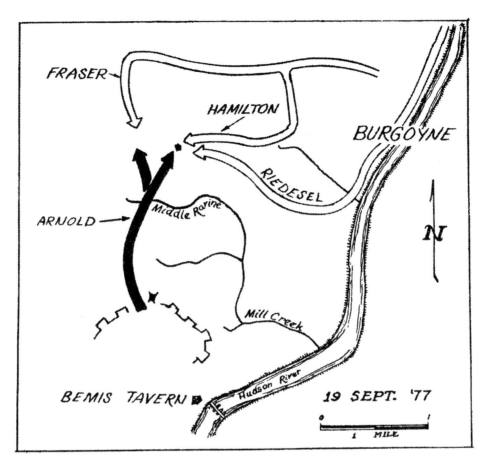

BATTLE OF SARATOGA. THE GALE GROUP.

the Twenty-first on the right, and the Sixty-second in the middle; the Ninth Foot continued as the reserve.

PHASE TWO

Morgan and Dearborn held positions along the southern edge of the clearing, and Arnold had already started at least seven of his regiments forward from Bemis Heights to support them. The First and Third New Hampshire Regiments, under Colonels Joseph Cilley and Alexander Scammell, were the first to arrive, and they formed to the left; others extended the line to the right as they arrived. Arnold arrive fairly soon, although charges and countercharges in his later argument with Gates have confused some historians on this point.

The fighting in the clearing became heavy at about 3 P.M. and continued until sunset. Each side advanced multiple times, but every advance was repulsed. Americans relied on numbers and accurate musket fire, the British on supporting artillery fire. It is a myth that this part of the engagement pitted inappropriate European tactics against American militiamen adept at frontier warfare. The heavy fighting at the clearing took place between two bodies of regular troops, both using linear tactics and both fully under the control of their officers.

PHASE THREE

Riedesel had heard the firefight start and sent two companies of the Rhetz Regiment forward to find out what lay in front; Phillips left to learn about the firing. On his own initiative he also called artillery forward, sent four guns to support Hamilton, and sent his aide to ask Burgoyne for orders. The latter returned around 5 o'clock with instructions to leave a force to defend the river road and bring the rest to attack the American east flank and take pressure off the center column. The buildup of American forces had required the three regiments at Freeman's Farm to thin out to prevent being overlapped, especially on their right. This left the Sixty-second Foot in the center in a particularly exposed position, especially when it surged forward in a counterattack. The center column was in a desperate situation when the Germans came to its support.

Riedesel, on the other hand, risked annihilation of his force on the river as well as loss of the vital bateaux and supply train he was protecting on that flank. But he accepted this risk and moved out with about five hundred infantry and two guns (his own regiment, the other two companies of the Rhetz, and six-pounders from the Hesse-Hanau Artillery Company). With the same vigor he had shown at Hubbardton in rescuing Fraser, the major general led the two Rhetz companies west along a road that he had previously reconnoitered. Reaching the top of a hill, he saw the desperate situation of the British and immediately committed the two companies without waiting for the rest of his men to catch up; as at Hubbardton, he ordered them to advance cheering and beating their drums.

The American right flank (the New Hampshire regiments and a detachment of Massachusetts Continentals) rested on the North Branch Ravine, which prevented their extending in Riedesel's direction. Instead, as fresh regiments came up from Bemis Heights, they reinforced the west end of the line. Furthermore, three hours of heavy combat left them tired and unable to devote any men to patrol beyond their flank. The sound of Riedesel's volley fire from this quarter took them by surprise. The Americans still outnumbered the enemy by about two to one and Hamilton's troops were almost fought out at this point, but Arnold was with Gates at Bemis Heights when the Germans arrived on the battlefield and was not in a position to exploit the situation; he had ridden back to get more troops. Gates did release Learned's Brigade, but it went to the west flank as well and engaged Fraser's wing, contributing nothing to the main fight at Freeman's Farm.

Burgoyne launched a counterattack when Riedesel's reinforcements were available. The Americans held their ground at first, but then started drawing back. Darkness was falling and they lacked unity of command.

Fraser had been off in the wilderness while Burgoyne and the center column fought for their lives. Late in the day his forward elements exchanged fire with those of Learned, but that was the extent of the action in this part of the battlefield.

NUMBERS AND LOSSES

Burgoyne lost about 160 men killed, 364 wounded and 42 missing. But they were not evenly distributed. The Germans only had eighteen men wounded, and Fraser's units also came out relatively unscathed. It appears that Hamilton's three regiments went into action with about 800 effectives and took 350 casualties (44 percent). The Sixty-second Foot alone went into action with 300; three officers and 50 men died and another eight officers and 101 enlisted men were wounded.

Americans suffered half as many casualties. Estimates vary—and because the troops engaged were from militia units or detachments, the number could be off—but casualties probably totaled 319: 8 officers and 57 men killed, 21 officers and 197 men wounded, and 36 reported missing.

SIGNIFICANCE

Burgoyne could and did claim the victory, since he camped on the battlefield. But he had no chance of defeating Gates before the battle began, and the day's losses doomed his expedition.

Gates's performance in the battle was cautious. Unwilling to risk an unnecessary defeat, he failed to see that he had an opportunity to crush Burgoyne on the spot by defeating the columns in detail. Suspicions that the personality conflict between Gates and Arnold played a large part in Gates's reluctance to give Arnold free rein are probably overstated. They fell apart after the action, not before.

Many historians refer to this engagement as the First Battle of Freeman's Farm, a more precise designation. But as in the case of Bunker Hill, Saratoga is more popular.

SEE ALSO *Arnold, Benedict; Bennington Raid; Burgoyne's Offensive; Dearborn, Henry; Defeat in Detail; Fraser, Simon (1729–1777); Hubbardton, Vermont; Learned, Ebenezer; Morgan, Daniel; Phillips, William; Riedesel, Baron Friedrich Adolphus; Scammell, Alexander.*

BIBLIOGRAPHY

Furneaux, Rupert. *Saratoga: The Decisive Battle.* London: Allen and Unwin, 1971.

Ketchum, Richard. *Saratoga: Turning Point of America's Revolutionary War.* New York: Holt, 1997.

Nickerson, Hoffman. *Turning Point of the Revolution; or, Burgoyne in America.* New York: Houghton Mifflin, 1928.

revised by Robert K. Wright Jr.

SARATOGA, SECOND BATTLE OF.

7 October 1777. Lieutenant General John Burgoyne held his first council of war in the evening of 4 October to discuss options with his key subordinates, a day after the British went on reduced rations after the damage they had suffered during the first battle of Saratoga (also called the battle of Freeman's Farm). At this point, it was clear that the American right was too strong to attack, and Burgoyne proposed moving with most of his troops to strike Gates's left. The other generals objected to the high risk of leaving only 800 men behind to guard the camp and escape route, pointing out that if the Americans struck them during the flanking maneuver, the whole force would be trapped. In a second meeting on the next night, Major General Friedrich Riedesel suggested falling back. Burgoyne rejected the idea of retreat but did agree to a compromise,

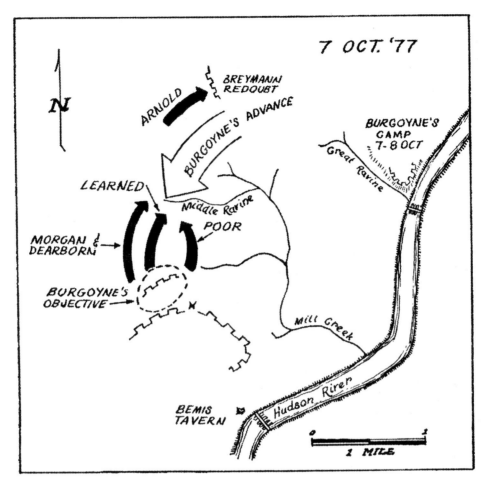

SECOND BATTLE OF SARATOGA. THE GALE GROUP

in which the British would conduct another reconnaissance in force on 7 October. For this second probe, Burgoyne planned to use 1,500 of his remaining regulars and all of the 600 auxiliaries remaining (50 Indians, 100 Canadians, and 450 Loyalists). The regulars would advance in three columns, while Captain Alexander Fraser with the auxiliaries and his marksmen swung west to screen the right column. If the effort discovered weakness, then a full attack would be made the next day. If it did not, then Burgoyne would begin withdrawing to the Batten Kill River on 11 October. To boost morale, rum was distributed to the troops on 6 October.

THE BATTLE: PHASE ONE

Between 11 P.M. and midnight, Captain Fraser's force set out to take up screening positions in the western hills. At about 1 A.M. the three columns started to advance southwest from their entrenchments, moving slowly to open roads for the artillery. After moving less than a mile, Burgoyne's main body formed a line 1,000 yards long on a gentle rise north of Mill Creek. While staff officers standing on the roof of an abandoned cabin tried unsuccessfully to locate Patriot general Horatio Gates's position with spyglasses, the men started digging in and a party was called up from the rear to collect forage in the 300-yard wide wheat field in front of the line. Major Alexander (Lindsay), Earl of Balcarres held the right (west) side of the line with his light infantry and the Twenty-fourth Foot; Riedesel took the center with a composite group of 500 Germans and two Hesse-Hanau six-pound cannons; on the left were the British grenadiers under Major John Acland.

By European standards it was a good position, although 1,000 yards of front overextended the 1,500 troops. It also furnished excellent observation and fields of fire to the front for the two German guns, and for a Royal Artillery force equipped with two twelve-pounders, four more six-pounders, and two howitzers. The defect of the position lay in the fact that woods on both flanks could provide cover for approaching Americans.

When Lieutenant Colonel James Wilkinson returned from checking outpost reports that the enemy was forming along Mill Creek, Gates—who apparently had learned something from the previous battle (at Freeman's Farm)—accepted Colonel Daniel Morgan's suggestion that his riflemen move out against the British west flank. "Order on Morgan to begin the game," is the theatrical quote attributed to Gates, by historian Richard Ketchum (*Saratoga*, p. 394). While Morgan worked around the high ground to turn Burgoyne's west flank, Major General Benedict Arnold (suspended from command earlier) arrived and asked Gates for permission to move forward and check if the 300-man picket needed help. Gates reluctantly agreed, but sent Major General Benjamin Lincoln along as well. They came back in a half-hour and reported that the British were maneuvering in strength against the west flank. Arnold became agitated and was sent away, but Lincoln talked Gates into sending Brigadier General Enoch Poor, with three regiments from his brigade, to reinforce Morgan. This was a modest part of the 12,000-man army in the American camp (half of them Continentals), but it was a significant challenge for Burgoyne's reconnaissance party.

The battle actually started when Poor's Continental regiments under Colonels John Cilley (First New Hampshire), Nathan Hale (Second New Hampshire), and Alexander Scammell (Third New Hampshire) reached Burgoyne's left (east) flank and formed up about 2:30 P.M. They coolly ignored twelve-pounder artillery fire and started forward against Acland's grenadiers, who were posted on higher ground. Major Acland mistakenly ordered a bayonet charge that Poor shattered with accurate fire; the major himself went down with wounds in both legs and was captured. The disorderly retreat of his men threw the adjacent German troops into confusion as well. The New Hampshire veterans also overran the four British guns on this flank before the British could fire a shot. Meanwhile, American reinforcements started arriving to build up the firing line and extend it to the west.

The collapse of so many of the British and German infantrymen turned the cabin, which the British had hastily augmented with earthworks, into a semi-isolated strongpoint. The British twelve-pounders and the two Hesse-Hanau six-pounders carried the burden of holding this improvised fort, with the assistance of pockets of musketmen who were still putting up resistance. The gunners drove back two American charges, expending three wagon-loads of ammunition in the process, before the cannon became too hot to touch and mounting casualties made their position untenable. They had to abandon all the guns in order to get away.

Meanwhile Morgan had also been in action. After first routing Captain Fraser's flank security in the woods, Morgan swung around and came in to hit Balcarres' end of the British line in the flank and rear. As the British light infantry were changing forward to meet his attack, Lieutenant Colonel Henry Dearborn's own light infantry arrived routed them with devastating musket fire. Balcarres rallied his men a short distance to the rear, but was unable to hold his position. Burgoyne sent his aide, Captain Sir Francis Carr Clerke, forward to order the last of the reconnaissance force to withdraw, but Clerke was mortally wounded and captured before he could complete the mission. Brigadier General Ebenezer Learned's brigade now came onto the field between Morgan and Poor, further tipping the scales in favor of the Americans. The opening round to the action ended as Arnold, who had no official standing whatsoever, appeared and led Learned's men directly at Lieutenant Colonel Ernst von Speth's German reinforcements. Speth stood his ground to cover the British withdrawal into the formidable earthworks known as the Balcarres and Breymann redoubts, and then fell back himself.

British General Simon Fraser had been conspicuous throughout the action. Now he committed his own regiment, the Twenty-fourth Foot, which was still relatively fresh, in attempt to cover the light infantry survivors. Either Arnold or Morgan recognized that Fraser's inspired leadership was a decisive factor holding the British together. Orders were given to rifleman Timothy Murphy to take him out. Murphy climbed up a tree to get into a better firing position, and with his third shot hit Fraser in the stomach. As their general was carried off the field, the British delaying position collapsed. Further strengthening the Patriot forces were Brigadier General Abraham Ten Broeck's 1,800 militiamen, who now arrived to augment Arnold's force.

PHASE TWO

At this point in the action, the Americans had accomplished their original objective of driving back Burgoyne before he could gain any information about Gates's main line of resistance on Bemis Heights, New York, and they had inflicted punishing casualties on the enemy, but Arnold was not satisfied. Drawing in elements from two Massachusetts Continental brigades—Brigadier General John Glover's Second and Brigadier General John Paterson's Third—he resumed the attack in an effort to make this battle the decisive one of the campaign. His assault on the Balcarres redoubt got through the abatis (defensive shields made of felled trees and brush) but was stopped by the light infantry and other survivors of the initial action who had taken refuge here and driven back.

Leaving men behind to keep this outpost neutralized, Arnold raced off to see what could be done elsewhere. Finding Learned's Fourth Massachusetts Brigade arriving on the field, Arnold led it in an attack that cleared several stockaded cabins that covered the gap between the

Balcarres and the Breymann redoubts. Then he took men through the newly created hole and overran Lieutenant Colonel Heinrich Breymann's position from the rear. Arnold himself went down with a wound—this was the third time in the war that his leg had been hit. Breymann was killed—tradition holds that one of his own men killed him for using his sword on the grenadiers to keep them from fleeing. Darkness and exhaustion brought the battle to an end.

NUMBERS, LOSSES, AND SIGNIFICANCE

Gates's losses were estimated at about 30 killed and 100 wounded. Burgoyne's troops suffered much worse. His losses numbered 184 killed, 264 wounded, and 183 captured. Thirty one of his officers were casualties, including Fraser, who died from his wounds. Riedesel's Germans had 94 killed, 67 wounded, and 102 prisoners of war. Loyalists, Indians, and Canadians appear to have suffered relatively few losses. While not all of these casualties were from the actual reconnaissance force, Burgoyne's "butcher's bill" represented a total equal to more than half of the number he had committed to action that morning.

It is hard to rate this engagement as decisive, since Burgoyne was already effectively doomed and Gates merely had to hold on and wait for starvation to eliminate the invaders. Nor did it make much sense from the British point of view, as Burgoyne had nothing to gain even if the reconnaissance had been unopposed. However, it did have enormous political consequences for the victors, for it helped enormously in gaining support both within the Americas and abroad. Arnold's role was controversial on that day, and has remained so ever since, thanks to the Gates–Schuyler Controversy: General Philip Schuyler supporters in the summer political dispute over who would command the Northern Department tend to exaggerate Arnold's impact (he was on Schuyler's side), while Gates's advocates went to the other extreme.

Personalities aside, the deeper impact of the campaign in general, and this battle in particular, came in the struggle that winter for the future course of the Revolution's military institutions. The more radical Whig politicians and many subsequent historians portrayed the militia as playing a critical role, and therefore thought that Washington's insistence on a large, well-trained regular army was excessive and potentially anti-democratic. A close examination of the day's events, however, shows very clearly that virtually the entire combat on the American side was carried out by the Continentals: Morgan's rifle corps, the New Hampshire Brigade, and the three Massachusetts Brigades, with their supporting artillery. The militia had been invaluable in isolating the battlefield but it was the regulars who had to carry the fight.

SEE ALSO *Burgoyne's Offensive; Gates-Schuyler Controversy; Saratoga, First Battle of.*

BIBLIOGRAPHY

Furneaux, Rupert. *Saratoga: The Decisive Battle.* London: George Allen & Unwin, Ltd., 1971.

Ketchum, Richard M. *Saratoga: Turning Point of America's Revolutionary War.* New York: Holt, 1997.

Mintz, Max M. *The Generals of Saratoga: John Burgoyne and Horatio Gates.* New Haven: Yale University Press, 1990.

Nickerson, Hoffman. *The Turning Point of the Revolution; or, Burgoyne in America.* Boston: Houghton Mifflin Co., 1928.

revised by Robert K. Wright Jr.

SARATOGA SURRENDER. 17 October

1777. On 13 October, John Burgoyne's officers unanimously agreed he should treat for surrender on honorable terms, and Burgoyne sent an officer to Horatio Gates proposing to begin negotiations. Gates consented, and the next day Major Robert Kingston, Burgoyne's adjutant general, was led blindfolded to the American headquarters. To the amazement of the British emissary (as well as Gates's aide, James Wilkinson), Gates immediately produced from his pocket a paper saying that only unconditional surrender would be considered. While this has sometimes been called a blunder, Gates was simply following classic European protocol. Burgoyne countered with an equally conventional response: in addition to demanding the honors of war, he now proposed that his command be paroled "upon condition of not serving again in North America during the present contest." This was a technical distinction, but one of great consequences that had been last used by a British commander at Kloster-Campen during the Seven Years' War. The men of the defeated force did not become prisoners of war, but rather would be allowed to depart the theater of war and fight elsewhere—or to release British troops in European garrisons, which would then come to America and fight. Uncertainty as to the status of Clinton's expedition and unwillingness to risk casualties in a frontal assault on the British defenses led Gates to agree to the outline of the terms on the 15th, provided that Burgoyne signed the capitulation by 2 P.M.

This last proviso was a blunder. Although Burgoyne had no hope of escape, he interpreted from the urgency of this time schedule that his adversary was worried about the British forces from the south. So Burgoyne agreed "in principle" but insisted on more time to work out details. Both commanders then appointed representatives with full powers to negotiate for them: Wilkinson and militia brigadier general William Whipple (a Signer of the Declaration of Independence) were the Americans;

Surrender of General Burgoyne at Saratoga (1820–1821). *John Trumbull's painting of General John Burgoyne's surrender at Saratoga in October 1777 dramatizes the moment when Horatio Gates rebuffs Burgoyne's offer to turn over his sword.* NATIONAL ARCHIVES AND RECORDS ADMINISTRATION

Lieutenant Colonel Nicholas Sutherland and Captain James Craig were their counterparts. They met between the lines and drew up articles of capitulation that all four signed at 8 P.M. At 11 o'clock that night Wilkinson was given a letter from Craig saying Burgoyne would sign the agreement if it were termed a convention rather than a capitulation. Gates promptly sent his consent, incorrectly feeling that there was no material distinction between the words.

On this same evening (the 15th) Burgoyne learned from a Loyalist messenger that Clinton's forces had taken the Highlands, had reached Esopus, and had probably gotten to Albany. He called a council of war to consider this development. His officers voted 14 to 8 that he could not honorably withdraw from a treaty he had promised to sign and, by the same majority, that the favorable terms should not be thrown away on the strength of the Tory's dubious report. Burgoyne now seemingly attempted to out-blunder Gates. He announced that he was not bound by these votes and, to stall for time, on 16 October he informed Gates he had learned that the

latter had detached a considerable force, which meant that the Americans might no longer have the numerical superiority that had persuaded him to start negotiations. Burgoyne, therefore, wanted to verify the remaining American strength. Gates sent Wilkinson to ask Burgoyne if he intended to resume hostilities. Faced with the possibility of being crushed, Burgoyne finally agreed at 9 A.M. on the 17th.

Riding forward on 17 October in a splendid uniform, Burgoyne was introduced by Wilkinson to a small, plainly clad American general. "The fortune of war, General Gates, has made me your prisoner," the Englishman reportedly said. "I shall always be ready to testify that it has not been through any fault of your Excellency," Gates is supposed to have replied. Burgoyne handed Gates his sword and Gates returned it to Burgoyne. The senior officers of both sides then went to dinner while Burgoyne's men laid down their arms, as the terms specified, under their own officers' orders. Under the agreement, officers would retain their side arms and the Convention Army would be allowed to march to Boston under guard to await the arrival of transports to take them to Europe. Meanwhile, as required by honors of war, American musicians played British or German marches to show respect for the defeated, and British and German musicians played American tunes.

A political firestorm erupted when Washington and Congress learned of the terms of the surrender. Washington correctly recognized that the British could simply rotate troops and make good the supposed losses. More to the point, the Virginian knew that the British had renounced the Kloster-Kampen agreement as soon as their men were out of French custody, and he feared similar duplicity.

SEE ALSO *Burgoyne, John; Burgoyne's Offensive; Clinton's Expedition; Convention Army; Gates, Horatio; Honors of War; Parole; Whipple, William; Wilkinson, James.*

BIBLIOGRAPHY

Nelson, Paul David. *General Horatio Gates: A Biography.* Baton Rouge: Louisiana State University Press, 1976.

Nickerson, Hoffman. *The Turning Point of the Revolution; or, Burgoyne in America.* New York: Houghton Mifflin, 1928.

revised by Robert K. Wright Jr.

SAUCISSON. A large fascine.

SEE ALSO *Fascine.*

SAVANNAH, GEORGIA SEE *Hutchinson's Island.*

SAVANNAH, GEORGIA. 29 December 1778. British capture. Determined to reclaim the southern colonies for the Crown, Lord George Germain (then Secretary of State for the American colonies) ordered Sir Henry Clinton to focus his energies on Georgia and the Carolinas. Clinton selected Lieutenant Colonel Archibald Campbell to lead this operation. On 27 November 1778 Campbell left Sandy Hook with 3,500 troops escorted by a squadron under Commodore Hyde Parker. On 23 December the expedition anchored off Tybee Island at the mouth of the Savannah River. Meanwhile, Clinton had ordered General Augustine Prevost, commander of British forces in East Florida, to move north to cooperate with Campbell in the capture of Savannah and take overall command. Major General Robert Howe, whom the

government of Georgia blamed for the failed revel invasion of Florida earlier that year, was waiting for his replacement, General Benjamin Lincoln, to arrive. Howe commanded the rebel's southern army, and was stationed at Charleston, South Carolina. Once Howe determined that Savannah was a likely target, he hurried south with the two inexperienced South Carolina regiments, led by Colonel Isaac Huger and Lieutenant Colonel William Thompson. Howe was joined by Colonel Samuel Elbert and his Georgia Continentals, bringing his total force to some 900 Continentals and 150 militia. Howe's forces established themselves at Sunbury, about twenty miles south of Savannah.

Lacking information on which to plan his actions, Campbell sent Grenadier Captain Sir James Baird ashore on the night of 25–26 December with a light infantry company. Baird picked up two men, one of them a slave who furnished what Campbell called "the most satisfactory intelligence concerning the state of matters at Savannah." This information convinced the British commander that he and Parker could capture the town without waiting for Prevost. The closest high ground for a landing between Tybee and Savannah was at Girardeau's Plantation, about two miles below the town. Parker's ships reached the area about 4 o'clock on the afternoon of 28 December and drove off two rebel galleys, but could not put the troops ashore until the following morning. About daybreak of 29 December, Lieutenant Colonel John Maitland went ashore with the light infantry of the Seventy-first Regiment, and a few Loyalist New York Volunteers, totaling 120 men. From the levee on which they landed, a narrow causeway led 600 yards across flooded rice lands to Brewton's Hill where Captain John C. Smith was posted with fifty South Carolina Continentals, Howe calculating that this attack was a feint by the British. The Continentals held a strong position among a group of buildings. Their famed marksmen opened fire on the advancing British, who rushed forward with bayonets. The Continentals retreated in good order, having killed Captain Charles Cameron, who was leading the attack, and two of his men. The Highlanders secured the beachhead, allowing the rest of Campbell's force to land.

Leaving 200 Continentals at Sunbury, Howe moved his remaining forces into Savannah. The old fortifications of the town were untenable, having been allowed to fall into disrepair, so Howe established his main line of defense a mile southeast of the town, to cover the road that led from the enemy landing site. This road crossed a marshy stream by a causeway and was flanked on the river side by the rice swamps of Governor James Wright's Plantation and by wooded swamps on the other side. The American left, extending from the road to the rice swamps, was held by a mixed force of 200 Georgia militia and Continentals under Colonel Elbert. On the right were Huger's Fifth South Carolina Regiment and Thompson's

Third South Carolina Rangers, totaling nearly 470 men. Colonel George Walton (a signer of the Declaration of Independence) was posted toward the rear in some buildings ("the new barracks") with 100 Georgia militia and a cannon. Another gun was on the left flank, and two more were in the center of the main line, on the road. Howe had additional militia covering his flanks. This line was 100 yards behind the stream mentioned earlier. The bridge at that point was destroyed, and halfway between this stream and the American line a trench was dug at what Campbell called "a critical spot between [the] two swamps." Although outnumbered four to one, the Americans appeared to be in a good position that left the enemy no choice but to make a costly frontal assault.

About 3 P.M. on 29 December the British light infantry advance guard halted and formed on the river side of the road, 800 yards from the American line. The main body of the British force halted on open ground, 200 yards to the rear. "I could discover from the movements of the enemy that they wished and expected an attack upon their left," says Campbell in his report, "and I was desirous of cherishing the opinion." But Campbell was approached by an old slave named Quamino Dolly, who told him of an obscure path through the swamps and around the American right.

Campbell skillfully used both this intelligence and the ground, while taking advantage of Howe's preconceptions, to achieve surprise. He sent Baird's light infantry forward to convey the impression that he was preparing an attack on the American left. Then, using a "happy fall of ground," he had Baird and 350 of his men follow Quamino Dolly to the rear of the rebel forces and circle around to execute the turning movement. Colonel George Turnbull's New York Volunteers, 180 strong, fell in behind the light infantry to reinforce their maneuver.

Innocent of the real danger, Howe ineffectively cannonaded Campbell's line. Baird reached the White Bluff road undetected and pressed on to wipe out Walton's Georgia unit by an attack from their flank and rear, taking Walton prisoner. At the sound of this action, Campbell had his cannon run forward from concealed positions to open on the American line, and his infantry charged with fixed bayonets. Howe ordered a general retreat across the Musgrove Swamp causeway, west of the town, but his men had to fight their way through enemy forces that had gotten there first. The retreat became a rout. The American right and center got across with difficulty, few of them having fired a shot and many throwing their muskets aside as they rushed to get away. Elbert's Georgians were cut off from the causeway and had to retreat through flooded Musgrove Swamp—many drowned and others were captured. Only thirty escaped. Colonel Huger managed a heroic rearguard action, aided by Colonel Owen Roberts, who managed to rescue three of the rebel's artillery

pieces. Howe camped for the night at Cherokee Hill, eight miles away, as Campbell swept into Savannah. He then retreated to General Lincoln's camp at Purysburg, on the South Carolina side of the Savannah River.

In this, the second battle of Savannah, Georgia, the Americans lost eighty-three killed or drowned and 453 (including thirty-eight officers) captured. The whole campaign cost the British three killed and seventeen wounded; none of the dead falling in the main attack. In Savannah the British took three ships, three brigs, eight smaller craft, forty-eight cannon, twenty-three mortars, and large quantities of supplies. They also captured 817 muskets, small arms the rebels could ill afford to lose. As for numbers involved, Campbell's strength of 3,500 is accepted but is somewhat academic, since Baird's light infantry and the Highlanders did almost all the fighting. Howe had 700 Continentals, counting the 200 in reserve, and 150 militia in the action. But in reality Few of these forces did any fighting.

Although a court of inquiry cleared Howe of blame for the defeat, his career as a field commander was over. Strategically, he was blamed for attempting a stand with untrained troops against superior numbers when he could have retreated to join Lincoln, after which a strengthened American army could have returned to take Savannah. Tactically, he was criticized for not challenging Campbell's landing, not launching a counterattack immediately after the landing, and failing to guard the route by which he was turned. Campbell, on the other hand, deserves the highest praise for his strategy and tactics; as a result of his success Savannah and most of Georgia remained under British control until almost the end of the Revolution. Nonetheless, the British high command refused to promote Campbell for several years.

SEE ALSO *Southern Theater, Military Operations in.*

BIBLIOGRAPHY

Commager, Henry Steele, and Richard B. Morris. *The Spirit of Seventy-Six.* Cambridge, Mass.: Da Capo Press, 1995.

Wilson, David K. *The Southern Strategy: Britain's Conquest of South Carolina and Georgia, 1775–1780.* Columbia: University of South Carolina Press, 2005.

revised by Michael Bellesiles

SAVANNAH, GEORGIA. 9 October 1779.

Franco-American fiasco. After the British capture of Savannah, Georgia, on 29 December, 1778, and subsequent actions that occurred in the southern theater, both sides suspended operations during the intensely hot and unhealthful summer months. Charleston, South Carolina, was still in American hands, but the British held Savannah

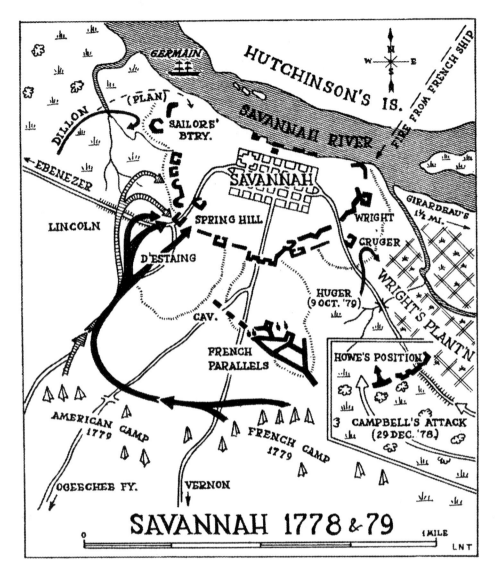

THE GALE GROUP

and several outposts. Sir James Wright returned from England on 20 July to resume his post as royal governor in Savannah, where General Augustine Prevost, military commander in the south, also had his headquarters. The town was garrisoned by about 2,400 troops, a large percentage of whom were Loyalists.

WAITING FOR D'ESTAING

Admiral-General Count Charles-Hector Théodat d'Estaing had sailed to the West Indies after the disappointing allied effort against Newport in August 1778. He had discretionary orders to aid the rebels if circumstances permitted, and had promised to return in May 1779. British and American commanders in North America were therefore anxiously anticipating his reappearance,

although they had no idea where he might appear. From Charleston, General Benjamin Lincoln and the French council appealed for d'Estaing's assistance, and although Commander in Chief George Washington had plans for combined operations in the north, the independent Frenchman decided to strike the British in the south.

Sending five ships ahead to notify Charleston of his coming, d'Estaing followed with thirty-three warships (totaling more than 2,000 guns) and transports bearing over 4,000 troops. His appearance off the Georgia coast on 4 September was so unexpected that he easily captured the fifty-gun *Experiment*, the frigate *Ariel*, and two store ships. He also captured Brigadier General George Garth, on his way to succeed Prevost as military commander, and £30,000 for the Savannah garrison's payroll. When news of d'Estaing's return reached New York City on 8 October, there was much consternation as to where the French would strike. General Charles Cornwallis was just about to leave with 4,000 men for the defense of Jamaica. His departure was stopped, and Sir Henry Clinton evacuated the British garrison from Rhode Island to New York. While Clinton waited and worried about Georgia, Washington was hoping for reports of French sails off Sandy Hook.

When the French fleet disappeared the evening of 4 September, Prevost hoped he was safe from attack. He sent his chief engineer, Captain James Moncrieff, with 100 infantry to reinforce the outpost on Tybee Island, in the mouth of the Savannah River. But the French reappeared on the 6th, and three days later started landing troops on the south side of the island. Moncrieff spiked his guns and withdrew. British ships moved into the river, and six of them were sunk to bar the channel. Lieutenant Colonel John Cruger was ordered to bring his battalion back to Savannah from Fort Sunbury, and Lieutenant Colonel John Maitland was ordered to bring his 800 men back from Beaufort on Port Royal Island.

While his fleet blockaded the coast, d'Estaing started landing troops on 12 September at Beaulieu, a point some fourteen miles south of Savannah. When he had gotten ashore with 1,500 men, bad weather set in and he was left in this vulnerable situation for several days, until the rest of his landing force and the supplies could join him. The next morning, advance American units under General Lachlan McIntosh and General Casimir Pulaski met with d'Estaing and advised him that the main body of Continental forces were still on their way from Charleston.

THE RUN-UP TO BATTLE

General Lincoln and his army had still not arrived by the morning of 16 September. General McIntosh advised d'Estaing attack Savannah immediately, as the British were still preparing their defenses. However, the French artillery had not yet landed, so d'Estaing instead called on Prevost to surrender. Playing for time, Prevost requested and was granted twenty-four hours to consider. During this truce Maitland reached Savannah with his troops from Beaufort, after a remarkable movement through swamps and streams to elude the French blockade and the American forces on the mainland. Since Cruger had already arrived from Sunbury, Prevost now had 3,200 regulars, plus a considerable number of Loyalists and slaves who would be useful in the defense. Prevost sent word he would fight.

Lincoln joined d'Estaing the evening of 16 September, swelling the American ranks to 1,500 (600 Continentals, Pulaski's 200 cavalry, and 750 militia). Unfortunately for the allies, there was a notable coolness between d'Estaing and Lincoln which undermined coordination. Lincoln was furious that d'Estaing had granted Prevost a 24-hour truce,

giving the British time to finish their defensive perimeter. The French commander in turn treated Lincoln with cold contempt, failing to keep him informed of French intentions. Continental officers found the French arrogant, while their French counterparts were particularly unimpressed with the militia, who were untrained, poorly armed, and had a habit of fleeing in the face of the enemy.

Although many Continental officers hoped for an immediate assault on Savannah, d'Estaing decided—apparently with Lincoln's agreement—to undertake a siege. Since guns and supplies had to be hauled fourteen miles from the landing site, and heavy rains delayed operations, regular approaches were not started until the night of 23–24 September, and the bombardment did not begin until the night of 3–4 October. Meanwhile, d'Estaing was under pressure from his naval captains to abandon the expedition. The fleet was in need of repairs, the hurricane season was approaching, they were vulnerable to attack by the British fleet, and their men were dying of scurvy at the rate of thirty-five men each day. D'Estaing had agreed to stay ashore only ten or fifteen days, which his engineers said would be enough time to capture the city. But when ten days had elapsed and his engineers estimated they would need ten more, he refused to delay further. After a council of war on 8 October, d'Estaing ordered an attack to be made the next day at dawn.

BRITISH DISPOSITIONS

With the excellent engineering services of James Moncrieff, Prevost had constructed a line of field fortifications in a rough half-circle to cover the land approaches to Savannah. The five-day bombardment had damaged many of the 430 houses in the town and had inflicted casualties among noncombatants, but the earthworks were virtually unscathed. Prevost realized that the right half of his line was the most vulnerable, and organized his defenses accordingly. The wooded marshes to the west, known as Yamacraw Swamp, would give an enemy concealment to within fifty yards of his fortifications in this area, and to cover this threat Moncrieff constructed the Sailors' Battery (see sketch), which was manned by sailors with nine-pound cannon. Additionally, the armed brig *Germain* was stationed in the river to deliver enfilade fire along this northwest flank.

The broad finger of flat ground leading toward Spring Hill from the southwest was recognized as excellent terrain for the type of open-field operations preferred by European commanders. A strong redoubt was therefore built on Spring Hill and manned initially by dismounted dragoons and supported by a regiment of South Carolina Loyalists. Along the quarter-mile that separated Spring Hill from the Sailors' Battery were two more redoubts and a second battery. Smaller fortifications and outposts covered the

Attack on Savannah, 8 October 1779. *American and French forces staged an unsuccessful attempt to capture Savannah from the British in October 1779. The attack is depicted here in an early twentieth-century illustration by A. I. Keller.* PICTURE COLLECTION, THE BRANCH LIBRARIES, THE NEW YORK PUBLIC LIBRARY, ASTOR, LENOX AND TILDEN FOUNDATIONS

gaps, and a strong line of earthworks protected the right flank of the Spring Hill (or Ebenezer Road) redoubt.

Continuing counterclockwise around Prevost's perimeter, a fourth redoubt, commanded by Cruger, covered the road leading to Savannah from the south; a fifth redoubt, commanded by Major James Wright, the governor's son, was situated on the northeast end of the line. Lesser defensive works were located along the entire line, most of which was fronted by a ditch and abatis. The regular regiments and the better Loyalist units were deployed to the rear.

THE ATTACK

The allies planned their main attack just where Prevost says he expected it—against Spring Hill. A secondary attack by General Arthur Dillon's Irish Regiment (serving in the French army) was to move secretly from the northwest and follow a defiladed route that would enable it to turn the enemy's right near the Sailors' Battery. General Isaac Huger prepared to lead 500 militia from the south toward Cruger's redoubt. His mission was to make a feint that would draw the enemy's attention away from the main effort, and to break through the defenses if this appeared to be possible.

All the flanking operations failed. Dillon's column lost its way in the swamp, emerged in plain view of the enemy's lines, fought fiercely, and was driven back by fire. Huger's command was also forced to withdraw without getting close enough to threaten the British left flank.

The attack on Spring Hill was supposed to be made by three French and two American columns. To get into position, the French had to march about half a mile west to the American camp and then move north to the line of departure. Here they would deploy along the edge of a woods in a "line of columns" and be prepared on signal to attack in a northeastly direction, across about 500 yards of open ground toward Spring Hill. Two American columns were to form on their left and attack Spring Hill from the west. These preliminary movements were supposed to take place so that a coordinated attack could be made at dawn, which was about 5 A.M.

The French were late getting started, and when the first French column reached its position on the right flank of the line of departure at around dawn, d'Estaing led it forward without waiting for the others to file off to the left. This column was assailed by grapeshot as they moved across the open space and by musket fire when they reached the abatis, with d'Estaing himself being twice wounded. The French columns quickly broke apart, with most of the troops making for the safety of the woods to their left.

In the American zone, Pulaski's 200 horsemen were supposed to lead the approach, pull off to the left, wait for the abatis to be breached, and charge through the gap. Colonel John Laurens would lead the Second South Carolina Continentals and the First Battalion of Charleston militia against the Spring Hill redoubt while General McIntosh brought up the rear with the First and Fifth South Carolina Continentals and some Georgia regulars. Colonel Francis Marion's Second South Carolina Continentals spearheaded the attack through heavy frontal and enfilade fire from an enemy that was now thoroughly alerted. They crossed the open area, swarmed over the ditch, hacked their way through the abatis, and planted their Crescent Flag and the French flag on the parapet of the Spring Hill redoubt. This marked the high tide of their attack, however, and the South Carolina troops were unable to press on any further. Both the French and Continental color guards were killed. A Lieutenant Gray replaced the flags and was killed in turn. Sergeant William Jasper, of Fort Sullivan fame, was mortally wounded while putting the flags up for a third time.

As Laurens's men began their retreat, the British counterattacked with the grenadiers of the Sixtieth Regiment and a small company of marines. Major Beamsley Glazier led this sortie and in fierce, hand-to-hand fighting drove back the French and Americans who had clung to their forward positions.

While this fight was going on, Pulaski was trying to force his way between Spring Hill and the works to its west. Cavalry is unsuited for an attack against organized defenses, and the infantry had not carried out the plan of breaching the abatis for him. The gallant Polish volunteer nevertheless led his troopers forward. They were caught in the abatis and badly shot up by well-organized enemy fire that covered this obstacle. When Pulaski was carried, mortally wounded, from the field, Colonel Daniel Horry took command and tried to continue the attack, but the cavalry fell back before this strong British position.

McIntosh arrived to meet a scene of bloody confusion. The retreating cavalry had swept away part of Laurens's command as they moved into Yamacraw Swamp, and Laurens had lost effective control of his scattered and disorganized units. The wounded d'Estaing was trying to rally the French troops, and when McIntosh asked him for instructions he was told to circle left so as not to interfere with the French reorganization. The fresh American column was consequently diverted into Yamacraw Swamp, where its left flank came under fire from the *Germain*, and was still floundering there when the sounds of battle died down. Major Thomas Pinckney went forward on reconnaissance and returned to report that not an allied soldier was left standing in front of Spring Hill. McIntosh therefore ordered his column to withdraw, and the battle ended.

NUMBERS, LOSSES, AND AFTERMATH

A combined force of 3,100 Americans and 4,500 French faced 4,813 British, German, and Loyalist troops in the Savannah operations. Of these, about 3,500 French and 1,500 American troops took part in the battle of 9 October. The rebels lost fifty-eight killed and 181 wounded, the French suffered fifty-nine killed and 526 wounded, for a total of 824 casualties. In contrast the British lost sixteen killed and thirty-nine wounded. This accounts for the majority of losses during the whole campaign, which lasted from 15 September through 9 October. The allies suffered an estimated 940 total casualties, and the British forces had 296 killed and wounded. The Continentals could bring just ten cannon to bear, while the French had forty-nine and the British some eighty-five pieces of artillery.

Although Lincoln urged d'Estaing to continue the siege, the French commander determined that this operation was hopeless. On 20 October the French returned to their ships and Lincoln was then obliged to retreat to Charleston. The Americans were bitter about the impotency of the French alliance and almost uniformly blamed d'Estaing for the failure of the Savannah campaign; but they had all underestimated the British strength and the effectiveness of Moncrief's defenses. Discouragement naturally was strongest in the south, and the militia which had been gathering at Charleston started melting home.

General Sir Henry Clinton was greatly encouraged by the failure of the allied attack on Savannah. With d'Estaing's failure, he was now free to undertake his long-considered return to Charleston.

SEE ALSO *Clinton, Henry; Estaing, Charles Hector Théodat, Comte d'; French Alliance; Southern Theater, Military Operations in.*

BIBLIOGRAPHY

Lawrence, Alexander. *Storm over Savannah.* Athens: University of Georgia Press, 1951.

Wilson, David K. *The Southern Strategy: Britain's Conquest of South Carolina and Georgia, 1775–1780.* Columbia: University of South Carolina Press, 2005.

revised by Michael Bellesiles

Death of Colonel Scammell at the Siege of Yorktown. *Alexander Scammell was inspecting his line during the siege of Yorktown in 1781 when he was surprised by a British detail and suffered a gunshot wound from which he later died. The scene is depicted in this engraving by J. Halpin after a nineteenth-century painting by Alonzo Chappel.* PICTURE COLLECTION, THE BRANCH LIBRARIES, THE NEW YORK PUBLIC LIBRARY, ASTOR, LENOX AND TILDEN FOUNDATIONS

SAVANNAH, GEORGIA (BRITISH OCCUPATION).

29 December 1778–11 July 1782. The town of Savannah, Georgia, was occupied by the British for three and one-half years. Except for the joint French-American effort to recapture the city in 1779, the British rule was largely peaceful.

revised by Michael Bellesiles

SCAMMELL, ALEXANDER.

(1747–1781). Continental officer. Massachusetts. Having come from Portsmouth, England, his parents settled in Mendon (later Milford), Massachusetts, about 1737. Alexander's father was a prominent and well-to-do doctor who died when the boy was six years old. Graduating from Harvard in

1769, Alexander taught school, worked as a surveyor, and then studied law in the office of John Sullivan in Durham, New Hampshire. In December 1774 he joined with Sullivan in the raid on Fort William and Mary to obtain powder for the local militia. He was appointed a major in the New Hampshire militia in April 1775 and brigadier major of Sullivan's brigade on 21 September 1775, serving at Bunker Hill, in the Boston Siege, and in Canada. He returned to New York City with Sullivan, was appointed his aide-de-camp on 14 August 1776, and as acting aide-de-camp to Washington made a mistake that might have lost the War of Independence for the Americans. At 2 A.M. on the morning of 30 August Scammell relayed to General Thomas Mifflin what he understood to be Washington's order to immediately move to the boats waiting to ferry Mifflin's force from Brooklyn Heights on Long Island to New York City on Manhattan. This caused Mifflin's force to be ahead of its scheduled evacuation, upsetting

Washington, but, more importantly, also leaving dangerously exposed the outposts that Mifflin's men had been guarding. This did not slow his military advancement; on 29 October he was made a brigadier major in Charles Lee's division, and on 8 November 1776 he took over as colonel of the Third New Hampshire Regiment and was with Washington at the Delaware crossings in December 1776 and January 1777. Returning to the Northern Department following the battles at Trenton and Princeton, he was present when St. Clair evacuated Ticonderoga on 5 July 1777 and led his regiment in the two Battles of Saratoga; in one of the latter actions he was slightly wounded.

On 5 January 1778 he succeeded Timothy Pickering as Washington's adjutant general, in which capacity it was his duty to arrest Charles Lee and, curiously, to execute his British counterpart, John André. It was during this period that Scammell worked with Steuben to standardize the army's paperwork and general administration. On 16 November 1780 Scammell submitted his resignation as adjutant general to take command of the First New Hampshire, but it was not until 1 January 1781 that he actually left Washington's staff. He commanded 400 light infantry in the preliminary operations against Manhattan in July 1781. At the siege of Yorktown, Scammell was inspecting his line when he was surprised by a detail of the enemy. Despite his surrender, he suffered a gunshot wound. Released and taken to Williamsburg in hopes of recovery, he died there on 6 October 1781. There can be no doubt as to his popularity; many late-eighteenth-century diarists and letter writers commented on the sad event. New Hampshire named a significant bridge near Portsmouth in his honor.

SEE ALSO *Long Island, New York, Evacuation of.*

BIBLIOGRAPHY

Kelley, Gail. "Alexander Scammell." In *New Hampshire: Years of Revolution, 1774–1783.* Edited by Peter E. Randall. Portsmouth: Profiles Publishing, 1976.

Kidder, Frederic. *History of the First New Hampshire Regiment in the War of the Revolution.* 1868. Reprint, Portsmouth, N.H.: Peter E. Randall, 1973.

Potter, Chandler E. *The Military History of the State of New Hampshire, 1623–1861.* 1868. Reprint, Baltimore: Genealogical Publishing, 1972.

Wright, Robert K., Jr. *The Continental Army.* Washington, D.C.: Center of Military History, 1983.

revised by Frank C. Mevers

SCHAFFNER, GEORGE.

Continental officer. Pennsylvania. Little is known of Schaffner's early life. He enrolled as a private in Abraham de Huff's company of Atlee's Pennsylvania musket battalion of militia in March 1776. Promoted to sergeant, he went with his unit to Philadelphia and reached Amboy on 21 July and New York City on 11 August. Eight days later he was promoted to ensign, and on 25 August he fought in General Alexander's right wing at Long Island. Remnants of his unit were incorporated into Samuel Miles's regiment for the march to Fort Lee and then to the Delaware. As part of Hand's brigade, Schaffner fought at Trenton and Princeton. On 4 February 1777 he became a second lieutenant in John Paul Schott's company of Ottendorf's battalion, which was soon incorporated into the First Battalion, Continental Partisan Legion, commanded by Colonel Armand-Tuffin. Schaffner fought at Short Hills, Brandywine, and Germantown. On 8 February 1778 he was promoted to captain, and to major on 1 December. He was honorably discharged on 25 November 1783.

Having become an intimate friend of the remarkable Armand-Tuffin, he accompanied the latter to France. He supported Tuffin in the Brittany uprising and was arrested on 24 August 1792 but released a few days later. From December 1792 to January 1793 he visited London as Tuffin's liaison officer to the émigrés. Learning that friends of his were being executed, Schaffner returned to France, joined the Vendée counterrevolutionaries, and disappeared. According to Lenôtre, he was captured in an action on the Loire and died in the *noyades* (judicial drownings).

SEE ALSO *Tuffin, Marquis de La Rouerie Armand-Charles.*

revised by Michael Bellesiles

SCHELL'S BUSH, NEW YORK.

6 August 1781. Donald McDonald, with sixty Indians and Loyalists, surprised this small community while its inhabitants were working in the fields. Most settlers ran for Fort Dayton, five miles to the south, but John Christian Schell, a wealthy German, made a stand in his fortified home. Two sons who had been with him in the fields were captured, but Schell, his wife, and six other sons made it to the blockhouse and held off the raiders, who were unable to set the place on fire. McDonald was wounded and dragged inside after trying to force the door with a crowbar; he died the next day. The frustrated enemy finally withdrew. Patriots claimed that eleven assailants were killed and six wounded, and the captured boys said another nine died of wounds before reaching Canada. The defenders suffered no casualties. John Schell was mortally wounded and one of his sons killed a short time later while in their fields.

SEE ALSO *Border Warfare in New York.*

revised by Robert K. Wright Jr.

SCHOENBRUNN, OHIO TERRITORY

SEE *Gnadenhutten Massacre, Ohio.*

SCHOHARIE VALLEY, NEW YORK.

15–19 October 1780. Sir John Johnson led a force of between eight hundred and fifteen hundred Loyalists, British regulars, and Indians into the Schoharie Valley from the southwest on 15 October. That night he bypassed the Upper Fort and, burning farms as he went, approached the Middle Fort early on 16 October. Major Melancthon Woolsey, commanding Middle Fort, sent out a 40-man reconnaissance force which withdrew before Johnson's forces. The garrison of 150 "three-months men" and 50 militia found themselves besieged by a vastly superior enemy possessing artillery in the shape of a grasshopper (a three-pound brass cannon).

Major Woolsey was ready to discuss surrender. But when a flag of truce started forward, Timothy Murphy fired on it. Woolsey and his officers were outraged at this breach of etiquette and discipline but failed to prevent Murphy from repeating the performance twice more. When Woolsey ordered a white flag raised, Murphy threatened to kill the man who moved to comply. While the militia in the fort argued among themselves, Johnson's raiders pillaged and burned everything in the area. They finally abandoned the siege and continued down the Schoharie, burning nearly every building in the valley before crossing the Mohawk. Schoharie Valley had been an important source of provisions for the Continental army; Washington wrote that it had furnished eighty thousand bushels of grain for public use. A strong west wind fanned the fires started by the raiders, and by the time Johnson's column cleared the Lower Fort, at 4 P.M. on the 17th, the prosperous valley was in flames. Informed that "the enemy have burnt the whole of Schohary," General Robert Van Rensselaer gathered a force to meet Johnson, but Van Rensselaer arrived well after the British and Loyalists had left the area. Loyalist houses left by the invaders were destroyed by the Patriots.

SEE ALSO *Border Warfare in New York; Johnson, Sir John; Klock's Field, New York; Murphy, Timothy.*

BIBLIOGRAPHY

Thomas, Earle. *Sir John Johnson: Loyalist Baronet.* Toronto: Dundurn Press, 1986.

revised by Michael Bellesiles

SCHUYLER, HON YOST. A mentally disturbed nephew of General Herkimer whom Benedict

Arnold used to panic the Indians around Fort Stanwix by spreading rumors of a vast American army approaching their positions. As his Indian allies fled, St. Leger's Expedition collapsed.

SEE ALSO *St. Leger's Expedition.*

revised by Michael Bellesiles

SCHUYLER, PHILIP JOHN. (1733–1804). Continental general. New York. Scion of one of New York's most ancient, honorable, and well-heeled Dutch families, Philip Schuyler was connected by marriage to just about all the others. Born in Albany, New York, 10 November 1733, Schuyler was commissioned as a captain at the beginning of the Seven Year's War, fought at Lake George on 8 September 1755, and almost immediately thereafter showed the military inclinations that were to characterize his Revolutionary War career—he became a logistician.

Even before 1755 Schuyler had had his first attack of rheumatic gout, a hereditary disease that troubled him throughout his life and that may well have inclined him toward army administration rather than field commands. After the action at Lake George, he was detailed to escort the French prisoners of war to Albany. Having handed over the prisoners, he married Catherine Van Rensselaer on 17 September, and then rejoined his unit. He established a military depot at Fort Edward, and the next spring served under Colonel John Bradstreet in carrying provisions to Oswego. Resigning his commission in 1757, he kept up his commissary interests and derived a substantial income from provisioning the army. In 1758 he returned to military service as deputy commissary with the rank of major, taking part in the unsuccessful attack on Fort Ticonderoga and the capture of Fort Frontenac. During 1759–1760 he operated from Albany, provisioning General Jeffery Amherst's forces. Schuyler had become a close friend of Bradstreet, with whom he sailed to England in February 1761 to settle his accounts with the War Office. At the end of the last colonial war, he was therefore a man with rich experience in provisioning field forces.

Coincident with the Peace of Paris in 1763, Schuyler settled his father's estate, inheriting thousands of acres in the Mohawk and Hudson valleys. In addition he received from his uncle, Philip, the old Schuyler homestead near West Troy and, his favorite heritage, lands in the Saratoga patent (a territory measuring about six square miles along the Hudson River). He became an efficient manager of these lands and a happy family man.

Elected to the state assembly in 1768, Schuyler proved to be an ardent Patriot but an opponent of the radical Sons

Philip Schuyler. *The American statesman and Continental Army officer who helped delay the British advance in New York in 1777, in a portrait (1792) by John Trumbull.* © **NEW-YORK HISTORICAL SOCIETY, NEW YORK/BRIDGEMAN ART LIBRARY**

of Liberty and other advocates of mob action. Because he was a commissioner in the boundary dispute with Massachusetts and New Hampshire over the region that later became Vermont (which always found in favor of the large New York landowners), many of his fellow New Englanders came to distrust Schuyler as a self-interested elitist. When the Continental Congress started naming generals, one of the top ones had to be from New York, and on 15 June 1775 Schuyler became a major general and commander of the Northern Department. Of Commander in Chief George Washington's generals, only Artemas Ward and Charles Lee ranked above Schuyler.

In preparing for the invasion of Canada, this austere Dutch patrician showed his good and bad qualities as a senior commander. Knowing the importance of logistics, he was slow getting started, and he had only the half-hearted support of the New Englanders at the outset. He further alienated these republicans by his personal manner and by his insistence on discipline. When he finally took the field to lead his troops down Lake Champlain into Canada, he almost immediately was prostrated by rheumatic gout. General Richard Montgomery took command of the field army, and Schuyler directed the forwarding of supplies from Albany. He also negotiated the neutrality of

the Indians who comprised the Six Nations, an important requisite to the invasion of Canada.

The events leading to Schuyler's downfall at the hands of Congress started on 9 January 1777, when the delegates voted to dismiss Dr. Samuel Stringer, who served as the director of hospitals in the Northern Department. Schuyler vehemently protested this interference in his command. Congress reprimanded Schuyler in an insulting fashion and ordered Horatio Gates north to take over as commander of the American forces then (March 1777) at Ticonderoga. Schuyler visited Washington's headquarters early in April to protest this action, and then went to Philadelphia, where he won the first round of this dispute with Congress As a result, that body clarified Gates's status as subordinate to Schuyler. Given the alternative of accepting this position or resuming his post of adjutant general, Gates left the Northern Department and rushed to Congress to lodge his own complaint.

Schuyler returned to find his army weak and demoralized. Except for his indecisiveness in connection with the defense of Ticonderoga, Schuyler's generalship in the initial stages of General John Burgoyne's offensive was sound. After abandoning Ticonderoga to the British, Schuyler sent Benedict Arnold to lift the siege of Fort Stanwix, acted with intelligence to slow down Burgoyne's advance, and frantically attempted to raise troops to confront the British. But the loss of Ticonderoga was enough to rally his enemies in Congress. On 4 August 1777 the delegates ordered Gates to relieve Schuyler. It was more than a year before Schuyler had the satisfaction of being acquitted by a court-martial (in October 1778) of charges of incompetence. On 19 April 1779 he resigned his commission.

Although he left the army under humiliating circumstances, Schuyler continued to serve the American cause. He remained on the Board of Commissioners for Indian Affairs and performed valuable service in reducing the ravages of the border warfare along the Iroquois frontier. In 1779 he advised Washington on the campaign by Generals John Sullivan and George Clinton against the Iroquois. The British thought highly enough of his work at negating their Indian alliances that they made three attempts at kidnapping Schuyler.

Having already served in the Second Continental Congress (1775) and again in 1777, Schuyler returned as a delegate from New York in 1779–1780. Near the end of this service, he prepared a report on depreciated currency and the issue of new bills of credit that was adopted with only slight modifications. From 13 April until 11 August 1780 he was chairman of a committee at Washington's headquarters, assisting the latter in reorganizing the army's staff departments and working out a scheme for effective cooperation with the French expeditionary forces. From 1780 until 1798 he held public office continuously at the state and federal level, highlighted by two short terms in the first U.S. Senate (1789–1791, 1797–1798). As an

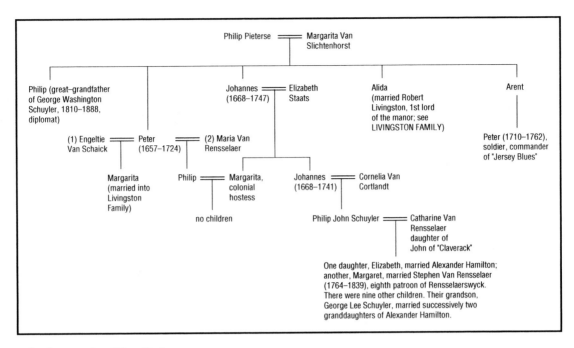

Schuyler Family of New York. THE GALE GROUP

adherent of a strong central government, Schuyler supported the federal Constitution as well as New York's abandonment of its claims to Vermont. During his many terms in the state senate, he firmly advocated internal improvements that would enhance New York's commercial development, serving as the president of the state's canal company from 1792 until his death on 18 November 1804.

SEE ALSO *Burgoyne's Offensive; Canada Invasion; Gates, Horatio.*

BIBLIOGRAPHY
Bush, Martin A. *Revolutionary Enigma: A Reappraisal of General Philip Schuyler of New York.* Port Washington, N.Y.: I. J. Friedman, 1967.
Gerlach, Don R. *Philip Schuyler and the American Revolution in New York, 1733–1777.* Lincoln: University of Nebraska Press, 1964.
———. *Proud Patriot: Philip Schuyler and the War of Independence, 1775–1783.* Syracuse, N.Y.: Syracuse University Press, 1987.
Tuckerman, Bayard. *Life of General Philip Schuyler, 1733–1804.* Freeport, N.Y.: Books for Libraries Press, 1969.

revised by Michael Bellesiles

SCHUYLER FAMILY OF NEW YORK.

Philip Pieterse Schuyler (pronounced "sky-ler") emigrated from Amsterdam and first appears in the records of Albany on the occasion of his marriage, in 1650, to the daughter of the resident director of Rensselaerswyck. He was a merchant and held offices under both the Dutch and English governments of the colony. His second son, Peter, married Engeltie Van Schaick, and their daughter Margarita married the nephew of the first Robert Livingston. Her sons were the soldiers in the Canada branch of the Livingston family, and her granddaughter tightened the Schuyler-Livingston bonds by marrying the first Robert R. Livingston. Peter's second wife Maria was the daughter of Jeremias Van Rensselaer, a son of the first patroon of Rensselaerswyck. In 1720 Peter and Maria's son Philip married his cousin Margarita, a remarkable woman who helped rear her nephew Philip John Schuyler, the Revolutionary War general.

SEE ALSO *Livingston Family of New York; Schuyler, Philip John; Van Rensselaer Family of New York.*

revised by Harold E. Selesky

"SCOTCH WILLIE" SEE *Maxwell, William.*

SCOTT, CHARLES. (1739–1813). Continental

general. Virginia. Born near Richmond, Virginia, in 1739, Scott served as a noncommissioned officer under Washington in Braddock's expedition. At the start of the

Revolution, he raised the first volunteer troops south of the James River in Virginia and commanded a company at Williamsburg in July 1775. On 13 February 1776 he was commissioned lieutenant colonel of the Second Virginia Regiment, on 7 May he became colonel of the Fifth Virginia, and on 12 August 1776 he took command of the Third Virginia. He led this regiment well at Trenton and as part of the covering force that so effectively delayed the British advance before Washington scored his victory at Princeton on 3 January 1777. Promoted to brigadier general on 2 April at Washington's urging, he and the brigade of William Woodford constituted General Adam Stephen's division. He was heavily engaged at Brandywine, facing the British turning column before Washington reinforced that flank. As part of Greene's column he saw action at Germantown, where his performance was severely criticized in a letter from Stephen to Washington on 7 October 1777. After spending the winter at Valley Forge he had a prominent role in the Monmouth campaign, first as commander of a large detachment and finally as part of Charles Lee's command in the battle of 28 June. He is responsible for the dubious but beloved story of Washington's cursing out Lee, and he testified effectively against the latter at the Lee court-martial.

Scott spent 1779 recruiting troops in Virginia. Ordered south to reinforce Lincoln, he was captured at Charleston on 12 May 1780, paroled, and exchanged for Lieutenant Colonel Lord Francis Rawdon in February 1782. He was brevetted major general on 30 September 1783.

In 1785 he moved to Kentucky. He was a representative in the Virginia assembly from Woodford County in 1789 and 1790. In April 1790 he took part in Harmar's unsuccessful expedition. The next year he was brigadier general of Kentucky levies and, with Colonel James Wilkinson as second-in-command, led them against the Indians on the Wabash River (23 May–4 June). In October 1793 he joined Anthony Wayne for an expedition against the Indians, but it was abandoned. On 20 August 1794 he led about fifteen hundred mounted volunteers in Wayne's victory at Fallen Timbers, though his own troops failed to arrive in time for the battle. Scott served as governor of Kentucky in 1808–1812, vigorously preparing Kentucky for war with Britain and promoting the career of William Henry Harrison. He died at his plantation in Clark County, Kentucky, on 22 October 1813.

SEE ALSO *Brandywine, Pennsylvania; Germantown, Pennsylvania, Battle of; Monmouth, New Jersey; Princeton, New Jersey.*

BIBLIOGRAPHY

Ward, Harry M. *Charles Scott and the "Spirit of '76."* Charlottesville: University Press of Virginia, 1988.

revised by Michael Bellesiles

SCOTTISH LEGION SEE *British Legion.*

SEARS, ISAAC. (1730?–1786). Privateer, New York City radical leader.

Both Sears's date and place of birth remain contested. He became a seaman and during the French and Indian War established a reputation as a privateer that made him a recognized leader of the sailors and shopkeepers of the New York City waterfront. As a Son of Liberty, "King" Sears was a leader of nearly every crowd action in New York City for ten years. He was wounded on 11 August 1766 in events related to the suspension of the New York assembly. In 1774 he led the Sons of Liberty in turning back the first tea ship and dumping the cargo of the second into the water. Having worked with John Lamb and Joseph Allicocke in 1765 to propose that the Sons of Liberty be organized into a continental military union, he worked with Alexander McDougall in 1774 in proposing to the Boston Committee of Correspondence that a meeting be held of delegates from the principal towns. This led indirectly to the first Continental Congress and showed the considerable scope of Sears as a revolutionary leader.

Arrested on 15 April 1775 for calling on the public to procure arms, he was rescued at the prison door by his supporters. When news of Lexington and Concord reached the city on 23 April, he and John Lamb led 360 men in scattering Loyalist leaders and officials, seizing arms from the arsenal, taking over the customs house, and preventing vessels from leaving. Sears also initiated the regular military training of his followers. The commander of the British ship *Asia* threatened to shell his house, persuading Sears to retreat to New England. In November 1775 he returned to lead crowds that burned a naval supply ship, captured prominent Loyalists, and wrecked James Rivington's press. He was commissioned by Charles Lee in January 1776 to administer the oath of allegiance to Loyalists on Long Island, raise volunteers in Connecticut, and capture British supplies for the army. With New York City under British control, Sears removed to Boston and returned to privateering from 1777 to 1783, at which he was very successful. Returning to New York City when the British left at the end of 1783, Sears led the effort to punish former Loyalists. Sears died on 28 October 1786 of fever aboard the *Empress of China* during its historic first journey to Canton, China.

SEE ALSO *New York Assembly Suspended.*

BIBLIOGRAPHY

Christen, Robert Jay. "King Sears: Politician and Patriot in a Decade of Revolution." Ph.D. diss., Columbia University, 1968.

revised by Michael Bellesiles

SECONDARY ATTACK.

A commander normally groups his forces so as to provide for a main attack, secondary attack, and reserve. The secondary attack is allocated minimum essential combat power and has the missions of deceiving the enemy as to the location of the main attack, of forcing him to commit his reserve prematurely and at the wrong place, and of fixing enemy troops in position so they cannot be shifted to oppose the main attack. By the use of his reserve or by other means, the commander may convert his secondary attack into a main attack.

Mark M. Boatner

SECRET COMMITTEE OF CONGRESS.

Congress created this standing committee (sometimes confused with the Committee of Secret Correspondence) on 18 September 1775 with responsibility for organizing the procurement of war supplies. Given wide powers, large sums of money, and authorization to keep its proceedings secret—it destroyed many of its records—the Secret Committee was effective largely because of its first chairman, Thomas Willing, who was succeeded in December 1775 by his business partner, Robert Morris. (On 30 January 1776, the latter was appointed also to the other secret committee.) Other original members were Benjamin Franklin, Silas Deane, Robert R. Livingston, John Alsop, John Dickinson, Thomas McKean, John Langdon, and Samuel Ward. The members of this committee tended to be men experienced in foreign trade, leading to some serious conflicts of interest. The biggest contracts went to the firm of Willing and Morris; to relatives and friends of Deane; and to firms connected with Alsop, Livingston, and Francis Lewis (who subsequently joined the committee). Criticism of the committee's activities increased as the war progressed, with the Adamses and Lees unsuccessfully demanding an investigation into war profiteering.

Authority of the Secret Committee soon was extended to include supplies other than guns and ammunition. In January 1776 it was asked to import medicines, surgical instruments, blankets, cotton goods, and various metals. Soon it controlled virtually all foreign trade. One of the most questionable operations of the committee started in January 1776, when Congress voted it forty thousand pounds for the importation of Indian gifts; contracting merchants were allowed a commission of 5 percent, and the government insured their vessels against British seizures. Three of the four contracting merchants were members of the Secret Committee: Morris, Alsop, and Lewis. The other was Philip Livingston, a cousin of another member of the committee. In April the Secret Committee was empowered to arm and man vessels in foreign countries for the work of Congress, thereby becoming involved in privateering.

The body launched itself boldly into the field of foreign affairs when, in conjunction with the Committee of Secret Correspondence, it sent Silas Deane to France. Affairs of the two secret committees became hopelessly scrambled early in 1777 when Franklin, Deane, and Arthur Lee began their duties as peace commissioners. The name of the Secret Committee was therefore changed in July 1777 to the Committee of Commerce, which later evolved into the Department of Commerce, and the Committee of Secret Correspondence became the Committee on Foreign Affairs on 17 April 1777.

SEE ALSO *Alsop, John; Committee of Secret Correspondence; Deane, Silas; Dickinson, John; Franklin, Benjamin; Hortalez & Cie; Langdon, John; Lewis, Francis; Livingston, Philip; Livingston, Robert R.; McKean, Thomas; Morris, Robert (1734–1806); Privateers and Privateering; Ward, Samuel.*

BIBLIOGRAPHY

Horgan, Lucille E. *Forged in War: The Continental Congress and the Origin of Military Supply and Acquisition Policy.* Westport, Conn.: Greenwood Press, 2002.

Nuxoll, Elizabeth. *Congress and the Munitions Merchants: The Secret Committee of Trade during the American Revolution, 1775–1777.* New York: Garland, 1985.

revised by Michael Bellesiles

SENTER, ISAAC.

(1755–1799). Army physician, diarist. New Hampshire and Rhode Island. Born in New Hampshire, Isaac Senter went to Newport, Rhode Island, early in life and studied medicine under Dr. Thomas Moffat. At the age of twenty he joined the Boston army as a surgeon and volunteered for Benedict Arnold's march to Quebec.

In November 1775 Senter became surgeon of the Third Rhode Island Regiment, a position he held until March 1776. Subsequently he was hospital surgeon from 20 July 1776 to April 1779, and surgeon-general of the Rhode Island Militia from 1779 to 1781. He established a private practice in Pawtucket, but later moved to Newport, Rhode Island, becoming an eminent surgeon there. An honorary member of the medical societies of London, Edinburgh, and Massachusetts, he was president of the Rhode Island Society of the Cincinnati for many years. He died in Newport on 20 December 1799.

SEE ALSO *Medical Practice during the Revolution.*

BIBLIOGRAPHY

Senter, Isaac. "The Journal of Isaac Senter, M.D., on a Secret Expedition against Quebec, 1775." *The Magazine of History* 42 (1915).

revised by Michael Bellesiles

SERLE, AMBROSE.

SERLE, AMBROSE. (1742–1812). Devotional writer, colonial official, and naval officer. An evangelical Anglican, he became undersecretary to William Legge, earl of Dartmouth, in 1772, went to America in 1774, and was in New York from 1776 to 1778. There he acted as William Lord Howe's secretary, for a time controlled the local press, and published a religious argument against the Revolution, *Americans against Liberty* (1775). His letters and journal, edited by E. H. Tatum and published by the Huntington Library as *The Journal of Ambrose Serle, Secretary to Lord Howe, 1776–1778,* (1940), are invaluable sources for historians.

revised by John Oliphant

SEVEN YEARS' WAR.

SEVEN YEARS' WAR. 1756–1763. All four of the major European wars between 1689 and 1763 also involved conflict among the imperial powers in North America and the West Indies. The first three (the War of the League of Augsburg, the War of the Spanish Succession, and the War of the Austrian Succession) began in Europe and spread across the Atlantic. The final conflict in this sequence was unique in that it began in the Ohio Valley and then spread to the European Continent. Known, confusingly, in America as "the" French and Indian War (1754–1763), this conflict is known in Europe by its duration, the roughly seven years between 18 May 1756 (when Britain declared war against France) and 10 February 1763 (when the Peace of Paris was signed).

Although Britain had hoped to confine to North America its fight to remove what it considered to be French encroachments on lands it claimed in the Ohio Valley, events beyond its control ensured that this would not happen. Since 1689, Britain had followed a national security policy of joining with other European powers to curb the efforts of France to dominate the Continent. Pursuing this policy required Britain's leaders to strike a balance between committing troops to campaigns against French armies and crippling the French economy by using its naval superiority to cut off France's overseas trade while simultaneously subsidizing its allies to do the actual fighting on the Continent. By the middle of the eighteenth century, this "blue-water strategy" of relying on allies and the Royal Navy had become more feasible. French overseas commerce had grown into a substantial part of the overall French economy, while despite the tug of the Hanoverian connection on George II (who was simultaneously Elector of Hanover), there was a growing reluctance on the part of British politicians to be drawn into struggles on the European Continent. Britain had supported Austria with money and troops during the War of the Austrian Succession (1740–1748) and was trying to re-knit an alliance structure that would keep the balance of power stable through money and diplomacy.

France, too, wanted to concentrate on events overseas, but both powers were drawn into a European war when Frederick II of Prussia attacked Saxony in an effort to preempt a new grand alliance of Austria, Russia, and a reluctant France from squeezing him back to being a secondary power. Britain had no choice but to ally with Frederick and send troops and subsidies to the Continent. Although the British army initially performed badly in Germany, Frederick managed to hold off encirclement by hard marching and heavy casualties. British performance improved, culminating in a tactical triumph over the French at Minden on 1 August 1759, but by that time the bulk of Britain's money, troops, and attention had been shifted to North America. The death of the anti-Prussian czarina of Russia on 6 January 1762 ultimately broke the alliance and saved Frederick. After several years of frustration in North America, the combination of British naval superiority and a series of slow but steady land campaigns that culminated in James Wolfe's lucky victory at the Plains of Abraham in Quebec on 13 September 1759 capped an *annus mirabilus* (year of miracles) that left Britain dominant at sea and in North America.

Even before the Peace of Paris ratified Britain's tremendous success, its leaders were grappling with the problems of how to pay the expenses incurred during the war and how to reorder the newly expanded empire. Their choices precipitated the War for American Independence.

SEE ALSO *Colonial Wars; French and Indian War; Minden, Battle of; Pitt, William (the elder); Plains of Abraham (13 September 1759).*

BIBLIOGRAPHY

Clayton, T. R. "The Duke of Newcastle, the Earl of Halifax, and the American Origins of the Seven Years' War." *Historical Journal* 24 (1981): 571–603.

Higgonet, Patrice. "The Origins of the Seven Years' War." *Journal of Modern History* 40 (1968): 57–90.

Middleton, Richard. *The Bells of Victory: The Pitt-Newcastle Ministry and the Conduct of the Seven Years' War, 1757–1762.* Cambridge, U.K.: Cambridge University Press, 1985.

Schweizer, Karl W. *Frederick the Great, William Pitt, and Lord Bute: The Anglo-Prussian Alliance, 1756–1763.* New York: Garland, 1991.

Showalter, Dennis E. *The Wars of Frederick the Great.* London: Longman, 1996.

revised by Harold E. Selesky

SEVIER, JOHN.

(1745–1815). Pioneer, militia officer, first governor of Tennessee. Born near the site of New Market, Virginia, on 23 September 1745, Sevier worked at farming, trading, tavern keeping, and surveying before moving southward in 1773 along the mountain valleys to the Holston settlements.

In 1776 Sevier joined in petitioning that North Carolina extend its jurisdiction over the Watauga and Holston settlements, and when this request was granted he became first a representative to the Provincial Congress and then lieutenant colonel of the militia. In 1777 he was promoted to colonel. Until 1780, however, Sevier took no active part in military operations. At the head of 240 Over Mountain Men, Sevier became one of the heroes of Kings Mountain in South Carolina on 7 October 1780. Immediately after his return from that victory, he started his career as leader of punitive expeditions against the Cherokees, or to be more specific, against the Chickamauga element of that tribe. In 1781 he again moved eastward across the mountains, this time with two hundred men, to support American regulars and militia against the British and Loyalist forces, though seeing little action.

When the war ended, Sevier entered into a project to establish a colony at Muscle Shoals, and he was so engaged when his Holston and Watauga neighbors started a movement to become a separate state. He was elected governor of the state of Franklin in 1785. Three years later this "state" collapsed, and Sevier was arrested for treason. North Carolina chose the path of reconciliation, pardoning Sevier, making him a brigadier general of the militia, and accepting him into the senate upon his election from Greene County that same year. The next year he was elected to Congress. When Tennessee was admitted as a new state he became its first governor, serving from 1796 to 1801 and holding this post again from 1803 to 1809. Two years later he was reelected to Congress and served until his death near Fort Decatur on 24 September 1815.

SEE ALSO *Indians in the Colonial Wars and the American Revolution; Kings Mountain, South Carolina; Over Mountain Men.*

BIBLIOGRAPHY

Driver, Carl. *John Sevier, Pioneer of the Old Southwest.* Chapel Hill: University of North Carolina Press, 1932.

revised by Michael Bellesiles

SHARON SPRINGS SWAMP, NEW YORK.

10 July 1781. Colonel Marinus Willett was in command of the force of New York state troops that took over responsibility for the defense of the Mohawk Valley from the Continentals at the beginning of July 1781. He set up headquarters at Fort Rensselaer (locally known as Fort Plain, later as Canajoharie) and immediately received word that large forces were moving against the settlements. On 9 July, Willett detected smoke rising in the southeast and assumed that the raiders were attacking Currytown, about eleven miles away. Earlier that morning Willett had sent out a thirty-five-man patrol under Captain Gross to Thurlough, but on seeing the smoke he sent a messenger to redirect the patrol towards Currytown. Willett also sent Captain Robert McKean with sixteen more of the state troops in the same direction, telling him to collect all the local militiamen he could as he advanced. McKean arrived in time to help the inhabitants put out burning buildings. Willett himself assembled a pursuit force and set out at dusk, picking up the two captains' detachments. By this time he had learned that the enemy was camped for the night about eighteen miles away in Sharon Springs Swamp (as it was subsequently called). The Americans (now numbering about 170 men) kept moving through the night, hoping to surprise the enemy soldiers at dawn before they were alert. However, his guide got lost for a while in the dark, and as a consequence, Willett arrived at 6 A.M. on the 10th to find the two hundred Indians and Loyalists formed up on high ground.

Willett determined to engage them, since the two forces were about equal in numbers, but as he was completing his deployment the Indians charged. The disciplined Americans repulsed the first attack in the center and then used their reserves under McKean to throw back a second charge on the American right flank. After an hour and one-half of combat, the Indians broke contact and withdrew by breaking into small parties. Willett said that he lost five killed and nine wounded, including the mortally wounded McKean, who died on the way back to Fort Rensselaer. He estimated the Indian losses at around forty based on the large number of dead left on the battlefield. The victory bought the valley several months of quiet. The city council of Albany voted the freedom of the city to Willett in honor of this action.

SEE ALSO *Border Warfare in New York; Currytown, New York.*

BIBLIOGRAPHY

Roberts, Robert B. *New York's Forts in the Revolution.* Rutherford, N.J.: Fairleigh Dickinson University Press, 1980.

Willett, William M. *A Narrative of the Military Actions of Colonel Marinus Willett.* 1831. Reprint, New York: New York Times, 1969.

revised by Robert K. Wright Jr.

SHAW, SAMUEL. (1754–1794). Continental officer. Massachusetts. Born at Boston on 2 October 1754, Samuel Shaw was the son of a prominent merchant and went to work in a countinghouse. As a lieutenant in Colonel Henry Knox's Continental Artillery Regiment from 10 December 1775, he served in the siege of Boston, the New York campaign (for a time at Fort Washington), and the Battles of Trenton and Princeton. He was regimental adjutant from May 1776. He was promoted to captain lieutenant in Colonel John Crane's Third Continental Artillery on 1 January 1777 and to captain on 12 April 1780. He was present at Brandywine, Germantown, and Monmouth. He spent most of his time as a staff officer, as brigade major of Knox's artillery brigade from 10 May 1777 to 31 December 1779, and thereafter until November 1783 as aide-de-camp to Knox with the rank of major (in the Corps of Artillery after 17 June 1783). His *Journals* are a particularly valuable source of information on the events surrounding the Mutiny of the Pennsylvania Line in January 1781 and the Newburgh Addresses in March 1783. He was with Washington's army when it reoccupied New York City on 25 November 1783 and assisted in disbanding the Continental army thereafter. He helped Knox organize the Society of the Cincinnati. When he left the service, Washington commended him for his intelligence, energy, and courage.

On 22 February 1784 he sailed from New York City as supercargo on the *Empress of China,* the first American ship to engage in the China trade. He arrived home on 11 May 1785 with a valuable cargo of tea, silk, and other commodities. Later that year Knox appointed him to a clerkship in the War Department, but he resigned when Congress made him the first American consul in Canton (January 1786). He sailed from New York City on 4 February 1786 and returned home on 17 July 1789. He was reappointed by President Washington and returned to China, where he served from March 1790 to January 1792. He married at Boston on 21 August 1792. Washington renewed his appointment and he sailed for China a fourth time. Delayed at Bombay because of typhoons, he contracted a liver disease and did not reach Canton until 2 November 1793. He left China on 17 March 1794 and died near the Cape of Good Hope on 30 May 1794. He was buried at sea.

SEE ALSO *Mutiny of the Pennsylvania Line; Newburgh Addresses.*

BIBLIOGRAPHY

Quincy, Josiah, ed. *The Journals of Major Samuel Shaw, the First American Consul at Canton: With a Life of the Author.* Boston: William Crosby and H. P. Nichols, 1847.

revised by Harold E. Selesky

SHAWNEE. The Shawnee Indians were a large and strategically significant Algonkian-speaking Indian nation that dominated the Ohio River Valley during the eighteenth century. The Shawnee were generally hostile to British and then American incursions into the Ohio Valley during the middle decades of the eighteenth century. During the War of the American Revolution and its immediate aftermath, the Shawnee would lead armed resistance against American settlements in Virginia's Kentucky District. Shawnee warriors, notably Tecumseh, would continue to fight against the United States intermittently through the end of the War of 1812.

During the seventeenth and eighteenth centuries, the Shawnee were a mobile and divided people. The Shawnee were divided into five units, or divisions, each centered on a town named after the division. The five divisions were Chillicothe, Thawekila, Maquachake, Kispoki, and Piqua, although transliterations of these names vary from source to source. The Shawnee had close relationships with the Creek, the Delaware, and the Iroquois League, although relations with the Iroquois League were often hostile, with the Iroquois pushing the Shawnee out of the Ohio Valley during the Beaver Wars of the seventeenth century. By the middle of the eighteenth century, the Shawnee had returned to the Ohio Valley, migrating from modern-day Pennsylvania to modern-day Ohio. Shawnee towns oscillated between alliance with the French and the English during the 1750s, but most Shawnee ultimately fought on the British side during the Seven Years' War.

After the Treaty of Fort Stanwix (1768), in which the Iroquois League sold to Virginia title to the Ohio Valley (claiming ownership of the land by right of conquest from its seventeenth century victories over the Shawnee), Virginian settlers began moving through the Cumberland Gap and into Kentucky in the early 1770s. Kentucky, although not home to Shawnee towns, was a prime hunting ground, and Virginian settlements threatened to disrupt Shawnee subsistence. The Shawnee actively sought to push Virginian settlers out of the Ohio Valley. The culmination of this incipient conflict was Lord Dunmore's War (1774), in which Virginia's governor backed the initiatives of settlers and speculators to claim Ohio Valley lands. No other Indian nation would ally with the Shawnee during Lord Dunmore's War, and Shawnee leaders were forced to accept the Ohio River as a boundary between Indian and European settlement. Tensions between settlers in Kentucky and the Shawnee towns in Ohio never really abated.

Many Shawnee hoped to remain neutral during the American Revolution, but violence perpetrated by American settlers pushed the Shawnee to the British side. One of the loudest advocates for peace and neutrality was the Maquachake chief, Cornstalk, who corresponded regularly with Congressional Indian agent George Morgan. Cornstalk and other Maquachake leaders were so committed to neutrality that they announced plans to separate their peace faction and found a new town. In October 1777, Cornstalk led a peace delegation to Fort Randolph on the Kanawha River. There he was captured and detained by the fort commander, Captain Matthew Arbuckle. Captain Arbuckle then imprisoned Cornstalk's son, Elinipsico, who had come to Fort Randolph to inquire about his father's condition. The Shawnees remained imprisoned through early November 1777, when a party of local militia, seeking retaliation for the death of a white settler, broke into the fort and killed all of the Shawnee under guard, including Cornstalk.

While Cornstalk's death was officially denounced by Congress, Pennsylvania, and Virginia, Shawnee outrage at the chief's killing fueled a wave of retaliation and pushed most Shawnee away from the American side, at least during the Revolutionary war. One noted battle that occurred in the wake of Cornstalk's death was a raid by a Chillicothe war chief, Black Fish, in which he captured Kentucky settler Daniel Boone. Interestingly, Cornstalk's Maquachakes continued to pursue a policy of peace and neutrality with the Americans and the British. Most of the other Shawnee towns relocated closer to Sandusky and Detroit after the winter of 1777–1778. Beyond a faction of the Maquachakes, led by Chief Moluntha, most Shawnee sided with the British.

After the Peace of Paris, most Shawnee kept the United States at arm's length. The Shawnee did not join in the Treaty of Fort McIntosh (1785) and resoundingly rejected the "conquest theory" formulation of sovereignty that the Confederation Congress put forward in 1784 and after. While some Shawnee leaders (mostly Maquachake, Cornstalk's heir as the advocate for peace and coexistence) signed the subsequent Treaty of Fort Finney (1786), the majority still did want a treaty with the Americans. Their forbearance was understandable. As later in 1786,

Kentucky militiamen attacked the Maquachake towns and killed chief Moluntha. During the 1790s, the Shawnee formed a large part of the pan-Indian resistance to the federal government led by the Miami chief, Little Turtle. In 1795, the Shawnee signed the Treaty of Greenville, terminating the resistance. However, a minority of the Shawnee, driven primarily by the Kispoki leader, Tecumseh, and his brother Tenskwatawa, would continue the resistance against the Americans until Tecumseh's death in Ontario at the battle of the Thames River (1813) during the War of 1812. After the War of 1812, the Shawnee were removed west of the Mississippi by the United States government, with most ending up in Oklahoma.

SEE ALSO *French and Indian War; Indians in the Colonial Wars and the American Revolution.*

BIBLIOGRAPHY

Callender, Charles. "Shawnee." *Handbook of North American Indians.* Edited by Bruce G. Trigger. Vol. 15: *Northeast,* general editor William C. Sturtevant. Washington, D.C.: Smithsonian Institution, 1978.

Calloway, Colin G. *The American Revolution in Indian Country: Crisis and Diversity in Native American Communities.* Cambridge, U.K.: Cambridge University Press, 1995.

Hoxie, Frederick E., Ronald Hoffman, and Peter J. Albert, eds. *Native Americans and the Early Republic.* Charlottesville: University Press of Virginia, 1999.

Prucha, Francis Paul. *American Indian Treaties: The History of a Political Anomaly.* Berkeley: University of California Press, 1994.

Leonard J. Sadosky

SHAYS, DANIEL.

SHAYS, DANIEL. (1747–1825). Continental officer, insurrectionist. Massachusetts. Born in Hopkinton, Massachusetts, Daniel Shays (the spelling varies) had married and moved to Shutesbury before the Revolution. Shays marched on the Lexington alarm as a sergeant in Captain Reuben Dickinson's company of minutemen in Colonel Benjamin Ruggles Woodbridge's Hampshire County regiment of minutemen, and he served for eleven days. Shays was promoted to second lieutenant in Dickinson's company of Woodbridge's regiment, now enlisted for eight months of service to besiege Boston, and he behaved well at the Battle of Bunker Hill. He served as a lieutenant in Colonel James M. Varnum's Ninth Continental Regiment (Rhode Island) in the New York and New Jersey campaigns of 1776. He was promoted to captain in Colonel Rufus Putnam's Fifth Massachusetts Regiment on 1 January 1777 and served at Ticonderoga and Saratoga, where he again distinguished himself. He was detached to the corps of light infantry, a temporary unit raised for the campaigning season, in 1779 and again in 1780 He participated in Anthony Wayne's attack at Stony Point on 16 July 1779. In May 1780 the senior light infantry officers each received a sword from the marquis de Lafayette, the new commander; Shays sold this gift, probably because he already owned a serviceable weapon and needed the money. A man of humble origin, he was a brave and efficient officer who was considerate of his subordinates and popular with his men.

He resigned on 14 October 1780 and settled as a farmer in Pelham, where he sat on the local committee of safety in 1781 and 1782. He is remembered for lending his name to Shays's Rebellion of 1786–1787, although others were as active as he was in this popular uprising against what some residents in central and western Massachusetts perceived as oppression by eastern monied interests. Shays fled to Vermont until he was pardoned in June 1788. After the pardon he moved to Schoharie County, New York, and then to Sparta, New York, where he died in September 1825.

SEE ALSO *Shays's Rebellion; Stony Point, New York.*

revised by Harold E. Selesky

SHAYS'S REBELLION.

31 August 1786– 4 February 1787. As the American states struggled with the problems of establishing a viable economy despite a postwar depression, the collapse of the currency, and an aversion to taxation rooted in their colonial past, an armed revolt against constituted authority arose in central and western Massachusetts. A grassroots insurgency movement with many local leaders, the so-called rebellion came to be known by the name of one of its leaders, Daniel Shays (1747–1825), who had returned to his farm in Pelham, Massachusetts, after retiring from the Continental army in 1781 as a captain in the Fifth Massachusetts Regiment. Those who had so recently united in revolt against British authority were now divided in opinion as to whether the "right of revolution" could be exercised any time citizens objected to governmental authority. Many small farmers in towns across central and western Massachusetts objected to the General Assembly's decision that debts had to be paid in specie, a position supported by the mercantile elites in coastal towns but that posed a significant hardship in agricultural regions that lacked ready access to hard money. They also objected to the mounting number of farm and home foreclosures that threatened to strip them of the economic independence that was a central pillar of their political independence.

Mob actions started on 31 August 1786, when armed men prevented the Hampshire county court from sitting at Northampton. After similar events took place at Worcester, Concord, and Great Barrington, Governor James Bowdoin sent William Shepard (formerly colonel of the Fourth Massachusetts Regiment and now a militia major general) with six hundred militiamen to protect the state's Supreme Court, then sitting at Springfield. Five hundred insurgents confronted the militia on 26 September and obliged the court to adjourn. Because Springfield was the site of a federal arsenal, Congress, under the Articles of Confederation, on 20 October authorized the raising of 1,340 federal troops, mostly in Massachusetts and Connecticut, ostensibly for service against the Indians in the Ohio Valley but which could also be used against the insurgents. However, the slow process of raising this force meant that suppressing the insurgency depended on the willingness of Massachusetts state militiamen to act effectively against their fellow citizens.

Toward the end of 1786, as the insurgency collapsed in other parts of the state, Shays marched on Springfield the day after Christmas with some twelve hundred men to reinforce those already there under Luke Day (formerly a captain in the Seventh Massachusetts Regiment). While Shepard's small militia force continued to guard the arsenal and on 25 January 1787 repulsed a mismanaged attack by the insurgents, Governor Bowdoin called forty-four hundred militiamen into service (mainly from eastern counties) and placed at their head Major General Benjamin Lincoln, who, as Washington's second-in-command, had accepted the British surrender at Yorktown on 19 October 1781. When official funds were not rapidly forthcoming, Lincoln raised twenty thousand dollars from private sources to pay the troops. Lincoln's little army arrived at Springfield on 27 January, dispersed the force under Day, and pursued Shays toward Petersham through a blizzard. Early on 4 February, Lincoln completed a vigorous night march to surprise the insurgents, capturing 150 men and scattering the rest. By the end of February, the insurgency had been suppressed.

Acting quickly to calm public anger and quench any remaining embers of armed resistance, the Massachusetts government offered pardons to all but Shays, Day, and two others; it finally pardoned Shays, who had fled to upper New York State, on 13 June 1788, when it was clear that the violence was finished. While some looked on the insurgency as evidence that a republican form of government was too weak to be feasible, the majority interpreted the experience to mean that a stronger central government was necessary, in part to provide the means to suppress such uprisings but, better still, to prevent them by enacting measures that would improve economic conditions so that a state would not have to adopt policies that set one group of its citizens against another. Thus, Shays's Rebellion strengthened the arguments of those who sought to create a new national government and helped to speed the movement toward the creation and adoption of a new federal Constitution. The rebellion also had an immediate impact that brought relief to those who had undertaken armed resistance: the Massachusetts legislature postponed imposition of a direct tax and limited the liability of debtors, exempting tools and certain personal effects from sale to satisfy creditors. It was a small victory, but sufficient to tamp down resentment.

SEE ALSO *Lincoln, Benjamin; Shays, Daniel; Shepard, William.*

BIBLIOGRAPHY
Richards, Leonard L. *Shays's Rebellion: The American Revolution's Final Battle.* Philadelphia: University of Pennsylvania Press, 2002.

Szatmary, David P. *Shays' Rebellion: The Making of an Agrarian Insurrection.* Amherst: University of Massachusetts Press, 1980.

Taylor, Robert J. *Western Massachusetts in the Revolution.* Providence, R.I.: Brown University Press, 1954.

revised by Harold E. Selesky

SHELBURNE, WILLIAM PETTY FITZMAURICE, EARL OF.

(1737–1805). British politician and prime minister. Born in Dublin, Fitzmaurice (later Petty) joined the Twentieth Regiment and served at Rochefort (1757), Minden (1759), and Kloster Kamp (1760). He was promoted colonel and appointed aide-de-camp to George III in 1760, and in 1761 he succeeded his father as earl of Shelburne. In 1763 he became president of the Board of Trade under George Grenville, fruitlessly challenging Lord Egremont's control of American policy and demanding equal access to the king. Quarreling with Lord Halifax, the other secretary of state, over the prosecution of John Wilkes, he tired of his position and resigned after only four months. Now an acolyte of William Pitt, earl of Chatham, in 1766 he supported the repeal of the Stamp Act, opposed the Declaratory Act, and became secretary of state for the Southern Department in Chatham's second ministry. In cabinet he unsuccessfully resisted Charles Townshend's duties and the persecution of Wilkes: when Chatham resigned in 1768, Shelburne went too. In opposition he spoke against the deployment of troops in Boston (1768), the Coercive Acts, and, at least at first, the war in America. However, his frequently declared opposition to American independence made him acceptable to George III as secretary of state in the second Rockingham government. He

quarreled with Charles Fox, the other secretary, over the peace negotiations, and sent his own representative to Paris. When Rockingham died, Shelburne became prime minister. He concluded a separate peace with the Americans but at the price of accepting both independence and the American refusal to compensate Loyalists. These issues did not prevent ratification, but they brought his ministry down early in 1783. He did not return to office under William Pitt the younger in 1784 but was raised to marquess of Lansdowne.

SEE ALSO *Chatham, William Pitt, First Earl of; Declaratory Act; Fox, Charles James; Intolerable (or Coercive) Acts; Stamp Act; Townshend Acts; Townshend, Charles; Wilkes, John.*

revised by John Oliphant

SHELBY, ISAAC.

(1750–1826). Militia leader, first governor of Kentucky. Born near Hagerstown, Maryland, on 11 December 1750, Isaac Shelby moved with his family to the Holston settlements in what was then the westernmost part of Virginia, and in 1774 he served in his father's Fincastle County militia company as a lieutenant. He distinguished himself in the battle of Point Pleasant, West Virginia, on 10 October 1774. Until July 1775 he was second in command of the garrison at Point Pleasant. After surveying lands in Kentucky for the Transylvania Company—and for himself—he was appointed captain of a company of Virginia militia in July 1776. For the next three years he was engaged in providing supplies for various frontier garrisons and for the expeditions of Lachlan McIntosh (1778) and George Rogers Clark (1779). In 1779 he was elected to the Virginia legislature for Washington County.

Early in 1780 he was appointed colonel of militia in Sullivan County, North Carolina. In July 1780 he joined General Charles McDowell with about 600 "Over Mountain Men" and helped in the capture of Thicketty Fort, in South Carolina. He then combined forces with Elijah Clarke to repulse a Loyalist attack at Cedar Springs, South Carolina, on 8 August, and to win the engagement at Musgrove's Mill ten days later.

Shelby figured prominently in the victory at Kings Mountain, South Carolina, on 7 October 1780. He was also present for the victory at Cowpens, also in South Carolina. Fear of the Cherokee kept Shelby's troops close to home until a treaty was negotiated on 20 July 1781. With 200 men Shelby joined Colonel Hezekiah Maham to capture a British post at Fair Lawn, near Monck's Corner, South Carolina, on 27 November 1781. While engaged in this expedition, Shelby was elected to the North Carolina legislature. He attended its sessions in December 1781 and, re-elected, he sat in the sessions held at Hillsboro in April 1782.

In 1783 Shelby moved to Kentucky, where he was a member of the conventions of 1787, 1788, and 1789 that prepared the way for statehood. On 4 June 1792 he took office as the state's first governor, but four years later he declined re-election and devoted the next 15 years to his private affairs. In August 1812 he again became governor, and the next year led 4,000 volunteers north to take part in the victory over the British at the Thames River, near Ontario, on 5 October 1813. In March 1817 he declined the portfolio of Secretary of War, which was offered to him by President James Monroe. Shelby died at his home in Lincoln County, Kentucky, on 18 July 1826.

SEE ALSO *Dunmore's (or Cresap's) War; Kings Mountain, South Carolina; Over Mountain Men.*

BIBLIOGRAPHY

Wrobel, Sylvia, and George Grider. *Isaac Shelby: Kentucky's First Governor and Hero of Three Wars.* Danville, Ky.: Cumberland Press, 1974.

revised by Michael Bellesiles

SHELDON, ELISHA. (1740–1796). Colonel of the Second Dragoons. Connecticut. Little is known of Sheldon's early life other than that he was born in Lyme, Connecticut, 6 Mar 1740. After commanding a battalion of Connecticut light cavalry from June 1776, he was commissioned as a colonel on 12 December 1776 and commanded the Second Dragoons, known as "Sheldon's Light Dragoons," from then until the end of the war. In the Philadelphia Campaign of 1777 he performed the normal cavalry tasks of reconnoitering the enemy's movements. Thereafter he served on the east side of the Hudson River. General Banastre Tarleton made an unsuccessful attempt to defeat him at Poundridge, New York, on 2 July 1779. As part of his preparations to give West Point to the British, Benedict Arnold had to hoodwink Sheldon into permitting "John Anderson" (John André) to enter the American lines. Sheldon had been temporarily succeeded by his lieutenant colonel, John Jameson, when "John Anderson" arrived.

Sheldon was brevetted as a brigadier general on 30 September 1780. In the operations against Manhattan preceding the Yorktown campaign, Sheldon took part in the unsuccessful attempt on 3 July 1781 to surprise Oliver De Lancey's Loyalist forces near Morrisania, New York. When the allies marched to Virginia he remained under William Heath, serving in in the Highlands Department

(around the Hudson River). After the war Sheldon moved to Vermont, where the town of Sheldon Springs was named in his honor.

SEE ALSO *Arnold's Treason; Poundridge, New York.*

revised by Michael Bellesiles

SHEPARD, WILLIAM. (1737–1817). Continental officer. Massachusetts. Born in Westfield, Massachuetts, William Shepard was the son of a tanner and deacon of the local Congregational church. He enlisted as a private in a Massachusetts provincial regiment at the age of seventeen, in 1755. By the end of the final French and Indian war, he was a captain with six years of valuable military experience. A farmer, selectman, and member of the Westfield Committee of Correspondence prior to the Revolution, he led his company of Colonel Timothy Danielson's minuteman regiment in response to the Lexington alarm in April 1775, and was elected lieutenant colonel of Danielson's regiment in May 1775, while serving in the New England army besieging Boston. On 1 January 1776 he was named lieutenant colonel of the Third Continental Infantry (Massachusetts), was wounded at the battle of Long Island on 27 August, and was promoted to colonel on 2 October, with seniority from 4 May. He performed well, but was wounded again, at Pell's Point, New York, on 18 October 1776. On 1 January 1777 he took command of the Fourth Massachusetts and led his regiment in the battles around Saratoga as part of John Glover's Second Massachusetts Brigade. After spending the winter at Valley Forge, he went on recruiting duty around Springfield, Massachusetts. By the time he retired from the army, on 1 January 1783, he had fought in twenty-two separate engagements. Breveted a brigadier general on 30 September 1783, he returned to his farm at Westfield.

As a major general of militia in Hampshire County in 1786, Shepard defended the federal court at Springfield during Shays's Rebellion. Starting on 25 January 1787, he held off Shays's attack on the arsenal until General Benjamin Lincoln arrived with a relief force. He was never fully reimbursed for public expenditures from his own pocket, and some of his personal property was destroyed by Shays's sympathizers. In addition to other public offices, he served in the House of Representatives for three two-year terms, starting in March 1797. He spent his last fifteen years quietly on his farm.

SEE ALSO *Lincoln, Benjamin; Pell's Point, New York.*

revised by Harold E. Selesky

SHERBURNE'S REGIMENT. Commanded by Colonel Henry Sherburne, it was one of the sixteen "additional Continental regiments." Lieutenant Colonel Return J. Meigs served with it 22 February–22 May 1777, and Major William Bradford served 12 January 1777–1 January 1781.

Mark M. Boatner

SHERMAN, ROGER. (1722–1793). Statesman and Signer. Massachusetts and Connecticut. Roger Sherman epitomizes the self-made man. Educated in country schools near his father's farm at Stoughton (now Sharon), Massachusetts, just south of Boston, he had a natural thirst for knowledge and a methodical approach to self-education. He read widely in history, law, politics, mathematics, and theology. Apprenticed as a cobbler, he is said to have worked with an open book always before him. In June 1743, after the death of his father, he moved to New Milford, Connecticut, where his elder brother had settled. Tradition says that he walked the entire distance, some 170 miles by road, with his cobbler's tools on his back. He had tremendous energy and versatility. His interest in mathematics led to his appointment as Litchfield County surveyor (1745–1758), and to the creation of a series of almanacs based on his own astronomical calculations (1750–1761). Interested in fiscal stability, he published in 1752 a pamphlet entitled *A Caveat Against Injustice, or an Enquiry into the Evil Consequences of a Fluctuating Medium of Exchange.*

He was admitted to the bar in 1754, held many of public offices (including delegate to the Assembly and commissary for the Connecticut provincial troops during the final French and Indian war), and made a good deal of money, not only as a multiple officeholder but also as a prominent local merchant. He moved to New Haven, Connecticut, in 1760 to enhance his mercantile prospects. He was elected treasurer of Yale College in 1765, a post he held until 1776, when politics began to consume most of his time and energy. He had been elected to the General Assembly from New Milford (1755–1761) and also from New Haven (1764–1766). In May 1766 his opposition to the Stamp Act led voters to elevate him to the governor's council, where he served for the next nineteen years.

By experience and temperament, Sherman was well qualified to represent Connecticut in the Continental Congress. He served as a delegate from September 1774 to November 1781, and again for the first six months of 1784. Perhaps because of his undramatic personality and lack of oratorical skill, he is not remembered as the author of any particular act of that body, but the stern old Puritan

was, in the words of John Adams, "honest as an angel and as firm in the cause of American independence as Mount Atlas." Sherman accumulated more legislative experience than any other delegate. He served on the committee to draft the Declaration of Independence, on various ways and means committees, on the boards of war and ordnance, on the treasury board, and on the committee on Indian affairs. With Yankee standards of frugality, and based on his considerable fiscal experience before and during the war, Sherman defied popular opinion to argue for sound currency, minimum government borrowing, and higher taxes. He also disregarded the vested interests of friends and former business associates to advocate Connecticut's cession of western land claims.

In addition to his extensive congressional duties, he also undertook important state business. He served on the Connecticut council of safety (1777–1779, 1782), and in 1783 he and Richard Law worked five months to revise the state's statutory laws. In the federal convention of 1787 he introduced and took the leading part in promoting the so-called Connecticut Compromise, whereby smaller states retained an equal voice in the Senate to balance the predominance of the more populous states in the House of Representatives. He served in the House from 1789 to 1791, and in the Senate from 1791 to 1793. He has the distinction of being the only man to sign four of the great documents of the Continental Congress: the Articles of Association of 1774, the Declaration of Independence in 1776, the Articles of Confederation in 1779, and the federal Constitution in 1787.

SEE ALSO *Continental Congress.*

BIBLIOGRAPHY

Collier, Christopher. *Roger Sherman's Connecticut.* Middletown, Conn.: Wesleyan University Press, 1971.

Rommel, John G. *Connecticut's Yankee Patriot.* Hartford, Conn.: American Revolution Bicentennial Commission of Connecticut, 1980.

revised by Harold E. Selesky

SHIP OF THE LINE. A "ship of the line" was a warship that was sufficiently large and well-armed so that it could lie in line of battle, where its guns, mounted in broadside, could bear on the enemy. A system of six "rates" was introduced by Lord George Anson, first lord of the Admiralty in the early 1750s, that grouped warships according to how many guns they carried. Only the first three rates were considered to be ships of the line. A "first-rate" carried upwards of one hundred guns, a "second-rate" from eighty-four to one hundred guns, and a "third-rate" from seventy to eighty-four guns. During

the War for American Independence, a third-rate of seventy-four guns was the most common type.

SEE ALSO *Line.*

revised by Harold E. Selesky

SHIPPEN FAMILY OF PHILADEL-PHIA.

Edward Shippen (1729–1806), in the fourth generation of a wealthy and powerful Philadelphia Quaker family, became chief justice of Pennsylvania after the Revolution. He attained this post despite the fact that he had been a moderate Loyalist and that his daughter Margaret (Peggy) was married to Benedict Arnold.

William Shippen (1736–1808), Edward's cousin and son of Dr. William Shippen II (a delegate to the Continental Congress in 1779–1780), was a physician and pioneer teacher of anatomy and midwifery. About 1760 he married Alice Lee, sister of Richard Henry, Francis Lightfoot, William, and Arthur Lee. After studying under William Hunter in London, Shippen started teaching anatomy in Philadelphia on 16 November 1762. Despite popular objections to his use of human bodies, which included attacks on his surgery, Shippen became professor of surgery and anatomy in the newly established medical school of the College of Philadelphia in 1765. He was also one of the few doctors in America to teach midwifery to both men and women.

In July 1776 William Shippen was appointed chief physician of the Continental army hospital in New Jersey, and in October he became director general of all hospitals west of the Hudson. On 11 April 1777 he succeeded John Morgan as chief physician and director general of all Continental army hospitals. His appointment undoubtedly was earned to a large extent by the plan for reorganization of the medical service that he had submitted to Congress in March 1777 and that was adopted almost in its entirety. Morgan, who had once been a close friend, accused Shippen of engineering his discharge and Benjamin Rush charged him with inefficiency. Shippen was arrested in October 1780 and charged with speculating in hospital stores and incompetence. He admitted the former but fought the latter, being acquitted by a bitterly divided court-martial and barely escaping censure by Congress. On 3 January 1781 he resigned from the army and continued his career as a teacher and practitioner. The scandals that drove him from his position with the army did not harm his later career, as he became a prominent professor at the University of Pennsylvania and president of the College of Physicians of Philadelphia from 1805 until his death on 11 July 1808.

SEE ALSO *Arnold, Benedict; Lee Family of Virginia; Morgan, John; Rush, Benjamin.*

BIBLIOGRAPHY

Klein, Randolph S. *Portrait of an Early American Family: The Shippens of Pennsylvania across Five Generations.* Philadelphia: University of Pennsylvania Press, 1975.

revised by Michael Bellesiles

SHIRLEY, WILLIAM.

(1694–1771). Colonial governor of Massachusetts. Son of a London merchant who died when he was only seven, William Shirley grew up amidst aristocratic connections but without the financial means for the life to which he aspired. He was graduated from Cambridge University, was admitted to the bar in 1720, and practiced law in London for the next eleven years. During this time he increased his circle of influential connections but not his financial status. Deciding to emigrate to America, he reached Boston in 1731 with a letter of introduction to Governor Jonathan Belcher from the duke of Newcastle, who was an acquaintance of the family and Shirley's lifelong patron. A long period of place-hunting was marked by his appointment as judge of the vice-admiralty court in New England in 1733 and, soon thereafter, as advocate general (prosecutor) of the court. In his search for higher office, Shirley undertook to undermine the already shaky reputation of Belcher, and on 25 May 1741 succeeded him as governor of Massachusetts.

Faced with the problem of liquidating various banking schemes that made the finances of the colony unstable, and with the need to strengthen military defenses because war with France appeared to be inevitable, Shirley restored public credit by closely regulating the use of tax money to redeem paper currency and by holding out the prospect of increased trade and a larger empire when French ambitions were defeated. He proved himself an able and tactful administrator. Shortly after Britain declared war on France in late 1744, Shirley proposed an expedition to capture Louisbourg, the French fortress that threatened the New England fisheries, and in early 1745 he secured from the Massachusetts General Court and from neighboring colonies approval for his scheme. Shirley's popularity soared when, on 17 June 1745, Louisbourg surrendered to an expeditionary force of New Englanders under William Pepperell and the supporting British fleet under Commodore Peter Warren. He made sure that the specie that Parliament voted in 1748 to reimburse Massachusetts for its expenses in the Louisburg expedition was used to reestablish the finances of the province on a firm basis. Shirley was in Paris from 1749 to 1753 as a commissioner to establish the boundary between New England and

French Canada. On his return to Massachusetts, he worked to prepare for the expected renewal of hostilities with the French in America.

In April 1755 Edward Braddock, the new British commander in North America, appointed Shirley as his second in command and gave him the task of mounting an expedition against Fort Niagara. Logistical obstacles prevented Shirley from ever reaching his target. One of his sons died of fever on this expedition, and his eldest son was killed at the Monongahela on 9 July while serving as Braddock's secretary. Shirley became British commander in chief in North America after Braddock's death, but his indecisiveness led to the loss of Oswego in 1756. He was succeeded by the Earl of Loudoun in July 1756, when the home authorities became dissatisfied with his conduct of military affairs. Loudoun developed an intense dislike for Shirley, who was finally recalled to England to face charges not only of mismanagement of military strategy and organization but also of irregularities in his financial accounts. It was his misfortune to arrive just as the tenure of the duke of Newcastle was ending, but in the fall of 1757 the War Office was forced to drop its court-martial charges for lack of evidence. Meanwhile, Thomas Pownall took office as governor of Massachusetts. Promoted to lieutenant general, Shirley became governor of the Bahamas in 1761, after having been denied the governorship of Jamaica. In 1767 he relinquished the governorship to his only surviving son, Thomas, and two years later he returned to his home at Roxbury, Massachusetts, where he died in March 1771.

SEE ALSO *Belcher, Jonathan; Pownall, Thomas.*

BIBLIOGRAPHY

Lincoln, Charles H., ed. *Correspondence of William Shirley, 1731–1760.* 2 vols. 1912.

Schutz, John A. *William Shirley: King's Governor of Massachusetts.* Chapel Hill, N.C.: Institute of History and Culture at Williamsburg, Virginia, 1961.

revised by Harold E. Selesky

SHIRTMEN.

A term for American riflemen, it appears to have been coined by the British and applied originally to the Virginia riflemen. In his entry of 20 July 1775, Thacher speaks of the arrival of Pennsylvania and Maryland riflemen in the Boston lines: "They are dressed in white frocks, or rifle-shirts, and round hats."

SEE ALSO *Great Bridge, Virginia; Riflemen.*

Mark M. Boatner

SHOEMAKER'S HOUSE
SEE *Butler, Walter; German Flats, New York.*

SHORT HILLS (METUCHEN), NEW JERSEY.

26 June 1777. During the "June Maneuvers" of the Philadelphia Campaign, Lieutenant General William Howe maintained strong forces in the Brunswick-Amboy area close to the shore and yet in a position to carry out foraging activities. Washington concentrated his main force in an excellent defensive position on the high ground around Quibble Town (modern New Market) and Bound Brook. To hold the foragers in check he pushed forward a task force built around a division consisting of the New Jersey Brigade and Conway's Third Pennsylvania Brigade, led by William Alexander (known as Lord Stirling). Relying on his men's knowledge of the local area, Alexander camped near Metuchen Meeting House, about five miles northwest of Amboy. While in this position Howe made his last effort to bring Washington to decisive battle in the New York area before sailing to Philadelphia. At 1 A.M. on 26 June, the British moved out in two columns. Howe planned to annihilate Alexander and then capture the passes to Middle Brook, which would force Washington into the open. The movement of such a large force could not be hidden, and Washington easily fell back to a more secure location.

The British boasted of defeating Alexander, and historians have often depicted the operation as an example of the inferiority of the Continentals' training. However, the reality is more complex. Alexander's troops displayed great coolness in forming for battle and staged a successful withdrawal while covering Washington. The British pursued some five miles without being able to cut him off. Casualties were light, but Alexander's rear guard lost three field guns. The next day Howe withdrew to Amboy and embarked on 30 June, having accomplished nothing from this affair.

Although "Short Hills" is used here to designate the affair, the name is confusing because the Short Hills Meeting House (Milburn, New Jersey) was actually near Springfield, more than twelve miles away. The incident might more logically be called the Affair at Metuchen Meeting House.

SEE ALSO *Philadelphia Campaign; Springfield, New Jersey, Raid of Knyphausen.*

revised by Robert K. Wright Jr.

SHORT HILLS (7–23 JUNE 1780)
SEE *Springfield, New Jersey, Raid of Knyphausen.*

SHREVE, ISRAEL. (?–1799). Continental

officer. New Jersey. Lieutenant colonel of the Second New Jersey on 31 October 1775, he was colonel on 28 November 1776 and served until he retired on 1 January 1781 when the reorganization of the New Jersey Line took effect, but stayed on duty long enough to deal with the mutiny of the New Jersey Line of 20–27 January 1781. When George Washington wrote Shreve for an explanation of his failure to put in an appearance on 27 January, Shreve mentioned nothing about being out of the service but said, "[I] thought it best to not go to camp until the matter was over, as those who suffered might look up to me for to intercede for their pardon." Washington did not learn until 7 February that Shreve had left the service when the New Jersey Brigade was reorganized as of 1 January 1781. Elias Dayton theoretically moved from command of the Third New Jersey to succeed Shreve as commander of the Second New Jersey.

A loyal Patriot who had been impoverished by his long war service, the immensely fat Shreve was an incompetent officer. His slim prospects for promotion to brigadier general were killed by Washington's statement in December 1780 that "here I drop the curtain." (Van Doren, p. 209).

During his six years of service, Shreve fought in skirmishes in New Jersey, the invasion of Canada in 1776, and the battles of Monmouth and Springfield. A farmer after the war, he moved to western Pennsylvania, where he died the same day as Washington.

SEE ALSO *Dayton, Elias; Mutiny of the New Jersey Line; New Jersey Line.*

BIBLIOGRAPHY

Thompson, William Y. *Israel Shreve, Revolutionary War Officer.* Ruston, La.: McGinty Trust Fund Publication, 1979.

Van Doren, Carl. *Mutiny in January: The Story of a Crisis in the Continental Army.* New York: Viking, 1943.

Ward, Harry M. *William Maxwell and the New Jersey Continentals.* Westport, Conn.: Greenwood Press, 1997.

revised by Harry M. Ward

SHURTLEFF, ROBERT. Alias under which

Deborah Sampson enlisted in the Continental Army.

SEE ALSO *Sampson, Deborah.*

Mark M. Boatner

SIGNERS. In American history, a "signer" is one of

the fifty-six members of the Second Continental Congress who signed the Declaration of Independence on or after 2 August 1776. The document was officially adopted on 4 July 1776, but it was signed only after it was engrossed on parchment (written out in a large, clear hand), a process that was completed on 2 August. On that date John Hancock of Massachusetts, the president of Congress, signed first, followed by forty-nine other delegates, beginning below and to the right of the text, in geographic order of the states from north to south. Six more delegates signed after 2 August, one of whom, Thomas McKean of Delaware, claimed to have signed before the end of the year but in fact had not done so by 18 January 1777 and may not have signed until 1781. All of the delegates signed, not as individuals, but in their capacity as members of a state delegation.

The signers were those men who happened to be delegates on 2 August. Of the fifty-six signers, fourteen had not been present on 2 July, when Richard Henry Lee's resolution declaring independence was adopted, or on 4 July, when the Declaration itself was approved. Eight delegates who were present on 2 or 4 July did not sign the engrossed copy of the Declaration, including John Dickinson of Pennsylvania and Robert R. Livingston of New York, who both thought independence premature, although Livingston had been a member of the committee to draft the Declaration. Opponents of the document who nevertheless signed it on 2 August were Carter Braxton of Virginia, Robert Morris of Pennsylvania, George Read of Delaware, and Edward Rutledge of South Carolina. Among the delegates no longer in Congress, and who therefore could not sign, were George Washington of Virginia, John Sullivan of New Hampshire, and George Clinton of New York, all of whom were in active military service, and Christopher Gadsden of South Carolina and Patrick Henry of Virginia, who were active in the governments of their home states. Men prominent in later years, including James Madison, Alexander Hamilton, and James Monroe, had not yet been elected to Congress.

The fifty-six signers were nearly all well educated and prosperous and represented a cross-section of the elite leadership of the rebellion. Benjamin Franklin of Pennsylvania was the oldest (seventy years old) and the American with the greatest international reputation. Edward Rutledge of South Carolina was the youngest (twenty-six years old). Most were in their thirties and forties. Charles Carroll of Carrollton, Maryland, lived the longest, dying at the age of ninety-five in 1832. All but eight signers had been born in the colonies; the eight immigrants had been born in the British Isles. Two were bachelors—Caesar Rodney and Joseph Hewes—while Carter Braxton was the father of eighteen children. Francis Hopkinson was a musician and poet, Lyman

Hall and John Witherspoon were clergymen. Lawyers predominated (twenty-four of fifty-six). Sixteen signers also signed the Articles of Confederation, and six also signed the federal Constitution. Only Roger Sherman of Connecticut and Robert Morris of Pennsylvania signed the Declaration, the Articles, and the Constitution.

Delegates not present on 2 or 4 July, who signed on 2 August:

- William Williams, Connecticut
- Lewis Morris, New York
- Benjamin Rush, Pennsylvania
- George Clymer, Pennsylvania
- James Smith, Pennsylvania
- George Taylor, Pennsylvania
- George Ross, Pennsylvania
- Samuel Chase, Maryland
- Charles Carroll of Carrollton, Maryland
- William Hooper, North Carolina

Delegates not present on 2 or 4 July, who signed after 2 August:

- Oliver Wolcott, Connecticut
- Mathew Thornton, New Hampshire
- Richard Henry Lee, Virginia
- George Wythe, Virginia

Delegates present on 2 or 4 July, who signed after 2 August:

- Elbridge Gerry, Massachusetts
- Thomas McKean, Delaware

Delegates present on 2 or 4 July, who did not sign:

- John Alsop, New York
- George Clinton, New York
- Robert R. Livingston, New York
- Henry Wisner, New York
- John Dickinson, Pennsylvania
- Charles Humphreys, Pennsylvania
- Thomas Willing, Pennsylvania
- John Rogers, Maryland

Considering the bleak outlook for the American cause in August 1776, the signers are particularly to be admired for signing a document for which they would have been hung as traitors and rebels had Britain won the war and reestablished royal control of the colonies. The danger to the signers was so great that their names were held secret until 18 January 1777, when the victories at Trenton and Princeton prompted Congress to take the bold step of ordering an authenticated copy of the Declaration of Independence and the names of the signers to be sent to each state. Although no signer died directly at the hands of the British, Francis Lewis of New York and Richard Stockton of New Jersey each suffered a particularly hard fate at the their hands. Both had their homes destroyed, and Lewis's wife and Stockton suffered a captivity that ruined their health. John Hart of New Jersey saw his farm destroyed, and he and his wife had to hide in the woods for months, ruining her health. Elbridge Gerry of Massachusetts and Thomas Jefferson of Virginia escaped capture by minutes, and another six were fortunate enough to avoid being taken by enemy forces sent in their pursuit. Homes of fifteen signers were destroyed.

A list of the fifty-six signers, arranged both alphabetically and by state, is contained in the Appendices. All are sketched individually in this book.

SEE ALSO *Continental Congress; Declaration of Independence; Independence.*

BIBLIOGRAPHY
Ferris, Robert G., ed. *Signers of the Declaration: Historic Places Commemorating the Signing of the Declaration of Independence.* Washington, D.C.: National Park Service, 1973.

Malone, Dumas. *The Story of the Declaration of Independence.* New York: Oxford University Press, 1954.

Smith, Paul H. et al., eds. *Letters of Delegates to Congress, 1774–1789.* Vols. 1–4. Washington, D.C.: Library of Congress, 1976–1979.

United States Congress. *Biographical Directory of the United States Congress, 1774–1989.* Washington, D.C.: U.S. Government Printing Office, 1989.

revised by Harold E. Selesky

SIGN MANUAL. The term "sign manual" had two meanings in the eighteenth century. In one sense, it meant the signature of the sovereign on a document to signify royal authentication. It also meant the regulations governing naval tactics contained in a manual (small book) of signals (signs) that would be flown from the flagship to direct an engagement.

revised by Harold E. Selesky

SILLIMAN, GOLD SELLECK. (1732–1790).

Militia general. Connecticut. Born at Fairfield, Gold Selleck Silliman was the son of Ebenezer Silliman (1707–1775), who was a member of the governor's council from 1739 to 1765 and a judge of the superior court from 1743 to 1765. Gold Selleck was graduated from Yale College in 1752, and eventually became an attorney. Captain of a militia troop of horse in May 1769, he was appointed major of the local militia regiment in January 1774, lieutenant colonel in November, and colonel in May 1775. Silliman led his militia regiment to New York on temporary duty in March 1776, and returned in early July as colonel of the newly-raised First Connecticut Battalion, one of seven the General Assembly had created to reinforce Commander in Chief George Washington's army. During the New York campaign he commanded his regiment at Long Island (it had rotated to the rear on the day of the battle, 27 August), in the evacuation of New York City on 15 September, and at White Plains on 28 October, where he distinguished himself. He returned home by 25 December. The Assembly had already appointed him brigadier general of the Fourth Militia Brigade, in southwestern Connecticut closest to the British at New York City. In addition to dealing with a constant stream of raids and counter-raids across the no-man's land on land and sea that separated the antagonists, Silliman saw action in the Danbury Raid of 24–26 April 1777 and led 1,800 militiamen to the Hudson Highlands in October 1777 in response to Sir Henry Clinton's attack. Captured by Loyalists on 1 May 1779, he was paroled on Long Island and exchanged a year later for a Yale contemporary, the Loyalist judge Thomas Jones, taken on 9 November 1779 to force Silliman's release. The exchange took place in the middle of Long Island Sound on 27 April 1780. He returned home broken in health and impoverished. He resumed his legal career, but resigned his commission at the end of 1781. He died at his home in Fairfield. His sons and grandsons became famous as scientists and lawyers.

SEE ALSO *Danbury Raid, Connecticut; Jones, Thomas.*

BIBLIOGRAPHY

Buel, Joy Day, and Richard V. Buel, Jr. *The Way of Duty.* New York: Norton, 1984.

revised by Harold E. Selesky

SILVER BULLET TRICK.

Messengers or spies would sometimes carry a message in a hollow, silver bullet that could be swallowed to prevent incrimination if they were captured. In his journal entry of 14 October 1777, Dr. James Thacher wrote:

> After the capture of Fort Montgomery, Sir Henry Clinton dispatched a messenger by the name of Daniel Taylor to Burgoyne with the intelligence; fortunately he was taken on his way as a spy, and finding himself in danger, he was seen to turn aside and take something from his pocket and swallow it. General George Clinton, into whose hands he had fallen, ordered a severe dose of emetic tartar to be administered. This produced the happiest effect as respects the prescriber; but it proved fatal to the patient. He discharged a small silver bullet, which being unscrewed, was found to enclose a letter from Sir Henry Clinton to Burgoyne (p. 106).

The spy was tried, convicted, and executed. It is not known how common was this method of secreting messages.

SEE ALSO *Clinton's Expedition.*

BIBLIOGRAPHY

Thacher, James. *A Military Journal during the American Revolutionary War, from 1775–1783.* Boston: Cottons and Barnard, 1827.

revised by Michael Bellesiles

SIMCOE, JOHN GRAVES. (1752–1806).

British commander of the Queen's Rangers. Son of a Royal Navy captain who died at Quebec in 1759, John Simcoe was schooled at Exeter Grammar School, Eton College, and Merton College, Oxford, before becoming an ensign in the Thirty-Fifth Foot on 27 April 1770. He served as adjutant from 27 March 1772, and was promoted lieutenant (by purchase) on 12 March 1774. In April 1775 he embarked with his regiment from Cork as part of the first reinforcement for the army at Boston, where he arrived two days after the battle of Bunker Hill. He saw active service around Boston for the remainder of the year. On 27 December 1775 he purchased a captaincy in the Fortieth Foot, and served with his new regiment in the New York campaign in 1776 and the Philadelphia campaign in 1777. He was severely wounded at the Brandywine River on 11 September 1777, and on 15 October was given the provincial rank of major and named commander of the Queen's Rangers. "He wanted to form a combined light corps which would be especially suited for service in America but would also introduce a more general reform of British military practice. Their training gave little attention to formal drill, but insisted on physical fitness, rapid movement, bayonet fighting, and most particularly, discipline in the field" (S. R. Mealing in

DCB). He led this Loyalist legion of light horse and foot troops in the skirmishes at Quintan's Bridge and Hancock's Bridge, both in New Jersey, in March 1778, and in the action at Crooked Billet, Pennsylvania, on 1 May, before taking part in the Monmouth campaign and winning promotion to the provincial rank of lieutenant colonel commandant in June. He took part in the foraging expedition that led to the Tappan massacre in New York on 28 September 1778, but was not engaged in the action itself. On 1 June 1779 his rangers took part in the capture of Stony Point and Verplanck's Point, and they raided Poundridge, New York, on 2 July 1779. He narrowly escaped death when he was ambushed, wounded, and captured with four of his men on 17 October after a successful raid from Amboy to Somerset Court House, New Jersey. He was exchanged on 31 December 1779. "As contemptuous of the military capacity of his adversaries as he was of their republicanism, his leadership made the Queen's Rangers the most successful of the American loyalist corps" (John A. Houlding in ODNB).

When the traitor Benedict Arnold was sent to raid Virginia a year later, Sir Henry Clinton included these instructions (14 December): "Having sent Lieutenant Colonels Dundas and Simcoe (officers of great experience and much in my confidence) with you, I am to desire that you will always consult those gentlemen previous to your undertaking any operation of consequence." Highlights of Simcoe's operations in Virginia were his rout of the militia defenders of Richmond on 5 January 1781, his surprise and rout of another militia concentration by a night raid to Charles City Court House on 8 January, his part in the attack at Petersburg on 25 April, his raid to scatter Friedrich Steuben's command at Point of Fork on 5 June, and his battle at Spencer's Tavern on 26 June. During the Yorktown siege he was posted on the north bank of the York River at Gloucester, and surrendered there with the rest of Cornwallis's army on 20 October 1781.

Promoted to brevet lieutenant colonel in the British Army on 19 December 1781 and invalided home the same month, he married in 1782 and until 1790 divided his time between London and his family estate in Devon. He then entered parliament. On the division of Canada in 1791 he was appointed the first lieutenant governor of Upper Canada, under Governor-General Sir Guy Carleton. He and his family arrived at Quebec on 11 November 1791, where they wintered. He arrived at Newark, the temporary capital of Upper Canada (now Niagara-on-the-Lake, Ontario), on 26 July 1792. While his plans "to create a bastion of social and political conservatism and to prevent the emergence of American-style frontier democracy" (ODNB) were beyond his capacity to accomplish in the short term, "he gave both expression and impetus to the blend of conservatism, loyalty, and emphasis on economic progress that was to dominate the province after the War of 1812. The most persistently energetic governor sent to British North America after the American Revolution, he had not only the most articulate faith in its imperial destiny but also the most sympathetic appreciation of the interest and aspirations of its inhabitants" (DCB). Ill health forced his resignation in the summer of 1796.

On 10 November 1796 he was appointed commander of the recently captured island of San Domingo. He returned to England in July 1797, again in ill health. In 1801 he commanded at Plymouth when Napoleon's invasion was expected. In July 1806 he was named commander in chief in India but, his health broken, he took sick on the way out, returned home, and died at Exeter on 26 October 1806.

Simcoe's self-published *Journal of the Operations of the Queen's Rangers*, released in Exeter in 1787) was "the outstanding tactical study of the *petite guerre* to emerge from the eighteenth-century American wars, an invaluable training and tactical manual for officers soon to be engaged with the light forces of the French revolutionary armies" (ODNB). It is also a valuable historical account, particularly for the host of skirmishes in which he participated.

BIBLIOGRAPHY
Riddell, W. R. *The Life of John Graves Simcoe.* Toronto: Mclelland and Stewart, 1926.

revised by Harold E. Selesky

SIMITIERE, PIERRE-EUGÈNE DU.

(1736–1784). Artist. Switzerland Born in Geneva, Switzerland, in 1736, Simitiere went to the West Indies when he was about fourteen years old. He settled in Philadelphia in 1766. Around 1779 he drew the portraits of Commander in Chief George Washington, Friedrich Wilhelm Augustus von Steuben, Silas Deane, Joseph Reed, Gouverneur Morris, John Dickinson, Benedict Arnold, and many other prominent Americans. Engraved in Paris, published there in 1781, pirated in England (1783), and reprinted many times, Simitiere's engravings became the standard visual portraits of the Revolutionary leadership. Simitiere was an avid collector of natural curiosities, books, and pamphlets. In 1782 he opened his celebrated collection to the public as the "American Museum" in Philadelphia, where he died in October 1784.

BIBLIOGRAPHY
Sifton, Paul G., ed. *Historiographer to the United States: The Revolutionary Letterbook of Pierre Eugène Du Simitière.* New York: Vantage Press, 1987.

The Simitiere Papers. Philadelphia, Pa. and Washington, D.C.: Library Company of Philadelphia and Library of Congress.

revised by Michael Bellesiles

SIMSBURY MINES, CONNECTICUT.
Abandoned copper mines, ten miles northwest of Hartford, where Loyalist prisoners were incarcerated.

Mark M. Boatner

SKENE, PHILIP. (1725–1810). Loyalist. Born in London on 9 January 1725, Skene entered the First Royal Regiment in 1741 and was in the Battles of Cartagena, Porto Bello, Dettingen, Fontenoy, and Culloden, where he was wounded. In 1750 he was promoted to lieutenant and in 1756 to captain. He served under William Lord Howe in the failed attack on Ticonderoga in 1758, again being wounded. The following year he acted with great heroism during General Jeffrey Amherst's capture of Ticonderoga and prevented the explosion of the fort's powder magazine. For this action he was promoted to major and took part in the subsequent operations against Martinique and Havana. In 1762 he was made provost marshal of Havana.

With Amherst's support, Skene in 1759 received the first of several land grants that would eventually total fifty thousand acres on Lake Champlain. In 1763 he brought 270 veterans of the Cuban campaign to Wood Creek, settling them as his tenants. He founded Skenesboro (later Whitehall), New York, in 1765 and was named colonel of militia in 1768, selling his British officer's commission the following year. Part of his domain lay in the Hampshire Grants (later Vermont), and in the controversy between New York and the region's settlers, Skene sided with New York. In this matter he shared cause with Philip Schuyler, whom he had known during the campaigns of 1758. By 1774 he had a flourishing little wilderness empire with sawmills, foundries, and shipyards, and he planned to end the land dispute in the Green Mountains by creating a new colony based at Skenesboro. Skene went to England that year, gaining appointment as lieutenant governor of Ticonderoga and Crown Point as the first step toward the creation of a new province.

But events interfered with his plans. After Ethan Allen captured Ticonderoga on 10 May 1775, he sent a force to seize Skenesboro, taking Skene's son and daughters prisoner. When Skene landed in Philadelphia in June 1775, he was immediately arrested and sent to internment in Connecticut. He was exchanged in October 1776 and returned to England, then coming back to join Burgoyne's offensive on Lake Champlain. Although he expected to assume his duties as governor of the region, he became Burgoyne's principal Loyalist adviser and in this capacity—much resented by the other Loyalists—he took part in subsequent military operations. Skene gave Burgoyne two disastrous pieces of advice: that most New Yorkers were loyal to the crown and would rise up to join Burgoyne as he advanced, and that the British forces should march overland to the Hudson via Skenesboro rather than taking the quicker and easier route on Lake George. Many contemporaries became convinced that Skene made the latter recommendation in order for Burgoyne's forces to build a road from Ticonderoga to Skenesboro. The ensuing military route through the woods and swamps became known as Skene's Road. He accompanied the Bennington raid in August 1777 and showed personal courage in the portion of that operation known as Breymann's defeat, escaping in the confusion and finding his way back to Burgoyne's main force.

Skene was paroled in 1778 and returned to England. The following year New York confiscated his property, for which he received £20,350 from the crown. Skene spent the remainder of his life in England, dying there on 9 June 1810.

SEE ALSO *Bennington Raid; Burgoyne's Offensive; Ticonderoga, New York, American Capture of.*

BIBLIOGRAPHY

Morton, Doris Begor. *Philip Skene of Skenesborough.* Granville, N.Y.: Grastorf Press, 1959.

revised by Michael Bellesiles

SKENESBORO, NEW YORK. Later Whitehall, New York. 6 July 1777. After John Burgoyne closed in on Ticonderoga on 2–5 July, Arthur St. Clair evacuated the position during the night of 5–6 July. He led the main body of American troops overland to Castleton, intending to continue to Skenesboro. Colonel Pierce Long commanded those retreating by water directly to Skenesboro using the five armed vessels that remained of the Champlain squadron and 220 small boats. Long had some 450 effectives escorting the invalids and all stores and artillery that could be saved. Leaving Ticonderoga shortly after midnight, he made two tactical errors that jeopardized his operation: (1) assuming that the boom and bridge between Ticonderoga and Mount Independence would delay pursuit, he took his time sailing up the lake;

and (2) he made no attempt to set up positions along the winding watercourse to check the enemy's advance.

Burgoyne needed less than half an hour to shoot his way through the undefended obstacle, and by 3 P.M. his pursuing squadron was only three miles from Skenesboro, where Long had landed two hours earlier. In a piecemeal commitment, Burgoyne put three regiments (the Ninth, Twentieth, and Twenty-first Foot) ashore in South Bay to move overland and cut off Long's retreat south from Skenesboro; he then continued with the rest of his force by water to attack Skenesboro from the north by way of Wood Creek. But since Burgoyne did not give the enveloping force enough time to get into position, Long escaped the trap. Setting fire to everything that would burn, Long hurried south toward Fort Anne with the 150 men of his rear guard as Burgoyne approached Skenesboro. This moment marked the end of the American naval presence on the lakes during the war. The British captured the galley *Trumbull* (10 guns) and schooner *Revenge* (8), but Long was able to successfully burn or blow up the sloop *Enterprise* (12), the schooner *Liberty* (8), and the galley *Gates* (4).

Early on 7 July, Lieutenant Colonel Hill pursued with his Ninth Regiment. That led to its near annihilation at Fort Anne on 8 July.

Long's poor management of his part of the evacuation from Ticonderoga deprived the Americans of time they should have been able to gain in delaying Burgoyne's offensive. It also forced St. Clair to make a seven-day detour with the main body to bypass captured Skenesboro.

SEE ALSO *Burgoyne, John; Burgoyne's Offensive; Champlain Squadrons; Fort Anne, New York; St. Clair, Arthur; Ticonderoga, New York, British Capture of.*

BIBLIOGRAPHY

Ketchum, Richard M. *Saratoga: Turning Point of America's Revolutionary War.* New York: Holt, 1997.

Nickerson, Hoffman. *The Turning Point of the Revolution; or, Burgoyne in America.* New York: Houghton Mifflin, 1928.

revised by Robert K. Wright Jr.

SKINNER, CORTLANDT. (1728–1799).

Loyalist officer. New Jersey. Related to prominent families of New Jersey and New York, Skinner served briefly as attorney general of New Jersey in 1775. As speaker of the assembly, he cast the deciding vote to petition King George for a redress of grievances in an effort to avoid more radical measures. As a major of Loyalist troops he was captured, and in September 1776 he and Governor Montfort Browne of New Providence in the Bahamas were exchanged for General William Alexander. The British

then made him a brigadier general of provincials, and he was authorized to raise a body of Loyalists. These were organized into the several battalions of Skinner's Brigade (one commanded by Lieutenant Colonel Abram Van Buskirk). After the war he was put on half pay as a brigadier general for life. Skinner died in Bristol, England, in 1799. One of his daughters married Sir William Robinson, commissary general of the British army, and another married Field Marshal Sir George Nugent. His son, Philip Kearny Skinner, was a British lieutenant general in 1825.

SEE ALSO *Cowboys and Skinners.*

revised by Michael Bellesiles

SKINNERS SEE *Cowboys and Skinners.*

SMALLWOOD, WILLIAM. (1732–1792). Continental general. Maryland. Born in Charles County, Maryland, in 1732, William Smallwood went to school in England and served in the Seven Years' War. In 1761 he was a delegate from Charles County to the Maryland assembly, where he served until 1774, doing particularly important work on the Arms and Ammunition Committee. A staunch patriot, Smallwood attended the Maryland Provincial Congresses of 1774, 1775, and 1776.

On 14 January 1776 Smallwood was commissioned as a colonel and raised the unit that was to become famous as Smallwood's Maryland Battalion (or Regiment). Smallwood and his unit left Annapolis on 10 July 1776 and marched to join Washington's army in New York. Smallwood's troops distinguished themselves in the battle of Long Island on 27 August, fighting under General William Alexander on the American right flank, but was, at the time, under the leadership of Mordecai Gist. (Smallwood himself was absent on court-martial duty in New York City during this action, which established the reputation of his regiment). Smallwood was wounded while leading his battalion at White Plains on 28 October, where the troops again distinguished themselves in several phases of that battle.

Promoted to brigadier general on 23 October, Smallwood's had not recovered from his wounds in time for him to take part in the New Jersey campaign, and in December he was sent to raise new levies in Maryland and Delaware, and to suppress a Loyalist uprising on the Eastern Shore in Virginia. His brigade was left south of the Schuylkill River in September 1777, with orders to cooperate with General Anthony Wayne's Brigade in retarding the British advance on Philadelphia, but Wayne's disaster at Paoli, Pennsylvania, on 21 September, ended this strategy before it could start.

In the battle of Germantown, Pennsylvania, on 4 October, Smallwood commanded a militia force that he criticized bitterly for lacking skill and discipline. When the army went into winter quarters at Valley Forge, Smallwood was given command of General John Sullivan's division and ordered to Wilmington, Delaware, with the mission of protecting supplies at Head of Elk (a settlement in Maryland). In addition, he was ordered to observe British movements in the Chesapeake Bay. In April 1780 he marched with Johann de Kalb's command to take part in operations in the Southern theater. In reserve at the start of the disastrous battle of Camden, South Carolina, on 16 August 1780, he was separated from his brigade and swept to the rear by the flood of fugitives. With de Kalb's death, Smallwood became division commander, and was appointed major general on 15 September. When General Freidrich von Steuben was made his immediate commander, Smallwood objected to serving under a foreigner and threatened to resign. General Nathanael Greene solved the problem by sending Smallwood to Maryland to raise troops and assemble supplies, and Smallwood won praise for his energy in both these tasks. He remained in the service until 15 November 1783. He declined to accept when he was elected as a delegate to Congress on 4 December 1784, but was elected governor the next year and served three consecutive one-year terms. In 1791 he was elected to the state senate, serving as its president until his death on 14 February 1792.

SEE ALSO *Long Island, New York, Battle of; White Plains, New York.*

BIBLIOGRAPHY

Kimmel, Ross M. *In Perspective: William Smallwood.* Annapolis: Maryland Department of Natural Resources, 1976.

Papenfuse, Edward C. "General Smallwood's Recruits: The Peacetime Career of the Revolutionary Private." *William and Mary Quarterly*, 3rd series, 30 (1973): 117–132.

revised by Michael Bellesiles

SMITH, FRANCIS. (1723–1791). British officer.

Commissioned lieutenant in the Royal Fusiliers on 25 April 1741, he became captain in the Tenth Foot on 23 June 1747 and on 16 January 1762 became brevetted lieutenant colonel of the regiment. The next month he was promoted to lieutenant colonel, and in 1767 he took the regiment to America. Known for his girth and caution,

Smith was promoted to brevetted colonel on 8 September 1775. His seniority in the Boston garrison seems to have been his only qualification for selection to command the expedition to Lexington and Concord. Having received a serious leg wound in the action at Fiske Hill, outside Concord, on 19 April 1775, he applied for retirement in August but was retained in the service and promoted. Before the end of the year he became colonel and aide-de-camp to the king. As a local brigadier general he showed as little skill at Dorchester Heights in March 1776 as he had at Concord. He commanded a brigade at Long Island in August 1776 and at Quaker Hill in the Battle of Rhode Island in August 1778. Before the end of the year his regiment returned to England to recruit and reform. He was promoted to major general in 1779 and lieutenant general in 1787. The unanswered question is why.

SEE ALSO *Dorchester Heights, Massachusetts; Lexington and Concord; Newport, Rhode Island (29 July–31 August 1778).*

BIBLIOGRAPHY

Fisher, David Hackett. *Paul Revere's Ride.* New York: Oxford University Press, 1994.

revised by Michael Bellesiles

SMITH, JAMES. (1719–1806). Signer. Ireland–

Pennsylvania. Born in Ireland, 17 Sept. 1719, Smith and his family settled in York Co., Pennsylvania in 1729. James was schooled in Philadelphia, admitted to the bar in 1745, and soon thereafter he became a lawyer and surveyor on the frontier near Shippensburg. Four or five years later he returned to York, which remained his home for the rest of his life. Although the only lawyer in town until 1769, he found little legal work and in 1771 he launched an unsuccessful iron manufacturing business that cost him £5,000 before he sold out in 1778. Meanwhile he had become a leader of the backcountry and Patriot causes. In July 1774 he read his "Essay on the Constitutional Power of Great Britain over the colonies in America" to the provincial conference. He also urged nonimportation and advocated that a general congress of the colonies be called. Returning to York full of revolutionary zeal, in Dec. 1774 he raised a volunteer company, was elected its captain, expanded this unit into a battalion, and accepted the honorary title of colonel. He was a delegate to the provincial congresses of Jan. 1775, June 1776, and in the constitutional convention of 1776 he was on the committee that drafted a state constitution. On 20 July, before the state convention had been in session a week, he was elected to the

Continental Congress where he signed the Declaration of Independence. He did not return to Congress for the next session, but was re-elected on 10 December 1777 and sat as a delegate the next year. He declined re-election, but thanks to the efforts of General Howe the Continental Congress came to him, and while that body met in York the board of war held its meetings in Smith's office.

He held a number of political posts after the war, was brigadier general of militia in 1782, and was counselor for his state in the Wyoming Valley controversy. Between 1781 and his retirement in 1801 he acquired a substantial estate through the practice of law. He died in York, 11 July 1806.

revised by Michael Bellesiles

SMITH, JOSHUA HETT. (1736–1818).

Lawyer. New York. A son of William Smith, Joshua Smith was a successful lawyer in the tradition of his father and elder brother, Chief Justice William Smith. Although his father and brother were suspected of having Loyalist sympathies, Joshua was an active Patriot, a member of the New York Provincial Congress, and a member of the militia. His wife was from South Carolina, and he had met General Robert Howe in Charleston in 1778. When the latter assumed command at West Point, Smith directed Howe's secret service. When Arnold succeeded Howe, he asked Smith to continue his intelligence work. Thus it was that Smith became—apparently in all innocence—a key actor in the events connected with Arnold's treasonous activities. Although acquitted of any part in Arnold's treason on 26 October 1780, Smith was imprisoned by New York authorities as a suspected Loyalist. In May 1781 he escaped from the Goshen jail, reached New York City the next month, and was given a stipend of one dollar a day by the British. Late in November 1783 he went to England, and in 1801 he returned to the United States. Although his property had not been confiscated, he had lost most of his fortune. Though returning to his legal practice, he never attained much prominence, and he died in New York City in 1818.

SEE ALSO *Arnold's Treason; Smith, William (I); Smith, William (II).*

BIBLIOGRAPHY

Van Doren, Carl. *Secret History of the American Revolution.* Garden City, N.Y.: Garden City Publishing, 1941.

revised by Michael Bellesiles

SMITH, WILLIAM (I). (1697–1769).

Colonial jurist. New York. Born in Buckinghamshire on 8 October 1697, Smith was the son of a tallow chandler who brought his family from England to New York in 1715. Smith graduated from Yale in 1719 and three years later received his master of arts degree. He remained at Yale as a tutor until April 1724, when he turned down the position of rector and moved to New York, becoming a member of the bar. Smith became a prominent attorney and ally of the Livingstons, joining their battle against the governor's authority and the De Lancey family. His most famous case was that of the printer John Peter Zenger from 1734 to 1736. For his role in defending Zenger's right to publish, Smith and his partner, James Alexander, were disbarred, leaving Zenger to look outside New York for his next attorney, Andrew Hamilton of Philadelphia. It took two years, but Smith and Alexander finally won readmission to the bar through the intercession of the assembly. In 1760 he declined the office of chief justice of New York, since it was to be held at the pleasure of the governor, but was associate justice of the supreme court from 1763 until his death in New York City on 22 November 1769. By his first wife, Mary, daughter of René and Blanche (Du Bois) Het, he had fifteen children, including William (II) and Joshua Hett Smith.

SEE ALSO *Smith, Joshua Hett; Smith, William (II).*

BIBLIOGRAPHY

Bonomi, Patricia U. *A Factious People: Politics and Society in Colonial New York.* New York: Columbia University Press, 1971.

Smith, William. Papers. New-York Historical Society, New York City.

revised by Michael Bellesiles

SMITH, WILLIAM (II). (1728–1793).

Jurist, historian, Loyalist. Eldest son of William Smith (I), he graduated from Yale in 1745, studied law in his father's office with William Livingston, was admitted to the bar in 1750, and in partnership with Livingston became a highly successful lawyer. At the request of the state authorities, he and Livingston compiled the *Laws of New-York from the Year 1691 to 1751, Inclusive (1752)* and *Laws of New-York . . . 1752–1762 (1762)*; these were the first two digests of New York statutes. With Livingston and John Morin Scott, he wrote *A Review of the Military Operations in North America: From . . . 1753, to . . . 1756 (1757)*; reprinted in 1801, this was a defense of Governor William Shirley and a criticism of James De Lancey, Thomas Pownall, and Sir

William Johnson. Smith is best-known for his *History of the Late Province of New York* (2 vols., 1829), which evolved from his *History . . . of New-York to the Year 1732* (1757), and to which Smith subsequently added a continuation to the year 1762. His "Historical Memoirs," which extend to the year 1783 and exist in six manuscript volumes in the New York Public Library, have been said by the historian Richard B. Morris to be essential for comprehending New York's situation at the time of the Revolution.

The chief justice of New York from 1763 to 1782 (nominally), and his father's successor on the royal council in 1767, Smith had a career during the Revolution that Morris has described as politically unique. When in 1777 he refused to give the test oath, he was ordered to Livingston Manor on the Hudson, and when he again refused the next year, he was banished to British-occupied New York City.

Smith was the most original and subtle of the Loyalist political thinkers. From 1767 until 1778 he positioned himself as "a loyal Wigg, one of King William's Wiggs, for Liberty and the Constitution," knowing full well that in the colonies Whigs were, at the minimum, staunch opponents of taxation by Parliament and executive undermining of provincial self-government (Upton, p. 110). He pursued a two-pronged strategy to preserve both liberty and empire.

First, he devised and privately circulated a constitutional treatise proposing that the British Constitution, as applied to the colonies, "ought to bend and sooner or later will bend" to accommodate the political maturity and continental extent of British North America. Projecting from Benjamin Franklin's work on colonial demography and predicting that the American population would double every generation, he anticipated the moment, sometime in the mid-nineteenth century, when the capitol of the empire would move west from London to New York. Counseling patience, he argued for awaiting that eventual shift in the balance of power within the empire.

The second prong of his loyal Whiggery was to become, as a member of the royal council, the gray eminence behind New York's royal governor, William Tryon. In that role he detached Tryon from the De Lancey faction in the distribution of land grants and then guided Tryon through the Tea Act crisis without violence.

In January 1776 he admitted the collapse of both strategies. No colonial politician or British statesman embraced his proposals for constitutional reform of the empire. Smith's "Thoughts as a Rule for My Own Conduct at This Melancholy Hour of Approaching Distress" condemned both British policy and American rebelliousness. His behind-the-scenes role exhausted, he told his neighbors on the Haverstraw, New York, Committee of Safety on 4 July 1776 that he could not endorse the measures of the Second Continental Congress

because "I persuade myself that Great Britain will discern the propriety of negotiating for a pacification."

Patriot officials in New York waited until 1778 to force the issue, and when the summons came to commit himself, Smith slipped quietly into the New York City garrison town where Lord North's negotiators on the Carlisle Peace Commission were sampling opinion on the subject of reconciliation. One of the commissioners took the measure of Smith's character and politics: "he is subtle, cool & persuasive [but] he may be secured [to the British side] by an application to his ambition."

General Henry Clinton tried, but Smith remained elusive. Nonetheless, and in contrast with his friend and fellow moderate, William Samuel Johnson, who made peace with the Connecticut state government in 1779, Smith had already burned his bridges. General Guy Carleton, Clinton's successor in 1782, shared Smith's hope for an eleventh-hour reconciliation, but nothing came of it, and in 1783 Smith went into exile in England. The ministry rewarded him with the chief justiceship of Quebec, where he died in 1793. Joshua Hett Smith was a brother of William (II).

SEE ALSO *Carleton, Guy; Clinton, Henry; De Lancey, James; Johnson, Sir William; Livingston, William; Pownall, Thomas; Shirley, William; Smith, Joshua Hett; Smith, William (I); Test Oath.*

BIBLIOGRAPHY

Benton, William A. *The Whig-Loyalists: An Aspect of Political Ideology in the American Revolutionary Era.* Philadelphia: University of Pennsylvania Press, 1965.

Smith, William. Historical Memoirs. 6 vols. New York Public Library, New York, N.Y.

Upton, L. F. S. *The Loyal Whig: William Smith of New York and Quebec.* University of Toronto Press, 1969.

revised by Robert M. Calhoon

SMITH'S POINT, LONG ISLAND, NEW YORK

SEE *Fort George, Long Island, New York.*

SOLDIERS' RATIONS.

Prussian King Frederick the Great wrote in 1747, "The foundation of an army is the belly." Major General Henry Knox weighed in on the subject in 1781: "To subsist an Army well, requires the utmost attention and exertion. Unless an Army is properly fed, all calculations and schemes of enterprize are in vain. . . . Experience has often convinced us of the truth of this assertion, and some times at too dear a rate." These lessons were quickly learned by Revolutionary soldiers. Private Joseph Plumb Martin recalled an incident while serving in the Connecticut militia in New York in 1776: "Having had nothing to eat for forty-eight hours . . . one of the men . . . complained of being hungry. The colonel, putting his hand into his coat pocket, took out a piece of an ear of Indian corn burnt as black as a coal. 'Here,' said he . . . 'eat this and learn to be a soldier.'" Later, Martin happily devoured broiled fresh beef "black as coal on the outside and . . . raw on the inside," a meal that, Delaware Captain Enoch Anderson noted, "to hungry soldiers . . . tasted sweet." But poor or inadequate provisions were hardly the everyday lot, and commanders did all they could to provide troops decent, sustaining food.

DIET

A British memorandum found at at Yorktown, Virginia, in October 1781, listed Major General Charles Lord Cornwallis's soldiers' daily allowance: one pound beef or nine ounces pork, one pound of flour or bread, three-sevenths pint of peas, and one-sixth quart "Rum or Spirits." A half pint of oatmeal or rice and 6 ounces of butter for seven days was also issued. The document also noted, "Since the troops have been upon this island, spruce beer has been issued at 8 quarts for 7 days. N.B. When the small species are not delivered, 12 oz of pork are allowed." "Small species" for British troops at Yorktown included sugar, chocolate, and coffee. Sauerkraut was also issued on occasion to British troops to minimize the effects of scurvy for soldiers in garrison or winter quarters.

Continental army rations mirrored the British model, but provisions were constantly modified. In July 1777 Major General William Heath ordered that rations include beer, butter, and "1 Jill of Rum Pr. Man each Day on Fatigue" as well as "Vinegar occasionally." After a winter at Valley Forge spent eating mostly meat and flour, in April fish, bacon, and "Pease, or Beans" were added to the daily ration; four months later both soft and hard breads (biscuit), as well as butter, were being issued. For seven months in 1780, New Jersey troops received extraordinary state stores consisting of rum, sugar, and coffee in substantial quantities and small amounts of chocolate, tea, pepper, and vinegar.

Further variation in the soldiers' diet was possible through the purchase of foodstuff from sutlers or local farmers at camp markets. George Washington noted in the summer of 1777 that "nothing can be more comfortable and wholesome to the army than vegetables, [and] every encouragement is to be given to the Country people, to bring them in." A large variety of items were available at these markets for those soldiers who had money to spend or items to barter. An August 1777 document listed "the Prices

of Articles sold in Camp," among them butter, "Mutton & Lamb," veal, milk, potatoes, squashes, "Beans or Peas in the Pod," cucumbers, "Pig[s] for roasting," and "Turnips Carrits & Beets." A 1779 order regulating "the prises of fresh Provisions, spirits, and shugar, and so forth, Hereafter to be given to farmers and others, seling to the army," included many of the items above, as well as turkeys; geese; ducks; "Dunghill fowls"; chickens; cheese; eggs; cabbage heads; "Sallets, Carrats, Pasnips"; lump, loaf, and brown sugar; honey; and vinegar plus a variety of beverages.

Foraging, authorized or not, was always an option. In 1778 at the Gulph in Pennsylvania, orders for Jackson's Additional Regiment stated, "Complaint has been made by many of the Inhabitants near this post of their Spring Houses being broke open & large quantities of Butter, Cheese, Bread & many other valuable articles stole from them, and it is strongly suspected these Robberies have been committed by some of the soldiers." From near Woodbridge, New Jersey, Colonel Israel Shreve wrote his wife: "I Rode All over this Village through the Gardens in search of Asparigas [but] found none, All the Beds being Cut that Day by the soldiers."

COOKING METHODS

Early in the war, General Washington set forth what he considered proper cooking methods:

> Head-Quarters, Middle-Brook [New Jersey], June 2, 1777. . . . Each regiment, or corps to appoint, by rotation, a regimental officer of the day . . . to inspect the food of the men, both as to the quality and the manner of dressing it, obliging the men to accustom themselves more to boiled meats and soups, and less to broiled and roasted, which as a constant diet, is destructive to their health. (Fitzpatrick, ed. *Writings,* 8, p. 171)

The only army-issue cooking and eating utensils were tin or sheet-iron camp kettles, with one wooden bowl per kettle, iron pots and wooden trenchers for garrison quarters or barracks, and usually inadequate supplies of spoons. In January 1777 Colonel Timothy Pickering described a typical kettle-cooked meal: "for two thirds of the week flour was dealt out, which the soldiers made, some into cakes, and some into dumplings, boiled with their meat."

Lacking kettles, soldiers were forced to prepare their rations crudely. Private Elijah Fisher recounted in November 1777 that

> we had no tents nor anithing to Cook our Provisions in and that was Prity Poor for beef was very leen and no salt nor any way to Cook it but to throw it on the Coles and brile it and the warter we had to Drink and to mix our flower with was out of a brook that run along by the Camps and so many dippin and washin [in] it maid it very Dirty and muddy. (p. 7)

The same month Connecticut surgeon Jonathan Todd described the firecake commonly eaten in such circumstances: "Our Flower we Wet with Water & Roll it in dirt & Ashes to bake it in a Horrible Manner."

British and German troops cooked the same way when campaigning. A British officer told of raw beef being issued the men under Major General John Burgoyne in New York during 1777, "which they eat, dressed upon wood ashes, without either bread or salt." German Sergeant Berthold Koch of the Regiment Von Bose, described the period following the Battle of Guilford Courthouse in 1781:

> We remained on the battlefield for three days, under the open skies without tents ... each man, officers as well as privates, received four measures of corn instead of bread and for meat, such cattle as the enemy had left behind.... We placed the corn on the fire to cook it. Then it was taken from the container and eaten. The meat was either boiled or roasted on sticks and eaten.... On 20 March we began our withdrawal.... We marched eighteen miles each day.... At evening we camped and the royal militia brought us cattle and some flour. The cattle were slaughtered and the meat was cooked or roasted and the flour made into cakes and cooked on a board in the fire. (Burgoyne, *Enemy Views*, pp. 450–451)

They marched north, and "on 5 April we went to Williamsburg in Virginia.... We received a double ration of rum each day at that place and our full provision of meat and ship's bread."

BIBLIOGRAPHY

Anburey, Thomas. *Travels Through the Interior Parts of America in a Series of Letters by an Officer.* New York: New York Times and Arno Press, 1969.

Burgoyne, Bruce E. *Enemy Views: The American Revolutionary War as Recorded by the Hessian Participants.* Bowie, Md.: Heritage Books, 1996.

Commager, Henry Steele, and Richard B. Morris. *The Spirit of 'Seventy-Six: The Story of the American Revolution as Told by Its Participants.* New York and London: Harper and Row, 1975.

Fisher, Elijah. *Elijah Fisher's Journal While in the War for Independence . . . 1775–1784.* Edited by William B. Lapham. Augusta, Maine: Badger and Manley, 1880.

Fitzpatrick, John C., ed. *The Writings of George Washington from the Original Manuscript Sources 1745–1799.* Vol. 8. Washington, D.C.: Government Printing Office, 1933.

Frederick II of Prussia. "The Instruction of Frederick the Great for His Generals." In *Roots of Strategy.* Edited by Thomas R. Phillips. Harrisburg, Pa.: Stackpole Books, 1985.

Rees, John U. "'The Foundation of an Army is the Belly:' North American Soldiers' Food, 1756–1945." *ALHFAM: Proceedings of the 1998 Conference and Annual Meeting* 21 (1999): 49–64.

Also available online at http://revwar75.com/library/rees/belly.htm.

———. "'To Subsist an Army Well ...:' Soldiers' Cooking Equipment, Provisions, and Food Preparation during the American War for Independence." *Military Collector and Historian* 53, 1 (Spring 2001): 7–23.

———. "Addendum: Brass Kettles." *Military Collector and Historian* 53, 3 (Fall 2001): 118–119.

John U. Rees

SOLDIERS' SHELTER.

Tents were the preferred method for sheltering troops in moderate weather during the Revolutionary War. They were described by Quartermaster General Timothy Pickering as "the most expensive & essential article of camp equipage," and tent size, quality, and availability were important considerations for both sides throughout the war.

British army tents were more or less standardized, as was the number of soldiers apportioned to a tent. Lewis Lochee's *Essay on Castrametation* (1778) noted British soldiers' tents "are large enough to lodge 5 men" and stated their size as "about 6 feet high ... [and] about 7 feet long." Lochee's camp layout indicates a common tent length of nine feet, perhaps adding two extra feet for a belled storage extension at the tent's rear. British officers preferred marquee or wall tents, but on campaign many used common tents or brush wigwams.

Following chronic standardization problems, in January 1781 the Continental army "Soldiers Tent" dimensions were set at "7 Feet Square [and] 7 Feet Height." The next year large numbers of French tents were imported; French common tents being larger, they were able to house eight or nine men. Most often used were common tents for the rank and file (and occasionally officers), horseman's and wall tents (usually for staff and company officers), and marquee tents (for generals and field officers). Several other variations, such as half-wall, square, and bell (for musket storage) tents, were used to a lesser degree.

In August 1777 Major General John Sullivan apportioned to his division "a tent to each Field officer, one to two Commissioned & Staff officers, one to 4 Serjts & one to 6 Privates including Corporals, as Well as Waggoners weomen &c." The American army allotment of May 1779 was even more detailed:

- One Markee and one Horseman's tent for the Field Officers.

- One horseman's tent for the officers of each company.

- One Wall'd tent for the Adjutant.

- One ditto for the Quarter Master.

- One ditto for the Surgeon and Mate.

- One ditto for the Pay-Master.

- One common tent for Serjeant Majr. and Qr. Mastr. Serjeant.

- One ditto for the Fife and Drum Major.

- One ditto for the non commissioned officers of each company

- and one for every six privates including Drums and Fifes. (*Writings of George Washington*, pp. 162–163)

Soldiers occasionally built makeshift shelters when tents were unavailable due to supply shortages or lack of transportation. American soldiers' names for such dwellings included "brush Hutt," "bush housen," and "hemlock bowhouses." While differences in construction existed among them, all the aforesaid shelters were enclosed lodgings with frames made of cut trees or tree limbs and covered with leafy branches or pine boughs. There were other shelter types. A "booth" seems to have referred to an open lean-to; sheds were similar in construction to brush huts but covered with milled lumber, fence rails, cornshocks, or straw. Bowers were flat-topped structures used primarily for sun protection, though there are indications some bowers were built as lean-tos for both overnight shelter and shade. British soldiers began using ad hoc campaign shelters as early as 1776, building them more often and relying upon their shelter for longer periods (for example, in the Philadelphia campaign of 1777 and late-war southern campaigns) than did their Continental army counterparts. British troops used both bowers and "wigwams," the latter a popular appellation probably begun as a derogatory term for any ad hoc shelter; as the war progressed, wigwams (usually some form of brush hut) became customarily adopted as a useful and acceptable alternative to tents.

In wintertime both armies resorted to soldier-built log huts, with barracks and local civilian housing used as occasion allowed. The Valley Forge huts varied in design but were supposed to adhere to stipulated measurements. New Jersey Ensign George Ewing described the living quarters:

> the huts eighteen by sixteen feet long six feet to the eves built of loggs and covered with staves / the chimney in the east end the door in the South side / the Officers huts in the rear of the mens / twelve men in each hut and two cores of Officers in a hut. (*Military Journal*, pp. 25–26)

A study of two Continental soldiers' diaries covering the years from 1776 to 1781 gives some idea of campaign shelter trends. On 979 days shelter was mentioned (not including winter camps). Of these, on 699 nights (71 percent) tents were used, while the men slept in buildings for 111 nights (11 percent). Of the rest, 98 nights (10 percent) were spent in the open, 36 (4 percent) were spent in makeshift shelters, and 35 (4 percent) were spent on shipboard. The light troops of both sides tended to live without tents more often than other troops.

BIBLIOGRAPHY

Ewing, George. *The Military Journal of George Ewing (1754–1824), a Soldier of Valley Forge.* Yonkers, N.Y.: privately printed, 1928.

Fitzpatrick, John C., ed. *The Writings of George Washington from the Original Manuscript Sources 1745–1799.* Vol. 15. Washington, D.C.: Government Printing Office, 1936.

Rees, John U. "'We . . . Got ourselves Cleverly Settled for the Night': Soldiers' Shelter on Campaign during the War for Independence." Pt. 1, "'The Most Expensive & Essential Article of Camp Equipage': Tents in the Armies of the Revolution." *Military Collector and Historian* 49, no. 3 (Fall 1997), 98–107. Pt. 2, "'The Allowance of Tents Is Not Sufficient . . .': An Overview of Tents as Shelter." Military Collector and Historian 49, no. 4 (Winter 1997): 156–168. Pt. 3, "'The Camps . . . Are as Different in Their Form as the Owners Are in Their Dress . . .': Shades, Sheds, and Wooden Tents, 1775–1782." *Military Collector and Historian* 53, no. 4 (Winter 2001–2002): 161–169. Pt. 4, "'We Are Now . . . Properly . . . Enwigwamed': British Soldiers and Brush Huts, 1776–1781." *Military Collector and Historian* 55, no. 2 (Summer 2003): 89–96. Pt. 5, "'We Built up Housan of Branchis and Leavs . . .': Continental Army Brush Shelters, 1775–1777." *Military Collector and Historian* 55, no. 4 (Winter 2003–2004): 213–223. Pt. 6, "'We Built up Housan of Branchis and leavs . . .': Continental Army Brush Shelters, 1778–1782." *Military Collector and Historian* 56, no. 2 (2004): 98–106.

John U. Rees

SOLEMN LEAGUE AND COVENANT.

The Boston Committee of Correspondence, headed by Samuel Adams, sent a circular letter to Massachusetts towns dated 8 June 1774, in which it asked all adults "to suspend all commercial intercourse" with Britain from 31 August until the Boston Port Act (by which Britain had closed the port of Boston for all shipping) was repealed. To emphasize the seriousness of the matter, and in an appeal to memories of the religious covenants to which the first settlers had subscribed, the committee dubbed its request a "solemn league and covenant," and threatened to publish the names of those people who did not comply, whom it termed "protesters." Merchants throughout Massachusetts objected to the committee's request, because they could not stop the shipment of goods from their British suppliers in time to meet the deadline and would thus be stuck with merchandise they could not sell. The request failed to garner widespread support, forcing Adams and the Boston radicals to defer the issues of nonimportation and nonconsumption to the Continental Congress, which was scheduled to meet at Philadelphia in September 1774.

SEE ALSO *Adams, Samuel.*

BIBLIOGRAPHY

Knollenberg, Bernard. *Growth of the American Revolution, 1766–1775.* Indianapolis, Ind.: Liberty Fund, 2002.

revised by Harold E. Selesky

SOMERSET COURTHOUSE.

On the Millstone River about halfway between Morristown and Trenton, Somerset Courthouse (later Millstone) figured prominently in New Jersey's military operations. Washington's army spent the night there after the Princeton victory on 3 January 1777, skirmishes took place there while the rebels were in their Morristown Winter Quarters from January to May 1777, and British forces occupied the village during their perplexing "June Maneuvers" of the Philadelphia campaign of 1777. More notably, on 20 January 1777, General Philemon Dickinson led New Jersey militia in a daring encounter with Cornwallis's troops. On 17 June 1777 Colonel Daniel Morgan's riflemen and other light troops attacked the British redoubts being built at that time. John Simcoe conducted a successful raid against this place but was captured on 17 October 1779 as he withdrew.

SEE ALSO *Dickinson, Philemon; Philadelphia Campaign; Simcoe, John Graves.*

revised by Michael Bellesiles

SONS OF LIBERTY.

When colonists came together in 1765 to protest and nullify the Stamp Act, they called their organization the Sons of Liberty. They took their name from Isaac Barré's speech of 6 February 1765 in the House of Commons opposing that act. Barré had closed his remarks with a reference to the colonists as "the sons of liberty."

In the name of liberty, the Sons were responsible for many acts of mob violence aimed at intimidating those who wished to remain loyal to the king, including the

application of hot tar and feathers to the bodies of those whose conception of liberty did not suit their own. A mob inspired by, although not operating under the direction of, the Boston Sons of Liberty on 26 August 1765 burned the records of the local vice admiralty court, ransacked the homes of the comptroller of the currency, and looted the home and library of Governor Thomas Hutchinson. The effectiveness of this sort of intimidation, even when threats were not accompanied by violence, is shown by the fact that all stamp agents in the colonies had resigned before the Stamp Act was supposed to become law (1 November 1765).

SEE ALSO *Tar and Feathers.*

revised by Harold E. Selesky

SOUTH AMBOY, NEW JERSEY SEE *Amboy, New Jersey.*

SOUTH CAROLINA, FLAG OF.

"As there was no national flag at the time [Sept. 1775]," wrote William Moultrie in his *Memoirs*, "I was desired by the [Charleston] Council of Safety to have one made, upon which, as the state troops were clothed in blue, and the fort [Fort Johnson on James Island] was garrisoned by the first and second regiments, who wore a silver crescent on the front of their caps, I had a large blue flag made, with a crescent in the dexter corner.... This was the first American flag displayed in the South."

BIBLIOGRAPHY

Lossing, Benson J. *The Pictorial Field Book of the Revolution; or, Illustrations, by Pen and Pencil, of the History, Biography, Scenery, Relics, and Traditions of the War for Independence.* 2 vols. New York: Harper & Bros., 1851-52.

Mark M. Boatner

SOUTH CAROLINA, MOBILIZATION IN.

When South Carolinians faced the imperial crisis of the 1770s, they did so as a divided people. South Carolina was geographically divided into two regions: a coastal low country of plantations worked by the colony's slave majority, where life centered on the social, cultural, and political capital, Charleston; and the back country, populated largely by recent immigrants from the northern colonies. Lacking proportional representation in the colonial assembly, and having belatedly received an effective judicial system, back country settlers harbored more grievances against low country Carolinians than they did against British rule.

In the low country resided the wealthiest men in the thirteen colonies. Though their wealth depended on rice and indigo, crops whose value was tied directly to British trade, these men resisted the tightening of imperial control with self-confidence born of their command over the environment, the colony, and their slaves.

It has been difficult for historians to determine why some Carolinians chose loyalty and others chose rebellion. Ethnicity played some role, as Scots in the low country and Germans in the back country tended to support royal rule. Before the disestablishment of the Anglican church, religious dissenters in the backcountry were skeptical of the Revolution. In the back country, the political decision of an influential man often meant the difference between the local population choosing to remain loyal or to embrace revolution. Some low country Carolinians supported opposition to parliamentary acts but not the independence that came in 1776. What is clear is that South Carolinians were more politically divided than most other Americans. After the British largely conquered the province in 1780, these divisions produced the bitterest fighting of the American Revolution.

SOUTH CAROLINA MOBILIZES (1775)

Revolutionary mobilization began in earnest when news of the battles of Lexington and Concord reached South Carolina. In response, the colony's Provincial Congress met from 1–22 June 1775. The provincial militia, divided into twelve infantry regiments drawn from different districts, provided a ready-made source of mobilization. Members of the congress, however, worried about the allegiance of some militia officers and units. These concerns eventually led to a decision to drop some officers and to draft volunteers to serve in the militia ranks. In the June session, these concerns led to the formation of a volunteer army led by appointed, gentleman officers. The resulting military establishment revealed the low country's political control—despite having less than forty percent of the province's population, the low country possessed seventy percent of the seats in congress. The congress established two 750-man infantry regiments in the low country, and a back country regiment of 450 mounted rangers.

Later in the session the congress opted to cut expenses, and reduced the infantry regiments to ten fifty-man companies and the regiment of rangers to nine thirty-man companies. To meet projected expenses for pay and supplies, the delegates opted to issue £1,000,000 currency rather than levy taxes. In other moves that placed the province on the path to military conflict with Britain, the congress authorized the seizure of weapons and gunpowder from the colony's magazine, and gunpowder from vessels headed to Georgia and East Florida. Before convening, the delegates left virtually unlimited executive authority in the hands of a thirteen-member Council of Safety, which oversaw regular and militia forces.

In July the Council of Safety ordered the seizure of arms and ammunition at Fort Charlotte, a post on the Savannah River. Though the operation was carried out successfully, loyal militia recaptured the arms. The Council of Safety first tried diplomacy to calm matters. Additional unrest in November produced a different response. The Provincial Congress, which was then in session, ordered the back country militia to embody and defeat the Loyalists. Colonel Ralph Richardson of Camden raised a force of 2,500 men, which included some North Carolina units, and conducted operations that ended the Loyalist threat in the back country for the next four years. The December "snow campaign" demonstrated that revolutionaries could quickly mobilize a sizable backcountry force, despite numerous Loyalists in the region.

FURTHER MOBILIZATION
(1775–1776)

While the Provincial Congress acted aggressively to end Loyalist unrest, it also made changes to its earlier military establishment. In November 1775, the representatives created the Fourth South Carolina Regiment of Artillery, a smaller regiment with three 100-man companies, to man the batteries at Charleston. Additional changes occurred three months later. On 22 February the congress authorized the original three regiments to augment their numbers until they reached full strength. The congress also established two new regiments of riflemen in the low country and back country respectively: The Fifth South Carolina, with seven 100-man companies, and the Sixth South Carolina, with five 100-man companies.

In 1776 the state's regiments were transferred to the Continental army, but only after negotiations with the Continental Congress. The state had already met Congress's quota of five infantry regiments, but complications over different enlistment periods and pay schedules compelled the Council of Safety to resist full incorporation of its army into the Continental line. In June 1776, Congress adopted South Carolina's regiments into the Continental army, but kept the soldiers under the state's articles of war and their original terms of enlistment. In a concession to concerns over the defense of South Carolina, more than one-third of its troops could not be sent outside the state without the prior approval of Congress.

A BRITISH ATTACK AND A CHEROKEE WAR (1776)

In June 1776, South Carolina's ability to mobilize faced a major test with the arrival of a British expeditionary force. Manning the defenses of Charleston were 6,500 soldiers, most of whom were South Carolina regulars and militia. On 28 June, the British directed a naval attack against Sullivan's Island, where the Carolinians had constructed a fort of palmetto logs and sand. The defenders of this fort, Colonel William Moultrie and 435 men of the Second South Carolina Regiment and the Fourth Regiment of Artillery, stood firm, inflicting major damage on the British ships. Charleston did not face another British attack for almost three years.

Soon after the British departed, a new threat broke out in South Carolina's interior. The Cherokees openly sided with the British and initiated a frontier war. Sensing an opportunity to eliminate the Cherokees, South Carolina's back country militia quickly mobilized. Joining this force were Carolinians who either had been neutral or slightly pro-British but now united against the threat back country settlers feared most. In August Colonel Andrew Williamson, at the head of about 1,200 militia, attacked and devastated the lower Cherokee towns. Williamson then joined militia from North Carolina and Virginia in laying waste to upper Cherokee towns. The Cherokees ceased to be a major threat. In 1777 they signed a treaty that ceded all their lands in South Carolina.

South Carolinians took great pride in the victories of 1776. Long an internal threat, the Cherokees had been eliminated. Despite the assistance of North Carolina Continentals and militia and the leadership of overall commander Major General Charles Lee, most of the forces defending Charleston had been South Carolina regulars and militia. The victory at Sullivan's Island resulted from equal parts British incompetence and Carolina pluck, but South Carolinians chose to remember the latter and forget the former. The ensuing period of relative quiet produced an apathy born of the certainty that they could again rise and meet threats when the need arose.

QUIET PRODUCES APATHY (1777–1778)

During the next two years, British ships patrolled the coast and disrupted the trade that was South Carolina's lifeline. The state responded by forming its own navy, which over the course of its checkered history numbered about one dozen vessels. The state's naval ships succeeded in capturing prizes, but were unable to drive British cruisers from Charleston. In 1778 the state legislature commissioned Commodore Alexander Gillon to purchase three frigates in Europe. Gillon leased a forty-four gun frigate, formerly owned by France, which he named *South Carolina*. The

frigate *South Carolina* did not depart Europe until the summer of 1781 and never reached South Carolina waters. This expensive venture cost about half a million dollars and involved the government in litigation with European claimants until the 1850s.

In 1778 a new state constitution provided for a governor and an advisory privy council, and a bicameral legislature composed of a senate and a house of representatives. It was left to this state government to deal with problems caused by dwindling enthusiasm for the war. Like Americans in other states, South Carolinians responded to the outbreak of hostilities with patriotic fervor that subsided over time. In 1776 more than 2,000 South Carolinians served as regular troops. Over the next two years, the state had difficulty meeting its quota of Continental soldiers, who dropped to 1,200. The General Assembly employed different expedients to increase the state's regular forces. In 1778, in an apparent act of desperation, the legislators authorized that vagrants be forcibly enlisted in the state's regiments. To attract volunteers, the representatives offered each enlistee 100 acres of land in the recently acquired Cherokee territory.

A military debacle in 1778 caused further problems. South Carolina contributed regular and militia troops to an invasion of British East Florida: Colonel Charles Cotesworth Pinckney commanded 600 soldiers from South Carolina's First, Third, and Sixth Regiments, and Colonel Andrew Williamson commanded 800 militia. Williamson's force arrived near the end of the expedition, which was marred by poor planning and squabbles between civilian and military authorities. Of Pinckney's troops, about 300 died or were hospitalized, South Carolina could ill afford this loss of manpower.

Manpower problems grew more serious in December 1778, when the British inaugurated their southern strategy with the capture of Savannah, Georgia. Once Georgia was secured, the British planned to invade South Carolina. The war had returned, this time with a vengeance.

A RENEWED BRITISH THREAT (1779)

Only 1,000 regulars remained to defend the state. Desiring Continental reinforcements, Governor John Rutledge dispatched Daniel Huger to Philadelphia to plead for aid. Huger testified before a committee of Congress that South Carolina had difficulties raising large numbers of militia because white men preferred to remain home and prevent their slaves from rebelling or fleeing to the British. With the concurrence of South Carolina delegates Henry Laurens and William Henry Drayton, Congress recommended that South Carolina and Georgia enlist 3,000 slaves as Continentals and promise them freedom in return for their service. Congress dispatched Lieutenant Colonel John Laurens, the originator of this plan, to South Carolina to persuade the state government to act.

When news of Congress's resolution reached South Carolina in late April 1779, the state already faced a British invasion. General Augustine Prevost had made a diversionary incursion into South Carolina to lure Major General Benjamin Lincoln, the new commander of the Southern Department, from an invasion of Georgia's backcountry. Finding the path to Charleston open, Prevost went beyond his original intent. By 11 May Prevost, with 2,500 troops, faced Charleston, which was defended by a comparable number of militia. Expecting reinforcements from Congress and receiving instead a recommendation to arm slaves, Governor Rutledge and the privy council offered to surrender Charleston in return for the state's neutrality. Prevost rejected the offer and retreated to avoid entrapment by Lincoln's force, which was returning from Georgia.

This brief crisis revealed the limits of the low country leadership's willingness to mobilize the state's population to win independence. They had no problem using slaves as laborers: In 1778 the General Assembly revised the militia law to use slaves in support roles. But the state's leaders refused to augment their dwindling regular forces by mobilizing slaves as soldiers. The crisis revealed other limits of mobilization. To meet the British threat, Governor Rutledge had hoped to mobilize 5,000 militia but raised only half that number. When Prevost threatened Charleston, numerous low country militia chose to desert and protect their homes rather than defend the state's capital.

With the British in Georgia, South Carolina's government needed to fill its Continental ranks and make changes in the disposition of its militia. Later that summer the General Assembly rejected Laurens's black regiment plan, but offered a 500-dollar bounty and 100 acres of land to every white man who enlisted, and an additional $2,500 at the end of 21 months of service. As for the militia, the legislators made decisions that seemed counterproductive. They refused to put the militia under the Continental articles of war, as requested by General Lincoln. Instead, they placed the militia into three classifications, each subject to successive terms of service limited to two months. None of these moves produced the mobilization of soldiers needed to defend the state.

Low country Carolinians were aroused in September, when a French fleet under Count Charles d'Estaing arrived to support combined operations against the British. South Carolina regulars and militia comprised most of the fifteen hundred soldiers Lincoln led in the siege of Savannah. On 9 October, in a desperate assault on the British defenses, 250 South Carolina Continentals were among the casualties.

After his return to South Carolina, Lincoln requested Continental reinforcements from the North. He now commanded a force of 3,600 soldiers, which included Continentals from Virginia and militia from North Carolina, and 800 South Carolina Continentals, as well as more than 1,000 low country militia. General George Washington responded by ordering North Carolina and Virginia Continentals to South Carolina.

THE SIEGE OF CHARLESTON (1780)

The British returned to Charleston in early 1780, bringing a larger fleet and army, along with a methodical approach that won them the success denied at Sullivan's Island. They faced an unprepared South Carolina. At the General Assembly meeting in January, Governor Rutledge acknowledged that the bounties approved the previous summer had attracted no new Continental enlistments. The Continental Congress responded to these declining numbers by ordering that South Carolina's four infantry regiments be consolidated into two. Nor had efforts to mobilize the militia been successful. The back country militia proved unwilling to leave home and defend the hot, humid, and unhealthy low country. The General Assembly again rejected Laurens's proposal that it arm slaves.

After a brave but hopeless defense, Charleston surrendered on 11 May. Of more than 5,500 American prisoners, 830 were South Carolina Continentals and 1,000 were Charleston militiamen. Facing its gravest crisis of the war, South Carolina managed to mobilize only one-third of the force that defended Charleston.

THE PARTISAN WAR (1780–1782)

With the surrender of Charleston, South Carolina's Continental line ceased to be. The full conquest of the state appeared only a matter of time. A series of counterproductive British actions, however, stimulated resistance and mobilization in the back country. Outraged by British and Loyalist punitive raids, and unwilling to abide a requirement that they swear allegiance and defend royal authority, Carolinians took up arms and fought as partisans (guerrillas). Mobile and flexible in numbers, partisan units operated in the back country under Thomas Sumter and Andrew Pickens, and in the low country under Francis Marion. These partisan bands engaged in hit-and-run raids that disrupted enemy supply lines and occupied the attention of large numbers of redcoats and Loyalist militia. The partisans, in effect, kept the Revolution alive in South Carolina during the summer and early fall of 1780.

Irregular forces played important roles in major battles that turned the tide of the war in the South. At Kings Mountain in October 1780, South Carolina back country militia, joined by "over-mountain" men from Virginia,

North Carolina, and what is now Tennessee, killed, captured, or wounded over 1,000 Loyalists. At Cowpens in January 1781, South Carolina militia and their counterparts from North Carolina and Virginia, under the astute leadership of Brigadier General Daniel Morgan, fought well alongside Continentals in a pitched battle that led to the total defeat of the British force.

Cowpens was the first major battle after Major General Nathanael Greene arrived to take command of the Southern Department. Greene coordinated the movements of his Continentals with militia and partisan forces. In the spring and summer of 1781, a combination of Continentals, militia, and partisans employed set battles, sieges, and guerrilla tactics to push the British back to Charleston. Controlling only Charleston and its environs, the British stayed put until they evacuated on 14 December 1782.

Because of the nature of the conflict, which often degenerated from a civil war between rebel and Loyalist Carolinians to a blood feud pitting neighbor against neighbor, it is difficult to assess the numbers of South Carolinians who mobilized to defeat the British and their Loyalist allies in 1780 and 1781. some measure of understanding of the activity of South Carolinians can be gained by examining the number of engagements where they fought without assistance from Continentals. From July to December 1780, South Carolina partisans fought twenty-six engagements against British or Loyalist forces. The partisans suffered over 800 casualties, but inflicted nearly 2,500 casualties on their enemies. In the following year, at least sixty-two battles or skirmishes were fought in South Carolina, and in forty-five of these engagements South Carolina partisans or militia fought without outside assistance. A low country elite led South Carolina into revolution, but back country settlers fought the battles that won independence.

THE LEGACIES OF WAR

The site of 137 battles, South Carolina was the major battleground of the War of Independence. The conflict's human and financial toll was immense. The human cost, in lives lost or affected by the war, was incalculable but enduring. The financial costs for the state were more accessible. While South Carolinians fought mainly at home, their state government contributed willingly to the financial needs of the common cause. In 1783 South Carolina was the only state to pay the full requisition of the Continental Congress. To win independence, South Carolina's government spent almost $5.4 million (comparable to about $89.2 million today), which, per capita, was the largest expense incurred by any state. One factor in South Carolina's support for the federal Constitution of 1787 was the belief that the state would become a creditor once its accounts were balanced. South

Carolina's representatives strongly supported Alexander Hamilton's plan to assume state debts. During debate, an opponent of assumption argued that it was unfair for other states to pay South Carolina's debts, for they were incurred in part because of its dubious naval expenditures.

Events late in the war foreshadowed the settlement of differences between the low country and back country (later called the upcountry). In January 1782, the General Assembly met for the first time in two years. With the British still holding Charleston, legislators considered ways to raise regular troops. They again rejected forming black regiments, but found another use for slaves: White men who enlisted as soldiers would receive one slave for each year of service. This plan mirrored Thomas Sumter's policy of offering captured slaves as a bounty to his soldiers. Slave ownership eventually linked the wealthy planters of the state's two regions, especially after cotton became a staple crop in the upcountry.

South Carolinians were justifiably proud of their contributions to winning the War of Independence. They tended to glorify their partisans, downplay Greene's Continentals, and gloss over the debacles of 1779 and 1780. Congressman Aedanus Burke probably spoke for many Carolinians when he hotly responded to Treasury Secretary Alexander Hamilton's eulogy of Nathanael Greene. Hamilton called the militia "the mimicry of soldiership." Speaking before the House of Representatives and Hamilton, Burke lauded the militia's contributions and called the treasury secretary a liar. The two men avoided a duel but the incident revealed a final legacy of mobilization during the Revolution. South Carolinians were defensive of their revolutionary heritage, which was inextricably bound with their sense of honor.

SEE ALSO *Charleston Raid of Prevost; Charleston Siege of 1780; Cherokee War of 1776; Cowpens, South Carolina; Drayton, William Henry; Estaing, Charles Hector Théodat, Comte d'; Huger, Daniel; Laurens, Henry; Lincoln, Benjamin; Marion, Francis; Moultrie, William; Pickens, Andrew; Pinckney, Charles Cotesworth; Prevost, Augustine; Provincial Military Organizations; Rutledge, John; South Carolina Line; Sullivan's Island; Sumter, Thomas; Williamson, Andrew.*

BIBLIOGRAPHY

Borick, Carl P. *A Gallant Defense: The Siege of Charleston, 1780.* Columbia: University of South Carolina Press, 2003.

Chesnutt, David R., and C. James Taylor, eds., *The Papers of Henry Laurens.* Vols. 10–16. Columbia: University of South Carolina Press, 1985–2003.

Edgar, Walter. *South Carolina: A History.* Columbia: University of South Carolina Press, 1998.

Gordon, John W. *South Carolina and the American Revolution: A Battlefield History.* Columbia: University of South Carolina Press, 2003.

Haw, James. *John and Edward Rutledge of South Carolina.* Athens, Ga., and London: University of Georgia Press, 1997.

Hemphill, William Edwin, and Wylma Anne Wates, eds. *Extracts from the Journals of the Provincial Congresses of South Carolina, 1775–1776.* Columbia: South Carolina Archives Department, 1960.

Hemphill, William Edwin, Wylma Anne Wates, and R. Nicholas Olsberg, eds. *Journals of the General Assembly and House of Representatives, 1776–1780.* Columbia: University of South Carolina Press, 1970.

Klein, Rachel N. *Unification of a Slave State: The Rise of the Planter Class in the South Carolina Backcountry, 1760–1808.* Chapel Hill: University of North Carolina Press, 1990.

Lambert, Robert Stansbury. *South Carolina Loyalists in the American Revolution.* Columbia: University of South Carolina Press, 1987.

Massey, Gregory D. *John Laurens and the American Revolution.* Columbia: University of South Carolina Press, 2000.

McCrady, Edward. *The History of South Carolina in the Revolution, 1775–1780.* New York: The Macmillan Company, 1901; New York: Russell & Russell, 1969.

———. *The History of South Carolina in the Revolution, 1780–1783.* New York: The Macmillan Company, 1902.

Nadelhaft, Jerome J. *The Disorders of War: The Revolution in South Carolina.* Orono: University of Maine at Orono Press, 1981.

Weir, Robert M. *Colonial South Carolina: A History.* Millwood, N.Y.: KTO Press, 1983.

Gregory D. Massey

SOUTH CAROLINA LINE.

South Carolina's Continental army contingent spent a large part of its existence being torn between the demands of the state government and the directions of the Continental Congress—more so than any other state's Line. It began on 4 June 1775, when the Provincial Congress reacted to the news of Lexington by creating three regiments: two of infantry and a third of "horse rangers." The rangers were recruited in the frontier zone, and had a minor mutiny because of the officers' personal disputes and some latent Loyalist tendencies. The Provincial Congress added a fourth regiment, of artillery men, on 12 November 1775 to defend Charleston. Meanwhile, on 4 November, the Continental Congress had authorized the recruitment of three infantry regiments as South Carolina's quota. This caused the Provincial Congress to pass a comprehensive defense bill on 22 February 1776 which retained the existing regiments and added a new, fifth regiment as riflemen. It rejected the Continental Congresss's offer

with thanks. Six days later it added a second rifle regiment. On 25 March 1776 the Continental Congress increased its authorization for South Carolina's military units to five regiments, but not until 18 June did it finally resolve the status issue to the state's satisfaction. The compromise accepted all six regiments as raised by the state (over time the tables of organization were brought into conformity), but promised that no more than a third of the men could be sent outside the boundaries of South Carolina without a specific authorizing resolution. This news did not reach Charleston until after the first British attack on the city so, in the eyes of the state, the defense of Fort Moultrie was carried out by state troops who had only temporarily accepted the orders of the Continental army generals. Recruiting lagged due to lingering friction between the two governments, and on 11 February 1780 the Line was reduced to three infantry regiments plus the artillery regiment. All were captured at Charleston on 12 May of that year, and were formally disbanded on 1 January 1781, except for the First South Carolina Regiment. It remained a paper organization until the winter of 1782–1783, when three companies were formed from its members. These were furloughed when the British evacuated Charleston, and were finally disbanded on 15 November 1783. The South Carolina Line was unique in having its artillery regiment legally acknowledged as part of the line.

SEE ALSO *South Carolina, Mobilization in.*

BIBLIOGRAPHY

De Saussure, Wilmot Gibbes, comp. *The Names, as Far as Can Be Ascertained, of the Officers Who Served in the South Carolina Regiments on the Continental Establishment; of the Officers Who Served in the Militia; of what Troops were upon the Continental Establishment; and of what Militia Organizations Served; Together with some Miscellaneous Information.* Columbia: South Carolina General Assembly, 1886.

Gibbes, R. W., ed. *Documentary History of the American Revolution.* 3 vols. Columbia and New York: Banner Steam-Power Press and D. Appleton & Co., 1853–1857.

McCrady, Edward. *The History of South Carolina in the Revolution.* 2 vols. New York: Macmillan Co., 1902.

Moss, Bobby Gilmer, comp. *Roster of South Carolina Patriots in the American Revolution.* Baltimore: Genealogical Publishing Co., 1983.

Moultrie, William. *Memoirs of the American Revolution, So Far as It Related to the States of North and South Carolina, and Georgia, Compiled from the Most Authentic Materials, the Author's Personal Knowledge of the Various Events, and Including an Epistolary Correspondence on Public Affairs, with Civil and Military Officers of that Period.* 2 vols. New York: David Longworth, 1802.

Salley, A. S., comp. *Records of the Regiments of the South Carolina Line in the Revolutionary War.* Edited by Alida Moe. Baltimore, Md.: Genealogical Publishing Co., 1977.

Robert K. Wright Jr.

SOUTHERN CAMPAIGNS OF NATHANAEL GREENE. December 1780– December 1781.

Following Horatio Gates's defeat at Camden, South Carolina, Washington's supporters in the Continental Congress allowed the commander in chief to select a new commanding general for the Southern Department, a break from its earlier insistence on reserving the choice of such important positions to civilian authority. Washington did not hesitate in picking Nathanael Greene, knowing that his experiences as both a combat commander and the quartermaster general made Greene the best choice to rebuild a shattered department. But he also ordered Inspector General Friedrich von Steuben to proceed south as well, informing him that he was to take over the department's base area in Virginia and begin passing supplies and reinforcements on to Greene. Greene moved rapidly southward, meeting with civilian leaders along the way, and reached Charlotte, North Carolina, on 2 December. He took command from Gates the next day.

GREENE SPLITS HIS FORCES

On paper, and in the eyes of the British, Greene's army was weak, demoralized, and poorly clothed and equipped. The theater of operations had few roads and limited agricultural resources, most of which lay in enemy hands. And civilian confidence in the Congress and the army lay at an all-time low. But he had several hidden advantages: the heart of his force consisted of veteran Continental infantry, artillery, and cavalry from Maryland, Delaware, and Virginia; his lines of communications northward were intact; and the majority of the population supported his cause. Greene felt confident that in time he could rebuild the department's field army into an effective fighting force but knew that he also had to restore the will to resist by avoiding the appearance of being on the defensive.

Greene's first decisions revealed pure military genius. One of Gates's final acts as department commander had been to detach a small mobile force under Daniel Morgan to probe along the inland routes toward the British outposts at Ninety Six and Augusta. Instead of following the conventional wisdom of recalling those troops, Greene did the exact opposite. Although the textbook solution called for an outnumbered general never to split his force in the face of a superior enemy, Greene actually reinforced Morgan. He fell back with his main body (about eleven hundred Continentals) to a camp selected by Thaddeus Kosciuszko near Cheraw, where he could regroup in some security and in a healthy environment. Morgan took six hundred of the best men to circle around the inland flank of Cornwallis (leading a four-thousand-man field army) and encourage the uprising of the militia of the Catawba district.

In a move that was to prove decisive in subsequent operations, Greene ordered his quartermaster general, Edward Carrington, to continue the mission Gates had previously given him to reconnoiter routes back to Virginia. Greene understood that in the Deep South, where roads were few and far apart, the rivers played a critical role. The waterways basically flowed from west to east, at right angles to the roads. While settlers had used them to push inland, from a military standpoint they actually became critically important obstacles. Close to the coast in the lowlands, they were numerous and frequently flooded, making the movement of large bodies of troops impossible. And in the Piedmont, where the climate was better for military operations, they could be crossed only at a relatively small number of ferries or fords. Furthermore, British seapower could not come far enough inland because of the fall line to land either troops or large quantities of supplies. Greene therefore instructed Kosciuszko and Edward Stevens not only to map the Yadkin and Catawba Rivers, identifying all the critical crossing points, but also to collect or construct boats that could be moved by wagon from one river line to another as a bridging train.

When this strategy revealed itself to Cornwallis, the British general was smart enough to see dangers in Greene's unorthodoxy that were not apparent to such subordinates as Banastre Tarleton—or to many later historians. The Napoleonic solution might seem to be for Cornwallis to use his interior lines for a defeat in detail of Greene's forces, which were eventually separated by about 120 miles (from Cheraw to Cowpens). But the realities of terrain and communications made such an approach risky. If Cornwallis moved in force against Cheraw, Morgan could attack Ninety Six and Augusta; if Cornwallis moved in force against Morgan, Greene could attack Charleston. If Cornwallis ignored Greene and Morgan to resume his invasion north, they would be a threat to his flanks and rear. If Cornwallis sat in Winnsboro and did nothing—which was highly unlikely—Greene's dual tasks of rehabilitation and harassment would be simplified. (This analysis of the situation is Greene's own.) Although Greene, who died in 1786, would never hear of Napoleon, who was born in 1769, he was taking advantage of his superior mobility to observe Napoleon's principle that an army must separate to live (off the country) but unite to fight.

Greene left Charlotte on 20 December and reached Cheraw on the 26th. His troops included 650 veteran Continentals plus almost as many Virginia and Maryland replacements, some of whom were also veterans who had reenlisted. They were soon reinforced by 400 more Virginia recruits under Colonel John Greene, the first of the detachments pushed forward by Steuben. Lee's Second Partisan Corps arrived on 13 January 1781, and

Nathanael Greene immediately sent it to support Marion (who raided Georgetown, South Carolina, on 24 January).

Morgan left Charlotte on 21 December with 320 Maryland and Delaware Continentals, 200 Virginia riflemen—all of the infantry under John Howard—and about 80 light dragoons under William Washington. He set off to join the North Carolina militia of General William Davidson and operate between the Broad and Pacolet Rivers to protect patriots of the region, harass the enemy, and gather supplies. Morgan had orders to rejoin the main army or harass the enemy's flank and rear if Cornwallis should advance in the direction of Greene's wing.

CORNWALLIS REACTS

Cornwallis received his last major reinforcements from Clinton in mid-December, when Major General Alexander Leslie landed in Charleston with fifteen hundred additional veteran troops. After calling them forward, Cornwallis began to assemble a field force of about four thousand men at Winnsboro. He counted on leaving about the same number behind to hold his scattered posts but recognized that they were less capable soldiers. Before Cornwallis could start taking the offensive again, he began getting disturbing intelligence of the American troop movements. Although he tended to discredit the early reports, by 26 December he was sufficiently alarmed to write Tarleton, who was about twenty miles west on the Broad River with some nine hundred men, to say that "Morgan and [William] Washington have passed Broad river" and asking that he "try to get all possible intelligence of Morgan." On the evening of 1 January 1781, Earl Cornwallis got unnerving reports from two different sources that Morgan was approaching Ninety Six with three thousand men. Cornwallis ordered Tarleton to protect this strategically important place and to find Morgan. "Let me know if you think that the moving the whole, or any part of my corps, can be of use," he told Tarleton.

Morgan had, in fact, reached the Pacolet River on Christmas after a tough fifty-eight-mile march across rain-soaked country. Two days later Washington rode south on his Hammond's Store Raid, which was the basis of the alarming, but incorrect, reports that Ninety Six was threatened.

Cornwallis was relieved by Tarleton's reports that although Morgan was not to be found, he was not around Ninety Six. The earl had confided to Tarleton on 27 December that he planned to resume the offensive northward, and Tarleton realized Cornwallis was reluctant to undertake this operation until Morgan was off his mind. On 4 January, therefore, Tarleton proposed a plan. He asked for reinforcements with which he would move to destroy Morgan or, more probably, drive him north toward Kings Mountain; the main army would advance simultaneously toward the latter point from Winnsboro to trap Morgan should he elude Tarleton. Cornwallis agreed and on the evening of 5 January wrote that he would head north on Sunday, 7 January. He also ordered the fifteen hundred troops of Major General Leslie to leave Camden on 9 January to join the main army on its march.

Meanwhile, Morgan had written Greene on 4 January that because of insufficient forage, he would have either to retreat or to move toward Georgia. Greene answered on 13 January, asking Morgan "hold your ground if possible . . . disagreeable consequences that will result from a retreat." If that was not possible, he suggested that Morgan move toward Ninety Six or elsewhere in the vicinity if this might alleviate his supply problem. (This is apparently the basis for the belief that Morgan's original directive told him to attack Ninety Six and Augusta.) "Colonel Tarleton is said to be on his way to pay you a visit," Greene concluded cheerily. "I doubt not but he will have a decent reception and a proper dismission."

Rain continued to impede operations, and Tarleton was stopped at Duggin's Plantation on Indian Creek between 6 and 9 January, waiting for a chance to continue north across the swollen Enoree. Cornwallis left Winnsboro on the 8th but took until the 16th to cover forty miles to Turkey Creek. During the critical period of 9–16 January, Cornwallis got only one message from Tarleton; as a result he did not know that on the 14th Tarleton had crossed the Enoree and the Tyger and was in hot pursuit of Morgan. Nor did Tarleton know that Cornwallis had slowed his own advance on the assumption that Tarleton was still being held back by swollen rivers. Too late to remedy matters, Tarleton sent this message from Pacolet at 8 o'clock on the morning of 16 January: "My Lord, I have been most cruelly retarded by the waters. Morgan is in force and gone for Cherokee Ford. I am now on my march. I wish he would be stopped."

On the 15th, when Morgan learned that Tarleton had crossed the Tyger with a force reported to number up to twelve hundred, Morgan wrote Greene: "My force is inadequate to the attempts you have hinted at" (see above). During the day of the 15th, Tarleton probed for a place to cross the Pacolet but found every ford guarded. That night he faked a march up the river toward Wofford's Iron Works and went silently into bivouac; after the Americans outposts had taken the bait and moved up the river opposite him, Tarleton countermarched and crossed the Pacolet, unopposed, six miles below Morgan at Easterwood Shoals. Morgan's scouts brought him this bad news as the Americans were preparing breakfast at about 6 A.M. on the 16th, and a half hour later the rebels were streaking north to put Broad River between them and their pursuers. After eating Morgan's breakfast, Tarleton sent the message quoted above. At Cowpens however, on

17 January, Morgan turned at bay to beat Tarleton in a little jewel of a battle.

HARE AND HOUNDS

Had Cornwallis been at Kings Mountain, as he had so optimistically planned, Greene's campaigns in the South might have ended here. But the realities of operations in adverse terrain and weather had left him still at Turkey Creek, thirty miles from Cowpens, when he learned on the evening of the 17th that Tarleton had been beaten. He had decided to wait there for Leslie who, ironically, arrived about the time "Bloody" Tarleton rode in with his two hundred survivors on the 18th.

Morgan wasted no time. Not more than two hours after the battle he marched east, crossed the Broad River, and camped six miles from the scene of his triumph. Early the next morning he was racing toward Ramseur's Mill (later Lincolnton). He crossed Sherrald's (or Sherrill's) Ford the morning of the 23rd and went into camp with the Catawba between him and pursuit. (He had unburdened himself of the prisoners by detaching Pickens with most of the militia and Washington's cavalry to escort them to Island Ford on the upper Catawba, where a commissary for prisoners sent them on to Virginia. Pickens rejoined Morgan's camp behind Sherrald's Ford.)

The first impact of Tarleton's defeat came from the way it crippled Cornwallis's reconnaissance and intelligence capabilities. He did not take up the pursuit until 19 January. Then, apparently thinking Morgan might still be around Cowpens, his force of almost 3,000 trudged northwest toward Kings Mountain. Two days later, after Tarleton finally was able to scout west of the Broad, Cornwallis corrected his course and picked up the trail. But the two lost days kept the British from reaching Ramseur's Mill until about 7 A.M. on the 25th. At this point, as it had earlier in the war in December 1776, Cornwallis's youth and inexperience led him to make a terrible mistake. Frustrated by the slow pace of march and unaware that it was caused by the weak nature of the British logistical structure coupled with the terrain and the lack of civilian support, the British commander now decided to convert his entire command into light troops in order to run Morgan to ground. He ordered all impedimenta destroyed, and during the next two days at Ramseur's Mill, his troops burned all their tents and all the wagons except the minimum number needed for ammunition, salt, medical supplies, and casualties; all the provisions that could not be packed into haversacks were destroyed, even the rum. The historian Christopher Ward has suggested in *War of the Revolution* (1952) that this may explain the 250 desertions at Ramseur's.

This dramatic move proved futile and, in the long run, disastrous. Cornwallis misread his opponents and instinctively sought to apply the same boldness that had worked against Lincoln and Gates. He should now have remembered the mission that Clinton had given him when placing him in command in the South and that Germain had assigned in the original instructions for a southern campaign. British forces first had to secure the agricultural resources needed to supply the West Indies, and they were to do it by organizing the Loyalists behind a secure screen of regular troops. For Cornwallis in January of 1781, North Carolina was to be invaded only if South Carolina and Georgia were properly secured; Cornwallis had abandoned his first invasion when Ferguson was destroyed at Kings Mountain and should again have done so when Tarleton met so similar a fate.

When Greene received word on 23 January of Morgan's victory, he was, naturally, delighted, but he also realized the mortal danger his army now faced. From the beginning Greene's southern campaign assumed that he might have to retreat, and he now profited from the careful plans of the previous weeks. As soon as he realized that Cornwallis was going to advance, Greene began carefully to trade space for time. Huger was directed to move his wing of the army from Cheraw toward Salisbury, on Morgan's line of retreat, as soon as possible. Commissaries at Salisbury and Hillsboro were told to get ready to move their prisoners and stores into Virginia. Carrington was told to assemble boats on the Dan. On 28 January, Greene left Cheraw with a small escort for a hazardous cross-country ride of 125 miles to join Morgan on his line of retreat. The same day Huger started his march, having previously sent nonessential baggage, the weakest horses, and the worst wagons to Hillsboro.

Greene joined Morgan in his camp behind the Catawba on 30 January. He found that Morgan, the Old Wagoner, thought the entire army should retreat west into the mountains. But Greene correctly interpreted Cornwallis's baggage-burning as an indication that the British would try to stabilize the situation in South Carolina by intercepting American men and supplies in North Carolina. By choosing to fall back in front of the British, Greene knew that he could draw Cornwallis further away from his bases while simultaneously shortening the Americans' lines of supply. At some point along that path Greene knew that a British mistake might give him the opportunity to turn the tables. Greene issued orders for Lee's Legion to rejoin him from the lower Peedee, where it had been operating with Marion. He wrote Huger of the ambitious new plan and urged him to hurry to effect a junction with Morgan. Although he first intended using Morgan's men to delay the enemy's crossing of the swollen Catawba, when the river started going down he ordered Morgan to continue his retreat to Salisbury, where he hoped Huger would soon arrive.

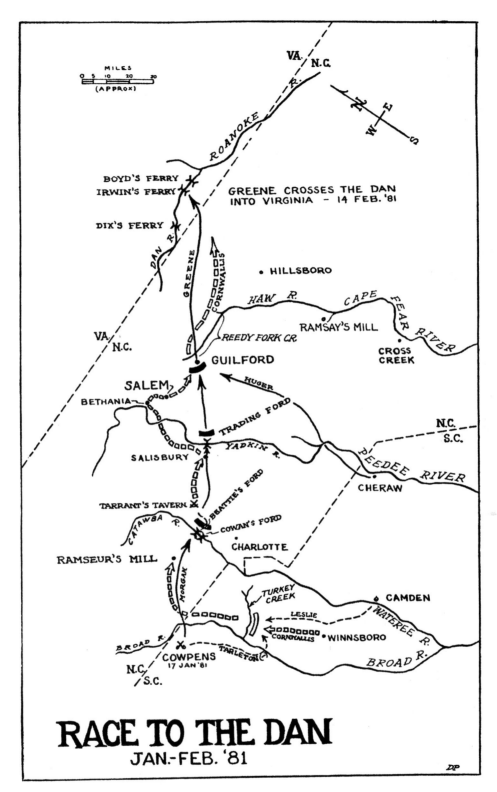

MILES
0 5 10   20   20
(APPROX)

VA. N.C.

ROANOKE R.

BOYD'S FERRY
IRWIN'S FERRY

GREENE CROSSES THE DAN
INTO VIRGINIA – 14 FEB. '81

DIX'S FERRY

DAN R.

GREENE

CORNWALLIS

• HILLSBORO

HAW R.   CAPE FEAR RIVER

REEDY FORK CR.

RAMSAY'S MILL

VA./N.C.

GUILFORD

CROSS CREEK

SALEM

HUGER

BETHANIA

TRADING FORD

N.C. S.C.

SALISBURY

YADKIN R.

PEEDEE RIVER

CHERAW

TARRANT'S TAVERN

BEATTIE'S FORD

CATAWBA R.

COWAN'S FORD

CHARLOTTE

RAMSEUR'S MILL

MORGAN

TURKEY CREEK

• CAMDEN

LESLIE

WATEREE R.

CORNWALLIS   • WINNSBORO

BROAD R.

COWPENS
17 JAN '81

TARLETON

BROAD R.

N.C.
S.C.

RACE TO THE DAN
JAN.-FEB. '81

DP

ACTION ON THE CATAWBA

General William Davidson had turned out eight hundred North Carolina militia and more were supposed to be coming. In Greene's master plan, as in Morgan's tactical plan at Cowpens, the militia forces played a valuable economy-of-force role, screening the Continentals from having to engage the British prematurely and wearing Cornwallis down. Greene planned to use Davidson's men to cover the four crossing sites along a thirty-mile front where Cornwallis might move. Shortly after 2 P.M. on the 31st, when Morgan's troops had already started toward the Yadkin, Greene met with Davidson, Morgan, and William Washington at Beattie's Ford on the Catawba to plan the defense of that obstacle. (Details of this commanders' conference are given because they clear up considerable confusion as to who was where at this important moment.) The British had been camped across the river for two days waiting for the water to go down, and an advance guard of four hundred or five hundred men appeared on the hill overlooking the stream as this twenty-minute conference started. When the meeting broke up, Morgan and Washington rode off to join their troops (temporarily commanded by Howard), Greene left with one aide to help assemble North Carolina militia a few miles behind the river, and Davidson made final arrangements to defend the fords.

Two fords had been obstructed with felled trees and could be held by small detachments. Davidson ordered patrols to watch most of the river during the night and concentrated the bulk of his militia around the remaining two crossing points. Beattie's Ford had not been obstructed because civilian refugees were still using it; about three hundred men took up defensive positions there. Four to six miles downstream, at a private crossing called Cowan's, Davidson put about the same number.

Thinking Morgan's troops were around Beattie's, Cornwallis planned a demonstration there, to consist only of an artillery bombardment; Lieutenant Colonel James Webster would command this operation. Cornwallis would lead the main body across Cowan's Ford at dawn and encircle Morgan at the principal ford. The troops turned out at 1 A.M. on 1 February and moved toward the river. The demonstration fizzled out in the rain. But Cornwallis was able to force a crossing at Cowan's Ford led by the heroics of the Guards Brigade. General Davidson fell in this action, and without his leadership the militia scattered. Webster crossed later in the day without opposition. At Tarrant's Tavern, about ten miles beyond the river, Tarleton scattered another militia group. Although Cornwallis had not come close to catching Morgan, the defeats temporarily demoralized the North Carolina militia. Greene wrote on 13 February that all but about eighty had deserted him, which was an

exaggeration, but the rest of his retreat took place with less support than before.

OPERATIONS ON THE YADKIN

From Salisbury, where he arrived alone during the early hours of 2 February, Greene sent word to Huger to rendezvous with Morgan at Guilford Courthouse unless he was within twenty-four hours of Salisbury. When Morgan reached the Yadkin on 2 February, boats were waiting, and he crossed at Trading (Trader's) Ford during the night. The British advance guard under General O'Hara arrived too late to accomplish anything more than rout the militiamen who were guarding a few wagons left by fleeing civilians.

Having been frustrated at the Catawba and the Yadkin, Cornwallis still hoped to catch Greene before he could reach the Dan. Greene's movement north from Trading Ford the evening of 4 February supported Cornwallis's belief that the Americans lacked the necessary boats to cross the lower Dan and would head for the fords upstream. But the rebels turned east a few miles before reaching Salem and, after a march of forty-seven miles in forty-eight hours, camped near Guilford Courthouse on the 7th. On this day they were joined by Huger and Lee. Huger's troops had completed a remarkable march under adverse weather conditions and with pitifully inadequate clothing—many of them barefooted—without the loss of a man.

RACE TO THE DAN

Greene studied the ground and gave serious consideration to making a stand at Guilford, but a council of officers persuaded him not to do so. Tradition holds that Greene hoped to fight there to encourage the militia but chose not to when relatively few of them mobilized. The truth is probably that Greene correctly assessed that the tables had not yet turned. His fifteen hundred or so reliable Continentals were still outnumbered by the enemy's estimated twenty-five hundred regulars, so Greene kept falling back. Henry Lee gave this explanation of Greene's plans for further retreat:

> The British general was 25 miles from Guilford Court-House; equally near with Greene to Dix's Ferry on the Dan, and nearer to the upper shallows or points of that river, which were supposed to be fordable, notwithstanding the late swell of water. Lieutenant Colonel Carrington, quartermaster-general, suggested the propriety of passing at Irwin's Ferry, 17 [this should be 70] miles from Guilford Court-House, and 20 below Dix's. Boyd's Ferry was four miles below Irwin's; and the boats might be easily brought down from Dix's to assist in transporting the army at these near and lower ferries. The plan of Lieutenant Colonel Carrington was adopted, and that officer charged with the requisite preparations. (*Memoirs*, p. 236)

A 700-man light corps, including all the cavalry and the best infantry troops, was organized to serve as rear guard and also to draw the enemy away from Greene's line of retreat. William Washington commanded the mounted element, 240 men, which included his own dragoons and the cavalry of Lee's Partisan Corps. John Howard commanded the infantry element, which included his 280-man battalion, Lee's 120 foot troops, and 60 Virginia militia armed with rifles.

Morgan was asked to command this body, but he declined on grounds of bad health and intimated that he would like to retire. Lee says he was asked to persuade Morgan to "obey the universal wish" and even argued that "the brigadier's retirement at that crisis might induce an opinion unfavorable to his patriotism." Although this almost swayed the Old Wagoner, on 10 February, Greene granted him his requested leave of absence. Morgan was suffering from sciatica, rheumatism, and a less delicate ailment "so that I scarcely can sit upon my horse," as he wrote Greene on the 5th. (There is no reason to believe, as some have charged, that his real reason for leaving was to dissociate himself from a strategy he considered too hazardous.) Command of the rear guard fell into the capable hands of Otho Williams.

Cornwallis, still blocked at Trading Ford by high water and a lack of boats, and still holding his preconceived idea of Greene's route, sent Tarleton with his cavalry and the Twenty-third Foot up the Yadkin toward Shallow Ford, twenty-five miles north. Meeting no resistance, Tarleton crossed on the 6th, and Cornwallis left Salisbury with his main body on the 7th and entered Salem on the 9th. Greene left Guilford with the main body on the 10th and headed for Carrington's crossing sites, seventy miles beeline to the northeast. Williams got in front of Cornwallis this same day, with the immediate result that the British checked their advance to close up ranks and reconnoiter. The British then started a vigorous pursuit of Williams, who succeeded for about two days in drawing them in the desired direction. Through intermittent rain and snow, over red clay roads that were churned into mud during the day and frozen into the thus-distorted surface at night, the armies struggled along on three parallel routes. Williams kept on the middle route, with the enemy to his left rear. Lee's cavalry had the particularly exhausting and nerve-racking mission of bringing up the rear and of watching for any indication that Cornwallis might have discovered the true situation. Lee had to keep the enemy advance guard from circling to the right to get between him and Williams; the latter had to avoid being cut off from Greene by the same maneuver. This meant that half of Lee's troopers were on duty every night and got only six hours' rest out of forty-eight. Lee pointed out, however, that the enemy cavalry "although more numerous . . . was far inferior in regard to size, condition, and activity of their horses."

Before dawn of the 13th, Tarleton informed Cornwallis that Greene's main body was headed for the lower Dan. Ordering his van to proceed as if the army were still following the former route, Cornwallis started on a forced march and soon found a causeway that led to the road Williams had been following with his infantry. As on previous days, the Americans had broken camp at 3 A.M., marched rapidly, and stopped for their one meal of the day. Mounted outposts covered the rear and reported that the enemy was moving forward in the normal manner. Having completed his preparations along the Dan, Quartermaster General Carrington was commanding the dragoon detachment in contact with the British van. His periodic reports informed Lee that the enemy was advancing at the usual pace. Suddenly, an excited civilian appeared to report that Cornwallis was on the other road and less than four miles away. Williams had ordered Lee to send a cavalry detachment back with this man to check on this report, and soon after Captain James Armstrong departed on this mission, a report from Carrington, saying that the enemy to his front had slowed down, confirmed the previous intelligence. Williams then ordered Lee to reinforce Armstrong and to take command.

This led to a clash in which eighteen of Tarleton's troopers were killed. Lee was about to hang the enemy commander, Captain Thomas Miller, in reprisal for the cold-blooded killing of his unarmed, teenage bugler by Miller's men, when the enemy van approached. (The boy, whose name was Gillies, had been ordered to lend his horse to the civilian when the latter was sent forward with a dragoon patrol. Lee then led his detachment off to the side of the highway and the boy was sent back to tell Williams no contact had yet been made. The dragoon patrol soon reappeared with the enemy hard on its heels. Not seeing Lee's detachment and unable to overtake the American patrol, some enemy dragoons ran down the unarmed bugler and sabered him as he lay on the ground. Lee then descended on the British, killed eighteen, and captured Miller and all but two of his men as they tried to escape. Miller argued that since he was on an intelligence mission, he had tried to save the boy's life, and he was not hanged.)

The Americans then resumed their retreat with Lee bringing up the rear and looking for a chance to chop off the head of Cornwallis's advance guard should they made the mistake of getting beyond supporting distance. "The skilful enemy never permitted any risk in detail, but preserved his whole force for one decisive struggle," said Lee. As the day of 13 February wore on—and both sides would have approved that choice of verb—Williams decided he had accomplished his mission by luring Cornwallis toward Dix's Ferry. Ordering Lee to continue screening to the rear with a small force, Williams led his main body onto a more direct route toward Irwin's Ferry. Cornwallis soon detected this change of route and came close to surprising Lee's men when they pulled off onto what they hoped was an obscure side road for the breakfast they had missed. A moment's hesitation by the British point and the superiority of the Americans' horses enabled them to escape. In his *Memoirs,* Lee called his momentary but near-fatal lapse of judgment "criminal improvidence!"

Cornwallis felt that he was coming close to his objective and pushed his men even harder into the night. The Americans had a bad moment about 8 P.M., when they saw campfires and thought they marked Greene's bivouac, but to their immense relief they found he had left this camp two days earlier and that a handful of local inhabitants were keeping the fires going to guide Williams's men. When the British stopped, so did the rebels, but at midnight the race was on again. They were still forty miles from the Dan. At night the combination of wet and cold added a crust of frost to the deep mud of the road. On the 14th, both sides stopped for only one hour to rest during the morning. At about noon came a message from Greene: "All our troops are over.... I am ready to receive you and give you a hearty welcome." It was dated 5:12 P.M. of the preceding day.

O'Hara's British vanguard heard the Americans cheer and made one final rush in an attempt to trap the rebels against the river. But although the British marched forty miles in those last twenty-four hours, the Americans covered the distance in sixteen hours. Thus, Greene was able to drop Lee off at about 3 P.M. some fourteen miles from the river and continue safely to Boyd's Ferry. The infantry reached the bank before sunset to find boats waiting. Lee's cavalry arrived between 8 and 9 P.M. and crossed on the same boats (the horses swimming, as was normal practice). "In the last boat, the quarter-master-general, attended by Lieutenant-Colonel Lee and the rear troop, reached the friendly shore," said Lee in his *Memoirs.*

Thus ended Greene's first campaign in the South. Part of his army had won a battle against Tarleton and then all of it had run two hundred miles for dear life. For the first time in the war not a single Continental soldier held any of the territory south of Virginia. Greene's pleasure over this apparent defeat and Cornwallis's bitter disappointment over this apparent triumph illustrate a fundamental principle of war—no matter how much territory you occupy, you have not won until you destroy the enemy's armed force. Washington had been proving this in the North; now his disciple Greene was doing it in the South.

The what-ifs of the Race to the Dan have tantalized historians ever since 1781. If Cornwallis had caught and destroyed Greene's army, one line goes, he would have been able to link up with Benedict Arnold (then carrying out a raid along the James River) and swell their combined force by liberating the Convention Army and the Cowpens prisoners. As a consequence, this scenario goes, all four southern provinces would have come back under royal authority. That is wishful thinking, however, because it ignores the reality of logistics and numerical strength. Cornwallis had quite literally run his small army into the ground, and as it lay panting on the south bank of the Dan, he had to start worrying about finding a way to get back to some safe location to resupply and refit his men.

WINNING THE CAROLINAS

Now what? Cornwallis lacked the boats to follow Greene. He could not maneuver upstream to cross at the fords because Greene could too easily counter such moves. He could not go downstream, as the terrain in that direction became more swampy. Nor could he rest in place. Winnsboro lay 250 miles to the rear as the crow flies, and Charleston was another 125 miles beyond. Every round of ammunition and every morsel of food would have to be transported along that tortured route, open to raiding attack by militia, and there were not enough British, German, or Loyalist troops in the South to secure it, nor were there wagons and horses to transport the supplies. In effect, since crossing the Catawba, every step Cornwallis took had overextended the British and increased American resistance by compressing the Patriots like a spring toward the bases in Virginia.

Cornwallis had no alternative but to withdraw, and on 17 February 1781 he started moving slowly toward Hillsboro, North Carolina. Here he issued a proclamation inviting "faithful and loyal subjects" to escape "the cruel tyranny under which they have groaned for many years"; they could save themselves by rallying around the royal standard with their arms and ten days' supply of groceries. Ironically, the "raising of the royal standard" in this case, as in others during the war, merely tempted locals with Loyalists sympathies into revealing themselves. When the royal troops marched away, as they inevitably did, the Patriots took their revenge. After this pattern had happened a few times, no more supporters of the crown could be found who were willing to speak up. Germain and Clinton's hopes for a secure South were slowly crushed by the tactical requirements of Cornwallis's movements.

Greene's situation was by no means rosy. His Continentals troops had also been worn down during the retreat, and the North Carolina militia was disorganized and demoralized. The Virginia militia was beginning to turn out, however, and Greene discovered that Steuben's efforts had assembled supplies and new recruits for him in Virginia. Greene shifted his main body to Halifax Court House, which became his new base. But he also pushed his light elements across the river a day after the British left it.

On 18 February, Lee's Partisan Corps, supported by two companies of Maryland Continentals, crossed the

Dan to operate with Pickens and his seven hundred newly raised militia. Colonel Otho Williams crossed two days later with the light infantry that had comprised a rear guard less than a week before. As soon as he was joined by six hundred Virginia militia under General Edward Stevens, Greene himself moved into North Carolina. His plan was to keep as much pressure on Cornwallis as possible—cutting up his foraging parties and discouraging the Loyalists from rising—while continuing to build his own army up with recruits and mobilized militia. The water level in the Dan was falling rapidly, and Greene did not want to give his opponent a chance either to resume the offensive or to escape.

In an action known as Haw River (Pyle's Defeat), on 25 February, Lee surprised and destroyed a Loyalist force with a violence reminiscent of The Waxhaws. The totality of that defeat, made possible by the fact that Pyle mistook the green of Lee's uniforms for those of the Provincials, effectively ended North Carolina's Tory militia. After some replenishment, Cornwallis took the field again and tried for several weeks to bring Greene to battle. Superior American mobility enabled Greene to maneuver away from danger and avoid a general engagement under any conditions that would have favored the British. The opposing forces did have one sharp skirmish at Wetzell's Mill on 6 March. Finally, in mid-March, Greene felt that he had attracted as many men as he could sustain and accepted the fight that Cornwallis sought.

At Guilford Courthouse on 15 March 1781, Cornwallis attacked and scored a hard-won tactical victory. But it was a strategic defeat, since it bled him dry and left him with no alternative but retreat.

CORNWALLIS WITHDRAWS TO WILMINGTON

Although Camden, South Carolina, the second most important British post in the South after Charleston, was closer than Wilmington, North Carolina, by forty miles, retreat to Camden would have meant the failure of Cornwallis's entire campaign. Instead, he opted to head toward the British coastal base at Wilmington on the Cape Fear River. Here he could be supplied by sea. Furthermore, Cornwallis believed that Greene would follow him. If Greene did so, it would keep the American field army away from South Carolina and Georgia. Wilmington had many features of a flanking position, but Greene quickly demonstrated that it lacked the essential one.

Giving his men two days' rest and abandoning his wounded, Cornwallis started withdrawing on 18 March; Greene followed immediately. On the 28th, Greene had an opportunity to hit the enemy forces while they were astride the Deep River at Ramsay's Mill, but he lacked the strength to assure success. In keeping with the fundamental concept behind the whole campaign, Greene refused to risk a devastating defeat for the chance of a decisive blow. He knew that time and attrition worked for the Americans as long as the Southern Department's field army remained intact. Cornwallis withdrew unmolested to Cross Creek (later Fayetteville). Since supplies he had ordered sent to this place were not there, he continued on to Wilmington, arriving on 7 April. (On the 24th he marched north to Virginia.)

GREENE VERSUS RAWDON

The Virginia and North Carolina militias had completed their six weeks' service, and Greene released them with thanks. Although some had run at Guilford, others had stood firm and softened up the redcoats for the Continentals in the main line. More to the point, the citizen soldiers had made that battle possible and had fulfilled their mission. Rather than overextending them, Greene chose to simplify his own logistics by sending them home. After remaining at Ramsay's Mill from 29 March until 5 April, Greene headed for South Carolina.

The two commanders reviewed the lessons of the preceding months and drew different conclusions. As the next stage unfolded, the failure of Cornwallis's strategic conception became as apparent as the soundness of Greene's vision. Determined to replace Clinton's defensive policy with an aggressive one, Cornwallis became fixated on the Southern Department's apparent ability to keep rising again. He kept searching for a way to press the offensive in an effort to cut off the rebels from their northern sources of support, first by pressing to Camden, then to North Carolina, and now by striking against the base areas in Virginia. Each time he compounded his errors; each time he proved to be incapable of looking beyond the battlefield to see the whole of the theater of operations. This lack of vision would be a critical factor in how Britain lost the war. As for the immediate operational situation, however, withdrawing to Wilmington—rather than dropping back to Camden, where Rawdon was located with almost 2,000 troops—surrendered the initiative. He had, in effect, abandoned Rawdon to fend for himself. Ramsay's Mill (where Greene stopped his pursuit), Wilmington, and Camden form an equilateral triangle, the points being about 120 miles apart. If Cornwallis had had the strength in Wilmington to threaten Greene's line of communications as the latter operated toward Camden, then the earl would have had the flanking position mentioned earlier. But he did not. Greene, knowing this, turned his back on Wilmington to hunt down Rawdon. In failing to follow, Cornwallis had made a gambler's desperate wager that he could conquer Virginia before the relentless American pressure ground down his subordinates in South Carolina and Georgia.

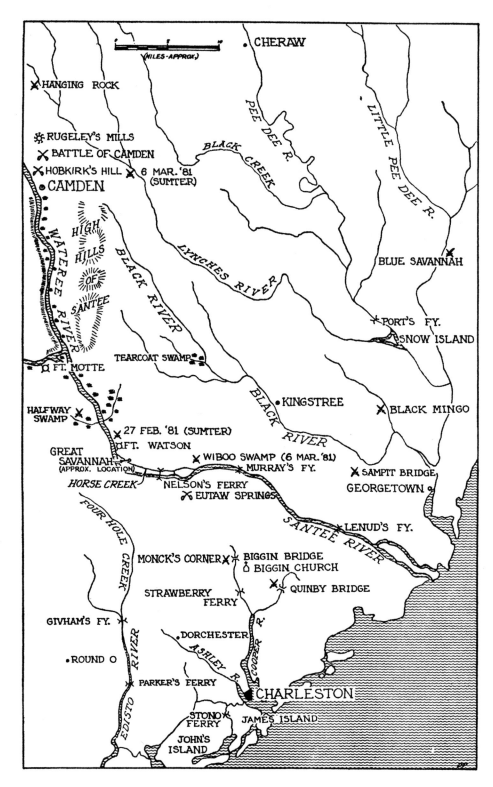

SOUTHERN CAMPAIGNS OF NATHANAEL GREENE. THE GALE GROUP.

Greene's army now contained a solid, veteran Continental cadre over fifteen hundred strong. One brigade comprised the reconstituted First and Second Virginia battalions, the other the First and Second Maryland. Rounding out the heart of the army were artillerymen from the First Continental Artillery Regiment, William Washington's dragoons (now a composite force of the First and Third Legionary Corps), and the combined arms team of Lee's Second Partisan Corps. Partisan forces of Marion in the Peedee swamps, Sumter on the Broad River, and Pickens in western South Carolina had been harassing the British and could now join forces with Greene as he marched south. Even more importantly, militia forces from Virginia and North Carolina had discovered a successful technique for making a contribution. Mobilizing only as needed for decisive engagement (thereby simplifying Greene's supply problems) and using former Continental officers like Stevens and Lawson and a healthy leavening of Valley Forge veterans as a cadre, they provided a far more effective battlefield force than the militia that had appeared earlier in the war. With a little lead time, this "surge" capacity enabled Greene to achieve the principle of mass at the point of his own choosing.

The youthful but capable Rawdon had on paper a strength of 8,141 British regulars, German regulars, and Provincials with which to hold an area of about 25,000 square miles—that is, a rough parallelogram measuring approximately 120 miles on a side. Rawdon himself held Camden, which would inevitably be Greene's first major objective and which was the northernmost point of the parallelogram, with almost a quarter of his total strength. Along the coast were the major posts of Charleston and Savannah along with the less important one at Georgetown. Far to the interior were Augusta, Ninety Six, and Fort Granby. These bases played an important role in maintaining Loyalist support and preserving any hope of coordination with pro-British Indian tribes. Orangeburg, Fort Watson, and Fort Motte served as connecting links between Charleston and these more distant strongpoints.

When Greene advanced on Camden he initiated a coordinated strategy worked out with the partisan leaders. Pickens threatened Ninety Six to keep reinforcements from being detached from that place. Greene called Sumter to the field army near Camden. Marion's mission was to move out of his Peedee swamps and join Henry "Light-Horse Harry" Lee in an attack on Fort Watson. Lee's primary mission at the onset of the offensive was to screen against a possible move by Cornwallis from Wilmington; as soon as it could be determined that Cornwallis was not heading south, he raced to join Marion.

The successful siege of Fort Watson on 15–23 April ended with the capture of that place and its garrison by Lee

and Marion with only minor losses. The action is more significant, however, for the light it sheds on the new tactics of cooperation employed in the Southern Department. These were built upon earlier experiments in the north but reached new heights of success during 1781 in South Carolina and Georgia. They relied on an experienced cadre of local partisans, under charismatic leaders, to maintain constant pressure on British lines of communication and to develop combat intelligence. When opportunities arose, the much larger number of part-time militia could rapidly assemble, relying on horses for mobility while fighting dismounted. And for important targets the partisans would be reinforced by Lee's Second Partisan Corps, which was specifically tailored to carry out deep operations. Combining the strengths of different groups made the resulting strike force much more flexible. An example of the creative ability to solve problems came immediately from the invention of the Maham Tower, first used in attacking Fort Watson. The man for whom the fort was named, British Colonel John Watson, had been detached from Camden earlier with five hundred of Rawdon's Tory troops to look for Marion in the vicinity of Georgetown (that is, the Peedee swamps), and uncertainty as to his location played a significant part in the operations around Camden as well as at Fort Watson.

At Hobkirk's Hill on 25 April, just outside of Camden, Rawdon defeated Greene in an action that left Greene "almost frantic with vexation and disappointment" (Alden, p. 263). (It was on this occasion that Greene made the statement that summarizes his southern campaigns: "We fight, get beat, rise, and fight again.") Greene's problems in coordinating his strategy against the various enemy posts, and also in Rawdon's success at making the best of his scattered dispositions, are clearly visible in the action around Camden. Greene had given the partisan chiefs assignments largely intended to isolate Rawdon so that the Continental field force could crush him. But Pickens was unable to threaten Ninety Six enough and Rawdon got reinforcements from that place. Sumter, the Gamecock, simply ignored the request that he join Greene near Camden (see below). Marion and Lee were supposed to join Greene, or at least to keep Watson from joining Rawdon; although Watson did not reach Camden until after the battle (7 May), he kept Marion and Lee so busy chasing him that they were not present at the Battle of Hobkirk's Hill.

On the other hand, Rawdon could not profit from his temporary victory and had to fall back. Sumter then took Orangeburg on 11 May. Marion and Lee took Fort Motte on 12 May, and Lee took Fort Granby on 15 May.

"With his usual rather arrogant independence," as the historian Christopher Ward had put it, the Gamecock had gone off to attack Fort Granby instead of joining Greene outside of Camden. He had then broken off this attack to take Orangeburg, about thirty miles south-southeast; he then retraced his steps to find that Fort Granby had already surrendered to Lee. At this point, the historian Francis Vinton Greene has written:

> Sumter felt that Lee had stolen his glory and complained to [Nathanael] Greene of Lee's conduct, stating that he considered it "for the good of the public to do it without regulars." Greene replied that Lee had acted in accordance with his orders; whereupon Sumter sent in his resignation. Greene diplomatically persuaded him to withdraw it, and he afterward rendered excellent service, in co-operation with Lee, in the vicinity of Charleston. (*Revolutionary War*, p. 249)

Greene's leadership ability in managing to hold together a collection of difficult personalities is reminiscent of Eisenhower's performance during World War II.

ROUND TWO

On 10 May, Rawdon abandoned Camden. Taking a more realistic view of the military situation than his patron, Cornwallis, he tried at least to accomplish the ministry's basic orders to hold on to the rice-producing coastal region by concentrating his resources. His own battered force reached Monck's Corner on the 24th. Georgetown's garrison, under pressure from Marion, evacuated by sea on the 23rd. Rawdon also ordered Fort Granby and Ninety Six abandoned, but they did not get the word in time.

Greene moved against Ninety Six on 9 May and detached Lee with some newly raised militia to join Pickens around Augusta. The siege of of Augusta on 22 May–5 June led to the surrender of Lieutenant Colonel Thomas Brown's 630-man garrison of regulars and Georgia Tories after stubborn resistance. The siege of Ninety Six during 22 May–19 June did not end with equal success. Greene broke of his attack just as the rebels appeared to be on the point of a hard-won success against the die-hard garrison of Lieutenant John Cruger. Rawdon had just received three fresh regiments from Ireland, the last reinforcements sent out to North America in the war. He was able to assemble a relief column of 2,000, elude Sumter's delaying force, and move rapidly to Cruger's support. Greene wisely avoided the risk of a decisive action in the field and retreated on 20 June. Rawdon pursued about 25 miles but turned back when Greene headed for safety behind the Broad River.

Rawdon ordered Ninety Six abandoned, leaving the place himself on 3 July and withdrawing through Fort Granby to Orangeburg. Here he was joined by Cruger from Ninety Six and by Lieutenant Colonel Alexander Stewart and his Third Regiment from Charleston. Greene withdrew his Continental regiments into the

Santee Hills to wait out the worst of the summer heat in a relatively healthy location. Rawdon left Stuart at Orangeburg and returned to Charleston with five hundred men; Marion, Sumter, and Lee dogged his heels to within five miles of the city. This ended the second phase. In less than eight months Greene had won back almost the entire South except for footholds around Savannah and Charleston. His little army had marched 950 miles, fought three battles and numerous minor engagements, captured 9 posts, and taken nearly 3,000 prisoners.

ROUND THREE

During the six weeks his army spent in the Santee Hills, Greene drew a stream of reinforcements that pushed his Continental infantry total to over two thousand. Sumter spent this period around Fort Granby, while Marion was at Nelson's Ferry and Pickens was in his home territory around Ninety Six. Rawdon fell ill and sailed (he was captured en route) home to recuperate, leaving Stuart in command. The latter moved up from Orangeburg to a position sixteen miles from Greene, with the flooded Congaree River between them, and could not be tricked out of position when Greene sent raids all the way to the outskirts of Charleston.

On 22 August 1781, Greene resumed the offensive. High water levels on the Santee and Wateree made him take a long detour through Camden to get at Stuart, and the latter withdrew to Eutaw Springs, where he could be supplied better from Charleston. On 7 September, Greene was joined by Marion, bringing his strength up to about twenty-four hundred. The next morning Stuart was surprised to find Greene on top of him, but he formed in time to meet Greene's attack. The Battle of Eutaw Springs of 8 September left Stuart in possession of the hotly contested field but so weakened that he had to withdraw to Monck's Corner. Greene had lost his fourth battle but had practically won his campaign.

The little southern army withdrew back into the Santee Hills again for badly needed rest and recuperation. Within ten days Greene had only one thousand men fit for duty as sickness and expiration of militia services thinned his ranks. The end of active campaigning gave men time to worry about their arrears in pay, inadequate clothing, and other grievances. A mutiny was brewing when one Timothy Griffin staggered onto the parade ground as the Maryland Continentals were being admonished by their officers for recent lax discipline. "Stand to it, boys!" shouted Griffin. "Damn my blood if I would give an inch!" This happened on 21 October, and the rest of Greene's command watched him shot the next afternoon for encouraging mutiny and desertion, which discouraged the others.

Cornwallis had surrendered three days earlier, and General Arthur St. Clair soon started south with two thousand Pennsylvania and Virginia regulars to reinforce Greene. Before he arrived on 4 January 1782, however, the southern army had to take the field to quell a Tory uprising that followed Fanning's Hillsboro Raid on 12 September. The attack on Dorchester on 1 December forced the last British outpost back into Charleston.

On 9 December, Greene joined the rest of his army at the place called Round O, about thirty-five miles west of Charleston, and St. Clair's troops arrived there on 4 January 1782. Wilmington having been evacuated in November, the British in the South were now confined to Charleston and Savannah.

Most accounts of the Revolution in the South end at this point with a general statement that it was over. The following military events are, however, worth recording: Johns Island on 28–29 December 1781; the Mutiny of Cornell on April 1782; the Georgia expedition of Anthony Wayne; and Combahee Ferry on 27 August 1782. The British evacuated Savannah on 11 July 1782 and Charleston on 14 December 1782.

Greene remained at Charleston until August 1783, after news of the peace treaty had arrived. He then returned to Rhode Island, being hailed along the way with the respect and admiration he had earned. After two years of getting his tangled personal affairs in order, he moved to an estate that the Georgia legislature had given him near Savannah. But his days were limited.

SIGNIFICANCE

The reputation Nathanael Greene won in his southern campaigns has worn well in the hands of historians. Initial writers emphasized the role of the Continentals; the generation of historians writing in the twentieth century shifted the attention to the irregulars, sometimes forgetting that Marion and Sumter in fact had been trained as Continental officers. The more modern interpretation tends to emphasize that both groups played important parts, with Greene emerging as the man who found a way to make them work together. It is clear that the Patriots of the Lower South, although they might have been able to continue guerrilla fighting indefinitely, could hardly have dealt effectively with the British and their Tory allies without the assistance of the regulars from the Upper South (Virginia and Maryland) and Delaware. On the other hand, Greene could hardly have kept the field without the aid of Davidson, Marion, Sumter, Pickens, Clarke, and their partisan bands.

Nor was the glory monopolized by the American Patriots. Rawdon, O'Hara, Cruger, Webster, and others had shown magnificent leadership; Camden, Cowan's Ford, and Guilford are names of which the British army is proud. Cruger's defense of Ninety Six and Rawdon's relief of that place were splendid military accomplishments.

SEE ALSO *Augusta, Georgia (22 May–5 June 1781); Carrington, Edward; Combahee Ferry, South Carolina; Convention Army; Cowans Ford, North Carolina; Cowpens, South Carolina; Cruger, John Harris; Davidson, William Lee; Defeat in Detail; Dorchester, South Carolina; Eutaw Springs, South Carolina; Flanking Position; Fort Granby, South Carolina; Fort Motte, South Carolina; Fort Watson, South Carolina (15–23 April 1781); Gates, Horatio; Georgetown, South Carolina (24 January 1781); Georgia Expedition of Wayne; Graham, Joseph; Greene, Nathanael; Guilford Courthouse, North Carolina; Hammonds Store Raid of William Washington; Haw River, North Carolina; Hillsboro Raid, North Carolina; Hobkirk's Hill (Camden), South Carolina; Howard, John Eager; Interior Lines; Johns Island, South Carolina (28–29 December, 1781); Kosciuszko, Thaddeus Andrzej Bonawentura; Leslie, Alexander; Morgan, Daniel; Ninety Six, South Carolina; Orangeburg, South Carolina; Point; Rawdon-Hastings, Francis; Southern Theater, Military Operations in; Steuben, Friedrich Wilhelm von; Stewart, Alexander; Tarleton, Banastre; Tarrant's Tavern, North Carolina; Watson, John Watson Tadwell; Wetzell's Mills, North Carolina; Williams, Otho Holland; Yorktown Campaign; Yorktown, Siege of.*

BIBLIOGRAPHY

Alden, John R. *The South in the Revolution, 1763–1789.* Baton Rouge: Louisiana State University Press, 1957.

Bass, Robert D. *The Green Dragoon: The Lives of Banastre Tarleton and Mary Robinson.* New York: Holt, 1957.

Buchanan, John. *The Road to Guilford Courthouse: The American Revolution in the Carolinas.* New York: Wiley, 1997.

Davis, Burke. *The Cowpens-Guilford Courthouse Campaign.* Philadelphia: Lippincott, 1962.

Dederer, John Morgan. *Making Bricks without Straw: Nathanael Greene's Southern Campaign and Mao Tse-tung's Mobile War.* Manhattan, Kans.: Sunflower University Press, 1983.

Edgar, Walter. *Partisans and Redcoats: The Southern Conflict That Turned the Tide of the American Revolution.* New York: Morrow, 2001.

Greene, Francis Vinton. *The Revolutionary War and the Military Policy of the United States.* New York: Scribner's Sons, 1911.

Greene, Nathanael. *The Papers of General Nathanael Greene.* 12 vols. Edited by Richard K. Showman. Chapel Hill: University of North Carolina Press, 1976–2002.

Lee, Henry. *Memoirs of the War in the Southern Department of the United States.* Rev. ed. New York: University Publishing, 1869.

Lumpkin, Henry. *From Savannah to Yorktown: The American Revolution in the South.* Columbia: University of South Carolina Press, 1981.

Pancake, John S. *This Destructive War: The British Campaign in the Carolinas, 1780–1782.* University: University of Alabama Press, 1985.

Schenck, David. *North Carolina, 1780–'81: Being a History of the Invasion of the Carolinas by the British Army under Lord Cornwallis*. Raleigh, N.C.: Edwards and Broughton, 1889.

Tarleton, Banastre. *A History of the Campaigns of 1780 and 1781, in the Southern Provinces of North America*. Dublin: n.p., 1787.

Ward, Christopher. *The War of the Revolution*. 2 vols. New York: Macmillan, 1952.

Weigley, Russell F. *The Partisan War: The South Carolina Campaign of 1780–1782*. Columbia: University of South Carolina Press, 1970.

revised by Robert K. Wright Jr.

SOUTHERN THEATER, MILITARY OPERATIONS IN.

The primary focus of military operations in the Revolutionary War was the North until after the Battle of Monmouth, New Jersey, 28 June 1778. Then, as the British adopted a southern strategy, the conflict moved south and ended, to all intents and purposes, at Yorktown, Virginia, 19 October 1781.

1775: SOUTHERN REBELS GAIN CONTROL

With major military events taking place around Boston and in Canada, the British sent few regulars to support the embattled Loyalists in the South. The year ended with the rebels generally in control of all four southern provinces. As in all the colonies, most initial actions involved the seizure of British munitions and posts. For instance, the South Carolina militia under Major James Mayson seized Fort Charlotte and its military supplies on 12 July 1775, only to immediately surrender the position to Loyalist militia under Captain Moses Kirkland. Most of these seizures of arms and ammunition did not involve bloodshed. That situation changed in October 1775 with the battle of Hampton, Virginia. Five more battles followed that year in the South: Kemp's Landing, Virginia, in early November, in which Governor John Murray, Lord Dunmore, scattered the Virginia militia (leading to his proclamation offering freedom to the slaves at that site on 7 November); the Hog Island Channel Fight, South Carolina, of 11–12 November; Ninety Six, South Carolina, 19–21 November; Great Bridge, Virginia, 9 December; and Cane Brake (Reedy River), South Carolina, 22 December. Each of these actions involved Patriot and Loyalist militia, giving a preview, albeit a tame one, of the civil war nature of the fighting that was to rage later in the South.

1776: THE REBELS MAINTAIN CONTROL

The London authorities counted strongly on Loyalist support in putting down the rebellion, but they sorely misunderstood the ability of the Loyalists to sustain a military presence on their own. They also generally believed their own misinformation on the number of Loyalists in the South; the majority of whites, it appears, would have preferred for both sides to just leave them alone. Frustrated around Boston and encouraged by reports of the fugitive governors from the Southern provinces, the British launched the Charleston Expedition of General Sir Henry Clinton in 1776. But before the British could get going with this operation their hopes for Loyalist support were crushed at Norfolk, Virginia, 1 January, and Moores Creek Bridge, North Carolina, 27 February. After a humiliating defeat at Charleston, 28 June, the British expedition limped back to join General Sir William Howe on Staten Island for the New York Campaign. The only other significant actions in the South during the year were at Hutchinson's Island, Georgia, 7 March; Gwynn Island, Virginia, 8–10 July; Rayborn Creek, South Carolina, 15 July; and Essenecca Town, South Carolina, 1 August 1776; and a number of naval encounters in the Chesapeake.

1777–1779: AFTER QUIET, THE WAR MOVES SOUTH

While decisive events took place in other theaters, armed actions in the South in 1777 were limited to some minor skirmishes and the battles at Fort McIntosh, Georgia, 2–4 February, and Fort Henry, Virginia, 1 September.

The French Alliance, signed in Paris on 6 February 1778, changed, in theory, the entire complexion of the Revolutionary War. In addition to the free flow of munitions and other supplies to the rebels and the addition of thousands of professional soldiers, France's entry into the war challenged the naval supremacy that had given the British such great strategic flexibility: the ability to move large bodies of troops along the coasts and up the rivers of America. Actually, the British had not capitalized fully on this advantage, and it was almost three years before the French fleet made any decisive contribution to American strategy; but this new element figured prominently in British planning.

Major General Robert Howe was the first commander of the rebel Southern army, and in the spring of 1778 he endeavored to mount an expedition to invade East Florida, where General Augustine Prevost was reported to be receiving British reinforcements. With about 550 Continental troops and the militia commands of Colonels Charles Cotesworth Pinckney, Stephen Bull, Andrew Williamson, and Governor John Houstoun (of Georgia) numbering an addition 1,500 men, as well as naval units commanded

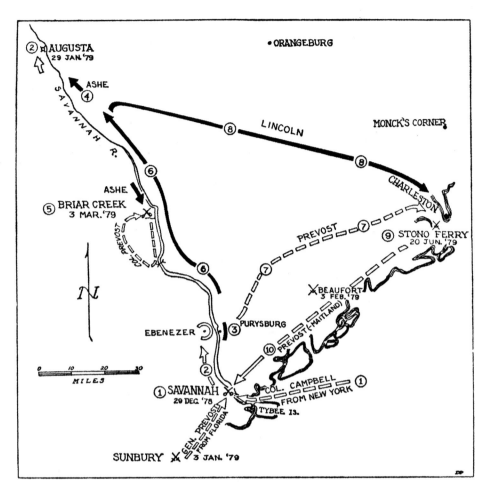

Southern Theater. THE GALE GROUP

by Commodore Oliver Bowen, Howe reached the Altamaha River on 20 May. Here his proposed attack on St. Augustine aborted because Houstoun and Williamson refused to take orders from Howe. Dissolution of the expedition was speeded by hunger and sickness.

The British then undertook operations that resulted in the capture of Savannah, 29 December 1778, by Lieutenant Colonel Archibald Campbell's expedition from New York. Prevost marched north to take Sunbury, Georgia, 9 January 1779, and assumed command of British operations in the South. These campaigns reflected a new British strategy which sought to reclaim the southern colonies one by one for British rule. The first indication of the success of this policy was the restoration of James Wright as governor of Georgia in July 1779.

LINCOLN'S OPERATIONS

Major General Benjamin Lincoln was appointed commander of the Southern Department in September 1778 while Howe was operating in Georgia. When Howe

retreated from Savannah he joined forces with Lincoln, who had moved south to Purysburg, on the South Carolina side of the Savannah River. The Americans then numbered 1,121 Continentals and 2,518 militia; but only 2,428 were fit for duty, and the militia demonstrated a lack of military ability. Prevost moved up to face Lincoln across the river with just under 1,000 British regulars, 700 Germans, some 100 Creeks, and 600 Loyalists. Campbell went inland to take Augusta, 29 January, with virtually no opposition.

As the two main armies faced each other across the formidable barrier of the swamp-bordered Savannah River, Prevost capitalized on his available naval forces to make the first move: he sent a force of about 200 men to take Port Royal Island. This turning movement was frustrated by General William Moultrie at Beaufort, South Carolina, 3 February 1779.

Moultrie's success swelled Lincoln's ranks with militia reinforcements, and he undertook a counteroffensive to recover Georgia. General Andrew Williamson moved with

1,200 men to a position across the river from Campbell's isolated force in Augusta. General Griffith Rutherford led 800 men to Black Swamp, about ten miles upstream from Purysburg. General John Ashe was then sent with 1,500 to join Williamson opposite Augusta. After Ashe crossed the river and started down the right bank in the tracks of Campbell, who had evacuated Augusta the evening before, Colonel Andrew Pickens won his victory at nearby Kettle Creek, Georgia, 14 February. The British under Lieutenant Colonel Mark Prevost executed a brilliant little operation that destroyed Ashe's column at Briar Creek, Georgia, 3 March. But Campbell had to pull his forces back from Augusta, as there was no general rising of Loyalists and he feared being cut off by the Patriot militia from Savannah.

Despite Campbell's retreat, the victory at Briar Creek made the recovery of Georgia for the Patriots that year highly unlikely, most particularly as they now were running dangerously low of arms and ammunition. Nonetheless, Lincoln remained optimistic, especially after a supply of firearms arrived from the Dutch West Indies in mid-April. Leaving Moultrie with 1,000 men at Purysburg and Black Swamp, Lincoln marched up the left bank of the river toward Augusta with the remaining 4,000. Lincoln's goal remains unclear, since Campbell's troops had already retreated to the coast and there were few active Loyalists left in the area of Augusta. Apparently he hoped to give the Georgia legislature, which was reconvening in Augusta, a needed morale boost. Prevost countered with the indirect strategy of pushing through Moultrie's covering force to bring Lincoln back by threatening Charleston. Lincoln recognized this as a diversion and continued his march toward Augusta, but Prevost met so little resistance that he moved on to threaten Charleston, 11–12 May. Lincoln stopped his advance at Silver Bluff, South Carolina, about ten miles short of Augusta, and came puffing back toward Charleston. Prevost withdrew by way of the coastal islands. In a mismanaged attempt to destroy the British rear guard of Lieutenant Colonel John Maitland, the rebels were beaten at Stono Ferry, 20 June 1779. Maitland was left with a strong outpost on Port Royal Island, and Prevost withdrew his main body to Savannah.

The Franco-American attempt to recapture Savannah, 9 October 1779, not only left the place in British hands but also generated more Loyalist support, dropped Patriot morale to a new low, and further disillusioned the Americans about the value of the French alliance.

1780: THE SOUTH BECOMES A MAJOR THEATER

The Charleston Expedition of Clinton in 1780 brought the Revolutionary War south to stay. The surrender of Lincoln's army on 12 May was the greatest British triumph of the war. This campaign also brought into prominence a British cavalry leader, Lieutenant Colonel Banastre Tarleton, whose victories—at Monck's Corner, 14 April; Lenud's Ferry, 6 May; and at the Waxhaws, 29 May—wiped out all organized Patriot resistance in South Carolina that had not been destroyed at Charleston.

When Clinton left for New York on 5 June with about a third of the troops he had brought on this expedition, General Charles Cornwallis was left with 8,345 men to maintain and extend British control of the South. With his main body at Charleston, and strong detachments at Savannah, Augusta, and Ninety Six, Cornwallis established a forward base at Camden and pushed outposts to Rocky Mount, Hanging Rock, and Cheraw. Another post was established at Georgetown, near the mouth of the Peedee River. Within this arc of over 350 miles were many other posts needed to secure lines of communications and rally Loyalists. The latter were counted on to hold this vast area of some 15,000 square miles. Once more the British miscalculated Loyalist strength.

During the three months that followed the surrender of Charleston, the Carolinas were the scene of skirmishes between bands of patriots and Loyalists. Pickens, Francis Marion, and Thomas Sumter emerged as the most prominent partisans in the actions against Loyalist forces, including those led by the British officers Tarleton and Major Patrick Ferguson. Many of these skirmishes were connected with the campaigns leading to the battles of Camden and Kings Mountain. Others took place at Ramseur's Mill, North Carolina, 20 June; Williamson's Plantation, South Carolina, 12 July; Rocky Mount, South Carolina, 30 July, Green Spring, South Carolina, 1 Aug., and Hanging Rock, South Carolina, 6 and 12 August. The Revolution in the south in the years 1779 to 1781 became a civil war, with all the cruelty and bitterness that tends to mark such conflicts.

AMERICAN REGULARS RETURN

Early in 1780 the French government warned Congress that the Patriots must do more for themselves and rely less on the French Alliance to win the war for them. Washington sent General Johann de Kalb south in April with a small body of Continental troops around whom they hoped the Southern militia would rally. Lincoln's surrender at Charleston shook patriot resolve, and Congress recognized the necessity of a major success in that theater of operations. Over Washington's recommendation of General Nathanael Greene, they turned on 13 July to the victor of Saratoga, General Horatio Gates, to serve as commander of the Southern Department.

Kalb, meanwhile, had left Morristown on 16 April with the Maryland and Delaware Continental contingents that constituted the main portion of the Southern army throughout most of the subsequent campaigning. The First Brigade, commanded by Brigadier General William Smallwood, was composed of the First, Third, Fifth, and Seventh Maryland. The Second Brigade of General Mordecai Gist comprised the Second, Fourth, and Sixth Maryland, and the Delaware Regiment. Kalb also had Colonel Charles Harrison's First Continental Artillery Regiment with its eighteen cannon. Marching through Philadelphia to Head of Elk, the infantry proceeded by water to Petersburg, Virginia, and the artillery continued by land. From Petersburg Kalb moved at the rate of fifteen to eighteen miles a day. On 20 June he learned of Charleston's surrender five weeks earlier (12 May). Because the purpose of his expedition was to help defend Charleston, Kalb was faced with a decision as to what he should do next. The hoped-for militia reinforcements failed to arrive in any appreciable numbers while he camped at Parson's Plantation, North Carolina, about thirty-five miles northeast of Hillsboro. Showing the initiative and resolution that were lacking in so many native-born Patriots during the Revolution, he led his regulars farther southwest. He reached Hillsboro on 22 June. Despite the heat, insects, lack of adequate equipment, and almost total lack of provisions, the expedition struggled on to Buffalo Ford on Deep River, about fifty miles north-northeast of the enemy post at Cheraw, South Carolina. Here he was joined by 120 survivors of Pulaski's Legion, now commanded by Colonel Charles Armand. But the large force of well-fed North Carolina militia under Major General Richard Caswell refused to join him, and he was unable to make contact with the Virginia forces of General Edward Stevens and Colonel Charles Porterfield, who were known to be in the field. During the two weeks he camped at Buffalo Ford, Kalb learned of Gates's appointment. His persevering efforts having gone almost completely unrewarded, the giant Bavarian moved his camp along Deep River to Hollingsworth's Farm and surrendered command to Gates on the latter's arrival on 25 July.

In the Camden Campaign, July–August 1780, Gates ignored the good advice of Kalb and several of the southern militia commanders, leading his army to a disaster that almost equaled Lincoln's surrender at Charleston. Kalb died of multiple wounds in the Battle of Camden, 16 August, while Gates fled the field and Tarleton wiped out Sumter's detachment at Fishing Creek, 18 August.

REORGANIZATION AFTER CAMDEN

Realizing that their previous three choices to command the Southern army—Generals Howe, Lincoln, and Gates—had proven less than stellar, Congress resolved on 5 October 1780 that General Washington should select the new commanding general. Washington immediately

chose General Nathanael Greene, with General Friedrich von Steuben as second in command.

Before Greene arrived at Charlotte, North Carolina (2 December) to take command, however, Gates had reorganized the puny remnants of his army. Of four thousand that had constituted this force before Camden, only about seven hundred made their way back to Hillsboro, North Carolina Most of them lacked weapons, having thrown them aside so as to not impede their flight. Congress resolved to forward food and other supplies, but none were forthcoming. The militia presented no problem of reorganization given that few, if any, of those from North Carolina showed up, and the fleet-footed Virginia militiamen who found their way to the rendezvous soon went home. This left only the regulars, and what was left of two brigades had to be consolidated to form a single regiment of two battalions. A third regiment was constituted a short time later when Colonel Abraham Buford arrived with the portion of his Third Virginia Continentals that had survived the Battle of the Waxhaws (29 May) plus two hundred recruits; fifty of Porterfield's light infantry also came into camp. Early in October, Gates organized a corps of light troops by taking selected men from the regiments; this formed the nucleus of General Daniel Morgan's division, which played a pivotal role in Greene's operations.

OPERATIONS AFTER CAMDEN

Cornwallis did not wait for Greene's arrival to take the field. Clinton had left Cornwallis with instructions to make the security of South Carolina his primary objective, but the ambitious earl also got authority to communicate directly with the London authorities, and the latter endorsed his more aggressive strategy to extend British control into North Carolina. On 8 September 1780, therefore, he started an offensive.

At Kings Mountain, South Carolina, 7 October, the Patriots won a victory over Major Patrick Ferguson. Clinton later called this victory "the first link of a chain of evils that followed each other in regular succession until they at last ended in the total loss of America."

In response to direction from London, where Cornwallis's strategy was favored over his own, Clinton had ordered Major General Alexander Leslie to move from New York with 2,500 troops to the Chesapeake; here he was to link up with Cornwallis as the latter pushed into Virginia, or at least to block movement of American reinforcements south. Leslie sailed from New York on 16 October with the British Guards, Eighty-second and Eighty-fourth Regiments, the Bose's German Regiment, and Loyalist units commanded by Lieutenant Colonels Edmund Fanning and John W. T. Watson. Although the Kings Mountain disaster had already occurred

(7 October), Leslie landed at Portsmouth, Virginia, as originally planned. Here he received orders from Lieutenant Colonel Francis Rawdon, who was acting commander while Cornwallis was incapacitated by fever, to bring his force to Charleston. Leslie sailed from Portsmouth on 23 November, reached Charleston on 16 December, and marched inland with 1,500 troops to arrive at Camden on 4 January 1781. The Eighty-second and Eighty-fourth stayed in Charleston, and Fanning went to Georgetown.

Cornwallis, meanwhile, had retreated from Charlotte to Winnsboro, South Carolina, which he reached in late October 1780. While the bulk of his army remained inactive he devoted his attention to suppressing the partisans. Marion's raids on the line of communications between Charleston and Camden were particularly troublesome. Marion sallied forth from his camp at Snow Island and routed a body of Loyalist militia under Lieutenant Colonel Samuel Tynes at Tearcoat Swamp, 26 October. Then he materialized out of the Black River swamps to cross the High Hills of Santee and camp astride the British supply line at Singleton's Mills. Cornwallis gave Tarleton permission to take most of his Legion off to catch Marion, but Tarleton was led a merry chase during which he never caught sight of Marion's men. A frustrated Cornwallis ordered Tarleton to turn his attention instead to Sumter, who had just defeated Major James Wemyss at Fishdam Ford, South Carolina, 9 November 1780. This victory brought swarms of Patriots to Sumter's camp and seriously alarmed Cornwallis about the safety of his rear area, particularly Ninety Six. On 20 November Tarleton finally brought Sumter to ground at Blackstock's Plantation, South Carolina, a hard-fought skirmish of which it is difficult to say who won.

GREENE TAKES THE OFFENSIVE

Greene assumed command on 3 December and almost immediately took the offensive in an extraordinarily unorthodox manner. The highlights include Morgan's brilliant victory over Tarleton at Cowpens, South Carolina, 17 January 1781; Greene's masterful retreat to the Dan River; his return to North Carolina and tactical defeat but strategic victory at Guilford Courthouse, 15 March; Cornwallis's retreat to Wilmington; Rawdon's victory over Greene at Hobkirk's Hill (Camden), South Carolina, 25 April; Greene's mopping up in the Carolinas; and the final major engagement, at Eutaw Springs, South Carolina, 8 September 1781.

Meanwhile, Virginia was the scene of devastating raids as the British shifted troops into that area from the stalemated north. Lafayette was sent there with an expeditionary force, and Cornwallis appeared from Wilmington. At first Cornwallis pursued Lafayette, hoping to crush his small army, but as the American force grew in size,

Lafayette cleverly outmaneuvered Cornwallis and began his retreat to the Chesapeake that culminated in the confrontation at Yorktown.

SEE ALSO *Beaufort, South Carolina; Blackstock's, South Carolina; Briar Creek, Georgia; Camden Campaign; Charleston Expedition of Clinton in 1776; Charleston Raid of Prevost; Cherokee War of 1776; Cowpens, South Carolina; Eutaw Springs, South Carolina; Fishdam Ford, South Carolina; Fishing Creek, North Carolina; Fort McIntosh, Georgia; Great Bridge, Virginia; Green (or Greene's) Spring, South Carolina; Guilford Courthouse, North Carolina; Gwynn Island, Virginia; Hampton, Virginia; Hanging Rock, South Carolina; Hutchinson's Island, Georgia; Kettle Creek, Georgia; Kings Mountain, South Carolina; Lenud's Ferry, South Carolina; Monck's Corner, South Carolina; Moores Creek Bridge; Ninety Six, South Carolina (19 November 1775); North Carolina, Mobilization in; Ramseur's Mill, North Carolina; Reedy River, South Carolina; Rocky Mount, South Carolina; Savannah, Georgia (29 December 1778); Savannah, Georgia (9 October 1779); Southern Campaigns of Nathanael Greene; Stono Ferry, South Carolina; Sunbury, Georgia (9 January 1779); Virginia, Military Operations in; Waxhaws, South Carolina; Wheeling, West Virginia; Williamson's Plantation, South Carolina; Yorktown Campaign.*

BIBLIOGRAPHY

Gordon, John W. *South Carolina and the American Revolution: A Battlefield History.* Columbia: University of South Carolina Press, 2003.

Hoffman, Ronald, Thad W. Tate, and Peter J. Albert, eds. *An Uncivil War: The Southern Backcountry during the American Revolution.* Charlottesville: University Press of Virginia, 1985.

Smith, Page. *A New Age Now Begins: A People's History of the American Revolution.* New York: McGraw-Hill, 1976.

Treacy, M. F. *Prelude to Yorktown: The Southern Campaign of Nathanael Greene, 1780–1781.* Chapel Hill: University of North Carolina Press, 1963.

Wilson, David K. *The Southern Strategy: Britain's Conquest of South Carolina and Georgia, 1775–1780.* Columbia: University of South Carolina Press, 2005.

revised by Michael Bellesiles

SOWER, CHRISTOPHER. (1754–1799).

Loyalist. Pennsylvania. Born on 27 January 1754 at Germantown, Pennsylvania, Sower (Sauer) was the grandson and son of prominent printers of the same name, all three of whom operated a German language press. The father, a bishop of the Dunkards, a pacifist denomination, had all his property, worth more than ten thousand pounds, confiscated by Pennsylvania for his views. The younger Christopher Sower and his brother Peter published the *Germantowner Zeitung,* which published articles disrespectful of the Patriot cause. In 1776 Pennsylvania ordered the suspension of the newspaper. When the British arrived, Sower moved to Philadelphia in September 1777 and continued his paper under the title of *Staats Courier.* On 5 December 1777 he was wounded and captured at Germantown (presumably in connection with the affair of Whitemarsh) and on 10 January 1778 was exchanged. He went to New York City when the British evacuated Philadelphia in June 1778.

In New York City he became the link between Sir Henry Clinton and the Pennsylvania Loyalists in the frontier counties of Lancaster, Northumberland, and York. During the next three years he was the principal agent for William Rankin, working as well with Major John André. When the British evacuated New York City in 1783 he went to England, where he was granted £1,289 to cover his war losses by confiscation. Two years later he went to New Brunswick as the king's printer and deputy postmaster general, publishing the *Royal Gazette.* In 1799 he returned to the United States, dying at the home of his brother Samuel in Baltimore on 3 July 1799.

SEE ALSO *Rankin, William; Whitemarsh, Pennsylvania.*

BIBLIOGRAPHY

Hocker, E. W. *The Sower Printing House of Colonial Times.* Norristown: Pennsylvania German Society, 1948.

revised by Michael Bellesiles

SPALDING, SIMON. (1742–1814). Continental officer. Connecticut–Pennsylvania. Born in Plainfield, Connecticut, on 16 January 1742, Spalding moved to the Wyoming Valley in 1772. On 26 August 1776 he became a second lieutenant of Ransom's Wyoming Valley company. Promoted to first lieutenant on 1 January 1777, he saw action at Bound Brook, New Jersey, on 13 April 1777, where he was given credit for effecting the successful retreat of the American forces. Promoted to captain on 24 June 1778, he led Connecticut troops to reinforce the Wyoming Valley but was nearly fifty miles away when the Wyoming Valley massacre took place on 3–4 July 1778. He commanded his company with distinction in Sullivan's expedition against the Iroquois in 1779. Transferred to the First Connecticut on 1 January 1781, he retired two years later. On 30 May 1783 he moved up the Wyoming Valley to settle at

Shesequin, where he eventually became brigadier general of militia. He died there on 24 January 1814.

SEE ALSO *Wyoming Valley Massacre, Pennsylvania.*

revised by Michael Bellesiles

SPANGENBERG, AUGUSTUS SEE *Moravian Settlements.*

SPANISH PARTICIPATION IN THE AMERICAN REVOLUTION.
Spain played a signal role in the American Revolution as a supply source for munitions and other material for the Americans. After 1779, Spain's military forces won significant victories against Great Britain, thereby helping to bring the war towards a conclusive defeat of the British. Spain, along with her ally France, had been a traditional and long-standing international rival of the British since the beginnings of the colonial era. These powers had fought a series of European intercolonial wars from the late 1680s until the 1760s. This heritage of warfare guaranteed that Spain would view the American Revolution as an opportunity to weaken, if not destroy, the British Empire. However, as a major colonial power herself, Spain had no sympathy for the rebel goals. The Spanish king and his ministers absolutely did not support the concept of colonials who might revolt against the authority of a sovereign. Spain therefore adopted a bifurcated policy: she would support the American cause as a mechanism to damage the British Empire; but she would not form an alliance with the infant United States until after the American Revolution. Given this policy, Spanish involvement in the American Revolution fell into two distinct eras. First, from 1775 until 1779, Spain secretly furnished badly needed supplies to the Americans in order to animate them in their revolt against British colonial authority, but in so doing refused to ally with the rebels. Second, after the summer of 1779, Spain entered the wider European war as a combatant against the British, but did not sign an alliance with the Continental Congress or coordinate her military campaigns with those of the infant United States.

LOUISIANA AND CUBA
Spanish Louisiana and Cuba served as important centers for Spain's participation in the Revolution, especially regarding the respective cities of New Orleans and Havana. Spanish officials in both ports played significant roles at every stage of Spain's involvement in the revolt.

Louisiana, along with its capital New Orleans, had only recently become a Spanish colonial possession when the French king transferred it to his Bourbon cousin at the treaty negotiations that occurred during the Peace of Paris in 1763. As part of this settlement, the Isle of Orleans which contained the province's capital, along with all lands on the west bank of the Mississippi River, became part of the new colony of British West Florida after 1763, with its capital at Pensacola. This meant that towns north of New Orleans, including Baton Rouge and Natchez, became British, along with Mobile and the other settlements along the Gulf Coast. Respective colonies in North America belonging to Spain and Great Britain thus touched as contiguous territories along the lower Mississippi for the very first time since the beginnings of European colonization in the New World. This geographical reality would have profound implications for Spanish participation in the American Revolution. A Spanish governor based at New Orleans served as the civil and military commander of the colony, serving in that regard as the subordinate of the Captain-General of Cuba. Located at Havana, the Captain-General commanded all of Spain's military forces throughout the Gulf of Mexico and the Caribbean, making him an important figure in Spain's involvement in the American Revolution.

MOUNTING COLONIAL UNREST

Both of these Spanish officials became aware of the governmental problems in British America during the late 1760s and early 1770s as controversy brewed between the English colonists on the Atlantic coast and the home government in London. The governor of Louisiana, Luis de Unzaga y Amezaga, routinely heard reports about events in America from his neighbors in West Florida. He dutifully passed this news on to his superiors in Cuba and Spain, where the highest level of policy makers in the king's inner circle of advisors considered this information. In addition, the Captain-General of Cuba regularly heard reports about the growing crisis in the British colonies from the maritime traffic in the region.

By 1770, these two officials had decided to create a secret intelligence network in the lower Mississippi valley, along the Gulf Coast, and in the Caribbean for the purpose of gathering news and information about the expanding crisis in the British colonies. They did so with the full approval of the Spanish court, where the king and his ministers were primarily concerned about the military defense of Spain's colonies in the face of an open colonial war in British North America. As part of this espionage network, the Captain-General routinely dispatched Cuban fishing boats to the South Atlantic coast in order to scout the sea-lanes and talk to the masters of ships sailing to and from ports in the British colonies. He also recruited two Spanish subjects who were living in British West Florida to provide regular intelligence about English naval and troop movements in the region. One of them, Father Pedro Camps, was a Roman Catholic Priest living at New Smyrna. While the other, Luciano Herrera, resided at St. Augustine.

Herrera, a Spanish merchant who continued to reside in East Florida after the British took it over, had many contacts among English officials and residents in the city. Both of these men proved to be fruitful sources for Spain about events in North American all during the course of the Revolution. While the Captain-General was occupied with the sea lanes around East Florida, the governor of Louisiana continued to monitor events in West Florida while he routinely interviewed English ship captains passing New Orleans on the Mississippi about occurrences in the British colonies of the Atlantic coast. He also permitted Louisiana merchant vessels to call at Pensacola and Mobile under the guise of conducting illegal trade, with their true purpose to gather information of events in the British colonies. In 1772, Governor Unzaga dispatched a confidential agent from Louisiana to New York and Philadelphia for the secret purpose of learning about recent events there. This person, Juan Surriret, was a prosperous merchant who had many commercial ties to mercantile houses in major ports of the Atlantic coast. Surriret employed these contacts as sources of information while he visited with them under the ruse of conducting private commerce. Returning en route to New Orleans from the east coast, he stopped at Pensacola, observing much British naval activity that proved useful to the Spanish. Surriret's mission was a great success.

By the time of Lexington and Concord (April 1775), Spanish officials in North America and in Spain had become reasonably well-informed about the unrest in the British colonies. Governor Unzaga at New Orleans heard early reports of the outbreak of fighting in Massachusetts within weeks of the events while the Captain-General quickly confirmed these reports as both men continued to gather news about the revolt during the ensuing months and years. By mid-1775, all of the information from the rebellious colonies had permitted the Spanish king and his ministers to craft a well-reasoned, official foreign policy and international response to the American Revolution. The Spanish would remain neutral in the ensuing conflict, and openly refused to engage in any action that might cause the British to turn their wrath against Spain or her new world colonies. The king and his ministers did not believe that their military had been adequately prepared for war. They feared that the rebellious British colonies might well lose their revolt, thus freeing a mobilized English army and navy to attack Spain or her possessions, especially if Spain politically supported the rebel colonists. Neutrality would give Spain the opportunity to prepare her military for eventual participation, should the opportunity for open conflict with Great Britain later present itself. At the same time, however, Spanish officials, including King Charles III, secretly wished for a rebel American victory, since such an occurrence would seriously damage the rival British Empire. For that reason, the Spanish decided to assist the rebels with all possible secrecy and confidentiality. The Spanish king's resolve to follow this risky policy increased when he learned that France had also decided on a similar response to events in British North America.

OPPORTUNITIES TO ASSIST

An unexpected opportunity for Spain to assist the American rebels came in the summer of 1776, when Captain George Gibson arrived at New Orleans in command of a company of soldiers from Virginia. They had floated down the Ohio and Mississippi Rivers under the pretense of being merchants engaged in frontier trade. They carried a confidential letter from General Charles Lee, who served as George Washington's second-in-command. Lee, who pointed out that, since Spain was Britain's long-standing international enemy, the Spanish might furnish a stream of badly needed supplies, including weapons, munitions, medicines, and other items. These could be shipped to New Orleans where they would be transferred to boats that would be poled up the inland rivers to Fort Pitt. Governor Unzaga, who had no instructions from Spain on these matters, quickly reported this request while he temporized with Captain Gibson, permitting the American officer to purchase gunpowder and other materials already on hand in the Louisiana capital.

While making his purchases, Captain Gibson made contact with Oliver Pollock, a Scot-Irish merchant who lived in New Orleans. A native of Ulster, Pollock had migrated first to Pennsylvania and then, in 1762, to Havana, where he found great prosperity as a merchant. He moved to New Orleans in the late 1760s, took Spanish citizenship, and had become one of the wealthiest merchants in Louisiana by the time of the American Revolution. Pollock quickly embraced the rebel cause, for which he manifested a great fervor and enthusiastic support. Pollock eagerly sold Captain Gibson the desired supplies and arranged for them to be shipped to Fort Pitt. Pollock also wrote a letter to the Continental Congress, which accompanied the shipment of supplies, in which he pledged his support for the Revolution and offered his services as the American supply agent at New Orleans. The Secret Committee of Correspondence of the Congress accepted Pollock's offer and, in the following year, appointed him as its official supply agent at New Orleans. For the next several years, Pollock shipped dozens of boatloads of material up the rivers to Fort Pitt while he liberally paid for much of this merchandise with personal drafts on his own accounts, pending eventual reimbursement from the Congress.

In the meantime, Unzaga's sending of Gibson's letter to his superiors in Madrid set in motion a larger, centrally directed effort by which Spain began to supply the Americans surreptitiously. A meeting of the king and the Spanish council of ministers resolved to create a regularized supply network in order to assist the rebel Americans. They dispatched a Cuban, Miguel Antonio Eduardo, to New Orleans with additional military supplies that soon found their way into American hands. The Spanish court also enlisted the services of a Spanish merchant from Bilbao, Diego de Gardoqui, who spoke fluent English and who had extensive mercantile experience in trading with the British Atlantic ports.

At the suggestion of the Spanish chief minister, Gardoqui formed a dummy merchant house under the guise of seeking quick profits from private trade with the rebels. In reality, all of the military supplies that his firm shipped to the rebellious Americans through Havana and other ports in the Caribbean were secretly supplied from the Spanish government as unofficial aid to the American cause. An additional chance to assist the Continental Congress occurred when an American envoy, Arthur Lee, appeared in Spain. The Marquis de Grimaldi, the Spanish minister of state, met secretly with Lee and publicly rebuffed his requests for aid, in keeping with Spain's official policy of neutrality. In secret, however, Grimaldi arranged for an under-the-table loan in the amount of one million dollars, which the Americans used to purchase additional supplies from other European sources.

Spanish espionage efforts also continued as supplies began to flow from Spain. Both the governor of Louisiana and the Captain-General of Cuba sent additional agents to various locations on the Atlantic coast to gather information about the revolt. Juan de Miralles, a Cuban merchant from Havana, proved to be the most important of these confidential agents. At the specific request of the Spanish court at Madrid, the Captain-General dispatched Miralles to Philadelphia to report on events at the Continental Congress. He left Havana in late 1777, landed at Charleston, and visited along the route with various American leaders as he traveled to the meeting place of the Congress. Miralles claimed to be a private merchant interested in fostering trade relations with the infant United States. His distinguished demeanor, official bearing, and extensive correspondence with individuals in Spain and Cuba, however, made his true status obvious to Congress and its members.

As the months progressed, the Americans increasingly treated Miralles as if he were Spain's unofficial envoy in the United States capital, which increasingly became an accurate description of Miralles's true role in Philadelphia. By 1778, the Spaniard enjoyed in a *de facto* manner all the rights and privileges normally accorded to an authorized diplomatic envoy. Miralles obliged by speaking for Spain at the Continental Congress, while he continued to fulfill his initial mission by sending a steady stream of news and information to his superiors.

THE REVOLUTION MOVES SOUTH

While Miralles established himself at the Congress, the American Revolution came to the lower Mississippi valley when a rebel expedition floated down the river to attack British West-Florida. Early in 1778, Pennsylvania Captain James Willing led a company of armed men on an attack against British settlements along the river. He took the town of Natchez, captured British ships that were plying the Mississippi, and sacked plantations belonging to West Floridian residents.

Willing arrived at New Orleans in the mid-spring of 1778, anxious to sell his plunder in order to raise money for the United States. Oliver Pollock, as the congressional agent in the city, eagerly assisted in the sales and, importantly, convinced the governor to offer Willing and his men protection. Louisiana had a new governor, Bernardo de Gálvez, who was very much a partisan of American independence. The son of a powerful Spanish family, Governor Gálvez saw the revolt as a way to defeat the British and end the centuries-old rivalry with them. He therefore welcomed the American expedition to New Orleans and rebuffed British complaints about the courtesies he extended to Willing and his men. Gálvez's support ensured that Oliver Pollock would be able to increase the amount of supplies being shipped from New Orleans, and that city became an important supply depot for the American cause.

CHALLENGING SPAIN'S NEUTRALITY POLICY

The Franco-American Alliance of February, 1778 (which partially resulted from the victory at Saratoga), radically changed the nature of Spanish participation in the Revolution. France, a European power traditionally allied with Spain, joined the conflict as an official ally of the United States and as a belligerent to Great Britain. This development forced Spain to continue its policy of neutrality alone. High-ranking ministers at the Spanish court therefore debated during the spring of 1778 about joining France and declaring war on Great Britain. After lengthy discussion, the Spanish king and his ministers decided to continue their neutral policies. They reasoned that the Spanish army and navy was not yet ready to achieve the specific war goals they wished to gain in a conflict with Great Britain. Specifically, Spain wanted to regain possession of Gibraltar, drive the British from both East and West Florida, sweep the English settlements from the Logwood coasts of Central America and end definitively the special trading concessions for British merchants in

some Spanish colonies which had been a provision of the Peace of Paris, 1763.

Spain would thus only enter the conflict when her ministers and king believed the military was strong enough to achieve these objectives. Even then, Spain might not risk a formal diplomatic alliance with the United States, as France had done when it entered the conflict. Important figures at the Spanish court, including the powerful Conde de Floridablanca who served as chief minister of the state, worried that the westward expanding young United States would replace Great Britain as a territorial rival for Spain in North America. Floridablanca, as Spain's highest ranking royal advisor, resolved that even if his nation entered the conflict as a belligerent, it would not sign a treaty of amity or commerce with the United States.

The successful campaigns of George Roger Clark in the Illinois country of the Mississippi valley confirmed these fears for Spain. Floating down the Ohio during the summer of 1778, Clark and his men won a series of victories at Kaskaskia, Cahokia, and Vincennes that swept the British from the region by early 1779. These conquests would not have been possible without the aid and support provided to Clark by Oliver Pollock at New Orleans. He liberally supplied anything the American general requested to hold the Illinois country, to the point of making possible the first settlement by the United States on the Mississippi River. This was at Fort Jefferson, established in 1780 near the confluence point of the great river with the Ohio on the northern edge of Spanish Louisiana. Spain's reaction to George Rogers Clark's conquest of western territory became apparent at Philadelphia in late 1779, when Juan de Miralles began to argue informally that, should the United States win the war, Spain might not grant it free navigation rights on the Mississippi as had been the case for Great Britain.

Nonetheless, Clark's victories in the Mississippi valley served as a motivating factor that pushed Spain towards declaring war on Great Britain. In the late spring of 1779, the Spanish colonial minister warned Louisiana governor Gálvez to prepare for an imminent declaration of war, which came officially on 21 June. True to established policy, Spain declared war against Great Britain, but did not recognize the United States as an ally. Nonetheless, both nations agreed to exchange informal envoys who would serve as the recognized spokespersons of their respective governments. Juan de Miralles became the recognized "Spanish observer" at the Continental Congress, while that body dispatched a New Yorker, John Jay, to Spain as its envoy. Jay had instructions to negotiate an alliance with Spain, but no such treaty came to pass during the two years of his residence at Madrid because the Spanish court refused to consider it.

Spain's entrance into the war began a series of military victories between 1779 and 1781 that fulfilled many of its war goals, especially along the Gulf coast and the lower Mississippi valley. Bernardo de Gálvez had astutely prepared the Spanish military forces in Louisiana for successful attacks on West Florida. During the fall of 1779, Governor Gálvez and his forces captured the British post at Baton Rouge. Natchez surrendered soon thereafter. The following spring Mobile fell to the Spanish. Then, in the spring of 1781, Gálvez led a combined army and navy attack against Pensacola, the British colonial capital. Spain also enjoyed successes further to the north when, in 1780, the Commander turned back a British attack on St. Louis. Spain's efforts to block additional British attacks on the Mississippi valley met with further good fortune when a Spanish force captured Fort St. Joseph in present-day Michigan, thereby thwarting additional English incursions into the region from Detroit.

Spain also met with limited success in dislodging the British from their establishments in Central America. In 1779, an army commanded by Matias de Gálvez, the father of the Louisiana governor, captured the British posts at Belize and Rotan. He also withstood an English counter-attack against Spanish positions in modern Nicaragua. In the Caribbean, a 1782 Spanish naval expedition commanded by Juan María de Cagigal forced the British surrender of New Providence Island.

In spite of these victories, however, Spain failed to achieve her major goal of reacquiring Gibraltar. In cooperation with French forces, Spain laid siege to the British fortress at Gibraltar in June of 1779, as soon as war had been declared. More than five thousand British forces, led by General George Elliot, held the great rock's impenetrable defenses with steadfast resolution. The British could easily secure needed foodstuffs and supplies from Moroccan smugglers from across the Straits, which ensured that the siege of Gibralter would be the longest running military engagement of the American Revolution.

AFTER THE WAR

The siege lasted until 1783, and Spain proved incapable of dislodging the British from their Mediterranean stronghold. By 1782, the Spanish king and his ministers were growing weary anyway of continuing major military operations against the British. The surrender at Yorktown had effectively settled the outcome of the Revolution in favor of the Americans. Thereafter, Floridablanca and his fellow Spanish ministers mostly fretted about the potential of the United States to become a new rival on the borders of Spanish America. For that reason, Spain began to plan her diplomacy to gain as much as possible from the forthcoming peace negotiations that would end the worldwide conflict in 1783.

The fact that each participating nation signed a separate, bilateral treaty at the Peace of Paris of that year was a diplomatic development that worked to Spain's advantage. Her diplomats at Paris were able to obscure the boundaries between Spanish Florida and the territories to the north that were claimed by the United States. The border asserted by Spain in its treaty with the United States placed the boundary line at one place while Spain's accord with Great Britain, the previous maser of the whole territory, drew it at another latitude. This gave Spain the opportunity after the war to maintain a large hegemony in the lower Mississippi valley and Gulf Coast regions than would have been the case had the treaties been more straightforward.

Hence, during the years following the American Revolution, Spain maintained cordial, yet less that cooperative, relations with the United States. In the year after the Peace of Paris, 1783, Spanish officials closed the free navigation of the Mississippi River to United States citizens. The arrival of Diego de Gardoqui, in his capacity as Spain's first accredited Charge d'Affairs at Philadelphia in 1785, did not result in a formal treaty between Spain and the United States over western boundary issues and American navigation rights on the Mississippi. An accord on these matters did not come until the Treaty of San Lorenzo in 1795. This agreement finally did settle the boundary question, permitted United States citizens free navigation of the great river, and granted them the "right of deposit" at New Orleans coming down the river for transshipment to international markets.

Nonetheless, the secret support that Spain gave to the United States during the American Revolution proved to be a decisive factor in sustaining the rebel cause. Once the Spanish entered the conflict in 1779, their campaigns also assisted the United States, even though the two nations never coordinated their military actions. The pressure of Spain's attacks against the British in the Mississippi valley, the Gulf coast and the Caribbean, along with the siege of Gibraltar. diverted British military resources that otherwise would have been directed against the rebel Americans and the fighting that took place in North America.

S E E A L S O *Pensacola, Florida; Pollock, Oliver.*

BIBLIOGRAPHY

Beerman, Eric. *España y la independencia de los Estados Unidos.* Madrid: Editorial MAPFRE, 1992.

Boeta, José Rudolfo. *Bernardo de Gálvez.* Madrid: Publicaciones Españoles, 1977.

Caughey, John Walton. *Bernardo de Gálvez in Louisiana 1776–1783.* Berkeley: University of California Press, 1934.

Chavez, Thomas E. *Spain and the Independence of the United States: An Intrinsic Gift.* Albuquerque: University of New Mexico Press, 2002.

Cummins, Light T. *Spanish Observers and the American Revolution.* Baton Rouge: Louisiana State University Press, 1991.

James, James Alton. *Oliver Pollock: The Life and Times of an Unknown Patriot.* New York: Appleton-Century, 1937.

Morales Padron, Francisco, ed. *Participación de España en la independencia política de los Estado Unidos.* Madrid: Publicaciones Espanolas, 1952.

Reparaz, Carmen de. *Yo Solo: Bernardo de Gálvez y la toma de Panzacola en 1781.* Barcelona: Ediciones de Serbal, 1986.

Ruigómez de Hernández, María Pilar. *El gobierne español del despotismo ilustrado ante la independencia de los Estados Unidos de América: una nueva estructura de la política internacional (1773–1783).* Madrid: Ministerio de Asunto Exteriores, 1978.

Starr, J. Barton. *Tories, Dons, and Rebels: The American Revolution in British West Florida.* Gainesville: University Press of Florida, 1976.

Yela Utrilla, Juan Francisco. *España ante la independencia de los Estados Unidos.* Lérida, Spain: Gráficos Academia Mariana, 1925

Light Townsend Cummins

SPANISH SUCCESSION, WAR OF THE.

1701–1714. After Carlos II, the last Habsburg king of Spain, died without issue in 1700, Louis XIV of France accepted the Spanish throne on behalf of his Bourbon nephew. A coalition of Protestant powers led by England's William III had already fought one war to curb Louis's ambitions, and now William's successor, his sister-in-law, Queen Anne, led another coalition with the same objective. The fighting in North America that pitted British colonists against the French in New France and the Spanish in Florida was called Queen Anne's War (1702–1713), and is covered under Colonial Wars.

SEE ALSO *Colonial Wars; League of Augsburg, War of the; Queen Anne's War.*

revised by Harold E. Selesky

SPECIE.

The term "specie" is used to denote metal coin, or "hard money," as opposed to paper money.

SEE ALSO *Continental Currency; Money of the Eighteenth Century.*

revised by Harold E. Selesky

SPENCER, JOSEPH.

(1714–1789). Continental general. Connecticut. Born in East Haddam,

Connecticut, Joseph Spencer was a prominent farmer, merchant, and attorney in the lower Connecticut valley. He was first elected as a deputy to the General Assembly in 1750, and served until he was elected to the governor's council as an opponent of the Stamp Act in May 1766. Major of the Twelfth Militia Regiment in October 1757, he served as a major (1758) and lieutenant colonel (1759 and 1760) in Connecticut's provincial regiments during the colony's years of maximum effort during the final French and Indian War. Appointed lieutenant colonel (1764) and then colonel (1766) of the Twelfth Militia, Spencer led a militia company from East Haddam to Boston after the Lexington alarm, and stayed for two weeks. The Assembly appointed the sixty-year-old politician and veteran as first brigadier general of Connecticut troops in April 1775, and he recruited and led the Second Regiment (of which he was simultaneously colonel) to Boston to join the New England army besieging the town.

On 20 June 1775 Congress ignored his Connecticut seniority by making him as a brigadier general while appointing Israel Putnam, his Connecticut subordinate, a major general. Incensed at this affront, Spencer went home. His conduct provoked a storm of criticism. Silas Deane, one of Connecticut's delegates to the Continental Congress at Philadelphia, wrote on 20 July that "the voice here is that he acted a part inconsistent with the character either of a soldier, a patriot, or even of a common gentleman to desert his post in an hour of danger, to sacrifice his country, which he certainly did as far as was in his power, and to turn his back sullenly on his general [Washington]." Connecticut's senior leaders, not wanting to lose the services of an important political figure or further divide a cause whose only hope of success lay in unity, had already acted. On the morning of 13 July, Governor Jonathan Trumbull and his council sent two of their number (Samuel Huntington and William Williams) to talk to Spencer at Gray's Tavern and persuade him to reconsider. That afternoon, they all met with Spencer "on the subject matter of his being superceded by the General Congress, ... which he thinks very hard of and resents," and persuaded him "to return to the army and not at present quit the service.". Spencer served through the rest of the siege, and then went south with the army to New York City. On 9 August 1776 he was promoted to major general.

At a council of war on 8 September, Spencer voted with George Clinton and William Heath not to evacuate the army from New York City, at the southern tip of Manhattan Island. Events proved that the trio was too sanguine about the possibility of holding the city. When the British subsequently landed at Kips Bay, on the east side of the island several miles north of the city, the American troops remaining in New York were lucky to escape. But Alexander McDougall was too harsh, when, years later, he labeled the trio as "a fool, a knave and an honest, obstinate man." In December 1776 Spencer was ordered to New England and established his headquarters at Providence, Rhode Island, where he worked to contain the British who had just taken Newport. In September 1777 he organized an amphibious attack from Tiverton against the island of Rhode Island, but canceled the operation after the troops had loaded into boats, when he learned that the plan had been compromised. Indignant about a proposed inquiry by Congress into the cause of this failure, Spencer requested a court of inquiry and was exonerated. He resigned his commission on 13 January 1778 and returned to Connecticut. He immediately became, again, a prominent figure in state government. He was named to the Council of Safety, elected to the Assembly (May 1778), re-elected to the governor's council (May 1779), and elected by the Assembly to Congress, where he served from June through September 1779. Historian Douglas Freeman's comment that neither William Heath nor Spencer "had done anything more than discharge routine duties without displaying such scandalous incompetence or sloth as to make their removal a public necessity" (*Washington*, IV, p. 367) overlooks the extent to which the war was directed from the American side by local politicians whose appreciation of military realities was limited.

SEE ALSO *New York.*

BIBLIOGRAPHY
Freeman, Douglas Southall. *George Washington.* Vol. IV. Scribner, New York: 1948–1957
Lossing, Benson J. *The Pictorial Field Book of the Revolution.* Vol. II. New York: Harper and Brothers, 1860

revised by Harold E. Selesky

SPENCER'S REGIMENT.

Spencer's Regiment, commanded by Colonel Oliver Spencer, was one of the sixteen "additional Continental regiments."

SEE ALSO *Additional Continental Regiments.*

Mark M. Boatner

SPENCER'S TAVERN, VIRGINIA.

26 June 1781. (VIRGINIA MILITARY OPERATIONS.) When reinforcements joined Lafayette, Cornwallis retreated slowly through Richmond, arriving at Williamsburg on 25 June, where he would remain until 4 July. Lafayette

followed at a respectable distance, remaining wary of a trap, and on 26 June was at Tyree's Plantation, some 20 miles from Williamsburg. Meanwhile, Simcoe had separated from the main British column on 23 June with his Queen's Rangers, one light three-pounder, and some Hessian jägers to destroy rebel stores on the Chickahominy River. Lafayette countered by detaching Colonel Richard Butler with his Pennsylvania Regiment, Majors Call and Willis with a body of Virginia riflemen, and Major William McPherson with 120 mounted troops to intercept Simcoe on his return. After an all-night march, they surprised Simcoe seven miles northwest of Williamsburg at Spencer's Tavern (or Ordinary). At sunrise McPherson had mounted 50 light infantrymen double with 50 of his dragoons to speed up the pursuit, and this detachment closed in for a brief hand-to-hand action while the main bodies came forward. Simcoe's Rangers drove McPherson back, but Call and Willis came up and were hotly engaged with Simcoe's infantry when his dragoons hit their flank and pushed them back on Butler's Pennsylvania Continentals. Simcoe briefly had the advantage in the confused fighting that followed, but fearing that Lafayette's entire army might be at hand, he took the first opportunity to break off the action and fall back to Williamsburg. Since Cornwallis was moving forward with a strong reinforcement, Butler was equally anxious to see this skirmish end.

The Americans lost nine men killed, 14 wounded, and 13 missing. Cornwallis reported 33 casualties; this figure is accepted by historians, although Lafayette thought the enemy lost 60 men killed and 100 wounded. A more reasonable calculation put Simcoe's losses at 11 dead and 26 wounded). Simcoe describes the action in detail and claims it was a sizable engagement won by his generalship (Simcoe, *Operations of Queen's Rangers*, 236; Johnston, Yorktown, 56 n.), yet he left the field and his wounded in the hands of the enemy. In point of fact it tended to bolster American morale and provided Cornwallis with a reason to decline Clinton's request to transfer men back to New York.

revised by Robert K. Wright Jr.

SPLIT ROCK (LAKE CHAMPLAIN), NEW YORK.

13 October 1776. Brigadier General Benedict Arnold's battered squadron, fleeing south after the battle of Valcour Island, was overtaken just south of Split Rock. The galley *Washington* was captured; the galley *Congress* and three gondolas (*Boston, New Haven, Connecticut,* and *Spitfire*) beached at Ferris Bay (now Arnold's Bay, Vermont) and were set on fire to prevent

capture. A different Split Rock figured in the action at Pell's Point (now in Pelham Bay Park, the Bronx).

SEE ALSO *Valcour Island.*

BIBLIOGRAPHY

Lunderberg, Philip K. *The Continental Gunboat* Philadelphia *and the Northern Campaign of 1776*. Washington, D.C.: Smithsonian Institution, 1966.

revised by Robert K. Wright Jr.

SPONTOON. The espontoon, spontoon, or half pike was a badge of officer's rank that evolved from the halberd, and until a few years before the American Revolution it was carried by all foot officers of all armies. It was replaced by the fusil, the change taking place in France in 1754 and in England in 1786. British troops in America started abandoning spontoons much earlier, however. Braddock ordered them left behind in 1755 when he departed Alexandria, Virginia, for his defeat in the wilderness, and almost all British regiments abandoned them for active field service during the American Revolution.

SEE ALSO *Fusils and Fusiliers.*

BIBLIOGRAPHY

Peterson, Harold L. *Arms and Armor in Colonial America, 1526–1783*. Harrisburg, Pa.: Stackpole, 1956.

Mark M. Boatner

SPRINGFIELD, NEW JERSEY, RAID OF KNYPHAUSEN. 7–23 June 1780. Prior to the return of Clinton from his Charleston expedition, General William Knyphausen (who was temporarily in command in New York) received reports that Washington's army was mutinous and might be won over. Being led to believe also that the civil population might rally to support him, Knyphausen organized a force of five thousand for a large-scale raid, landed it at De Hart's Point, near Elizabethtown, and on 7 June marched toward Morristown. Washington received this disturbing information the evening of the 7th, but when he reached Short Hills the next day he learned that Colonel Elias Dayton's regiment of Maxwell's brigade, promptly reinforced by neighborhood militia, had so successfully blocked the enemy advance that it had gotten only as far as Springfield Bridge and had then pulled back and started

entrenching. Knyphausen's position on the afternoon of 7 June was on high ground northwest of Connecticut Farms (later Union, New Jersey), a settlement about two and a half miles southeast of Springfield.

British intelligence had obviously erred badly: the natives not only were hostile but efficient. General Thomas Stirling, who commanded Knyphausen's vanguard, was wounded. At Connecticut Farms, the rebels held off the Hessian vanguard with fixed bayonets. The invaders burned about thirty buildings in Connecticut Farms and, to the mystification of Washington, withdrew during the night of 8–9 June to De Hart's Point and dug in. It was a peculiar situation: Knyphausen had withdrawn simply because his original mission, based on faulty intelligence, obviously could not be accomplished. Washington, on the other hand, had no way of knowing that the explanation for the enemy's peculiar conduct was this simple—he suspected they were up to something logical, such as feinting in New Jersey before making a main effort up the Hudson. "Our situation," said Washington on the 14th, "is as embarrassing as you can imagine," and then he had to add: "When they unite their force, it will be infinitely more so." He recalled Henry Lee's Light Horse (which had received orders on 30 March to prepare to move to South Carolina), sent for other mounted troops to perform the reconnaissance missions that were now so important, and organized a force of five hundred men under Brigadier General Edward Hand to harass the enemy position at De Hart's Point.

When Washington learned on 20 June that six British warships had sailed up the Hudson to Verplancks Point and, "with as little apparent reason for going as for coming, had dropped down the river again," (Freeman, vol. 5, p. 172) he had to redeploy his forces so as to meet an attack against West Point and also to watch for a main effort in New Jersey. So he moved his main body to Pompton, where it would be closer to West Point yet still within sixteen miles of Springfield, and he left Nathanael Greene at the latter place with about one thousand Continental troops to watch Knyphausen. General Maxwell's Continentals and General Philemon Dickinson's militia were still in the field to support Greene.

Clinton had reached Sandy Hook on 17 June. Learning then of Knyphausen's operation and its lack of success, he also received information from Benedict Arnold (dated 12 June) that the French expeditionary force of comte de Rochambeau would soon reach Newport, Rhode Island. The British commander realized that by committing troops to support Knyphausen's stalled offensive against Washington, he would leave New York City open to a possible French attack. The mysterious British movement up the Hudson (see above) had been prompted by Clinton's fear that Washington might try to cross the river and join forces with the French, a movement Washington actually did not make until 31 July. (The French did not actually reach Newport until 12 July, and Clinton did not get word of their arrival until the 18th.)

A SECOND ATTACK

Meanwhile, Clinton prepared to advance into Westchester County, and Knyphausen built a pontoon bridge between Elizabethtown and Staten Island for a rapid junction with the main army after the British learned of Washington's movement toward West Point. Clinton and Knyphausen therefore organized a feint against Springfield and a stronger effort against Morristown on 23 June. Although one reason might have been to save face, Knyphausen's new thrust was ordered by Clinton to retard Washington's suspected movement of his entire army up the Hudson and to gain time for the troops just returning from Charleston to be transported up the Hudson to block Washington.

At 6 A.M. on 23 June, Washington heard the sound of cannon on Greene's front, and in midmorning he received an alarming report from Greene: "The enemy are out on their march towards this place [Springfield] in full force, having received a considerable reenforcement last night" (Freeman, 5, p. 173). According to the Hessian officer Carl Leopold Baurmeister, Knyphausen's original expedition had consisted of the British Guards; the Twenty-second, Thirty-seventh, Thirty-eighth, Forty-third, and Fifty-seventh Regiments; two battalions of Cortland Skinner's West Jersey Volunteers; two Anspach regiments; the entire Anspach and Hessian Jäger Corps; the Seventeenth Light Dragoons; von Diemar's Hussars; the mounted Queen's Rangers (Simcoe's); the Leib Regiment; and the Landgraf, Donop, Bünau, and Bose Regiments. Brigades were commanded by Generals von Lossberg, von Hachenberg, Mathew, Skinner, and Thomas Stirling. James Robertson, commandant of New York, and Governor Tryon accompanied Knyphausen as volunteers. The reinforcements mentioned by Greene were the Forty-second Regiment and the rest of Simcoe's Rangers. The Leib regiment and Jäger Corps returned to Staten Island to resupply their ammunition after the action of 7 June and, presumably, returned to New Jersey

The enemy's second advance on Springfield was, like the first, contested by Maxwell's brigade. Greene positioned his regulars and Dickinson's militia to cover the bridge at Springfield, and Lee's dragoons operated with Maxwell's delaying force. On approaching Springfield, Knyphausen sent half his force to envelop Greene's left by way of the Vauxhall Bridge and to get to his rear at Chatham. Lee's dragoons and Dayton's Third New Jersey delayed the enveloping column under General Edward Mathew at Vauxhall Bridge and then dropped back to hold another position on the Vauxhall Road to protect

Greene's left. Knyphausen's frontal attack was held up for forty minutes by Colonel Israel Angell's Rhode Island Regiment, which then dropped back to a new position with Colonel William Shreve's New Jersey militia. Greene reinforced Lee with two regiments of regulars (Colonel Henry Jackson's Massachusetts and Colonel S. B. Webb's Connecticut) to block Mathew, and he concentrated the rest of his command on high ground behind Springfield. Knyphausen was reluctant to attack Greene and broke off the action. After burning all but four of the fifty houses in Springfield, he withdrew during the afternoon and crossed his bridge to Staten Island. Washington had had no alternative but to start back from Pompton to support Greene and to order supplies evacuated from Morristown, but he covered only five or six miles on 23 June and that night received the good news that Greene would not need his help after all.

New Jersey had once more been cleared of British troops. Jerseyites, far from being swayed back toward King George, were aroused by the destruction of Connecticut Farms and Springfield. They were particularly outraged by the Patriot propaganda which claimed that the Reverend James Caldwell's wife, killed at Connecticut Farms on 7 June, had been shot by an enemy soldier as she sat by a window with her children.

NUMBERS AND LOSSES

Patriot losses on 7 June were about fifteen killed and forty wounded, according to Colonel Sylvanus Seeley of the New Jersey militia. Major Baurmeister estimated that the eight hundred men under General Maxwell in Elizabethtown had been reinforced by militia and regulars to a total of twenty-five hundred by the time they withdrew to Springfield Bridge. Army surgeon Dr. James Thacher said the rebels took twenty prisoners in this first action, but enemy killed and wounded are not reported by either side.

According to Douglas S. Freeman, on 23 June the rebels lost fifteen killed, forty-nine wounded, and nine missing. This may, however, be the total casualties for the period 7–23 June, since it bears a strange similarity to the figures already quoted for the 7th, and in *The War of the Revolution* (vol. 2, 1952), Christopher Ward says American losses for the entire period were thirteen killed, sixty-one wounded, and nine missing. Seeley, however, is specific in saying that fifteen were killed and forty wounded on 7 June. Knyphausen's losses on the 23rd are not known; Thacher said American troops found fifteen bodies and several fresh graves, and that the inhabitants reported seeing eight or ten wagon loads of dead and wounded. Enemy strength on the 23rd was between five and six thousand. Greene had about one thousand at Springfield, and Maxwell may have had almost that many troops, including militia harassing the enemy's advance.

SEE ALSO *Maxwell, William.*

BIBLIOGRAPHY

Fleming, Thomas. *The Battle of Springfield.* Trenton: New Jersey Historical Commission, 1976.

———. *The Forgotten Victory: The Battle for New Jersey, 1780.* New York: Reader's Digest Press, 1973.

Freeman, Douglas Southall. *George Washington.* Vol. 5. New York: Scribner, 1952.

Lundin, Leonard. *Cockpit of the Revolution: The War for Independence in New Jersey.* Princeton, N.J.: Princeton University Press, 1940.

Ward, Christopher. *The War of the Revolution.* Vol. 2. New York: Macmillan, 1952.

Ward, Harry M. *General William Maxwell and the New Jersey Continentals.* Westport, Conn.: Greenwood Press, 1997.

revised by Harry M. Ward

SPRINGFIELD, NEW YORK.

May 1778. In the spring of 1778, after the repulse of St. Leger's expedition, Joseph Brant returned with his Indian troops and a large number of Loyalists to Oquaga. After sending out parties to attack isolated farms, he carried out his first large-scale raid in the Mohawk Valley in May. His objective was Springfield, at the head of Lake Otsego, a little less than ten miles west northwest of Cherry Valley and somewhat more than that distance south of Fort Herkimer. Brant took the town without loss of life and burned all the houses but one, moving all the women and children into that house for safety. Several men and a considerable amount of property were evacuated to Oquaga, while eighty refugees from the town made their way to Schenectady.

SEE ALSO *Oquaga; St. Leger's Expedition.*

revised by Michael Bellesiles

SPRUCE BEER.

Part of the American ration, it was made by boiling an extract from leaves and branches of the spruce fir with sugar or molasses and fermenting with yeast.

Mark M. Boatner

SPUYTEN DUYVIL, NEW YORK.

Probably a corruption of the Dutch for "in spite of the Devil," this creek marks the northern boundary of Manhattan Island. The Post Road crossed it at the Kings Bridge, which made the latter of great strategic importance: Along with the Freebridge, it was the island's only link to the mainland. As Douglas Southall Freeman has noted, "there is always a question where Spuyten Duyvil ends and Harlem Creek, now the Harlem River, begins" (vol. III, p. 470 n.), because the two constituted in 1776, as they do today, a continuous waterway between the Hudson and East Rivers. The British used this route in moving troops from the Hudson into the Harlem River to attack Fort Washington, 16 November 1776.

The sinuous creek was straightened and parts of it filled in during the completion of the Harlem River Ship Canal in 1923. The Marble Hill neighborhood was cut off from Manhattan. The site of the Kings Bridge is now on dry land, lying north of the canal near West 231st Street and Marble Hill Avenue.

SEE ALSO *Harlem Heights, New York.*

BIBLIOGRAPHY

Freeman, Douglas Southall. *George Washington.* 7 vols. New York: Scribner, 1948–1957.

revised by Barnet Schecter

SQUAW CAMPAIGN.

February 1778. "Squaw campaign" was the derisive name given to Edward Hand's unsuccessful expedition from Fort Pitt (later Pittsburgh, Pennsylvania) against British-held Detroit.

SEE ALSO *Hand, Edward.*

revised by Harold S. Selesky

STAFF OFFICERS.

Over the course of the war, the American concept of the military staff was influenced by three traditions of how the administration and management of armies ought to be organized and ought to function. Not surprisingly, at the start of the war the Congress and General Washington adopted the British model, the fundamentals of which had been laid down by the duke of Marlborough during the War of the Spanish Succession (1702–1713) and with which the colonists had become familiar during the French and Indian War (1754–1763). In each army, British and American, the principal staff officers involved in preparing the army for operations were the adjutant general, the quartermaster general, and the commissary general. The adjutant general recorded and transmitted orders from the commander in chief to the army, maintained the records of musters that told the commander how many soldiers were ready to fight, and handled all the paperwork on personnel matters. The quartermaster general organized the acquisition and transportation to camp of all the material goods the army needed to fight effectively, established and managed the camps that sheltered the soldiers, and oversaw just about everything else connected with operations. The commissary general was responsible for all matters involving food and forage.

THE CONTINENTAL STAFF

Congress began the long process of evolving the staff of the Continental Army on 16 June 1775, when it created five senior staff positions at the same time that it appointed the army's first general officers, but it did not fill all the slots immediately. It appointed Horatio Gates as adjutant general on 17 June and continued Richard Gridley, the officer Massachusetts had appointed as its chief engineer. It waited until 19 July to appoint Joseph Trumbull as commissary general, the same day it authorized, at Washington's request, a wagon master and a commissary of artillery stores; Washington appointed John Goddard and Ezekiel Cheever to fill these positions. The last days of July saw a spate of appointments. Congress named Benjamin Church as director general and chief of the medical department on 25 July, and on 27 July it appointed James Warren as paymaster general and Robert Erskine as geographer and surveyor to the army. Two days later it created the office of judge advocate and named William Tudor to the post; in 1776 the title was changed to judge advocate general. (Tudor was succeeded by John Laurance on 11 April 1777; Laurance served until 3 June 1782, when Colonel Thomas Edwards was appointed to the office.) Stephen Moylan was named commissary general of musters on 11 August, and finally, on 14 August, Washington appointed Thomas Mifflin as quartermaster general.

Most of the army's high-level administrative work was accomplished by these staff officers, who oversaw the implementation of orders from Washington and the Congress by their deputies and assistant deputies. During the first years of the war, the army was administered through its regiments, which were also its principal combat organizations. Regimental staff typically included an adjutant, a quartermaster, a commissary, a paymaster, a surgeon and surgeon's mate, and a chaplain. The first four of these positions were generally filled by line officers, who thus bore dual responsibilities in their regiments. (On 29 July 1775, Congress made provision to pay chaplains, turning volunteer clergymen into formal members of regimental and brigade staffs.) Regiments were always brigaded together under a brigadier general, but these groupings were initially ad hoc formations whose composition could change rapidly. Beginning with the enlistment of men into the army for three years or the duration of the war (1 January 1777), brigade composition became more stable, and more staff work was accomplished at the brigade level, under the supervision of the brigade major. Eighteenth-century armies did not have standing corps and divisions; these additional layers of operational control were institutionalized in the much larger armies that European states fielded around the turn of the nineteenth century.

OTHER INFLUENCES

As the war continued, the American understanding of the military staff was influenced by aspects of the French staff system, especially the concept of an inspector general that was brought to America by the many French volunteers who served in the American army. By 1777 the Continental army was maturing as an institution, and both Congress and General Washington saw the need to improve the competence and professionalism of a force that was clearly going to exist for several more years. Congress appointed Colonel Augustin Mottin de la Balme as inspector general of cavalry on 8 July 1777, and on 11 August named Philippe Tronson de Coudray a "major general of the staff" and inspector general of ordnance and military stores, more to quiet this troublesome Frenchman than out of respect for his abilities.

On 26 October 1777, as he contemplated how to dislodge the British from Philadelphia, Washington sent a circular letter to his generals, asking them for, among other things, a recommendation on whether an inspector general should be appointed to establish uniformity in drill, troop training, and command procedure, "as the time of the Adjutant General seems to be totally engaged with other business." Washington wanted the office to be filled by an acceptable, professionally trained foreign officer who would act as an overall inspector general, and he later indicated that the idea of an inspector general had originated with Henry, Baron d'Arendt. The generals concurred with Washington's proposal on 29 October, but before Washington could find time from the press of field duties to get congressional approval, the delegates acted. On 13 December 1777 Congress created the post of inspector general, directed that this officer report directly to it, and appointed Brigadier General Thomas Conway as "Inspector General of the Army," which some delegates meant as criticism of Washington's leadership. The commander in chief deftly parried this insult, and the French-Irish troublemaker never functioned as inspector general.

The Continental army's first actual inspector general was Friedrich Steuben, whom Congress appointed on

5 May 1778. Steuben had already acted as a de facto inspector general during the winter encampment at Valley Forge, where his modesty, sincerity, and earnest attention to training soldiers in an adaptation of Prussian drill fulfilled the requirements set out by Washington and his generals in October 1777. Aspects of the Prussian staff model, which was becoming highly influential as armies digested the success of Frederick the Great in the Seven Years' War, were adapted by Steuben for the Continental army after he became inspector general. His efforts to standardize the equipment and training of the army was intended to produce more uniform regiments that would be under greater central control and approach interchangeability on the battlefield. A formal complaint against "the progressive encroachment of a new-fangled power" was submitted by Brigadier General James M. Varnum, a Rhode Islander who was "filled with horror" when Steuben's inspectors called for reports on men fit for duty (Hittle, pp. 179–180).

The northern and southern military departments had staff officers corresponding to those in Washington's main army or those answerable directly to Congress. Each department had, for example, a deputy quartermaster general, and each brigade an assistant deputy quartermaster general. The same nomenclature applied generally to the adjutant general, the inspector general, and other staff positions. Although Edward Carrington was technically a deputy quartermaster general, as the quartermaster general of Major General Nathanael Greene's Southern Department in 1780–1781, he can sensibly be referred to as "Greene's quartermaster general."

Another category of staff officer contributed significantly to the administration and operation of the Continental army. It had long been a tradition in the British army for senior officers to rely heavily on their aides-de-camp and military secretaries to help them conduct business and operate their command. When he was appointed commander in chief, Washington requested and Congress approved the appointment of three aides-de-camp and a secretary. It was only with the help of these men, a total of thirty-two over the course of the war, that Washington was able to transmit orders, manage an enormous correspondence (some twelve thousand letters and orders went out at his direction or over his signature during eight years of war, the vast majority produced by his secretaries), and keep himself informed of the daily activities of the forces under his command as well as understand what was going on in theaters far removed. Not formally vested with specific responsibilities, the men who served as aides-de-camp to general officers had to have the intelligence, talent, and experience to deal with whatever task needed to be accomplished. Washington generally chose his aides well; they tended to leave his

military family, as the close-knit group of trusted aides around the general was called, only when they needed respite from the burden of work or wanted to serve more actively in a line command. Washington's military family, with the general acting in the role of *pater familias*, was the operational heart of the main Continental army.

SEE ALSO *Adjutants; Church, Benjamin; Conway Cabal; Conway, Thomas; Engineers; Erskine, Robert; Gates, Horatio; Gridley, Richard; Laurance, John; Medical Practice during the Revolution; Mifflin, Thomas; Mottin de La Balme, Augustin; Moylan, Stephen; Steuben, Friedrich Wilhelm von; Supply of the Continental Army; Tronson du Coudray, Philippe Charles Jean Baptiste; Trumbull, Joseph; Warren, James.*

BIBLIOGRAPHY

Chase, Philander D., et al., eds. *The Papers of George Washington*. Vols. 12 and 13. Charlottesville: University Press of Virginia, 2002–2003.

Hittle, James. *The Military Staff: Its History and Development*. 3rd ed. Harrisburg, Pa.: Stackpole Book, 1961.

Lefkowitz, Arthur S. *George Washington's Indispensable Men: The 32 Aides-de-Camp Who Helped Win American Independence*. Harrisburg, Pa.: Stackpole Books, 2003.

Risch, Erna. *Supplying Washington's Army*. Washington, D.C.: Center of Military History, 1981.

revised by Harold E. Selesky

STAMP ACT.

(22 March 1765–18 March 1766) and Stamp Act Congress (7–25 October 1765). The Stamp Act was one of the measures Parliament enacted in the wake of the final French and Indian War to increase imperial supervision of and control over the existing British colonies, the French territories conquered during the war, and the Native Americans in the Ohio Valley who faced a rising tide of encroachment by colonial settlers. Imperial officials decided to keep in North America some of the regular troops who had spearheaded the conquest of New France, initially at least to keep the peace in the areas formerly under French control, especially west of the Appalachians. While not a clearly thought through part of the plan, regular troops would also serve to support imperial authority by reminding restive American colonists of the power and reach of the British Empire.

Supporting this military establishment was expensive. Since imperial officials faced a vastly increased national debt at home and believed that the troops protected (and thus benefited) the colonies, they not unreasonably expected Americans to help pay part of the cost. Prime Minister George Grenville intended the Stamp Act to raise a revenue of £60,000 a year in the colonies to pay part of the estimated £350,000 cost of maintaining 10,000 British troops in North America. The act, which passed through Parliament with little debate and no understanding that it would meet colonial resistance, extended to the colonies a form of taxation already in use in Britain. (Imperial officials were not deterred by the fact that a similar tax that had been enacted earlier by the colonial legislatures in New York and Massachusetts had proved so unpopular that it was quickly abandoned.) Taking effect on 1 November 1765, the Stamp Act taxed various types of printed matter (newspapers, broadsides, pamphlets), all types of legal documents, and even included dice and playing cards. Taxes were to be paid in specie (a significant problem in societies where hard money was scarce), transactions made in violation of the act would be deemed invalid, and penalties for infringements could be imposed by vice-admiralty courts as well as by colonial common law courts. In an attempt to win support for the act in the colonies, Grenville appointed Americans as stamp agents. Richard Henry Lee and other prominent colonists eagerly sought the posts, which paid £300 a year and offered patronage possibilities.

The Stamp Act was the first direct tax Parliament had levied on the colonies. Since it followed other measures (the Sugar Act and the Currency Act) and contained provisions like expanded jurisdiction for the vice-admiralty courts, many Americans came to believe that the new era of increased imperial supervision would restrict their economic freedom and curtail their civil liberties. They contended that they had contributed significant financial resources to Britain's victory in the final French and Indian War (thereby ignoring substantial subsidies the colonies had received from Parliament), and they believed that because they were suffering through a postwar depression partly because of those exertions, they would be unable to pay such a tax. More troubling was Parliament's assumption that it had a right to impose taxes on the colonies without the consent of their local legislative assemblies, a position opponents summarized in the slogan "taxation without representation is tyranny." Moreover, the authority granted to the vice-admiralty courts to decide customs enforcement cases without trial by jury seemed to pose a serious threat to civil liberties. The Stamp Act generated opposition in all geographical sections of America and from many diverse and influential groups, including lawyers (whose business would be particularly hard hit), printers, tavern keepers, land speculators, merchants, and shipowners. The fact that Grenville proposed the stamp tax almost a year before Parliament enacted it gave colonial leaders additional time to think about the nature of the colonies' relationship with the mother country.

Opponents of increased imperial supervision moved swiftly to organize resistance. They took to the public prints to explain their objections and to generate support. Attorney Daniel Dulany of Maryland argued in *Considerations on the Propriety of Imposing Taxes in the British Colonies* (1765) that the act was illegal because the colonies were not actually represented in Parliament. Other activists took a stand in their legislative assemblies. Patrick Henry first rose to prominence when he introduced the Virginia Resolves into the House of Burgesses in May 1765. John Adams, too, gained notoriety by drafting instructions that his home town of Braintree, Massachusetts, gave to its assembly delegates to object to the Stamp Act. Still others acted extralegally in ways that were a familiar part of the political process. They gathered together in groups called the Sons of Liberty and were not averse to using intimidation and mob action to force all the stamp agents to resign their commissions in the autumn of 1765. The opponents were so successful that only in Georgia, whose governor was the remarkable Sir James Wright, was the Stamp Act ever put into effect, and there it was only enforced to a limited degree. Elsewhere, colonial courts initially closed rather than use the stamps, and they later resumed business without stamps, an open violation of the act. In Rhode Island, where the governor refused to execute the Stamp Act, the courts never closed.

Opposition to the Stamp Act forced colonists to consider their place in the empire, and perhaps most importantly in the long term, broke down intercolonial differences by promoting communication and cooperation among like-minded leaders in all colonies. A significant step in that process was initiated by James Otis of Massachusetts, who, understanding that the colonies' objections would be taken more seriously if they acted together, proposed that each colonial assembly send delegates to meet in a congress and explore the possibility of concerted opposition. His proposal won the support of the Massachusetts assembly and was endorsed by the assemblies in South Carolina, Rhode Island, Connecticut, Pennsylvania, and Maryland; these six colonies sent official delegates to the Stamp Act Congress. The assemblies in New Jersey, Delaware, and New York took no formal action, but did send delegates. Virginia, New Hampshire, North Carolina, and Georgia did not participate.

Twenty-seven delegates from nine colonies met in the Stamp Act Congress at New York City on 7–25 October 1765. They formulated fourteen resolutions in a Declaration of Rights and Grievances (drafted by John Dickinson) that denied Parliament's right to tax the colonies and condemned the extension of vice-admiralty-court jurisdiction. The Congress delivered its resolutions in the form of petitions to the king and both houses of Parliament. None of these appeals caused imperial officials to rethink their position that Parliament had a fundamental right to legislate in all matters for the colonies, including the right to impose taxes to support regular troops and imperial administrators.

In Britain, doubts about the wisdom of the Stamp Act had been building even before it took effect. Grenville advocated the enforcement of his act by military force, but he had been replaced as prime minister in July 1765, and the new prime minister—the marquis of Rockingham—was reluctant to support such a drastic and expensive response. In December 1765 Parliament received numerous petitions for repeal from British merchants, who feared a loss of trade with the colonies as a result of nonimportation and an American austerity program. In January 1766 William Pitt, the single most influential political figure in Parliament, called for repeal of the Stamp Act, but at the same time he expressed the widely held opinion that Parliament ought to assert its "sovereign authority over the colonies ... to extend to every point of legislation whatsoever, that we may bind their trade, confine their manufactures, and exercise every power whatsoever, except that of taking their money out of their pockets without their consent." Benjamin Franklin, then a colonial agent in London, gave Commons cogent testimony in February 1766 that the colonies not only should not but could not pay, and he warned that military action might cause rebellion.

Repeal of the Stamp Act received royal assent on 18 March, to take effect on 1 May 1766. Opponents of increased imperial control rejoiced when the news reached American shores on 26 April. They overlooked or ignored the significance of the position outlined by Pitt. Those ideas had been forcefully expressed in the Declaratory Act, which Parliament had passed as a prelude to repealing the Stamp Act.

SEE ALSO *Adams, John; Admiralty Courts; Declaratory Act; Dulany, Daniel; Grenville, George; Henry, Patrick; Nonimportation; Otis, James; Pontiac's War; Sons of Liberty; Taxation without Representation Is Tyranny; Virginia Resolves of 1765; Wright, Sir James, Governor.*

BIBLIOGRAPHY

Knollenberg, Bernhard. *The Origin of the American Revolution: 1759–1766.* New York: Macmillan, 1960.

———. *Growth of the American Revolution, 1766–1775.* New York: Free Press, 1975.

Morgan, Edmund S., and Helen M. Morgan. *The Stamp Act Crisis: Prologue to Revolution.* Chapel Hill: University of North Carolina Press, 1953.

Thomas, P. D. G. *British Politics and the Stamp Act Crisis: The First Phase of the American Revolution, 1763–1767.* Oxford and New York: Clarendon Press, 1975.

revised by Harold E. Selesky

STANSBURY, JOSEPH. (c. 1742–1809).

Loyalist secret agent, poet. England-Pennsylvania. Son of a London haberdasher, Stansbury immigrated to Philadelphia in 1767, opening a china store. He became well-known for his humorous and satirical songs. Although he sympathized with the Patriots, he opposed separation from the empire and in 1776 was briefly imprisoned for his Loyalist sentiments. He held several minor British posts during the occupation of Philadelphia, signed the oath of allegiance to the Patriot cause after the British left, paid for substitutes in the Pennsylvania militia, and remained in the city until he was arrested for treason in 1780. After six months in jail he was permitted to leave the city with his family for New York City, the Patriots remaining ignorant of his role in Arnold's treason.

In New York he continued to write political songs and satirical prose. Stansbury's writings lacked the bitterness and anger that marked the works of the other Loyalist poet, Jonathan Odell. In August 1783 Stansbury went to Nova Scotia for a year and then to England, where the commission on Loyalist claims disallowed his appeal for one thousand pounds on the grounds that his loyalty had been too flexible. In November 1785 he resumed his business in Philadelphia, but in 1793 he gave up and moved back to New York City, where he was secretary of the United Insurance Company until his death in 1809.

SEE ALSO *Arnold's Treason; Odell, Jonathan.*

BIBLIOGRAPHY

Sergent, Winthrop, ed. *The Loyal Verses of Joseph Stansbury and Doctor Jonathan Odell.* Albany, N.Y.: J. Munsell, 1860.

revised by Michael Bellesiles

STARK, JOHN. (1728–1822). Continental general. New Hampshire. Son of a Scots–Irishman who came to New Hampshire in 1720, he was a woodsman and Indian fighter. In 1755 he participated in the operations leading to the defeat of Baron Dieskau and then served as a lieutenant and captain of rangers led by Robert Rogers. In January 1757 he walked forty miles through deep snow to bring assistance to the wounded, having previously been engaged in a day of fighting and an all-night march. After taking part in Amherst's campaign against Ticonderoga and Crown Point in 1759, he returned to central New Hampshire, where he helped establish a new township, originally called Starksville and later renamed Dunbarton.

On 23 April 1775 the New Hampshire house appointed Stark colonel of the first New Hampshire Regiment. He quickly raised fourteen companies, which he led to join Washington's army at Medford, Massachusetts. In the battle on 17 June he led his men and others under the command of Colonel James Reed to hold the American Line along the famous "rail fence" at Bunker Hill. Following the British evacuation of Boston in March 1776, Colonel Stark obeyed orders to lead his men to New York where, as colonel of the Fifth Continental, he helped prepare the defenses of New York City. In May he went with reinforcements to Canada, where he was in command at Montreal for a brief time during the summer. In early fall he marched his troops back to Crown Point, then to Ticonderoga, and then on to Pennsylvania, where he again joined Washington's camp as part of General John Sullivan's brigade. Stark's regiment participated in the crossing of the Delaware on 26 December 1776 and in the subsequent victorious battle at Trenton. While some New Hampshire men went home at the end of 1776, Stark crossed the Delaware again with Washington on 2 January 1777 and again faced the British at Trenton and on to secure Princeton, taking a significant number of Hessian prisoners. When Congress appointed Enoch Poor as its brigadier general from New Hampshire early in 1777, Stark felt that his previous experience, his age, and his seniority of command had been ignored. Stark returned to the state legislature meeting at Exeter, New Hampshire, in April, where he appeared before that body to resign his command.

As the British under General John Burgoyne threatened New England from Canada, the New Hampshire legislature on 18 July 1777 called upon Stark to accept the state rank of brigadier general to lead one of its two militia brigades to Vermont to stop the redcoats. Between 19 July and 24 July, Stark raised fifteen hundred men with whom he crippled Burgoyne at Bennington on 16 August 1777 and helped force British capitulation at Saratoga. At Bennington, Stark won one of the most spectacular and decisive successes of the Revolution.

When he left his post and returned to New Hampshire, after others whom he considered less qualified were promoted over him, Congress first to reprimanded him for his insubordination and then appointed him brigadier general on 4 October 1777. In the final stage of Burgoyne's offensive, he led the force that cut off Gentleman Johnny's last escape route. John Stark had an uncanny way of being at the critical and unexpected place to ruin British plans, first at Bunker Hill, then at Bennington, and finally at Saratoga. He remained on active duty for the rest of the war, twice commanding the Northern Department, being involved in the planned Canada invasion of 1778, serving under Gates in Rhode Island in 1779, and taking part in New Jersey operations in the summer of 1780. While serving at West Point, he sat on André's board of inquiry. Suffering from arthritis,

he spent much time over the next few years at home in Dunbarton. Breveted major general on 30 September 1783, he retired from the army on 3 November of that year and went home. Unlike other war heroes, he stayed out of public life, finding enough to do managing his large farm and eleven children. He lived to be ninety-three years old, expiring on 8 May 1822 at home.

A man of medium height, bold features, keen light blue eyes, and compressed lips, John Stark was a man who generated legends. Most of them appear to have a kernel of truth. One rare quality that emerges from his picturesque battlefield remarks is an appreciation of the human factor in war. When he refused to hurry his men through an artillery barrage because "one fresh man in action is worth ten fatigued men," he not only was saving energy but was calming down a body of inexperienced officers and men who were on the verge of panic. When he said, "Boys, aim at their waistbands," he was enunciating more military wisdom than meets the eye for an era when European soldiers usually aimed only in the general direction of the enemy. (In addition, the men would not fire too early if they waited until they could see their enemies' waistbands.)

At Bennington he reportedly said, "We'll beat them before night, or Molly Stark will be a widow." He apparently had a gift for making such memorable remarks. To Stark's discredit it must be said that except at Bunker Hill, he showed a consistently insubordinate character; but for his incredible luck, he would not be the national hero he remains. He refused to join the Order of the Cincinnati owing to his opposition to military organizations in principle.

A brother, William (1724–c.1776), served in Rogers's Rangers, fighting at Ticonderoga, Louisburg, and Quebec. He defected to the enemy when the Americans would not give him command of a regiment at the start of the Revolution and died after a fall from his horse. A son, Caleb (1759–1838), was a fifteen-year-old ensign in his father's regiment at Bunker Hill and finished the war as a brigade major. After becoming a Boston businessman, he moved to Ohio in 1828.

SEE ALSO *Bennington Raid; Bunker Hill, Massachusetts; Burgoyne's Offensive.*

BIBLIOGRAPHY

Fischer, David Hackett. *Washington's Crossing.* New York: Oxford University Press, 2004.

Kidder, Frederick. *History of the First New Hampshire Regiment in the War of the Revolution.* 1868. Reprint, Portsmouth: Peter E. Randall, 1973.

Resch, John. *Suffering Soldiers: Revolutionary War Veterans, Moral Sentiment, and Political Culture in the Early Republic.* Amherst: University of Massachusetts Press, 1999.

Stark, Caleb. *Memoir and Official Correspondence of General John Stark.* 1860. Reprint, Boston, Gregg Press: 1972.

Upton, Richard Francis. *Revolutionary New Hampshire.* 1936. Reprint, New York: Octagon Books, 1971.

Wright, Robert K., Jr. *The Continental Army.* Washington, D.C.: Center of Military History, 1983.

revised by Frank C. Mevers

STARS AND STRIPES SEE *Flag, American.*

STATEN ISLAND, NEW YORK.

22 August 1777. Sullivan's raid. Once Lieutenant General William Howe set sail, Washington started the bulk of the main army south to protect Philadelphia. Major General John Sullivan, in command of the division composed of the First and Second Maryland Brigades, lagged behind. On 3 August Washington told Sullivan to hold in place at Hanover, New Jersey, where the division could move north to reinforce the Hudson Highlands or south to Philadelphia once the situation clarified. The Americans sought to keep Sir Henry Clinton, left by Howe as the British commander in New York, immobilized by giving indications that they would attack the city's defenses at Kings Bridge, Long Island, and Staten Island. The first two threats turned out to be feints, but Sullivan actually landed on Staten Island with his division. According to Clinton, they

> effected an almost total surprise of two provincial battalions belonging to Skinner's Brigade, and after setting fire to the magazines at Decker's Ferry were on their march to Richmond; while another corps, that had landed on the west part of the island for the purpose of cutting off three other provincial battalions, had taken Lieutenant Colonel Lawrence, with the great part of his battalion, prisoners, and only missed the remainder by Lieutenant Colonels Dongan and Allen having the presence of mind to throw them into some old rebel works at Prince's Bay. (*American Rebellion,* 68 n.)

Despite Sullivan's initial success, Brigadier John Campbell used the regular regiments stationed on the island, especially the Fifty-second Foot and the Waldeck Regiment, to stop him cold. The Americans rapidly lost cohesion and withdrew to the Jersey shore with the loss of between somewhere between 170 and 259, mostly troops captured during the withdrawal.

American histories of the war usually pass over this action rather casually as an embarrassingly inept sideshow for which Sullivan was court-martialed and acquitted. Clinton on the other hand obsessed over the tenuous nature of his hold on New York and believed that the defeat prevented Washington from taking advantage of Howe's departure to make a major attack. In reality, the greatest impact of the operation was political. The middle states' delegates in Congress used the defeat to attack the New Englander, Sullivan, in retaliation for the New England delegates' role in replacing General Philip Schuyler with Horatio Gates.

SEE ALSO *Philadelphia Campaign.*

BIBLIOGRAPHY

Clinton, Sir Henry. *The American Rebellion: Sir Henry Clinton's Narrative of His Campaigns, 1775–1782, with an Appendix of Original Documents.* Edited by William B. Willcox. Hamden, Conn.: Archon Books, 1971.

Pearce, Steward. "Sullivan's Expedition to Staten Island in 1777." *Pennsylvania Magazine of History and Biography* 3 (1879): 167–173.

Whittemore, Charles P. *A General of the Revolution: John Sullivan of New Hampshire.* New York: Columbia University Press, 1961.

revised by Robert K. Wright Jr.

STATEN ISLAND EXPEDITION OF ALEXANDER.

14–15 January 1780. The winter of 1779–1780 was the coldest in New York City's recorded history, with ice making water communications between Manhattan and Staten Island all but impossible by mid-January, and allowing heavy artillery pieces to be pulled across the Hudson River to Paulus Hook by teams of horses. At the same time General Henry Clinton was in South Carolina with a large portion of the British forces stationed in North America. Major General James Pattison commanded at New York in his absence, and feared that Washington would take advantage of the two unique situations to attack. Although the weather was too severe for a major operation, on the night of 14–15 January, General William Alexander (known as Lord Stirling) led three thousand men across the ice from Elizabethtown Point to Staten Island. The defenders spotted the move and took cover in their fortifications. After spending a miserable twenty-four hours in the subzero weather and deep snow, the Americans withdrew with seventeen prisoners and a small quantity of loot. Alexander had six men killed and about five hundred "slightly frozen" (in the words of a contemporary). In a classic example of the bitterness of the between-the-lines raiding during the time the British held New York, New Jersey militia on this raid stripped Loyalists' farms; the British retaliated ten days later by burning the academy at Newark and the courthouse and meeting house at Elizabethtown.

BIBLIOGRAPHY
Nelson, Paul David. *William Alexander, Lord Stirling.* University: University of Alabama Press, 1987.

revised by Robert K. Wright Jr.

STATEN ISLAND PEACE CONFERENCE SEE *Peace Conference on Staten Island.*

STEDMAN, CHARLES. (1753–1812).

British officer, historian. Born in Philadelphia, Stedman studied at William and Mary College and took the British side at the start of the Revolution, serving as commissary under Sir William Howe. Fluent in German, he was liaison to the German troops serving with the British. Twice wounded during Howe's and Cornwallis's campaigns, Stedman was also twice taken prisoner, escaping from the same jail that held Major André. After the war he served on the commission established to examine Loyalist claims. His *History of the Origin, Progress, and Termination of the American War* (2 vols., 1794) became the standard British work on the Revolution, sparking a lively dispute with Sir Henry Clinton over a number of petty details. In his later years, Stedman was a deputy comptroller of the British stamp office.

revised by Michael Bellesiles

STEPHEN, ADAM. (c. 1721–1791). Con-

tinental general. Virginia. Educated as a surgeon in Scotland and England and a former naval surgeon, Stephen emigrated to Virginia in 1748. Finding too many physicians in Virginia and ambitious to enter the ranks of the gentry, he acquired a huge plantation in the Shenandoah Valley and produced flour and livestock, among other commodities; during the Revolutionary War he established an arms manufactory on his property. While serving in the French and Indian War, Stephen—as a lieutenant colonel—was second in command to George Washington in the Virginia Regiment. Thus, he participated in the clashes with French and Indian troops at Little

Meadows and Great Meadows in 1754, the ill-fated Braddock expedition of 1755, and in the Forbes expedition of 1758. He himself conducted the heroic defense of Fort Ligonier in July 1759. Stephen commanded the Virginia Regiment in operations against the Cherokees in 1761. During the war Washington was almost always absent from his troops, who were stationed at Forts Cumberland and Loudoun and elsewhere, and hence Stephen had the responsibility of immediate command. Washington early developed a dislike of Stephen, considering him conniving and insubordinate. The relationship became somewhat humorous. The two men ran against each other for a seat in the House of Burgesses from Frederick County, Virginia; Washington accused Stephen of engaging in dirty politics, while the future commander in chief was doing much the same thing.

Appointed colonel of the Fourth Virginia Regiment on 13 February 1776 and brigadier general on 4 September 1776, Stephen jeopardized Washington's Trenton raid by sending an unauthorized patrol across the Delaware on Christmas Day, coming across Stephen's wandering troops after he himself had crossed the Delaware. Washington turned on Stephen in one of his occasional bursts of flaming temper. "You sir," said Washington, "may have ruined all my plans." As it was, the premature crossing worked in favor of the Americans; the Hessian commander at Trenton mistook this episode as the one reported to him in intelligence of an American crossing, and therefore took no further precautions to impede an American attack.

As a major general (appointed 19 February 1777), Stephen sent troops on missions of his own devising and submitted exaggerated reports of their success. On 10 May he attempted to surprise the Forty-second Highlanders at Piscataway, New Jersey. Although repulsed and driven back toward his own camp, he reported a gallant success in which at least two hundred of the enemy were killed. Washington questioned Stephen's veracity and pointed out to Stephen that "your account . . . is favorable, but I am sorry to add, widely different from those I have had from others."

The divisions of Stephen and Wayne collided during the Battle of Germantown on 4 October 1777, a misfortune that probably caused the panic of Washington's attacking force. Shortly afterwards, Stephen was brought before a court of inquiry and then a court-martial, where in the latter he was charged with "unofficerlike behaviour" in the march from northern New Jersey preliminary to the Philadelphia campaign and during the battles of Brandywine and Germantown and also charged with "drunkenness." He was found guilty for not restraining retreating soldiers at Germantown and also for being "frequently intoxicated since in the service." Despite his appeal of the verdict to Congress, Stephen was "dismissed" (not cashiered) from the army. The case against Stephen had not been strong. Working against him was his advanced age (fifty-six years), flamboyance, and outspokenness. Upon Stephen's removal, Washington assigned Stephen's division to Lafayette.

Stephen retired to his plantation in western Virginia. He founded Martinsburg (later in West Virginia), which was incorporated in 1778, and reestablished his residence there at an eight-room stone house finished in 1789. The house and grounds became an historical park with a small museum. Evidence that his dismissal from the army was considered an injustice is his service in the Virginia House of Delegates from 1780 to 1785 and in the state convention for ratifying the U.S. Constitution in June 1788. Stephen never married but had a daughter by his mistress; the daughter, Ann, married Alexander Spotswood Dandridge, brother-in-law of Patrick Henry and second cousin of Martha Washington.

BIBLIOGRAPHY

Mish, Mary V. "General Adam Stephen, Founder of Martinsburg, West Virginia." *West Virginia History* 28 (1961): 63–75.

Stephen, Adam. "Colonel Stephen's Life Written by Himself for B. Rush in 1775." *Pennsylvania Magazine of History and Biography* 18 (1894): 43–50.

Van Metre, Thomas E. "Adam Stephen—the Man." *Berkeley Journal* (Fall 1970): 12–21.

Ward, Harry M. *Major General Adam Stephen and the Cause of American Liberty.* Charlottesville: University Press of Virginia, 1989.

revised by Harry M. Ward

STEUBEN, FRIEDRICH WILHELM VON.

(1730–1794). Inspector General of the Continental Army. Friedrich Wilhelm von Steuben was the grandson of Augustin Steube, a minister of the German Reformed Church. The grandfather inserted the "von" in the family name about 1708 as a sign of aristocratic status, although he technically had no right to do so. The man who became the foremost military instructor of the American Revolution was born in Magdeburg, Germany, while his father, Wilhelm Augustus von Steuben, an engineer lieutenant in the Prussian army, was stationed there. His early youth was spent in Russia. At the age of ten he returned to Germany with his parents, was schooled by Jesuits in Breslau, and at seventeen became a Prussian officer with the rank of ensign. During the Seven Years' War, from 1756 to 1763, he served first as a lieutenant in an infantry

regiment and then as adjutant of a partisan corps. Later in the war he was promoted to captain and was made an assistant quartermaster at the general headquarters. Captured by the Russians in the fall of 1762, he was released a short time later, and the following spring he carried a diplomatic dispatch from Czar Peter III to Frederick the Great.

Although Steuben never held the high rank and influential positions in Prussian service that he later claimed, his early military training and experience should not be undervalued. As a junior officer, he mastered the rigorous Prussian drill system that was respected throughout Europe for its efficiency and effectiveness, and as an adjutant and an assistant quartermaster, he became proficient in every phrase of military administration from supply to battlefield organization and discipline. His skills and knowledge fitted him almost perfectly to become the sort of chief of staff that George Washington needed to help make the Continental army a more fully competent and stable professional force.

Steuben was discharged from the Prussian army in 1763, at the age of only 33, for reasons that are obscure. The next year he became chamberlain (*hofmarschall*) at the court of Hohenzollern-Hechingen, a small south German principality, where he subsequently assumed his title of baron (*freiherr*). When his prince closed the court in 1771 and went incognito to France, where he hoped to live more economically, Steuben accompanied him. In 1774 they were back in Germany, having failed to achieve solvency. One year later Steuben was beset by rumors that were never proven or subsequently revived of behaving inappropriately with young boys. He was forced to seek other employment.

After several unsuccessful attempts to enter European armies (France, Austria, Baden), Steuben met a friend of Benjamin Franklin who suggested to the latter, then one of the American commissioners in Paris, that Steuben could render valuable service in America. Having pursued this lead to Paris, where he arrived during the summer of 1777, Steuben had the good fortune of being endorsed by the French minister of war, Claude-Louis, comte de St. Germain, who recognized the value of his Prussian military training. Pierre-Augustin Caron de Beaumarchais, the French playwright who was secretly aiding the Americans, advanced travel funds from his company, Roderique Hortalez et Cie, and on 4 September 1778 the resourceful Franklin penned a letter introducing Steuben to Washington as "a Lieutenant General in the King of Prussia's Service." With all these bogus credentials, Lieutenant General Baron von Steuben left Marseilles on 26 September. He arrived at Portsmouth, New Hampshire, on 1 December, and after spending several weeks at Boston being royally entertained, he reached York, Pennsylvania, where the Continental Congress was then sitting, on about

Baron von Steuben. *The Prussian-born director of training and inspector general of the Continental Army, in a copy of a portrait (c. 1780) by Ralph Earl.* LANDOV

5 February 1778. Congress, he learned, had already accepted the offer made in his letter to Congress of 6 December to serve for the time being as an unpaid volunteer, and on 23 February 1778 he reported to Washington at Valley Forge.

At Washington's request, Steuben began a comprehensive new program of drill instruction for the Contintental army in late March 1778. Although he at first spoke only German and French, Steuben drafted a series of lessons that skillfully adapted Prussian methods to American needs and temperament, employing the assistance of his English-speaking, French aide-de-camp, Pierre Etienne Du Ponceau. He started with a model company of about 150 hand-picked men. and spread his instruction in a sort of geometric progression through the little army. An essential element of his successful formula was Steuben's picturesque personality. He stood before the ill-clad Continentals in a magnificent uniform, and put on a show worthy of paid admission. According to Du Ponceau, when Steuben could no longer curse his awkward pupils in German and French, he would call on both Du Ponceau and his French-speaking American aide, Captain Benjamin Walker, "to come and swear for me in

English, these fellows won't do what I bid them." Ponceau went on to observe that "a good natured smile then went through the ranks, and at last the maneuver or the movement was properly perfomed."

The drill improvements that Stueben began introducing at Valley Forge did much more than simply make the Continentals look better on the parade ground. In the methodical brand of warfare that was practiced in the eighteenth century, the soldiers' ability to march in large formations on the battlefield with precision and discipline often made the difference between victory and defeat. Steuben's achievement was not in teaching the Continentals how to march—something that most of them already could do—but in enabling them to march together in brigades and divisions with greater efficiency by instituting a uniform and innovative, army-wide drill system. Although the stalemate that generally prevailed in the northern states after the spring of 1778 meant that the results of Steuben's work were never fully tested in open battle, they were partially displayed at Barren Hill on 20 May 1778, and at Monmouth, on 28 June 1778, where the troops' new training significantly aided Continental officers in maintaining control under dangerous circumstances. Washington was sufficiently pleased with the progress that had been made within a few weeks time that, on 30 April 1778, he recommended Steuben's appointment as inspector general of the army with the rank of major general, and on 5 May Congress confirmed the promotion.

During the Monmouth campaign, the new inspector general served in Washington's headquarters, and in the final phase of the battle of 28 June, he helped collect some of the disorganized American units. A few weeks later, during his court-martial for misconduct at Monmouth Court House, Charles Lee referred to Steuben as one of "the very distant spectators of the manoeuvres" on that day. The Prussian subsequently challenged Lee to a duel over his remarks, but was satisfied when Lee explained that he meant no offense.

After temporarily commanding the right wing of the Continental Army in July 1778, Steuben spent much of the rest of the year training troops and negotiating with Congress over the organization and powers of the inspector general's department. The next winter he prepared his *Regulations for the Order and Discipline of the Troops of the United States*, which became known as the "Blue Book." Serving as the principal military guide not only for the Continental army but also for the first generation of United States Army officers and soldiers, this manual contained both a revamped version of the drill system that Steuben had devised at Valley Forge and a compendium of the latest administrative practices used in European armies. Continuing his duties of training and instilling discipline in 1779 and 1780, Steuben began making regular inspections of the regiments, and he set up a badly needed system of property accountability. During the winter of 1779–1780 he was Washington's representative to Congress on matters of army reorganization.

When Nathanael Greene was given command of the Southern Department in the fall of 1780, Steuben went along, and since most of Greene's support—personnel as well as provisions—would come from Virginia, he stayed there. Bluntly insistent that democratic procedures be sacrificed to military expediency, Steuben was ill suited to deal with Governor Thomas Jefferson and the Virginia legislature. As the senior Continental officer in the Old Dominion during the winter and early spring of 1781, Steuben commanded the pitifully small Continental contingent and the hastily assembled militiamen who tried unsuccessfully to check Benedict Arnold's and William Phillips's raids in force up the James River.

When the Marquis de Lafayette arrived in Virginia at the end of April, Steuben yielded his command to the newcomer and focused on the job of gathering reinforcements and supplies for Greene's army in the Carolinas. Steuben encountered a firestorm of public criticism in June 1781 when, during General Charles Cornwallis's invasion of Virginia, he failed to save the supply depot at Point of Fork from enemy raiders and then began marching his detachment of about five hundred Continental recruits south to join Greene. Realizing his mistake only after several days, he reversed his march, delivered his recruits to Lafayette, and took an extended sick leave. Steuben rejoined the army for the Yorktown campaign, taking command of one of the three divisions of Washington's force and giving the benefit of his experience in siege warfare. This was the closest he came to realizing his long cherished desire for a prestigious field command suited to his rank.

Steuben continued serving as inspector general during the last two years of the war. In the spring of 1783 he assisted Washington in planning for the demobilization of the Continental army and the future defense of the United States. He also was actively involved in the creation of the Society of the Cincinnati, and warmly approved of its controversial provision for hereditary membership. In August 1783 he went to Canada to receive the surrender of British frontier posts, but found that Canadian governor, Frederick Haldimand, had no authority to treat with him. Steuben resigned his commission on 21 March 1784.

Having become an American citizen by an act of the Pennsylvania legislature in March 1783 and the New York legislature in July 1786, Steuben established residence at the "Louvre," a country estate on Manhattan Island, and became a prominent and popular social figure. He lived far beyond his means, however, and was soon in serious financial straits. In June 1790 the new federal government granted him a yearly pension of $2,500 instead of a lump sum settlement of his Revolutionary War claims, and it was only the following October, when Alexander Hamilton and other friends got him a "friendly mortgage" on the 16,000 acres given him by New York in 1786, that Steuben's financial affairs were straightened out. During his last years, the old bachelor spent summers on his Mohawk Valley property north of Utica (near modern Remsen), New York, and his winters in New York City. He willed his property to his former aides, William North and Benjamin Walker.

Steuben's legacy to the American people was the high standard of professional military discipline and efficiency that he managed to introduce within the larger framework of liberty and independence—a standard that sustained the Continental army through five years of war following Valley Forge and won it the respect of its French allies. Steuben never claimed to have worked miracles on the drill field. "I leave it to your other Correspondents," he wrote Benjamin Franklin on 28 September 1779, "to give you an Account of the present State of our Army; If they tell you that our Order & Discipline Equals that of the French and Prussian Armies, do not believe them, but do not believe them neither, if they compare our Troops to those of the Pope, & take a just medium between those two Extremes." Steuben knew, however, the practical value of what he accomplished, as did the Continental officers and soldiers who were his students. A master teacher by any measure, Steuben did not rely on rote leassons taken from an old drill book of his youth, but rather he borrowed freely from the newest sources of military knowledge available—Prussian, Austrian, French, and British—to create a strong but flexible system of command and control designed to enable Americans to deal effectively with the various military situations that they faced in winning their freedom and consolidating their hold over almost half a continent.

SEE ALSO *Valley Forge Winter Quarters, Pennsylvania.*

BIBLIOGRAPHY

Chase, Philander D. "Baron von Steuben in the War of Independence." Ph.D. diss., Duke University, 1973.

Clary, David A., and Joseph W. A. Whitehorne. *The Inspectors General of the United States Army, 1777–1903.* Washington, D.C.: Office of the Inspector General and Center of Military History, United States Army, 1987.

Du Ponceau, Pierre Etienne. "The Autobiography of Peter Stephen Du Ponceau." Edited by James L. Whitehead. *Pennsylvania Magazine of History and Biography*, 63 (1939): 189–227, 311–343, 432–461; 64 (1940): 97–120, 243–269.

Franklin, Benjamin. *The Papers of Benjamin Franklin.* Edited by Leonard W. Labaree et al. 37 vols. to date. New Haven, Conn.: Yale University Press, 1959–.

Jefferson, Thomas. *The Papers of Thomas Jefferson.* Edited by Julian P. Boyd et al. 31 vols. to date. Princeton, N.J.: Princeton University Press, 1950–.

North, William. "Baron Steuben." Edited by William L. Stone. *Magazine of American History with Notes and Queries,* 8 (1882): 187–199.

Palmer, John McAuley. *General von Steuben.* New Haven, Conn.: Yale University Press, 1937.

Steuben, Friedrich Wilhelm von. *The Papers of General Friedrich Wilhelm von Steuben, 1777–1794.* Edited by Edith von Zemenszky and Robert J. Schulmann. Millwood, N.Y.: Kraus International Publications, 1984. Microfilm.

Washington, George. *The Papers of George Washington, Revolutionary War Series.* Edited by Philander D. Chase et al. 14 vols to date. Charlottesville, Va.: University of Virginia Press, 1985–.

Wright, Robert K., Jr. *The Continental Army.* Washington, D.C.: Center of Military History, 1983.

revised by Philander D. Chase

STEVENS, EDWARD.

(1745–1820). Militia general. Virginia. Born in Culpeper County, Virginia, in 1745, Stevens commanded a militia battalion at Great Bridge, Virginia, in December 1775 and became colonel of the Tenth Virginia Continentals on 12 November 1776. Joining Washington's army in New Jersey, he took part in the Battles of Brandywine and Germantown. Stevens resigned from the Continental Army on 31 January 1778 and was appointed brigadier general of the Virginia militia in 1779. He joined Gates's army with seven hundred militia at Rugeley's Mills on 14 August 1780. Although he showed personal courage at the battle of Camden, two days later his troops disgraced themselves. After discharging these men on the expiration of their enlistments, Stevens rejoined Greene before the latter retreated across the Dan River and was appointed by Greene to command the Halifax County militia. He and his irregulars distinguished themselves at Guilford, where he was wounded severely. Three months later he commanded one of the three Virginia brigades that joined Lafayette, and he led his brigade of 750 men in the Yorktown campaign. Promoted to major general of militia, he also served as state senator from the adoption of the Virginia constitution of 1776 until 1790.

SEE ALSO *Camden Campaign; Guilford Courthouse, North Carolina; Yorktown Campaign; Yorktown, Siege of.*

revised by Michael Bellesiles

STEWART, ALEXANDER.

(1741–1794). British army officer in the South. He entered the army as an ensign in the Thirty-seventh Foot on 8 April 1755 and remained with it until he was promoted lieutenant colonel of the Third Foot (the "Buffs") on 7 July 1775. He reached Charleston on 4 June 1781 and took over command of the field force at Orangeburg, South Carolina, from Francis Rawdon. He was not, however, in overall command in the South or even in South Carolina, where his superior was Colonel Paston Gould. At Eutaw Springs on 8 September, Stewart won a hard-fought victory in the last major engagement of the war. However, losses on both sides were high—the highest in terms of numbers engaged of any battle in the war—and the British, less able than their foes to withstand such attrition, had to withdraw toward Charleston. At Monck's Corner on 12 September 1781, he met the Thirtieth Foot led by Gould, to whom he handed over command. Stewart subsequently commanded the troops defending Charleston Neck. He was promoted colonel on 16 May 1782 and major general on 25 April 1790.

SEE ALSO *Eutaw Springs, South Carolina; Gould, Paston; Monck's Corner, South Carolina; Orangeburg, South Carolina.*

BIBLIOGRAPHY

Mackesy, Piers. *The War for America, 1775–1783.* London: Longman, 1964.

revised by John Oliphant

STEWART, WALTER.

(1756–1796). Continental officer. Pennsylvania. At the start of the Revolution he raised a company for the Third Pennsylvania Battalion, was commissioned captain on 5 January 1776, became aide-de-camp to Gates on 26 May, and was promoted to major on 7 June 1776. Commissioned colonel of a Pennsylvania state regiment (militia) on 17 June 1777, he left Gates and assumed command on 6 July to take part in Washington's Philadelphia campaign. His green regiment distinguished itself at Brandywine, where as part of Weedon's brigade (with Edward Stevens's Tenth Virginia) it held a defile near Dilworth until the main army could make good its retreat. In the action at Germantown he fought on Washington's left wing. The next month, on 12 November 1777, his regiment joined the Continental army as the Thirteenth Pennsylvania. This unit was not with the army in the Valley Forge winter quarters but was part of Lee's command in the Battle of Monmouth on 28 June 1778. Bringing up the rear of the retreat with

Nathaniel Ramsey's Third Maryland, it was halted by Washington, faced about, and used as a delaying force until the main battle position was organized. On 1 July the regiment was merged with the Second Pennsylvania under Stewart's command.

Colonel Stewart has been described by Freeman as "an officer of fine presence and persuasive manner" (Freeman, vol. 5, p. 165). He was regarded as one of the handsomest men in the American army. The young colonel also appears to have been an outstanding mediator: he intervened to make peace between Gates and Wilkinson (in connection with the Conway Cabal) in February 1778; stepped in to help dissolve the mutiny of the Connecticut Line on 25 May 1780; and had a prominent part in helping Wayne settle the mutiny of the Pennsylvania Line on 1–10 January 1781. He marched south under Wayne to take part in Lafayette's operations against Cornwallis and was engaged at Green Spring, Virginia, on 6 July 1781. He served under Wayne in Steuben's division during the Yorktown campaign. Stewart retired on 1 January 1783 and went to Philadelphia. At the insistence of Washington, he was recalled as inspector general of the Northern Department. He agitated the discontent that led to the Newburgh Addresses. Breveted brigadier general on 30 September 1783, he became a prominent merchant in Philadelphia and major general of militia.

SEE ALSO *Green Spring (Jamestown Ford, Virginia); Mutiny of the Connecticut Line; Mutiny of the Pennsylvania Line; Newburgh Addresses; Virginia, Military Operations in; Virginia, Military Operations in; Yorktown Campaign.*

BIBLIOGRAPHY

Freeman, Douglas Southall. *George Washington.* Vols 4–5. New York: Scribner, 1951–1952.

Stillé, Charles J. *Major General Anthony Wayne and the Pennsylvania Line in the Continental Army.* Port Washington, N.Y.: Kennikat Press, 1968.

Trussell, John B. B. *The Pennsylvania Line: Regimental Organization and Operations, 1776–1783.* Harrisburg, Pa.: Pennsylvania Historical and Museum Commission, 1977.

Wildes, Harry E. *Anthony Wayne: Troubleshooter of the American Revolution.* Westport, Conn.: Greenwood Press, 1990.

revised by Harry M. Ward

STILES, EZRA. (1727–1795). Clergyman, scholar, and president of Yale College. Born in North Haven, Connecticut, Stiles was graduated from Yale College in 1746. Although he studied theology and was licensed to preach on 30 May 1749, he remained at Yale as an instructor (called tutor). He delayed entering actively into the ministry until 1755 when he was ordained as pastor of the Second Congregational Church at Newport, Rhode Island, where he remained for twenty-two years. A man of omnivorous curiosity, he accumulated information and correspondents in enormous quantities. Among other activities, he kept a meteorological notebook (taking temperature readings with a thermometer given him by Benjamin Franklin), experimented with the growing of silk worms (to provide a luxury commodity with which to redress the balance of payments deficits with Britain), accumulated population statistics, studied Hebrew and the Kabala, and closely followed the development of and resistance to British imperial policy in the 1760s and 1770s, all while ministering to an active congregation. His "Stamp Act Notebook" is an important source of information about colonial resistance to that measure. He corresponded with a host of luminaries in the colonies and across the Atlantic, and became so well known that the University of Edinburgh awarded him an honorary doctorate in 1765. Driven out of his ministry by the British occupation of Newport in December 1776, he and his family became refugees in Tiverton, Rhode Island. In the spring of 1778 he accepted the presidency of Yale College, an office he discharged with great devotion and ability during a particularly difficult period. College administrator, intellectual, and minister, the physically delicate Stiles showed tremendous energy and ability in a great variety of pursuits. He died at 68 of "bilious fever."

SEE ALSO *Franklin, Benjamin.*

BIBLIOGRAPHY

Dexter, Franklin B., ed. *The Literary Diary of Ezra Stiles.* 3 vols. New York: Scribners Sons, 1901.

Morgan, Edmund S. *The Gentle Puritan: A Life of Ezra Styles, 1727–1795.* New York: Norton, 1984.

Selesky, Harold E., ed. The Stiles papers (microfilm, with guide). Yale University, New Haven, Connecticut.

Stiles, Ezra. *Extracts from the Itineraries and Other Miscellanies.* New Haven, Conn.: Yale University Press, 1916.

revised by Harold E. Selesky

STILLWATER, NEW YORK. On the west bank of the Hudson, about eleven miles below Saratoga, this was the place to which General Phillip Schuyler withdrew his army before Burgoyne's offensive on 3 August 1777. He then retreated a further twelve miles south, to the mouth of the Mohawk River. After General Horatio Gates relieved Schuyler as commander of the Northern army on 19 August, Gates moved back to Stillwater on

8 September. Four days later the Northern army moved three miles north to occupy defensive positions at Bemis Heights. The decisive battles that then took place in this area on 19 September and 7 October are known variously by the names of Stillwater, Bemis Heights, Freeman's Farm, and Saratoga. Purely for the purpose of grouping the descriptions and maps of these actions, they are referred to here as the First and Second Battles of Saratoga.

SEE ALSO *Saratoga, First Battle of; Saratoga, Second Battle of.*

revised by Michael Bellesiles

STIRLING, LORD SEE *Alexander, William.*

STOCKTON, RICHARD. (1730–1781). Signer, lawyer. New Jersey. Born in Princeton, New Jersey, on 1 October 1730, Stockton graduated from the College of New Jersey at Newark in 1748, was admitted to the bar in 1754, and within ten years was recognized as one of the most eloquent lawyers in the middle colonies. Among the prominent lawyers he trained were Elias Boudinot and Joseph Reed. In 1766 he went as a trustee of his alma mater to Scotland to offer its presidency to John Witherspoon.

While in Britain, Stockton was received by the king and by Lord Rockingham (Charles Watson-Wentworth), and he was given the freedom of the city of Edinburgh. Returning to America in 1767, he entered politics, and the next year was named to the provincial council. He originally advocated conciliation with Great Britain, but opposed their taxing powers, even when Governor William Franklin appointed him to the New Jersey Supreme Court in 1774. Late in 1774 he sent Lord Dartmouth (William Legge) a plan for settlement on the basis of continued allegiance to the crown but freedom from parliamentary control. Sent to the Continental Congress, he took his seat on 1 July 1776, voting for independence on the following day and signing the Declaration of Independence On 30 August he tied with William Livingston for Governor of New Jersey and the next day, after the latter was chosen for the office by a single vote, Stockton declined the post of chief justice to remain in Congress. After serving on many important committees, on 26 September he and George Clymer were appointed to inspect the Northern army, which was then reorganizing after failure of the Canada invasion. Returning home as the British invaded New Jersey, he evacuated his family safely to the home of a friend in Monmouth County, but there he was betrayed by a Loyalist and captured on 30 November

1776. Taken first to Perth Amboy and then imprisoned in the infamous provost jail in New York City, he was subjected to cruel treatment that broke his spirit and led him to sign the amnesty proclamation declaring his loyalty to the king, making him the only signer of the Declaration of Independence to renounce his vote. Meanwhile, his home had been pillaged and his library burned. On 3 January 1777 Congress formally protested to the British and made efforts to secure his exchange. When he finally was liberated Stockton's health was shattered, his home, "Morven," was destroyed, and he found himself shunned by former friends. He died on 28 February 1781 after a long bout with cancer.

SEE ALSO *Witherspoon, John.*

BIBLIOGRAPHY

Bill, Alfred H. *A House Called Morven: Its Role in American History, 1701–1954.* Princeton, N.J.: Princeton University Press, 1954.

revised by Michael Bellesiles

STONE, THOMAS. (1743–1787). Signer. Maryland. Born in Charles County, Maryland, 1743, Stone studied law with Thomas Johnson in Annapolis, was admitted to the bar in 1764, and four years later married the wealthy Margaret Brown. In 1771 he bought land near Port Tobacco, Charles County, and established a successful legal practice. In 1774, Stone was one of the sheriff's lawyers who prosecuted Thomas Johnson, Samuel Chase, and William Paca for contesting the legality of poll taxes for supporting the clergy. Although a conservative, Stone sided with the Patriots when the break came with England. He served in the Continental Congress from 13 May 1775 until October 1778, except for a portion of 1777, when he declined re-election. Fellow signers of the Declaration of Independence from Maryland were Chase and Paca, and Johnson also served in Congress with Stone.

Stone also served in the Maryland Convention of 1775–1776, and in the state senate from 1776 to 1791, becoming known mostly for his silence. He appears to have retained his moderate views toward war with England, and one of his few recorded speeches advocated coming to terms with Lord Richard Howe in September 1776. He resumed his seat in Congress on 26 March 1784. Toward the end of this session he was named president pro tempore, but he declined re-election to Congress and resumed his law practice. He was named to the federal Constitutional Convention in Philadelphia, but declined to serve on account of his wife's illness. She died in June 1787 Stone gave up his work and died of "melancholy" on 5 October 1787.

SEE ALSO *Chase, Samuel; Paca, William.*

BIBLIOGRAPHY
Vivian, Jean H. "Thomas Stone and the Reorganization of the Maryland Council of Safety, 1776." *Maryland History Magazine* 69 (1974): 271–278.

revised by Michael Bellesiles

STONE ARABIA, NEW YORK. A

Mohawk Valley settlement burned on 19 October 1780 in Tory raid.

SEE ALSO *Fort Keyser, New York.*

Mark M. Boatner

STONO FERRY, SOUTH CAROLINA.

20 June 1779. General Augustine Prevost withdrew from Charleston, 11–12 May, and headed toward Savannah. When he reached Johns Island he left Lieutenant Colonel John Maitland in command of a 900-man rear guard to cover Stono Ferry, which connected Johns Island with the mainland. Maitland hastily built three redoubts and an abatis on the mainland side of the ferry to cover the position. On his left he placed his German troops with the North and South Carolina Loyalists holding the redoubts to the left and the center under Lieutenant Colonel John Hamilton, while the right consisted of his Seventy-first Highlands Regiment commanded by Major Duncan McPherson. He had six artillery pieces.

General Benjamin Lincoln had about 6,500 troops in Charleston and decided to attack this isolated British outpost with a force of 1,200. He personally led the main effort, which crossed the Ashley River about midnight and undertook an eight-mile approach march to hit the enemy position on James Island around dawn. General William Moultrie was supposed to support this operation by a secondary attack against Johns Island to keep Maitland from moving reinforcements across Stono Inlet to the bridgehead, but he failed to cross the river. Lincoln's main body was organized into a right wing of South and North Carolina militia troops under General Jethro Sumner with two cannon and General Casimir Pulaski's Legion, a left wing of Continental troops and four cannon under General Isaac Huger, a Virginia militia force with two cannon under Colonel David Mason in reserve, light

infantry companies covering each flank (Lieutenant Colonel Francis Malmedy on the right and Lieutenant Colonel John Henderson on the left), and a rear guard of Lieutenant Colonel David Horry's South Carolina cavalry.

Henderson's flank patrol made contact first. Maitland thought these forces were just more of the skirmishers who had harassed his line for the past two days and sent two companies of Highlanders to drive them away. Henderson ordered a bayonet charge that killed or wounded nearly half their number and drove them back into their defenses. The rebels advanced to within sixty yards of the abatis on the right when the British opened fire. Disobeying orders to press forward with their bayonets, the Patriots began exchanging fire with the British. On the British right, the Germans broke before a fierce assault and fled. Maitland shifted part of the Seventy-first to stop the advancing rebels and rallied the Germans to return to the fight. Maitland then started bringing reserves over from Johns Island; Lincoln ordered a retreat, which was effectively covered by his cavalry and the Virginia militia.

American losses in this poorly conceived operation were heavy: 146 killed or wounded (including 24 officers) and 155 missing. Most of the latter were deserters, since the British apparently took no prisoners. The British lost 26 killed, 103 wounded, and 1 missing.

The only thing Lincoln achieved by his attack was to speed up the course of action already agreed on by the British commander. Prevost returned with the main body of troops to Savannah while Maitland abandoned his bridgehead on 23 June and retreated to Beaufort (Port Royal Island), where he established a defensive position.

SEE ALSO *Charleston Raid of Prevost; Lincoln, Benjamin; Maitland, John; Prevost, Augustine.*

revised by Michael Bellesiles

STONY POINT, NEW YORK. 16 July

1779. Anthony Wayne's coup de main. After a quiet winter and spring, on 28 May 1779 a large British expedition started north from Kings Bridge in four columns supported by vessels in the Hudson River. General Clinton's objective was to cut the primary route used by the Americans to move provisions from New England to West Point and its supporting forts, forcing the supplies to take a lengthy detour. The lines of communications crossed the Hudson River at Kings Ferry, the southern entrance to the Hudson Highlands, about fifteen miles below West Point. Easily defended hills anchored both ends of the ferry: Stony Point on the west and Verplanck's Point on the east. The former was lightly held, but Fort

Lafayette stood on Verplanck's. The next day an expedition returning from a raid on Virginia sailed up the river to cooperate. Some of the British landed on 30 May and started working overland; the rest stayed on the transports and landed farther north the next day. Stony Point was taken without a shot on the afternoon of 31 May when its forty-man garrison withdrew to avoid being cut off. The British immediately landed some heavy artillery, including a ten-inch mortar and an eight-inch howitzer, and moved the pieces to the top from which they opened fire on Verplanck's. The seventy-five North Carolina troops holding Fort Lafayette were trapped; surrender was their only option.

Since 1778 Washington had considered the West Point complex to be the "key to the Continent" and maneuvered his field forces both to support the garrison there and to use the Highlands complex as a strategic pivot. When Clinton set out, most of Washington's brigades shifted north. The primary road from New Jersey to West Point ran through a valley known as Smith's Clove; Washington initially put his headquarters at the southern end by Smith's Tavern, although he later shifted to a safer position at New Windsor. Within a few days the Americans could see that Clinton did not intend to advance up the Hudson but only to build more formidable defenses to hold the ferry.

During June the Americans kept a close watch on the British progress. On 15 June Washington told Major Henry Lee to gather information about the Stony Point position and on 2 July Lee sent Captain Allen McLane into the works disguised as a local farmer. On 28 June Washington directed Brigadier General Anthony Wayne to study the possibilities of retaking Kings Ferry with his newly assembled light infantry corps. Washington personally reconnoitered Stony Point with Wayne on 6 July, covered by Lee's light dragoons and McLane's attached infantry company, and Wayne briefed him on a plan for a surprise night attack. Based largely on McLane's information that the works were incomplete, Washington approved. To keep the plan simple the Americans would not make a simultaneous attack on Verplanck's Point but instead would move troops into a position to do so if the more dominant Stony Point fell.

The Hudson at the ferry is only a half-mile wide and is actually an estuary subject to the tides. Just south of the ferry landing, a sharp hill rose 150 feet above the water. Marshes surrounded the north, west, and south sides of the hill, and the river covered the east. Two separate lines of abatis further obstructed the slopes, the first at the base of the hill, the second about 200 yards away protecting the crest. A semi-enclosed fort at the crest contained the bulk of the garrison, with three nearby batteries dominating the river. Trees had been cleared in front of the forward abatis, and some outworks covered the most likely avenue

of approach where the ferry road crossed a causeway. Lieutenant Colonel Henry Johnson held the position with the battalion companies of his Seventeenth Foot, the two grenadier companies of the Seventy-first Foot (Highlanders), a 60-man detachment of the Loyal Americans, a composite 51-man detachment of the Royal Artillery, and 15 guns; total strength was about 625.

Wayne's recently assembled light infantry corps consisted of the light companies detached from their parent regiments and now formed a large 1,200-man brigade. Colonel Christian Febiger (a Dane) commanded the First Regiment drawn from Virginia and Pennsylvania units, assisted by Lieutenant Colonel François Louis de Fleury and Major Thomas Posey. Colonel Richard Butler's Second Regiment with companies from Delaware, Maryland, and Pennsylvania had Lieutentenant Colonel Samuel Hay and Major John Stewart as battalion commanders. The Third Regiment, all Connecticut men, was commanded by Colonel Return Meigs, Lieutenant Colonel Isaac Sherman and Captain Henry Champion. The Fourth Regiment had not completely formed yet but contained Massachusetts troops under Major William Hull and North Carolinians under Major Hardy Murfree. Captains James Pendleton and Thomas Barr accompanied the expedition with twenty-four gunners and two small pieces, but did not take part in the attack. Supporting troops in reserve included Lee's contingent and three hundred infantry under Brigadier General John Peter Muhlenberg.

About noon on 15 July the American light infantry and the two guns started a fifteen-mile approach march from their camp near Fort Montgomery. They swung inland to avoid detection, at one point taking a trail so primitive the men had to move single file. Around 8 P.M. they reached the final assembly area a mile and a half west of Stony Point at a place called Springsteel's and ate dinner. Because surprise was essential, Wayne prescribed strict security measures: Lee cleared civilians and dogs from the line of march and kept Johnson's positions under observation; only a few officers knew the objective; and guards surrounded the final assembly area to prevent a last-minute deserter from alerting the British. Wayne also issued orders forbidding the men (except a designated covering force under Murfree) from loading their muskets; attacking with just fixed bayonets would ensure that an accidental discharge could not give warning.

A dark night and high tide favored the attackers as they started forward about 11:30 P.M. Wayne planned to penetrate the enemy's defenses at two points, one column hitting on the north, near the ferry landing, and the other to the south, where the defenses were closest to the main enemy works. Each of the two assault columns had the same arrangement. In the lead came a 20-man "forlorn

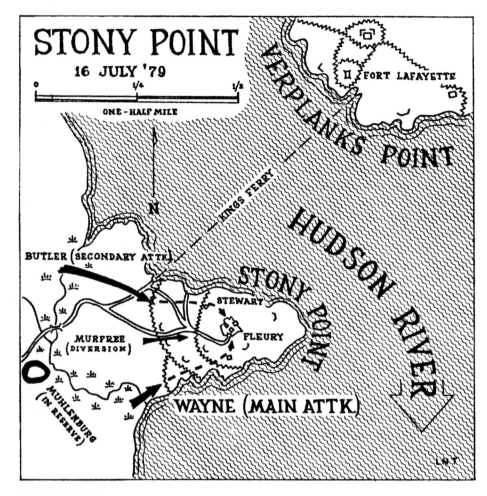

STONY POINT
16 JULY '79

ONE - HALF MILE

N

VERPLANKS POINT

FORT LAFAYETTE

KINGS FERRY

HUDSON RIVER

STONY POINT

BUTLER (SECONDARY ATTK.)

STEWART

FLEURY

MURFREE (DIVERSION)

MUHLENBURG (IN RESERVE)

WAYNE (MAIN ATTK.)

THE GALE GROUP

hope" to hack through the abatis; then an advance party of 150 men under selected officers followed to immediately exploit the breakthrough; and finally the third element was the main body to keep up the momentum of the attack and push on to the objective. The third force in Wayne's plan was Major Murfree's covering party, who would open fire on the British center by the causeway at the start of the attack as a diversion with Lee in support; his men were the only ones authorized to fire during the operation.

Wayne personally led the larger south column since it would make the main effort. It waded through marsh and along the bank of the river on the downstream side and turned ashore after passing the first line of abatis. Fleury's advance party estimated that they waded through water four feet deep, while Meigs led the main body. Butler's left column used a similar technique but entered the water well north of the causeway and also bypassed the first line of defense.

Schematically, the attack formation was as follows in table 1.

Shortly after midnight the two attack columns made contact, almost simultaneously, and the British sentries opened fire. The light infantry pressed forward without shooting back. The forlorn hopes chopped and clawed through a few minor obstacles and rushed for the second abatis with the advance parties on their heels. Murfree started his demonstration in the center and immediately succeeded in achieving his mission. Johnson charged down the hill with half his garrison—six companies of the Seventeenth—to repel the attack he thought was coming over the causeway.

Although most of the British firing was directed at shadows, the musketry began to take a toll of those at the front. Wayne went down briefly when a ball grazed his head but revived and maintained command. Four other officers from Meigs's regiment of the main column were hit. Fleury caught up with Lieutenant George Knox's forlorn hope and became the first man to enter the works, with Knox a close second and three sergeants following in order: Baker and Spencer from Virginia and

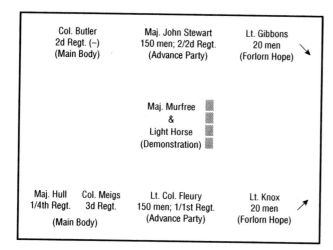

Col. Butler 2d Regt. (–) (Main Body)	Maj. John Stewart 150 men; 2/2d Regt. (Advance Party)	Lt. Gibbons 20 men (Forlorn Hope)
	Maj. Murfree & Light Horse (Demonstration)	
Maj. Hull Col. Meigs 1/4th Regt. 3d Regt. (Main Body)	Lt. Col. Fleury 150 men; 1/1st Regt. (Advance Party)	Lt. Knox 20 men (Forlorn Hope)

Table 1. *American Attack Formation at Stony Point.*
THE GALE GROUP

Donlop from Pennsylvania. This sequence is a matter of exact record because cash prizes of $500 to $100 had been announced for the first five to enter the works. Fleury personally pulled down the British flag.

The left column had farther to go, and also took casualties on the final approach, including wounds to Febiger and Hay. Lieutenant James Gibbons spearheaded their attack and took seventeen casualties out of his twenty men, but Major Stewart was right behind him with the advance party. In company with Colonel Butler the left column reached the fort only a few minutes after the right.

When Johnson heard the sounds of the battle he tried to move back up to the fort but was cut off and captured by Febiger's regiment. Posey's battalion overwhelmed the other two companies of the Seventeenth Foot in the fort, and Meigs's regiment captured the Loyalist detachment on the east side of the hill. Thirty minutes after the columns crossed the beach, the fight was over, and without any of the British being killed while attempting to surrender. A British officer, Commodore George Collier, entered this comment in his journal:

> The rebels had made the attack with a bravery they never before exhibited, and they showed at this moment a generosity and clemency which during the course of the rebellion had no parallel. There was light sufficient after getting up the heights to show them many of the British troops with arms in their hands; instead of putting them to death, they called to them 'to throw their arms down if they expected any quarter. (Quoted in Johnston, *The Storming of Stony Point*, p. 135.)

NUMBERS AND LOSSES

Wayne lost 15 killed and 84 wounded out of a total force engaged that probably amounted to 1,350. Johnson's official after-action report listed 22 killed, 74 wounded, and 472 captured; he also reported 58 missing, and only one of them is known to have actually escaped to safety. So an accurate estimate of total British casualties would be 626.

The Americans also captured a significant amount of equipment, stores and ammunition, and the fifteen guns the British had emplaced. Washington sent vessels down from West Point to take the items away, but British warships damaged the galley *Lady Washington,* which had the brass artillery on board. Her crew ran the vessel ashore and burned her.

SEQUEL

The attack on Stony Point alerted Verplanck's Point, and Clinton reacted swiftly to reinforce Fort Lafayette. Guns on Stony Point were at least 1,500 yards from the east bank, too far for bombardment to have any effect. British warships prevented any kind of attack from the river and made it impossible for troops to cross from the west bank without going far upriver first. And the terrain at Verplanck's worked in Clinton's favor.

Washington wisely decided the defense of Stony Point would require more men than it was worth, so he ordered the works destroyed, and on 18 July Wayne's troops were withdrawn. Clinton reoccupied the place the next day; he then established a stronger garrison and rebuilt the defenses—only to abandon Kings Ferry altogether in the fall. He realized that if the river froze it would prevent supply or reinforcement.

For this brilliant exploit Congress voted its thanks to Wayne and a gold medal. Fleury and Stewart were voted silver medals; Lieutenants Gibbons and Knox got brevet promotions.

SIGNIFICANCE

The operation had little strategic value, but it was a morale builder for the American army and people; it had the opposite effect on the British, but to a lesser degree. For Clinton the attack's immediate impact stemmed from the loss of the Seventeenth Foot and the grenadier companies of the Seventy-First as combat elements for the rest of the war. Stony Point's greatest impact came in its validation of the level of tactical training instituted by Washington and "Baron" Friedrich Steuben's "Blue Book." The first copies of the manual reached the Highlands in time for the light infantry to use them in their final preparations.

S E E A L S O *Hudson River and the Highlands; McLane, Allan.*

BIBLIOGRAPHY

Johnston, Henry P. *The Storming of Stony Point on the Hudson, Midnight, July 15, 1779: Its Importance in the Light of Unpublished Documents.* New York: James T. White, 1900.

Anthony Wayne at Stony Point. *General Wayne leads American troops into battle in July 1779 at Stony Point near the Hudson River in New York. Although the operation at Stony Point had little strategic value, it was a morale builder for the American army.*
© BETTMANN/CORBIS

Palmer, Dave Richard. *The River and the Rock: The History of Fortress West Point, 1775–1783.* New York: Greenwood, 1969.

Sklarsky, I. W. *The Revolution's Boldest Venture: The Story of "Mad Anthony" Wayne's Assault on Stony Point.* Port Washington, N.Y.: Kennikat Press, 1965.

Stillé, Charles J. *Major-General Anthony Wayne and the Pennsylvania Line in the Continental Army.* Philadelphia: Lippincott, 1893.

revised by Robert K. Wright Jr.

STORMONT, DAVID MURRAY, SEVENTH VISCOUNT. (1727–1796).

British ambassador to Versailles, 1772 to March 1778. Through an efficient net of informers, Stormont's task was to monitor secret French aid to the American rebels, while postponing open war for as long as possible. He made frequent protests against such aid and against the use of French posts by American privateers. As secretary of state for the Northern Department (October 1779–March 1782) and virtually foreign minister, he competently directed Britain's European affairs until the end of the war.

SEE ALSO *French Covert Aid.*

revised by John Oliphant

STRATEGIC ENVELOPMENT. A turning movement.

SEE ALSO *Turning Movement.*

STUART, SIR CHARLES. (1753–1810).

British officer. Born in London in January 1753, Stuart was the son of the future prime minister, the earl of Bute. The younger Stuart became an ensign in 1768, purchasing the rank of lieutenant of the Seventh Regiment in 1770 and of captain of the Thirty-seventh Regiment in 1773.

Sent to America with his regiment in 1775, Stuart saw action at Bunker Hill that year and then in Howe's New York campaign of 1776, during which he was elected to Parliament for Bossiney. He earned promotion to lieutenant colonel of the Twenty-sixth Regiment in 1777. Critical of the conduct of the war, Stuart left America in 1779. His opposition to the policies of George Germain prevented his gaining a command outside of America, while King George's hostility to Stuart's father, the king's one-time mentor but now a loathed reminder of past failures, frustrated his efforts to become a diplomat. The war with France revived his military career as he was given command of the army in Corsica, where he won praise for his bravery at the Battle of Calvi. In 1797 he commanded British forces in Portugal. The following year his brilliantly executed capture of Minorca led to his being made a knight of the Bath and governor of Minorca. His inability to get along with his superiors led to his resignation in April 1800 with the rank of lieutenant general. He died at his home in Surrey on 25 March 1801.

BIBLIOGRAPHY

Wortley, Violet S., ed. *A Prime Minister and His Son: From the Correspondence of the 3rd Earl of Bute and of Lt-General the Hon. Sir Charles Stuart.* London: J. Murray, 1925.

Michael Bellesiles

STUART, JOHN. (1718–1779).

British superintendent of Indian affairs. The son of a merchant and magistrate, John Stuart was born in Inverness on 25 September 1718. Educated at Inverness grammar school, at the age of seventeen he took a position in a London mercantile business that traded with Spain. His business was interrupted by the War of Jenkins's Ear (1739), which in 1740 merged into the War of Austrian Succession. Stuart then circumnavigated the globe with Commodore George Anson's expedition to the Pacific, serving as clerk, purser and midshipman. In 1748 Stuart emigrated to Charleston, South Carolina, where he married, had two children, failed in an initial mercantile venture, and gradually established himself as a prominent citizen. It may have been in this period that he first came into contact with the Cherokees and other Native American nations of the hinterland.

During the early part of the Seven Years War, while serving at Fort Loudoun in the Overhill country of what is now Tennessee, Stuart established himself as a trusted friend of the Cherokees. In 1759, when that fort was starved into surrender and some of the garrison was massacred, Stuart not only survived but was allowed to escape from captivity. Stuart disliked the genocidal blood-

lust that gripped Charleston during the Anglo-Cherokee War that followed, and supported his fellow Scot, Lieutenant Colonel James Grant, when he ended the conflict on terms far more generous than those demanded by South Carolina. Stuart's conviction that only a strong imperial authority could impose a stable and just frontier settlement probably dates from this period. So too, do the beginnings of a fracture in South Carolina between those who supported Grant and Stuart and the many who resented imperial interference in the colony's affairs.

In 1762 Stuart succeeded the deceased Edmund Atkin as superintendent of Indian affairs for the southern department. Lord Egremont (Charles Windham), the new secretary of state, was already mapping out an imperial plan for frontier management, including a fixed boundary line between white and Indian territories and a closely regulated Indian trade. His scheme was given official form in the Proclamation of 1763, which prohibited colonial expansion beyond the frontier, and gave Stuart a degree of autonomy of which his counterpart in the northern department, Sir William Johnson, could only dream (Johnson's efforts were frequently frustrated by the clumsy intervention of Jeffery Amherst, the British commander in chief in North America and technically his superior. At the Congress of Augusta in November 1763, Stuart was able to promise the suspicious Indian nations of the southern department security for their lands and an adequate trade, He also distributed presents—paid for by Egremont—on an unprecedented scale. He followed this up with a series of smaller local conferences which gradually established the line of the fixed boundary. Thereafter he urged the imperial government to take direct control of the frontier areas, forbidding private land sales and closely regulating traders. He received limited support until the very eve of war; but because his policy ran counter to aggressive powerful economic and expansionist interests, by early 1775 opinion in the south was polarised over frontier issues. Men like Henry Laurens, who had supported Grant and Stuart in 1761, were now revolutionaries.

In 1775 he was very quick to move against his American rivals for influence in the Indian nations, exploiting the fact that British control of the seas and the Floridas allowed him to promise more and better trade goods than the rebels could provide. Moreover, in time of war he could compensate friendly warriors far more generously with presents—a crucial point for peoples who stood to lose not only their winter hunting but their crops and homes as well. Forced to flee from Charleston in September 1775, when the royal government collapsed, he moved first to Georgia, then to St. Augustine in June 1776, and later to Pensacola, which became his permanent base of operations. Fearing that indiscriminate attacks would only alienate potential Loyalists, Stuart responded cautiously to General Thomas Gage's orders to encourage the Indian nations to take up arms, though carefully concerted operations against specific targets would be another matter. He did not always succeed in restraining his Native American protégés, and their operations against the colonies were not always successful—the Cherokee war of 1776 being a key example. However, with generous backing from London, and his own high personal standing among them, Stuart managed to keep the vast majority of southern Indians friendly or neutral. In February 1778 he sent emissaries to obtain Cherokee and Seminole support for the coming attacks on Georgia, and in March he sent small mixed forces to the lower Mississippi. The work he had done lived on long after his death in Pensacola on 21 March 1779.

Stuart has been accused of being an extremist and, by neglecting the Americans' perspectives and interests, of pushing otherwise well-disposed colonists into the arms of revolution. On the other hand, Stuart like most southern Indians, understood that the aims of colonial assemblies, frontier traders, and rogue settlers were incompatible with those of the Indians, and therefore with a stable frontier. The only alternative was tough imperial control, and there is something to be said for Stuart's complaint that there was not enough of it at a sufficiently early stage. Whether the eighteenth century British empire was capable of exerting such authority is another question.

SEE ALSO *Cherokee; French and Indian War; Southern Theater, Military Operations in.*

BIBLIOGRAPHY

Alden, J. R. *John Stuart and the Southern Colonial Frontier: A Study of Indian Relations, War, Trade, and Land Problems in the Southern Wilderness, 1754–1775.* Ann Arbor: University of Michigan Press, 1944.

Braund, K. E. H. *Deerskins and Duffels: Creek Indian Trade with Anglo-America, 1685–1815.* Lincoln: University of Nebraska Press, 1993.

Hatley, Tom. *The Dividing Paths: Cherokees and South Carolinians through the Era of Revolution.* New York: Oxford University Press, 1993.

Oliphant, John. *Peace and War on the Anglo-Cherokee Frontier, 1756–1763.* Basingstoke, U.K.: Palgrave, 2001.

Snapp, J. Russell. *John Stuart and the Struggle for the Southern Colonial Frontier.* Baton Rouge, La. and London: Louisiana State University Press, 1996.

Van Doren, Carl. *Secret History of the American Revolution: An Account of the Conspiracies of Benedict Arnold and Numerous Others.* New York: Viking, 1941.

revised by John Oliphant

SUFFOLK RESOLVES.

9–17 September 1774. Delegates from towns across Massachusetts met in county conventions in early September 1774 to coordinate their opposition to the Intolerable Acts. The Suffolk county convention adopted a set of resolves on 9 September, drafted by Joseph Warren, that summarized the state of the imperial relationship as seen from Massachusetts. While acknowledging George III as king "agreeable to compact," the resolves rejected the Intolerable Acts as "gross infractions of those rights to which we are justly entitled by the laws of nature, the British constitution, and the charter of this province" and denounced them "as the attempts of a wicked administration to enslave America" (Knollenberg, p. 312). They recommended a stoppage of trade with Britain and the withholding of taxes from the Crown until the acts were repealed, and urged the citizens of Massachusetts to "use their utmost diligence to acquaint themselves with the art of war as soon as possible" (Knollenberg, pp. 312–313).

A copy of the resolves was rushed by Paul Revere to the Massachusetts delegates attending the first Continental Congress at Philadelphia. Revere arrived on 16 September, and the next day the Massachusetts delegates presented the resolves to Congress for approval. While more conservative delegates from other colonies had no sympathy for the acts, they were initially reluctant to endorse such militant resolves. But, not wanting to seem to question the need to resist the acts, they finally voted with their colleagues to endorse the resolves. The vote gave important support to the radicals in Massachusetts and made reconciliation with the imperial government even more difficult to achieve.

SEE ALSO *Continental Congress; Intolerable (or Coercive) Acts; Warren, Joseph.*

BIBLIOGRAPHY

Jensen, Merrill, ed. *English Historical Documents.* Volume IX: *American Colonial Documents to 1776.* David C. Douglas, general editor. New York: Oxford University Press, 1955.

Knollenberg, Bernard. *Growth of the American Revolution, 1766–1775.* Indianapolis, Ind.: Liberty Fund, 2002.

revised by Harold E. Selesky

SUFFREN DE SAINT TROPEZ, PIERRE ANDRÉ DE.

(1729–1788). French admiral. Born to a noble family in Provence, he entered the Naval Guards in October 1743 and served the next year off Toulon on the *Solide,* on which he participated in the Battle of Cape Sicié in February 1744. Next he served in the West Indies and in 1746 took part in the expedition of D'Anville in Acadia. The following year he was captured by the British in the Bay of Biscay. He was promoted to ship's ensign in 1748 and participated in galley duty from 1749 to 1751. He was promoted to ship's lieutenant in 1756, commanded the *Singe* in Duchaffault's squadron in the Larache affair in 1765, became a frigate captain in 1767, and *capitaine de vaisseau* in 1772. He became commander of the *Fantasque* in 1777.

When France declared war on England, Suffren served as commander of the same vessel under Estaing in 1778–1779. On 5 August 1778 he distinguished himself at Newport, where he forced entry into the harbor and hastened the torching of five English vessels. In action against Admiral Byron off Grenada, he held the line despite the loss of sixty-two men aboard his ship. He strongly disapproved of the restrained tactics of Estaing and made this known in official communications to his admiral. The latter nevertheless recommended that Suffren be given command of the *Héros* and a division of five vessels that the French planned to send to help the Dutch defend their Cape of Good Hope colony against an expected British attack. On 22 March 1781 Suffren sailed from Brest with Grasse to the Azores and went on toward southern Africa. On 16 April he successfully attacked the English expedition under Admiral Johnstone upon finding it anchored off the Cape Verde Islands, technically in the neutral waters of Portugal. After saving the Cape Colony from capture, Suffren continued on to India where, in a series of four savage actions at Sadras, Provedien, Negapatam, and Trincomalé, he fought Sir Edward Hughes to a standstill. He was promoted to lieutenant general in February 1783, returned to Toulon in March 1784, and was promoted to vice admiral in April. As Anglo-French tensions were increasing in 1787, he was given command of the squadron at Brest. He died suddenly at Paris in December 1788.

SEE ALSO *Estaing, Charles Hector Théodat, Comte d'; Newport, Rhode Island (29 July–31 August 1778).*

BIBLIOGRAPHY

Cavaliero, Roderick. *Admiral Satan: The Life and Campaigns of Suffren.* London: I. B. Tauris Publishers, 1994.

Mackesy, Piers. *The War for America, 1775–1783.* Cambridge, Mass.: Harvard University Press, 1965.

Moran, Charles. "Suffren, the Apostle of Action." *United States Naval Institute Proceedings* 64 (1938): 313–325.

Taillemite, Etienne. *Dictionnaire des Marins Français.* Paris: Editions Maritimes et d'Outre-Mer, 1982.

revised by Robert Rhodes Crout

SUGAR ACT.

The Revenue Act of 1764, usually known as the Sugar Act, had two purposes. First, it was intended to raise money from trade to and between the British colonies in America. It levied import duties on a list of enumerated commodities (including sugar, indigo, coffee, wine, and various cloths) and made the Molasses Act of 1733 perpetual, although it cut the duty on molasses in half, from six pence to three pence per gallon, to make evasion of the tax less attractive. Monies raised in America were reserved "to be from time to time disposed of by Parliament towards defraying the necessary expenses of defending, protecting, and securing the British colonies and plantations in America" (section 11). Second, it revamped and reinvigorated the customs service charged with the collection of these import duties. Two provisions attracted the most colonial opposition. By the terms of the first, legal cases in which the validity of seizures of ships and goods were determined could now be adjudicated in a new vice-admiralty court in Halifax, Nova Scotia, instead of in local colonial courts that were more susceptible to popular pressure. By virtue of the second, customs officials were relieved of liability for unlawful seizures if "the judge or court indicates there was probable cause for seizure" (section 46).

SEE ALSO *Grenville Acts; Vice-Admiralty Courts.*

BIBLIOGRAPHY

Jensen, Merrill, ed. *English Historical Documents.* Vol. 9: *American Colonial Documents to 1776.* New York: Oxford University Press, 1955.

Thomas, Peter D. G. *British Politics and the Stamp Act Crisis: The First Phase of the American Revolution, 1763–1767.* Oxford: Oxford University Press, 1975.

revised by Harold E. Selesky

SULLIVAN, JOHN.

(1740–1795). Continental general. New Hampshire. Born of parents who had arrived about 1723 as redemptioners from Ireland, he became an "able, if somewhat litigious, lawyer" practicing in Durham, New Hampshire. In 1772 he was a major in his local New Hampshire militia unit and in September 1774 was seated in the Continental Congress. Home in December, he and John Langdon led a group of volunteers that captured Fort William and Mary at the entrance to Portsmouth harbor. He took his seat in the Second Continental Congress on 10 May 1775 and was appointed a Continental brigadier general on 22 June. During the Boston siege he commanded a brigade at Winter Hill, except for a period in October 1775 when he organized the defenses of Portsmouth. After the British evacuation of Boston he led a column of reinforcements to join the Canada invasion. Reaching St. Johns on 1 June 1776, he assumed command of the army when General John Thomas died the next day. Without adequate intelligence of enemy strength or position, Sullivan allowed Brigadier General William Thompson to join the force of Arthur St. Clair to attack a British force at Trois Riviéres. Thompson lost the element of surprise and, with most of his force, was taken prisoner. After the defeat at Trois Rivières on 8 June, Sullivan ordered the retreat up Lake Champlain.

NEW YORK

His army was at Crown Point when Gates superseded him in command. Sullivan left the theater of operations with threats of resignation and took his grievance to Congress. He was prevailed on to remain in service, reached New York City on 21 July, and was appointed major general on 9 August 1776. On 20 August he succeeded Greene as commander on Long Island, but four days later Washington put Israel Putnam in top command. Captured in the Battle of Long Island on 27 August, Sullivan went to Philadelphia with a message for Congress from British General William Howe that led to the fruitless peace conference of 11 September 1776. He was exchanged for General Richard Prescott about 25 September and was back at Washington's headquarters on the 27th. Given command of a division, he took part in the remaining phase of the New Yorkcampaign.

NEW JERSEY AND PENNSYLVANIA

At the start of the New Jersey campaign, Sullivan's division was on the Hudson as part of General Charles Lee's command. He succeeded Lee when the latter was captured and joined Washington west of the Delaware on 20 December with the remaining two thousand of the five thousand troops with which Lee had started. At Trenton he led the right column and rendered valuable service in the American victory. He commanded the main body in the advance on Princeton but contributed nothing significant to that success.

While the army was in winter quarters around Morristown during the first part of 1777, Sullivan commanded forces on outpost duty and was in the exposed position at Princeton when the British undertook the mystifying "June maneuvers" that started the Philadelphia campaign. He led an unsuccessful operation against Staten Island on 22 August and then hurried south in time to fight at Brandywine on 11 September. Meanwhile, he had made enemies in Congress by joining Greene and Knox in threatening to resign over the Tronson de Coudray affair, an action that politicians considered an attempt by generals to "dictate" to civil authority. In September 1777 a proposal was advanced in Congress to suspend him from command while an inquiry was made into his failure at Staten Island, and

John Sullivan. *The Continental general and governor of New Hampshire, in a mezzotint (1776) attributed to C. Corbutt.* THE LIBRARY OF CONGRESS

delegate Thomas Burke of North Carolina charged him with misconduct at Brandywine. Washington refused to relieve Sullivan, whom he regarded as one of his more valuable commanders, and Sullivan led a column at Germantown on 4 October. Meanwhile, he was cleared of charges in connection with the Staten Island expedition.

NEWPORT AND THE IROQUOIS

He spent the winter at Valley Forge. Sullivan may have been to some degree involved in the Conway Cabal. Freeman has said that Sullivan's "love of popularity had led him to seek the good will of parties to the controversy" (Freeman, vol. 4, p. 608). Early in 1778 he was named to succeed General Joseph Spencer as commander in Rhode Island, "not because of any special fitness for the post," according to Freeman, "but because the New Hampshire General happened to be more readily available than any other officer of appropriate rank" (*ibid.*, vol. 4, p. 613). He turned out to be singularly unqualified for what Freeman has called the "puzzling experiment in cooperation," the Franco-American operation against Newport on 29 July–31 August 1778.

Perhaps in testimony to his previously good record, not to mention his political connections in New England, Sullivan's military career survived the Newport affair. In March 1779 he left Providence and led a force of 2,300 from its gathering place of Easton, PA, on 31 July 1779 on a punitive expedition against the Six Nations. Following the Susquehanna River to Wyoming, then to Tioga, they reached Chemung on 11 August joining an army under General James Clinton on 22 August. Sullivan's expedition fought its largest battle at Newtown where most of the enemy retreated successfully to the west. The army continued its march, destroying villages and crops in its wake, going northwest to Genesee Castle before returning to Easton on about 12 October. Indian raids continued much as they had prior to the expedition leading historians, like the Continental Congress, to question the value of the expedition. His health impaired by this experience in the out-of-doors, he resigned from the army on 30 November 1779. The canny Irishman did not leave his last command without, however, securing a semipolitical endorsement of his Iroquois expedition from his officers.

LATER CAREER

Sullivan promptly secured reelection to Congress. He was chairman of the committee appointed on 3 January 1781 to represent Congress in settling the mutiny of the Pennsylvania Line. During this term in Congress his brother Daniel, who was fatally ill from his mistreatment on a British prison hulk, brought him a peace feeler from the enemy. Sullivan refused to have anything to do with the communication but referred it to La Luzerne, the French minister to the United States. Since Sullivan had borrowed money from the minister, post mortem charges were made that the general had been paid for this service. This accusation, however, has been completely discredited.

In 1782 Sullivan was a member of his state's constitutional convention, was elected attorney general, and was also elected as a member of the New Hampshire assembly; he was elected speaker of the assembly in the spring of 1785. In spring elections in 1786 he was elected President of the State and handled the paper money riots of that year firmly but coolly. Elected governor of New Hampshire in 1786, 1787, and 1789, he actively supported adoption of the federal Constitution. The last years of Sullivan's life were spent as a federal judge. He died on 23 January 1795. Sullivan's brother, James (1744–1808), was one of the most prominent lawyers in Massachusetts and a political figure of great power and wealth.

SEE ALSO *Brandywine, Pennsylvania; Canada Invasion; Conway Cabal; Germantown, Pennsylvania, Battle of; Long Island, New York, Battle of; Mutiny of the* *Pennsylvania Line; New Jersey Campaign; Newport, Rhode Island (29 July–31 August 1778); Peace Conference on Staten Island; Philadelphia Campaign; Princeton, New Jersey; Staten Island, New York; Sullivan's Expedition against the Iroquois; Trenton, New Jersey; Tronson du Coudray, Philippe Charles Jean Baptiste.*

BIBLIOGRAPHY

Amory, Thomas C. *The Military Services and Public Life of Major-General John Sullivan of the American Revolutionary Army.* 1968. Reprint, Port Washington, N.Y.: Kennikat Press, 1968.

Daniell, Jere R. *Experiment in Republicanism: New Hampshire Politics and the American Revolution, 1741–1794.* Cambridge, Mass.: Harvard University Press, 1970.

Fischer, Joseph. *A Well-Executed Failure: The Sullivan Campaign against the Iroquois, July–September 1779.* Columbia: University of South Carolina Press, 1997.

Freeman, Douglas Southall. *George Washington.* 7 vols. New York: Scribner, 1951–1952.

Sullivan, John. *Letters and Papers of Major-General John Sullivan, Continental Army.* 3 vols. Edited by Otis G. Hammond. Concord: New Hampshire Historical Society, 1930–1939.

Upton, Richard Francis. *Revolutionary New Hampshire.* 1936. Reprint, New York: Octagon Books, 1971.

———. "John Langdon and John Sullivan: A Biographical Essay." In *New Hampshire: The State That Made Us a Nation.* Edited by William M. Gardner, Frank C. Mevers, and Richard F. Upton. Portsmouth: New Hampshire Bicentennial Commission on the United States Constitution and the New Hampshire Humanities Council, 1989.

Whittemore, Charles P. *A General of the Revolution: John Sullivan of New Hampshire.* New York: Columbia University Press, 1961.

Wright, Robert K., Jr. *The Continental Army.* Washington, D.C.: Center of Military History, 1983.

revised by Frank C. Mevers

SULLIVAN'S EXPEDITION AGAINST THE IROQUOIS.

The Sullivan expedition, or the Sullivan-Clinton expedition, is the name given to the Continental army's invasion of the Iroquois homeland, conducted between May and November 1779. George Washington designed the campaign to punish the British-allied Iroquois nations for a series of frontier raids the year before (including the Wyoming Valley massacre) and to force the Iroquois out of the war. Major General John Sullivan commanded the main body of the troops, which entered Iroquoia via the Susquehanna Valley, while a smaller column of troops under Brigadier General James Clinton entered Iroquoia through the

Mohawk Valley. After defeating the only organized resistance it faced at Newtown, the Sullivan expedition proceeded to destroy Iroquois towns and cornfields. The expedition devastated the Iroquois League and, because of the tactics used, remains controversial into the twenty-first century.

ORIGINS AND PLANNING

In the summer of 1778, British irregulars under John Butler and British-allied Iroquois warriors launched a series of raids against Patriot communities on the Pennsylvania and New York frontiers, including the Wyoming Valley massacre (June 1778) and the Cherry Valley massacre (November 1778). Accounts of the massacres circulated widely on the American side, and public pressure on the Continental army to respond to these attacks was high. In the winter of 1778–1779, Washington began to plan a campaign to take Fort Niagara. Its strategic significance was multifold: it controlled a major choke point between British Canada and the United States and it also served as a main distribution point for British trade goods and arms to their Iroquois allies. Washington soon realized that taking Niagara would probably be beyond the realm of possibility for the operation he was planning. Because of the constraints of manpower and supply, he planned a more modest expedition that would attack the British-allied Iroquois directly. Attacking Niagara was retained as a secondary objective.

Washington initially offered the command of the Iroquoia invasion to Major General Horatio Gates, who turned it down on account of his age. Washington's offer then went to New Hampshire's Major General John Sullivan in March 1779. Washington made the ultimate objectives of Sullivan's operations clear in a letter of 31 May 1779. Sullivan was to attack "the hostile tribes of the Six Nations" and insure "the total destruction and devastation of their settlements and the capture of as many prisoners of every age and sex as possible." Washington also explained to Sullivan that it was "essential to ruin their crops now in the ground" and to prevent them from "planting more." Washington suggested that Sullivan enter Iroquoia through the Susquehanna Valley, establish a fort at Tioga (at the confluence of the Chemung and Susquehanna Rivers), and then proceed into the lands of the Seneca following the Chemung River. Washington also ordered Brigadier General James Clinton to the town of Canajoharie, in the Mohawk Valley, to support Sullivan's operations. Initial planning envisioned Clinton entering Iroquoia from the east, but he moved his troops through Otsego Lake into the Susquehanna Valley and rendezvoused with Sullivan at Tioga. A five-hundred-man force under Colonel Gose Van Shaick did use the eastern route, however. Van Shaick left Fort Stanwix in April

1779 and attacked and destroyed the town of Onondaga. Finally, Washington ordered the commander at Fort Pitt, Colonel Daniel Brodhead, to lead a small body of troops up the Allegheny River to harass Iroquois communities on the northern stretches of the river. Although Washington doubted that Brodhead could rendezvous with Sullivan and Clinton, he kept that option open.

THE ARMIES ADVANCE

Sullivan's troops began assembling at Easton, Pennsylvania, in early May; Sullivan arrived there on 7 May. His troops did not begin to move until 18 June and did not leave the Wyoming Valley until 31 July. Sullivan reached Tioga on 10 August 1779 and immediately began the construction of Fort Sullivan. A small party under Captain John Cummings traveled up the Chemung River and reconnoitered the Iroquois village of Chemung on 11 August. A somewhat larger detachment under General Edward Hand attacked and destroyed the village the next day. (The village had been evacuated by the Iroquois and the British before Hand's arrival.) Clinton began his preparations in June, completing his portage from the Mohawk Valley to Lake Otsego on 17 June. Clinton departed Otsego on 9 August, made contact with General Enoch Poor (whom Sullivan had ordered up the Susquehanna to find Clinton) on 19 August, and arrived at Tioga on 22 August.

Combined at Tioga, Sullivan's and Clinton's forces numbered about six thousand combatants and support personnel. Combat troops number about four thousand. The troops were composed of fifteen regiments of infantry and one regiment of artillery. The sixteen regiments were organized into four brigades under the command of Clinton, Hand, Poor, and General William Maxwell. The expedition included a small cavalry division of about seventy-five horses, commanded by Colonel Thomas Proctor. The expedition also employed a small number of Oneida, Tuscarora, and Stockbridge Mochian Indians as guides and scouts. The expedition's numbers were further augmented by noncombat support personnel, estimated to be two thousand in number. These included the "women of the army" (often called camp followers), whose numbers included nurses, cooks, and washerwomen. The expedition also employed boat crews, engineers, chaplains, surveyors, pioneers, and teamsters. The expedition carried its boats and other equipment with it. All of this served to slow its pace.

BRITISH PREPARATIONS

John Butler, the British commander at Fort Niagara, was aware of all aspects of the expedition: Van Schaick's April raid; the movement of Brodhead up the Allegheny; and the advance of Sullivan's columns to Tioga. Lacking a regular army of any size in his department, Butler could do little to halt Sullivan's advance. Butler consulted with Mohawk leader Joseph Brant and planned to gather a force of British rangers, Loyalists, and British-allied Iroquois warriors to harass Sullivan's column as it moved up the Chemung River. Butler was astonished by the size of Sullivan's expeditionary force, and he feared that Fort Niagara was Sullivan's ultimate target. Butler and Brant planned to make their first attempt to slow Sullivan at Newtown (modern Elmira, New York).

THE BATTLE OF NEWTOWN

The size of Sullivan's force dictated slow and deliberate movement. His full force left Tioga on 26 August, traveled up the Chemung River and camped at the ruins of Chemung on 28 August, and finally approached the village of Newtown on the morning of 29 August. Newtown was located at a bend in the Chemung River below a substantial hill; the ground was suitable for an ambush. Butler's Iroquois were stationed in an ambuscade on a small hill outside Newtown. The Iroquois attempted to lure Sullivan's men into an ambush, but the first parties to encounter them—Major James Parr's riflemen and infantry under General Hand—did not give chase. Sullivan then ordered Colonel Thomas Proctor's artillery regiment forward. Proctor's artillery devastated the Iroquois position, precipitating the retreat of Butler's forces from the battlefield and from Newtown itself. Their withdrawal was so precipitous that the brigades of Poor and Clinton, attempting a flanking maneuver, did not have time to get into position before the British-Iroquois retreat. Sullivan had won what would be the one pitched battle of the entire invasion of Iroquoia. Newtown was burned to the ground after the battle was over.

FURTHER OPERATIONS

For the remainder of their campaign, Sullivan's troops would not meet the kind of organized, sustained resistance they encountered at Newtown. In keeping with Iroquois traditions of war making, in which pitched battles were to be avoided and casualties minimized, the British-allied Iroquois opted to remove from their towns with the plan to return after the Americans had passed through. The move kept casualties to a minimum but gave Sullivan free reign to destroy towns and cornfields. Fearing that Sullivan's ultimate objective was Niagara, Butler attempted to organized additional ambuscades to slow Sullivan. However, the extended nature of Sullivan's supply lines and the consequent slowness of his march always gave the Iroquois time to retreat further.

Sullivan's troops destroyed the Seneca settlement called Catherine's Town, south of Seneca Lake, on 1 September. By 7 September, Sullivan's forces had reached the northern end of Seneca Lake, where they occupied and destroyed the village of Candasaga, or Seneca Castle. Sullivan's troops then moved westward to attack the Seneca town of Genesee Castle, also known as Little Beard's Town. On the night of 12–13 September, a party under Lieutenant Thomas Boyd, sent to reconnoiter the area near Genesee Castle, was ambushed by the Senecas. Most of the party, which numbered twenty-three men, were killed; only Boyd and a private were captured alive, and they were killed the next day. The destruction of Boyd's party caused the highest number of losses suffered by Sullivan during any one engagement of the expedition. On 14 September, Sullivan entered Genesee Castle without opposition and burned it to the ground the following day.

Sullivan then turned his expedition back east. Between his departure from Genesee Castle and his arrival back at Tioga on 30 September, Sullivan sent several detachments of his forces through Iroquoia to commit further acts of destruction. William Butler was dispatched to destroy the towns of the Cayuga along Cayuga Lake. Colonel Peter Gansevoort was sent eastward into the Mohawk country to destroy the Lower Mohawk Castle on his way to Albany. Smaller detachments were dispatched to destroy villages throughout the Finger Lakes region. The total devastation was enormous. Numbers vary from account to account, but at least 40 Iroquois villages were burned to the ground and at least 160,000 bushels of Iroquois corn were destroyed. Sullivan's troops destroyed the fort at Tioga on 3 October and arrived in the Wyoming Valley on 8 October.

AFTERMATH AND CONCLUSIONS

Although casualties suffered by both sides during the Sullivan expedition itself were fairly light, a severe impact on the Iroquois was felt soon after. The winter of 1779–1780 was exceptionally cold and harsh, and with most of their food stores destroyed, the British-allied Iroquois found subsistence a difficult prospect. Many did not survive the winter. Most Iroquois reconstituted their villages around Fort Niagara. The destruction of their home villages prompted many Iroquois to leave New York altogether and resettle inside Canada. Governor Haldimand endorsed this migration when he granted Mohawk leader Joseph Brant rights to a large reserve along Ontario's Grand River in 1784.

Although Sullivan succeeded in bringing devastation to Iroquoia, this destruction did not achieve the goal of knocking the Iroquois out of the war. Ironically, since the British-allied Iroquois removed to the area near Niagara after the expedition, the effect was to push them into closer alliance with the British. By late 1780, Iroquois were fighting alongside British troops in the western theater once more. Modern military historians have seen the Sullivan expedition as a failure, since it did not accomplish its strategic objectives. Modern American Indian historians have been even less generous, lamenting the destruction of Iroquois culture and civilization the Sullivan Expedition exacerbated. Although the Six Nations survived the Revolutionary War, they never regained the preeminent political and diplomatic position they had held for over a century before the American Revolution. Finally, the Sullivan expedition, and the orders of George Washington that set it into motion, remain a source of controversy and anger for many modern members of the Iroquois nations. For most Americans, George Washington is remembered as the "father of the country," but for most Iroquois, he is known as the "town destroyer" because of the actions wrought by the Sullivan expedition.

SEE ALSO *Butler, John; Clinton, James; Newtown, New York; Sullivan, John.*

BIBLIOGRAPHY

Fisher, Joseph R. *A Well-Executed Failure: The Sullivan Campaign against the Iroquois, July–September 1779.* Columbia: University of South Carolina Press, 1997.

Spiegelman, Robert, et al. "The Sullivan-Clinton Campaign, 1779–2005." Website, CD-ROM, and book. http://sullivanclinton.com.

Wittemore, Charles P. *A General of the Revolution: John Sullivan of New Hampshire.* New York: Columbia University Press, 1961.

revised by Leonard J. Sadosky

SULLIVAN'S ISLAND, SOUTH CAROLINA.

June 1776 and May 1780. The site of Fort Sullivan, which was renamed Fort Moultrie, this island was successfully defended against the Charleston expedition of Clinton in 1776 and fell to the British without resistance during the Charleston expedition of Clinton in 1780.

SEE ALSO *Charleston Expedition of Clinton in 1776; Charleston Expedition of Clinton in 1780.*

revised by Carl P. Borick

SUMNER, JETHRO.

(1735–1785). Continental general. Virginia and North Carolina. Sumner served in the Virginia militia throughout the Seven Years' War, becoming a paymaster and commander of Fort Bedford in 1760. Four years later he moved to North Carolina, married Mary Hurst, and with a large inheritance from his wife became a planter and tavern owner at the seat of what became Warren County. He became a justice of the peace in 1768 and was county sheriff from 1772 to 1777. He was elected to the Third Provincial Congress in 1775, which appointed him major of the Halifax County militia. He went north to support the Virginians at Norfolk during the last two months of the year, became a colonel of the Third Battalion of the North Carolina Continentals on 15 April 1776, and participated in the defense of Charleston in June. In September he was detached from the forces moving toward Florida and sent to raise supplies in North Carolina. The next spring he led his unit north, fought at Brandywine and Germantown, and spent the winter at Valley Forge. Early in 1778 he was invalided home and spent the summer recruiting regulars. Promoted to brigadier general on 9 January 1779, he led his new Continental brigade at Stono Ferry, South Carolina, on 20 June 1779, but illness again forced him home.

After spending more than a year recruiting in North Carolina, he commanded a militia brigade in opposing the advance of General Charles Cornwallis to Charlotte, North Carolina, in September 1780. When William Smallwood was given command of state troops in October, Sumner refused to continue serving in the field. In February 1781 he acceded to Nathanael Greene's request to return to active duty, even while continuing his recruiting efforts, at which he excelled. His major combat service of the Revolution came as commander of three small small North Carolina Continental battalions at Eutaw Springs, South Carolina, on 8 September 1781. Here his men performed with great credit. He was in command of military forces in North Carolina for the remainder of the war, taking part in small actions, and on 3 November 1783 he retired. He died at his home 18 March 1785.

SEE ALSO *Eutaw Springs, South Carolina; Norfolk, Virginia; Stono Ferry, South Carolina.*

BIBLIOGRAPHY

Rankin, Hugh F. *The North Carolina Continentals.* Chapel Hill: University of North Carolina Press, 1971.

revised by Michael Bellesiles

SUMTER, THOMAS.

(1734–1832). Militia general. South Carolina. Thomas Sumter was born on 14 August 1734 near Charlottesville, Virginia. He served as a sergeant of Virginia troops in the 1761 campaign against the Cherokees. At the end, of that campaign he escorted a troop of Cherokee leaders to England and back. On their return to the Cherokee nation, Sumter fought a French officer, the Baron des Jonnes, whom he found attempting to recruit the Cherokee. He emerged victorious, and took the baron prisoner.

Sumter was jailed for debt in Staunton, Virginia, in 1765, but he escaped and fled to South Carolina. There he opened a store near Eutaw Springs and married a wealthy widow, Mary Cantey Jameson, in 1767. By 1775 he owned thousands of acres, mills, and many slaves. Sumter was elected to the first and second provincial congresses, which became the new state assembly in 1776. He also captained a company of mounted rangers under Colonel Richard Richardson, defeating a group of Loyalists in the "snow campaign" of December 1775 (so called because of the record fifteen inches of snow that had just fallen). The following year he was promoted to lieutenant colonel of the Second (later Sixth) Rifle Regiment that formed part of the defense of Charleston against General Henry Clinton's attack in July 1776. Sumter's regiment became part of the Continental army, participating in some minor skirmishes against the Cherokee and in limited military operations in South Carolina and Georgia. In 1778 Sumter joined with General Robert Howe in planning the aborted invasion of Florida, but contracted malaria and resigned on 19 September 1778. When parts of his plantation were burned and his slaves were liberated by Captain Charles Campbell of Banastre Tarleton's Legion in 1780, Sumter headed for the Patriot stronghold west of the Catawba River and started raising volunteers. He was soon joined by a number of other officers seeking to resist the successful British forces.

Sumter's partisans struck first at Williamson's Plantation, on 12 July 1780, gaining a victory that brought him more volunteers. Repulsed at Rocky Mount on 1 August, Sumter went on to success at Hanging Rock on 6 August. His lack of strategic sense first showed itself in the Camden campaign. On 18 August, after General Horatio Gates accepted his request for a reinforcement and just before the main army advanced to defeat at Camden, Sumter was badly beaten by Tarleton at Fishing Creek. He soon resumed operations, however, and on 6 October was named senior brigadier general of the South Carolina militia. Although the action at Fishdam Ford, on 9 November, was a draw, he foiled an attempt by the notorious Major James Wemyss to annihilate him and inspired a Patriot uprising that panicked Cornwallis. Sumter fought Tarleton to a bloody standstill at Blackstocks on 20 November, but was badly wounded.

By this time Sumter was known as "The Carolina Gamecock," for the cock's feather he wore in his hat. Sending word for Francis Marion to join forces with

Thomas Sumter. *Known as the "Carolina Gamecock" for the cock's feather he wore in his hat, Thomas Sumter was a bold and imaginative partisan leader, but a less effective tactical commander. Nineteenth-century engraving by George Parker after a portrait by Charles Willson Peale.* © **STAPLETON COLLECTION/CORBIS**

him, Sumter started down the Congaree River on 16 February 1781 in hopes of inspiring more enlistments as he made his way to the Santee River. He would support this operation logistically by capturing the enemy base of Fort Granby. Marion knew that the British were reinforcing the posts along their line of communications and was pessimistic about the success of Sumter's strategy, but being the junior brigadier general, he prepared to join Sumter. Sumter launched his attack on Fort Granby before dawn on 19 February, before Marion could arrive. The next day he had to retreat as Colonel Welbore Doyle's New York Volunteers approached to relieve the garrison. The partisans moved 35 miles downriver and surprised the post at Belleville, but had to withdraw when enemy forces approached from Camden. On 28 February he launched an attack against Fort Watson without having properly reconnoitered the outpost, and therefore suffered a costly repulse.

When he learned that Colonel John Watson was preparing to attack him with overwhelming force, Sumter moved to his plantation to pick up his paralytic wife and young son, and started withdrawing northward. After moving some 40 miles to the Bradley Plantation, between the Black and Lynches rivers, he waited until

6 March before giving up hope of seeing Marion and then continued his retreat northward. On that same day, Major Thomas Fraser's Loyal South Carolina Regiment attacked Sumter's force, the partisans escaping with the loss of ten killed and about forty wounded. His own ill-advised campaign was over, but as Nathanael Greene's army approached he ignored the latter's requests to join him in an attack on Francis Rawdon's principal post.

Sumter wanted to fight his own little war. When Greene needed his support at Hobkirk's Hill, Sumter struck at Fort Granby, instead. He broke off that attack, however, to capture Orangeburg on 11 May, and then threatened to resign from the army because Henry Lee had taken Granby while he was otherwise occupied. Greene placated Sumter, who then came up with his controversial plan of raising troops by "Sumter's law": to recruit dependable mounted militia for ten months, Sumter proposed paying them in plunder taken from Loyalists in a sort of "pay as you go" scheme. He succeeded in assembling men, but touched off a renewed wave of vicious civil war and earned a disreputable reputation that dogged him to the grave. When he finally moved south to support Greene, his strategic blunders contributed to the American failure at Ninety Six.

Sumter then got Marion and Lee put under his command and launched a campaign that ended in the mismanaged attack at Quinby Bridge on 17 July. On the 25th he sent a force to plunder Loyalists in Georgetown. The British retaliated by virtually destroying Georgetown on 2 August. Perceiving Sumter's policies as counterproductive, Governor John Rutledge, who had just arrived to restore civil government in South Carolina, issued a proclamation terminating "Sumter's law" by prohibiting plundering. This action also ended Sumter's military career. Bothered by his wound, exhausted by his campaigns, and with his name "almost universally odious" (as Henry Lee put it), Sumter retired to his plantation. Sumter was elected state senator, and sat in the assembly that met 8 January 1782 at Jacksonboro. He resigned his military commission the next month.

After the war he was given the thanks of the South Carolina senate and a gold medal. Sumter served many terms in the South Carolina statehouse. After an investigation into his use of "Sumter's law," Sumter was exonerated, and the legislatures of North and South Carolina forbade state courts to entertain damage suits connected with this matter. He founded Stateburg, South Carolina, which he attempted to have made the state capital, without success. An anti-federalist, he voted against the Constitution in the South Carolina ratifying convention. Elected to the First Congress, he worked to limited federal powers. Suspected of speculation in government paper, he was defeated for re-election in 1793 but returned to Congress in 1796 as an adherent of Thomas Jefferson's. He served in the House of Representatives until elected to the Senate in December 1801 and resigned from Congress in December 1810. For the next 22 years he was harried by litigation and creditors. In 1827 the South Carolina legislature granted him a lifetime moratorium for his debt to the state bank. He lived to be 98, the oldest surviving general of the war, dying 1 June 1832.

SEE ALSO *Blackstock's, South Carolina; Camden Campaign; Carolina Gamecock; Fishdam Ford, South Carolina; Fishing Creek, North Carolina; Hanging Rock, South Carolina; Hobkirk's Hill (Camden), South Carolina; Ninety Six, South Carolina; Orangeburg, South Carolina; Rocky Mount, South Carolina.*

BIBLIOGRAPHY

Bass, Robert D. *Gamecock: The Life and Campaigns of General Thomas Sumter.* New York: Holt, Rinehart and Winston, 1961.

Gregoire, Anne King. *Thomas Sumter.* Columbia, S.C.: R. L. Bryan, 1931.

Smith, Harry A. M. "General Thomas Sumter." *Magazine of History* 9–10 (1908): 160–167, 336–340; (1909): 17–22, 80–85, and 165–170.

Sumter, Thomas. Thomas Sumter papers. Madison: Wisconsin State Historical Society.

revised by Michael Bellesiles

SUNBURY (FORT MORRIS), GEORGIA.

25 November 1778. Lieutenant Colonel Lewis V. Fuser's effort to take this position was foiled by firm resistance from the rebel commander.

SEE ALSO *McIntosh, John.*

revised by Michael Bellesiles

SUNBURY (FORT MORRIS), GEORGIA.

9 January 1779. British capture. Major Joseph Lane was left with two hundred Continentals to defend this place when the rest of General Robert Howe's Southern army left for the operation that ended in the British capture of Savannah, 29 December 1778. General Augustine Prevost left St. Augustine on 23 December with about two thousand men and attacked Sunbury on 6 January. Three days later the British got their artillery into position, and Lane surrendered. American casualties were four killed and seven wounded; the British captured twenty-four cannon and a quantity of stores, losing one man killed and three wounded.

SEE ALSO *Savannah, Georgia (29 December 1778).*

revised by Michael Bellesiles

SUPPLY OF THE CONTINENTAL ARMY.

The American rebels started the war with almost none of the supplies required to arm, clothe, shelter, or otherwise equip, maneuver, and support army or naval forces. They lacked powder, muskets, cannon, lead, bayonets, cartridge boxes, cartridge paper, textiles, entrenching tools, and such camp equipment as kettles. The supplying of food was less of a problem while the army was stationary around Boston, but the shortage of salt meant that meat and fish could not be preserved. Manufacturing in America was undeveloped when the war started and never was built up to a point where it contributed significantly to the war effort; virtually all the shortages had to be made up by captures from the British or by purchase on credit from friendly powers (France, Spain, and the Netherlands).

The basic structure of American procurement was adapted from the way the British army organized and administered its supply system. On 16 June 1775, Congress created two supply offices, the quartermaster general and the commissary general of stores and purchases, both of which were required to report to the delegates. But since these departments began operating from a standing start in an economy much less well developed and flexible than Britain's, their efforts were often ad hoc and had about them an air of desperation. Given the difficulties they faced, American supply officers in most cases accomplished great feats in keeping the Continental army in the field and able to fight.

QUARTERMASTER GENERAL

Until the reorganization of 1780, the American quartermaster general had duties and responsibilities far beyond those of the modern quartermaster. In addition to the procurement and distribution of supplies other than food and clothing, he was the principal staff officer involved in the movement of troops and therefore responsible for route reconnaissance; the repair and maintenance of roads and bridges; the layout, organization, and construction of camps; and the supply and maintenance of wagons and teams and of boats for water movement. Washington therefore felt the need for this key staff officer soon after assuming command at Boston and asked for authority to make his own appointment. When this was granted on 19 July 1775, Washington named Thomas Mifflin of Pennsylvania to the post on 14 August. Stephen Moylan took over the office in June 1776 but proved unequal to the task, and four months later Mifflin was back. He was seldom at Washington's headquarters in 1777, but his duties were performed by three subordinates: Joseph Thornsbury, whom Washington appointed wagonmaster general in May; Clement Biddle, appointed commissary general of forage on 1 July; and Colonel

Henry Emanuel Lutterloh (or Lutterlough), an officer who had served as a quartermaster in the army of the duke of Brunswick, whom, at Washington's suggestion, Mifflin made his deputy.

Quartermaster operations, severely strained in 1776, suffered further dislocation in 1777, primarily in the field of transportation and distribution. Congress detained Mifflin in Philadelphia over matters of reorganization, and he remained in the city to stimulate recruiting and later to move stores out of the way of the British threat. On 8 October 1777 he submitted his resignation on grounds of ill health, but Congress, whose indecision and neglect had contributed to the collapse of the supply system, did not accept the resignation until 7 November. Then, the next day, the delegates asked Mifflin to carry on until they could get around to picking his successor. Mifflin, who had been appointed to the new Board of War, retaining the rank but not the pay of a major general, simply told his deputy, Lutterloh, to take over as quartermaster general. This shuffling of personnel came at a time when defeats in the field, and the need to keep operating in the face of the British occupation of Philadelphia, had already dislocated the supply system and contributed to the army's suffering during the winter encampment at Valley Forge, Pennsylvania.

With the lament that "No body ever heard of a quarter Master in history as such," the capable Major General Nathanael Greene of Rhode Island reluctantly accepted the noncombatant office of quartermaster general on 2 March 1778 and held it until 5 August 1780. Two able men were prevailed on to be his deputies: John Cox was to make all purchases and examine all stores; Charles Pettit would keep the books and the cash. Congress put Greene and his deputies on a commission system, whereby they could retain one percent of the money spent by the Quartermaster Department. The three men agreed to divide this amount equally.

COMMISSARY GENERAL

On 19 July 1775, Congress appointed Joseph Trumbull, the son of Connecticut governor Jonathan Trumbull, as commissary general. His department, charged with feeding the army, functioned well until the war moved from the Boston area to New York and New Jersey, when it faced the unprecedented challenges of reconnecting logistical arrangements in a war that went from the defense of extended positions to the near chaos of defeat and retreat.

After the disasters of 1776—the loss of New York City and the retreat through New Jersey—Congress was seized by what Richard Henry Lee would later call a veritable "rage for reformation," most of which was directed against the Commissary Department. On the recommendation of the Board of War, and in line with

Wagon Train. *In this nineteenth-century engraving General Washington and his staff welcome a wagon train carrying supplies for the Continental Army.* THE GRANGER COLLECTION, NEW YORK

Washington's ideas, the delegates split Trumbull's office into a commissary general of purchases and a commissary general of issues. Fully a year before Congress made the decision, Trumbull had wholeheartedly supported this division of his office but made a strong argument that he and his deputies be taken off a fixed salary. He reiterated an earlier proposal that he receive a one-half of one percent commission on all money passing through his hands, and that 2.5 percent be retained by the deputies purchasing subsistence. The morale of Trumbull's assistants was low because of criticism and because Congress had been so slow to prescribe regulations for the department.

On 10 June 1777 Congress finally produced a long, detailed set of regulations prescribing how records would be kept, how government animals would be branded, and other minutiae. On 18 June it elected officers for the new organization. Although he apparently was not officially notified until 5 July, Trumbull was retained in the establishment as commissary general of purchases, and his deputies were William Ayless, William Buchanan, Jacob Cuyler, and Jeremiah Wadsworth. The second post was given to Charles Stewart (who retained it until the end of the Yorktown campaign), and his deputies were William

Mumford, Matthew Irwin, and Elisha Avery. Congress paid little attention to Trumbull's recommendations, particularly with regard to his proposal about commissions. Trumbull tried to hold his department together while he argued with Congress on modification of its plan, but the delegates refused to yield ground and Trumbull's deputies began to resign. On 19 July, Trumbull submitted his resignation with the request that it be effective 20 August 1777. Buchanan was named (5 August) to succeed him. After Buchanan's resignation on 23 March 1778, Jeremiah Wadsworth took over the office on 9 April. After Wadsworth resigned on 1 January 1780, Ephraim Blaine became commissary general of purchases and held the post until it was abolished after the Yorktown campaign, in October 1781.

CLOTHIER GENERAL

Although the supply of clothing fell in the domain of the commissary general, the quartermaster general, Mifflin, had temporarily handled this responsibility in 1775. When Congress got around to reorganizing the supply services after the evacuation of New York City, its first act was to create the office of commissary of clothing. This official would submit regimental clothing to the states and receive and pay for deliveries; regimental paymasters then would receive the clothing, make issue to the troops, and deduct the costs from the soldiers' wages. George Measam was appointed to this post in the southern army on 16 October 1776, a week after Congress created it, and at the same time Washington was authorized to fill the post in his own army. On 20 December, Washington wrote Congress to recommend that a clothier general for the Continental army (rather than one for each field army) be appointed, and a week later the delegates agreed, although they did not prescribe his authority.

James Mease, a Philadelphia merchant and former butler who had been commissary to Pennsylvania troops since 25 January 1776 and who had executed supply orders for Congress, asked Washington for this post on 6 January 1777 and received it four days later. He reported to Washington's camp in February 1777. On 19 July, Washington reported that "I have no reason to accuse the Clothier General of inattention to his department, and therefore, as his supplies are incompetent to the wants of the army, I am to suppose his resources are unequal." Shoes were a particular problem, the shortage rendering some organizations, in Washington's words on 23 June, "almost entirely incapable of doing duty." Congress had established a Hide Department (22 November 1776) to take custody of the original wrappings of cattle slaughtered for the army. Now it directed the commissary of hides to exchange these for tanned leather or for shoes; if this proved unfeasible, the commissary of hides could set up the tanyards, secure the other necessary materials and workmen, and produce the shoes, or he could contract for their manufacture. The Hide Department was then put under the Board of War, which directed that it make deliveries of leather to the commissary of military stores for the production of other equipment. Six weeks after the man selected by Congress declined to serve as commissary of hides, George Ewing was appointed to the post on 5 August 1777. He resigned on 20 April 1779, and the Board of War came up with a new plan under which five commissioners were appointed: William Henry for Pennsylvania, Maryland, and Delaware; John Mehelm for New Jersey; Moses Hatfield for New York; Robert Lamb for Massachusetts; and George Starr for Connecticut.

Washington had meanwhile grown increasingly dissatisfied with Mease's performance. In April 1778 he asked Congress to investigate, and on 4 August he wrote that Mease was unfit for the post. Mease's functions were reduced as clothing started to arrive from France, the states were directed to supply their own troops, and the Board of War took over the purchase of items for the Continental army. Late in 1778 Washington told a visiting congressional committee that a reorganization of the Clothing

Department was still necessary, and on 23 March 1779 the delegates got around to acting. Mease had submitted his resignation in December 1777, offering to stay in office until a successor was named, but on grounds of ill health he left the main army and operated from Lancaster, Pennsylvania. After two others had declined the new office as set up in March 1779, James Wilkinson accepted on 24 July. He was to take orders from Washington and the Board of War, and each state would appoint its own clothier.

EXPANDING THE QUARTERMASTER DEPARTMENT

In 1775 the quartermaster general had operated with two assistants and some forty clerks, laborers, wagonmasters, and superintendents. By 1780 the quartermaster general and his two assistants had 28 deputies and 109 assistant deputies plus many storekeepers; clerks; barrackmasters; express riders; laborers; and superintendents of government property, roads, stables, woodyards, and horseyards. The forage branch had a commissary general and assistant, 25 deputies, and 128 assistant deputies as well as clerks, forage masters, measurers, collectors, weighers, stackers, superintendents, and laborers. The wagon branch had a wagonmaster general, eleven deputies, plus many wagon masters, wagoners, packhorse masters, and packhorsemen. The boat department had superintendents, masters of vessels, mates, and boatmen. In 1780 the Quartermaster Department employed almost 3,000 people at an estimated monthly payroll of $407,593, a sum that excluded the commissions paid to the quartermaster general, his assistants, and the commissary general of forage but included those paid to some, but not all, of their deputies.

In 1779 the operations of the quartermaster general and the commissary general came under mounting criticism. Expenditures of the two departments had more than quadrupled, from $9,272,534 in 1776 to $37,202,421 in 1778, and in May 1779 Congress's committee on the treasury estimated that at least $200 million would have to be spent that year by the two departments unless finances could be put on a firmer basis. The larger problem, of course, was the extraordinary depreciation of the Continental currency. The extremely severe weather, the suffering of the army at its winter encampment at Morristown, New Jersey, during 1779–1780, and the suspicion that all purchasing agents were getting rich on the commission system all brought such animosity against the two department heads that Greene and Wadsworth both threatened to resign. Only Congress's public statement of confidence in their activity kept them in office until the fall, when both officials tendered their resignations. Congress accepted Wadsworth's on 1 January 1780 and Greene's on 5 August 1780.

THE WAR'S LAST YEARS

Greene's successor, Timothy Pickering, the former adjutant general and member of the Board of War, was named to the position on 5 August but did not wind up his affairs in Philadelphia and report for duty until late September; he would hold the office until 25 July 1785. Pickering operated under the reorganization plan Congress had implemented on 15 July 1780. For the first time, the duties of the quartermaster general no longer included any of the operational functions inherited with the model adopted from the British army. Pickering and all subsequent quartermasters general of the American army have been concerned only with supply. With much noise about "four years of wasteful profusion," Pickering undertook to eliminate the "superfluities" in his department and "lop them off" (Risch, *Supplying*, p. 62). But the real requirement was money to make the supply system work, and this was not available in sufficient quantities to buy food and clothing or to transport what little was received. The situation was so desperate that Washington had to furlough many troops for want of food and clothing when he went into winter quarters in December 1780, and Greene's southern army also went threadbare and hungry. These shortages, plus pay and enlistment grievances, contributed significantly to the troop mutinies of 1781.

In the spring of 1781 the New England states again came through with provisions, thanks largely to the efforts of Major General William Heath, whom Washington sent to request help. Congress then established a new system whereby private contractors, instead of the states, procured, delivered, and issued the rations. Robert Morris, the newly appointed superintendent of finance, worked out the details and raised the cash. It took the combined and cooperative efforts of the quartermaster general, the state deputy quartermasters, and the superintendent of finance to provide Washington with the means to move the Franco-American army from the Hudson Valley southward 450 miles to the James River and defeat Earl Cornwallis, a prodigious achievement accomplished between 14 August and 19 October 1781.

After the victorious Yorktown campaign, Quartermaster General Pickering took charge of all arrangements for returning American troops to the North. He also took charge of much of the captured British matériel, sending some of it to Greene in the South. He provided wood and straw for the army hospitals at Williamsburg and Hanover, Virginia; handled claims for damages and debts incurred by the allied armies in Virginia; and during the winter of 1781–1782 was involved in settling the transportation accounts arising from the campaign.

As early as 1781 Morris, whose role in restructuring and sustaining the finances of the Revolution made him increasingly prominent in matters of army supply, was responsible for purchasing clothing. Soon he was making all contracts for supplies, and on application of the clothier general was providing funds to pay for the manufacture of clothing. Wilkinson resigned as clothier general on 27 March 1781 and was succeeded by John Moylan, a brother of Stephen.

As the year 1781 ended, Morris had taken over the duties of the commissary generals of purchases and of issues, both Blaine and Stewart relinquishing their posts without waiting for Congress to accept their resignations. Morris, by one means or another, furnished clothes for the army, "not as fully as Washington desired but nevertheless more adequately than in earlier years of the war" (Risch, *Supplying*, p. 71). Elimination of the commissary departments made it possible to consolidate many supply functions and to reduce overhead, an economy measure that Pickering heartily supported. Congress put other reforms into effect, and before the end of 1782, Pickering's staff was reduced to ten officers. On 25 July 1785 it abolished the office of the quartermaster general.

The remarkable and unsung Edward Carrington served as Greene's quartermaster general in the Southern Department. His success in equipping and feeding the troops under extraordinarily difficult circumstances earned him a lasting reputation; Alexander Hamilton nominated him to be quartermaster general of the U.S. Army in the mobilization for the Quasi-War against France in 1798.

SEE ALSO *Board of War; Carrington, Edward; Continental Currency; Greene, Nathanael; Heath, William; Manufacturing in America; Mifflin, Thomas; Morris, Robert (1734–1806); Morristown Winter Quarters, New Jersey (1 December 1779–22 June 1780); Moylan, Stephen; Pay, Bounties and Rations; Pickering, Timothy; Salt; Valley Forge Winter Quarters, Pennsylvania.*

BIBLIOGRAPHY

Chase, Philander D., et al., eds. *The Papers of George Washington.* Vols. 10 and 12. Charlottesville: University Press of Virginia, 2000, 2002.

Risch, Erna. *Quartermaster Support of the Army: A History of the Corps, 1775–1939.* Washington, D.C.: U.S. Government Printing Office, 1962.

———. *Supplying Washington's Army.* Washington, D.C.: Center of Military History, 1981.

Showman, Richard K., et al., eds. *The Papers of Nathanael Greene.* Vol. 3. Chapel Hill: University of North Carolina Press for the Rhode Island Historical Society, 1983.

revised by Harold E. Selesky

SUTHERLAND, WILLIAM.

British officer. A Lieutenant William Sutherland of the Thirty-eighth Foot Brigade took part in the expedition to Lexington and

Concord (Massachusetts), and his account is in the papers of Thomas Gage that are held by the Clements Library at Ann Arbor, Michigan. It is likely, but not certain, that this is the same William Sutherland who served as captain of the 55th Foot Brigade and adjutant and aide-de-camp to General Henry Clinton in 1778. This latter Sutherland raised and commanded a light infantry unit that may have become the cadre for the British Legion. He also saved Clinton's life at Monmouth and commanded the Corps of Invalids that reached Bermuda on 2 November 1778 to constitute the first garrison of that place during the Revolution. He may also be the unlucky commander of Paulus Hook during the operations there on 19 August 1779, and subsequently court-martialed for his conduct. To further confuse the identification, there was a Lieutenant Colonel Sutherland commanding a force comprising the Ninth and Forty-seventh Regiments in the final phase of Burgoyne's offensive in 1777.

SEE ALSO *British Legion; Burgoyne's Offensive; Invalid; Paulus Hook, New Jersey.*

revised by Michael Bellesiles

SWAMP FEVER. Malaria.

SWAMP FOX. Francis Marion.

SEE ALSO *Marion, Francis.*

SWAN SHOT. Large shot, but smaller than buckshot, used for hunting large fowl and small game and occasionally used in battle.

Mark M. Boatner

SWIFT, HEMAN. Continental officer. Connecticut. Heman Swift enlisted as a private in the Fourth Connecticut Provincial Regiment in September 1755, was a corporal in the militia sent to reinforce Fort William Henry when it was besieged by the French in August 1757, and was appointed a lieutenant in the provincial regiments for the three years of Connecticut's maximum effort during the final French and Indian war (1758–1760). He was elected a deputy to the General Assembly from Cornwall, in the far northwest corner of Connecticut, in the early 1770s. In June 1776, the Assembly appointed him colonel of a Connecticut state regiment, one of two such regiments it authorized to reinforce the Northern Department. The regiments were stationed at Fort Ticonderoga and came home in November. He became colonel of the Seventh Connecticut Regiment in the Continental Army on 1 January 1777 and served with it as part of the main army throughout the war. On the consolidation of the Connecticut Line on 1 January 1781, he was transferred to command the Second Connecticut Regiment. On 28 September 1781 he was sent from the Hudson Highlands with 300 infantry and some light artillery to Ramapo, New Jersey, to support the militia against a possible British raid from Staten Island. In June 1783 he was retained as colonel of the last consolidated Connecticut regiment. On 30 September, he was breveted brigadier general and in December 1783 retired from the army.

SEE ALSO *Fort William Henry (Fort George), New York; Hudson River and the Highlands.*

BIBLIOGRAPHY
Heath, William. *Memoirs of Major-General Hetah, Containing Anecdotes, Details of Skirmishes, Battles, and other Military Events During the American War.* New York: New York Times, 1968.

revised by Harold E. Selesky

T

TACTICS AND MANEUVERS.

Revolutionary-era battle tactics depended largely on disciplined troops maneuvering in compact formations that were able to deploy quickly from column into line and deliver massed volleys of musketry or execute a bayonet charge. Artillery supported infantry formations, occasionally delivering a massed cannonade in field battles or serving in its classic siege role of destroying enemy fortifications and the will to resist. Cavalry operated only in small bodies, occasionally as shock troops but more often in reconnaissance and the pursuit of a demoralized enemy.

Building on experiences in the Seven Years' War in Europe and America, light troops and innovative battle formations were increasingly used, and commanders gained invaluable experience with both. The early British adoption in 1776 of a two-rank, open-order line of battle for all infantry units was in response to the broken, wooded North American terrain and was made possible by British troop discipline, small numbers of opposing cavalry, and American inexperience. Later in the war, notably at Cowpens, the drawbacks of such loose formations were made apparent when faced and occasionally overthrown by veteran Continental regiments.

On 21 September 1777, Brigadier General Thomas Conway described problems poorly trained Continental troops experienced at the Battle of Brandywine that year: "Troops of this Army . . . Appear to Manoeuvre upon false principles . . . I Could not Discover . . . the Least notion of displaying Columns & forming [line] briskly upon all Emergencies" (Continental Congress, *Papers,* reel 178, p. 71). These deficiencies were rectified with the armywide adoption in the spring of 1778 of Major General Friedrich Wilhelm de Steuben's uniform system of maneuver. Steuben's system introduced standard marching rates and methods of changing formation, simplifying command and control, and improving army cohesion. These innovations were set within a closely monitored training program that ensured minimum variation in interpreting the new instructions. The first real combat test came at the Battle of Monmouth on 28 June 1778, where the newly trained troops performed well. The fact that much of the burden was successfully borne by provisional battalions of picked men from different regiments, sometimes operating under unfamiliar officers, is a tribute to the efficacy of Steuben's work.

Both armies' tactical systems were based on the latest European military practice, including theories concerning the primacy of columns over lines (or vice versa) when attacking. Both formations were used in line of battle during the war, with linear formations preferred for forward regiments, while supporting units remained in easily maneuvered columns ready to deploy when needed.

Irregular warfare played a part, too. Early on, General George Washington's forces often relied on hit-and-run tactics. A French volunteer said of the American army in 1777, "The maneuver that it executes best . . . A regiment places itself behind some . . . bushes and waits, well hidden, for the enemy. They stick their muskets through the bushes, take careful aim, fire, and fall back . . . a quarter of a league. . . . If the enemy appears, they repeat the same maneuver several times" (Idzerda, ed., *Lafayette,* 1, p. 81). The practice continued into 1778, when Brigadier General William Maxwell noted on 19 June, "The Enemy . . . is coming on the Road to EvesHam. They got a full fire from Captain Ross [Third New Jersey] this morning with 50 men which threw them into a great confusion. He came off some distance & Post[ed] them to give them More in a nother place" (*Presidential Papers Microfilm*, series 4, reel 50).

Militia units fought in line of battle, but they were better known for less formal warfare. Hessian Captain Johann Ewald asked,

> What can you do to those small bands who have learned to fight separate, who know how to use any molehill for their protection, and who, when attacked, run back as fast as they will approach you again . . .? Never have I seen these maneuvers carried out better than by the American militia, especially that . . . of Jersey. If you were forced to retreat through these people you could be certain of having them constantly around you. (*Treatise*, p. 115)

SEE ALSO *Steuben, Friedrich Wilhelm von.*

BIBLIOGRAPHY

Continental Congress. *Papers of the Continental Congress.* Washington, D.C.: National Archives Microfilm, 1958.

Ewald, Johann. *A Treatise on Partisan Warfare by Johann von Ewald.* Translated by Robert A. Selig and David Curtis Skaggs. Westport, Conn.: Greenwood Press, 1991.

Gruber, Ira D. "The Education of Sir Henry Clinton." *Bulletin of the John Rylands University Library of Manchester* 72, no. 11 (Spring 1990): 131–153.

Idzerda, Stanley J., ed. *Lafayette in the Age of the American Revolution: Selected Letters and Papers, 1776–1790.* Vol. 1. Ithaca, N.Y.: Cornell University Press, 1977.

Presidential Papers Microfilm. Washington, D.C.: Library of Congress, 1961.

John U. Rees

TALLMADGE, BENJAMIN, JR. (1754–
1835). Continental officer, manager of Washington's secret service. Born in Brookhaven, New York, on 25 February 1754, Tallmadge graduated from Yale in 1773 and became superintendent of the high school at Wethersfield, Connecticut. He left this post to fight in the Revolution, being made lieutenant and adjutant in Chester's Connecticut State Regiment on 20 June 1776, captain on 14 December 1776, and major on 7 April 1777 and was brevetted lieutenant colonel on 30 September 1783. He saw action at Long Island, White Plains, Brandywine, Germantown, and Monmouth. For his raid to Fort George, Long Island, on 21–23 November 1780, he was commended by Washington and Congress. During the period 1778–1783, after the cessation of major military operations in the North, Tallmadge was primarily occupied with the management of Washington's secret service. His initiative after the capture of "John Anderson" led to the exposure of Arnold's treason. He was in charge of John André while the latter was a prisoner. He developed a deep affection for André and found his execution deeply troubling.

After the war Tallmadge was a businessman in Litchfield, Connecticut. In 1800 he was elected as a Federalist to Congress and served until 1817. He died in Litchfield on 7 March 1835.

SEE ALSO *Arnold's Treason; Fort George, Long Island, New York.*

BIBLIOGRAPHY

Hall, Charles S. *Benjamin Tallmadge: Revolutionary Soldier and American Businessman.* New York: Columbia University Press, 1943.

revised by Michael Bellesiles

TAPPAN MASSACRE, NEW JERSEY.
28 September 1778. Once Admiral Howe's fleet returned from ending the threat from d'Estaing's squadron, Major General Henry Clinton could risk sending large foraging parties to sweep through Westchester County and northern New Jersey. On the night of 21–22 September Major General Charles Cornwallis crossed to Bergen on the west side of the Hudson with some 5,000 men (Wilhelm Knyphausen would start a similar operation on the east side with 3,000 on 30 September). As Cornwallis established a forward base on the site of Fort Lee, Washington augmented the screening forces and told Major General Anthony Wayne to try and limit the depredations. Wayne posted the New Jersey militia of General William Winds at New Tappan while the Third Continental Light Dragoons of Colonel George Baylor occupied Old Tappan, two and a half miles away. Cornwallis aggressively sought ways to cut off and annihilate small parties and focused on Tappan, where he thought about seven hundred militia lay. During the night of 27–28 September he sent out two columns. Cornwallis himself led the right; Major General Charles "No-flint" Grey of Paoli the left. Deserters warned Winds in time to pull back, but Grey learned that Baylor was nearby and switched objectives. After a successful approach under cover of darkness, undoubtedly with the assistance of Loyalist guides, Grey's men silenced a twelve-man guard and surrounded three barns in which about 120 troopers slept. The Second Light Infantry Battalion charged in with the bayonet and smashed the regiment as a fighting force without firing a shot. Even

Kemble felt that the British troops got out of control and killed men trying to surrender.

NUMBERS AND LOSSES

Baylor lost about 120 men, of whom Grey killed about 50 and captured about 50. Baylor was among the prisoners. Major Alexander Clough and seven other officers were mortally wounded.

SIGNIFICANCE

The operation had no impact on operations other than forcing Washington to send the survivors back to Virginia under Lieutenant Colonel William Washington to recover, and thus made a key player available for later campaigns in the south. But the "massacre" did inflame the Patriots. More important, Baylor's failure to provide adequate security did not obscure a fundamental weakness in using mounted units in such missions without giving them infantry support. Washington learned this lesson: in January 1781 the light dragoon regiments converted into combined arms legions.

SEE ALSO *Paoli, Pennsylvania.*

BIBLIOGRAPHY

Leiby, Adrian C. *The Revolutionary War in the Hackensack Valley: The Jersey Dutch and the Neutral Ground, 1775–1783.* New Brunswick, N.J.: Rutgers University Press, 1980.

Mazur, D. Bennett, and Wayne Daniels. *Baylor's Dragoons Massacre, September 28, 1778.* N.p. 1968.

Weskerna, Eleanor, and F. W. William Maurer. *"The Flower of the Virginian" and the Massacre Near Old Tappan, September 28, 1778.* River Vale, N.J.: Baylor's Dragoons Memorial Committee, 1978.

revised by Robert K. Wright Jr.

TAPPAN SEA.

12–18 July 1776. The Tappan Sea, now called Tappan Zee, is the widest stretch of the Hudson River, to the north of Manhattan. On 12 July, 10 days after the British troop build-up started on Staten Island, the warships *Phoenix* (forty guns) and *Rose* (twenty guns), along with a schooner and two tenders, ran the American batteries that were supposed to be guarding the entrance to the Hudson and sailed forty miles upstream to anchor, virtually unscathed, in the Tappan Sea. On 3 August Lieutenant Colonel Benjamin Tupper led five small boats in a gallant but unsuccessful attack against the flotilla. On 16 August an attack by fire rafts also failed, although the Phoenix was seriously threatened and the British commander was so alarmed by this attempt that he withdrew. Rerunning the gauntlet, he rejoined the fleet on 18 July.

This naval demonstration demoralized the Americans, showing that British ships could move at will against the flanks and rear of the main army in and around New York City. Commander in Chief George Washington and his generals were further bewildered as to Howe's strategy—where would he move from Staten Island? As for the immediate purpose of the naval demonstration, other than testing American defenses, and preparing for a link-up with General John Burgoyne's expected advance from Canada, Washington supposed that it was to cut the flow of American supplies by water and land along the Hudson, or to supply arms to Loyalists in the region.

One serious aspect of the affair was the ludicrously poor performance of many American troops. Not more than half the artillerists went to their guns, and these scored only a few insignificant hits, although they fired almost 200 shots at close range. Several men were killed or wounded because they carelessly failed to sponge their guns, while hundreds of troops neglected their duties to play spectator.

SEE ALSO *New York Campaign.*

revised by Barnet Schecter

TAR AND FEATHERS.

A form of punishment in which the victim is coated with molten pitch or tar and then covered with feathers. Although it was an official punishment in England as early as the twelfth century, it is associated in America with mob action. The Sons of Liberty used the punishment against Loyalists and crown officials; a Boston rebel got the treatment in 1755. In the opening scenes of the historical novel *Oliver Wiswell* (1940), Kenneth Roberts gives a vivid and horrible picture of a man tarred, feathered, and ridden on a rail.

Mark M. Boatner

TARLETON, BANASTRE.

(1754–1833). Baronet, British army officer and politician. Tarleton, born in Liverpool on 21 August 1754, was the son of a merchant and ship owner in the sugar and slave trades who became mayor of the city in 1764. Banastre entered the Middle Temple, a leading London law school, in April 1770 and matriculated at University College, Oxford, in November 1771. It seems likely that he was destined for a legal career in conjunction with the family business. When his father died in 1773, however, he inherited £5,000 and proceeded to gamble it away. On 20 April 1775, to evade ruin he bought, with his mother's assistance, a cornetcy in the First Dragoon Guards. After training he volunteered for service in America, reaching Cape Fear with Charles Cornwallis's troops on 3 May 1776.

Tarleton took part in the unsuccessful Charleston Expedition before serving in New York. Attached to the Sixteenth Light Dragoons when they arrived from Britain, he took part in the surprise attack that captured rebel general Charles Lee at Basking Ridge, New Jersey, on 13 December 1776. He was promoted captain in January 1777 and served in the Pennsylvania campaign. On 8 January 1778 he was made captain in the Seventy-ninth Foot but continued to make his mark as a daring and energetic cavalry commander. He also acquired a reputation for ruthlessness toward suspected civilian rebels, an attitude apparently sharpened by the acute supply difficulties faced by the British army in America. As he wrote to John André on 19 February 1779, "Coolness Apathy & Civil Law will never supply Hussars with Horses." To what extent he acted on his words is another matter.

Later in the year he became the lieutenant colonel commandant of Cathcart's Legion, soon renamed the British Legion, a Loyalist cavalry and mounted infantry formation which often operated with the Seventeenth Dragoons. On 2 July 1779 he led 360 cavalry against Poundridge, New York, where he failed to capture Major Ebenezer Lockwood. Sent south with Clinton's Charleston expedition in 1780, on 23 March his Legion routed a body of rebel militia and dragoons and captured some badly needed horses. Three days later he was worsted in a skirmish around Rutledge's Plantation, which almost led to Clinton's capture; but his greatest triumphs were yet to come. On 14 April Tarleton took Monck's Corner on the Cooper River, thus completing the isolation of Benjamin Lincoln's army in Charleston. Charleston surrendered on 12 May and with it Lincoln's entire force. On 6 May he surprised a rebel force at Lenud's Ferry on the Santee River, and on 29 May he annihilated a rebel force twice the size of his own at Waxhaws.

Here there occurred an incident that seemed to confirm Tarleton's reputation as a ruthless commander. In the final charge, Tarleton cut down an American officer as he struggled to raise a white flag. At that moment Tarleton's horse was shot from under him and he went down. Seeing their commander fall, his soldiers went berserk, killing every rebel they could reach until they were brought back under control. Although it better illustrated the Legion's brittle discipline than any personal vindictiveness by Tarleton, rebel propaganda quickly branded him "Bloody Tarleton" and coined the term "Tarleton's quarter." Though no more justified than the opprobrium flung

under similar circumstances at Charles "No-flint" Grey, the story may have blackened the British cause in the eyes of southern civilians, and was certainly used to justify American outrages later on.

At Camden, South Carolina, on 16 August he was loosed to drive Thomas Gage's broken army from the battlefield, after which Cornwallis sent him in pursuit of Thomas Sumter. Two days later, Tarleton surprised and destroyed his quarry at Fishing Creek, North Carolina. Although Sumter himself escaped, 150 Americans were killed, 300 taken, and numerous British prisoners and supply wagons recaptured.

It is a measure of Tarleton's leadership that the Legion was far less successful when, as at Williamson's Plantation on 12 July, he was not in direct command. Soon after Fishing Creek he fell seriously ill with a fever and in subsequent actions at Wahab's Plantation (21 September) and Charlotte (26 September), the Legion did badly. Tarleton's illness was also partly responsible for Cornwallis's failure to send help to Patrick Ferguson in time to prevent the disaster at Kings Mountain, South Carolina, on 7 October. Tarleton rose from his sickbed to track Francis Marion through the lower Peedee swamps; but before he could catch him, Cornwallis recalled him to deal with Sumter, who was threatening Ninety Six, South Carolina. At Blackstocks on 20 November 1780 Tarleton, with only 270 men engaged, fought 1,000 rebels to a standstill, badly wounded Sumter, and deflected the threat to Ninety Six. Despite his heavy losses, it was a striking success.

Tarleton's reputation as a light cavalry and counter-partisan leader now stood very high. However, he turned out to be less successful as a conventional battlefield commander, leading a balanced force of cavalry, infantry, and artillery against Daniel Morgan at Cowpens on 17 January 1781. Tarleton launched a well-conceived attack which nearly succeeded. However, Morgan had chosen a position that forced his shaky militia to stand and fight, and had deployed his riflemen in depth to slow down the British advance. When the attacking troops were exhausted he counterattacked, the British force broke, and two-thirds were killed or taken. Tarleton rallied some dragoons, burned his baggage, and fought a personal duel with William Washington before escaping with about 300 men. His Legion, lacking his personal direction, had done badly, and his name for generalship was severely damaged. Although Cornwallis defended his performance, he never gave Tarleton another independent command, and their earlier free and easy relations came to an end. However, that was not the end of Tarleton's career, reputation, or successes.

At Tarrant's Tavern on 1 February 1781, he surprised and dispersed a numerically superior force so successfully that few militia turned out against Cornwallis as he marched deeper into North Carolina. He provided vigorous support for the infantry Cornwallis sent to surprise Greene's advance guard at Wetzell's Mills on 6 March. Nine days later at Guilford Courthouse, he fought a heavy advance guard action and suffered a wound that later cost him two fingers. At the end of the day he led his cavalry against the American rear guard and was wounded again. He marched into Virginia with Cornwallis and on 4 June raided on Charlottesville, capturing seven members of the legislature, narrowly missing Thomas Jefferson himself, and destroyed a thousand muskets and four hundred barrels of gunpowder. From 9 to 24 July he carried out a long-range raid against enemy stores, covering over two hundred miles, outrunning all pursuit and news of his position. It was a brilliant feat, although results were relatively insignificant compared with his losses in skirmishes and from the heat. During the final stages of the campaign, he joined Thomas Dundas at Gloucester Point across the river from Yorktown, where on 3 October he was pinned under his fallen horse and almost taken by advancing French cavalry. When Cornwallis surrendered two weeks later, Tarleton became a prisoner of war.

Returning home on parole in January 1782, Tarleton found himself a national hero. Befriended by the Prince of Wales and painted in Legion uniform by Sir Joshua Reynolds and Thomas Gainsborough, the foremost portrait painters of the day, he began a five-year-long affair with Perdita (Mrs. Mary Robinson), an actress, poet, and ex-mistress of the prince. He lived extravagantly and gambled heavily. In 1787, embroiled in a dispute about his conduct at Cowpens, he published his *History of the Campaigns of 1780 and 1781, in the Southern Provinces of North America* (1787), a usefully detailed but self-serving account which attacked Cornwallis. It may have also been intended to further his political ambitions. In 1790, following a narrow defeat in 1784, he became the Foxite member of Parliament for Liverpool. In Parliament he spoke on military matters and, reflecting his constituents' concerns, in defense of the slave trade. He became a major general in 1794, lieutenant general in 1801, and full general in 1812, but, apart from a brief assignment in Portugal in 1798, he never held another active command. He married Priscilla Susan Bertie in 1798 and became a baronet in 1816. He died in Hertfordshire on 23 January 1833.

Tarleton was probably the finest commander of light cavalry on either side in the War of American Independence. Such success so young probably went to his head and his reputation for vanity was probably well earned. His own utterances and the criticisms of fellow officers give some colour to accusations of ruthless brutality. However, the direct evidence against him is thin and should be understood in the context of the brutalising partisan war, in which both sides committed outrages.

The vilification of "Bloody Tarleton" probably owes more to his military skills than to his vices.

SEE ALSO *Blackstock's, South Carolina; British Legion; Camden Campaign; Charleston Expedition of Clinton in 1776; Charleston Expedition of Clinton in 1780; Cowpens, South Carolina; Fishing Creek, North Carolina; Guilford Courthouse, North Carolina; Kings Mountain, South Carolina; Lee, Charles (1731–1782); Lenud's Ferry, South Carolina; Monck's Corner, South Carolina; Morgan, Daniel; Tarleton's Quarter; Tarleton's Virginia Raid of 9–24 July 1781; Tarrant's Tavern, North Carolina; Wahab's Plantation, North Carolina; Washington, William; Waxhaws, South Carolina; Wetzell's Mills, North Carolina; Williamson's Plantation, South Carolina.*

BIBLIOGRAPHY

Bass, R. D. *The Green Dragoon: The Lives of Banastre Tarleton and Mary Robinson.* 2nd ed. Columbia, S.C: Sandlapper, 1973.

Mackesy, Piers. *The War for America, 1775–1783.* London: Longman, 1964.

Wickwire, F. B., and M. B. Wickwire. *Cornwallis and the War of Independence.* London: Faber and Faber, 1971.

revised by John Oliphant

TARLETON'S LEGION SEE *British Legion.*

TARLETON'S QUARTER.

This cynical term for "no quarter" was coined after Tarleton's victory at the Waxhaws in South Carolina on 29 May 1780.

SEE ALSO *Waxhaws, South Carolina.*

Mark M. Boatner

TARLETON'S VIRGINIA RAID OF 9–24 JULY 1781.

Intent on destroying the rebels' public and private stores, Cornwallis ordered Tarleton to ride through Prince Edward Court House to New London, Virginia, more than 150 miles west of Cornwallis' new base at Suffolk on the south side of the James River. Tarleton left Cobham (opposite Jamestown Island) on 9 July and rode through Petersburg, Amelia Court House, Prince Edward Court House, Charlotte, New London, and Bedford. Here he camped in the rich grasslands at the foot of the Blue Ridge Mountains for two days and collected some of the finest horses in America. Task forces of this type were too strong to be opposed by the Virginia militia which by this point in the war lacked adequate arms. But Lafayette sent Wayne into Amelia County with his Pennsylvania Continentals to try to intercept Tarleton on his return. Morgan was assembling a second strong force at Goode's Bridge, near Petersburg, for the same purpose. Learning of this threat, Tarleton burned his three light wagons and returned by a more southerly route through Lunenburg County. Despite intense July heat, which limited his movement to the early morning and late afternoon, Tarleton covered 30 or 40 miles a day and outran all news of his location; he was never in danger. On 24 July he returned to Suffolk, having covered 400 miles in 15 days. It was a remarkable performance, but Tarleton noted that:

> The stores destroyed, either of a public or private nature, were not in quantity or value equivalent to the damage sustained in the skirmishes on the route, and the loss of men and horses by the excessive heat of the climate.

SEE ALSO *Virginia Military Operations.*

revised by Robert K. Wright Jr.

TARRANT, CAESAR. (c. 1740–1797). Patriot

seaman. Born a slave in Virginia around 1740, Caesar took the last name of his owner, Carter Tarrant. Acquiring the unusual skill of river pilot, a knowledge generally denied to slaves for fear that they would use it to escape, Tarrant saw the American Revolution as a chance to gain his freedom. Though Virginia's royal governor, Lord Dunmore, promised freedom to slaves who joined his forces, Tarrant offered his skills to the Patriots and was named a pilot in the Virginia navy in 1775. Over the next three years he guided ships through the state's coastal waters and become a trusted pilot. In 1777 a small fleet under the command of Commodore Richard Taylor gave battle to the *Lord Howe.* Piloting the *Patriot,* Tarrant rammed it into the larger British ship. In the ensuing battle, Tarrant acted with great courage, earning his captain's praise. He behaved similarly in a number of other encounters with the British, for which the Americans rewarded him by returning him to slavery. In 1789, five years after the death of Carter Tarrant, the Virginia assembly finally corrected this injustice by granting Tarrant his freedom, paying Mary Tarrant recompense. Tarrant devoted the rest of his life to attempting to purchase his family's freedom, buying his wife and one daughter in 1793 but leaving two other children enslaved. He clearly earned the respect of his fellow pilots, who petitioned the

assembly in 1791 to grant qualified free blacks like Tarrant pilot licenses. He died in Hampton, Virginia, in 1797.

SEE ALSO *African Americans in the Revolution.*

Michael Bellesiles

TARRANT, SARAH SEE *Salem, Massachuesetts.*

TARRANT'S TAVERN, NORTH CAROLINA. 1 February 1781. After Cornwallis crossed

the Catawba River at Cowan's Ford, Lieutenant Colonel Banastre Tarleton, who had already crossed at Beattie's Ford, moved swiftly to this place, about ten miles from the river, to strike a body of some two hundred North Carolina militia assembling there. Although outnumbered, Tarleton risked an attack. Stung by their commander's taunt to "Remember the Cowpens," Tarleton's dragoons charged and routed the militia, whose muskets were mostly soaked by the rain and inoperable. Tarleton doubled the number of Patriot militia in his account of the battle and exaggerated its casualties, but the victory was definitely quick and easy, the Patriots losing ten dead without firing a shot. The North Carolina militia was dispersed and demoralized by its defeat. What Tarleton did not know was that he had narrowly missed capturing General Nathanael Greene in his pursuit immediately after the action.

SEE ALSO *Torrence's Tavern, North Carolina.*

revised by Michael Bellesiles

TAXATION, EXTERNAL AND INTERNAL. Before 1765, Americans had not clearly

thought through an answer to the question of Parliament's right to levy taxes on the colonies. There was general agreement that Parliament had the right to regulate trade, a consequence of which might be the raising of a revenue through customs duties on imports. The imperial government's attempt to tax Americans directly with the Stamp Act forced the colonists to clarify their thinking. In the process, a significant number of them came to believe that Parliament did not have the right to lay any tax on Americans, even to regulate trade. However, in order to facilitate repeal of the Stamp Act by

Parliament, several influential individuals on both sides of the Atlantic—including William Pitt and Benjamin Franklin—introduced the idea that the colonists objected only to internal taxes, such as those prescribed by the Stamp Act, but conceded Parliament's right to raise a revenue through trade regulation. The stance was disingenuous at best, since most Americans made no distinction between external and internal taxes, and it introduced confusion into both policy decisions at the time and accounts of later historians. Charles Townshend, chancellor of the exchequer, cleverly constructed his revenue act in 1767 to avoid levying internal taxes, thereby "honoring" the colonists' distinction while also taking advantage of their failure to adopt a strong position prior to 1765 against all forms of parliamentary taxation. The purpose of the Massachusetts Circular Letter was to organize American resistance to all forms of parliamentary taxation, whether external or internal.

SEE ALSO *Declaratory Act; Massachusetts Circular Letter; Stamp Act; Townshend Revenue Act; Townshend, Charles.*

BIBLIOGRAPHY

Morgan, Edmund S., and Helen M. Morgan. *The Stamp Act Crisis: Prologue to Revolution.* Chapel Hill: University of North Carolina Press, 1953.

Thomas, Peter D. G. *British Politics and the Stamp Act Crisis: The First Phase of the American Revolution, 1763–1767.* Oxford: Oxford University Press, 1975.

———. *The Townshend Duties Crisis: The Second Phase of the American Revolution, 1767–1771.* Oxford: Oxford University Press, 1987.

revised by Harold E. Selesky

American colonists generally rejected the notion of "virtual representation." (The most notable argument was put forward by Daniel Dulany, an attorney from Maryland.) Their view of representation was based on the idea that delegates elected by voters to the local legislative assembly should "represent" the concerns of their constituents in a particular geographic locality. Since no men elected in North America sat in Parliament, that body could not fairly represent the colonists and thus could not levy taxes on people it did not represent.

Parliament had levied customs duties on parts of American trade before 1764, but that form of taxation had not become a widespread grievance because the duties were relatively easy to evade. In that year, however, imperial officials signaled that they were going to enforce a revised customs schedule and intended to levy a direct stamp tax on the colonists. These decisions generated an unprecedented level of resentment in the colonies, as much because Parliament was unilaterally changing the existing system as because of the tax itself. Many Americans concluded that taxing them in these ways was unconstitutional and "tyrannical." The slogan, "Taxation without representation is tyranny," summarized these beliefs, and variations on it became a powerful means of spreading the patriot message in 1764–1765. (John Adams remembered that James Otis had used the phrase in his famous oration against the writs of assistance on 24 February 1761, but Adams's memory was not always accurate.)

SEE ALSO *Dulany, Daniel.*

revised by Harold E. Selesky

TAXATION WITHOUT REPRESENTATION IS TYRANNY.

There was no disagreement in Britain or America about the basic truth of this idea, first used by John Hampden in 1637 against Charles I, but by the middle of the eighteenth century "representation" had come to mean different things on opposite sides of the Atlantic. In theory, Parliament had the right to levy taxes in Britain because its members acted in the name and for the interest of the entire realm. Every Englishman was "virtually" represented in Parliament, whether or not he had actually participated in choosing its members. After the final French and Indian War, imperial officials who wanted to increase Britain's control over its colonies argued that the interests of the American colonists were represented in Parliament in the same way, and that Parliament thus had the right to levy taxes on the colonists to support the greater good of the whole empire.

TAYLOR, GEORGE.

(1716?–1781). Signer. Ireland-Pennsylvania. What is reasonably certain about Taylor's early life is that he settled in East Nantmeal, Pennsylvania, in 1736, became clerk in an iron works, rose to the position of manager, and in 1742 married his boss's widow, whose legacy hastened his success. Around 1754 he moved to Durham, Pennsylvania, opened a successful ironworks, and settled in Easton, Pennsylvania, in 1764, being elected that year to the first of five one-year terms in the provincial assembly. He became a leader of the proprietary party, opposing Franklin and those who favored crown rule. He was a member of the local committee to choose delegates for the Stamp Act Congress, and he later was chairman of the Northampton County meeting to protest the Boston Port Bill in 1774. After being named to the county committee of correspondence, in July 1775 he became colonel of the Third Battalion of the Bucks County militia, and on 20 July 1776 he became a delegate to the Continental Congress when it was decided to replace the representatives who refused to sign the Declaration of Independence. He became a Signer on 2 August but resigned from Congress in March 1777 having taken no other part in the business of Congress other than to treat with the Susquehanna Indians in January 1777 at the Easton conference. Nor did he take any active part as a militia officer, although he retained the title of colonel.

He sat briefly in the Supreme Executive Council of his state in 1777 but retired for ill health after six weeks. He spent the next several years overseeing the production of cannonballs at his Durham foundry and another in Greenwich, New Jersey. He died in Durham on 23 February 1781, leaving behind a number of illegitimate children.

revised by Michael Bellesiles

TEA ACT.

TEA ACT. 10 May 1773. Colonial Americans drank lots of tea. From 1764 through 1768, exports of tea from England to the colonies averaged nearly 565,000 pounds a year. But, with the adoption of nonimportation by the colonies, that average dropped to less than 215,000 pounds a year from 1769 to 1772. To save the corrupt and mismanaged East India Company from bankruptcy, Parliament authorized it to send half a million pounds of tea to America for sale with payment of only the nominal 3 pence a pound in American duty, and with reimbursement for the British duty previously paid. This meant that East India Company tea could undersell smuggled Dutch tea as well as legally imported tea. Consignees were designated in New York, Charleston, Philadelphia, and Boston to receive the shipment.

The Philadelphia consignees were forced to resign by a committee that had been appointed for this purpose by a mass meeting on 16 October 1773. The New York consignees resigned after harbor pilots were warned not to board the tea ships and the Sons of Liberty branded tea importers as enemies of America. The Charleston tea ship arrived on 2 December, but the consignees were forced to resign the next day, and the tea was impounded after the lapse of the prescribed twenty-day waiting period. (In July 1776 it was auctioned by the Revolutionary government.)

In Boston, a town meeting on 5 and 6 November endorsed the Philadelphia resolves, but the consignees would not resign. Local radicals decided to destroy the tea, which they accomplished at the Boston Tea Party on 16 December 1773.

SEE ALSO *Boston Tea Party; Nonimportation.*

BIBLIOGRAPHY

Jensen, Merrill, ed. *English Historical Documents.* Volume IX: *American Colonial Documents to 1776.* David C. Douglas, general editor. New York: Oxford University Press, 1955.

Knollenberg, Bernard. *Growth of the American Revolution, 1766–1775.* Indianapolis, Ind.: Liberty Fund, 2002.

Labaree, Benjamin W. *The Boston Tea Party.* New York: Oxford University Press, 1964.

revised by Harold E. Selesky

TEARCOAT SWAMP, SOUTH CAROLINA.

TEARCOAT SWAMP, SOUTH CAROLINA. 25 October 1780. Also known as Tarcote and Tarcot Swamp. With instructions from General Horatio Gates to continue his harassment of the enemy's rear, Lieutenant Colonel Francis Marion established a base at Port's Ferry. On 24 October he learned that Lieutenant Colonel Samuel Tynes was assembling Loyalist militia near Tearcoat Swamp, in the vicinity of where U.S. Highway 301 now crosses Black River. Marion was able to arm his 150 recruits with British firearms he had seized from the Loyalists at Nelson's Ferry. Marching quickly, Marion's force surprised the Loyalists shortly after midnight. Tynes apparently failed to post sentries, allowing the rebels to rush into the Loyalist camp firing their weapons. They received no return fire and routed the Loyalists, who lost 3 dead, 14 wounded, 23 prisoners, 80 good horses captured with their bridles, saddles, and blankets, and 80 new British muskets. More important, however, Loyalist activities in the area of the Santee and Peedee Rivers of South Carolina were completely squelched, and many Loyalists joined Marion.

SEE ALSO *Marion, Francis; Port's Ferry, Pee Dee River, South Carolina.*

revised by Michael Bellesiles

TEISSÈDRE DE FLEURY, FRANÇOIS LOUIS.

TEISSÈDRE DE FLEURY, FRANÇOIS LOUIS. (1749–before 1814). (Viscomte de.) French volunteer. Born at Saint-Hippolyte, Aveyron, he was a volunteer in the infantry regiment of Roergue starting 15 May 1768, had become a *sous lieutenant* by August, and was promoted to *sous aide major* on 5 February 1772. He was made First Lieutenant in 1777 and left for America with Tronson du Coudray. When Congress refused to employ Coudray and his officers, Fleury joined the army as a volunteer. In the affair of Piscataway, New Jersey, on 10 May 1777, he distinguished himself, and Congress commissioned him captain of engineers on 22 May.

On 3 October 1777, Washington appointed Fleury brigade major to Pulaski with the comment that he was "to be respected as such." Serving at Fort Mifflin as an engineer, he came into conflict with the fort's commander, Lieutenant Colonel Samuel Smith, whom Washington eventually ordered "to make the best arrangement." Because of what Congress termed his "disinterested gallantry," they breveted Fleury a lieutenant colonel on 26 November. During January and February 1778, Congress had hoped he would set fire to British shipping on the Delaware River, but he was not able to carry out his project. This plan was interrupted by his desire to join Lafayette for the expedition to Canada; Fleury had sought to command a corps of French Canadians there, but Lafayette's Canadian campaign was cancelled later in February. In April 1778, in the absence of an army assignment, Washington sent Fleury temporarily as subinspector under Steuben to maneuver and discipline the troops of Brigadier General Smallwood. In June he was attached to General Lee's division but the following month was sent as Washington's representative with Hamilton to Estaing in Newport. As Fleury's furlough from the French army was running out, he requested Congress on 29 November to intercede directly with French minister Gérard, but Washington opposed congressional intervention with foreign powers. Washington again ordered Fleury to assist in battalion training in late April 1779.

Fleury's performance in the attack on Stony Point on 16 July 1779 eclipsed his other achievements. He was the first to enter and took its flag. When he requested the flag from Congress, it balked and voted him one of eight congressional medals bestowed during the nine years of the war. Hamilton even suggested that he become secretary to La Luzerne. Congress granted him leave on 27 September to return to France and commended him further on 1 October 1779, which caused him to delay his plans and to consider joining Estaing in South Carolina. He left for France shortly afterward. In response to a recommendation from Vergennes, he was promoted on 19 March 1780 to major in the Saintonge Regiment and in 1781 was made a chevalier in the Order of Saint Louis. Rushing to join his regiment, he asked Franklin to send the medal to his father and returned under Rochambeau to America. On 22 May 1780 Congress extended his leave to enable him to serve with the French forces, but in January 1781 it suspended his pay and benefits during his absence from the American army. He returned as a major in the Saintonge regiment of Rochambeau's army and distinguished himself at the siege of Yorktown. In October 1782 Rochambeau put Fleury in command of a French force stationed in Portsmouth, New Hampshire, to repulse a possible British attack. Following his return to France in June 1783, Franklin presented him with a duplicate medal in gold on 15 August 1783.

On 16 January 1784, Fleury was appointed colonel of the Pondichéry Regiment and made commandant of Ile-de-France and Ile-de-Bourbon in 1785. In April 1790 he returned to France and on 30 June 1791 was promoted to *maréchal de camp*. On 30 April 1792 he was wounded in the retreat from Mons when he tried to rally the rear guard. His ill health forced his resignation on 24 June 1792, and he retired to Rebais. In 1799 he was living in Grenoble and appears to have died in Paris sometime before 1814.

SEE ALSO *Estaing, Charles Hector Théodat, Comte d'; Fort Mifflin, Pennsylvania; Gérard, Conrad Alexandre; Hamilton, Alexander; La Luzerne, Anne-César de; Lee, Charles (1731–1782); Medals; Smallwood, William; Steuben, Friedrich Wilhelm von; Stony Point, New York.*

BIBLIOGRAPHY

Bodinier, André. *Dictionnaire des officiers de l'armée royale qui ont combattu aux Etats-Unis pendant la guerre d'Indépendance 1776–1783.* Vincennes, France: Service historique de l'armée, 1982.

Contenson, Ludovic de. *La Société des Cincinnati de France et la Guerre d'Amérique.* Paris: Editions Auguste Picard, 1934.

Ford, Worthington C., et al., eds. *Journals of the Continental Congress, 1774–1789.* 34 vols. Washington, D.C.: U.S. Government Printing Office, 1904–1937.

Franklin, Benjamin. *Papers of Benjamin Franklin.* Edited by Leonard W. Labaree, et al. 37 vols. to date. New Haven, Conn.: Yale University Press, 1959–.

Lafayette, Gilbert du Motier de. *Lafayette in the Age of the American Revolution: Selected Letters and Documents, 1776–1790.* Edited by Stanley J. Idzerda, et al. 5 vols. to date. Ithaca, N.Y.: Cornell University Press, 1977–.

Laurens, Henry. *The Papers of Henry Laurens.* Edited by Philip M. Hamer, et al. 16 vols. Columbia: University of South Carolina Press, 1968–2003.

Rice, Howard C., Jr., and Anne S. K. Brown, eds. and trans. *The American Campaigns of Rochambeau's Army: 1780, 1781, 1782, 1783.* 2 vols. Princeton, N.J.: Princeton University Press, 1972.

Smith, Paul H., et al., eds. *Letters of Delegates of the Continental Congress, 1774–1789.* 26 vols. Washington: U.S. Government Printing Office, 1976–2000.

Stevens, Benjamin Franklin, comp. *B. F. Stevens' Facsimiles of Manuscripts in European Archives Relating to America, 1775–1783.* 24 vols. London: Malby, 1889–1895.

Teissèdre de Fleury, François Louis. Journal. George Washington Papers. Library of Congress, Washington, D.C.

Washington, George. *Writings of George Washington.* Edited by John C. Fitzpatrick. 39 vols. Washington: U.S. Government Printing Office, 1931–1944.

———. *The Papers of George Washington, Revolutionary War Series.* Edited by Philander Chase, et al. 14 vols. to date. Charlottesville: University Press of Virginia, 1985–.

revised by Robert Rhodes Crout

TEMPLE, JOHN. (1732–1798). British official.

Born in Boston in 1732, Temple went to London in 1761 in search of preferment. Aided by family connections, which included Earl Temple and future prime minister George Grenville, he was named lieutenant governor of New Hampshire and surveyor general of customs. Temple earned the approval of colonial merchants for his fair implementation of the tax laws; his not very secret opposition to the Stamp Act; and his bitter dispute with the Massachusetts governor, Francis Bernard, whom he accused of fraud. In 1767 he further cemented his warm relations with Boston Patriots by marrying Elizabeth Bowdoin, daughter of James Bowdoin. Appointed to the Board of Customs that same year, Temple was the only one of the five commissioners not driven out of Boston by an angry crowd. Using Temple's local approval against him, Governor Bernard succeeded in getting Temple fired.

Back in England in 1771, Temple—unable to regain his position—turned to extortion, threatening to publish his correspondence unless new employment was found for him. Lord North gave in, making Temple surveyor general of customs for England. The publication of Governor Thomas Hutchinson's letters in 1772 cast suspicion on Temple as the source of these documents, leading to a duel with William Whately in which the latter was wounded. Temple again lost his position, even after Benjamin Franklin admitted that he had leaked the letters. In 1778 Lord North sent Temple to Boston as a gesture towards reconciliation with the Patriots, but Congress refused to listen to him, and he returned to England the following year. In 1785 he was named the first British consul to the United States. He died in New York City on 17 November 1798.

SEE ALSO *Hutchinson Letters Affair.*

BIBLIOGRAPHY

Bowdoin-Temple Papers. Massachusetts Historical Society, Boston.

Michael Bellesiles

TERNAY, CHARLES LOUIS D'ARSAC, CHEVALIER DE. (1722–1780). French

admiral. Of an old Breton family with a naval tradition, he entered the French naval school in 1738. After taking part in the unsuccessful defense of Louisburg in 1757, he commanded a division of gunboats on the St. Lawrence. Promoted to captain, he participated in a raid that captured Saint John, New Brunswick, on 2 June 1762. After the peace of 1763 he served on the Leeward Islands station and later was promoted to brigadier general of the naval forces. In 1772 he retired as *chef d'escadre* and was appointed governor general of the island of Bourbon. He left this post in 1779 to reenter the active service.

Early in 1780 he organized the fleet that was to escort the expeditionary force of the comte de Rochambeau to America. With eight ships of the line, two frigates, and two *bomb-galliots,* he arrived off Newport on 10 July 1780, just three days before a British fleet under Admiral Thomas Graves arrived off Sandy Hook to give the British an advantage of thirteen more powerful ships of the line against Ternay's eight. (One of Ternay's ships was being used as a transport.) Lafayette as Washington's representative met with Ternay and Rochambeau on 30 July. While Ternay expressed a willingness to take naval action when there was naval superiority, he and Rochambeau agreed that without it, no action would occur. That was in line with their instructions. As a senior officer, however, Ternay took a quick dislike to the opinions of the young Lafayette. The British eventually bottled up Ternay's fleet in Newport. The Americans, on the other hand, were bitterly disappointed to find that they had to spend an inactive season because the French could not achieve the all-important naval superiority. Ternay died on 15 December 1780 in Newport of a fever. Upon reflection after Ternay's death, Lafayette wrote that "he was ill-tempered and stubborn, but firm, clear-sighted, and intelligent, and all things considered, his death is a loss to us." Following Ternay's death, the French fleet was commanded by Destouches until the arrival of Barras in May 1781.

SEE ALSO *Graves, Thomas; Lafayette, Marquis de; Rochambeau, Jean Baptiste Donatien de Vimeur, comte de.*

BIBLIOGRAPHY

Donoil, Jean Henri. *Histoire de la participation de la France à l'établissement des Etats-Unis d'Amérique.* 5 vols. Paris: Imprimerie Nationale, 1884–1899.

Kennett, Lee. *The French Forces in America, 1780–1783.* Westport, Conn.: Greenwood Press, 1977.

Lafayette, Gilbert du Motier de. *Lafayette in the Age of the American Revolution: Selected Letters and Documents, 1776–1790.* Edited by Stanley J. Idzerda, et al. 5 vols. to date. Ithaca, N.Y.: Cornell University Press, 1977–.

Linyer de la Barbée, Maurice. *Le Chevalier de Ternay: Vie de Charles Henry Louis d'Arsac de Ternay, chef d'escadre des armées navales, 1723–1780.* 2 vols. Grenoble, France: Editions des Quatre Seigneurs, 1972.

revised by Robert Rhodes Crout

TEST OATH. To force a declaration of principles from those who were indifferent or were secret enemies of the Revolution, state legislatures enacted "test" laws. The

oath demanded by these laws varied in the different colonies that adopted the laws, but in general they prescribed loyalty to the Patriot cause, disloyalty to the British government, and a promise not to aid and abet the enemy. In the test acts passed before the Declaration of Independence, "the oath of abjuration and allegiance was omitted" (Van Tyne, p. 131). The British offered various inducements to Americans to swear an oath of allegiance. These included the Peace Commission of the Howes and their offer of 30 November 1776 and the efforts of Patrick Ferguson during the Kings Mountain campaign.

SEE ALSO *Kings Mountain, South Carolina; Peace Commission of the Howes.*

BIBLIOGRAPHY

Van Tyne, Claude H. *The Loyalists in the American Revolution.* New York: P. Smith, 1929.

Mark M. Boatner

THACHER, JAMES. (1754–1844). Continental surgeon and diarist. Massachusetts.

James Thacher was the son of a poor farmer who had the good fortune to be apprenticed at the age of sixteen to Abner Hersey, the leading physician in Thacher's hometown of Barnstable, where he received five years of arduous training. When the war began, Thacher applied to serve in the provincial hospital at Cambridge, was accepted by the medical examiners on 10 July and started his duties five days later. In an account of the examination of another candidate he recorded in his *Military Journal,* Thacher reported that the candidate, asked how he would induce a sweat in a patient to remedy rheumatism, replied that "I would have him examined by a medical committee."

In February 1776 Thacher was named surgeon's mate of Colonel Asa Whitcomb's Sixth Continental Infantry (Massachusetts), then recruiting at its camp on Prospect Hill. He marched with the regiment to Canada and took part in the retreat from Ticonderoga. On 1 April 1777 he was assigned as surgeon's mate to the General Hospital at Albany but went with the regiment when it moved to West Point. He returned to the field as surgeon of the First Virginia State Regiment on 10 November 1778 and spent the winter in quarters at Middlebrook, New Jersey. He transferred in June 1779 to Colonel Henry Jackson's Additional Continental Regiment, then stationed in Providence, Rhode Island, and marched with it to Boston, where it embarked on transports to reinforce the Penobscot expedition. Delayed by contrary winds, the transports put into Portsmouth, New Hampshire, thereby enabling the regiment to escape capture at Penobscot. He spent the arduous winter of 1779–1780 in New Jersey and witnessed the execution of Major John André on 1 October 1780. When his regiment (designated the Sixteenth Massachusetts beginning 23 July 1780) was absorbed in the reduction of the Massachusetts Line on 1 January 1781, he remained as surgeon of the Ninth Massachusetts. On 17 July 1781 he was detached as surgeon to the elite battalion of light infantry led by Colonel Alexander Scammell and served through the Yorktown campaign. He retired on 1 January 1783.

Thacher is famous for the *Military Journal* he kept during the Revolutionary War, first published in 1823, with a second edition in 1827 and many reprints thereafter. He wrote his journal in a lively style and included valuable information on army life and senior commanders, particularly Washington, Lafayette, and Steuben. His account of military medicine is regrettably slender. He "failed to give many details of his hospital experiences, except in regard to smallpox inoculation, which he carried out on a large scale" (Henry R. Viets in DAB). Since he wrote about matters about which he had no firsthand knowledge, it is important to distinguish that information from episodes in which he personally participated.

After the war he became a prominent physician in Plymouth. "Small of stature, light and agile in movements, Thacher was fond of social intercourse, yet regularly studious" (DAB). An astute observer, he produced important books on medicine and contemporary medical biography, including *The American Medical Biography* (1828). He also wrote on orchards (1822, 1825), bees (1829), ghosts (1831), and the history of the town of Plymouth (1832, 1835).

SEE ALSO *Additional Continental Regiments; Canada Invasion; Penobscot Expedition, Maine.*

BIBLIOGRAPHY

Thacher, James. *A Military Journal during the American Revolutionary War, from 1775 to 1783.* 2d ed. Boston: Cottons and Barnard, 1827.

revised by Harold E. Selesky

THICKETTY FORT (FORT ANDERSON), SOUTH CAROLINA. 30 July 1780.

In one of the actions that preceded the Battle of Kings Mountain, Lieutenant Colonel Isaac Shelby led six hundred men against the Loyalist post at Thicketty Fort, on the headwaters of the Pacolet, ten miles southeast of Cowpens, and without firing a shot persuaded the garrison to surrender.

SEE ALSO *Kings Mountain, South Carolina.*

revised by Michael Bellesiles

THOMAS, JOHN. (1724–1776). Continental

general. Massachusetts. Born in Marshfield, Massachusetts, John Thomas studied medicine under Dr. Simon Tufts in Medford. Thomas began his military career on 1 March 1746, when Governor William Shirley appointed him as a surgeon's mate to the garrison at Annapolis Royal. He served the next year under General Samuel Waldo in Nova Scotia, and returned to the region in 1755 as a lieutenant and again in 1759–1760 as colonel of a provincial regiment. In the summer of 1760 he commanded a provincial regiment in Sir Jeffrey Amherst's advance down Lake Champlain, and led the left wing of Colonel William Haviland's detachment that joined in the capture of Montreal on 8 September 1760. Thomas spent the next 15 years engaged primarily in the practice of medicine at Kingston, Massachusetts. When the revolutionary movement started, he joined the Sons of Liberty. As the siege of Boston began, the Massachusetts Provincial Congress needed to bring order to the army, so it appointed this experienced senior officer as colonel of a regiment raised in Plymouth County, and on 25 May 1775 named him lieutenant general (second-in-command) of all Massachusetts troops. He commanded the right wing of the army at Roxbury, facing the British across Boston Neck.

In his fiftieth year, he stood six feet tall, had a distinguished face, and a commanding presence. When Congress prepared its first list of eight brigadier generals (22 June 1775), it did not fully consider military seniority at the state level, and appointed the mediocre William Heath and the superannuated Seth Pomeroy over the capable Thomas. On 10 July, in his first detailed report to Congress about conditions around Boston, General George Washington hinted broadly that Congress should remedy the situation. When Pomeroy declined his appointment, Congress made Thomas the senior brigadier general. Meanwhile, Thomas had conducted himself with decorum and had demonstrated his superiority as a military leader. Washington gave him the job of occupying Dorchester Heights, and on the evening of 4 March 1776 Thomas led 3,000 men across Dorchester Neck to take possession of this critical hill overlooking Boston Harbor. The successful completion of this critical operation gained him even higher esteem in the eyes of Washington and the Boston army.

On 6 March 1776 Thomas was promoted to major general and ordered north, where disaster had already struck during the invasion of Canada. He left Roxbury on 22 March, reached Albany on the 28th, and on 1 May took command of the American army around Quebec. The very next day he got the bad news that a British relief expedition was coming up the St. Lawrence River, and on 6 May he had to start a demoralized and disorganized retreat toward Montreal. He contracted the smallpox that was decimating his army and died on 2 June at Sorel.

SEE ALSO *Canada Invasion; Dorchester Heights, Massachusetts.*

BIBLIOGRAPHY
Coffin, Charles. *The Life and Services of Major General John Thomas.* New York: Egbert, Hovey, and King, 1844.
Thomas Papers. Boston: Massachusetts Historical Society.

revised by Harold E. Selesky

THOMPSON, BENJAMIN COUNT

RUMFORD. (1753–1814). Colonial administrator, physicist, Loyalist. Massachusetts-New Hampshire. Born in Woburn, Massachusetts, on 26 March 1753, Thompson—famous as one of America's leading scientists and a mean-spirited social climber—was self educated, only attending a few lectures at Harvard in 1770. In 1771 he became a schoolteacher in Concord, New Hampshire, where he met and, the following year married, the widow Sarah Walker Rolfe, the largest landholder in the region. They separated in 1775, but Thompson was able to hold on to a great deal of his wife's wealth. Through her, Thompson met Governor John Wentworth, who appointed the twenty-year-old teacher with no military background a major of militia in 1773. Though the Patriots suspected Thompson of favoring the crown as early as 1774, the smooth-talking major persuaded two inquiries of his patriotism. He associated with Patriots in Massachusetts, gaining information about the Continental army encircling Boston and passing on what he learned to General Thomas Gage. In October 1775, suspecting his cover was blown, he joined the British in Boston, sailing from there to England in March 1776. There he became a favorite of Lord George Germain, who appointed him to the sinecure of secretary of Georgia. In September 1780 Thompson became undersecretary of state for the Northern Department, and in October 1781 he returned to America as lieutenant colonel of the King's American Dragoons, seeing some action around Charleston in March 1782 and commanding a regiment on Long Island, in New York, until April 1783.

In August 1783, having returned to England, he was made colonel of the King's American Dragoons and was retired on half pay. He was knighted on 23 February 1784 and for the next eleven years he served the elector of Bavaria as minister of war, minister of police, and grand chamberlain. In addition to reforming the Bavarian army, Thompson conducted important research in these years on the nature of heat and light and introduced the potato to central Europe. In 1791 he was made count of the Holy Roman Empire and chose his title of Rumford from the township of his wife, though he had not seen her since 1775. Thompson returned to England in 1795, inventing the famous Rumford Lamp, a more efficient oil lamp, sometime thereafter. In 1796 he published his *Essays, Political, Economical, and Philosophical* and gave one thousand pounds to the Royal Society and five thousand dollars to the American Academy of Arts and Sciences to award Rumford Medals for distinguished work on heat or light. He did some of the first research into air pollution and nutrition and developed a nonsmoking and highly efficient fireplace known as the Rumford Roaster that came into extensive use in Great Britain and America.

In 1802 he settled in Paris, where in 1805 he married Marie Anne Pierrette, the widow of the eminent chemist Antoine Lavoisier; they separated four years later. He died at Auteuil on 21 August 1814, leaving funds to create the Rumford professorship of physics at Harvard University.

revised by Michael Bellesiles

THOMPSON, WILLIAM. (1736?–1781).

Continental general. Pennsylvania. Born in Ireland, Thompson settled near Carlisle and became a surveyor and justice of the peace. He served as a captain under John Armstrong Sr. in the expedition of Pennsylvania troops against the Indian settlements at Kittanning, Pennsylvania, on 8 September 1756 and after the Seven Years' War took part in locating lands granted to officers on the western frontier of the province. Appointed commander with the rank of colonel of one of Pennsylvania's battalions raised in response to the news of Lexington, Thompson arrived in Cambridge, Massachusetts, in early August 1775. His unit, known as Thompson's Pennsylvania Rifle Battalion (or Regiment) until the reorganization of 1 January 1776, when it became the First Continental Infantry, was appraised as more trouble than it was worth in the Boston siege. Thompson commanded the attack on Lechmere Point on 9 November 1775, and although he was commended the next day in general orders, Washington subsequently realized that the operation had been less admirable than indicated by the first reports.

The historian Douglas Freeman has said, "Washington privately opposed an excessively responsible assignment for William Thompson, whose seniority seemed to him to be more fortuitously conferred than valiantly earned" (Freeman, vol. 4, pp. 73 and 84). Congress, however, appointed him brigadier general on 1 March 1776 before receiving Washington's views. He was named to command the first reinforcements sent to Canada, and on 21 April he sailed up the Hudson with the regiments of Bond, Greaton, Paterson, and Poor. Thompson commanded the disastrous attack at Trois Rivières on 8 June 1776 and was taken prisoner. Although back in Philadelphia on parole two months later, it was four years before his exchange was effected. Meanwhile, he became so offensive in accusing Congressman Thomas McKean of hindering his exchange that he was censured by Congress on 23 November 1778. Thompson apologized to Congress, but McKean pressed a libel suit, was awarded damages of £5,700, and then released Thompson from payment. Thompson died near Carlisle on 3 September 1781, less than a year after being exchanged for Baron Riedesel.

SEE ALSO *Lechmere Point, Massachusetts; Riflemen; Trois Rivières.*

BIBLIOGRAPHY
Freeman, Douglass Southall. *George Washington.* 7 vols. New York: Scribner, 1948–1957.

revised by Michael Bellesiles

THOMPSON'S PENNSYLVANIA RIFLE BATTALION.

Although the Continental Congress called for only six companies of riflemen from Pennsylvania, so many volunteers presented themselves that they were formed into nine companies and organized as a battalion under the command of Colonel William Thompson. The unit was created on 25 June 1775. It was reorganized on 1 January 1776 as the First Continental Infantry and as the First Pennsylvania on 1 January 1777 (Heitman, *Historical Register,* p. 47). Edward Hand was lieutenant colonel of the first organization, and Robert Magaw was its major.

SEE ALSO *Riflemen; Thompson, William.*

BIBLIOGRAPHY
Heitman, Francis B. *Historical Register of Officers of the Continental Army.* Revised edition. Washington, D.C.: Rare Book Shop Pub. Co., 1914.

Mark M. Boatner

THORNTON, MATTHEW. (1714–1803).

Signer. Ireland–Massachusetts–New Hampshire. Born in Ireland of Scots-Irish ancestry, he came to America with his parents around 1718 and lived in Maine before moving to the neighborhood of Worcester, Massachusetts. He completed his medical studies in 1740 and started a practice in the Scots-Irish colony of Londonderry, New Hampshire. In 1745 he took part in the Louisbourg expedition as an "under-surgeon." In 1758 Londonderry elected him to the provincial assembly. He was commissioned a militia colonel in 1770 and sent off troops to Massachusetts in April 1775. His militia commission was reinstituted by the provincial congress of New Hampshire, but Thornton, over sixty years old, saw no further active military duty.

In 1775 he was elected president of the provincial congress, which the same year selected him as chairman of the committee of safety that was, in effect, the local Patriot government. From 1776 to 1782 he was an associate justice of the superior court. During the war years he served as speaker of the house, member of the executive council, and president of the state constitutional convention.

He served one term in Congress (1776–1777) and is believed to have been the last delegate to sign the Declaration of Independence, in November 1776, as it lay on the table. In 1780 he moved to Merrimack County where he practiced politics but not medicine. He served in the newly created state senate in 1784–1786.

He had married Hannah (Jack) about 1760. They had five children. Dr. Thornton died on 24 June 1803 while visiting his daughter in Newburyport, Massachusetts.

BIBLIOGRAPHY

Estes, J. Worth. "Honest Dr. Thornton." In *Physician Signers of the Declaration of Independence.* Edited by George E. Gifford Jr. New York: Science History Publications, 1976.

Randall, Peter E. "Matthew Thornton." In *New Hampshire: Years of Revolution.* Edited by Peter E. Randall. Portsmouth, N.H.: Profiles Publishing, 1976.

revised by Frank C. Mevers

THREADWELL'S NECK SEE *Treadwell's Neck, Long Island, New York.*

THREE-SIDED STATES.

"Three-sided states" were those that, as colonies, had sea-to-sea charters or some other claim to western land. The four-sided or nonlanded states were New Hampshire, Rhode Island, New Jersey, Pennsylvania, Delaware, and Maryland. The latter states strongly supported the idea that Congress should have the power to establish the boundaries of the "landed" states; this issue held up ratification of the Articles of Confederation.

SEE ALSO *Articles of Confederation.*

Mark M. Boatner

THROG'S NECK, NEW YORK. 12–18

October 1776. Throg's Neck (or Point) was also known as Frog's or Throck's Point. It was apparently named after John Throgmorton (or Throckmorton) who settled there in 1643. Known today as Throg's Neck, it is now also known as Schuyler Park, located in the southeast corner of the Bronx.

To avoid American General George Washington's strong defenses on Harlem Heights, British General William Howe planned an amphibious envelopment with most of his forces. The exceptions were one brigade of Hessians and two of British, all under the command of Lord Hugh Percy, who would hold the lines around McGown's Pass to cover New York City. At 9 A.M. on 12 October about 4,000 British started landing, unopposed, at Throg's Neck from 80 vessels that had left Kips Bay the night before. Thick fog in the dangerous waters of Hell Gate nearly turned the expedition into a disaster, but Admiral Richard Howe and his officers managed to get through with minimal losses. By afternoon, most of General Howe's force was ashore. He did not know, however, that Throg's Neck was virtually an island, being surrounded by water at high tide. As soon as the British started inland, they found a marshy creek that could be crossed in only two places: a causeway and bridge on one side, and a ford on the other. Colonel Edward Hand's thirty-man guard from his First Pennsylvania Rifle Regiment (William Heath's Division), firing from concealed positions, stopped them cold.

Reinforcements soon arrived to swell the defenders' ranks to 1,800 and bottle up Howe's force. These reinforcements were Prescott's Massachusetts Continental Regiment and a three-pounder (cannon) at the causeway, and John Graham's New York Continental Regiment, with a six-pounder at the ford. Further reinforcements, in the form of Alexander McDougall's brigade, arrived the evening of 12 October. Frustrated, Howe took six days to prepare for his next move, the landing at Pell's Point. It is interesting to speculate on what would have resulted had Howe forced his way through Hand's thirty riflemen and moved against the Kings Bridge, eight miles away.

SEE ALSO *Pell's Point, New York.*

revised by Barnet Schecter

THRUSTON, CHARLES MYNN.

(1738–1812). Continental officer. Virginia. Born in Gloucester County, Virginia, in 1738, Thruston graduated from William and Mary and studied theology in England. Returning to Virginia after ordination in the Church of England, he settled in the Shenandoah Valley. For his service as a militia lieutenant in 1754 he was given title to two thousand acres in Fincastle County, but in 1770 he became so discouraged about the prospects of actually getting this land that he sold his claim for £10 to a former companion in arms named George Washington. The "warrior parson," as he was known, raised a company of volunteers at the beginning of the Revolution, was commissioned a captain, was badly wounded at Trenton, and subsequently was appointed colonel of an "additional continental regiment" on 15 January 1777. Thruston lost an arm at Amboy on 8 March 1777 and resigned from the army on 1 January 1779. After the war Thruston was a judge and member of the legislature. In 1808 he moved to Louisiana and died four years later near New Orleans.

SEE ALSO *Additional Continental Regiments.*

revised by Michael Bellesiles

THRUSTON'S REGIMENT. Thruston's

Regiment was one of the sixteen "additional Continental regiments."

SEE ALSO *Additional Continental Regiments.*

Mark M. Boatner

TICONDEROGA, NEW YORK. 1755–

1759. In October 1755 the Marquis de Lotbinière started construction of a fort the French called Carillon at the place later known as Ticonderoga. The fort was an outpost for Fort St. Frederick (Crown Point). Montcalm was defending Fort Carillon with 3,526 men on 8 July 1758 when Abercromby attacked with a force of 16,000. Instead of taking his time and bringing up heavy artillery, Abercromby launched a direct assault. In one of their costliest failures of the century, the British lost almost 2,000 killed and wounded while inflicting under 400 casualties on the French. Lord George Howe, Abercromby's popular second in command and the elder brother of Richard and William, died on 6 July in a preliminary skirmish. On 26 July 1759 the French blew up the fort when its capture by General Jeffrey Amherst was inevitable.

SEE ALSO *Colonial Wars.*

BIBLIOGRAPHY

Anderson, Fred. *Crucible of War: The Seven Years' War and the Fate of Empire in British North America, 1754–1766.* New York: Knopf, 2000.

revised by Robert K. Wright Jr.

TICONDEROGA, NEW YORK, AMERICAN CAPTURE OF. 10 May

1775. Captured by the Americans. The idea of capturing this strategically located post and its deposit of military stores appeared obvious to many of the Patriot leaders in April 1775. The old French works were occupied by a small British garrison under Captain William Delaplace. Early in 1775 this officer reported suspicious activity around his isolated post to General Gage, assuming that there might be an attempt from the settlers in the New Hampshire Grants to steal some of his ammunition. He promised Gage that he would take "every necessary precaution to frustrate their designs." Still, as the leader of the Green Mountain Boys, Ethan Allen, discovered, Delaplace remained completely unaware of the worsening relations between the colonists and Britain. Governor Guy Carleton in Canada planned to reinforce the fort in the months ahead but made no effort to inform Delaplace about the war that broke out in Massachusetts on 19 April.

ALLEN AND ARNOLD

In Hartford, Samuel H. Parsons, Silas Deane, and others organized an expedition that was a private enterprise but that had the tacit approval of the Connecticut assembly. After sending a proposal to Ethan Allen at Bennington to gather some Green Mountain Boys for the operation, the first of the Connecticut group left Hartford on 28 April and were followed the next day by others. About twenty Connecticut men were joined in Pittsfield, Massachusetts, by James Easton and John Brown, who had assembled about fifty Massachusetts volunteers. At Castleton on 7 May, they joined one hundred Green Mountain Boys raised by Allen, with another one hundred on the way. The next day they chose a Committee of War, chaired by Edward Mott of the Hartford Committee of Safety, elected Ethan Allen commander, and drew up their plan of attack. Allen, who had stationed guards on all the roads leading to the fort to keep information of the war from filtering through to Delaplace, sent Noah Phelps inside, pretending to be a hunter in need of a haircut and shave. Phelps reported that, incredibly, the British still had no idea that they were at war. If alerted, they could put up a stiff resistance, being well supplied with munitions and artillery. On 9 May, Allen moved with the main body to Hand's Cove, a point on Lake Champlain's east shore just over a mile from Fort Ticonderoga (at modern Orwell, New York, then called Shoreham.) Allen sent Samuel Herrick with a thirty-man detachment to Skenesboro to seize Colonel Philip Skene> and a large schooner for use in the crossing to Fort Ticonderoga. Asa Douglass was sent to Crown Point to hire that garrison's boats for use in the attack.

Meanwhile, Captain Benedict Arnold had persuaded the Massachusetts Committee of Safety to let him lead an expedition against Ticonderoga, receiving authorization on 3 May to raise up to four hundred men. Three days later, however, he learned of Allen's undertaking and rushed to Castleton, accompanied by only a servant, arriving the evening of 9 May. He immediately claimed command of the operation. Colonels Allen and Easton asked the assembled men for their judgment, which was that they would go home rather than accept Arnold's command. Allen soothed Arnold's injured pride by offering to let the captain march at his side at the head of the column. Arnold, who added only himself to the unit's strength, accepted.

Shortly before the dawn of 10 May, nearly three hundred men were at Hand's Cove waiting for boats. Two scows finally arrived, one brought by two boys who had heard of the operation and the other brought by Asa Douglass. Realizing the importance of surprise, Allen decided not to wait any longer for the boats from Skenesboro, packed eighty-five men into the available boats, and headed for the opposite bank. Squalls of wind and rain had made the two-mile crossing hazardous but probably benefited the attackers by covering their noise.

THE CAPTURE

The Green Mountain Boys rushed up the path from the cove below the fort, with Allen and Arnold quick stepping at their head in a race to be first to the narrow covered way with a small gate leading into the fort. Allen won. A British sentry's musket misfired as he sought to shoot Allen, who knocked him aside and then hit a second sentry with the flat of his sword. The huge Allen grabbed this sentry and forced him to act as a guide to the officers' quarters as his men swarmed into the fort behind him. As his men ran for the barracks, Allen banged on the commandant's door, shouting, "Come out of there, you damned British rat!" Lieutenant Jocelyn Feltham, who had arrived twelve days previously with the advance element of a twenty-man reinforcement Carleton was sending to Delaplace from Canada, appeared at the door wearing his coat and carrying his breeches.

Thinking Feltham was Captain Delaplace, Allen called on him to surrender the fort. When the lieutenant demanded to know by what authority he had entered the king's fort, Allen responded, "In the name of the great Jehovah and the Continental Congress." At this point Delaplace, who had taken the time to dress fully, appeared and, seeing his sleepy and unarmed soldiers being herded out of their barracks, surrendered the fort. Allen immediately sent Seth Warner and Levi Allen with one hundred men to capture Crown Point.

Prisoners consisted of two officers and forty-eight men, many of them invalids, as well as twenty-four women and children. Captured matériel at Ticonderoga and Crown Point included at least seventy-eight serviceable cannon out of more than two hundred taken, six mortars, three howitzers, thousands of cannon balls, thirty thousand flints, some twenty casks and powder, and other stores.

In a small schooner and several bateaux captured at Skenesboro, Arnold led a successful raid to St. Johns, Canada, on 17 May. Allen followed and made an ill-advised and unsuccessful attempt to hold this last post against British reinforcements from nearby Chambly.

AFTERMATH

When Congress learned 18 May that Ticonderoga had been taken, it ordered the fort abandoned and all the military stores carefully inventoried and evacuated to the south end of Lake George. An absolute refusal from Allen, followed by protests from New York and New England, forced Congress to pass a resolution on 31 May that Fort Ticonderoga and Crown Point be held. Arnold considered himself in command of these two places, creating enormous difficulties for the rebels. A Massachusetts committee, however, arrived to inform him that he was to be second in command to Colonel Benjamin Hinman, who had been sent with fourteen hundred Connecticut men to garrison the captured posts. Arnold resigned his Massachusetts commission and left the service with his first of a succession of grievances.

SEE ALSO *Crown Point, New York; Deane, Silas; Green Mountain Boys; Invalid; Knox's "Noble Train of Artillery"; Skene, Philip; St. John's, Canada (14–18 May 1775).*

BIBLIOGRAPHY

Bellesiles, Michael. *Revolutionary Outlaws: Ethan Allen and the Struggle for Independence on the Early American Frontier.* Charlottesville: University Press of Virginia, 1993.

Martin, James K. *Benedict Arnold: Revolutionary Hero.* New York: New York University Press, 1997.

revised by Michael Bellesiles

TICONDEROGA, NEW YORK, BRITISH CAPTURE OF.

2–5 July 1777. Captured by the British during Burgoyne's offensive. After the Americans evacuated Crown Point in July 1776, they accelerated efforts to strengthen Fort Ticonderoga. Much of the work was planned by young John Trumbull, and the professional engineering talent was furnished by Thaddeus Kosciuszko. The old fort was partially repaired and blockhouses were erected, the old French earthworks that barred an approach from the northwest were improved, and a new barbette battery was constructed on Mount Hope. Mount Independence was fortified and a bridge of boats spanned the quarter-mile water gap between it and Ticonderoga, while a barrier of log booms and iron chains was constructed north of the bridge. Trumbull pointed out to his skeptical commander that artillery from a hill known as Mount Defiance would threaten the main defenses, and with Wayne and Arnold he climbed the eight-hundred-foot hill to prove that the crest was accessible. The American General Arthur St. Clair, the commander, had only one-fifth of the troop strength needed to man existing works properly, and he left Mount Defiance undefended.

It was apparent to Trumbull and most of the other officers that there was little hope of defending Ticonderoga with such a small force against Burgoyne's army. Schuyler's suggestion that only Mount Independence be occupied was twice approved by Congress. But the popular image of Ticonderoga as impregnable and a symbol of security precluded its immediate abandonment. As General Gates pointed out, the boom was an essential feature of the defenses, and unless it was defended at both ends, the enemy could break through and turn Mount Independence. On 20 June, Schuyler and the four generals on the spot decided to hold Ticonderoga as long as possible and then defend Mount Independence.

AMERICAN DISPOSITIONS

St. Clair had taken command at Ticonderoga on 12 June, less than a month before the attack. His three senior subordinates, Brigadier Generals Matthias Fermoy, John Paterson, and Enoch Poo, failed to gain distinction during the war. St. Clair's 2,500 troops included 10 Continental and 2 militia regiments, 250 artillerymen, 124 artificers, and some scouts; however, they were an ill-disciplined group.

British forces totaled about seven thousand regulars and another twenty-five hundred or so white and Indian auxiliaries. The troops were well equipped, well disciplined, and well led, excepting Burgoyne.

THE ATTACK

British General Simon Fraser's Advance Corps left Crown Point on 26 June and was two miles from Ticonderoga when the rest of Burgoyne's force landed behind him. The German Wing debarked on the east shore, and the British Wing landed on the other. On 2 July, Fraser cautiously took possession of Mount Hope, cutting off the American route to Lake George. St. Clair's outpost set fire to its works at 9 A.M. and then retreated, the enemy arriving four hours later. The British moved cautiously along the peninsula, making contact with the main defenses at about 3 P.M. American officers watched this advance while their men, on St. Clair's orders, held their fire. When Colonel James Wilkinson saw an enemy skirmisher stop a mere forty paces away, he ordered a sergeant to pick him off, touching off an unauthorized fire from the rest of the waiting rebels. As U.S. officers ran around trying to stop the firing, the enemy dropped back out of range, leaving the prostrate form of the man Wilkinson had ordered shot—a drunken member of the Forty-Seventh Regiment, who was unscathed. In addition to eight cannon, the Americans had fired an estimated three thousand rounds from one thousand muskets at less than one hundred yards, demonstrating their marksmanship by hitting just three of their targets.

The Germans on the other side of the lake had meanwhile pushed forward to East Creek. There, the advance elements under Breymann drew artillery fire from Mount Independence.

From a prisoner, St. Clair learned the extent of Burgoyne's numbers. The Americans' situation was not yet critical, however, since their line of communication by water to Skenesboro was still open and the threat of a German envelopment of the Mount Independence position was considerably reduced by the obstacle of East Creek and its swamps. St. Clair hoped that Burgoyne would make the error of a frontal attack against Ticonderoga from the northwest

On 3 July, Burgoyne occupied Mount Hope in force, and a relatively harmless artillery exchange ensued. Gall's brigade was taken from Riedesel to reinforce the right wing, and some Canadians and Indians, along with Captain Fraser's light infantry company, were shifted across the lake to Riedesel. The latter was given the mission

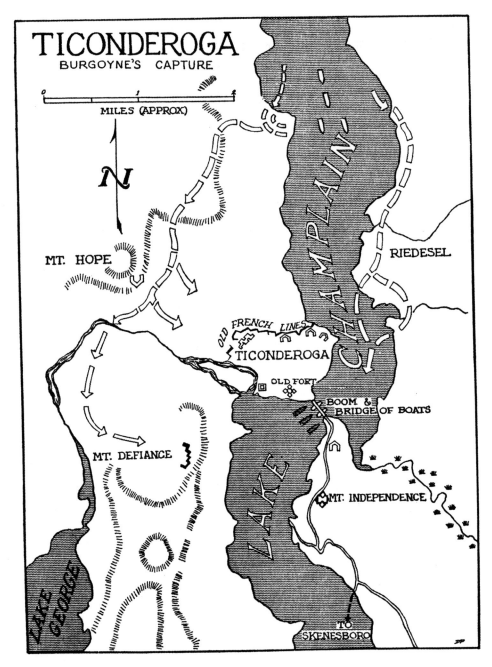

TICONDEROGA
BURGOYNE'S CAPTURE

0   1   2
MILES (APPROX)

N

MT. HOPE

LAKE CHAMPLAIN

RIEDESEL

OLD FRENCH LINES

TICONDEROGA

OLD FORT

BOOM & BRIDGE OF BOATS

MT. DEFIANCE

LAKE

LAKE GEORGE

MT. INDEPENDENCE

TO SKENESBORO

THE GALE GROUP

of turning the Mount Independence position and cutting the line of communication to Skenesboro.

On 4 July, Burgoyne's chief engineer, Lieutenant Twiss, reconnoitered Mount Defiance, reporting that the hill was within effective artillery range of Ticonderoga and Mount Independence and that the necessary roadwork to get guns into position could be done within twenty-four hours. The energetic Major General William Phillips took command of the operation with the comment, "Where a

goat can go, a man can go; and where a man can go he can haul up a gun." Four twelve-pounders were in position, ready to open fire at noon of 6 July.

The significance of these guns was not that they could deliver a fire of sufficient intensity and accuracy to make the American positions untenable; the range, about twenty-two hundred yards, was too great for precision fire with the guns of the day, and the improvised road up the northwest slopes of Mount Defiance would not permit

ENCYCLOPEDIA OF THE AMERICAN REVOLUTION

the ammunition supply needed for sustained fire. On the other hand, the guns could threaten the bridge and wreak havoc among boats brought up to evacuate the garrison. Perhaps the most significant threat was to the morale of the defenders. The British made the mistake of letting the Americans see their preparations on 5 July. St. Clair called a council of war at 3 P.M., which ended with a unanimous decision to pull out.

TICONDEROGA ABANDONED

The heavy American cannonade at dusk on 5 July should have tipped Burgoyne off to American plans but did not. After carrying as much matériel down to the boats as possible, some four hundred to five hundred troops commanded by Colonel Pierce Long left Ticonderoga with the artillery, supplies, and wounded shortly after midnight and headed for Skenesboro. The rest of the garrison headed across the bridge of boats about two hours later. Since there was no road south along the lake, St. Clair planned to lead the main body by way of Castleton to join Long at Skenesboro.

A well-planned retreat was marred by a series of mishaps. First, General Fermoy went to sleep without giving the withdrawal orders to all his troops on Mount Independence. Then, when he got ready to leave at about 3 A.M., he set fire to his quarters, contrary to St. Clair's orders, illuminating the scene for Riedesel, who sent troops by boat to harass the withdrawal. Finally, the four gunners posted to deliver enfilade fire along the bridge got drunk and went to sleep; an Indian with the party that captured them almost did their duty for them when he accidentally touched off one of the cannon with a slow match, but the shot passed harmlessly over the heads of the British troops on the bridge.

Burgoyne himself did not learn until dawn that St. Clair had slipped away, but he then reacted with exceptional vigor. Ordering General Fraser to march quickly to overtake the main body that was moving overland, he personally led the pursuit by water. Burgoyne caught up with Long at Skenesboro on 6 July and pushed his pursuit to Fort Anne on 8 July. Fraser surprised the rear guard of St. Clair's column at Hubbardton on 7 July, where he won a costly victory with Riedesel's timely support.

COMMENT

The fall of Ticonderoga depressed the spirits of Americans and sent those of their enemy soaring. King George rushed into the queen's dressing room shouting, "I have beat them! I have beat all the Americans!" A court-martial acquitted St. Clair with honor; forced by political considerations to bait the Ticonderoga trap, he saved his army.

Burgoyne, on the other hand, revealed his mediocrity. He had opened the attic door of the American colonies, but by failing to annihilate its defenders had won what Napoleon called an ordinary victory.

SEE ALSO *Burgoyne's Offensive; Fermoy, Matthias Alexis de Roche; Fort Anne, New York; Hubbardton, Vermont; Kosciuszko, Thaddeus Andrzej Bonawentura; Marksmanship; Paterson, John; Poor, Enoch; Skenesboro, New York; Trumbull, John.*

BIBLIOGRAPHY

Bobrick, Benson. *Angel in the Whirlwind: The Triumph of the American Revolution.* New York: Penguin, 1997.

Ketchum, Richard M. *Saratoga: Turning Point of America's Revolutionary War.* New York: Holt, 1997.

Mintz, Max M. *The Generals of Saratoga: John Burgoyne and Horatio Gates.* New Haven, CT: Yale University Press, 1990.

revised by Michael Bellesiles

TICONDEROGA RAID. September 1777.

After the British capture of Ticonderoga on 5 July, Major General Benjamin Lincoln was ordered to Vermont to organize and command New England militia being raised in the region. One of his missions was to threaten Burgoyne's long lines of communication to Canada, and in September, after the Battle of Bennington, Lincoln saw his chance. Remaining at Pawlet with five hundred troops, Lincoln sent three five-hundred-man detachments to disrupt British supply lines. The principal effort was assigned to Colonel John Brown, who was to attack Ticonderoga from the west. Colonel Samuel Johnson was to support him by a diversion against Mount Independence, across the lake. Colonel Ruggles Woodbridge was to occupy Skenesboro, which the British had abandoned, and move south through Fort Anne to Fort Edward.

British Brigadier General Henry Powell commanded Ticonderoga and its outposts. Apparently feeling secure, he had disposed his nine hundred soldiers carelessly and had not posted adequate security detachments. Brown was therefore able to spend two days undetected in the area before attacking at daybreak on 18 September. Rushing the Lake George landing (at the outlet from that lake into Lake Champlain) and overwhelming the sergeant's guard on Mount Defiance, the Americans had little difficulty in gaining control of everything on the west shore except the French stone fort and the Grenadier's Battery at the tip of the peninsula. Brown also freed over one hundred American prisoners while capturing three hundred of the enemy. However,

Johnson reached Mount Independence too late in the day to surprise the Prince Frederick Regiment stationed there. Powell refused to surrender Ticonderoga, which was defended by the Fifty-third Regiment, and Brown lacked the heavy artillery and other supplies needed to reduce it. The Americans cannonaded the positions for four days and then withdrew.

Using captured boats, Brown moved up Lake George with 420 men, planning to surprise the British post at Diamond Island, 25 miles south of Ticonderoga, at dawn on the 23rd. He was frustrated by adverse winds, and by the time he could launch his attack, at about 9 A.M. on 24 September, the two companies that constituted the British garrison had been warned of his approach by a paroled Loyalist. Brown soon saw that the artillery on his boats was no match for enemy guns firing from breastworks, and he withdrew after a short bombardment. The Americans landed on the east shore, burned their boats, and rejoined Lincoln.

Although short of complete success, the raid was strategically important. Brown brought back information that Burgoyne had provisions for no more than four weeks. The confidence of the British was shaken by this unexpected threat to their lines of communication, and news of the raid was received in Gates's camp on 21 September with prolonged cheering and a thirteen-gun salute. A few days later Burgoyne, whose troops were close enough to hear the celebration on Bemis Heights, got the bad news from a prisoner released precisely to report the ill tidings.

SEE ALSO *Bennington Raid; Burgoyne's Offensive.*

BIBLIOGRAPHY

Ketchum, Richard M. *Saratoga: Turning Point of America's Revolutionary War.* New York: Holt, 1997.

revised by Michael Bellesiles

TILGHMAN, TENCH. (1744–1786). Aide-de-camp and military secretary to Washington. Maryland-Pennsylvania. Born in Talbot County, Maryland, on 25 December 1744, Tilghman graduated in 1761 from what became the University of Pennsylvania and became a merchant in Philadelphia. On the eve of the Revolution, and in opposition to his Loyalist father, he liquidated his business and in 1775 was secretary and treasurer of the Continental Congress's commissioners to the Iroquois. In July 1776 he was commissioned captain of an independent company that subsequently joined a Pennsylvania battalion of the Flying Camp. On 8 August 1776 he began his duties in Washington's headquarters as a volunteer

military secretary. On 1 April 1777 he was given the rank of lieutenant colonel, but his volunteer status without pay was continued until the Continental Congress responded favorably to Washington's personal appeal of 11 May 1781 that Tilghman receive a formal commission.

Honored by Washington with the mission of taking news of the Yorktown surrender to the Continental Congress, Tilghman reached Philadelphia at 3 A.M. on 22 October 1781. A week later the delegates resolved that he be given a sword and horse in gratitude for his service. Tilghman served as Washington's personal secretary for seven years, longer than any of the other thirty-two aides, becoming a close friend of the commander in chief. On 9 June 1783 Tilghman married his cousin, Anna Maria, younger daughter of Matthew Tilghman (1718–1790), a powerful Maryland political figure and member of Congress. Two years after entering into a business association in Baltimore with Robert Morris, Tilghman died on 18 April 1786.

BIBLIOGRAPHY

Harrison, S. A., ed. *Memoir of Lieutenant Colonel Tench Tilghman, Secretary and Aid to Washington.* Albany, N.Y.: J. Munsell, 1876.

Shreve, L. G. *Tench Tilghman: The Life and Times of Washington's Aide-de-camp.* Centreville, Md.: Tidewater, 1982.

revised by Michael Bellesiles

TONYN, PATRICK. (1725–1804). British officer, governor of East Florida. Born in Ireland in 1725, Tonyn, the son of Lieutenant Colonel Charles William Tonyn (d. 1754), joined his father's regiment, the Sixth (Inniskilling) Dragoons on 16 March 1744 and was promoted to captain on 10 May 1751. After seeing action in Germany in 1758, on 12 August 1761 he became lieutenant colonel of the 104th Foot. On 1 March 1774 he reached East Florida to succeed John Moultrie as governor, and he held this post until 1785, coming into repeated conflict with the region's settlers and his fellow officials but keeping the province in the empire. Tonyn made East Florida a haven for southern Loyalists, raised the East Florida Rangers to harass the Patriots in Georgia and South Carolina, and enlisted Seminole and Creek support for the British. With his province returned to Spain in the peace treaty ending the Revolution, Tonyn spent his last two years as governor seeing to the relocation of Loyalists and those inhabitants who wanted to leave, as well as the evacuation of military bases and the contentious transfer of authority to the Spanish. Meanwhile he had been promoted to colonel on 29 August 1777 and to

major general on 19 October 1781. In 1793 he became a lieutenant general, and on 1 January 1798 he was promoted to full general. He died on 30 December 1804 in London.

SEE ALSO *Moultrie, John.*

BIBLIOGRAPHY

Wright, J. Leitch, Jr. *Florida in the American Revolution.* Gainesville: University Presses of Florida, 1975.

revised by Michael Bellesiles

TORRENCE'S TAVERN, NORTH CAROLINA SEE *Tarrant's Tavern.*

TORY RANGERS SEE *Butler's Rangers.*

TOUSARD, ANN-LOUIS. (1749–1817).

French and U.S. officer. Born in Paris on 12 March 1749, Tousard, the son of a general, graduated from the French Artillery Academy and volunteered for service with the Americans in the Revolution. He arrived in America during April 1777 as part of the group led by Philippe Tronson du Coudray. After the latter's death in October, Tousard became a captain attached to the marquis de Lafayette's staff. After taking part in the Battles of Germantown and Brandywine, Tousard spent the winter of 1777–1778 at Valley Forge. In March 1778 he was appointed military adviser to allied Oneida Indians. He was present with the Oneidas when they covered Lafayette's retreat before a far superior British force at the Battle of Barren Hill on 21 May 1778. Tousard then transferred to the staff of General John Sullivan for the unsuccessful French-American campaign against Newport, Rhode Island. Tousard lost his right arm during the Battle of Quaker Hill on 28 August 1778. His heroic performance in that battle earned him promotion to lieutenant colonel of the Continental army on 29 October 1778. Returning to France, he received the Royal Order of St. Louis on 3 July 1779 and was made a major of artillery on 5 April 1780.

In 1784 Tousard was promoted to lieutenant colonel in the French army and stationed on Saint-Domingue (Haiti). In the slave revolt led by Toussaint L'Ouverture,

Tousard in 1791–1792 commanded troops battling the slaves and attempted to persuade the local government to arm free blacks but was ignored. Nonetheless, he was blamed for the failure of the colonial officials to obey orders from France in this regard and was arrested and imprisoned. U.S. pressure effected his release in February 1793, and he settled on a farm outside Wilmington, Delaware.

In April 1795 President George Washington appointed Tousard a major in the Corps of Artillerists and Engineers, beginning a period in which he had enormous influence on the U.S. military. After supervising the construction of several significant fortifications, he restructured the U.S. artillery service on the French model, bringing uniformity to its use of cannon. In 1798 he laid out the plans for what would become the Military Academy at West Point. Also, his *American Artillerists Companion* (1809) became the standard text for the instruction of artillery use in the United States. Along the way he aided Eleuthère Irénée du Pont in establishing gunpowder mills in Delaware, which would prove vital to American interests. After being named inspector of artillery in 1800, Tousard became commander of the Second Artillery Regiment in January 1801. Incredibly, when the Academy at West Point was completed in 1802, President Thomas Jefferson passed over Tousard for superintendent because he was French. Tousard resigned in March 1802, returning to the French army as a battalion commander in General Victor Leclerc's failed attempt to conquer Haiti. Tousard served as a French consul in the United States during 1805–1816, returning in the latter year to France, where he died in Paris on 10 April 1817.

BIBLIOGRAPHY

Tousard, Ann-Louis. Tousard Papers. William L. Clements Library. University of Michigan, Ann Arbor.

Michael Bellesiles

TOWNSHEND, CHARLES. (1725–

1767). British politician. Second son of the third Viscount Townshend, he was educated at Clare College, Cambridge, Leiden University, and Lincoln's Inn, and was called to the bar in 1747. In the same year he was elected to Parliament for Great Yarmouth, and in 1748 he became a member of the Board of Trade. Here he impressed the president, Lord Halifax, whose intelligence and energy had considerable influence on colonial policy, and under him acquired considerable knowledge of imperial affairs. By 1753 he was thinking in terms of giving governors and other officials permanent financial independence of the colonial assemblies. At about this time he began to emerge as an impressive debater in the House of Commons, and in 1754 he moved to the Admiralty.

In 1755 he married the wealthy and influential widow of the earl of Dalkeith, so achieving considerable political independence. He now declared his opposition to the Duke of Newcastle's Europe-centered foreign policy and what he saw as neglect of American defense. He remained out of office from the formation of the first ministry of William Pitt, earl of Chatham, in 1756 until after George III's accession in 1760, partly because he was distrusted, partly because he was too clever for comfort. In March 1761 he became secretary at war but complained that he was not made leader of the House of Commons as well. Having now, like Pitt, reversed his earlier position, he urged the government to remain involved in the war in Germany: a commitment Lord Bute and George III were anxious to end. In December he resigned, apparently in protest over the terms of the Peace of Paris, which, to general confusion, he then defended in debate.

In March 1763, having at last obtained the presidency of the Board of Trade, he unsuccessfully proposed a measure that anticipated the Sugar Act of 1764. Although initially excluded from George Grenville's ministry, he supported the Stamp Act in February 1765 and was rewarded with the office of paymaster on 24 May. The following year he opposed the repeal of the Stamp Act. In 1766 he became Chatham's chancellor of the exchequer. Townshend then took advantage of Chatham's illness to prevent a government takeover of Bengal, while at the same time speculating with government money in East India stock.

He also carried the most moderate of the three suggested punishments for New York's defiance of the 1765 Mutiny Act: a temporary suspension of the colonial assembly's right to legislate. The cabinet, already committed to colonial taxation for military purposes, was now considering ways and means. Townshend persuaded ministers to widen the aim to giving colonial officials financial independence of the assemblies, the idea he had first proposed in 1753. By selecting customs duties he exploited the American distinction between internal and external taxes, not realizing that the real objection was *any* revenue-raising measure, as opposed to one designed to manage trade. A deficit arising from a ministerial defeat on the land tax was made up by thorough auditing and had nothing to do with the Townshend duties.

Townshend died suddenly on 4 September 1767. Although a brilliant speaker, he had never inspired confidence, and his frequent changes of allegiance deservedly earned him the nickname "the shuttlecock," or, as he expressed it in his "Champagne speech" on the East India Company measures, "the weathercock." He spent years in relatively minor offices and was chancellor only for a matter of months. Yet in that office he was assiduous and able, and his attitude toward American problems remained consistent and sincere from 1753 to his death.

SEE ALSO *Chatham, William Pitt, First Earl of; Grenville, George; Newcastle, Thomas Pelham Holies, Duke of; Stamp Act; Townshend Acts.*

BIBLIOGRAPHY

Christie, I. R. *Wars and Revolutions: Britain 1760–1815*. London: Edward Arnold, 1982.

Namier, Lewis, and John Brooke. *Charles Townshend*. London: Macmillan, 1964.

Thomas, Peter D. G. *British Politics and the Stamp Act Crisis: The First Phase of the American Revolution, 1763–1769*. Oxford: Oxford University Press, 1975.

revised by John Oliphant

TOWNSHEND ACTS.

1767. These were the Townshend Revenue Act, an act establishing a new system of customs commissioners, and an act suspending the New York assembly. The Farmer's Letters expressed colonial objection to the acts.

SEE ALSO *Customs Commissioners; Farmer's Letters; New York Assembly Suspended; Townshend Revenue Act.*

BIBLIOGRAPHY

Commager, Henry Steele. *Documents of American History*. 5th ed. New York: Appleton-Century-Crofts, 1949.

Mark M. Boatner

TOWNSHEND REVENUE ACT.

26 June 1767. Charles Townshend, who became chancellor of the exchequer on 2 August 1766, renewed the imperial government's efforts to raise revenue in America with the Revenue Act of 1767, passed by the House of Commons on 26 June 1767. Customs duties levied on glass, lead, painters' colors, paper, and, especially, tea imported into the colonies were expected to raise £40,000 annually. In raising revenue via customs duties, a supposedly "external" tax, Townshend sought to cloak taxation with the mantle of trade regulation, thus avoiding colonial opposition to an "internal" tax like the stamp tax of 1765.

The duties were to be paid in specie (metal currency), a requirement that put a drag on colonial economies that lacked adequate circulating currencies, but the manner in which the monies were raised proved to be less controversial than the uses to which Townshend proposed to put them. The funds would be used first to pay for "defraying the charges of the administration of justice, and the support of the government" in the colonies (Section 5 of the Act), including the payment of fixed salaries to royal officials. Any remaining funds would be devoted to paying British military expenses in the colonies. Since the colonial assemblies had fought long and successfully to maintain the power of the purse and to frustrate royal attempts to establish a fixed civil list in the colonies, it was the loss of control over the salaries of royal officials that particularly alarmed them. Many Americans believed that colonial governors would be bolder in violating colonial rights and trampling on American liberty, now that they were freed from the need to conciliate the local assemblies who had formerly paid their salaries.

To provide for efficient collection of the new duties, the Townshend Revenue Act and a companion measure generally legalized writs of assistance, extended the system of vice-admiralty courts, and set up a new American Board of Customs Commissioners. Receiving royal assent on 29 June, the act was to take effect on 20 November 1767. Townshend died on 4 September, leaving his successors the task of enforcing his act. Americans countered the act by reviving nonimportation. Their resistance proved so successful that on 12 April 1770 the House of Commons voted to repeal all the Townshend duties, effective 1 December 1770, except the one on tea.

SEE ALSO *Customs Commissioners; Massachusetts Circular Letter; Nonimportation; Royal Government in America; Townshend, Charles; Vice-Admiralty Courts; Writs of Assistance.*

BIBLIOGRAPHY

Jensen, Merrill, ed. *English Historical Documents.* Volume IX: *American Colonial Documents to 1776.* David C. Douglas, general editor. New York: Oxford University Press, 1955.

Knollenberg, Bernard. *Growth of the American Revolution, 1766–1775.* Indianapolis, Ind.: Liberty Fund, 2002.

Thomas, Peter D. G. *The Townshend Duties Crisis: The Second Phase of the American Revolution, 1767–1771.* Oxford, U.K.: Oxford University Press, 1987.

revised by Harold E. Selesky

TRADE, ACTS OF SEE *Navigation Acts.*

TRADE, THE BOARD OF. 1696–1782.

In 1696 William III created "A Board of Commissioners for Trade and Plantations" (the Board of Trade) as the principal manager of colonial affairs. Headed by a president who was also the first lord of trade, the Board had eight paid members and seven senior political officials who reviewed and reported to the Privy Council on colonial legislation, and recommended appointments of colonial officials. The activity of the Board varied according to the energy and interest of the first lord, reaching a high point when George Montagu Dunk, the earl of Halifax, became president in 1748 and going into a decline during the final French and Indian war (1756–1763). After Wills Hill, the earl of Hillsborough, became secretary of state for the American colonies and president of the Board of Trade in 1768, a single person continued to hold both positions until the board was abolished in 1782.

The Treasury Board also played a prominent part in colonial affairs because the Navigation Acts, particularly that of 1673, gave it authority over the Customs Commissioners, who had jurisdiction over collectors, searchers, and surveyors of customs in the colonies.

SEE ALSO *Background and Origins of the Revolution; Customs Commissioners; Disallowance; Germain, George Sackville; Royal Government in America; Vice-Admiralty Courts.*

revised by Harold E. Selesky

TRAINBAND OR TRAIN-BAND.

Appearing in 1630, the word is a clipped form of "trained band" and meant "militia."

BIBLIOGRAPHY

Onions, C. T., ed. *Oxford University Dictionary on Historical Principles.* 3rd ed. Oxford: Oxford University Press, 1955.

Mark M. Boatner

TRANSATLANTIC COMMUNICATION SEE *Atlantic Crossing.*

TRANSPORT. Wheeled vehicles, the mainstay of transport, were needed to move large quantities of military goods for the Revolutionary armies. A Continental army Wagon Department, subordinate to the quartermaster

general, was created in 1777 to deal with increasingly complex transportation needs. Headed by a wagonmaster general, deputies were assigned to the main army and each regional military department. The Northern Department's deputy wagonmaster general alone had five wagonmasters under his direction; they, in turn, each had charge of one or more wagon brigades, comprising ten to twelve vehicles and drivers. The historian Erna Risch has noted, "The [1777] regulation establishing the Wagon Department remained in effect until 1780, when Congress drastically reorganized the Quartermaster's Department following the adoption of the system of specific supplies [via state governments]" (*Supplying Washington's Army, p. 71*).

Large numbers and various types of vehicles were needed for both the supply lines and army carriage. An October 1780 Continental army "Estimate of Waggons" listed "Total waggons for a regiment" as four "4 horse close covered waggons," one "2 horse close covered waggon or tumbril," six "4 horse open waggons," and one "2 horse open waggon or tumbril." Another document included brigade support vehicles, namely one covered wagon for the brigade quartermaster and stores, four open wagons for the commissary and provisions, two open wagons for the foragemaster, two open wagons for the commissary of military stores "for spare ammunition and arms," one traveling forge, and two covered wagons for ammunition. "Close" covered wagons had a canvas tarpaulin fitting snugly over the vehicle's load. Other wagons were topped with a high-standing, cloth-covered frame or bonnet. Depending on circumstances, American and British forces also used sleds and often packhorses.

Finding suitable wagons was a concern of Francis Rush Clark, "Inspector and Superintendent of His Majesty's Provision Train of Wagons and Horses," who wrote of British transport in 1776 and 1777

> The English Waggons, sent over for the use of the Army, were undoubtedly much heavyer, than was either necessary or proper ... [and] Orders were given, to hire Country Waggons in preference.... Nothing of this sort could be constructed more unfit for an Army. They are so slight, as to be perpetually in want of repair.... These were taken pro miscuously from the Farmers on Long Island & Staten Island, & some from the Jerseys. Many of them in a wretch'd Condition, & none having any Cover[s].

Clark's solution was to devise an "English reduced" wagon, having "One of the English Waggons ... alter'd & set up upon the same principle, & reduced in Weight from 1350 lb to 900 lb, & made up very serviceable, & with some still lighter."

Both sides procured civilian wagons, and some, such as the large but serviceable Pennsylvania Conestogas, were used predominantly as long-distance carriers rather than for regimental baggage. Suitability for campaign use was based on a vehicle's balance of endurance, capacity, and weight. One Conestoga example, dating to about 1762, had a bed four feet wide by fourteen feet long (comparable in size to the cumbersome "English Waggons"), and a June 1781 Continental artillery transport estimate called for "Waggons or carts well coverd each to carry about 1400 lbs." According to Superintendent Clark, the "large English" wagon was about the same weight as a "Philadelphia Waggon" (1,350 pounds, 12 feet 3 inches long). Among the several vehicle types noted by Clark were the "Dutch or American" wagon (700 to 800 pounds, 9 feet 10 inches long), the "English reduced" (850 pounds), and the 700-pound "new Waggon with Rope Sides & Bottom, [that] runs light & handy." Clark stated this last vehicle "has been greatly approved by all that have seen it, as the best & most fit for American Service":

> The Body of this Waggon is 10 Feet long, & 3 Feet 6 Inches wide, The Sides are 18 Inches high, & turn down with hinges; a Box before, a hind Board framed light, to take off at pleasure, The Hind Wheels 4 Feet 8 Inches high, & the Fore Wheels 3 Feet 8 Inches high.... This Waggon is made 4 Inches lower before than behind, which greatly facilitates the draught & light going, & the floor & Sides are made of Rope, spun of old Cordage, as few or no boards are to be purchased in these times ... if thought better, the floor & sides might be made with thin, light battins, flat hoops or twisted hay (ibid).

Army trains could be inordinately long, and that of Lieutenant General Sir Henry Clinton's during the Monmouth campaign was likely the war's largest, with 1500 wagons taking up "near twelve miles" of road.

BIBLIOGRAPHY

Clark, Francis Rush. Papers. Sol Feinstone Collection. David Library of the American Revolution, Washington Crossing, Pa.

Greene, Nathanael, "Estimate of Teams to be employed in transporting Provisions and Forage from Trenton to Kings Ferry," 19 October 1778, George Washington Papers, Presidential Papers Microfilm, Washington: Library of Congress, 1961, series 4, reel, reel 53.

Rees, John U. "'Employed in Carrying Cloathing & Provisions': Wagons and Watercraft during the War for Independence." Part 1: "'Country Waggons,' 'Tumbrils,' and 'Philadelphia Carts': Wheeled Transport in the Armies of the Revolution." *The Continental Soldier* 12, no. 2 (Winter 1999): 18–25.

Risch, Erna. *Supplying Washington's Army*. Washington: Government Printing Office, 1981.

Shumway, George, Edward Durell, and Howard C. Frey. *Conestoga Wagon 1750–1850*. York, Pa.: George Shumway, 1964.

John U. Rees

TRANSPORTS, HORRORS OF BRITISH SOLDIER LIFE ABOARD

S E E *Atlantic Crossing.*

TRAVERSE.

A wall or other structure across the approach to a fortification or across an interior portion to cut off a part. It also meant right angles in the trace of a trench or parapet to minimize enfilade. See maps accompanying Saratoga battles.

S E E A L S O *Enfilade; Fort Mercer, New Jersey; Saratoga Surrender; Saratoga, First Battle of; Saratoga, Second Battle of.*

Mark M. Boatner

TREADWELL'S NECK, LONG ISLAND, NEW YORK.

10 October 1781. At 4 A.M. Major Lemuel Trescott attacked Fort Slongo with 150 dismounted troopers of the Second Continental Dragoons and took the Tory garrison without losing a man. After destroying the blockhouse he withdrew across Long Island Sound with twenty-one prisoners and captured matériel.

Mark M. Boatner

TREATIES.

Treaties are alphabetized by—or cross-referenced from—the identifying name of where they were concluded.

Mark M. Boatner

TRENTON, NEW JERSEY.

26 December 1776. Trenton was held by the Hesse-Cassel brigade of Colonel Johann Rall, which had distinguished itself during the battles at White Plains and Fort Washington. The brigade consisted of three regiments—the experienced Füsilier-Regiment von Lossburg and the Füsilier-Regiment von Knyphausen, along with the Landgrenadiere Regiment von Rall. This latter unit was formed in 1776 by splitting a two-battalion regiment (the other battalion stayed in Germany). In peacetime it maintained lower tables of organization than the other field regiments, meaning

that it had absorbed many new replacements in the spring and lacked the quality and cohesion of normal Hessian units. All three regiments had absorbed relatively heavy casualties already, and many of the officers who had been wounded were still in New York receiving medical attention. The brigade had six artillery pieces (two per regiment) with their gun crews, a detachment of jägers, and a small detachment of British light dragoons.

Rall himself was a commander with important political connections and great personal bravery. However, he had certain shortcomings that combined to produce spectacular failure at Trenton: like General Edward Braddock in the French and Indian War, he had a very conventional tactical sense and he severely underestimated his opponents. His superiors understood his inexperience at independent command, but the four senior officers who would normally have commanded the brigade were all ill. Although relatively isolated from the other garrisons at Princeton and Bordentown, he saw no need to construct fortifications, but he did establish some outposts and conducted morning and evening patrols of the nearby countryside. Near dusk on Christmas day Rall personally led one such patrol, which skirmished with an unauthorized American patrol. The brigade had gone into winter quarters and occupied various buildings in Trenton, a policy that kept them protected from the miserable wet and cold weather but required the regiments to take time to assemble in the event of an emergency. Also, the wear and tear of constant small skirmishing and nightly alerts had worn them down. On Christmas night a howling northeaster finally gave them a chance to relax a bit, since it was clear to all that the Americans would be quiet for a change.

WASHINGTON'S PLAN

Selecting the isolated post of Trenton as his objective, Washington—on the west bank of the Delaware River—devised a scheme of maneuver utilizing three separate groups. Brigadier General James Ewing would cross the Delaware with eight hundred militia at Trenton Ferry and occupy the south bank of Assunpink Creek to block the enemy's retreat in that direction. Colonel John Cadwalader was to lead eighteen hundred men—his Philadelphia Associators, supported by Colonel Daniel Hitchcock's Continental brigade—across the river at Burlington and block the garrison at Bordentown from reinforcing Trenton. Weather, particularly the ice on the river, prevented the supporting attacks from taking place. Ewing never got across the river; Cadwalader only got the van of his force over before conditions deteriorated and he had to pull them back.

The main body under Washington's personal command planned to cross at McKonkey's Ferry (later Washington Crossing), nine miles upstream, and separate

The Passage of the Delaware *(1819) by Thomas Sully.* *On Christmas night 1776, General Washington led American troops across the cold, icy Delaware River before marching toward Trenton.* THE PASSAGE OF THE DELAWARE, 1819 (OIL ON CANVAS) BY SULLY, THOMAS (1783–1872) © MUSEUM OF FINE ARTS, BOSTON, MASSACHUSETTS/BRIDGEMAN ART LIBRARY

into two columns. Major General John Sullivan's (Brigadier General Arthur St. Clair's, Colonel John Glover's, and Colonel Paul D. Sargent's brigades) would advance along the River Road. Washington and Major General Nathanael Greene would lead the brigades of Brigadier Generals Hugh Mercer, Adam Stephen, Lord Stirling, and Matthias Roche de Fermoy inland and attack down the Pennington Road. Washington allocated a total of eighteen cannon to these two columns, about three times the ratio of guns normally found in European warfare. Four accompanied each lead brigade, with three others at the head of each of the supporting brigades and two with each column's trail brigade. The plan called for the two columns to synchronize watches and strike the village from the north before dawn, which would come about 5 A.M.

THE ATTACK

Washington's column got off late and only reached the assembly area starting at 6 P.M. The men embarked in the

dark in Durham boats and assorted other river craft manned by Glover's Fourteenth Continental Regiment, watermen from the Philadelphia Associators, and the local ferrymen. In a remarkable feat, the force crossed eight hundred feet to the east bank in the face of the strong current; floating ice; bitter cold; and a storm of wind, hail, rain, and snow that started about 11 P.M. Not a man was lost, and the artillery and horses also made it, but way behind schedule. Although the debarkation was supposed to be accomplished by midnight, leaving five hours to reach Trenton before daybreak, the last man was not landed until 3 A.M., and the troops were not ready to start marching for another hour.

Despite the delays, a number of events combined to favor the American attack. British intelligence had been collecting information from Loyalist sympathizers, but reports back estimated that only American raiding patrols would cross the river. That had been the experience of a week or more, and on the morning of the 25th, Rall himself had led a sweep that clashed with an unauthorized probe by Captain Richard Clough Anderson of the Fifth Virginia Regiment and later in the day with a second raiding party from the Fourth Virginia Regiment under Captain George Wallis. Each morning Rall had his pickets make a dawn sweep of the immediate vicinity, which normally returned about sunrise (on the 26th at about 7:20 A.M.). By moving later than they had planned, the Americans avoided this patrol and therefore remained undetected.

At Birmingham, about four miles from its landing, the attacking force split into its two columns. Turning left to pick up the Pennington Road so as to approach Trenton from the north, Greene had Stephen's Virginia Continental brigade in the lead, followed by Mercer and Stirling and the Philadelphia Light Horse. Its vanguard consisted of forty men from the Third Virginia Regiment under Captain William Washington and Lieutenant James Monroe. Washington accompanied this column as did Fermoy's brigade, which would peel off and hold the Princeton road to prevent reinforcement of the Hessians. Sullivan continued down the River Road with the troops of St. Clair in front, followed by Glover and then Sargent. They would approach Trenton from the northwest. Captain John Flahaven led the vanguard of this column with forty men from the First New Jersey Regiment.

At about 7:30 A.M., American scouts located the Hessian outposts about a mile from the center of town. Fifty jägers under Lieutenant Friedrich von Grothausen covered the more dangerous River Road while a smaller force under Lieutenant Johann Andreas Wiederhold of the Knyphausen regiment held a building at the intersection of the Scotch and Pennington Roads, with about twenty assorted men; similar small detachments watched the Princeton Road and the bridge over the Assunpink, with the British dragoons further downstream. Washington therefore had Greene stop and deploy under the cover of woods into three brigade-sized columns before making their final advance. Wiederhold's men spotted them at the last second and got off a few shots about 8 A.M. Then they fell back on the billets of Captain Ernst von Altenbockum's No. 3 Company of Lossburg; that force fell out and also put up a brief resistance before falling back. Three minutes after Wiederhold was engaged, the artillery leading Sullivan's column opened fire on the outpost at the River Road.

Despite the myths, Rall was not drunk when the shooting started. But because the Hessians had gone into winter quarters, the companies were billeted in multiple buildings and required considerable time to assemble into regimental formations capable of actually fighting, a process complicated by the fact that the officers had to turn the five administrative companies into eight firing platoons before it could engage. The Rall and Lossburg regiments were generally situated in the north end of town, while Knyphausen's was in south end. Each day one regiment was designated as the "alert" regiment and kept under tighter control so that it could assemble first and give the other two more time. Rall's had assumed that duty at 4 P.M. on Christmas Day and was to form up on King Street. The Lossburg was supposed to use Queen Street, and the Knyphausen would form along the creek.

Although the Hessians turned with a reasonable amount of speed, Washington's posting of artillery in the van enabled the gunners to enfilade the regiments by firing down the street. Captain Alexander Hamilton's company broke up Rall's regiment as it was trying to sort itself out, and—together with Captain Thomas Forrest's guns firing down Queen Street—silenced the four Hessian guns in the center of town. The infantry followed with a charge, since the wet conditions limited the men's ability to reload their muskets effectively. William Washington and Monroe were both wounded as they overran the Lieutenant Johannes Englehard's two cannon supporting Rall's regiment in King Street. Sullivan's troops, meanwhile, had penetrated the south end of the village led by St. Clair's brigade and drove back the Knyphausen regiment before it could effectively organize. Several hundred of the jägers and Knyphausen men escaped over the bridge across the Assunpink because Ewing's force was not there to block them. Glover's brigade pushed directly on to finally seal the bridge, while Sergeant's concentrated on securing the old barracks building.

From the Hessian point of view the scene was one of indescribable confusion. Converging American columns pushed forward on their designated lines of advance and drove the Germans into the open east of town. Rall's remnants took shelter in an apple orchard, where they were joined by most of the Lossburg (without their cannon, which had become bogged down in low ground). Two counterattacks simply never made any headway and the two regiments were pounded by artillery fire. The Knyphausen regiment fought a separate battle in the south end of town and was similarly driven into fields near the creek without its guns. Efforts to find a route to escape proved useless, and as casualties began to mount (Rall himself went down mortally wounded), the senior officer still on his feet, Lieutenant Colonel Franziscus Scheffer of Lossburg, ordered the survivors to give up. Stirling's brigade took the surrender of the Rall-Lossburg force, while the Knyphausen element ground its arms to Sullivan slightly later, at about 9:30 A.M. Overall, the engagement lasted roughly ninety minutes from first skirmish to last surrender; heavy fighting lasted only from thirty to forty-five minutes. This variation explains the discrepancies in different accounts.

AMERICAN WITHDRAWAL

The inability of Ewing and Cadwalader to accomplish their missions made it out of the question for

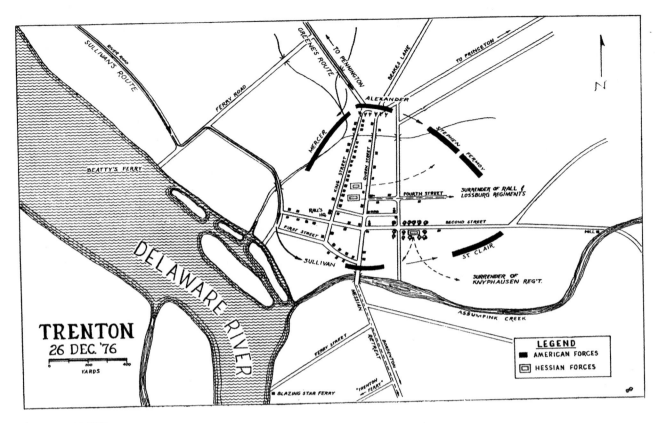

Washington to continue his offensive to Princeton and Brunswick. With a large body of prisoners to evacuate, his own men exhausted, and knowing that other enemy forces were nearby, Washington had no choice but to withdraw. The return proved even more arduous than the advance because the icing had gotten worse. Evacuation started at noon, and the rear guard did not reach its bivouacs until noon on the 27th.

NUMBERS AND LOSSES

While most sources state that Washington crossed with about twenty-four hundred troops and eighteen guns, a more accurate estimate can be made from the returns compiled on 22 December. (St. Clair's brigade was not included in the return.) Green's column had around three thousand officers and men and Sullivan over thirty-five hundred. The two American casualties that are positively known are William Washington and James Monroe, both wounded. Washington also reported one or two privates wounded in the action, and probably several more men died as a result of exposure.

Of the 1,400 Hessians, 106 were killed or wounded (5 officers, 17 men killed; 6 officers, 78 men wounded). Including wounded prisoners, 918 Hessians were captured (32 officers, 92 noncommissioned officers, 29 individuals in such categories as musician and surgeon's mate, 25 servants, and 740 rank and file). The rest escaped. None of the handful of British light dragoons was a casualty.

SIGNIFICANCE

It is hard to overstate the importance of this battle to the American cause. It started the reversal of fortunes that kept the Revolution alive and began the erosion of the Germans' reputation of invincibility that culminated the following autumn at Red Bank. Americans no longer feared them, and the British started to relegate them mostly to garrison activity. And, most significantly, the experimental use of combined arms brigades in this battle convinced Washington to adopt that formation permanently.

SEE ALSO *Alexander, William; Cadwalader, John; Durham Boats; Fermoy, Matthias Alexis de Roche; Fort Washington, New York; Glover, John; Greene, Nathanael; Hamilton, Alexander; Mercer, Hugh; Monroe, James; New Jersey Campaign; Rall, Johann Gottlieb; St. Clair, Arthur; Stephen, Adam; Sullivan, John; Washington, William; White Plains, New York.*

BIBLIOGRAPHY

Fischer, David. *Washington's Crossing.* New York: Oxford University Press, 2004.

Stryker, William S. *The Battles of Princeton and Trenton.* Boston: Houghton, Mifflin, 1898.

revised by Robert K. Wright Jr.

TRESCOTT, LEMUEL. (1751–1826).

Continental officer, Massachusetts. Born at Dorchester, Massachusetts, on 23 March 1751, Trescott was commissioned as a captain in Colonel John Brewer's Massachusetts Regiment on 19 May 1775. He held this rank in the Sixth Continental Regiment (Massachusetts) in 1776, and in Colonel David Henley's Additional Continental Regiment in 1777. On 20 May 1778 he was promoted to major, and on 22 April 1779 was transferred to Colonel Henry Jackson's Additional Continental Regiment, which was designated the Sixteenth Massachusetts on 23 July 1780. Major Trescott was transferred to the Ninth Massachusetts on 1 January 1781 and led the raid on Treadwell's Neck, 10 October 1781. As the Massachusetts Line shrank through two successive reorganizations, he became major of the Seventh Massachusetts on 1 January 1783 and, nominally, of the Fourth Massachusetts on 12 June 1783. On furlough in Connecticut from 24 April 1783, he remained on the rolls until the Continental Army was disbanded in November 1783. On 4 March 1791, he returned to military service as major of the Second United States Infantry, serving until he resigned on 28 December 1791. He settled on Passamaquoddy Bay, Maine, and engaged in lumbering with Colonel John Crane, formerly of the Continental artillery. He died at Lubec, Maine, on 13 August 1826.

SEE ALSO *Long Island, New York; Treadwell's Neck.*

revised by Harold E. Selesky

TROIS RIVIÈRES.

8 June 1776. Canada Invasion. An American defeat during the Canada invasion. When American reinforcements under Generals John Sullivan and William Thompson assembled at St. Johns on 1 June, they learned of the shattered condition of the army that General John Thomas had led back from Quebec. American authorities still hoped to hold Canada as the fourteenth colony, and to further that goal, the Canadian Department field army would attempt to push back toward Quebec. Sullivan directed Thompson to take two thousand of the best troops to attack Trois Rivières as a staging area. This town lay on the north bank of the St. Lawrence, about halfway between Montreal and Quebec, and was believed by Sullivan to be held by only four hundred men. Actually, General Burgoyne's regulars had started arriving there by ship, and the place was defended by about six thousand men under Brigadier General Simon Fraser.

Starting on 6 June, Thompson dropped down the river in bateaux to a point 10 miles from his objective. Moving by water again the next night, he landed at 3 A.M. on the morning of the 8th about 3 miles away. Here he left 250 men to guard the boats and started forward in four columns led by Arthur St. Clair, William Irvine, William Maxwell, and Anthony Wayne. (Thompson and these four subordinates all were outstanding commanders.) A plan calling for multiple elements moving in the dark over unfamiliar terrain to strike a target simultaneously was probably beyond the troops' abilities. Trouble started when their guide got lost and the men spent hours floundering in a swamp, which exhausted the troops. When they finally reached the river road shortly before dawn, three British warships chased them back into the cover of the swamp.

That firing of the warships alerted the British. Troops in the town moved into defensive positions, while those still on shipping poured ashore. Combat patrols sent out soon made contact with the American advance and identified the threat. About 7 A.M. Anthony Wayne led two hundred men in an attack that routed a patrol, and Thompson followed with the rest of the command to continue the pursuit. But the Americans then hit a line of entrenchments manned by vastly superior forces and covered by guns from the river. Unaware of the true odds, Thompson attacked and was repulsed. With a misguided courage he tried to organize another attempt, but his command was too scattered, and nothing more than an irregular patter of musketry could be delivered. In a matter of minutes the battle was over and the Americans found themselves in a race to escape capture.

Carleton pursued but used caution. He also took advantage of having absolute control of the sea (in this case, the river) and sent his armed vessels upstream to cut Thompson off. The boat guard escaped with its bateaux, but the rest of the Americans had to make their way out through swamps in great hardship and under constant threat of attack by Indians or Canadian Loyalists. The last of the eleven hundred survivors straggled into Sorel the evening of 11 June.

Total American losses were about four hundred, mostly prisoners. Thompson was one of the captives. The British lost five killed and fourteen wounded.

SEE ALSO *Canada Invasion; Irvine, William; Maxwell, William; St. Clair, Arthur; Sullivan, John; Thomas, John; Thompson, William; Wayne, Anthony.*

BIBLIOGRAPHY

Digby, William. *The British Invasion from the North: Digby's Journal of the Campaigns of Generals Carleton and Burgoyne from Canada, 1776–1777.* New York: Da Capo, 1970.

Stillé, Charles J. *Major-General Anthony Wayne and the Pennsylvania Line in the Continental Army.* Philadelphia: Lippincott, 1893.

revised by Robert K. Wright Jr.

TRONSON DU COUDRAY, PHILIPPE CHARLES JEAN BAPTISTE.

(1738–1777). Continental general. France. Born in Reims, he became an artillery lieutenant in 1760 and a captain in 1766. On 14 September 1768 he was promoted to *chef de brigade*. His brother, Alexandre, was lawyer to Marie Antoinette. He tutored the king's brothers, the comte d'Artois and the duc de Chartres, in the art of war and was technical adviser to several ministers of war, including Saint Germain. He was also a prolific writer. Selected to cull the arsenals for matériel that might be sent covertly to America without impairing French combat effectiveness, he worked with the great Gribeauval, whose new system of artillery had just been adopted in France. He also supervised the selection of artillery and engineer officers who would go to America as technical advisers. Gribeauval, Beaumarchais, and Silas Deane were impressed not only by his zeal and professional competence but also by his spirit of cooperation. On 11 September 1776 Deane signed an agreement that du Coudray would accompany a shipment of officers, men, and matériel to America and would then be commissioned major general with the title of general of artillery and ordnance, and that he would have "the direction of whatever relates to the Artillery and Corps of Engineers."

Du Coudray reached America in May 1777. Although Deane had exceeded his authority, Congress had to treat du Coudray with respect for fear of alienating powers near the French throne. John Adams expressed the quandary in two letters of June 1777. To Nathanael Greene, he swore that a foreigner such as du Coudray "shall never have my consent to be at the head of the artillery." Yet to James Warren he wrote, "His interest is so great and so near the throne, that it would be impolitick not to avail ourselves of him." Greene, Knox, and Sullivan threatened Congress in a letter read on 5 July that they would resign if du Coudray were made senior to them. Congress responded on 7 July by denouncing their threats as an "invasion of the liberties of the people." Four other French engineers who had arrived before him—Duportail, Gouvion, Laumoy, and La Radière—complained that he was not even in the French Royal Corps of Engineers. On 11 August, Congress voted a solution that at least satisfied the disgruntled American generals. They made du Coudray a major general "of the staff," as they later did with Conway, so he had no command authority over the major generals "of the line." Instead, they declared him inspector general of ordnance and military manufactories. Congress still had contrived nothing more than an interim solution, but the problem soon resolved itself. On 15 September 1777, he rode his horse onto the Schuylkill Ferry; the horse was spooked and rode out the other end and into the river. Du Coudray was drowned. He was buried that afternoon in Philadelphia.

SEE ALSO *Adams, John; Beaumarchais and the American Revolution; Conway, Thomas; Deane, Silas; Duportail; Gouvion, Jean Baptiste; Greene, Nathanael; Laumoy, Jean Baptiste Joseph, Chevalier de.*

BIBLIOGRAPHY

Adams, John. *Diary and Autobiography.* Edited by Lyman H. Butterfield. 4 vols. Cambridge, Mass.: Harvard University Press, 1961.

———. *Papers of John Adams.* Edited by Robert J. Taylor, et al. 10 vols. to date. Cambridge, Mass.: Harvard University Press, 1977–.

Ford, Worthington C., et al., eds. *Journals of the Continental Congress, 1774–1789.* 34 vols. Washington, D.C.: U.S. Government Printing Office, 1904–1937.

Washington, George. *The Papers of George Washington, Revolutionary War Series.* Edited by Philander Chase, et al. 14 vols. to date. Charlottesville: University Press of Virginia, 1985–.

revised by Robert Rhodes Crout

TRUMBULL, BENJAMIN. (1735–1820).

Clergyman and historian. Connecticut. Eldest son of Benjamin Trumbull Sr., Trumbull was graduated from Yale College in 1759 and studied theology under Eleazar Wheelock. On 24 December 1760 he became pastor of the Congregational Church in New Haven, where, save for six months in 1776, he served continuously until his death sixty years later. His single absence was to serve as chaplain of Wadsworth's Brigade from 24 June to 25 December 1776. At the urging of prominent citizens of Connecticut, including Governor Jonathan Trumbull, he undertook to write the history of his state. Without neglecting his pastoral duties, and working under great difficulties, it took him more than 20 years to publish his *Complete History of Connecticut from 1630 to 1713* (1797). An expanded, two volume edition appeared in 1818: *Complete History of Connecticut . . . to the Year 1764.* His *General History of the United States . . . 1492–1792* was to be a three-volume work, but he lived to complete only the first volume, to the year 1765, which appeared in 1810. He published 16 other pamphlets and books, three of them political and the others religious in nature. From material collected by Trumbull, *A Compendium of the Indian Wars in New England*, edited by F. B. Hartranft, was published in 1924. Trumbull's faithful chronicle of events in Connecticut retains considerable historical value.

SEE ALSO *Trumbull Family; Trumbull, John.*

revised by Harold E. Selesky

TRUMBULL, JOHN. (1756–1843). "The painter of the Revolution." Connecticut. The youngest of six children of Governor Jonathan Trumbull, John was a sickly child who had severe convulsions caused by overlapping bones of the skull. This defect healed in his third year, but he severely injured his left eye about a year later. Interested in drawing early in life, he was prevented by his father from studying under John Singleton Copley in Boston. He was sent instead to Harvard College, from which he graduated in 1773. He started teaching school in Lebanon, and continued to teach himself art. When the war began John was appointed adjutant to General Joseph Spencer, and on 27 July 1775 became an aide to General George Washington, who had seen some of Trumbull's drawings of enemy positions and thought he could put his talents to military use. Trumbull did not feel at ease in this post, however, and he accepted a commission as brigade major on 15 August 1775. He took part in the action on Dorchester Heights, went with the army to New York City, and on 28 June 1776 became deputy adjutant general to Horatio Gates, with the rank of colonel. He resigned on 19 April 1777 and spent time in Boston studying art before volunteering as an aide to John Sullivan for the actions around Newport, Rhode Island, between July and August 1778. In May 1780 he sailed for France and, with the help of Benjamin Franklin and John Temple, got himself accepted as a pupil by Benjamin West in London. On 19 November 1780 he was arrested on suspicion of treason and ultimately released through the efforts of Charles Fox and Edmund Burke. He moved to the Continent, attempted to raised a loan for Connecticut through his father's Dutch bankers, and then returned to Boston.

By December 1783 Trumbull was back in London at the studio of West. After two years painting classical subjects, he turned to the history of the American Revolution. The first paintings in this series, the "The Death of General Warren at the Battle of Bunker's Hill" and "The Death of General Montgomery in the Attack of Quebec," were done under the direction of West and were heavily influenced by West's own "Death of General Wolfe at

Quebec" (1772). They were completed in the spring of 1786. Trumbull started "The Declaration of Independence." This work took eight years to complete, in part because thirty-six of the forty-eight portraits in it were done from life. His "The Surrender of Lord Cornwallis at Yorktown," "The Death of General Mercer at the Battle of Princeton," and "The Capture of the Hessians at Trenton" were also done in West's studio. Meanwhile he had gone to Paris to have his first two American works published as engravings. Finding that his American subjects were not particularly relished in England, he painted a British success, "Sortie Made by the Garrison at Gibraltar." In 1787 and 1789 he revisited Paris to paint portraits of French and British officers. He stayed with Jefferson, who offered him a post as private secretary, but Trumbull declined and in 1789 returned to America.

In Philadelphia Trumbull did a number of portraits, starting with Washington. In 1793 he became private secretary to John Jay, and used the opportunity to return to Europe to supervise the engraving of the work he had already completed. He performed his official duties with distinction, and returned to America in the spring of 1804 with a pretty English wife, Sarah Hope, neé Harvey. He resumed his painting, but his art had declined. In March 1817 he was commissioned by Congress to do four life-size, 12-by-18-foot paintings for the Capitol, which was being restored after suffering damage during the War of 1812. Working in New York City from miniatures previously executed, he took seven years to complete the canvases, for which he was paid $8,000 apiece. The paintings—"The Surrender of General Burgoyne at Saratoga," "The Surrender of Lord Cornwallis at Yorktown," "The Declaration of Independence," and "The Resignation of Washington"—were controversial. The one-eyed Trumbull's greatest skill was as a miniaturist; he had not done large figures well even during his prime.

In 1831 he gave his unsold paintings to Yale College in return for an annuity, and designed a building to hold them, thus creating the first college-affiliated art gallery in the United States. Becoming cantankerous and haughty as disappointments and waning talent clouded his old age, Trumbull published his *Autobiography* in 1841. He died two years later at the age of 87. The art historian Theodore Sizer concludes that ". . . no schoolboy but sees the Revolution through his eyes. His 250 to 300 faithful representations, drawn from life, of the principal actors and actions of the Revolution make him at once the chief, the most prolific, and the most competent visual recorder of that heroic period."

SEE ALSO *Trumbull Family.*

The Sortie Made by the Garrison at Gibraltar *(1789).* *Trumbull painted this scene of a famous episode in British history when he discovered that his American subjects were not particularly relished in England.* © GEOFFREY CLEMENTS/CORBIS

BIBLIOGRAPHY

Jaffe, Irma B. *Patriot Artist of the American Revolution.* Boston: New York Graphic Society, 1975.

Sizer, Theodore. *Works of Colonel John Trumbull, Artist of the American Revolution.* New Haven: Yale University Press, 1950.

Trumbull, John. *The Autobiography of Colonel John Trumbull, Patriot Artist, 1756–1843.* Edited by Theodore Sizer. New Haven: Yale University Press, 1953.

revised by Harold E. Selesky

TRUMBULL, JOHN (THE POET).

(1751–1831). Connecticut. A second cousin of the painter John Trumbull, this John Trumbull is remembered for his comic epic, *M'Fingal,* the narrative of a Tory squire's misfortunes. "Reprinted more than 30 times between 1782 and 1840, it was the most popular American poem of its length before Longfellow's Evangeline" (Alexander Cowie in DAB). "It borrowed much of its style from the seventeenth-century English versifier, Samuel Butler, the author of *Hudibras.* Hudibrastic satire, crude but sometimes effectively epigrammatic, was popular in America at this time as a vehicle for the expression of political grievances" (Dennis R. Dean in ODNB). Trumbull wanted to pioneer an independent American aesthetic in poetry, but it was a goal he did not achieve. "He could not conceive of poetry in forms not established by English predecessors. In politics as in literature, Trumbull was fundamentally conservative"(ibid.).

Tremendously precocious, he passed the entrance examination to Yale College at the age of seven but was forced to wait until the more mature age of thirteen before being allowed to enter. He was graduated in 1767 and received his master's degree in 1770. In 1773 he passed his bar examination and moved to Boston, where he continued his studies under John Adams. When Adams left Boston in August 1774, Trumbull moved to New Haven, which he left in 1777 for the relative safety of his native Westbury (later in Watertown), Connecticut

Although he was a Patriot and had been writing clever satire since his college days, Trumbull's work had little popular appeal during the war. *M'Fingal* was published early in 1776, almost simultaneously with Thomas Paine's *Common Sense*; it had only three editions during the war, whereas 120,000 copies of *Common Sense* were sold within less than three months. Not until after the war was *M'Fingal* accepted as an important literary achievement. Although Trumbull was the leader of an important group of writers and poets called the Connecticut (or Hartford) Wits, after 1782 his main interest turned to law and politics. He held his first office in 1789, when he became state's attorney for Hartford County. Appointed judge of the Connecticut superior court in 1801 and judge of the supreme court of errors in 1808, he lost these positions for political reasons in 1819. The next year, *The Poetical Works of John Trumbull* was published in two volumes. Five years later he moved to Detroit, where he died after living there six years.

SEE ALSO *M'Fingal; Salem, Massachusetts; Trumbull Family.*

revised by Harold E. Selesky

TRUMBULL, JONATHAN, SR.

(1710–1785). Governor of Connecticut. The great-grandson of the founder of the Trumbull Family in Connecticut, Jonathan changed the spelling of his name from Trumble in 1766. Having graduated from Harvard College in 1727, he was preparing for the ministry when his elder brother, Joseph, died in 1731. Joseph had been their father's associate in a large mercantile business in Lebanon, Connecticut, and Jonathan felt it was his duty to succeed him in this responsibility. By 1760 he was a major figure in the commerce of the colony, but a credit crisis during the depression that followed the final French and Indian war left him virtually bankrupt in 1762. His economic travails did not affect his standing with the voters of Connecticut, however. He rose steadily in politics, and in 1766 he became deputy governor and chief justice. On the death of Governor William Pitkin in October 1769, Trumbull succeeded to the governorship, an office to which he was re-elected annually until his voluntary retirement in 1784, the year before his death.

A strong supporter of colonial rights and an early advocate for independence, Trumbull was a pillar of the Patriot cause. He was the only colonial governor to retain his office even after the colony gained its independence and became a state, and the only governor to serve throughout the war. Connecticut was a major source of

war materiel, especially during the first two years of the conflict. Trumbull's main contribution to the war effort was organizing its resources of food, clothing, and munitions for use by General George Washington's army, a job for which his experience and connections as a merchant prepared him well. He was such an important figure that he received an average of three letters a month from Washington during this period. (Washington's first commissary general was the governor's son, Joseph Trumbull, and the second was another Connecticut man, Jeremiah Wadsworth. The Connecticut Coast Raid of July 1779 was prompted by a desire of the British to end the state's contributions to the rebel army.)

Trumbull had to cope with political opposition at home, where his policies seemed to favor mercantile and commercial groups over farmers and artisans. It was also rumored that he was secretly trading with the enemy. In the gubernatorial elections of 1780 through 1783 his popular majority was reduced to a mere plurality, but the General Assembly voted to retain him in office each year. In January 1782 he demanded a legislative investigation. He was completely vindicated, and the investigation found evidence that the rumors were enemy-inspired. He was about 5 feet 7 inches in height, austere in dress and manner, and very much what the French traveler, the Marquis de Chastellux, called "the great magistrate of a little republic."

Writing in the *Dictionary of National Biography*, historian Bruce C. Daniels notes the following:

> Instead of courting voters and listening to their opinions, he expected the deference he felt he had earned through a lifetime of service. More dignified and reserved than haughty, Trumbull nevertheless appeared remote and cold to the new type of participatory voter who emerged during the revolutionary era–a great leader of a movement whose inner vitality tragically escaped his knowledge.

Trumbull retired in May 1784 in the face of certain electoral defeat. He spent his last fifteen months straightening out his long-neglected personal affairs.

> In the nineteenth century, several biographers erroneously claimed that Trumbull was the prototype for "Brother Jonathan," the name invented by whig historians to describe their ideal of the simple citizen of the fledgling republic. Few images of Trumbull could be further from the truth.

SEE ALSO *Connecticut Coast Raid; Trumbull Family; Trumbull, Joseph; Wadsworth, Jeremiah.*

BIBLIOGRAPHY

Buel, Richard V., Jr. *Dear Liberty: Connecticut's Mobilization for the Revolutionary War.* 1980.

Roth, David M. *Connecticut's War Governor.* Chester, Conn.: Pequot Press, 1974.

Shipton, Clifford K. *Biographical Sketches of Those Who Attended Harvard College,* 8. Boston: Massachusetts Historical Society, 1951.

Weaver, Glenn. *Jonathan Trumbull: Connecticut's Merchant Magistrate.* Hartford: Connecticut Historical Society, 1956.

revised by Harold E. Selesky

TRUMBULL, JONATHAN, JR.

(1740–1809). Paymaster General, comptroller of the treasury, military secretary to Washington. Connecticut. Son and namesake of Governor Jonathan Trumbull Sr. and kin to other famous members of the Trumbull Family, Jonathan Jr. entered Harvard College at the age of 15 and graduated in 1759. Like his older brother, Joseph, he joined the family mercantile business in Lebanon, Connecticut, and ran it after 1767 when their father became more involved in the politics of resisting British imperial policies. His neighbors elected him a town selectman in 1770, and sent him to the General Assembly in 1774 and 1775. On 28 July 1775 Congress named him paymaster general of the Northern Department, a difficult office that he held until 29 July 1778. At that time he resigned to settle the accounts of his brother, Joseph, who had been commissary general of the Continental Army and who had died on 23 July.

On 3 November 1778 Congress unanimously elected him as the first comptroller of the treasury, and he served for six months until resigning in April 1779. In November he declined the office of commissioner of the board of the treasury. When Alexander Hamilton asked to leave General George Washington's staff in February 1781, Washington chose Trumbull as Hamilton's successor. Appointed lieutenant colonel and military secretary on 8 June 1781, Trumbull served through the Yorktown Campaign and to the end of the war. He resigned on 23 December 1783 and returned to Lebanon to take care of his personal affairs.

A strong supporter of the federal Constitution, Trumbull was elected to the first three congresses of the new government and became speaker of the House of Representatives in October 1794. He served three years in the Senate (1794–1796), resigning in June 1796 when elected deputy governor of Connecticut. He succeeded the late Governor Oliver Wolcott in December 1797, and held the post until he died of dropsy on 7 August 1809. Among his last political acts was his refusal to authorize the use of Connecticut militia to enforce the Embargo Act, which closed all American ports to foreign trade. Although a strong nationalist, in January of 1809 he defied the Act of Congress (1807) because he considered it a violation of states' rights. The act was repealed in March 1809.

SEE ALSO *Hamilton, Alexander; Trumbull Family.*

BIBLIOGRAPHY

Ikovic, John. *Connecticut's Nationalist Revolutionary.* Hartford, Conn.: American Revolution Bicentennial Commission of Connecticut, 1977.

———. *Jonathan Trumbull, Junior: A Biography.* New York: Arno Press, 1982.

revised by Harold E. Selesky

TRUMBULL, JOSEPH.

(1738–1778). First commissary general of the Continental army. Connecticut. Eldest son of Governor Jonathan Trumbull and brother of the younger Jonathan Trumbull and of the painter John Trumbull, Joseph graduated from Harvard College in 1756. After studying the law, he joined his father's mercantile firm in Lebanon, one of the most important retail and wholesale businesses in eastern Connecticut. As one of Lebanon's representatives in the General Assembly after 1767, he shared his family's dislike of British colonial policies. In May 1773 the Assembly appointed him a member of its Committee of Correspondence, and in August 1774 elected him to the first Continental Congress as an alternate to Roger Sherman, but he did not get the opportunity to take a seat. Although he had served as captain of his local militia company in Lebanon, the Assembly selected him in April 1775 to be commissary general of the Connecticut forces at the Boston Siege because of his extensive mercantile and political connections. Impressed by his performance, and fully aware of the important role Governor Trumbull played in supporting the cause and the army, Commander in Chief George Washington on 10 July urged Congress to appoint Joseph as commissary general of the Continental Army. On 19 July 1775 the delegates complied with this request, giving Trumbull the rank and pay of a colonel and the job of feeding the army.

Logistics can be an overwhelming task in a modern army, but for Trumbull it was a pioneer effort in which he was handicapped not only by his own lack of logistical experience but also by lack of funds, lack of transportation, lack of support from jealous state and Congressional authorities, and lack of qualified subordinates. He was charged with dishonesty, but an inquiry directed by Washington in December 1775 exonerated him. In 1776

General Phillip Schuyler challenged his authority to control the provisioning of the Northern army, but Congress and Washington upheld Trumbull's position. His performance had not been perfect, however. The inquiry in December 1775 found fault with the prices he fixed for provisions, although it held that no fraud was involved, and his conduct in the clash with Schuyler had reflected the ill-tempered rivalry between New York and New England. In the spring of 1777 an impatient Congress approved an ill-advised reorganization that split Trumbull's job in two: one commissary general for purchases and another for issues. Trumbull refused the purchasing post because his deputies would report directly to Congress rather than to him. He pronounced the system unworkable and resigned on 2 August 1777. (When Congress re-established in the spring of 1778 the system under which Trumbull had operated, Jeremiah Wadsworth became commissary general.) Appointed by Congress to the new Board of War on 27 November 1777, he was forced by ill health to resign on 18 April 1778. Worn down by his labors, he died 23 July 1778 at the age of 41. Faced by the complexity of supplying an army of unprecedented size that operated over vast distances, a problem exacerbated by the structural impediments, inefficiencies, inelasticity, and inexperience that were endemic in the late colonial economy, Trumbull did a masterful job of providing the material resources that enabled the American army to fight.

SEE ALSO *Trumbull Family; Wadsworth, Jeremiah.*

BIBLIOGRAPHY

Buel, Richard V., Jr. *In Irons: Britain's Naval Supremacy and the American Revolutionary Economy.* New Haven: Yale University Press, 1998.

Risch, Erna. *Supplying Washington's Army.* Washington, D.C.: Center of Military History, United States Army, 1981.

revised by Harold E. Selesky

TRUMBULL FAMILY.

John Trumble founded the American branch of the Trumbull family when he emigrated from England to Roxbury, Massachusetts, in 1639. The spelling "Trumbull" was adopted in 1766 by John's great-grandson Jonathan (1710–1785) and by other branches of the family about two years later. Several members of the family were famous during the Revolutionary era. Jonathan was governor of Connecticut from 1769 to 1784. His sons also had notable careers: Jonathan Jr. was governor of Connecticut from 1797 to 1809, Joseph was the first commissary general of the Continental Army, and John painted portraits of many

important figures of the revolutionary era. Two other Trumbulls were the sons of two first cousins of Jonathan the elder, and therefore were second cousins of the three brothers just mentioned. These cousins are Benjamin (1735–1820), a clergyman and historian, and John (1751–1831), a poet, wit, and jurist.

SEE ALSO *Trumbull, Benjamin; Trumbull, John; Trumbull, John (the poet); Trumbull, Jonathan, Jr.; Trumbull, Jonathan, Sr.; Trumbull, Joseph.*

revised by Harold E. Selesky

TRUMBULL–IRIS ENGAGEMENT.

9 August 1781. Captain James Nicholson departed the Delaware Capes on 8 August, escorting a twenty-eight-sail convoy to the West Indies with his own twenty-eight-gun *Trumbull* and two privateers. The *Trumbull*, the last of the original Continental Navy frigates, had a crew composed for the most part of British deserters. The next day three British vessels gave chase, and the convoy scattered. The *Trumbull* was pulling away when a squall tore way part of two of her masts and left the rigging in shambles. Unable to get away, Nicholson tried to jettison the guns; but most of the crew refused to come on deck. The lead British frigate came up, the thirty-two-gun *Iris.* This vessel was the Continental Navy's *Hancock*, captured in 1777 by the *Rainbow* and taken into the Royal Navy under a new name. Nicholson, Lieutenants Richard Dale and Alexander Murray, and a small minority of the crew resisted for an hour and a half before being captured. The eighteen-gun *General Monk* came up at the end of the action but did not get a share of the prize money. Ironically, she had formerly been the American privateer *General Washington.*

SEE ALSO *Trumbull–Watt Engagement.*

BIBLIOGRAPHY

Fowler, William M., Jr. *Rebels under Sail: the American Navy during the Revolution.* New York: Scribners, 1976.

United States Navy. Naval Historical Division. *Dictionary of American Naval Fighting Ships.* 8 vols. Washington, D.C.: U.S. Government Printing Office, 1959–1981.

revised by Robert K. Wright Jr.

TRUMBULL–WATT ENGAGEMENT.

1 June 1780. In May 1780 the last of the original Continental Navy frigates, the twenty-eight-gun

Trumbull, finally got to sea from New London, Connecticut, on her maiden voyage. On 1 June, about 250 miles north of Bermuda, Captain James Nicholson detected a sail and turned to investigate. The vessel was a thirty-two-gun ship from Liverpool, the *Watt,* sailing under a letter of marque and reprisal and commanded by John Coulthard. About twelve hours later, at 1 P.M., Nicholson cleared for action, and shortly thereafter the vessels engaged. In one of the hottest engagements of the naval war, they hammered away at each other at a range of fifty to eighty yards for two and a half hours, then separated. The *Watt* limped away to New York; the *Trumbull* had sustained so much damage that she could not catch up and headed for Boston. Nicholson's green crew had about 40 casualties out of 199 men; Watt had about 90 killed and wounded.

SEE ALSO Trumbull–Iris *Engagement.*

BIBLIOGRAPHY

Fowler, William M., Jr. *Rebels under Sail: The American Navy during the Revolution.* New York: Scribners, 1976.

United States Navy. Naval Historical Division. *Dictionary of American Naval Fighting Ships.* 8 vols. Washington, D.C.: U.S. Government Printing Office, 1959–1981.

revised by Robert K. Wright Jr.

TRYON, WILLIAM. (1729–1788). Royal

governor of North Carolina and New York, British general. Well born, Tryon used his family connections to secure a lieutenancy in the prestigious First Regiment of Foot Guards in 1751. He was promoted to the rank of captain the same year. In 1757, he married Margaret Wake, heiress of a fortune and a relative of Lord Hillsborough (Wills Hill). Tryon saw military service during the Seven Years' War, during which he was in the Cherbourg-St. Malo operation (1758) and was almost killed. Also in 1758, he was promoted to lieutenant colonel. Through the influence of Hillsborough, he was appointed lieutenant governor of North Carolina in 1764. A year later, when Governor Arthur Dobbs died, he was appointed governor.

Proving himself a successful administrator, Tryon reorganized the province's taxes; established the Anglican Church and a postal system; improved defenses; erected "Tryon Palace," a new governor's mansion at New Bern; drew a boundary between North and South Carolina; and attempted, unsuccessfully, to get London's approval for a provincial currency. He sympathized with the Carolinians in their opposition to the Stamp Act in 1765 and the Townshend Duties in 1769, but nevertheless attempted to enforce the measures. His final act as governor of North Carolina was to defeat the frontiersmen known as Regulators in the battle of the Alamance on 16 May 1771.

Replacing Lord Dunmore (John Murray) as governor of New York in late 1771, Tryon had difficulties with frontiersmen there as well. He became embroiled in a border controversy between New York and New Hampshire over the region that became Vermont. He got into difficulties with London when he granted enormous tracts of land to colonial aristocrats, and to himself. His avowed aim, as he explained to the British ministry, was to counteract "the general leveling spirit" that prevailed in many of England's American colonies, by imposing aristocratic landlords on tenants. In 1772 he also fostered hierarchy by establishing a militia system that granted all officers' commissions to "Gentlemen of first families" and created several independent companies for the provinces' richest citizens,

When Tryon was confronted in the mid-1770s with radical New Yorkers' resistance to the Tea Act, he attempted to isolate the protesters from the rest of the population. At the same time, he implored the ministry in London to end attempts to tax Americans. Failing in both these matters, he fled on 19 October 1775 to a British ship in New York harbor. Although he retained the governorship for the remainder of his tenure in the colonies, he concentrated on service in the British army. Having been promoted colonel in 1772, he used his military authority to organize Loyalist militias in New York. He welcomed General William Howe's army in July 1776, and acted as Howe's adviser during the fighting for the remainder of the year. On 1 January 1777 he was commissioned a major general in America and given command of Loyalist regiments in Howe's army. In April he led a successful raid against Danbury, Connecticut, and in October he joined Sir Henry Clinton in attacking the Highland Forts on the Hudson River. In 1778, he was appointed colonel of the Seventieth Regiment.

A year later, Tryon conducted savage attacks against Horseneck, New Haven, and Norwalk, all in Connecticut. Practicing what he called "desolation warfare," he unleashed merciless operations against both civilians and soldiers in an attempt to break their will to resist. In 1780, convinced that the war was unwinnable, he abandoned this policy. After serving in operations against Connecticut Farms and Springfield, New Jersey, in June 1780, he resigned his civil and military offices and returned to England. There he lived quietly and comfortably with his family until his death on 17 January 1788.

Before the War for America commenced in 1775, Tryon had sided with the colonists in opposing parliamentary taxes, even though he favored social hierarchy and believed the Americans were too democratic. Hence, he was generally popular. But his advocacy of sanguinary warfare after that time destroyed his popularity and convinced the rebels that he was a brutal despot. By his own lights a friend of America, he found himself in an impossible situation, for Britain refused to make timely and necessary concessions in the early 1770s. Through no fault of his own, he was a victim of forces over which he exerted no control.

SEE ALSO *Dunmore's (or Cresap's) War; Regulators.*

BIBLIOGRAPHY

Nelson, Paul David. *William Tryon and the Course of Empire: A Life in British Imperial Service.* Chapel Hill: University of North Carolina Press, 1990.

Powell, William S., ed. *The Correspondence of William Tryon and Other Selected Papers*, 2 vols. Raleigh, N.C.: Division of Archives and History, 1980–1981.

revised by Paul David Nelson

TRYON COUNTY, NEW YORK.

The half of New York province bordering on Canada and the Iroquois country was taken from Albany County in 1772 and named Tryon County in honor of Governor. William Tryon. It comprised all the Mohawk Valley from a point about ten miles west of Schenectady and contained all the colonial settlements west and southwest of that place. (The main settlements of the Schoharie Valley were in Albany County.) It was renamed Montgomery County in 1784.

Sir William Johnson dominated the affairs of Tryon County until his death in 1774, when Guy Johnson became the leader of the Loyalist element. The latter group was driven into exile and returned to ravage the Mohawk Valley; the region, in fact, was subject to violent civil war between Patriot and Loyalist forces through much of the Revolution, with occasional incursions by Indians, British, and Continental troops.

SEE ALSO *Border Warfare in New York; Johnson, Guy; Johnson, Sir William; Tryon, William.*

BIBLIOGRAPHY

Campbell. William W. *Annals of Tryon County; or, The Border Warfare of New York during the Revolution.* 4th ed. New York: Dodd, Mead, 1924.

revised by Michael Bellesiles

TRYON COUNTY, NORTH CAROLINA.

Named for Governor William Tryon in 1769, it was located in the southwest part of the province and was a Loyalist stronghold for much of the Revolution. In 1779 the North Carolina legislature terminated Tryon County, forming the area into Rutherford and Lincoln Counties.

SEE ALSO *Kings Mountain, South Carolina; Tryon, William.*

revised by Michael Bellesiles

TUFFIN, ARMAND CHARLES, MARQUIS DE LA ROUËRIE.

(1750–1793). French volunteer. Known in America as Colonel Armand, this wealthy nobleman was born at Fougères, France. Flag ensign in the French Guard in 1766, he was promoted to first ensign in 1771 and *sous lieutenant* on 9 April 1775. He seriously wounded the king's cousin, the comte de Bourbon-Besset, in a duel and was exiled from court. Toward the end of 1776 he sailed for America on the *Morris*. When three British warships pursued it into Chesapeake Bay, he and his companions defended themselves until forced to run the ship aground, abandon and destroy it, and escape overland on 11 April 1777.

On 10 May Robert Morris wrote a letter of introduction for Armand to Washington in which he stated that the Frenchman brought credit from "a Gentn to whom America is under the most important obligations." In fact, Congress's initial decision to appoint him a major was quickly modified on 10 May to the rank of colonel. Armand would become one of the few foreign officers who impressed Washington.

For what must have been their first action, at Short Hills on 26 June 1777, Armand's men fought against great odds; the unit lost thirty killed out of eighty engaged, and Armand saved a gun by his personal courage. He also exhibited great skill at Head of Elk; Brandywine; Whitemarsh; and, particularly, for his attack against Cornwallis's rear guard while serving as Lafayette's second in command in New Jersey. He was at Valley Forge and Monmouth and then engaged in partisan operations in Westchester County, New York, and Connecticut.

On 27 December 1777, Armand proposed creation of a partisan force, an idea that Lafayette supported in a deluge of letters. Washington at first strongly opposed the inclusion of British deserters, who he feared would be "debauching our own men" but later preferred it as a means of employing foreign officers. Congress eventually relented and on 25 June 1778 authorized a unit of Free and Independent Chasseurs.

Congress rejected Armand's request for promotion to brigadier general. When he then requested a leave of absence to return to France, Congress complied (probably to his surprise) on 5 February 1779 but commended him for his "disinterested zeal & services." He decided to delay his departure, and Congress complied by modifying the leave until the end of the next campaign.

On 18 January 1780 the Board of War supported Armand's promotion before Congress, but Washington opposed it as fomenting "jealousies and discontents" among the other officers. Armand requested his transfer to the Southern Department and the merger of his corps with Pulaski, which Washington endorsed on 6 February 1780. He joined de Kalb in North Carolina in July 1780, after the fall of Charleston. The next month Armand's troops were given an improper mission by Gates and performed poorly at Camden. On 21 October 1780 the old Pulaski Legion was redesignated Armand's Partisan Corps. Again in November 1780, Congress denied his request for promotion to Brigadier General. In February 1781 he received six months' leave to return to France to obtain clothing and equipment for his corps at his own expense, but he returned in time for the final operations in Virginia Some forty survivors of his unit joined Lafayette in May 1781 and fought at Green Spring on 6 July. On 13 February 1782 Washington sent Armand and his legion to South Carolina, where he remained until recalled to the main army in September. On 26 March 1783 he was appointed brigadier general and chief of cavalry. Having been highly commended by Congress for his war service, Armand was discharged on 25 November 1783. Washington glowingly detailed his record of service in a letter of 15 December 1783. When Armand petitioned Congress on 22 January 1784 for an advance, Congress responded by simply commending him on 27 February 1784 for his "bravery, activity and zeal." He embarked from Philadelphia for France on 18 May 1784 after severely criticizing the French minister, Barbé de Marbois. On 8 April 1784, Congress authorized the issuing of notes to pay Armand.

Armand received the cross of the Order of Saint Louis in 1781, but upon his return to France, he did not receive command of a regiment. Instead he was offered the rank of colonel and command of command of the cavalry battalion of Le Roussillon, which he refused. He joined a group of other Breton nobles who carried the complaints of those nobles to the king and who were imprisoned in the Bastille in July 1788 for their insolence. In 1791 he headed a secret organization stretching from Brittany through Anjou and Poitou to act with emigré armies. He died the night of 29–30 January 1793 at the Chateau of Guyomarais.

SEE ALSO *Brandywine, Pennsylvania; Camden, South Carolina; De Kalb, Johann; Green Spring (Jamestown Ford, Virginia); Monmouth, New Jersey; Morris, Robert (1734–1806); Short Hills (Metuchen), New Jersey; Valley Forge Winter Quarters, Pennsylvania; Whitemarsh, Pennsylvania.*

BIBLIOGRAPHY

Bodinier, Gilbert. *Dictionnaire des officiers de l'armée royale qui ont combattu aux Etats-Unis pendant la guerre d'Indépendance, 1776–1783.* Vincennes, France: Ministère de la defense, Etat-Major de l'Armée de terre, Service historique, 1982.

Ford, Worthington C., ed. *Journals of the Continental Congress.* 39 vols. Washington, D.C.: Government Printing Office, 1904–1933.

Mohrt, Michel. *Tombeau de La Rouerie.* Paris: Gallimard, 2002.

Smith, Paul H., ed. *Letters of the Delegates to Congress, 1774–1789.* 26 vols. Washington, D.C.: Government Printing Office, 1976–2000.

Stutesman, John H. "Colonel Armand and Washington's Cavalry." *New-York Historical Society Quarterly* 45 (1961): 5–42.

Tuffin, Armand Charles, Marquis de La Rouërie. "Letters of Colonel Armand." *New-York Historical Society Collections* (1878): 287–396.

Washington, George. *Writings of George Washington.* Edited by John C. Fitzpatrick. 39 vols. Washington, D.C.: U.S. Government Printing Office, 1931–1944.

Whitridge, Arnold. "The Marquis de La Rouërie, Brigadier General in the Continental Army." *Proceedings of the Massachusetts Historical Society* 79 (1967): 47–63.

revised by Robert Rhodes Crout

TUPPER, BENJAMIN.

(1738–1792). Continental officer. Massachusetts. Born in Stoughton (later Sharon), Massachusetts, on 11 March 1738, Tupper's father died when he was young, and after a common school education, the boy was apprenticed to a Dorchester tanner until he was sixteen years old. During the French and Indian War he served in the company commanded by his uncle, Captain Nathaniel Perry, and became a sergeant in 1759. After a few years as a schoolteacher in Easton, Massachusetts, he married in 1762, and moved to Chesterfield, in the western part of the province, two years later. In 1774 he served as a militia lieutenant in ridding his area of Tory influence. On 25 April 1775 he became major of Colonel John Fellows's Massachusetts Regiment. Early on the morning of 8 July, he and Captain John Crane led a party of volunteers and two guns in a raid that routed the British from an outpost on Boston Neck. On 31 July he led a highly successful raid to Great

Brewster Island to destroy the Boston lighthouse. He was promoted to lieutenant colonel on 4 November, and in the reorganization of 1 January 1776, he became lieutenant colonel of the Twenty-first Continental Regiment. Commanding a flotilla of gunboats and galleys on the Hudson River, on 3 August he attacked the British ships that had penetrated to the Tappan Sea on 12–18 July. After taking part in the Battle of Long Island on 27 August, he was named lieutenant colonel of the Second Massachusetts Regiment on 1 November 1776 and colonel of the Eleventh Massachusetts Regiment on 7 July 1777.

He fought in the campaign against Burgoyne as part of John Paterson's Third Massachusetts Brigade and spent the winter of 1777–1778 with the main army at Valley Forge. He participated in the Monmouth Campaign (June 1778), worked on the defenses of West Point, and served on the New York frontier. In the reorganization of 1 January 1781 he assumed command of the Tenth Massachusetts, and in the reorganization of 1 January 1783 he was transferred to the Sixth Massachusetts. He retired from the army on 12 June and was breveted brigadier general on 30 September 1783.

Returning to Chesterfield, he was elected to the state legislature. During Shays's Rebellion of 1786–1787 he had an active part in the defense of nearby Springfield. Having signed the Newburgh Petition of 1783 asking Congress to give western lands to veterans, he was intimately involved during the last ten years of his life with the westward movement. He represented Massachusetts in the corps of state surveyors under Thomas Hutchins sent west by Congress in 1785 and joined Rufus Putnam in forming the Ohio Company of Associates in January 1786. In early 1788 they led the first settlers to what became Marietta, Ohio. Both veterans took a leading part in the affairs of the new settlement. Tupper died at Marietta on 7 June 1792.

S E E A L S O *Great Brewster Island, Massachusetts.*

revised by Harold E. Selesky

TURNBULL, GEORGE. Loyalist officer.
Credited as the first into Fort Montgomery on 6 October 1777, Captain Turnbull of De Lancey's Loyal American Regiment was promoted for his heroism and given command of one of the battalions. The following year he went south with the expedition of Lieutenant Colonel Archibald Campbell that captured Savannah on 29 December 1778. As part of General James Paterson's command, Turnbull—now a lieutenant colonel—participated in the Charleston expedition in 1780 and remained

with the main British army while the other De Lancey battalion, commanded by J. Harris Cruger, was stationed at Ninety Six. As part of the defenses of Camden, Turnbull commanded the outpost at Rocky Mount. From here he sent out the expedition that came to grief at Williamson's Plantation on 12 July 1780, and he successfully held out in the face of Sumter's attack against Rocky Mount on 1 August 1780.

S E E A L S O *Rocky Mount, South Carolina; Savannah, Georgia (29 December 1778); Williamson's Plantation, South Carolina.*

revised by Michael Bellesiles

TURNING MOVEMENT. A wide (strate-
gic) envelopment that avoids the enemy's main battle position and by threatening some vital point to his rear forces him to leave his original position either to defend that vital point or to take some other course of action. The term comes from its effect of turning the enemy out of his position, not because it is executed by one's turning around (enveloping) him. The term is employed in its correct sense in military works but is too esoteric for most popular writers, who incorrectly use it to mean any kind of envelopment, tactical or strategic. Howe's maneuver at Brandywine and Washington's at Princeton are examples of turning movements.

S E E A L S O *Brandywine, Pennsylvania; Princeton, New Jersey.*

Mark M. Boatner

TURTLE BAY, NEW YORK. Turtle Bay
was a small, rock-bound cove in the East River at the foot of today's 47th Street in Manhattan. The area has been reclaimed and is now covered by the United Nations Park, which is located north of the United Nations building. While the cove once did contain turtles, its name is more probably a corruption of its early Dutch name, Deutal Bay, because it was shaped like a knife-blade, *deutal* in Dutch.

The cove was the site of a British storehouse that was captured at midnight on 20 July 1775. This coup was led by John Lamb, Isaac Sears, Alexander McDougall, and Marinus Willett, all of whom were New York Sons of Liberty who later became famous in the Revolution. The raiders left Greenwich, Connecticut, in a sloop, passed through Hell Gate at twilight, and surprised the guard at midnight. The storehouse was still standing seventy-five years later, and is the subject of a sketch by Benson J. Lossing. Part of General George Washington's army was posted here in September 1776 before the British landed at nearby Kips Bay (which was located at present-day 34th Street in Manhattan).

SEE ALSO *New York Campaign.*

BIBLIOGRAPHY

Lossing, Benson J. *The Pictorial Field Book of the Revolution.* 2 vols. New York: Harper and Brothers, 1851.

revised by Barnet Schecter

TWO PENNY ACTS **SEE** *Parson's Cause.*

U

UNADILLA, NEW YORK.

6–8 October 1778. On the boundary line fixed in the Treaty of Fort Stanwix in 1768 between the Iroquois Confederation and colonial settlements of Tryon County, Unadilla was inhabited by whites when the Revolution started. In June 1777 Joseph Brant arrived with about seventy-five Indians, demanding provisions. The inhabitants, hoping to avoid conflict, gave him what he demanded, but when the Indians returned two days later for a forced requisition of livestock, the inhabitants decided it was time to leave for a more secure location. General Nicholas Herkimer marched to Unadilla in July with 380 militia and met with Brant. The Mohawk chief apparently was feuding with Guy Johnson, superintendent of Indian affairs and Loyalist leader, at the time and sought to negotiate neutrality for provisions. When Brant and Herkimer could come to no understanding, the latter withdrew, leaving Brant in control of Unadilla, which he made his headquarters. Located on the Susquehanna about twenty miles above Oquaga and forty miles south of Lake Otsego, Unadilla was a natural assembly area for attacks on the settlements in Mohawk Valley. After Brant had used it for precisely this purpose, raiding German Flats on 13 September 1778, the rebels countered with a punitive expedition against Unadilla.

Lieutenant Colonel William Butler left Schoharie on 2 October with his Fourth Pennsylvania Continentals, a detachment of Morgan's riflemen, and a small body of rangers. Moving down the upper reaches of the Delaware, he spent sixteen days destroying Indian posts around Unadilla. Brant was raiding Cookhouse, on the Delaware due east of Oquaga, when his stores at the latter place were destroyed and he was forced to return to Unadilla. He retaliated with the Cherry Valley Massacre on 11 November 1778.

SEE ALSO *Border Warfare in New York; Cherry Valley Massacre, New York; German Flats, New York.*

BIBLIOGRAPHY

Kelsay, Isabel T. *Joseph Brant, 1743–1807: Man of Two Worlds.* Syracuse, N.Y.: Syracuse University Press, 1984.

revised by Michael Bellesiles

UNIFORMS OF THE REVOLUTION.

Military apparel of standard material, cut, color, and appearance came into widespread use only about a century before the American Revolution. Several trends influenced the adoption of uniforms. Because regimental commanders in European armies were required to furnish their men with clothing, and clothing was cheaper to buy in bulk, "uniformity" had an economic basis. Properly cut and sewn, uniforms gave the soldier a set of clothes in which he could fight and work effectively. Uniforms could be adorned in various ways, which was both a way to identify leaders within a unit and a means of distinguishing among units. Distinctive uniforms helped to raise morale, make recruiting easier, and identify units on the battlefield.

DISTINCTIVENESS IN UNIFORMS

Because uniforms were first introduced when European armies fought each other at close range on compact battlefields, with infantrymen arrayed shoulder to shoulder in the linear tactics of the period, uniforms were designed to be distinctive and visible. Rather than the dull colors and camouflage patterns that have been synonymous with soldiers' clothing since the late nineteenth century, uniforms in the eighteenth century were generally meant to be seen. Certain uniform colors became associated with particular states: white with France; blue with Prussia; and none more so than scarlet with Britain, although there was enough variation within armies and coalition partners so that a commander on a swirling battlefield would have been unwise to assume that he could always distinguish friends from foes by the color of their uniforms.

Soldiers received only one set of clothes, which, when complete, might comprise a coat of relatively heavy fabric (usually with long tails that were normally turned up), a lighter-weight waistcoat, a linen shirt, a pair of coarse breeches (or gaiters or overalls, as available), a pair of short linen stockings, and rough leather shoes. Various buckles and buttons kept the clothing in place, along with the accoutrements that hung on leather belts from the soldier's shoulders and waist. Adornments in the British army included such details as lace around the coat's buttonholes, burnished coat buttons bearing the regimental number, and pressed metal helmet plates on the tall caps of the elite grenadiers that carried distinctive devices of king and country. The chief means of distinguishing among similarly uniformed British regiments were the coat's facings, the contrasting colors of cloth turned up at the collar, cuffs, and lapels that were set by royal warrant in 1768.

As a mark of special favor, usually to recall some battlefield achievement, certain British regiments bore the adjective "royal" in their name and were allowed to wear blue facings, as, for example, the 7th (Royal Fusiliers), the 23rd (Royal Welsh Fusiliers), the 42nd (Royal Highland Regiment), and the 60th (Royal American Regiment). Other facing colors included variations on yellow (buff for the 3rd, 14th, and 22nd; pale yellow for the 20th, 26th, and 30th; and just yellow for the 9th and 38th), orange (35th), gosling green (5th), willow green (24th), black (50th and 58th), white (43rd and 47th), and even red (33rd). Perhaps the least uniform aspect of British army clothing were the kilts worn first by the 42nd Highlanders and subsequently by all newly raised Highland Scots regiments. Uniforms were paid for by deductions from the soldiers' wages and were replaced only when they wore out.

During the War for American Independence, British redcoats fought alongside two other groups of soldiers with different uniform traditions. Of the contingents of line infantry hired from six German states to augment the British forces, five followed the dominant Prussian uniform style in color (blue) and cut. Only the Anhalt-Zerbst troops were uniformed in white coats in the more ornate Austrian style. Loyalist units, when uniformed, received green coats early in the war and red coats after 1778. The most effective and renowned of the German and Loyalist units were the light troops, mounted and on foot, all of whom wore green coats during the war. The jägers from Hesse-Cassel wore grass green coats, faced and lined with crimson red, and black felt bicorne hats, similar in style to the Prussian jägers on which they were modeled. John Graves Simcoe's Queen's Rangers and Banastre Tarleton's British Legion retained their green uniforms after 1778. Both units were so active and tenacious that the color green earned them their opponents' fear and respect. The Rangers' silver crescent moon, worn points up on the front of their light infantry caps, was the most distinctive, and distinguished, Loyalist military insignia of the war.

AMERICAN UNIFORMS TO 1779

American soldiers had been raised in the British uniform tradition during the colonial period, but their sources of supply were so haphazard and varied that their appearance in the field was usually anything but uniform. Regulations during the French and Indian War had generally called for provincial troops to be outfitted in blue coats. George Washington, for instance, had a formal portrait painted by Charles Willson Peale in April 1772 in which he wore the blue coat with red facings of the Virginia Regiment. In May 1775 he wore to sessions of the Continental Congress the blue coat with buff facings of the Fairfax Independent Company, blue and buff being the traditional colors of the Whigs who opposed royal tyranny. Since the motives for joining the militia were social and political as well as martial, some militia units, particularly in urban areas like New York City, Philadelphia, and Charleston, had uniforms. Otherwise, militia units in all regions throughout the war turned out in their own civilian clothing, with their own weapons and accoutrements. A few units raised after the outbreak of hostilities were well uniformed in blue, notably Captain John Chester's company from Wethersfield, Connecticut, at the siege of Boston, and Colonel John Haslett's Delaware Battalion, the "blue hen's chicks," that marched from Wilmington for the defense of New York City in 1776. Regiments raised in New York and Pennsylvania in 1775 and 1776 wore a mix of blue, green, and brown coats, the last two colors being popular because the dyes were locally available. Some officers from New England wore their old uniforms from the French and Indian War, but most soldiers across the colonies went to war in what amounted to a combination of their everyday work clothes and a uniform coat.

Washington, who understood the morale value of a good uniform, made every effort to acquire appropriate clothing for his troops. When the Virginia and

Pennsylvania riflemen arrived at Cambridge wearing hunting shirts, a garment well-known to Washington, the commander in chief recommended to Congress that, because "the army in general, and the troops raised in Massachusetts in particular, [are] very deficient in necessary clothing,... I am of the opinion that a number of hunting shirts not less than 10,000 would in a great degree remove this difficulty in the cheapest and quickest manner." Hunting shirts were relatively easy to make, being, according to Silas Deane, who had seen Pennsylvania riflemen in Philadelphia, a piece of stout linen cloth dyed the color of "a dry or fading leaf" that is made into a "kind of frock ... reaching down below the knee, open before, with a large cape," wrapped "around them tight" and tied "with their belt in which hangs their tomahawk" (Smith, *Letters of Delegates*, 1, pp. 436–438). Washington wanted the shirts in order to give the army a uniform appearance and "abolish those provincial distinctions which lead to jealousy and dissatisfaction," but he was also aware of the psychological value of the hunting shirt, since the British would prudently assume that any American wearing one might be a crack shot. Congress agreed with Washington's suggestion and directed him to buy tow cloth (made of short, broken fibers from flax, hemp, or jute) in Rhode Island and Connecticut, but when the cloth proved to be unavailable, the idea was abandoned.

The Continental army retained a motley appearance as long as it relied on domestic cloth production (linen was woven at home, but wool and woolen cloth were scarce), British uniforms found in supply ships captured by American privateers, or contracts made with European suppliers by American purchasing agents overseas. For his additional Continental Regiment, Colonel Samuel Blatchley Webb commandeered scarlet coats intended for British regiments in Canada that had been captured at sea in December 1776. The Second Pennsylvania, while at Valley Forge, received royal blue coats with scarlet facings, part of an order for thirty thousand uniforms placed with French manufacturers by Silas Deane and Benjamin Franklin, the American commissioners to France. The Fourth New York in late 1778 received white coats faced with red from Boston suppliers. Colonel George Baylor outfitted his Third Regiment of Light Dragoons in 1778 in white coats with blue facings.

AMERICAN UNIFORMS FROM 1779

Only in the wake of the formal alliance with France did the Americans have access to sufficient stocks of uniforms for Washington to designate blue as the official army uniform color on 2 October 1779. The regulations specified that Continental infantry regiments from New England would wear blue faced with white; those from New York and New Jersey blue faced with buff; those from Pennsylvania, Delaware, Maryland, and Virginia blue faced with red; and those from North Carolina, South Carolina, and Georgia blue faced with blue. The artillery would wear blue faced with scarlet, and the light dragoons blue faced with white. Even after these regulations were promulgated, the uniforms of many units escaped standardization. When sent south in October 1780, Lee's Legion, for example, wore short green jackets resembling those worn by the Queen's Rangers and the British Legion.

In fact, Continental army units were lucky to get any clothing and shoes at all. The modern renderings of such superb artists and researchers as Charles M. Lefferts, H. Charles McBarron Jr., Frederick P. Todd, John R. Elting, Rene Chartrand, Peter F. Copeland, Eric I. Manders, Frederic Ray Jr., Herbert Knotel, Frederick T. Chapman, Clyde A. Risley, Eugene Leliepvre, Don Troiani, and a host of others suggest, for purposes of illustration, a uniformity that rarely existed during the war. All armies had supply problems, and soldiers always had to accept what they could get.

BIBLIOGRAPHY

Abbot, W. W., et al., eds. *The Papers of George Washington, Revolutionary War Series*. Vol. 1, *June–September 1775*. Charlottesville: University Press of Virginia, 1985.

Elting, John R., ed. *Military Uniforms in America: The Era of the American Revolution, 1755–1795, from the Series Produced by the Company of Military Historians*. San Rafael, Calif.: Presidio Press, 1974.

Fitzpatrick, John C., ed. *The Writings of George Washington*. Vol. 16: *July 29, 1779–October 20, 1779*. Washington, D.C.: Government Printing Office, 1937.

Lefferts, Charles M. *Uniforms of the American, British, French, and German Armies in the War of the American Revolution*. New York: New-York Historical Society, 1926.

Smith, Paul H., ed. *Letters of Delegates to Congress, 1774–1789*. 26 vols. Washington, D.C.: Library of Congress, 1976–2000.

Troiani, Don, Earl J. Coates, and James J. Kochan. *Don Troiani's Soldiers in America, 1754–1865*. Harrisburg, Pa.: Stackpole Books, 1998.

revised by Harold E. Selesky

UNITED STATES OF AMERICA. This

name first appears in the Declaration of Independence, which is headed "The Unanimous Declaration of the Thirteen United States of America." Elsewhere in the document, the "united" is not capitalized, although the last paragraph states, "these United Colonies are, and of Right ought to be, Free and Independent States...." On the same day that they adopted the Declaration of Independence, 4 July 1776, the delegates first used the name of the new nation in their Journals when John

Adams, Benjamin Franklin, and Thomas Jefferson were elected to a committee "to bring in a device for a seal of the United States of America" (*Journals of the Continental Congress 1774 to 1789*, vol. 5, p. 518). The phrase "United States of North America" appeared in the Franco-American treaties of 1778 and occasionally was employed in official pronouncements. Congress resolved on 11 July 1778 that "United States of America" would be used on its bills of exchange, and it has been used since as the official name.

BIBLIOGRAPHY

Journals of the Continental Congress 1774 to 1789. 34 vols. Washington, D.C.: Government Printing Office, 1904-1937.

revised by Michael Bellesiles

UNITY OF COMMAND.

One principle of war on which strategists still disagree is the method whereby the essential "unity of effort" is to be achieved in military operations, particularly when one is dealing with a military force of different services (for example, army and navy) and of different nationalities. The American army feels that unity of command means that "for every task there should be unity of effort under one responsible commander." Other services contend that this "unity of effort" can be achieved by "cooperation" among commanders, and that there is no necessity to go so far as to put "one responsible commander" in overall charge. There was a time in the history of war when various "arms"—such as infantry, artillery, and cavalry—refused to serve under the overall command of one officer from one arm. As late as the American Revolution, there was some question as to whether a British artillery general had the authority to command a force that included other arms. During the Revolution, the British had separate army and navy commanders in chief in America: Gage, William Howe, and Clinton were commanders in chief of the British army in America; they could ask the commander in chief of the Royal Navy in American waters to cooperate, but they could not order him to follow a certain course of action. The objections to unity of command—in the early twenty-first century and in the eighteenth—are that one service does not want to surrender control of its forces to a commander of another service, who might misuse them; the navy, for example, does not trust an army general to take the proper care of an expensive fleet in the support of land operations. Thus, there was no unity of command in the allied operations at Newport in 1778 or at Leyte Gulf (Philippine Islands) in 1944. There was, rather, "cooperation."

SEE ALSO *Newport, Rhode Island (29 July–31 August 1778).*

Mark M. Boatner

V

VACANT REGIMENT. German regiments (or battalions) were so called when the colonel by whose name they had been known was no longer in command. Baurmeister, for example, refers in a letter of 2 June 1777 to "the Regiment vacant Rail." The latter unit was commanded in turn by Rall, Woellwarth, Trumbach, and d'Angelli; it was a "vacant regiment" during the intervening periods.

Mark M. Boatner

VALCOUR ISLAND. 11–13 October 1776. Upon collapse of the ill-fated Canada invasion, the British prepared a counteroffensive. In June 1776 they forced the Americans to withdraw from Canada, pursuing them as far as Fort Chambly on the Richelieu River. Control of Lake Champlain was critical to operations in northern New York because the only passable road hugged the western shore of the lake and troops or supplies moving along it would be vulnerable to waterborne attack. Thus, both sides hastened to assemble fleets.

Major General Sir Guy Carleton established a base at St. Johns on the Richelieu River and spent the summer constructing vessels, while the Americans did the same at Skenesboro at the southern end of Lake Champlain. On 10 September, Carleton's army, including Major General von Riedesel's five thousand German mercenaries, began moving southward. Leaving four regiments and part of a fifth with some artillery to secure St. Johns and Fort

Chambly, Carleton sent a younger brother, Lieutenant Colonel Thomas Carleton, south with four hundred Indians in canoes; these were reinforced later with one hundred Canadian volunteers and thirteen hundred Germans. Brigadier General Simon Fraser went into position about five miles north of the New York state line with the light infantry, grenadiers, and the Twenty-fourth Foot. Ile aux Noix, which the British had taken in August and later organized into a fortified base, was occupied by Burgoyne with six regiments (the Ninth, Twenty-first, Thirty-first, Forty-seventh, Riedesel, and Hanau). Captain Thomas Pringle, Carleton's naval commander, set sail with twenty-five vessels on 3 October, the day after work was completed on the sloop of war *Inflexible*. On 14 October, Burgoyne and Fraser started forward with all but two of Carleton's British regiments (the Twentieth and Sixty-first garrisoned Ile aux Noix). (All German troops were left in Canada except the Hanau artillery, which was on the *Thunderer*.)

THE BATTLE

Having left Crown Point on 24 August with the ten craft that were ready, Brigadier General Benedict Arnold moved north to Windmill Point, near the Canadian border. Threatened in these narrow waters by some of Carleton's Indians, he had withdrawn to the vicinity of Cumberland Head by 19 September. Then, having taken soundings of the half-mile channel between rocky Valcour Island and the west shore, Arnold skillfully anchored his ships in a crescent-shaped formation across the channel on the 23rd. The day of the battle he had fifteen vessels under his command: the sloop *Enterprise*; the schooners *Royal Savage* and *Revenge*; the galleys

The Battle of Valcour Island. *This naval battle, pictured here in a contemporary engraving published by William Faden, was fought in October 1776 near Valcour Island on Lake Champlain.* AP/WWP/SPECIAL COLLECTIONS UVM LIBRARIES

Congress, Trumbull, and *Washington*; the cutter *Lee*; and eight gundalows. (The Gates galley was still under construction at Ticonderoga, the schooner *Liberty* had been sent after supplies, and there is no record of a ninth gundalow, *Success,* being present.)

Carleton sailed southward cautiously until 11 October, when he rounded Cumberland Head with a strong wind behind him and overshot his quarry by two miles before he realized it. The *Revenge* sighted the oncoming British fleet as it cleared Cumberland Head at 8 A.M. and scurried into Valcour Channel to inform Arnold, who quickly assembled his commanding officers on the *Congress,* went over his brilliantly unorthodox plan, and exhorted them to put up a "resolute" defense. When Brigadier General David Waterbury, his second in command, advised executing a fighting retreat to Ticonderoga, Arnold overruled him, explaining that given the uncertainty of winds and inexperience of his crews, such a maneuver would be more dangerous than making a stand. Arnold ordered the *Revenge* to sail toward the enemy until spotted, then return and join the line of battle; ordered his four fastest vessels, *Royal Savage, Congress, Trumbull,* and *Washington,* to sally forth to inflict what damage they might, but also to draw the enemy into the southern end of the channel and minimize the chance that Carleton might be smart enough either to anchor out of range and await a southern wind or return up the lake to come around the northern end of Valcour; and ordered his (Arnold's) other craft to form a line of battle across the channel, facing south.

When Arnold and his galleys and schooners withdrew, beating against the wind, the British impetuously gave chase. Caught by winds made treacherous by the cliffs and tall timber along the shorelines, the *Royal Savage* grounded on the southwest tip of Valcour Island. The British schooner *Carleton* (armed with twelve cannon that fired six-pound shot), which aggressively led the attack, blasted the unfortunate *Royal Savage* with a crippling broadside and was passing, with all sails set, along the American front when it was suddenly betrayed by the same wind and whirled straight toward the American boats. Under heavy musket and cannon fire, Lieutenant James Dacres, its commander, anchored the *Carleton* and then, with a spring in its cable, swung it into position to fire broadside. British gunboats moved to support Dacres, but four of the five larger vessels were prevented by the northerly wind from entering the fray. By 12:30 P.M., a general engagement was in progress. At a range of 350 yards, with observation impeded by a haze of gun smoke, the two forces hammered away. In the absence of trained gunners, Arnold personally pointed most of the cannon fired from the *Congress.*

After about an hour, the spring was shot away from the battered *Carleton,* which then turned on the anchor to face helplessly toward the converging fire of Arnold's fleet. When Pringle signaled it to withdraw, nineteen-year-old Midshipman Edward Pellew, in command since Dacres and the next-senior officer had been knocked out of action, climbed onto the bowsprit and tried to make a jib draw into the northeast wind and bring it about to sail away. Unsuccessful, he remained a conspicuous target of massed cannon and musket fire until he could throw a line to two boats that came up to tow the *Carleton* to safety.

The chagrined crew of the *Royal Savage* manned its guns until driven off by gunfire. A crew from the *Thunderer* boarded it and manned the guns until driven off by American fire. When the Americans tried to return, a crew from the *Maria* beat them to it and set the vessel afire. After dark, the *Royal Savage* exploded when the flames reached its magazine.

The British gunboats withdrew as dusk fell (around 5 o'clock) and continued their fire until dark from a line six hundred to seven hundred yards farther south. About the same time, the *Inflexible* managed to come up and deliver five broadsides that silenced Arnold's guns.

Carleton's Indian auxiliaries had landed on both shores of Valcour Channel and began to deliver They delivered a harassing, but generally ineffective, musket fire from the trees.

THE PURSUIT

The British thought they had Arnold trapped and expected to destroy him the next day in Valcour Channel, but Arnold had not finished outgeneraling Carleton. Aided by a northeast breeze, a dark night, dense fog, and Carleton's fear of the shoals along the shoreline, Arnold's battered flotilla escaped by rowing with muffled oars single file between the western end of the British line and the shore. Colonel Edward Wigglesworth led with the *Trumbull* at 7 P.M.; the *Congress* and *Washington* brought up the rear. (Two vessels remained in the channel: the *Royal Savage*, which was on fire, and a gundalow, the *Philadelphia*, which sank an hour after the battle ended.) By midnight the last vessel had passed the British. Unfortunately, the slight north wind that had aided their escape turned, and by dawn their ten hours of backbreaking rowing and pumping had taken the last five of Arnold's battered craft a mere eight miles. At Schuyler's Island, desperate attempts at repair were made. The gundalows *Providence* and *New York* were unsalvageable, so their equipment was removed and they were scuttled in fifty fathoms. The *Jersey* foundered on a rock and, being too waterlogged to burn, had to be abandoned. At about 1:30 P.M. the hastily repaired *Congress* and *Washington* started rowing south.

When dawn revealed Arnold's escape, Carleton sent scouts to track him, set out in pursuit himself, and then returned to his starting point to relay orders to the army to move southward. This allowed the Americans to keep ahead of their hunters on 12 October, but the next day the British closed the gap. At dawn on the 13th, after creeping six miles in sixteen hours, Arnold and his last two vessels were abreast of Willsborough, twenty-eight

miles from Crown Point. When the wind turned to the northeast the British benefited first and got to within a mile before the sails of the slower-moving American vessels began to fill. At 11 A.M. at Split Rock, the end came quickly. The *Maria*, followed by the *Inflexible* and the *Carleton*, forced Waterbury to surrender the *Washington* and his 110 men. The *Lee* ran ashore and was abandoned. The *Congress* and four gundalows (that had fallen back from Wigglesworth's group) kept up a running fight against the three enemy ships, which used their speed and maneuverability to rake the Americans at point-blank range. In a final act of defiance, the die-hard Arnold signaled his ships to windward, a maneuver the British could not follow, and the Americans rowed for Buttonmould Bay on the east (Vermont) shore. Here he beached and burned his wrecks with their colors still flying. That night Arnold reached Crown Point (ten miles away) with two hundred men, having escaped an Indian ambush en route. At Crown Point, Arnold found the *Trumbull, Enterprise, Revenge, Liberty,* and (according to some reports) "one gundalow."

Unable to hold Crown Point against such heavy odds, Arnold burned its buildings. He then withdrew to Fort Ticonderoga with his survivors of Valcour Island and with Lieutenant Colonel Hartley's garrison of the Sixth Pennsylvania.

CONCLUSIONS

Benedict Arnold's name is forever linked to treason, but on Lake Champlain, against all odds, he constructed a squadron that may well have saved the American Revolution by delaying the British invasion of 1776 until it was too late in the season for Carleton to press further southward. Arnold had lost the entire squadron, but the stout resistance of his men led Carleton to fear that if the defenders of Fort Ticonderoga fought as tenaciously, then winter would close in before it could be taken. Thus, on 2 November he began withdrawing to Canada.

NUMBERS AND LOSSES

Of the eighteen or nineteen vessels comprising Arnold's portion of the Champlain squadrons, he lost eleven of the fifteen that probably were present at Valcour Island. The day of the battle he lost 60 killed and wounded out of some 750 present (assuming absence of the 16th vessel, the *Success*). Two days later on 13 October, he lost another twenty killed and wounded and the entire crew of the Washington galley was captured; some of the twenty killed and wounded were undoubtedly among the latter. The *Congress* lost twenty-seven out of a crew of seventy-three. Carleton paroled Brigadier General Waterbury and the rest of the prisoners from the *Washington*, who arrived at Fort Ticonderoga with such praise of Carleton's generous treatment that they were immediately sent home to prevent their lowering the will of others in the American camp to resist.

Aside from the *Carleton* and, toward the end, the *Inflexible*, the only British ships engaged in the battle of Valcour Island were the seventeen to twenty gunboats. Total British strength, including those on ships that did nothing more than shell from a distance, was 670 seamen and four companies of the Twenty-ninth Regiment (serving as marines on the four larger vessels). Since the inexperienced American gunners failed to sink any of the gunboats or damage the *Carleton* enough to keep it out of action on the pursuit, British losses must have been light.

SEE ALSO *Arnold, Benedict; Canada Invasion; Carleton, Guy; Champlain Squadrons; Champlain, Lake; Fraser, Simon (1729–1777); Maxwell, William; Riedesel, Baron Friedrich Adolphus.*

BIBLIOGRAPHY

Fowler, William M., Jr. *Rebels under Sail: The American Navy during the Revolution.* New York: Scribner, 1976.

Mahan, A. T. "The Naval Campaign of 1776 on Lake Champlain." *Scribner's Magazine* 23 (1898): 147–160.

Martin, James Kirby. "The Battle of Valcour Island." In *Great American Naval Battles.* Edited by Jack Sweetman. Annapolis, Md.: Naval Institute Press, 1998.

Miller, Nathan. *Sea of Glory: The Continental Navy Fights for Independence.* New York: McKay, 1974.

Paul David Nelson, "Guy Carleton versus Benedict Arnold: The Campaign of 1776 in Canada and on Lake Champlain." *New York History* 57 (1976): 147–160.

revised by James C. Bradford

VALENTINE'S HILL, NEW YORK.

Just north of Spuyten Duyvil, this was the site of Fort Independence.

SEE ALSO *Fort Independence Fiasco, New York; Spuyten Duyvil, New York.*

Mark M. Boatner

VALLEY FORGE, PENNSYLVANIA.

18 September 1777. In 1777 the Continental Army maintained a small depot at Valley Forge, using it to store bread, flour, and grain and iron tools and equipment, mostly products of Colonel William Dewees's iron forge. The British advance toward Philadelphia threatened the depot. In the afternoon of 18 September Lieutenant Colonel Alexander Hamilton, Captain Henry Lee, and eight dragoons arrived to assist Dewees in removing the materiel. At this point General William Howe arrived at Tredyffrin, four miles away. Informed of the depot by a local Loyalist sympathizer, he detached Lieutenant Colonel William Harcourt with part of the Sixteenth Light Dragoons and three companies of light infantry to capture it. A small skirmish took place as Lee retreated west and Hamilton crossed the Schuylkill in a scow. One American was killed and another man wounded; Hamilton's and British major Peter Craig's horses were also shot. Most of the supplies fell into Howe's hands, but the incident is significant primarily because it was the largest military engagement to take place at the famous site.

SEE ALSO *Philadelphia Campaign.*

BIBLIOGRAPHY

McGuire, Thomas J. *The Battle of Paoli.* Harrisburg, Pa.: Stackpole Books, 2000.

revised by Robert K. Wright Jr.

VALLEY FORGE WINTER QUARTERS, PENNSYLVANIA.

19 December 1777 to 19 June 1778. The men that marched into Valley Forge, and into legend, on 19 December 1777 were tired, hungry, and very poorly clad. They had lost the battles of Brandywine and Germantown, and seen their capitol occupied, but had just faced down General William Howe at Whitemarsh (5–8 December 1777), daring him to assault. Carried with them was a "collective intransigence" that held the force together against the enemy, even in the face of neglect by their fellow Americans. General George Weedon wrote on 17 December 1777 that the men's zeal for their country was unabated and that they seemed determined to turn hardships into diversion. The day after arriving at Valley Forge, General Jedediah Huntington wrote "the Army is well disposed and will try to make the best of it." More than a quarter of the army was now composed of New England brigades, whose morale was high, for they had seen the greatest American triumph to date—the surrender of Burgoyne at Saratoga.

Winter quarters had been discussed at a council of war on 29 October 1777, but a decision regarding their establishment was deferred. The commander in chief, General George Washington, never wrote his reasons for choosing Valley Forge as the winter quarters for his army, but he had held several councils of war considering the options of staying in the field, attacking the British, or going into quarters. The last was the eventual selection, but his generals mostly favored wintering at Wilmington, Delaware, or pulling back into Pennsylvania to a line from Reading to Lancaster. This would have exposed much of the productive part of the state to enemy ravaging, angered both the state and Continental governments, and been difficult with the number of refugees and army sick already in those areas.

Wilmington could be surprised by British forces coming down the river, or Howe could move westward into Pennsylvania, cutting off supply stores and easily capturing thousands of Americans in hospitals. The British general might even move into Chester County and isolate the Continental force in the Delmarva peninsula. Despite this, Washington decided to split his force, and on 19 December he sent William Smallwood with two brigades to Wilmington, where they remained until late May 1778.

On making the decision for Valley Forge, Washington sent his men to a relatively unsettled triangular area of small farms and woodlands, about two miles long and a mile and a quarter wide. About eighteen miles in a straight line to Philadelphia but longer by road, the high ground could be fortified and would serve to protect most of the state from the ravages of the enemy. It was well located, strategically, and out of the way of the bulk of the civilian population. These sterling military qualities were lost on the troops who huddled in makeshift shelters until they could complete their log huts. On 25 December Major General Johann de Kalb called it the worst part of Pennsylvania, and considered that the advice to station the army there arose from a private interest, or people whose intention was the ruin of the cause.

In the view of the troops, they lacked everything they needed, except trees to cut for shelters, but even axes were in short supply. Washington ordered that the camp be carefully laid out and that log huts, measuring fourteen by sixteen feet, be constructed for every twelve enlisted men. These were mostly completed by the middle of January 1778. However, archeological work has discovered that many of the huts were not constructed in accordance with Washington's instructions.

LOGISTICS

According to historian John Buchanan: "At Valley Forge the problem was the all-important logistical system" which had disintegrated so pitifully that the "army almost perished at Valley Forge" (pp. 286–287). The soldiers had been hungry for weeks and poorly clad for months. The reasons for this were many, but a series of failures by the Continental Congress were at the forefront. It can be fairly said that throughout the war, the army suffered more by neglect from fellow Americans than from any enemy activities.

The major responsibility of the quartermaster department was to meet the army's transportation needs, but Congressional price restrictions made private teamsters reluctant to haul cargoes for the army. In October 1777, Quartermaster General Thomas Mifflin resigned, and his post was left empty for nearly five months. His chief deputy was incapable of bringing order as winter came on and roads were turned into quagmires.

The commissary department purchased food, and the clothier department purchased and distributed clothing. Both departments were dependent on the quartermaster department for transportation of their goods. Congress had reorganized the commissary department in the summer of 1777, and Joseph Trumbull, then the highly competent commissary. resigned—as did most of his deputies. Trumbull's replacement, William Buchanan, tried and failed to fulfill the office, and after another Congressional reorganization of the department, Buchanan was replaced with Jeremiah Wadsworth in April 1778, who was far more effective.

Clothier General James Mease also failed to produce the desired results. His performance is shown by the phrase that was coined in the army to describe the chronic disease of inadequate clothing: "the Meases." Alexander Hamilton noted that, as early as September 1777, Washington had sent him to collect blankets and clothing from citizens as the "distressed situation of the army for want of blankets and many necessary articles of clothing, is truly deplorable... if unremoved, would involve the ruin of the army, and perhaps the ruin of America" (*Hamilton Papers*, vol. 1, pp. 330–331). Things were much worse in December, and the storied "bloody footprints" in the snow were a reality. Although imports, captures, and domestic production reduced the clothing problems, as late as 6 June 1778 there were still 805 men in camp "destitute of Cloaths & Necessaries."

The army went through two starving times: right after they arrived at Valley Forge, and mid-February 1778, which was the worst. The average daily consumption in December was over 33,600 pounds of bread and flour and 34,500 pounds of meat. All of this had to be purchased at varying distances from camp, then transported via wagon or on the hoof to the army through roads that were almost impassable. The shortage of grain meant that the animals got only such grain that the men didn't eat, and hard work and lack of adequate forage therefore killed hundreds of horses, worsening the transportation problems.

Mid-February marked the most desperate time in the camp. On 16 February Washington wrote to Governor George Clinton that "For some days past, there has been little less than a famine in camp. A part of the army has been a week, without any kind of flesh, and the rest three or four days. Naked and starving as they are, we cannot enough admire the incomparable patience and fidelity of the soldiery." On that same day a delegate to Congress,

Washington and Lafayette at Valley Forge, Pennsylvania. *George Washington and the Marquis de Lafayette stand amongst shivering soldiers during the harsh winter of 1777 to 1778, in a nineteenth-century engraving by Henry Bryan Hall after a painting by Alonzo Chappel.* NATIONAL ARCHIVES AND RECORDS ADMINISTRATION

Francis Dana, reported: "Sunday morning colonel Brewer's regiment rose in a body and proceeded to general Patterson's quarters . . . laid before him their complaints, and threatened to quit the army. By a prudent conduct he quieted them. . . . The same spirit was rising in other regiments, but has been happily suppressed for the present by the prudence of some of their officers. But no prudence or management, without meat, can satisfy the hungry man."

Henry Lee, Nathanael Greene, and Anthony Wayne were sent out on major foraging expeditions to find what they could in New Jersey, Southeastern Pennsylvania, Delaware, and Maryland. Had it not been for the food supplies they brought in, the army would almost certainly have dissolved. Better weather, the appointment of Greene as quartermaster general in March, and the arrival of food supplies from more distant states, after repeated appeals from Washington, eased the supply problems. Also by April, Congress realized that its parsimony the year before had nearly wrecked the army,

and moved to the other extreme of pouring money into supply operations.

The 1777 campaign had produced thousands of wounded and sick soldiers. These were sent to temporary hospitals and then on to makeshift facilities, often in church buildings in Pennsylvania and New Jersey. On 22 December, reports showed 3,948 men as sick absent. While the majority of the absentees were in Pennsylvania or New Jersey, many were from the brigades who joined after Saratoga and had been left in other states. As late as 6 June 3,158 ailing men were present at Valley Forge. A high proportion of those had been made ill from the ongoing smallpox inoculation program that Washington had initiated in January.

The hospital department was also short of food and clothing and lacked medical supplies. The total number of soldiers who died during the six month encampment will never be accurately known, but it was approximately 1,800 to 1,900. Most died at hospitals miles or states away from Valley Forge. Poor recordkeeping stifled accuracy. The records of the Reading, Pennsylvania, hospital from September 1777 through 16 April 1778 showed 132 men "dead and deserted" without specifying which had occurred in any individual instance.

As soon as the 1777 campaign ended, hundreds of officers submitted requests to resign, some from camp, others from their hometowns, to which they had returned on furloughs. Many were in poor health or had significant personal issues, but some just wanted to get out of the army. Numerous resignations were accepted, which allowed the winnowing out of the weak and half-hearted, leaving a more professional corps of officers. As most regiments were grossly short of privates, the loss of many officers did not seem to have had serious consequences. The officers who remained were cheered when, on 15 May, Congress promised those who continued until the end of the war would receive half-pay for seven years after the end of the struggle.

DISCIPLINE

The Continental Army has sometimes been depicted as so ignorant of military training that they had to walk into Valley Forge in Indian file. This was far from accurate. The troops had been training since the beginning of the war, and Washington regularly emphasized to the officers they were to oversee training every day the weather allowed. Yet despite this training, different officers used different methods and techniques of maneuver, which led to confusion and inefficiency in maneuvers.

The contributions of Friedrich Steuben have sometimes been magnified, but his arrival at Valley Forge on 23 February was a major turning point. A soldier of fortune, he initially impressed Washington because he did not demand pay or rank. All he asked was that his expenses be paid. After a few weeks of review, Steuben began to train a model company consisting of the commander in chief's Guard of Virginians, with 100 men from other states annexed to it. On 8 April Adjutant General Alexander Scammell wrote

> He [Steuben] has undertaken the Discipline of the army & shows himself to be a perfect Master of it, not only in the grand manieuvres but in every Minutia—to see ... with a grace particular to himself, to take under his direction, a Squad, or ten or twelve men in Capacity of a Drill [Sergeant] induce the Officers & men to admire him—and improve exceeding fast under his Instructions.

The men and officers learned the new close order drill that Steuben introduced, and this was followed by the manual of arms and use of the bayonet. The seasoned and dedicated veterans understood the need for firm leadership and coordinated responses to orders, which probably helped the successful spread of the discipline. Washington was so impressed that he recommended

Steuben be appointed inspector general with the rank of major general, and Congress agreed with alacrity.

Though some historians believe that the Battle of Monmouth was did not prove the efficacy and importance of Steuben's reforms, his contemporaries showed great respect for the training he provided and the improvements he accomplished. On 6 December 1785, Horatio Gates wrote to Steuben regarding his plans to leave America. "I am distressed at your determination to leave this country. The soldiers part with their military father, when you go from them; they never knew a regular system of discipline until you came and taught it them."

"JOY SPARKLES IN EVERY EYE"

Washington was blessed by the relative inactivity of the enemy. For all of March the army could not muster 4,000 privates fit for duty. The low point was on 7 March, when only 3,301 rank and file were available, another 3,796 soldiers who were sick but present for duty, and 2,028 were unfit for duty due to lack of shoes and clothing. Had Howe attacked with his superior numbers, the main Continental army would likely have suffered a stunning defeat. The British did send out regular patrols, particularly to protect citizens bringing food into the city to sell, and also to cut wood and forage for themselves. There were frequent skirmishes and several small-scale actions: at Quinton's Bridge, New Jersey, on 18 March; Hancock's Bridge, New Jersey, on 21 March; and Crooked Billet, Pennsylvania on 1 May 1778, but there were no major engagements.

By April things were much improved at Valley Forge and the best news of all arrived in early May, when news of the treaties with France arrived. Washington stated "I believe no event was ever received with more heartfelt joy." The treaty of amity and commerce, which opened French ports and several in the West Indies to American ships, and the treaty of alliance had been signed on 6 February. French recognition of American independence made war with Britain inevitable, and it was so by mid-June. This brought into effect the treaty of alliance, the purpose of which was to maintain the independence of the United States.

An elaborate ceremony was planned for 6 May with a *feu de joie*—three volleys of musket fire by the complete army, three rounds of artillery fire, and, as Private Elijah Fisher recounted it, "three Chears for the King of France and three for the Friendly Powers of Europe and three Chears for the Thirteen United States of Amarica." All American prisoners in the provost jail were released, and all the officers were invited by Washington to dine with him. The afternoon was spent in joviality and toasts.

Two weeks later the Marquis de Lafayette led a detachment of several thousand men out of camp, and narrowly escaped annihilation at Barren Hill, Pennsylvania, but Steuben's training program bore its first fruit and the force evaded the enemy. When the British abandoned Philadelphia in June, Washington led a revitalized army from Valley Forge to chase Henry Clinton across New Jersey in the Monmouth campaign.

The renewed army enchanted Chaplain David Griffith, who returned from furlough and wrote on 3 June "The Army is . . . but very differently circumstanced; things seem much mended for the better. Everything wears the appearance of neatness and order. . . . The strictest attention is paid to discipline since the appointment of the new Inspector-General, the Baron Steuben (A Prussian), and I think the whole army is much improved in that particular."

SEE ALSO *Commissaries of the Continental Army; Steuben, Friedrich Wilhelm von; Washington, George.*

BIBLIOGRAPHY

Benninghoff, Herman O. *Valley Forge, A Genesis for Command and Control Continental Army Style.* Gettysburg, Pa.: Thomas Publications, 2001.

Bodle, Wayne. "Generals and 'Gentlemen': Pennsylvania Politics and the Decision for Valley Forge." *Pennsylvania History* 62 (1995): 59–89.

———. *The Valley Forge Winter: Civilians and Soldiers in War.* University Park: The Pennsylvania State University Press, 2002.

——— and Jacqueline Thibaut. *Valley Forge Historical Research Report.* 3 vols. Valley Forge, Pa.: Valley Forge National Historical Park, 1980–1982.

Boyle, Joseph Lee, ed. *My Last Shift Betwixt Us & Death: The Ephraim Blaine Letterbook, 1777–1778.* Bowie, Md.: Heritage Books, 2001.

———. *Writings From the Valley Forge Encampment of the Continental Army.* 5 vols. Bowie, Md.: Heritage Books, 2000–2005.

Branch, John P. *The John P. Branch Papers.* Randolph-Macon College, Ashland, Va., 1901.

Buchanan, John. *The Road to Valley Forge: How Washington Built the Army That Won the Revolution.* Hoboken, N.J.: John Wiley & Sons, 2004.

Greene, Nathanael. *The Papers of General Nathanael Greene.* Edited by Richard K. Showman. Vols. 1–2. Chapel Hill: University of North Carolina Press, 1976–1980.

Jackson, John W. *With the British Army in Philadelphia, 1777–1778.* San Rafael, Calif.: Presidio Press, 1979.

———. *Valley Forge: Pinnacle of Courage* Gettysburg, Pa.: Thomas Publications, 1992.

Lafayette, Marquis de. *Lafayette in the Age of the American Revolution: Selected Letters and Papers, 1776–1790.* Edited by Stanley K. Idzerda. Vols. 1–2. Ithaca, N.Y.: Cornell University Press, 1979.

Newcomb, Benjamin. "Washington's Generals and the Decision to Quarter at Valley Forge." *Pennsylvania Magazine of History and Biography* 117 (1993): 309–329.

Pancake, John S. *1777: The Year of the Hangman,* Tuscaloosa: The University of Alabama Press, 1977.

Reed, John Ford. *Campaign to Valley Forge, July 1, 1777–December 19, 1777.* Philadelphia: University of Pennsylvania Press, 1965; reprint, Pioneer Press, 1980.

Selesky, Harold E. *A Demographic Survey of the Continental Army that Wintered at Valley Forge, Pennsylvania, 1777–1778.* Valley Forge, Pa.: 1987.

Smith, Paul H. et. al., eds. *Letters of Delegates to Congress, 1774–1789.* Vols. 8–10. Washington, D.C.: 1981–1983.

Taaffee, Stephen R. *The Philadelphia Campaign, 1777–1778.* Lawrence: University Press of Kansas, 2003.

Trussell, John B. B., Jr. *Birthplace of an Army: A Study of the Valley Forge Encampment.* Harrisburg, Pa.: Commonwealth of Pennsylvania, Pennsylvania Historical and Museum Commission, 1976.

Washington, George. *The Papers of George Washington: Revolutionary War Series.* Vols. 12–14. Edited by Philander D. Chase, et al. Charlottesville: University Press of Virginia, 2002–2004.

revised by Joseph Lee Boyle

VAN CORTLANDT, PHILIP. (1749–1831). Continental officer. New York. Born in New York City on 21 August 1749 to great privilege, Van Cortlandt was the eldest son of Pierre Van Cortlandt (1721–1814), who was the first lieutenant governor of New York (elected in 1777 and periodically reelected for eighteen years), and Joanna Livingston. Van Cortlandt spent the ten years preceding the Revolution on the family estate, where he surveyed, disposed of tracts of land that had been part of the original manor, and operated mills for his father. In April 1775 he attended the Provincial Convention and the next month was selected as a representative from Westchester County to the first Provincial Congress of New York.

Commissioned lieutenant colonel of the Fourth New York Regiment on 18 June 1775, he reached Albany about the end of August with four companies but was prevented by sickness from participating in Montgomery's wing of the Canada invasion. He served on Washington's staff for a short time before being commissioned colonel of the Second New York Continental Regiment on 21 November 1776. This vacancy resulted from the defection of Rudolph Ritzema to the British. Philip joined his unit at Trenton the day after the battle and commanded it the rest of the war. Ordered to Peekskill, he was moving north to oppose St. Leger's expedition when Benedict Arnold's success in August 1777 led to his being attached instead to the main northern army. His regiment took part in both Battles of Saratoga, coming up among the last to reinforce Arnold at Freeman's Farm and serving in Poor's brigade in the

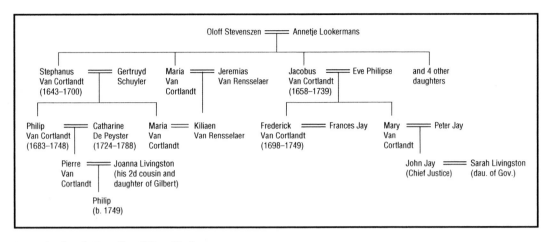

Van Cortlandt Family of New York. THE GALE GROUP

battle of 7 October. He rejoined the main army for winter quarters at Valley Forge. His regiment was stationed in Ulster County, New York, and as part of Clinton's division accompanied Sullivan's expedition against the Iroquois in 1779. He sat on the court-martial of Arnold (26 December 1779–26 January 1780) and, in disagreement with the majority sentence of a reprimand, felt that Arnold should be dismissed from the service. In the spring of 1780 he was sent to Fort Edward, New York, and later in the year was ordered to Schenectady, where the Second, Fourth, and Fifth New York Continentals were consolidated under his command. In June 1781 he was ordered south to join the forces preparing to march against Cornwallis in Virginia, and in the Yorktown campaign he was conspicuous for bravery and resourcefulness while serving under the Marquis de Lafayette. He was breveted brigadier general on 30 September 1782 for his performance at Yorktown.

After the war, Van Cortlandt was a commissioner of the appropriation of Loyalist lands in New York. As a delegate to the Poughkeepsie convention in 1788, Van Cortlandt opposed his father and his political ally, Governor George Clinton, and voted for ratification of the federal Constitution. After sitting in the state assembly in 1788–1790 and the state senate in 1791–1793, he entered the U.S. House of Representatives in December 1793 and served seventeen years, though—having become a Jeffersonian and supporter of slavery—he won some narrow victories, one by just thirteen votes. Undistinguished as a congressman, he lost his seat in the 1808 election after he had first voted for and then against Jefferson's Embargo Act. He emerged from retirement to accompany Lafayette on a large part of his triumphal tour in 1824 and died at his manor on 5 November 1831.

SEE ALSO *Arnold, Benedict; Border Warfare in New York; Ritzema, Rudolphus.*

BIBLIOGRAPHY

Judd, Jacob, ed. and comp. *The Van Cortlandt Family Papers.* 4 vols. Tarrytown, N.Y.: Sleepy Hollow Restorations, 1976–1981.

revised by Michael Bellesiles

VAN CORTLANDT FAMILY OF NEW YORK.

Oloff Stevenszen (1600–1684) was born and reared in the Netherlands. He came to New Amsterdam in 1638 and in 1643 adopted the surname Van Cortlandt, probably because he came from the small village of Cortlandt in the province of Utrecht. His eldest child, Stephanus (1643–1700), became a prominent merchant and colonial official; his great-grandson was Philip Van Cortlandt. Oloff's youngest child, Jacobus (1658–1739), was a wealthy merchant and landholder in Westchester County whose estate in New York City became Van Cortlandt Park. John Jay was his grandson.

SEE ALSO *Jay, John; Van Cortlandt, Philip.*

revised by Harold E. Selesky

VANDEWATER'S HEIGHTS.

Later called Morningside Heights, this place figured in the Battle of Harlem Heights in Manhattan on 16 September 1776.

SEE ALSO *Harlem Heights, New York.*

Mark M. Boatner

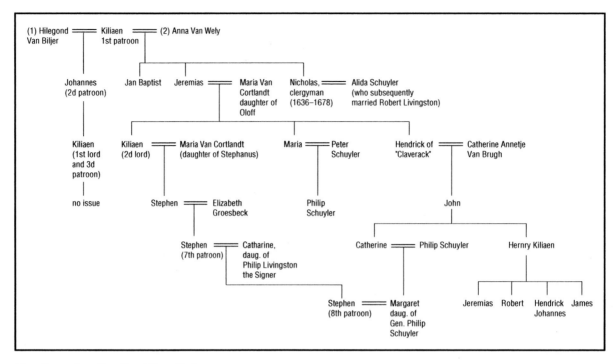

Van Rensselaer Family of New York. THE GALE GROUP

VAN RENSSELAER FAMILY OF NEW YORK.

Kiliaen van Rensselaer (1595–1644) was first patroon (lord) of Rensselaerswyck, a manor on the Hudson River around Albany that was the first and the only successful patroonship in New Netherland. His son Nicholas (1636–1678), a clergyman who came to New York in 1674, married Alida Schuyler, who, after his death in 1678, married Robert Livingston. Kiliaen's other son, Jeremias (1632–1674), married Maria, the daughter of Oloff Van Cortlandt. Their son Kiliaen (or Killian), the second lord, married his first cousin Maria Van Cortlandt (1643–1700). Their grandson was Stephen Van Rensselaer, the seventh patroon, who married Catharine Livingston, daughter of Philip Livingston, the Signer. Their son Stephen, the eighth patroon (1764–1839), married Margaret Schuyler, daughter of Major General Philip Schuyler.

SEE ALSO *Livingston Family of New York; Schuyler Family of New York; Schuyler, Philip John; Van Cortlandt Family of New York.*

revised by Harold E. Selesky

VAN SCHAICK, GOSE. (1736–1789).

Continental officer. New York. Also known as Goosen and Gosen. Van Schaick was born in Albany on 15 September 1736. He was the son of Sybrant Van Schaick, Albany's mayor from 1756 to 1761. A lieutenant in the Crown Point expedition of 1756 and a militia captain with Bradstreet in the capture of Fort Frontenac in 1758, he was promoted to lieutenant in 1760. He served first with the Second New York Provincials and then with the First New York Regiment in the final operations of the Seven Years' War.

Van Schaick was a member of the Albany Committee of Safety at the beginning of the Revolution. He was commissioned colonel of the Second New York on 28 June 1775, joining Montgomery on Lake Champlain with four hundred men in September for the Canada invasion, though they were limited to outpost duty. The next spring he was stationed at Johnstown in the Mohawk Valley as commander of the First New York. He was wounded at Ticonderoga on 6 July 1777. In the Battle of Monmouth in New Jersey on 28 June 1778, he commanded a brigade under William Alexander.

The operation for which he is best known is the raid against the Onondagas in April 1779, which preceded Sullivan's expedition. He left Fort Stanwix with 550 men and in a march of 180 miles in five and a half days destroyed a neutral Onondaga village of about 50 houses, took 37 prisoners, killed 15 Indians, picked up 100 muskets, and returned without losing a man. For this achievement in defeating a previously nonhostile group of Indians, he was given the "Thanks of Congress" on 10 May 1779. He was in command at Albany while General

James Clinton accompanied Sullivan's expedition. As part of Clinton's division, he marched south for the Yorktown campaign. Van Schaick spent much of the war arguing questions of seniority and seeking promotion. On 10 October 1783 he was brevetted brigadier general, and the next month he retired from the Continental army. He died of facial cancer in Albany on 4 July 1789.

SEE ALSO *Sullivan's Expedition against the Iroquois.*

BIBLIOGRAPHY

Egly, T. W., Jr. *Goose Van Schaik of Albany, 1736–1789: The Continental Army's Senior Colonel.* United States: T.W. Egly, 1992.

revised by Michael Bellesiles

VAN WART, ISAAC.

VAN WART, ISAAC. (1760–1828). A captor of John André. New York. A Westchester County farmer, he took part with John Paulding and David Williams in the capture of John André. He had no other known military career. Like his two cohorts in the capture of André, he received from Congress a silver medal and a small pension.

SEE ALSO *Arnold's Treason.*

revised by Michael Bellesiles

VARICK, RICHARD.

VARICK, RICHARD. (1753–1831). Continental officer. New York. Born in Hackensack, New Jersey, on 25 March 1753, Varick studied law in New York City, establishing a practice with John Morin Scott just as the Revolution started. On 28 June 1775 he was made captain in the First New York Regiment, becoming military secretary to General Schuyler the following month and gaining a reputation for efficiency in adverse situations. On 25 September he was made deputy muster master general of the Northern army, and on 10 April 1777, following the reorganization of the Muster Department, he became lieutenant colonel and deputy commissary of musters, a position he held until June 1780, when the department was terminated.

In August 1780 he became aide-de-camp to General Arnold at West Point, Varick having become a friend and supporter of Arnold during the Saratoga campaign. Both Varick and the other aide, Franks, soon became uneasy about their general's activities as the new commander of West Point, but they thought that he was engaged in nothing more dishonorable than profiteering. Duped not only by his chief but also by the latter's lovely young wife,

Colonel Varick was cleared by a court of inquiry that met on 2 November 1780 at West Point. He nevertheless remained under some suspicion, and although he wished to remain in the army, he was left without military employment. In May 1781 he was selected by Washington as his confidential secretary to supervise a staff of writers in the arrangement, classification, and copying of all the correspondence and other papers of the Continental army located at Washington's headquarters. This helped to restore Varick's reputation. Establishing his office at Poughkeepsie, Varick and his assistants spent more than two years in compiling the forty-four folio volumes known as the Varick Transcripts, later deposited in the Library of Congress and of great value to historians.

In 1784 Varick became the recorder of New York City. With Samuel Jones he codified New York State's statutes enacted since the Revolution in *Laws of the State of New York* (2 vols., 1789). Speaker of the New York assembly in 1787–1788, attorney general in 1788–1789, he then served as mayor from 1789 until 1801, when Aaron Burr's new machine swept the Federalists out of power. A founder of the American Bible Society, he was its president from 1828 until his death in Jersey City, New Jersey, on 30 July 1831.

SEE ALSO *Arnold's Treason; Burr, Aaron.*

BIBLIOGRAPHY

Rommel, John G., Jr. "Richard Varick: New York Aristocrat." Ph.D. dissertation, Columbia University, 1966.

revised by Michael Bellesiles

VARNUM, JAMES MITCHELL.

VARNUM, JAMES MITCHELL. (1748–1789). Continental general. Massachusetts–Rhode Island. Born at Dracut, Massachusetts, on 17 december 1748, Varnum entered Harvard College in 1765 and remained until April 1768, his junior year, When he was asked to leave after leading a protest against the college tutors. He entered Rhode Island College (now Brown University) and graduated with honors in its first class in 1769. He was admitted to the Rhode Island bar in 1771, and rapidly became a successful lawyer renowned for his courtroom oratory. A physically powerful man who was interested in gymnastics and military drill, he was elected captain of the Kentish Guards, an elite militia unit in which his friend Nathanael Greene served as a private.

Before dawn on the day of Lexington and Concord (19 April 1775), Varnum was awakened at Dracut by the alarm gun at Tewksbury, where Paul Revere's message had been received at 2 A.M. He was commissioned colonel of the First Rhode Island Regiment on 3 May, and marched to the Boston siege, where he and his regiment served on the right wing of the army in a brigade commanded by Greene, his former subordinate. Varnum re-raised the regiment, now called the Ninth Continental Regiment (Rhode Island) for 1776, and let it go to New York, where it helped to erect fortifications around Brooklyn Heights. The regiment fought in the Battles of Long Island, Harlem Heights (though Varnum was absent), and White Plains. Dissatisfied with his prospects for promotion to brigadier general, he left the continental service in mid-December after the Rhode Island Assembly named him brigadier general of the state militia. On 1 January 1777, he was appointed colonel of the First Rhode Island for 1777, but it was death of his rival Daniel Hitchcock, wounded at Princeton and dead a weak later, that cleared the way for his promotion to brigadier general on 21 February and his return to the continental service. He spent the winter recruiting and overseeing smallpox inoculations, and had just rejoined Washington's army when the British undertook their perplexing "June maneuvers" of the Philadelphia campaign. His brigade of Connecticut and Rhode Island troops was not formally assigned to a division, and he did not receive an order to attack the retreating British forces around Brunswick on 22 June. After taking part in the Battle of Germantown, he displayed personal heroism in the failed defense of Forts Mercer and Mifflin.

He took a dim view of Valley Forge. "The situation of the camp is such that in all human probability the army must soon dissolve," he wrote Greene on 12 February 1778 from that dismal encampment. "It is unparalleled in the history of mankind to establish winter quarters in a country wasted and without a single magazine." After having an active part in the Monmouth campaign, serving in Lee's division, he marched under Lafayette to support General John Sullivan at Newport in July–August 1778. In Rhode Island he advocated that an African American unit be raised, and the battalion that was created performed well in the action of 29 August.

A mutiny broke out in Varnum's brigade in early 1779. After Varnum expressed sympathy for his unpaid troops, he entered into an extended controversy with Sullivan that led to Varnum's resignation from the Continental army on 5 March 1779. Returning to his law practice, Varnum was named major general of the Rhode Island militia in April 1779. In this capacity he supported the French army of Rochambeau in July and August 1780. He was elected in May 1780 to the Continental Congress, serving in 1780–1782 and 1786–1787. In August 1787 Varnum, a director of the Ohio Company (its mandate being to purchase Northwest Territory lands west of the Seven Ranges), was appointed a judge for the Northwest Territory. Although in poor health, he rode on horseback to Marietta, Ohio, arriving on 5 June 1788. He had an active role in framing a code of territorial laws before his death there on 9 January 1789.

SEE ALSO *Greene, Nathanael; Monmouth, New Jersey; Newport, Rhode Island (29 July–31 August 1778); Philadelphia Campaign.*

BIBLIOGRAPHY

Greene, Nathanael. Papers. Vols. 1 to 4. Edited by Richard K. Showman et al. Chapel Hill: University of North Carolina Press for the Rhode Island Historical Society, 1976–1986.

Shipton, Clifford K. *Biographical Sketches of Those Who Attended Harvard College*, 17. Boston: Massachusetts Historical Society, 1975.

Varnum, James M. *The Varnums of Dracutt in Massachusetts.* Boston: David Clark, 1907.

Walker, Anthony. *So Few the Brave (Rhode Island Continentals, 1775–1789)*. Newport: Seafield Press for the Rhode Island Society of the Sons of the American Revolution, 1981.

revised by Michael Bellesiles

VAUGHAN, JOHN. (c. 1731–1795). British general. John Vaughan, the second son of the Third Viscount Lisburne, became a lieutenant of marines in 1746 and transferred to a cornetcy in the Tenth Dragoons in 1748. Propelled by a combination of ability and family influence, he quickly rose to lieutenant (1751) and captain (1754). After serving in Germany in the early years of the Seven Years War, he raised the Ninety-fourth Foot in 1759 and became its lieutenant colonel in 1760. He led the regiment in North America and the West Indies, distinguishing himself at the taking of Martinique in 1762. On 25 November, when the regiment disbanded, Vaughan took over the Sixteenth Regiment, serving with it in America until 1767 and in Ireland thereafter. In 1772 he was promoted to colonel and in 1774 he entered Parliament, representing Berwick-on-Tweed.

In 1775 Vaughan moved to the Forty-sixth Foot Regiment, and embarked with them for America in 1776. Arriving with General Charles Cornwallis's reinforcements from Ireland, he took part in the abortive Charleston expedition as a brigadier general before moving on to New York. He led attacks at Long Island (Brooklyn) on 27 August and at Kips Bay on 15 September, and was wounded in the thigh at White Plains on 28 October.

Vaughan, now known as a valiant commander, briefly visited Britain with Cornwallis before returning to America and being promoted major general on the regular establishment on 29 August 1777. He had a horse shot from under him at the storming of Fort Montgomery in the Hudson Highlands in October 1777, and led the 2,000 troops that were carried up river by Sir James Wallace in a vain attempt to reach General John Burgoyne. During this raid, Vaughan burnt the settlement of Aescopus (later Kingston) as well as farms and settlements to within forty-six miles of Albany, earning from the rebels the hostile epithet "General Aescopus." In 1779 he was back with General Henry Clinton's second Hudson expedition, capturing Verplanck's Point on 1 June 1779. In December he embarked for Britain, where he was given a dormant commission as British commander in the southern colonies, should Cornwallis refuse to return there.

When Cornwallis did return, Vaughan was made commander in chief of the Leeward Islands. Reaching Barbados in February 1780, he abandoned Grant's basically defensive approach and gathered troops for assaults on the French islands. However, he had reckoned without Admiral George Rodney's failure to win supremacy at sea and could do nothing until he and Rodney took St. Eustatius from the Dutch in February 1781. Vaughan later denied in parliament that he had profited from this operation; but he had substantial wealth from unknown sources even before the war, and his large disbursements afterward still require explanation.

On 20 November 1782 Vaughan was promoted to lieutenant general and retired from active service. In parliament he tried unsuccessfully to bargain his vote for a colonial governorship from the administrations of the Earl of Shelburne and William Pitt, but he did at last obtain a knighthood in 1792. Recalled to active duty in 1793, he was sent to succeed Sir Charles Grey in the Windward Islands in 1794. There he was beset by lack of troops, fever, and French-inspired slave and Carib risings. The government contributed to his difficulties by refusing to allow him to raise black troops, a prohibition that Vaughan at times defied. He died unmarried, probably of a bowel complaint, possibly of poison, at Martinique on 30 June 1795.

SEE ALSO *Charleston Expedition of Clinton in 1776; Clinton, Henry; Cornwallis, Charles.*

BIBLIOGRAPHY

Mackesy, Piers. *The War for America 1775–1783.* London: Longman, 1964.

revised by John Oliphant

VENCE, JEAN GASPARD. (1747–1808).

French privateer, admiral. Son of a merchant marine captain, he was born in Marseilles. In 1762 he sailed to the West Indies. The following year he served aboard the warship *Protecteur* in combat against English privateers. In 1777 he went to Martinique, was commissioned as a privateer, and in May sailed in the *Tigre*. In 40 actions before the war, he took 211 prizes.

On 6 September 1778 Vence took part in the capture of Dominique and Governor General Bouillé breveted him *lieutenant de frégate*. In December he saw action aboard the *Truite* off Saint Lucia. He then served aboard the *Cérès* and subsequently on the *Languedoc*, Admiral d'Estaing's flagship. On 4 July 1779 he spearheaded the French attack at Grenada, taking the main enemy battery, cutting down the Union Jack, and holding his position against heavy odds until d'Estaing arrived with the main body. Promoted to *lieutenant de vaisseau*, he led an attack at Savannah that got into the British works before being driven back. He was made chevalier in the Order of Saint Louis in 1780 and was later admitted to the Society of the Cincinnati.

Made captain of the port of Grenada in 1780, he served in 1782 on the *Terrible* in the Franco-Spanish squadron at Cadiz. *Capitaine de vaisseau* in November 1792 and commanding the *Duquesne*, he campaigned in the Mediterranean and at Tunis. On 10 March 1793 he was given command of the *Heureux* and on 16 November became vice admiral. In 1800, as maritime prefect of Toulon, he commanded an armed squadron at Brest whose duty was to protect the anticipated invasion of England. His criticism of the project drew the ire of Naval Minister Decrès, and he was retired on 16 October 1803.

SEE ALSO *Estaing, Charles Hector Théodat, Comte d'.*

BIBLIOGRAPHY

Contenson, Ludovic de. *La Société des Cincinnati de France et la Guerre d'Amérique.* Paris: Editions Auguste Picard, 1934.

Lasseray, André. *Les Français sous les treize étoiles (1775–1783).* 2 vols. Macon: Imprimerie Protat Frères, 1935.

Lawrence, Alexander A. *Storm over Savannah: The Story of Count d'Estaing and the Siege of the Town in 1779.* Athens: University of Georgia Press, 1951.

Loir, Maurice. *Jean-Gaspard Vence, corsaire et amiral, 1747–1808.* Paris: Baudoin, 1894.

Taillemite, Etienne. *Dictionnaire des Marins Français.* Paris: Editions Maritimes et d'Outre-Mer, 1982.

revised by Robert Rhodes Crout

VERGENNES, CHARLES GRAVIER, COMTE DE. (1717–1787).

French foreign minister. Born at Dijon, he started his diplomatic career under his uncle, Chevignard de Chavigny, at Lisbon and at Frankfort (1740–1745) and then represented the French monarchy at the courts of Trier (1750), Constantinople (1754–1768), and Stockholm (1771–1774). When Louis XVI ascended the throne in 1774, Vergennes became foreign minister. With a desire to restore France to its status as preeminent European power by reducing English power, organizing a tier of client states in alliance with France, and renewing an alliance with the Swiss cantons (1777), he sought to aid the Americans clandestinely until French military and naval strength could be restored and the king could be convinced to undertake a formal war against England. He proceeded with much greater caution than an earlier foreign minister, Choiseul.

Events of 1775 in America led Vergennes to believe that the colonists were serious about resisting the British government. The danger to France was that after committing themselves against the British, the latter might quickly settle the problem in America—by diplomacy or arms—and then turn their entire strength against France. Having previously refused to act on hints from American agents (for example, Arthur Lee in London) that the colonists would welcome aid from their traditional enemy, France, should a shooting war develop with England, Vergennes now agreed to the exploratory mission of Achard de Bonvouloir. At the same time Vergennes undertook a study of secret aid that led to establishment of Beaumarchais's Hortalez & Cie.

French statesmen were faced with the problem of when it would be wise to fight England, even with that country being handicapped by its war in America. Turgot, controller general of finances, was opposed for a number of reasons but finally agreed to secret aid. The other problem was that of getting support from Spain, a country with grave fears that the success of revolution in the thirteen colonies of North America might inspire Spanish colonies to revolt.

Vergennes succeeded first in getting his own government and that of Spain to support the plan for secret aid through Hortalez & Cie. In the summer of 1776, Vergennes was ready to go to war against Britain if Spain would join in, but upon learning of the British victory at Long Island, he decided it would be better for France to restrict assistance to secret aid until it could be sure the Americans could continue the war long enough for open assistance to do them any good. Two months before Burgoyne's defeat at Saratoga and influenced largely by Washington's brilliant riposte in the Trenton-Princeton campaign, Vergennes in July 1777 again officially proposed armed intervention by France and Spain. France had lost the restraining influence of Turgot, but Spain had a new foreign minister, the Conde Floridablanca, who lacked the enthusiasm of his predecessor, Grimaldi, for participation in a shooting alliance. Spanish hesitancy to agree to Vergennes's plan as well as reports of Burgoyne's initial successes in his invasion from Canada led the French foreign minister to delay his schemes. Lord Stormont, the British ambassador in Paris, had meanwhile succeeded in seriously embarrassing Vergennes by finding out details of the latter's secret aid and making official protests, an embarrassment to the French king.

The Saratoga surrender, Germantown, and Franklin's diplomacy in Paris led ultimately to the French alliance, which Congress ratified on 4 May 1778. Vergennes's policy partially prevailed, to the benefit of the Americans—who probably never could have achieved independence without active French participation in the war in America. In 1784 Vergennes wrote to Louis XVI that England was "bent under the weight of an enormous debt which is crushing her." However, the burdens of the global war and active intervention with its client states had also overburdened the French economy and accelerated the financial crisis that would lead to the French Revolution. Vergennes sought to tie England to France through a commercial treaty in 1786. Exhausted by the efforts, he died during deliberations.

SEE ALSO *Achard de Bonvouloir et Loyauté, Julien Alexandre; Choiseul, Etienne François, Comte de Stainville; French Alliance; Germantown, Pennsylvania, Battle of; Hortalez & Cie; Lee, Arthur.*

BIBLIOGRAPHY

Dull, Jonathan R. *A Diplomatic History of the American Revolution.* New Haven, Conn.: Yale University Press, 1985.

Hardman, John, and Munro Price, eds. *Louis XVI and the Comte de Vergennes: Correspondence, 1774–1787.* Oxford: Voltaire Foundation, 1998.

Murphy, Orville T. "The View from Versailles: Charles Gravier Comte de Vergennes's Perceptions of the American Revolution." In *Diplomacy and Revolution: The Franco-American Alliance of 1778.* Edited by Ronald Hoffman and Peter J. Albert. Charlottesville: University Press of Virginia, 1981.

———. *Charles Gravier, Comte de Vergennes: French Diplomacy in the Age of Revolution, 1719–1787.* Albany: State University of New York Press, 1982.

———. "A la sublime porte: La preparation de Vergennes au ministère." *Revue d'Histoire Diplomatique* 101 (1987): 227–237.

Price, Munro. *Preserving the Monarchy: The Comte de Vergennes, 1774–1787.* Cambridge, U.K.: Cambridge University Press, 1995.

revised by Robert Rhodes Crout

VERMONT.

Vermont was a largely unsurveyed wilderness in the mid-eighteenth century, except for Fort Dummer in the southeast and some Abenaki villages to the north. The area was claimed by New York, Massachusetts, and New Hampshire, but none of these provinces seemed interested in settling the region, even after New Hampshire's Governor Benning Wentworth granted a patent for a township in 1749, which he named Bennington in his own honor. By 1764, over the strenuous objections of New York's government, Wentworth had issued the rights to 129 townships west of the Connecticut River, and settlement had begun in what became known as the New Hampshire Grants. That same year the king issued a royal proclamation setting the Connecticut River as the border between New Hampshire and New York, thereby officially voiding the existence of all the Grants towns. New York immediately began carving the region up into large land grants shared among the province's leading families. In 1770 the Green Mountain Boys under Ethan Allen started resisting the civil power of New York. Royal Governor William Tryon and then Patriot Governor George Clinton opposed the Grants' claims to sovereignty, but without success. General Philip Schuyler of New York sided with his government, which was one of the reasons why New Englanders resented being under his command during the Revolution. In 1777 the Grants declared independence, becoming the state of Vermont. New York consistently opposed the new state, with Governor Clinton twice threatening to abandon the Revolution if Congress recognized Vermont. In 1790 New York formally relinquished claim to the region, and in 1791 Vermont became the fourteenth state.

SEE ALSO *Allen, Ethan; Skene, Philip; Tryon, William.*

BIBLIOGRAPHY

Bellesiles, Michael A. *Revolutionary Outlaws: Ethan Allen and the Struggle for Independence on the Early American Frontier.* Charlottesville: University Press of Virginia, 1993.

revised by Michael Bellesiles

VERMONT, MOBILIZATION IN.

On 21 April 1775, angry settlers living along the west side of the Connecticut River met in convention in the town of Westminster. Their outrage grew from what quickly became known as the Westminster Massacre, an effort by New York to assert its authority to a territory occupied mostly by people whose land grants came from the colony of New Hampshire. New York's officials had been too energetic, killing two men and wounding ten more. These settlers looked for leadership to an imposing figure from the other side of the Green Mountains, Ethan Allen. Allen gave eloquent voice to their claims to the land they worked and to the authority of their traditional New England town structures. What they all feared was ending up like the poor tenant farmers of New York, "peasants" tied to land they could never own in a political system dominated by the great landlords. Even as Allen was writing their public protest against the tyranny of New York, word arrived that galvanized the convention and the region they called the New Hampshire Grants and redirected their energy toward a new enemy.

What the Westminster Convention heard was that just two days earlier, British regulars had fired on American farmers at Lexington. There was little doubt in the minds of those attending the convention that resistance to ministerial authority had now become war. They also shared deep misgivings about their degree of preparation for a conflict with the world's most powerful empire.

Rushing back over the mountains, Allen called together a hasty meeting of militia officers and town leaders who decided to stand with the rest of America against the British "and thereby annihilate the old quarrel with the government of New-York by swallowing it up in the general conflict for liberty." They assumed that once the Grants settlers demonstrated their loyalty to the common cause that Congress would not "in any manner countenance their being deprived of their liberty by subjecting them under the power of a government [New York] which they detest more than that of the British" (Walton, ed., *Records*, pp.447–448).

Deciding for war required that they confront a number of difficult issues. Allen and his fellow officers understood that they needed four things for war: money, munitions, men, and motivation. In 1775 the New Hampshire Grants possessed the last two of these but had little hope for money and munitions. The Grants had one major advantage over the rest of the American colonies—they had been in open rebellion for five years, but against New York rather than Britain. The Grants had no legal existence. The British king had given the Green Mountains region by colonial charters to New York, New Hampshire, and Massachusetts. As a consequence, all three colonies issued land grants in the area, New York to wealthy, politically connected absentee owners, the other two states to anyone willing to pay their low fees. When the British Privy Council decided that New York held the right to all the land west of the Connecticut River and north of the Massachusetts border, the other governments abandoned those living in the Grants to their own devices. New York's officials proceeded to evict the settlers they saw as nothing but squatters.

MILITARY AND CIVILIAN STRUCTURES

At this juncture, in 1770, the extended Allen family settled in the Grants. In July 1770 Ethan Allen, the head of this clan, called a meeting at Stephen Fay's Catamount Tavern in Bennington and organized an extralegal militia company, the Green Mountain Boys. Over the next four years, eight companies with some three hundred men organized on the west side of the Green Mountains. Anyone could claim membership in the Green Mountain Boys by sticking a fir twig in his hat or hair. Its loose structure formed the primary strength of the organization, drawing ever more of the community into the resistance movement. Membership was entirely voluntary, as was showing up; but their "colonel commandant," Ethan Allen, had a notable ability to arouse the settlers to turn out for service.

Later observers such as Generals Philip Schuyler and Richard Montgomery; Governor Guy Carleton; and even Allen's bitter rival, Benedict Arnold, acknowledged his charismatic skill as a recruiter. Allen excelled at what he called "preaching politics."

Motivation required organization to be effective. In 1774 the region's towns organized committees of correspondence to strengthen their link with the rest of the American colonies. They were quickly followed by a series of conventions of the region's towns, the struggle against British authority thus reinforcing their search for autonomy. On the west side of the Green Mountains, these conventions built upon the preexisting structure of the Green Mountain Boys and committees of correspondence. On the east side, the conventions met as the result of individual initiative. Theirs was a fluid authority, as town meetings simply adjourned in order to reconstitute themselves as committees of safety to oversee a temporary crisis. In 1775 the crisis seemed to become permanent.

CAPTURING TICONDEROGA

Motivated by a fear of losing all they had built in the Green Mountains, the region's settlers willingly appeared for service in support of their rebellion. But they seriously lacked the material by which they could expect to engage in war against the British Empire. All those who visited the Grants noted their poverty. Noah Phelps, who reconnoitered the area for Connecticut, reported on its destitution to the General Assembly, doubting that the settlers could sustain any military action without external assistance. For munitions the Grants had to rely mostly on what the settlers had brought with them, primarily old muskets from the Seven Years' War or earlier. For gunpowder they needed to turn to the distant markets of Albany or Montreal. There were no local manufacturers of either guns or powder, and only a few of either in the whole of the American colonies. Ironically, the American colonies' prime source for munitions prior to 1775 was exactly the country against which they were now revolting. Not surprisingly, then, the Green Mountain Boys looked to the same source for the arms and ammunition they would need to launch their war against Britain. They looked west, to a fort sitting on a high bluff above Lake Champlain.

Fort Ticonderoga loomed large in the imagination of the American colonists. It was at this stone bastion that Montcalm had inflicted his notorious defeat on Abercrombie's superior force of fifteen thousand British and American troops in 1758. The fort, which passed into British hands with the Treaty of Paris in 1763, acquired the reputation of being the key to control of the northern colonies. To attack such an imposing fort seemed the height of folly. But in the last days of April, that was exactly what Ethan Allen proposed to do.

Allen ordered the mobilization of the Green Mountain Boys and the stationing of guards on all the roads leading to Fort Ticonderoga, successfully isolating the British and keeping information of Lexington from them. The Grants benefited from having an experienced and organized military force with a clearly established chain of command. Within seventy-two hours of Allen's mobilization order, all eight companies of Green Mountain Boys had appeared for duty.

For money the Grants turned to the other provinces. Allen sent his brothers Heman and Levi to Hartford to seek financial support. They returned with three hundred pounds "borrowed" from the Connecticut treasury. (Connecticut would eventually spend fifteen hundred pounds on the campaign.) Allen sent two men to Albany with this money to purchase gunpowder and other supplies for his troops.

An ad hoc council or war met in Castleton on 8 May and planned the attack on Fort Ticonderoga. Clearly, surprise was essential. The following night two hundred men gathered at Hand's Cove just a mile from the fort. For some reason Canada's governor Carleton did not see fit to inform Captain William Delaplace of the threat he faced, guaranteeing the operation's success; Delaplace surrendered his sword to Allen without any idea that Britain was at war with anyone. The American haul was enormous. In addition to their 50 prisoners, the Americans seized 120 iron and 2 brass cannon, 50 swivel guns, 2 10-inch mortars, 10 barrels of musket balls, 3 cartloads of flints, 30 gun carriages, 10 casks of powder, hundreds of shells, materials for a boat, food stuffs, and a large supply of rum "for the refreshment of the fatigued soldiery" (Allen to Delaplace, 10 May 1775, Stevens Papers).

Allen immediately sent Seth Warner and Levi Allen north to capture Crown Point, where the Americans gained an additional 113 cannon, hundreds of muskets, and numerous casks of powder. While most of the other munitions went to the Continental Army, the Green Mountain Boys armed themselves with sufficient muskets and ammunition to last them for the next two years of war. The material captured on Lake Champlain in those first days of the northern campaign also supplied the Green Mountain Regiment organized in July 1775 under the command of Seth Warner.

The major stumbling block to mobilization was fear. Many hesitated to act, including the Continental Congress. The capture of Ticonderoga had been the first obviously offensive act of the war, and many patriots remained uncertain of its wisdom. Congress apologized to the Canadian people for the unfortunate seizure of the fortress and ordered Allen to move the cannon and other supplies at Ticonderoga to the far end of Lake George to await a peace settlement with England. Allen ignored

Congress's order, firing off an angry letter reminding that body that it was at war and needed to act quickly.

Yet the commanders of these volunteer forces had little or no experience keeping troops in the field. Provisioning alone was a daunting task. After having seized the British garrisons on Lake Champlain, Allen realized that he was not in the least aware how to maintain his troops in their positions there. He wrote the Albany Committee of Safety that his men only had enough food for four days and that most of the cannon were not mounted. Thus, the arrival of Generals Schuyler and Montgomery was an enormous relief to all the officers except Arnold, who first refused to give up his command and then resigned in a huff. The two generals were experienced officers who knew what to do and could take responsibility for organizing the next step of the campaign. The inexperienced Grants officers would learn the necessary skills as they went along.

FORMING A STATE GOVERNMENT

Despite all the initiative they had demonstrated in the first months of the Revolution, the Grants settlers lacked a preexisting political structure. Whereas the other colonies all had legislatures and court systems upon which they could build their new republican governments, the Grants had to create it all from scratch. It should not be too surprising then that their town meetings served as the building blocks and model for the state they created.

At first the region operated as it had prior to April 1775, relying on local committees of safety to address matters dealing with the Revolutionary struggle. These were supplemented by a number of ad hoc committees and the occasional convention addressing regional issues. But as New York refused to abandon its pre-Revolutionary claims to the territory, the Grants settlers found it necessary to create their own state to secure their revolution.

The war itself mobilized the Grants and crafted the kind of republic it became. In a series of six conventions between April 1775 and January 1777, the Grants moved slowly toward unification and independence. The earliest conventions concentrated almost entirely on military matters, postponing political disputes in the name of a requisite unity. For a time it seemed that the east-side towns would sit out the Revolution, only Townshend sending a representative to any of the first four conventions. Attempting to overcome this coolness, the Dorset Convention of July 1776 produced an "Association" for submission to the people, claiming to act for Congress, which had requested "that every honest Friend to the Liberties of America ... should subscribe an Association, binding themselves as Members of some Body or Community" (Walton, ed., *Records*, 1, pp. 21–22). Signers of the Dorset Association swore to protect the United States, but as inhabitants of the Grants, not as New Yorkers. Emphasizing its jurisdiction,

the Dorset Convention appointed a committee of war responsible for military procurement and oversight of the local committees of safety. The convention charged the committees with policing anyone who refused to sign the association as an enemy of the people.

Despite the military disasters of 1776, most of the region's inhabitants chose to identify with the Revolutionary struggle. The Grants leaders took these affirmations as excuse enough to call another convention at Westminster in January 1777. The convention voted unanimously that the Grants become "a new and separate state; and for the future conduct themselves as such," legitimating its action with John Adams's congressional resolution of 10 May 1776 (Proctor, p. 63). This resolution recommended that "where no government sufficient to the exigencies of their affairs has been hitherto established," that the inhabitants should "adopt such government as shall in the opinion of the Representatives of the people best conduce to the happiness and safety of their constituents"— an exact description of the Grants, the convention asserted (Walton, ed., *Records*, 1, pp. 40–44). The convention closed its business by applying for admission to Congress and voting to raise more troops for Warner's regiment, which it claimed as its own.

By the time the constitutional convention opened its meeting in Windsor on 2 July 1777, the state had a new name, Vermont. The state also had a spur to act quickly, as the northern defenses crumbled before General John Burgoyne's onslaught. Over the next week, the convention, guided by Ira Allen and Thomas Chittenden, wrote the most democratic constitution of its time. It also launched the structure by which Vermont would meet its enemies on the field of battle, leaving most authority in the towns, though granting strong executive powers to a governor and council elected directly by the people. On 8 July, during the last reading of the constitution, news arrived of Ticonderoga's fall and Warner's defeat at Hubbardton. The enemy had overrun the homes of many delegates and threatened to make the convention's proceedings moot. It passed the constitution unanimously, arranged for a statewide election in December, appointed a Council of Safety to oversee the war effort until the new government was approved by the people. The delegates then scattered to their militia units.

OPPOSING BURGOYNE'S INVASION

The newly constituted Vermont Council of Safety's first action was to call out the Green Mountain Boys to resist Burgoyne's invasion. They followed this up with an appeal to New Hampshire and Massachusetts for assistance, a step that had not occurred to any of the Continental army's generals. When Burgoyne sent Lieutenant Colonel Frederick Baum to Bennington, the gathered militiamen rejected General Benjamin Lincoln's claim to command and his order that they march to the Hudson. Instead, they turned to Colonel Warner and Colonel John Stark of New Hampshire. The complicated plan devised by these two commanders succeeded beyond their expectations, defeating both Baum's regiment and the relief force under Lieutenant Colonel Henrick von Breymann on 16 August 1777. In addition to seven hundred prisoners, the New Englanders also captured four brass cannon and hundreds of high-quality muskets that would serve the region's militia well in the years ahead.

Rearmed and invigorated by its triumph, Vermont's militia was sent by the Council of Safety on a campaign of harassment, breaking Burgoyne's lines of communication and retreat, driving the British into their defenses at Ticonderoga and Mount Independence, seizing Skenesboro and Mount Defiance, and capturing hundreds of prisoners and most of the supplies bound for the dispirited British army. General Horatio Gates finally persuaded the Council of Safety to send its troops beyond its borders. In early October the Vermont militia settled on the heights above Fort Edward. When Burgoyne finally attempted his retreat in mid-October he found his way blocked and his army completely encircled. Vermont had demonstrated an ability to overcome its many shortfalls to field an effective military force.

The war brought the Vermont towns together in battle, intensifying each participant's identification with the new state and nation. Town militia acted as coherent units, and battles were often family affairs with sons and fathers, brothers and cousins standing side by side. Unlike in other states where the poorest were generally sent to serve, sparsely populated Vermont called on most of its citizens to participate in the war effort. The loss of a family member or neighbor further personalized the conflict. Militia companies thus served as what the historian John Shy has called "the infrastructure of revolutionary government" and also as sources of political education (*A People Numerous and Armed*, p. 177). Risking one's life for a cause made political goals all the more personal.

STATE FINANCES

Even while the Council of Safety worked to maintain its security against external threats, it turned on internal enemies. In July 1777, Ira Allen oversaw the creation of a commission of confiscation to seize the property of Loyalists, finding precedent in New York's commissioners of sequestration. Identifying and punishing the enemies of the people not only removed a potential threat to the state's security, it also increased the state's wealth from the auction of seized property. The state used the funds raised from the rent or sale of confiscated property to pay for its military. As Allen honestly admitted, "In consequence of internal divisions, and to make government popular, it was thought good policy not to lay any taxes on the people but to raise a sufficient revenue out of the

property confiscated" (Allen, *Natural and Political History*, p. 111). The assembly supplemented these funds by authorizing itself to sell off all unappropriated lands in northern Vermont, tens of thousands of acres with which to meet government expenses while attracting new settlers. Most of Vermont's income between 1777 and 1786 came from land sales: £190,433 from confiscated lands, £66,815 from land grants, and £44,948 from taxes. Comparing this with the tax burden common in the other states, it is clear that Vermont's citizens had a solid financial incentive to support their government.

Thomas Chittenden, governor throughout the Revolutionary period, and his council oversaw the daily operation of the state and its war effort. No detail appeared too trivial for the council, from determining the ownership of a specific firearm to locating American prisoners of war held in Canada to providing aid during the winter to the families of those manning the state's forts. The state felt free to deal with these matters in practically any way it saw fit. As Governor Chittenden wrote, the Constitution "placed no embarrassing restrictions on the power of the legislature respecting the finances" of Vermont. Towns held a similar authority. In 1780 the legislature declared that town meetings might impose whatever taxes they felt necessary.

CONGRESS REFUSES TO HELP

Despite the boon gained from selling confiscated lands, the Revolution proved a significant drain on Vermont's limited resources. Bordering Canada, facing persistent invasion threats, uncertain of its own legitimacy, Vermont spent most of the war in a state of war readiness. The state's Board of War, which overlapped with the governor's council, proclaimed a defensive line across the center of the state in 1779, relocating women and children to homes in the safer southern districts. Ethan Allen, who chaired the board, oversaw the construction and manning of a series of garrisons across the state. The militia was kept in constant readiness, being called out several times in 1780 in response to British probes. The only help Vermont got from the rest of the United States was orders of Congress in 1779 and 1780 that it cease to exist.

The Vermonters learned that they could not rely on the rest of America for aid; they had to find their own way. For example, in 1779 Chittenden requested ammunition for the state militia from Isaac Tichenor, commissary general of the Continental army's Bennington arsenal. Backed by Congress, Tichenor refused this request, leaving Allen to rush to Connecticut and purchase munitions with his personal credit.

NEGOTIATING WITH THE BRITISH

Allen understood that if the British again invaded from Canada that the Continental army would do nothing until the enemy troops entered New York. The Royalton raid of October 1780 clarified Vermont's isolation, as Indians and Loyalists burned the town, killed two people, and took thirty-two captives. Under these circumstances, Allen felt justified in concocting a separate peace.

When Major Charles Carleton descended Lake Champlain with one thousand British troops in the fall of 1780, Governor Chittenden responded to the appeal of New York's Governor Clinton for help by calling out the state's militia. As the British burned Fort Edward, the New York militia refused to march. Allen shadowed the British, waiting for assistance that never came. Allen never admitted it in public, but he and his Board of War knew that a British attack would be a losing proposition for Vermont. For this reason, and to avoid bankruptcy from the state's being on a constant war footing, Allen sought the alternative path of negotiation. His discussions with the British, in which he hinted that Vermont might be interested in becoming a British province if Congress continued to ignore it, led to a truce in December 1780 that held on the Champlain frontier through the rest of the Revolution. In an ironic twist, Allen refused to agree to a ceasefire unless New York was included. Even Governor Clinton had to admit in an angry letter to Washington that Allen had saved New York from invasion.

VERMONT BATTLES NEW YORK

Congress might continue to deny the existence of Vermont, but the state was an established fact by 1781. The state's solidity was clearly demonstrated in the last military encounter of the Revolution on the northern frontier, though in the "Battle" of Walloomsac, Vermont's troops defended their state against an invasion from New York rather than Canada. As 1781 drew to a close and the Lake Champlain truce held, Governor Clinton decided it was time to move against his breakaway northeastern counties. Clinton ordered General Peter Gansevoort to call out the northern militia of New York and march on Bennington, expecting that this show of force would be sufficient to put an end to the so-called state of Vermont. Though only two hundred militia turned out for service, Gansevoort followed his orders and led them east. Governor Chittenden ordered out the Bennington militia, which also numbered two hundred men. On 20 December 1781 the two miniature armies met at the Walloomsac. After exchanging insults and threats, the two sides settled in, each claiming to lay siege to the other. General Allen, who had been in Castleton, mobilized more state forces and rushed south with these reinforcements and an old cannon taken from Ticonderoga back in 1775. The New York militia took one look at the superior forces arriving on the other side of the meandering creek and went home. Vermont won its

final victory of the war without firing a shot. The state's ability to call out its troops and their actually showing up proved sufficient to sustain its independence until Congress finally acknowledged reality and welcomed Vermont into the union as the fourteenth state in 1791.

SEE ALSO *Allen, Ethan; Allen, Ira; Hubbardton, Vermont; Warner, Seth.*

BIBLIOGRAPHY
Allen, Ethan. *A Vindication of the Opposition of the Inhabitants of Vermont to the Government of New-York.* Bennington, Vt.: Alden Spooner, 1779.

Allen, Ira. *The Natural and Political History of the State of Vermont.* London: J. W. Meyers, 1798.

Arnold, Benedict. "Benedict Arnold's Regimental Memorandum Book." *Pennsylvania Magazine of History and Biography* 8 (1884): 363–376.

Bellesiles, Michael A. *Revolutionary Outlaws: Ethan Allen and the Struggle for Independence on the Early American Frontier.* Charlottesville: University Press of Virginia, 1993.

Buel, Richard, Jr. *Dear Liberty: Connecticut's Mobilization for the Revolutionary War.* Middletown, Conn.: Wesleyan University Press, 1980.

Force, Peter, ed. *American Archives.* 9 vols. Washington, D.C.: n.p., 1837–1853.

Proctor, Redfield, ed. *Records of the Conventions of the New Hampshire Grants for the Independence of Vermont, 1776–1777.* Washington, D.C.: n.p., 1904.

Shy, John. *A People Numerous and Armed: Reflections on the Military Struggle for American Independence.* New York: Oxford University Press, 1976.

Stevens Papers. Vermont State Archives, Montpelier, Vt.

Walton, E. P., ed. *Records of the Governor and Council of the State of Vermont.* 8 vols. Montpelier: J. & J. M. Poland, 1873–1880.

Michael Bellesiles

VERNIER, PIERRE-JEAN-FRANÇOIS.

(1736–1780). Officer in Pulaski's Legion. Born at Belfort, France, he became a volunteer in the Fischer corps in 1752, was made lieutenant in a regiment of foreign volunteers of Tirant in 1756, took part in the action at Saint Cast on 11 September 1758, and received a gunshot wound in the thigh at Vildungen on 25 July 1760. He was taken into the Legion of Conflans in 1763, retired on 1 January 1768, and was assigned to the Invalides in Paris.

Having been recommended by Franklin along with others in the Marquis de Brétigney's party in June 1777, he was captured that year by the English and imprisoned at Saint Augustine with Brétigney. He eventually made his way to America with Brétigney, and Congress appointed him a major in Pulaski's Legion on 23 February 1779.

According to Johann Ewald's diary, he was mortally wounded in a surprise attack by Tarleton's cavalry near Monck's Corner, South Carolina on 14 April 1780. His last name is often spelled "Vernie." In *Dictionnaire des officiers de l'armée royale* (1982), Bodinier lists his given names as "Jean François" or "François Jean."

SEE ALSO *Franklin, Benjamin; Monck's Corner, South Carolina (14 April 1780); Tarleton, Banastre.*

BIBLIOGRAPHY

Bodinier, André. *Dictionnaire des officiers de l'armée royale qui ont combattu aux Etats-Unis pendant la guerre d'Indépendance, 1776–1783*. Vincennes, France: Service historique de l'armée, 1982.

Ford, Worthington C., et al., eds. *Journals of the Continental Congress, 1774–1789*. 34 vols. Washington, D.C.: U.S. Government Printing Office, 1904–1937.

Franklin, Benjamin. *Papers of Benjamin Franklin*. Edited by Leonard W. Labaree, et al. 37 vols. to date. New Haven, Conn.: Yale University Press, 1959–.

Uhlendorf, Bernhard A., ed. and trans. *The Siege of Charleston with an Account of the Province of South Carolina: Diary and Letters of Hessian Officers*. Ann Arbor: University of Michigan Press, 1938.

revised by Robert Rhodes Crout

VERNON, EDWARD.

(1685–1757). British admiral. In 1740 Vernon, popularly known as "Old Grog" from his grogram cloak, ordered that the daily rum issue in his squadron be diluted with three parts water—hence the naval name "grog" for watered-down rum. Vernon's capture of Porto Bello in 1739 made him famous, and his reputation survived the disastrous attempt on Cartagena in 1741. Lawrence Washington, the half-brother from whom George Washington inherited his estate, named Mount Vernon in his honor.

revised by John Oliphant

VERPLANCK'S POINT.

On the east bank of the Hudson River, with Stony Point it covered King's Ferry at the southern approach to the Hudson Highlands. On 1 June 1779 the British captured Fort Lafayette, which had been built on this place, in the operations preceding the action at Stony Point on 16 July 1779.

SEE ALSO *Stony Point, New York.*

Mark M. Boatner

VICE-ADMIRALTY COURTS.

The branch of Anglo-American law dealing with maritime matters is known as admiralty law. The High Court of Admiralty was created in England in the fourteenth century, and spawned regional tribunals known as vice-admiralty courts. Because the imperial government did not establish vice-admiralty courts in the colonies at the start of settlement, most admiralty cases were tried in civil courts. The Navigation Act of 1696 systematically established vice-admiralty courts in the American colonies, with a jurisdiction broader than that of their English counterparts, in order to enable them to enforce the Navigation Acts. Cases involving the seizure of ships at sea during wartime were placed under the jurisdiction of these courts in 1708, as were cases involving the sequestration of timber for use by the Royal Navy in 1722. The Townshend Acts of 1767 extended the system by establishing vice-admiralty courts at Halifax, (Nova Scotia), Boston (Massachusetts), Philadelphia (Pennsylvania), and Charleston (South Carolina). The older courts continued to function, but the new ones took over appellate jurisdiction, although further appeal to the Privy Council was permitted.

Vice-admiralty courts were unpopular with Americans because their purpose was to enforce Britain's control over the colonial economy. It was particularly galling that the courts were staffed by imperial placemen who exercised summary jurisdiction over local merchants. The absence of trial by jury reduced local influence on the courts and allowed them more latitude in helping Customs Commissioners prosecute smugglers and collect the fees levied by the various acts of trade.

SEE ALSO *Customs Commissioners; Townshend Acts.*

revised by Harold E. Selesky

VIGO, JOSEPH MARIA FRANCESCO.

(1747–1836). Spanish officer, frontier merchant. Born in Mondovi, Italy, Vigo joined the Spanish army as a young man, being stationed in Cuba and then New Orleans in the 1760s. Leaving the military around 1770, he entered into the fur trade, working closely with Native Americans and French traders. In 1772 he settled in the new Spanish post of St. Louis, eventually establishing a partnership with the lieutenant governor of Louisiana, Fernando de Leyba. The latter secretly encouraged Vigo to assist Colonel George Rogers Clark in his 1778 campaign against British outposts in the Old Northwest. Vigo responded with financial aid, which proved essential since Clark had no other way of purchasing supplies from the Spanish or the French in Vincennes. After loaning Clark nearly ten thousand dollars, Vigo set out for Vincennes, which had just been captured by Henry Hamilton's British forces. Unaware of Spanish sympathy for the Americans, Hamilton let Vigo leave, the latter traveling to Kaskaskia, where Clark was stationed. Guided by Vigo's thorough intelligence on the British position, Clark launched his surprising and successful winter attack on Vincennes in February 1779. After the Revolution, Vigo moved to Vincennes, marrying an American woman, Elizabeth Shannon. He continued to be active in the fur trade and to supply American forces with goods. He also was an agent for the Miami Company. Named a colonel of militia in 1790, he acted on behalf of the United States in negotiations with various Indians nations over the next fifteen years. The decline of the fur trade in the early 1800s and his inability to obtain payment for the funds he had advanced to the Americans during the Revolution led to Vigo's economic failure. He died in Vincennes homeless and poor on 22 March 1836.

BIBLIOGRAPHY

Roselli, Bruno. *Vigo: A Forgotten Builder of the American Republic.* Boston, Mass.: Stratford, 1933.

Vigo, Joseph. Joseph Maria Francesco Vigo Papers. Indiana Historical Society, Indianapolis.

Michael Bellesiles

VINCENNES, INDIANA.

This French settlement on the Wabash shifted allegiance to Virginia on 20 July 1778, was retaken by the British on 17 December, and capitulated to the Americans on 24–25 February 1779.

SEE ALSO *Western Operations.*

Mark M. Boatner

VIOLENCE.

It goes without saying that violence played a significant role in the outbreak and over the course of the American Revolution. It was, after all, a *war* for American independence. The nature and meaning of that violence, however, demands interpretation. Perhaps the foremost task in the interpretation of revolutionary-era violence, whether protest or war, is to understand it from the perspective of contemporaries. With regard to war, for example, contemporaries understood that war naturally carried with it death and destruction. The killing of hundreds or thousands in the context of the battlefield excited no repugnance or outrage—fear, worry, desperation, yes, but not outrage. However, acts considered atrocities or, more simply, behavior outside accepted norms for wartime violence, did inspire outraged reaction, and the political consequences could be significant. Again, whether referring to the riots of the prewar period of imperial tension, or to the acts of competing armies, historians have confronted a similar question: what in fact was the relationship between violence and political reaction? Did it provide a "liberating" quality that fostered democratization, or did it simply inspire fear and thus a conservative reaction? Perhaps violence led to both outcomes in different circumstances, and the trick is to find the source of the difference.

RIOT AND PROTEST

At one level colonists saw violence as simply one more tool in the arsenal of political protest. As tensions in the imperial relationship rose and fell, violence as a way of communicating discontent always existed as an option. This understanding of protest violence as communicative is crucial. It reminds us that late eighteenth-century colonial protestors and rioters were hoping for a response—an alteration in existing conditions or relationships. They were not trying to destroy or fundamentally rewrite the nature of society. As a result of this overall intention, they structured their violent behavior in such a way as to convey both their intent and their sense of their own legitimacy in so acting. Communicative rioters (as opposed to the riots of the truly hopeless, which are usually much more violent) are playing to audiences: themselves, their opponents, and, crucially, the undecided.

In the eighteenth century that desire to convey legitimacy led rioters to lean on precedent. They acted violently in ways calculated to seem familiar; much of their violence, such as mock trials and mock hangings, for example, simulated penal measures. Riots were also in part public festivals, drawing on imagery and practices from more peaceful kinds of festivals. Of particular importance in Boston, for example, was the annual Pope's Day (transmuted from England's Guy Fawkes Day) festival (5 November), which provided much of the structure for political riots there during the 1760s and 1770s. Because rioters also intended to correct problems, they often focused on particular persons with whom they had a grievance. Mock trials and hangings incorporated the shaming qualities of many judicial punishments of the era, thus putting public pressure on the targeted individual. Not all scholars are comfortable with this limited characterization of eighteenth-century American rioting as communicative in nature; yet that characterization is hard to dispute for those protests most closely associated with the colony-mother country relationship.

In contrast, local riots, especially over the access to land, could be much less restrained, especially when they were less public; some were not even "riots" so much as a raid on someone else's home. Violent behavior that remained within expectations about rioting, conforming to penal and festive traditions without seeming too greatly to threaten the social order, were generally tolerated; the "audience" understood them as forms of communication. Authorities, whether local or imperial, usually reacted by at least appearing to fix the problem, while also publicly deploring the violence and officially asserting the sanctity of the state and the social hierarchy. Behavior that seemed outside the expected norms generated much more stringent reactions.

This basic understanding of protest violence can be found operating from the earliest clashes of the revolutionary era right up to the outbreak of war. The Stamp Act riots are exemplary. Colonists around the continent began their protests almost as soon as the law's passage became known. Crucially, however, they began their protests in writing, fulfilling a standard "requirement" prior to a riot: the need to petition peacefully for redress. The first act of violence hit Boston on 14 August 1765, when the South End mob, spurred on by Samuel Adams and the Loyal Nine, hanged an effigy of the new stamp distributor, Andrew Oliver, paraded the effigy through town, and then tore down the stamp distribution building as well as Oliver's house. Oliver promptly resigned his distributorship. The Boston violence peaked eleven days later when the rioters pillaged and destroyed the mansion of Lieutenant Governor Thomas Hutchinson. Word of Boston's riots spread quickly around the colonies, and as 1 November (the date for the law to take effect) approached, riots broke out in nearly every colony. In most of them the violence remained confined to the most visible symbols of the act: forcing distributors to resign, preventing the landing of the stamps, or tearing up customs records. The rioters effectively nullified the act, and Parliament got the message. Parliament repealed the act in early 1766, at least momentarily confirming for Americans the effectiveness of their actions.

Although many observers considered the destruction of Hutchinson's house to be excessive, for the most part rioters around the colonies worked hand in glove with local elites and were specific and discriminatory in their violence, while fully adhering to the penal and festive traditions of riot. Some scholars have even argued that the colonists understood such corrective riots aspart of a legal process of popular enforcement. Events in New York City were in marked contrast to the Boston riots. There the Stamp Act riots quickly spun out of control, gripping the city for a full twelve months. The scholar Philip Ranlet has argued that this experience of excessive protest violence energized moderate and conservative forces within the city's leadership and led New York in the succeeding years to be among the most reluctant of the revolutionary colonies.

The Stamp Act episode set another precedent that would contribute strongly to the character of later imperial riots. The intercolonial Stamp Act Congress, with its call for a boycott of English goods, set a precedent for future cooperation among the colonies, and the boycott required enforcement. Rioters thus found a further basis for their legitimacy as popular enforcers of a local congress's decrees. Violence came part and parcel with the developing notion of popular sovereignty—with the people's will defined in extralegal conventions and conferences, and enforced in the streets.

The almost refined quality of the protest riots, and the increasing control over the rioters' behavior exercised by an elite committed to principles of preserving property, culminated in the Boston Tea Party. This was a highly controlled protest exercise that in fact generated little to no actual violence. In Boston the "rioters" even replaced a broken padlock and punished those few who tried to steal tea for personal use. During a similar tea dumping in New York "persons of reputation" stationed themselves on the ship to make sure that the crowd only dumped tea. The British reaction, however, was of a different order. Despite a clearly expressed colonial restraint, Parliament and the ministry saw only the destruction of valuable property and retaliated with a series of punitive acts, the Intolerable (or Coercive) Acts. Britain's outraged response would eventually create the circumstances for the march on Concord, and the violence there would lead to war.

Violence as a component of the protests between 1765 and 1774 advanced the level of friction and disgust on both sides of the Atlantic, and thus helped lead to revolution. This was true in part because violence as a tool of communication is an awkward medium, easily misunderstood and frequently hard to keep "on message" when passions of the moment break free of control. The infamous Boston Massacre represents a good example. The poorer workers of urban Boston had grown to resent moonlighting British regulars and had begun insulting and challenging them in the streets. On that particular March night in 1770 the resentments of the workers spiraled out of control, and their taunts and rocks finally led a small, scared troop of soldiers to open fire. Passion and fear ended up dictating the violence on both sides, and no clear message emerged except for the propagandized version later constructed by the Whig leadership: the redcoats were in Boston to impose tyranny. It was easy to take rhetorical advantage of violence.

Imperial protest violence had other effects. The consistent use of riot as a means of popular expression over a long period of time helped widen the political public. As large numbers of people participated in political action in the streets, they felt included in the wider discussion, and this helped create an expectation that they would be included in all political discussions. Furthermore, American militia laws (in most colonies) that nominally required all free men to own weapons meant that a riot always held the menace, and sometimes the actual presence, of armed force. In many circumstances, in fact, the militia formed the nucleus of a body of protestors. In the minds of the colonists, such a body of men, in their ranks with their officers at their head, did indeed represent the political will of the people. From a British perspective, such a body of men represented a dramatic escalation away from traditionally structured riots and toward something that looked much more like a rebellion.

WAR

Eighteenth-century Americans were no less cognizant than we that war inevitably entailed a certain amount of indiscriminate destruction and death. War, and the violence therein, carried with it a certain legitimacy. That legitimacy did not extend to acts seen as outside the bounds of acceptable wartime behavior. The issue of the legitimacy of wartime violence, especially in terms of the political effect of that violence, was most pertinent in the interactions of armies and civilians. Eighteenth-century European armies, although still highly cosmopolitan and international, were nevertheless uniformed, and the distinction between soldier and civilian was at least theoretically clear. During the Revolution, as civilians suffered from the actions of soldiers who were clearly soldiers, or from the actions of irregulars pretending to be soldiers, or as soldiers suffered from the actions of guerrillas not in uniform, resentment and anger built, leading to an escalation and intensification of violence.

The War of Independence was in fact an ideal arena for an escalation of violence based on perceptions of illegitimacy. First of all, it had begun with an act widely perceived as an atrocity: American propagandists portrayed the British march on Concord, and especially British actions on the march back, as unprovoked attacks on civilians, women, and children. Reports of Lexington and Concord played a major role in spurring the *rage militaire*—the filling of the ranks of the Continental Army and the militias during 1775 and 1776. As for the British, they initially conceived of the war as a rebellion; both by tradition and by recent codification (in the juristic works of Hugo Grotius and Emmerich de Vattel), rebels in arms merited no restraint. This attitude plagued British planners and officers throughout the war, as they never consistently settled on a policy of fire-and-sword destruction (as appropriate to a rebellion) versus one of conciliation and counterrevolution. Even those counterrevolutionary activities that the British did undertake—supporting Loyalists, encouraging slave revolt, and leaning on Indian allies—were all seen by colonists as acts outside the bounds of legitimacy, and thus all were used as excuses for intensifying violence. Finally, and perhaps most significant in terms of day-to-day activity over an eight-year war, were logistical difficulties for both sides—for the British, the Atlantic Ocean; for the Americans, financial and demographic shortfalls. These

difficulties led to a nearly constant reliance on the populace for supply, and the impressment of supplies from locals has ever been fraught with the potential for violence. Such violence might be considered the collateral damage of an early modern army on the move, but by the late eighteenth century it had come to be regarded as illegitimate.

Historians have approached the topic of wartime violence in various ways. Nineteenth-century folklorists tended to exaggerate the level of British and Loyalist atrocity, and their accounts held sway for many years. Later historians preferred to avoid the subject in favor of a cleaner political or military narrative. Some scholars have begun to move past nineteenth-century assumptions to ask just how bad the violence was. More significantly, other historians have returned to the issue of violence as part of an effort to understand the experience of the home front, both for its own sake and for its possible radicalizing influence on postwar popular politics. Some scholars have used the contours of the violence (who used violence, against whom, and how) to examine issues of regional and social relationships. Following one such approach, historians have argued that the violence represented a continuation of prewar social struggles exacerbated by the elite-led revolutionary government. The alternative argument contends that localism and a desire for order were more central and that, in the end, the Whig government was the most effective in meeting those demands for order.

Just how bad was the wartime violence? There is no general consensus on the issue. The answer depends on perspective—whether you were an Indian, a Tory, a householder in a theater of operations, a British soldier, or a Continental Army soldier. The war was fought on a continental scale, with operations of varying intensities in widely dispersed locales; all had consequences for residents in the area. Whether driven by an ideological belief in the cause or by an intensely localist instinct for self-preservation, much of the unconventional violence of the war followed the patterns of violence in other "people's wars" in its intensity and in its tendency to escalate through upward spiraling rounds of retaliation. It is also true, however, that despite Whig propaganda to the contrary, much of the conventional confrontation between British forces and Washington's Continentals tended to follow eighteenth-century prescriptions for restraint in war. There were glaring exceptions, especially by the British, perhaps most famously the poor conditions and treatment of American prisoners of war, or such events as the 1780 massacre of surrendering Continentals at Waxhaws, South Carolina, by Banastre "Bloody" Tarleton. Washington, for his part, was largely successful in containing the worst effects of an army on the move—never perfectly, but nevertheless impressively.

The conflicts between Whig and Loyalist adherents generated significantly more violence, and in some regions apparently deteriorated into widespread destruction and vigilantism. Even in this environment of civil war, however, both sides sought to clothe their actions in legitimacy either through pretensions at judicial forms or with reference to the Law of Retaliation. The famous hanging of Loyalist prisoners taken after battle at Kings Mountain, South Carolina, for example, followed not only a consultation of the North Carolina law for the establishment of a court, but also a trial, complete with references to retaliation for Loyalist violence in South Carolina. In the end only nine of some six hundred prisoners were hanged. The remainder were marched away and for the most part forced to enlist in the Patriot militia. In one sense, the easiest way to acknowledge the restraint that persisted even in the worst episodes of Whig–Tory violence is to compare it to the kind of warfare waged against Indian enemies. In the campaigns against the Cherokees or against the Iroquois, the precedents of white–Indian war and the all-consuming desire for land required little to no restraint. Few rules applied, and women, children, the old, and the towns and crops themselves were all regarded as legitimate targets.

Even more elusive is a consensus on the political ramifications of the experience of violence. Indeed, the debate on the political ramifications of the Revolution as a whole still rages on, and the impact of violence alone is a mere subset of the larger question. The historian Richard Maxwell Brown has suggested that the whole experience of resistance and war contributed to an expansion of the expectations of popular sovereignty. John Shy and Alan Kulikoff each have gone farther, arguing that military participation and the widespread violence of the war deepened democratic impulses. Contradicting Shy and Kulikoff, Sung Bok Kim has argued that sheer exhaustion from the high level of violence in Westchester County, New York, in fact brought about a depoliticization. A. Roger Ekirch has argued that the level of violence in North Carolina inspired a demand for a return to older standards of order and thus won support in the countryside for the order-imposing Whigs. It is possible to see a trend toward greater centralized control of the militias, at least in North and South Carolina, as a response to the unconstrained militias who were sowing violence in the countryside. The conservative reaction of the late 1780s is usually blamed on the experience of a weak central government during the war. Its inefficacy in raising money and running a war frustrated many, and led some leaders (including George Washington and Alexander Hamilton) to demand a more powerful government. The experience of violence may have had a similar effect on a more popular, visceral level. Some revolutionary leaders had lost their confidence in the ability of republican virtue to contain excessive violence and now instead looked to establish stronger forms of authority. Other colonists, having engaged in violence during the war, expected a similar freedom to be violent in the early republic.

SEE ALSO *Boston Massacre; Boston Tea Party; Guerrilla War in the North; Intolerable (or Coercive) Acts; Kings Mountain, South Carolina; Stamp Act; Tarleton, Banastre; Waxhaws, South Carolina.*

BIBLIOGRAPHY

Brown, Richard Maxwell. "Violence and the American Revolution." In *Essays on the American Revolution.* Edited by Stephen Kurtz and James H. Hutson. Chapel Hill: University of North Carolina Press, 1973.

————. *Strain of Violence: Historical Studies of American Violence and Vigilantism.* New York: Oxford University Press, 1975.

Ekirch, A. Roger. "Whig Authority and Public Order in Backcountry North Carolina, 1776–1783." In *An Uncivil War: The Southern Backcountry during the American Revolution.* Edited by Ronald Hoffman, Thad W. Tate, and Peter J. Albert. Charlottesville: University Press of Virginia, 1985.

Gilje, Paul A. *The Road to Mobocracy: Popular Disorder in New York City, 1763–1834.* Chapel Hill: University of North Carolina Press, 1987.

Greene, Jack P. "From the Perspective of Law: Context and Legitimacy in the Origins of the American Revolution." *South Atlantic Quarterly* 85 (1986): 56–77.

Hoerder, Dirk. *Crowd Action in Revolutionary Massachusetts, 1765–1780.* New York: Academic Press, 1977.

Kim, Sung Bok. "The Limits of Politicization in the American Revolution: The Experience of Westchester County, New York." *Journal of American History* 80 (1993): 868–889.

Kulikoff, Allan. "Revolutionary Violence and the Origins of American Democracy." *Journal of the Historical Society* 11 (2002): 229–260.

Lee, Wayne E. *Crowds and Soldiers in Revolutionary North Carolina: The Culture of Violence in Riot and War.* Gainesville: University Press of Florida, 2001.

————. "From Gentility to Atrocity: The Continental Army's Ways of War." *Army History* 62 (2006).

Maier, Pauline. *From Resistance to Revolution.* New York: Knopf, 1972.

Ranlet, Philip. *The New York Loyalists.* Knoxville: University of Tennessee Press, 1986.

Shy, John. "The Military Conflict Considered as a Revolutionary War." In *A People Numerous and Armed.* Rev. ed. Ann Arbor: University of Michigan Press, 1990.

Slaughter, Thomas P. "Crowds in Eighteenth-Century America: Reflections and New Directions." *Pennsylvania Magazine of History and Biography* 115 (1991): 3–34.

Van Buskirk, Judith L. *Generous Enemies: Patriots and Loyalists in Revolutionary New York.* Philadelphia: University of Pennsylvania Press, 2002.

Ward, Harry M. *Between the Lines: Banditti of the American Revolution.* Westport, Conn.: Praeger, 2002.

Wood, Gordon S. "A Note on Mobs in the American Revolution." *William and Mary Quarterly,* 3rd series, 23 (1966): 635–642.

Wayne E. Lee

VIRGINIA, MILITARY OPERATIONS

IN. Like Massachusetts, Virginia's Whigs took steps to prepare for possible armed conflict before the fighting actually began at Lexington. In late 1774 and early 1775 volunteer companies outside the militia system appeared. The first extra-legal Virginia Convention met from 20 to 27 March 1775 to take the place of the House of Burgesses when the royal governor (John Murray, the Fourth Earl of Dunmore) refused to call it into session. In spite of Patrick Henry's impassioned "liberty or death" speech, the convention rejected his call to raise troops. Then, on 20 April, Dunmore had a party come ashore before dawn and move the colony's gunpowder and store of arms from the Williamsburg magazine to the Royal Navy's schooner *Magdalen* in the James River. This action infuriated the Whigs and many of the volunteer companies quickly assembled in Williamsburg. Cooler heads avoided violence, but the political situation continued to deteriorate and on 8 June 1775 the Governor fled to the *Magdalen*, which was now anchored off Yorktown, and shifted his activities to Norfolk where Loyalist sentiment was stronger.

By the time the second Virginia Convention assembled in Richmond on 17 July 1775, the representatives knew that the war had started and that the Continental Congress had raised troops, including two companies of riflemen in Virginia. Two days later it voted to raise troops. By the time the convention adjourned on 26 August, it had expanded its military actions to include forming two full-time regiments to confront Dunmore and a number of separate companies to occupy frontier forts in case the Indians attacked. It had also taken control of the militia structure and supplemented the local defense force with a set of minute battalions to replace the volunteer companies. The minutemen undertook extra training, and provided a force that could mobilize quickly and move to a threatened location outside its own immediate area. Patrick Henry, despite a lack of military experience, became the colony's commander in chief.

Confrontation finally erupted in Hampton between 24 and 27 October. One of Dunmore's tenders had gone aground and was destroyed by the militia. In retaliation, Dunmore sent parties ashore to destroy several houses, and the troops who were camped in Williamsburg on the grounds of the college responded. A skirmish resulted, marking the first engagement of the war in Virginia. The following month a second area of confrontation developed on the south side of the James River, and both sides established outposts near Great Bridge, with more skirmishing on 15 November at Kemp's Landing. In his report to London on 6 December, Dunmore claimed that popular support for this minor engagement led him to "erect the King's Standard." This phrase describes a formal step

in the suppression of rebellion, requiring all residents to assemble under arms to defend the Crown and making a refusal to comply an act of treason punishable by death. He also used his authority as the captain-general of the colony to raise two groups of Provincial forces—the Queen's Own Loyal Virginia Regiment and Lord Dunmore's Ethiopian Regiment. The latter unit consisted of slaves who had left their masters to join the British, serving under white officers and noncommissioned officers.

After some further skirmishing, Colonel William Woodford moved a force of the regulars (who would become Continentals on 28 December 1775) and minutemen. They defeated the governor's forces at Great Bridge on 9 December, and occupied Norfolk five days later. Crowded aboard ships in the Elizabeth River and unable to get provisions, Dunmore turned the guns of his small squadron on Norfolk on 1 January 1776. Destruction of the largest town in Virginia completed the polarization of the colony and eroded much of the remaining Loyalist support. Dunmore had to evacuate the lower Hampton Roads area and tried to set up a new base in Chesapeake Bay, but was driven from Gwynn Island on 8–10 July 1776. The forces that survived this defeat and a smallpox epidemic sailed further up the bay to the Potomac River. After burning several plantations and engaging militia from both Virginia and Maryland, Dunmore finally put out to sea on 7 August 1776.

BRITISH RAIDS, 1779–1781

Virginia was spared any further military action east of the mountains during the three years following Dunmore's departure. The state supported the 1776 defense of Charleston, South Carolina, but sent most of its Continentals north to fight in George Washington's main army. Then, on 4 December 1779, the Continental Congress (at Washington's suggestion) ordered the Virginia moved to the Southern Department, where it would spend the rest of the war. Meanwhile the Chesapeake Bay had emerged as a critical component of the American economy because the tobacco from Virginia and Maryland had become the cash export crop which propped up the foreign credit needed to import military supplies and manufactured goods. Destroying that trade played a very important role in George Sackville Germain's "southern strategy," which was adopted after the French entered the war. In addition to a loose naval blockade, General Henry Clinton undertook a series of raids as soon as he could spare the resources.

Mathew-Collier raid, 1779. The first of these amphibious operations departed from New York on 4 May 1779 under Commodore Sir John Collier and Major General Edward Mathew. It was a relatively modest expedition, with three regiments (one each of Highlanders, Germans, and Loyalists) and several flank companies. The troops were

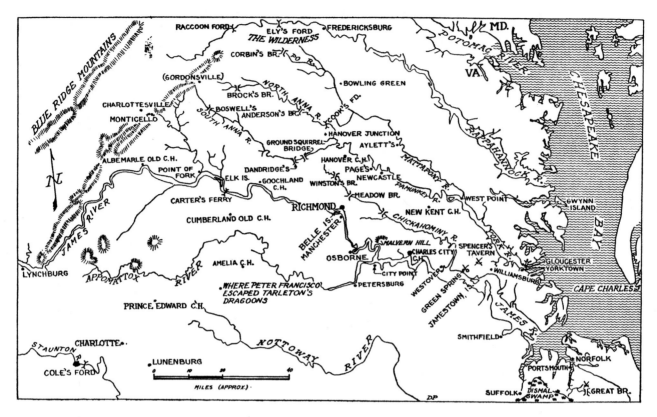

Virginia Military Operations: 1. THE GALE GROUP

on board 22 transports, escorted by one ship of the line, one frigate, four smaller warships, and four privateers. They entered Chesapeake Bay on 8 May and came to in Hampton Roads on the next day. On the 10th the expedition crossed over to the mouth of the Elizabeth River and took Fort Nelson before moving on to nearby Portsmouth. Over the course of several days the invaders captured or destroyed ships, supplies, and tobacco in the various communities within reach of the water, penetrating as far as Suffolk. They finally departed the Bay on 26 May, having inflicted major damage with almost no casualties, and reached New York on the 29th.

Leslie's raid, 1780. On 12 October 1780 Clinton issued orders to Major General Alexander Leslie to take a 2,500-man task force to the Chesapeake Bay and try to carry out a diversionary operation to take pressure off of Lieutenant General Charles Cornwallis in North Carolina. While giving Leslie a free hand to pick the best way of accomplishing his task, Clinton recommended that he sail up the James River and destroy the magazines at Petersburg and Richmond, and then fall back to set up a base on the Elizabeth River. Once in the bay, Leslie's force would fall under Cornwallis's operational control. Leslie's key units were the Guards Brigade, the Eighty-second Foot, the

Hesse-Cassel Regiment von Bose, and several Loyalist units. It put out from Sandy Hook on the 17th with two frigates and a sloop as escorts and quickly reached the Chesapeake, putting troops ashore at Portsmouth on the evening of 22 October. From there, raiding parties struck Hampton, Newport News, and Nansemond County. Meanwhile, Leslie received word from Colonel Francis Rawdon telling him that Cornwallis would prefer that the expedition move on to the field force in North Carolina. Up until this point, the limited state and Continental forces in Virginia under Brigadier General Peter Muhlenberg could only watch from a safe distance. Acting on Rawdon's information, Leslie embarked on 11 to 16 November and sailed south on 22 November, when winds finally permitted them to sail. The raid itself was more of a nuisance than a real threat to the state, but Leslie's report to Clinton set the stage for future actions. He said that he had left his fortifications at Portsmouth intact, and he recommended that future operations in the Chesapeake Bay employ shallow-draft craft to carry out economic raids throughout the bay's watershed.

Arnold's raid, 1781. The third attack on Virginia came as the result of Clinton's continuing desire to interrupt the state's support for Major General Nathanael Greene's operations against Cornwallis in the Carolinas. On 20 December 1780 Benedict Arnold, now a British general, sailed from New York with about 1,600 troops and supporting warships to conduct amphibious operations. On 30 December they reached Hampton Roads and found that the state authorities did not have the resources to put up much of a defense. Arnold moved up the James River with his remaining 1,200 men in captured American vessels. They destroyed the battery at Hood's Point on 3 January 1781 and occupied Richmond on 5–6 January. After destroying the important Westham Foundry, burning tobacco, supplies, and some buildings, Arnold withdrew to Westover. Lieutenant John Graves Simcoe broke up a militia concentration at Charles City Courthouse on the 8th, and then the force embarked and slowly worked its way back downriver. On 23 January, from a base at Portsmouth, Arnold sent word to Clinton that he and his subordinates believed that the ability to exploit their control over the Virginia waterways would enable a relatively small force to negate the huge manpower advantage of the American militia. They merely felt that there were better places than Portsmouth to use as the base.

Lafayette's expedition, 1781. Although Virginia itself lacked the resources to defend itself, and Governor Thomas Jefferson did not possess the expertise to deal with Arnold, Washington stepped in. While the prospect of capturing the traitor was appealing, the American leaders and their French allies in Newport, Rhode Island, saw the exposed nature of the Portsmouth base as an opportunity to crush an isolated British force. He picked Major General Lafayette (Marie Joseph Paul Yves Roch Gilbert du Montier) to lead an elite force south, and asked the French to provide a naval force to prevent Arnold's escape. On 19 February, Washington's main army's light infantry companies assembled at Peekskill as three regiments, commanded by Joseph Vose, Jean-Joseph de Gimat, and Francis Barber. The assembled force included four artillery companies under Lieutenant Colonel Ebenezer Stevens. With three light infantry regiments drawn from the New England and New Jersey Continentals, Lafayette's command was about 1,500 officers and men when it started south.

The companion French effort bogged down when it ran into a streak of bad luck. A storm scattered the British squadron watching Newport, enabling a ship of the line, two frigates, and a cutter to get to sea on 9 February 1781. These ships entered the Chesapeake Bay on 13 February. Although they captured eleven British vessels, including the forty-four-gun frigate *Romulus*, they could not trap Arnold because the French ships drew too much water to work their way up the Elizabeth River to Portsmouth. The task force returned to Newport on 24 February. A much larger task force, including nearly 1,200 troops, sailed under the command of Captain Charles Destouches on

8 March, five days after Lafayette reached Head of Elk on his overland march to Annapolis (the designated rendezvous point). Admiral Marriott Arbuthnot started out thirty-six hours behind the French, but actually arrived ahead of them. The French had seven ships of the line, two frigates, and an armed storeship; Arbuthnot had seven ships of the line, one fifty-gun ship, and three frigates. The squadrons engaged just outside the mouth of Chesapeake Bay on 16 March. Destouches emerged from this fight, which lasted an hour and Forty-five minutes, in slightly better shape than his adversary, but he abandoned the expedition because he could not put his troops ashore. Arbuthnot limped into the Chesapeake and made contact with Arnold.

With the sea routes now open, Clinton sent Major General William Phillips with 2,000 more troops to reinforce Arnold and to assume command. His orders, issued on 10 March, gave Phillips the task of holding a Chesapeake base (Portsmouth, or some other port) and destroying American magazines at Petersburg, Appomattox, or along the James River. Phillips's convoy anchored in Hampton Roads on 25 March, bringing the total Crown force in Virginia to at least 3,000 men, and he assumed command two days later. Major General Frederick Steuben was the Continental army commander opposing Phillips, having been assigned to the state by Greene to organize the flow of replacements and supplies to the south. While there were relatively few Continentals available, mostly green troops, Brigadier Generals Muhlenberg, Thomas Nelson, and George Weedon had built up some 4,000 militia and state troops in the general area. This mix could not pose a threat of assaulting Portsmouth, but they were strong enough to limit the ability of the British to penetrate very far inland. Lafayette's far more dangerous light infantry command was still in Maryland, more than 150 miles from Richmond.

Meanwhile, Phillips did not sit idle. As soon as he felt the defenses of Portsmouth were completed, he started sending out raiding parties. The first departed on 18 April and went up the James River; Arnold led one division ashore near Williamsburg, while a second party landed above. The goal was to trap the Americans occupying the town, but the force failed in that object and pushed on into Yorktown on the other side of the Peninsula, where it destroyed the abandoned American defenses. A brief skirmish took place at Burrell's Ferry. The British then resumed their movement upriver, with the objective of confronting the Americans who had concentrated at Petersburg. Phillips landed at City Point on 24 April and, despite brief resistance by Steuben, took Petersburg on 25 April. Phillips then took part of the force on to Chesterfield Courthouse, while Arnold detoured to destroy the remnants of the Virginia state navy at Osborne's on 27 April. The columns reunited and continued on to Manchester on the south bank of the James opposite Richmond. Arriving in the morning of the 30th,

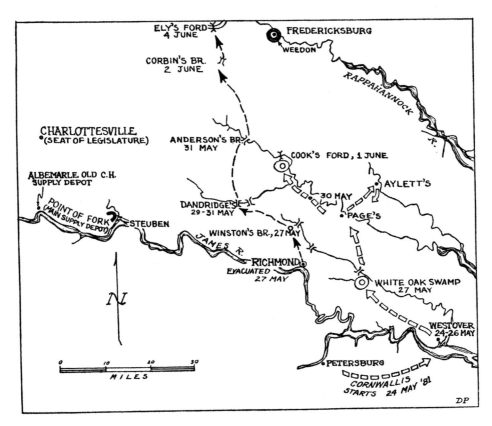

Virginia Military Operations: 2. THE GALE GROUP

they discovered that Lafayette had arrived in Richmond the evening before with his Continental light infantry.

LAFAYETTE'S MARCH TO RICHMOND

The inability of the French Rhode Island squadron to reach Virginia, combined with Phillips's expedition, altered the nature of Lafayette's expedition. Instead of waiting for transports, he moved overland with the mission of keeping the British from interfering with the southern army's lines of communications. In Baltimore Lafayette borrowed £2,000 from the merchants to buy material for summer clothing to replace the winter uniforms of his troops. Expecting the British to head for Richmond, Lafayette left his tents and artillery to follow at their own pace and, moving by forced marches; he left Baltimore on 19 April, moving through Alexandria, Fredericksburg, and Bowling Green to reach Richmond the evening of the 29th, a few hours ahead of Phillips. Surprised by this speed, Phillips withdrew to the vicinity of Jamestown Island. Learning on 7 May that Cornwallis was moving to join him at Petersburg, Phillips re-entered that place on the 10th. Cornwallis arrived on the 20th, seven days after Phillips died of a sudden illness. Later, additional troops (the Seventeenth and Forty-third Foot and the two

Anspach-Bayreuth regiments) from Clinton landed at Portsmouth.

CORNWALLIS VS. LAFAYETTE

British strategy in Virginia failed in one of its main objectives: to help Cornwallis hold the Carolinas and Georgia. In complete defiance of Clinton's instructions to make the security of South Carolina and Georgia his primary mission, Cornwallis had chosen to invade Virginia, leaving Rawdon to try and keep Greene at bay. After assuming command at Petersburg, Cornwallis controlled about 7,200 British, German, and Loyalist troops, of whom some 5,300 were rank-and-file soldiers that Clinton considered fully fit for duty.

Lafayette, meanwhile, had assumed command from Steuben as the senior Continental officer in Virginia. His troops consisted of his three light infantry regiments, 500 eighteen-month-service Virginia Continental recruits assembled by Steuben into provisional battalions, the remnants of Armand's First Partisan Corps, some Virginia state troops, and two companies of volunteer horsemen under John Mercer and Nicholas Moore. Working to assemble and hold together several thousand militia were Muhlenberg and Weedon (both Virginia

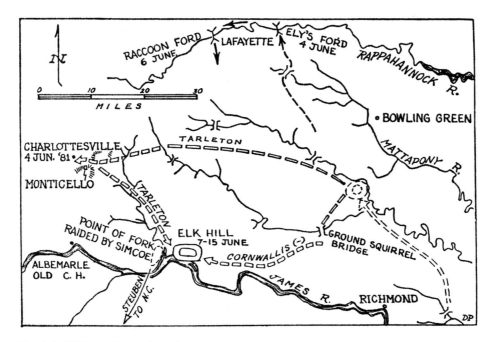

Virginia Military Operations: 3. THE GALE GROUP

Continental officers), state Brigadier Generals Robert Lawson and Edward Stevens (two former Continental colonels), and Thomas Nelson, the brigadier general who had just succeeded Thomas Jefferson as governor. Riflemen from the western counties were requested, but they did not arrive until relatively late in the campaign. The critical reinforcement whose delayed arrival shaped Lafayette's strategy was the body of Pennsylvania regulars under Anthony Wayne.

Cornwallis left Petersburg on 24 May, crossed the James River at Westover, and camped at Hanover Junction on 1 June. (Arnold left for New York on the 6th, taking two Loyalist regiments.) Lafayette fell back from Winston's Bridge, eight miles north of Richmond, on 28 May, and covered 70 miles in seven days. To keep in a position to be reinforced by Wayne and Steuben, he retreated north through the wilderness to Ely's Ford on the Rapidan River, 20 miles above Fredericksburg. Cornwallis pursued only 30 miles, stopping on the North Anna River. Unable to catch the Americans and force them to give battle, he now turned his attention to destroying materiel. General Banastre Tarleton led a raid to Charlottesville on 4 June, and Simcoe led another to Point of Fork on 5 June. Meanwhile, Cornwallis moved slowly toward Point of Fork, about 45 miles up the James River from Richmond, and established a camp at Elk Hill after brushing aside Steuben's token resistance. His raiders joined him here on 9 June, and he prepared to send Tarleton to raid the supply point at Albemarle Old Courthouse (on the James, 20 miles west of Elk Hill).

Cornwallis cancelled this new operation when he learned that Wayne had finally joined Lafayette and that their combined forces were moving toward Elk Hill. Wayne's departure from York, Pennsylvania, had been delayed by lack of supplies and unsatisfied payrolls. He was about to start when his troops, most of whom had been reorganized after the mutiny of the Pennsylvania Line, showed signs of another mutiny. (This time they were dissatisfied about being paid in Continental currency without the depreciated value added.) Wayne showed no leniency, and executed seven ringleaders of the rebellion. Leaving York the morning of 26 May, Wayne's troops marched into Lafayette's camp on 10 June. Wayne himself had ridden ahead to meet Lafayette about three days earlier. Numbering about 1,000 good troops, Wayne's corps consisted of three provisional Pennsylvania infantry regiments under Richard Butler, Walter Stewart, and Richard Humpton, supported by a detachment of the Fourth Continental Artillery, with six guns.

While this reinforcement did not increase Lafayette's strength enough to risk a major battle, it did enable him to move closer and thereby stop the unopposed raiding. As soon as the forces joined, the Americans moved south from Raccoon Ford on the Rapidan River and, by the morning of 12 June, Lafayette held an excellent defensive position behind Mechunck Creek. There he blocked any British move on Charlottesville (13 miles to the west) and Staunton, where the Americans had moved the stores from Albemarle Old Courthouse. There he was joined

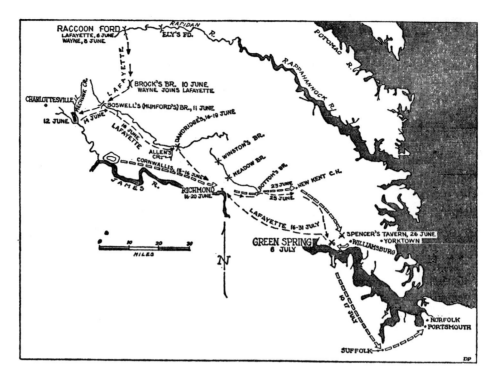

Virginia Military Operations: 4. THE GALE GROUP

by 600 of the frontier riflemen led by William Campbell. Meanwhile, Cornwallis had begun getting letters from Clinton demanding that he pull into a defensive shell and return 3,000 troops to help protect New York City from the Franco-American attack that Clinton was convinced was coming. Although not immediately apparent, the tide had turned. On 15 June Cornwallis left Elk Hill and fell back, reaching Richmond on the 16th. Four days later he started down the Virginia peninsula to Williamsburg, with Lafayette cautiously following and looking for chances to nibble away at the rear guard.

Cornwallis reached Williamsburg on 25 June and remained there until 4 July. The first skirmish between the Marquis de Lafayette and the Earl of Cornwallis came on 26 July at Spencer's Tavern (called Spencer's Ordinary in the eighteenth century), seven miles from Williamsburg. A more serious engagement came when Cornwallis left Williamsburg and began crossing to the south side of the James River near the site of the Jamestown settlement. Cornwallis deliberately tried to lure Lafayette into a trap at Green Spring on 6 July, but the Americans fell back after some heavy fighting. Lafayette withdrew to Malvern Hill; Cornwallis continued east to Suffolk. He then moved to the Portsmouth base, which he didn't like. (The 3,000-man detachment he expected never was sent.) Tarleton's Virginia Raid, which took place from 9–24 July 1781, was a dramatic cavalry operation, but it was meaningless. The stage was now set for the Yorktown Campaign.

SIGNIFICANCE

Governor Thomas Nelson summarized the impact of the war's Virginia campaigns in a letter he sent from Richmond to Washington on 27 July 1781. He wrote that they (the campaigns) "have made Whigs of Tories." By this, Nelson meant that each appearance by the Crown's forces prompted Loyalists to reveal themselves; and each time, when the British left, the Loyalists had to leave as well, or suffer the wrath of their neighbors. Other sympathizers turned against the king's men when they saw indiscriminate destruction and plundering. By the summer of 1781, very few Loyalists remained in the Old Dominion. Nelson also pointed out that each invasion saw a sea-borne force arrive and strike at areas which were lightly defended and then withdraw as the Americans assembled troops. It became clear that, sooner or later, British luck would run out.

SEE ALSO *Arnold's Raid in Virginia; Chesapeake Bay; Great Bridge, Virginia; Hampton, Virginia; Henry, Patrick; Lafayette, Marquis de; Murray, John; Virginia, Mobilization in.*

BIBLIOGRAPHY

Clark, William Bell, et al., eds. *Naval Documents of the American Revolution.* 11 vols. to date. Washington: Government Printing Office, 1964–.

Cometti, Elizabeth. "Depredations in Virginia During the Revolution." In *The Old Dominion: Essays for Thomas Perkins*

Abernathy. Edited by Darret B. Rutman. Charlottesville: University Press of Virginia, 1964: 135–151.

Eckenrode, Hamilton J. *The Revolution in Virginia.* Boston: Houghton Mifflin Co., 1916.

———. *The Story of the Campaign and Siege of Yorktown.* Washington, D.C.: Government Printing Office, 1931.

Fleming, Thomas J. *Beat the Last Drum: The Siege of Yorktown, 1781.* New York: St. Martin's Press, 1963.

Johnston, Henry P. *The Yorktown Campaign and the Surrender of Cornwallis, 1781.* New York: Harper and Brothers, 1881.

Kemble, Stephen. "Journal of Lieutenant Colonel Stephen Kemble, 1773–1789; and British Army Orders: General Sir William Howe, 1775–1778; General Sir Henry Clinton, 1778; and General Daniel Jones, 1778." *New-York Historical Society Collections for 1884.*

McIlwaine, Henry Read, ed. *Official Letters of the Governors of the State of Virginia.* 3 vols. Richmond: Virginia State Library, 1926–1929.

Selby, John E. *The Revolution in Virginia, 1775–1783.* Charlottesville: University Press of Virginia, 1988.

Simcoe, John Graves. *Simcoe's Military Journal. A History of the Operations of a Partisan Corps, Called the Queen's Rangers, Commanded by Lieutenant Colonel J. G. Simcoe, During the War of the American Revolution.* New York: Bartlett & Welford, 1844.

Stevens, Benjamin Franklin, editor. *The Campaign in Virginia 1781. An exact Reprint of Six rare Pamphlets on the Clinton-Cornwallis Controversy with very numerous important Unpublished portions of the letters in their Appendixes added from the Original Manuscripts.* 2 vols. London: Privately printed, 1888.

Tartar, Brent, ed. "The Orderly Book of the Second Virginia Regiment, September 27, 1775–April 15, 1776." *Virginia Magazine of History and Biography* 85 (April, July 1977): 156–183, 302–336.

Van Schreevan, William J., et al., eds. *Revolutionary Virginia: The Road to Independence.* 7 vols. Charlottesville: University Press of Virginia for the Virginia Independence Bicentennial Commission, 1973–1983.

revised by Robert K. Wright Jr.

VIRGINIA, MOBILIZATION IN.

In 1775 Virginians began an eight-year-long war with Britain that they had neither predicted nor desired. What became the War for Independence was one of the longest, most divisive, and deadliest conflicts since the colony's founding and would at times bring the Old Dominion to its knees. Mobilization for the Revolutionary War strained the resources even of Virginia, the most valuable British mainland colony, and as in many other colonies, it exacerbated preexisting social tensions and created new divisions—mainly over the important questions of who should serve and who should pay for the costs of war. But mobilization in Virginia was also hampered in significant and sometimes surprising ways by the presence of hundreds of thousands of enslaved workers in the colony. In the end, the demands of war in a slave society would prove crippling as Virginia struggled throughout the conflict to mobilize effectively.

Though Virginians had participated in the colonial protests over British imperial measures since the mid-1760s—and, indeed, had been at the forefront of many of them—Patriot leaders stepped up their resistance once the British response to the Boston Tea Party became clear. The more militant Patriot leaders throughout the eastern seaboard circulated plans for a continental congress and a plan of association that included a boycott of trade between Britain and the mainland colonies. As the summer progressed, however, there were growing fears that more than just economic resistance might be necessary to counter the British; indeed, the Boston Port Act in particular was seen by some as an invasion, and from the middle of 1774, many travelers in Virginia began to note the increased militancy of many Virginians.

INDEPENDENT COMPANIES

At first, Patriot leaders began organizing themselves into Independent Companies of Gentlemen Volunteers. That is because the established militia was still technically under the control of the royal governor, Lord Dunmore. Moreover, the militia had played a diminishing role in the lives of most Virginians over previous decades, and Patriot leaders were still unclear how their fellow white Virginians would react to a general call for mobilization. The Independent Companies would allow Patriot leaders to present a show of militancy to both British officials and to the increasingly restive slaves of Virginians; ready Patriots for possible conflict; and provide a training ground for gentlemen, who could then become officers if resistance escalated. Though few ordinary Virginians seemed interested in the Independent Companies, Governor Dunmore became increasingly irritated by their presence.

Only two days after General Gage marched out and provoked the famous confrontations at Lexington and Concord—an event still unknown to Virginians—Governor Dunmore made a move against militants in his colony, seizing gunpowder from the Williamsburg public magazine in the early hours of 21 April 1775. Unlike Gage's ill-fated expedition, however, there was no bloodshed in Virginia. Dunmore claimed that he had removed the powder because of rumors that Virginia's enslaved population intended to rise up against its white masters. At the same time, Dunmore warned that he would arm enslaved Virginians if Patriot leaders did not curb the militants in the Independent Companies. Given that many slaves had already begun making their way to the governor with offers of help, moderates feared that Dunmore's threats were not idle ones.

Dunmore's actions and threats stirred up a hornet's nest, and thousands of white Virginians flew to arms. While moderate Patriot leaders appealed for calm and tried to avert civil war, ordinary Virginians swelled the ranks of the Independent Companies, elected their own officers, and debated whether to march against the governor. After several weeks of aggressive posturing and skirmishing, and after hearing of news of the Battle of Breed's Hill outside Boston, militants forced Dunmore to flee for safety on board one of the royal ships in the Chesapeake Bay. Though the perceived erosion of political rights helped convince some Virginians to mobilize for possible conflict, particular local issues—especially threats of armed insurrections by enslaved Virginians—helped spur mobilization on a broader scale, which in turn contributed to the rapid deterioration of imperial relations in the colony. Dunmore's flight from Williamsburg on 8 June 1775, at least in retrospect, signaled the end of royal government in Virginia.

Faced with almost inevitable war against Britain and anxious to reassert control over the increasingly anarchic situation in Virginia, Patriot leaders quickly moved to curb the militancy of the autonomous Independent Companies by replacing them with a more structured, hierarchical, and responsive military organization, one that fused elements of old and new military thinking. In the third Virginia Convention in July 1775, Patriot leaders devised a three-tiered military organization. Drawing on past military experience—most recently in the Seven Years' War—they ordered the creation of two regiments of regular troops that would serve as Virginia's contingent of Continental soldiers but act as a permanent home guard. Patriot leaders also resurrected the militia, in which all white males between the ages of eighteen and fifty would be enrolled. Finally, Patriot leaders also called for the recruitment of sixteen battalions of elite militia, called the minutemen, who would serve as a first line of defence for the colony against the British. Patriot leaders hoped that such a system would not only protect them from the British, but that it would also deter black Virginians from taking advantage of the civil war and making their own bids for freedom. To ensure this dual role, Patriot leaders gave commanding officers in the militia new powers to appoint and lead slave patrols and exempted from service altogether all overseers of at least four enslaved Virginians.

If these initial proposals reflected a concern about race and slavery within Virginia, they also reflected Patriot leaders' class-based perspectives on mobilization. For it was clear from the outset that most of these leaders believed that the two regiments of Continental soldiers should and would be composed of men similar in social standing as those drafted to serve in regular units in the Seven Years' War—the poor and marginal. Many gentlemen warned their sons to stay clear of the regular service and not to serve as mere "common Soldiers." Instead, many secured appointments as officers in the service. But if service in the regular army proved unattractive for gentlemen and their sons, service in the minutemen proved unattractive for many ordinary white Virginians. Having elected their own officers in the Independent Companies, few former volunteers were happy about having appointed officers imposed on them from above and paid much more than enlisted men. And while they acted spontaneously in the Independent Companies, most would-be minutemen were reluctant to spend any unnecessary time away from their farms training in the new service as required by law. Finally, many poorer or smallholding militiamen particularly resented the exemptions allowed in the militia. They believed the exemption of overseers shielded wealthier slave owners from military service at the expense of nonslaveholders. Patriot leaders wanted a disciplined armed force that they could control; ordinary white Virginians wanted a greater say in return for the sacrifices they were being asked to make.

RECRUITING THE POOR

By choosing order over democracy, Patriot leaders quashed enthusiasm for the cause. In the end, too few Virginians stepped forward to make the minutemen service a viable defense force. Incredibly, the minutemen service stalled even after Governor Dunmore had upped the ante in Virginia in November 1775 by declaring the slaves and servants of rebel masters free if they could reach his lines and join him to fight against the Patriot forces. Even the renewed threat of racial war failed to mobilize middling white Virginians in sufficient numbers, and not for the last time in the conflict. Consequently, by December 1775 Patriot leaders had all but scrapped the minutemen service and, in desperation, instead called for a vastly enlarged regular service that they hoped would serve as a permanent wartime professional army for the protection of the state. At the same time, they also pleaded with Congress to include this contingent as part of Virginia's contribution to the Continental army. In doing so, the leading Patriots signaled that they would not rely on middling citizens in the militia for the colony's defense; instead, they would award generous enlistment bounties and regular pay to anyone who would give up their independence and submit to the more onerous regulations governing the Continental army. To put it another way, as early as the end of 1775, Virginia's leaders had concluded that it was better to pay the poor to fight on behalf of taxpaying citizens and the ruling class than to send the sons of the elite and middling classes to war and risk social upheaval.

Initially, this policy enjoyed some success. Enlistments for the newly enlarged regular army were brisk throughout the early months of 1776. But as bad news from the northern theater began to reach Virginia in the early summer, enlistments began to fall off. And as Washington called for increasing numbers of soldiers to stave off British advances around New York, fewer Virginians stepped forward as it looked more and more likely that they would be sent northward, far from their homes and families. In turn, Patriot leaders began thinking about new ways of "encouraging" enlistments into the army, revealing more explicitly their thinking about who ought to serve. At the end of 1776, for example, the assembly gave justices of the peace and the governor wide powers to imprison and ultimately impress "rogues and vagabonds" into the armed services. By the spring of 1777, the assembly also sanctioned the recruitment of free blacks into the army.

With still only as little as one-quarter of its new quota raised by May 1777, Virginia also succumbed to pressure from Washington and Congress and instituted a draft for soldiers. But contrary to congressional recommendations that men be drafted universally, Virginia legislators decided that draftees would be those who could "be best spared, and will be most serviceable," to be decided by the field officers and the top four magistrates of the county. Virginia's Revolutionary leaders, then, fell back on a colonial strategy of targeting the more vulnerable in society. As one recruiting officer put it later in the year, the draft was designed to force the "expendables" into service, or more explicitly, according to one Virginian, the "Lazy fellows who lurk about and are pests to Society."

If Revolutionary leaders and middling Virginians were content to shift the burden of fighting, the lower sort upon whom that burden fell were quick to fight back. Would-be recruits forced Patriots to raise bounty money, bargained with their neighbors for their services, and resisted and evaded the draft when coerced into service. In some places, they violently resisted any and all attempts to conscript soldiers. In other places, once drafted they simply deserted and found refuge, usually with friends and family. Lower-class resistance was so vehement that, by early 1778, Virginia legislators were forced to abandon the idea of raising men by a draft altogether and turned instead to high bounties and short terms of service. When the assembly made economic enticements the sole inducement to join the army in 1778 and 1779, the inflation of bounty rewards accelerated. By the fall of 1779, the sums given to recruits for the army had reached critical and crippling proportions. Because of rising inflation, Edmund Pendleton thought that almost every man enlisted had cost, on average, about five thousand pounds each.

Some Virginians, of course, were happy to serve on any terms. Many men, for example, were willing to exchange one kind of bondage for another. In 1775 the third Virginia Convention had forbidden recruiters to enlist any servants at all unless they were apprentices who had the written consent of their masters. Yet desperation drove recruiters to enlist anyone who seemed willing to serve. Indentured and convict servants took full advantage. But enslaved Virginians also took advantage of the desperate need for soldiers by offering themselves to recruiters under the guise of being freemen. The prohibition of 1775 against enlisting servants presumably applied to enslaved Virginians, for on that front the Convention was completely silent. However, at some point between 1775 and early 1777, desperate recruiters began allowing free blacks into the Virginia line. But enslaved Virginians knew that in the face of a shortage of white enlistments, recruiters were more likely to enlist blacks whether enslaved or free. By the middle years of the war, blacks constituted a significant minority in Virginia's line in the Continental army. Because middling and upper-class whites refused to fight for themselves, and because even lower-class whites only reluctantly joined the army, necessity forced white Virginians to rely on blacks for their defense.

The end result of lower-class resistance through the middle years of the war was that the war effort simply ground to a halt. Despite the pleas of Continental officials, Virginia legislators failed to put teeth into their recruiting laws through the latter part of 1778, throughout 1779, and into 1780. The returns of the First Virginia Regiment, probably the strongest regiment from the state at any given moment during the war, showed the shortcomings of Virginia military policy in the war's midyears. In September 1776 there were 590 men enrolled in the regiment (though only 406 were present and fit for duty). By the end of 1779, even after being reinforced with remnants of the Ninth and Tenth Virginia Regiments, the First consisted of only 295 men, most of whose terms of service were expiring. Finally, just before its capture at Charleston, South Carolina, in May 1780, the strength of the Regiment was listed at just 195 effective men. "Virginia," wrote one army chaplain definitively, "makes the poorest figure of any State in the Recruiting way."

THE WAR MOVES SOUTHWARD

While Virginians divided among themselves and hoped for peace, the British began moving to bring the war to the South and open up a new front in the stagnating conflict. With the British believing themselves to be at a stalemate in the North, the southern colonies began to look more inviting to them by 1778–1779. It was not until British strategy shifted southward that state leaders again took the war seriously—only, in fact, when Virginia lost the remnants of its contingent of Continental soldiers at the fall of Charleston in 1780. The members of the assembly, under mounting pressure from Congress and from officers such as Washington, finally expanded their mobilization efforts. They did so by putting increased pressure on the middling classes, both by requiring from them more extensive militia service and by reinstituting and expanding the draft, this time to include all men.

Calls on the militia for more frequent service in Virginia and in neighboring states escalated after 1778 in the face of British raids. But the more the assembly and governor called on the militia, the more middling white Virginians protested. Ordinary farmers and planters demanded that calls be limited, for short terms of service, and for service only close to home. Most were adamant that they would not serve outside the state, and particularly in the hotter climates of the states to the south of them. But middling men in the militia were equally insistent that their taxpaying status should exempt them from fighting altogether and that the state ought to spend their tax money on raising a proper army and filling it with their lower-class neighbors. Petitioners in the militia claimed that full citizens of the new Republic had the right not to serve but to pay others to do it for them. Only by pushing lower-class men into a permanent army, they warned, could the government quell the "great uneasiness and disquiet in the Country" caused by militia call outs and high taxes.

SLAVERY AND RECRUITMENT

But middling Virginians were equally concerned about serving in the military because of the shadow of slavery. The presence of a large number of enslaved Virginians in the state affected mobilization in several significant ways. In the first place, many slaveholders were worried about losing their valuable property amidst the British raids and invasion. But many white Virginians also harbored a deep-seated fear that Virginia's enslaved population might do more than just take the opportunity to escape to the British. With first-hand accounts raising alarms, they feared that Virginia's slaves would revolt and kill their masters. Such worries, perhaps predictably, kept many militia at home when the British invaded the state.

Slavery also had a less obvious impact on mobilization in Virginia. Though many historians have assumed that slavery helped unify white communities in times of trouble, the ownership of enslaved Virginians actually aggravated deep divisions among whites. Nonslaveholders, for example, were quick to claim that military service for slaveholders was much less of a burden than for those without slaves. Slaveowners still had someone to labor for them in their absence. Moreover, many nonslaveholders believed that slaveholders had enjoyed too many exemptions from fighting altogether. Under the strain of war, resentments became glaring divides. In the midst of one British raid up the Potomac, for example, many of the militia of the Northern Neck refused to serve, declaring

"the Rich wanted the Poor to fight for them, to defend there property, whilst they refused to fight for themselves." Slaveholding, then, particularly towards the end of the war, increasingly became the touchstone for class divisions among white Virginians.

Given these seemingly intractable considerations, Patriot leaders were forced into thinking about some revolutionary proposals. In the fall of 1780, Virginia legislators announced a radical new plan to raise a more permanent army. They proposed offering volunteers, in addition to the Continental bounty (which still included a parcel of land), an enslaved Virginian between the ages of ten and forty years old. After years of resistance and holding out for the best leverage for their services, lower-class Virginians were finally able to extract a huge windfall in return for serving in the military. Not only would they get enough land to vote, but they would also receive money enough to establish themselves and even an enslaved Virginian to make that land more productive. And legislators may have hoped that in addition to raising a more permanent army, they were also making a judicious move to shore up what was clearly a tenuous alliance between poor whites and wealthy slave owners to resist the British invasion.

Significantly, Revolutionary leaders stopped short of making the most obvious move of enlisting slaves rather than using them as part of the bounty to enlist poor whites. James Madison, for example, thought it would be much better if Patriot leaders in Virginia took the more obvious step and allow enslaved Virginians themselves to serve. He thought that such a move would "certainly be more consonant to the principles of liberty which ought never to be lost sight of in a contest for liberty." Most of Madison's elite colleagues in the assembly, however, were not prepared to move so far. The war had already chipped away at the institution of slavery on a number of different fronts. Many gentlemen believed that officially arming enslaved Virginians and offering them their freedom would amount to a virtual emancipation call across the state. Patriot leaders were not going to go that far, regardless of the costs.

INVASION OF VIRGINIA

As it turned out, the new recruiting law was undermined by a fresh British offensive in the state that began in January 1781. Increased militia call outs and general protests against the new law ensured that it was ineffective. Few recruits actually stepped forward, and many counties refused to implement the recruiting law in sympathy with their militia or in fear of what might happen if they did. Worse, though, when local officials tried forcibly to draft men, it caused widespread unease, discontent, and in some cases collective and violent resistance. As for the permanent army Washington wanted, in 1781 Virginia managed to scrape up just 773 men, or a mere 24 percent of the 3,250 men for whom Washington had called. Pressure from below thoroughly disabled mobilization for the regular army in 1781. Though repeated British invasions helped undermine the draft in Virginia, the militia's sometimes intense, sometimes passive, but persistent local resistance to state laws had brought recruiting to a halt.

Nor did white Virginians do much better in rallying themselves to the battlefield as militia. As the British made further inroads into the state, Virginians seemed powerless to stop them, and many militiamen throughout Virginia actually rioted in protest against both the draft for Continental soldiers and the militia call outs. In the end, while Washington and Lafayette hurried to Virginia with the remains of the Continental army in the hopes of trapping Cornwallis at Yorktown, white Virginians divided among themselves. The end of the war came at Yorktown, but with only an indifferent contribution from Virginians. Even the best estimates of the number of militia at Yorktown show that perhaps no more than 3,000 Virginia militia out of a potential 50,000 participated in some way; 7,800 French troops and over 5,000 Continental troops—mainly from states north of Virginia—played the greatest role. In the critical year of 1781, Revolutionary leaders in Virginia reaped the fruits of the divisive policies they had sown over the preceding years of war.

AFTER THE WAR

Close attention to mobilization, then, reveals that like many other states, Virginia was wracked by internal divisions and conflicts, often over the all-important question of who should serve or at least bear the burden of the costs of the war. Such conflicts continued in the postwar era but significantly, most protagonists then rested the legitimacy of their arguments on their wartime sacrifices, however great or small. Middling Virginians, for example, complained about and evaded high postwar taxes by claiming that they had already made tremendous sacrifices during the war. They also fundamentally changed the tax structure of the new state by continuing to argue that all men ought to bear a share of the costs of the war in proportion to their wealth. Though poorer Virginians and even blacks joined the army and helped win the war, middling militia who stayed at home claimed the fruits of the Revolution. Indeed, slaveholding Virginians even used enslaved Virginians' resistance to justify continued bondage and used their own wartime sacrifices and military service, however limited they may have been, to justify their efforts to keep a tenacious hold on their human property. In doing so, slaveholders used Revolutionary principles and their Revolutionary participation to legitimate the continued enslavement of black Virginians.

Moreover, wartime divisions took on particular importance in America because the war was so central to the political settlement that occurred in many states during the war and, shortly thereafter, at a national level. For example, precisely because so many people defended their own interests and refused to fight the war on terms proposed by elites, elites themselves in turn began thinking about new ways of organizing society and politics to protect the fragile republican experiment of which they were only nominally in charge by the end of the war. Indeed, the divisive and crippling experience of the war helped produce a small group of committed nationalists—including George Washington and many other Continental army officers who had been frustrated by the conflicts at the state level that had undermined the war effort. At the same time, many state leaders believed that Virginia had been abandoned by its northern neighbors in the latter stages of the war and blamed their internal problems on the lack of cooperation between the states. Thus, the political issues that divided Americans in the run-up to the passage of the Constitution and that continued to plague national politics in the 1790s and beyond may, in part at least, be traced to the problems faced by the different states in mobilizing for the War for Independence.

SEE ALSO *Virginia, Military Operations in.*

BIBLIOGRAPHY

Evans, Emory G. "Trouble in the Backcountry: Disaffection in Southwest Virginia during the American Revolution." In *An Uncivil War: The Southern Backcountry during the American Revolution.* Edited by Ronald Hoffman, Thad W. Tate, and Peter J. Albert. Charlottesville: University of Virginia Press, 1985.

Frey, Sylvia R. *Water from a Rock: Black Resistance in a Revolutionary Age.* Princeton, N.J.: Princeton University Press, 1991.

Goldenberg, Joseph A., Eddie D. Nelson, and Rita Y. Fletcher. "Revolutionary Ranks: An Analysis of the Chesterfield Supplement." *Virginia Magazine of History and Biography* 87 (1979): 182–189.

Hast, Adele. *Loyalism in Revolutionary Virginia: The Norfolk Area and the Eastern Shore.* Ann Arbor: University of Michigan Press, 1982.

Holton, Woody. *Forced Founders: Indians, Debtors, Slaves, and the Making of the American Revolution in Virginia.* Chapel Hill: University of North Carolina Press, 1999.

Isaac, Rhys. *The Transformation of Virginia, 1740–1790.* Chapel Hill: University of North Carolina Press, 1982.

McDonnell, Michael A. "Popular Mobilization and Political Culture in Revolutionary Virginia: The Failure of the Minutemen and the Revolution from Below." *Journal of American History* 85 (1998): 946–981.

Sargent, Walter, and John P. Resch, eds. *Revolutionary War and Society.* Dekalb: Northern Illinois University Press, 2006.

Selby, John E. *The Revolution in Virginia, 1775–1783.* Williamsburg, Va.: The Colonial Williamsburg Foundation, 1988.

Shea, William L. *The Virginia Militia in the Seventeenth Century.* Baton Rouge: University of Louisiana Press, 1983.

Tillson, Albert H., Jr. *Gentry and Common Folk: Political Culture on a Virginia Frontier, 1740–1789.* Lexington: University Press of Kentucky, 1991.

Titus, James. *The Old Dominion at War: Society, Politics, and Warfare in Late Colonial Virginia.* Columbia: University of South Carolina Press, 1991.

Van Atta, John R. "Conscription in Revolutionary Virginia: The Case of Culpeper County, 1780–1781." *Virginia Magazine of History and Biography* 92 (1984): 263–281.

Wood, Peter. "'Liberty Is Sweet': African-American Freedom Struggles in the Years before White Independence." In *Beyond the American Revolution: Explorations in the History of American Radicalism.* Edited by Alfred F. Young. Dekalb: Northern Illinois University Press, 1993.

Michael A. McDonnell

VIRGINIA LINE.

VIRGINIA LINE. Along with Massachusetts, Virginia was one of the most populous of the original thirteen states and, as such, both Massachusetts and Virginia each furnished the largest of the state Lines. While the first Virginia Continental units were the two rifle companies formed in June 1775, these were never part of the Line. The state's infantry force began on 21 August 1775 as two full-time regiments, created by the Virginia Convention as part of a comprehensive defense program. This program also included independent frontier guard companies, minutemen, and a reorganized militia. These units were transferred to the Continental army on 1 November. On 28 December the Continental Congress asked Virginia to increase the force to six regiments, but the Convention actually voted instead to raise a total of nine regiments on 11 January 1776. This brought the first two up to a uniform strength and added seven new ones, including one (the Eighth) recruited primarily from the ethnic German settlers in the northwestern part of the colony, and another (the Ninth) raised mostly in the Delmarva Peninsula ("Eastern Shore"). The Continental Congress accepted all nine into their service. A final six regiments were added when the Army was expanded for 1777, producing four Virginia brigades formed into two divisions.

Although Virginia raised the regiments with relative ease, the state had a much harder time keeping them up to strength and making good the losses from combat and by the expiration of the original enlistments. Two consecutive temporary consolidations took place in 1778 in an effort to keep all active units at effective strength for combat, with surplus officers returning home to try to recruit. The state government even loaned its own two infantry battalions to General George Washington to help offset the losses. Finally, on 12 May 1779, Washington faced the fact that his native state just could not provide all the troops he needed, and he reluctantly reorganized and renumbered the Line's regiments to a total of eleven units. When the Line was sent in December of that year to reinforce the Southern Department, it carried out another temporary reorganization by transferring the enlisted men into the three senior regiments and promising to organize contingents of new men or veterans who would reenlist if given a furlough to follow.

The first two of those detachments joined the regiments in Charleston in time to be captured; the third was destroyed by Banastre Tarleton at the Waxhaws soon thereafter. Major General Frederick Steuben accompanied Nathaniel Greene to the south at the end of 1780 and remained in Virginia to organize the efforts to rebuild a semblance of a Line. More provisional battalions were formed in time to either join Greene in the Carolinas or help at Yorktown; and for the remainder of the war only provisional formations remained. There was one exception to this provisional approach—the Virginia contingent at Fort Pitt. In May 1778 the Thirteenth Virginia Regiment (which came from the frontier) was sent there, and the regiment remained there despite being renumbered first as the Ninth and then as the Seventh, until it was disbanded on 1 January 1783. The official Virginia quota of regiments dropped to six in 1781 and to two in 1783 before being disbanded on 15 November 1783.

In addition to the Line itself, Virginia also contributed half of the Maryland and Virginia Rifle Regiment, the majority of the First Continental Artillery Regiment, the First and Third Continental Light Dragoons, most of Henry Lee's Second Partisan Corps, and a special unit to guard the prisoner of war facilities in Charlottesville (the Regiment of Guards). It also recruited large elements of Grayson's, Gist's, and Thruston's Additional Continental Regiments.

SEE ALSO *Southern Campaigns of Nathanael Greene.*

BIBLIOGRAPHY

Burgess, Louis A., comp. *Virginia Soldiers of 1776: Compiled from Documents on File in the Virginia Land Office Together with Material found in the Archives Department of the Virginia State Library, and other Reliable Sources.* 3 vols. Richmond, Va.: Richmond Press, 1927–1929.

Cecere, Michael. *They Behaved Like Soldiers: Captain John Chilton and the Third Virginia Regiment 1775–1778.* Bowie, Md.: Heritage Books, 2004.

Eckenrode, Hamilton J. *The Revolution in Virginia.* Boston: Houghton Mifflin Co., 1916.

Flagg, C. A., and W. O. Waters. "A Bibliography of Muster and Pay Rolls, Regimental Histories, etc., with Introductory and Explanatory Notes." *Virginia Magazine of History and Biography* 19 (October 1911): 402–414; 20 (January, April, July 1920): 52–68, 181–194, 267–281; 22 (January 1914): 57–67.

Graham, James. *The Life of General Daniel Morgan of the Virginia Line of the Army of the United States, with Portions of His Correspondence.* New York: Derby & Jackson, 1856.

Gwathmey, John H. *Historical Register of Virginians in the Revolution: Soldiers, Sailors, Marines 1775–1783.* Richmond, Va.: Dietz Press, 1938.

Lewis, Virgil A. *The Soldiery of West Virginia in the French and Indian War; Lord Dunmore's War; the Revolution; the Later Indian Wars; the Whiskey Insurrection; the Second War with England; the War with Mexico. and Addenda relating to West Virginians in the Civil War.* Charleston, W.Va.: Third Biennial Report of the Department of Archives and History, State of West Virginia, 1911.

McDonnell, Michael A. "The Politics of Mobilization in Revolutionary Virginia: Military Culture and Political and Social Relations, 1774–83." Ph.D. dissertation, Oxford University, 1996.

Minnis, M. Lee. *The First Virginia Regiment of Foot 1775–1783.* Lovettsville, Va.: Willow Bend Books, 1998.

Sanchez-Saavedra, E. M. *A Guide to Virginia Military Organizations in the American Revolution, 1774–1787.* Richmond: Virginia State Library, 1978.

Sellers, John Robert. "The Virginia Continental Line, 1775–1780." Ph.D. dissertation, Tulane University, 1968.

Taliaferro, Benjamin. *The Orderly Book of Captain Benjamin Taliaferro: 2d Virginia Detachment, Charleston, South Carolina, 1780.* Edited by Lee A. Wallace Jr. Richmond: Virginia State Library, 1980.

Van Schreevan, William J., et al., ed. *Revolutionary Virginia: The Road to Independence.* 7 vols. Charlottesville: University Press of Virginia for the Virginia Independence Bicentennial Commission, 1973–1983.

"Virginia Officers and Men in the Continental Line." *Virginia Magazine of History and Biography* 2 (January, April 1895), pp. 241–258, 357–370.

Robert K. Wright Jr.

(Only 39 burgesses remained in Williamsburg, the rest of the 116 members having already gone home.) The next day, conservative burgesses forced the House to rescind the fifth resolution. But then an extraordinary thing happened, as described by the historians Edmund and Helen Morgan: "Henry and his friends, having failed to secure the passage of their most radical items in the House of Burgesses, were able to get them passed unanimously in the newspapers: every newspaper which carried the resolutions printed the fifth, sixth, and seventh as though they had been adopted" (*Stamp Act Crisis,* p. 102). Beginning with the *Newport Mercury* of Rhode Island on 24 June, the printing of the final three resolutions made the House of Burgesses appear to be much more radical than it actually was. These inaccurate reports lifted the spirits of Stamp Act opponents throughout the colonies and gave new life to the movement to resist imperial control.

SEE ALSO *Henry, Patrick; Stamp Act.*

BIBLIOGRAPHY

Morgan, Edmund S., ed. *Prologue to Revolution: Sources and Documents on the Stamp Act Crisis, 1764–1766.* Chapel Hill: University of North Carolina Press, 1959.

Morgan, Edmund S., and Helen M. Morgan. *The Stamp Act Crisis: Prologue to Revolution.* Chapel Hill: University of North Carolina Press, 1953.

Van Schreeven, William J., comp. *Revolutionary Virginia: The Road to Independence.* Edited by Robert L. Scribner. Vol. 1: *Forming Thunderclouds and the First Convention, 1763–1774, A Documentary Record.* Charlottesville: University Press of Virginia, 1973.

revised by Harold E. Selesky

VIRGINIA RESOLVES OF 1765.

Patrick Henry, who had been a member of the House of Burgesses for nine days, introduced on 29 May 1765, in the last days of the session, perhaps as many as seven resolutions that expressed opposition to the Stamp Act. The resolutions were debated on the 30th, during which Henry made allusions that, since Caesar had his Brutus and Charles II his Cromwell, he hoped that "some good American would stand up, in favour of his country," for which hint of treason he was reprimanded by the speaker, and after which he apologized for his remarks (Morgan, p. 46). The first four resolutions were passed, "the greatest majority being 22 to 17." The fifth resolution, declaring that the Burgesses "have the only and sole exclusive right and power to lay taxes and impositions upon the inhabitants of this colony," passed by 20 to 19 (ibid., pp. 47–48).

VIRGINIA RESOLVES OF 1769. 16

May 1769. Framed by George Mason, introduced in the House of Burgesses by Washington on 16 May, and unanimously adopted the same day, these resolutions asserted that only the governor and the provincial legislature had the right to lay taxes in Virginia. They implied censure of the British ministry's denunciation of the Virginia and Massachusetts circular letters, and they condemned the Parliamentary proposal that an ancient law of Henry VIII be revived to bring American malcontents to England for trial. Governor Norborne Berkeley, baron de Botetourt, promptly dissolved the assembly, but the Burgesses met informally and on 18 May adopted the Virginia Association.

SEE ALSO *Association; Massachusetts Circular Letter.*

BIBLIOGRAPHY

Van Schreeven, William J., comp. *Revolutionary Virginia: The Road to Independence.* Edited by Robert L. Scribner. Vol. 1: *Forming Thunderclouds and the First Convention, 1763–1774: A Documentary Record.* Charlottesville: University Press of Virginia, 1973.

revised by Harold E. Selesky

VOLUNTEERS OF IRELAND.

This Provincial regiment was created by Sir Henry Clinton in the summer of 1778 at the behest of Lord George Germain. In a letter to Germain on 23 October, Clinton stated that he wanted "to try all means . . . to draw off from the American army the number of Europeans which constituted its principal force" ("On-Line Institute"). Although based on a smug misreading of the composition of the American army, the effort produced an effective regiment. In his memoirs, Clinton recalled the difficulties he had in implementing Germain's suggestion. Regretting that "no very large portion of the friendly colonists who had taken refuge within our posts seemed much inclined to add to their other sufferings those of a military life," he nevertheless

> had recourse to those sources from whence the rebels themselves drew most of their best soldiers—I mean the Irish and other Europeans who had [recently] settled in America. As it was difficult, however, to hold forth terms of sufficient advantage to these emigrants to incite them to quit their present service [i.e., desert] without running a risk of giving umbrage to the natives of America who had, with voluntary zeal, entered into the first provincial corps that had been raised, I made use of another lure, which I thought might prove equally effectual. This was to endeavor to work upon the national attachment of the Irish by inviting them into a regiment whose officers should all be from that country, and placing at its head a nobleman of popular character and ability. Accordingly, before I left Philadelphia [16 June 1778], I began to form such a corps, under the title of the Volunteers of Ireland and the command of Lord Rawdon, whose zeal I knew would lead him to spare neither [personal] expense nor pains to complete its numbers and render it useful and respectable.

The Volunteers "afterward filled fast and, being employed on active service the rest of the war, had frequent opportunities of signalizing themselves."

In May 1779 the Volunteers were placed on the American Establishment as the Second American Regiment (Volunteers of Ireland) and joined the expedition sent to Virginia for the Mathew-Collier Raid. The next year they arrived with the reinforcements from New York to take part in the final operations of the Charleston campaign of 1780. At Hobkirk's Hill, South Carolina, on 25 April 1781, they particularly distinguished themselves under the overall command of their founder. In his report of the action to Earl Cornwallis, Rawdon, in command of the British occupation of South Carolina, wrote on 26 April 1781:

> We were so fortunate in our march [against Nathanael Greene's position outside Camden] that we were not discovered till the flank companies of the Volunteers of Ireland, which led our column, fell in with Greene's pickets. The pickets, though supported, were instantly driven in and followed to their camp. . . . I had ordered Lieutenant Colonel Campbell to lead the attack with the Sixty-third and King's American Regiments, which he performed with great spirit. The extent of the enemy's line soon obliged me to throw forward the Volunteers of Ireland also. Those three corps quickly gained the summit of the hill; and, giving room for the rest of our force to act, the rout of the enemy was immediately decided.

The Volunteers were placed on the British Establishment on Christmas Day 1782, as the 105th Regiment of Foot. In April 1783 the officers and non-commissioned officers were sent to Ireland to raise a new regiment, and the men were transferred to other Provincial regiments then serving at Charleston, effectively disbanding the Volunteers. The 105th Regiment was disbanded in Britain in January 1784.

SEE ALSO *Charleston Expedition of Clinton in 1780; Clinton, Henry; Hobkirk's Hill (Camden), South Carolina; Rawdon-Hastings, Francis; Virginia, Military Operations in.*

BIBLIOGRAPHY

Clinton, Henry. *The American Rebellion: Sir Henry Clinton's Narrative of His Campaigns, 1775–1782.* Edited by William B. Willcox. New Haven, Conn.: Yale University Press, 1954.

Cole, Nan, and Todd Braisted. "The On-Line Institute for Advanced Loyalist Studies." Available online at http://www.royalprovincial.com.

Mills, T. F. "Land Forces of Britain, the Empire, and Commonwealth: The Volunteers of Ireland (2nd American Regiment) [105th Regiment of Foot]." Available online at http://regiments.org.

Smith, Paul H. "The American Loyalists: Notes on Their Organization and Numerical Strength." *William and Mary Quarterly,* third series, 25 (1968): 259–277.

revised by Harold E. Selesky

VON STEUBEN SEE *Steuben, Friedrich Wilhelm von.*

VOSE, JOSEPH. (1738–1816). Continental officer. Massachusetts. Eldest brother in a large, extended kinship of Voses in Milton, Massachusetts, Joseph was major in General William Heath's Massachusetts Regiment from 1 May to December 1775, serving with his brothers, Captain Elijah Vose and Lieutenant Bill Vose. Joseph distinguished himself in the raid on Great Brewster Island on 21 July, and his promotion to lieutenant colonel was backdated to 1 July. In the army's reorganization of 1 January 1776 he became lieutenant colonel of Colonel John Greaton's Twenty-Fourth Continental Regiment, and served with it in the Canada campaign. By 8 December, he was at Peekskill, New York, on his way to join General George Washington's main army, in command of a single unit made up of the remnants of the Twenty-Fourth, Colonel William Bond's Twenty-Fourth Continental Regiment, and Colonel Elisha Porter's Massachusetts state regiment. In the next reorganization (1 January 1777), he was named lieutenant colonel of the First Massachusetts (6 November 1776) and promoted to colonel on 22 April 1777 when the original colonel, John Paterson, became a brigadier general. He was rejoined in the regiment by his brother Elijah (now a lieutenant colonel); brother Bill continued as a staff officer (paymaster). The First Massachusetts Regiment was part of John Glover's Second Massachusetts Brigade that held the American right flank at Saratoga, after which Vose led it south to join the main army for the winter of 1777–1778 at Valley Forge. He took part in the Monmouth, New Jersey, campaign of June–July 1778, and then marched east for the operations under John Sullivan at Newport, Rhode Island, the next month. He was back in the Hudson Highlands in the summer of 1779.

On 17 February 1781, "the eight eldest companies" (in the words of William Heath) of the Massachusetts line were formed into a battalion under Colonel Vose and Major Caleb Gibbs (*Memoirs*, p. 288). This elite unit formed part of the Marquis de Lafayette's force that marched south from West Point for Military operations in Virginia in the summer of 1781. During the Yorktown campaign it was in John P. G. Muhlenberg's First Brigade of Lafayette's light infantry division. In the reorganization of 13 June 1783 Vose was continued in command of one of the four Massachusetts regiments formed of men whose enlistments had not expired. As a brevet brigadier general (promoted to the rank on 30 September 1783), he led his unit into New York City on Evacuation Day, 25 November 1783. After the war he returned to his farm in Milton, Massachusetts.

SEE ALSO *Great Brewster Island, Massachusetts.*

BIBLIOGRAPHY
Heath, William. *Memoirs of Major General William Heath.* Boston: I. Thomas and E. T. Andrews, 1798.

revised by Harold E. Selesky

W

WADSWORTH, JEREMIAH. (1743–1804).

Commissary general of the Continental army and congressman. Connecticut. Jeremiah Wadsworth went to sea at the age of 18 to improve his health. He started as a common sailor aboard one of the ships owned by his uncle, Matthew Talbott, rose to the rank of ship captain, and by 1771 was a wealthy man. In April 1775 the General Assembly appointed him as one of nine merchants to serve as commissaries for the Connecticut forces at New York and Boston. Commissary General Joseph Trumbull chose him to serve as commissary for the Eastern Department in 1776, and on 18 June 1777 Congress elected him deputy commissary general of purchases. He resigned this post in August 1777. When Congress re-established the previous system under which Joseph Trumbull had operated, Wadsworth again became commissary general and held this post from April 1778 until he resigned on 4 December 1779. Operating under circumstances that were both extraordinary and unprecedented, Wadsworth earned General George Washington's commendation for managing to keep the Continental army supplied. He also worked well with Nathanael Greene, the army's quartermaster, who became his partner in private mercantile ventures from 1779 to 1785. Wadsworth was commissary for the comte de Rochambeau's army from its arrival at Newport in 1780 until it departed for home in 1782, and in the summer of 1783 he went to Paris to settle accounts. Like Robert Morris, Wadsworth made a substantial personal profit from his public activities. He was a delegate to the Confederation Congress in 1788, and the same year supported ratification of the federal Constitution in the Connecticut state convention. A Federalist member of the first Congress, he supported Alexander Hamilton's scheme for the federal assumption of state debts from the Revolution. He resigned in March 1795. A pioneer in American business, banking, insurance, and cattle breeding, he died at Hartford, Connecticut.

SEE ALSO *Trumbull, Joseph.*

BIBLIOGRAPHY

East, Robert A. *Business Enterprise in the American Revolutionary Era.* New York: Columbia University Press, 1938.

Risch, Erna. *Supplying Washington's Army.* Washington, D.C.: Center of Military History, United States Army, 1981.

revised by Harold E. Selesky

WAGONER, OLD. Nickname of Daniel Morgan.

SEE ALSO *Morgan, Daniel.*

WAHAB'S PLANTATION, NORTH CAROLINA. 21 September 1780.

Tarleton's Legion, reinforced, moved on the left (west) of the British army that advanced toward Charlotte. During this advance, Tarleton came down with yellow fever and command passed to Major George Hanger. Acting on intelligence reports that the Legion was camped at Wahab's Plantation, home of Captain James Wahab of the rebel militia, Colonel William Davie approached the plantation with eighty mounted partisans and seventy riflemen in two small companies under Major George Davidson at around sunrise on 21 September. Oblivious to the presence of enemy troops nearby, the British had called in their sentries and more than sixty men were now sitting their horses on a road near one of the plantation houses. Davie's force, guided by Captain Wahab, broke into two units; one, under Davidson, seized the plantation house, while the mounted troops used a cornfield as cover to emerge on the road below the Loyalists.

When Davie attacked up the road at the same moment that Davidson's men stormed the house, the Loyalists were caught completely by surprise. In just a few minutes, fifteen or twenty Loyalists were killed, forty were wounded, and rest of the Loyal Legion fled in disorder. There was only one American casualty, and this a man who was wounded during the pursuit when mistaken for an enemy. The rebels carried off 96 fully equipped horses and 120 stand of arms, retreating before a British relief force. Davie returned to camp at Providence after covering sixty miles in less than twenty-four hours. The British responded by burning Wahab's house. Davie and Hanger met next at Charlotte, North Carolina, on 26 September.

SEE ALSO *Charlotte, North Carolina; Kings Mountain, South Carolina.*

revised by Michael Bellesiles

WALLABOUT BAY, BROOKLYN, NEW YORK.

The site of what would become the New York Naval Shipyard, this is where the *Jersey* and other British prison ships were moored and where the British dumped the bodies of thousands of dead prisoners. Nathanael Greene oversaw the construction of Fort Putnam, which overlooks the bay, in 1776.

SEE ALSO *Prisons and Prison Ships.*

revised by Michael Bellesiles

WALLACE, SIR JAMES. (1731–1803).

British naval officer. Wallace entered the Royal Naval Academy at Portsmouth in 1746. He fought in the Seven Years' War and was promoted post-captain on 10 January 1771. In November he was given the frigate *Rose* (twenty guns), which he took to North America in 1774. Based at Newport in 1775–1776, he vigorously conducted raids on rebel-held coastal towns and harbors. In July 1776 he was given *Experiment* (fifty guns), and in January 1777

carried despatches home to Britain, where he was knighted on 13 February. In July he returned to the North American station and in October took part in Henry Clinton's expedition to the Highlands, pushing on with John Vaughan to Kingston and beyond. In 1778 *Experiment* took part in the relief of Newport and in August evaded capture by sailing into Long Island Sound and through Hell Gate, a passage previously thought impossible for a two-decker. In December she was severely damaged by a storm off Virginia, and Wallace took her home for repairs. Sailing with Marriot Arbuthnot's squadron in May 1779, he took part in the relief of Jersey in the English Channel and destroyed the French squadron in Cancale Bay in northwest France. Rejoining Arbuthnot in Torbay in southwest England, he returned with him to New York. Sent south with pay for the troops in Georgia, in September 1779 he ran into part of comte d'Estaing's squadron and was captured. Acquitted at the ensuing court martial, he took command of *Nonsuch* (sixty-four guns) in March 1780, and in July captured the corvette *Hussard* and the frigate *Belle Poule*. In 1781 he took part in George Darby's relief of Gibraltar and on the return voyage engaged and severely damaged an eighty-gun ship. In January 1782 he sailed in the *Warrior* (seventy-four guns) with George Rodney to the West Indies, where he took part in the battle of the Saints. He returned to Britain in 1783 and served as commander in chief in Newfoundland from 1793 to 1796.

SEE ALSO *Arbuthnot, Marriot; Clinton's Expedition; Kingston, New York.*

revised by John Oliphant

WALLIS, SAMUEL. (?–1798).

Loyalist secret agent. Born in Maryland of Quaker descent, he became a substantial Philadelphia merchant, shipper, and speculator long before the War of American Independence. An investor in frontier lands, he took advantage of the 1768 Treaty of Fort Stanwix to build a substantial house in Muncy, Pennsylvania, on the west branch of the Susquehanna River, about twenty-five miles north of Fort Augusta at Sunbury. He used to spend the summers there, returning to Philadelphia for the winter. When the British arrived in Pennsylvania in 1777–1778, he worked secretly for them and helped to organize Loyalist raids on the frontier. In 1778, during a major Indian raid, nearby settlers took refuge in Wallis's stone dwelling before moving on to Sunbury. Afterward, Wallis had the effrontery to demand a garrison of Continental troops to supplement the useless militia. In August a detachment of the Sixth Pennsylvanian Regiment was posted close by. Later he was asked to draw up a map of the Iroquois country for use by Sullivan in his expedition in 1779. He is supposed to have supplied a false map—intended to send Sullivan a hundred miles astray—while providing the British with an accurate one. Unfortunately, as neither map has ever been found, and Sullivan did not stray out of his way, the story may be untrue.

Wallis used his house as a rendezvous for British and Loyalist frontier agents, and he was one of the spies who reported to John André and George Beckwith, Henry Clinton's intelligence chiefs in New York. André made use of him in mid-1779 when Benedict Arnold was making overtures from Philadelphia. Beckwith tried to get Wallis to exploit the mutiny of the Pennsylvania Line (1–10 January 1781), but the opportunity passed before anything could be done. He continued to send intelligence and food shipments to the British army until 1782, all the time keeping up close personal contacts with the Continental Congress and posing as a Whig. In 1782 he moved permanently to Muncy, expanded his land holdings to about seven thousand acres, and—especially as the agent of the Holland Land Company—became a major speculator in lands farther west. He died of smallpox in Philadelphia in 1798; his fortune, possibly owing to the concurrent financial crisis, was lost.

So good was Wallis's cover that his Loyalist activities went unsuspected until the Clinton and Arnold papers reached the public domain in the early twentieth century. His significance lies less in the damage he may have caused the rebels—which in the nature of things is hard to evaluate—but as a rare known example of the operations of a British agent. Many others, like Wallis, must have contributed to the jigsaw André and Beckwith labored to assemble for Clinton. Like him, too, they may have honestly worked for a British victory while taking care to be on the winning side in the end.

SEE ALSO *André, John; Arnold's Treason; Beckwith, George; Clinton, Henry; Fort Stanwix, Treaty of; Sullivan's Expedition against the Iroquois.*

BIBLIOGRAPHY

Van Doren, Carl. *Secret History of the American Revolution: An Account of the Conspiracies of Benedict Arnold and Numerous Others.* New York: Viking, 1941.

revised by John Oliphant

WALPOLE, HORACE OR HORATIO.

(1717–1797). Diarist, author, politician, patron of the arts, and fourth earl of Orford. Walpole, the youngest child of Sir Robert Walpole, left an immense volume of letters and diaries that provide a fertile source for historians studying the eighteenth century. His waspish and often prejudiced observations must be treated with caution, but the memoirs in particular contain a great deal of accurate political information. The first letters were published in 1798, soon after his death, as *The Works of Horatio Walpole, Earl of Orford,* in five volumes edited by Robert Walpole and Mary Berry. The *Reminiscences written by Mr Horace Walpole in 1788,* originally published in 1819, were reedited by Paget Toynbee and published by Clarendon Press in 1924. *Memoirs of the Reign of King George II* first appeared in 1822 and were published again, in an edition by John Brooke, by Yale University Press, in 1985. *Memoirs of the Reign of King George III* followed in 1845; these were reedited by Derek Jarrett and published by Yale University Press in 2000. *The Last Journals of Horace Walpole* appeared in 1859, followed by a revised edition in 1910. Although he entered Parliament in 1754, his political activities were marginal.

SEE ALSO *Walpole, Sir Robert.*

revised by John Oliphant

WALPOLE, SIR ROBERT. (1676–1745).

British politician. Often described as the first "prime minister," he dominated British politics for over twenty years and was once regarded as the architect of Georgian stability. A masterly parliamentary manager with the full confidence of George I and George II, his sheer political longevity shaped the office he held. Horace (or Horatio) Walpole, the diarist, was his son.

SEE ALSO *Walpole, Horatio (or Horace).*

revised by John Oliphant

WALTON, GEORGE. (c. 1749–1804).

Signer, governor of Georgia. Virginia and Georgia. Born in Cumberland County, Virginia, George Walton was orphaned and apprenticed to a carpenter. At the end of his apprenticeship, in 1769, he moved to Savannah, studied law, and was admitted to the bar in 1774. As early as July of that year he was one of the local Patriots urging action against Britain, and he had a leading role in putting Georgia in the Patriot camp. Named a delegate to the Continental Congress on 2 February 1776, he sat for the periods 1776–1777 and 1780–1781.

On 9 January 1778 he was named a colonel of militia, and he was severely wounded in the thigh and captured during the unsuccessful defense of Savannah, Georgia, on 29 December 1778.. He was exchanged in Sept. 1779, during the unsuccessful siege of Savannah by rebel and French troops. General Benjamin Lincoln urged him to establish a constitutional government in Augusta, thus replacing the unconstitutional supreme executive council currently functioning there., Walton complied with Lincoln's suggestion. Although Walton's newly established government was not considered any more constitutional than its previous form, Walton nonetheless held the position of governor between November 1779 and January 1780. In this capacity he sent a request to the Continental Congress for the transfer of General Lachlan McIntosh, which bore the fraudulent signature of William Glascock, speaker of the assembly. Congress complied with Walton's request; however, in 1781 they repealed the resolution.

Walton was not returned to Congress after his 1781 term, and he remained in Philadelphia with his family until late 1782. Although the 1783 Georgia assembly censured him for the forgery on his request to have McIntosh removed, they elected him chief justice, an influential position he filled for six years. After serving as governor in 1789, he became a district superior-court judge under the new state constitution. In late 1795 he filled the unexpired U.S. Senate term of James Jackson, but was not returned to the Senate.

SEE ALSO *McIntosh, Lachlan.*

BIBLIOGRAPHY

Buell, Richard. *Securing the Revolution: Iideology in American Politics, 1789–1815.* Ithaca, N.Y.: Cornell University Press, 1972.

Jackson, Harvey H. "Georgia Whiggery: The Origins and Effects of a Many-Faceded Movement." In *Forty Years of Diversity: Essays on Colonial Georgia.* Edited by Harvey H. Jackson and Phinizy Spalding. Athens: University of Georgia Press, 1984.

revised by Leslie Hall

WARD, ARTEMAS. (1727–1800).

American politician and Continental general. Massachusetts. Artemas Ward was born in Shrewsbury, Massachusetts, and was graduated from Harvard College in 1748. He opened a retail store in his home town, married, and became a prominent figure in local political and judicial affairs. Appointed a major in the local militia regiment on 28 January 1755, Ward turned out with his men in August 1757 when the French took Fort William Henry at the head of Lake George. The next year he was appointed major in Colonel William Williams's Massachusetts provincial regiment, was promoted lieutenant colonel on 3 July 1758, and five days later participated in James Abercromby's disastrous attack on Ticonderoga. He returned from that campaign with his health permanently impaired.

A strong and vocal supporter of colonial rights, he worked with Samuel Adams and other leaders to oppose the Stamp Act in 1765. In retaliation, the royal governor, Francis Bernard, removed him from the colonelcy of the local militia regiment to which he had been appointed on 1 July 1762. From that point on, Ward was a principal leader of the resistance in Worcester County. He believed that Providence had blessed Massachusetts and its inhabitants as the chosen people, and that British policies were interfering with that happy relationship. The Massachusetts Provincial Congress appointed him a brigadier general on 26 October 1774, and promoted him to senior major general on 15 January 1775. Sick in bed when news of the Lexington alarm (19 April) reached him, he rode at dawn the next day to assume command of the forces around Boston, and directed operations until Washington arrived on 2 July. On 19 May the provincial congress named this stern-looking man of medium height, heavy in body and slow of speech (Freeman, *George Washington,* III, p. 477), as commander in chief of the Massachusetts army. In that position, Ward also exercised significant coordinating authority over the contingents from other colonies. Involved in planning the occupation of the Charlestown peninsula in mid-June 1775, he ably funneled men and material to the battle of Bunker Hill (17 June) from his headquarters at Cambridge.

On the same day, in Philadelphia, the Continental Congress appointed Ward the senior major general of the Continental army, second only to George Washington as commander-in-chief. Washington and Ward had a sometimes tense working relationship. Although Washington placed Ward in command of the important right wing of the American army at Roxbury, Ward, understandably, was disappointed about being superseded as commander-in-chief. He also resented Washington's evident conviction that troops of the Boston army, including those from Massachusetts, left something to be desired in the way of military proficiency.

After the British evacuated from Boston, Ward submitted his resignation (22 March), withdrew it, and then resubmitted it on 12 April. On 23 April Congress accepted it with little appearance of reluctance, but at Washington's request Ward retained his post until the end of May, until the problem of a replacement could be solved. Tensions exploded when Washington wrote Ward that he had been informed that troops performing outpost duty on Bunker Hill and Dorchester Neck were being excused from work on the city's fortifications. Ward fired back on 9 May that this information was an "injurious falsehood" and complained that "because 1,500 men could not throw up the works as fast as 6,000 or 7,000 had done in time past, there appeared to some an unaccountable delay." When he learned that Ward had withdrawn his original resignation, Washington wrote Charles Lee that Ward probably wanted to stay by "the smoke of his own chimney." The Massachusetts authorities had begun to indicate some dissatisfaction with Ward's performance, and when this was reported to Washington he asked (13 May), "If General W is judged an improper person to command five Regiments in a peaceful camp or garrison ... why was he appointed to the first military command in the Massachusetts government?" After giving up direct responsibility for the defense of Boston, Ward remained as commander of the Eastern Department until succeeded by William Heath on 20 March 1777.

Ward remained an important leader in Massachusetts civil government, to the extent his poor health would allow. He was a member of the Executive Council (1778 and 1780-1782), a delegate to the Continental Congress (1780–1781), and a member of the state legislature (1782–1787). He strongly opposed Shays's Rebellion, to the point of standing before insurgent bayonets on 5 September 1786 in an unsuccessful attempt to keep the Worcester County courts open. A Federalist, he sat in the House of Representatives from 1791 until illness forced him to resign in 1795. He died at his home (still standing) in Shrewsbury, Massachusetts.

Of this austere, unsympathetic Yankee who might well have had Washington's task, Douglas S. Freeman has this epitaph: "Perhaps he deserved more credit than he received. He kept the Army together in front of Boston until Washington came, and after that, however much he felt aggrieved, he did not add to his successor's difficulties by organizing the discontented" (*George Washington*, III, p. 495a). Ward's papers are scattered among the Massachusetts Historical Society, the Massachusetts State Archives, and the American Antiquarian Society.

SEE ALSO *Boston Siege; Washington, George.*

BIBLIOGRAPHY

Freeman, Douglas Southall. *George Washington.* 7 vols. New York: Scribner, 1948-57.

Martyn, Charles. *The Life of Artemas Ward.* New York: A. Ward, 1921.

revised by Harold E. Selesky

WARD, SAMUEL. (1725–1776). Governor of

Rhode Island, member of Continental Congress. Born in Newport, Rhode Island, on 27 May 1725, Ward was son of a prosperous merchant who was governor of Rhode Island from 1740 to 1742. Samuel himself was elected governor in 1762, 1765, and 1766. In Rhode Island politics, Ward was leader of the conservative group centered around the merchants of Newport, while Stephen Hopkins was the more successful champion of the Providence radicals, though Ward had led the opposition to the Stamp Act while he was governor. In 1774 the former political enemies were united as delegates to the first Continental Congress. In the Second Congress, Ward presided frequently over the Committee of the Whole, becoming a firm advocate of independence before Hopkins. He died of smallpox in Philadelphia on 26 March 1776. He was the father of Samuel Ward Jr.

SEE ALSO *Hopkins, Stephen; Stephen, Adam; Ward, Samuel, Jr.*

BIBLIOGRAPHY

Lovejoy, David S. *Rhode Island Politics and the American Revolution, 1760–1776.* Providence, R.I.: Brown University Press, 1958.

Ward Papers. Rhode Island Historical Society, Providence, Rhode Island.

revised by Michael Bellesiles

WARD, SAMUEL, JR. (1756–1832). Con-

tinental officer. Rhode Island. Second son of Governor Samuel Ward of Rhode Island, Ward graduated with honors in 1771 from what became Brown University. On 3 May 1775 he was commissioned captain in the First Rhode Island Regiment, and on 31 December he was taken prisoner at Quebec. Exchanged in August 1776, he returned from Canada and on 12 January 1777 was promoted to major, First Rhode Island. He was with the main army at Morristown and then went north to oppose Burgoyne's offensive. After spending the winter at Valley Forge, he fought at Newport (July–August 1778), and on 12 April 1779 he was promoted to lieutenant colonel. He resigned his army commission on 1 January 1781 and started a business career that led him to travel extensively. In 1788 he became one of the first American merchants to visit the Far East. He was in Paris when Louis XVI was sentenced to death in January 1793.

SEE ALSO *Ward, Samuel.*

revised by Michael Bellesiles

WARNER, SETH. (1743–1784). Militia offi-

cer. Vermont. Born in Woodbury (later Roxbury), Connecticut, on 6 May 1743, Warner moved with his family to Bennington, Vermont, in 1763 and became a leader of the Green Mountain Boys. On 9 March 1774 he was outlawed by New York, and a reward was offered for his arrest. He took part in the capture of Ticonderoga on 10 May 1775 and occupied Crown Point two days later. At a council held at the latter the next month, he and Ethan Allen were named to ask Congress to create a Green Mountain regiment in the Continental army. Their mission was successful, and on 26 July, Warner was elected commander with the rank of lieutenant colonel.

Returning to Lake Champlain, he joined Montgomery's wing of the Canada invasion and fought at Longueuil on 31 October 1775, defeating a far superior British force. In the retreat from Canada he commanded rear guard actions and also raised reinforcements in Vermont. At Hubbardton on 7 July 1777, his rear guard was surprised and defeated. Rallying his forces, Warner arrived for the final and decisive phase of the Battle of Bennington on 16 August 1777. In October the Green Mountain Regiment joined the forces of General Horatio Gates at Stillwater. On 20 March 1778 he was promoted to brigadier general of Vermont militia, having been given the grade of colonel of one of the Additional Continental Regiments on 5 July 1776. Warner and his regiment spent the rest of the war at various northern outposts. In 1780 he was wounded during a skirmish with Indians on Lake George.

Warner's constant hard service left him in declining health. He and his regiment were retired on 1 January 1783. He died at his home in Woodbury on 26 December 1784.

SEE ALSO *Additional Continental Regiments; Bennington Raid; Crown Point, New York; Gates, Horatio; Green Mountain Boys; Hubbardton, Vermont; Longueuil, Canada; Ticonderoga, New York, American Capture of.*

BIBLIOGRAPHY

Bellesiles, Michael. *Revolutionary Outlaws: Ethan Allen and the Struggle for Independence on the Early American Frontier.* Charlottesville: University Press of Virginia, 1993.

Chipman, Daniel. *The Life of Colonel Seth Warner.* Burlington, Vt.: C. Goodrich, 1858.

revised by Michael Bellesiles

WARNER'S REGIMENT. Warner's regi-
ment was organized on 5 July 1776 and in 1777 became one of the sixteen "additional Continental regiments."

SEE ALSO *Additional Continental Regiments.*

Mark M. Boatner

WARRANT MEN. Six fictitious persons in almost all British foot regiments whose pay was distributed as follows: the pay of two men went to widows of regimental officers; the pay of the others went to reimburse the colonel for deserters' clothing, for recruiting, and for the personal use of the colonel and regimental agent.

SEE ALSO *Contingent Men.*

BIBLIOGRAPHY

Curtis, Edward P. *The Organization of the British Army in the Revolution.* New Haven, Conn.: Yale University Press, 1926.

Mark M. Boatner

WARREN, JAMES. (1726–1808). Political leader. Massachusetts. The eldest son of James and Penelope (Winslow) Warren, he was not related to Joseph and John Warren, who also achieved some fame during the Revolutionary War era. Born at Plymouth, James was graduated from Harvard College in 1745, succeeded his father as Plymouth county sheriff in 1757, and pursued careers as a merchant and gentleman farmer. In 1754 he married the sister of James Otis; Mercy Otis Warren (1728–1814) is remembered as a poet and one of the most perceptive of the first generation of historians of the Revolution.

James sat in the lower house of the Massachusetts General Court and the Provincial Congress from 1766 until 1778. He was speaker in 1769 and 1770, and helped to establish the local Committee of Correspondence. He was a close friend of John and Samuel Adams, and succeeded Joseph Warren as president of the Provincial Congress. He became speaker of the House of Representatives in the new General Court. Between 27 July 1775 and 19 April 1776 he was paymaster general of the Continental army, and from 1776 to 1781 he was on the Navy Board for the Eastern Department. When, in September 1776, the General Court designated him one of three major generals to lead a force into Rhode Island, he was unwilling to serve under a Continental officer of lesser rank and excused himself on the grounds of a recent illness. The next year he resigned his commission to avoid another such situation, and his political enemy, John Hancock, used this to undermine his reputation to such a degree that Warren failed to be re-elected to the legislature in 1778. In 1779 he won re-election, but was unable to win again until 1787. He held a number of offices after the war, but was unable to amass the political power needed to compete with such antagonists as Hancock. "I am content to move in a small sphere," he had written to John Adams in 1775. "I expect no distinction but that of an honest man who has exerted every nerve." Yet when he later sought and failed to achieve such distinctions as the office of lieutenant governor and member of Congress he was resentful. "His mind has been soured, and he became discontented and querulous," wrote John Quincy Adams. He opposed ratification of the federal Constitution in 1788, believing that it would lead to a dissolution of the state governments, and became an Anti-Federalist.

SEE ALSO *Hancock, John.*

BIBLIOGRAPHY
Shipton, Clifford K. *New England Life in the 18th Century: Representative Biographies from "Sibley's Harvard Graduates."* Cambridge: Belknap Press of Harvard UniversityPress, 1963.

revised by Harold E. Selesky

WARREN, JOHN.

WARREN, JOHN. (1753–1815). Continental surgeon. Massachusetts. After studying under his elder brother, Joseph Warren, John became a successful doctor in Boston. In 1773 he joined Colonel Timothy Pickering's regiment as a surgeon, and on hearing of his brother Joseph's death at Bunker Hill, he volunteered for service in the ranks. At the age of just twenty-two, however, he became senior surgeon of the hospital at Cambridge. In 1776 he was transferred to New York and was appointed surgeon of the general hospital on Long Island. After serving with Washington's army at Trenton and Princeton, he returned to Boston in April 1777 to resume his medical practice while performing the duties of a military surgeon in the army hospital there. He became one of the leading New England surgeons of his day, performed one of the first abdominal operations in America, and was a founder of the Harvard Medical School.

SEE ALSO *Warren, Joseph.*

revised by Harold E. Selesky

WARREN, JOSEPH.

WARREN, JOSEPH. (1741–1775). Patriot leader killed at Bunker Hill. Massachusetts. Born at Roxbury, Joseph Warren distinguished himself at Harvard College, from which he graduated in 1759, and became a successful medical doctor in Boston. His willingness to inoculate patients against smallpox during an outbreak of the disease established his reputation as the foremost physician in Massachusetts. John Adams was one of his patients, and he was closely associated with Samuel Adams during the Stamp Act crisis. In the political turmoil of Boston he distinguished himself as a political writer, orator, and organizer, along with Samuel Adams, John Hancock, and James Otis. In 1770 he was a member of the committee to demand the removal of British troops from Boston after the "Massacre," and in 1772 and 1775 he delivered celebrated commemorative addresses on the anniversary of the event. He drafted the Suffolk Resolves in 1774, and succeeded Samuel Adams as head of the committee of safety.

On the eve of Lexington and Concord he remained in Boston, despite the danger to himself, and sent out his friend Paul Revere (and William Dawes) to warn the Patriots. He left Boston the next morning and took an active part in the day's fighting. Succeeding John Hancock as president of the Massachusetts Provincial Congress on 23 April 1775, on 20 May he became head of the committee to organize the army in Massachusetts. In both positions Warren did more than any other leader to transform the mob of minuteman and militia that had sent the British scurrying back to Boston into an army capable of maintaining the siege of Boston.

In the early stages of the siege Warren proved to be a savvy and aggressive leader, so aggressive that on several occasions he accompanied American forces skirmishing with the British, despite having no military rank. On 14 June he was elected major general of the militia, having declined the post of physician general, but he had not received his commission when he went to fight on the Charlestown peninsula, and therefore he technically had no official military rank. On the night of 16–17 June he sat with the Provincial Congress at Watertown, on the morning of the 17th he met with the Committee of Safety at Cambridge, and that afternoon he went out to Bunker Hill, where the battle was about to start. Israel Putnam offered to turn over his command, but Warren said, with apparent sincerity, but disingenuously since he was the most important Patriot leader in New England, that he had come as a volunteer to serve where he would be most useful. Proceeding to the redoubt on Breed's Hill, Warren again declined to assume the command from William Prescott, who now faced the British assault with Warren at his side. In the final phase of the action Warren was shot in the face and died instantly, one of only thirty Americans who were killed in the redoubt.

Warren was buried on Bunker Hill with the other American dead in an unmarked grave. When the British left Boston nine months after the battle, his body was positively identified by the two artificial teeth Revere had made for his friend shortly before his death. This was one of the first recorded instances of identifying a corpse by its dental records.

SEE ALSO *Lexington and Concord; Revere, Paul; Suffolk Resolves.*

BIBLIOGRAPHY

Cary, John H. *Joseph Warren: Physician, Politician, Patriot.* Urbana: University of Illinois Press, 1961.

Frothingham, Richard. *Life and Times of Joseph Warren.* Boston: Little, Brown, and Company, 1865.

revised by Harold E. Selesky

WARREN OR WHITE HORSE TAV- ERN, PENNSYLVANIA.

16 September 1777. Five days after the Battle of the Brandywine, the opposing armies converged on White Horse Tavern (in latter-day Planebrook, Pennsylvania) and on the Admiral Warren Tavern (three miles east in latter-day Malvern).

Each commander learned early in the day of the other's approach and both prepared for a major engagement. Pulaski was sent forward with the American cavalry and three hundred supporting infantry as a delaying force, but the infantry ran as soon as fired on, and Pulaski had to retreat before the advancing British.

At about 1 P.M. the brigades of Wayne and Maxwell met Knyphausen's column near Boot Tavern and almost cut off a reconnaissance party of jägers commanded by Colonel von Donop, but the Americans were soon forced back by jäger reinforcements and Hessian grenadiers. The main bodies were squaring off for a major battle when nature intervened.

A heavy rain drenched both armies. As one German officer wrote: "I wish I could give a description of the downpour which began during the engagement and continued until the next morning. It came down so hard that in a few moments we were drenched and sank in mud up to our calves" (Baurmeister, *Revolution*, p. 114).

Because of defective cartridge boxes—the leather tops did not extend sufficiently to keep out the rain—the Americans lost, according to General Henry Knox, four hundred thousand rounds, and many regiments were unable to fire a shot. The British, on the other hand, lost little ammunition and Washington had no choice but to retreat.

SEE ALSO *Philadelphia Campaign.*

BIBLIOGRAPHY

Bauermeister, Carl Leopold. *Revolution in America: Confidential Letters and Journals, 1776–1784.* Translated by Bernhard A. Uhlendorf. New Brunswick, N.J.: Rutgers University Press, 1957.

Reed, John F. *Campaign to Valley Forge, July 1, 1777–December 19, 1777.* Philadelphia: University of Pennsylvania Press, 1965.

revised by Michael Bellesiles

Porthole Portrait of George Washington *(1795).* *The Continental commander and first president of the United States in a portrait by Rembrandt Peale.* © **BUTLER INSTITUTE OF AMERICAN ART, YOUNGSTOWN, OH/BRIDGEMAN ART LIBRARY**

WASHINGTON, GEORGE.

(1732–1799). Commander in chief of the Continental army, first president of the United States. Virginia. Born on 11 February 1732, George Washington was the first child of Augustine Washington (1694–1743) by his second wife, Mary Ball (c.1708–1789), who then lived on the family plantation near Pope's Creek, by the Potomac River, in Westmoreland County, Virginia. On the death of Augustine Washington in 1743, the family estate passed to George's elder half-brother, Lawrence (c.1718–1752). Lawrence settled at Mount Vernon, Virginia, an estate that was named for the British admiral under whom Lawrence had served in a British expedition against Carthagena (now in Colombia) in 1740.

Washington was taught by private tutors at home until he was fifteen, excelling at mathematics, which would serve him well as a surveyor. His education prepared him for the role of a Virginia gentleman, and he worked to meet the standards of civility and conduct that such a station would imply. This striving for acceptance was a lifelong feature of his character, evolving from a quest for economic advantage in his youth to a prickliness about his reputation as an adult. As a young man, Washington learned how to face adversity, take corrective action, and emerge chastened and more determined.

In 1748, Lawrence Washington's connections gained George an appointment as surveyor of the Northern Neck Proprietary, a huge area of land claimed by Lord Thomas Fairfax. In 1751 Lawrence, whose already delicate health had been ruined at Carthagena, went to Barbados in the West Indies to seek relief from what was probably tuberculosis. His brother George accompanied him on this trip. When Lawrence died on 26 June 1752, his will made George executor of his estate and residuary heir of Mount Vernon. George's feet were now firmly planted among the aristocrats of Virginia.

SEVEN YEARS' WAR

French claims to the Ohio River Valley worried many Virginians, who viewed those lands as prime territory for their own speculation and settlement. On 28 August 1753, the British government ordered Lieutenant Governor Robert Dinwiddie to investigate the French incursions and, if necessary, "to drive them off by force of arms" (Abbot, *Washington Papers, Colonial*, 1, p. 57). Washington volunteered to warn the French to abandon their new posts. He left Fort Le Bouef on 31 October 1753 on the first mission of his military career. With a small party guided by the frontiersman Christopher Gist, Washington delivered his message to the French and returned to Williamsburg with the scornful reply.

Appointed lieutenant colonel at the age of twenty-two, Washington was given command of the force Dinwiddie ordered to expel the French from their western posts. Washington reached the Great Meadows (present day Union Town, Pennsylvania) on 24 May 1754, and began construction of Fort Necessity. Learning of the approach of French troops, Washington led a mixed force of forty Virginians and a dozen Native American allies to ambush the French on the morning of 28 May. His troops killed thirteen Frenchmen, including their commander, Ensign Joseph Coulon de Jumonville. He was apprised by scouts that seven hundred more Frenchmen and Indians were advancing toward him, led by Jumonville's elder brother. Washington retreated to the Great Meadows, where his four hundred men were surrounded on 1 July. Because Fort Necessity was incomplete and badly sited, Washington signed a surrender written in French (which he did not speak) admitting culpability for Jumonville's "assassination." The surrender, and its imputation of dishonorable conduct in Jumonville's death, was a bitter humiliation that Washington never forgot.

Washington's defeat was the opening engagement in what became known as the Seven Years' or French and Indian War. Even before receiving news of the debacle at Fort Necessity, the British government decided to remove the French from the western frontier, appointing Major General Edward Braddock as commander in chief for North America. Braddock arrived in Virginia in February 1755 with two regiments that were to form the core of an expedition to oust the French from the Forks of the Ohio River, where the Allegheny and the Monongahela meet to form the Ohio. Washington was with Braddock on 9 July when nearly nine hundred French and Indian fighters surprised Braddock's army ten miles east of Fort Duquesne. Washington, who had been ill with a fever, distinguished himself in the intense combat that killed or wounded two-thirds of the Anglo-American force. He helped carry the mortally wounded Braddock away from the battle, and led the shattered army in its humiliating retreat.

Appointed colonel of the Virginia Regiment on 14 August 1755, Washington devoted the next two years to coping with the problems of commanding seven hundred soldiers strung out along a 350-mile frontier. He gained valuable, if frustrating, experience in dealing with obtuse officers, recalcitrant soldiers, intractable logistical problems, and demanding civilian superiors. He also confronted the elitism of the British high command. In February 1756 Washington went to Boston to meet with William Shirley, the Royal governor of Massachusetts and Braddock's successor as commander in chief. At this meeting, Washington proposed making the Virginia Regiment—and its commander—part of the regular British army. Shirley rejected the idea out of hand. The failure of these efforts to gain imperial preferment convinced Washington that his future lay with Virginia rather than with the wider empire.

When William Pitt became prime minister of Britain in 1757, he included in his grand plans for 1758 an expedition to reduce Fort Duquesne and so avenge Braddock's defeat. Pitt named Brigadier General John Forbes to lead the campaign, and Forbes shrewdly persuaded Washington to remain in service, thereby retaining his unparalleled expertise in frontier warfare. Serving under Forbes gave Washington an important opportunity to work with and observe a British professional officer, one more capable than Braddock. Forbes moved slowly but inexorably forward with his five thousand provincials and seventeen hundred regulars. With their position in the Ohio valley collapsing, and Forbes just twelve miles away by 23 November—Washington's First Virginia Regiment led the advance guard—the French evacuated and blew up Fort Duquesne. With the frontier now secure and land speculation beckoning, Washington resigned his commission in December 1758, and on 6 January 1759 married the wealthy widow Martha Dandridge Custis (1732–1802). The twenty-six-year-old Virginian emerged from his first period of military service with a reputation as a brave, ambitious, and hard-driving officer. In terms of the breadth of his experience and the length of his service,

Washington was, at that point, the foremost colonial American soldier.

ROAD TO REVOLUTION

Washington, his wife, and his two step-children settled down at Mount Vernon. With Martha's property added to his own inheritance, he was now one of the richest planters in Virginia, though, like most wealthy planters, he carried an enormous debt. Washington spent sixteen years (1759–1775) focused on his personal economy. He decided on what to grow in which fields (he moved in 1765–1766 from cultivating tobacco to growing wheat), managed his largely slave labor force (216 workers and their families in February 1786, and 317 by July 1799), marketed his crops, kept his accounts, speculated in western lands, and renovated his mansion. As a member of the elite he also served in the House of Burgesses, gaining the respect of his peers, though not rising to leadership positions in the colony.

Washington viewed the Stamp Act of 1765 as bad economic policy, but played no significant role in the opposition to this or other British legislation until 1769. Then he promoted the non-importation association designed to force repeal of the Townshend Acts. When the Royal governor, Norborne Berkeley, baron de Botetourt, dissolved the House of Burgesses on 9 May 1769, Washington was among the members who reconvened at Williamsburg's Raleigh Tavern. He was named to the committee that, on the next day, presented George Mason's non-importation plan for adoption by the extra-legally assembled burgesses. Siding with the radicals, Washington opposed making petitions to the king and parliament, not only because they would be scorned, but because he did not believe in begging for rights. His response in June 1774 to "the oppressive and arbitrary act of Parliament for stopping up the port" of Boston, reflects his mature judgment:

> the ministry may rely on it that Americans will never be taxed without their own consent, that the cause of Boston ... now is and ever will be considered as the cause of America (not that we approve their conduct in destroying the tea), and that we shall not suffer ourselves to be sacrificed by piecemeal (*ibid.*, 10, pp. 95–96).

His letters show that he comprehended the political course the Patriots were taking and recognized that the course led to war with Britain.

The next step in Washington's carefully considered support for American rights came in August 1774, when he accepted the Virginia Convention's appointment as delegate to the first Continental Congress, where his participation was not remarkable. He urged that military preparations get under way, personally drilled volunteers, and sat on the Virginia Convention's committee "to

prepare a plan for embodying, arming and disciplining" men who would be able "immediately" to put the colony "into a posture of defence" (*ibid.*, p. 309). On 25 March, the Convention elected him as a delegate to the Second Continental Congress, where he was conspicuous as the only member habitually to attend sessions dressed in a military uniform. With no recorded dissent, the delegates decided to adopt a European-style military organization, one that derived from the colonies' own military experience, as the principal vehicle for the armed defense of their rights. On 15 June 1775, on the motion of John Adams of Massachusetts, Washington was unanimously selected by Congress as commander in chief of this force, newly styled the Continental Army, which, at that point, comprised only the recently raised regiments of the four New England colonies.

The choice of Washington for this unprecedented position was both shrewd and nearly inevitable. A prominent member of the ruling class in the most powerful and important colony, Washington was clearly an ardent defender of colonial rights and possessed more military experience than anyone else in Congress. Washington brought many skills, some not yet evident, to his new responsibility. Perhaps the most important of these was his thoroughgoing belief in the subordination of the military to civilian control. The irony in Washington's position was that he was being called upon to establish and command an Americanized version of the standing army that was regarded as the principal threat to American liberty.

THE FIRST CAMPAIGN

Commissioned on 19 June 1775, Washington departed for Cambridge four days later. He reached New York City on 25 June, and there began two streams of communication that he would faithfully continue, and that would consume an enormous amount of his time and energy, for the rest of the war. He wrote the first in a long series of letters to Congress to explain the situations he encountered, the steps he had taken, and the actions he thought Congress should take. Congress and its principal military officer were breaking new ground with every decision they made, and they had to communicate, and negotiate, about nearly everything. Washington believed that he owed his colleagues in Congress, and the political leaders at state and local levels with whom he also regularly corresponded, his best advice about how to manage the armed resistance to Britain, its policies, and supporters. So far as operational necessity allowed, he left the final decision up to civilian policy makers.

The second line of correspondence was equally important. He began to correspond with the commander of the New York Department, Major General Philip Schuyler, who led the only American forces then in the field, apart from the main army around Boston.

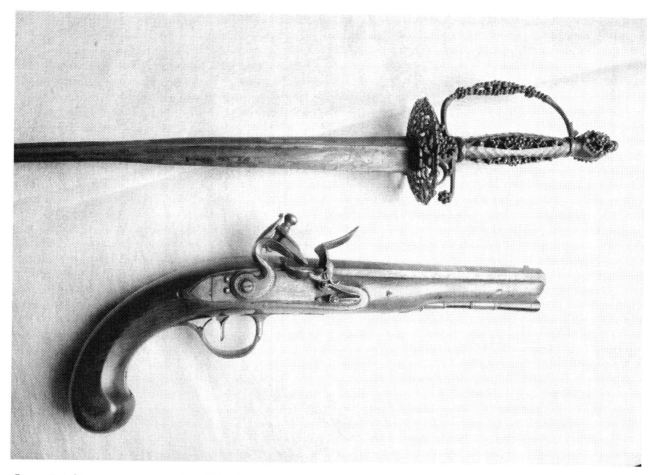

George Washington's Dress Sword and Pistol. *This sword and pistol are now held by the New York State Archive and the New York State Library, along with numerous other items related to Washington and the American Revolution.* **AP/WIDE WORLD PHOTOS**

Washington did this, in part, to exercise the oversight he believed was required of a commander in chief. However, he also sought to keep himself apprised of developments in other theaters that could affect the overall war effort and his own direction of the main American army. His instructions to Schuyler to obey the orders of Congress "with as much precision and exactness as possible" (*ibid.*, p. 37) reflected the fact that time and distance would not allow him to exercise close control over forces elsewhere.

Washington arrived at Cambridge on 2 July 1775, and took formal command the next day of the New England troops besieging Boston. He faced two immediate and ongoing problems, one administrative and organizational, the other operational. His principal challenge was to prepare American recruits to face in battle, and to defeat, the soldiers of an army that was better trained, better equipped, and more responsive to its officers than was his own force. By temperament and experience a believer in social hierarchy, Washington also knew that military success would hinge on how well he and his officers could command soldiers who were unused to

military discipline. To set a good example of the care and attention he expected from his officers, Washington immediately began the practice of riding around the army each morning. He was thereby able to observe and be observed by his troops. Since he was an excellent horseman, the display presented by the tall, powerfully built, and well-accoutered general riding by in firm control of a strong horse must have had a positive effect on the army.

Administrative minutiae consumed much of Washington's time. He put in place the new people and procedures established by Congress to feed, pay, and supply the soldiers. He paid particular attention to imposing order, discipline, and central control on an army created just eleven weeks earlier. He had to know the state of the army—especially how many men were fit for duty—and to ensure that the soldiers had enough food, shelter, and equipment (clothing, arms, and gunpowder) so that they were a viable force. Tasks that were routine in the British army had to be explained to American soldiers, none perhaps more essential than the proper management of latrines. In his first set of general orders (4 July), he included an exhortation to unity: "it is hoped that all distinctions of colonies will be laid aside, so that one and the same spirit may animate the whole, and the only contest be, who shall render ... the most essential service to the great and common cause in which we are all engaged" (*ibid.*, p. 54).

As the military leader of a coalition, Washington had to exercise tact in dealing with governments, officers, and soldiers alike. In public and to Congress he told the truth, but remained upbeat. On 10 July, he told John Hancock that he took "a sincere pleasure in observing that there are materials for a good army, a great number of able-bodied men [who are] active [and] zealous in the cause and of unquestionable courage" (*ibid.*, p. 91). In private, to his cousin and business manager Lund Washington, he was less sanguine. On 20 August he observed of the Massachusetts troops: "their officers generally speaking are the most indifferent kind of people I ever saw.... I daresay the men would fight very well (if properly officered), although they are an exceeding dirty and nasty people" (*ibid.*, pp. 335–336). When the Connecticut regiments, whose enlistments expired on 1 December, chose to leave camp and march home, an enraged Washington could do nothing to stop them.

Washington's second major problem was deciding what to do with the army, which reached a peak strength of nearly 19,000 officers and men fit for duty in August 1775, once he was satisfied it was ready to fight. He had to find the best use of the military means at hand to reverse British oppression before the cost of the army—the strain it placed on the lines of authority in society as much as the expense of raising, paying, feeding, and equipping it—proved more than the colonies could bear.

Washington, who was deliberative and cautious most of the time, also possessed a streak of aggressiveness that was fueled by an ever-growing anxiety about the expense of, and social dangers posed by, keeping soldiers idle under arms for long periods. These considerations found expression in his continuing desire to use the army for offensive action that was sometimes fantastically over-ambitious. On 8 September, with winter on the horizon and, more importantly, the enlistments of the bulk of his army set to expire by 1 January, Washington asked his generals—all New Englanders—if an assault on the British in Boston by boat was advisable. Unsurprisingly, they decided the project was "not expedient." Then, after going through the trauma and anxiety of seeing the 1775 army dissolve away and being forced to raise the 1776 army in the face of the enemy, he proposed on 16 February 1776 to attack Boston across the ice of Back Bay. Again, his generals vetoed the idea, and Washington admitted that "perhaps the irksomeness of my situation led me to undertake more than could be warranted by prudence" (*ibid.*, 3, p. 370). The arrival of Colonel Henry Knox with heavy artillery from Fort Ticonderoga allowed Washington to speed the

British evacuation from Boston without having to risk his authority by ordering an assault his men might have refused to undertake.

In his first campaign as commander in chief, Washington faced nearly all the issues that would plague him for the next eight years. He had to keep Congress informed about the military situation and seek its sanction for measures he knew were important but about which his former colleagues often held different views. He also had to maintain good relations with local leaders while keeping his eye on the central issue—building and maintaining an army that could defeat the British. This often meant denying requests to disperse soldiers from his army for local defense. If he wanted to undertake a particular course of action, he knew he had to seek the advice of his subordinates, the men who would know best whether or not the soldiers might obey his orders. To his credit, Washington listened carefully to his generals and often deferred to their arguments. Because the army had not been enlisted for the duration of the war—Americans could not have been persuaded in 1775 to enlist in what was in effect a standing army—he had to manage the dissolution of one army and the raising of its successor, knowing that the British might at any moment take advantage of the opportunity to cripple his force. Nearly every decision he made established new traditions, sometimes on the remnants of prior colonial experience, but in circumstances made new and more dangerous by the need for larger numbers of troops. He gained vivid experience in the reality of something he already well understood: commanding an army in America was as much a political process as a military one. His actions cannot therefore be evaluated exclusively, or even primarily, from a military point of view.

MANEUVER WAR IN 1776

After the British evacuated Boston in March 1776, Washington moved his army toward New York City, the most obvious place where the enemy would strike next. The decision to defend New York City was made for political reasons because, militarily, the area was so laced by rivers and estuaries that it was nearly indefensible with land forces. Without naval forces capable of contesting control of the water with the Royal navy, Washington convinced himself that shore batteries could so command the water passages around Manhattan Island and the western quarter of Long Island that fending off the British forces might be possible. With an army composed of half-trained Continentals and untrained militia, and, most importantly, an officer corps—up to and including Washington—that was utterly inexperienced in maneuver warfare, the Americans stood on the defensive.

By early July 1776, Washington had over 12,000 men in the area. Continentals from New England, New York, Maryland, and Delaware formed the core of the army, their numbers augmented by militia and flying camp units that continued to come in even as the Howe brothers (William and Richard) massed the largest expeditionary force Britain had ever sent overseas to take back the city and begin the reconquest of America. Washington made a mistake by dividing his forces, sending part of his army to oppose William Howe on Long Island in August. An unsettled command structure, faulty reconnaissance, and widespread inexperience in making and interpreting decisions amid the chaos of battle deprived the American army of any chance of success. With the concurrence of a council of war composed of his surviving generals, Washington decided on 29 August to evacuate Long Island. He was very lucky to get his army back to Manhattan, an accomplishment made possible only by an extraordinary effort by men determined to escape the trap and General William Howe's failure to pursue the Americans vigorously. Howe hesitated, offering the carrot of a political solution in tandem with the stick of a military beating. Washington always deferred Howe's overtures to Congress.

Washington then prepared to defend Manhattan Island, a decision again based on political rather than military logic. When the British landed at Kips Bay on 15 September, all of Washington's personal efforts to stem the flight of several Connecticut state regiments defending the landing beach were for naught. The American army was saved once more by Howe's deliberate pace. Although American rangers bloodied the nose of the British pursuit at Harlem Heights the next day, by the end of the month Washington's army was being consistently pushed around and beaten by a British army far superior at maneuver warfare.

On 25 September, while staying at Colonel Roger Morris's house on Harlem Heights, Washington made his case to John Hancock, then president of Congress, for the kind of army he needed to defeat the British. Written under the pressure of impending defeat, the arguments are among his most candid remarks about the character of his officers and soldiers, and the paramount importance of proper leadership. With the enlistment of his troops set to expire at year's end, Washington wrote:

> We are now as it were, upon the eve of another dissolution of our army. The remembrance of the difficulties which happened upon that occasion last year, . . . satisfy me, beyond the possibility of a doubt, that unless some speedy and effectual measures are adopted by Congress, our cause will be lost.

The bounties and pay offered by Congress convinced him that only a "triffling" number would reenlist. The core issue before Congress, Washington argued, was retaining experienced soldiers and officers. Doing so required that Congress recognize that the members of the army are motivated, like most others, by self-interest.

> The few, therefore, who act upon principles of disinterestedness, are, comparatively speaking, no more than a drop in the ocean. It becomes evidently clear then, that as this contest is not likely to be the work of a day, as the war must be carried on systematically, and to do it, you must have good officers, there are, in my judgment, no other possible means to obtain them but by establishing your army upon a permanent footing, and giving your officers good pay. . . . nothing but a good bounty can obtain them [the soldiers] upon a permanent establishment, and for no shorter period than the continuance of the war ought they to be engaged, as facts incontestably prove, that the difficulty and the cost of enlistment, increase with time.

He went on to argue that Congress must act on these recommendations despite the cost. "[H]owever high the mens' pay may appear, it is barely sufficient in the present scarcity and dearness of all kinds of goods, to keep them in cloths, much less afford support to their families" (Twohig, *Washington Papers*, 6, pp. 394–396).

Washington asserted that, if pay and bounties were raised to attract the right sort of officers and men, he would soon have an army capable of beating British regulars. Because he believed a long-service, and therefore well-trained, standing army was absolutely necessary, he downplayed the fear that such a force might destroy civil liberties, which was the great bugbear of Whig political philosophy: "The jealousies of a standing army, and the evils to be apprehended from one, are remote, and in my judgment, situated and circumstanced as we are, not at all to be dreaded; but the consequence of wanting one . . . is certain, and inevitable ruin" (*ibid.*, p. 397). Washington accepted responsibility for his inability to defeat the British, but felt success was impossible "unless there is a thorough change in our military system" (*ibid.*, p. 400).

Washington's analysis was accurate on nearly every point, but Congress never followed his advice so completely that he could build the army he wanted. One of his greatest military attributes was a willingness and ability to create a viable military force from the materials his civilian superiors and American society gave him. His other great military attribute was an indomitable spirit. On one key point, however Washington was wrong. Although prospects looked dim, and got worse, the cause was not lost, in large part because Washington himself refused to give up.

As Howe continued to outflank the Americans and force their retreat, Washington concluded by mid-October that his position on the north end of Manhattan

Island was untenable. He withdrew north to Westchester County, but decided, on Nathanael Greene's advice, to leave a strong garrison behind at Fort Washington. It was a decision based more on pride than military reality, and it cost the Americans dearly. Howe decided after the battle at White Plains (28 October) not to chase the Americans further north. Instead, he turned back south and, on 16 November, took the fort, along with its stockpile of weapons and ammunition. Washington's reputation sank to a new low as he led his army west over the Hudson and across northern New Jersey.

The flight of the American army was precipitous and, as militia went home and detachments left to cover other possible British targets, the main army was reduced on 22 December to less than 6,100 effective men. Washington did not panic. He sent parties ahead to gather up all the boats on the Delaware River. He thought that "the design of General Howe is to possess himself of Philadelphia this winter, if possible" (*ibid.*, p. 381). As he told Hancock on 20 December, "in truth, I do not see what is to prevent him, as ten days more will put an end to the existence of our army" (*ibid.*, p. 382). He understood that Howe's larger objective was to keep pressure on the Continentals in order to prevent recruitment for the following year. "If every nerve is not strained to recruit the new army with all possible expedition, I think the game is pretty near up" (*ibid.*, p. 370).

Because of the gravity of the military situation, Washington asked Congress for an extraordinary grant of power. Speed in decision-making was essential: if "every matter that in its nature is self evident, is to be referred to Congress, . . . so much time must necessarily elapse as to defeat the end in view." He understood that "It may be said that this is an application for powers, that are too dangerous to be entrusted. I can only add, that desperate diseases require desperate remedies" (*ibid.*, p. 382). On 27 December, Congress granted, for a term of six months, Washington's request for extraordinary powers to sustain the army under his command. By that time, Washington had already acted with the remnant of the 1776 army to rescue the American cause from the brink of extinction. It must have given him enormous satisfaction to know that, on the same day that Congress acted, he had dispatched to Hancock his account of the success at Trenton on Christmas Day.

Washington's decisions to attack the British outpost at Trenton on 25–26 December 1776, and to follow up that success with a spoiling attack on the British pursuit at Princeton on 3 January 1777, were his most important of the war. Few commanders could have achieved offensive maneuvers of this type in the dead of winter, with demoralized, starved, and ill supplied troops. The riposte had military value—it pushed in the British outpost line and

saved Philadelphia—but its transcendent impact was on the psychology of the war. The British army under Howe pushed aside the American forces defending New York City, reestablished British control over important areas, and began a cascade of defections from the rebel cause. But Howe was too enamored of positional warfare, so he failed to realize that his true target ought to have been the destruction of Washington's army. When Washington demonstrated in convincing fashion at Trenton and Princeton that the American army was still alive and dangerous, he won for the American cause the opportunity to continue the fight into 1777.

SURVIVAL

The 1776 campaign had been so disruptive that it took Washington and his officers well into the new year to organize a new army. The disasters of 1776 persuaded Congress that Washington was right to advocate longer enlistments. It therefore authorized recruiting soldiers for three years of service, or for the duration of the war. Many veterans re-enlisted, but it took until mid-year for them to recuperate physically and be joined by sufficient new recruits to make a respectable army. Fortunately for Washington, the British also needed several months to ready their forces.

Skirmishing in northern New Jersey had convinced Howe that an overland campaign against Philadelphia would be too costly, so he decided to transport his army by sea to attack the American capital. Recognizing that Howe was his most dangerous opponent, but not knowing exactly where or when he would strike, Washington gambled by sending some of his best troops to reinforce the northern army, which faced John Burgoyne's troops who were advancing south from Montreal. With that help, and an abundance of militia flowing in from New England and New York, the northern army stopped Burgoyne's advance and forced him to surrender at Saratoga on 17 October 1777. Meanwhile, in early August, the British fleet carrying Howe's army had already been spotted at the mouth of the Delaware River. Although it put out to sea and disappeared, by the time it reappeared in the Chesapeake and began disembarking the invasion force on 22 August, Washington had his hands full directing the defense of Philadelphia.

As had been the case with New York City in 1776, Washington had to defend Philadelphia for political reasons, although the city's setting afforded the Americans a greater chance for success in 1777. By threatening the American capital, Howe sought both to discredit the rebel government and to pin Washington's army to its defense, thus affording the British forces an opportunity to destroy it. When Washington took up a position behind Brandywine Creek, thirty miles west of the city, he was fully aware that Howe might seek to outflank him, as he had done so often in 1776. The fog of war made British movements difficult to confirm, and, despite hard fighting and improved tactical control, the ensuing battle (11 September) once again showed the immaturity of the Continental Army's command structure and its lack of battle management skills. The army escaped the British pincers, but could not prevent the enemy from occupying Philadelphia on 23 September.

Washington still thought he might be able to force Howe out by holding several forts on the Delaware below the city, thus preventing the British from readily supplying the city by water. To help distract the British from concentrating on reducing the forts, Washington launched on 4 October an overly complicated, four-pronged attack on British defenses five miles north of the city, at Germantown. Chronic difficulties in command were exacerbated by a literal fog that covered the battlefield. Washington accepted Henry Knox's advice that the Americans reduce a British fortified post at the Chew House (in Germantown) before advancing further, a decision which slowed the momentum of the American advance and contributed significantly to the failure of the attack. The American forts on the Delaware held out until the third week of November, but could not prevail against the full weight of British land and sea power.

INTERLUDE AT VALLEY FORGE

Having failed to hold the capital, Washington set about containing the military damage to the cause. After considering several potential encampments at a greater distance from Philadelphia, he chose a position at Valley Forge, twenty-five miles west of the city. From here he could closely observe the British and respond quickly to any foray into the countryside. The army went into winter quarters on 11 December 1777, very late in the season, and suffered enormously from a logistics crisis that had been building for several months. Valley Forge became the archetype of Revolutionary War winter encampments, although the suffering endured in 1776–1777 and 1780–1781 was probably more intense and widespread.

Washington's unceasing efforts to remedy the supply problems did much to cement his reputation with the army. Concentrating the troops further dislocated the logistics system, but gave Washington an opportunity for training that he and the army had not had in 1775–1776 or 1776–1777. Baron Friedrich Wilhelm Augustus von Steuben arrived in camp on 24 February 1778, and began the process of standardizing the training and regularizing the drill of the army. His efforts helped veteran officers and men better understand what was expected of them on the battlefield, and gave Washington for the first time a reason to expect that his orders might be carried out in a similar way across the army. Steuben's efforts as inspector general also helped to give the commander in chief more uniform tactical combat units, thus potentially increasing the flexibility of the army on the battlefield.

At the same time that the army was maturing, Washington faced the most notorious, if perhaps not the most serious, attempt to unseat him. In the autumn of 1777, Brigadier General Thomas Conway, a French volunteer of Irish descent and no discernable ability, became the vehicle for discontent with the state of the war. Conway was a public critic of Washington's leadership, and the efforts of some Congressional delegates to promote him to major general over the heads of the other brigadiers sparked in Washington the suspicion of a conspiracy directed against him. Washington was insistent as any of his subordinates that proper respect be paid to seniority, and more sensitive, in private, about his reputation than most of them. Therefore, the news of Conway's ascendancy provoked Washington to write a sharp letter to Richard Henry Lee on 16 October. Calling Conway an officer whose merit "exists more in his own imagination than in reality," he told Lee that "I have been a slave to the service. I have undergone more than most men are aware of, to harmonize so many discordant parts, but it will be impossible for me to be of any further service if such insuperable difficulties [as Conway's promotion] are thrown in my way" (*ibid.*, 11, pp. 529–530). Conway was not the only man proposed to replace Washington at the head of the army. Some delegates to Congress supported Horatio Gates, the victor over Burgoyne. In effect, he forced Congress to choose between him and someone else (Gates may have been the candidate of some delegates), a response that, coming in the wake of the defeat at Germantown, reflected his own uncertainty and frustration about the loss of Philadelphia. The fact that he continued to try to root out conspirators into February 1778 (long after Conway's resignation showed the depth of his anger at being under-appreciated).

RETURN TO BATTLE

The newly refurbished Continental Army, 12,000 men now healthy and well-supplied, left Valley Forge on 18 June 1778, in pursuit of the British army retreating overland from Philadelphia to New York City. Washington saw an opportunity to land a hard blow on his nemesis, the British army, and he dispatched a strong advance guard, five thousand men under Charles Lee, to harass the British and bring them to bay before they reached the safety of their fleet at Sandy Hook.

Lee, to whom Washington had not given more than general instructions, found his force overextended when the British rear guard turned to fight at Monmouth Court House on 27 June. As the American advance guard retreated, under pressure but in good order on a day when the temperature soared to 110 degrees, Washington came up with the main army and encountered Lee, who could not give a coherent account of the whereabouts of his troops. Some observers remembered that Washington, who was extremely anxious about losing an unprecedented opportunity to hurt the British army, lost his temper and berated Lee. If so, he quickly recovered his self-control and spent the rest of the day stemming the retreat and establishing a defensive position. He was unceasingly active and repeatedly exposed himself to enemy fire, reaching a pinnacle of effective battle management of the best army America had yet fielded. When the British rear guard broke off the encounter, having successfully covered the retreat of the army, Washington's men were so spent that they could not offer pursuit.

Monmouth Court House was the last battlefield on which Washington would exercise overall field command. The character of the war was changing—news of the French alliance had been received and celebrated on 6 May, before the army left Valley Forge—and Washington's role would also change. His contributions to this point had been crucial. More than any other individual, he had turned the army kicked out of New York City in 1776 into a competent fighting force, achieving his goal of creating a force able to match the British army. By building and preserving the army, he had, in effect, kept the Americans from losing the war. But Britain was not yet ready to concede the political independence of its colonies, even though its failure to suppress the rebellion had blossomed into another world war against its ancient enemy, France.

Having managed not to lose the war militarily, Washington now faced the equally formidable task of applying military power to induce Britain to recognize American independence. Washington's new task was two-fold: keeping the Continental army in a state of readiness, while learning to cooperate with new allies—Spain and, most particularly, France—to achieve victory. French land forces were only potentially significant, but Washington understood that French naval power was crucial to transforming the outcome of the conflict from 'not losing' to 'winning.'

STALEMATE AND FRENCH AID

Washington's immediate challenge after 1778 was to hold the army together. As the British shifted the main theater of operations to the south, Washington's army continued to hold a wide perimeter around British-occupied New York City. Lacking the means to assault the British defenses, Washington was reduced to fighting what he called a "war of posts," a term that described on-going, small-scale fighting between detachments of the main armies. The Americans had, of course, engaged in this sort of partisan war since 1775, but now supporting it became the principal activity of the main army.

Historians have applied the adjective "Fabian" to much of Washington's strategy, because his efforts to avoid allowing the British to trap his army into fighting at a disadvantage echoed what Quintus Fabius Maximus had done to preserve Rome against the Carthaginian army under Hannibal Barca during the second Punic war (218–202 B.C.). In doing so, they have underestimated the extent to which Washington wanted to act aggressively to end a financially ruinous and socially disruptive war as quickly as possible. They overlook the fact that this "Fabian" style was imposed upon him by Britain's efforts to end the war quickly and by the manifest deficiencies of his army to meet and defeat that challenge. When, after Valley Forge, Washington at last had an army capable of beating the British in battle, he found that the enemy had shifted the battleground and refused to fight the war for which he was now better prepared.

Holding an army together required more than the endless paperwork that consumed much of Washington's time and energy. Washington knew that the fighting skills of an idle army would erode almost as fast as its discontent would grow. He kept his troops busy drilling, skirmishing, and building encampments. He drew together in the summer of 1779 an elite force of light infantry that stormed the British outpost of Stony Point on 16 July, and sent another force to raid Paulus Hook on 19 August. The bulk of the campaigning that summer was done away from the main army by Continental troops that Washington sent in May under John Sullivan to ravage the British-allied Iroquois Confederacy. The expedition reduced the danger to American settlers along the frontier in New York and Pennsylvania, but it held no prospect of ending the stalemate with Britain.

With the enlistments of many of his soldiers set to expire starting on 1 January 1780, Washington faced yet again the prospect of re-creating the Continental Army, the third time he had to undertake that unsettling job since 1775. By the early fall of 1780, more than 12,000 men who had enlisted for three years of service would complete their obligation, leaving Washington with a nominal strength of only the 15,000 men who had enlisted for the duration of the war. Although he had been a consistent and persistent advocate of longer enlistments, he now saw that annual enlistments, with the states' drafting their quota of soldiers if necessary, was "the surest and most certain if not the only means left us, of maintaining the army on a proper and respectable ground" (Fitzpatrick, *Washington Writings*, 17, p. 127). It was a policy he had first advocated as a stop-gap in February 1778, but now it became the centerpiece of his efforts to keep an army in the field during the war's fifth year. Despite considerable grumbling among New England troops about when, exactly, their enlistments expired—the discontent reached mutiny among some Massachusetts troops on 1 January 1780 and affected Connecticut troops on 25 May—he managed to re-create a smaller army around a core of veterans.

As Washington watched events in the south unfold disastrously during the summer of 1780, he could take comfort in the fact that a French expeditionary force was making its way to America. Its commander, the comte de Rochambeau, arrived at Newport, Rhode Island, on 10 July, and Washington went to Hartford to meet with him on 22 September to press his plan to attack New York City. For this plan, the support of French naval power was crucial. He candidly told Rochambeau that his army was on the eve of another reorganization, and that without a decision from a dithering Congress on how to augment the army, he would have only six thousand men available after 1 January 1781, too few for the contemplated attack. He asked if the French could augment their land forces to fifteen thousand men, and thus bear the brunt of the fighting. His plans remained in abeyance when he left Hartford to return to the Hudson Highlands and rode into the worst nightmare of the war.

No event shocked Washington and the rebel cause more than the treason of Benedict Arnold and his attempt to turn over the key post of West Point to the British. The loss of West Point would have forced Washington to retreat north from the Highlands and impeded east-west communication and transportation across the Hudson River. But without a strong follow-up by the British—an impossibility given their commitments further south—these military consequences could have been mitigated and endured. Washington called Arnold's conduct "so villainously perfidious, that there are no terms that can describe the baseness of his heart" (*ibid.*, 20, p. 213). Arnold's treason was so serious because it highlighted how fragile the Patriot cause might be, raising the specter that it might collapse from within. Washington, as usual, put the best public face that he could on the events. He congratulated the army, saying that its ability had caused the British to despair "of carrying their point by force" and forced them into "practicing every base art to effect by bribery and corruption what they cannot accomplish in a manly way" (*ibid.*, p. 95). To Rochambeau, he struck a more worldly pose: "traitors are the growth of every country and in a revolution of the present nature, it is more to be wondered at, that the catalogue is so small than that there have been found a few" (*ibid.*, p. 97).

The fall and winter of 1780–1781 was the nadir of the American military effort. There was no settled plan on how to use French help, treason had been detected but was still hanging in the air, and, early in January, the largest mutinies ever to erupt in the Continental Army, broke out among Pennsylvania troops at Morristown, New Jersey, spreading to New Jersey soldiers stationed at Pompton three weeks later. The same point Washington made

about Arnold's treason could be applied to the army. Given the string of continuing deprivation, recent idleness, doubts about the terms of their enlistment, and endless unfulfilled promises of support from Congress and the states, it is a wonder that the soldiers did not mutiny more often than they did. Washington, who was fully aware of the state of the army, knew he had to move carefully to restore discipline without spreading the discontent and turning the army into a dangerous mob of armed men. He could not leave his headquarters at New Windsor, New York, until he was assured that the West Point garrison, which had shown "some symptoms of a similar intention," would not also mutiny (*ibid.*, 21, p. 65). Washington left it to Anthony Wayne, the commander of the Pennsylvania Division, and other influential officers to quell the mutiny. To Wayne, he observed (8 January) that "such measures founded in justice, and a proper degree of generosity, as will have a tendency to conciliate" the men would be most appropriate, a concise statement of what it took to be a leader of American soldiers, then and now (*ibid.*, p. 71).

In his general orders of January 1781, Washington exhorted the army to endure in the face of adversity. His words summarize his views about the course of the war to that point:

> We began the contest for liberty and independence ill provided with the means of war, relying on our own patriotism to supply the deficiency. We expected to encounter many wants and distresses, and we should neither shrink from them when they happen nor fly in the face of law and government to procure redress.... [I]t is our duty to bear present evils with fortitude, looking forward to the period when our country will have it more in its power to reward our services (Fitzpatrick, *Washington Writings*, 21, p. 159).

Americans' self-image of the virtue of their actions was at stake. In public, Washington blamed the British for appealing to the weaknesses of the average American soldier, blaming them for the recent mutinies. In private, however, he admitted that the men had been driven to extremes by the neglect of the civilian authorities. They were not traitors—he early laid to rest the suspicion that they might join the enemy—but men with legitimate grievances. Far more than his pious words, it was the reputation that Washington, and many of his officers, had earned as paternal advocates of their men that prevented the mutinies from so crippling the army that the British might have had an opportunity at the eleventh hour to crush the rebellion.

Instead, it was Washington who, as the war entered its sixth year, had the chance to win the victory. On 22 May 1781, he met with Rochambeau at Wethersfield, Connecticut, to push his plan to attack the British garrison at New York City, which had been weakened when it sent detachments to the southern theater. To Washington, New York City was the best target for a joint Franco-American operation. By early August, however, and after having probed its outer defenses, he reluctantly acknowledged that it was still too strongly held. At a conference with Rochambeau at Dobb's Ferry on 19 July, he proposed sending a joint force to oppose British operations in Virginia, thus putting aside his earlier objections to campaigning so far from New York City and in a climate less healthy for his troops.

On 14 August, Washington learned that the French West Indies fleet, sailing under the comte de Grasse, was headed to the Chesapeake. Then, in a decision that ranks second in importance and audacity only to the attack on Trenton in 1776, and which together marks him as the most audacious gambler in the history of American arms, Washington decided to shift the theater of war from the Hudson to the Chesapeake. Although previous joint ventures with the French—at Newport and Savannah—had failed, he realized that he had to take advantage of when and where the French chose to employ their naval power if he were to have any chance of breaking the military stalemate. With great secrecy about its final destination, the allied army—the French expeditionary corps and the best of the reorganized American army—began moving west across the Hudson and then southward on 18 August. Organizing that transit was a masterstroke of military logistics, the most impressive achievement of its kind to that date. The arriving troops tipped the balance against the British field army under Earl Cornwallis, but it was the draw earned by the French fleet at the Battle of the Chesapeake Capes on 5 September that ensured the success of Washington's gamble.

THE WAR WINDS DOWN

The surrender of Cornwallis's army at Yorktown on 19 October 1781 ultimately made Britain's political leaders realize they did not have the resources to re-conquer their North American colonies by force of arms. It was not, however, the end of war. Washington wanted to continue the successful Franco-American partnership into the following year. To this end, he wrote to de Grasse on 28 October proposing a rendezvous with the fleet in the Chesapeake in 1782, when a decision would be made to move against either New York City or Charleston, South Carolina. De Grasse was understandably non-committal. Nevertheless, as the Continental troops made their way north to the Hudson for the winter, Washington's hopes for such an alliance were high, raised no doubt by his first visits to Mount Vernon since the war began (9–12 September on the march south, 13–20 November on the way north). He wintered at Philadelphia, but had returned to the Highlands by the time he received news that George

Rodney's destruction of the French fleet at the Saintes (near Martinique) in early April had scuttled his plans for 1782.

Holding the army together while the political and diplomatic process wound its way to a final peace treaty was Washington's main preoccupation after Yorktown. The army's continued existence signified American willingness to continue military operations if necessary. Instead of a year of victory, however, 1782 turned into a year of frustration, with no significant military activity to relieve the main army's idleness.

The men endured, but by early 1783, some officers had had enough of Congress's failure to carry through on its promise of pay and rewards. A dissident group circulated two petitions, the gist of which was a threat to use force to make Congress comply. The Newburgh Addresses, named for the location of the headquarters of the army, constituted the most serious challenge to Washington's leadership since the "Conway Cabal" in 1777. They also represented the most dangerous attempt during the Revolution by military officers to dominate the civilian leadership, a circumstance that gave credence to those who thought the Continental Army a dangerous standing army. Washington put a quick and effective end to these efforts at a meeting of his officers on 15 March.

Four days later, on 19 March 1783, Washington received news that the preliminary articles of peace had been signed in Paris on 20 January. Ever cautious, he kept a much reduced Continental Army together over the summer, its strength eroded by his liberal use of furloughs to send men home and reduce the expense to the public of maintaining them. On 8 June he sent to the states a circular letter that distilled the lessons he had learned during his command of the Continental Army, an intrusion into the nexus between civilian and military that all his recipients did not appreciate. The most important point, "essential to the well being, I may even venture to say, to the existence of the United States as an independent power" was "an indissoluble union of the states under one federal head" (*ibid.*, 26, p. 487). Washington thus staked out a position as a strong nationalist, an unsurprising position considering his experience in command of the army.

Washington disbanded the last major units of the Continental Army on 3 November, keeping under arms less than a thousand men, whose principal service was to reclaim and occupy New York City on 25 November. It was an emotional month for Washington, returning in triumph to the scene of his earlier defeat. On 4 December, the day the last British ship sailed from the harbor, he bid farewell to his officers at Fraunces Tavern. On this occasion he was, for once, rendered speechless by the depth of his feelings for the men he had led since July 1775. On 23 December he returned his commission as commander in chief to Congress, then meeting in the

General George Washington Resigning his Commission *(1783) by John Trumbull.* *Washington submitted his resignation as commander in chief to Congress at the Maryland State House in Annapolis on 23 December 1783. Trumbull's painting shows Thomas Jefferson, James Madison, James Monroe, and Martha Washington in attendance.* **LANDOV**

Maryland State House in Annapolis, and returned to Mount Vernon.

POST-WAR, PRESIDENCY, AND RETIREMENT

Washington's stature and reputation meant that he continued to be involved in public affairs, even as he set about restoring his plantations after an absence of more than eight years. Always interested in western lands, he was involved in shaping the Northwest Ordinance of 1787. More aware than anyone else of the perils of a weak central government, he supported efforts to strengthen the federal union that culminated in the Philadelphia Constitutional Convention of 1787, over which he presided.

After the Constitution was ratified, Washington was the unanimous choice for president, taking office on 30 April 1789 in New York City. He was re-elected in 1792, and in 1796 he refused to stand for a third term. During his presidency, he supported the financial plans of Alexander Hamilton to stabilize the new nation's currency and credit, maintained United States' neutrality during the European war that broke out in 1793, upheld federal

authority to impose an excise tax during the Whiskey Insurrection in 1794, and endorsed Jay's Treaty by which the British finally evacuated posts in the Northwest Territory in 1795. In addition, he appointed Anthony Wayne to command the Legion of the United States, which defeated the Indians at the battle of Fallen Timbers on 20 August 1794, thus opening the Northwest Territory to unrestricted white settlement.

Washington's two terms as president were not without controversy, nor did his great reputation protect him from personal criticism. Rejecting the need for party politics in a republic, he attempted to balance one faction against the other in his cabinet, and concluded his presidency with his "Farewell Address" warning against foreign entanglements. In 1798, President John Adams named Washington as commander in chief of the provisional army that was raised for the expected war with France. Washington's will, dated 9 July 1799, provided, after the death of his wife, for the manumission and financial support of his slaves. He died on 14 December 1799 at Mount Vernon, where he was buried.

Standing well over six feet tall, strongly built, and weighing about 210 pounds, Washington was an imposing physical presence. Except for bad teeth and bouts of debilitating gastrointestinal tuberculosis during the Seven Years' War, he enjoyed remarkably vigorous health until his final illness (a throat infection of some sort). He and Martha, who had spent every possible moment of the war with her husband, had no children, probably because tuberculosis had made Washington infertile. He regarded her two surviving children with her first husband as his own. Prior to her own death, on 22 May 1802, Martha destroyed all but three of the letters George had sent to her.

ASSESSMENT

Washington's military abilities have earned few accolades from historians. Mark Boatner, for example, in the first edition of this encyclopedia, said he had "character and fortitude but a lack of real genius," and regarded Washington's performance at Trenton and Princeton as "his only flash of strategic genius." In terms of battles won, number of troops under his personal direction, or depth of military thinking, Washington does not rank among history's great military leaders. But, although he served under arms longer than anyone else in his generation, he did not consider himself to be a professional soldier, and he cannot be judged by the standards that subsequent generations developed to evaluate success in that field. Rather, he was the quintessential American soldier, a person for whom military service was a central part of his definition of what it meant to be a citizen in his society. In terms of what he accomplished in using force of arms to protect and defend that society, he ranks as the most adroit manipulator of armed force in American history.

Interested in military glory from an early age, Washington managed to survive and—more importantly—to learn from his experiences in the Seven Years' War. In the fifteen years thereafter, he matured and crafted the public face by which we know him best. He channeled his ambitions into paths that were socially acceptable in Virginia society, and won what he always craved—the admiration of his peers. He remained vain and sensitive to criticism of his character and motives, and seems to have adopted a reserved manner to shield himself from insult. With the characteristics of his personality fully in place, Washington in 1775 was a middle-aged man of wealth and stature who believed the society he knew and loved was under attack, and who also believed that it was his obligation as a member of that society to devote his skills and energy to its preservation.

The value of Washington's contribution to winning the war for American Independence and establishing the new nation cannot be overstated. Nearly everything he did as commander in chief of the Continental Army established precedents for the principal American military force

fighting the British. His extraordinary talents as a military administrator helped to sustain the army physically, and his abilities as spokesman for its interests helped to sustain its morale. Two dimensions of his character were especially vital to his success. First, he refused to give up the struggle, even in the darkest days of the war. Second, he never wavered from the principle of civilian control of the military, even to the point of straining the war effort almost to the breaking point. In the end, he accomplished what he had set out to do. He compelled Britain by force of arms to acknowledge the political independence of its former colonies, without sending those colonies into a spiral of political chaos and social disorder. Remarkably, circumstances gave Washington the opportunity to repeat this performance as president of the new United States. He well merited the oft-quoted words of Henry Lee in his funeral oration before members of Congress: "first in war, first in peace, first in the hearts of his countrymen."

SEE ALSO *Braddock, Edward; Conway Cabal; Forbes's Expedition to Fort Duquesne; French Alliance; French and Indian War; Mason, George; Stamp Act; Townshend Acts; Valley Forge Winter Quarters, Pennsylvania.*

BIBLIOGRAPHY

Abbot, W. W., Dorothy Twohig, Philander D. Chase, Beverly H. Runge, and Frederick Hall Schmidt, eds. *The Papers of George Washington, Colonial Series,* 10 vols. Charlottesville: University Press of Virginia, 1983–1995.

Alderman Library. *The Papers of George Washington.* University of Virginia. Online at gwpapers.virginia.edu.

Amory, John K. "George Washington's Infertility: Why Was the Father of Our Country Never a Father?" *Fertility and Sterility* 81, no. 3 (March 2004): 495–499.

Anderson, Fred W. *Crucible of War: The Seven Years' War and the Fate of Empire in British North America, 1754–1766.* New York: Alfred A. Knopf, 2000.

Anderson, Fred W. "The Hinge of Revolution: George Washington Confronts a People's Army. July 3, 1775." *Massachusetts Historical Review* 1 (1999): 21–50.

Chase, Philander D., ed. *The Papers of George Washington, Revolutionary Series,* 14 vols. to date. Charlottesville: University Press of Virginia, 1985–.

Cunliffe, Marcus. "George Washington: George Washington's Generalship." In *George Washington's Generals.* Edited by George Athan Billias. New York: William Morrow and Company, 1964.

Ellis, Joseph J. *His Excellency: George Washington.* New York: Alfred A. Knopf, 2004.

Ferling, John. *The First of Men: George Washington.* Knoxville: University of Tennessee Press, 1988.

Fitzpatrick, John C., ed. *The Writings of George Washington from the Original Manuscript Sources, 1745–1799.* 39 vols. Washington, D.C.: Government Printing Office, 1931–1944.

Flexner, James T. *George Washington.* 4 vols. Boston, Mass.: Little, Brown and Company, 1965–1972.

Freeman, Douglas S. *George Washington: A Biography.* 7 vols. New York: Charles Scribner's Sons, 1948–1957.

Frothingham, Thomas. *Washington: Commander in Chief.* Boston, Mass.: Houghton Mifflin and Company, 1930.

Higginbotham, R. Don. *The War of American Independence: Military Attitudes, Policies, and Practices, 1763–1789.* New York: Macmillan Company, 1971.

———. *George Washington and the American Military Tradition.* Athens: University of Georgia Press, 1985.

———, ed. *George Washington Reconsidered.* Charlottesville: University Press of Virginia, 2001.

Knollenberg, Bernhard. *Washington and the American Revolution: A Reappraisal.* New York: Macmillan Company, 1940.

Lengel, Edward G. *General George Washington: A Military Life.* New York: Random House, 2005.

Longmore, Paul K. *The Invention of George Washington.* Berkeley: University of California Press, 1988.

Middlekauf, Robert. *The Glorious Cause: The American Revolution, 1763–1789.* Revised edition. New York: Oxford University Press, 2005.

Morgan, Edmund S. *The Meaning of Independence: John Adams, George Washington, and Thomas Jefferson.* Charlottesville: University of Virginia Press, 1976.

———. *The Genius of George Washington (The Third George Rogers Clark Lecture).* New York: W. W. Norton and Company, 1980.

Palmer, David R. *The Way of the Fox: American Strategy in the War of Independence.* Westport, Conn.: Greenwood Press, 1975.

Rhodehamel, John, ed. *Writings of George Washington.* New York: Library of America, 1997.

Shy, John. "George Washington Reconsidered." In *The John Biggs Cincinnati Lectures in Military Leadership and Command.* Edited by Henry S. Bausum. Lexington, Va.: VMI Foundation, 1986–1988.

Wills, Garry. *Cincinnatus: George Washington and the Enlightenment.* Garden City, N.Y.: Doubleday and Company, 1984.

revised by Harold E. Selesky

WASHINGTON, WILLIAM. (1752–1810).

Continental officer. Virginia. Born 28 February 1752 on his family's plantation in Stafford County, Virginia, Washington was studying for the ministry when the Revolution started. On 25 February 1776 he was commissioned captain in the Third Virginia Continentals, in which he served during the New York and New Jersey campaigns, seeing combat for the first time at Harlem Heights. Leading the attack on cannon in King Street with Lieutenant James Monroe at Trenton, he was wounded in the hand by a musket ball. Promoted to major in the Fourth Continental Dragoons on 27 January 1777, Washington served at the Battles of Brandywine, Germantown, and Monmouth. After the Tappan massacre in New Jersey on 28 September 1778 that decimated the Third Dragoons of Colonel George Baylor, Washington's cousin—General George Washington—put him in command of the remnants on 20 November 1778.

Late in 1779 Washington moved south with his rebuilt regiment. During the initial phase of the Charleston campaign Washington skirmished with Tarleton on several occasions, getting the better of him at Rantowles on 27 March after also defeating the North Carolina Loyalists under Colonel John Hamilton. Washington was lucky to escape with his life at Monck's Corner and then Lenud's Ferry a few weeks later. After Charleston fell, Washington and Lieutenant Colonel Anthony White (of Moylan's regiment) withdrew into eastern North Carolina to recover and recruit.

Washington scored a clever victory at Rugeley's Mills, South Carolina, on 4 December 1780 and struck next in his Hammond's store raid on 27–31 December. This was the start of operations that led to Morgan's victory at Cowpens on 17 January 1781, where Washington distinguished himself in the battle and closed the action with a dramatic personal encounter with Tarleton witnessed by John Marshall. In the "Race to the Dan" and Greene's counteroffensive, Washington's cavalry was prominent, bringing up the rear of the retreat or leading the advance. After performing with valor at Guilford and Hobkirk's Hill (where only fifty-six of his remaining eighty-seven men were mounted), he was wounded and captured in the Battle of Eutaw Springs on 8 September 1781. While a prisoner in Charleston, Washington married Jane Elliott and stayed in the city after the British left at the end of 1783. He served seventeen years in the South Carolina legislature but refused to consider running for governor. On 19 July 1798, during the French crisis, he was commissioned brigadier general and served until 15 June 1800. He died at his home in Charleston on 6 March 1810.

SEE ALSO *Cowpens, South Carolina; Eutaw Springs, South Carolina; Guilford Courthouse, North Carolina; Hammonds Store Raid of William Washington; Hobkirk's Hill (Camden), South Carolina; Lenud's Ferry, South Carolina; Monck's Corner, South Carolina; Rugeley's Mills; Tappan Massacre, New Jersey; Tarleton, Banastre.*

BIBLIOGRAPHY

Haller, Stephen E. *William Washington: Cavalryman of the Revolution.* Westminster, Md.: Heritage Books, 2001.

revised by Michael Bellesiles

WASHINGTON'S "DICTATORIAL POWERS."

27 December 1776–27 June 1777. When the British advance reached the Delaware River in December 1776, Congress fled from Philadelphia to Baltimore (26 December) and the fate of the Revolution appeared to rest solely in military hands. Before Congress adjourned, it resolved "that, until the Congress shall otherwise order, General Washington be possessed of full power to order and direct all things relative to the [military] department, and to the operations of the war" (*Journals*, 6, p. 1027). Writing on 20 December that "ten days more will put an end to the existence of our army" unless drastic measures were accepted, Washington asked for more sufficient and specific authority to deal with the military emergency. He pointed out that if

> every matter that in its nature is self-evident, is to be referred to Congress, at a distance of 130 or 40 miles [to Baltimore], so much time must necessarily elapse, as to defeat the end in view. It may be said, that this is an application for powers, that are too dangerous to be entrusted. I can only add that, desperate diseases require desperate remedies and with truth declare, that I have no lust after power. (Twohig, ed., 7, p. 382)

Robert Morris carried the burden of administration until 21 December, when Congress appointed George Clymer and George Walton of Georgia to join him in a three-man committee "with powers to execute such continental business as may be proper and necessary to be done at Philadelphia" (*Journals*, 6, p. 1032). Washington dealt with this committee as he planned the counteroffensive that resulted in the brilliant victory at Trenton on Christmas Day. On the evening of 31 December, an express reached his headquarters with a congressional resolution adopted in Baltimore on 27 December:

> This Congress, having maturely considered the present crisis; and having perfect reliance on the wisdom, vigour, and uprightness of General Washington, do, hereby, Resolve, That General Washington shall be, and he is hereby, vested with full, ample, and complete powers to raise and collect together, in the most speedy and effectual manner, from any or all of these United States, sixteen battalions of infantry, in addition to those already voted by Congress; to appoint officers for the said battalions; to raise, officer, and equip three thousand light horse; three regiments of artillery, and a corps of engineers, and to establish their pay; to apply to any of the states for such aid of the militia as he shall judge necessary; to form such magazines of provisions, and in such places, as he shall think proper; to displace and appoint all officers under the rank of brigadier general, and to fill up all vacancies in every other department in the American armies; to take, wherever he may be, whatever he may want for the use of the army, if the inhabitants will not sell it, allowing reasonable price for the same; to arrest and confine persons who refuse to take the continental currency, or are otherwise disaffected to the American cause; and return to the states of which they are citizens, their names, and the nature of their offences, together with the witnesses to prove them: That the foregoing powers be vested in General Washington, for and during the term of six months from the date hereof, unless sooner determined by Congress. (*ibid.*, 6, pp. 1045–1046)

The delegates were obviously breathing more easily in Baltimore when, after Washington's Trenton victory, they felt some further statement as to their position was in order. In a circular letter of 30 December 1776, it informed the thirteen states that:

> Congress would not have Consented to the Vesting of such Powers in the military department . . . if the Situation of Public Affairs did not require at this Crisis a Decision and Vigour, which Distance and Numbers Deny to Assemblies far Remov'd from each other, and from the immediate Seat of War. (*ibid.*, 6, p. 1053)

It is evident from the wording of the 27 December resolve that the powers granted Washington were far from "dictatorial." When he used his authority to make all citizens who had taken the British offer of protection surrender the papers they had accepted or move within the British lines, Congress violently criticized this policy. He has been criticized by historians for failing to use fully his power to take provisions for his army from the profiteering inhabitants of New Jersey. Yet in January 1777, thanks largely to his new, temporary authority, Washington was able to start rebuilding a real army.

When in the fall of 1777 the British army again approached Philadelphia, Congress again evacuated the capital, heading through Lancaster to York, Pennsylvania, and again it gave Washington "dictatorial" powers. This time it was for a six-day period only, and he used the authority sparingly.

SEE ALSO *Continental Congress; New Jersey Campaign; Philadelphia Campaign; Princeton, New Jersey; Trenton, New Jersey.*

BIBLIOGRAPHY

Ford, Worthington C., ed. *Journals of the Continental Congress, 1774–1789.* Vol. 6: *October 9–December 31, 1776.* Washington, D.C.: Library of Congress, 1906.

Lengel, Edward G. *General George Washington: A Military Life.* New York: Random House, 2005.

Twohig, Dorothy, et al., eds. *The Papers of George Washington, Revolutionary War Series.* Vol. 7: *October 1776–January 1777.* Edited by Philander D. Chase. Charlottesville: University Press of Virginia, 1997.

revised by Harold E. Selesky

WATERCRAFT. Revolutionary North America was a region of crude road networks and rigorous terrain intersected by hundreds of waterways. While watercraft played a secondary role on the military supply lines and during many campaigns, it was a crucial one.

British and American forces used numerous vessel types. Sloops, schooners, shallops, and pettiaugers (not to be confused with the similarly named log canoes, called periaugers, pettiaguas, or pettiaugers) were sailing vessels used to transport troops and supplies. Gunboats, galleys, and xebecs were oar-driven craft for river and lake defense. Ferryboats, Durham boats, scows, barges, bateaux, and other flat-bottomed craft carried troops and supplies up and down rivers and lakes or ferried them across bodies of water. Other small vessels, particularly whaleboats, filled important roles as attack craft, guard boats, and logistical support.

By the time of the Revolution the British navy was adept at amphibious operations, and the Royal Navy King's Boat was much used on the lower Hudson, in the Chesapeake, and along the Atlantic coastline. They were propelled with twenty oars, crewed by twenty-five men, and carried as many as fifty troops, though for various reasons the craft were often loaded to only 50 or 70 percent of passenger capacity. These craft were effective troop carriers, though barely seaworthy, difficult to row and maneuver, and detested by Royal Navy personnel. Major General William Phillips suggested building a modified design for use on the northern inland campaign:

> June 3rd 1776. Lieutenant Twiss is to proceed to Three Rivers and give his directions for constructing of Boats the description . . . is, a Common flat Bottom called a Kings Boat or Royal Boat calculated to Carry from 30 to 40 men with Stores and Provisions, with this only difference, that the Bow of each Boat is to be made square resembling an English punt for the conveniency of disembarking the Troops by the means of a kind of Broad Gang board with Loop-holes made in it for musquetry, and which may serve as a mantlet when advancing towards an Enemy, and must be made strong accordingly. (Hagist, "Extracts," p. 23)

It is not known if Phillips's vessels were ever built and used.

Of all the watercraft that served the armies, none were more important or ubiquitous than flat-bottomed boats. Among those craft, bateaux were foremost. Inexpensive to build, crude but effective, bateaux were also clumsy and leaky. Quartermaster General Timothy Pickering described them in 1782, "The common batteaux being built with pine boards, are of course very tender, and altogether unsuitable for the rough services to which those in common use are applied: they require, besides, at least five hands to work them to advantage" (*George Washington Papers,* series 4, reel 83). Bateaux were particularly useful in northern New York and Canada, where waterways provided the only reliable transportation network. Used in large numbers during the French and Indian War, they conspicuously served on General Benedict Arnold's march to Quebec in 1775, again in the Saratoga campaign of 1777, and as wagon boats (large bateaux mounted on carriages) in the Carolina and Yorktown campaigns.

Quartermaster General Thomas Mifflin noted several Continental flatboat types at Coryell's Ferry, Pennsylvania, in June 1777:

> We have here 3 large Artillery Flats, [and] four Scows, each of which will carry a loaded Wagon with Horses, 4 flat boats, each to carry 80 Men, 13 Boats on Wagons at this place and 5 others on the Way 6 Miles from this Ferry each of which Wagon Boats will carry 40 Men[,] All which will transport 3 p[ieces]. Artillery with Matrosses & Horses, 4 Wagons & Horses, and 1000 Men at a Try. (*George Washington Papers* series 4, reel 42)

Transporting large quantities of men and materiel across waterways, while a common event, was a complicated affair. The difficulties of a Hudson River crossing in December 1780 were described by Richard Platt: "By 12 [noon] our van was at Kings ferry - [but] found only one sloop, a scow & five flat boats" (*War Department Collection,* reel 82, no. 23737). A large portion of the baggage for two Massachusetts brigades

> was embarked by 4 P.M. & [the] vessel saild - the same Night the Baggage Waggons & Horses of the Conn[ecticu]t Line crossd - yesterday (tho not till late) a reinforcement of sloops & 3 or 4 small Batteaux arrived - the Conn[ecticu]t Division, Artillery, Ammunition Waggons & Horses belonging were put over & a sloop loaded with M[assachusetts]. Baggage - last Night Col Baldwin's Corps [of Artificers] & apparatus helped themselves across - and [the] light waggons of ye. 4th. M[ass].B[rigade]. & many of the 3rd. by the Assistance of Col Sprout's men were transported. (ibid.)

After all this labor there was still more to do: "This morning remains to be unloaded two sloops containing Jersey Baggage & the same Vessels to take in the remainder of the Massachusett's Baggage & whatever Hutting tools &c Major Kiers has to send (ibid.)."

BIBLIOGRAPHY

Hagist, Don N. "Extracts from the Brigade Orders of Major General Phillips in Canada." *Brigade Dispatch* 29, no. 2 (Summer 1999): 23.

Miffllin, Thomas to George Washington, 8 June 1777, *George Washington Papers, Presidential Papers Microfilm.* Washington, D.C.: Library of Congress, 1961.

Pickering, Timothy to George Washington, 3 March 1782, *George Washington Papers, Presidential Papers Microfilm.* Library of Congress: Washington, D.C., 1961, series 4, reel 83.

Rees, John U. "'Employed in Carrying Clothing & Provisions': Wagons and Watercraft during the War for Independence." Part 2: "Sloops, 'Scows,' 'Batteaux,' and 'Pettyaugers': Continental Army Rivercraft, 1775–1782." *Continental Soldier* 13, no. 1 (Winter/Spring 2000): 34–46.

———. "'The Enemy Was in Hackansack Last Night Burning & Destroing . . .': British Incursions into Bergen County, Spring 1780." Part 1: "'So Much for a Scotch Prize': Paramus, New Jersey, 23 March 1780." Available online at http://www.continentalline.org/articles/article.php?date=0502&article=050201.

War Department Collection of Revolutionary War Records 1775–1790's. Washington, D.C.: National Archives, 1971.

John U. Rees

WATEREE FERRY, SOUTH CAROLINA.

15 August 1780. After Major General Horatio Gates approved General Thomas Sumter's secondary efforts against British communications in the action known as the Camden campaign, Sumter asked for reinforcements to attack a post guarding the Wateree River ferry crossing connecting Camden with Ninety Six. Gates detached one hundred Maryland Continentals, two guns, and three hundred North Carolina militia, under Lieutenant Colonel Thomas Woolford of the Fifth Maryland Regiment, who joined Sumter on 14 August.

The British garrisoned a small redoubt called Fort Cary, named after Loyalist Colonel James Cary (Carey) who commanded it, at the west end of Wateree Ferry, On 15 August, the day after Woolford joined him, Sumter sent Colonel Thomas Taylor, with his Kershaw District militiamen, to surprise Fort Cary. Taylor captured Colonel Cary, thirty men, and thirty-six wagons loaded with clothing, food, and rum. Later that day, fifty-six more wagons with supplies and baggage, seventy British invalid soldiers, and a cattle herd coming from Ninety Six were taken.

Sumter initially wanted to hold the river crossing, but started withdrawing up the Wateree's west bank after he learned that the British were preparing to cross the river and retrieve their prisoners and stores. After hearing the fighting at the battle of Camden (16 August), and then learning of Horatio Gates's defeat shortly thereafter, Sumter moved further north. He made camp at Fishing Creek on 18 August. His encampment was inadequately secured, however, and his troops were surprised by the enemy. His 800-man command was annihilated and the supplies they carried were retaken by Lieutenant Colonel Banastre Tarleton with only 160 dragoons and light infantry.

SEE ALSO *Camden Campaign; Fishing Creek, North Carolina; Sumter, Thomas.*

BIBLIOGRAPHY

Kirkland, Thomas J., and Robert M. Kennedy. *Historic Camden.* Part I. Camden, S.C.: Kershaw County Historical Society, 1968.

Tarleton, Banastre. *A History of the Campaigns of 1780 and 1781 in the Southern Provinces of North American.* Reprint. Spartanburg, S.C.: Reprint Company, 1967.

revised by Lawrence E. Babits

WATSON, JOHN WATSON TADWELL.

(1748–1826). British officer. Born in London in 1748, Watson entered the Third Foot Guards in April 1767 and on 20 November 1778 became captain and lieutenant colonel of that regiment. On 16 October 1780 he sailed from New York in the expedition of General Leslie that was diverted from Virginia to reinforce Cornwallis in the Carolinas. While Cornwallis was pursuing Greene, Watson was instructed to secure his lines of supply. Identifying Francis Marion as a major threat to continued British control of South Carolina, Watson took five hundred picked men and went in pursuit. He left Fort Watson on 5 March 1781 and started down the Santee, but in a brilliant series of guerrilla actions, Marion blocked Watson's advance and drove him into the British base at Georgetown. Marion then joined "Light Horse Harry" Lee to capture Fort Watson on 15–23 April. His force much weakened by battle losses, sickness, and the detachment of troops to strengthen the Georgetown garrison, Watson rejoined Rawdon at Camden on 7 May. He was too late to take part in the battle of Hobkirk's Hill on 25 April, but incorrect information about his movements affected American actions at that battle.

Watson was promoted to colonel in 1783 and became a full general in April 1808. He died in Calais, France, on 11 June 1826.

S E E A L S O *Fort Watson, South Carolina (15–23 April 1781); Hobkirk's Hill (Camden), South Carolina; Marion, Francis.*

revised by Michael Bellesiles

WAUCHOPE S E E *Wahab's Plantation, North Carolina.*

WAWARSING, NEW YORK. 22 August 1781. About four hundred Tories and Indians under Captain William Caldwell appeared in Ulster County and destroyed isolated settlements before the militia, under Colonel Albert Pawling, turned out and drove the raiders off with considerable losses. The principal action took place at Wawarsing, on the southern edge of the Catskills about twenty miles west of the Hudson.

S E E A L S O *Border Warfare in New York.*

Mark M. Boatner

WAXHAWS, SOUTH CAROLINA. 29 May 1780. Marching to reinforce Charleston during Clinton's siege of 1780, Colonel Abraham Buford's Third Virginia Continentals could get no closer than Lenud's Ferry (Santee River), since British forces under Cornwallis had already established control of the intervening forty miles. When Charleston surrendered on 12 May, Buford's regiment and a few cavalry survivors of the skirmishes at Lenud's Ferry and Monck's Corner were the only organized American military troops left in South Carolina. Huger therefore ordered Buford to withdraw to Hillsborough, and Cornwallis—with twenty-five hundred men—started in pursuit from Huger's Bridge on 18 May. Realizing that his foot troops could not overcome Buford's ten-day lead, Cornwallis turned this mission over to Tarleton, whose dragoons had been sweeping the country toward Georgetown.

On 27 May, Tarleton—with 40 men of the Seventeenth Dragoons and 130 cavalry and 100 infantry of the Legion (many of them riding double with the horsemen)—left Cornwallis's command at Nelson's Ferry and started in hot pursuit. Although the weather was oppressively hot and the men and horses were already tired from vigorous campaigning, Tarleton's Tories and British dragoons had covered the 60 miles to Camden by the next afternoon. They already knew that Governor John Rutledge was traveling with Buford's command, and at Camden they learned that on 26 May, Buford had left Rugeley's Mill, only 12 miles away. Tarleton rested his troops and mounts until 2 A.M. on the 29th, and by early afternoon his leading element had closed in on Buford's rear guard. The British had covered 105 miles in 54 hours, although they had ridden many horses to death and Tarleton's column was badly strung out.

Warned of this pursuit, Rutledge rode ahead to safety. Buford's supply train and field guns were also ahead of the column, and his 350 or so Virginia Continentals were moving on the double. Tarleton first sent an officer forward under a flag of truce to demand surrender; this, he claimed candidly, was a stratagem to deceive Buford into thinking that British numbers were greater and, therefore, to induce him to consider surrender.

About 3 P.M., the British advance guard attacked and badly chopped up the small rear guard commanded by Lieutenant Pearson, and Buford turned to face the enemy. Holding out a small reserve, he formed his available infantry and cavalry in a single line near the road in an open wood. Tarleton deployed in three elements: Major Cochrane with sixty dragoons and about fifty infantry on his right to move forward first and "gall the enemy's flank"; thirty selected dragoons and some infantry, Tarleton's left wing, which he would personally lead against Buford's right and rear; and the Seventeenth Dragoons with the rest of the available infantry to attack the American center. The British commander, with an eye not only for sound tactical deployment but also for psychological effect, selected a small hill opposite the enemy center, in plain view of it, and ordered the rest of his command to form there as they reached the battlefield.

Since the American artillery was not in position, the British formed within three hundred yards of Buford's line without drawing any fire. Tarleton then launched his attack. When his troopers had charged to within fifty paces, they were astounded to hear Continental officers order their men to hold their fire until the British were nearer! The volley they fired came too late to check the rush of horses, and within moments, the cavalry broke the Patriot line and went to work with their sabers.

"TARLETON'S QUARTER"

When Buford saw he was being surrounded, he sent a flag of truce to Tarleton. The officer carrying the flag seems never to have reached Tarleton, however, possibly because the British commander had his horse killed from under him near this point in the action. Before he could mount another, "a report amongst the cavalry that they had lost their commanding officer ... stimulated the soldiers to a vindictive asperity not easily restrained" (Tarleton, pp. 30–31).

NUMBERS AND LOSSES

Patriot accounts claimed that Tarleton's men inhumanly butchered Continentals who were in the process of surrendering. Although evidence of British and Loyalist troops murdering soldiers who had thrown down their arms is sketchy, American casualties bear out the one-sided nature of the action. Their losses were 113 killed and 203 captured; 150 of the latter were too badly wounded to be moved, and most of the other 53 prisoners were wounded. Buford and a few other mounted men escaped from the battlefield. The only other survivors were 100 infantry who had been at the head of the retreat and were not in the action.

Tarleton's account indicates that about 200 of his 270 troops were on hand for the attack. He gave his casualties as 19 men and 31 horses killed or wounded.

COMMENT

The propaganda-inspired uproar about a "massacre" has obscured the brilliance of Tarleton's pursuit and attack. With professional detachment he credited his opponent with blunders that made the victory possible. Even allowing for poor discipline and low morale, Buford should have been able to fight off a tired enemy he outnumbered two to one. Although he did not have time to find good defensive terrain, he might have formed his wagons into a defensive perimeter and used his guns and infantry in a "hedgehog" the enemy would not have been able to successfully attack. Ordering his men to hold their fire was a case of applying a sound military principle at the wrong time. Tarleton suggested that a fire by platoons or battalions beginning at a greater range would have been much more effective.

As for the morality displayed by the victor, a successful cavalry charge exploited by a bayonet attack is bound to be messy, and the dividing line between military success and slaughter depends on which side one is on. While scholars have debated whether the Waxhaws was in fact a massacre, the important point is that Patriots perceived that Tarleton's men had acted viciously. Commanders at Kings Mountain, Cowpens, and other battles throughout the South would use the exaggerated accounts of Tarleton's cruelty to motivate their men.

Unknown at home prior to the action at Waxhaws, Tarleton was now a British hero. But to the American army,

"Tarleton's quarter" became a synonym for the butchery of surrendered men, and "Bloody Tarleton" is a name more familiar in America today than it is in England.

SEE ALSO *Carter, John Champe; Lenud's Ferry, South Carolina; Monck's Corner, South Carolina (14 April 1780); Paoli, Pennsylvania.*

BIBLIOGRAPHY

Tarleton, Banastre. *A History of the Campaigns of 1780 and 1781 in the Southern Provinces of North America.* 1787. Reprint, Ayer Company Publishers, Inc. North Stratford, N.H.: 2001.

revised by Carl P. Borick

WAYNE, ANTHONY. (1745–1796).

Continental general. Anthony Wayne was born at the family estate of Waynesborough in Chester County, Pennsylvania. He was the son of Isaac Wayne, a prosperous farmer and tanner. At an early age, he challenged his father's authority by resisting farm work. Hence, the elder Wayne enrolled him in a school run by his uncle, Gilbert Wayne. There, he did well in mathematics. After studying for two years at Philadelphia Academy, he became a surveyor in Chester County at the age of eighteen. In 1765, he was hired by a land company to survey and settle a tract of land in Nova Scotia. On 25 March 1766 he married Mary Penrose; they had two children. Later he was estranged from his wife and took up with a Wilmington socialite named Mary Vining. When his father died in 1776 he inherited Waynesborough.

SERVICE IN THE REVOLUTION

As antagonisms grew between Britain and America in the 1770s, Wayne emerged as a leader of Pennsylvania Patriots. He was a sturdy, handsome, well-educated, and established citizen. Though given to swearing, bombast, vanity, and impulsiveness, he was admired and respected by his neighbors. In 1774 he was elected chairman of the Chester County Committee of Safety and to a term in the Provincial Assembly. During the following year he turned his attention to things martial, helping to organize and drill militiamen. Appointed colonel of the Fourth Pennsylvania Battalion on 3 January 1776, he marched with his soldiers in mid-May to the Continental army's encampment at New York. From there he almost immediately proceeded to reinforce an American army that was withdrawing from Canada. At Trois Rivières on 8 June, while serving under the command of General William Thompson, he was involved in a hot battle with the British and received a slight wound in the leg. After withdrawing into New York, he was given command of Fort Ticonderoga. During the following

Anthony Wayne. *Wayne, who came to be known as "Mad Anthony" during the war, was a handsome, well-educated, and established Pennsylvania citizen, much admired and respected by his neighbors. Nineteenth-century engraving by John Francis Eugene Prud'Homme after a painting by John Trumbull.*
THE LIBRARY OF CONGRESS

winter, he battled cold, lack of provisions, and near-mutiny among his disgruntled soldiers.

On 21 February 1777 Wayne was promoted brigadier general. Rejoining the main Continental army at Morristown, New Jersey, on 20 May, he was given command of the Pennsylvania Line, even though he did not receive the commensurate rank of major general. In the battle of the Brandywine on 11 September, General George Washington posted him at Chadd's Ford, in command of the army's left wing. He performed with zeal and competence, covering the army's retreat after Washington's right wing was routed. On 18 September he was detached with 1,500 men to harass the British army's rear as it marched toward Philadelphia. On the evening of 20 September, he was surprised in camp at Paoli by General Charles Grey, who commanded 5,000 soldiers. Routed from the field, he suffered 200 men killed and another 150 wounded. His opponent, Grey, had only ten casualties. Wayne was charged with negligence, and although acquitted by a court-martial, he was haunted long thereafter by accusations of military ineptitude. In the battle of Germantown on 4 October, he avenged his insult at Paoli by leading his Pennsylvanians in furious assaults against the enemy. On the brink of victory, he descried musket fire at his rear and was forced to retreat. Soon Washington's army was in flight, with Wayne once more covering the withdrawal.

For some months afterward, as he lived through the travails of the army's winter encampment at Valley Forge, Wayne was disgusted with Washington's leadership. At the battle of Monmouth on 28 June 1778 he was given a large role by Washington. Fighting furiously, he earning the military glory that he cherished. His confidence in Washington restored, he served on a court-martial of Charles Lee, who was charged with military incompetence and insubordination. He also came close to fighting a duel with Lee over these matters. On 21 June 1779 Washington gave him command of an elite corps of Continental light infantry, numbering 2,000 men. These troops he led on the night of 15 July against Stony Point, a strategically important British post on the Hudson River below West Point. Overwhelming the defenders, he received a slight wound to the head and immortality as a soldier. Shortly thereafter, the light infantry corps was disbanded. On 20 July 1780 he commanded an unsuccessful assault against a British blockhouse at Bull's Ferry, New Jersey. Two months later, he frustrated Benedict Arnold's attempt to deliver West Point into enemy hands by marching his soldiers quickly to the defense of that post.

On 1 January 1781 Wayne's Pennsylvania troops mutinied, after months of discontented grumbling. In a display of good sense and courage, he managed to placate the soldiers while presenting their demands to Congress. By the end of January, many of his troops had been discharged. In May, Wayne and the remaining 800 troops were ordered to join the Marquis de Lafayette's army in Virginia. After quelling two more mutinies, Wayne proceeded southward and, on 6 July, audaciously attacked Lord Charles Cornwallis's entire army at Green Spring. Only his steely fearlessness managed to extricate him from this dangerous predicament. Thereafter, he was known as "Mad Anthony" Wayne.

Wounded in the leg by an American sentry on 2 September, he was not present at General Charles Cornwallis's surrender at Yorktown on 19 October. In early 1782 he assumed command of American forces in Georgia, and for the next seven months battled British Loyalists, Creeks, and Cherokees. After the enemy evacuated Savannah in 11 July, Wayne joined Nathanael Greene in South Carolina. There he fell ill with a fever that nearly killed him. On 14 December the British withdrew from Charleson, South Carolina, and eight months later Wayne returned to Pennsylvania. He was promoted brevet major general on 30 September 1783, and on 3 November resigned from the army.

COMMAND OF THE LEGION

In late 1783 Wayne was elected to the Pennsylvania Council of Censors and the Assembly. He served as an assemblyman for two years, and in 1787 was a member of the Pennsylvania convention that ratified the new Constitution. Given a rice plantation by Georgia for his wartime services there, he went deeply in debt in a futile effort to make it pay. Finally he had to sell the plantation. In 1791 he was elected to Congress in Georgia, but served only seventeen days before his seat was declared vacant because of election irregularities. On 5 March 1792 he was appointed commander of the American army that was fighting Indians in the Northwest, with the rank of major general. He replaced Arthur St. Clair, who had been defeated in battle the year before. Taking command at Pittsburgh, he devoted the next two years to the careful training of his army in the use of the bayonet and musket. He marched northward from Cincinnati into Indian country, establishing military posts as he went. On 20 August 1794, on the Maumee River, he routed an Indian army in the battle of Fallen Timbers, and broke the will of the natives to resist American hegemony. In 1795 he negotiated the Treaty of Greenville, thus confirming the submission of the Northwest Indians. Praised for his exploits, he was touted in the east as a possible secretary of war, but never got the appointment. He died of gout on 15 December 1796 at Presque Isle, and was buried there. On 3 October 1809 he was exhumed, then reinterred at St. David's Church near Waynesborough on 3 October 1809. A courageous and intelligent military leader, Anthony Wayne deserves his reputation as one of America's great soldiers.

SEE ALSO *Chadds Ford, Pennsylvania; Green Spring (Jamestown Ford, Virginia); Stony Point, New York.*

BIBLIOGRAPHY

Knopf, Richard C., ed. *Anthony Wayne, A Name in Arms: Soldier, Diplomat, Defender of Expansion Westward of a Nation: The Wayne-Knox-Pickering-McHenry Correspondence.* Pittsburgh: University of Pittsburgh Press, 1960.

Nelson, Paul David. *Anthony Wayne: Soldier of the Early Republic.* Bloomington: Indiana University Press, 1985.

Rankin, Hugh F. "Anthony Wayne: Military Romanticist." In *George Washington's Generals.* Edited by George A. Billias. New York: William Morrow and Company, 1964.

Stillé, Charles Janeway. *Major-General Anthony Wayne and the Pennsylvania Line in The Continental Army.* Philadelphia: J.B. Lippincott Company, 1893.

Tucker, Glen. *Mad Anthony Wayne and the New Nation: The Story of Washington's Frontline General.* Harrisburg, Pa.: Stackpole Books, 1973.

Wildes, Harry Emerson. *Anthony Wayne: Trouble Shooter of the American Revolution.* New York: Harcourt, Brace and Company, 1941.

revised by Paul David Nelson

WAYNE'S LIGHT INFANTRY. Relying

on small partisan corps, including Major Henry Lee's legion, for outpost duty early in the campaigning season, General Washington waited until 15 June 1779 to reconstitute the Corps of Light Infantry. Colonel Richard Butler of Pennsylvania supervised the assembly of the four battalions at Fort Montgomery, in the Hudson Highlands, until Washington directed Brigadier General Anthony Wayne of Pennsylvania to assume command of the Continental Army's elite light infantry corps on 1 July. The composition of his twelve-hundred-man force is given in the entry on the attack on Stony Point (16 July 1779), the most famous engagement in the history of the Continental Army's light infantry and one that demonstrated that at least some American soldiers were now mature professionals. On 30 November orders were issued for the corps to disband but for the companies to be ready to reassemble on one day's notice. Before these orders had been completely executed, several companies were retained around West Point to meet any movements the British might make up the Hudson. Washington wrote to Wayne on 28 December ordering all companies to return to their parent organizations, adding: "Before the separation of the corps, I beg the favor of you to present my warmest thanks to the officers and men and assure them that I have a high sense of the zeal, gallantry, and good conduct of the former and of the bravery and fidelity of the latter" (Washington, 17, p. 329).

SEE ALSO *Butler, Richard; Lee, Henry ("Light-Horse Harry"); Light Infantry; Stony Point, New York; Wayne, Anthony.*

BIBLIOGRAPHY

Washington, George. *The Writings of George Washington, from the Original Manuscript Sources.* Vol. 15: *May 6, 1779–July 28, 1779.* Edited by John C. Fitzpatrick. Washington, D.C.: U.S. Government Printing Office, 1936.

————. *The Writings of George Washington, from the Original Manuscript Sources.* Vol. 17: *October 21, 1779–February 9, 1780.* Edited by John C. Fitzpatrick. Washington, D.C.: U.S. Government Printing Office, 1937.

revised by Harold E. Selesky

WAYNE'S PENNSYLVANIA LINE IN VIRGINIA. After the reorganization following

the mutiny of the Pennsylvania Line, General Anthony Wayne left York, Pennsylvania, on 26 May 1781 with the Second, Fifth, and Sixth Pennsylvania Regiments (about 1,000 infantry in all), and Proctor's Fourth Continental

Artillery (6 cannon and 90 men). He joined Lafayette on 10 June 1781.

SEE ALSO *Mutiny of the Pennsylvania Line; Virginia, Military Operations in.*

revised by Michael Bellesiles

WEATHER GAUGE.

In the days of fighting sail, maneuvering to obtain and to hold the weather gauge was of prime importance in naval engagements because it allowed the ship that possessed it to dictate the terms of the engagement. A ship was said to have the weather gage, or "the advantage of the wind," when she could steer straight for an opponent while the latter would have to tack into the wind.

revised by Harold E. Selesky

WEBB, SAMUEL BLATCHLEY.

(1753–1807). Continental officer. Connecticut. Born on 15 December 1753 at Wethersfield, Connecticut, Webb was the stepson of Silas Deane and became his stepfather's private secretary. Both men were involved in the colonial resistance to increased imperial control. When the General Assembly elected Deane a delegate to the first Continental Congress, Webb accompanied him to Philadelphia in September 1774. Webb marched with his militia company to Boston in the aftermath of the Lexington alarm (April 1775) and was commissioned first lieutenant of Captain John Chester's Wethersfield company of Joseph Spencer's Second Connecticut Regiment on 1 May 1775. He was wounded in the Battle of Bunker Hill (17 June 1775), and five days later, thanks to his stepfather's influence, he became aide-de-camp to Major General Israel Putnam, with the rank of major.

On 21 June 1776 he was promoted to lieutenant colonel and became aide and private secretary to Washington. With Joseph Reed and Henry Knox, in July he met the British officer who was attempting to deliver a letter addressed to "George Washington, Esq. etc. etc" from the Howes as part of their peace efforts. He was present at the Battle of Long Island (27 August 1776), was wounded at White Plains (28 October 1776) and again at Trenton (2 January 1777), and was present at Princeton (3 January 1777). On 11 January 1777 Webb was commissioned colonel of one of the sixteen Additional Continental Regiments, and he served in the Hudson Highlands during that summer's

campaigns. Along with part of his regiment, he was captured in the unsuccessful attack against Long Island, New York, on 10 December 1777, and not exchanged until January 1781. His regiment was transferred to the Connecticut Line in June 1780 as the Ninth Connecticut. On 1 January 1781 it was consolidated with the Second Connecticut, and the combined unit was redesignated the Third Connecticut. Webb commanded this regiment through a further consolidation on 1 January 1783 and until it was disbanded in June. He left the service on 3 June 1783 and was breveted brigadier general on 30 September 1783. From 1789 until his death on 3 December 1807, he lived at Claverack, New York.

SEE ALSO *Additional Continental Regiments; Long Island, New York, Battle of; Peace Commission of the Howes.*

BIBLIOGRAPHY

Ford, Washington C., ed. *The Correspondence and Journals of Samuel Blatchley Webb.* 3 vols. Lancaster, Pa.: Wickersham Press, 1893.

revised by Harold E. Selesky

WEBB, THOMAS.

(1725–1796). British officer and evangelist. Born in England on 31 May 1725, Webb became quartermaster of the Forty-eighth Regiment on 29 October 1754, and he was promoted to lieutenant on 9 November 1755. After serving at the siege of Louisburg in 1758, he was seriously wounded at the Battle of Montmorency on 31 July 1759. He settled in Albany, marrying an American woman and writing *Military Treatise on the Appointments of the Army* (1760). This small book pointed out the difficulties of supplying troops with sufficient weaponry in America and the inadequacy of British weapons for that service, recommending lighter guns. After his wife died, Webb returned to Britain to sell his commission, falling into a depression that ended with a vision of Christ in March 1765. Becoming a Methodist itinerant, he traveled through England and New York in his British uniform, employing his military persona and rhetoric to maximum effect. His vigorous style attracted attention and money, the latter helping to build churches in New York City, Philadelphia, Baltimore, and New Jersey. He also aroused a great deal of skepticism from those, such as Charles Wesley, who thought his stories unlikely and his visions slightly unnerving. Webb was a regular correspondent of the earl of Dartmouth, keeping the colonial secretary advised of events in America. These exchanges led to Webb's being arrested on suspicion of spying, and he was jailed at Bethlehem, Pennsylvania.

Webb's second wife, Grace Gilbert, personally persuaded General Washington to free her husband on condition that he return to England, which he and his family did in August 1778. Webb continued to preach around England, finally settling in Bristol, where he died on 20 December 1796.

BIBLIOGRAPHY

Baker, Frank. *From Wesley to Asbury: Studies in Early American Methodism.* Durham, N.C.: Duke University Press, 1976.

Michael Bellesiles

WEBB'S REGIMENT. Webb's regiment, under Colonel Samuel B. Webb, was one of the sixteen "additional Continental regiments."

SEE ALSO *Additional Continental Regiments.*

Mark M. Boatner

WEBSTER, JAMES. (1743?–1781). British officer. Webster became a lieutenant in the Thirty-third Foot (West Riding) on 10 May 1760 and was promoted to captain in 1763, to major in 1771, and to lieutenant colonel on 9 April 1774. Cornwallis commanded the Third-third from March 1766 until he was promoted to major general in 1775, when Webster took over command as lieutenant colonel, continuing to serve under Cornwallis in the New York and New Jersey campaigns. In the Philadelphia campaign, the Thirty-third was in Grey's brigade of Cornwallis's command. In the Battle of Monmouth on 28 June 1778, it was Webster who came onto the field in the final stage of the action to make it possible for Clinton to extricate the light infantry.

Webster was promoted to brigadier in 1779. When Clinton withdrew forces from the Hudson Highlands and Rhode Island for Governor Tryon's Connecticut coast raid (July 1779), he left the Thirty-third Foot, Robinson's Loyal American Regiment, and half of Ferguson's corps to hold Fort Lafayette at Verplanck's Point under Webster's command.

Sailing south on 26 December 1779 with Clinton's Charleston expedition, Webster commanded a task force of fourteen hundred men that operated against Lincoln's line of communications from Charleston. Commanding a brigade composed of his own regiment, three light infantry companies, and the Twenty-third Fusiliers, he distinguished himself at Camden, where he was slightly wounded. In the unsuccessful pursuit of Greene to the Dan River, Webster commanded the force that conducted

the demonstration against Beattie's Ford when Cornwallis made his main crossing of the Catawba at Cowan's Ford, 1 February 1781. He defied American marksmanship to lead his brigade forward at Wetzell's Mills, North Carolina, on 6 March 1781.

At Guilford on 15 March 1781, Webster particularly distinguished himself from the opening movement of the battle to the end. Mortally wounded in this action, he died a fortnight later.

SEE ALSO *Camden Campaign; Charleston Expedition of Clinton in 1780; Cornwallis, Charles; Guilford Courthouse, North Carolina; Marksmanship; Monmouth, New Jersey; Southern Campaigns of Nathanael Greene; Wetzell's Mills, North Carolina.*

revised by Michael Bellesiles

WEEDON, GEORGE. (1730–1793). Continental general. Virginia. A Fredericksburg innkeeper and prewar acquaintance of Washington, he served in the French and Indian War, rising to captain. He was characterized in 1774 by an English visitor as "very active in blowing the seeds of sedition." He became lieutenant colonel of the Third Virginia on 13 February 1776 and colonel on 13 August, joined Washington's army in mid-September with slightly more than six hundred men, and took part in the New York and New Jersey campaigns. On 20 February 1777 he became acting adjutant general to Washington and on 21 February was promoted to brigadier general. After a long leave of absence he rejoined the army at Morristown in time for the Philadelphia campaign. Leading Greene's division, he reached the Plowed Hill at Brandywine just as the American defenses were collapsing; his men calmly opened ranks to let the fugitives pass and reformed to check the enemy. As part of Greene's column he participated in the attack at Germantown and expressed the (questionable) view that the Americans were within fifteen minutes of victory when their attack collapsed. He was among the nine brigadier generals who memorialized Congress against General Thomas Conway's promotion and has been characterized with General John Peter Muhlenberg and William Woodford as one of the "jealous, ambitious men" competing for promotion (Freeman, vol. 4, p. 613 n.). On 18 August 1778 he appealed to Congress to be put on the inactive list; by November "Weedon had gone home and kept both his complaint and his commission" as a Continental brigadier general (ibid, 5, p. 79). In the Virginia military operations that followed, Weedon helped organize military resistance to the British raids and in the Yorktown campaign commanded the militia investing Gloucester.

"Joe Gourd," as the tavern-keeping general was known to his soldiers, idolized the former patron who became commander in chief. On 14 April 1777 he wrote John Page,

> no other man but our present General, who is the greatest that ever did or ever will adorn our earth, could have supported himself under the many disappointments and disgraces he was subjected to from this singular system of carrying on a war against the most formidable enemy in the world (ibid., 4, p. 411 n.).

He died in November 1793. Weedon was the brother-in-law of General Hugh Mercer. Weedon's wife, Catherine, raised Mercer's two sons after Mercer's death at the Battle of Princeton.

SEE ALSO *Virginia, Military Operations in.*

BIBLIOGRAPHY

Ford, Allyn K. Weedon Correspondence Collection. Minnesota Historical Society, St. Paul, Minnesota.

Freeman, Douglas Southall. *George Washington.* Vols. 3–5. New York: Scribner, 1951–1952.

Ward, Harry M. *Duty, Honor, or Country: General George Weedon and the American Revolution.* Philadelphia: American Philosophical Society, 1979.

Weedon, George. *Valley Forge Orderly Book of General George Weedon.* New York: Arno Press, 1971.

Weedon Correspondence collection. American Philosophical Society, Philadelphia, Pennsylvania.

Weedon Correspondence collection. Brown University, Providence, Rhode Island.

revised by Harry M. Ward

WEEMS, MASON LOCKE PARSON.

(1759–1825). Clergyman, bookseller, writer. Born in Anne Arundel County, Maryland, on 11 October 1759, Weems studied medicine at the University of Edinburgh and returned to Maryland sometime during the Revolution. Weems went to England in 1782 seeking ordination in the Church of England, but he had to wait until 1784 for Parliament to pass an act allowing for the ordination of ministers who would not take the oath of allegiance to the king. He was finally ordained on 12 September 1784, when he returned to his home county. He quit the ministry in 1792 to act as an agent for publisher Mathew Carey, a career he followed during the rest of his life, becoming a highly successful editor and writer. His *A History of the Life and Death, Virtues and Exploits of General George Washington,* published in 1800, went through some seventy editions in his lifetime. It is primarily a work of fiction and was responsible for some of the iconic tales of Washington and the American Revolution. They included the highly dubious cherry tree story, which appeared in the fifth edition (1806). He wrote biographies of several other Revolutionary figures, as well as some of the first temperance books published in the United States. He died at Beaufort, South Carolina, on 23 May 1825.

BIBLIOGRAPHY

Ford, Paul Leicester, and Emily Ellsword Ford Skeel, eds. *Mason Locke Weems.* 3 vols. New York: Richmond Mayo-Smith, 1928–1929.

Leary, Lewis. *The Book-Peddling Parson.* Chapel Hill, N.C.: Algonquin Books, 1984.

revised by Michael Bellesiles

WELZELL'S MILLS, NORTH CAROLINA SEE *Wetzell's Mills, North Carolina.*

WEMYSS, JAMES.

British officer. An ensign in the Fortieth Foot on 6 April 1766, he was promoted to captain in that regiment on 14 March 1771 and commanded the Loyalist Queen's Rangers at Brandywine on 11 September 1777. On 10 August 1778 he was promoted to major of the Sixty-third Foot. With the start of major British military operations in the South, he became second only to Tarleton as the object of hatred among Patriots. He was defeated, wounded, and captured by Sumter at Fishdam Ford, South Carolina, on 9 November 1780. On 22 August 1783 he became a major in the army and on 20 September 1787 was promoted to lieutenant colonel of the Sixty-third Foot. Two years later he disappeared from the Army Lists.

SEE ALSO *Brandywine, Pennsylvania; Fishdam Ford, South Carolina.*

revised by Michael Bellesiles

WENTWORTH, PAUL.

(c. 1736–1793). Double spy. New Hampshire. Probably born in Barbados, Wentworth claimed kinship with anyone having the same last name, including Governor Benning Wentworth of New Hampshire. He moved to Portsmouth in the 1750s, gaining the governor's patronage. Around 1760 he moved to Surinam, where he married a rich widow, inheriting her sugar plantation when she died shortly thereafter. In 1766 Wentworth went to London, setting himself up as a stock speculator and becoming friends with John Wentworth. When the latter succeeded his uncle as governor of New Hampshire, he appointed Paul Wentworth the province's agent to Parliament and a member of the council, even though the two offices required that he be on opposite sides of the Atlantic. Wentworth determined that the crown offered greater preferment than the patriots could ever hope to match, and in 1772 began feeding information to the king's secret service.

At the beginning of the Revolution, Sir William Eden, head of the British secret service, granted Wentworth a salary of five hundred pounds per year. As soon as Congress sent Silas Deane to Paris in 1776, Eden instructed Wentworth to spy on the American delegation to the French court. Since Deane and Benjamin Franklin were both old friends of his, Wentworth found it easy to establish the necessary connections. On Franklin's recommendation Edward Bancroft, whom Wentworth had hired as a doctor for his Surinam plantation in 1764, was added to the American mission in Paris. Wentworth now recruited him to spy for the British in December 1776. The two men also used their inside information from both sides of the war to speculate with some success on the stock market.

When, after Burgoyne's surrender, the British felt they could offer the Americans some terms short of complete independence, Wentworth was selected to feel out the American commissioners in Paris. He had to wait almost four weeks there before the suspicious Benjamin Franklin agreed to a meeting on 6 January 1778. Secretary Eden had given Wentworth a letter to show Franklin that came with an assurance that it was from a source close to the throne; the letter said that England would fight another ten years to prevent American independence. Franklin said that America would fight fifty years to win it and that both countries would be better off when they were bound only by peaceful commerce. Not only did Wentworth's mission fail to do any good for England, but Vergennes used it to accelerate the French Alliance by pointing out to the kings of France and Spain that the Americans might be making peace with Great Britain. Louis XVI consented to the Franco-American treaty the day after Wentworth saw Franklin.

Hoping that a British victory would save him his New Hampshire estates and aspiring to a title, a seat in Parliament, and an important office, Wentworth appointed and directed spies, used their reports to furnish military intelligence to the British, and in various disguises made frequent trips to the European Continent. After his visit to Franklin, however, he was so well known to French police that he had to remain in London.

Wentworth's rewards were meager: only a seat in Parliament in 1780, which he held just six weeks before being defeated in the general election of that year. George III had little confidence in Wentworth's reports and disapproved of his stock speculation. After failing in his political career, Wentworth retired to his Surinam plantation and died there in December 1793.

BIBLIOGRAPHY

Augur, Helen. *The Secret War of Independence*. New York: Duell, Sloan and Pearce, 1955.

revised by Michael Bellesiles

WEST CANADA CREEK, NEW YORK

SEE *Jerseyfield, New York.*

WESTERN OPERATIONS.

The Western Theater was comprised of the area lying north and west of the Ohio River, south of the Great Lakes, and east of the Mississippi River. Just as Niagara was the British base for raids against American border settlements in New York and eastern Pennsylvania, Detroit became headquarters for British operations against Patriot settlements in western Pennsylvania, Virginia, and Kentucky. American officials established their base of operations at Fort Pitt (Pittsburgh).

Military planners on both sides of the war realized that the contest would neither be won nor lost in the west. Separated from supplies and reinforcements by the Appalachian Mountains, British officials at Detroit and their counterparts in Pittsburgh watched as the war turned into an unending series of raids and counter raids. These marauds, any of which could be brutal in the extreme, were never strong enough nor sustained for a sufficient period of time to inflict a fatal blow upon the enemy. Nonetheless, the theater remained an actively contested zone throughout the war.

THE NATIVE AMERICAN QUESTION

Although British forces employed Indian allies against the Americans in the East as early as 1775, as the war began in the West, both sides attempted to secure Native American neutrality. Sir Guy Carleton, the commander of British forces in Canada, feared that an overt military alliance with the region's Indians would fuel widespread resentment against Crown interests, and emphatically opposed the use of Native American forces against Americans from 1775 throughout much of 1777.

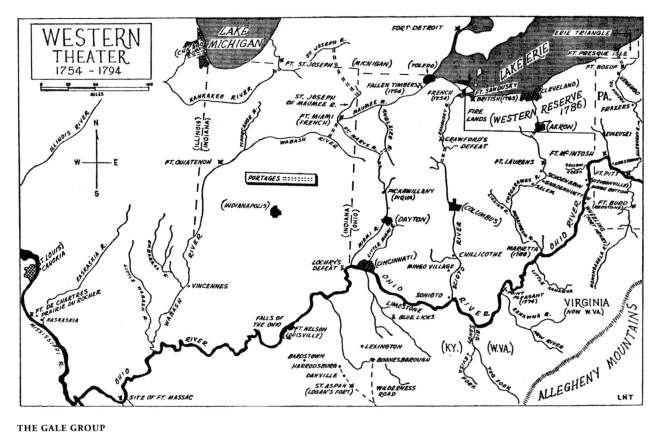

WESTERN THEATER 1754–1794

British officials attempted to sway Native sentiment by reaffirming the Proclamation of 1763, signed at the conclusion of the French and Indian War. Under this treaty, the Crown recognized Native American territorial claims within the region and promised to enforce a ban on American settlement beyond the crest of the Appalachian Mountains. Likewise, American authorities held a series of councils with the Ohio Country Indian nations that concluded with the signing of the Treaty of Pittsburgh in October 1776. In exchange for Native American neutrality, American officials acknowledged Indian sovereignty and also recognized Native American territorial claims north and west of the Ohio River.

Despite American efforts, after the outbreak of hostilities, Native American sympathies gravitated generally toward the British. Native American resentment was real. The American invasion of Canada in 1775 and 1776 greatly diminished the flow of British trade goods to the west. Further, Americans had become increasingly insistent in violating the settlement boundary established in 1763 and had established permanent settlements in Kentucky, at Harrodsburg in 1774 and at Boonesborough and St. Asaph in 1775.

In June 1777, British colonial secretary Lord George Germain ordered Carleton and Henry Hamilton, the British colonial governor at Detroit, to establish a formal military alliance with the region's Indian nations and employ them against American settlements throughout the Ohio Valley. In July, fifteen parties from Detroit conducted extensive raids along the Pennsylvania and Virginia frontiers. Americans were outraged and claimed that Hamilton had deliberately ordered the murder of defenseless women and children. The charge was untrue, but among Americans, Hamilton became one of the most despised figures along the western border.

In January 1778, Patriot forces in Pittsburgh launched an ambitious raid against British holdings along the lower Mississippi. Commanded by James Willing, the American force, consisting of an armed flatboat and twenty-six soldiers, descended the Ohio and Mississippi Rivers for the purpose of apprehending British supplies and disrupting British operations wherever possible. A short distance below the Wabash, Willing captured a large bateau containing furs bound for Cahokia. The following day, he also commandeered a second craft carrying a cargo of brandy. Once on the Mississippi, Willing surprised a British detachment near Walnut Hills; captured Anthony Hutchins, a well-known

Loyalist living along the river and then ransacked the Hutchins estate; plundered Natchez; looted Manchak; and seized two British vessels, the *Rebecca* and *Neptune,* before reaching port at New Orleans in late February. The Willing raid was a bold stroke that broadly diminished British influence in the region. Moreover, it also promised to destabilize Great Britain's political and commercial alliances with the region's Indians if Crown authorities did not respond aggressively.

Hamilton was alarmed both by the Willing raid and the Americans' continuing infringement into Kentucky and western Virginia. Convinced that the rebels' ability to penetrate the Ohio Country would eventually pose a direct threat to Detroit, he organized a strike against Pittsburgh. Hamilton sent the plan to Carleton for approval in late July, but on 8 August he learned that an American frontiersman, George Rogers Clark, and a small force of backwoods irregulars had crossed deep into the Illinois country and taken possession of Vincennes on the Wabash River in present-day southwestern Indiana. Clark's advance put an end to the planned action against Fort Pitt.

CLARK'S 1778 CAMPAIGN FOR VINCENNES

Born near Charlottesville, Virginia, in 1752, Clark became a surveyor while a young man. When the Revolution began, he was living in Kentucky, at the time still part of Virginia. Clark was appointed a lieutenant colonel in the Virginia militia in 1777. In the wake of escalating Indian violence that year, Clark devised a plan to take offensive action against the British and their Native American allies north of the Ohio River. Virginia officials, including Governor Patrick Henry, Thomas Jefferson, and George Mason, approved the proposal in early 1778. The scheme called for Clark to raise a small force, descend the Ohio River, and occupy Kaskaskia, a French village near the Mississippi River in southern Illinois. However, the Virginia Assembly's instructions gave Clark wide latitude in conducting his campaign and urged him to consider moving against other settlements within the region, including Vincennes and Detroit, if circumstances permitted.

Clark began his expedition in May 1778. After descending the Ohio from Pittsburgh, Clark established his base camp on Corn Island at the falls of the Ohio River (Louisville, Kentucky). He spent a brief time training his men, then began his thrust against the British on 24 June. The American force was small, consisting of about 180 men divided into four companies commanded by Captains John Montgomery, Joseph Bowman, Leonard Helm, and William Harrod.

Navigating the Ohio in flatboats, Clark reached the mouth of the Tennessee River on 28 June. That evening his guards apprehended a group of American hunters who had been in Kaskaskia only eight days before. They reported that the British commander at Kaskaskia, Philippe de Rastel, chevalier de Rocheblave, had placed the village's militia on alert and sent spies to the Ohio and Mississippi Rivers to watch for any approach by American forces. But they also claimed that the militia was weak and untrained, and that if Clark could approach the town undetected, he could seize the village before the residents could mount a resistance. As a result of this intelligence, the following day Clark decided to land his force at Fort Massiac, an abandoned British outpost a few miles below the Tennessee River opposite present-day Paducah, Kentucky, and use an old buffalo trace or hunters' road that ran from that location to Kaskaskia (a distance of about 120 miles) to attack the settlement from the southeast.

The Americans reached Kaskaskia after nightfall on 4 July. Clark divided his men into two columns to seize the town and safeguard the approaches leading into the village, and sent a third group of spies, led by Simon Kenton, directly to de Rocheblave's residence. De Rocheblave was quickly arrested and the village subdued without incident. The following day, Clark sent an emissary to open communication with Spanish officials across the Mississippi River and successfully deployed a thirty-man detachment accompanied by a small French delegation from the village to secure Prairie du Rocher, fifteen miles north of Kaskaskia. The detachment also secured Philippi, a smaller settlement nine miles further up the Mississippi River, and Cahokia, fifty miles north of Kaskaskia, opposite present-day St. Louis.

After consolidating his gains, Clark opened negotiations with the region's Indians, and sent two French envoys from Kaskaskia, Father Pierre Gibault and Dr. Jean Baptiste Laffont, to Vincennes. Skillful diplomacy convinced the various tribes to remain neutral, and Gibault and Laffont's efforts prompted Vincennes's residents to join the American cause. As a result, Clark placed Captain Leonard Helm in command of Fort Sackville at Vincennes. By early August, the peaceful conquest of the Illinois country was complete and had provided Clark with a strong forward base from which he could threaten Detroit.

THE BRITISH RETAKE VINCENNES

British authorities reacted immediately once they learned of Clark's incursion. In Detroit, Hamilton prepared an expedition to the Wabash River to repatriate the occupied settlement. Hamilton's force, consisting of forty British regulars, 125 French militia, and approximately seventy Native American allies, set out from Detroit on 7 October 1778. Traveling the length of the Maumee River, the raiding party then portaged to the Wabash River and proceeded directly to Vincennes, gathering additional

Indian support along the way. As Hamilton approached his objective, his force numbered more than 500 men.

Vincennes and the small American garrison at Fort Sackville surrendered at once when confronted by the over-whelming British force. But at this critical juncture, Hamilton made a series of errors that led ultimately to the mission's failure. Concerned about his ability to conduct a winter offensive, Hamilton declined to move immediately against Kaskaskia and Cahokia, electing instead to winter at Fort Sackville before resuming operations the following spring. Secondly, he allowed most of his Indian allies to depart and permitted most of his militia to return to Detroit. Lastly, he seriously underestimated Clark's resourcefulness and resolve.

Clark learned of Hamilton's arrival on 29 January 1779 and quickly determined to undertake a daring mid-winter attack to reclaim Vincennes. On 4 February, Clark deployed a small vessel, the *Willing,* carrying forty-six soldiers and a small artillery piece, down the Mississippi and up the Ohio and Wabash Rivers. He ordered the company to halt at the White River below Vincennes, and waited while Clark personally led the main force overland. The following day, Clark and between 130 and 170 men, nearly half of whom were French volunteers, set out from Kaskaskia for Vincennes.

Clark's journey would be arduous. An unusually mild and wet winter had flooded much of southern Illinois. Although Clark easily traversed the first 100 miles, when he entered the Wabash watershed on 15 February, he discovered that much of his route was covered by two to four feet of water. The flooding reduced the supply of game in the area, and Clark's men soon found themselves without rations. Further, the weather turned frigid. Clark's men were wet, cold, exhausted, and on the verge of starvation. Nonetheless, Clark pushed on, arriving outside of Vincennes shortly after dark on 23 February.

Clark quickly obtained the allegiance of the town's French citizens and commenced the attack on Fort Sackville that evening. Through a series of deceptive displays, Clark convinced Hamilton that his force was much larger than it actually was, and in a personal negotiation with the British commander, Clark implied that if the Americans stormed the fort, the British could expect no quarter. Convinced that he was facing a superior force and with grave doubts concerning the continued loyalty both of his Indian allies and the French militia within his fort, Hamilton surrendered the following day.

Clark's activity in the Illinois country was the most successful American campaign in the west during the Revolution. Hamilton's capture diminished British influence, provided an important psychological boost to American forces throughout the Ohio Valley, and prompted a new wave of settlement into western Virginia and Kentucky. However, Clark was never able to capitalize on his victory and strike directly at Detroit. He planned expeditions in 1779, 1780, and 1781, but never was given the means for the operations and, instead, spent the remainder of the war countering a renewed wave of British-led assaults against American settlements.

BRITISH OPERATIONS

Hamilton's capture was a serious, but not catastrophic blow to British efforts in the West. Clark's dramatic ree-mergence on the Wabash rekindled fears of an American offensive against Detroit, and British officials redoubled their efforts to reenergize their alliance with the western nations.

In early spring 1780, Hamilton's successor, Major Arent DePeyster, proposed an offensive against a string of stockaded civilian settlements, or stations, in Kentucky, hoping to divert American attention from Detroit, demoralize the western settlements, and encourage the Crown's Native American allies to renew their allegiance. DePeyster ordered Captain Henry Bird to lead the expedition, and placed Indian agent Alexander McKee in charge of the force's Native American contingent.

Bird left Detroit on 25 May 1780 with 150 soldiers, two small caliber cannon, and nearly 100 Indians. As the expedition moved southward, additional Indians joined the force and eventually numbered in excess of 850. Bird directed his command against Martin's and Ruddell's Stations on the Licking River in northern Kentucky. Both communities had been founded in 1775 and were each home to about twenty families.

Bird attacked and reduced Ruddell's Station on 24 June and Martin's Station the following day. Lacking the provisions and supplies to continue, Bird withdrew from Kentucky and returned safely to Detroit in early August with nearly 300 prisoners and a great deal of personal property. The expedition successfully demonstrated British resolve to the region's Indians and proved that British forces could attack settlements deep within Kentucky virtually unmolested.

In 1781 Clark attempted to form an expedition against Detroit and raised four hundred volunteers at Pittsburgh. Clark and his command departed Fort Pitt down the Ohio River for Fort Nelson, at the falls on the Ohio River, in early August and sent word to his second–in-command, Captain Archibald Lochry, to follow with additional troops. Lochry, however, was never able to overtake the senior officer. Spies and deserters had informed British officials of Clark's expedition, and a large party of Indians led by the Mohawk chief, Joseph Brant, was waiting in ambush for the Americans at the mouth of the Great Miami River. Brant's men were unable to attack Clark's force as he passed, but shortly afterwards they captured an American officer and seven of Lochry's men, an advance guard sent by Lochry to convince Clark to stop and consolidate his force. Using the prisoners as decoys, Brant lured the main body of Lochry's troops ashore on 24 August. The ambush destroyed the American detachment, killing Lochry and thirty-seven others, and capturing every other member of the 101-man expedition.

In late-summer 1782, McKee and Captain William Caldwell led a second raid into Kentucky. Thirty rangers and nearly 300 Indians attacked Bryant's Station, on the Elkhorn River near present-day Lexington, on 12 August. The Americans had been warned of the British approach and repulsed the attack. At the end of the siege's second day, Caldwell destroyed the settlement's crops and livestock and withdrew to the Blue Licks on the Licking River.

Soon, 182 Kentucky militia, led by John Todd and including Daniel Boone and his son Israel, were in pursuit. At the Blue Licks, Todd permitted his men to be drawn into an ambush. In the fierce battle that followed, nearly seventy of the Americans were killed, including Israel Boone and Thomas Boone, Daniel's nephew. Caldwell remained at Blue Licks one more day, hoping to lure a second American patrol into the same trap. When the Kentuckians did not advance, Caldwell withdrew back to Detroit.

AMERICAN OPERATIONS

In 1778 American officials at Fort Pitt began a second offensive against Detroit. The plan called for General Lachlan McIntosh to lead an expedition into Ohio, constructing a string of forts as he advanced westward. These posts would serve as forward bases from which to attack Detroit, discourage Native Americans loyal to the British from attacking frontier settlements in Pennsylvania and western Virginia, and reassure neutral Christian Delawares living in eastern Ohio.

McIntosh began the invasion in the fall of 1778. The Americans constructed Fort McIntosh at the mouth of Beaver Creek near Beaver, Pennsylvania, and advanced to the Tuscarawas River near present-day Bolivar, Ohio. In December, McIntosh halted for the winter and constructed Fort Laurens, naming the post for Henry Laurens, then President of the Continental Congress. After the post was finished, McIntosh and most of his command returned to Pittsburg, leaving 172 troops from Pennsylvania and Virginia under the command of Colonel John Gibson.

British officials were aware of the American advance, and in January 1779 a reconnaissance party led by Simon Girty attacked a small party from the fort, killing two and capturing another. On 22 February 1779, a larger British force commanded by Captain Henry Bird laid siege to the post. McIntosh attempted to reinforce the beleaguered garrison, but was unsuccessful. The British forced the

Americans to undergo a season of deprivation, and the Americans became so desperate they were reduced to boiling their moccasins for stew. Nonetheless, the British could not force the garrison's surrender. On 22 March they lifted the siege and returned to Detroit. In the wake of the attack, American officials concluded that the post could not serve its purpose and abandoned the fort on 2 August 1779.

In May 1779 John Bowman led an expedition from Kentucky against Shawnee villages clustered along the Little Miami River in Ohio. The attack was poorly orchestrated and his command was more concerned with acquiring plunder than fighting. Bowman's men put the Shawnee villages to the torch and accumulated more than 180 horses and other property, but at the cost of nine dead and several wounded. A few defenders were killed, but most escaped and approximately forty Shawnee adults and boys were able to harass Bowman's nearly 300-man force along its entire retreat to the Ohio River. While revealing the Shawnees' vulnerability to attack, the raid was a tactical failure and had little lasting effect.

In 1780 Clark undertook a punitive expedition against the Ohio Indian nations in retaliation for Bird and McKee's raid against Martin's and Ruddell's Stations. Clark learned of the Bird invasion in early June. By July, he had determined to strike against Chillicothe and Pickaway, Shawnee settlements on the Miami River in Ohio. Assembling nearly 1,000 Kentucky troops near the mouth of the Licking River near present-day Covington, Kentucky, Clark began his advance on 2 August.

Clark reached Chillicothe on 6 August, but found that the Shawnees had burned and then evacuated the town in anticipation of Clark's arrival. The Americans destroyed anything left standing, cut down several hundred acres of corn, and moved against Pickaway the following day. The Shawnees were prepared and had constructed what Clark described as "strongholds," "works," and a "very strong" blockhouse enclosed by a triangular stockade with which to meet the attackers.

Clark commenced a general engagement in late afternoon. Strong Indian resistance stalled the Americans' advance, and the battle did not conclude until evening, when Clark deployed two small caliber cannon against the Shawnees. The Kentuckians took possession of the village, but most of the defenders slipped away. The following day, Clark's men destroyed approximately 800 acres of crops containing an estimated 36,000 bushels of corn. On 9 August, the army began its withdrawal. Clark reached the Ohio River on 14 August and, following an auction of Shawnee plunder, disbanded his force.

The attack heightened growing tension between Crown officials and their allies, who claimed that Detroit was slow to send troops and other support in the days leading up to the engagement. Further, the loss of such a prodigious supply of food placed a serious burden on British officials as they attempted to provision the Shawnees throughout the following winter and spring. Ultimately, however, the raid had inflicted few casualties and diminished neither the Shawnees' willingness nor ability to continue the war.

In March 1782 Pennsylvania irregulars led by Colonel David Williams undertook an expedition against Gnadenhutten on the Tuscarawas River in Ohio. The Indian village was home to a congregation of Moravian Delawares. Williamson believed, incorrectly, that the Delawares had participated in several raids against western Pennsylvania. By feigning friendship, the Pennsylvanians lured nearly 100 of the Delaware into two cabins, after which Williamson and his men bludgeoned ninety-six men, women, and infants to death. The massacre was the worst atrocity perpetrated during the war.

On 25 May 1782, 400 Pennsylvania troops commanded by Colonel William Crawford began an expedition against Wyandot and Delaware towns located on the Sandusky River near present-day Upper Sandusky, Ohio. Among the Americans were Williamson and several other Gnadenhutten murderers. Crawford encountered stiff resistance near the Sandusky River on 6 June, losing nearly 50 men in the engagement. The following day, the Indians renewed the attack, capturing Crawford and scattering his army. Crawford was tortured and killed in revenge for the Gnadenhutten massacre. Ironically, Williamson escaped and returned safely to Pennsylvania. The Crawford expedition marked the last campaign in the Western Theater.

CONCLUSIONS

The campaigns fought in the West had little impact on the outcome of the conflict. However, Clark's success in Illinois allowed American negotiators to claim control over the region during peace negotiations at war's end. The Treaty of Paris, which ended the conflict in 1783, awarded the territory to the United States. The region's Indians continued to resist expansion into the region until the battle of Fallen Timbers in 1794 and the subsequent Treaty of Greenville, signed in August 1795. The pact led to the eventual admittance of Ohio, Michigan, Indiana, Illinois, and Wisconsin into the federal union.

SEE ALSO *Clark, George Rogers; Indians in the Colonial Wars and the American Revolution; Shawnee; Vincennes, Indiana.*

BIBLIOGRAPHY

Allen, Robert S. *His Majesty's Indian Allies: British Indian Policy in the Defence of Canada, 1774–1815.* Toronto and Oxford: Dundurn Press, 1992.

Barr, Daniel. *The Ends of the American Earth: War and Society on the Pittsburgh Frontier.* Kent, Ohio: Kent State University Press, 2007.

Butterfield, Consul Willshire. *An Historical Account o the Expedition against Sandusky under Colonel William Crawford in 1782.* Cincinnati, Ohio: Robert Clarke & Co., 1873.

———. *History of the Girtys: Being a Concise Account of the Girty Brothers . . .* Cincinnati, Ohio: Robert Clarke & Co., 1890.

Calloway, Colin G. *The American Revolution in Indian Country: Crisis and Diversity in Native American Communities.* Cambridge: Cambridge University Press, 1995.

Carstens, Kenneth C. and Nancy Son Carstens, eds. *The Life of George Rogers Clark, 1752–1818: Triumphs and Tragedies.* Westport, Conn.: Greenwood Publishing, 2004.

Harrison, Lowell H. *George Rogers Clark and the War in the West.* Lexington: University Press of Kentucky, 1976.

Hinderaker, Eric. *Elusive Empires: Constructing Colonialism in the Ohio Valley, 1673–1800.* Cambridge: Cambridge University Press, 1997.

Nelson, Larry L. *A Man of Distinction among Them: Alexander McKee and the Ohio Country Frontier, 1754–1799.* Kent, Ohio, and London: Kent State University Press, 1999.

Perkins, Elizabeth A. *Border Life: Experience and Memory in the Revolutionary Ohio Valley.* Chapel Hill, N.C., and London: University of North Carolina Press, 1998.

Pieper, Thomas I. and James B. Gidney. *Fort Laurens, 1778–1779: The Revolutionary War in Ohio.* Kent, Ohio: Kent State University Press, 1976.

Skaggs, David Curtis, ed. *The Old Northwest in the American Revolution: An Anthology.* Madison: State Historical Society of Wisconsin, 1977.

Skaggs, David Curtis and Larry L. Nelson, eds. *The Sixty Years' War for the Great Lakes, 1754–1814.* East Lansing: Michigan State University Press, 2001.

Smith, Thomas, ed. *Ohio in the American Revolution.* Columbus: Ohio Historical Society, 1975.

revised by Larry L. Nelson

WESTERN RESERVE. About three million
acres in the northeast corner of modern Ohio were reserved by Connecticut when that state surrendered claims to all other western lands in 1786. A 500,000-acre tract known as the Fire Lands (later the counties of Huron, Erie, and the eastern tip of Ottawa) was used to repay citizens of Danbury, Fairfield, Norwalk, New Haven, and New London for war losses.

Mark M. Boatner

WEST INDIES IN THE REVOLUTION. The West Indies were a major theater of
the American Revolutionary War. This was because they were divided among the colonial powers of Britain,

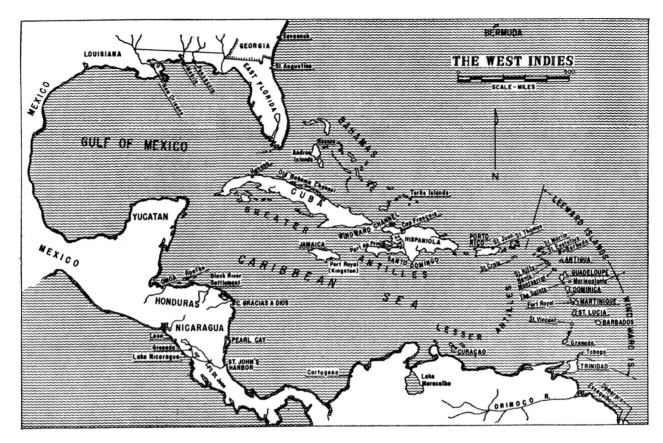

France, Spain, and the Netherlands, all of whom were belligerents at some stage of the Revolutionary War. Furthermore, they were economically important as the principal market for the slave trade in the Americas and as the primary source of the sugar and rum consumed in Europe and America.

The six British colonies in the Caribbean—Jamaica; Grenada, which included Tobago; Barbados; the Leeward Islands; St. Vincent; and Dominica—did not ally themselves with the thirteen mainland colonies, even though they were tied closely to the rebel colonies by trade before the war. Their political systems, including elected assemblies, were similar to those of the mainland colonies, and their plantation systems shared much in common with the southern mainland colonies, especially South Carolina. Nevertheless, they did not unite in even a limited campaign of opposition to Britain or engage in a pamphlet war with Britain. They continued to affirm their belief in parliamentary sovereignty. Unlike Bermuda, they did not send delegates to the Continental Congress. It was only on the eve of the war that they made sympathetic gestures to the mainland cause, but this sudden change of tone was motivated primarily by their desire to prevent a war that was likely to have adverse economic consequences for the

British West Indies. Their loyalty during the imperial crisis was based on their reliance upon the home government for defense owing to their greater vulnerability to slave revolts and foreign attack. In addition, they were economically dependent upon their monopoly of the sugar market in Britain. The white colonists on the islands were also more closely connected with the mother country; many of the elite returned to Britain for their education and even settled there as wealthy absentees.

From the outset, the Revolutionary War involved the West Indies. The islands became an essential channel of gunpowder and military supplies provided by the French and Dutch for the state militias and the Continental army. American privateers were also active in attempting to destroy Britain's lucrative trade with the Caribbean. The British islands did not initially face a threat of invasion, although privateers raided Nassau (New Providence) in the Bahamas in 1776 and twice attacked Tobago in 1777. The first foreign salute of the American flag occurred in the Caribbean in 1776 in the Danish island of St. Croix in October and by the Dutch Fort Orange at St. Eustatius, which saluted the flag flying from a ship of the Continental navy, the *Andrew Doria,* on 16 November. General Sir William Howe attempted with little success to obtain troops from Jamaica and supplies from Barbados. He did not receive the troops from Jamaica, where their embarkation coincided with a major slave revolt that an inquiry by the local assembly concluded to be inspired by the anticipated withdrawal of the troops. Howe received some food provisions from Barbados, but the island was on the verge of famine. In the Leeward Islands, which had previously relied on food imports from British North America, there were such shortages that an estimated one-fifth of the slave population died in Antigua. Agents of the Continental Congress and the state governments were dispersed throughout the French and Dutch islands, including William Bingham, who operated in Martinique. His mission was not only to procure supplies and to assist privateers but also to create incidents likely to provoke war between Britain and France.

STRATEGY PRIORITIES

The war in the West Indies was transformed by the entry into the war of France in 1778 and Spain in 1779. The islands became a major theater of the conflict and the relative strength of the respective navies became critical. The British navy was overstretched, with often fewer ships than islands in the eastern Caribbean. The navy had to provide convoys for merchants ships in both the Indian Ocean and the Atlantic. It not only had to protect the home waters and to blockade the coast of North America, but also to defend British colonies in the Mediterranean, India, and the Caribbean along with slave trading posts on the west coast of Africa. The colonists in the British islands regarded the navy as their only means of defense and were inclined to submit to invasion rather than risk the destruction of their plantations. The reliance on the navy was greater still owing to the inadequacy of the size of the army garrisons. However, the earl of Sandwich, the first lord of the Admiralty, was primarily concerned with the defense of Britain. His strategy was largely reactive, with British fleets countering their opponents by shadowing and pursuing enemy fleets. His caution was due to the uncertainty about whether the destination of the enemy fleets was the Indian Ocean, the Atlantic, the North Sea, the Mediterranean, or the English Channel. The danger of this policy was that a superior enemy fleet might gain naval superiority for sufficient time to inflict a major blow before the arrival of the pursuing British fleet.

The climate and wind directions also presented particular problems for strategy in the West Indies. The fleets were unsafe in the islands during the hurricane months from the beginning of August to early November. It was therefore customary to leave only a minimal presence during the hurricane season. The trade winds blew from east to west for much of the year, which had the effect of dividing the small islands of the eastern Caribbean, known

as the Lesser Antilles, which included the Leeward and Windward Islands, from the large islands to the west, the Greater Antilles, which included Cuba, Puerto Rico, St. Domingue (Haiti), Santo Domingo, and Jamaica. A ship could sail from Barbados to Jamaica in about a week, but the return journey against adverse winds might take as long as a voyage across the Atlantic. The possession of the most easterly islands was therefore particularly desirable. The primary naval bases of Britain and France were in the Lesser Antilles, at English Harbour in Antigua and Fort Royal in Martinique.

France was more concerned with strategic objectives in the Caribbean than in North America. On the outbreak of war with Britain in 1778, it seized the initiative in the Caribbean, where the marquis de Bouillé, the governor of Martinique, conquered Dominica in September. The small local defense force was easily overwhelmed by an invasion army of two thousand. There were no casualties on either side. The French conquered the island before news of the expedition reached the British admiral in the eastern Caribbean, who was unable to come to the rescue because of orders to remain in Barbados, where he was to join a secret expedition for the conquest of St. Lucia. The fall of Dominica enabled the French to consolidate their own colonial possessions and to divide the British islands in the eastern Caribbean. The British, however, more than compensated themselves for this loss by capturing St. Lucia.

Britain persisted in the war for America partly in the belief that the loss of the thirteen colonies might be followed by the loss of the British West Indies. George III regarded the possession of the island colonies as essential for generating the wealth to wage the war and to preserve national greatness. There was even discussion within the cabinet of withdrawing from America to launch an offensive war in the Caribbean. The strategic importance of the islands explains why the British temporarily subordinated military activities in North America for objectives in the West Indies in 1778. The government withdrew five thousand troops from New York for the conquest of St. Lucia, a strategic priority given its fine harbor at Gros Islet Bay, which enabled the British navy to observe the movements of the French navy around the neighboring island of Martinique. However, the divisions within the government about strategic priorities and the fatal delays in mounting the expedition allowed France to take Dominica before the arrival of the expedition from New York.

EARLY FRENCH VICTORIES

The war in the Caribbean gradually deteriorated for the British during 1779. In the summer, France again seized the initiative in the West Indies. On 18 June, St. Vincent surrendered without a shot fired to Admiral Charles D'Estaing and four hundred troops under the chevalier du Romain. There was not a single British artillery officer on the island nor anyone else with knowledge of artillery. There was virtually no gunpowder or provisions in the islands. The French landed less than two miles from Kingston, where there were forty-four British soldiers and the governor was only able to assemble an additional thirty-five militiamen. Less than a month later on 4 July, the French seized Grenada, the largest sugar producer after Jamaica in the British West Indies. Governor Lord Macartney attempted to defend the island with a force of only 150 regulars and 300 militia against 3,000 French troops. The predominantly French free black and free colored population hastened his surrender by deserting the garrison.

The British loss of St. Vincent and Grenada illustrated the problems facing the Royal Navy in the Caribbean. Vice Admiral John Byron had to leave Barbados and St. Lucia twice in a month to go to the defense of St. Kitts, which was under apprehension of an attack by the French Admiral D'Estaing. It was while he was escorting the homeward-bound convoy from St. Kitts that D'Estaing attacked St. Vincent and Grenada. Byron was unable to reach Grenada until two days after the surrender. The French, in the meantime, had gained naval supremacy with reinforcements from Commodore la Motte-Picquet in June. Off Grenada, the inferior fleet of Byron fought an indecisive sea battle against D'Estaing's fleet and then returned to St. Kitts with 183 killed and 340 wounded, as well as considerable damage to masts and rigging. The condition of the British fleet left the way open for D'Estaing to attack the remaining British colonies in the Caribbean. The latter were under constant apprehension of an invasion throughout the rest of the summer. In September, the importance of the islands to Britain was demonstrated by the willingness of Sir Henry Clinton to send Lord Cornwallis and four thousand troops to the defense of Jamaica in response to an invasion scare. The expedition was called off when the alarm proved false; D'Estaing intended instead to retake Georgia.

SPAIN IN THE WAR

The entry of Spain into the war further expanded British operations in the Caribbean in 1779. There were informal British settlements along the coasts of Nicaragua and the Gulf of Honduras. In retaliation for a raid by the Spanish, the British seized the port of Omoa in the Gulf of Honduras. The success of the assault, which included the capture of large amounts of bullion, emboldened more ambitious plans that were attempted in 1780. The object was no less than to divide the Spanish Empire in the Americas and to open commercial routes with the Pacific by an expedition along the San Juan River through Lake Nicaragua to Grenada andLeón. The plan was conceived by the governor of Jamaica, Major General John Dalling. On 3 February 1780 a force of four hundred regulars

under Captain Polson sailed from Jamaica. They were accompanied by HMS *Hinchinbrook,* commanded by Captain Horatio Nelson, the future victor of Trafalgar. The enterprise proved a fiasco. It succeeded in the capture of Fort St. Juan but failed to reach the lake and was called off in May. The fort was subsequently evacuated and partly demolished on 4 January 1781.

BRITISH SUCCESS AND FAILURE

The French were less successful in 1780. In the last week of March, Admiral De Guichen arrived at Martinique with large reinforcements to take command of French forces in the West Indies. The British, meanwhile, had appointed Major General John Vaughan to be commander in chief in the Leeward Islands. A veteran of campaigns in America, he arrived in Barbados on 14 February. De Guichen attempted to attack St. Lucia with twenty-one ships of the line, but Sir Hyde Parker's sixteen ships and Vaughan's defenses forced him to abandon the attempt and return to Martinique. On 17 April, Admiral Sir George Rodney fought an indecisive naval battle with twenty ships of the line against De Guichen's superior French fleet of twenty-three. Although outnumbered, he regarded the battle as a great missed opportunity to defeat the French. He variously blamed some of his captains for failing to follow his orders during the battle and the Dutch at St. Eustatius who refitted the French fleet but refused the British. Rodney confronted De Guichen again with similarly inconclusive exchanges between the two fleets during 15–20 May. After De Guichen sailed for Europe, Rodney left for New York.

Rodney returned to St. Lucia in December. On the 16th he sailed for St. Vincent with a force of soldiers under Vaughan, but the French defenses were found to be too strong for any prospect of a successful attack. On 27 January 1781, Rodney and Vaughan received orders for the immediate capture of St. Eustatius; they carried out the attack before the inhabitants were even aware of the outbreak of war between Britain and the Netherlands. The war was partly motivated by British anger at the assistance given by the Dutch to the rebel cause in America through St. Eustatius. On 3 February 1781, St. Eustatius surrendered unconditionally to the combined British forces. The island was incapable of resistance, with a garrison of less than sixty men and a single frigate against fifteen British warships and three thousand troops. The British proceeded to capture most of the remaining Dutch territories in the Caribbean, including the islands of St. Martin and Saba, and the South American colonies of Demerara and Essequibo (Guyana). They also took French St. Bartholomew.

The British successes in the Caribbean were short lived. Rodney failed to mount any more offensives but instead spent weeks presiding over the indiscriminate plunder of St. Eustatius. He treated all the inhabitants, who included some British subjects, as smugglers, pirates, and traitors and therefore denied them the usual protection of their private property according to the laws of war. The episode caused an outcry, led in Parliament by Edmund Burke. In the meantime, Rodney delegated the task of intercepting the arrival of the French fleet of Admiral De Grasse to Admiral Sir Samuel Hood off Martinique. De Grasse, the new French commander in chief, avoided the British fleet and sailed his ships into Fort Royal on 29 April, where they joined four other ships that the British had blockaded at Martinique. On the night of the 10 May, the French again attempted St. Lucia but reembarked after finding it too well defended. A few days later, De Grasse sent a small squadron and twelve hundred troops to Tobago; they landed unopposed on the 23rd and forced its surrender on 2 June. Rodney appeared two days later but was unable to reverse the victory. De Grasse avoided a naval engagement and sailed via St. Domingue to play a critical role at the Battle of Yorktown.

AFTER YORKTOWN

The British defeat at Yorktown in October 1781 marked an escalation of the war in the Caribbean, leaving the French to resume the offensive. France and Spain planned to attack Jamaica. While awaiting the return of De Grasse from Virginia, the marquis de Bouillé seized the opportunity to recapture the British-occupied Dutch islands of St. Martin and Saba. On 15 November he also recaptured St. Eustatius from the British. Unable to land his 2,000 troops owing to a heavy surf, he made a bold surprise attack with only 300 men against a garrison of 723 troops under Colonel Cockburn and captured prizes of two million livres, including pay for the British army in North America. In the meantime, De Grasse had declined the request of George Washington that he and the French fleet remain in North America and assist in an attack on Charleston. He had already overstayed his orders to return to the Caribbean with the object of a combined attack with the Spanish fleet against Jamaica. De Grasse reached Martinique the day after De Bouillé's capture of St. Eustatius. While waiting for reinforcements and the juncture of the Spanish fleet, he made several attempts on British islands in the Lesser Antilles, but bad weather foiled his designs on Barbados and a determined defense twice repulsed his efforts to take St. Lucia. Accompanied by the same victorious French army and commanders that had served at Yorktown, De Grasse landed at St. Kitts on 11 January 1782, but he faced a determined opposition from the garrison of Brimstone Hill and did not secure the surrender of the island until 11 February. The fall of St. Kitts was quickly followed by Nevis and Montserrat and then Demerara and Essequibo.

The Caribbean became the main theater of military operations in the final year of the war. Hood's fleet was reinforced by Rodney on the 25th, preceding the departure of De Grasse from Martinique for St. Domingue, where he planned to join the Spanish fleet and to embark French troops for the invasion of Jamaica. With additional reinforcements, Rodney enjoyed naval superiority with thirty-seven ships of the line against De Grasse's thirty-three effective sail of the line and two fifty-gun ships. On 12 April 1782, in a passage of islands between Dominica and Guadeloupe called the Saintes, he encountered Rodney and the British fleet in what proved to be one of the most decisive British naval victories before Trafalgar. During the Battle of the Saintes, Rodney captured the French flagship, the *Ville de Paris*, together with Admiral de Grasse and four ships carrying the siege artillery intended for Jamaica.

Rodney consequently became one of the few heroes of the Revolutionary War, although there was some criticism of his failure to continue the pursuit of the French fleet after the battle. The victory did not allay fears of an Franco-Spanish invasion of Jamaica. While Rodney sailed for Jamaica in May, a Spanish force captured the Bahamas. The British, therefore, continued to prepare for the continuation of the war and even sent orders to Guy Carleton, the commander in chief in America, to move to the Caribbean. Nevertheless, the only significant action was the recapture of Honduras by the British in October. The peace preliminaries in Europe ended the military preparations for new campaigns in the Caribbean. Rodney's victory helped Britain obtain generous terms from France and Spain at the Treaty of Paris in 1783. The British had lost seven islands and made only one conquest, but they were forced by the terms of the peace to cede only Tobago and St. Lucia to France and the coastal settlements along the shore of Nicaragua to Spain.

ASSESSMENTS

The war in the Caribbean was inextricably linked with the war in North America. Rodney and Clinton had even suggested a supreme commander in chief for both the Caribbean and North America. Many British officers who served in North America also served in the Caribbean, including Colonel Archibald Campbell, Major John Dalrymple, Colonel William Dalrymple, Major General George Garth, Major General James Grant, Lieutenant Colonel Stephen Kemble, Major General Alexander Leslie, Lieutenant Colonel Thomas Musgrave, Major General Charles O'Hara, Lord Charles Montagu, Major General Edward Mathew, Major General Robert Prescott, Major General Augustine Prevost, and Major General John Vaughan.

The defense of the West Indies contributed to the British defeat in North America. Britain had to deploy resources in the former that might otherwise have served in the latter. These included naval convoys to protect merchant ships against privateers and enemy fleets. In 1778 Sir Henry Clinton withdrew from Philadelphia to free five thousand troops for the conquest of St. Lucia, together with an additional three thousand troops for service in Florida and Canada. Clinton resented their loss, particularly because the German mercenary regiments were debarred by their contracts from serving in the Caribbean, which forced him to send British regiments that he regarded as much superior. Clinton was promised the return of the troops from the Caribbean, and he later blamed their absence for his subsequent failure to aggressively engage the Continental army. Historians have long criticized Lord George Germain or the commanding officers in the Caribbean for the dispersion of these troops throughout the Leeward Islands, but the British had little choice, since the islands had insufficient garrisons to withstand attacks and the cabinet was under constant political pressure for better protection from the opposition parties and the powerful West India lobby in London.

The troops that served on other campaigns in the West Indies might similarly have reinforced Clinton. Furthermore, the British regiments in the islands had to be continually replenished owing to the high mortality rates due primarily to malaria. During the American War, 11 percent of the troops died on the voyage to the Caribbean. The annual mortality rate of soldiers in the Caribbean was 15 percent, compared to 6 percent for those stationed in New York and 1 percent in Canada. Without a single short being fired, the British lost 3,500 troops in three and one-half years in Jamaica. Of the 1,008 men of the Seventy-eighth Regiment stationed at Kingston in 1779, only 18 were still alive in 1783. Of 7,000 troops sent to Jamaica, only 2,000 were fit for duty in April 1782.

Rodney's failure to intercept the arrival of De Grasse's fleet at Martinique before the Battle of Yorktown had the greatest strategic implications for the British war in America. Sir Henry Clinton and Lord Cornwallis were led to expect by the ministry in London that Rodney would either check De Grasse in the Caribbean or follow him to North America. Rodney instead spent three months presiding over the sale of goods at St. Eustatius and left Hood to prevent De Grasse's entry into Martinique. Hood argued with Rodney about his orders for positioning the British fleet outside Martinique, orders that he believed were motivated by Rodney's greater interest in protecting prize convoys from St. Eustatius to Britain than in inhibiting the movements of De Grasse. Rodney compounded the failure by not following De Grasse to America, which again delegated the responsibility of the pursuit to Hood. Rodney instead pleaded ill-health and returned to England, where his first priority was to defend himself in Parliament against critics like Edmund Burke, who were demanding an inquiry into his behavior at St. Eustatius. His departure contributed to the numerical inferiority of the British fleet at the Battle of the Virginia Capes (in the Chesapeake), which sealed the fate of Cornwallis. His absence also deprived the navy of the most brilliant and the most senior British naval commander in the Americas.

SEE ALSO *Estaing, Charles Hector Théodat, Comte d'; French Alliance; Grasse, François Joseph Paul, Comte de; Jamaica (West Indies); Naval Operations, French; Nicaragua; Rodney, George Bridges; Spanish Participation in the American Revolution; St. Eustatius; St. Kitts, Captured by the French; St. Lucia, Captured by the British; Vaughan, John.*

BIBLIOGRAPHY

Alberts, Robert C. *The Golden Voyage: The Life and Times of William Bingham, 1752–1804.* Boston: Houghton-Mifflin, 1969.

Carrington, Selwyn H. H. *The British West Indies during the American Revolution.* Dordrecht, Netherlands: Foris, 1988.

Dull, Jonathan R. *The French Navy and American Independence: A Study of Arms and Diplomacy, 1774–1787.* Princeton, N.J.: Princeton University Press, 1975.

Hurst, Ronald. *The Golden Rock: An Episode in the American War of Independence, 1775–1783.* London: Leo Cooper, 1996.

Mackesy, Piers. *The War for America, 1775–1783.* London: Longmans, 1964.

Makinson, David H. *Barbados: A Study of North-American-West Indian Relations, 1739–1789.* The Hague, Netherlands: Mouton, 1964.

Metcalf, George. *Royal Government and Political Conflict in Jamaica, 1729–1783.* London: Longmans, 1965.

O'Shaughnessy, Andrew Jackson. *An Empire Divided: The American Revolution and the British Caribbean.* Philadelphia: University of Pennsylvania Press, 2000.

Ragatz, Lowell. *The Fall of the Planter Class in the British Caribbean, 1763–1833.* 1928. Reprint, New York: Octagon Books, 1963.

Robertson, Eileen A. *The Spanish Town Papers.* London: Cresset Press, 1959.

Sheridan, Richard B. "The Crisis of Slave Subsistence in the British West Indies during and after the American Revolution." *William and Mary Quarterly*, third series, 33 (1976): 615–641.

Singh, R. John. *French Diplomacy in the Caribbean and the American Revolution.* Hicksville, N.Y.: Exposition Press, 1977.

Toth, Charles W., ed. *The American Revolution and the West Indies.* Port Washington: Kennikat Press, 1975.

Tuchman, Barbara. *The First Salute: A View of the American Revolution.* New York: Knopf, 1988.

Whitson, Agnes. "The Outlook of the American Colonies on the British West Indies, 1760–1775." *Political Science Quarterly* 45, no. 1 (1930): 56–86.

revised by Andrew Jackson O'Shaughnessy

WESTMORELAND, PENNSYLVANIA.

Township into which Wyoming Valley settlements were incorporated by Connecticut in January 1774.

SEE ALSO *Wyoming Valley Massacre, Pennsylvania.*

Mark M. Boatner

WEST POINT, NEW YORK.

Located on the west side of a sharp bend of the Hudson River seven miles below Fishkill, West Point was not fortified until after Clinton's expedition of October 1777 demonstrated the inadequacy of the Patriots' existing defenses. It became, in Washington's words, the "key to America," and was to have been the prize of Arnold's treason. From the completion of its works in 1778, Washington made it the center of his defensive lines against the British in New York. Many scholars hold that it served effectively to bottle the British into their positions in New York City, while others find it insignificant to the total war effort. With patrols ranging widely from this base, the Americans were able to put serious pressure on the British supply system.

A detachment of the Corps of Invalids was assigned there in 1781 to instruct officer candidates, but the plan did not materialize. Washington first proposed the establishment of a military academy at this site in 1783. Instead, Congress terminated the Continental army the next year (2 June 1784), replacing it the following day with the miniscule U.S. Army. West Point was garrisoned by fifty-five men under a captain who were charged with maintaining the decaying fort. Later it was home for the Corps of Artillerists and Engineers established on 9 May 1794, and on 4 July 1802 the U.S. Military Academy started operating with ten cadets present. West Point is the oldest continuously garrisoned U.S. military post.

SEE ALSO *Arnold's Treason; Clinton's Expedition; Corps of Invalids; Hudson River and the Highlands.*

revised by Michael Bellesiles

WETHERSFIELD CONFERENCE, CONNECTICUT.

21 May 1781. In a historic meeting at Wethersfield between Washington and the comte de Rochambeau, commander of the French forces, a plan was made for an all-out attack on the British in New York City, which Washington hoped would be the decisive campaign of the war. (This was not the genesis—except indirectly—of the Yorktown campaign, as has been frequently claimed.) After the meeting, Washington wrote to all the New England assemblies requesting more than six thousand militia to supplement his forces for the upcoming attack on General Clinton. The very next day, Rochambeau's senior officers persuaded him to switch their campaign to the Chesapeake; Washington insisted on the original proposal to which Rochambeau had agreed, but the French eventually persuaded the Americans to head south.

The Wethersfield Plan was potentially compromised on 3 June when Sir Henry Clinton received a captured copy and became aware of the Washington's plan of operation. The oldest permanently inhabited township in Connecticut, Wethersfield became a suburb of Hartford.

SEE ALSO *Yorktown Campaign.*

revised by Michael Bellesiles

WETZELL'S MILLS (OR MILL), NORTH CAROLINA.

6 March 1781. The day after General Charles Cornwallis started withdrawing from the Dan River toward Hillsboro, North Carolina (17 February 1781), General Nathanael Greene sent over his advance elements with the intention of harassing the British until he had received reinforcements and could face Cornwallis in a pitched battle. The opposing forces clashed first at Clapp's Mills, 2 March. At 3 A.M the morning of 6 March, Cornwallis undertook a movement by which he hoped to surprise Colonel Otho Williams's advance element, which was guarding a large supply of food at Wetzell's Mills on the Reedy Fork, and draw Greene into a general engagement. By 8 A.M. the British were within two miles of Colonel William Campbell's detachment of about 150 Virginia militia when their presence was detected. Sending Lieutenant Colonel Henry Lee's Legion and Colonel William Washington's dragoons to support Campbell, Williams started withdrawing along Reedy Fork from his camp at High Rock Ford to the ford at Wetzell's Mills.

Lieutenant Colonel Banastre Tarleton's cavalry and a thousand infantry of Lieutenant Colonel James Webster's Brigade (Twenty-third, Thirty-third, Seventy-first, Light Infantry Company of the Guards, and some jägers) pushed forward aggressively, while Cornwallis followed with the main body. Colonel William Preston commanded a covering force of Virginia militia while Campbell, Lee, and Washington made good their retreat across the ford at Wetzell's Mills. Seeing that the numerically superior

British had too many opportunities to turn him out of a defensive position along Reedy Fork, Williams ordered Campbell, Lee, and Washington to delay as long as possible at Wetzell's Mills while the rest of the light corps continued their retreat toward Greene's camp. The delaying force was directed to withdraw when faced with the danger of being overwhelmed.

Lee posted a company of Preston's riflemen to cover the ford, deployed the Legion infantry in a line parallel to the creek, and placed Campbell's men and the remainder of Preston's in some heavy woods so that their left flank tied in with the right flank of the Legion infantry. Lee's cavalry were to the rear where they could protect the militia horses and also be prepared to cover the retreat of the first line.

The Guards led Webster's Brigade in an attempt to force a crossing of the creek at the ford. When they were driven back by well-aimed fire from Preston's riflemen, Webster rode up to lead them across. The British infantry then stormed the high bank on which the defenders were deployed, and Tarleton's cavalry splashed across the ford and got into a position to cut off the Americans if they did not withdraw promptly. Covered by the Legion cavalry, the delaying force withdrew five miles while the British maintained pressure. Cornwallis then accepted the fact that his attempt had failed and withdrew. Williams had been able to extract his entire force from a well-coordinated British attack and to bring away all the foodstuffs stored at Wetzell's for use by the Continentals. Greene had marched the main body to the ironworks on Troublesome Creek.

Losses were about fifty killed and wounded on each side. The next encounter between Greene and Cornwallis was the major engagement at Guilford Courthouse, 15 March 1781.

SEE ALSO *Clapp's Mills, North Carolina; Guilford Courthouse, North Carolina; Marksmanship; Southern Campaigns of Nathanael Greene.*

revised by Michael Bellesiles

WHALEBOAT WARFARE. Whaleboat
warfare was the name given to the water-borne guerrilla operations and small-boat privateering that was waged across Long Island Sound and along the New Jersey coast (including Staten Island) between the British and the rebels after Sir William Howe captured New York City in September 1776. The name derives from the fact that the raiders typically used whaleboats—sturdy but handy and relatively capacious wooden boats, propelled generally by oarsmen, that had been developed to hunt whales along

the New England coast—to sneak across the water quickly and quietly under cover of night.

SEE ALSO *Blue Mountain Valley off Sandy Hook, New Jersey; Hyler, Adam; London Trading; Marriner, William; Meigs, Return Jonathan; Tallmadge, Benjamin, Jr.*

revised by Harold E. Selesky

WHEELING, WEST VIRGINIA. 31
August–1 September 1777 and 11–13 September 1782. This site on the Ohio River was first settled in 1769 by Ebenezer Zane. During Dunmore's War, Fort Fincastle was built there in 1774 by William Crawford; in 1776 it was renamed Fort Henry for Patrick Henry. The exposed and isolated settlement in the Dark and Bloody Ground was often the target of Indian raids. On the last day of August 1777, however, it was attacked by almost four hundred Indians and besieged for twenty-three hours. Colonel Sheppard lost twenty-three men of his forty-two-man garrison in preliminary skirmishes during the early morning hours, yet refused to surrender, withstanding a six-hour fire delivered from the cover of the abandoned cabins. After a lull the Indians resumed their attack at 2:30 P.M. The next morning at 4 A.M, Colonel Swearingen got into the fort with fourteen reinforcements and Major McCulloch arrived later with forty mounted men. After burning the settlement and killing what livestock they could find, the Indians withdrew. None of the defenders was killed after the initial attack.

In what may technically be the last battle of the war (the alternative being at Johns Island, South Carolina, on 4 Nov. 1782), Fort Henry held off 250 Indians and 40 Loyalists during 11–13 September 1782. It was probably during the latter action that Elizabeth Zane performed her feat of valor: during a lull in the battle, she volunteered to leave the fort and get a keg of badly needed powder from her brother Ebenezer's cabin, sixty yards away across open ground. Zane argued that the Indians might be so surprised to see a woman walking out of the fort that they would be slow to fire. Either through shock or respect, the Indians did not fire on Zane as she strolled to the cabin. However, they did begin shooting when she emerged with the powder keg. Defying myths of eagle-eyed shots, not a single shot hit Zane as she raced across the open ground just a few feet from the Indians' position, reaching the fort unscathed.

SEE ALSO *Crawford, William; Dark and Bloody Ground; Johns Island, South Carolina (4 November 1782); McCulloch's Leap.*

BIBLIOGRAPHY
Schneider, Norris F., and G. M. Farley. *Betty Zane, Heroine of Fort Henry.* Williansport, Md.: Zane Grey Collector, 1969.

revised by Michael Bellesiles

SEE ALSO *George III.*

revised by Harold E. Selesky

WHIGS AND TORIES.

The names "Whigs" and "Tories" were applied from the middle of the seventeenth century to political groupings in Parliament that were held together by shifting combinations of patronage, personal loyalties, special interests, and political principles; they were not organized political parties in the modern sense. The names continued to be used even as the people and issues changed over time. The Whigs, broadly, supported Parliamentary supremacy and commercial expansion. From the Revolution of 1688, they tarred the Tories with the stain of royal absolutism. Toryism finally collapsed after extreme elements tried to overthrow the Hanoverian succession in 1715. Politics during the reigns of George I and II (1714–1760) became a contest about who would wield power and patronage. Issues of principle were still hotly debated, but the main fight was for preferment within an established system of politics based on the supremacy of the king-in-Parliament, what Englishmen called mixed government. With the accession of George III, some groups of Whigs supported the right of the king to be more assertive in choosing and controlling his ministers, provided he had the support of a majority in the House of Commons. Other Whigs contended that Parliament alone, which they intended to dominate, should select and control the ministers. George and his supporters, called the "king's friends," jostled for a greater role for the king during the 1760s, at enormous cost for the consistency of colonial policy. With the appointment of Lord North in 1770, George finally had a prime minister with whom he could work.

Americans who objected to increased imperial control of the colonies adopted the name "Whig" to denote their commitment to legislative supremacy, in this case to the supremacy of their own local legislatures over ministers, Parliament, and eventually a king who they believed were exercising arbitrary and tyrannical power over them. Using this name also connected them in spirit to the long list of people who had opposed conspiracies against the rights of Englishmen. The fact that George and his ministers had the approval of their own legislature—and were themselves staunch defenders of legislative supremacy—was not something American whigs chose to acknowledge. Consistent with this point of view, after 1775 American Whigs labeled those who continued to support the king "Tories." Supporters of the king called themselves "Loyalists."

WHIPPLE, ABRAHAM.

(1733–1819). Continental naval officer. Rhode Island. Born in Providence, Rhode Island, on 26 September 1733, Whipple married Sarah Hopkins, the sister of Esek and Stephen Hopkins, in 1761. During the Seven Years' War he served as a privateer, first under Esek Hopkins's command and then as captain of the *Game Cock.* With the latter he captured twenty-three French vessels in 1759–1760, earning a reputation as the colony's most experienced sea captain. In 1772 he led the attack on the British schooner *Gaspée,* becoming a hero among American radicals.

Whipple was appointed commodore of the little (two-ship) Rhode Island fleet when it was organized in 1775. On 15 June 1775, the day he received his commission, he captured a British tender, the first official American prize of the Revolution. One of the first captains of the Continental navy, he commanded the *Columbus* (twenty guns) in the first naval operation of the war. In 1778 he took the *Providence* (twelve guns) to Europe, was presented to the French king, and took a few prizes. In mid-July 1779, while his *Providence* was cruising with Rathbun's *Queen of France* and the *Ranger,* he had the good fortune of drifting into a British convoy of heavily laden East Indiamen off Newfoundland in a heavy fog. Thanks largely to the initiative of Rathbun, he cut eleven of the ships out of the convoy and got eight of them safely to Boston. Sold for one million dollars, they constituted one of the richest single captures of the war.

Later in the year he reached Charleston with four Continental vessels and was given responsibility for the naval defense of the doomed city. He became a prisoner on 12 May 1780, when the city was surrendered to Clinton, and for the remainder of the war he was on parole at Chester, Pennsylvania.

Returning to Providence in 1783, Whipple decided in 1788 to move west to Marietta, Ohio. He died there on 27 May 1819.

SEE ALSO *Hopkins, Stephen; Naval Operations, Strategic Overview; Rathbun, John Peck.*

BIBLIOGRAPHY
Morgan, William James. *Captains to the Northward: The New England Captains in the Continental Navy.* Barre, Mass.: Barre Gazette, 1959.

Whipple, Abraham, Papers. Rhode Island Historical Society, Providence, Rhode Island.

revised by Michael Bellesiles

WHIPPLE, WILLIAM. (1730–1785).
Signer. Maine-New Hampshire. A descendant of Matthew Whipple, who came to America from England prior to 1638, William was born on 14 January 1730 in Kittery (in what became Maine). After attending local schools he went to sea, was made master of a vessel while still in his early twenties, and engaged in slave trading. He left the sea in 1760 when he entered a business partnership with his brother, Joseph, at Portsmouth, New Hampshire, a short distance from his birthplace. After playing a prominent part in the Revolutionary politics of his region, he was elected to the Continental Congress in 1776 and remained a delegate until he declined reelection in 1780. He signed the Declaration of Independence, was active in committees, and showed an exceptionally realistic attitude on such vital matters as the need for heavy taxation to finance the struggle, the need for reforms in the commissary and recruiting systems, the importance of naval operations, and the requirement for military success in America rather than diplomatic cleverness in Europe to win the war. He left Congress temporarily to serve as a brigadier general (appointed by the New Hampshire state legislature on 18 July 1777) in command of the First Brigade of the state militia in the two Battles of Saratoga and in Sullivan's Newport operations in 1778. He and General Glover commanded the troops that escorted Burgoyne's captured army to Cambridge. During the period 1780–1784 Whipple sat in the state assembly, and from 1782 until his death in 1785, he was associate justice of the New Hampshire superior court. Only fifty-five years old when he died on 28 November 1785, he had been performing his arduous duties for several years while in bad health and with the belief—confirmed by autopsy—that he was in danger of sudden death. Whipple had married Catherine Moffatt in 1767, and they had lived in a house owned by her family that overlooked Portsmouth Harbor.

BIBLIOGRAPHY

Adams, Steve. "William Whipple." In *New Hampshire: Years of Revolution, 1774–1783*. Edited by Peter Randall. Portsmouth: New Hampshire Profiles, 1976.

Estes, J. Worth. *Hall Jackson and the Purple Foxglove: Medical Practice and Research in Revolutionary America, 1760–1820*. Hanover, N.H.: University Press of New England, 1979.

Potter, Chandler E. *The Military History of the State of New Hampshire, 1623–1861*. 1868. Reprint, Baltimore: Genealogical Publishing, 1972.

Upton, Richard Francis. *Revolutionary New Hampshire*. 1936. Reprint, New York: Octagon Books, 1971.

revised by Frank C. Mevers

WHITCOMB, JOHN. (1713–1785). Militia general. Massachusetts. Older brother of Asa Whitcomb, John Whitcomb (also spelled Whetcomb) served as a field officer in the Massachusetts provincial regiments during several campaigns of the final French and Indian war (1755, 1758, and 1760). After the war he became a prominent political leader in Bolton, Massachusetts, and was commissioned brigadier general by the Massachusetts Provincial Congress on 15 February 1775. As colonel of the local Worcester County minuteman regiment, he participated in the pursuit of the British after Lexington and Concord, 19 April 1775. He was elected first major general of the Massachusetts provincial army on 13 June 1775, and commanded at Lechmere Point during the battle of Bunker Hill. Passed over by Congress in the first round of appointments, he was elected a brigadier general on 5 June 1776, but declined the commission because of his age.

SEE ALSO *Lexington and Concord.*

revised by Harold E. Selesky

WHITEFIELD, GEORGE. (1714–1770).
Anglican evangelist. George Whitefield (pronounced Whitfield) was closely identified with John and Charles Wesley, the founders of Methodism, until 1741 when he began to espouse Calvinistic views. Whitefield made seven trips to America before the Revolution. He was appointed minister of Savannah, in the newly founded colony of Georgia, and in 1739 established an orphanage called Bethesda some ten miles from the city. He toured the colonies from Georgia to New Hampshire several times, with the avowed purpose of raising money for his orphanage. Hugely popular on his first itinerancy in 1740–1741, he preached to enormous numbers of people in the open air, and sparked what contemporaries believed was a revival of interest in religion so overwhelming that it could properly be called a "great awakening." His popularity declined as the number of new souls to be saved diminished, and as some established clergy came to view his revivals as overwrought displays of emotion and enthusiasm. Nonetheless, if we believe the figures he gave for the numbers who heard him preach, he was seen by more people in more places than anyone before him in British

ENCYCLOPEDIA OF THE AMERICAN REVOLUTION

colonial America. By showing people in widely distant places that they shared an interest in the revival of religion, he contributed to eroding the insularity and provincialism that had hitherto isolated colonial Americans.

BIBLIOGRAPHY

Lambert, Frank. *"Pedlar in Divinity:" George Whitefield and the Transatlantic Revivals, 1737–1770*. Princeton, N.J.: Princeton University Press, 1994.

revised by Harold E. Selesky

WHITEHAVEN, ENGLAND. 22–23

April 1778. On 10 April Captain John Paul Jones sailed in the eighteen-gun sloop *Ranger* from Brest, France. He was under the orders of the American commissioners in Paris to attack British commercial shipping in the Irish Sea and along Britain's west coast. After taking a number of prizes, including the revenue cutter *Hussar*, Jones headed for Whitehaven, a small port on the west coast of England, roughly due east of Belfast. The target had no particular value, but it was a location Jones knew intimately from his youth. Winds failed while the *Ranger* was far outside the harbor, requiring Jones to have his ships' boats row for three hours to reach their objective late on 22 April. Jones spiked the few guns and burned some small craft, and departed in the morning. Although there had been minimal physical damage, the psychological impact on the nation was enormous, as this marked one of the few times in a century when an enemy had actually landed in England. Jones then crossed to St. Mary's Island on the other side of Solway Firth, hoping to kidnap the earl of Selkirk (to exchange for captured American seamen); but his landing party learned that the nobleman was not home. The next day, back in Belfast Lough, he captured the fourteen-gun Royal Navy sloop *Drake* off Carrickfergus. Jones arrived at Brest with his prizes on 8 May.

SEE ALSO *Jones, John Paul.*

BIBLIOGRAPHY

Fowler, William M., Jr. *Rebels under Sail: The American Navy during the Revolution*. New York: Scribners, 1976.

revised by Robert K. Wright Jr.

WHITE HORSE TAVERN, PENN-SYLVANIA. 21 September 1777. John Kerlin's

White Horse Tavern was located about eight miles east of Downingtown, Pennsylvania, in what is now East Whitehead Township. During the Philadelphia Campaign it served as an important landmark because it lay at the junction of six important roads. During the night of 20–21 September, Brigadier General William Smallwood led 2,100 Maryland militia down the road from Downingtown, trying to get past the British in the dark and link up with Brigadier General Anthony Wayne's Pennsylvania Continentals in nearby Paoli. Shortly after midnight, as they were moving east along what is now King Road, a patrol from Major John Maitland's Second Battalion of Light Infantry opened fire. This was a violation of Major General Charles Grey's direct orders to Maitland to have his men move with unloaded muskets. An American fell, and the bulk of the militia stampeded to the rear. Very soon after, Major Caleb North arrived from Wayne with orders telling Smallwood to fall back to White Horse. Smallwood, North, and Colonel Mordecai Gist had a narrow escape in the dark during the retreat when a group of militia mistook them for British cavalry and opened fire, killing a private from the First Continental Light Dragoons. American losses were three killed and three wounded; no British were hurt.

SEE ALSO *Philadelphia Campaign.*

BIBLIOGRAPHY

McGuire, Thomas J. *The Battle of Paoli*. Harrisburg, Pa.: Stackpole Books, 2000.

revised by Robert K. Wright Jr.

WHITEMARSH, PENNSYLVANIA.

5–8 December 1777. George Washington kept his headquarters in Whitemarsh from 2 November to 10 December 1777 as the final struggle for control of the Delaware River played out. There, he began staff discussions to decide where to establish winter quarters. Before he could fall back or winter weather could prevent further action, Sir William Howe determined to make one more effort to bring his opponent to battle. But American intelligence reports kept Washington alert. For example, Mrs. Lydia Darragh (according to tradition) overheard British plans and sent word out of the city that a large British force would move during the night of 4–5 December to strike the American camp. As he so often did during the campaign, Howe marched in two columns, one primarily British and the other mostly German. Charles Lord Cornwallis's element marched directly along the Germantown Road. That movement was detected by Captain Allan McLane's outpost around 3 A.M. at Beggarstown (later Mount Airy), and the patrol immediately alerted Washington. British light infantry in Cornwallis's van kept going to Chestnut Hill and then halted there at dawn while the commanders pushed ahead to inspect the American positions.

Finding the Americans already deployed, Cornwallis opted for caution and waited at Chestnut Hill for Wilhelm Knyphausen to arrive with the other column. By midmorning Washington had sent out a strong combat patrol to obtain exact information on the enemy's size, location, and intentions. Brigadier General James Irvine, now leading Pennsylvania militia but formerly an experienced Continental officer, tangled with the light infantry for about twenty minutes. The militia withdrew after a wounded Irvine and about sixteen of his men had been captured. Howe spent the next two days cautiously probing but concluded that Washington's defenses were too strong and returned to Philadelphia. Although there were several more foraging operations by the British before the end of the year, the Whitemarsh probe marked the end of the campaign.

Howe's force probably approached ten thousand men; Washington most likely had slightly more men available. American losses seem to have been about forty, only six of whom were killed. British casualties were lighter, apparently amounting to one officer killed and a dozen men wounded on the 5th, although more men seem to have been picked off or to have deserted during the maneuvering.

SEE ALSO *Cornwallis, Charles; Howe, William; Irvine, James; Knyphausen, Wilhelm; Washington, George.*

BIBLIOGRAPHY
Martin, David G. *The Philadelphia Campaign: June 1777–July 1778*. Conshohocken, Pa.: Combined Books, 1993.

revised by Robert K. Wright Jr.

WHITE PLAINS, NEW YORK.

During the American retreat from northern Manhattan to Westchester County on 18–22 October, Washington knew that his forces would be surrounded if Major General William Howe reached White Plains first and proceeded westward to the Hudson River for a rendezvous with his brother's fleet at Tarrytown. If the Americans arrived first, the hills around White Plains would provide a strong defensive position. In addition, a substantial depot had already been established there with supplies sent from Connecticut. Washington ordered Major General William Alexander (Lord Stirling) to hurry ahead and secure the depot.

AMERICAN DISPOSITIONS

Stirling arrived on 21 October and Washington followed later that day. Immediately entrenching his forces in a three-mile line, Washington secured his flanks with the steep and wooded Chatterton's Hill on the right and a nearby lake on the left. Chatterton's Hill was separated from the American right wing by the Bronx River, but Washington occupied it to prevent the British from mounting artillery there. He sent his chief engineer, Colonel Rufus Putnam, and four regiments of levies—two from Massachusetts, one from New York, and one from New Jersey—to fortify the hill; and General Alexander McDougall's regiment was assigned to defend it, with orders to retreat, if necessary, to the American right wing. Washington later added Colonel Rudolphus Ritzema's Third New York, Colonel William Smallwood's Maryland Continental regiment, Colonel Charles Webb's Nineteenth Continental Connecticut regiment, and Colonel John Haslet's Delaware Continental regiment for a total of 1,600 two thousand troops and two fieldpieces on the hill.

BRITISH DELAYS

Howe had lost three days at New Rochelle waiting for eight thousand Hessian reinforcements under Lieutenant General Wilhelm von Knyphausen, who finally joined him on 22 October. Howe proceeded north to Mamaroneck, where he paused for another four days while sending Clinton ahead to reconnoiter the ground within three miles of the American position. Clinton recommended the same kind of tactics that had succeeded on Long Island: extensive reconnaissance; diversionary detachments; and, finally, marching all night to attack the American lines at dawn. Howe initially agreed, but he changed his mind on the 27th and sent Clinton forward to determine if an immediate attack seemed feasible. Clinton recommended against it, since Washington's flanks were protected by the Bronx River and the hills, enabling him to retreat whenever he chose.

THE BRITISH ATTACK

Nonetheless, on the cold, bright morning of 28 October, Howe ordered a frontal attack on the American lines. The fourteen thousand British troops were arrayed in several columns, as Clinton recommended, and he led the one farthest to the right, assigned to outflank the Americans while they fought the British column on the left. Washington and his generals were on horseback that morning, discussing which of the surrounding hills should be occupied, when they learned that the British were advancing. General Spencer, with eight hundred Connecticut men, was sent to confront the British vanguard. They crossed the Bronx River and gathered behind a stone wall to await the enemy. They skirmished with some Hessians across an apple orchard until Clinton's flanking column forced them to retreat from the stone wall with heavy losses.

FIGHT FOR CHATTERTON'S HILL

The Americans retreated across the Bronx River and up Chatterton's Hill with the Hessians in pursuit. General McDougall's troops, shielded by a stone wall at the crest of the hill and supported by Captain Alexander Hamilton's artillery company, poured a volley into the Hessian column, inflicting numerous casualties and sending them back down the hill in disorder. The Hessians regrouped and, with reinforcements, made a second attempt, but McDougall's men "gave them a second warm reception" (Tallmadge, p. 14).

However, the column of eight regiments on the British left began crossing the Bronx River, sending three Hessian regiments to some ridges half a mile south of Chatterton's Hill. From there and from the east, the British began to pound the hill with their artillery. The militia panicked and tried to flee, but then they were rallied and put on the right flank behind Smallwood.

While additional Hessian units paused to build a bridge and were attacked by Smallwood and Ritzema, General Alexander Leslie's regiments forded the river further south and, supported by the cannonade from a dozen guns, charged up the steep, densely wooded slope. The dry autumn leaves and branches, ignited by British artillery shells, created a screen of smoke and fire that partially concealed Leslie's men during their ascent. However, the British gunners had to desist when the soldiers neared the top for fear of hitting them, and Leslie's troops fell back with heavy losses.

Undeterred, the rest of the British column crossed the river, formed a line, and swept up the hill under a hail of musket fire and grapeshot. Attacked by the Hessians under Colonel Johann Rall, the militia bolted, exposing the American right flank. Haslet's and Smallwood's troops put up stiff resistance, exacting an exorbitant price in British and Hessian lives before they retreated. The Americans suffered 175 casualties in the fight for Chatterton's Hill, later called the Battle of White Plains, but even by Howe's official estimate, they had inflicted more than 200 on the British. Including the Hessians, that number rose to 313.

FURTHER BRITISH DELAYS

The carnage on Chatterton's Hill discouraged Howe from further attacks on the American lines. With Bunker Hill, Long Island, Harlem Heights, and now White Plains, a pattern had emerged: after a show of American resistance, Howe refrained from a frontal assault—even when he had the advantage. Instead, on 28 October both sides hunkered down for a heavy exchange of artillery fire that continued throughout the day. British forces on Chatterton's Hill augmented the American fortifications, while Howe once again waited for reinforcements, losing two more critical days in which he might have stormed Washington's lines.

Six regiments of Hessians and one of Waldeckers newly arrived from Germany were brought to White Plains from Staten Island by Lord Percy on 30 October. Howe was finally ready to renew the offensive on 31 October, but a heavy rainstorm lasting twenty-hours forced a delay. The next day Howe's forces moved forward, only to find that Washington had moved out of reach, into the higher and steeper hills of North Castle Heights.

SEE ALSO *New York Campaign.*

BIBLIOGRAPHY

Tallmadge, Benjamin. *Memoir of Colonel Benjamin Tallmadge.* 1858. Reprint, New York: New York Times, 1968.

Washington, George. *The Papers of George Washington, Revolutionary War Series.* 14 vols. Edited by Philander D. Chase. Charlottesville: University Press of Virginia, 1985–2004.

Barnet Schecter

WICKES, LAMBERT. (1742?–1777). Continental naval officer. Maryland. Born at Eastern Neck Island, Maryland, perhaps in 1742, Wickes went to sea early in life. By 1769 he had become a ship's captain, and by 1774 he was part owner of a ship, the *Neptune*. While in London in December of that year, he discovered that his ship was carrying tea. He ordered it put off and sailed for America. The ship that took his consignment, the *Peggy Stewart*, was burned along with its tea when it arrived in Annapolis.

Wickes's courageous devotion to the Patriot cause and acquaintance with Robert Morris were factors in his getting command of the Continental armed ship *Reprisal* (eighteen guns) in March 1776. On 3 July he sailed from Cape May after a sharp engagement in which his brother Richard was killed, and on 27 July he appeared off Martinique after sending three prizes back to Philadelphia. Defeating HMS *Shark* outside the harbor of St. Pierre, the first American naval battle in foreign waters, Wickes reached Philadelphia in September with a valuable cargo of powder, five hundred muskets, and clothing. He sailed secretly from Philadelphia on 26 October with Benjamin Franklin aboard and reached France on 28 November, having taken two English prizes en route. In January 1777 he took five British prizes in the Channel.

In April the American commissioners in Paris put him in command of a small force comprising his ship and those of Captains Henry Johnson and Samuel Nicholson. Under orders from Franklin and Deane to carry out a cruise in the Irish Sea, Wickes sailed from France on 28 May. Circling around Ireland, the captains entered the Irish Channel from the north, captured eighteen small merchantmen (eight were kept as prizes, the rest destroyed), and escaped through the British forces guarding the south end of the channel. When almost back to France, the American raiders sighted a huge enemy warship that turned out to be the *Burford* (seventy-four guns). Wickes signaled for Johnson, Nicholson, and the prizes accompanying them to scatter and fly for safety while he tried to escape from the faster, more heavily armed ship of the line. The chase started shortly before noon on 27 June 1777, and the *Reprisal* managed to keep just out of range until 7 P.M., when the *Burford* got close enough to start dropping gunshot on the deck. Wickes jettisoned all his cannon and swivels and raced away from the British.

Lord Stormont protested so vigorously with the French government for allowing American ships to use their ports that Wickes was detained at St. Malo until 14 September, when he sailed for America. His ship foundered off the Banks of Newfoundland on 1 October 1777 in a heavy storm, and only the cook survived.

S E E   A L S O   *Conyngham, Gustavus.*

BIBLIOGRAPHY

Clark, William Bell. *Lambert Wickes, Sea Raider and Diplomat.* New Haven, Conn.: Yale University Press, 1932.

revised by Michael Bellesiles

WILKES, JOHN.

(1725–1797). British politician. Wilkes was born in Clerkenwell, London, on 17 October 1725, the second son of a malt distiller. Educated at a Hertford school from 1734, in 1744 he entered the University of Leiden. Here he rebelled against his mother's Presbyterianism with endless bouts of womanizing and drinking. His arranged marriage in 1747 to Mary Mead, puritanical and ten years his senior, had no effect on his behavior. However, her dowry, the manor of Aylesbury in Buckinghamshire, secured Wilkes's status as a landed gentleman. He joined Sir Francis Dashwood's "Monks of Medmenham," a secret society that met at the ruins of Medmenham Abbey to engage in obscene parodies of Roman Catholic ritual. In 1754 he composed an obscene *Essay on Woman*, a satire on Alexander Pope's *Essay on Man*; fatefully, he had thirteen copies printed for private circulation. Meanwhile his life as a witty and generous man about town, combined with his first attempts to enter politics, proved enormously expensive. In 1758 he

was permanently separated from his wife, to whom he paid £200 a year in return for possession of the manor.

In 1757, with the support of his neighbors the Grenvilles—Richard Grenville, first Earl Temple, and his brother, George Grenville (who was the brother-in-law of William Pitt)—he was elected member of Parliament for Aylesbury. However, Wilkes was a poor and infrequent speaker and of little use to the ministry. Consequently his ambitious requests to be appointed to the Board of Trade, ambassador to Constantinople, and governor of Quebec fell on deaf ears. Under Temple's patronage, Wilkes spoke up for Pitt after the latter's resignation in October 1761 but made little impression. He had finally to accept that he was no orator and could not hope to make his way in the House of Commons.

Wilkes, funded by Temple, now turned to journalism. The new Lord Bute ministry was negotiating peace on terms unacceptable to Pitt and his allies, and badly needed a pen to counter Bute's journal *The Briton*, edited by the Scottish novelist Tobias Smollett. After writing a few articles for existing journals, on 6 June 1762 Wilkes founded *TheNorth Briton*, the title being an ironic reference to the Scot Bute's supposed takeover of English politics. Wilkes reminded readers of the ancient Franco-Scots alliance against England and falsely hinted that Bute owed his position to a liaison with the king's mother. The claim rightly angered George III, but it went down very well with the London crowds: a gibbet bearing a top boot and a petticoat became a familiar symbol in popular demonstrations. Although this gutter journalism soon alarmed Pitt and Temple, they were not inclined to stop it, and Wilkes cleverly avoided giving grounds for prosecution. Private victims were less restrained: in 1763 the artist William Hogarth published a savage caricature which has ever since perpetuated an image of Wilkes as surpassingly ugly.

Bute, wearied and distressed by such attacks, resigned on 8 April 1763 to be succeeded by George Grenville, who had fallen out with Temple and Pitt in 1761. Grenville ended the parliamentary session with a king's speech praising the peace settlement, and on 23 April Wilkes struck. Number 45 of *The North Briton* attacked the treaties and suggested that the king had lied on his prime minister's instructions. This was enough to goad ministers into bringing a charge of seditious libel. The problem was that the articles in number 45 were anonymous, and, although everyone knew Wilkes had written them, there was no legal proof of authorship. Lord Halifax, secretary of state for the north, therefore issued a general warrant for the arrest of the unnamed authors, printers, and publishers. Most of those arrested were quickly released, but crucially they provided firm evidence that Wilkes had wielded the offending pen. Halifax could then have issued a warrant naming Wilkes. Instead, he took legal advice as to whether Wilkes could be arrested on the existing general warrant. The reply was that Wilkes's parliamentary privilege protected him from arrest except on charges of treason, felony, or actual breach of the king's peace; number 45 tended to a breach of the peace and for that the general warrant would suffice. Reassured, on 30 April Halifax and his colleagues had Wilkes arrested and his papers seized.

This was a disaster. Although there were plenty of precedents for ministers using general warrants, their legality was uncertain and had already been questioned. Moreover, the view that Wilkes was guilty of a breach of the peace was open to question. Temple at once obtained a writ of habeas corpus, and on 6 May Chief Justice Sir Charles Pratt, a supporter of Pitt, heard the case in the Court of Common Pleas. In his defense Wilkes claimed that he was acting for those who had no political voice-and at least some spectators thought he meant it. When he was freed on grounds of parliamentary privilege the crowd in Westminster Hall, thinking he had been acquitted, raised the cry "Wilkes and liberty!"

Wilkes and his friends now counterattacked, bringing a series of prosecutions for wrongful arrest and seizure against the ministers, their undersecretaries, and king's messengers who had executed the warrant. Their cause was assisted by the now widespread concern about the principle of general warrants, even among those who despised Wilkes as a man. On 3 December Pratt ruled that general warrants could not be used to authorize searches of unspecified buildings and awarded Wilkes £4,000 in damages against the government. In January 1764 the Commons expelled Wilkes without a vote; but on 17 February the government survived a motion condemning general warrants only by begging to await the courts' decisions. On 18 June 1764 and 8 November 1765, Lord Chief Justice Mansfield ruled that general warrants could not be used against persons. Finally, Pratt (now Lord Camden) found that, except in cases of treason, secretaries of state could not issue warrants for even named persons. In this way Wilkes's scurrilous opportunism produced landmark protection for the liberty of the subject, the freedom of the press, and private property. Wilkes, however, was not there to see the fullness of his triumph: by then he was an exiled outlaw in France.

Shortly after the case against Wilkes collapsed, the ministry's agents had obtained one of the printed copies of *Essay on Woman*, which (the print claimed) had been edited by a bishop. Ribald mirth greeted the earl of Sandwich, secretary of state for the northern department, when he read it to the Lords on 15 November 1763. Nevertheless, the peers promptly declared it blasphemous. On the same day the Commons resolved that number 45 was a seditious libel and that seditious libels were not protected by parliamentary privilege. During this debate Samuel Atkins, the secretary to the treasury, called Wilkes

a coward, and in the ensuing pistol duel Wilkes was severely wounded in the stomach. He still had the crowd on his side: when, on 3 December, number 45 was to be ceremonially burned in Cheapside, the crowd attacked the sheriffs, rescued the papers, and burned a top boot in its place. However, it could do him little good. Too ill to attend Parliament or court, and unwilling to face the inevitable prosecutions, Wilkes decamped to France on 25 December 1763. When he repeatedly failed to appear in King's Bench, he was outlawed in November 1764. He remained abroad for four years, writing, traveling in France and Italy, getting robbed by a teenage mistress and by his English agent, and failing to live within his precarious means. In the end his French debts forced him to flee to Leiden, where he enrolled in his old university as a precaution against prosecution.

He returned to Britain in 1768, hoping for a pardon and, lacking a patron, for popular election to a seat in Parliament. Promising to surrender when the court of King's Bench next met, he was triumphantly returned as member for Middlesex, where he had attracted hordes of skilled workers pressed by high prices and lack of work. In spite of almost nightly demonstrations in his favor, Wilkes took care not to use the crowd as a weapon. He surrendered to the court and—his outlawry being quashed on a technicality—accepted two years' imprisonment for seditious libel and blasphemy. Now a political martyr, Wilkes lived comfortably in prison and continued his political activity. On 3 February 1769 the Commons voted to expel him, but at the ensuing Middlesex election he was returned unopposed. Once again he was expelled, the House declaring him incapable of election: and once again he was re-elected without a contest. Yet again he was expelled. This time the ministry put up its own candidate, Colonel Luttrell, who, though defeated by a landslide vote, was nevertheless declared elected. This blatant attack on the principle of representation, even though aimed at an obnoxious individual, united the opposition leaders in January 1770. The prime minister, the duke of Grafton, was forced to resign. But Wilkes and the opposition had not triumphed: Lord North's new ministry declined to unseat Luttrell in favor of Wilkes.

Wilkes now turned to building up a power base in the City of London, where he had been elected alderman in January 1769. In 1771 he orchestrated a successful City challenge to the ban on parliamentary reporting, advocated annual parliamentary elections, and was elected sheriff. In 1774 he became lord mayor, and Middlesex re-elected him to Parliament. In the House he advocated the parliamentary reform and full civil rights for Dissenters and Catholics.

From the beginning of the colonial troubles, Wilkes was opposed to American independence. In 1765 he thought the Stamp Act riots little short of rebellion.

However, public adulation in America, he was persuaded, sincerely or otherwise, to exploit the idea of a trans-Atlantic plot to subvert English liberties. By 1767 he was praising the resistance to the Townshend duties, and in 1768 he denounced the deployment of troops against civilians in Boston. From then until 1774 Wilkes had little use for American issues as his Middlesex election and City politics provided plentiful antigovernment ammunition. Although he organized petitions against the Coercive Acts and denounced parliamentary taxation of the colonies, he did not oppose parliamentary supremacy until October 1775. By 1777 he was arguing that the war was bloody and futile and recommended conciliation. On 10 December, after news of Saratoga, he moved for the repeal of the Declaratory Act only as a last-ditch means of persuading the rebels to forgo independence. Not until the failure of the 1778 Carlisle Peace Commission was Wilkes induced to speak for independence, and then only as an expedient to end an unwinnable war. Even this position was so unpopular that his radical power base in City politics wasted away. It was further weakened by his part in suppressing the anti-Catholic Gordon Riots in 1780. By the end of the war the once terrible Wilkes had become respectable, and in1790 he abandoned his Middlesex seat without a contest. He died in London on 26 December 1797.

Whatever popular legend might say, his espousal of American causes was at best lukewarm and always subservient to his domestic and personal agenda. However, at first for his own ends, later also from reasons of principle, Wilkes had campaigned for traditional liberties for over two decades. His career had seen the demise of general warrants, the establishment of the supremacy of electors over parliamentary privilege, and vindication of the right to report debates. Politics was no longer a closed world, and the way was paved for reform, which followed in the nineteenth century. Above all he had shown how an unsavory personality might be a powerful vehicle for lofty causes.

SEE ALSO *Bute, John Stuart, Third Earl of; Chatham, William Pitt, First Earl of; Gordon Riots; Grafton, Augustus Henry Fitzroy; Grenville, George; Intolerable (or Coercive) Acts; Sandwich, John Montagu, fourth earl of; Stamp Act; Townshend Acts.*

BIBLIOGRAPHY

Christie, I. R. *Wars and Revolutions: Britain 1760–1815.* London: Edward Arnold, 1982.

Thomas, Peter D. G. *John Wilkes: A Friend to Liberty.* Oxford and New York: Oxford University Press, 1996.

Williamson, A. *Wilkes.* London: Allen and Unwin, 1974.

revised by John Oliphant

WILKINSON, JAMES. (1757–1825).

Continental officer, scoundrel. Maryland. Wilkinson, who was born in Benedict, Maryland, had just finished his medical studies and opened a practice in Monocacy, Maryland, when the war began. As a volunteer in William Thompson's Pennsylvania Rifle Regiment from 9 September to 1775 to March 1776, he joined the forces investing Boston, where be volunteered to join Benedict Arnold's march to Quebec. In the course of the march he became friends with Arnold. Having been promoted to captain of the Second Continental Infantry in March 1776, Wilkinson remained with Arnold until December 1776, when the latter had reached Albany after the retreat from Canada. Briefly a member of General Horatio Gates's staff, Wilkinson was again promoted, this time to lieutenant colonel of Thomas Hartley's Continental Regiment on 12 January 1777 and served as deputy adjutant general of the Northern Department from 24 May 1777 to 6 March 1778. He figured in the actions at Ticonderoga in July 1777 and Saratoga on 7 October 1777.

Named by Gates to take the news of the Saratoga surrender to Congress, Wilkinson did not reach York, Pennsylvania, until 31 October, and did not make up his written report until 3 November 1777. The 20-year-old aide had stopped off in Reading, Pennsylvania, for some courting, and while at the headquarters of General William Alexander he dropped a bit of gossip that brought the Conway Cabal to a head. Wilkinson's degree of personal involvement in the cabal is not known.

Young Wilkinson was an unpopular man in York for having kept Congress writhing on a rack of suspense. They took a dim view of Gates's request that he be breveted brigadier general, but on 6 November they granted the request and tried to calm the outraged uproar in the army by appointing him secretary to the new Board of War In an effort to vindicate himself from the accusation of betraying the confidence of Gates, Wilkinson threatened to fight a duel with General Alexander, and a duel with Gates was called off at the last minute. Wilkinson resigned from the Board of War on 29 March 1778. His letter of resignation was so insulting to Gates that Congress ordered it destroyed.

Appointed clothier-eneral of the Continental army on 24 July 1779, Wilkinson resigned on 27 March 1781 because of irregularities in his accounts. While in uniform Wilkinson had proved himself guilty of intrigue and excessive drinking; now he added greed to the list of his vices. Just before resigning, he married Ann Biddle, daughter of the wealthy Quaker merchant, John Biddle.

After the war, Wilkinson entered into intrigue on an interstate and even international scale. He moved to Kentucky in 1784, using his wife's money to purchase land. He soon became prominent in trade and politics, supplanting George Rogers Clark as leader in that region.

In the Spanish Conspiracy—the purpose of which may have been to set up a separate republic in the West allied to Spain, or may have been a plot to force the admission of Kentucky to the United States—he appears to have intrigued both with and against Spain. Wilkinson swore allegiance to the king of Spain, for which he received an annual pension of $2,000. Thinking they were aiding his efforts to attach Kentucky to their empire, the Spanish opened the Mississippi River to American traffic. In 1791 Wilkinson applied for a military commission, was made lieutenant colonel commanding the Second U.S. Infantry on 22 October 1791, and served as second-in-command to Anthony Wayne in his operations against the Indians. Appointed brigadier general on 5 March 1792, he intrigued against Wayne even while serving under his command during the campaign that culminated in the battle of Fallen Timbers (30 August, 1794), where Wilkinson demonstrated bravery. Wilkinson succeeded Wayne as commander in chief on Wayne's death in 1796, passing on information to the Spanish while commanding the American army. As governor of Louisiana (1805) he became involved in the Aaron Burr conspiracy, disclosed the plot in which he was an accomplice if not the originator, evaded the persistent efforts of Congress to prove his complicity, and in 1811 won acquittal at a court-martial (an outcome regretted by President James Madison). Restored to command, he was made a major general on 2 March 1813, but so mishandled the northern campaign of the War of 1812 that he was called before a court of inquiry. In 1815 he was exonerated, although not returned to duty, and on 15 June 1815 was honorably discharged.

Wilkinson settled in New Orleans after the war, where he ran through his remaining resources. In 1822 he went to Mexico City as an agent for the American Bible Society, but was actually seeking land grants in Texas. Wilkinson died there on 28 December 1825. As one writer put it: "It is not certain whether the Mexican climate or the use of opium did more to hasten his end" (Nickerson, p. 428).

SEE ALSO *Arnold, Benedict.*

BIBLIOGRAPHY

Hay, Thomas R., and M. R. Werner. *The Admirable Trumpeter: A Biography of General James Wilkinson.* Garden City, N.Y.: Doubleday, Doran, & Company, 1941.

Jacobs, James. *Tarnished Warrior: Major General James Wilkinson.* Freeport, N.Y.: Books for Libraries Press, 1972.

Nickerson, Hoffman. *The Turning Point of the Revolution.* Boston: Houghton Mifflin, 1928.

Shreve, Royal O. *The Finished Scoundrel.* Indianapolis, In.: Bobbs-Merrill, 1933).

The Wilkinson Papers. The Chicago Historical Society.

revised by Michael Bellesiles

WILLETT, MARINUS. (1740–1830). Continental officer. New York.

Born near Jamaica, New York, on 31 July 1740, Willett was a cabinetmaker in New York City who joined the militia during the Seven Years' War. In 1758 he was named a lieutenant in Oliver De Lancey's New York Regiment in 1758 and served on the unfortunate expedition of James Abercromby to Ticonderoga as well as in Bradstreet's capture of Frontenac. During the years leading up to the Revolution he was a fiery and effective Son of Liberty, taking part in numerous crowd actions, including the attack on the New York City arsenal on 23 April 1775, and preventing the British from evacuating five wagonloads of weapons and ammunition when they left the city on 6 June. On the 28th he became captain in Alexander McDougall's First New York Regiment; joined Montgomery's wing of the Canada invasion; and on 3 November 1775 was left in command of St. Johns, returning with his men to New York City when their enlistments ended in May 1776. He led militia units at the Battle of Long Island on 27 August 1776 and was active in the ensuing encounters around New York City. On 21 November he became lieutenant colonel of the Third New York and was put in command of Fort Constitution opposite West Point, driving the British away in the Peekskill raid of 23 March 1777.

On 18 May 1777 he was transferred to Fort Stanwix, where he had served briefly in 1758. Here, as second in command to Peter Gansevoort, he distinguished himself in stopping St. Leger's expedition of June–September 1777. For his gallant sortie on 6 August he was voted "an elegant sword" by Congress. He served under Charles Scott at Monmouth in June 1778 and then took part in the raid against the Onondagas before joining Sullivan's expedition of May–November 1779. On 1 July 1780 he was appointed lieutenant commanding the Fifth New York and in November was promoted to colonel. When the five New York regiments were consolidated into two on 1 January 1781, Willett retired, but he soon accepted Governor Clinton's request to command New York levies and militia in the border warfare of 1781. In that fighting he did a remarkable job in driving Loyalist and Indian raiders out of the Mohawk Valley. In February 1783 he led an abortive attempt to attack Oswego by a midwinter advance on snowshoes.

Elected to the state assembly in 1783, he vacated his seat to become sheriff of New York City and County, serving seven years in this post in 1784–1788 and 1792–1796. In 1790 he was highly successful as Washington's personal representative in making a peace treaty with the Creeks. Willett became wealthy on confiscated Loyalist estates, served briefly as mayor of New York City in 1807–1808, and remained active in local politics. He died on 22 August 1830.

SEE ALSO *Border Warfare in New York; Peekskill Raid, New York; St. Leger's Expedition.*

BIBLIOGRAPHY

Thomas, Howard. *Marinus Willett, Soldier-Patriot, 1740–1830.* Prospect, N.Y.: Prospect Books, 1954.

revised by Michael Bellsiles

WILLIAMS, DAVID. (1754–1831). A captor

of John André. New York. Enlisting in 1775, he served in the operations against St. Johns and Quebec in 1775 and 1776. In 1779 he left the army. The following year he was one of André's three captors. After the war he bought a farm near the Catskill Mountains that had belonged to Daniel Shays.

SEE ALSO *Arnold's Treason.*

revised by Michael Bellesiles

WILLIAMS, OTHO HOLLAND.

(1749–1794). Continental general. Maryland. Born in Prince Georges County, Maryland, in March 1749, Williams worked in the county clerk's office at Baltimore from 1767 until 1774, when he returned to his home in Frederick to start a commercial career. The Revolution interfered with those plans. On 22 June 1775 he became lieutenant in Captain Thomas Price's Frederick City Rifle Corps and marched with it to join the Boston army. When the Virginia and Maryland riflemen were combined to form Colonel Hugh Stephenson's regiment on 27 June 1776, Williams was made major of that unit and after Stephenson's death that August succeeded him as commander. At Fort Washington, New York, on 16 November 1776, he received a serious wound in the groin and was taken prisoner. He was initially on parole in New York City but was confined on suspicion of secretly corresponding with Washington. Sharing a cell with Ethan Allen, he was not exchanged until 16 January 1778, by which time his health had been permanently impaired by inadequate food and harsh treatment. Meanwhile, however, he had been promoted to colonel of the Sixth Maryland on 10 December 1776, and he led that unit in the Monmouth campaign.

On 16 April 1780 he left Morristown, New Jersey, with the force of Continental troops being led by De Kalb into the southern theater. As a result of the Camden campaign of July and August, Colonel Williams became

well-known not only as an outstanding combat commander but also as the author of the informative and well-written *Narrative of the Campaign of 1780,* published in 1822. Serving as assistant adjutant general to Gates, he performed brilliantly at Camden on 16 August. In the reorganization preceding the arrival of Greene, Williams was put in command of a special corps of light troops. Greene made him adjutant general, however, and Williams was with the left wing of the army at Cheraw when Daniel Morgan led the light troops on the maneuver that resulted in the victory at Cowpens.

When Morgan declined to take command of the rear guard of elite troops that Greene formed to cover his race for the Dan, Williams was given this vital duty. Williams accomplished his hazardous mission brilliantly. He then led the return of Greene's army into North Carolina, frustrating an attempt by Cornwallis to surprise and annihilate him at Wetzell's Mills on 6 March 1781. He played a distinguished part in the Battles of Guilford on 15 March, Hobkirk's Hill on 25 April, and particularly at Eutaw Springs on 8 September 1781. Although he commanded a brigade of Continentals in each of these three major engagements, he was not promoted to brigadier general until 9 May 1782. He retired on 16 January 1783, having been elected naval officer of the Baltimore district on the 6th. He became collector of the port of Baltimore and a successful merchant. In May 1792 he declined the post of second-in-command of the U.S. Army with the rank of brigadier general because of ill health. He died on 15 July 1794 at Miller's Town, Virginia.

SEE ALSO *Camden Campaign; Eutaw Springs, South Carolina; Guilford Courthouse, North Carolina; Hobkirk's Hill (Camden), South Carolina; Southern Campaigns of Nathanael Greene; Southern Theater, Military Operations in; Wetzell's Mills, North Carolina.*

BIBLIOGRAPHY

Williams, Otho, Papers. Maryland Historical Society, Baltimore, Maryland.

revised by Michael Bellesiles

WILLIAMS, WILLIAM. (1731–1811).

Signer. Connecticut. William Williams was born at Lebanon, Connecticut, on 18 March 1731. He graduated from Harvard College in 1751; studied theology under his father, a Congregational minister; and in 1755 served on the staff of his cousin, Ephraim Williams, during William Johnson's expedition against Crown Point during the

French and Indian War. Returning home, he went into business and launched a long and distinguished career in public service. He was a selectman of Lebanon (1760–1785), town clerk (1752–1796), representative in the assembly (1757–1776 and 1781–1784), member of the governor's council (1776–1780 and 1784–1803), probate judge (1775–1809), and judge of the Windham county court (1776–1806). His political career was undoubtedly helped by his marriage on 14 February 1771 to Mary, the daughter of Governor Jonathan Trumbull and sister of the younger Jonathan Trumbull.

Religious faith was at the center of Williams's character and was the source of his unwavering devotion to the cause of American rights. Less cosmopolitan than most senior Connecticut leaders, he made his most important contributions at the state level. He helped his father-in-law with numerous state papers and also contributed essays to local newspapers supporting the American cause. As speaker of the assembly after October 1774, he played a major role in preparing Connecticut for war and in establishing the Council of Safety, the executive body that advised the governor between sessions of the assembly. In May 1775 he financed on his personal credit the dispatch of Connecticut troops to Ticonderoga. Commissioned colonel of the Twelfth Militia Regiment the same month, he resigned a year later to sit in the Continental Congress. He served two terms (July–November 1776 and June–December 1777). As a delegate, on 2 August he signed the Declaration of Independence, a document he had played no role in drafting or adopting since he had not arrived in Philadelphia until 28 July. Williams helped draft the Articles of Confederation, and he served on the Board of War from October to December 1777. In 1779 he offered a quantity of his own hard cash in exchange for virtually worthless Continental paper money so that supplies could be purchased for the army, one of many instances in which he sacrificed his own resources for the American cause and one of the reasons why he was left in penury at war's end He demonstrated his personal courage by riding twenty-three miles in three hours to volunteer his services in repelling Benedict Arnold's New London raid on 6 September 1781.

Politically active after the war, Williams supported local interests rather than a strong central government, opposed half-pay and commutation for Continental officers, and distrusted the Society of the Cincinnati. But at the Connecticut ratifying convention in January 1788, he voted to support the federal Constitution, thus violating the instructions he had received from his home town. He remained on the Council until 1803, and served as a judge until 1810. He died at Lebanon on 2 August 1811.

SEE ALSO *New London Raid, Connecticut.*

BIBLIOGRAPHY
Stark, Bruce P. *Connecticut Signer: William Williams.* Chester, Conn.: Pequot Press for the American Revolution Bicentennial Commission of Connecticut, 1975.

revised by Harold E. Selesky

WILLIAMSON, ANDREW. (1730–1786). Turncoat militia general. South Carolina. Born in Scotland, Williamson came to South Carolina with his family some time before 1750, making his living driving cattle. In 1760 Williamson was commissioned lieutenant of militia, and he served in James Grant's Cherokee expedition of 1761. Four years later he was established as a store owner and planter near Ninety Six, and in July 1768 he joined other local Regulators in a petition to the legislature. When the Revolution started he was a major of militia and leading Patriot. In November 1775 he held off the Loyalists besieging his fort at Ninety Six for three days and then participated in the "Snow Campaign" that captured Loyalists hiding in Cherokee country. The following summer he led close to two thousand militia and Indians in the Cherokee War of 1776 and was promoted to state brigadier general in 1778. (Andrew Pickens succeeded him as colonel.) He also served in South Carolina's first and second Provincial Congresses in 1775 and 1776 and in the assembly from 1776 to 1780. Taking part in the expedition of General Robert Howe against Florida in the spring of 1778, his refusal to take orders from Howe contributed to the American failure. In the unsuccessful operations of Lincoln against Prevost, Williamson commanded twelve hundred men opposite Augusta and helped force back the British at Briar Creek on 3 March 1779. In October 1779 Williamson took part in the unsuccessful Franco-American assault on Savannah. During the Charleston campaign the next year his militia refused to participate and Williamson himself, with some three hundred men, remained idle at Ninety Six.

Initially announcing his intention to continue the fight against the British, he suddenly surrendered the fort. Released by the British, Williamson traveled about the western part of the state encouraging his one-time followers to give up the fight. Accused of treason, he was kidnapped by some friends who tried to determine his loyalties, but he remained obscure. Released, he went straight to Charleston, settling under British rule.

Recaptured in July 1781 by Colonel Isaac Hayne, Williamson was promptly rescued by the British, who hanged Hayne. Williamson was blamed for Hayne's hanging, and in 1782 the legislature confiscated his property. As the war came to an end, General Nathanael Greene informed the South Carolina legislature that

Williamson had risked his life in passing information to the Americans. The legislature returned his property, and he died at his plantation in St. Paul's Parish on 21 March 1786.

SEE ALSO *Briar Creek, Georgia; Cherokee Expedition of James Grant; Hayne, Isaac; Regulators.*

revised by Michael Bellesiles

WILLIAMSON'S PLANTATION, SOUTH CAROLINA.

12 July 1780. Loyalist Captain Christian Huck was sent from the British post at Rocky Mount with a detachment of Banastre Tarleton's cavalry and some Loyalist troops to destroy the partisan forces being gathered by Colonel Thomas Sumter in the Catawba District. Huck's force of thirty-five cavalry, twenty mounted infantry of the New York Volunteers, and sixty other Loyalists reached James Williamson's plantation (now Brattonville) on 11 July. At the house of Captain James McClure, Huck caught the younger James McClure and his brother-in-law, Edward Martin, melting pewter dishes to make bullets. He looted the house, announced that he would hang the two rebels the next day, and slapped Mary McClure with the flat of his sword when she pleaded for their lives. The raiders then looted the house of Colonel William Bratton before camping at the plantation half a mile away. Mary McClure slipped off and rode thirty miles to Sumter's camp, where she informed her father of the raid. Bratton and McClure started off with 150 mounted volunteers and were joined by another 350 under Captain Edward Lacey Jr., Colonel William Hill, and Colonel Andrew Neal. But a great number of these men, more than half, left the column before they reached their goal.

During the approach, Lacey had posted a guard around his own house to keep his Loyalist father from alerting the enemy; the enterprising old gentleman escaped, was recaptured, and the son ordered him tied to his bed. When the column reached Bratton's house, a quarter of a mile from Huck's camp, they found that the enemy had pitched their tents between the rail fences that lined the road to Williamson's house.

Taking advantage of Huck's lack of security and his vulnerable situation, the rebels launched a surprise attack at dawn. They approached in two groups from opposite sides so as to cut the enemy off from their horses. Reveille came as the Americans opened fire at seventy-five yards. The Loyalists tried to fight back, but the rail fences kept them from charging with their bayonets and the rebel fire inflicted heavy casualties. Huck was mortally wounded when he rushed from the house and tried to rally his troops. Only 12 of the Legion cavalry and about the same number of others escaped from the force of about 115 Loyalists in the camp. The rebels had one man killed. Young McClure and Martin were found tied in a corncrib and freed.

Tarleton was in Charleston when this action took place. His violent reaction to the misuse of his Legion by Lieutenant Colonel Francis Rawdon in such dangerous piecemeal operations led General Charles Cornwallis to write Rawdon a sharp note. This episode was the beginning of Tarleton's bitterness not only toward Rawdon but also toward Cornwallis.

The rebels' success greatly assisted Sumter's recruiting and enabled him to attack Rocky Mount, 1 August 1780.

SEE ALSO *Huck, Christian; Rawdon-Hastings, Francis; Rocky Mount, South Carolina; Tarleton, Banastre.*

revised by Michael Bellesiles

WILLIAMSON'S PLANTATION, SOUTH CAROLINA

SEE *Hammond's Store Raid of William Washington.*

WILMINGTON, NORTH CAROLINA.

1 February–18 November 1781. British occupation. To provide a closer supply port for his operations into North Carolina, General Charles Cornwallis directed Lieutenant Colonel Nisbet Balfour, commandant at Charleston, to send a force to seize and hold Wilmington. Major James H. Craig took the town with four hundred regulars on 1 February, meeting little resistance. He captured the prominent patriots John Ashe and Cornelius Harnett, both of whom died in captivity, and won so much Loyalist support that the rebel leader, Colonel Joseph Hawkins, subsequently found it almost impossible to raise troops or supplies in Duplin County. Cornwallis retreated to Wilmington after the Battle of Guilford Courthouse, arriving 7 April and leaving eighteen days later for Virginia. In July Craig commissioned David Fanning a colonel with orders to rally North Carolina's Loyalists, and this remarkable partisan leader subsequently used Wilmington as a sort of administrative base.

With a well-mounted and well-led body of regulars, mostly from his Eighty-second Regiment, and supported by local partisans, Craig himself conducted raids that compared favorably in speed of execution with those of

Lieutenant Colonel Banastre Tarleton. One of the most devastating of these raids was launched against New Bern in August 1781. During his occupation of Wilmington, Craig converted the Episcopal church into a citadel. The British commander prudently evacuated the town on 18 November 1781 to avoid being cut off by the column of regulars General Arthur St. Clair was leading south to reinforce General Nathanael Greene after the Yorktown surrender. Craig also evacuated all the region's Loyalists who asked to leave with the British to Charleston.

SEE ALSO *Craig, James Henry; Hillsboro Raid, North Carolina; New Bern, North Carolina.*

revised by Michael Bellesiles

WILMOT, WILLIAM. (c. 1745–1782).
Continental officer. Maryland. Often called the last casualty of the Revolution, he was commissioned first lieutenant in the Third Maryland on 10 December 1776. He was promoted to captain on 15 October 1777, transferred to the Second Maryland on 1 January 1781, and killed in a British ambush at Johns Island, South Carolina, on 4 November 1782.

SEE ALSO *Johns Island, South Carolina (4 November 1782).*

revised by Michael Bellesiles

WILSON, JAMES. (1742–1798). Signer, jurist,
speculator. Scotland and Pennsylvania. Born in Carskerdo, Scotland, on 14 September 1742, Wilson studied at St. Andrews, Glasgow, and Edinburgh (1757–1765). While learning accounting in the latter city, Wilson suddenly decided to move to America. He reached Philadelphia in the middle of the Stamp Act crisis and immediately began tutoring Latin at the College of Philadelphia. The following year, 1766, he abandoned teaching to study law under John Dickinson. Admitted to the bar in 1767, he practiced briefly at Reading, Pennsylvania, before moving to the Scots-Irish community of Carlisle and married Rachel Bird. Here he quickly became the leading lawyer and acquired a taste for land speculation. Having also taken an active part in Patriot politics, on 12 July 1774 he became chairman of the local Committee of Correspondence and was elected to the first Provincial Congress.

That same year, 1774, Wilson published *Considerations on the Nature and Extent of the Legislative Authority of the British Parliament,* which argued that Parliament had no authority of any kind over the colonists and advocated that America become an independent state within the British empire. Even more dramatically, Wilson insisted that legitimate authority derived solely from the people. This pamphlet was widely read, and it immediately marked Wilson as a leading intellectual in the Patriot struggle.

On 3 May 1775 Wilson was elected colonel of the Fourth Battalion of the Cumberland County associators, and served as commissioner and superintendent of Indian affairs for the Middle Department in 1775, although an Indian conference at Pittsburgh was fruitless. Elected to the Continental on 6 May 1775, Wilson was quickly recognized as an able writer, and he was called on to draft a number of papers. Early in 1776 he was directed to craft an address to the people, to prepare them for the idea of independence, but Thomas Paine's *Common Sense* made Wilson's task unnecessary; it was never published. Although Wilson believed in independence for America, he shared the convictions of conservatives such as John Dickinson, Edward Rutledge, and Robert R. Livingston, that neither the American people nor their government were capable at that time of making this jump. Wilson and James Duane led the opposition against John Adams and Richard Henry Lee in the four-day debate on the preamble to the Congressional resolution in favor of independence (May 1776). "Before we are prepared to build the new house," Wilson asked, "why should we pull down the old one, and expose ourselves to the inclemencies of the season?" After continuing to oppose the Declaration of Independence in the debate of 8 June, Wilson joined Benjamin Franklin and John Morton in voting for it on 2 July, and eventually signed the finished document. Wilson's heated opposition to the new state constitution resulted in his being removed from the Pennsylvania delegation to Congress on 14 September 1777. This ended his congressional career during the war, but he returned to Congress in 1783 and for the period 1785–1787.

Wilson's conservative views and his continued opposition to the state constitution, which he considered too "democratic," made him so unpopular in Philadelphia that he had to spend the winter of 1777–1778 in Annapolis, Maryland. When he returned to the city he had to barricade his house for protection against the mob. Though Wilson supported independence and the war effort, and his wife Rachel raised more money for the troops than anyone else, he allied himself with the state's financial elite, apparently not hiding his desire to become one of them. As a consequence, he was identified with the conservative opposition to the more democratic impulses of the Revolution. Wilson compounded this negative image by defending Loyalists in court. In October 1779 "Fort Wilson" was attacked by a militia force in response to a handbill of 4 October calling on them to "drive off from the city all disaffected persons and those who supported them." Wilson and his friends were rescued by the timely arrival of the First City Troop and President Joseph Reed (the title of president was accorded to the head of the Pennsylvania government at the time).

In the last years of the Revolution, Wilson took part in many speculative schemes, and he became legal adviser to Robert Morris in the formation of the Bank of America in 1780. Wilson borrowed heavily from the bank to finance his other investments, particularly in land. Wilson's postwar congressional career was highlighted by his proposal to erect states in the western lands (9 April 1783) and the major part he played in the adoption of the Constitution. Wilson sought a strong central government that could promote national economic development. He favored proportional representation, opposed slavery, and generally demonstrated a greater commitment to democracy than most of the other delegates. On the other hand, he did not completely trust the people, proposing a powerful President with an absolute veto over all legislation. Ultimately, though, Wilson went along with the Convention and helped craft the final wording of the Constitution, taking an active part in gaining its ratification. Wilson modeled Pennsylvania's state constitution of 1790, which he largely wrote, on the federal constitution. Replacing the democratic constitution of 1776, Wilson's frame of government sought a careful balance between the three branches of government.

Wilson sought the office of chief justice of the United States in 1789, writing to President George Washington to apply for the position. The President was a bit taken aback, but did name him an associate justice on the first court. On 17 August 1789, Wilson was appointed to the chair of law at the College of Philadelphia. Alert to the possibilities of establishing a new system of American jurisprudence, he launched a series of lectures in which he departed from Blackstonian views and contended instead that law was the rule of the individual, "whose obedience the law requires." Blackstone had defined law as the rule of a sovereign superior and maintained that revolution was illegal, whereas Wilson maintained that sovereignty resided in the individual and used this as the basis for legally justifying the American Revolution. Wilson's call for an American common law fell on deaf ears, most American jurists preferring statute and constitutional law as the nation's legal basis.

Wilson's early interest in land speculation continued throughout his life, and ultimately led to his destruction. Having been interested in various western land companies in 1785—he was president of the Illinois and Wabash Company—in 1792 he involved the Holland Land

Company in unwise purchases in Pennsylvania and New York, and three years later he bought a large interest in one of the Yazoo companies which were later shown to be involved in a massive land-fraud scheme in Georgia. In 1797 the bubble of speculation burst as Wilson was launching into a grandiose plan for immigration and colonization. That summer he moved to Burlington, New Jersey, to avoid arrest for debt, but he retained his supreme court seat despite talk of impeachment. His mind began to break under the stress of this financial and professional failure. Early in 1798 he moved to the home of a friend in Edenton, North Carolina, and on 21 August he died of what was called a "violent nervous fever."

SEE ALSO *Independence.*

BIBLIOGRAPHY

McCloskey, Robert G., ed. *The Works of James Wilson.* 2 vols. Cambridge, Mass.: Harvard University Press, 1967.

Seed, Geoggrey. *James Wilson.* Millwood, N.Y.: KTO Press, 1978.

Smith, Page. *James Wilson, Founding Father 1742–1798.* Chapel Hill: University of North Carolina Press, 1956.

revised by Michael Bellesiles

WINN, RICHARD. (c. 1750–c. 1824). Militia

officer. Born in Fauquier County, Virginia, around 1750, Winn went to South Carolina in 1768, working as a surveyor and becoming a large landowner. With the start of the Revolution, he received a lieutenant's commission in Colonel William Thompson's rangers. During General Henry Clinton's assault on Charleston in 1776, Winn's unit prevented the landing of British troops before Fort Sullivan. Promoted to captain, he was placed in command of Fort McIntosh in southeast Georgia, which was overwhelmed by Loyalists and Indians on 4 February 1777. Paroled to his home, Winn served in the legislature from 1779 to 1786 and trained militia until the British capture of Charleston on 12 May 1780, when he was promoted to major and raised militia to contest British control of South Carolina. On 29 May 1780 his volunteers defeated a Loyalist company at Moberley's Meetinghouse before crossing over to North Carolina to join General Griffith Rutherford's forces in their significant victory over the Loyalists at Ramsour's Mill on 20 June 1780. While Winn was engaged in this campaign, British troops burned his Winnsboro home. Promoted to colonel of militia, he served under General Thomas Sumter, leading his troops to several more minor victories and displaying particular heroism at the battle of Hanging Rock on 6 August 1780, in which he was wounded. After another fierce engagement at Fishdam Ford on 9 November 1780, Winn fought his last, inconclusive battle against Lieutenant Colonel Banastre Tarleton's Loyalist cavalry at Blackstocks, South Carolina, on 20 November 1780. Made brigadier general at the war's end, Winn served in the U.S. House of Representatives in 1793–1797 and 1803–1813 and as lieutenant governor in 1800–1802. He was also major general of the Second Division of the South Carolina militia from 1800 to 1811. In 1812 he moved with his family to Tennessee, dying there at Winnsborough, perhaps in 1824.

BIBLIOGRAPHY

Chappell, Buford S. *The Winns of Fairfield County: Colonel John Winn, William Winn, General Richard Winn.* Columbia, S.C.: Buford, 1975.

Michael Bellesiles

WINTER OF 1779–1780.

The winter of 1779–1780 has been called among the harshest in the eighteenth century. A total of twenty-eight snowstorms hit the United States, some dropping snow for several days in succession. The temperature rarely rose above freezing as the Delaware and Hudson Rivers froze over. Sledges moved regularly across ten miles of ice between Annapolis and the opposite shore of the Chesapeake. Wild animals were almost exterminated. General Alexander (Lord Stirling) marched over a saltwater channel to make his unsuccessful Staten Island raid—even his artillery passed over the six miles of open water safely. Washington's main army suffered much more, because of this weather, in their Morristown winter quarters than they had at Valley Forge two years earlier, with snow lying six feet deep. The British in New York suffered almost as much as the economy of the United States ground to a halt and food became scarce everywhere. As inflation took off, Washington found it ever more difficult to obtain much needed supplies for his shrinking army.

SEE ALSO *Morristown Winter Quarters, New Jersey (1 December 1779–22 June 1780); Staten Island, New York.*

revised by Michael Bellesiles

WITHERSPOON, JOHN. (1723–1794).

Signer, clergyman, college president, member of Congress. Scotland–New Jersey. Born in Gifford, Scotland, on 5 February 1723, Witherspoon was the son of a minister and followed his father's calling. At the early age of sixteen he earned a master of arts degree from the University of Edinburgh, getting his divinity degree in 1743. Ordained on 11 April 1745, he became minister to Beith in Ayrshire. That same year he raised troops to oppose Charles Stuart, was taken prisoner at the Battle of Falkirk, and suffered a brief but harsh imprisonment in Castle Doune before Stuart was defeated. Witherspoon became well-known as a leader of the Popular Party in the Church of Scotland, which argued for the right of congregations to pick their own ministers and against the secular ways of the Moderates. In 1757 he became pastor in Paisley, and his fame spread to America. Richard Stockton was sent from New Jersey in 1766 to offer Witherspoon the presidency of the College of New Jersey (later called Princeton). But Witherspoon's wife, Elizabeth Montgomery, did not want to leave Scotland. Two years later Benjamin Rush, who was studying medicine in Edinburgh, made a personal appeal to the Witherspoons, winning them both over. They arrived in Princeton on 12 August 1768.

As president of the College of New Jersey, Witherspoon infused new life into the institution, building up its endowment, its faculty, and its student body until the military events of 1776 interfered. Before the war broke out he had introduced the study of philosophy, French, history, and oratory. Not a profound scholar himself but with the ability of a real educator, he deplored book learning for its own sake, discouraged pure scholarship, and worked on the theory that an education should make a man useful in public life.

Although he disapproved of ministers taking part in politics, he quickly gravitated to the Patriot camp, awarding honorary degrees to John Dickinson, Joseph Galloway, and John Hancock for their defense of liberty. In 1774 he became a member of the Somerset County Committee of Correspondence, attended provincial conventions, and took a prominent part in the imprisonment of the Loyalist governor William Franklin. On 22 June 1776 he was chosen as a delegate to the Continental Congress, arriving in time to vote for independence and to sign the Declaration. He remained a delegate until November 1782, serving on more than one hundred committees, including the committee on secret correspondence for foreign affairs, and on the Board of War. He also worked to silence the Loyalist publishers Benjamin Towne of Philadelphia and James Rivington of New York, as well as writing pamphlets in opposition to the issue of paper money.

After leaving Congress, Witherspoon was elected to the New Jersey legislature in 1783 and 1789 and was a federalist member of the New Jersey ratifying convention in 1787. He devoted most of his energies until his death on 15 November 1794 to rebuilding the College of New Jersey.

Witherspoon also left his mark on American religion. He had reached America at a time when the Presbyterian

Church was badly divided between the New and Old Side elements engendered by the Great Awakening of the 1740s. He played a key role in unifying America's Presbyterians and was closely identified its growth in the mid-Atlantic states and on the frontier. By 1776, with the help of a large influx of Scots–Irish, the church was firmly entrenched in the new country. From 1785 to 1789 Witherspoon helped organize the church nationwide, assisting in the crafting of its catechisms, confessions of faith, and government.

SEE ALSO *Stockton, Richard.*

BIBLIOGRAPHY

Collins, Varnum L. *President Witherspoon: A Biography.* 2 vols. Princeton, N.J.: Princeton University Press, 1925.

Green, Ashbel, ed. *Works of the Rev. John Witherspoon.* 4 vols. Philadelphia: Woodward, 1802.

revised by Michael Bellesiles

WOEDTKE, FREDERICK WILLIAM, BARON DE. (1740?–1776). Continental general.

Prussia. Born in Prussia, perhaps in 1740, Woedtke claimed to have been a major in the Prussian army. In early 1776 he appeared in Philadelphia with a strong letter of recommendation from Benjamin Franklin. Congress commissioned him brigadier general on 16 March 1776 and assigned him to the Northern Army. He is known to have attended the council of war at Crown Point on 5 July and to have died at Lake George on 28 July 1776. James Wilkinson characterized both Matthias Fermoy and Woedtke as worthless drunkards, one of the few subjects on which one feels historically safe in accepting Wilkinson's testimony.

SEE ALSO *Canada Invasion; Fermoy, Matthias Alexis de Roche.*

revised by Michael Bellesiles

WOLCOTT, ERASTUS. (1722–1793).

Militia general and judge. Connecticut. Elder brother of Oliver Wolcott, Erastus rose to prominence in his family's ancestral home town of Windsor (East Windsor after 1768), Connecticut, and was first elected to the General Assembly in 1758. The Assembly named him to its nine-member Committee of Correspondence in May 1773, and chose him as a delegate to the first Continental Congress in September 1774, but then and later he declined to serve politically outside Connecticut. In late

April 1775, the Assembly sent him, along with the pro-British William Samuel Johnson, to confer with General Gage in Boston about a cessation of hostilities, but they achieved nothing of note. He was elected Assembly speaker in May 1776.

Wolcott led Connecticut troops in the field on several occasions. Colonel of his local militia regiment from October 1774, he led a reinforcement of militia to Boston early in January 1776 to help General George Washington hold the lines while the Continental Army of 1776 was recruited. As colonel of a regiment of state troops, he commanded the New London forts during the summer of 1776. Named brigadier general of the first brigade of the reorganized Connecticut militia in December 1776, he acted principally to draft and equip men to reinforce state and continental forces, but commanded a militia detachment on the Hudson River from April to June 1777. An occasional member of the state's Council of Safety, he resigned his militia rank in January 1781 in protest over Governor Jonathan Trumbull's direction of the war effort. After the war he became a judge of the Connecticut supreme court.

SEE ALSO *Trumbull, John.*

revised by Harold E. Selesky

WOLCOTT, OLIVER. (1726–1797). Signer,

militia general. Connecticut. Oliver Wolcott, the youngest son of Governor Roger Wolcott (1679–1767), was a scion of one of Connecticut's most prominent families. He was graduated from Yale College in 1747 and immediately took up a commission to raise and command a volunteer company on the New York frontier during the French and Indian Wars. After the end of the war (1748) he studied medicine with his brother Alexander, but in October 1751 he became a merchant at Litchfield, the seat of a new county in northwest Connecticut where his father owned property. Over the next twenty-five years he became the most important man in the region. His father named him county sheriff in 1751, an office he held for twenty years. His neighbors elected him to the Connecticut Assembly in 1764, and voters across the colony elected him to the Governor's Council in 1771. Other important offices followed: judge of the local probate court in May 1772, and county judge and colonel of the local militia regiment in May 1774. A strong supporter of colonial rights, and ultimately of independence, he was moderator of the Litchfield town meeting that condemned the Intolerable Acts, and later served on town and county committees of inspection and safety.

Wolcott played a larger role in Connecticut than he did nationally. After serving as one of the nine commissioners to procure supplies for Connecticut forces, in July 1775 Congress appointed him as one of five commissioners of Indian affairs for the Northern Department. Elected to the Continental Congress in October 1775, he had to leave Philadelphia because of illness just before the Declaration of Independence was signed; he signed the document on 1 October 1776, after his return. On his way home in late June 1776 he brought to Litchfield the equestrian statue of George III that had been torn down by a New York City mob, and oversaw its transformation into over 42,000 lead bullets. Elected a delegate to Congress through 1783 (except in 1779), his participation was not noteworthy, in part because he was absent for six to nine months every year on other business. In August 1776 he commanded (as a brigadier general) the fourteen militia regiments sent to reinforce General Israel Putnam on the Hudson River. In December 1776 he was named to command the Litchfield county militia brigade, and in September 1777 he led several hundred volunteers to oppose General John Burgoyne's invasion. He was promoted to major general commanding the Connecticut militia in May 1779 and directed, with limited success, resistance to the Connecticut Coast Raids in July of that year. He was also a member of the state's Council of Safety (1780–1783).

After the war Wolcott helped to negotiate two treaties that opened Indian land to white settlement, with the Iroquois at Fort Stanwix in 1784 and with the Wyandottes five years later, that cleared title to the Western Reserve. He supported the federal Constitution and voted for it as a member of Connecticut's ratifying convention. Lieutenant governor from May 1787, he became governor when Samuel Huntington died in January 1796. He died in office less than two years later.

His son and namesake (1760–1833) saw service as a volunteer in 1777 and 1779. Declining a commission in the army, he served in the Quartermaster Department as storekeeper in the depot at Litchfield. He was later U.S. Secretary of the Treasury (1795–1800) and governor of Connecticut (1817–1827).

SEE ALSO *Connecticut Coast Raid; Western Reserve.*

revised by Harold E. Selesky

WOLFE, JAMES. (1727–1759). British general.
Born on 2 January 1727, Wolfe was commissioned second lieutenant in the First Marines in 1741 and exchanged into the Twelfth Foot in 1742. At Dettingen (Germany) on 27 June 1743 he came to the attention of the Duke of Cumberland (Prince William Augustus). Wolfe's subsequent promotions, to lieutenant (July 1743), captain in the Fourth Foot (1744), and brigade major in Flanders (1745), were due to the duke's patronage. Wolfe served as a staff officer against the Jacobites in the battles of Falkirk and Culloden, and was badly wounded in the battle at Laffeld on 21 June 1746. He became a major in the Twentieth Foot in 1749 and its lieutenant colonel in March 1750.

As commandant of the Twentieth Foot, Wolfe developed an improved, simplified system of platoon firing. He also introduced a new bayonet technique, in which the musket with the fixed blade was not hefted overhead but levelled at the hip, thus making it an effective offensive weapon. Noticing that French military writers were interested in the technique of attacking in massed column, Wolfe worked out the most effective defence against it: a massed battalion volley delivered in line, followed by a bayonet charge. These innovations, adopted for the whole army in 1764, were to have a significant impact on the infantry's performance in the War of American Independence and beyond. In 1757, returning from a staff posting with the failed expedition against Rochefort, on the French coast, he began to work out a manual for combined operations, drawing on his recent experience of what not to do.

On 23 January 1758 Wolfe was made brigadier general in North America to serve under Jeffery Amherst in the Louisburg expedition. Wolfe led the light infantry assault that enabled the army to get safely ashore, and his brigade's batteries made the breach that forced the garrison to surrender on 27 July. It was now too late in the year to move on Quebec, and the news of General James Abercromby's fiasco at Ticonderoga sent Amherst hurrying back to New York. Wolfe promptly took himself home and obtained command of the Quebec expedition, with the rank of major general in North America, on 30 December 1758. At the siege of Quebec he displayed major weaknesses in troop management, and the difficulties of implementing his initial plan of attack made him look hesitant and uncertain.

However, Wolfe's death in battle on 13 September 1759, after the famous night climb to the Heights of Abraham, made him an iconic national hero. Two dramatic, but historically inaccurate paintings depicted his death, and his statue still looks out over Greenwich in London, where he was buried. Yet his most important legacy was his system of battlefield tactics, which carried the British Army through the American Revolution and at last immortalized a far greater commander: Arthur Wellesley, the Duke of Wellington and victor of Waterloo.

SEE ALSO *Abercromby, James (1706–1781); Plains of Abraham (13 September 1759).*

BIBLIOGRAPHY

Houlding, J. A. *Fit for service: the Training of the British Army, 1715–1795*. Oxford: Oxford University Press, 1981.

Stacey, C. P. *Quebec: The Siege and the Battle*. Toronto: Robin Brass Studio, 2002.

revised by John Oliphant

WOODFORD, WILLIAM. (1734–1780).

Continental general. Virginia. Son of Major William Woodford, an Englishman who settled in Caroline County and grandson of Dr. William Cocke, secretary of the colony, he received the normal education for a young Virginian of the better class and served as a militia officer in the French and Indian War. In 1774 he was a member of the county committee of correspondence and of the committee to enforce the Association. The next year he sat as Edmund Pendleton's alternate in the Virginia Convention from 17 July to 9 August.

On 5 August he was appointed colonel of the Third Regiment and at Hampton on 24–25 October 1775, Great Bridge on 9 December, and Norfolk on 1 January 1776, he had a leading role in the fight that drove Lord Dunmore out of the province. In the closing months of 1775, when he was given the mission of opposing Dunmore around Norfolk, Woodford got into a warm dispute with Patrick Henry over the scope of their respective commands. As colonel of the First Regiment, Henry was the senior officer and would normally have had the honor given to Woodford in making the principal military effort in the colony. On 13 February 1776 Woodford became colonel of the Second Virginia Continental Regiment. Woodford resigned in September because Andrew Lewis had been promoted over him, but Woodford returned when Congress appointed him brigadier general on 21 February 1777. He was wounded in the hand at Brandywine but fought at Germantown three weeks later (4 October 1777). During the army's encampment at Valley Forge he quarreled over the relative rank of Muhlenberg, Weedon, and himself in what Douglas Freeman has referred to as a "clash of jealous and ambitious men" (Freeman, vol. 4, p. 613 and n.). He took part in the Monmouth campaign and subsequent operations in New Jersey. On 13 December 1779 he received orders to lead 750 Virginia Continentals to the relief of Charleston. After marching 500 miles in 28 days during the dead of winter, his column arrived on 6 April 1780.

Taken prisoner with the Charleston garrison on 12 May 1780 and sent to New York, Woodford died in captivity on 13 November 1780 and was buried in Old Trinity Church Yard. Woodford County, Kentucky, was named for him in 1789.

SEE ALSO *Charleston Siege of 1780; Great Bridge, Virginia; Hampton, Virginia; Norfolk, Virginia.*

BIBLIOGRAPHY

Freeman, Douglas Southall. *George Washington*. Vols. 3–5. New York: Scribner, 1951–1952.

Stewart, Catesby Willis. *The Life of Brigadier General William Woodford of the American Revolution*. 2 vols. Richmond, Va.: Whittet and Shepperson, 1973.

Ward, Harry M. *Duty, Honor or Country: General George Weedon and the American Revolution*. Philadelphia: American Philosophical Society, 1979.

revised by Harry M. Ward

WOODHULL, NATHANIEL. (1722–1776).

Militia general. New York. A major under Abercromby in the Ticonderoga and Crown Point operations of 1758, he accompanied Bradstreet's expedition against Fort Frontenac and was a colonel under Amherst in 1760. A wealthy landowner, he was active in Patriot politics, serving as president of the New York Provincial Congress in 1775 and 1776. Appointed brigadier general of the militia in Suffolk and Queens Counties in October 1775, he was surprised at Jamaica on 28 August 1776 and wounded in the arm. He died on 20 September of gangrene after his arm was removed by a surgeon.

SEE ALSO *De Lancey, Oliver (1749–1822); Jamaica (Brookland), New York.*

revised by Michael Bellesiles

WOOSTER, DAVID. (1711–1777).

Continental general. Connecticut. Born at Stratford, Connecticut, on 2 March 1711, the son of a mason, Wooster was graduated from Yale College in 1738. He was appointed lieutenant of the Connecticut armed sloop *Defense* in 1741 and the next year was promoted to its captain. In 1745 Wooster was one of eight captains in the Connecticut regiment on the Louisburg expedition, and on 4 July he sailed for France with French prisoners for exchange. He was commissioned on 24 September 1745 as a captain in the new British provincial regiment of Sir William Pepperrell, in garrison at Louisburg, but retired on half pay in 1748 when the fortress was returned to the French at the Treaty of Aix-la-Chapelle. He married the daughter of Thomas Clap, the president of Yale College, in March 1746, became a merchant at New Haven, and in 1750 helped to organize one of the first lodges of Free

Masons in Connecticut. During the French and Indian War, he was colonel of a Connecticut provincial regiment in 1756 and again in 1758–1760, taking part in the attack on Ticonderoga in 1758 and in later operations under Jeffrey Amherst. In 1763 he became customs collector at New Haven.

In April 1775 the General Assembly appointed this sixty-four-year-old veteran of two colonial wars as its major general of the six regiments to be raised for "the safety and defence of the colony." In conformity with Connecticut practice, he was simultaneously colonel of the First Regiment (raised in New Haven County) and captain of the regiment's first company. At the request of the New York assembly, the Connecticut governor's council ordered Wooster on 19 June to march with his regiment and Colonel David Waterbury's Fifth Regiment (raised in Fairfield County) to New York City. During the summer of 1775 he commanded Connecticut troops on Long Island and at Harlem. Congress named Wooster as the fourth brigadier general of the Continental army on 22 June. He was the only major general of militia not given the equivalent rank in the Continental army and was piqued at being passed over by younger men with less military experience, as well as by Israel Putnam, formerly subordinate in Connecticut rank but who was now a Continental major general. Ordered to report to Major General Philip Schuyler in the Northern Department, he left New York City on 28 September. Although Wooster quarreled with Schuyler during the Canada invasion, he took part in the siege and capture of St. Johns and remained commandant at Montreal when Richard Montgomery moved against Quebec. On Montgomery's death on 1 January 1776, Wooster assumed command in Canada. On 2 April, Wooster reached the outskirts of Quebec, where he quarreled with Benedict Arnold, but was succeeded on 1 May by John Thomas.

Wooster's service in Canada confirmed his incapacity for high command. "A general . . . of a hayfield," is Justin H. Smith's characterization of him (vol. 2, p. 230). He was "dull and uninspired, garrulous about his thirty years of service . . . tactless, hearty rather than firm with his undisciplined troops who adored him, at times brutal towards the civilian population of Montreal" (Stanley M. Pargellis in DAB). The death of Thomas on 2 June 1776 again left Wooster as senior officer in Canada but Congress, informed by its commissioners in Montreal of his incompetence, recalled him immediately. An official inquiry exonerated him of misconduct and kept him on the rolls as a brigadier general without employment—he was given no further assignment in the Continental army.

He was reappointed major general of Connecticut militia on 23 October 1776 and that winter commanded a small force on the border with New York. He joined William Heath for the mismanaged diversion against Fort

Independence, New York, on 17–18 January 1777. Mortally wounded on 27 April at Ridgefield while opposing William Tryon's Danbury raid, he died on 2 May at Danbury. Congress voted him a monument but never got around to having it built. The Masons erected a monument to Wooster at Danbury in 1854.

SEE ALSO *Canada Invasion; Danbury Raid, Connecticut; Fort Independence Fiasco, New York.*

BIBLIOGRAPHY
Smith, Justin H. *Our Struggle for the Fourteenth Colony: Canada, and the American Revolution.* New York: G. P. Putnam's Sons, 1907.

revised by Harold E. Selesky

"WORLD TURNED UPSIDE DOWN, THE."

The 1828 edition of Garden's *Anecdotes of the Revolution* is responsible for the much-repeated statement that, following surrender, the forces of British General Charles Cornwallis marched out of Yorktown, Pennsylvania, with their bands playing a piece called "The World Turned Upside Down," and implied that the tune was played frequently throughout the war years. The only thing that can be said with certainty is that a piece of music by this name did exist—in fact, there were several tunes known by this name—and that at least one of them was popular during the Revolution. It also seems certain that various pieces of music were played during the surrender ceremonies, and that bands and pipers participated, not just drummers.

Commager and Morris report that "[t]he version which has the strongest support in tradition and which . . . we would like to believe was played appeared in the *Gentleman's Magazine* of 1766, beginning 'Goody Bull and her daughter fell out'" (where the words are reproduced but not the music). Nothing about "the world turned upside down" appears in the words of this song, however. The same authorities give another song for which a case has been made, and in which the words do appear:

> If Buttercups buzzed after the bee,
> If boats were on land, churches on sea,
> ***
> [If] Summer were spring and the t'other way
> round,
> Then all the world would be upside down.

Freeman has examined this mystery with assistance from the Music Division of the Library of Congress. He reproduces the score of a piece titled "When the King

Enjoys His Own Again," from which numerous other songs and ballads were adapted, including one called "The World Turned Upside Down." According to the Library of Congress, Freeman's suggested score is generally assumed to be the tune played at the Yorktown surrender, and Freeman furnishes additional support for this theory (pp. 388–389).

According to Bass, the British soldiers were amused by this choice of music, "for they knew the tune as the old Jacobite serenade to Prince Charlie: 'When the King Enjoys His Own Again'!" (p. 4). The British are also supposed to have played this tune when they retreated from Salem, Massachusetts, on 26 February 1775.

SEE ALSO *Culloden Moor, Scotland.*

BIBLIOGRAPHY
Bass, Robert D. *The Green Dragoon: The Lives of Banastre Tarleton and Mary Robinson.* New York: Holt, 1957.

Commager, Henry Steele, and R. B. Morris. *Spirit of 'Seventy-Six.* New York: Crown, 1958.

Freeman, Douglas Southall. *George Washington.* New York: Scribner, 1948–1957.

Garden, Alexander. *Anecdotes of the American Revolution.* Charleston, S.C.: A. E. Miller, 1828.

revised by Harold E. Selesky

WRIGHT, GOVERNOR SIR JAMES.

(1716–1785). Royal governor of Georgia. South Carolina-Georgia. Often confused with his son, Major Sir James Wright, the senior Wright was born in London on 8 May 1716, moving with his family to Charleston in 1730 when his father, Robert, became chief justice of South Carolina. Wright studied law and became South Carolina's attorney general in 1739. In 1757 he went to London as the province's agent. On 13 May 1760 he was appointed lieutenant governor of Georgia, becoming governor the following year.

Most of Wright's governorship was devoted to maintaining peace between the Indians and the people he called "Crackers," aggressive settlers who violated English laws and Indian property rights in their move westward. Though there were protests against the Stamp Act, Georgia was the only colony in which they were sold. On 2 January 1766 Wright led a detachment of mounted rangers to break up a crowd of two hundred men in the port who were threatening to seize and destroy the recently arrived stamps. On 4 February he defied a body of three hundred armed countrymen who came into Savannah to make him stop the issue of the stamps, and public opinion finally rallied to his defense of law and order.

Governor Wright performed his duties capably and without any further serious challenge to his authority. In 1773 he won a high degree of popularity in the province when he negotiated a new Indian treaty that opened up more lands to white settlement, effectively negating the Proclamation Line of 1763. His handling of the Creek War of 1773–1774 was brilliant, using trade sanctions rather than violence to bring the Creek to negotiate an end to the conflict. The crown rewarded Wright on 8 December 1772 by making him a baronet. News of Lexington and Concord changed the situation in Georgia. The Liberty Boys of Savannah, led by young Joseph Habersham, defied royal authority and, on 11 May, seized five hundred pounds of powder from the provincial magazine. On 2 June they spiked a battery in Savannah; three days later they erected the first liberty pole in the province and paraded with fixed bayonets. On 4 July the Provincial Congress met and took control of the province. Wright remained another six months, hoping for the armed assistance needed to restore his authority, but when two warships and a troop transport arrived in January 1776, the Patriots promptly arrested Wright to keep him from rallying the Loyalists around this nucleus of regulars. Held incommunicado for a month, he finally escaped and took refuge aboard a warship. He made an unsuccessful attempt to take Savannah by force but in February 1776 gave up hope of restoring control and sailed for Halifax; two months later he left Halifax for England.

In 1779, after the British had recaptured Savannah, Wright returned to his former post, arriving 14 June and convening a Loyalist assembly. Wright and General Augustine Prevost defended Savannah against a Franco-American siege in September-October 1779. Over the next year Georgia and South Carolina were restored to British authority. Wright opposed Cornwallis's policy of pushing north from South Carolina, leaving the two southern states exposed to attack. Lee took Augusta in June 1780, and Savannah was isolated until the British surrendered the city in July 1782, contrary to Wright's wishes. Losing eleven plantations and more than five hundred slaves to confiscation by the victorious Patriots, Wright headed the commission that awarded compensation for Loyalist losses during the Revolution. Wright received nothing from his commission, though he estimated his loss at thirty-three thousand pounds. However, the government gave him an annual pension of five hundred pounds. He died in Westminster on 20 November 1785.

Governor Wright's brother Jermyn commanded a Loyalist strongpoint on the St. Mary's River in East Florida that the Patriots attacked several times without success. The governor's son, Sir James Wright (d. 1816), inherited the title on the death of his father. Commissioned a major in 1779, he commanded the

Georgia Loyalists at the defense of Savannah. In 1782 this unit became part of the King's (Carolina) Rangers.

SEE ALSO *Hutchinson's Island, Georgia.*

BIBLIOGRAPHY

Candler, A. D., et al., eds. *The Colonial Records of the State of Georgia.* 26 vols. Atlanta: various state printers, 1904–1916.

Coleman, Kenneth. *Colonial Georgia: A History.* New York: Scribner's, 1976.

revised by Michael Bellesiles

BIBLIOGRAPHY

Jensen, Merrill, ed. *English Historical Documents.* Volume IX: *American Colonial Documents to 1776.* David C. Douglas, general editor. New York: Oxford University Press, 1955.

Knollenberg, Bernard. *Growth of the American Revolution, 1766-1775.* Indianapolis, Ind.: Liberty Fund, 2002.

———. *Origin of the American Revolution, 1759–1766.* 1960. Revised, Indianapolis, Ind.: Liberty Fund, 2002.

Thomas, Peter D. G. *British Politics and the Stamp Act Crisis: The First Phase of the American Revolution, 1763–1767.* Oxford, U.K.: Oxford University Press, 1975.

revised by Harold E. Selesky

WRITS OF ASSISTANCE.

Writs of assistance were general search warrants that authorized customs officers to search private warehouses and homes for contraband during daylight hours, and to call on provincial officers for assistance. The imperial government authorized their use in the colonies in 1755 to combat widespread smuggling to the French West Indies and the evasion of the Molasses Act of 1733, but they were not widely used until 1760, when customs officers began a wide-scale seizure of illicit cargoes in Boston.

Writs of assistance were valid only during the reign of the incumbent monarch (George II) and expired on his death in October 1760. Customs officials applied for a renewal of these general search warrants, but Boston merchants opposed a renewal and retained James Otis Jr., and Oxenbridge Thacher to represent them in a suit before the Massachusetts Superior Court. Otis made the most important argument against the writs, on constitutional grounds. If the writs were made legal by act of Parliament, then the act of Parliament was wrong because Parliament could not make any act that violated a citizen's natural rights. The argument, while unsuccessful, helped to lay the foundation for the transfer of the locus of sovereignty from statute law to a more nebulous concept of natural law, which Americans would refine and draw on for the next thirty years. The controversy over the legality of these writs was so toxic that customs officials never again applied for a general writ of assistance in Massachusetts.

The imperial government extended the use of the general writs of assistance to the other colonies in Section 10 of the Townshend Revenue Act of 1767, but colonial courts narrowly construed the provision to require only the granting of so-called particular or special writs that specified the object of the search. This way of finessing the law allowed the other colonies to avoid the situation Massachusetts had faced in 1760 and 1761.

SEE ALSO *Otis, James; Townshend Revenue Act.*

WYANDOT.

A remnant of the once large and powerful Huron Indian nation, the Wyandot Indians were a small but strategically significant Indian nation who, during the eighteenth century, inhabited the southern Great Lakes basin. The Wyandot were British allies during the War of the American Revolution.

In the early seventeenth century, the Huron Indians inhabited a region (Huronia) on the south end of the Georgian Bay, in modern-day Ontario. The Huron spoke a northern Iroquoian language and subsisted through a combination of agriculture, hunting, and farming. The Huron, along with their neighbors and close relatives the Petun, may have numbered between eighteen thousand and thirty thousand in the 1610s and 1620s. The Huron were decimated by epidemics of European diseases in the 1630s and then fared poorly in the Beaver Wars against the Iroquois League after 1640. The community that became the Wyandot opted to leave Huronia in the 1650s. (The Huron called themselves the Wendat.) It was likely a small community, as eighteenth-century accounts of the Wyandot population fix the number of Wyandot warriors between 150 and 250.

The Wyandot migrated throughout the northern Great Lakes during the second half of the seventeenth century and eventually settled in the area around Detroit after 1701. The Wyandot were one of many Indian nations to establish communities near the French post at Detroit. The Wyandot ranged into modern-day Ohio to hunt and began to establish contact with British traders in the mid-1740s. French agents strengthened their alliance with the Wyandot (and other Indians) and the Wyandot fought on the French side in the Seven Years' War, participating in the 1755 defeat of Edward Braddock. After participating in Pontiac's Rebellion, the Wyandot committed themselves to alliance with the British. They remained on the British side during the American Revolution. From their community at Sandusky, on Lake Erie, the Wyandot were active in the harassment of the communities of the Pennsylvania frontier. They were part of the force that defeated the William Crawford expedition of 1782 and that famously captured Crawford and burned him at the stake.

The Wyandot were part of the Ohio Valley alliance that resisted the United States until Anthony Wayne's victory at Fallen Timbers (1794). The Wyandot signed the Treaty of Greenville (1795). After a series of subsequent treaties, the Wyandot were eventually removed west of the Mississippi —first to Kansas (1843) and then to Oklahoma (between 1855 and 1870)—where they remain today.

SEE ALSO *Braddock, Edward; Crawford, William; Crawford's Defeat; Indians in the Colonial Wars and the American Revolution; Pontiac's War; Wayne, Anthony.*

BIBLIOGRAPHY

Heidenreich, Conrad E. "Huron." In *Handbook of North American Indians.* Vol. 15: *Northeast.* Edited by William C. Sturtevant. Washington: Smithsonian Institution, 1978–.

Hinderaker, Eric. *Elusive Empires: Constructing Colonialism in the Ohio Valley, 1673–1800.* Cambridge, U.K.: Cambridge University Press, 1997.

Tooker, Elisabeth. "Wyandot." In *Handbook of North American Indians.* Vol. 15: *Northeast.* Edited by William C. Sturtevant. Washington: Smithsonian Institution, 1978–.

White, Richard. *The Middle Ground: Indians, Empires, and Republics in the Great Lakes Region, 1650–1815.* Cambridge, U.K.: Cambridge University Press, 1991.

revised by Leonard J. Sadosky

WYOMING VALLEY MASSACRE, PENNSYLVANIA.

3–4 July 1778. Although the name was applied to most of the northern quarter of Pennsylvania, the Wyoming Valley of the Revolution was the twenty-five-mile stretch of the Susquehanna River below the mouth of the Lackawanna River, including modern Wilkes-Barre. "Wyoming" comes from the Delaware Indian name M'cheuwómink, "upon the great plain." The Wyoming Valley Massacre had its origins partially in local disputes. Conflicting claims of Connecticut and Pennsylvania resulted in regular clashes after the original Connecticut settlement in 1753. In January 1774 the Connecticut General Assembly, defying Pennsylvania's claims, incorporated the settlement into a chartered township called Westmoreland. By 1775 the three thousand inhabitants of the isolated valley split between the more numerous "Yankees" and the "Pennamites," although the two groups shared a strong attachment to the Patriot cause. But a number of Loyalist families began moving into the area from the Hudson and Mohawk Valleys, most prominently the Wintermoot family.

In response to this influx of new settlers, who made no apologies for their loyalty to the king, the original settlers formed committees of vigilance. They arrested several of the newcomers and sent them off to Connecticut, where many ended up in the Connecticut Mines or Simsbury Prison. The Wintermoots had purchased land toward the head of the valley and proceeded to construct a fort. This was common sense in a region vulnerable to Indian raids, but under the circumstances the Patriot settlers thought it wise to start throwing up some forts of their own. About two miles above the Wintermoots they built Fort Jenkins. Forty Fort, a blockhouse whose name came from the first forty Connecticut pioneers, was strengthened. Plans were made to build and renovate other posts.

Meanwhile, the valley sent off two companies of regulars, eighty-two men each, to join Washington. Also, Patriot committees continued their vigilance, sending more accused Tories to the mines and further alienating neighbors with differing political views.

War had lurked around the edges of Wyoming Valley for some months. During St. Leger's expedition in June–Sept. 1777, stray Indians appeared. In January 1778, twenty-seven suspected Tories were arrested and eighteen were sent to prison in Connecticut. The other nine fled, probably to Niagara, and were followed by many other Loyalists from the Wyoming region. At British headquarters in Niagara, meanwhile, Major John Butler was preparing another series of raids against the exposed U.S. frontier.

THE BRITISH APPROACH WYOMING

Butler left Niagara in June 1778 with his Rangers, a detachment of Johnson's Royal Greens, and an assortment of volunteers from Pennsylvania, New Jersey, and New York, about four hundred loyalists in all. As deputy of the Indian forces, Butler had the support of about five hundred Iroquois, mainly Senecas and Cayugas, under the command of a chief named Gi-en-gwahtoh. Though the strength of Butler's command remains in dispute, his forces definitely outnumbered the militia he encountered in Wyoming Valley.

The invasion route was eastward toward Tryon County, southward along Seneca Lake, and on to Tioga. The latter was roughly fifty miles up the Susquehanna River from the head of Wyoming Valley. While waiting for boats and rafts to be built, Butler sent raiding parties to the West Branch of the Susquehanna. On 27 June his entire force reached Wyalusing, and the next day the men camped at a rebel mill about twenty miles from their objective. Lacking provisions, Butler welcomed the arrival of several Wintermoots with fourteen cows and an offer to surrender their fort if promised safety.

The Wintermoots also supplied valuable intelligence, informing Butler that, though the Patriots expected a raid, the Continental army had been unable to spare any troops for their defense, Washington being in the midst of the Monmouth campaign during 16 June–5 July. The local defense was a hastily assembled company of from forty to sixty men at Forty Fort, commanded by Captain Detrick Hewett. Colonel Zebulon Butler (no relation to Major John Butler), a Continental officer home on leave, was given overall command of the situation and called on the militia to turn out. Many of the local militia insisted on staying at the seven other forts that extended ten miles on both sides of the river. Colonel Butler was able to raise some three hundred militia to reinforce Hewett's volunteers and arrived at Forty Fort on 1 July. Major John Butler's forces entered the valley from the west and quickly took possession of Fort Jenkins and a little fort called Exeter. He established headquarters at Wintermoot's fort (as his blockhouse was known). The Patriots clashed with an Indian patrol that surprised and murdered some men working in a field near Fort Jenkins; the Patriots then withdrew to Forty Fort.

THE BATTLE OF WYOMING

On 3 July, Colonel Zebulon Butler fell for one of the oldest tricks in the book. Major John Butler had Fort Wintermoot set on fire and pretended to retreat, drawing Colonel Butler and his militia out of Forty Fort. Rather than proceeding cautiously and sending out scouts to determine the exact movements of the Loyalists and Indians, Colonel Butler rushed forward, apparently shouting taunts at what he took to be the retreating British forces. The Patriots were scattered over an open field, with Butler commanding the right, Colonel Nathan Denison the left, and Hewett's volunteers in the center. Major Butler anchored his left flank on Wintermoot's fort, where he personally commanded his Rangers, deploying the Indians on the opposite flank, and placing the Greens in the center. When the Patriots returned the fire of Butler's troops, the Indians rushed upon them with axes, knives, and hatchets before they could reload. The Patriots fled in panic, many of them throwing down their muskets and several dozen leaping into the Susquehanna in an effort to swim to safety. The Indians pursued the latter into the water, killing most of them. Many of the Patriots ran for Forty Fort but were intercepted by Butler's Loyalists.

The exact number killed in this battle is unknown, but at least twenty militia officers and three Continental officers were killed, including Hewett. Major Butler claimed to have killed 227 patriots while losing just two Rangers and one of his Indian allies. Only 60 patriots escaped the vigorous pursuit, and Denison led some of these back to Forty Fort to protect the women and children. Zebulon Butler was less heroic, not stopping until he reached Fort Wyoming at Wilkes-Barre, where he gathered such regulars as he could and withdrew from the valley. The slaughter of fugitives and torture of prisoners continued through the night of 3–4 July. J. Hector St. John Crèvecoeur wrote, "It is said that those who were then made prisoners were tied to small trees and burnt the evening of the same day" as the battle (Smith 2: 1157) Some accounts say that prisoners were thrown into a fire and held there by pitchforks.

During the night a few reinforcements under John Franklin reached Forty Fort, but Denison accepted John Butler's surrender terms the next morning. These terms required the people of the Wyoming Valley to not take up arms again during the war, demolish their garrisons, and spare loyalists from further persecution while restoring their lost property.

For the Loyalists, the battle at Forty Fort was a great victory. As Richard McGinnis described events, "Thus did loyalty and good order that day triumph over confusion and treason, the goodness of our cause, aided and assisted by the blessing of Divine Providence, in some measure help to restore the ancient constitution of our mother country, governed by the best of kings" (Commager and Morris, p. 1007).

The Patriots, of course, had a very different view. Atrocity tales quickly circulated and multiplied until not a single inhabitant of the Wyoming Valley, it seemed, remained alive. Newspapers throughout America reported on the Loyalists refusing quarter to rebel brothers, the roasting of prisoners, the slaughter of babies, and several instances of parricide. Revenge was called for and promised.

Major Butler withdrew from the Wyoming Valley on 8 July, having accomplished his primary purposes of destroying a Patriot stronghold and spreading terror throughout the U.S. frontier. He reported the destruction of one thousand houses and the capture and evacuation of one thousand head of cattle, as well as large numbers of sheep and pigs. Butler reached Tioga on 10 July, and four days later he started for Niagara. Small bands of Indians continued to roam the defenseless settlement, however, destroying crops, burning buildings, and menacing the remaining inhabitants.

A relief column of Connecticut troops led by Captain Simon Spalding was nearly fifty miles away from Wilkes-Barre the day of the battle. When Spalding got within twelve miles of the valley, his scouts reported the enemy was still there in strength, so he wisely withdrew to Stroudsburg. Colonel Butler assembled some settlers and troops and returned to Wilkes-Barre on 3 August. Colonel Thomas Hartley arrived with the Eleventh Pennsylvania Regiment to protect the valley until the crops were salvaged and the enemy threat was gone.

In September came the first of the promised reprisals as 130 patriots under Hartley and Denison, who broke his parole in volunteering to serve, moved up the East Branch of the Susquehanna destroying several Indian villages and taking a few prisoners. They withdrew upon learning that the Indians were massing under Joseph Brant around Unadilla. A few settlers strove to get crops planted even though the season was well advanced, and several were killed in isolated attacks by Indians. It was not until 22 October that the rebel dead were collected on the battle-ground and buried in a common grave.

COMMENTS

Major John Butler deserves his due as a military commander. This fifty-three-year-old officer led his mixed force almost two hundred miles through the wilderness from Niagara, achieving a highly effective surprise. Patriot authorities, civil and military, local and elsewhere, failed to do what they could with available resources, and the militia showed no spirit of courage or sacrifice in organizing its own security before John Butler reached Tioga in overwhelming strength. Zebulon Butler's handling of the situation on 3 July was singularly inept: he and Denison herded their troops forward to be slaughtered by an enemy superior in numbers and quality. John Butler's vigorous pursuit resulted in the tactician's dream: a battle of annihilation. In justice to the officers and men who tried to defend Wyoming Valley on 3 July, it must be reiterated that it was already too late to overcome Butler's tactical surprise.

John Butler always denied that any massacre occurred. In his report, written 12 July at Tioga, he concluded: "But what gives me the sincerest satisfaction is that . . . not a single person was hurt except such as were in arms, to these in truth the Indians gave no quarter" (Swiggett, p. 133). However, the treatment of prisoners after the battle, though grotesquely exaggerated, spread the perception of barbaric treatment and fed popular demands for retribution. The virulence of frontier warfare accelerated after July 1778.

SEE ALSO *Butler, John; Butler, Zebulon; Denison, Nathan; Monmouth, New Jersey; Spalding, Simon; St. Leger's Expedition.*

BIBLIOGRAPHY

Calloway, Colin G. *The American Revolution in Indian Country: Crisis and Diversity in Native American Communities.* New York: Cambridge University Press, 1995.

Commager, Henry Steele, and Richard B. Morris, eds. *The Spirit of 'Seventy-Six: The Story of the American Revolution as Told by Participants.* New York: Harper and Row, 1967.

Mancall, Peter C. *Valley of Opportunity: Economic Culture along the Susquehanna, 1700–1800.* Ithaca, N.Y.: Cornell University Press, 1991

Smith, Page. *A New Age Now Begins.* 2 vols. New York: McGraw-Hill, 1976.

Swiggett, Howard. *War out of Niagara: Walter Butler and the Tory Rangers.* New York: Columbia University Press, 1933.

revised by Michael Bellesiles

WYTHE, GEORGE. (1726?–1806).

Signer, statesman, jurist, law professor. Virginia. Born on the family plantation in Elizabeth City County, Virginia, perhaps in 1726, Wythe was educated by his mother. After studying law with his uncle, he was admitted to the bar in 1746. In 1753 he replaced Peyton Randolph as Virginia's attorney general. After receiving only one vote when he ran for the Burgesses from his home county, Wythe moved to Williamsburg, representing the town in the assembly in 1754–1755.

Wythe's brilliant career was closely related to those of several exceptional men who were his intimate friends or, later, students. In 1758, after being admitted to the bar of the General Court, he started a profitable friendship with the new lieutenant governor, Francis Fauquier. Another close friend at this time was William Small, professor of mathematics and natural philosophy at William and Mary. Later he was to be a friend and teacher of Thomas Jefferson, James Monroe, and Henry Clay.

During the years leading up to the break with England, Wythe was a representative in the House of Burgesses (1754–1755, 1758–1768), clerk of that body, 1769–1775, and mayor of Williamsburg (1768). In the controversy leading to Patrick Henry's triumph in the Parson's Cause, Wythe presided over the court that upheld Virginia's action against the claim of the Reverend Thomas Warrington for damages. In 1764 he drafted a protest to the Stamp Act (1765) that so far exceeded most of his colleagues' ideas of permissible candor that they toned it down considerably before adoption. In 1774 he served on the Williamsburg committee that enforced the nonimportation agreements.

In 1775 Wythe showed a wisdom surpassing that of the political majority when he recommended that Virginia organize a regular army and not a militia. As a delegate to the Continental Congress in 1775–1776, he ably supported Richard Henry Lee's resolution for independence and signed the Declaration. With Jefferson and Edmund Pendleton, he accomplished the monumental task of revising the laws of Virginia; their committee reported 126 bills in 1779, though the assembly rejected many of them. Meanwhile, Wythe was speaker in the House of Delegates in 1777 and the next year assumed the title of chancellor when he became one of three judges in the state's high court of chancery. Like most states, Virginia had a bicameral assembly, the House of Delegates and the Senate, the names they still use today. On 4 December 1779 he was named to a chair of law at William and Mary, the first chair of law established in an American college. He held the position until 1790.

Though elected to the Constitutional Convention in 1787, Wythe had to resign his seat and return home due to the fatal illness of his wife. The following year he was elected to Virginia's ratifying convention, even though he did not run for the office. His influence at the convention in favor of the Constitution is often credited with swaying many votes. His opinion that slavery violated the Virginia bill of rights received a less favorable hearing.

His death was tragic and bizarre. Wythe had moved to Richmond in 1791. In his will he left most of his estate to his only sister's grandson, George Wythe Sweeney, with a legacy for a servant that was to pass to Sweeney if the servant died. In 1806, tired of waiting for his inheritance, Sweeney poisoned some coffee with arsenic in order to kill both the servant and Wythe. The servant died first, but Wythe lived long enough to disinherit Sweeney. The latter escaped conviction for murder since the testimony of the principal witness, Wythe's freedwoman cook, was not admissible in court since she was black.

SEE ALSO *Parson's Cause; Virginia, Military Operations in.*

BIBLIOGRAPHY

Blackburn, Joyce. *George Wythe of Williamsburg.* New York: Harper and Row, 1975.

Dill, Alonzo T. *George Wythe: Teacher of Liberty.* Williamsburg: Virginia Independence Bicentennial Commission, 1979.

revised by Michael Bellesiles

Y-Z

YAGERS SEE *Jägers.*

"YANKEE DOODLE."

Of unknown origin and existing in almost countless versions, this song is generally attributed to a British surgeon in Lord Amherst's army named Richard Shuckburgh, who supposedly wrote it in 1755 to ridicule provincial troops. It was first used as a marching song by the British and appeared in Andrew Barton's 1767 play, *The Disappointment*. It is known that by 1768 crowds partying in Boston sang "Yankee Doodle" in celebration. The British played it when they left the surrender field at Saratoga, not in derision but because they had been instructed to play something light. By that time it was a song closely identified with the Patriots.

BIBLIOGRAPHY

Silverman, Kenneth. *A Cultural History of the American Revolution: Painting, Music, Literature, and the Theatre in the Colonies and the United States.* New York: Columbia University Press, 1987.

revised by Michael Bellesiles

YANKEE HERO–MILFORD ENGAGEMENT.

7 June 1776. While making a quick dash from Newburyport to Boston with a skeleton crew, the American privateer *Yankee Hero* ran into the British warship *Milford* off Cape Ann. Captain James Tracy's fourteen-gun brig was badly overmatched by Captain John Burr's twenty-eight-gun frigate. The British accounts say there was a short engagement, ending with Tracy's surrender at 5:50 P.M.; the American version says Tracy and his men put up gallant defense for over two hours. The Americans had sixteen or seventeen casualties, including Tracy who was wounded; the British admitted to having only one marine wounded.

revised by Robert K. Wright Jr.

YORKTOWN, SIEGE OF.

September–October 1781. Admiral Francois Jean Paul, Comte de Grasse's twenty-eight ships of the line arrived at the mouth of the Chesapeake River on 30 August 1781. The fleet, serving the Patriot cause, caught two British frigates at anchor, capturing one and sending the other into the York River. As a result, the Royal navy in New York received no notice that De Grasse was in Virginia. De Grasse brought 3,300 French troops from the West Indies, commanded by Major General Claude-Anne, marquis de Saint-Simon, Montbléru.

While Saint-Simon's troops were landing at Jamestown on 5 September 1781, Lieutenant General Charles Lord Cornwallis had one last chance to fight his way up the peninsula to Richmond and retreat into the Carolinas. The commander of American troops in Virginia, Major General the Marquis de Lafayette anxiously deployed his forces so as to block this route. After some probing, Cornwallis declined to make the attempt. Confidently expecting the Royal navy would rescue him, Cornwallis continued to fortify his positions at Yorktown and Gloucester Point to await their arrival. This opportunity closed when Admiral de Grasse's fleet drove the Royal navy off in the battle of the Chesapeake Capes, and Admiral Jacques Melchior Saint-Laurent Barras brought his squadron from Newport into the bay while the two fleets were still at sea. Meanwhile, the Franco-American armies commanded by Major General George Washington and Lieutenant General the comte de Rochambeau (Jean Baptiste Donatiatien de Virneur) progressed from New York towards the Chesapeake. As he moved southward, Washington picked up new troops, such as the Third and Fourth Regiments of the Maryland Line, which had recently been recruited at Baltimore. Joining them in Virginia were that commonwealth's militiamen, who were commanded by Virginia's governor, Thomas Nelson. The Chesapeake encirclement was complete when all these troops arrived at Williamsburg by 26 September.

As he withdrew within Yorktown, Lord Cornwallis faced a severe moral dilemma. While his troops marched through Virginia they were viewed as liberators to thousands of African American slaves, who flocked to their columns and provided domestic labor for the troops, intelligence information for the staff, and geographic familiarity with the countryside that proved particularly useful. According to Hessian Captain Johann Ewald, every officer had four to six blacks and a similar number of horses, as well as one or two "Negresses for cook and maid." Every soldier's woman had a couple of black servants and eventually every enlisted man had "his Negro, who carried his provisions and bundles." For the enslaved, a red coat was a symbol of liberty. They brought with them foodstuffs, horses, cattle, sheep, and poultry. Estimates of the number of blacks with Cornwallis start at 3,000 and go to many times that number.

The hard hand of war inflicted by the British and their black Loyalist allies impoverished the Lower Neck and Southside Virginia. But close confinement within British fortifications at Portsmouth and Yorktown contributed to the spread of the dreaded smallpox, typhus, and typhoid, which apparently killed many of the self-made freedmen. Although their labor contributed significantly to the construction of fortifications at both places, in the end they died or were among the approximately 2,000 blacks that Cornwallis ultimately expelled from Yorktown. Their story is one of the great tragedies of the Yorktown siege.

BRITISH DEFENSES

Cornwallis established his main line of defense close to the town, with an average depth of only 400 yards between the river and the line of fortifications, and with a width of only 1.200 yards. Yorktown was not selected as a place for withstanding a protracted siege and did not provide good defensive terrain. It was flat, offering little defilade and depriving the defenders of the other advantages of high ground (observation, fields of fire). Yorktown Creek and Wormley Creek would have furnished excellent natural obstacles on which to organize a defense if the British garrison had been large enough to cover such a long perimeter, but this was beyond their capability, particularly in the absence of naval superiority.

The inner line of fortifications comprised ten batteries, some sixty-five guns, and eight redoubts. The principal strongpoint was known as the "horn work," and was located astride the road from Hampton. Forward of this position, to defend the half-mile of flat ground between the heads of the two creeks, were several outworks. This area, part of which was known as Pigeon Quarter, was the principal approach for an attacker. Along the river, west of Yorktown and covering the Williamsburg Road where it entered from that direction, was a strong position called the Fusilier Redoubt, since it was held by a detachment from the Royal Welch Fusiliers (Twenty-third Regiment). On the opposite flank were the detached Redoubts Nine and Ten.

Gloucester Point was important not only in connection with Cornwallis's original mission of establishing a naval station but also as a base for foraging. The position was commanded by Lieutenant Colonel Thomas Dundas, and its fortifications included four redoubts, three batteries, and a line of entrenchments.

ORDER OF BATTLE

On 27 September Washington organized the American Continentals into three divisions of two brigades each. These were commanded by the Marquis de Lafayette, Benjamin Lincoln, and Baron Friedrich Wilhelm Augustus von Steuben. The artillery brigade, small troops of cavalry, and detachments of sappers and miners rounded out the regular units. The total strength of the Continental troops approximated 5,500. Additionally, Governor Thomas Nelson of Virginia commanded a division of militiamen of approximately 3,500. Governor Nelson personally financed many of the Virginia militiamen, and the failure of the Commonwealth to reimburse him contributed to his subsequent financial difficulties.

Rochambeau's contingent was made up of the four regiments that had marched from Newport (the Regiments Bourbonnais, Royal Deux-Ponts, Soissonais, Saintonge) and the three that had come with de Grasse (Regiments Agenais, Gâtinais, and Touraine) plus 600 artillerymen, the Duke de Lauzun's Legion (comprising horse and foot soldiers), and marines detached for operations against Gloucester. Total French ground forces amounted to approximately 8,600, to which must be added at least 19,000 French sailors who manned the ships blockading the entrance to the Chesapeake and the mouth of the York

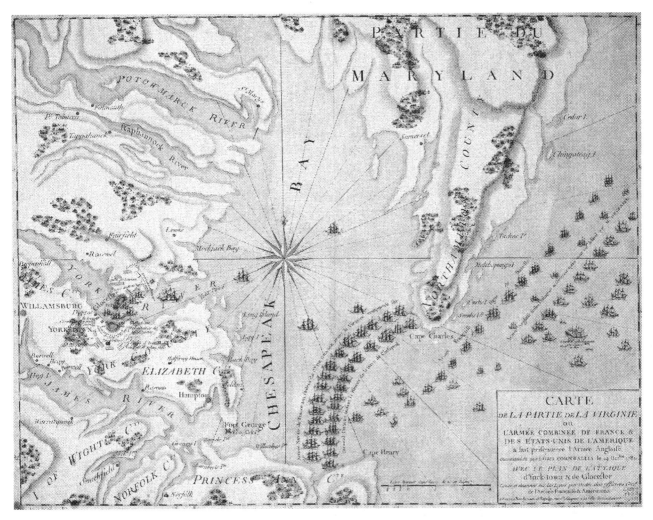

The Battle of Yorktown. *This French map (1781) shows the positions of troops and ships in Washington's victory over Cornwallis at Yorktown.* © **CORBIS**

River from British relief efforts. Obviously, the French contribution to the victory vastly outnumbered that provided by the Americans. Nonetheless, Washington commanded the allied ground forces.

To defend Yorktown and Gloucester, Cornwallis had what historian Henry P. Johnston terms "the élite of the King's army in America." He had brought the following units from the Carolinas: the Brigade of Guards, the Twenty-third, Thirty-third, and Seventy-first Foot Regiments, the light infantry company of the Eighty-second Regiment, Banastre Tarleton's British Legion, the North Carolina Volunteers, and the German Bose Regiment. The remainder of his troops had come south with Benedict Arnold and William Phillips: two battalions of light infantry, the Seventeenth, Forty-third, Seventy-sixth and Eightieth Regiments, the Queen's Rangers, two Anspach Battalions, the Hessian Regiment Prince Hereditaire, and a jäger company. These were

supplemented by a Royal artillery detachment, in addition to naval guns and gunners. About 800 marines were also on hand, plus pioneers and other detachments. Total ground forces totaled approximately 8,900 before the siege began. The Royal navy forces included approximately 850 sailors and ten naval vessels plus several dozen transports, victuallers, and privateers. Cornwallis had the heavy guns from the ships installed in the Yorktown fortifications. There was dearth of senior officers, however. Brigadier General Charles O'Hara was the only other general, and among the field grade officers there were only two colonels, twelve lieutenant colonels, and twelve majors.

PRELIMINARY MOVEMENTS

The American allied forces started from Williamsburg on the morning of 28 September and moved to within a mile of

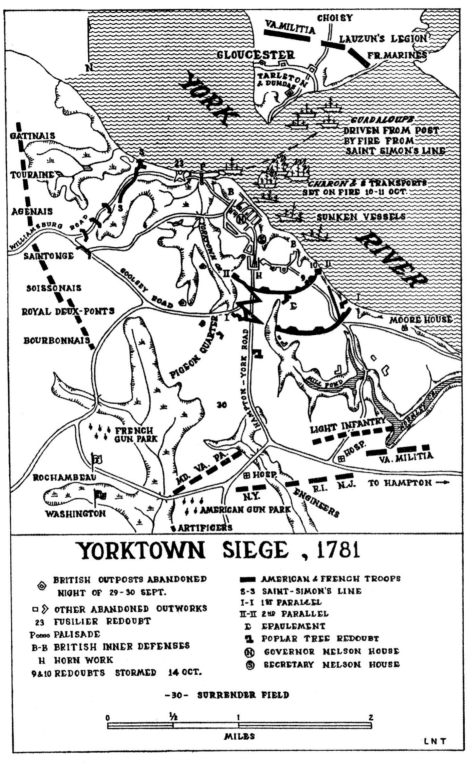

YORKTOWN SIEGE, 1781

◈ BRITISH OUTPOSTS ABANDONED
NIGHT OF 29-30 SEPT.

▢◇ OTHER ABANDONED OUTWORKS

23 FUSILIER REDOUBT

Pᵒᵒᵒᵒ PALISADE

B-B BRITISH INNER DEFENSES

H HORN WORK

9&10 REDOUBTS STORMED 14 OCT.

▬▬ AMERICAN & FRENCH TROOPS

S-S SAINT-SIMON'S LINE

I-I 1ˢᵗ PARALLEL

II-II 2ⁿᵈ PARALLEL

E EPAULEMENT

⚑ POPLAR TREE REDOUBT

Ⓝ GOVERNOR NELSON HOUSE

Ⓢ SECRETARY NELSON HOUSE

-30- SURRENDER FIELD

0   ½   1   2
MILES

LNT

the Yorktown defenses by dark. The light infantry of Lieutenant Colonel Robert Abercromby was on the British right, but withdrew as the French wing advanced in that sector, and Tarleton's mounted troops withdrew to the Moore House when the American wing arrived to the southeast of Yorktown. Cornwallis sought to pollute area wells by having animal carcasses and the bodies of deceased african americans thrown into them. He began forcing his black refugees out of the little town. On 29 September Washington and his officers examined the enemy position while their troops deployed to invest Yorktown. Orders were issued for the siege artillery and stores to move up from Trebell's Landing on the James River—a difficult operation because sufficient draft animals were not available and the heavy guns had to be moved over ten miles of sandy roads.

De Grasse stationed Admiral Barras and ships of the line off Cape Henry at the mouth of Chesapeake Bay, and ordered several frigates to lie off Old Point Comfort (modern Fort Monroe), while the remainder of the French naval forces blockaded the British naval vessels in the York River. A British attempt on 21 September to employ several merchantmen as fireships against the French had failed to dislodge the enemy. By early October ten merchantmen had been sunk in front of Yorktown in an effort to impede the French men-of-war.

On Sunday morning, 30 September, the Americans and their allies were pleasantly surprised to discover that the enemy had abandoned the three outposts covering the approach from the southwest—the two astride Goosley Road in the Pigeon Quarter and another one to the north covering a road across the top of Yorktown Creek. Although Cornwallis has been severely criticized for his failure to hold these positions to buy time, his decision was sound in the light of the information available to him. He had received word from Sir Henry Clinton on the 29th that a fleet would leave New York for his relief on about 5 October. Since the three abandoned outposts were vulnerable to envelopment by the superior allied force, Cornwallis believed he could best employ his limited forces in a defense of the inner line during the week or so it would take for relief to arrive.

At Gloucester, General George Weedon's Virginia militia, which opposed the British garrison under Lieutenant Colonel Thomas Dundas, were reinforced on 28 September by Lauzun's Legion. On 1 October, General Claude-Gabriel, marquis de Choisy assumed overall command and, about the same time, 800 French marines were detached for service on this front. Tarleton's Legion joined Dundas on 2 October. After a spirited clash at Gloucester on 3 October, Choisy kept the British bottled up until the end of the campaign.

REGULAR APPROACHES STARTED

Washington and Rochambeau wasted no time undertaking the siege of Cornwallis's position. On 6 October the main allied force opposite Yorktown was ready to break ground for their formal siege operations. Following techniques developed by French marshal Sébastien Le Prestre de Vauban early in the century, French engineers directed the implementation of his principles of investiture, circumvallation, countervallation, bombardment, and excavation of parallel entrenchments that went ever closer to the British lines. While the French pushed forward on the left, driving the pickets into the Fusilier Redoubt and forcing the Royal Welch Fusiliers to make a stubborn defense of their position, the Americans began edging closer on the right.

To divert attention from the main effort, Saint-Simon's troops started a Flying Sap toward the Fusilier's Redoubt. Meanwhile, the trace of the 2,000 yard-long first parallel was staked out by engineers and well-organized work parties moved forward after dark to dig. Favored by a dark, rainy night and sandy soil, some 1,500 men shoveled enough dirt to have protection in their trench and four redoubts before daylight. Saint-Simon's diversion started drawing enemy fire about 9 P.M. (a French deserter had alerted the British), but the working parties were subjected to little shelling during the night. Cornwallis probably did not realize that the first parallel had been started until the morning of 7 October, when his troops could see it at a distance of 600 to 800 yards from their positions.

On 9 October the first allied batteries were ready to start the bombardment. To divert British attention from the allied right, Washington gave Saint-Simon the honor of opening the show at 3 P.M. on the opposite flank. Early the next day another four batteries were in action—two French and two American—bringing the total to at least 46 pieces. By 10 A.M allied fire had inflicted such damage that the British could return only about six rounds per hour. The superiority of French artillery and the expertise of French engineers proved decisive in the prosecution of the siege.

On 10 October the battery commanded by Captain Thomas Machin began a bombardment of the town with targeting advice from Governor Thomas Nelson, who directed fire against his uncle's house because he thought it was the location of Cornwallis's headquarters. Actually the British general was in a bunker near the hornwork.

French artillery hot shot set the British frigate *Charon* on fire during the night of 10–11 October, and another three or four vessels were also destroyed by hot shot from Saint-Simon's guns. The British moved the remainder of their vessels closer to Gloucester to evade the French artillerymen. *Charon* was the largest of vessels in the York River which were either destroyed, scuttled, or surrendered by the British. Meanwhile De Grasse sent planned to send *Le Vaillant* (sixty-four guns) and *L'Expériment* (fifty guns) up the York to bombard the town and fleet from the river. This never happened due to the surrender.

ASSAULT OF REDOUBTS NINE AND TEN

Work had been started on the second parallel on 11 October, but two detached British works, Redoubts Nine and Ten, had to be reduced before the American end of this parallel could be completed. As a preliminary step in the reduction of these two positions, French engineers directed construction of an *epaulement* (a raised defensive wall or elevation) on the eastern end of the second parallel as close to the redoubts as this work could be accomplished. Digging started at dusk on 11 October. All possible allied artillery was brought to bear on the two redoubts, and on 14 October Washington was told that an assault was now feasible.

Redoubt Number Ten was closer to the York River, and Alexander Hamilton claimed the honor of leading the American assault there. Grenadiers and chasseurs of the Gâtinais and Royal Deux-Ponts would make a simultaneous attack on Redoubt Number Nine. It would be commanded by Colonel Guillaume, comte de Deux-Ponts with Colonel Claude, Baron d'Estrade as second in command.

Saint-Simon and Choisy started were to conduct diversionary demonstrations on the Allied left wing and at Gloucester, but these efforts began after the redoubts had fallen. At 7:00 P.M, Hamilton and Deux-Ponts sent their troops forward silently into the darkness. The Americans had their muskets unloaded, and they took Redoubt Ten by the bayonet.

The French column had advanced about 120 yards when they were challenged by a sentry from the parapet of Redoubt Number Nine. The 120 British and Hessian defenders under Lieutenant Duncan McPherson then opened fire as the French rushed forward. While the pioneers worked to clear obstructions so that the entire column could scale the parapet, other officers and men went up without waiting for support.

After inflicting heavy losses on the French before they scaled the parapet, the defenders tried to take refuge behind a line of large casks within the redoubt. The French fired into the huddled mass, and then prepared to close with cold steel. The British and Hessians threw down their arms and surrendered. General Antoine-Charles, baron de Vioménil, who had over-all command of the French attack, arrived and ordered Deux-Ponts to consolidate his position and prepare for a counterattack from the main enemy lines. This threat, however, did not materialize.

Hamilton's attack took place simultaneously, and the Americans were fired on shortly after the Hessian sentinel challenged the French column, some 200 yards away. Lieutenant John Mansfield led his forlorn unit of twenty men from the Fourth Connecticut Regiment into the redoubt, and was supported immediately by the leading battalion. The attack was a brilliant success, costing the Americans only nine killed and twenty-five wounded. The French lost fifteen killed and seventy-seven wounded. In Redoubt Number Ten the enemy had six officers and sixty-seven men captured; eighteen were killed and fifty captured in Redoubt Number Nine.

Cornwallis did not counterattack, but he massed all possible guns against the captured works. The allies moved working parties out immediately to throw up a protective wall of dirt at the back of the redoubts and to incorporate them into the already completed portion of the second parallel.

ABERCROMBY'S SORTIE AND ESCAPE FAILURE

Completion of the second parallel had not only the obvious effect of moving allied guns within closer range of the enemy lines, but it also permitted batteries to enfilade the defenders. The standard reaction to such a threat is for the defenders to sally forth and spike the most dangerous guns. Therefore, at about 4 A.M. on 16 October, Lieutenant Colonel Robert Abercromby led 350 hand-picked British troops out on this mission. Hitting near the boundary between French and American troops in the second parallel, and near two unfinished batteries where no working parties were then located, Abercromby led his raid westward along the trench. Pretending to be an American detachment, he surprised an element of the Agenais Regiment, most of whom were asleep. After spiking four guns he continued down the trench until he sighted another position. Louis-Marie, count de Noailles discovered the British and started a fight that drove them back to their lines. The raiders had nonetheless spiked two of the American guns before withdrawing. However, the guns had been ineffectually spiked with bayonet points, and the allies had them back in action within six hours.

On the night of 16–17 October, Cornwallis tried to ferry his effective troops across the river, with a view to fighting his way to New York via the Gloucester lines. Insufficient boats and an exceptionally severe storm frustrated this effort. On 17 October, the fourth anniversary of General John Burgoyne's surrender at Saratoga (New York), the allied artillery started the heaviest bombardment yet delivered. According to some estimates, more than one hundred artillery pieces were in action.

SURRENDER

Sometime between 9 and 10 A.M. on 17 October, a British drummer appeared on the parapet of the horn work. A redcoated officer then came out in front of the lines with a white handkerchief. The guns gradually fell silent. An American ran out, blindfolded the officer, and led him into the lines. The British officer bore a message from Cornwallis to Washington proposing surrender.

The British commander asked for a 24-hour truce to work out terms. Washington gave him two hours to submit

The Surrender of Yorktown. *The siege left Yorktown in a state of ruin. The surrendered forces remained two days before leaving under militia escort for camps in Maryland and Virginia. During this time, trenches were filled in to prevent their use by a returning enemy force.*
THE SURRENDER OF YORKTOWN, 19TH OCTOBER 1781 (OIL ON CANVAS) BY BLARENBERGHE, LOUIS NICOLAS VAN (1716–94)
CHATEAU DE VERSAILLES, FRANCE / GIRAUDON / BRIDGEMAN ART LIBRARY

his proposals. The latter were received about 4:30 P.M., and commissioners met the next morning (18 October) at the Moore House (home of Augustine Moore) to settle details. Dundas and Major Alexander Ross represented Cornwallis; Noailles and John Laurens represented the allies. Washington had stated that "The same Honors will be granted to the Surrendering Army as were granted to the –Garrison of Charles Town," but British appeals and objections resulted in a prolonged and heated session at the Moore House. Washington's representatives could show him only a rough draft by midnight, but the morning of 20 October he had written his comments on the draft, had the surrender document transcribed, and sent it to Cornwallis to be signed by 11 A.M. Cornwallis was also informed that Washington expected the garrison to march out at 2 P.M. to surrender. Between 11 A.M. and noon the document was back, bearing the signatures of Cornwallis and Captain Thomas Symonds, who was the senior British naval officer present. Washington, Rochambeau, and Barras signed for the allies.

Except for the article based on British precedent at Charleston, that "The troops shall march out, with colors cased, and drums beating a British or a German march,"

the surrender terms were honorable. Cornwallis and his principal officers could return to Europe on parole or go to an American port in British hands. The sloop *Bonetta* was put at the temporary disposal of Cornwallis "to receive an Aid de Camp to carry dispatches to Sir Henry Clinton; and such soldiers as he may think proper to send to New York." This last provision was a device for getting rid of American deserters to whom Washington could not grant prisoner-of-war status and with whose disciplining he did not wish to be burdened. The troop capacity of the *Bonetta* was 250, and most of those who reached New York on 2 November aboard her were deserters and Loyalists. Surrender terms permitted the British officers to retain their side arms and all personnel to keep their personal effects. The infantry of the Gloucester garrison grounded their arms there, but the John Graves Simcoe's and Tarleton's cavalry capitulated with their swords drawn and their trumpets sounding.

At noon two detachments of 100 men each—one French, one American—occupied two British redoubts southeast of Yorktown. The rest of the victorious army formed on both sides of the Hampton road, along which the vanquished would march to the surrender field, about a mile and a half south of Yorktown. At 2 P.M. the British troops came slowly down the road, allegedly to the tune of "The World Turned Upside Down," but contemporary accounts mention only "melancholy marches."

The man most intimately responsible for their predicament was not, however, at their head. Cornwallis was "sick," so General Charles O'Hara of the Guards acted as his deputy. An interesting scene of military etiquette resulted when O'Hara asked his French escort to point out Rochambeau and the Guardsman then raced ahead to present himself to this officer. With a devastating savoir faire, Rochambeau pointed across the road to Washington. The ruddy Irishman bowed and turned about to face Washington, with an apology for his "mistake." Seeing that Cornwallis would not appear, Washington directed O'Hara to his second in command, General Benjamin Lincoln. A persistent myth is that Lincoln received the surrender in compensation for his surrender at Charleston; However, it was a matter of military etiquette that Washington sent the British general to his American counterpart.

Between lines of finely dressed French troops and shabbily dressed American ones, the British and German regiments arrived one by one to present arms; ground their weapons, accoutrements, and cased colors; and return to Yorktown. Some of the prisoners threw their muskets onto the ground in an effort to damage them. There are no authentic details on the surrender of the colors.

NUMBERS AND LOSSES

Of the 16,600 allied ground forces in Yorktown and Gloucester, casualties did not exceed 400. Cornwallis had an initial strength of at least 9,750. A total of 8,087 soldiers and sailors surrendered. Surrendered troops would subsequently be marched to camps in Virginia, Maryland, and Pennsylvania.

Captured British property included 244 pieces of artillery, at least 2,857 small arms, 24 transports (many of which were small craft), 40 wagons and teams, 260 horses, a military chest of £2,116, and 24 regimental standards, plus ammunition and stores. Cornwallis had surrendered one fourth of the total British military strength in America. Prior to the surrender, the British scuttled most of their naval and cargo vessels.

SEQUEL

By mid-September, Henry Clinton had decided to send a relief expedition to Yorktown, but there were numerous delays even after the arrival of Admiral Robert Digby (who was to transport Clinton's troops) and the repair of damages inflicted by De Grasse off the Chesapeake Capes on 5 September. Clinton sighted the capes on 24 October but, as a French officer put it, "il était trop tard.

La Poule était mangée" ("Too late. The hen had been eaten"). Learning of the surrender, Clinton returned to New York without a fight. Even if he had arrived earlier, De Grasse's foresight in bringing his entire fleet from the West Indies virtually assured that Graves, Digby, and Hood would not have been able to fight their way through and land Clinton's troops at Yorktown.

Washington did his utmost to persuade De Grasse to remain long enough to support operations against the Southern ports. The admiral reluctantly refused, however. His refusal was the consequence of his agreement with the Spanish authorities as to when they might expect his return to the West Indies. On 5 November he sailed away, but he promised to return the following summer.

The siege left Yorktown in a state of ruin from which it never recovered. The surrendered forces remained two days before leaving under militia escort for camps in Maryland and Virginia, and during this time their officers were treated to a series of dinners. Trenches were filled in to prevent their use by a returning enemy force, and the allied army was dispersed. General Arthur St. Clair started south with 2,000 Pennsylvania, Maryland, and Delaware regulars, to reinforce General Nathanael Greene. Washington led the rest of the Americans back to their posts on the Hudson River. Rochambeau's troops remained in Virginia until spring, and on 23 June 1782 started their march back to Newport, Rhode Island.

Congress learned of the victory at Yorktown when Tench Tilghman reached Philadelphia at 3 A.M. on 22 October. As the news traveled north and south there were celebrations throughout the new nation. The fateful news arrived in London about noon on Sunday, 25 November. Frederick Lord North, then prime minister of Britain, who had retained his aplomb through previous disasters, is reported to have received this last intelligence with, "Oh God! It is all over!" The coordinated campaign strategy, the tactical victory of De Grasse's French naval forces over the British fleet, combined with the skillful prosecution of the siege, produced the most decisive military victory of the American war. Historian Jerome Greene concludes: "Contrasted with the British facility for ineptitude and mismanagement, the Allies exhibited a cohesion of purpose paralleled by an admirable ability to coordinate their maneuvers toward the desired objective." Although it would take two years more to conclude the Peace of Paris, after 19 October 1781 the independence of the United States of America was never in doubt.

SEE ALSO *Chesapeake Capes; Flying Sap; Gloucester, Virginia; O'Hara, Charles; World Turned Upside Down.*

BIBLIOGRAPHY

Bonsal, Stephen. *When the French Were Here.* Garden City, N.Y.: Doubleday, 1945.

Greene, Jerome A. *The Guns of Independence: The Siege of Yorktown, 1781.* New York: Savas Beatie, 2005.

Johnston, Henry P. *The Yorktown Campaign and the Surrender of Cornwallis, 1781,* New York: Harper & Brothers, 1881.

Pybus, Cassandra. "Jefferson's Faulty Math: The Question of Slave Defections in the American Revolution." *William and Mary Quarterly,* 62 (April 2005): 243–264.

Sands, John O. *Yorktown's Captive Fleet.* Charlottesville: University Press of Virginia, 1983.

Urwin, Gregory J. W. "Cornwallis and the Slaves of Virginia: New Look at the Yorktown Campaign." In *ACTA: International Commission of Military History, XXVIII Congress: Coming to the Americas.* Edited by John A. Lynn. Wheaton, Ill.: United States Commission on Military History and the Cantigny First Division Foundation, 2003.

David Curtis Skaggs

YORKTOWN CAMPAIGN.

May–October 1781. Patriot fortunes were at particularly low ebb during the winter and spring of 1781. Finances had finally collapsed completely. The British were firmly established in the far south, and Virginia's military operations had left that state ravaged by enemy raiders. Mutiny erupted in the unpaid, ill-fed, badly clothed, sickly, and seemingly forgotten Continental army. The alliance with the French, now in its third year, had been a big disappointment.

EUROPEAN PRELIMINARIES

General George Washington discouragingly wrote in his diary that May:

> In a word—instead of having everything in readiness to take the Field, we have nothing—and instead of having the prospect of a glorious offensive campaign before us, we have a bewildered, and gloomy defensive one—unless we should receive a powerful aid of Ships—Land Troops and Money from our generous allies & these, at present, are too contingent to build upon.

Troops, ships, and money from the French allies that was a key to victory, but there also had to be a decisive and coordinated point of attack. Where would that be?

To Paris went the Donatien-Marie-Joseph de Vimeur, vicomte de Rochambeau, son of the commander of 5,500 French troops at Newport, Rhode Island. With him went John Laurens, aide-de-camp to Washington and son of the former president of the Continental Congress (now imprisoned in the Tower of London), bearing a letter from the Marquis de Lafayette. All beseeched their European allies for monetary, military, and naval assistance.

As the collapse of the American resistance seemed imminent, the French and Spanish governments made significant efforts to support the colonial revolt and bolster their own strategic objectives in the New World. In the first months of 1781 they developed a series of strategic decisions that impacted upon the American quest for independence in a dramatic fashion. Paris and Madrid officials decided to concentrate their resources in the Caribbean, and French naval assistance was sent to North American in the autumn of 1781. The principal Franco-Spanish objective was Jamaica, but islands in the Lesser Antilles and the Floridas also invited their attention. From France sailed an armada, commanded by Admiral François-Joseph-Paul, comte de Grasse, bound for the West Indies. A sub-division, commanded by the Bailli de Suffren, headed for the Indian Ocean. The Spanish Council of the Indies dispatched Don Francisco Saavedra de Sangronis as commissioner regius to push a more activist policy among the sometime reluctant military and naval commanders headquartered in Havana. He was also charged to support Louisiana Governor Bernardo de Gálvez's plan to drive the British from West Florida.

For the British there was a sense of elation and desperation. On the one hand, the American revolt seemed about to implode in a burst of exhaustion, financial distress, and military failures. On the other, the British faced problems of strategic overreach, thinly dispersed forces, and uncooperative leadership. They concentrated their American army at New York, but had separate expeditionary forces in the Caribbean, the Floridias, the Carolinas, and Virginia. Should they lose naval superiority, any one of these forces might find itself entrapped by a superior Franco-American or Franco-Spanish combined operation. All sides concentrated their naval forces in the West Indies, where the lucrative sugar islands proved inviting targets of opportunity.

COMMAND CONFERENCES

The key to understanding the Yorktown campaign can be found in three critical allied commander conferences and a series of contradictory, confused, and contrary decisions by semi-independent British commanders that collectively led to the most daring, dramatic, and successful combined arms victory in the age of fighting sail. The first conference occurred in February 1781 when Saavedra met with Spanish army and navy commanders in Havana and secured a reluctant agreement to support Gálvez's expedition against Pensacola. Of particular importance here was the willingness of Commodore the chevalier de Monteil to employ his French naval squadron (temporarily in Havana) in support of this expedition. The agreement brought into being a degree of inter-allied cooperation not seen previously in the Caribbean.

The British surrender of Pensacola in May earned Gálvez a promotion to field marshal and his designation as commander of Spanish ground forces in the Caribbean. He then dispatched his long-time friend, Saavedra, to sail with Monteil to Saint-Domingue (now Santo Domingo, capital of the Dominican Republic) to coordinate operations with De Grasse, who was expected from France. The battle for Pensacola exposed the vulnerability of isolated British garrisons to combined operations that secured local naval control. The French and Spanish understood this, but British leadership ignored the lessons of West Florida and the near loss of Savannah in 1779. Meanwhile, the picture for the Americans suddenly brightened. First, in March, at Guilford Courthouse in North Carolina, Major General Nathanael Greene lost a battle to General Charles Lord Cornwallis. This nominal defeat, however, so depleted the British general's forces that he withdrew to Wilmington to resupply his troops. This withdrawal to the coast uncovered the Carolinas for possible reconquest by Greene's Continental and militia troops.

The second conference occurred in mid-May, when Commodore Jacques-Melchior-St. Laurent, comte de Barras arrived in Boston on the frigate *Concorde*. He did not bring with him the hoped-for second division of French troops to Newport, Rhode Island, but he provided Lieutenant General Jean-Baptiste-Donatien de Vimeur, Comte de Rochambeau a confidential letter indicating that De Grasse was to come to the North American coast during the Caribbean hurricane season. Although not yet authorized to give this last important piece of news to Washington, Rochambeau did propose that the two senior commanders meet to decide what might be done with the forces at hand. The American commander understood the criticality of naval superiority to military success, but had experienced disappointment after disappointment with the French Navy's inability to secure dominance at crucial points along the North American coast in previous years. The latest example came in March 1781, when Captain Charles-René-Dominique Gochet, the chevalier des Touches secured a tactical victory over a Royal navy squadron off the Virginia coast and then threw away the opportunity to isolate a British raiding party in the Chesapeake by returning to Rhode Island.

General Sir Henry Clinton was in and around New York City with about 10,500 rank and file troops, whereas Washington had 3,500 Continentals in the Hudson Highlands. The French fleet was bottled up at Newport with about 5,000 French troops. Lafayette was in Virginia with a sizable detachment of Continental troops, prepared to oppose the British raiding parties in that region, and Anthony Wayne was preparing to add his support with more regulars. Greene was doing what he could to contain the forces of Cornwallis in the Carolinas. What Cornwallis would do from his Wilmington base was unknown.

Enemy forces were also known to be coming up Lake Champlain from Canada, and an invasion of northern New York was a possibility.

Washington and Rochambeau conferred at Wethersfield, Connecticut, on 22 May 1781, with this strategic situation as the backdrop for their deliberations. They also shared the disappointing knowledge that Barras lacked the naval strength to join in amphibious operations unless he received huge reinforcements. Washington therefore proposed a joint Franco-American ground operation against New York City. The American commander believed New York was the decisive point of attack, and that it would be extremely hazardous to march 450 miles to the Chesapeake Bay in a hot summer under the possibility of securing French naval superiority (never before achieved) against a mere raiding party. Rochambeau objected strenuously, realizing that the British had spent five years fortifying the New York islands and possessed army and naval superiority and interior lines to thwart any attack. He also understood that it would be extremely difficult for the deep-draft, heavily armed French vessels to cross the bar at Sandy Hook and enter New York harbor.

Washington obstinately stuck to the idea of a New York campaign, and Rochambeau reluctantly agreed that the proposed plan was the best possible option, at least for the time being. However, Rochambeau asked what might be done later, if naval reinforcements from the West Indies happened to become available? It is important to note that Rochambeau was not authorized at this time inform Washington that De Grasse actually was under orders to effect such cooperation. It is therefore incorrect to say, as many writers have, that the "Wethersfield Plan" visualized the strategy of the Yorktown Campaign. Washington's restrained reply was that, with effective French naval support, the strategic possibilities would be almost unlimited. The two commanders decided at Wethersfield that De Grasse should be asked to come north as soon as possible, and that Rochambeau would move his army towards New York, where they would probe Clinton's position.

Back in Newport on May 28, Rochambeau wrote to De Grasse a critical letter that undercut much of what Washington desired. He painted a gloomy picture of the situation and urged the admiral to bring money, soldiers, and ships northward as soon as possible. While acknowledging that he and Washington had agreed in choosing New York as the primary target, he also noted that the "southwesterly winds and the state of distress in Virginia will probably make you prefer the Chesapeake Bay." Enclosed in this epistle was a copy of a letter from Anne César, chevalier de La Luzerne, then serving as French ambassador to the United States. The letter, addressed to Barras and Rochambeau, stated that it appeared "imperative to take into the Chesapeake all the naval forces of the king along with whatever land forces the generals judge suitable." This enclosure was critical to the operational decision that was made in the West Indies. Nearly important was a second letter, dated 6 June, in which Rochambeau reported that the funds necessary to pay and to supply the French army would dry up by mid-October unless De Grasse brought with him 1,200,000 livres in specie.

LORD CORNWALLIS'S FATAL DECISION

Meanwhile, in the south, Cornwallis devised an operational plan that made the Chesapeake option much more inviting to America and its allies than it had been when Washington and Rochambeau met in Wethersfield. When Clinton left Cornwallis to command British forces in the South after the capture of Charleston (12 May 1780), Clinton instructed his subordinate to make the security of South Carolina his primary concern. Clinton's over-all strategy for the prosecution of the war in America was, for the time being, defensive. He planned to hold the vital bases at New York, Charleston, and Savannah until the government furnished the reinforcements he considered necessary for further offensive operations. Although Sir Henry has never been called a military genius, his estimate of the situation was sound. He called for 10,000 more troops and the assurance of continued naval supremacy for operations in 1781. Most historians agree with the soundness of this assessment.

The zealous Cornwallis, however, had other ideas. The best way to defend South Carolina, he proposed, was to attack into North Carolina and destroy what little American armed strength was located there. Clinton had no objection, provided that Cornwallis remembered his primary mission. Since New York was too far away for Clinton to control the operations of Cornwallis, the latter was granted the authority to communicate directly with London. While Cornwallis was preparing for his move into North Carolina he learned that American General Horatio Gates was advancing against his forward bases. Ignoring the odds, Cornwallis took the offensive, and brilliantly defeated Gates at Camden on 16 August 1780. Some have said that this victory cost the British the war.

Cornwallis sent his aide-de-camp, Captain Alexander Ross, to carry the news of the victory at Camden to London. When he returned from England in December, Ross informed Cornwallis that he had the favor of Lord George Germain, the American Secretary. Dazzled by the Camden victory, Germain virtually gave Cornwallis free rein in the south. As a result, Cornwallis's attitude toward Clinton was no longer that of a subordinate to a superior. Germain thought he found in the relatively youthful Cornwallis a general who would implement what historian John W. Fortescue has called Germain's "insane schemes of conquest without garrisons and of invasions without communications" (*History*, III, p. 358).

Despite the British disasters at Kings Mountain (7 October 1780), and Cowpens (17 January 1781), and the failure of expected Loyalist support in North Carolina, Cornwallis followed Gates's successor, Major General Nathanael Greene to the Dan River. He ignored Clinton's instructions to make the security of South Carolina his primary concern, and refused to withdraw from an untenable position around Hillsboro, North Carolina. His Pyrrhic victory at Guilford Courthouse on 15 March 1781 forced him to withdraw, but instead of falling back to Camden, South Carolina, he moved to Wilmington, North Carolina. Furthermore, he so misrepresented the facts of the Guilford engagement that Clinton and the London authorities were led to believe he had gained control of North Carolina. By the time they knew the truth, Cornwallis was marching to Virginia and Greene was moving against the scattered British forces of the young Francis Lord Rawdon in South Carolina.

When Clinton received the incredible news that Cornwallis had abandoned the Carolinas and arrived at Petersburg, Virginia, he expressed his disapproval. However, he was presented with a *fait accompli*, and so he acquiesced in the Virginia move. Exasperated by Lord George Germain's meddling and by the government's support of Cornwallis's strategy in the Carolinas, which favored expansion over pacification, Clinton decided to resign "the instant I could with propriety." Consequently, Clinton gave his subordinate complete freedom of action, even though he wished Cornwallis was back in South Carolina. Fortescue says that Clinton "kept Cornwallis close at hand in order to resign the command to him, instead of sending him back, as he ought, to Carolina" (*History.*, III, p. 391).

The famed Hessian jäger commander, Johann Ewald, could not understand why Cornwallis would throw away hard won ground in the Carolinas for less acreage in Virginia. Shortly after allied commanders returned from Wethersfield to their camps to prepare for the coming campaign, they learned that Cornwallis had reached Virginia. This meant Lafayette was in a dangerous position, and that plans for the diversion against New York would have to be speeded up in the hope that Clinton might reduce his forces in Virginia to defend his main North American base. It also meant that the Chesapeake option contained a much more inviting target than existed at the time of the Wethersfield meeting.

ALARMING DEVELOPMENTS FOR THE ALLIES

The Americans and their allies were now faced with certain alarming developments. The most serious was that the Wethersfield plan had been compromised. On 3 June, Clinton received an intercepted copy of the plan. This was ironic, for the intercept persuaded Clinton of a Franco-American attack on New York to such an extent that Washington and Rochambeau were in Philadelphia before Clinton began to anticipate a possible switch to the Chesapeake strategy.

The next bad news came from Commodore Barras. He was under orders to withdraw from Newport to provide greater base security at Boston once Rochambeau's army left Rhode Island. If he did so, he could have undertaken a profitable raiding campaign in the Bay of Fundy and Gulf of St. Lawrence during the summer. In a delicate negotiation, however, Rochambeau persuaded Barras to stay in Newport under the protection of a few French troops and American militiamen. If he remained, operations could be more easily coordinated between Barras, Rochambeau, and De Grasse, and Barras would be more readily available to transport the siege artillery left in Newport to whatever location in which it might be needed. However, Washington also received news that British forces had pushed up Lake Champlain to Crown Point, and he had to resist the proposal that he detach regulars to meet a possible invasion of northern New York.

DECISIONS IN THE WEST INDIES

On 20 June the *Concorde* sailed out of Boston for the West Indies carrying messages from Barras, Rochambeau, and La Luzerne to Admiral De Grasse, along with several pilots who had knowledge of navigation in American waters. A few days later, Saavedra accompanied Monteil's squadron heading for Cap Français, Saint-Domingue (modern Cap Haitien, Haiti). Both awaited De Grasse—he arrived on 16 July. After reading the dispatches from the north, De Grasse decided that the Chesapeake Bay would be his destination. De Grasse then met with Saavedra on board *La Ville de Paris* in the third and most crucial allied conference of the year. After several days of discussions, they concluded a Franco-Spanish concord known as the De Grasse-Saavedra Agreement.

This document permitted a most critical element in the Chesapeake encirclement. Both men concluded that the onset of the hurricane season required them to postpone any invasion of Jamaica until early 1782. This understanding freed ground and naval forces for use in operations elsewhere. Although De Grasse desired Spanish ships to accompany him northward, Saavedra knew that the Spanish government could not endorse the direct support of the United States that such a move would constitute. Instead, they compromised. De Grasse would surprise everyone and take all his ships of the line to North America, whereas Saavedra promised to send four Spanish naval vessels from Havana to Cap Français to protect the French merchantmen anchored there. Later, in Havana, a very frustrated Saavedra would be unable to convince Admiral José de Solano to honor this commitment, but fortunately, the Spanish ships were not needed. Saavedra also agreed to release a French army force that had been stationed at

Saint-Domingue and allocated to Gálvez's command for the Jamaica invasion. These troops were made available to De Grasse for employment on the American coast. As a consequence, De Grasse would bring with him approximately 3,300 infantry, 100 artillerymen, 100 dragoons, 10 field pieces, and a few siege guns and mortars.

De Grasse and Saavedra then turned to a consideration of future operations. De Grasse promised that he would return to the West Indies in October. He further agreed that the French would allow Gálvez to command ground forces in attacks on the British Windward Islands, should the Spanish desire to make this a combined operation. (As it turned out this winter campaign was solely a French one.) It was understood that Gálvez would command the ground troops and De Grasse the naval vessels during the Jamaica campaign.

The single element remaining on the agenda concerned the money Rochambeau requested to support the proposed operations. Much to De Grasse's disgust, the French merchants and planters on Saint-Domingue refused to loan money to this purpose, and he was forced to go begging to Saavedra. The Spaniard agreed to seek funds in Havana. This decision forced De Grasse to make another choice. Instead of sailing east of the Bahama Islands toward the American coast, he would have to negotiate the shallow Bahama Channel between those islands and Cuba so that he could pick up any funds Saavedra might acquire. The Spaniard sailed ahead, and in Havana he secured overnight loans from local citizens amounting to 1.2 million livres. These funds were forwarded to De Grasse near Matanzas, on the northeast Cuban coast. This, too, was ironic. Forced to sail in the Bahama Channel, rather than directly into American coastal waters, De Grasse evaded any British sighting of his fleet. This permitted him to sail toward the Chesapeake without his opponent knowing the strength of his forces or his destination. Meanwhile, the *Concorde* sailed northward with news of De Grasse's intentions for the anxious Washington, Rochambeau, and Barras.

The British failed to understand the size of De Grasse's fleet and the risks the French admiral would take. This incomprehension contributed to the inadequate force deployment by Admiral Sir George Rodney, commander of the Royal navy fleet in the Caribbean. Rodney made three conventional assumptions about French naval behavior, based on past experience, and these assumptions proved totally wrong in this instance. His first error was in assuming that part of De Grasse's fleet would be diverted from military action to serve as escorts to convey homeward the merchantmen in port in the West Indies. His second mistake was to assume that some of De Grasse's fleet would remain in the West Indies, which led to his third erroneous assumption, that only about ten French ships of the line would make the trip to North America. Rodney made no

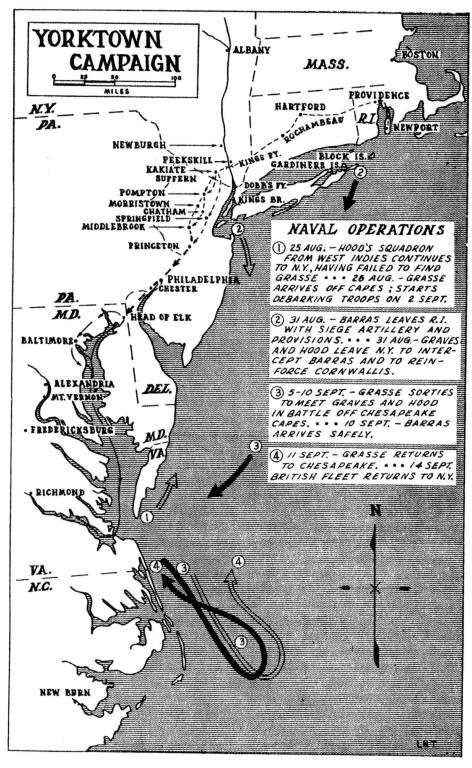

YORKTOWN CAMPAIGN

NAVAL OPERATIONS

① *25 AUG.* — HOOD'S SQUADRON FROM WEST INDIES CONTINUES TO N.Y., HAVING FAILED TO FIND GRASSE • • • *26 AUG.* - GRASSE ARRIVES OFF CAPES ; STARTS DEBARKING TROOPS ON 2 SEPT.

② *31 AUG.* - BARRAS LEAVES R.I. WITH SIEGE ARTILLERY AND PROVISIONS. • • • *31 AUG.* - GRAVES AND HOOD LEAVE N.Y. TO INTERCEPT BARRAS AND TO REINFORCE CORNWALLIS.

③ *5-10 SEPT.* - GRASSE SORTIES TO MEET GRAVES AND HOOD IN BATTLE OFF CHESAPEAKE CAPES. • • • *10 SEPT.* - BARRAS ARRIVES SAFELY.

④ *11 SEPT.* - GRASSE RETURNS TO CHESAPEAKE. • • • *14 SEPT.* BRITISH FLEET RETURNS TO N.Y.

THE GALE GROUP

effort to ascertain the accuracy of these conclusions. For instance, he did not order any of his frigates to shadow De Grasse's movements. Instead, the ailing Rodney took three ships of the line with him to convoy British merchantmen home and sent three more in a convoy to Jamaica. Two of these were to sail to New York, but they did not arrive in time. Finally, he sent Admiral Sir Samuel Hood with fourteen to join Admiral Thomas Graves in New York. In addition, he sent a dispatch to Graves directing him to meet Hood at the Chesapeake, but the French captured the ship carrying this message. Thus, De Grasse's audacity was rivaled by British complacency and misfortune.

De Grasse left Saint-Domingue on 5 August, and sailed slowly through the Bahama Channel with Spanish pilots. The twenty-eight French liners spent one day loading the 1,200,000 livres from Havana before proceeding northward. Hood and his fourteen ships left Antigua on 10 August. Because they sailed east of the Bahamas, they missed sighting De Grasse's fleet. Sir Samuel arrived at the Chesapeake Capes on 25 August, and found neither Admiral Graves, whom he expected, nor the French, whom he anticipated. He therefore continued north to New York where, on 28 August, he alerted Graves of the danger to Cornwallis. Royal naval forces numbered nineteen ships of the line, compared to De Grasse's twenty-eight. Neither British admiral realized that their French opponents overmatched them in fleet strength.

OPERATIONS AGAINST MANHATTAN

The junction of Rochambeau's forces with those of Washington did not take place until six weeks after plans were made at Wethersfield. The French infantry left Newport on 9 June and moved twenty-five miles north, to Providence. On 18 June the French troops started west. Washington, meanwhile, reorganized his own forces, and by 24 June he was camped near Peekskill, New York, awaiting Rochambeau's arrival. On the 28th, however, he conceived the ambitious plan of capturing the British posts on the north end of Manhattan Island so as to speed up subsequent operations against Clinton.

Major General Benjamin Lincoln was given 800 good troops for this surprise attack—400 light infantry under Colonel Alexander Scammell, the battalion of Lieutenant Colonel Ebenezer Sprout, and a detachment of artillery. They were to descend the Hudson River from Peekskill on the night of 2–3 July, capture the works around Kings Bridge, and raid Forts Tryon and Knyphausen (formerly Fort Washington). If this plan did not turn out to be feasible, Lincoln was to land above Spuyten Duyvil and support an attack by the duc de Lauzun's Legion, and the Connecticut militia against the Tory troops of Oliver De Lancey Jr., who were deployed around Morrisania, northeast of Kings Bridge. The complicated plan was coordinated with Rochambeau, who gave his full cooperation, Washington personally supervised most of the preparations, but everything went wrong.

Washington had advanced with the rest of his force to Valentine's Hill, four miles above Kings Bridge, to support Lincoln, and Rochambeau was asked to hurry toward the same point. After spending the day of the 3 July reconnoitering for further operations against Manhattan, Washington withdrew his entire force to Dobb's Ferry on 4 July, and the French joined him there on the 6th.

During the four days starting 21 July, 5,000 French and American troops pushed out to form a screen while Washington and Rochambeau, with an escort of 150 Continentals, thoroughly reconnoitered the northern defenses of Manhattan. This convinced them that an attack would require formal siege operations, which they lacked the means to undertake. Allied plans now hung on word from De Grasse. There was still no suspicion that the closing scene of the American Revolution would be enacted at a place called Yorktown, Virginia.

CONFUSION IN VIRGINIA

After failing in his efforts to trap Lafayette, Cornwallis reached Williamsburg, Virginia, on 25 June. There he received Clinton's letter of 11 June, which said: "I beg leave to recommend it to you, as soon as you have finished the active operations you may be now engaged in, to take a defensive station in any healthy situation you choose, be it at Williamsburg or Yorktown." Clinton also requested that a major portion of Cornwallis's force be sent to New York, to defend against the expected allied attack. Another letter, received this same day, was dated 15 June. This one added Portsmouth and Old Point Comfort, both in Virginia, to possible locations for Cornwallis's base. It also informed him of the possibility that De Grasse was moving his French fleet from the West Indies to attack New York.

The ever-eager Cornwallis, who thought operations in Virginia were so important that Clinton should abandon New York to provide the necessary strength to support them, now made the startling request that he be allowed to return to Charleston. He also decided that he could not hold a position on the peninsula after sending a detachment of troops to New York, and made plans to cross the James River to reach Portsmouth. He skillfully lured Lafayette into the action at Green Spring, 6 July, but failed to follow up on his advantage. If he had, he might well have crippled the American army to such an extent that he could maintain his position on the peninsula. Instead, he crossed the James and immediately (8 July) received instructions from Clinton to send 2,000 or 3,000 troops to Philadelphia, instead of New York. On the 12th he received another letter, this one changing the destination of the reinforcements back to New York. Finally, on 20 July, he was told to keep all his troops and establish a naval station on the tip of the peninsula at Old Point Comfort. This last directive reflected Admiral Graves's desire for an ice-free, winter anchorage at Hampton Roads.

This tangle of orders and counter-orders resulted from Clinton's efforts to direct Cornwallis with instructions that

Washington Before Yorktown *(1824), by Rembrandt Peale.*
Washington achieved an astounding strategic success at Yorktown. While luck figured prominently, the American commander showed skill of the highest order in planning and executing the campaign.
REMBRANDT PEALE, *WASHINGTON BEFORE YORKTOWN,* (AMERICAN, 1779–1860) OIL ON CANVAS, 137.5 X 120 IN. GIFT OF THE MOUNT VERNON LADIES ASSOCIATION, MOUNT VERNON, VIRGINIA. 44.1. CORCORAN GALLERY OF ART, WASHINGTON, D.C./CORBIS.

took eight days to arrive, while Germain was trying to direct both of them from across the Atlantic. All three agreed that major operations should be undertaken in the Chesapeake, but they disagreed on the timing. Clinton wanted to establish a post at the mouth of the Chesapeake that would immediately serve as a base for naval operations and later, when the necessary reinforcements were available, as a base for land operations in the Middle Colonies. Cornwallis wanted to move on the Middle Colonies operations immediately, even if it meant abandoning New York. Historian Fortescue suggests that Germain "desired to combine both designs after some incomprehensible fashion of his own," and accuses Germain of "ill-timed interference . . . in every respect fatal" (*History*, p. 391). According to Fortescue, noting that Clinton's demand for reinforcements from Cornwallis was almost immediately contradicted by a letter from Germain that prohibited the withdrawal of troops from the Chesapeake:

> This was nothing less than the rejection of the Commander-in-chief's scheme in favour of his subordinate's; yet by the irony of fate Clinton

had hardly received this order before Germaine [sic] repented of it, and wrote again, though of course too late, to approve of Clinton's original plan (*History*, p. 390, citing Germain to Clinton, 7 and 14 July 1781).

Historian John Tilly shares in this judgment, and concludes:

> The combination of Cornwallis's presence in Virginia, Graves's desire to winter at Hampton Roads, Germain's dispatch, and the rebel and French threat to New York forced Clinton to compromise. . . . The gist of Clinton's decision was simple: Cornwallis was to set up, somewhere in the vicinity of Hampton Roads, a 'post' suitable for the protection of a squadron of ships of the line (*British Navy*, 247).

Clinton's final order, which told Cornwallis to establish the base at Old Point Comfort (modern Fort Monroe, Virginia), also authorized Cornwallis to occupy Yorktown, if this would contribute to the security of his main position. However, Cornwallis's engineers advised him that the former site was unsuitable. They judged that the channel was too wide to be covered by shore batteries, there would be inadequate protection for shipping, and enemy vessels could closely approach the post and bombard it. Cornwallis therefore picked Yorktown for his main base, and established a supporting position across the York River at Gloucester Point. Although Clinton later insisted that this was a violation of his orders, he tacitly acquiesced in this arrangement. Cornwallis might have been better served had he returned across the James River and taken a position at Portsmouth, where fortifications had already been erected and from which he might have more easily escaped to the Carolinas. These considerations notwithstanding, by 22 August Cornwallis had moved his entire command into the two posts that they would eventually leave only as prisoners of war.

THE ALLIED CONCENTRATION BEGINS

On 14 August Washington and Rochambeau received the news that shaped the decisive operation of the war: De Grasse was sailing for the Chesapeake with 28 warships and more than 3,000 troops. He would remain available for combined operations until 15 October, and then he would return to the West Indies. Moreover, German reinforcements reached New York in early August, bringing Clinton's total strength to over 15,000 rank and file troops. This seemingly negated any chance of a successful assault on the now well-defended New York. Additionally, probes at Clinton's defenses proved their impregnability, at least by the forces currently at hand.

Washington's course of action was now obvious, but he remained obsessed with New York even though,

Washington and his Generals at Yorktown (c. 1784). *This painting by Charles Willson Peale depicts General Washington near Yorktown with a group of senior officers that includes the comte de Rochambeau, the Marquis de Lafayette, and Tench Tilghman.* PRIVATE COLLECTION, © CHRISTIE'S IMAGES/BRIDGEMAN ART LIBRARY

as early as 2 August, he had expressed growing support for the Chesapeake option. Washington believed Cornwallis would escape any trap in the Chesapeake region before the army could arrive. In addition, he had been disappointed too many times by the French navy to depend on it now. He also realized that most of his New England troops would not go so far southward.

Further complicating allied planning was the distinct possibility that the British navy would interfere with any operation in the Chesapeake. For instance, Commodore Barras could be spotted and attacked by the British fleet before reaching the Peninsula with the French siege artillery and the Americans' reserve of salted provisions from Newport. Natural disaster also loomed, in the form of a hurricane that might strike the French fleet either en route to the Chesapeake or after it arrived. Additional concerns revolved around the possibility that Clinton might attack the strung out Franco-American columns along the

Hudson, or that he might strike out against Philadelphia, or toward the fortress of West Point.

Finally, with a decisiveness that does credit to his reputation as a great captain, Washington abandoned his preference for New York and started planning the strategy dictated by De Grasse's Chesapeake decision. Rochambeau directed Barras to take the siege guns and supplies from Newport to the Chesapeake. Barras left Newport on 25 August, forcing British Admiral Graves to contend with two French fleets at sea whose size and destination he did not know. Washington directed General William Heath to remain on the Hudson with half the army, including most of its New Englanders, and charged him with three tasks. Heath was to cover the passage of the Virginia expedition across the river, feign a move towards Staten Island to confuse Clinton, and then withdraw to the Hudson Highlands. Washington called to duty thousands of militiamen from Pennsylvania to Connecticut should Clinton sortie from his

New York defenses. As a consequence Clinton remained behind his New York entrenchments and frittered away an opportunity to redeem some of the losses that the British had already sustained in the Carolinas. The importance of this rear guard of American troops to the whole plan is neglected in most of the historical literature on the campaign.

The Americans crossed the Hudson River by Kings Ferry to Stony Point on 20–21 August, and the French completed their crossing on the 25th. Clinton was puzzled by this movement, but not worried. He knew De Grasse was expected, but he had been assured that Rodney would send a superior force, and he was confident that the Royal navy would retain command of the Atlantic coastal waters. On the latter assumption, therefore, Clinton ruled out the possibility that Washington would march to Virginia. Far from concerned about the indications that the Americans were preparing to attack Staten Island—his spies duly reported the presence of boats with the American army—Clinton was planning an attack on Rhode Island. Fortescue assesses the situation in the following terms:

> It was not until the 2nd of September [when the allied army reached Philadelphia] that Clinton realized that Washington was actually on the march for Virginia, but still he felt little anxiety. He wrote to Cornwallis that Admiral Robert Digby's squadron was expected shortly, and that he himself would send reinforcements and make a diversion from New York, adding, in tragic ignorance of the true state of affairs, that as Graves had sailed Cornwallis need fear nothing (*History*, p. 393).

Admiral Digby's three ships did not arrive in time to accompany Admirals Graves and Hood to their fateful encounter with De Grasse in the battle of the Chesapeake Capes on 5 September. The French navy's tactical victory was a strategic triumph of enormous proportions that not only sealed Cornwallis's fate but also that of most of the British empire in North America.

THE ALLIED MARCH SOUTH

After crossing the Hudson, the allies followed three roughly parallel routes to Princeton, New Jersey. The American light infantry moved on the left, through Paramus, to simulate an attack in the direction of Staten Island, and the entire army halted in the vicinity of Chatham and Springfield (due west of New York City) during 28 August in order to heighten the deception and also to close up the columns. On the 29th the columns still marched as if heading for Sandy Hook to link up with the French fleet, but on the next day they abandoned the deception and openly headed for Princeton.

The leading elements of Washington's army reached Princeton on the 30th, and Washington rode ahead with Rochambeau to enter Philadelphia the same day. The

American troops passed through Philadelphia on 2 September and continued straight on to reach Head of Elk on 6 September. They found time, however, to let Congress know that, despite the lawmakers' problems of higher finance, they wanted a month's pay before they continued their patriotic steps southward, and they wanted it in hard money. Robert Morris had to raise the funds by borrowing from Rochambeau's war chest. French troops entered the American capital in two divisions on 3 and 4 September, dazzling the provincials with their brilliant uniforms, their bands, and their military precision.

After struggling with problems of transportation and hoping for news of the two French fleets, Washington had left Philadelphia on 5 September. At Chester, that afternoon, he received the joyful intelligence that De Grasse had reached the Chesapeake safely. Now all he had to worry about was whether Barras would get through with the siege guns and whether Lafayette and the troops brought by De Grasse would be able to keep Cornwallis from escaping up the Peninsula and into the Carolinas.

While their troops waited at Head of Elk, Baltimore, and Annapolis for transportation, Washington and Rochambeau rode ahead with their staffs. From 9 to 12 September they stopped at Mount Vernon, Washington's home, which he had not seen for six years. They reached the Peninsula on 14 September. Although Cornwallis had not tried to escape the Chesapeake region, the naval situation was still fraught with suspense. Washington had learned on 12 September that de Grasse's fleet had sailed away to meet a British fleet that was approaching the Chesapeake, and there was still no news about Barras. By the morning of the 15th, however, word came that De Grasse was back and that Barras had arrived safely. The noose encircled Cornwallis's neck, although the trap door had not yet been sprung.

CONCLUSION

With the Yorktown campaign, Washington achieved an astounding strategic success. While luck figured prominently, the American commander showed skill of the highest order in planning and executing this concentration of allied forces. The odds against all of this coming together successfully were astronomical, but they had been overcome.

Still, one must not laud the American general too much. As his biographer Joseph J. Ellis notes, Washington's "subsequent distortion of the historical record" (he indicated that he had advocated the Chesapeake idea in the fall of 1780) "was designed to make the Yorktown victory a possibility he saw early on, whereas his correspondence reveals that New York had dominated his mind's eye for so long that he only gave it up grudgingly and gradually" (p. 133). In allocating praise for the success of the Yorktown campaign, the strategic contributions of Rochambeau, De Grasse, Barras, and Saavedra should never be overlooked, nor should the exertions of thousands of French and American sailors and soldiers, who collectively turned paper plans into physical reality, be ignored. All these participants contributed to an outcome in which, according to Washington biographer James T. Flexner, "the curtain fell on the greatest defeat which the European aristocratic way of life had so far suffered" (p. 464).

SEE ALSO *Cornwallis, Charles; Clinton, Henry; Finances of the Revolution; French Alliance; Wethersfield Conference, Connecticut.*

BIBLIOGRAPHY

Breen, Kenneth. "A Reinforcement Reduced? Rodney's Flawed Appraisal of French Plans, West Indies, 1781." In *New Interpretations in Naval History: Selected Papers from the Ninth Naval History Symposium.* Edited by William R. Roberts and Jack Sweetman. Annapolis, Md.: Naval Institute Press, 1991.

———. "Sir George Rodney and St. Eustatius in the American War: A Commercial and Naval Distraction, 1775–1781." *Mariner's Mirror,* 84 (May 1998): 192–203.

Chávez, Thomas E. *Spain and the Independence of the United States.* Albuquerque: University of New Mexico Press, 2002.

Dull, Jonathan R. *The French Navy and American Independence.* Princeton, N.J.: Princeton University Press, 1975.

Ellis, Joseph J. *His Excellency George Washington.* New York: Knopf, 2004.

Flexner, James Thomas. *George Washington in the American Revolution.* Boston: Little, Brown, 1968.

Fortescue John W. *History of the British Army.* 14 vols. London: Macmillan, 1911–1935.

———. *The War of Independence.* London: Greenhill, 2001.

Freeman, Douglas Southall. *George Washington: A Biography.* 7 vols. New York: Scribner, 1948–1957.

Gottschalk, Louis. *Lafayette and the Close of the American Revolution.* Chicago: University of Chicago Press, 1942.

Johnston, Henry P. *The Yorktown Campaign and the Surrender of Cornwallis, 1781.* New York: Harper & Brothers, 1881.

Larrabee, Harold A. *Decision at the Chesapeake.* New York: Clarkson N. Potter, 1964.

Lewis, Charles Lee. *Admiralde Grasse and American Independence.* Annapolis, Md.: Naval Institute Press, 1945.

Lewis, James A. "Las Damas de la Havana, El Precursor, and Francisco de Saavedra: A Note on Spanish Participation in the Battle of Yorktown." *The Americas* 37 (July 1981): 83–99.

Mackesy, Piers. *War for America, 1775–1783.* Cambridge, Mass.: Harvard University Press, 1965.

Padron, Francisco Morales, ed. *Journal of Don Francisco Saavedra de Sangronis.* Gainesville: University of Florida Press, 1989.

Rice, Howard C., Jr., and Anne S. K. Brown, eds., *American Campaigns of Rochambeau's Army, 1780, 1781, 1782, 1783.* 2 vols. Princeton, N.J. and Providence, R.I.: Princeton University Press and Brown University Press, 1972.

Skaggs, David Curtis. "Decision at Cap Français: Franco-Spanish Coalition Planning and the Prelude to Yorktown." In *New Interpretations in Naval History: Selected Papers from the Thirteenth Naval History Symposium.* Edited by William M. McBride. Annapolis, Md.: Naval Institute Press, 1998.

Syrett, David. *Royal Navy in American Waters, 1775–1783.* Brookfield, Vt.: Gower Publishing, 1989.

Washington, George. *The Diaries of George Washington.* 4 vols. Edited by Donald Jackson. Charlottesville: University Press of Virginia, 1976–1979.

Whitridge, Arnold. *Rochambeau: Neglected Founding Father.* New York: Collier Books, 1965.

Wickwire, Franklin B., and Mary Wickwire. *Cornwallis: The American Adventure.* Boston: Houghton Mifflin, 1970.

Willcox, William B. "The British Road to Yorktown: A Study in Divided Command," *American Historical Review* 52 (October 1946): 1–35.

———. *Portrait of a General: Sir Henry Clinton in the War of Independence.* New York: Knopf, 1964.

David Curtis Skaggs

YOUNG'S HOUSE, NEW YORK.

(Four Corners). 3 February 1780. The "Neutral Ground" was the term used to describe the zone around New York City lying outside the permanent control of either side. Both the Americans and the British patrolled aggressively all year long, seeking opportunities to overpower small parties, inflict casualties, and damage enemy morale. The regions within the Neutral Ground became hunting grounds for elite units, and both sides sought to employ their best officers as commanders there. The heart of the zone lay in Westchester County, in the region between the Hudson River and Bedford and between White Plains and the Croton River. For the Americans, this sector fell under the supervision of the Highlands Department, which had its headquarters at West Point. In the winter of 1779–1780 Major General William Heath, the departmental head, placed Lieutenant Colonel Joseph Thompson (Tenth Massachusetts Regiment) on duty with a detachment of five Massachusetts companies— about 250 men.

Thompson violated a cardinal rule by remaining in one location for several days. Alerted by an active intelligence network, the British launched an expedition from Fort Knyphausen (previously Fort Washington) against him. Thompson learned of the enemy's advance but, perhaps deceived by the extreme winter weather, thought he had only to deal with a mounted patrol. In reality he was the target of Lieutenant Colonel Chaple Norton with 450 infantry and 100 mounted men. The core of the task force consisted of the two grenadier and two light companies of the Guards Brigade, augmented by detachments from two Hesse-Cassel infantry regiments, some mounted and dismounted jägers, and forty Loyalists from Colonel James De Lancey's Westchester Refugees (The Cowboys).

Norton's mounted vanguard overwhelmed a nine-man outpost and then opened a long-range fire on Thompson, who had three of his companies in position at the crossroad. Around 9 A.M. Norton's main body came up and the opposing forces spent fifteen minutes in a hot firefight. Some of the Americans broke and the rest withdrew, covered by a fourth company that came up. A few took refuge in the house of Joseph Young, which was captured and burned.

The Americans lost fourteen killed, fourteen wounded, and ninety-five captured, including Thompson. Norton admitted losing five killed and eighteen wounded.

BIBLIOGRAPHY

Heath, William. *Heath's Memoirs of the American War.* 1798. Reprint, Freeport, N.Y.: Books for Libraries Press, 1970.

Hufeland, Otto. *Westchester County during the American Revolution, 1775–1783.* New York: Knickerbocker Press, 1926.

revised by Robert K. Wright Jr.

ZANE, EBENEZER. (1747–1812). Pioneer.

Virginia. Born near modern Moorefield, West Virginia, he explored and surveyed lands in the Ohio country with his brothers Silas and Jonathan, claiming thousands of acres in the process. During Dunmore's War he was the disbursing agent of the Virginia militia, in which he held the rank of colonel, and in 1774 he supervised the construction of Fort Fincastle (later Fort Henry). During the Revolution he took part in the defense of Fort Henry in both 1777 and 1782. His brother Jonathan was present at Crawford's defeat in 1782, and his sister Elizabeth became a heroine of the Revolution. As a member of the Virginia ratifying convention of 1788, Zane supported the Constitution. In 1793 he laid out the town of Wheeling and began selling lots. In 1796 Ebenezer got permission from Congress to open a road from Wheeling to Limestone (Maysville), Kentucky, when southern Ohio was opened for settlement by the Treaty of Greenville. This became the famous "Zane's Trace," and Zanesville (originally Westbourne) was established on a section of land granted to Zane where his road crossed the Muskingum. Zane died in Wheeling on 19 November 1812.

SEE ALSO *Crawford's Defeat; Wayne, Anthony; Wheeling, West Virginia.*

revised by Michael Bellesiles

ZEISBERGER, DAVID. (1721–1808).

Moravian missionary. Born in Bohemia, he followed his parents to Georgia a year after they had established the first of the Moravian settlements there in 1736. In 1745 Zeisberger became a missionary among the Indians, earning the trust of the Iroquois and the enmity of many whites. Present as an interpreter for several treaty negotiations, he helped the Delawares build the town of Friedenshuetten in the Wyoming Valley in 1767 and aided in the establishment of the missionary communities of Schoenbrunn Gnadenhutten, Salem, and Lichtenau in Ohio between 1771 and 1774. Until 1782 Zeisberger secretly supplied information to the Patriots, talking his way out of a number of difficult encounters with pro-British Indians. But after the Gnadenhutten massacre, he ended his political involvement. He continued to live among Indians and established new settlements in Michigan, Ohio, and Canada, earning a reputation as one of the most successful and honest Christian missionaries in North America. In 1798, encouraged by Congress, Zeisberger returned to Ohio and established a mission at Goshen, where he died on 17 November 1808.

SEE ALSO *Gnadenhutten Massacre, Ohio; Moravian Settlements.*

revised by Michael Bellesiles

ZÉSPEDES Y VELASCO, VINCENTE MANUEL DE. (1720–1794). Spanish officer and

official. Born in Spain in 1720, Zéspedes entered the military in 1734, serving in several postings in North Africa, South America, and Cuba. Named captain of grenadiers, he was sent in 1761 to Pensacola, Florida, which he successfully defended against the Creeks, receiving a royal citation for his performance. In 1768 he was sent to New Orleans to put down French resistance to Spanish control. When Spain and England went to war in 1779, Zéspedes was promoted to colonel and placed in command of the Havana Regiment, serving as interim governor in 1782. With the end of the American Revolution, he was promoted to brigadier general and made governor of East Florida, overseeing the transfer of authority from Britain to Spain. Zéspedes's primary duty was to protect Spanish territory from the encroachment of the new United States. Toward this end, he entered into a number of mutually beneficial treaties with the Indian nations of the region and supplied the Creeks with arms and ammunition for their struggle against Georgia. He also established an extensive intelligence network through which he could keep the Spanish government aware of American expansionism. In 1790 he returned to Havana, where he died on 21 July 1794.

BIBLIOGRAPHY

Tanner, Helen Hornbeck. *Zéspedes in East Florida, 1784–1790.* Coral Gables, Fla.: University of Miami Press, 1963.

Michael Bellesiles

Appendices

Appendix I: Signers of the Declaration of Independence

	State	Birthdate	Birthplace	Age at Signing	Occupation	Death Date	Age at Death
Adams, John	MA	10/30/1735	Quincy, MA	40	Lawyer	7/4/1826	90
Adams, Samuel	MA	9/27/1722	Boston, MA	53	Politician	10/2/1803	81
Bartlett, Josiah	NH	11/21/1729	Amesbury, MA	46	Physician	5/19/1795	65
Braxton, Carter	VA	9/10/1736	Newington, VA	39	Planter Merchant, Planter	10/10/1797	61
Carroll, Charles (of Carrollton)	MD	9/19/1737	Annapolis, MD	38		11/14/1832	95
Chase, Samuel	MD	4/17/1741	Somerset Co., MD	35	Lawyer	6/19/1811	70
Clark, Abraham	NJ	2/15/1726	Elizabethtown, NJ	50	Surveyor	9/15/1794	68
Clymer, George	PA	3/16/1739	Philadelphia, PA	37	Merchant	1/24/1813	73
Ellery, William	RI	12/22/1727	Newport, RI	48	Lawyer, Merchant	2/15/1820	92
Floyd, William	NJ	12/17/1734	Brookhaven, NY	41	Land Speculator	8/4/1821	86
Franklin, Benjamin	PA	1/17/1706	Boston, MA	70	Printer, scientist	4/17/1790	84
Gerry, Elbridge	MA	7/17/1744	Marblehead, MA	32	Merchant	11/23/1814	70
Gwinnett, Button	GA	1735	Gloucester, England	41	Merchant, Planter	5/15/1777	42
Hall, Lyman	GA	4/12/1724	Wallingford, CT	52	Physician, Minister	10/19/1790	66
Hancock, John	MA	1/12/1737	Quincy, MA	40	Merchant	10/8/1793	56
Harrison, Benjamin	VA	4/7/1726	Charles City Co., VA	65	Planter	4/24/1791	65
Hart, John	NJ	1714	Hopewell, NJ	62	Landowner	5/11/1779	65
Hewes, Joseph	NY	1/23/1730	Kingston, NJ	46	Merchant	10/10/1779	49
Heyward, Thomas	SC	7/28/1746	St. Helena Parish, SC	30	Lawyer, Planter	3/6/1809	62
Hooper, William	NC	6/17/1742	Boston, MA	34	Lawyer	10/14/1790	48
Hopkins, Stephen	RI	3/7/1707	Providence, RI	69	Merchant	4/13/1785	78
Hopkinson, Francis	NJ	10/2/1737	Philadelphia, PA	38	Lawyer, Composer	5/9/1791	53
Huntington, Samuel	CT	7/3/1731	Windham, CT	45	Lawyer	1/5/1796	64
Jefferson, Thomas	VA	4/13/1743	Albemarle Co., VA	33	Lawyer, Planter	7/4/1826	83
Lee, Francis Lightfoot	VA	10/14/1734	Mt. Pleasant, VA	41	Planter	1/11/1797	62
Lee, Richard Henry	VA	1/20/1732	Stratford, VA	44	Planter	6/19/1794	62
Lewis, Francis	NY	3/21/1713	Llandaff, Wales	63	Merchant	12/30/1802	89
Livingston, Philip	NY	1/15/1716	Albany, NY	60	Merchant	6/12/1778	62
Lynch, Thomas, Jr.	SC	8/5/1749	Winyah, SC	26	Lawyer	1779	30
McKean, Thomas	DE	3/19/1735	Chester Co., PA	42	Lawyer	6/24/1817	83
Middleton, Arthur	SC	6/26/1742	Charleston, SC	34	Planter	1/1/1787	44
Morris, Lewis	NY	4/8/1726	Westchester Co., NY	50	Landowner	1/22/1798	71
Morris, Robert	PA	1/31/1734	Liverpool, England	42	Merchant	5/8/1806	72
Morton, John	PA	1725	Tinicum, PA	51	Farmer, Lawyer	4/1/1777	52
Nelson, Thomas, Jr.	VA	12/26/1738	Yorktown, VA	37	Merchant, Planter	1/4/1789	50
Paca, William	MD	10/31/1740	Abington, MD	35	Lawyer, Planter	10/13/1799	58
Paine, Robert Treat	MA	3/11/1731	Boston, MA	45	Lawyer	5/12/1814	83
Penn, John	NC	5/6/1740	Carolina Co., VA	36	Lawyer	9/14/1788	48
Read, George	DE	9/18/1733	Cecil Co., MD	42	Lawyer	9/21/1798	65
Rodney, Caesar	DE	10/7/1728	Dover, DE	47	Landowner	6/29/1784	55
Ross, George	PA	5/10/1730	New Castle, DE	46	Lawyer	7/14/1779	49
Rush, Benjamin	PA	1/4/1746	Philadelphia, PA	30	Physician	4/19/1813	67
Rutledge, Edward	SC	11/23/1749	Christ Church Parish, SC	26	Lawyer, Planter	1/23/1800	50
Sherman, Roger	CT	4/19/1721	Newton, MA	55	Surveyor, Merchant	7/23/1793	72
Smith, James	PA	9/17/1719	Ireland	57	Lawyer	7/11/1806	87
Stockton, Richard	NJ	10/1/1730	Princeton, NJ	45	Lawyer	2/28/1781	50
Stone, Thomas	MD	1743	Durham Parish, MD	33	Lawyer	10/5/1787	44
Taylor, George	PA	1716?	Ireland	60	Ironmaster	2/23/1781	65
Thornton, Matthew	NH	1714?	Ireland	62	Physician	6/24/1803	89
Walton, George	GA	1749?	Cumberland Co., VA?	27	Lawyer	2/2/1804	55
Whipple, William	NH	1/14/1730	Kittery, ME	46	Merchant	11/28/1785	55
Williams, William	CT	3/18/1731	Lebanon, CT	45	Merchant	8/2/1811	80
Wilson, James	PA	9/14/1742	Carskerdo, Scotland	33	Lawyer	8/21/1798	55
Witherspoon, John	NJ	2/5/1723	Gifford, Scotland	53	Minister	11/15/1794	71
Wolcott, Oliver	CT	11/20/1726	Windsor, CT	49	Lawyer	12/1/1797	71
Wythe, George	VA	1726?	Elizabeth City Co., VA	50	Lawyer	6/8/1806	80

Appendix II: Delegates to the Continental Congress

Member	Years served
CONNECTICUT	
Andrew Adams	1778–1782
Josiah P. Cooke	1784–1785, 1787–1788
Silas Deane	1774–1776
Eliphalet Dyer	1774–1779, 1782–1783
Pierrepont Edwards	1788
Oliver Ellsworth	1778–1783
Titus Hosmer	1778
Benjamin Huntington	1780, 1782–1783, 1788
Samuel Huntington	1776, 1778–1781, 1783
William S. Johnson	1785–1787
Richard Law	1781–1782
Stephen M. Mitchell	1785–1788
Jesse Root	1778–1782
Roger Sherman	1774–1782, 1784
Joseph Spencer	1779
Jonathan Sturges	1786
James Wadsworth	1784
Jeremiah Wadsworth	1788
William Williams	1776–1777
Oliver Wolcott	1776–1778, 1781–1783

Elected from Connecticut but did not serve: Joseph Trumbull, Erastus Wolcott, Jedediah Strong, John Treadwell, William Pitkin, William Hillhouse, John Canfield, Charles Church Chandler, John Chester.

Member	Years served
DELAWARE	
Gunning Bedford, Jr.	1783–1785
John Dickinson	1779
Philemon Dickinson	1782–1783
Dyre Kearny	1787–1788
Eleazer McComb	1783–1784
Thomas McKean	1774–1776, 1778–1782
Nathaniel Mitchell	1787–1788
John Patten	1786
William Peery	1786
George Read	1774–1777
Caesar Rodney	1774–1776
Thomas Rodney	1781–1782, 1786
James Tilton	1783–1784
Nicholas Van Dyke	1777–1781
John Vining	1784–1785
Samuel Wharton	1782–1783

Elected from Delaware but did not serve: John Evans, James Sykes, Henry Latimer, John McKinly, Samuel Patterson, Isaac Grantham.

Member	Years served
GEORGIA	
Abraham Baldwin	1785, 1787–1788
Nathan Brownson	1777
Archibald Bulloch	1775
William Few	1780–1782, 1786–1787
William Gibbons	1784
Button Gwinnett	1776
John Habersham	1785
Lyman Hall	1775–1777
John Houstoun	1775
William Houstoun	1784–1786
Richard Howley	1781
Noble Wymberly Jones	1781–1782
Edward Langworthy	1777–1779
William Pierce	1787
Edward Telfair	1778, 1780–1782
George Walton	1776–1777, 1780–1781
John Walton	1777
Joseph Wood	1777–1778
John J. Zubly	1775

Elected from Georgia but did not serve: Joseph Clay, Benjamin Andrew, Samuel Stirk, Lachlan McIntosh.

Member	Years served
MARYLAND	
Robert Alexander	1776
William Carmichael	1778–1779
Charles Carroll of Carrollton	1776–1778
Daniel Carroll	1781–1783
Jeremiah T. Chase	1783–1784
Samuel Chase	1774–1778
Benjamin Contee	1788
James Forbes	1778–1780
Uriah Forrest	1787
Robert Goldsborough	1774–1776
John Hall	1775
John Hanson	1780–1782
William Harrison	1786
William Hemsley	1782–1783
John Henry	1778–1780, 1785–1786
William Hindman	1785–1786
John E. Howard	1788
Daniel of St. Thomas Jenifer	1779–1781
Thomas Johnson	1774–1776
Thomas Sim Lee	1783
Edward Lloyd	1783–1784
James McHenry	1783–1785
Luther Martin	1785
William Paca	1774–1779
George Plater	1778–1780
Richard Potts	1781
Nathaniel Ramsey	1786–1787
John Rogers	1775–1776
David Ross	1787–1789
Benjamin Rumsey	1777
Joshua Seney	1788
William Smith	1777
Thomas Stone	1775–1778, 1784
Matthew Tilghman	1774–1776
Turbutt Wright	1782

Elected but did not serve: Richard Ridgely, Gustavus Scott, Edward Giles

Member	Years served
MASSACHUSETTS	
John Adams	1774–1778
Samuel Adams	1774–1782
Thomas Cushing	1774–1776
Francis Dana	1777–1778, 1783–1784
Nathan Dane	1785–1788
Elbridge Gerry	1776–1780, 1783–1785
Nathaniel Gorham	1783, 1786–1788
John Hancock	1775–1778
Stephen Higginson	1783
Samuel Holten	1778–1780, 1783–1785, 1787
Jonathan Jackson	1781–1782
Rufus King	1784–1787
James Lovell	1777–1782
John Lowell	1782
Samuel Osgood	1781–1784
Samuel A. Otis	1787–1789
Robert Treat Paine	1774–1776
George Partridge	1779–1782, 1787
Theodore Sedgwick	1785–1786, 1788
George Thatcher	1788–1789
Artemas Ward	1781

Elected from Massachusetts but did not serve: James Sullivan, James Bowdoin, Timothy Edwards, Caleb Strong, Timothy Danielson, Tristram Dalton.

Member	Years served
NEW HAMPSHIRE	
Josiah Bartlett	1775–1778
Jonathan Blanchard	1783–1784
Nathaniel Folsom	1774, 1777–1780

Member	Years served
NEW HAMPSHIRE [CONTINUED]	
Abiel Foster	1783–1785
George Frost	1777–1779
John Taylor Gilman	1782–1783
Nicholas Gilman	1787–1789
John Langdon	1775–1776, 1786–1787
Woodbury Langdon	1779–1780
Samuel Livermore	1780–1783, 1785–1786
Pierse Long	1784–1786
Nathaniel Peabody	1779–1780
John Sullivan	1774–1775, 1780–1781
Matthew Thornton	1776–1777
John Wentworth, Jr.	1777
William Whipple	1776–1779
Phillips White	1782–1783
Paine Wingate	1788–1789

Elected from New Hampshire but did not serve: Ebenezer Thompson, Timothy Walker, Jr., Joshua Wentworth, George Adkinson, Benjamin Bellows, Moses Dow, Elisha Payne.

Member	Years served
NEW JERSEY	
John Beatty	1783–1785
Elias Boudinot	1778,1781–1783
William Burnet	1780–1781
Lambert Cadwalader	1784–1787
Abraham Clark	1776–1778, 1780–1783, 1786–1788
Silas Condict	1781–1783
Stephen Crane	1774–1776
Jonathan Dayton	1787–1788
John De Hart	1774–1776
Samuel Dick	1783–1785
Jonathan Elmer	1777–1778, 1781–1783, 1787–1788
John Fell	1777–1780
Frederick Frelinghuysen	1779, 1783
John Hart	1776
Francis Hopkinson	1776
Josiah Hornblower	1785–1786
William C. Houston	1779–1781, 1784–1785
James Kinsey	1774–1775
William Livingston	1774–1776
James Schureman	1786–1787
Nathaniel Scudder	1778–1779, 1781
Jonathan D. Sergeant	1776–1777
Richard Smith	1774–1776
John Stevens	1784
Charles Stewart	1784–1785
Richard Stockton	1776
John C. Symmes	1785–1786
John Witherspoon	1776–1782

Elected from New Jersey but did not serve: John Cooper, John Neilson, William Paterson.

Member	Years served
NEW YORK	
John Alsop	1774–1776
Egbert Benson	1784, 1787–1788
Simon Boerum	1774–1775
George Clinton	1775–1776
Charles De Witt	1784
James Duane	1774–1779, 1781–1783
William Duer	1777–1778
William Floyd	1774–1776, 1779–1783
Leonard Gansevoort	1788
David Gelston	1789
Alexander Hamilton	1782–1783, 1788
John Haring	1774, 1785–1787
John Jay	1774–1779, 1784

Member	Years served
NEW YORK [CONTINUED]	
John Lansing, Jr.	1785
John Lawrance	1785–1787
Francis Lewis	1775–1779, 1781–1783
Ezra L'Hommedieu	1779–1783, 1788
Philip Livingston	1775–1778
Robert R. Livingston	1775–1776, 1779–1781, 1785
Walter Livingston	1784–1785
Isaac Low	1774
Gouverneur Morris	1778–1779
Lewis Morris	1775–1777
Alexander McDougall	1781
Ephraim Paine	1784
Philip Pell	1789
Zephaniah Platt	1785–1786
Philip Schuyler	1775, 1777, 1779–1780
John Morin Scott	1780–1782
Melancton Smith	1785–1787
Henry Wisner	1775–1776
Abraham Yates	1787–1788
Peter W. Yates	1786

Elected from New York but did not serve: none.

Member	Years served
NORTH CAROLINA	
John B. Ashe	1787
Timothy Bloodworth	1786
William Blount	1783, 1786–1787
Thomas Burke	1777–1781
Robert Burton	1787
Richard Caswell	1774–1775
William Cumming	1785
Cornelius Harnett	1777–1779
Benjamin Hawkins	1782–1783, 1787
Joseph Hewes	1774–1777, 1779
Whitmill Hill	1778–1780
William Hooper	1774–1777
Samuel Johnston	1780–1782
Allen Jones	1779–1780
Willie Jones	1780–1781
Abner Nash	1782–1783
John Penn	1775–1780
William Sharpe	1779–1781
John Sitgreaves	1784–1785
Richard D. Spaight	1783–1785
John Swann	1787–1788
James White	1786–1788
John Williams	1777–1779
Hugh Williamson	1782–1785, 1787–1788

Elected from North Carolina but did not serve: Ephraim Brevard, Adlai Osborn, Thomas Person, Charles Johnson, Joseph McDowell, Nathaniel Macon, Alexander Martin, Thomas Polk, Benjamin Smith, John Stokes.

Member	Years served
PENNSYLVANIA	
Andrew Allen	1775–1776
John Armstrong	1779–1780, 1787–1788
Samuel J. Atlee	1778–1782
John B. Bayard	1785–1786
Edward Biddle	1775
William Bingham	1786–1788
William Clingan	1777–1779
George Clymer	1776–1778, 1780
Tench Coxe	1788–1789
John Dickinson	1774–1776
Thomas FitzSimons	1782–1783
Benjamin Franklin	1775–1776
Joseph Galloway	1774
Joseph Gardner	1784–1785

Member	Years served
PENNSYLVANIA [CONTINUED]	
Edward Hand	1784–1785
William Henry	1784–1785
Charles Humphreys	1774–1776
Jared Ingersoll	1780
William Irvine	1787–1788
David Jackson	1785
James McClene	1779–1780
Timothy Matlack	1781
Samuel Meredith	1786–1788
Thomas Mifflin	1774–1775, 1783–1784
John Montgomery	1782–1784
Joseph Montgomery	1781–1782
Cadwalader Morris	1783–1784
Robert Morris	1776–1778
John Morton	1774–1776
Frederick Muhlenberg	1778–1780
Richard Peters	1782–1783
Charles Pettit	1785–1787
Joseph Reed	1778
James R. Reid	1787–1789
Samuel Rhoads	1774
Daniel Roberdeau	1777–1779
George Ross	1774–1777
Benjamin Rush	1776–1777
Arthur St. Clair	1786–1787
James Searle	1778–1780
William Shippen	1779–1780
James Smith	1776–1778
Jonathan B. Smith	1777–1778
Thomas Smith	1781–1782
George Taylor	1776
Thomas Willing	1775–1776
James Wilson	1775–1777, 1783, 1785–1787
Henry Wynkoop	1779–1782

Elected from Pennsylania but did not serve: Matthew Clarkson, William Montgomery.

Member	Years served
RHODE ISLAND	
Jonathan Arnold	1782–1784
Peleg Arnold	1787–1789
John Collins	1778–1783
Ezekiel Cornell	1780–1782
William Ellery	1776–1785
John Gardiner	1788–1789
Jonathan J. Hazard	1788
Stephen Hopkins	1774–1777
David Howell	1782–1785
James Manning	1785–1786
Henry Marchant	1777–1779
Nathan Miller	1785–1786
Daniel Mowry, Jr.	1781
James M. Varnum	1781, 1787
Samuel Ward	1774–1776

Elected from Rode Island but did not serve: none.

Member	Years served
SOUTH CAROLINA	
Robert Barnwell	1788–1789
Thomas Bee	1780–1782
Richard Beresford	1783–1784
John Bull	1784–1787
Pierce Butler	1787–1788
William H. Drayton	1778–1779
Nicholas Eveleigh	1781–1782
Christopher Gadsden	1774–1776
John L. Gervais	1782–1783
Thomas Heyward, Jr.	1776–1778

Member	Years served
SOUTH CAROLINA [CONTINUED]	
Daniel Huger	1786–1788
Richard Hutson	1778–1779
Ralph Izard	1782–1783
John Kean	1785–1787
Francis Kinloch	1780
Henry Laurens	1777–1780
Thomas Lynch, Sr.	1774–1776
Thomas Lynch, Jr.	1776
John Mathews	1778–1782
Arthur Middleton	1776–1777, 1781–1782
Henry Middleton	1774–1776
Isaac Motte	1780–1782
John Parker	1786–1788
Charles Pinckney	1784–1787
David Ramsay	1782–1783, 1785–1786
Jacob Read	1783–1785
Edward Rutledge	1774–1776
John Rutledge	1774–1775, 1782–1783
Thomas T. Tucker	1787–1788

Elected from South Carolina but did not serve: Paul Trapier, Rawlins Lowndes, Alexander Gillon, William Moultrie, Thomas Sumter.

Member	Years served
VIRGINIA	
Thomas Adams	1778–1779
John Banister	1778
Richard Bland	1774–1775
Theodorick Bland	1781–1783
Carter Braxton	1776
John Brown	1787–1788
Edward Carrington	1785–1787
John Dawson	1788
William Fitzhugh	1779
William Fleming	1779–1780
William Grayson	1785–1787
Cyrus Griffin	1778–1780, 1787–1788
Samuel Hardy	1783–1785
Benjamin Harrison	1774–1777
John Harvie	1777–1779
James Henry	1780–1781
Patrick Henry	1774–1775
Thomas Jefferson	1775–1776, 1783–1784
Joseph Jones	1780–1783
Arthur Lee	1782–1784
Francis Lightfoot Lee	1775–1779
Henry Lee	1786–1788
Richard Henry Lee	1774–1780, 1784–1787
James Madison	1780–1783, 1787–1788
James Mercer	1779–1780
John F. Mercer	1783–1784
James Monroe	1783–1786
Thomas Nelson, Jr.	1775–1777, 1779
Mann Page	1777
Edmund Pendleton	1774–1775
Edmund Randolph	1779, 1781–1782
Peyton Randolph	1774–1775
Meriwether Smith	1778–1781
John Walker	1780
George Washington	1774–1775
George Wythe	1775–1776

Elected from Virginia but did not serve: Gabriel Jones, John Blair.

Appendix III: Members of the British Cabinet

	Period of service
First Lord off the Treasury (Prime Minister)	
Thomas Holles, Duke of Newcastle	June 1757–May 1762
John Stuart, Earl of Bute	May 1762–April 1763
George Grenville	April 1763–July 1765
Charles Wentworth, Marquis of Rockingham	July 1765–July 1766; March–July 1782
William Pitt, Earl of Chatham	August 1766–October 1768
Augustus FitzRoy, Duke of Grafton	October 1768–January 1770
Frederick, Lord North	February 1770–March 1782
William Petty, Earl of Shelburne	July 1782–March 1783
William Bentinck, Duke of Portland	April–December 1783
Lord President of the Council	
John Carteret, Earl Granville	1751–January 1763
John Russell, Duke of Bedford	September 1763–July 1765
Daniel Finch, Earl of Winchilsea and Nottingham	July 1765–July 1766
Robert Henley, Earl of Northington	July 1766–December 1767
Granville, Lord Gower	December 1767–November 1779
Henry, Earl Bathurst	November 1779–March 1782
Charles Pratt, Lord Camden	March 1782–March 1783
David Murray, Viscount Stormont	April–December 1783
Secretary of State for the Northern Department	
Robert D'Arcy, Earl of Holderness	1754–March 1761
John Stuart, Earl of Bute	March 1761–May 1762
George Grenville	May–October 1762
George Dunk, Earl of Halifax	October 1762–September 1763; January–June 1771
John Montagu, Earl of Sandwich	September 1763–July 1765
Augustus FitzRoy, Duke of Grafton	July–May 1765
General Henry S. Conway	May 1766–January 1768
Thomas Thynne, Viscount Weymouth	January–October 1768
William van Zuylestein, Earl of Rochford	October 1768–December 1770
Henry Howard, Earl of Suffolk	June 1771–March 1779
David Murray, Viscount Stormont	October 1779–March 1782
Secretary of State for the Southern Department	
William Pitt, Earl of Chatham	1757–October 1761
Charles Wyndham, Earl of Egremont	October 1761–August
George Dunk, Earl of Halifax	September 1763–July 1765
General Henry S. Conway	July 1765–May 1766
Charles Lennox, Duke of Richmond	May–July 1766
William Petty, Earl of Shelburne	August 1766–October 1768
Thomas Thynne, Viscount Weymouth	October 1768–December 1770; November 1775–November 1779
William van Zuylestein, Earl of Rochford	December 1770–October 1775
Wills Hill, Earl of Hillsborough	November 1779–March 1782
Secretary of State for the American Colonies	
Wills Hill, Earl of Hillsborough	January 1768–August 1772
William Legge, Earl of Dartmouth	August 1772–Novermber 1775
George Germain, Viscount Sackville	November 1775–February 1782
Welbore Ellis	February–March 1782
Secretary of State for Home and Colonial Affairs	
William Petty, Earl of Shelburne	March–July 1782
Thomas Townshend, Baron Sydney	July 1782–April 1783
Frederick, Lord North	April–December 1783
"Secretary of State for Foreign Affairs"	
Charles James Fox	March–July 1782; April–December 1783
Thomas Robinson, Baron Grantham	July 1782–April 1783

	Period of service
Lord Chancellor	
Robert Henley, Earl of Northington	1757–July 1766
Charles Pratt, Lord Camden	July 1766–January 1770
Charles Yorke	January 1770
Henry, Earl Bathurst	January 1771–April 1778
Edward, Lord Thurlow	June 1778–1792
Chancellor of the Exchequer	
Henry B. Leffe	1757–March 1761
William, Viscount Barrington	March 1761–May 1762
Francis Dashwood, Baron Le Despencer	May 1762–April 1763
George Grenville	April 1763–July 1765
William Dowdeswell	July 1765–July 1766
Charles Townshend	July 1766–September 1767
William Murray, Earl of Mansfield	September–October 1767
Frederick, Lord North	October 1767–March 1782
Lord John Cavendish	April–July 1782; April–December 1783
William Pitt	July 1782–April 1783
First Lord of the Admiralty	
George, Baron Anson	March 1761–June 1762
George Dunk, Earl of Halifax	June 1762–January 1763
George Grenville	January–April 1763
John Montagu, Earl of Sandwich	April–September 1763; January 1771–March 1782
John Perceval, Earl of Egmont	September 1763–September 1766
Sir Charles Saunders	September–December 1766
Sir Edward Hawke	December 1766–January 1771
Augustus, Viscount Keppel	March–December 1782; April–December 1783
Richard, Earl Howe	January–April 1783
Commander in Chief	
John, Earl of Ligonier	1759–August 1766
John Manners, Marquess of Granby	August 1766–January 1770
Jeffrey, Baron Amherst	January 1778–March 1782
General Henry S. Conway	March 1782–December 1783
Master General of the Ordnance	
John, Earl of Ligonier	1759–1763
John Manners, Marquess of Granby	July 1763–January 1770
George, Marquess Townshend	1772–March 1782
Charles Lennox, Duke of Richmond	March 1782–1795
Secretary at War	
William, Viscount Barrington	1755–March 1761; July 1765–December 1778
Charles Townshend	March 1761–December 1762
Welbore Ellis	January 1763–July 1765
Charles Jenkinson	December 1778–March 1782
Thomas Townshend, Viscount Sydney	March–July 1782
Sir George Yonge	July 1782–April 1783
Richard Fitzpatrick	April–December 1783
President of the Board of Trade	
George Dunk, Earl of Halifax	October 1757–March 1761
Samuel, Baron Sandys	March 1761–March 1763
Charles Townshend	March–April 1763
William Petty, Earl of Shelburne	April–September 1763
Wills Hill, Earl of Hillsborough	September 1763–July 1765; August–December 1766; January 1768–August 1772
William Legge, Earl of Dartmouth	July 1765–August 1766; August 1772–November 1775
Robert C. Nugent, Viscount Clare	December 1766–January 1768
George Germain, Viscount Sackville	November 1775–November 1779
Frederick Howard, Earl of Carlisle	November 1779–September 1780
Thomas Robinson, Baron Grantham	December 1780–June 1782

Appendix IV: Continental Army, General Offices

		Appointed		End of Service	
General in Chief					
Washington, George	Virginia	15–Jun–75		23–Dec–83	resign
Major Generals					
1. Ward, Artemas	Massachusetts	17–Jun 75		23–Apr 76	resign
2. Lee, Charles	Virginia	17–Jun 75		10–Jan 80	resign
3. Schuyler, Philip John	New York	19–Jun 75		19–Apr 79	resign
4. Putnam, Israel	Connecticut	19–Jun 75		3 Jun 83	resign
5. Montgomery, Richard	New York	9 Dec 75	from 3 bg	31–Dec 75	killed
6. Thomas, John	Massachusetts	6 Mar 76	from 2 bg	2 Jun 76	died
7. Gates, Horatio	Virginia	16–May 76	from 1 bg	3 Nov 83	resign
8. Heath, William	Massachusetts	9 Aug 76	from 5 bg	3 Nov 83	resign
9. Spencer, Joseph	Connecticut	9 Aug 76	from 6 bg	13–Jan 78	resign
10. Sullivan, John	New Hampshire	9 Aug 76	from 7 bg	30–Nov 79	resign
11. Greene, Nathanael	Rhode Island	9 Aug 76	from 8 bg	3 Nov 83	resign
12. Arnold, Benedict	Connecticut	17–Feb 77	from 10 bg	25–Sep 80	traitor
13. Alexander, William (Lord Stirling)	New York	19–Feb 77	from 15 bg	15–Jan 83	resign
14. Mifflin, Thomas	Pennsylvania	19–Feb 77	from 18 bg	25–Feb 79	resign
15. St. Clair, Arthur	Pennsylvania	19–Feb 77	from 22 bg	3 Nov 83	resign
16. Stephen, Adam	Virginia	19–Feb 77	from 26 bg	20–Nov 77	resign
17. Lincoln, Benjamin	Massachusetts	19–Feb 77		29–Oct 83	resign
18. Lafayette, Marquis De	France	31–Jul 77		3 Nov 83	resign
19. Tronson de Coudray, Philippe	France	11–Aug 77		15–Sep 77	drowned
20. De Kalb, Johann	France	15–Sep 77		19–Aug 80	killed
21. Howe, Robert	North Carolina	20–Oct 77	from 16 bg	3 Nov 83	resign
22. McDougall, Alexander	New York	20–Oct 77	from 23 bg	3 Nov 83	resign
23. Conway, Thomas	France	13–Dec 77	from 50 bg	28–Apr 78	resign
24. Steuben, Friedrich	Germany	5 May 78		15–Apr 84	resign
25. Smallwood, William	Maryland	15–Sep 80	from 31 bg	3 Nov 83	resign
26. Parsons, Samuel Holden	Connecticut	23–Oct 80	from 24 bg	22–Jul 82	resign
27. Knox, Henry	Massachusetts	15–Nov 81	from 34 bg	20–Jun 84	resign
28. LeBegue DePresle Duportail, Louis	France	16–Nov 81	from 53 bg	10–Oct 83	resign
29. Moultrie, William	South Carolina	15–Oct 82	from 28 bg	3 Nov 83	resign
Brigadier Generals					
1. Gates, Horatio	Virginia	17–Jun 75		16–May 76	to 7 mg
2. Thomas, John	Massachusetts	22–Jun 75		6 Mar 76	to 6 mg
3. Montgomery, Richard	New York	22–Jun 75		9 Dec 75	to 3 mg
4. Wooster, David	Connecticut	22–Jun 75		2 May 77	died
5. Heath, William	Massachusetts	22–Jun 75		9 Aug 76	to 8 mg
6. Spencer, Joseph	Connecticut	22–Jun 75		9 Aug 76	to 9 mg
7. Sullivan, John	New Hampshire	22–Jun 75		9 Aug 76	to 10 mg
8. Greene, Nathanael	Rhode Island	22–Jun 75		9 Aug 76	to 11 mg
9. Frye, Joseph	Massachusetts	10–Jan 76		23–Apr 76	resign
10. Arnold, Benedict	Connecticut	10–Jan 76		17–Feb 77	to 12 mg
11. Armstrong, John Sr.	Pennsylvania	1 Mar 76		4 Apr 77	resign
12. Thompson, William	Pennsylvania	1 Mar 76		3 Sep 1781	died
13. Lewis, Andrew	Virginia	1 Mar 76		15–Apr 77	resign
14. Moore, James	North Carolina	1 Mar 76		9 Apr 77	died
15. Alexander, William (Lord Stirling)	New York	1 Mar 76		19–Feb 77	to 13 mg
16. Howe, Robert	North Carolina	1 Mar 76			to 21 mg
17. Woedtke, Frederick, Baron De	France				
18. Mifflin, Thomas	Pennsylvania				to 14 mg
19. Mercer, Hugh	Virginia				
20. Reed, James	New Hampshire				
21. Nixon, John	Massachusetts				
22. St. Clair, Arthur	Pennsylvania				to 15 mg
23. McDougall, Alexander	New York				to 22 mg
24. Parsons, Samuel Holden	Connecticut				to 26 mg
25. Clinton, James	New York				
26. Stephen, Adam	Virginia				to 16 mg
27. Gadsden, Christopher	South Carolina				
28. Moultrie, William	South Carolina				to 29 mg
29. McIntosh, Lachlan	Georgia				
30. Maxwell, William	New Jersey				
31. Smallwood, William	Maryland				to 25 mg

Appendix IV: Continental Army, General Offices [CONT]

		Appointed	End of Service
32. Fermoy, Matthias	France		
33. Preudhomme DeBorre, Phillipe	France		
34. Knox, Henry	Massachusetts		to 27 mg
35. Nash, Francis	North Carolina		
36. Poor, Enoch	New Hampshire		
37. Glover, John	Massachusetts		
38. Paterson, John	Massachusetts		
39. Wayne, Anthony	Pennsylvania		
40. Varnum, James Mitchell	Rhode Island		
41. deHaas, John P.	Pennsylvania		
42. Woodford, William	Virginia		
43. Muhlenberg, John Peter Gabriel	Virginia		
44. Weedon, George	Virginia		
45. Clinton, George	New York		
46. Hand, Edward	Pennsylvania		
47. Scott, Charles	Virginia		
48. Learned, Ebenezer	Massachusetts		
49. Huntington, Jedidiah	Connecticut		
50. Conway, Thomas	France		to 23 mg
51. Pulaski, Casimir	Poland		
52. Stark, John	New Hampshire		
53. LeBegue DePresle Duportail, Louis	France		to 28 mg
54. Sumner, Jethro	North Carolina		
55. Hogun, James	North Carolina		
56. Huger, Isaac	South Carolina		
57. Gist, Mordecai	Maryland		
58. Irvine, William	Pennsylvania		
59. Morgan, Daniel	Virginia		
60. Williams, Otho Holland	Maryland		
61. Greaton, John	Massachusetts		
62. Putnam, Rufus	Massachusetts		
63. Dayton, Elias	New Jersey		
64. Armand, Charles	France		

Note: mg = Major General, bg = Brigadier General

Appendix V: British Regiments

Unit	Alternate unit name	Arrived in America			Left America	
		Date	Year	Location	Date	Fate/Destination
Guards (single battalion drawn from the three Guards regiments)						
1st Gds		July	1776	New York	1781	interned, Yorktown
2nd Gds	Coldstream	July	1776	New York	1781	interned, Yorktown
3rd Gds		July	1776	New York	1781	interned, Yorktown
Regiments of Foot						
3rd	Buffs	June	1781	Charleston	1782	West Indies
4th	King's Own	June	1774	Boston	1778	West Indies
5th		July	1774	Boston	1778	West Indies
6th		October	1776	New York	1776	drafted
7th	Royal Fusiliers	July	1773	Canada	1783	British Isles
8th	King's		1768	Canada	1785	British Isles
9th		May	1776	Canada	1777	interned, Saratoga
10th			1767	Canada	1778	drafted
14th			1766	Halifax	1777	drafted
15th		May	1776	Cape Fear	1778	West Indies
16th			1767	New York	1782	drafted
17th		December	1775	Boston	1781	interned, Yorktown
18th	Royal Irish		1767	Philadelphia	1775	drafted
19th		June	1781	Charleston	1782	West Indies
20th		May	1776	Quebec	1777	interned, Saratoga
21st	Royal North British Fusiliers	May	1776	Quebec	1777	interned, Saratoga
22nd		July	1775	Boston	1783	British Isles
23rd	Royal Welsh Fusiliers		1773	New York	1781	interned, Yorktown [1]
24th		May	1776	Quebec	1777	interned, Saratoga
26th	Cameronians		1767	New Jersey	1779	drafted
27th	Enniskillens	October	1775	Boston	1778	West Indies
28th		May	1776	Cape Fear	1778	West Indies
29th		May	1776	Quebec	1787	British Isles
30th		June	1781	Charleston	1782	West Indies
31st		May	1776	Quebec	1787	British Isles
33rd		May	1776	Cape Fear	1781	interned, Yorktown [1]
34th		May	1776	Quebec	1786	British Isles
35th		June	1775	Boston	1778	West Indies
37th		May	1776	Cape Fear	1783	left New York
38th		July	1774	Boston	1783	left New York
40th		1. June	1775	Boston	1778	West Indies
		2. September	1781	New York	1783	left New York
42nd	Royal Highland Regiment	July	1776	New York	1783	left New York
43rd		June	1774	Boston	1781	interned, Yorktown
44th		June	1775	Boston	1780	Canada
45th		July	1775	Boston	1778	drafted
46th		May	1776	Cape Fear	1778	West Indies
47th			1773	New Jersey	1777	interned, Saratoga
49th		June	1775	Boston	1778	West Indies
52nd		October	1774	Boston	1778	drafted
53rd		May	1776	Cape Fear	1777	interned, Saratoga
54th		May	1776	Cape Fear	1783	left New York
55th		December	1775	Boston	1778	West Indies
57th		May	1776	Cape Fear	1783	left New York
59th			1765	Halifax	1775	drafted
60th	Royal American Regiment: 1st Battalion 2nd Battalion 3rd Battalion, raised 1775 4th Battalion, raised 1775					
62nd		May	1776	Quebec	1777	interned, Saratoga
63rd		June	1775	Boston	1782	West Indies
64th			1768	Boston	1782	West Indies
65th			1768	Boston	1776	drafted
69th		September	1781	New York (6wks)	1781	West Indies
70th		August	1778	Halifax		

[1] Part not interned at Yorktown left Charleston in 1782: 23rd, 33rd, and 71st.

SOURCE: Anthony D. Darling, *Red Coat and Brown Bess*, Museum Restorationn Service (Ottawa, Ontario), 1970, pp. 55-57

Appendix V: British Regiments [CONT]

Unit	Alternate unit name	Arrival in America			Left America	
		Date	Year	Location	Date	Fate/Destination
Newly Raised						
71st	Fraser's Highlanders	1776	July	New York	1781	interned, Yorktown [1]
74th	Argyll Highlanders	1778	August	Halifax		
76th	MacDonald's Highlanders	1779		New York	1781	interned, Yorktown
80th	Royal Edinburgh Volunteers	1779		New York	1781	interned, Yorktown
82nd	Duke of Hamilton's Regiment	1778	August	Halifax	1781	interned, Yorktown 1co
					1782	left Charleston 3 cos
Newly Raised in America						
84th=1779	Royal Highland Emigrants 1st Battalion 2nd Battalion	1775		CANADA		
105th=1782	King's Irish Regiment	1778		AMERICA	1782	left Charleston
Light Dragoons						
16th LD	Queen's Light Dragoons	1776	July	New York	1778	drafted
17th LD		1775	June	Boston	1783	British Isles

[1] Part not interned at Yorktown left Charleston in 1782: 23rd, 33rd, and 71st.

SOURCE: Anthony D. Darling, *Red Coat and Brown Bess*, Museum Restorationn Service (Ottawa, Ontario), 1970, pp. 55-57

Appendix VI

1775

JANUARY	FEBRUARY	MARCH	APRIL	MAY	JUNE

JANUARY
S M T W T F S
1 2 3 4 5 6 7
8 9 10 11 12 13 14
15 16 17 18 19 20 21
22 23 24 25 26 27 28
29 30 31

FEBRUARY
S M T W T F S
        1 2 3 4
5 6 7 8 9 10 11
12 13 14 15 16 17 18
19 20 21 22 23 24 25
26 27 28

MARCH
S M T W T F S
        1 2 3 4
5 6 7 8 9 10 11
12 13 14 15 16 17 18
19 20 21 22 23 24 25
26 27 28 29 30 31

APRIL
S M T W T F S
                    1
2 3 4 5 6 7 8
9 10 11 12 13 14 15
16 17 18 19 20 21 22
23 24 25 26 27 28 29
30

MAY
S M T W T F S
    1 2 3 4 5 6
7 8 9 10 11 12 13
14 15 16 17 18 19 20
21 22 23 24 25 26 27
28 29 30 31

JUNE
S M T W T F S
                1 2 3
4 5 6 7 8 9 10
11 12 13 14 15 16 17
18 19 20 21 22 23 24
25 26 27 28 29 30

JULY
S M T W T F S
                        1
2 3 4 5 6 7 8
9 10 11 12 13 14 15
16 17 18 19 20 21 22
23 24 25 26 27 28 29
30 31

AUGUST
S M T W T F S
        1 2 3 4 5
6 7 8 9 10 11 12
13 14 15 16 17 18 19
20 21 22 23 24 25 26
27 28 29 30 31

SEPTEMBER
S M T W T F S
                    1 2
3 4 5 6 7 8 9
10 11 12 13 14 15 16
17 18 19 20 21 22 23
24 25 26 27 28 29 30

OCTOBER
S M T W T F S
1 2 3 4 5 6 7
8 9 10 11 12 13 14
15 16 17 18 19 20 21
22 23 24 25 26 27 28
29 30 31

NOVEMBER
S M T W T F S
            1 2 3 4
5 6 7 8 9 10 11
12 13 14 15 16 17 18
19 20 21 22 23 24 25
26 27 28 29 30

DECEMBER
S M T W T F S
                    1 2
3 4 5 6 7 8 9
10 11 12 13 14 15 16
17 18 19 20 21 22 23
24 25 26 27 28 29 30
31

1776

JANUARY
S M T W T F S
1 2 3 4 5 6
7 8 9 10 11 12 13
14 15 16 17 18 19 20
21 22 23 24 25 26 27
28 29 30 31

FEBRUARY
S M T W T F S
            1 2 3
4 5 6 7 8 9 10
11 12 13 14 15 16 17
18 19 20 21 22 23 24
25 26 27 28 29

MARCH
S M T W T F S
                1 2
3 4 5 6 7 8 9
10 11 12 13 14 15 16
17 18 19 20 21 22 23
24 25 26 27 28 29 30
31

APRIL
S M T W T F S
    1 2 3 4 5 6
7 8 9 10 11 12 13
14 15 16 17 18 19 20
21 22 23 24 25 26 27
28 29 30

MAY
S M T W T F S
            1 2 3 4
5 6 7 8 9 10 11
12 13 14 15 16 17 18
19 20 21 22 23 24 25
26 27 28 29 30 31

JUNE
S M T W T F S
                        1
2 3 4 5 6 7 8
9 10 11 12 13 14 15
16 17 18 19 20 21 22
23 24 25 26 27 28 29
30

JULY
S M T W T F S
    1 2 3 4 5 6
7 8 9 10 11 12 13
14 15 16 17 18 19 20
21 22 23 24 25 26 27
28 29 30 31

AUGUST
S M T W T F S
                1 2 3
4 5 6 7 8 9 10
11 12 13 14 15 16 17
18 19 20 21 22 23 24
25 26 27 28 29 30 31

SEPTEMBER
S M T W T F S
1 2 3 4 5 6 7
8 9 10 11 12 13 14
15 16 17 18 19 20 21
22 23 24 25 26 27 28
29 30

OCTOBER
S M T W T F S
            1 2 3 4 5
6 7 8 9 10 11 12
13 14 15 16 17 18 19
20 21 22 23 24 25 26
27 28 29 30 31

NOVEMBER
S M T W T F S
                    1 2
3 4 5 6 7 8 9
10 11 12 13 14 15 16
17 18 19 20 21 22 23
24 25 26 27 28 29 30

DECEMBER
S M T W T F S
1 2 3 4 5 6 7
8 9 10 11 12 13 14
15 16 17 18 19 20 21
22 23 24 25 26 27 28
29 30 31

1777

JANUARY
S M T W T F S
            1 2 3 4
5 6 7 8 9 10 11
12 13 14 15 16 17 18
19 20 21 22 23 24 25
26 27 28 29 30 31

FEBRUARY
S M T W T F S
                        1
2 3 4 5 6 7 8
9 10 11 12 13 14 15
16 17 18 19 20 21 22
23 24 25 26 27 28

MARCH
S M T W T F S
                        1
2 3 4 5 6 7 8
9 10 11 12 13 14 15
16 17 18 19 20 21 22
23 24 25 26 27 28 29
30 31

APRIL
S M T W T F S
            1 2 3 4 5
6 7 8 9 10 11 12
13 14 15 16 17 18 19
20 21 22 23 24 25 26
27 28 29 30

MAY
S M T W T F S
                1 2 3
4 5 6 7 8 9 10
11 12 13 14 15 16 17
18 19 20 21 22 23 24
25 26 27 28 29 30 31

JUNE
S M T W T F S
1 2 3 4 5 6 7
8 9 10 11 12 13 14
15 16 17 18 19 20 21
22 23 24 25 26 27 28
29 30

JULY
S M T W T F S
        1 2 3 4 5
6 7 8 9 10 11 12
13 14 15 16 17 18 19
20 21 22 23 24 25 26
27 28 29 30 31

AUGUST
S M T W T F S
                    1 2
3 4 5 6 7 8 9
10 11 12 13 14 15 16
17 18 19 20 21 22 23
24 25 26 27 28 29 30
31

SEPTEMBER
S M T W T F S
    1 2 3 4 5 6
7 8 9 10 11 12 13
14 15 16 17 18 19 20
21 22 23 24 25 26 27
28 29 30

OCTOBER
S M T W T F S
            1 2 3 4
5 6 7 8 9 10 11
12 13 14 15 16 17 18
19 20 21 22 23 24 25
26 27 28 29 30 31

NOVEMBER
S M T W T F S
                        1
2 3 4 5 6 7 8
9 10 11 12 13 14 15
16 17 18 19 20 21 22
23 24 25 26 27 28 29
30

DECEMBER
S M T W T F S
    1 2 3 4 5 6
7 8 9 10 11 12 13
14 15 16 17 18 19 20
21 22 23 24 25 26 27
28 29 30 31

1778

JANUARY
S M T W T F S
                1 2 3
4 5 6 7 8 9 10
11 12 13 14 15 26 17
18 19 20 21 22 23 24
25 26 27 28 29 30 31

FEBRUARY
S M T W T F S
1 2 3 4 5 6 7
8 9 10 11 12 13 14
15 16 17 18 19 20 21
22 23 24 25 26 27 28

MARCH
S M T W T F S
1 2 3 4 5 6 7
8 9 10 11 12 13 14
15 16 17 18 19 20 21
22 23 24 25 26 27 28
29 30 31

APRIL
S M T W T F S
                1 2 3 4
5 6 7 8 9 10 11
12 13 14 15 16 17 18
19 20 21 22 23 24 25
26 27 28 29 30

MAY
S M T W T F S
                    1 2
3 4 5 6 7 8 9
10 11 12 13 14 15 16
17 18 19 20 21 22 23
24 25 26 27 28 29 30
31

JUNE
S M T W T F S
    1 2 3 4 5 6
7 8 9 10 11 12 13
14 15 16 17 18 19 20
21 22 23 24 25 26 27
28 29 30

JULY
S M T W T F S
                1 2 3 4
5 6 7 8 9 10 11
12 13 14 15 16 17 18
19 20 21 22 23 24 25
26 27 28 29 30 31

AUGUST
S M T W T F S
                            1
2 3 4 5 6 7 8
9 10 11 12 13 14 15
16 17 18 19 20 21 22
23 24 25 26 27 28 29
30 31

SEPTEMBER
S M T W T F S
            1 2 3 4 5
6 7 8 9 10 11 12
13 14 15 16 17 18 19
20 21 22 23 24 25 26
27 28 29 30

OCTOBER
S M T W T F S
                    1 2 3
4 5 6 7 8 9 10
11 12 13 14 15 16 17
18 19 20 21 22 23 24
25 26 27 28 29 30 31

NOVEMBER
S M T W T F S
1 2 3 4 5 6 7
8 9 10 11 12 13 14
15 16 17 18 19 20 21
22 23 24 25 26 27 28
29 30

DECEMBER
S M T W T F S
            1 2 3 4 5
6 7 8 9 10 11 12
13 14 15 16 17 18 19
20 21 22 23 24 25 26
27 28 29 30 31

1779

JANUARY
S M T W T F S
                        1 2
3 4 5 6 7 8 9
10 11 12 13 14 15 16
17 18 19 20 21 22 23
24 25 26 27 28 29 30
31

FEBRUARY
S M T W T F S
    1 2 3 4 5 6
7 8 9 10 11 12 13
14 15 16 17 18 19 20
21 22 23 24 25 26 27
28

MARCH
S M T W T F S
    1 2 3 4 5 6
7 8 9 10 11 12 13
14 15 16 17 18 19 20
21 22 23 24 25 26 27
28 29 30 31

APRIL
S M T W T F S
                    1 2 3
4 5 6 7 8 9 10
11 12 13 14 15 26 17
18 19 20 21 22 23 24
25 26 27 28 29 30

MAY
S M T W T F S
                            1
2 3 4 5 6 7 8
9 10 11 12 13 14 15
16 17 18 19 20 21 22
23 24 25 26 27 28 29
30 31

JUNE
S M T W T F S
            1 2 3 4 5
6 7 8 9 10 11 12
13 14 15 16 17 18 19
20 21 22 23 24 25 26
27 28 29 30

JULY
S M T W T F S
                    1 2 3
4 5 6 7 8 9 10
11 12 13 14 15 16 27
18 19 20 21 22 23 24
25 26 27 28 29 30 31

AUGUST
S M T W T F S
1 2 3 4 5 6 7
8 9 10 11 12 13 14
15 16 17 18 19 20 21
22 23 24 25 26 27 28
29 30 31

SEPTEMBER
S M T W T F S
                1 2 3 4
5 6 7 8 9 10 11
12 13 14 15 16 17 18
19 20 21 22 23 24 25
26 27 28 29 30

OCTOBER
S M T W T F S
                        1 2
3 4 5 6 7 8 9
10 11 12 13 14 15 16
17 18 19 20 21 22 23
24 25 26 27 28 29 30
31

NOVEMBER
S M T W T F S
    1 2 3 4 5 6
7 8 9 10 11 12 13
14 15 16 17 18 19 20
21 22 23 24 25 26 27
28 29 30

DECEMBER
S M T W T F S
                1 2 3 4
5 6 7 8 9 10 11
12 13 14 15 16 17 18
19 20 21 22 23 24 25
26 27 28 29 30 31

Appendix VI [CONT]

1780

JANUARY

S	M	T	W	T	F	S
						1
2	3	4	5	6	7	8
9	10	11	12	13	14	15
16	17	18	19	20	21	22
23	24	25	26	27	28	29
30	31					

FEBRUARY

S	M	T	W	T	F	S
		1	2	3	4	5
6	7	8	9	10	11	12
13	14	15	16	17	18	19
20	21	22	23	24	25	26
27	28	29				

MARCH

S	M	T	W	T	F	S
			1	2	3	4
5	6	7	8	9	10	11
12	13	14	15	16	17	18
19	20	21	22	23	24	25
26	27	28	29	30	31	

APRIL

S	M	T	W	T	F	S
						1
2	3	4	5	6	7	8
9	10	11	12	13	14	15
16	17	18	19	20	21	22
23	24	25	26	27	28	29
30						

MAY

S	M	T	W	T	F	S
	1	2	3	4	5	6
7	8	9	10	11	12	13
14	15	16	17	18	19	20
21	22	23	24	25	26	27
28	29	30	31			

JUNE

S	M	T	W	T	F	S
				1	2	3
4	5	6	7	8	9	10
11	12	13	14	15	26	27
18	19	20	21	22	23	24
25	26	27	28	29	30	

JULY

S	M	T	W	T	F	S
						1
2	3	4	5	6	7	8
9	10	11	12	13	14	15
16	17	18	19	20	21	22
23	24	25	26	27	28	29
30	31					

AUGUST

S	M	T	W	T	F	S
		1	2	3	4	5
6	7	8	9	10	11	12
13	14	15	16	17	18	19
20	21	22	23	24	25	26
27	28	29	30	31		

SEPTEMBER

S	M	T	W	T	F	S
					1	2
3	4	5	6	7	8	9
10	11	12	13	14	15	16
17	18	19	20	21	22	23
24	25	26	27	28	29	30

OCTOBER

S	M	T	W	T	F	S
1	2	3	4	5	6	7
8	9	10	11	12	13	14
15	16	17	18	19	20	21
22	23	24	25	26	27	28
29	30	31				

NOVEMBER

S	M	T	W	T	F	S
			1	2	3	4
5	6	7	8	9	10	11
12	13	14	15	16	17	18
19	20	21	22	23	24	25
26	27	28	29	30		

DECEMBER

S	M	T	W	T	F	S
					1	2
3	4	5	6	7	8	9
10	11	12	13	14	15	16
17	18	19	20	21	22	23
24	25	26	27	28	29	30
31						

1781

JANUARY

S	M	T	W	T	F	S
	1	2	3	4	5	6
7	8	9	10	11	12	13
14	15	16	17	18	19	20
21	22	23	24	25	26	27
28	29	30	31			

FEBRUARY

S	M	T	W	T	F	S
				1	2	3
4	5	6	7	8	9	10
11	12	13	14	15	26	27
18	19	20	21	22	23	24
25	26	27	28			

MARCH

S	M	T	W	T	F	S
				1	2	3
4	5	6	7	8	9	10
11	12	13	14	15	26	27
18	19	20	21	22	23	24
25	26	27	28	29	30	31

APRIL

S	M	T	W	T	F	S
1	2	3	4	5	6	7
8	9	10	11	12	13	14
15	16	17	18	19	20	21
22	23	24	25	26	27	28
29	30					

MAY

S	M	T	W	T	F	S
		1	2	3	4	5
6	7	8	9	10	11	12
13	14	15	16	17	18	19
20	21	22	23	24	25	26
27	28	29	30	31		

JUNE

S	M	T	W	T	F	S
					1	2
3	4	5	6	7	8	9
10	11	12	13	14	15	16
17	18	19	20	21	22	23
24	25	26	27	28	29	30

JULY

S	M	T	W	T	F	S
1	2	3	4	5	6	7
8	9	10	11	12	13	14
15	16	17	18	19	20	21
22	23	24	25	26	27	28
29	30	31				

AUGUST

S	M	T	W	T	F	S
			1	2	3	4
5	6	7	8	9	10	11
12	13	14	15	16	17	18
19	20	21	22	23	24	25
26	27	28	29	30	31	

SEPTEMBER

S	M	T	W	T	F	S
						1
2	3	4	5	6	7	8
9	10	11	12	13	14	15
16	17	18	19	20	21	22
23	24	25	26	27	28	29
30						

OCTOBER

S	M	T	W	T	F	S
	1	2	3	4	5	6
7	8	9	10	11	12	13
14	15	16	17	18	19	20
21	22	23	24	25	26	27
28	29	30	31			

NOVEMBER

S	M	T	W	T	F	S
				1	2	3
4	5	6	7	8	9	10
11	12	13	14	15	26	27
18	19	20	21	22	23	24
25	26	27	28	29	30	

DECEMBER

S	M	T	W	T	F	S
						1
2	3	4	5	6	7	8
9	10	11	12	13	14	15
16	17	18	19	20	21	22
23	24	25	26	27	28	29
30	31					

1782

JANUARY

S	M	T	W	T	F	S
		1	2	3	4	5
6	7	8	9	10	11	12
13	14	15	16	17	18	19
20	21	22	23	24	25	26
27	28	29	30	31		

FEBRUARY

S	M	T	W	T	F	S
					1	2
3	4	5	6	7	8	9
10	11	12	13	14	15	16
17	18	19	20	21	22	23
24	25	26	27	28		

MARCH

S	M	T	W	T	F	S
					1	2
3	4	5	6	7	8	9
10	11	12	13	14	15	16
17	18	19	20	21	22	23
24	25	26	27	28	29	30
31						

APRIL

S	M	T	W	T	F	S
	1	2	3	4	5	6
7	8	9	10	11	12	13
14	15	16	17	18	19	20
21	22	23	24	25	26	27
28	29	30				

MAY

S	M	T	W	T	F	S
			1	2	3	4
5	6	7	8	9	10	11
12	13	14	15	16	17	18
19	20	21	22	23	24	25
26	27	28	29	30	31	

JUNE

S	M	T	W	T	F	S
						1
2	3	4	5	6	7	8
9	10	11	12	13	14	15
16	17	18	19	20	21	22
23	24	25	26	27	28	29
30						

JULY

S	M	T	W	T	F	S
	1	2	3	4	5	6
7	8	9	10	11	12	13
14	15	16	17	18	19	20
21	22	23	24	25	26	27
28	29	30	31			

AUGUST

S	M	T	W	T	F	S
				1	2	3
4	5	6	7	8	9	10
11	12	13	14	15	26	27
18	19	20	21	22	23	24
25	26	27	28	29	30	31

SEPTEMBER

S	M	T	W	T	F	S
1	2	3	4	5	6	7
8	9	10	11	12	13	14
15	16	17	18	19	20	21
22	23	24	25	26	27	28
29	30					

OCTOBER

S	M	T	W	T	F	S
		1	2	3	4	5
6	7	8	9	10	11	12
13	14	15	16	17	18	19
20	21	22	23	24	25	26
27	28	29	30	31		

NOVEMBER

S	M	T	W	T	F	S
					1	2
3	4	5	6	7	8	9
10	11	12	13	14	15	16
17	18	19	20	21	22	23
24	25	26	27	28	29	30

DECEMBER

S	M	T	W	T	F	S
1	2	3	4	5	6	7
8	9	10	11	12	13	14
15	16	17	18	19	20	21
22	23	24	25	26	27	28
29	30	31				

1783

JANUARY

S	M	T	W	T	F	S
			1	2	3	4
5	6	7	8	9	10	11
12	13	14	15	16	17	18
19	20	21	22	23	24	25
26	27	28	29	30	31	

FEBRUARY

S	M	T	W	T	F	S
						1
2	3	4	5	6	7	8
9	10	11	12	13	14	15
16	17	18	19	20	21	22
23	24	25	26	27	28	

MARCH

S	M	T	W	T	F	S
						1
2	3	4	5	6	7	8
9	10	11	12	13	14	15
16	17	18	19	20	21	22
23	24	25	26	27	28	29
30	31					

APRIL

S	M	T	W	T	F	S
		1	2	3	4	5
6	7	8	9	10	11	12
13	14	15	16	17	18	19
20	21	22	23	24	25	26
27	28	29	30			

MAY

S	M	T	W	T	F	S
				1	2	3
4	5	6	7	8	9	10
11	12	13	14	15	26	27
18	19	20	21	22	23	24
25	26	27	28	29	30	31

JUNE

S	M	T	W	T	F	S
1	2	3	4	5	6	7
8	9	10	11	12	13	14
15	16	17	18	19	20	21
22	23	24	25	26	27	28
29	30					

JULY

S	M	T	W	T	F	S
		1	2	3	4	5
6	7	8	9	10	11	12
13	14	15	16	17	18	19
20	21	22	23	24	25	26
27	28	29	30	31		

AUGUST

S	M	T	W	T	F	S
					1	2
3	4	5	6	7	8	9
10	11	12	13	14	15	16
17	18	19	20	21	22	23
24	25	26	27	28	29	30
31						

SEPTEMBER

S	M	T	W	T	F	S
	1	2	3	4	5	6
7	8	9	10	11	12	13
14	15	16	17	18	19	20
21	22	23	24	25	26	27
28	29	30				

OCTOBER

S	M	T	W	T	F	S
			1	2	3	4
5	6	7	8	9	10	11
12	13	14	15	16	17	18
19	20	21	22	23	24	25
26	27	28	29	30	31	

NOVEMBER

S	M	T	W	T	F	S
						1
2	3	4	5	6	7	8
9	10	11	12	13	14	15
16	17	18	19	20	21	22
23	24	25	26	27	28	29
30						

DECEMBER

S	M	T	W	T	F	S
	1	2	3	4	5	6
7	8	9	10	11	12	13
14	15	16	17	18	19	20
21	22	23	24	25	26	27
28	29	30	31			

Selected Bibliography

This compilation expands upon the on-line bibliographies of the U.S. Army's Center of Military History, which were in turn based on Robert K. Wright Jr's bibliography for his contribution to the Center's Army Lineage Series, The Continental Army *(Washington, D.C.: Center of Military History, 1983). In addition to updating the scholarship of these earlier works, this bibliography has added material on the U.S. Navy and maritime studies, as well as incorporating books and articles on social history, gender studies, racial relations, and other topics of interest to contemporary historians. A number of web sites offering accurate information and documents of value have been included. It is hoped that this bibliography will serve as a useful starting point from which the next generation may craft an independent interpretation of this seminal event in the creation of the United States.*

I. MANUSCRIPTS

Albany Institute of History and Art (Albany, New York).
  Online at www.albanyinstitute.org
  Schuyler, Philip John. Papers.

American Antiquarian Society (Worcester, Massachusetts).
  See [American Antiquarian Society], *The Catalogue of the Manuscripts Collections of the American Antiquarian Society,* 4 vols. (Boston, Mass.: G. K. Hall and Company, 1979).
  Online at www.americanantiquarian.org/manuscripts.
  Shays' Rebellion Collection.
  Washington, George. Papers.

American Philosophical Society (Philadelphia, Pennsylvania).
  Online at www.amphilsoc.org/library/mole.
  Franklin, Benjamin. Papers.
  Greene, Nathanael. Papers.
  Hand, Edward. Papers.
  Lee, Richard Henry. Papers.
  Peale, Charles Willson. Papers.
  Orderly Book Collection.
  Sol Feinstone Collection of the American Revolution.
  Weedon, George. Papers.

Bayerisches Hauptstaatsarchiv (München).
  Kriegsarchiv.
  Prechtel, Johann Ernst. Beschreibung derer Von 7. Mart: bis 9. Decembr: 1783.
  von Feilitzsch, Heinrich Karl Philipp. Diary, 7 March 1777– 3 June 1780.

Bayerisches Staatsarchiv (Nürnberg).
  Ansbacher Kriegsakten [Ansbach War Files].
  HStAM, IV, nr. 2: Diary of First Lieutenant Johann Ernst Prechtel.
  Stang, Georg Adam. March Ruthen für Georg Adam Stang, Haudtboist Bayreuth den 19t Januar 1784.

Boston Public Library (Boston, Massachusetts).
  See G. B. Warden, compiler, *Manuscripts of the American Revolution in the Boston Public Library: A Descriptive Catalog* (Boston, Mass.: G. K. Hall and Company, 1968).
  Online at www.bpl.org.
  Knox, Henry. Papers.
  Lincoln, Benjamin. Papers.

British Library (London).
  Online at molcat.bl.uk/msscat.
  Arundel Manuscripts.
  Auckland Papers.
  Bouquet Papers.
  Burney Manuscripts.
  Class 50: Military Manuscripts.
  Cottonian Manuscripts.
  Egerton Manuscripts.
  Haldimand Papers.
  Hardwick Papers.
  Harleian Manuscripts.
  Landsdowne Manuscripts.
  Liverpool, Lord (Charles Jenkinson). Papers.
  Montague Papers.
  Rainsford Papers. [Records of the British Commissary of Musters for the German auxiliary troops.]

Sloan Manuscripts.

Stowe Manuscripts.

Brown University (Providence, Rhode Island).
Online at www.brown.edu.
Anne S. K. Brown Collection.
Weedon, George. Papers.

Charleston Library Society (Charleston, South Carolina).
Online at sciway.net/lib.
Rutledge, John. Papers.

Chicago Historical Society (Chicago, Illinois).
Online at www.chicagohs.org.
Anton B. C. Kalkhorst Papers.
Weedon, George. Papers.

William L. Clements Library, University of Michigan (Ann Arbor, Michigan).
See Arlene Shy, editor, *Guide to the Manuscript Collections in the William L. Clements Library* (Boston, Mass.: G. K. Hall, 1978).
Online at www.clements.umich.edu.
Amherst, Jeffrey. Papers
Braddish Orderly Book (16 August 1778–3 April 1779)
Clinton, Henry. Papers.
Continental Army Returns.
Gage, Thomas. Papers.
Gates, Horatio. Papers.
Germain, George. Papers.
Greene, Nathanael. Papers.
Knox, William. Papers.
"Lord North's Confidential Reports on the Strength of the British Army."
Simcoe, John Graves. Papers.
Sumner, Jethro. Papers.
Sydney Papers.
Vaughan, John. Papers.
Von Jungkenn Papers.
Wray, George. Papers.

Colonial Williamsburg Foundation (Williamsburg, Virginia).
See Gregory Williams, compiler, *Guide and Inventories to Manuscripts in the Special Collections Section, John D. Rockefeller, Jr., Library* (Williamsburg, Va.: Colonial Williamsburg Foundation, 1992).
Online at research.history.org/JDRLibrary.
Headquarters Papers of the British Army in America.
[Photostatic copies of original documents presented to the Queen in 1957 and now Class 30/55 in the Public Record Office, London.]

Columbia University Library (New York, New York).
Online at www.columbia.edu/cu/lweb.
Hamilton, Alexander. Papers.
Jay, John. Papers.
Morris, Gouveneur. Papers.

Connecticut Historical Society (Hartford, Connecticut).
Online at www.chs.org.
American Revolution Collection.
Deane, Silas. Papers.
Farmington Manuscripts.
Hoadley Collection.
Huntington, Jedidiah. Papers.
Tallmadge, Benjamin. Papers.
Trumbull, David. Papers.

Trumbull, John. Papers.
Trumbull, Jonathan, Jr. Papers.
Trumbull, Jonathan, Sr. Papers.
Trumbull, Joseph. Papers.
Wadsworth, Jeremiah. Papers.
Williams, William. Papers.
Wolcott, Oliver, Jr. Papers.
Wolcott, Oliver, Sr. Papers.

Connecticut State Library (Hartford, Connecticut).
See Mark H. Jones et al., editors, *Guide to the Archives in the Connecticut State Library, 4th Edition* (Hartford, Conn.: Connecticut State Library, 2002).
Online at cslib.org/archives.
Boardman, William. Collection.   Connecticut Archives, 1629–1820: Revolutionary War. (Three Series.)
Fitch, John. Papers.
Fitz-Randolph, Nathaniel. Manuscripts.
Hubbard, Henrietta W. Collection.
Trumbull, Jonathan, Jr. Papers.
Trumbull, Jonathan, Sr. Papers.
Trumbull, Joseph. Papers.
Wadsworth, Jeremiah. Papers.

Dartmouth College Library (Hanover, New Hampshire).
Online at www.dartmouth.edu.
Bartlett, Josiah. Papers.
Bedel, Timothy. Papers.
Chase, Jonathan. Papers.
Hale Chandler Family Papers.
McClure Family Papers.
Wheelock, Eleazer. Papers.

David Library of the American Revolution (Washington Crossing, Pennsylvania).
Online at www.dlar.org.

Delaware State Archives (Dover, Delaware).
Online at www.state.de.us/sos/dpa/collections.
Executive Papers. Military.
Legislative Papers.

Duke University, Perkins Library (Durham, North Carolina).
Online at www.duke.edu.
Greene, Nathanael. Papers.
Habersham Family Papers.
Lawson, Robert. Papers.
Lincoln, Benjamin. Papers.
McIntosh, Lachlan. Papers.

Fort Ticonderoga Museum (Ticonderoga, New York).
Online at www.fort-ticonderoga.org.

Friends Historical Society, Swarthmore College (Swarthmore, Pennsylvania).
Biddle Manuscripts.

Georgia Department of Archives and History (Atlanta, Georgia).
Online at www.sos.state.ga.us/archives.
Georgia. Executive Department. Incoming Correspondence, 1754–1800.
Governors' Commissions.

Georgia Historical Society (Savannah, Georgia).
Online at www.georgiahistory.com.
Berrien-Burroughs Papers.
Bevan, Joseph Vallence. Papers.
Bulloch, Archibald. Papers.
Cate, Margaret Davis. Collection.

Houston, John. Papers.
McIntosh, Lachlan. Papers.
Sheftall, Mordecai. Papers.

Harvard University, Houghton Library (Cambridge, Massachusetts).
Online at hcl.harvard.edu/libraries. OASIS catalog.
Febiger, Christian. Papers.
Hamilton, Henry. Papers.
Lee, Arthur. Papers.
Sparks, Jared. Collection of American Manuscripts.
Stewart, Charles. Papers.
Talbot, Silas. Papers.

Historical Society of Delaware (Wilmington, Delaware).
Online at www.hsd.org.
Brown, H. F. Collection.
Dansey, William. Letters.
McLane, Allen. Papers.
Read, George. Papers.
Rodney, Caesar. Papers.

Historical Society of Pennsylvania (Philadelphia, Pennsylvania).
See [Richard N. Williams, II, director], *Guide to the Manuscript Collections of The Historical Society of Pennsylvania,* second edition (Philadelphia: The Historical Society of Pennsylvania, 1949).
Online at www.hsp.org.
Armstrong, William. Papers.
Balch Collection.
Baltzel, Charles. Orderbook.
Biddle, Clement. Papers.
Boudinot, Elias. Papers.
Bradford, Thomas. Papers.
Bradford, William. Papers.
Brodhead, Daniel. Letterbook.
Burnside, James. Letterbook.
Cadwallader, John. Papers.
Challoner and White Papers.
Chambers, James. Orderbooks.
Clymer, Daniel C. Papers.
Conarroe Authograph Collection.
Council of Safety Papers.
Dreer Collection.
Feltman, William. Military Journals.
Gratz, Simon. Collection.
Hand, Edward. Papers.
Hawkins, John. Journals and Orderbook.
Hazard, Samuel. Papers.
Hazen, Moses. Orderbooks.
Hildeburn, Charles R. Papers.
Hubley, Adam. Journal.
Humphreys, Joshua. Papers.
Irvine, William. Papers.
Jenkins, George. Orderbook.
Lacey, John. Correspondence.
Laurens, Henry. Correspondence.
Loxley, Benjamin. Journal.
Morris, Robert. Papers.
Morris-Hollingsworth Correspondence.
Nice, John. Papers.
Nichols, Francis. Journals.
Orderly Book Collection.
Pemberton Papers.

Potts, Jonathan. Papers.
Sproat, James. Journals.
Stewart, Walter. Orderly Book.
Watson, John Fanning. Manuscripts.
Wayne, Anthony. Papers.
Weiss, Jacob. Family Correspondence.

Henry E. Huntington Library (San Marino, California).
See [Mary L. Robertson, compiler], *Guide to American Historical Manuscripts in the Huntington Library* (San Marino, Calif.: Henry E. Huntington Library and Art Gallery, 1979); and [Mary L. Robertson, compiler], *Guide to British Historical Manuscripts in the Huntington Library* (San Marino, Calif.: Henry E. Huntington Library and Art Gallery, 1982).
Online at www.huntington.org.
Abercrombie Papers.
Amherst Papers.
Diary of an Unknown German Soldier.
Loudoun Papers.
Morris, Robert. Papers.
Schuyler, Philip John. Papers.

Indiana Historical Society. (Indianapolis, Indiana).
Online at www.indianahistory.org.
Posey, Thomas. Memorandum Book, 12 January 1776– 24 May 1777.

Indiana University, Eli Lilly Library (Bloomington, Indiana).
Online at www.indiana.edu.
Williams, Jonathan. Papers.

Lancaster County Historical Society. (Lancaster, Pennsylvania).
Online at www.lancasterhistory.org
Hand, Edward. Papers.

Landesbibliothek (Kassel).
4° Ms. hass. 186: Tagebuch des Obrist Lieutnants von Dinklage 1776–84.

Landeskirchliches Archiv (Nürnberg).
Militärkirchenbücher der Militärpfarrei bei St. Johannis, Ansbach. [Military Church Records of the Military Chaplaincy at St. Johannis Church, Ansbach.]

Library of Congress (Washington, DC).
See John R. Sellers et al., editors, *Manuscript Sources in the Library of Congress for Research on the American Revolution.* (Washington, DC: Library of Congress, 1975).
Online at www.loc.gov/rr/mss.
Blaine, Ephraim. Papers.
Force, Peter. Collection.
Greene, Nathanael. Papers.
Hughes, Hugh. Papers.
Stephen, Adam. Papers.
Stewart, Charles. Papers.
Stoddert, Benjamin. Collection.
Washington, George. Papers.
Microfilms and Photostats of Documents in German Repositories, including:
Bayerisches Kreisarchiv (Bamberg): Documents on Anspach-Bayreuth contingent. 3 rolls.
Bayerisches Staatsarchiv (Nürnberg): Documents on Ansbach-Bayreuth contingent prior to deployment. 3 rolls.
Geschichtsverein (Hanau): Miscellaneous materials primarily for Hesse-Hanau. 1 box.

Historischer Verein für Mittlefranken (Ansbach): Documents on Anspach-Bayreuth contingent. 2 rolls.

Historischer Verein für Oberfranken (Bayreuth): Documents on Anspach-Bayreuth contingent. 1 roll.

Landesarchiv (Oldenburg): Relating to Anhalt-Zerbst contingent. 3 rolls.

Landesbibliothek (Kassel): Includes manuscript diaries of Erbprinz, Mirbach, Lossburg regiments and Linsing battalion, and various paperwork from Mirbach's brigade. 2 boxes.

Landeshauptarchiv (Wolfenbüttel):
Acta Militaria. 15 rolls. Documents from Braunschweig-Lünenburg contingent.
Historische Handeschrift. 3 rolls.
Riedesel Papers. 57 rolls.

Preussisches Staatsarchiv (Hannover): General Kommando. 7 rolls.

Preussisches Staatsarchiv (Marburg):
Documents on Hesse-Cassel contingent, including three boxes from the Trenton court martial. 61 boxes.
Furstlich Waldeckisches Kabinett on 3rd Regiment Waldeck. 16 boxes.
Kriegsministerium (formerly Heeresarchiv) for Hesse-Cassel. 26 boxes.
Staatsarchiv (Hamburg): Ritzebuttel. 3 rolls.

Litchfield Historical Society (Litchfield, Connecticut).
Online at www.litchfieldhistoricalsociety.org.
Tallmadge, Benjamin. Papers.

Maine Historical Society (Portland, Maine).
Online at www.mainehistory.org.

Maine State Archives (Augusta, Maine).
Online at www.maine.gov/sos/arc.

Marietta College Library (Marietta, Ohio).
Putnam, Rufus. Papers.

Maryland Historical Society (Baltimore, Maryland).
Online at www.mdhs.org.
Gist, Mordecai. Papers.
Hanson, Alexander Contee. Papers.
Howard, John Eager. Papers.
McHenry, James. Papers.
Smallwood, William. Papers.
Smith, Samuel. Papers.
Stoddert, Benjamin. Papers.
Williams, Otho Holland. Papers.
Military Collection. Miscellaneous.
Revolutionary War Collection.
Revolutionary War Military Records.

Maryland State Archives (Annapolis, Maryland).
Online at www.mdarchives.state.md.us.
Revolutionary War Papers.

Massachusetts Archives (Boston, Massachusetts).
Online at www.state.ma.us/sec/arc.
Massachusetts Archives Collection:
Board of War Letters and Minutes. 6 vols.
Thomas Hutchinson. Correspondence and Papers. 7 vols.
Revolutionary Miscellaneous. 6 vols.
Revolution Council Papers. 16 vols.
Revolution Letters. 14 vols.
Revolution Loyalists. 2 vols.
Revolution Petitions. 9 vols.

Revolution Resolves. 34 vols.
Shays's Rebellion. 4 vols.
Continental Army Books. 21 vols.
Revolutionary Rolls. 77 vols.

Massachusetts Historical Society (Boston, Massachusetts).
Online at masshist.org/library_collections.
Gerry, Elbridge. Papers.
Heath, William. Papers.
Knox, Henry. Papers.
Lincoln, Benjamin. Papers.
Livingston, William. Papers.
Lovell, Solomon. Papers.
Paine, Robert Treat. Papers.
Palmer, Joseph. Papers.
Pickering, Timothy. Papers.
Revolutionary War Orderly Books.
Sullivan, John. Papers.
Thomas, John. Papers.
Tudor, William. Papers.
Ward, Artemas. Papers.
Weare, Meshech. Papers.

Montressor Family Archives (Kingsdown, Surry, England).

J. Pierpont Morgan Library (New York, New York).
Online at www.morganlibrary.org
Gilder-Lehrman Collection.

Morristown National Historic Park (Morristown, New Jersey).
Online at www.nps.gov/morr.
Hessischen Feld-Jäger-Corps Während der Campagnen der Königl. Grossbritannischen Armee in Nord-Amerika.
Lidgerwood Hessian Papers.
Manuscript Collection.
Seeley, Silvanus. Journals.

National Archives and Records Administration (Washington, DC).
See Howard H. Wehmann et al., editors, *A Guide to Pre-Federal Records in the National Archives* (Washington, DC: National Archives and Records Administration, 1989).
Naval Records Collection of the Office of Naval Records and Library (Record Group 45).
Records of the Continental and Confederation Congresses and the Constitutional Convention (Record Group 360).
Revolutionary War Pension Records (Record Group 15a).
War Department Collection of Revolutionary War Records (Record Group 93).

National Archives of Canada (Ottawa, Ontario).
Online at www.collectionscanada.ca.
Manuscript Group 9: Provincial, Local, and Territorial Records.
Manuscript Group 11: Colonial Office Records.
Manuscript Group 12: Admiralty Records.
Manuscript Group 13: War Office:
Amherst, Jeffrey. Papers.
Manuscript Group 14: Audit Office.
Manuscript Group 15: Treasury Office.
Manuscript Group 21: British Museum Papers:
Haldimand, Frederick. Papers.
Manuscript Group 23: Late 18th-Century Papers:
Carleton, Guy. Papers.
Moody, James. Papers.
Winslow, Edward. Papers.

Record Group 8: British Military, Ordnance, and Admiralty
Records, 1757–1903:
American Loyalist Regimental Muster Rolls.

National Archives of Scotland (Edinburgh, Scotland).
Online at www.nas.gov.uk.

National Library of Scotland (Edinburgh, Scotland).
Online at www.nls.uk.

New England Historical and Genealogical Society (Boston,
Massachusetts).
Online at www.newenglandancestors.org/libraries/manuscripts.
Diary Collection.
Order Book, 3rd Troop, 2nd Continental Light Dragoons,
June 1782.

New Hampshire Historical Society (Concord, New Hampshire).
Online at www.nhhistory.org.
Bartlett, Josiah. Papers.
Bedel Papers.
Boyd, George. Letterbook.
Currier Papers.
Hale Papers.
Langdon, John. Papers.
Livermore, Samuel. Papers.
Marston Papers.
Plummer Papers.
Stark, John. Papers.
Sullivan, John. Papers.
Thompson Papers.
Toscan Papers.
Walker Papers.
Weare, Meshech. Papers.
Wentworth Papers.

New Hampshire State Library/State Archives (Concord,
New Hampshire).
Online at www.sos.nh.gov/archives.
Bartlett, Josiah. Papers.
Continental Army Books.
Patten, Matthew. Papers.
Plumer Papers.
Provincial Records (to 1786).
Revolutionary War Miscellaneous Papers.
Weare, Meshech. Papers.
Wentworth, John. Papers.

New Haven Colony Historical Society (New Haven, Connecticut).
Fourth Connecticut Regiment Paybook. [September-October
1782.]

New Jersey Historical Society. (Newark, New Jersey).
Online at www.jerseyhistory.org.
Abeel, James. Papers.
Assembly Minutes.
Bloomfield, Joseph. Journal.
Clark, Joseph. Diary.
Craig, Charles. Orderbook.
Drury, Matthew. Orderbook.
Greene, Nathanael. Papers.
Piatt, Jacob. Orderbook.
Provincial Congress Manuscripts.
Revolutionary Documents.
Ross, Jonathan. Orderbook.
Speer, John. Orderbook.
Swan, Jedediah. Orderbook.

Tuttle, Timothy. Journal.

New Jersey State Archives (Trenton, New Jersey).
Online at www.state.nj.us/state/darm/archives.

New Jersey State Library (Trenton, New Jersey).
Online at www.njstatelib.org.
Department of Defense Collection.
Furman, Moore. Papers.
Revolutionary War Collection.

New-York Historical Society (New York, New York).
Online at www.nyhistory.org.
Alexander, William (Lord Stirling). Papers.
Bauman, Sebastian. Papers.
Clinton, James. Papers.
Duane, James. Papers.
Duer, William. Papers.
Early American Orderly Books, 1748–1817.
Erskine-DeWitt Map Collection.
Gates, Horatio. Papers.
Hand, Edward. Papers.
Hughes, Hugh. Papers.
Lamb, John. Papers and Letterbook.
Lee, Charles. Papers.
Livingston, Robert R., Jr. Papers.
Livingston, William. Papers.
Machin, Thomas. Papers.
McDougall, Alexander. Papers.
McIntosh, Lachlan. Papers.
McLane, Allen. Papers.
Morris, Gouveneur. Papers.
Steuben, Friedrich. Papers.
Stevens, Ebenezer. Papers.
Stewart, Walter. Papers.
Willett, Marinus. Papers and Orderly Book.

New York Public Library (New York, New York).
Online at www.nypl.org/research.
Adams, Samuel. Papers.
Arnold, Benedict. Papers.
Bancroft, George. Collection.
Chalmers, George. Papers.
Chase, Samuel. Papers.
Clinton, Henry. Deserter Intelligence Book, November
1780–July 1781.
Emmet, Thomas Addis. Collection.
North, William. Papers.
Frederick, Charles. Record Books.
Gansevoort, Peter. Military Papers.
Gansevoort-Lansing Collection.
Gist, Mordecai. Papers.
Hand, Edward. Papers.
Livingston, William. Papers.
Livingston family. Papers.
Morris, Robert. Papers.
Myers, Theodorus Bailey. Collection.
Morgan, Daniel. Papers.
Orderly Book Collection.
Schuyler, Philip John. Papers.
Van Cortlandt, Philip. Papers.
Ward, Artemas. Papers.
Wayne, Anthony. Papers. [Transcripts.]

New York State Historical Association (Cooperstown, New York).
  Online at www.nysha.org.
  Gilbert, Benjamin. Journal.
  Stewart, Charles. Papers.
New York State Library (Albany, New York).
  See Stefan Bielinski, editor, *Revolutionary War Manuscripts in the New York State Library* (Albany, N. Y.: New York State American Revolution Bicentennial Commission, 1976).
  Online at www.nysl.nysed.gov/research.
  Lewis, Morgan. Papers.
  Schuyler, Philip John. Papers.
North Carolina Department of Archives and History (Raleigh, North Carolina).
  See Beth G. Crabtree, editor, *Guide to Private Manuscript Collections in the North Carolina State Archives* (Raleigh: State Department of Archives and History, 1964).
  Online at www.ah.dcr.state.nc.us/archives.
  Brevard, Alexander. Papers.
  Burke, Thomas. Papers.
  Caswell, Richard. Papers.
  Dickson Manuscripts.
  Graham, Joseph. Papers.
  Nash, Abner. Papers.
  Robeson, John A. Collection.
  Schenck, David. Papers.
  Military Collection:
    Board of War Journals and Correspondence.
    Mecklenburg County Militia Records, 1771–1775.
    Miscellaneous Revolution Papers.
    Secretary of State's Office Papers.
    Troop Returns, 1747–1859.
Nova Scotia Archives and Records Management [Public Archives of Nova Scotia] (Halifax, Nova Scotia).
  Online at www.gov.na.ca/nsarm.
  Manuscript Group 12: Nova Scotia Military Records.
  Record Group 1: Commissioner of Public Records Collection.
Ohio State Historical Society (Columbus, Ohio).
  Online at www.ohiohistory.org.
  Sargent, Winthrop. Papers.
Oneida Historical Society (Utica, New York).
  King, Rufus. Papers.
  Steuben, Friedrich. Papers.
Oswego Historical Society (Oswego, New York).
  Laurance, John. Papers.
Pennsylvania State Archives (Harrisburg, Pennsylvania).
  See Harry E. Whipkey, compiler and editor, *Guide to the Manuscript Groups in the Pennsylvania State Archives* (Harrisburg, Penn.: Pennsylvania Historical and Museum Commission, 1976); George Dailey et al., editors, *Guide to the Microfilm of the Records of the Provincial Council, 1682–1776, in the Pennsylvania State Archive* (Harrisburg, Penn.: Pennsylvania Historic and Museum Commission, 1966); Roland M. Baumann et al., editors, *Guide to Microfilm of the Miscellaneous Manuscripts of the Revolutionary War Era, 1771–1791 (Manuscript Group No. 275), in the Pennsylvania State Archive* (Harrisburg, Penn.: Pennsylvania Historic and Museum Commission, 1978); Roland M. Baumann et al., editors, *Guide to the Microfilm of the Records of Pennsylvania's Revolutionary Governments,*

1775–1790 (Record Group No. 27), in the Pennsylvania State Archives (Harrisburg, Penn.: Pennsylvania Historic and Museum Commission, 1978).
  Online at www.phmc.state.pa.us.
  Delaware Fortification Accounts.
  Hand, Edward. Papers.
  Military Accounts.
  Minutes and General Correspondence of the Navy Board and Board of War.
  Records of Pennsylvania's Revolutionary Governments, 1775–1790.
Preussisches Staatsarchiv (Hannover).
  52 III, Nr. 29: Diarium (Briefe) des als Adjutant des englischen Generals Sir William Howe am Nordamerikanischen Freiheitskriege teilnehmenden Hauptmanns Friedrich v. Münchhausen an sienen Bruder Wilhelm v. M., Geh. Kriegsrat in Hannover 1776–8.
Preussisches Staatsarchiv (Marburg).
  Felzüg 1776–83: Abschrift B: Tagebuch des Pfarrers Kümmel Feldprediger bei den Fürstlich Hessichen Regimenter von Huyn und von Bünau.
  4° Ms. hess. 28: Journal of the Regiment jung-Lossberg (formerly Mirbach).
  4h.412 nr. 2: Journal of Regiment Prinz Karl.
  Kirchenbuch von hess. Truppenteilen a. d. amerik.
  12.11 I Ba 1: Journal of Regiment von Ditfurth.
  12.11 I Ba 2: Journal of Regiment von Lossberg.
  12.11 I Ba 3: Journal of Grenadier Regiment von Bischhausen (formerly Rall's).
  12.11 I Ba 4: Journal of Regiment Landgraf, later the Lieb-Infanterie-Regiment.
  12.11 I Ba 5: Journal of Regiment von Donop.
  12.11 I Ba 6: Journal of Regiment von Knyphausen.
  12.11 I Ba 7: Journal of Regiment von Bose.
  12.11 I Ba 9: Order Book of Regiment Mirbach.
  12.11 I Ba 10: Journal of Leib Regiment.
  12.11 I Ba 11: Journal of Regiment Prinz Friedrich (formerly Erbprinz).
  12.11 I Ba 12: Journal of Regiment von Wissenbach, later von Knoblauch.
  12.11 I Ba 13: Journal of Garrison Regiment von Huyn.
  12.11 I Ba 14: Journal of Block's Battalion.
  12.11 I Ba 15: Journal of Minnigerode's Battalion.
  12.11 I Ba 16: Journal of Grenadier Battalion von Platte.
  12.11 I Ba 17: Journal of Feldjägerkorps.
Princeton University, Firestone Library (Princeton, New Jersey).
  Online at www.princeton.edu
  Boudinot, Elias. Papers.
  de Coppet, Andre. Collection.
  Glyn, Thomas. Diary. [14 April 1776–17 August 1777.]
  Hunter, Andrew. Diaries.
  Ogden-Kennedy Collection.
Public Record Office [now National Archives] (London).
  Online at nationalarchives.gov.uk.
  Admiralty Papers.
  Colonial Office Papers:
    Class 5: America and West Indies, 1606–1807.
    CO 5/7: Materials for Raising Provincial Troops.
    CO 5/42: Burgoyne Expedition.
    CO 5/92–95: Correspondence between Germain and Howe.

CO 5/193: Materials Relating to German Mercenaries.

CO 5/229: Military Dispatches from America and West Indies.

CO 5/253: Materials on the Campaigns of 1776.

CO 5/263: Secret Dispatches to Commanders in Chief.

CO 5/542: Papers Laid before Commons Relative to American Campaigns.

CO 318/5–8: Correspondence of the Commander in the Lesser Antilles with Secretaries of State, 1778–1781.

Home Office Papers, Domestic and General.

Class 42: George III, 1782–1798. [Continuation of State Papers Class 37.]

Class 43: Entry Books, 1782–1798.

Class 50: Correspondence, Military, 1782–1840.

Class 51: Entry Books, 1758–1855. [Militia, Yeomanry, Volunteers.]

Paymaster General's Office Papers.

Class 2: Ledgers, 1757–1840.

Class 4: Half-Pay, 1737–1921.

Class 14: Miscellaneous Books, 1720–1861.

Public Record Office Lists and Indexes. [Includes Army Lists formerly in WO 64 and WO 65.]

Class 30/11: Cornwallis Papers.

Class 30/37: Ordnance Board Papers.

Class 30/55: Dorchester [Carleton] Papers. [See Colonial Williamsburg Foundation.]

State Office Papers.

Class 34: State Papers, Domestic, Anne, 1702–1714.

Class 35: State Papers, Domestic, George I, 1714–1727.

Class 36: State Papers, Domestic, George II, 1727–1760.

Class 37: State Papers, Domestic, George III, 1760–1782.

Class 41: State Papers, Domestic, Military, 1640–1782.

Class 44: Entry Books, 1661–1828.

Class 87: State Papers, Foreign, Military Expeditions, 1695–1763.

Various Papers.

War Office Papers.

Class 1: Letters-In, 1732–1868.

Class 2: Indexes of Correspondence, 1759–1858.

Class 4: Secretary's Letter Books, 1715–1782.

Class 7: Departmental Letter Books, 1715–1782.

Class 17: Muster Master General Monthly Returns.

Class 24: Establishment Warrants, 1661–1846.

Class 25: Registers, Various, 1660–1938. [Includes Embarkation Returns.]

Class 26: Miscellaneous Books.

Class 28: Headquarters Records, America, 1746–1785.

Class 34: Amherst Papers.

Classes 44–55: Ordnance Board Papers, 1568–1923.

Rhode Island Historical Society (Providence, Rhode Island).

Online at www.rihs.org.

Greene, Christopher. Papers.

Greene, Nathanael. Papers.

Hopkins, Esek. Papers.

Olney, Jeremiah. Papers.

Revolutionary Correspondence.

Revolutionary War Military Records.

Talbot, Silas. Papers.

Ward Manuscripts.

Rhode Island State Archives (Providence, Rhode Island).

Online at www.sec.state.ri.us/archives.

Revolutionary War Papers.

Royal Artillery Library (Woolwich, England).

Pattison, James. Papers.

Royal Engineers Library (Chatham, England).

Conolly Manuscripts.

Rutgers University Library (New Brunswick, New Jersey).

Online at www.libraries.rutgers.edu.

Egbert, Thomas. Memorandum Book.

Foreman, David. Papers.

Paterson, William. Papers.

Shreve, Israel. Papers.

Towne, Zaccheus. Diary.

South Carolina Department of Archives and History (Columbia, South Carolina).

Online at www.state.sc.us/scdah.

Gibbes Collection.

South Carolina Historical Society (Charleston, South Carolina).

Online at www.schistory.org.

Elliott, Barnard. Order Book.

Du Bose, Isaac. Order Book.

Horry, Harriott Pinckney. Papers.

Laurens, Henry. Papers.

Laurens, John. Papers.

Middleton Collection.

Moultrie-Lincoln Order Book.

Pinckney, Thomas. Papers.

Stadtsarchiv Bayreuth (Bayreuth).

Mss. 1000: Tagebuch des mark-gräflichen Jäger-leutnants Carl Philipp von Feilitzsch März.

Stadtsarchiv Frankfurt-am-Main (Frankfurt).

Depositum Adolf Reuber. Nr. 1: Tagebuch des Grenadiers Johannes Reuber.

State Historical Society of Wisconsin [Wisconsin Historical Society] (Madison, Wisconsin).

See Josephine L. Harper, *Guide to the Draper Manuscripts* (Madison, Wisc.: The State Historical Society of Wisconsin, 1983).

Online at www.wisconsinhistory.org.

Lyman C. Draper Manuscript Collection.

United States Army Center of Military History (Washington, DC).

Online at www.army.mil/cmh-pg/reference/revbib.

Blatsos, John. "Chronological Development and Combat Record of the New Hampshire Continental Brigade during the Revolutionary War."

United States Army Military History Institute (Carlisle Barracks, Pennsylvania).

Ninth Connecticut Regiment Orderly Book, 21 February–11 May 1780.

United States Military Academy (West Point, New York).

Online at www.library.usma.edu/archives/special.

University of Georgia, Hargrett Library (Athens, Georgia).

Online at www.libs.uga.edu.

Cuyler, Telamon. Collection.

Hargrett, Felix. Collection.

McIntosh, Lachlan. Papers.

Rare Map Collectdion.

Reid, Keith. Collection.

University of New Brunswick, Harriet Irving Library (Fredericton, New Brunswick).
　Online at www.hil.unb.ca
　Loyalist Collection.
　Winslow, Edward. Papers.
University of North Carolina, Southern Historical Collection (Chapel Hill, North Carolina).
　Online at www.lib.unc.edu/mss.
　Lenoir Family Papers.
　Lytle, W. F. Papers.
　North Carolina Historical Society Miscellaneous Papers.
　North Carolina State Papers.
　Revolutionary Papers.
University of South Carolina, South Caroliniana Library (Columbia, South Carolina).
　Online at www.sc.edu/library.
　Burke, Aedanus. Manuscripts.
　Butler, William. Manuscripts.
　Drayton, Stephen. Manuscripts.
　Hart, Oliver. Manuscripts.
　Laurens, John. Manuscripts.
　Marion, Francis. Manuscripts.
　Mayes Family Records.
University of Virginia, Alderman Library (Charlottesville, Virginia).
　Online at www.lib.virginia.edu/speccol.
　Lee, Henry. Papers.
　Revolutionary War Collections.
　Swearingen, Thomas. Journal.
　Wallace, A. D. Papers.
Vermont Historical Society (Montpelier, Vermont).
　Online at www.vermonthistory.org.
　Revolutionary War Papers.
Vermont State Archives (Montpelier, Vermont).
　Online at vermont-archives.org.
　Stevens Papers.
Virginia Historical Society (Richmond, Virginia).
　Online at www.vahistorical.org.
　Charles Campbell Collection of Theodoric Bland Papers.
　Dabney, Charles. Papers.
　Griffith, David. Papers.
　Keith of Woodbine Papers.
Virginia State Library [Library of Virginia] (Richmond, Virginia).
　Online at www.lva.lib.va.us.
　Cabell Papers.
　Fleming, William. Papers.
　Miscellaneous Revolutionary Manuscripts.
　Public Store Papers.
　Sergeant Long's Orderly Book of Captain John Belfield's Troop, First Continental Light Dragoon Regiment.
　War Office Papers.
Western Reserve Historical Society (Cleveland, Ohio).
　Online at www.wrhs.org.
　Cleveland, Moses. Papers.
Yale University Library, Manuscripts and Archives (New Haven, Connecticut).
　Online at www.yale.edu.
　Trumbull, John. Papers.
　Wadsworth Family Collection.

II. PUBLISHED SOURCES

Abbey, Kathryn T. "Efforts of Spain to Maintain Sources of Information in the British Colonies before 1779." *Mississippi Valley Historical Review*, 15 (June 1928), pp. 56–68.

———. "Peter Chester's Defense of the Mississippi after the Willing Raid." *Mississippi Valley Historical Review*, 22 (June 1935), pp. 17–32.

———. "Spanish Projects for the Reoccupation of the Floridas during the American Revolution." *Hispanic American Historical Review*, 9 (August 1929), pp. 265–285.

Abbot, Henry L., compiler. *The Beginnings of Modern Submarine Warfare under Captain-Lieutenant David Bushnell.* 1882. Reprint Edition, Hamden, Conn.: Archon Books, 1966.

Abernethy, Thomas J. "Crane's Rhode Island Company of Artillery, 1775." *Rhode Island History*, 29 (February–May 1970), pp. 46–51.

Abernethy, Thomas P. *Western Lands and the American Revolution.* New York: D. Appleton-Century Co., 1937.

Abu-Shumays, Mary D. "British Views of America and the American Revolution, 1774–1783." *Western Pennsylvania Historical Magazine*, 59 (July 1976), pp. 289–318.

Adams, Charles F. "The Battle of Bunker Hill." *American Historical Review*, 1 (April 1896), pp. 401–413.

———. "Cavalry in the War of Independence." *Proceedings of the Massachusetts Historical Society*, 43 (May 1910), pp. 547–593.

———. "Contemporary Opinion on the Howes." *Proceedings of the Massachusetts Historical Society*, 44 (November 1910), pp. 94–119.

———. *Studies Military and Diplomatic, 1775–1865.* New York: Macmillan Co., 1911.

Adams, John. *Adams Family Correspondence.* Edited by Lyman H. Butterfield, et al. Cambridge, Mass.: Harvard University Press, 1963.

———. *Diary and Autobiography of John Adams.* Edited by Lyman H. Butterfield, et al. Cambridge, Mass.: Harvard University Press, 1961.

Adams, Douglas N. "Jean Baptiste Ternant, Inspector General and Advisor to the Commanding Generals of the Southern Forces, 1778–1782." *South Carolina Historical Magazine*, 86 (July 1985), pp. 221–240.

Adams, Randolph G. *British Headquarters Maps and Sketches Used by Sir Henry Clinton While In Command of the British Forces Operating in North America.* Ann Arbor: William L. Clements Library, 1928.

———. "A View of Cornwallis' Surrender at Yorktown." *American Historical Review*, 37 (October 1931), pp. 25–49.

Adams, Thomas R. "The British Pamphlets of the American Revolution for 1774: A Progress Report." *Proceedings of the Massachusetts Historical Society*, 81 (1969), pp. 31–103.

Ahlin, John H. *Maine Rubicon: Downeast Settlers during the American Revolution.* Camden, Maine: Picton Press, 1966.

Aimone, Alan C., and Barbara A. Aimone. "'Brave Bostonians:' New Yorkers' Roles in the Winter Invasion of Canada." *Military Collector and Historian*, 36 (Winter 1984), pp. 134–150.

———. "Organizing and Equipping Montgomery's Yorkers in 1775." *Military Collector and Historian*, 28 (Summer 1976), pp. 53–63.

Aimone, Alan C., and Eric I. Manders. "A Note on New York City's Independent Companies, 1775–1776." *New York History*, 63 (January 1982), pp. 59–73.

Ainsley, Thomas. *Canada Preserved: The Journal of Captain Thomas Ainsley.* Edited by Sheldon S. Cohen. New York: New York University Press, 1968.

Akers, Charles W. "New Hampshire's 'Honorary' Lieutenant Governor: John Temple and the American Revolution." *Historical New Hampshire*, 30 (Summer 1975), pp. 78–99.

Alberts, Robert C. *George Rogers Clark and the Winning of the Old Northwest.* Washington, DC: National Park Service, 1975.

Albion, Robert G. *Forests and Sea Power: the Timber Problem of the Royal Navy, 1752–1862.* Cambridge, Mass.: Harvard University Press, 1926.

Alden, John R. *The American Revolution, 1775–1783.* New York: Harper & Brothers, 1954.

———. *General Charles Lee, Traitor or Patriot?* Baton Rouge: Louisiana State University Press, 1951.

———. *General Gage in America: Being Principally a History of His Role in the American Revolution.* Baton Rouge: Louisiana State University Press, 1948.

———. *George Washington: A Biography.* Baton Rouge: Louisiana State University Press, 1984.

———. *A History of the American Revolution.* New York: Alfred A. Knopf, 1969.

———. *John Stuart and the Southern Colonial Frontier: A Study of Indians Relations, War, Trade, and Land Problems in the Southern Wilderness, 1754–1775.* Ann Arbor: University of Michigan Press, 1944.

———. *The South in the American Revolution, 1763–1789.* Baton Rouge: Louisiana State University Press, 1957.

———. "Why the March to Concord?" *American Historical Review*, 49 (April 1944), pp. 446–454.

Alderman, Clifford L. *The War We Could Have Lost: The American Revolution.* New York: Four Winds Press, 1974.

Alexander, Arthur J. "Deserters: A British Source of Information during the American Revolution." *Journal of the Society for Army Historical Research*, 27 (Spring 1949), pp. 12–18.

———. "Desertion and Its Punishment in Revolutionary Virginia." *William and Mary Quarterly*, 3d Ser., 3 (July 1946), pp. 383–397.

———. "Exemptions from Military Service in the Old Dominion during the War of the Revolution." *Virginia Magazine of History and Biography*, 53 (July 1945), pp. 163–171.

———. "Exemptions from Militia Service in New York State during the Revolutionary War." *New York History*, 27 (April 1946), pp. 204–212.

———. "A Footnote on Deserters from the Virginia Forces during the American Revolution." *Virginia Magazine of History and Biography*, 55 (April 1947), pp. 137–146.

———. "How Maryland Tried to Raise Her Continental Quota." *Maryland Historical Magazine*, 37 (September 1942), pp. 184–196.

———. "Pennsylvania's Revolutionary Militia." *Pennsylvania Magazine of History and Biography*, 69 (January 1945), pp. 15–25.

———. "Service by Substitute in the Militia of Northampton and Lancaster Counties (Pennsylvania) during the War of the Revolution." *Military Affairs*, 9 (Winter 1945), pp. 278–282.

Alexander, C. B. "Richard Caswell." *North Carolina Historical Review*, 23 (1946), pp. 13–31, 119–141, 287–312.

Alexander, John K. "Forton Prison during the American Revolution: A Case Study of British Prisoner of War Policy and the American Prisoner Response to that Policy." *Essex Institute Historical Collections*, 103 (October 1967), pp. 365–389.

———. "The Fort Wilson Incident of 1779: A Case Study of the Revolutionary Crowd." *William and Mary Quarterly*, 3d Ser., 31 (October 1974), pp. 589–614.

Allard, Dean C. "The Potomac Navy of 1776." *Virginia Magazine of History and Biography* 84 (October 1976), pp. 411–430.

Allen, Gardner W. *Massachusetts Privateers of the Revolution.* Boston: Massachusetts Historical Society, 1927.

———. *A Naval History of the American Revolution.* 2 vols. Boston: Houghton Mifflin, 1913.

Allen, Penelope J., editor. *Tennessee Soldiers in the Revolution.* Bristol: King Printing Co., 1935.

Allyn, Charles. *The Battle of Groton Heights.* Revised Edition. New London: Charles Allyn, 1882.

Almeida, Dierdre. "The Stockbridge Indian in the American Revolution." *Historical Journal of Western Massachusetts*, 4 (Fall 1975), pp. 34–39.

"The American Revolution in the Hudson River Valley," *The Hudson River Valley Review*, 20 (Summer 2003), pp. 1–71.

Amerman, Richard H. "Treatment of American Prisoners during the Revolution." *Proceedings of the New Jersey Historical Society*, New Ser., 78 (October 1960), pp. 257–275.

Ammerman, David. *In the Common Cause: American Response to the Coercive Acts of 1774.* Charlottesville: University Press of Virginia, 1974.

ANB. *American National Biography.* John A. Garraty, and Mark C. Carnes, general editors. New York : Oxford University Press, 1999.

Anbury, Thomas. *With Burgoyne from Quebec: An Account of the Life at Quebec and of the Famous Battle of Saratoga.* Edited by Sydney Jackman. Toronto: Macmillan of Canada, 1963.

Anderson, Enoch. *Personal Recollections of Captain Enoch Anderson, an Officer of the Delaware Regiments in the Revolutionary War.* Edited by Henry Hobart Bellas. Wilmington: Historical Society of Delaware, 1896.

Anderson, Fred, and Andrew Cayton. *The Dominion of War: Empire and Liberty in North America, 1500–2000.* New York: Viking Press, 2005.

Anderson, John R. "Militia Law in Colonial New Jersey." *Proceedings of the New Jersey Historical Society*, 76–77 (October 1958–January 1959).

Anderson, Olive. "The Role of the Army in Parliamentary Management during the American War of Independence." *Journal of the Society for Army Historical Research*, 34 (December 1956), pp. 146–149.

———. "The Treatment of Prisoners of War in Britain during the American War of Independence." *Bulletin of the Institute of Historical Research*, 28 (May 1955), pp. 63–83.

Anderson, Troyer S. *The Command of the Howe Brothers during the American Revolution.* New York: Oxford University Press, 1936.

Anderson, William G. *The Price of Liberty: The Public Debt of the American Revolution.* Charlottesville: University Press of Virginia, 1980.

André, John. *Major André's Journal: Operations of the British Army under Lieutenant Generals Sir William Howe and Sir Henry Clinton June 1777 to November 1778. Recorded by Major John André, Adjutant General.* Edited by C. DeWitt Willcox. Tarrytown: William Abbatt, 1930.

Andreano, Ralph L., and Herbert D. Warner. "Charleston Loyalists: A Statistical Note." *South Carolina Historical and Genealogical Magazine*, 60 (July 1959), pp. 164–168.

Andresen, Karen E. "A Return to Legitimacy: New Hampshire's Constitution of 1776." *Historical New Hampshire*, 31 (Winter 1976), pp. 155–163.

Andrews, Charles M. *The Colonial Background of the American Revolution.* Revised edition. New Haven: Yale University Press, 1931.

———. *Guide to the manuscript materials for the history of the United States to 1783 in the British Museum, in minor London archives, and in the libraries of Oxford and Cambridge.* Washington: Carnegie Institution, 1908.

———. *Guide to the materials for the American History, to 1783, in the Public Record Office of Great Britain.* 2 vols. Washington: Carnegie Institution, 1912–1914.

Angell, Israel. *Diary of Colonel Israel Angell Commanding the Second Rhode Island Continental Regiment during the American Revolution 1778–1781.* Edited by Edward Field. Providence: Preston and Rounds, 1899.

Appel, John C. "Colonel Daniel Brodhead and the Lure of Detroit." *Pennsylvania History*, 38 (July 1971), pp. 265–282.

Applegate, Howard L. "The Medical Administration of the American Revolutionary Army." *Military Affairs*, 25 (Spring 1961), pp. 1–10.

Archdeacon, Thomas J. "American Historians and the American Revolution: A Bicentennial Overview." *Wisconsin Magazine of History*, 63 (Summer 1980), pp. 278–298.

Arena, Carmelo R. "Philadelphia-Spanish New Orleans Trade." Ph.D. dissertation, University of Pennsylvania, 1959.

Arndt, Karl J. R. "New Hampshire and the Battle of Bennington: Colonel Baum's Mission and Bennington Defeat As Reported by a German Officer under Burgoyne's Command." *Historical New Hampshire*, 32 (Winter 1977), pp. 198–227.

Arnold, Douglas M. *A Republican Revolution: Ideology and Politics in Pennsylvania, 1776–1790.* New York: Garland, 1989.

Ashe, Samuel A. *Rutherford's Expedition against the Indians, 1776,* by Captain S. A. Ashe. Raleigh: E. M. Uzzell & Co., 1904.

Ashmore, Otis, and C. H. Olmstead. "The Battles of Kettle Creek and Briar Creek." *Georgia Historical Quarterly*, 10 (June 1926), pp. 85–125.

Ashton, Rick J. "The Loyalist Congressmen of New York." *New-York Historical Society Quarterly*, 60 (July–October 1976), pp. 95–106.

Atkinson, Christopher T. "British Forces in North America, 1774–1781: Their Distribution and Strength." *Journal of the Society for Army Historical Research*, 16 (Spring 1937), pp. 3–23; 19 (Autumn 1940), pp. 163–166; 20 (Winter 1941), pp. 190–192.

———. "Material for Military History in the Reports of the Historical Manuscripts Commission." *Journal of the Society for Army Historical Research*, 21 (Spring 1942), pp. 17–34.

———, editor. "Some Evidence For the Burgoyne Expedition." *Journal of the Society for Army Historical Research*, 26 (Fall 1948), pp. 132–142.

Atwood, Rodney. *The Hessians: Mercenaries from Hessen-Kassel in the American Revolution.* New York: Cambridge University Press, 1980.

Auerbach, Inge, et al. *Hessen und die Amerikanische Revolution 1776.* Marburg: das Hessische Staatsarchiv, 1976.

Auerbach, Inge, Franz G. Eckhart, and Otto Frölich, editors. *Hessische Truppen im amerikanischen Unabhängigkeitskrieg [HETRINA].* 5 vols. Marburg: Veröttenlichungen der Archivschule Marburg-Institut für Archivwissenschaft, 1972–76.

Aussaresses, Paul. "L'Artillerie Française au siege de Yorktown (1781)." *Revue Historique de L'Armée*, 26 (#2, 1970), pp. 34–42.

Aykroyd, Elizabeth Rhoades. "Notes on the Raids on Fort William and Mary." *Historical New Hampshire*, 32 (Fall 1977), pp. 144–146.

Babits, Lawrence E. *A Devil of a Whipping: The Battle of Cowpens.* Chapel Hill: University of North Carolina Press, 1998.

———. "The 'Fifth' Maryland at Guilford Courthouse: An Exercise in Historical Accuracy." *Maryland Historical Magazine*, 84 (Winter 1989), pp. 370–378.

———. "Shoe Life in the 71st of Foot 1776–1777." *Military Collector and Historian*, 34 (Summer 1982), pp. 84–86.

———. *The Southern Campaigns of the American Revolution.* Washington, DC: Eastern National Parks, 2002.

Bailey, De Witt. *British Military Longarms, 1715–1815.* Harrisburg: Stackpole Books, 1971.

Bailyn, Bernard. *The Faces of Revolution: Personalities and Themes in the Struggle for American Independence.* New York: Alfred A. Knopf, 1990.

———. *Ideological Origins of the American Revolution.* Cambridge, Mass.: Harvard University Press, 1967.

———. *The Ordeal of Thomas Hutchinson.* Cambridge, Mass.: Harvard University Press, 1974.

———. "Political Experience and Enlightenment Ideas in Eighteenth-Century America." *American Historical Review*, 67 (January 1962), pp. 339–351.

Bakeless, John E. *Background to Glory: The Life of George Rogers Clark.* Philadelphia: J. B. Lippincott, 1957.

———. *Turncoats, Traitors and Heroes.* Philadelphia: J. B. Lippincott Co., 1960.

Baker, Mary Ellen, compiler. *A Bibliography of Lists of New England Soldiers.* 1910–1911. Boston, Mass.: New England Historical and Genealogical Society, 1977.

Baker, Norman. *Government and Contractors: The British Treasury and War Supplies, 1775–1783.* London: University of London, 1971.

Balderston, Marion. "Lord Howe Clears the Delaware." *Pennsylvania Magazine of History and Biography*, 96 (July 1972), pp. 326–345.

Balderston, Marion, and David Syrett, editors. *The Lost War: Letters from British Officers during the American Revolution.* New York: Horizon Press, 1975.

Baldry, W. Y. "Memorandum Relating to the Sortie, Gibraltar, 27th November, 1781." *Journal of the Society for Army Historical Research,* 15 (Summer 1936), pp. 145–151.

Baldwin, Jeduthan. *The Revolutionary Journal of Col. Jeduthan Baldwin 1775–1778.* Edited by Thomas William Baldwin. Bangor: De Burians, 1906.

Barck, Oscar T. *New York City during the War For Independence with Special Reference to the Period of British Occupation.* New York: Columbia University Press, 1931.

Bargar, B. D. "Charles Town Loyalism in 1775: The Secret Reports of Alexander Innes." *South Carolina Historical Magazine,* 63 (July 1962), pp. 125–136.

———. *Lord Dartmouth and the American Revolution.* Columbia: University of South Carolina Press, 1965.

Barker, John. *The British in Boston Being the Diary of Lieutenant John Barker of the King's Own Regiment from November 15, 1774 to May 31, 1776.* Edited by Elizabeth Ellery Dana. Cambridge, Mass.: Harvard University Press, 1924.

Barnhart, John D. "A New Evaluation of Henry Hamilton and George Rogers Clark." *Mississippi Valley Historical Review,* 37 (March 1951), pp. 643–652.

Barnsley, R. E. "The Life of an 18th Century Army Surgeon." *Journal of the Society for Army Historical Research,* 44 (September 1966), pp. 130–134.

Barnwell, Joseph W. "The Evacuation of Charleston by the British in 1782." *South Carolina Historical and Genealogical Magazine,* 11 (January 1910), pp. 1–26.

Barrington, William Wildman, Viscount. *An Eighteenth-Century Secretary at War: The Papers of William, Viscount Barrington.* Edited by Tony Hayter. London: The Army Records Society, 1988.

Barrow, Thomas C. "The American Revolution As a Colonial War for Independence." *William and Mary Quarterly,* 3d Ser., 25 (July 1968), pp. 452–464.

———. *Trade and Empire: the British Customs Service in Colonial America 1660–1775.* Cambridge, Mass.: Harvard University Press, 1967.

Barrs, Burton. *East Florida in the American Revolution.* Jacksonville: Guild Press, 1932.

Bartenstein, Fred, and Isabel Bartenstein. *New Jersey's Revolutionary War Powder Mill.* Mendham, N.J.: Privately printed, 1973.

Bartholomees, James B., Jr. "Fight or Flee: The Combat Performance of the North Carolina Militia in the Cowpens-Guilford Courthouse Campaign, January to March 1781." Ph.D. dissertation, Duke University, 1978.

Bartlett, John R., editor. *Records of the Colony of Rhode Island and Providence Plantations in New England.* 9 vols. Providence: Various publishers, 1856–1865.

Bartlett, Josiah. *The Papers of Josiah Bartlett.* Edited by Frank C. Mevers. Hanover: University Press of New England for the New Hampshire Historical Society, 1979.

Bass, Robert D. *Gamecock: The Life and Campaigns of General Thomas Sumter.* New York: Holt, Rinehart and Winston, 1961.

———. *The Green Dragon: The Lives of Banastre Tarleton and Mary Robinson.* New York: Henry Holt and Co., 1957.

———. *Ninety-Six: The Struggle for the South Carolina Back Country.* Lexington, South Carolina: Sandlapper Press, 1978.

———. *Swamp Fox: The Life and Campaigns of General Francis Marion.* New York: Henry Holt and Co., 1959.

Bast, Homer. "Creek Indian Affairs, 1775–1778." *Georgia Historical Quarterly,* 33 (March 1949), pp. 1–25.

Batchellor, Albert S. *The Ranger Service in the Upper Valley of the Connecticut and the Most Northerly Regiment of New Hampshire Militia in the Period of the Revolution.* Concord: Rumford Press, 1903.

Batt, Richard J. "The Maryland Continentals, 1780–1781." Ph.D. dissertation, Tulane University, 1974.

Baule, Steven M., and Stephen Gilbert. *British Army Officers Who Served in the American Revolution, 1775–1783.* Westminster, Maryland: Heritage Books, 2004.

Bauman, Sebastian. *Memoirs of Sebastian Beauman (sic) and His Descendants with Selections from His Correspondence.* Edited by Mary C. Doll Fairchild. New York: Privately printed, 1900.

Baxter, James P., editor. *Documentary History of the State of Maine.* 20 vols. Portland: Lefavor-Tower Co., 1910–1914.

Baxter, William T. *The House of Hancock: Business in Boston, 1724–1775.* New York: Russell and Russell, 1965.

Beane, Samuel C. "General Enoch Poor." *Proceedings of the New Hampshire Historical Society,* 3 (1895–1899), pp. 435–472.

Bearss, Edwin C. *The Battle of Cowpens: A Documented Narrative and Troop Movement Maps,* Washington, DC: National Park Service, 1967.

Beasley, Paul W. "The Life and Times of Isaac Shelby 1750–1826." Ph.D. dissertation, University of Kentucky, 1968.

Becker, Laura L. "The American Revolution As a Community Experience: A Case Study of Reading, Pennsylvania." Ph.D. dissertation, University of Pennsylvania, 1978.

———. "Prisoners of War in the American Revolution: A Community Perspective." *Military Affairs,* 46 (December 1982), pp. 169–173.

Becker, Robert A. *Revolution, Reform, and the Politics of American Taxation, 1763–1783.* Baton Rouge: Louisiana State University Press, 1980.

Beeman, Richard R. *The Evolution of the Southern Backcountry: A Case Study of Lunenburg County, Virginia 1746–1832.* Philadelphia: University of Pennsylvania Press, 1984.

Beerman, Eric. "José de Ezpeleta: Alabama's First Spanish Commandant during the American Revolution." *Alabama Review,* 29 (October 1976), pp. 249–260.

Beitzell, Edwin W. *St. Mary's County, Maryland in the American Revolution: Calendar of Events.* Leonardstown: St. Mary's County, Maryland, Bicentennial Commission, 1975.

Bell, Whitfield J., Jr. *Colonel Lewis Nicola: Advocate of Monarchy, 1782.* Philadelphia: Pennsylvania Society of the Cincinnati, 1983.

———. *John Morgan Continental Doctor.* Philadelphia: University of Pennsylvania Press, 1965.

Bellesiles, Michael A. *Arming America: The Origins of a National Gun Culture.* New York: Alfred A. Knopf, 2000.

————. *Revolutionary Outlaws: Ethan Allen and the Struggle for Independence on the Early American Frontier.* Charlottesville: University Press of Virginia, 1993.

Bemis, Samuel F. "British Secret Service and the French-American Alliance." *American Historical Review*, 29 (April 1924), pp. 474–495.

————. *The Diplomacy of the American Revolution.* Bloomington: Indiana University Press, 1965 (1935).

Bennett, Charles E., and Donald R. Lennon. *A Quest for Glory: Major General Robert Howe and the American Revolution.* Chapel Hill: University of North Carolina Press, 1991.

Benninghoff, Herman O., II. *Valley Forge: A Genesis for Command and Control.* Gettysburg, Pa.: Thomas Publications, 2001.

Benton, William A. "Pennsylvania Revolutionary Officers and the Federal Constitution." *Pennsylvania History*, 31 (October 1964), pp. 419–435.

————. *Whig-Loyalism: An Aspect of Political Ideology in the American Revolutionary Era.* Rutherford, N.J.: Fairleigh Dickinson University Press, 1969.

Beers, Henry P. "The Papers of the British Commanders in Chief in North America, 1754–1783." *Military Affairs*, 13 (Summer 1949), pp. 79–94.

Beresford, Marcus de la Poer. "Ireland in French Strategy during the American War of Independence, 1776–83." *Irish Sword*, 12 (Winter 1976), pp. 285–297; 13 (Summer 1977), pp. 20–29.

Berger, Carl. *Broadsides and Bayonets: The Propaganda War of the American Revolution* 96. Revised edition, San Rafael, California: Presidio Press, 1976.

Berkeley, Henry J. "Maryland Physicians at the Period of the Revolutionary War." *Maryland Historical Magazine*, 24 (March 1929), pp. 1–177.

Berlin, Ira and Ronald Hoffman, editors, *Slavery and Freedom in the Age of the American Revolution.* Charlottesville: University Press of Virginia, 1983.

Berlin, Robert H. "The Administration of Military Justice in the Continental Army during the American Revolution, 1775–1783." Ph.D. dissertation, University of California at Santa Barbara, 1976.

Bernard, Stuart L. "George Washington and the Genesis of American Military Discipline." *Mid-America*, 49 (April 1967), pp. 83–100.

Bernstein, David. "New Jersey in the American Revolution: The Establishment of a Government Amid Civil and Military Disorder, 1770–1781." Ph.D. dissertation, Rutgers University, 1969.

Bezanson, Anne. "Inflation and Controls, Pennsylvania, 1774–1779." *Journal of Economic History*, Supplement 8 (1948), pp. 1–20.

Bickford, Christopher P. "In the King's Pay: Two Customs Officials in New Haven, 1774–1776." *Connecticut Historical Society Bulletin*, 42 (January 1977), pp. 1–7.

Bielinski, Stefan, editor. *A Guide to the Revolutionary War Manuscripts in the New York State Library.* Albany: New York American Revolution Bicentennial Commission, 1976.

Bill, Alfred H. *The Campaign of Princeton, 1776–1777.* Princeton: Princeton University Press, 1948.

————. *New Jersey and the Revolutionary War.* Princeton: D. Van Nostrand Co., 1964.

————. *Valley Forge: The Making of an Army.* New York: Harper, 1952.

Bill, Shirley A., and Louis Gottschalk. "Silas Deane's 'Worthless' Agreement with Lafayette." *Prologue*, 4 (Winter 1972), pp. 219–223.

Billias, George A. "Beverly's Seacoast Defenses during the Revolutionary War." *Essex Institute Historical Collections*, 94 (April 1958), pp. 119–131.

————. *General John Glover and His Marblehead Mariners.* New York: Holt, Rinehart and Winston, 1960.

————, editor. *George Washington's Generals.* New York: William Morrow, 1964.

  Billias, George A. "Horatio Gates: Professional Soldier," pp. 79–108.
  Callahan, North. "Henry Knox: American Artillerist," pp. 239–259.
  Cunliffe, Marcus. "George Washington: George Washington's Generalship," pp. 3–21.
  Higginbotham, Don. "Daniel Morgan: Guerrilla Fighter," pp. 291–317.
  Peckham, Howard H. "Marquise de Lafayette: Eager Warrior," pp. 212–238.
  Pell, John H. G. "Philip Schuyler: The General As Aristocrat," pp. 54–78.
  Rankin, Hugh F. "Anthony Wayne; Military Romanticist," pp. 260–290.
  Shipton, Clifford K. "Benjamin Lincoln: Old Reliable," pp. 193–211.
  Shy, John. "Charles Lee: The Soldier As Radical," pp. 22–53.
  Thayer, Theodore. "Nathaniel [sic] Greene: Revolutionary War Strategist," pp. 109–136.
  Wallace, Willard M. "Benedict Arnold: Traitorous Patriot," pp. 163–192.
  Whittemore, Charles P. "John Sullivan: Luckless Irishman," pp. 137–162.

Billias, George A., editor. *George Washington's Opponents.* New York: William Morrow, 1969.

  Baugh, Daniel A. "Sir Samuel Hood: Superior Subordinate," pp. 291–326.
  Billias, George A. "John Burgoyne: Ambitious General," pp. 142–192.
  Gruber, Ira D. "Richard Lord Howe: Admiral As Peacemaker," pp. 233–259.
  Jones, Maldwyn A. "Sir William Howe: Conventional Strategist," pp. 39–72.
  Lloyd, Christopher. "Sir George Rodney: Lucky Admiral," pp. 327–354.
  Rankin, Hugh F. "Charles Lord Cornwallis: Study in Frustration," pp. 193–232.
  Shy, John. "Thomas Gage: Weak Link of Empire," pp. 3–38.
  Smith, Paul H. "Sir Guy Carleton: Soldier-Statesman," pp. 103–141.
  Willcox, William B. "Arbuthnot, Gambier, and Graves: 'Old Women' of the Navy," pp. 260–290.
  ————. "Sir Henry Clinton: Paralysis of Command," pp. 73–102.

————. "Pelham Bay: A Forgotten Battle." *New-York Historical Society Quarterly*, 42 (January 1958), pp. 20–38.

Billington, Ray A. "The Fort Stanwix Treaty of 1768." *New York History*, 25 (April 1944), pp. 182–194.

———, editor. *The Reinterpretation of Early American History*. San Marino, Calif.: Huntington Library, 1966.

Bird, Harrison. *March to Saratoga: General Burgoyne and the American Campaign*. New York: Oxford University Press, 1963.

Bishop, Morris. "Love on Parole, 1778–1780." *New York History*, 20 (January 1939), pp. 43–50.

Black, Jeremy. *The War for America: The Fight for Independence, 1775–1783*. New York: St. Martin's Press, 1991.

Blackmore, Howard L. *British Military Firearms, 1650–1850*. London: Herbert Jenkins, 1961.

Blanco, Richard L., editor. *The American Revolution, 1775–1783*. 2 vols. New York: Garland Publishing, 1993.

———. "Military Medicine in Northern New York, 1776–1777." *New York History*, 63 (January 1982), pp. 39–58.

———. *Physician of the American Revolution: Jonathan Potts*. New York: Garland STPM Press, 1979.

———. *The War of the American Revolution: A Selected Annotated Bibliography of Published Sources*. New York: Garland Publishing, 1984.

Bliven, Bruce, Jr. *Battle for Manhattan*. New York: Henry Holt and Co., 1955.

———. *Under the Guns. New York: 1775–1776*. New York: Harper & Row, 1972.

Bloomfield, Joseph. *Citizen-Soldier: The Revolutionary War Journal of Joseph Bloomfield*. Edited by Mark E. Lender and James K. Martin. Newark: New Jersey Historical Society, 1982.

Boatner, Mark M., III. *Encyclopedia of the American Revolution*. New York: David McKay Co., 1966.

Bobb, Bernard E. *The Viceregency of Antonio María Bucareli in New Spain, 1771–1779*. Austin: University of Texas Press, 1962.

Bodinier, Gilbert. *Dictionnaire des officiers de l'armee royale qui ont combattu aux Etats-Unis pendant la guerre d'Independance*. 3eme edition. Paris: Service Historique de l'Armée de terre, 2000.

———. *Les officiers de l'armée royale, combattants de la guerre d'indépendance des Etats-Unis de Yorktown à l'an II*. Paris: Service Historique de l'Armée de terre, Château de Vincennes, Paris, 1983.

Bodle, Wayne K. *The Valley Forge Winter: Civilians and Soldiers at War*. University Park: Pennsylvania State University Press, 2002.

Boehret, Paul C. *The Committee of Safety Musket*. N.P.: Privately printed, 1956.

Böhm, Uwe Peter. *Hessisches Militär Die Truppen der Landgrafschaft Hessen-Kassel, 1672–1806 [The Hessian Army: Troops of Hessen-Kassel County 1672–1806]*. Beckum: Herausgegeben im Auftrag der Deutschen Gesellschaft für Heereskunde [German Society for Military Studies], 1986.

Bolton, Charles K. *The Private Soldier under Washington*. New York: Charles Scribner's Sons, 1902.

Bonner, Frederick L. "Marinus Willett." *New York History*, 17 (July 1936), pp. 273–280.

Bonsal, Stephen. *When the French Were Here: The French Forces in America and Their Contribution to the Yorktown Campaign*. Garden City, New York: Doubleday and Company, 1945.

Bonwick, Colin. *The American Revolution*. Charlottesville: University Press of Virginia, 1991.

Borick, Carl P. *A Gallant Defense: The Siege of Charleston, 1780*. Columbia: University of South Carolina Press, 2003.

Boromé, Joseph A. "Dominica during French Occupation, 1778–1784." *English Historical Review*, 84 (January 1969), pp. 36–58.

Bostwick, Elisha. "A Connecticut Soldier under Washington: Elisha Bostwick's Memoirs of the First Years of the Revolution." Edited by William S. Powell. *William and Mary Quarterly*, 3d Ser., 6 (January 1949), pp. 94–107.

Boudriot, Jean. *John Paul Jones and the Bonhomme Richard: A Reconstruction of the Ship and an Account of the Battle with HMS Serapis*. Translated by David H. Roberts. Annapolis: Naval Institute Press, 1987.

Bouton, Nathaniel, et al., editors. *Documents and Records Relating to the Province, Towns and State of New Hampshire*. 40 vols. Concord, Nashua and Manchester: Various Publishers, 1867–1943.

Bowden, David K. *The Execution of Isaac Hayne*. Lexington, S.C.: Sandlapper Store, 1977.

Bowen, Joanne V. "A Study of Seasonality and Substance: Eighteenth Century Suffield, Connecticut." Ph.D. dissertation, Brown University, 1990.

Bowie, Lucy L. "German Prisoners in the American Revolution." *Maryland Historical Magazine*, 40 (September 1945), pp. 185–200.

———. "Maryland Troops in the Battle of Harlem Heights." *Maryland Historical Magazine*, 43 (March 1948), pp. 1–23.

Bowler, R. Arthur. "The American Revolution and British Army Administrative Reform." *Journal of the Society for Army Historical Research*, 58 (Summer 1980), pp. 66–77.

———. *Logistics and the Failure of the British Army in America, 1775–1783*. Princeton: Princeton University Press, 1975.

———. "Sir Guy Carleton and the Campaign of 1776 in Canada." *Canadian Historical Review*, 55 (June 1974), pp. 131–140.

———. "Sir Henry Clinton and Army Profiteering: A Neglected Aspect of the Clinton-Cornwallis Controversy." *William and Mary Quarterly*, 3d Ser., 31 (January 1974), pp. 111–122.

Bowling, Kenneth R. "New Light on the Philadelphia Mutiny of 1783: Federal-State Confrontation at the Close of the War for Independence." *Pennsylvania Magazine of History and Biography*, 101 (October 1977), pp. 419–450.

Bowman, Allen. "The Morale of the American Army in the Latter Half of 1776." *Virginia Magazine of History and Biography*, 40 (July 1931), pp. 193–205.

———. *The Morale of the American Revolutionary Army*. Washington: American Council on Public Affairs, 1943.

Bowman, Larry G. *Captive Americans: Prisoners during the American Revolution*. Athens: Ohio University Press, 1977.

———. "The Court-Martial of Captain Richard Lippincot." *New Jersey History*, 89 (Spring 1971), pp. 23–36.

———. "Military Parolees on Long Island, 1777–1782." *Journal of Long Island History*, 18 (Spring 1982), pp. 21–29.

———. "The Pennsylvania Prisoner Exchange Conferences, 1778." *Pennsylvania History*, 45 (July 1978), pp. 257–269.

———. "The Virginia County Committees of Safety, 1774–1776." *Virginia Magazine of History and Biography*, 79 (July 1971), pp. 322–337.

Boyd, George A. *Elias Boudinot: Patriot and Statesman, 1740–1821*. Princeton: Princeton University Press, 1952.

Boyd, Mark F., and José Navarro Latorre. "Spanish Interest in British Florida, and in the Progress of the American Revolution." *Florida Historical Quarterly*, 32 (October 1953), pp. 92–130.

Boyer, Charles S. *Early Forges and Furnaces in New Jersey*. Philadelphia: University of Pennsylvania Press, 1931.

Boyle, Joseph L., editor. *Writings from the Valley Forge Encampment of the Continental Army, 19 December 1777–19 June 1778*. 4 vols. Bowie, Maryland: Heritage Books, 2000–2003.

Bradford, James C., editor. *Command Under Sail, 1775–1850*. Annapolis: Naval Institute Press, 1985.

——— "The Navies of the American Revolution." In *In Peace and War, Interpretations of American Naval History*. 2d edition. Edited by Kenneth J. Hagan. Westport, Conn.: Greenwood Press, 1984.

Bradford, S. Sidney. "Discipline in the Morristown Winter Encampments." *Proceedings of the New Jersey Historical Society*, 80 (January 1962), pp. 1–30.

———. "Hunger Menaces the Revolution, December, 1779–January, 1780." *Maryland Historical Magazine*, 61 (March 1966), pp. 1–21.

Brady, William Y. "Brodhead's Trail up the Allegheny, 1779." *Western Pennsylvania Historical Magazine*, 37 (March 1954), pp. 19–31.

Brant, Irving. *James Madison*. 6 vols. Indianapolis: Bobbs-Merrill, 1941–1961.

Bratten, John R.. *The Gondola Philadelphia and the Battle of Lake Champlain*. College Station: Texas A&M University Press, 2002.

Bredenberg, Oscar R. "The American Champlain Fleet, 1775–77." *Bulletin of the Fort Ticonderoga Museum*, 12 (September 1968).

———. "The Royal Savage." *Bulletin of the Fort Ticonderoga Museum*, 12 (September 1966), pp. 128–149.

Brennan, Ellen E. *Plural Office-Holding in Massachusetts 1760–1780*. Chapel Hill: University of North Carolina Press, 1945.

Brenneman, Gloria E. "The Conway Cabal: Myth or Reality." *Pennsylvania History*, 40 (April 1973), pp. 169–177.

Brewer, John. *The Sinews of Power: War, Money, and the English State, 1688–1783*. Cambridge, Mass.: Harvard University Press, 1990.

Brewington, Marion V. "American Naval Guns, 1775–1785." *American Neptune*, 3 (January, April 1943), pp. 11–18, 148–158.

Bridenbaugh, Carl B. *Cities in Revolt: Urban Life in America, 1743–1776*. New York: Oxford University Press, 1955.

———. *The Spirit of '76: The Growth of American Patriotism before Independence*. New York: Oxford University Press, 1975.

Brooke, John L. "The Quiet of the People: Revolutionary Settlements and Civil Unrest in Western Massachusetts, 1774–1789." *William and Mary Quarterly*, 3d Ser., 46 (July 1989), pp. 425–462.

Brookhiser, Richard. *Founding Father: Rediscovering George Washington*. New York: Free Press, 1996.

Brown, Anne S. K. "Eighteenth Century Grenadier Caps." *Rhode Island History*, 12 (April 1953), pp. 44–49.

Brown, Gerald S. *The American Secretary: The Colonial Policy of Lord George Germain, 1775–1778*. Ann Arbor: University of Michigan Press, 1963.

Brown, Jared A. "A Note on British Military Theatre in New York at the End of the American Revolution." *New York History*, 62 (April 1981), pp. 177–187.

Brown, Lloyd A. *Loyalist Operations at New Haven*. Ann Arbor: William L. Clements Library, 1938.

Brown, M. L. *Firearms in Colonial America: Their Impact on History and Technology, 1492–1792*. Washington, DC: Smithsonian Institution Press, 1980.

Brown, Margaret L. "William Bingham, Agent of the Continental Congress in Martinique." *Pennsylvania Magazine of History and Biography*, 61 (January 1937), pp. 54–87.

Brown, Marvin L., Jr., editor. *Baroness von Riedesel and the American Revolution: Journal and Correspondence of a Tour of Duty 1776–1783*. Chapel Hill: University of North Carolina Press, 1965.

Brown, Parker B. "The Battle of Sandusky, June 4–6, 1782." *Western Pennsylvania Historical Magazine*, 65 (April 1982), pp. 115–151.

———. "The Fate of Crawford Volunteers Captured by Indians Following the Battle of Sandusky in 1782." *Western Pennsylvania Historical Magazine*, 65 (October 1982), pp. 323–340.

———. "Reconstructing Crawford's Army of 1782." *Western Pennsylvania Historical Magazine*, 65 (January 1982), pp. 17–36.

Brown, Ralph A. "Colonel Experience Storrs, Connecticut Farmer and Patriot." *Connecticut Historical Society Bulletin*, 19 (October 1954), pp. 118–121.

Brown, Richard M. *The South Carolina Regulators*. Cambridge, Mass.: Harvard University Press, 1963.

Brown, Robert M. "Revolutionary New Hampshire and the Loyalist Experience: 'Surely We Have Deserved a Better Fate.'" Ph.D. dissertation, University of New Hampshire, 1983.

Brown, Rodney H. *American Polearms, 1526–1865*. New Milford, Conn.: N. Fleyderman, 1967.

Brown, Wallace S. *The Good Americans: The Loyalists in the American Revolution*. New York: William Morrow, 1969.

———. *The King's Friends: The Composition and Motives of the American Loyalist Claimants*. Providence: Brown University Press, 1965.

———. "The View at Two Hundred Years: The Loyalists of the American Revolution." *American Antiquarian Society Proceedings*, New Ser., 80 (April 1970), pp. 25–47.

Brown, Weldon A. *Empire or Independence: A Study of the Failure of Reconciliation, 1774–1783.* Baton Rouge: Louisiana State University Press, 1941.

Brownlow, Donald G. *A Documentary History of the Battle of Germantown.* Germantown: Germantown Historical Society, 1955.

Bruce, Anthony. *The Purchase System in the British Army, 1600–1871.* London: Royal Historical Society, 1980.

Brumbaugh, Gaius M., and Margaret R. Hodges. *Revolutionary Records of Maryland.* 1924. Reprint, Genealogical Publishing Co., 1967.

Brumwell, Stephen. *Redcoats: The British Soldier and War in the Americas, 1755–1763.* New York: Cambridge University Press, 2001.

Bryant, G. J. "The East Indian Company and the British Army: The Crisis at Madras in 1783." *Journal of the Society for Army Historical Research,* 62 (Spring 1984), pp. 13–27.

Buchanan, John. *The Road to Guilford Courthouse: The American Revolution in the Carolinas.* New York: John Wiley, 1997.

Buel, Richard V., Jr. *Dear Liberty: Connecticut's Mobilization for the Revolutionary War.* Middletown: Wesleyan University Press, 1980.

———. *In Irons: Britain's Naval Supremacy and the American Revolutionary Economy.* New Haven: Yale University Press, 1998.

Buker, George E. *The Penobscot Expedition: Commodore Saltonstall and the Massachusetts Conspiracy of 1779.* Annapolis: Naval Institute Press, 2002.

Buker, George E., and Richard A. Martin. "Governor Tonyn's Brown-Water Navy: East Florida during the American Revolution, 1775–1778" *Florida Historical Quarterly,* 58 (July 1979), pp. 58–71.

Bull, Stewart Hastings. *The Queen's York Rangers: An Historic Regiment.* Erin, Ontario: Boston Mills Press, 1984.

Bullen, Ripley P. "Fort Tonyn and the Campaign of 1778." *Florida Historical Quarterly,* 29 (April 1951), pp. 253–260.

Bullion, John L. "British Ministers and the American Resistance to the Stamp Act, October–December 1765." *William and Mary Quarterly,* 3d Ser., 49 (January 1992), pp. 89–107.

———. *A Great and Necessary Measure: George Grenville and the Genesis of the Stamp Act, 1763–1765.* Columbia: University of Missouri Press, 1982.

———. "'Truly Loyal Subjects:' British Politicians and the Failure to Foresee American Resistance to Parliamentary Taxation, 1762–1765." *Connecticut Review,* 11 (Summer 1989), pp. 28–42.

Burgoyne, Bruce, translator and editor. *Defeat, Disaster, and Dedication* [two Hessian journals]. Bowie, Md.: Heritage Books, 1997.

———. *Diaries of Two Ansbach Jagers.* Bowie, Md.: Heritage Books, 1997.

———. *The Diary of Lieutenant von Bardeleben and Other von Donop regiment Documents.* Bowie, Md.: Heritage Books, 1998.

———. *A Hessian Officer's Diary of the American Revolution.* Bowie, Md.: Heritage Books, 1994.

———, compiler. *Waldeck Soldiers of the American Revolutionary War.* Bowie, Md.: Heritage Books, 1991.

Burnett, Edmund C. "Ciphers of the Revolutionary Period." *American Historical Review,* 22 (January 1917), pp. 329–334.

———. *The Continental Congress.* New York: Macmillan, 1941.

———. "The Continental Congress and Agricultural Supplies." *Agriculture History,* 2 (July 1928), pp. 111–128.

Burns, Brian. "Massacre or Muster? Burgoyne's Indians and the Militia at Bennington." *Vermont History,* 45 (Summer 1977), pp. 133–144.

Burns, R. E. "Ireland and British Military Preparations for War in America in 1775." *Cithara,* 2 (May 1963), pp. 42–61.

Burt, Alfred L. *Guy Carleton, Lord Dorchester, 1724–1808.* Revised Edition. Ottawa: Canadian Historical Association, 1955.

———. "The Quarrel between Germain and Carleton: An Inverted Story." *Canadian Historical Review,* 11 (September 1930), pp. 202–220.

Burton, I. F., and A. N. Newman. "Sir John Cope: Promotion in the Eighteenth-Century Army." *English Historical Review,* 78 (October 1963), pp. 655–668.

Butler, John P. *Index to the Papers of the Continental Congress, 1774–1789.* 5 vols. Washington: National Archives and Records Service, 1978.

Butler, Lindley S. *North Carolina and the Coming of the Revolution, 1763–1776.* Raleigh: North Carolina Department of Cultural Resources, 1976.

Butterfield, Lyman H. "Psychological Warfare in 1776: The Jefferson-Franklin Plan to Cause Hessian Desertion." *Proceedings of the American Philosophical Society,* 94 (June 1950), pp. 233–241.

Caemmerer, H. Paul. *The Life of Pierre Charles L'Enfant.* Washington: National Republic Publishing Co., 1950.

Calderhead, William L. "British Naval Failure at Long Island: A Lost Opportunity in the American Revolution." *New York History,* 57 (July 1976), pp. 321–338.

———. "Prelude to Yorktown: A Critical Week in a Major Campaign." *Maryland Historical Magazine,* 77 (June 1982), pp. 123–135.

———. "Thomas Carney: Unsung Soldier of the American Revolution." *Maryland Historical Magazine,* 84 (Winter 1989), pp. 319–326.

Caley, Percy B. "The Life Adventures of Lieutenant-Colonel John Connolly: The Story of a Tory." *Western Pennsylvania Historical Magazine,* 11 (1928), pp. 10–49, 76–111, 144–179, 225–259.

Calhers, Darryl I. "Powder to the People: The Revolutionary Structure behind the Attack on Fort William and Mary, 1774." *Historical New Hampshire,* 29 (Winter 1974), pp. 261–280.

Calhoon, Robert M. *The Loyalists in Revolutionary America, 1760–1781.* New York: Harcourt, Brace, Jovanovich, 1973.

———. *The Loyalist Perception and Other Essays.* Columbia: University of South Carolina Press, 1989.

Calhoun, George N. *Colonel William Bradford.* Philadelphia: Temple University Press, 1941.

Callahan, North. "Henry Knox, General Washington's General." *New-York Historical Society Quarterly,* 44 (April 1960), pp. 150–165.

———. *Henry Knox: George Washington's General.* New York: Rinehart, 1958.

———. *Royal Raiders: The Tories of the American Revolution.* Indianapolis: Bobbs-Merrill, 1963.

Calloway, Colin G. *The American Revolution in Indian Country: Crisis and Diversity in Native American Communities.* New York: Cambridge University Press, 1995.

———. "'We Have Always Been the Frontier:' The American Revolution in Shawnee Country." *American Indian Quarterly,* 16 (Winter 1992), pp. 39–52.

Calver, William L., and Reginald Bolton. *History Written with a Pick and Shovel: Military Buttons, Belt-Plates, Badges, and Other Relics Excavated from Colonial, Revolutionary, and War of 1812 Camp Sites.* New York: New-York Historical Society, 1950.

Campbell, Colin. "Lieutenant Colonel George Campbell, King's American Regiment." *New England Historical and Genealogical Register,* 137 (October 1983), pp. 306–316.

———. "The 71st Highlanders in Massachusetts, 1776–1780." *New England Historical and Genealogical Register,* 112 (July, October 1958), pp. 200–213, 265–275; 113 (January, April 1959), pp. 3–14, 84–94.

Camus, Raoul F. *Military Music of the American Revolution.* Chapel Hill: University of North Carolina Press, 1976.

Candler, Allen D., editor. *The Colonial Records of the State of Georgia.* 26 vols. Atlanta: C. P. Byrd, 1904–1926.

———, editor. *The Revolutionary Records of the State of Georgia.* 3 vols. Atlanta: Franklin-Turner Co., 1908.

Cann, Marvin L. "Prelude to War: The First Battle of Ninety-Six, November 19–21, 1775." *South Carolina Historical Magazine,* 76 (October 1975), pp. 197–214.

———. "War in the Backcountry: The Siege of Ninety Six, May 22–June 19, 1781." *South Carolina Historical Magazine,* 72 (January 1971), pp. 1–14.

Cappon, Lester J. et al., editors. *The Atlas of Early American History: The Revolutionary Era, 1760–1790.* Princeton University Press, 1976.

———. "Geographers and Map-makers, British and American, from about 1750 to 1789." *American Antiquarian Society Proceedings,* 81 (October 1971), pp. 243–271.

Carey, Arthur M. *American Firearms Makers: When, Where, and What They Made from the Colonial Period to the End of the Nineteenth Century.* New York: Thomas Y. Crowell, 1953.

———. *English, Irish, and Scottish Firearms Makers: When, Where, and What They Made, from the Middle of the Sixteenth Century to the End of the Nineteenth Century.* New York: Thomas Y. Crowell, 1954.

Carlson, Eric T. "Benjamin Rush on Revolutionary War Hygiene." *Bulletin of the New York Academy of Medicine,* 55 (July–August 1979), pp. 614–635.

Carman, W. Y. "Banastre Tarleton and the British Legion." *Journal of the Society for Army Historical Research,* 62 (Autumn 1984), pp. 127–131.

———. "The Uniform of the Queen's Rangers 1777–1783." *Journal of the Society for Army Historical Research,* 57 (Summer 1979), pp. 63–70.

Carp, E. Wayne. "Early American Military History: A Review of Recent Work." *Virginia Magazine of History and Biography,* 94 (July 1986), pp. 259–284.

———. "The Origins of the Nationalist Movement of 1780–1783: Congressional Administration and the Continental Army." *Pennsylvania Magazine of History and Biography,* 107 (July 1983), pp. 263–282.

———. *To Starve the Army at Pleasure: Continental Army Administration and American Political Culture, 1775–1783.* Chapel Hill: University of North Carolina Press, 1983.

Carrington, Henry B. *Battles of the American Revolution, 1775–1781. Historical and Military Criticism, with Topographical Illustration.* New York: A.S. Barnes & Co., 1781.

Carroll, Charles. *The Journal of Charles Carroll of Carrollton As One of the Congressional Commissioners to Canada in 1776.* Edited by Allan S. Everest. Fort Ticonderoga, N.Y.: Champlain-Upper Hudson Bicentennial Committee, 1976.

Carter, Clarence E. "The Significance of the Military Office in America, 1763–1775." *American Historical Review,* 28 (April 1923), pp. 475–488.

Caruana, Adrian B. *British Military Ammunition, 1780.* Bloomfield, Ont.: Museum Restoration Service, 1980.

———. *Grasshoppers and Butterflies: The Light 3 Pounders of Pattison and Townshend.* Bloomfield, Ont.: Museum Restoration Service, 1979.

———. *The Light 6-Pounder Battalion Gun of 1776.* Bloomfield, Ont.: Museum Restoration Service, 1976.

Cary, John H. *Joseph Warren: Physician, Politician, Patriot.* Urbana: University of Illinois Press, 1961.

———. "'The Juditious Are Intirely Neglected:' The Fate of a Tory." *New England Historical and Genealogical Register,* 134 (April 1980), pp. 99–114.

Cash, Philip. "The Canadian Military Campaign of 1775–1776: Medical Problems and Effects of Disease." *Journal of the American Medical Association,* 236 (5 July 1976), pp. 52–56.

———. *Medical Men at the Siege of Boston, April 1775–April 1776: Problems of the Massachusetts and Continental Armies.* Philadelphia: American Philosophical Society, 1973.

Cashin, Edward J. "'The Famous Colonel Wells': Factionalism in Revolutionary Georgia." *Georgia Historical Quarterly,* 58 (Supplement 1974), pp. 137–156.

———. *The King's Ranger: Thomas Brown and the American Revolution on the Southern Frontier.* Athens: University of Georgia Press, 1989.

———. "Nathanael Greene's Campaign for Georgia in 1781." *Georgia Historical Quarterly,* 61 (Spring 1977), pp. 43–58.

Cashion, Jerry C. "North Carolina and the Cherokee: The Quest for Land on the Eve of the American Revolution, 1754–1776." Ph.D. dissertation, University of North Carolina at Chapel Hill, 1979.

Casion, Joseph J. "Elizabethtown, 1782: The Prisoner-of-War Negotiations and the Pawns of War." *New Jersey History,* 102 (1984) pp. 1–35.

Cassell, Frank A. *Merchant Congressman in the Young Republic; Samuel Smith of Maryland, 1752–1839.* Madison: University of Wisconsin Press, 1971.

Caughey, John. "Bernardo de Gálvez and the English Smugglers on the Mississippi." *Hispanic American Historical Review,* 12 (February 1932), pp. 46–58.

———. *Bernardo de Gálvez in Louisiana 1776–1783*. Berkeley: University of California Press, 1934.

———. "The Natchez Rebellion of 1781 and Its Aftermath." *Louisiana Historical Quarterly*, 16 (January 1933), pp. 57–83.

———. "The Panis Mission to Pensacola, 1778." *Hispanic American Historical Review*, 10 (November 1930), pp. 480–489.

———. "Willing's Expedition down the Mississippi, 1778." *Louisiana Historical Quarterly*, 15 (January 1932), pp. 5–36.

Chadwick, French E., editor. *The [Thomas] Graves Papers and Other Documents Relating to the Naval Operations of the Yorktown Campaign July to October 1781*. New York: Naval Historical Society, 1916.

Chaffin, Robert J. "The Townshend Acts of 1767." *William and Mary Quarterly*, 3d Ser., 27 (January 1970), pp. 90–121.

Champagne, Roger J. *Alexander McDougall and the American Revolution in New York*. Schenectady: New York State American Revolution Bicentennial Commission, 1975.

———. "Liberty Boys and Mechanics of New York City, 1764–1774." *Labor History*, 8 (Spring 1967), pp. 115–135.

———. "The Military Association of the Sons of Liberty." *New-York Historical Society Quarterly*, 41 (July 1955), pp. 338–350.

———. "New York and the Intolerable Acts, 1774." *New-York Historical Society Quarterly*, 45 (April 1961), pp. 195–207.

———. "New York's Radicals and the Coming of Independence." *Journal of American History*, 51 (June 1964), pp. 21–40.

———. "The Sons of Liberty and the Aristocracy in New York Politics, 1765–1790." Ph.D. dissertation, University of Wisconsin, 1960.

Chaput, Donald. "Treason or Loyalty? Frontier French in the American Revolution." *Journal of the Illinois State Historical Society*, 71 (November 1978), pp. 242–251.

Chartrand, Rene. *The French Army in the American War of Independence*. London: Osprey Publishing, 1991.

Chase, Philander D. "Baron Von Steuben in the War of Independence." Ph.D. dissertation, Duke University, 1973.

Chitwood, Oliver P. *Richard Henry Lee, Statesman of the Revolution*. Morgantown: West Virginia University Press, 1967.

Christie, Ian R. *The End of North's Ministry, 1780–1782*. New York: St. Martin's Press, 1958.

Churchill, Edwin A. *Maine Communities and the War for Independence: A Guide for the Study of Local Maine History As Related to the American Revolution*. Augusta: Maine State Museum, 1976.

Cifelli, Edward M. *David Humphreys*. Boston: Twayne, 1982.

Clarfield, Gerard H. *Timothy Pickering and the American Republic*. Pittsburgh: University of Pittsburgh Press, 1980.

Clark, David S. *Index to Maps of the American Revolution in Books and Periodicals: Illustrating the Revolutionary War and Other Events of the Period, 1763–1789*. Westport, Conn.: Greenwood Press, 1974.

Clark, Donald F., editor. *Fort Montgomery and Fort Clinton: Several Contemporary Accounts of the Battle, Monday, 6 October 1777*. Fort Montgomery, N.Y.: Town of Highlands, 1952.

Clark, Dora Mae. "The British Treasury and The Administration of Military Affairs in America, 1754–1774." *Pennsylvania History*, 2 (October 1935), pp. 197–204.

Clark, George Rogers. *George Rogers Clark Papers 1771–1783*. Edited by James Alton James. 2 vols. Springfield: Illinois State Historical Library, 1912–1926.

Clark, H. C. "Report on Publication of Revolutionary Military Records." In the *American Historical Association Annual Report for 1915*, pp. 193–199.

Clark, Jane. "The Command of the Canadian Army for the Campaign of 1777." *Canadian Historical Review*, 10 (June 1929), pp. 129–135.

———, editor. "The Convention Troops and the Perfidy of Sir William Howe." *American Historical Review*, 37 (July 1932), pp. 721–723.

Clark, Lyman. "A Private's Diary of the Siege of Boston and the Canada Campaign, 1775–76." Edited by T. D. Seymour Bassett and J. Robert Maguire. *New England Historical and Genealogical Register*, 137 (April 1983), pp. 114–125.

Clark, Murtie J. *Loyalists in the Southern Campaign of the Revolutionary War*. Baltimore: Genealogical Publishing Co., 1981.

Clark, Raymond B. *Maryland Revolutionary Records: How to Find Them & Interpret Them*. St. Michaels, Md.: Clark, 1976.

Clark, Walter, et al., editors. *The State Records of North Carolina*. 16 vols. Winston and Goldsboro: Various publishers, 1895–1907.

Clark, William Bell. *Ben Franklin's Privateers: A Naval Epic of the American Revolution*. Baton Rouge: Louisiana State University Press, 1956.

———. *Captain Dauntless: The Story of Nicholas Biddle of the Continental Navy*. Baton Rouge: Louisiana State University Press, 1949.

———. *The First Saratoga, Being the Saga of John Young and His Sloop-of-War*. Baton Rouge: Louisiana State University Press, 1953.

———. *Gallant John Barry, 1745–1803: The Story of a Naval Hero of Two Wars*. New York: Macmillan, 1938.

———. *George Washington's Navy: Being an Account of His Excellency's Fleet in New England Waters*. Baton Rouge: Louisiana State University Press, 1960.

———. *Lambert Wickes, Sea Raider and Diplomat: The Story of a Naval Captain of the Revolution*. New Haven: Yale University Press, 1932.

———, et al., editors. *Naval Documents of the American Revolution*. 10 vols. Washington: Government Printing Office, 1964–1996.

Clarke, Ernest. *The Siege of Fort Cumberland, 1776*. Montreal: McGill-Queens University Press, 1995.

Clarke, William B., editor. "Col. John Brown's Expedition against Ticonderoga and Diamond Island, 1777." *New England Historical and Genealogical Register*, 74 (October 1920), pp. 284–293.

Clary, David A., and Joseph W. A. Whitehorne. *The Inspectors General of the United States Army, 1777–1903*. Washington, DC: Center of Military History, 1987.

Clements, S. Eugene Clements, and F. Edward Wright, editors. *Maryland Militia in the Revolutionary War*. Westminster, Maryland: Family Line Publications, 1987.

Clinton, George. *Public Papers of George Clinton, First Governor of New York.* Edited by Hugh Hastings and James Austin Holden. 10 vols. Albany: State Printers, 1899–1914.

Clinton, Henry. *The American Rebellion: Sir Henry Clinton's Narrative of His Campaigns, 1775–1782, with an Appendix of Original Documents.* Edited by William B. Willcox. New Haven: Yale University Press, 1954.

Clodfelter, Mark A. "Between Virtue and Necessity: Nathanael Greene and the Conduct of Civil-Military Relations in the South, 1780–1782." *Military Affairs*, 52 (October 1988), pp. 169–175.

Closen, Ludwig von. *The Revolutionary Journal of Baron Ludwig von Closen, 1780–1783.* Edited by Evelyn M. Acomb. Chapel Hill: University of North Carolina Press, 1958.

Coakley, Robert A. "Virginia Commerce during the American Revolution." Ph.D. dissertation, University of Virginia, 1949.

Coakley, Robert A. and Stetson Conn, *The War of the American Revolution.* 1975. Washington, DC: Center of Military History, 1992.

Coburn, Frank W. *The Battle of April 19, 1775.* 2d Edition. Lexington: Lexington Historical Society, 1922.

Cohen, Joel A. "Democracy in Revolutionary Rhode Island: A Statistical Analysis." *Rhode Island History*, 29 (February–May 1970), pp. 3–16.

———. "Lexington and Concord: Rhode Island Reacts." *Rhode Island History*, 26 (October 1967), pp. 97–102.

Cohen, Sheldon S. *Connecticut's Loyalist Gadfly: The Reverend Samuel Andrew Peters.* Hartford: American Revolution Bicentennial Commission of Connecticut, 1976.

———. "The Death of Colonel Thomas Knowlton." *Connecticut Historical Society Bulletin*, 30 (April 1965), pp. 50–57.

———. "Thomas Wren: Ministering Angel of Forton Prison." *Pennsylvania Magazine of History and Biography*, 103 (July 1979), pp. 279–301.

Coil, George L. "War Crimes of the American Revolution." *Military Law Review*, 82 (Fall 1978), pp. 171–198.

Coker, Kathy R. "The Punishment of Revolutionary War Loyalists in South Carolina." Ph.D. dissertation, University of South Carolina, 1987.

Coker, William S., and Hazel P. Coker. *The Siege of Mobile, 1780.* Pensacola: Perdido Bay, 1982.

Coker, William S., and Robert R. Rea, editors. *Anglo-Spanish Confrontation on the Gulf Coast during the American Revolution.* Pensacola: Gulf Coast History and Humanities Conference, 1982.

Colburn, H. Trevor. *The Lamp of Experience: Whig History and the Intellectual Origins of the American Revolution.* Chapel Hill: University of North Carolina Press, 1965.

Cole, David. "A Brief Outline of the South Carolina Militia System." *South Carolina Historical Association Proceedings for 1954*, pp. 14–23.

Cole, Richard C. "The Siege of Savannah and the British Press, 1779–1780." *Georgia Historical Quarterly*, 65 (Fall 1981), pp. 189–202.

Coleman, Francis X. J. "John Jay on War." *Journal of the History of Ideas*, 43 (January–March 1982), pp. 145–151.

Coleman, John M. "Joseph Galloway and the British Occupation of Philadelphia." *Pennsylvania History*, 30 (July 1963), pp. 272–300.

———. *Thomas McKean: Forgotten Leader of the Revolution.* Rockaway, N.J.: American Faculty Press, 1975.

Coleman, Kenneth. *The American Revolution in Georgia.* Athens: University of Georgia Press, 1958.

Coleman, Kenneth and Charles S. Gurr, editors. *Dictionary of Georgia Biography.* 2 vols. Athens: University of Georgia Press, 1983.

Collier, Christopher. *Connecticut in the Continental Congress.* Chester: Pequot Press, 1973.

Collins, James F. "Whaleboat Warfare on Long Island Sound." *New York History*, 25 (April 1944), pp. 195–201.

Cometti, Elizabeth. "Depredations in Virginia during the Revolution." In *The Old Dominion: Essays for Thomas Perkins Abernathy.* Edited by Darrett B. Rutman. Charlottesville: University Press of Virginia, 1964.

Commager, Henry S., and Richard B. Morris, editors. *The Spirit of 'Seventy-Six: As Told by Participants.* Bicentennial edition. New York: Harper and Row, 1975 (1958).

Connecticut Historical Society. *Collections,*
 vol. 7 (1899): "Orderly Books and Journals Kept by Connecticut Men while Taking Part in the American Revolution."
 vol. 8 (1901): "Rolls and Lists of Connecticut Men in the Revolution 1775–1783."
 vol. 12 (1909): "Lists and Returns of Connecticut Men in the Revolution 1775–1783."
 vol. 20 (1923): "Correspondence of the Brothers Joshua and Jedediah Huntington, 1771–1783."
 vol. 21 (1924): "Correspondence and Documents Chiefly of Descendants of Gov. George Wyllys of Connecticut 1590–1796."
 vol. 23 (1930): "[Silas] Deane Papers, 1771–1795."

Conover, Bettie J. "British West Florida's Mississippi Frontier Posts, 1763–1779." *Alabama Review*, 29 (July 1976), pp. 177–207.

Conrad, Dennis M. "Nathanael Greene and the Southern Campaigns, 1780–1783." Ph.D. dissertation, Duke University, 1979.

Conway, Stephen R. "British Army Officers and the American War for Independence." *William and Mary Quarterly*, 3d Ser., 41 (April 1984), pp. 265–276.

———. *The British Isles and the War of American Independence.* Oxford, England: Oxford University Press, 2000.

———. "'The Great Mischief Complain'd of:' Reflections on the Misconduct of British Soldiers in the Revolutionary War." *William and Mary Quarterly*, 3d Ser., 47 (July 1990), pp. 370–390.

———. "To Subdue America: British Army Officers and the Conduct of the Revolutionary War." *William and Mary Quarterly*, 3d Ser., 43 (July 1986), pp. 381–407.

———. *The War of American Independence, 1775–1783.* London: Arnold, 1995.

Cooch, Edward W. *The Battle of Cooch's Bridge, Delaware, September 3, 1777.* Wilmington: W. N. Cann, Inc., 1940.

Cook, Frederick, editor. *Journals of the Military Expedition of Major General John Sullivan against the Six Nations of Indians in 1779.* Auburn, N.Y.: Knapp, Peck & Thomson, 1887.

Cooke, Jacob E. *Alexander Hamilton.* New York: Charles Scribner's Sons, 1982.

———. "Tench Coxe: Tory Merchant." *Pennsylvania Magazine of History and Biography,* 96 (January 1972), pp. 48–88.

Cornwallis, Charles, Earl. *The Cornwallis Papers: Abstracts of Americana.* Edited by George H. Reese. Charlottesville: Virginia Independence Bicentennial Commission, 1970.

Corsar, Kenneth C., editor. "Letters From America, 1780 and 1781." *Journal of the Society for Army Historical Research,* 20 (Fall 1941), pp. 130–135.

Countryman, Edward. *The American Revolution.* New York: Hill and Wang, 1985.

———. *The People's American Revolution.* British Association of American Studies, 1983.

Cowen, David L. *Medicine in Revolutionary New Jersey.* Trenton: New Jersey Historical Commission, 1975.

———. "Revolutionary New Jersey." *Proceedings of the New Jersey Historical Society,* 71 (January 1953), pp. 1–23.

Cox, Caroline. *A Proper Sense of Honor: Service and Sacrifice in George Washington's Army.* Chapel Hill: University of North Carolina Press, 2004.

Cox, William E. "Brigadier-General John Ashe's Defeat in the Battle of Brier Creek." *Georgia Historical Quarterly,* 57 (Summer 1973), pp. 295–302.

Crackel, Theodore J. "Revolutionary War Records and Patterns of American Mobility, 1780–1830." *Prologue,* 16 (Fall 1984), pp. 155–167.

Crane, Elaine F. *A Dependent People: Newport, Rhode Island, in the Revolutionary Era.* New York: Fordham University Press, 1985.

Crary, Catherine S., editor. *The Price of Loyalty; Tory Writings from the Revolutionary Era.* New York: McGraw-Hill, 1973.

———. "The Tory and the Spy: The Double Life of James Rivington." *William and Mary Quarterly,* 3d Ser., 16 (January 1959), pp. 61–72.

Cress, Lawrence D. "An Armed Community: The Origins and Meaning of the Right to Bear Arms." *Journal of American History,* 71 (June 1984), pp. 22–42.

———. *Citizens in Arms: The Army and the Militia in American Society to the War of 1812.* Chapel Hill: University of North Carolina Press, 1982.

———. "Radical Whiggery on the Role of the Military: Ideological Roots of the American Revolutionary Militia." *Journal of the History of Ideas,* 40 (January–March 1979), pp. 43–60.

———. "Republican Liberty and National Security: American Military Policy As an Ideological Problem, 1783 to 1789." *William and Mary Quarterly,* 3d Ser., 38 (January 1980), pp. 73–96.

Crispin, Barbara. "Clyde Shipping and the American War." *Scottish Historical Review,* 41 (October 1962), pp. 124–133.

Crout, Robert R. "Pierre-Emmanuel de la Plaigne and Georgia's Quest for French Aid during the War of Independence." *Georgia Historical Quarterly,* 60 (Summer 1976), pp. 176–184.

Crow, Jeffery J. *The Black Experience in Revolutionary North Carolina.* Raleigh: North Carolina Department of Cultural Resources, 1977.

Crow, Jeffery J., and Larry E. Tise, editors. *The Southern Experience in the American Revolution.* Chapel Hill: University of North Carolina Press, 1978.

Ferguson, Clyde R. "Carolina and Georgia Patriot and Loyalist Militia in Action, 1778–1783," pp. 174–179.

Shy, John. "British Strategy for Pacifying the Southern Colonies, 1778–1781," pp. 155–173.

Cruikshank, Ernest A. "The King's Royal Regiment of New York." *Ontario Historical Society Papers and Records,* 27 (1931), pp. 193–323.

———. *The Story of Butler's Rangers and the Settlement of Niagara.* Welland, Ont.: Tribune Printing House, 1893.

Cubberly, Fred. "Fort George (St. Michael), Pensacola." *Florida Historical Quarterly,* 6 (October 1928), pp. 220–234.

Cummin, Katherine H. *Connecticut Militia General: Gold Selleck Silliman.* Hartford: American Revolution Bicentennial Commission of Connecticut, 1980.

Cumming, William P. *British Maps of Colonial America.* Chicago: University of Chicago Press, 1974.

Cummins, Light T. "Spanish Agents in North America during the Revolution, 1775–1779." Ph.D. dissertation, Tulane University, 1977.

Cuneo, John R. "The Early Days of the Queen's Rangers, August 1776–February 1777." *Military Affairs,* 22 (Summer 1958), pp. 65–74.

Cunliffe, Marcus. *George Washington: Man and Monument.* Boston: Little, Brown, 1957.

———. *Soldiers and Civilians: The Martial Spirit in America, 1775–1865.* Boston: Little, Brown, 1968.

Cunz, Dieter. *The Maryland Germans: A History.* Princeton: Princeton University Press, 1948.

Curry, Richard O. "Lord Dunmore and the West: A Re-evaluation." *West Virginia History,* 19 (July 1958), pp. 231–243.

———. "Loyalism in Western Virginia during the American Revolution." *West Virginia History,* 14 (April 1953), pp. 265–274.

Curtis, Edward E. *Organization of the British Army in the American Revolution.* New Haven: Yale University Press, 1926.

———. "The Recruiting of the British Army in the American Revolution." *American Historical Association Annual Report for 1922,* pp. 311–322.

DAB. *Dictionary of American Biography.* Comprehensive Index: Complete through Supplement Ten. New York : Charles Scribner's Sons, c. 1996.

Dabney, Charles W. "Colonel Charles Dabney of the Revolution: His Service As a Soldier and Citizen." *Virginia Magazine of History and Biography,* 51 (April 1943), pp. 186–199.

Dabney, William M. *After Saratoga: The Story of the Convention Army.* Albuquerque: University of New Mexico Press, 1954.

———. "Drayton and Laurens in the Continental Congress." *South Carolina Historical and Genealogical Magazine,* 60 (April 1959), pp. 74–82.

Dabney, William M., and Marion Dargan. *William Henry Drayton and the American Revolution.* Albuquerque: University of New Mexico Press, 1962.

Dandridge, Danske. *American Prisoners of the Revolution.* Charlottesville: Michie, 1911.

Dangerfield, George. *Chancellor Robert R. Livingston of New York, 1746–1813.* New York: Harcourt, Brace and World Co., 1960.

Daniell, Jere R. *Experiment in Republicanism, New Hampshire Politics and the American Revolution, 1741–1794.* Cambridge, Mass.: Harvard University Press, 1970.

Dann, John C., editor. *The Revolution Remembered: Eyewitness Accounts of the War for Independence.* Chicago: University of Chicago Press, 1980.

Darling, Anthony D. *Red Coat and Brown Bess.* Bloomfield, Ontario: Museum Restoration Service, 1970.

Daughters of the American Revolution, National Society. *Minority Military Service, 1775–1783.* Eight pamphlets. Washington, DC: Daughters of the American Revolution, 1988–1997.

Davidson, Chalmers. *Piedmont Partisan: The Life and Times of Brigadier-General William Lee Davidson.* Davidson, N.C.: Davidson College, 1951.

Davies, Kenneth G., editor. *Documents of the American Revolution, 1770–1783 (Colonial Office Series).* 21 vols. Shannon: Irish Universities Press, 1972–1981.

Davies, Kenneth G., and N. E. Evans. *Still in British Hands: Major Documents of the American Revolution in the British Public Record Office.* Mystic, Conn.: Pendragon, 1981.

Davies, Wallace E. "The Society of Cincinnati in New England 1783–1800." *William and Mary Quarterly,* 3d Ser., 5 (January 1948), pp. 3–25.

Davis, Burke. *The Campaign that Won America: The Story of Yorktown.* New York: Dial Press, 1970.

———. *The Cowpens-Guilford Courthouse Campaign.* Philadelphia: J. B. Lippincott Co., 1962.

Davis, Curtis C. "Helping to Hold the Fort, Elizabeth Zane at Wheeling, 1782: A Case Study in Renown." *West Virginia History,* 44 (Spring 1983), pp. 212–225.

Davis, Gherardi. *Regimental Colors in the War of the Revolution.* New York: Privately printed, 1907. Supplements in 1908 and 1910.

Davis, Robert S., Jr. "The British Invasion of Georgia in 1778." *Atlanta Historical Journal,* 24 (Winter 1980), pp. 5–25.

———. "The Invisible Soldiers: The Georgia Militia and the Siege of Savannah." *Atlanta Historical Journal,* 25 (Winter 1981), pp. 23–66.

———. "Lord Montagu's Mission to South Carolina in 1781: American POWs for the King's Service in Jamaica." *South Carolina Historical Magazine,* 84 (April 1983), pp. 89–109.

———. "The Loyalist Trials at Ninety-Six in 1779." *South Carolina Historical Magazine,* 80 (April 1979), pp. 172–181.

———. "New Research Materials on the American Revolution in Georgia." *Georgia Historical Quarterly,* 65 (Winter 1981), pp. 316–322.

———. "Thomas Pinckney and the Last Campaign of Horatio Gates." *South Carolina Historical Magazine,* 86 (April 1985), pp. 75–99.

Dawson, Henry B. *Westchester-County, New York, during the American Revolution.* Morrisania: Privately printed, 1886.

DCB. *Dictionary of Canadian Biography.* Toronto: The Macmillan Company of Canada, 1926, 1945, 1966.

Dearborn, Henry. *Revolutionary War Journals of Henry Dearborn, 1775–1783.* Edited by Lloyd A. Brown and Howard H. Peckham. 1939. New York: Da Capo Press, 1971.

Dearden, Paul F. *The Rhode Island Campaign of 1778: Inauspicious Dawn of Alliance.* Providence: Rhode Island Bicentennial Foundation, 1980.

———. "The Siege of Newport: Inauspicious Dawn of Alliance." *Rhode Island History,* 29 (February–May 1970), pp. 17–35.

Dederer, John M. "Making Bricks without Straw: Nathanael Greene's Southern Campaign and Mao Tse-Tung's Mobile War." *Military Affairs,* 47 (October 1983), pp. 115–121.

Delaware. *Delaware Archives. Military.* 5 vols. Wilmington: Public Archives Commission of Delaware, 1911–1919.

D'Elia, Donald J. "Dr. Benjamin Rush and the American Medical Revolution." *Proceedings of the American Philosophical Society,* 110 (August 1966), pp. 227–234.

Demarest, Thomas. "The Baylor Massacre—Some Assorted Notes and Information." *Bergen County History 1971 Annual,* pp. 29–93.

De Mond, Robert O. *The Loyalists of North Carolina during the Revolution.* Durham: Duke University Press, 1940.

Dendy, John O. "Frederick Haldimand and the Defense of Canada, 1778–1784." Ph.D. dissertation, Duke University, 1972.

Denn, Robert J. "Captivity Narratives of the American Revolution." *Journal of American Culture,* 2 (Winter 1980), pp. 575–582.

Denny, Ebenezer. *Military Journal of Major Ebenezer Denny.* 1859. New York: Arno Press, 1971.

De Paolo, William A., Jr. "The Establishment of the Nueva Vizcaya Militia during the Administration of Teodoro de Croix 1776–1783." *New Mexico Historical Review,* 48 (July 1973), pp. 223–249.

DePauw, Linda G. "Women in Combat: The Revolutionary War Experience." *Armed Forces and Society,* 7 (Winter 1981), pp. 209–226.

Deprez, J. H. "La prise de l'île de Sainte-Lucie par les Anglais en décembre 1778: Victoire militaire certaine, erreur stratégique probable." *Revue Historique des Armeés,* 6 (#2, 1979), pp. 19–33.

Destler, Charles M. "Colonel Henry Champion, Revolutionary Commissary." *Connecticut Historical Society Bulletin,* 36 (April 1971), pp. 52–64.

———. *Connecticut, The Provisions State.* Chester, Connecticut: Pequot Press for the American Revolution Bicentennial Commission of Connecticut, 1973.

Deutrich, Mabel E., and Howard Wehmann. *A Preliminary Inventory of the War Department Collection of Revolutionary War Records (Record Group 93).* Washington: National Archives, 1970.

DeVaro, Lawrence J., Jr. "The Gaspee Affair As Conspiracy." *Rhode Island History,* 32 (November 1973), pp. 107–121.

Devine, Francis E. "The Pennsylvania Flying Camp, July–November 1776." *Pennsylvania History*, 46 (January 1979), pp. 59–78.

Dexter, Franklin B. *Biographical Sketches of the Graduates of Yale College with Annals of the College History*. 6 vols. New York: Henry Holt and Co., 1885–1912.

Diamant, Lincoln. *Chaining the Hudson: The Fight for the River in the American Revolution*. New York: Lyle Stuart, 1989.

———. "First Blood for the Infantry—1776." *Military Affairs*, 15 (Spring 1951), pp. 16–24.

Dickerson, Oliver M. *The Navigation Acts and the American Revolution*. Philadelphia: University of Pennsylvania Press, 1951.

Dickinson, Harry T., editor. *Britain and the American Revolution*. London: Longmans, 1998.

Dickson, Paul D. "'We Prefer Trade to Dominion'—Imperial Policy and the Settlement of the King's Royal Regiment." *Ontario History*, 82 (June 1990), pp. 129–148.

Dill, Alonzo T. *Carter Braxton, Virginia Signer: A Conservative in Revolt*. Lanham, Md.: University Press of America, 1983.

Din, Gilbert C. "Protecting the 'Barrera:' Spain's Defenses in Louisiana, 1763–1779." *Louisiana History*, 19 (Spring 1978), pp. 183–211.

Dippel, Horst. "Sources in Germany for the Study of the American Revolution." *Quarterly Journal of the Library of Congress*, 33 (July 1976), pp. 199–217.

DNB. *Dictionary of National Biography*. London, Smith, Elder, & co., 1885–1901.

DNB (or ODNB). *The Dictionary of National Biography, 1986–1990,* with an index covering the years 1901–1990 in one alphabetical series. Edited by C.S. Nicholls; consultant editor, Sir Keith Thomas. New York: Oxford University Press, 1996.

Doblin, Helga. "The Case of the Musketeer Andreas Hasselmann." *Military Affairs*, 51 (April 1987), pp. 73–74.

Doblin, Helga, translator; and Mary C. Lynn, editor. *The American Revolution, Garrison Life in French Canada and New York: Journal of an Officer in the Prinz Friedrich Regiment, 1776–1783*. Westport: Greenwood Press, 1993.

Doerflinger, Thomas M. "Hibernia Furnace during the Revolution." *New Jersey History*, 90 (Summer 1972), pp. 97–114.

Döhla, Johann C. *A Hessian Diary of the American Revolution*. Translated and edited by Bruce E. Burgoyne. Norman: University of Oklahoma Press, 1990.

Doniol, Henri. *Histoire de la Participation de la France à l'établissement des États-Unis d'Amérique*. 5 vols. Paris, 1884–1892.

Donoghue, Bernhard. *British Politics and the American Revolution: The Path to War, 1773–75*. London: Macmillan, 1964.

Dornfest, Walter T. "British, Hessian and Provincial Troops at Paulus Hook, 18th–19th August, 1779." *Journal of the Society for Army Historical Research*, 45 (Winter 1967), pp. 177–182.

———. "Hanoverian Troops in the British Service 1775–1792." *Journal of the Society for Army Historical Research*, 61 (Spring 1983), pp. 58–61.

———. "The Royal Garrison Battalion 1778–1784." *Journal of the Society for Army Historical Research*, 47 (Spring 1969), pp. 55–69; 51 (Summer 1973), pp. 124–125.

Dorwart, Jeffery M. *Fort Mifflin of Philadelphia: An Illustrated History*. Philadelphia: University of Pennsylvania Press, 1998.

Doughty, Joshua, Jr. "Washington's March from Princeton to Morristown." *Proceedings of the New Jersey Historical Society*, New Ser., 5 (October 1920), pp. 240–246.

Downes, Randolph C. "George Morgan, Indian Agent Extraordinary, 1776–1779." *Pennsylvania History*, 1 (October 1934), pp. 202–216.

———. "Indian War on the Upper Ohio, 1779–1782." *Western Pennsylvania Historical Magazine*, 17 (June 1934), pp. 93–115.

Draper, Lyman C. *King's Mountain and Its Heroes: History of the Battle of King's Mountain October 7th, 1780*. Cincinnati: Peter G. Thomson, 1881.

Driver, Carl S. *John Sevier, Pioneer of the Old Southwest*. Chapel Hill: University of North Carolina Press, 1932.

Dull, Jonathan R. *A Diplomatic History of the American Revolution*. New Haven: Yale University Press, 1985.

———. "France and the American Revolution: Questioning the Myths." *Proceedings of the Western Society for French History*, 1 (March 1974), pp. 110–119.

———. *The French Navy and American Independence: A Study of Arms and Diplomacy, 1774–1787*. Princeton: Princeton University Press, 1975.

———. *The French Navy and the Seven Years' War*. Lincoln: University of Nebraska Press, 2005.

———. "Mahan, Sea Power, and the War for American Independence." *International Historical Review*, 10 (February 1988), pp. 59–67.

Duncan, Louis C. *Medical Men in the American Revolution, 1775–1783*. Carlisle Barracks, Pa.: Medical Field Service School, 1931.

Dunnigan, Brian L. "Fort Mackinac: A Revolutionary War Post in Michigan." *Military Collector and Historian*, 29 (Spring 1977), 15–21.

Dupuy, R. Ernest, and Trevor N. Dupuy. *The Compact History of the Revolutionary War*. New York: Hawthorne Books, 1963.

Du Roi, August Wilhelm. *Journal of Du Roi the Elder Lieutenant and Adjutant, in the Service of the Duke of Brunswick, 1776–1778*. Translated by Charlotte S. J. Epping. New York: D. Appleton and Co., 1911.

Dwight, C. Harrison. "Count Rumford: His Majesty's Colonel in Carolina." *South Carolina Historical Magazine*, 57 (January 1956), pp. 23–27.

Dwyer, William H. *The Day Is Ours! November 1776–January 1777: An Inside View of the Battles of Trenton and Princeton*. New York: Viking Press, 1983.

Dykeman, Wilma. *With Fire and Sword: The Battle of Kings Mountain, 1780*. Washington, DC: National Park Service, 1991.

East, Robert A. *Connecticut's Loyalists*. Chester, Conn.: Pequot Press, 1974.

East, Robert A., and Jacob Judd, editors, *The Loyalist Americans: A Focus on Greater New York*. Tarrytown: Sleepy Hollow Restorations, 1975.

Crary, Catherine S. "Guerrilla Activities of James Delancey's Cowboys in Westchester County: Conventional Warfare or Self-Interested Freebooting?" pp. 14–24.

Shy, John. "The Loyalist Problem in The Lower Hudson Valley: The British Perspective," pp. 3–13.

Echevarria, Durand, and Orville T. Murphy. "The American Revolutionary Army: A French Estimate in 1777." *Military Affairs*, 27 (Spring, Winter 1963), pp. 1–7, 153–162.

Eddis, William. *Letters from America.* Edited by Aubrey C. Land. Cambridge, Mass.: Harvard University Press, 1969.

Edgar, Walter B. *Partisans and Redcoats: The Southern Conflict That Turned the Tide of the American Revolution.* New York: William Morrow, 2001.

Edmonson, James H. "Desertion in the American Army during the Revolutionary War." Ph.D. dissertation, Louisiana State University, 1971.

Eelking, Max von. *German Allied Troops in the North American War.* Translated by J. G. Rosengarten. Albany: Joel Munsell's Sons, 1893.

Egleston, Thomas. *The Life of John Paterson: Major-General in the Revolutionary Army.* 2d Edition. New York: G. P. Putnam's Sons, 1898.

Egli, Clara, translator. "Diary of a Voyage from Stade in Hanover to Quebec in America of the Second Division of Ducal Brunswick Mercenaries." *Quarterly Journal of the New York State Historical Association*, 8 (October 1927), pp. 323–351.

Egly, Theodore W., Jr. *History of the First New York Regiment 1775–1783.* Hampton, N.H.: Peter E. Randall, 1981.

Eid, Leroy V. "Liberty: The Indian Contribution to the American Revolution." *Midwest Quarterly*, 22 (Spring 1981), pp. 279–298.

Ellefson, C. Ashley. "Loyalists and Patriots in Georgia during the American Revolution." *Historian*, 24 (May 1962), pp. 347–356.

Eller, Ernest M., editor. *Chesapeake Bay in the American Revolution.* Centreville, Md.: Tidewater Publishers, 1981.

Ellis, Joseph J. *His Excellency: George Washington.* New York: Alfred A. Knopf, 2004.

Ellis, K. L. "British Communications and Diplomacy in the Eighteenth Century." *Bulletin of the Institute of Historical Research*, 31 (November 1958), pp. 159–167.

Elting, John R., editor. *Military Uniforms in America: The Era of the American Revolution 1755–1795.* San Rafael, Calif.: Presidio Press, 1974.

English, Frederick. *General Hugh Mercer, Forgotten Hero of the American Revolution.* New York: Vantage Press, 1975.

Ernst, Robert. "Andrew Elliot, Forgotten Loyalist of Occupied New York." *New York History*, 57 (July 1976), pp. 285–320.

———. *Rufus King: American Federalist.* Chapel Hill: University of North Carolina Press, 1968.

———. "A Tory-Eye View of the Evacuation of New York." *New York History*, 64 (October 1983), pp. 377–394.

Essex Institute Historical Collections.

Ethridge, Harrison M. "Governor Patrick Henry and the Reorganization of the Virginia Militia, 1784–1786." *Virginia Magazine of History and Biography*, 85 (October 1977), pp. 427–438.

Evans, Emory. *Thomas Nelson and the Revolution in Virginia.* Richmond: Virginia Independence Bicentennial Commission, 1978.

Everest, Allan S. *Moses Hazen and the Canadian Refugees in the American Revolution.* Syracuse: Syracuse University Press, 1976.

Ewald, Johann. *Diary of the American War: A Hessian Journal.* Translated by Joseph P. Tustin. New Haven: Yale University Press, 1979.

Fagerstrom, Dalphy I. "Scottish Opinion and the American Revolution." *William and Mary Quarterly*, 3d Ser., 11 (April 1954), pp. 252–275.

Farley, M. Foster. "The South Carolina Negro in the American Revolution, 1775–1783." *South Carolina Historical Magazine*, 79 (April 1978), pp. 75–86.

Farmar, Robert. "Bernardo de Galvez's Siege of Pensacola in 1781 (As Related in Robert Farmar's Journal)." Edited by James A. Padgett. *Louisiana Historical Quarterly*, 26 (April 1943), pp. 311–329.

Farmer, John S. *The Regimental Recods of the British Army.* Bristol, England: Crecy Books, 1984.

Faye, Stanley. "The Arkansas Post of Louisiana: Spanish Domination." *Louisiana Historical Quarterly*, 27 (July 1944), pp. 629–716.

———. "British and Spanish Fortifications of Pensacola, 1781–1821." *Florida Historical Quarterly*, 20 (January 1942), pp. 277–292.

Fellows, Jo-Ann, editor. "A Bibliography of Loyalist Source Material in Canada." *American Antiquarian Society Proceedings*, 82 (1972), pp. 67–270.

Fenn, Elizabeth. *Pox Americana: The Great Smallpox Epidemic of 1775–1782.* New York: Hill and Wang, 2001.

Fenton, Walter S. "Seth Warner." *Vermont Historical Society Proceedings*, New Ser., 8 (December 1940), pp. 325–350.

Ferguson, Clyde R. "General Andrew Pickens." Ph.D. dissertation, Duke University, 1960.

Ferguson, E. James. "The Nationalists of 1781–1783 and the Economic Interpretation of the Constitution." *Journal of American History*, 56 (September 1969), pp. 241–261.

———. *The Power of the Purse: A History of American Public Finance, 1776–1790.* Chapel Hill: University of North Carolina Press, 1961.

Ferguson, Kenneth P. "Military Manuscripts in the Public Record Office of Ireland." *Irish Sword*, 15 (Winter 1982), pp. 112–115.

Ferling, John E. *The First of Men: George Washington.* Knoxville: University of Tennessee Press, 1988.

———. "Joseph Galloway's Military Advice: A Loyalist's View of the Revolution." *Pennsylvania Magazine of History and Biography*, 98 (April 1974), pp. 171–188.

———. *A Leap in the Dark: The Struggle to Create the American Republic,* New York: Oxford University Press, 2003.

———. *The Loyalist Mind: Joseph Galloway and the American Revolution.* University Park: Pennsylvania State University Press, 1977.

———. "The New England Soldier: A Study in Changing Perceptions." *American Quarterly*, 33 (Spring 1981), pp. 26–45.

———. "'Oh, That I Was a Soldier:' John Adams and the Anguish of War," *American Quarterly*, 36 (April 1984), pp. 258–275.

———. *Setting the World Ablaze: Washington, Adams, Jefferson, and the American Revolution.* New York, 2002.

————, editor. *The World Turned Upside Down: The American Victory in the War of Independence.* Westport: Greenwood Press, 1988.

Fernow, Berthold, editor. *New York in the Revolution.* Albany: Weed, Parsons and Co., 1887.

Fetter, Frank W. "Who Were the Foreign Mercenaries of the Declaration of Independence?" *Pennsylvania Magazine of History and Biography,* 104 (October 1980), pp. 508–513.

Filby, P. William, compiler. *A Bibliography of American County Histories.* Baltimore: Genealogical Publishing Co., 1985.

Fingerhut, Eugene R. "Uses and Abuses of the Loyalists' Claims: A Critique of Quantitative Analysis." *William and Mary Quarterly,* 3d Ser., 25 (April 1968), pp. 245–258.

Fischer, David H. *Paul Revere's Ride.* New York: Oxford University Press, 1994.

————. *Washington's Crossing.* New York: Oxford University Press, 2004.

Fischer, Joseph R. *A Well-Executed Failure: Sullivan's Campaign against the Iroquois, July–September 1779.* Columbia: University of South Carolina Press, 1997.

Fisher, John S. "Colonel John Armstrong's Expedition against Kittanning." *Pennsylvania Magazine of History and Biography,* 51 (1927), pp. 1–14.

Fithian, Philip V. *Journal, 1775–1776, Written on the Virginia-Pennsylvania Frontier and in the Army around New York.* Edited by Robert G. Albion and Leonidas Dodson. Princeton: Princeton University Press, 1934.

Flanagan, Vincent, and Gerald Kurland. "Stephen Kemble: New Jersey Loyalist." *New Jersey History,* 90 (Spring 1972), pp. 6–26.

Fleming, Thomas J. *The Battle of Springfield.* Trenton: New Jersey Historical Commission, 1975.

————. *The Forgotten Victory: The Battle for New Jersey—1780.* New York: E. P. Dutton & Co., 1973.

————. *Liberty: The American Revolution.* New York: Viking Press, 1997.

————. *Now We Are Enemies: The Story of Bunker Hill.* New York: St. Martin's Press, 1960.

————. *The Secret War in Morristown.* 2d edition. Morristown, New Jersey: Morris County Historical Society, 1980.

————. *1776: Year of Illusions.* New York: W. W. Norton & Co., 1975.

Flexner, James T. *George Washington.* 4 vols. Boston: Little, Brown, 1965–1972.

————. *The Traitor and the Spy, Benedict Arnold and John Andre.* New York: Harcourt, Brace and Co., 1953.

————. *The Young Hamilton, A Biography.* Boston: Little, Brown and Co., 1978.

Flick, Alexander C. "General Henry Knox's Ticonderoga Expedition." *Quarterly Journal of the New York State Historical Association,* 9 (April 1928), pp. 119–135.

————, editor. "New Sources on the Sullivan-Clinton Campaign in 1779." *Quarterly Journal of the New York State Historical Association,* 10 (July, October 1929), pp. 185–224, 265–317.

————. "The Sullivan-Clinton Campaign in 1779." *Proceedings of the New Jersey Historical Society,* New Ser., 15 (January 1930), 64–72.

Flood, Charles B. *To Rise and Fight Again: Perilous Times along the Road to Independence.* New York: Dodd, Mead & Co., 1976.

Flower, Milton E. *John Dickinson: Conservative Revolutionary.* Charlottesville: University Press of Virginia, 1983.

Floyd, Troy S. *The Anglo-Spanish Struggle for Mosquitia.* Albuquerque: University of New Mexico Press, 1967.

Folsom, William R. "The Battle of Hubbardton." *Vermont Quarterly,* New Ser., 20 (January 1952), pp. 3–18.

————. "The Battle of Valcour Island." *Vermont Quarterly,* New Ser., 19 (July 1951), pp. 133–146.

Foner, Eric. *Tom Paine and Revolutionary America.* Revised edition. 1976. New York: Oxford University Press, 2005.

Footner, Hulbert. *Sailor of Fortune: The Life and Adventures of Commodore Barney, U.S.N.* New York: Harper, 1940.

Force, Peter, editor. *American Archives: A Collection of Authentic Records, State Papers, Debates, and Letters and Other Notices of Public Affairs.* 9 vols. Washington: M. St. Clair Clarke and Peter Force, 1839–1853.

Ford, Corey. *A Peculiar Service.* Boston: Little, Brown, 1965.

Ford, Worthington C., compiler. *British Officers Serving in the American Revolution 1774–1783.* Brooklyn: Historical Printing Club, 1897.

————, editor. *Defences of Philadelphia in 1777.* Brooklyn: Historical Printing Club, 1897.

————, editor. *General Orders Issued by Major General William Heath When in Command of the Eastern Department, 23 May 1777–3 October 1777.* Brooklyn: Historical Printing Club, 1890.

————, editor. *The Journals of the Continental Congress, 1774–1789.* 34 vols. Washington, DC: Government Printing Office, 1904–1937.

————. "Parliament and the Howes." *Proceedings of the Massachusetts Historical Society,* 44 (November 1910), pp. 120–143.

Forry, Richard R. "Edward Hand: His Role in the American Revolution." Ph.D. dissertation, Duke University, 1976.

Fortescue, John W. *A History of the British Army.* Vol. 3. Second edition. London: Macmillan and Co., 1911.

Foster, Herbert D., and Thomas W. Streeter. "Stark's Independent Command at Bennington." *Manchester Historic Association Collections,* 4 (1910–1911), pp. 181–211.

Fowler, James H., II. "The Breakdown of Congressional Authority: A Study of the Relations between the Continental Congress and the States, 1780–1783." Ph.D. dissertation, Ohio State University, 1977.

Fowler, William M., Jr. *The Baron of Beacon Hill: A Biography of John Hancock.* Boston: Houghton, Mifflin, 1980.

————. *Rebels under Sail: The American Navy during the Revolution,* New York: Charles Scribner's Sons, 1976.

————. *Samuel Adams: Radical Puritan.* New York: Longmans, 1997.

————. "William Ellery: Making of a Rhode Island Politician." *Rhode Island History,* 30 (November 1971), pp. 125–135.

Fox, Dixon R. "Burgoyne, before and after Saratoga." *Quarterly Journal of the New York State Historical Association,* 10 (April 1929), pp. 128–137.

———. "Culture in Knapsacks." *Quarterly Journal of the New York State Historical Association*, 11 (January 1930), pp. 31–52.

Franklin, Benjamin. Papers of Benjamin Franklin. Edited by Leonard W. Labaree et al. 37 vols. to date. New Haven, Conn.: Yale University Press, 1959–.

Franklin, John H. "The North, the South, and the American Revolution." *Journal of American History*, 62 (June 1975), pp. 5–23.

Frantz, John, and William Pencak, editors. *Beyond Philadelphia: The American Revolution in the Pennsylvania Hinterland*. State College: Pennsylvania State University Press, 1998.

Franz, Eckhart G., and Otto Frölich, compilers. *Hessische Truppen im Amerikanischen Unabhängigkeitskrieg*. Marburg: 1972.

Fraser, Walter J., Jr. *Patriots, Pistols, and Pettycoats: "Poor Sinful Charles Town" during the American Revolution*. 2d edition. Columbia: University of South Carolina Press, 1993.

———. "Reflections of 'Democracy' in Revolutionary South Carolina? The Composition of Military Organizations and the Attitudes and Relationships of the Officers and Men, 1775–1780." *South Carolina Historical Magazine*, 78 (July 1977), pp. 202–212.

Freeman, Douglas S. *George Washington: A Biography*. 7 vols. New York: Charles Scribner's Sons, 1948–1957.

Freiberg, Malcolm. *Prelude to Purgatory: Thomas Hutchinson in Provincial Massachusetts Politics, 1760–1770*. New York: Garland, 1990.

French, Allan. "The British Expedition to Concord, Massachusetts, in 1775." *Military Affairs*, 1 (Spring 1937), pp. 1–17.

———. *The Day of Lexington and Concord, the Nineteenth of April, 1775*. Boston: Little, Brown, 1925.

———. *The First Year of the American Revolution*. Boston: Houghton Mifflin Co., 1934.

———. *General Gage's Informers: New Material upon Lexington & Concord, Benjamin Thompson As Loyalist and the Treachery of Benjamin Church, Jr.* Ann Arbor: University of Michigan Press, 1932.

———. *The Taking of Ticonderoga in 1775: The British Story, a Study of Captors and Captives*. Cambridge, Mass.: Harvard University Press, 1928.

French, Laura P. "The Wilmington Committee of Public Safety and the Loyalist Rising of February 1776." *North Carolina Historical Review*, 41 (June 1964), pp. 21–33.

Frey, Sylvia R. *The British Soldier in America: A Social History of Military Life in the Revolutionary Period*. Austin: University of Texas Press, 1981.

———. "The Common British Soldier in the Late Eighteenth Century: A Profile." *Societas*, 5 (Spring 1975), pp. 117–131.

———. *Water From the Rock: Black Resistance in a Revolutionary Age*. Princeton, N.J.: Princeton University Press, 1991.

Frothingham, Richard. "Bunker Hill." *Proceedings of the Massachusetts Historical Society*, 14 (June 1875), pp. 53–98.

———. *History of the Siege of Boston, and of the Battles of Lexington, Concord and Bunker Hill*. 4th Edition. Boston: Little, Brown and Co., 1873.

———, editor. "Letters Illustrating the Siege of Boston." *Proceedings of the Massachusetts Historical Society*, 14 (March 1876), pp. 275–285.

Frothingham, Thomas G. "The Military Test of the Spontaneous American Revolution." *Proceedings of the Massachusetts Historical Society*, 58 (November 1924), pp. 110–117.

———. *Washington: Commander in Chief*. Boston: Houghton Mifflin Co., 1930.

Fryer, Mary B. *The King's Men: The Soldier-Founders of Ontario*. Toronto: Dundurn Press, 1980.

Furlong, Patrick J. "Civilian-Military Conflict and the Restoration of the Royal Province of Georgia, 1778–1782." *Journal of Southern History*, 38 July 1972, pp. 415–442.

Gadsden, Christopher. *The Writings of Christopher Gadsden, 1746–1805*. Edited by Richard Walsh. Columbia: University of South Carolina Press, 1966.

Gage, Thomas. *The Correspondence of General Thomas Gage with the Secretaries of State 1763–1775*. Edited by Clarence E. Carter. 2 vols. New Haven: Yale University Press, 1931–1933.

Gallagher, John J. *The Battle of Brooklyn, 1776*. New York: Da Capo Press, 1995.

Gálvez, Bernardo de. "Bernardo de Gálvez's Combat Diary for the Battle of Pensacola, 1781." Edited by Maury Baker and Margaret Bissler Haas. *Florida Historical Quarterly*, 56 (October 1977), pp. 176–199.

———. "Diary of the Operations against Pensacola." Translated by Gaspar de Cusachs. *Louisiana Historical Quarterly*, 1 (January 1917), pp. 44–84.

Galvin, John R. *The Minute Men, the First Fight: The Myths and Realities of the American Revolution* (revised edition). McLean, Virginia: Pergamon-Brassey, 1989.

Ganyard, Robert L. "Threat from the West: North Carolina and the Cherokee, 1776–1778." *North Carolina Historical Review*, 45 (January 1968), pp. 47–66.

Gardner, C. Harvey, editor. *A Study in Dissent: The Warren-Gerry Correspondence 1776–1792*. Carbondale: Southern Illinois University Press, 1968.

Gates, David. *The British Light Infantry Arm*. London, Batsford, 1987.

Gee, Olive. "The British War Office in the Later Years of the American War of Independence." *Journal of Modern History*, 26 (June 1954), pp. 123–136.

George III. *The Correspondence of King George the Third from 1760 to December 1783*. Edited by John W. Fortescue. 2d Edition. 6 vols. London: Frank Cass & Co., 1967.

Gephart, Ronald M. *Periodical Literature on the American Revolution: Historical Research and Changing Interpretations 1895–1970, A Selective Bibliography*. Washington: Library of Congress, 1971.

———. *Revolutionary America 1763–1789: A Bibliography*. 2 vols. Washington: Library of Congress, 1984.

Gerlach, Don R. "The British Invasion of 1780 and 'A Character . . . Debased Beyond Description.'" *Bulletin of the Fort Ticonderoga Museum*, 14 (Summer 1984), pp. 311–321.

———. "The Fall of Ticonderoga in 1777: Who Was Responsible?" *Bulletin of the Fort Ticonderoga Museum*, 14 (Summer 1982), pp. 131–157.

———. "A Note on the Quartering Act of 1774." *New England Quarterly*, 39 (March 1966), pp. 80–88.

———. *Philip Schuyler and the American Revolution in New York, 1733–1777*. Lincoln: University of Nebraska Press, 1964.

———. *Philip Schuyler and the Growth of New York, 1733–1804*. Albany: Office of State History, 1968.

———. "Philip Schuyler and the New York Frontier in 1781." *New-York Historical Society Quarterly*, 53 (April 1969), pp. 148–181.

———. "Philip Schuyler and 'the Road to Glory:' A Question of Loyalty and Competence." *New-York Historical Society Quarterly*, 44 (October 1965), pp. 341–386.

———. *Proud Patriot: Philip Schuyler and the War of Independence, 1775–1783*. Syracuse: Syracuse University Press, 1987.

———. "Trial at Quaker-Hill: 'Justice to an Injured Country' or 'Justice to . . . Injured Gentlemen?'" *Bulletin of the Fort Ticonderoga Museum*, 14 (Fall 1983), pp. 250–259.

Gerlach, Larry R. "Connecticut and Commutation, 1778–1784." *Connecticut Historical Society Bulletin*, 33 (April 1968), pp. 51–58.

———. *Connecticut Congressman: Samuel Huntington, 1731–1796*. Hartford: American Revolution Bicentennial Commission of Connecticut, 1976.

———. "A Delegation of Steady Habits: The Connecticut Representatives to the Continental Congress, 1774–1789." *Connecticut Historical Society Bulletin*, 32 (April 1967), pp. 33–39.

———. "Firmness and Prudence: Connecticut, the Continental Congress, and the National Domain, 1766–1786." *Connecticut Historical Society Bulletin*, 31 (July 1966), pp. 65–78.

———. "Loyalist Studies in New Jersey: Needs and Opportunities." *New Jersey History*, 95 (Summer 1977), pp. 69–84.

———, editor. *New Jersey in the American Revolution, 1763–1783: A Documentary History*. Trenton: New Jersey Historical Commission, 1975.

———. *Prologue to Independence: New Jersey in the Coming of the American Revolution*. New Brunswick: Rutgers University Press, 1976.

———. *The Road to Revolution*. Trenton: New Jersey Historical Commission, 1975.

———. "Soldiers and Citizens: The British Army in New Jersey on the Eve of the Revolution." *New Jersey History*, 93 (Spring–Summer 1975), pp. 5–36.

———. *William Franklin: New Jersey's Last Royal Governor*. Trenton: New Jersey Historical Commission, 1975.

Gerson, Noel B. *The Man Who Lost America: A Biography of Gentleman Johnny Burgoyne*. New York: Dial Press, 1973.

Gibson, J. E. *Dr. Bodo Otto and the Medical Background of the American Revolution*. Springfield, Mass.: Charles C. Thomas, 1937.

Gibson, Marjorie H. *HMS Somerset, 1746–1778: The Life and Times of an Eighteenth-Century British Man-o-War and Her Impact on North America*. Cotuit, Massachusetts: Abbey Gate Press, 1992.

Gilbert, Arthur N. "An Analysis of Some Eighteenth Century Army Recruiting Records." *Journal of the Society for Army Historical Research*, 54 (Spring 1976), pp. 38–47.

———. "The Changing Face of British Military Justice, 1757–1783." *Military Affairs*, 49 (April 1985), pp. 80–84.

———. "Charles Jenkinson and the Last Army Press, 1779." *Military Affairs*, 42 (February 1978), pp. 7–11.

———. "Law and Honour among Eighteenth Century British Army Officers." *Historical Journal*, 19 (March 1976), pp. 75–87.

———. "Military and Civilian Justice in Eighteenth-Century England: An Assessment." *Journal of British Studies*, 17 (Spring 1978), pp. 41–65.

———. "Military Recruitment and Career Advancement in the Eighteenth Century: Two Case Studies." *Journal of the Society for Army Historical Research*, 57 (Spring 1979), pp. 34–44.

———. "Recruitment and Reforms in the East India Company's Army, 1760–1800." *Journal of British Studies*, 15 (November 1975), pp. 89–111.

———. "The Regimental Courts Martial in the Eighteenth Century British Army." *Albion*, 8 (Spring 1976), pp. 50–66.

———. "Why Men Deserted from the Eighteenth-Century British Army." *Armed Forces and Society*, 6 (Summer 1980), pp. 553–567.

Gilbert, Benjamin. *A Citizen-Soldier in the American Revolution: Diary, in Massachusetts and New York*. Edited by Rebecca Symmes. Cooperstown, N.Y.: New York State Historical Association, 1980.

———. *Winding Down: The Revolutionary War Letters of Lieutenant Benjamin Gilbert of Massachusetts, 1780–1783*. Edited by John Shy. Ann Arbor: University of Michigan Press, 1989.

Gill, Harold B., Jr. *The Gunsmith in Colonial Virginia*. Williamsburg: Colonial Williamsburg Foundation, 1974.

Gillett, Mary C. *The Army Medical Department, 1775–1818*. Washington: Government Printing Office, 1981.

Gil Munilla, Octavio. *Participación de España en la genesis histórica de los Estados Unidos*. Madrid: Publicaciones Españolas, 1952.

Gipson, Lawrence H. "The American Revolution As an Aftermath of the Great War for the Empire, 1754–1763." *Political Science Quarterly*, 65 (March 1950), pp. 86–104.

———. *The Coming of the Revolution, 1763–1775*. New York: Harper and Row, 1954.

———. *Jared Ingersoll: A Study of American Loyalism in Relation to British Colonial Government*. New Haven: Yale University Press, 1920.

Giunta, Mary A. et al., editors. *The Emerging Nation: The Documentary History of the Foreign Relations of the United States under the Articles of Confederation, 1780–1789*, Washington, DC: National Historic Publications and Records Commission, 1996.

Glascock, Melvin B. "New Spain and the War for America, 1779–1783." Ph.D. dissertation, Louisiana State University, 1969.

Glover, John. *General John Glover's Letterbook, 1776–1777*. Edited by Russell W. Knight. Salem: Essex Institute, 1976.

Glover, Michael. *General Burgoyne in Canada and America: Scapegoat for a System.* London: Gordon & Cremonesi, 1976.

Gluckman, Arcadi. *United States Muskets, Rifles and Carbines.* Harrisburg: Stackpole Co., 1959.

Godbold, E. Stanley, Jr., and Robert H. Woody. *Christopher Gadsden and the American Revolution.* Knoxville: University of Tennessee Press, 1982.

Godechot, Jacques. "L'Influence de la Tactique et de la Stratégie de la guerre d'indépendance Américaine sur la tactique et la stratégie française de l'armée de terre." *Revue Internationale d'Histoire Militaire,* 41 (1979), pp. 141–147.

Godfrey, Carlos E. *The Commander-in-Chief's Guard: The Revolutionary War.* Washington: Stevenson-Smith Company, 1904.

Gold, Robert L. "Governor Bernardo de Gálvez and Spanish Espionage in Pensacola, 1777." In *The Spanish in the Mississippi Valley 1762–1784.* Edited by John F. McDermott. Urbana: University of Illinois Press, 1974.

Goldenberg, Joseph A., Eddie D. Nelson, and Rita Y. Fletcher. "Revolutionary Ranks: An Analysis of the Chesterfield Supplements." *Virginia Magazine of History and Biography,* 87 (April 1979), pp. 182–189.

Goodrich, John E., compiler. *Rolls of the [Vermont] Soldiers of the Revolutionary War, 1775 to 1783.* Rutland: State of Vermont by the Tuttle Co., 1904.

Goodwin, Edmund P. *Colonel William Fleming of Botetourt, 1728–1795.* Roanoke, Va.: Roanoke Valley Historical Society, 1976.

Goold, Nathan. *Colonel James Scamman's 30th Regiment of Foot 1775.* Portland, Me.: Thurston Print, 1900.

———. *History of Colonel Edmund Phinney's 18th Continental Regiment Twelve Months' Service in 1776.* Portland, Me.: Thurston Print, 1898.

———. *History of Colonel Edmund Phinney's 31st Regiment of Foot Eight Months' Service Men.* Portland, Me.: Thurston Print, 1896.

———. *History of Colonel Jonathan Mitchell's Cumberland County Regiment Bagaduce Expedition, 1779.* Portland, Me.: Thurston Print, 1899.

Gordon, Colin. "Crafting a Usable Past: Consensus, Ideology, and Historians of the American Revolution." *William and Mary Quarterly,* 3d Ser., 46 (October 1989), pp. 671–695.

Gordon, John W. *South Carolina and the American Revolution: A Battlefield History.* Columbia: University of South Carolina Press, 2003.

Gordon, Maurice B. *Naval and Maritime Medicine during the American Revolution.* Ventnor, N.J.: Ventnor Publishers, 1978.

Gordon, William W. "Count Casimir Pulaski." *Georgia Historical Quarterly,* 13 (October 1929), pp. 169–227.

Gott, Joseph W. "Orange County in the Revolution." *Quarterly Journal of the New York State Historical Association,* 12 (October 1931), pp. 366–374.

Gottschalk, Louis. "The Attitude of European Officers in the Revolutionary Armies toward General George Washington." *Journal of the Illinois State Historical Society,* 32 (December 1939), pp. 20–50.

———. *Lafayette and the Close of the American Revolution.* Chicago: University of Chicago Press, 1942.

———. *Lafayette Comes to America.* Chicago: University of Chicago Press, 1935.

———. *Lafayette Joins the American Army.* Chicago: University of Chicago Press, 1937.

Gottschalk, Louis, and Josephine Fennell, editors. "Duer and the 'Conway Cabal.'" *American Historical Review,* 52 (October 1946), pp. 87–96.

Gould, Eliga. *The Persistence of Empire: British Political Culture in the Age of the American Revolution.* Chapel Hill: University of North Carolina Press, 2000.

Gradish, Stephen F. "The German Mercenaries in North America during the American Revolution: A Case Study." *Canadian Journal of History,* 4 (March 1969), pp. 23–46.

Graham, Gerald S. "Considerations on the War of American Independence." *Bulletin of the Institute for Historical Research,* 22 (May 1949), pp. 22–34.

Graham, John. "Journal of John Graham, South Carolina Militia, 1779." C. F. W. Coker, editor. *Military Collector and Historian,* 19 (Summer 1967), pp. 35–47.

Grant, Alastair M. *General James Grant of Ballindalloch, 1720–1806.* London: A. M. Grant, 1930.

Graves, Donald E. *French Military Terminology, 1670–1815. A Technical Glossary.* Saint John, N.B.: New Brunswick Museum, 1979.

Graydon, Alexander. *Memoirs of His Own Time. With Reminiscences of the Men and Events of the Revolution.* Edited by John Stockton Littell. Philadelphia: Lindsay and Blackiston, 1846.

Graymont, Barbara. *The Iroquois in the American Revolution.* Syracuse N.Y.: Syracuse University Press, 1972.

Greene, Christopher. "Crisis on the Sparkling Bay (Revolution in Rhode Island April 1775–April 1776)." *Military Collector and Historian,* 29 (Spring 1977), pp. 52–61.

Greene, Evarts B., and Virginia D. Harrington. *American Population before the Federal Census of 1790.* New York: Columbia University Press, 1932.

Greene, Jack P., editor. *The American Revolution: Its Character and Limits.* New York: New York University Press, 1987.

———. "The Plunge of Lemmings: A Consideration of Recent Writings on British Politics and the American Revolution." *South Atlantic Quarterly,* 67 (April 1968), pp. 141–175.

———. "The Social Origins of the American Revolution: An Evaluation and an Interpretation." *Political Science Quarterly,* 88 (March 1973), pp. 1–22.

———. "The South Carolina Quartering Dispute, 1757–1758." *South Carolina Historical Magazine,* 60 (October 1959), pp. 193–204.

———. *Understanding the American Revolution: Issues and Actors.* Charlottesville: University Press of Virginia, 1995.

Greene, Jerome A. *The Guns of Independence: The Siege of Yorktown, 1781.* New York: Savas Beatie, 2005.

Greene, Lorenzo J. "Some Observations on the Black Regiment of Rhode Island in the American Revolution." *Journal of Negro History,* 37 (April 1952), pp. 142–172.

Greene, Nathanael. *The Papers of General Nathanael Greene.* Edited by Richard K. Showman, et al. 12 vols. Chapel Hill: University of North Carolina Press for the Rhode Island Historical Society, 1976–2002.

Greene, Robert E. *Black Courage, 1775–1783: Documentation of Black Participation in the American Revolution.* Washington, D.C.: Daughters of the American Revolution, 1984.

Greenman, Jeremiah. *Diary of a Common Soldier in the American Revolution, 1775–1783: An Annotated Edition of the Military Journal of Jeremiah Greenman.* Edited by Robert C. Bray and Paul E. Bushnell. DeKalb: Northern Illinois University Press, 1978.

Greenwood, Isaac J. "The Stockbridge Indians during the American Revolution." *New England Historical and Genealogical Register,* 54 (April 1900), pp. 162–164.

Greenwood, John. *The Revolutionary Services of John Greenwood of Boston and New York, 1775–1783.* Edited by Isaac J. Greenwood. New York: DeVinne Press, 1922.

Greenwood, W. Bart, compiler and editor. *The American Revolution, 1775–1783: An Atlas of 18th Century Maps and Charts.* Washington, D. C.: Navy Department, 1972.

Grenier, John. *The First Way of War: American War-Making on the Frontier, 1607–1814.* New York: Cambridge University Press, 2005.

Griffenhagen, George B. "Drug Supplies in the American Revolution." *Contributions from the Museum of History and Technology [Smithsonian Institution],* 225 (1961), pp. 109–133.

Griffin, Martin I. J. *Stephen Moylan: Muster-Master General, Secretary and Aide-de-Camp to Washington.* Philadelphia: Privately printed, 1909.

Griffin, William D. "General Charles O'Hara." *Irish Sword,* 10 (Summer 1972), pp. 179–187.

Griffith, Lucille. "Peter Chester and the End of the British Empire in West Florida." *Alabama Review,* 30 (January 1977), pp. 14–33.

Gross, Robert A., editor. *In Debt to Shays: The Bicentennial of an Agrarian Rebellion.* Charlottesville: University Press of Virginia, 1993.

———. *The Minutemen and Their World.* Revised Edition. Hill and Wang, 2001.

———. "The Revolutionary Soldier." *Historical New Hampshire,* 36 (Summer/Fall 1981), pp. 202–208.

Gruber, Ira D. "The American Revolution As a Conspiracy: The British View." *William and Mary Quarterly,* 3d Ser., 26 (July 1969), pp. 360–372.

———. *The Howe Brothers and the American Revolution.* Chapel Hill: University of North Carolina Press, 1972.

———. "Lord Howe and Lord George Germain: British Politics and the Winning of American Independence." *William and Mary Quarterly,* 3d Ser., 22 (April 1965), pp. 225–243.

Guthorn, Peter J. *American Maps and Mapmakers of the Revolution.* Monmouth Beach, N.J.: Philip Freneau Press, 1966.

———. *British Maps of the American Revolution.* Monmouth Beach, N.J.: Philip Freneau Press, 1972.

———. "A Hessian Map from the American Revolution: Its Origin and Purpose." *Quarterly Journal of the Library of Congress,* 33 (July 1976), pp. 219–231.

———. "Revolutionary War Mapmakers." *Prologue,* 9 (Fall 1977), pp. 171–177.

Gutridge, George H. *English Whiggism and the American Revolution.* 2d edition. Berkeley: University of California Press, 1963.

———. "Lord George Germain in Office, 1775–1782." *American Historical Review,* 33 (October 1927), pp. 23–43.

Guzzardo, John C. "The Superintendant and the Ministers: The Battle for Oneida Allegiances, 1761–75." *New York History,* 57 (July 1976), pp. 255–283.

Gwathmey, John H. *Historical Register of Virginians in the Revolution: Soldiers, Sailors, Marines, 1775–1783.* Richmond: Dietz Press, 1938.

Haarmann, Albert W. "American Provincial Corps Authorized by Lord Dunmore, 1775." *Journal of the Society for Army Historical Research,* 52 (Winter 1974), pp. 254–255.

———. "The Anhalt-Zerbst Troops in British Service during the American War of Independence, 1776–1783." *Military Collector and Historian,* 32 (Fall 1980), pp. 115–116.

———. "British, German, and Provincial Uniforms in the Revolution: Some Notes from Rivington's North American History for 1783." *Military Collector and Historian,* 14 (Winter 1962), pp. 113–120.

———. "Contemporary Observations on the Hesse-Cassel Troops Sent to North America, 1776–1781." *Journal of the Society for Army Historical Research,* 54 (Autumn 1976), pp. 130–134.

———. "The Jamaica Volunteer Corps, 1779–1781." *Journal of the Society for Army Historical Research,* 49 (Winter 1971), pp. 249–250.

——— "Notes on the Brunswick Troops in British Service during the American War of Independence 1776–1783." *Journal of the Society for Army Historical Research,* 48 (Fall 1970), pp. 140–143; 51 (Summer 1973), p. 123.

———. "The Siege of Pensacola: An Order of Battle." *Florida Historical Quarterly,* 44 (January 1966), pp. 193–199.

———. "Some Notes on American Provincial Uniforms, 1776–1783." *Journal of the Society for Army Historical Research,* 49 (Autumn 1971), pp. 141–151.

———. "The Spanish Conquest of British West Florida, 1779–1781." *Florida Historical Quarterly,* 39 (October 1960), pp. 107–134.

Haarmann, Albert W., and Donald W. Holst. "The Friedrich von Germann Drawings of Troops in the American Revolution." Military Collector and Historian, 16 (Fall 1964), pp. 1–9.

———. "The Hesse-Hanau Free Corps of Light Infantry, 1781–1783." Military Collector and Historian, 15 (Summer 1963), pp. 40–42.

Haase, Carl. "Das militärgeschichtliche Archivgut im Niedersächsischen Staatsarchiv im Hannover." *Militärgeschichtliche Mitteilungen,* #1, 1969, pp. 155–164.

Hadden, James M. *Hadden's Journal and Orderly Books: A Journal Kept in Canada and upon Burgoyne's Campaign in 1776 and 1777.* Edited by Horatio Rogers. Albany: Joel Munsell's Sons, 1884.

Hale, Richard W. "New Light on the Naval Side of Yorktown." *Massachusetts Historical Society Proceedings*, 71 (1953–1957), pp. 124–132.

Hale, Richard W., Jr. "The American Revolution in Western Massachusetts." *New England Historical and Genealogical Register*, 129 (October 1975), pp. 325–334.

Hall, Charles S. *Benjamin Tallmadge: Revolutionary Soldier and American Businessman.* New York: Columbia University Press, 1943.

———. *Life and Letters of Samuel Holden Parsons, Major General in the Continental Army and Chief Judge of the Northwestern Territory, 1737–1789.* Binghamton, N.Y.: Otseningo Publishing Co., 1905.

Hall, Leslie. *Land and Allegiance in Revolutionary Georgia.* Athens: University of Georgia Press, 2001.

Hall, Wilbur C. "Sergeant Champe's Adventure." *William and Mary Quarterly*, 2d Ser., 18 (July 1938), pp. 322–342.

———. "Sergeant John Champe and Certain of His Contemporaries." *William and Mary Quarterly*, 2d Ser., 17 (April 1937), pp. 145–175.

Hambrick-Stowe, Charles E., and Donna D. Smerlas, editors. *Massachusetts Militia Companies and Officers in the Lexington Alarm.* Boston: New England Historic Genealogical Society, 1976.

Hamer, Philip M. "Henry Laurens of South Carolina—The Man and His Papers." Proceedings of the Massachusetts Historical Society, 77 (1965), pp. 3–14.

———. "John Stuart's Indian Policy during the Early Months of the American Revolution." *Mississippi Valley Historical Review*, 17 (December 1930), pp. 351–366.

Hamilton, Alexander. *The Papers of Alexander Hamilton.* Edited by Harold C. Syrett and Jacob E. Cook. 26 vols. New York: Columbia University Press, 1961–1979.

Hamilton, Edward P. "General John Thomas." *Proceedings of the Massachusetts Historical Society*, 84 (1972), pp. 44–52.

———. "Was Washington to Blame for the Loss of Ticonderoga in 1777?" *Bulletin of the Fort Ticonderoga Museum*, 11 (September 1963), pp. 65–74.

Hammon, Neal O., and Richard Taylor. *Virginia's Western War, 1775–1786.* Mechanicsburg, Pennsylvania: Stackpole Books, 2002.

Hammond, Otis G. *Tories of New Hampshire in the War of the Revolution.* Concord: New Hampshire Historical Society, 1917.

Hancock, Harold B. *The Delaware Loyalists.* Wilmington: Historical Society of Delaware, 1940.

———. "The Kent County Loyalists." *Delaware History*, 6 (March, September 1954), pp. 3–24, 92–139.

———. "The New Castle County Loyalists." *Delaware History*, 4 (September 1951), pp. 315–333.

———, editor. "Revolutionary War Period Material in the Hall of Records, 1775–1787: Four Little Known Sources." *Delaware History*, 17 (Spring–Summer 1976), pp. 54–85.

———. "Thomas Robinson: Delaware's Most Prominent Loyalist." *Delaware History*, 4 (March 1950), pp. 1–36.

Hand, Edward. *The Unpublished Revolutionary Papers of Major General Edward Hand of Pennsylvania, 1777–1784.* Edited by A. J. Bowden. New York: Privately printed, 1907.

Handlin, Oscar, and Mary F. Handlin. "Revolutionary Economic Policy in Massachusetts." *William and Mary Quarterly*, 3d Ser., 4 (January 1947), pp. 3–26.

Hanley, Thomas O. *Charles Carroll of Carrollton: The Making of a Revolutionary Gentleman.* Washington: Catholic University of America Press, 1970.

———. "The State and Dissenters in the American Revolution." *Maryland Historical Magazine*, 58 (December 1963), pp. 325–332.

Hanson, Willis T., Jr. *A History of Schenectady during the Revolution.* Brattleboro, Vt.: E. I. Hildreth & Co., 1916.

Haraszti, Zoltan. "Besieging Boston with a Dwindling Army; The Last Stages of the Siege of Boston." *More Books*, 7 (May, September 1932), pp. 123–138, 219–228.

Harding, Richard. "Sailors and Gentlemen of Parade: Some Professional and Technical Problems Concerning the Conduct of Combined Operations in the Eighteenth Century." *Historical Journal*, 32 (March 1989), pp. 35–56.

Hargreaves, Reginald. *The Bloodybacks: The British Serviceman in North America and the Caribbean, 1655–1783.* London: Rupert Hart-Davis, 1968.

Hargrove, Richard J., Jr. *General John Burgoyne.* Newark: University of Delaware Press, 1983.

Harkey, Joseph H. "Captain William Morgan's Berkeley County, Virginia, Militia Company." *West Virginia History*, 38 (October 1976), pp. 35–55.

Harley, J. B., Barbara B. Petchenik, and Lawrence W. Toner. *Mapping the American Revolutionary War.* Chicago: University of Chicago Press, 1978.

Harlow, Ralph V. "Aspects of Revolutionary Finance, 1775–1783." *American Historical Review*, 35 (October 1929), pp. 46–68.

Harris, P. M. G. "The Demographic Development of Colonial Philadelphia in Some Comparative Perspective." *Transactions of the American Philosophical Society*, 113 (June 1989), pp. 262–304.

Harrison, Lowell H. *George Rogers Clark and the War in the West.* Lexington: University Press of Kentucky, 1976.

Harrison, Richard A., editor. *Princetonians, 1769–1775: A Biographical Dictionary.* Princeton, N.J.: Princeton University Press, 1976.

Hart, Freeman H. *The Valley of Virginia in the American Revolution, 1763–1789.* Chapel Hill: University of North Carolina Press, 1942.

Haslewood, William. "Journal of a British Officer during the American Revolution." Edited by Louise Phelps Kellogg. *Mississippi Valley Historical Review*, 7 (June 1920), pp. 51–58.

Hassler, Warren W., Jr. "General Washington and the Revolution's Crucial Campaign." *Western Pennsylvania Historical Magazine*, 48 (July 1965), pp. 249–270.

Hast, Adele. *Loyalism in Revolutionary Virginia: The Norfolk Area and the Eastern Shore.* Ann Arbor: UMI Research Press, 1982.

Hastings, George E. *The Life and Works of Francis Hopkinson.* Chicago: University of Chicago Press, 1926.

Hatch, Charles E., Jr. "The 'Affair Near James Island' (or, 'The Battle of Green Spring') July 6, 1781." *Virginia Magazine of History and Biography*, 53 (July 1945), pp. 172–196.

———. *The Battle of Guilford Courthouse.* Washington, DC: National Park Service, 1971.

———. *The Battle of Moore's Creek Bridge,* Washington, DC: National Park Service, 1969.

———. "Gloucester Point in the Siege of Yorktown, 1781." *William and Mary Quarterly,* 2d Ser., 20 (April 1940), pp. 265–284.

Hatch, Charles E., Jr., and Thomas M. Pitkin, editors. *Yorktown, Climax of the Revolution.* Washington: Department of the Interior, National Park Service, 1941.

Hatch, Louis C. *The Administration of the American Revolutionary Army.* New York: Longmans, Green, and Co., 1904.

Hatch, Robert M. *Major John Andre: A Gallant in Spy's Clothing.* Boston: Houghton Mifflin, 1986.

———. *Thrust for Canada: The American Attempt on Quebec in 1775–1776.* Boston: Houghton Mifflin, 1979.

Haw, James. "Patronage, Politics, and Ideology, 1753–1762: A Prelude to Revolution in Maryland." *Maryland Historical Magazine,* 85 (Fall 1990), pp. 236–255.

Hawke David F. *Benjamin Rush; Revolutionary Gadfly.* Indianapolis: Bobbs-Merrill, 1971.

———. *Honorable Treason: The Declaration of Independence and the Men Who Signed It.* New York: Viking Press, 1976.

Hayes, John T. *Connecticut's Revolutionary Cavalry: Sheldon's Horse.* Chester, Conn.: Pequot Press, 1975.

Haynes, Robert V. "James Willing and the Planters of Natchez: The American Revolution Comes to the Southwest." *Journal of Mississippi History,* 37 (February 1975), pp. 1–40.

———. *The Natchez District and the American Revolution.* Jackson: University Press of Mississippi, 1976.

Hays, Louise F. *Hero of the Hornet's Nest: A Biography of Elijah Clark, 1733–1799.* New York: Stratford House, 1946.

Hayter, Tony. *The Army and the Crowd in Mid-Georgian England.* Totawa, N.J.: Rowman and Littlefield, 1978.

Heath, William. "The Heath Papers." *Massachusetts Historical Society Collections,* 5th Ser., 4 (1878), pp. 1–285; 7th Ser., 4 (1904) and 5 (1905).

———. *Memoirs of Major-General William Heath By Himself.* Edited by William Abbatt. New Edition. New York: William Abbatt, 1901.

Hecht, Arthur. "Lead Production in Virginia during the Seventeenth and Eighteenth Century." *West Virginia History,* 25 (April 1964), pp. 173–183.

Heidler, David S. "The American Defeat at Briar Creek, 3 March 1779." *Georgia Historical Quarterly,* 66 (Fall 1982), pp. 317–331.

Heitman, Francis B. *Historical Register of Officers of the Continental Army during the War of the Revolution April, 1775, to December, 1783.* Revised Edition. Washington: The Rare Book Shop Publishing Co., 1914.

Helgesen, M. P. "The British Army in Boston, June 1774 to March 1776." *Army Quarterly,* 78 (April 1959), pp. 99–113.

Hemphill, William E., and Wylma A. Waters, editors. *Extracts from the Journals of the Provincial Congresses of South Carolina, 1775–1776.* Columbia: South Carolina Archives Department, 1960.

———, et al., editors. *Journals of the General Assembly and House of Representatives, 1776–1780.* Columbia: University of South Carolina Press, 1970.

Henderson, H. James. *Party Politics in the Continental Congress.* New York: McGraw-Hill Book Co., 1974.

Henry, William W. *Patrick Henry: Life, Correspondence and Speeches.* 3 vols. New York: Charles Scribner's Sons, 1891.

Henshaw, William. *The Orderly Book of Colonel William Henshaw, of the American Amy, April 20–September 26, 1775.* Boston: A. Williams and Co., 1881.

———. *The Orderly Books of Col. William Henshaw, October 1, 1775, through October 3, 1776.* Worcester: American Antiquarian Society, 1948.

Herbert, Charles. "Coxheath Camp, 1778–1779." *Journal of the Society for Army Historical Research,* 44 (Fall 1967), pp. 129–148.

Heusser, Albert H. *George Washington's Map Maker: A Biography of Robert Erskine.* 1928. Reprinted and edited by Hubert Schmidt. New Brunswick: Rutgers University Press, 1966.

Hibbert, Christopher. *Redcoats and Rebels: The American Revolution through British Eyes.* New York: Avon Books, 1990.

Higginbotham, Don. "American Historians and the Military History of the American Revolution." *American Historical Review,* 70 (October 1964), pp. 18–34.

———. *Daniel Morgan: Revolutionary Rifleman.* Chapel Hill: University of North Carolina Press, 1961.

———. *George Washington and the American Military Tradition.* Athens: University of Georgia Press, 1985.

———, editor. *George Washington Reconsidered.* Charlottesville: University Press of Virginia, 2001.

———, editor. *Reconsiderations on the Revolutionary War: Selected Essays.* Westport, Conn.: Greenwood Press, 1978.

    Bowler, R. Arthur. "Logistics and Operations in the American Revolution," pp. 54–71.

    Kohn, Richard H. "American Generals and the Revolution: Subordination and Restraint," pp. 104–123.

———. *War and Society in Revolutionary America: The Wider Dimensions of Conflict.* Columbia: University of South Carolina Press, 1988.

———. *The War of American Independence: Military Attitudes, Policies, and Practice, 1763–1789.* New York: Macmillan Co., 1971.

Higgins, W. Robert, editor. *The Revolutionary War in the South: Power, Conflict, and Leadership: Essays in Honor of John Richard Alden.* Durham: Duke University Press, 1979.

High, John W., Jr. "The Philadelphia Loyalists, 1763–1783." Ph.D. dissertation, Temple University, 1975.

Higham, Robin, and Donald J. Mrozek, editors. *A Guide to the Sources of United States Military History.* Original and 4 supplements. Hamden, Conn.: Archon Books, 1975–1998.

Hinitt, Dorothy, and Frances Duncombe. *The Burning of Bedford [New York], July 1779.* Bedford, N. Y.: Historical Society, 1974.

Hirschfeld, Fritz, editor. "'Burnt All Their Houses': The Log of HMS *Savage* during a Raid up the Potomac River, Spring, 1781." *Virginia Magazine of History and Biography,* 99 (October 1991), pp. 513–530.

Historical Manuscripts Commission. *The Manuscripts of Captain Howard Vincente Knox.* London: His Majesty's Stationery Office, 1909.

———. *Report on American Manuscripts in the Royal Institution of Great Britain.* 4 vols. London: His Majesty's Stationery Office, 1904–1909.

———. *Report on the Manuscripts of Mrs. Stopford-Sackville, of Drayton House, Northamptonshire.* 2 vols. London: His Majesty's Stationery Office, 1904–1910.

Historical Society of Delaware. *Minutes of the Council of Delaware State, 1776–1792.* Wilmington: Historical Society of Delaware, 1887.

Hitchcock, Dan. "So Few the Brave (The Second Rhode Island 1777–1781)." *Military Collector and Historian*, 30 (Spring 1978), pp. 18–22.

Hoadley, Charles J., et al., compilers. *The Public Records of the State of Connecticut.* 11 vols. Hartford: Various publishers, 1894–1967.

Hocker, Edward W. *The Fighting Parson of the American Revolution: A Biography of General Peter Muhlenberg, Lutheran Clergyman, Military Chieftain, and Political Leader.* Philadelphia: Privately printed, 1936.

Hoffman, Ronald. *A Spirit of Dissension: Economics, Politics, and the Revolution in Maryland.* Baltimore: Johns Hopkins University Press, 1973.

Hoffman, Ronald, and Peter J. Albert, editors. *Arms and Independence: The Military Character of the American Revolution.* Charlottesville: University Press of Virginia, 1984.

———. *Diplomacy and Revolution: The Franco-American Alliance of 1778.* Charlottesville: University Press of Virginia, 1981.

———. *Peace and the Peacemakers: The Treaty of 1783.* Charlottesville: University Press of Virginia, 1986.

———. *Sovereign States in an Age of Uncertainty.* Charlottesville: University Press of Virginia, 1981.

Hoffman, Ronald, and Peter J. Albert, John J. McCusker, and Russell R. Menard, editors. *The Economy of Early America: The Revolutionary Period, 1763–1790.* Charlottesville: University Press of Virginia, 1988.

Hoffman, Ronald, and Peter J. Albert, and Thad W. Tate, editors. *An Uncivil War: The Southern Backcountry during the American Revolution.* Charlottesville: University Press of Virginia, 1985.

Holmes, Jack D. L. "Alabama's Bloodiest Day of the American Revolution: Counterattack at The Village, January 7, 1781." *Alabama Review*, 29 (July 1976), pp. 208–219.

———. *A Guide to Spanish Louisiana, 1762–1806.* New Orleans: Louisiana Collection Series, 1970.

———. "The Historiography of the American Revolution in Louisiana." *Louisiana History*, 19 (Summer 1978), pp. 309–326.

———. "Jose de Evia and His Activities in Mobile, 1780–1784." *Alabama Historical Quarterly*, 34 (Summer 1972), pp. 105–112.

———. "Juan de la Villebeuvre: Spain's Commandant of Natchez during the American Revolution." *Journal of Mississippi History*, 37 (February 1975), pp. 97–129.

———. "Robert Ross' Plan for an English Invasion of Louisiana in 1782." *Louisiana History*, 5 (Spring 1964), pp. 161–177.

Holton, Woody. *Forces Founders: Indians, Debtors, Slaves, and the Making of the American Revolution in Virginia.* Chapel Hill: University of North Carolina for the Institute of Early American History and Culture, 1999.

Honneywell, Roy J. *Chaplains of the United States Army.* Washington: Office of the Chief of Chaplains. 1958.

Horne, Paul A., Jr. "Forgotten Leaders: South Carolina's Delegation to the Continental Congress, 1774–1789." Ph.D. dissertation, University of South Carolina, 1988.

Horrell, Joseph, editor. "New Light on William Grayson: His Guardian's Account." *Virginia Magazine of History and Biography*, 92 (October 1984), pp. 423–443.

Houlding, John A. *Fit for Service: The Training of the British Army, 1715–1795.* Oxford: Clarendon Press, 1981.

Howard, Cary. "John Eager Howard: Patriot and Public Servant." *Maryland Historical Magazine*, 62 (September 1967), pp. 300–317.

Howard, Clinton N. "Colonial Pensacola: The British Period." *Florida Historical Quarterly*, 19 (October 1940–April 1941), pp. 109–127, 246–269, 368–401.

Hubbs, Valentine C., editor. *Hessian Journals: Unpublished Documents of the American Revolution [from the Von Jungkenn manuscripts at the William L. Clements Library].* Columbia, South Carolina: Camden House, 1981.

Huddleston, F. J. *Gentleman Johnny Burgoyne: Misadventures of an English General in the Revolution.* Indianapolis: Bobbs-Merrill Co., 1927.

Hufeland, Otto. *Westchester County during the American Revolution 1775–1783.* White Plains: Westchester County Historical Society, 1926.

Hughes, B. P. *British Smooth-Bore Artillery: The Muzzle Loading Artillery of the 18th and 19th Centuries.* London: Arms and Armour Press, 1968.

Hughes, Thomas. *A Journal by Thos: Hughes . . . (1778–1789).* Edited by E. A. Benians. Cambridge: Cambridge University Press, 1947.

Hull, N. E. H., Peter C. Hoffer, and Stephen L. Allen. "Choosing Sides: A Quantitative Study of the Personality Determinants of Loyalism and Revolutionary Political Affiliation in New York." *Journal of American History*, 65 (September 1978), pp. 344–366.

Hummel, William. "The Committee of Safety in Northumberland County During the American Revolution." *Pennsylvania History*, 11 (April 1944), pp. 145–148.

Humphreys, David. *David Humphreys' 'Life of General Washington' with George Washington's 'Remarks'.* Edited by Rosemarie Zagarri. Athens: University of Georgia Press, 1991.

Humphreys, R. A. "Richard Oswald's Plan For an English and Russian Attack on Spanish America, 1781–1782." *Hispanic American Historical Review*, 18 (February 1938), pp. 95–101.

Hunt, Richard I., Jr. "The Loyalists of Maine." Ph.D. dissertation, University of Maine, 1980.

Hunter, Lloyd A., editor. *Pathways to the Old Northwest: An Observance of the Bicentennial of the Northwest Ordinance.* Indianapolis: Indiana Historical Society, 1988.

Huntington, Ebenezer. *Letters Written by Ebenezer Huntington during the American Revolution.* New York: C. F. Heartman, 1914.

Hurt, N. Franklin. "Growth of Local Action during the British Military Rule at Detroit: 1760–1774." *Michigan History,* 40 (December 1956), pp. 451–464.

Huston, James A. "The Logistics of Arnold's March to Quebec." *Military Affairs,* 32 (December 1968), pp. 110–124.

———. *Logistics of Liberty: American Services of Supply in the Revolutionary War and After.* Newark: University of Delaware Press, 1990.

———. *The Sinews of War: Army Logistics 1775–1953.* Washington: Government Printing Office, 1966.

Huth, Hans. "Letters from a Hessian Mercenary." Translated by C. V. Easum. Pennsylvania Magazine of History and Biography, 62 (October 1938), pp. 488–501.

Hutson, James H. *John Adams and the Diplomacy of the American Revolution.* Lexington: University Press of Kentucky, 1980.

———. "The Partition Treaty and the Declaration of American Independence." *Journal of American History,* 58 (March 1972), pp. 877–896.

Hyatt, A. M. J. "The Origin of Napoleonic Warfare: A Survey of Interpretations." *Military Affairs,* 30 (Winter 1966), pp. 177–185.

Ifkovic, John W. *Connecticut's Nationalist Revolutionary: Jonathan Trumbull, Jr.* Hartford: American Revolution Bicentennial Commission of Connecticut, 1977.

Indiana Historical Society. *The French, The Indians, and George Rogers Clark in the Illinois Country: Proceedings of an Indiana American Revolution Bicentennial Symposium.* Indianapolis: Indiana Historical Society, 1977.

Ingrao, Charles W. "'Barbarous Strangers': Hessian State and Society during the American Revolution." *American Historical Review,* 87 (October 1982), pp. 954–976.

———. *The Hessian Mercenary State: Ideas, Institutions and Reform under Frederick II, 1760–1785.* Cambridge: Cambridge University Press, 1987.

Ippel, Henry P. "Jeffrey, Lord Amherst, British Commander-in-Chief, 1778–1782." Ph.D. dissertation, University of Michigan, 1957.

Iredell, James. *The Papers of James Iredell.* Edited by Don Higginbotham. Raleigh: Division of Archives and History, 1976–.

Ireland, Oliver. "Partisanship and the Constitution: Pennsylvania 1787." *Pennsylvania History,* 45 (October 1978), pp. 315–332.

Jackson, Harvey H., III. "The Battle of the Riceboats: Georgia Joins the Revolution." *Georgia Historical Quarterly,* 58 (Summer 1974), pp. 229–243.

———. "Button Gwinnett and the Rise of the 'Western Members': A Reappraisal of Georgia's 'Whig Excess.'" *Atlanta Historical Journal,* 24 (Summer 1980), pp. 17–30.

———. *Lachlan McIntosh and the Politics of Revolutionary Georgia.* Athens: University of Georgia Press, 1979.

Jackson, James B. "Our Forgotten Regiment: The Second Delaware Militia, 1780." *Delaware History,* 9 (April 1960), pp. 2–49.

Jackson, John W. *The Pennsylvania Navy 1775–1781: The Defense of the Delaware.* New Brunswick: Rutgers University Press, 1974.

———. *Whitemarsh, 1777: Impregnable Stronghold.* Fort Washington, Pennsylvania: Historical Society of Fort Washington, 1984.

———. *With the British Army in Philadelphia, 1777–1778.* San Rafael, Calif.: Presidio Press, 1979.

Jackson, Luther P. "Virginia Negro Soldiers and Seamen in the American Revolution." *Journal of Negro History,* 27 (July 1942), pp. 247–287.

Jackson, Melvin H., and Carel De Beer. *Eighteenth Century Gunfounding.* Washington: Smithsonian Institution Press, 1974.

Jacobs, James R. *Tarnished Warrior: Major-General James Wilkinson.* New York: Macmillan and Co., 1938.

Jacobs, Roberta T. "The Treaty and the Tories: The Ideological Reaction to the Return of the Loyalists, 1783–1787." Ph.D. Dissertation, Cornell University, 1974.

Jacobson, David L. *John Dickinson and the Revolution in Pennsylvania, 1764–1776.* Berkeley: University of California Press, 1965.

Jaffe, Irma B. *John Trumbull: Five Paintings of the Revolution.* Hartford: Wadsworth Athenaeum, 1976.

———. *John Trumbull: Patriot-Artist of the American Revolution.* Boston: New York Graphic Society, 1975.

James, James A. "Oliver Pollock, Financier of the Revolution in the West." *Mississippi Valley Historical Review,* 16 (June 1929), pp. 67–80.

———. "Spanish Influence in the West during the American Revolution." *Mississippi Valley Historical Review,* 4 (September 1917), pp. 193–208.

James, William M. *The British Navy in Adversity: A Study of the War of American Independence.* London: Longmans, Green, & Co., 1926.

Jameson, Hugh. "Equipment for the Militia of the Middle States, 1775–1781." *Military Affairs,* 3 (Spring 1939), pp. 26–38.

———. "Subsistence for Middle States Militia, 1776–1781." *Military Affairs,* 30 (Fall 1966), pp. 121–134.

Jameson, J. Franklin. "St. Eustatius in the American Revolution." *American Historical Review,* 8 (July 1903), pp. 683–708.

Jamieson, A. G. "War in the Leeward Islands, 1775–1783." Ph.D. Dissertation, Oxford University, 1981.

Jay, John. *The Correspondence and Public Papers of John Jay.* Edited by Henry P. Johnston. 4 vols. New York: G. P. Putnam's Sons, 1890–1905.

———. *John Jay: Unpublished Papers.* Edited by Richard B. Morris, et al. New York: Harper and Row, 1975 –.

Jefferson, Thomas. *The Papers of Thomas Jefferson .* Edited by Julian P. Boyd. Princeton: Princeton University Press, 1950–.

Jellison, Charles A. *Ethan Allen: Frontier Rebel.* Syracuse: Syracuse University Press, 1969.

Jellison, Richard M., editor. *Society, Freedom, and Conscience: The American Revolution in Virginia, Massachusetts, and New York.* New York: W. W. Norton and Co., 1976.

Jensen, Merrill. *The American Revolution within America.* New York: New York University Press, 1974.

———. *The Articles of Confederation: An Interpretation of the Social-Constitutional History of the American Revolution, 1774–1781.* Madison: University of Wisconsin Press, 1948.

———. *The Founding of a Nation: A History of the American Revolution, 1763–1776.* New York: Oxford University Press, 1968.

Johannesen, Stanley K. "John Dickinson and the American Revolution." *Historical Reflections,* 2 (Summer 1975), pp. 29–49.

Johnson, Cecil. *British West Florida. 1763–1783.* New Haven: Yale University Press, 1943.

Johnson, Elmer D. "David Ramsay: Historian or Plagiarist?" *South Carolina Historical Magazine,* 57 (October 1956), pp. 189–198.

Johnson, James M. "'Not a Single Soldier in the Province': The Military Establishment of Georgia and the Coming of the American Revolution." Ph.D. Dissertation, Duke University, 1980.

Johnson, Keach. "The Genesis of the Baltimore Ironworks." *Journal of Southern History,* 19 (May 1953), pp. 157–179.

Johnson, Victor L. The Administration of the American Commissariat during the Revolutionary War. Philadelphia: University of Pennsylvania, 1941.

———. "Robert Morris and the Provisioning of the American Army during the Campaign of 1781." *Pennsylvania History,* 5 (January 1938), pp. 7–20.

Johnston, Henry P. *Battle of Harlem Heights, September 16, 1776.* New York: Macmillan Co., 1897.

———. *Campaign of 1776 around New York and Brooklyn Including a New and Circumstantial Account of the Battle of Long Island and the Loss of New York.* Brooklyn: Long Island Historical Society, 1876.

———, editor. *Record of Service of Connecticut Men in the War of the Revolution, War of 1812, Mexican War.* Hartford: Case, Lockwood & Brainard Co. for the Adjutant General's Office, 1889.

———. *The Storming of Stony Point on the Hudson, Midnight, July 15, 1779.* New York: James T. White, 1900.

———. *Yale and Her Honor-Roll in the American Revolution 1775–1783.* New York: Privately printed, 1888.

———. *The Yorktown Campaign and the Surrender of Cornwallis, 1781.* New York: Harper and Brothers, 1881.

Johnston, James A. "The War Did Not End at Yorktown." *Virginia Magazine of History and Biography,* 60 (July 1952), pp. 444–457.

Jones, E. Alfred. "English Convicts in the American Army in the War of Independence." *Proceedings of the New Jersey Historical Society,* New Ser., 7 (October 1922), pp. 286–291.

Jones, Eldon L. "Sir Guy Carleton and the Close of the American War of Independence." Ph.D. dissertation, Duke University, 1968.

Jones, George F. "The Black Hessians: Negroes Recruited by the Hessians in South Carolina and Other Colonies." *South Carolina Historical Magazine,* 83 (October 1982), pp. 287–302.

———. "Sergeant Johann Wilhelm Jasper." *Georgia Historical Quarterly,* 65 (Spring 1981), pp. 7–15.

Jones, Gwynfor. "An Early Amphibious Operation: Danbury 1777." *Journal of the Society for Army Historical Research,* 46 (Summer 1968), pp. 129–131.

Jones, Lewis P. *The South Carolina Civil War of 1775.* Lexington, S.C.: Sandlapper Store, 1975.

Jones, Robert F. "William Duer and the Business of Government in the Era of the American Revolution." *William and Mary Quarterly,* 3d Ser., 32 (July 1975), pp. 393–416.

Jones, Thomas. *History of New York during the Revolutionary War, and of the Leading Events in the Other Colonies at that Period, by Thomas Jones, Justice of the Supreme Court of the Province.* Edited by Edward Floyd DeLancey. 2 vols. New York: New-York Historical Society, 1870.

Journal of the Johannes Schwalm Historical Association.

Journal of the Society for Army Historical Research.

Kahn, David. "Washington's New York Spy Net." *Military History,* 1 (December 1984), pp. 10, 56–57, 62.

Kail, Jerry, et al., editors. *Who Was Who during the American Revolution.* Indianapolis: Bobbs-Merrill Co., 1976.

Kalinoski, Sarah V. "Sequestration, Confiscation, and the 'Tory' in the Vermont Revolution." *Vermont History,* 45 (Fall 1977), pp. 236–246.

Kaminski, John P. *George Clinton: Yeoman Politician of the New Republic.* Madison, Wisconsin: Madison House, 1993.

Kammen, Michael. *Empire and Interest: The American Colonies and the Politics of Mercantilism.* Philadelphia: Lippincott, 1970.

———. *A Rope of Sand: The Colonial Agents, British Politics and the American Revolution.* Ithaca: Cornell University Press, 1968.

Kaplan, Lawrence S. "Toward Isolationism: The Jeffersonian Republicans and the Franco-American Alliance of 1778." *Historical Reflections,* 3 (Summer 1976), pp. 69–81.

Kaplan, Roger. "The Hidden War: British Intelligence Operations during the American Revolution." *William and Mary Quarterly,* 3d Ser., 47 (January 1990), pp. 115–138.

Kaplan, Sidney. "Pay, Pension, Power: Economic Grievances of the Massachusetts Officers of the Revolution." *Boston Public Library Quarterly,* 13 (January, April 1951), pp. 15–34, 127–142.

———. "Rank and Status among Massachusetts Continental Officers." *American Historical Review,* 56 (January 1951), pp. 318–326.

———. "Veteran Officers and Politics in Massachusetts, 1783–1787." *William and Mary Quarterly,* 3d Ser., 9 (January 1952), pp. 29–57.

Kashatus, William C., III. *Conflict of Conviction: A Reappraisal of Quaker Involvement in the American Revolution.* Lanham: University Press of America, 1990.

Katcher, Philip R. N. *Armies of the American Wars, 1753–1815.* New York: Hastings House, 1975.

———. "Loyalist Militia in the War of American Independence." *Journal of the Society for Army Historical Research,* 54 (Autumn 1976), pp. 136–139.

———. "The Provincial Corps of the British Army 1775–1783." *Journal of the Society for Army Historical Research,* 54 (Autumn 1976), pp. 164–171.

———. "'They Behaved Like Soldiers': The Third Virginia Regiment at Harlem Heights." *Virginia Cavalcade,* 26 (Autumn 1976), pp. 64–70.

———. *Uniforms of the Continental Army.* New York: George Shumway, 1981.

Kauffman, Henry J. *Early American Gunsmiths, 1650–1850.* Harrisburg: Stackpole Co., 1952.

———. *The Pennsylvania-Kentucky Rifle.* Harrisburg: Stackpole Co., 1960.

Keesey, Ruth M. "Loyalism in Bergen County, New Jersey." *William and Mary Quarterly,* 3d Ser., 18 (October 1961), pp. 558–576.

Kelby, William, editor. *Orderly Book of the Three Battalions of Loyalists Commanded by Brigadier-General Oliver De Lancey 1776–1778.* New York: New-York Historical Society, 1917.

Kellogg, Louise P., editor. *Frontier Advance on the Upper Ohio, 1778–1779.* Madison: Wisconsin Historical Society, 1916.

———, editor. *Frontier Retreat on the Upper Ohio, 1779–1781.* Madison: Wisconsin Historical Society, 1917.

Kemp, Franklin W. *A Nest of Rebel Pirates.* Egg Harbor City, N.J.: Laureate Press, 1966.

Kennedy, Benjamin, editor. *Muskets, Cannon Balls and Bombs.* Savannah: Beehive Press, 1973.

Kennett, Lee. *The French Forces in America, 1780–1783.* Westport, Conn.: Greenwood Press, 1977.

Kenney, Alice P. "The Albany Dutch: Loyalists and Patriots." *New York History,* 42 (October 1961), pp. 331–350.

———. *Stubborn for Liberty, The Dutch in New York.* Syracuse: Syracuse University Press, 1975.

Kenyon, Cecilia M. "Republicanism and Radicalism in the American Revolution: An Old Fashioned Interpretation." *William and Mary Quarterly,* 3d Ser., 19 (April 1962), pp. 153–182.

Kepner, Francis R., editor. "A British View of the Siege of Charleston, 1776." *Journal of Southern History,* 11 (February 1945), pp. 93–103.

Kerr, Wilfred B. *Bermuda and the American Revolution: 1760–1783.* Princeton: Princeton University Press, 1936.

Ketcham, Ralph L. "France and American Politics, 1763–1793." *Political Science Quarterly,* 78 (June 1963), pp. 198–223.

Ketchum, Richard M. *Decisive Day: The Battle for Bunker Hill.* Revised edition. Garden City: Doubleday, 1974.

———. *Divided Loyalties: How the Revolution Came to New York.* New York: Henry Holt and Company, 2002.

———. *Saratoga: Turning Point of America's Revolutionary War.* New York: Henry Holt and Company, 1997.

———. *Victory at Yorktown: The Campaign that Won the Revolution.* New York: Henry Holt and Company, 2004.

———. *The Winter Soldiers.* New York: Doubleday & Co., 1973.

Kevitt, Chester B., compiler. *General Solomon Lovell and the Penobscot Expedition, 1779.* Weymouth, Mass.: Weymouth Historical Commission, 1976.

Kidder, Frederick. *History of the First New Hampshire Regiment in the War of the Revolution.* Albany: Joel Munsell, 1868.

Kierner, Cynthia A. "Landlord and Tenant in Revolutionary New York: The Case of Livingston Manor." *New York History,* 70 (April 1989), pp. 133–152.

Killion, Howard Ray. "The Suffren Expedition: French Operations in India during the War of American Independence." Ph.D. Dissertation, Duke University, 1972.

Kim, Sung Bok. "Impact of Class Relations and Warfare in the American Revolution: The New York Experience." *Journal of American History,* 69 (September 1982), pp. 326–346.

Kinnaird, Lawrence, editor. *Spain in the Mississippi Valley, 1765–1794.* 3 vols. Washington: American Historical Association, 1949.

———. "The Spanish Expedition against Fort St. Joseph in 1781, A New Interpretation." *Mississippi Valley Historical Review,* 19 (September 1932), pp. 173–191.

———. "The Western Fringe of the Revolution." *Western Historical Quarterly,* 7 (July 1976), pp. 253–270.

Kipping, Ernst. *Die Truppen von Hessian-Kassel im Amerikanischen Unabhangigkeitskrieg, 1776–1783.* Darmstadt: Wehr und Wissen Verlagsgesellschaft M. B. H., 1965.

———. *The Hessian View of America, 1776–1783.* Translated by Bernhard A. Uhlendorf. Monmouth Beach, N.J.: Philip Freneau Press, 1971.

Kirkwood, Robert. *The Journal and Order Book of Captain Robert Kirkwood of the Delaware Regiment of the Continental Line.* Edited by Joseph Brown Turner. Wilmington: Historical Society of Delaware, 1910.

Kite, Elizabeth S. *Beaumarchais and the War of American Independence.* 2 vols. Boston: R. G. Badger, 1918.

———. *Brigadier-General Louis Lebègue Duportail, Commandant of Engineers in the Continental Army, 1777–1783.* Baltimore: Johns Hopkins Press for the Institut Français de Washington, 1933.

———. *Conrad Alexandre Gerard and American Independence.* Philadelphia: N.p., 1921.

———. "The Continental Congress and France: Secret Aid and the Alliance, 1776–1778." *American Catholic Historical Society Records,* 39 (June 1928), pp. 155–174.

———. "General Duportail at Valley Forge." *Pennsylvania Magazine of History and Biography,* 56 (1932), pp. 341–351.

Kitman, Marvin. *George Washington's Expense Account.* New York: Simon and Schuster, 1970.

Klein, Milton M. *The American Whig: William Livingston of New York.* New York: Garland, 1990.

———. "An Experiment that Failed: General James Robertson and Civil Government in British New York, 1779–1783." *New York History,* 61 (July 1980), pp. 228–254.

———. "Why Did the British Fail to Win the Hearts and Minds of New Yorkers?" *New York History,* 64 (October 1983), pp. 357–376.

Klein, Rachel N. *Unification of a Slave State: The Rise of the Planter Class in the South Carolina Backcountry, 1760–1808.* Chapel Hill: University of North Carolina Press, 1990.

Klingelhofer, Herbert E. "The Cautious Revolution: Maryland and the Movement toward Independence: 1774–1776." *Maryland Historical Magazine,* 60 (September 1965), pp. 261–313.

Klingle, Philip. "Soldiers of Kings." *Journal of Long Island History*, 12 (Spring 1976), pp. 23–35.

Knepper, George W. "The Convention Army, 1777–1783." Ph.D. dissertation, University of Michigan, 1954.

Knight, Betsy. "Prisoner Exchange and Parole in the American Revolution." *William and Mary Quarterly*, 3d Ser., 48 (April 1991), pp. 201–222.

———. "Thomas and William Woodford: The Travails of Two Maryland Brothers who Served in the South during the American Revolution." *Maryland Historical Magazine*, 84 (Winter 1989), pp. 379–386.

Knoblock, Glenn A. *Strong and Brave Fellows: New Hampshire's Black Soldiers and Sailors of the American Revolution, 1775–1784.* Jefferson, North Carolina: McFarland and Company, 2003.

Knollenberg, Bernhard. "Bunker Hill Re-viewed: A Study in the Conflict of Historical Evidence." *Proceedings of the Massachusetts Historical Society*, 72 (1957–1960), pp. 84–100.

———. "Did Samuel Adams Provoke the Boston Tea Party and the Clash at Lexington?" *Proceedings of the American Antiquarian Society*, 70 (October 1960), pp. 493–503.

———. *Growth of the American Revolution, 1766–1775.* New York: Free Press, 1975.

———. *Origin of the American Revolution, 1759–1766.* New York: Macmillan, 1960.

———. *Washington and the Revolution, A Reappraisal: Gates, Conway and the Continental Congress.* New York: Macmillan Co., 1940.

Knouf, Gregory T. *The Soldiers' Revolution: Pennsylvanians in Arms and the Forging of Early American Identity.* University Park: Pennsylvania State University Press, 2004.

Knox, Dudley W. *The Naval Genius of George Washington.* Boston: Houghton Mifflin Co., 1932.

Kohn, Richard H. *The Eagle and the Sword: The Federalists and the Creation of the Military Establishment in America 1783–1802.* New York: Free Press, 1975.

———. "The Inside History of the Newburgh Conspiracy: America and the Coup d'Etat." *William and Mary Quarterly*, 3d Ser., 27 (April 1970), pp. 187–220.

Koke, Richard J. "The Britons Who Fought at Stony Point: Uniforms of the American Revolution." *New-York Historical Society Quarterly*, 44 (October 1960), pp. 443–471.

———. "Forcing the Hudson River Passage, October 9, 1776." *New-York Historical Society Quarterly*, 36 (October 1952), pp. 459–466.

———. "The Struggle for the Hudson: The British Naval Expedition under Captain Hyde Parker and Captain James Wallace, July 12–August 18, 1776." *New-York Historical Society Quarterly*, 40 (April 1956), pp. 114–175.

———. "War, Profit, and Privateers along the New Jersey Coast: Letters of 1782 Relating to an Obscure Warfront of the American Revolution." *New-York Historical Society Quarterly*, 41 (July 1957), pp. 279–337.

König, Joseph. "Die militärgeschichtlichen Bestände des Niedersächsischen Staatsarchivs im Wolfenbüttel." *Militärgeschichtliche Mitteilungen*, No. 2, 1969, pp. 179–182.

Kopperman, Paul E. "The British High Command and Soldiers' Wives in America, 1755–1783." *Journal of the Society for Army Historical Research*, 60 (Spring 1982), pp. 14–34.

———. "Medical Services in the British Army, 1742–1783." *Journal of the History of Medicine and Allied Sciences*, 34 (October 1979), pp. 428–455.

Korn, E. *Fahnen und Uniformen der Landgräflich Hessen-Kasselschen Truppen im Amerikanischen Unabhängigkeitskrieg.* Kassel: 1977.

Kozy, Charlene J. "Tories Transplanted: The Caribbean Exile and Plantation Settlement of Southern Loyalists." *Georgia Historical Quarterly*, 75 (Spring 1991), pp. 18–42.

Krueger, John W. "Troop Life at the Champlain Valley Forts during the American Revolution." *Bulletin of the Fort Ticonderoga Museum*, 14 (Summer 1982; Fall 1983; Summer 1984).

Kurtz, Stephen G., and James H. Hutson, editors. *Essays on the American Revolution.* Chapel Hill: University of North Carolina Press, 1973.

Kwasny, Mark V. *Washington's Partisan War, 1775–1783.* Ohio: Kent State University Press, 1996.

Kyte, George W. "Francis Marion As an Intelligence Officer." *South Carolina Historical Magazine*, 77 (October 1976), pp. 215–226.

———. "General Greene's Plans for the Capture of Charleston, 1781–1782." *South Carolina Historical Magazine*, 61 (April 1960), pp. 96–106.

———. "General Wayne Marches South." *Pennsylvania History*, 30 (July 1963), pp. 301–315.

———. "Introduction to the Periodical Literature on Middle Colony Loyalists in the American Revolution." *Pennsylvania History*, 18 (April 1951), pp. 104–118.

———. "Plans for Reconquest of the Rebellious Colonies in America." *Historian*, 10 (Spring 1948), pp. 101–117.

———. "A Projected British Attack upon Philadelphia in 1781." *Pennsylvania Magazine of History and Biography*, 76 (October 1952), pp. 379–393.

———. "Strategic Blunder: Lord Cornwallis Abandons the Carolinas." *Historian*, 22 (February 1960), pp. 129–144.

———. "Thaddeus Kosciuszko at the Liberation of Charleston, 1782." *South Carolina Historical Magazine*, 84 (January 1983), pp. 11–21.

———. "Victory in the South: An Appraisal of General Greene's Strategy in the Carolinas." *North Carolina Historical Review*, 37 (July 1960), pp. 321–347.

Labaree, Benjamin W. *The Boston Tea Party.* New York: Oxford University Press, 1964.

———. "The Idea of American Independence: The British View, 1774–1776." *Proceedings of the Massachusetts Historical Society*, 82 (1970), pp. 3–20.

Labaree, Leonard W. *Royal Government in America, A Study of the British Colonial System Before 1763.* New Haven: Yale University Press, 1930.

———, editor. *Royal Instructions to British Colonial Governors, 1670–1776.* 2 vols. New York: D. Appleton-Century Co., 1935.

LaCrosse, Richard. *The Frontier Rifleman: His Arms, Clothing and Equipment during the Era of the American Revolution, 1760–1800.* Union City, Tenn.: Pioneer Press, 1989.

Lafayette, Marie Paul Joseph Roch Yves Gilbert Motier, marquis de. *Lafayette in the Age of the American Revolution: Selected Letters and Papers, 1776–1790.* Edited by Stanley J. Idzerda, et al. Ithaca: Cornell University Press, 1977.

———. *The Letters of Lafayette to Washington, 1777–1799.* Edited by Louis Gottschalk and Shirley A. Bill. Revised Edition. Philadelphia: American Philosophical Society, 1976.

Lafferty, Maude W. "Destruction of Ruddle's and Martin's Forts in the Revolutionary War." *Register of the Kentucky Historical Society,* 54 (October 1956), pp. 297–338.

Lamb, Roger. *An Original and Authentic Journal of Occurrences during the Late American War, from its Commencement to the Year 1783.* Dublin: Wilkinson & Courtney, 1809.

Lambert, Robert S. "The Repossession of Georgia, 1782–1784." *Proceedings of the South Carolina Historical Association for 1957,* pp. 14–25.

———. *South Carolina Loyalists in the American Revolution.* Columbia: University of South Carolina Press, 1987.

Lanctot, Gustave. *Canada and the American Revolution 1774–1783.* Translated by Margaret M. Cameron. Cambridge, Mass.: Harvard University Press, 1967.

Landers, H. L. *The Battle of Camden, South Carolina, 16 August 1780.* Camden, South Carolina: Kershaw County Historical Society, 1997 (1929).

———. *The Virginia Campaign and the Blockade and Siege of Yorktown, 1781.* Washington: Government Printing Office, 1931.

Larrabee, Harold A. *Decision at the Chesapeake.* New York: Clarkson N. Potter, Inc., 1964.

Laub, C. Herbert. "The Problem of Armed Invasion of the Northwest during the American Revolution." *Virginia Magazine of History and Biography,* 42 (January–April 1934), pp. 18–27, 132–144.

Lauber, Almon W., editor. *Orderly Books of The Fourth New York Regiment, 1778–1780; The Second New York Regiment, 1780–1783 by Samuel Tallmadge and Others with Diaries of Samuel Tallmadge, 1780–1782 and John Barr, 1779–1782.* Albany: University of the State of New York, 1932.

Launitz-Schurer, Leopold S., Jr. *Loyal Whigs and Revolutionaries: The Making of the Revolution in New York, 1765–1776.* New York: New York University Press, 1980.

Lawrence, Alexander A. "General Lachlan McIntosh and His Suspension from Continental Command during the Revolution." *Georgia Historical Quarterly,* 38 (June 1954), pp. 101–141.

———. "General Robert Howe and the British Capture of Savannah in 1778." *Georgia Historical Quarterly,* 36 (December 1952), pp. 303–327.

———. *Storm over Savannah: The Story of Count d'Estaing and the Siege of the Town in 1779.* Athens: University of Georgia Press, 1951.

Lawson, Cecil C. P. "Dress and Accoutrements of British Foot and Artillery in America, 1755–1783." *Military Collector and Historian,* 5 (June 1953), pp. 35–41.

———. "Uniforms and Equipment of the British Light Cavalry in America, 1775–1783." *Military Collector and Historian,* 5 (December 1953), pp. 87–90.

Leamon, James. *Revolution Downeast: The War for American Independence in Maine.* Amherst: University of Massachusetts Press, 1993.

Lee, Charles. "The Lee Papers." [4 vols.] *New-York Historical Society Collections* for 1871–1874.

Lee, Jean B. "Maryland's 'Dangerous Insurrection' of 1786." *Maryland Historical Magazine,* 85 (Winter 1990), pp. 329–344.

———. *The Price of Nationhood: The American Revolution in Charles County, Maryland.* New York: W. W. Norton and Company, 1994.

Lee, Wayne E. *Crowds and Soldiers in Revolutionary North Carolina: The Culture of Violence in Riot and War.* Gainesville: University Press of Florida, 2001.

Lefferts, Charles. *Uniforms of the American, British, French & German Armies in the War of the American Revolution, 1775–1783.* New York: New-York Historical Society, 1926.

Lefkowitz, Arthur S. *George Washington's Indispensable Men: The 32 Aides-de-Camp Who Helped Win American Independence.* Mechanicsburg, Pennsylvania: Stackpole Books, 2003.

Leiby, Adrian C. *The Revolutionary War in the Hackensack Valley: The Jersey Dutch and the Neutral Ground.* New Brunswick: Rutgers University Press, 1962.

Lemisch, Jesse "Listening to the 'Inarticulate': William Widger's Dream and the Loyalties of American Revolutionary Seamen in British Prisons." *Journal of Social History,* 3 (January 1969), pp. 1–29.

Lender, Mark E. "The Conscripted Line: The Draft in Revolutionary New Jersey." *New Jersey History,* 103 (1985), pp. 22–45.

———. *The New Jersey Soldier.* Trenton: New Jersey Historical Commission, 1975.

———. *The River War: The Fight for the Delaware, 1777.* Trenton: New Jersey Historical Commission, 1979.

———. "The Social Structure of the New Jersey Brigade: The Continental Line As an American Standing Army." In *The Military in America From the Colonial Era to the Present.* Edited by Peter Karsten. New York: Free Press, 1980.

Lengel, Edward G. *General George Washington: A Military Life.* New York: Random House, 2005.

Lenman, Bruce. *Britain's Colonial Wars, 1688–1783.* New York: Longman, 2001.

Lennon, Donald R. "'The Graveyard of American Commanders': The Continental Army's Southern Department, 1776–1778." *North Carolina Historical Review,* 67 (April 1990), pp. 133–158.

Leonard, Eugenie A. "Paper As a Critical Commodity during the American Revolution." *Pennsylvania Magazine of History and Biography,* 74 (October 1950), pp. 488–499.

Lesser, Charles H., editor. *The Sinews of Independence: The Monthly Strength Reports of the Continental Army.* Chicago: University of Chicago Press, 1975.

Lettieri, Ronald, and Charles Wetherell. "The New Hampshire Committees of Safety and Revolutionary Republicanism, 1775–1784." *Historical New Hampshire,* 55 (Fall 1980), pp. 241–283.

Leuthy, Ivor C. E. "General Sir Frederick Haldimand: A Swiss Governor-General of Canada (1777–1784)." *Canadian Ethnic Studies*, 3 (June 1971), pp. 63–75.

Leventhal, Herbert, and James A. Mooney, editors. "A Bibliography of Loyalist Source Material in the United States." *Proceedings of the American Antiquarian Society*, 85, 86, and 90 (1975, 1976, and 1980).

Lewis, Berkeley R. *Small Arms and Ammunition in the United States Service*. Washington: Smithsonian Institution, 1956.

Lewis, Charles L. *Admiral de Grasse and American Independence*. Annapolis: U.S. Naval Institute, 1945.

Lewis, George G., and John Mewha. *History of Prisoner of War Utilization by the United States Army, 1776–1945*. Washington: Department of the Army, 1955.

Lewis, James A. "New Spain During the American Revolution, 1779–1783: A Viceroyalty at War." Ph.D. dissertation, Duke University, 1975.

Lewis, Paul. *The Man Who Lost America. A Biography of Gentleman Johnny Burgoyne*. New York: Dial Press, 1973.

Lewis, Theodore B. "Was Washington Profane at Monmouth?" *New Jersey History*, 89 (Fall 1971), pp. 149–162.

Lightfoot, Marise P. *Let The Drums Roll: Veterans and Patriots of the Revolutionary War Who Settled in Maury County, Tennessee*. Nashville: Parthenon Press for the Maury County Historical Society, 1976.

Lincoln, Rufus. *The Papers of Captain Rufus Lincoln of Wareham, Mass.* Edited by James Minor Lincoln. N.P.: Privately printed, 1904.

Lipscomb, Terry W. *The Carolina Lowcountry, April 1775–June 1776, and the Battle of Fort Moultrie*. (2nd edition), Columbia: South Carolina Department of Archives and History, 1994.

Livingston, William. *The Papers of William Livingston*. Edited by Carl E. Prince, et al. 5 vols. Trenton: New Jersey Historical Commission, 1979–1988.

Lloyd, Malcolm, Jr., editor. "The Taking of the Bahamas by the Continental Navy in 1776." *Pennsylvania Magazine of History and Biography*, 49 (1925), pp. 349–366.

Lockyard, E. Kidd. "Some Problems of the Draft in Revolutionary Virginia." *West Virginia History*, 37 (April 1976), pp. 201–210.

Loescher, Burt Garfield. *Washington's Eyes: The Continental Light Dragoons*. Ft. Collins, Colo.: The Old Army Press, 1977.

Lofgren, Charles A. "Compulsory Military Service Under the Constitution: The Original Understanding." *William and Mary Quarterly*, 3d Ser., 33 (January 1976), pp. 61–88.

Logan, Gwendolyn E. "The Slave in Connecticut during the American Revolution." *Connecticut Historical Society Bulletin*, 30 (July 1965), pp. 73–80.

Lomask, Milton. *Aaron Burr: The Years from Princeton to Vice President, 1756–1805*. New York: Farrar, Straus, Giroux, 1979.

Long, John C. *Lord Jeffrey Amherst, a Soldier of the King*. New York: Macmillan, 1933.

Lopez, Claude-Ann. "The Man Who Frightened Franklin" *Pennsylvania Magazine of History and Biography*, 106 (October 1982), pp. 515–526.

Lord, Arthur. "Biographical Sketch of General John Thomas" *Proceedings of the Massachusetts Historical Society*, 38 (November 1904), pp. 419–432.

Lord, Philip, Jr. *War over Waloomscoick: Land Use and Settlement Pattern on the Bennington Battlefield, 1777*. Albany: New York State Education Department, 1990.

Lossing, Benson J. *The Pictorial Field-Book of the Revolution; or Illustrations, by Pen and Pencil, of the History, Biography, Scenery, Relics, and Traditions of the War for Independence*. 2 vols. New York: Harper & Brothers, 1859.

Lovell, Louise L. *Israel Angell, Colonel of the 2nd Rhode Island Regiment*. New York: Knickerbocker Press, 1921.

Lowell, Edward J. *The Hessians and Other German Auxiliaries of Great Britain in the Revolutionary War*. New York: Harper & Bros., 1884.

Lumpkin, Henry. *From Savannah to Yorktown: The American Revolution in the South*. Columbia: University of South Carolina Press, 1981.

Lundin, Leonard. *Cockpit of the Revolution: The War for Independence in New Jersey*. Princeton: Princeton University Press, 1940.

Lunt, James D. *John Burgoyne of Saratoga*. New York: Harcourt Brace and World, 1975.

Lutnick, Solomon N. "The American Victory at Saratoga: A View From the British Press" *New York History*, 44 (April 1963), pp. 103–127.

———. "The Defeat at Yorktown: A View from the British Press." *Virginia Magazine of History and Biography*, 72 (October 1964), pp. 471–478.

Lutz, Paul V. "Land Grants for Service in the Revolution." *New-York Historical Society Quarterly*, 48 (July 1964), pp. 221–235.

———. "A State's Concern for the Soldier's Welfare: How North Carolina Provided for Her Troops During the Revolution." *North Carolina Historical Review*, 42 (July 1965), pp. 315–318.

Luzader, John F. "The Arnold-Gates Controversy." *West Virginia History*, 27 (January 1966), pp. 75–84.

Luykx, John M. "Fighting for Food: British Foraging Operations at St. George's Island." *Maryland Historical Magazine*, 71 (Summer 1976), pp. 212–219.

Lynch, Barbara A., compiler. *The War at Sea: France and the American Revolution, A Bibliography*. Washington: Department of the Navy, 1976.

Lynd, Stoughton. "The Tenant Rising at Livingston Manor, May 1777." *New-York Historical Society Quarterly*, 48 (April 1964), pp. 163–177.

Maas, David E. *Divided Hearts: Massachusetts Loyalists, 1765–1790, A Biographical Directory*. Boston: New England Historic Genealogical Society, 1980.

———. *The Return of the Massachusetts Loyalists*. New York: Garland, 1989.

McAdams, Donald R. "The Sullivan Expedition: Success or Failure?" *New-York Historical Society Quarterly*, 54 (January 1970), pp. 53–81.

McAllister, J. T. *Virginia Militia in the Revolutionary War; McAllister's Data*. Hot Springs, Va.: McAllister Publishing Co., 1913.

McBride, John D. "The Virginia War Effort, 1775–1783: Manpower Policies and Practices." Ph.D. dissertation, University of Virginia, 1977.

McCall, Eltie T. *Roster of Revolutionary Soldiers in Georgia and Other States.* 3 vols. Baltimore: Genealogical Publishing Co., 1968–1969.

McCaughey, Elizabeth P. *From Loyalist to Founding Father: The Political Odyssey of William Samuel Johnson.* New York: Columbia University Press, 1980.

McClusker, John J. "The American Invasion of Nassau in the Bahamas." *American Neptune,* 25 (July 1965), pp. 189–217.

McCorison, Marcus A. "Bayley-Hazen Military Road." *Vermont History,* New Ser., 27 (January 1959), pp. 57–68.

McCowen, George S., Jr. *The British Occupation of Charleston, 1780–1782.* Columbia: University of South Carolina Press, 1981.

———. "The Charles Town Board off Police, 1780–1782: A Study in Civil Administration Under Military Occupations." *Proceedings of the South Carolina Historical Association for 1964,* pp. 25–42.

McCullough, David. *1776.* New York: Simon and Schuster, 2005.

McCurry, Allan J. "Joseph Hewes and Independence." *North Carolina Historical Review,* 40 (October 1963), pp. 455–464.

McDermott, John F. "The Battle of St. Louis, 25 May 1780." *Missouri Historical Society Bulletin,* 36 (April 1980), pp. 131–151.

McDermott, John F., editor. *The Spanish in the Mississippi Valley 1762–1784.* Urbana: University of Illinois Press, 1974.

McDevitt, Robert F. *Connecticut Attacked: A British Viewpoint, Tryon's Raid on Danbury.* Chester, Conn.: Pequot Press, 1974.

McDonald, Forrest. *E Pluribus Unum: The Formation of the American Republic 1776–1790.* Boston: Houghton Mifflin, 1965.

McDonnell, Michael A. "Popular Mobilization and Political Culture in Revolutionary Virginia: The Failure of the Minutemen and the Revolution from Below." *Journal of American History,* 85 (December 1998), pp. 946–981.

McDonough, Daniel J. "Christopher Gadsden and Henry Laurens: The Parallel Lives of Two American Patriots." Ph.D. dissertation, University of Illinois, Urbana-Champagne, 1990.

McDougall, William L. *American Revolutionary: A Biography of General Alexander McDougall.* Westport: Greenwood Press, 1977.

McEachern, Leora H., and Isabel M. Williams, editors. *Wilmington-New Hanover Safety Committee Minutes, 1774–1776.* Wilmington: Wilmington-New Hanover County American Revolution Bi-centennial Association, 1974.

McGinn, Robert, and Larry Vaden. "Michael Cresap and the Cresap Rifles." *West Virginia History,* 39 (July 1978), pp. 341–347.

McGrath, Stephen P. "Connecticut's Tory Towns: The Loyalty Struggle in Newtown, Redding, and Ridgefield 1774–1783." *Connecticut Historical Society Bulletin,* 44 (July 1979), pp. 88–96.

McGroarty, William B. "Captain Cameron and Sergeant Champe." *William and Mary Quarterly,* 2d Ser., 19 (January 1939), pp. 49–54.

McGuffie, Tom H. *The Siege of Gibraltar, 1779–1783.* London: B. T. Batsford, 1965.

McGuire, Thomas J. *The Battle of Paoli.* Mechanicsburg, Pennsylvania: Stackpole Books, 2000.

———. *The Surprise of Germantown, or the Battle of Cliveden, 4 October 1777.* Gettysburg, Pennsylvania: Thomas Publications, 1994.

MacKenzie, Frederick. *Diary of Frederick MacKenzie Giving a Daily Narrative of his Military Service as an Officer of the regiment of Royal Welch Fusileers during the Years 1775–1781 in Massachusetts, Rhode Island and New York.* 2 vols. Cambridge, Mass.: Harvard University Press, 1930.

Mackesy, Piers. "British Strategy in the War of American Independence." *Yale Review,* 71 (June 1963), pp. 539–557.

———. *The Coward of Minden: The Affair of Lord George Sackville.* New York: St. Martin's Press, 1979.

———. *The War for America, 1775–1783.* Cambridge, Mass.: Harvard University Press, 1964.

McKinney, Francis F. "The Integrity of Nathanael Greene." *Rhode Island History,* 28 (May 1969), pp. 53–60.

MacKinnon, Neil. *This Unfriendly Soul: The Loyalist Experience in Nova Scotia, 1783–1791.* Kingston: McGill-Queen's University Press, 1986.

McLarty, Robert N. "The Expedition of Major General John Vaughan to the Lesser Antilles, 1779–1781." Ph.D. dissertation, University of Michigan, 1951.

———. "Jamaica Prepares for Invasion, 1779." *Caribbean Quarterly,* 4 (January 1955), pp. 62–67.

McLaughlan, James, editor. *Princetonians, 1748–1768: A Biographical Dictionary.* Princeton: Princeton University Press, 1976.

Maclay, Edgar S. *A History of American Privateers.* New York: Appleton, 1899.

MacLennan, Alastair. "Highland Regiments in North America 1756–1783." *Bulletin of the Fort Ticonderoga Museum,* 12 (September 1966), pp. 118–127.

MacMillan, Margaret B. *The War Governors in the American Revolution.* New York: Columbia University Press, 1943.

McMurtrie, Douglas C. *The Proceedings of the Revolutionary Committee of the Town of Newbern, North Carolina, 1775.* Chicago: Chicago School of Printing, 1938.

Madariaga, Isabel de. *Britain, Russia, and the Armed Neutrality of 1780: Sir James Harris's Mission to St. Petersburg during the American Revolution.* New Haven: Yale University Press, 1962.

Maguire, J. Robert. "The British Secret Service and the Attempt to Kidnap General Jacob Bayley of Newbury, Vermont, 1782." *Vermont History,* 44 (Summer 1976), pp. 141–167.

Mahan, Alfred T. *The Major Operations of the Navies in the American War of Independence.* Boston: Little, Brown & Co., 1913.

Maier, Pauline. "Coming to Terms with Samuel Adams." *American Historical Review,* 81 (February 1976), pp. 12–37.

———. *From Resistance to Revolution: Colonial Radicals and the Development of An Opposition to Britain, 1765–1776.* New York: Alfred A. Knopf, 1972.

Main, Jackson T. *Political Parties before the Constitution.* Chapel Hill: University of North Carolina Press, 1973.

————. *The Upper House in Revolutionary America, 1763–1788.* Madison: University of Wisconsin Press, 1967.

Maine Historical Society. *Collections and Proceedings, 2d Ser.:* Porter, Joseph W. "Gen. David Cobb of Gouldsborough, Maine." 6 (1895), pp. 1–6.

Safford, Moses A. "General William Whipple." 6 (1895), pp. 337–357.

Malone, Dumas. *Jefferson and His Time.* Boston: Little, Brown, 1948.

Malone, Joseph J. *Pine Trees and Politics: the Naval Stores and Forest Policy in Colonial New England, 1691–1775.* Seattle: University of Washington Press, 1964.

Mancall, Peter C. "Notes on Troop Units in the Army at New York City, 1776." *Military Collector and Historian,* 26 (Summer 1974), pp. 86–97.

————. "The Revolutionary War and the Indians of the Upper Susquehanna Valley." *American Indian Culture and Research Journal,* 12 (1988), pp. 39–57.

Mandell, Daniel. "'To Live More Like My Christian English Neighbors': Natick Indians in the Eighteenth Century." *William and Mary Quarterly,* 3d Ser., 48 (October 1991), pp. 552–579.

Manders, Eric L. "Notes on Troop Units in the Cambridge Army, 1775–1776." *Military Collector and Historian,* 23 (Fall 1971), pp. 69–74.

————. "Notes on Troop Units in the Flying Camp, 1776." *Military Collector and Historian,* 26 (Spring 1974), pp. 9–13.

————. "Notes on Troop Units in the New York Garrison, 1775–1776." *Military Collector and Historian,* 25 (Spring 1973), pp. 18–21.

————. "Notes on Troop Units in the Northern Army." *Military Collector and Historian,* 23 (Winter 1971), pp. 117–120.

————. "Notes on Troop Units in the Northern Army." *Military Collector and Historian,* 27 (Spring, Fall 1975), pp. 9–12, 113–117.

Mann, David L. "Bennington: A Clash Between Patriot and Loyalist." *Historical New Hampshire,* 32 (Winter 1977), pp. 171–188.

Manucy, Albert. *Artillery Through the Ages: A Short Illustrated History of Cannon, Emphasizing Types Used in America.* Washington: National Park Service, 1949.

Mark, Edward M. "The Reverend Samuel Peters and the Patriot Mobs in Connecticut." *Connecticut Historical Society Bulletin,* 40 (July 1975), pp. 88–94.

Marraro, Howard R. "Unpublished Letters of Colonel Nicola, Revolutionary Soldier." *Pennsylvania History,* 13 (October 1946), pp. 274–282.

Marshall, Douglas W. "The British Engineers in America: 1755–1783." *Journal of the Society for Army Historical Research,* 51 (Autumn 1973), pp. 155–163.

Marshall, Douglas W. and Howard H. Peckham. *Campaigns of the American Revolution: An Atlas of Manuscript Maps.* Ann Arbor: University of Michigan Press, 1976.

Marshall, Peter J. "Colonial Protest and Imperial Retrenchment: Indian Policy 1764–1768." *Journal of American Studies,* 5 (April 1971), pp. 1–17.

————, editor. *The History of the British Empire: vol. 2: The Eighteenth Century.* New York: Oxford University Press, 1998.

Marston, Jerrilyn G. *The King and Congress: The Transfer of Political Legitimacy, 1774–1776.* Princeton, N.J.: Princeton University Press, 1987.

Martin, James K. *Benedict Arnold, Revolutionary Hero: An American Warrior Reconsidered.* New York: New York University Press, 1997.

————. *Men in Rebellion: Higher Governmental Leaders and the Coming of the American Revolution.* New Brunswick: Rutgers University Press, 1973.

Martin, James K. and Mark E. Lender. *A Respectable Army: The Military Origins of the Republic, 1763–1789.* Second Edition. Arlington Heights, Ill.: Harlan Davidson, 2006.

Martin, Joseph Plumb. *Private Yankee Doodle Being a Narrative of Some of the Adventures, Dangers and Sufferings of a Revolutionary Soldier. [1830].* Edited by George F. Scheer. Boston: Little, Brown and Co., 1962.

Martyn, Charles. *The Life of Artemas Ward The First Commander-in-Chief of the American Revolution.* New York: A. Ward, 1921.

Maryland Hall of Records Commission. *Calendar of Maryland State Papers.* 7 vols. Annapolis: State of Maryland, 1943–1958.

Maryland Historical Society. *Archives of Maryland.* 66 vols. Baltimore: Maryland Historical Society, 1883–1954.

Maslowski, Pete. "National Policy Toward the Use of Black Troops in the Revolution." *South Carolina Historical Magazine,* 73 (January 1972), pp. 1–17.

Mason, Bernard. *The Road to Independence: The Revolutionary Movement in New York, 1773–1777.* Lexington: University of Kentucky Press, 1966.

Mason, George. *The Papers of George Mason 1725–1792.* Edited by Robert A. Rutland. 3 vols. Chapel Hill: University of North Carolina Press, 1970.

Massachusetts. Secretary of the Commonwealth. *Massachusetts Soldiers and Sailors of the Revolutionary War; A Compilation from the Archives.* 17 vols. Boston: Wright 1908.

Massay, Glenn F. "Fort Henry in the American Revolution." *West Virginia History,* 24 (April 1963), pp. 248–257.

Massey, Gregory D. "The British Expedition to Wilmington, January-November 1781." *North Carolina Historical Review,* 66 (October 1988), pp. 387–411.

Masterson, William H. *William Blount.* Baton Rouge: Louisiana State University Press, 1954.

Mathews, Alice. *Society in Revolutionary North Carolina.* Raleigh: North Carolina Department of Cultural Resources, 1976.

Mattern, David B. *Benjamin Lincoln and the American Revolution.* Columbia, South Carolina: University of South Carolina Press, 1995.

Matthews, William. *British Diaries: An Annotated Bibliography of British Diaries Written Between 1442–1942.* Berkeley: University of California Press, 1950.

Matthews, William and Roy Harvey Pearce. *American Diaries: An Annotated Bibliography of American Diaries Written Prior to the Year 1861.* Boston: J. S. Canner, 1959.

Maurer, Maurer. "Military Justice Under General Washington." *Military Affairs*, 28 (Spring 1964), pp. 8–16.

May, Robin, and Gerry Embleton. *The British Army in North America, 1775–1783*. London: Osprey Publishing, 1997.

May, W. E. "The *Gaspee* Affair." *Mariner's Mirror*, 63 (May 1977), pp. 129–136.

Mayer, Henry. *A Son of Thunder: Patrick Henry and the American Republic*. New York: Watts, 1986.

Mayer, Holly. *Belonging to the Army: Camp Followers and Community during the American Revolution*. Columbia: University of South Carolina Press, 1996.

Mayo, Lawrence S. "Colonel John Stark at Winter Hill, 1775." *Proceedings of the Massachusetts Historical Society*, 57 (April 1924), pp. 328–336.

————. *John Langdon of New Hampshire*. Concord: Rumford Press, 1937.

Mekeel, Arthur J. "The Relation of the Quakers to the American Revolution." *Quaker History*, 65 (Spring 1976), pp. 3–18.

Meleney, John C. *The Public Life of Aedanus Burke: Revolutionary Republican in Post-Revolutionary South Carolina*. Columbia: University of South Carolina Press, 1989.

Meng, John J., editor. *Dispatches and Instructions of Conrad Alexandre Gerard, 1778–1780: Correspondence of the First French Minister to the United States with the Comte de Vergennes*. Baltimore: Johns Hopkins University Press, 1939.

Merony, Geraldine M. "William Bull's First Exile from South Carolina, 1777–1781." *South Carolina Historical Magazine*, 80 (April 1979), pp. 91–104.

Merrens, Harry R. *Colonial North Carolina in the Eighteenth Century: A Study in Historical Geography*. Chapel Hill: University of North Carolina Press, 1964.

Merriam, John M. "The Military Record of Brigadier General John Nixon of Massachusetts." *American Antiquarian Society Proceedings*, New Ser., 36 (April 1926), pp. 38–70.

Merrick, Samuel F. "Medicine in the Canadian Campaign of the Revolutionary War: The Journal of Doctor Samuel Fisk Merrick." Edited by David B. Davis. *Bulletin of the History of Medicine*, 44 (September-October 1970), pp. 461–473.

Merritt, Elizabeth. "The Lexington Alarm, April 19, 1775: Messages Sent to the Southward After the Battle." *Maryland Historical Magazine*, 41 (June 1946), pp. 89–114.

Metzger, Charles H. *The Prisoner in the American Revolution*. Chicago: Loyola University Press, 1971.

Meyer, Mary K., and Virginia B. Bachman. "The First Battalion of Maryland Loyalists." *Maryland Historical Magazine*, 68 (Summer 1973), pp. 199–210.

Middlebrook, Louis F. *History of Maritime Connecticut during the American Revolution, 1775–1783*. Salem, Mass.: Essex Institute, 1925. 2 vols.

————. *Salisbury Connecticut Cannon*. Salem, Mass.: Newcomb & Gauss Co., 1935.

Middlekauff, Robert. *The Glorious Cause: The American Revolution 1763–1789*. Revised edition. New York: Oxford University Press, 2005.

————. "Why Men Fought in the American Revolution." *Huntington Library Quarterly*, 43 (Spring 1980), pp. 135–148.

Middleton, Richard D. "British Historians and the American Revolution." *Journal of American Studies*, 5 (April 1971), pp. 43–58.

Military Collector and Historian, vol. 1(1949) to vol. 58 (2006). [www.revwar75.com provides an updated list of articles on the War for American Independence.]

Miller, John C. *Alexander Hamilton: Portrait in Paradox*. New York: Harper & Brothers, 1959.

————. *Origins of the American Revolution*. Boston: Little, Brown and Co., 1943.

————. *Sam Adams, Pioneer in Propaganda*. Boston: Little, Brown and Co., 1936.

————. *Triumph of Freedom, 1775–1783*. Boston: Little, Brown, 1958.

Miller, Nathan. *Sea of Glory: The Continental Navy Fights for Independence, 1775–1785*. New York: David McKay Co., 1974.

Miller, Randall M., editor. "A Backcountry Loyalist Plan to Retake Georgia and the Carolinas, 1778." *South Carolina Historical Magazine*, 75 (October 1974), pp. 207–214.

Mills, Borden H. "Albany County's Part in the Battle of Saratoga." *Proceedings of the New York State Historical Association*, 15 (1916), pp. 204–224.

Mills, Leon and James L. Kochan. *Guide to Hessian Documents of the American Revolution, 1776–1782*. Boston: G. K. Hall and Co., 1989.

Milsop, John, and Steve Noon. *The Continental Infantryman of the American Revolution*. Oxford, England: Osprey Publishing, 2004.

Mintz, Max M. *The Generals of Saratoga: John Burgoyne and Horatio Gates*. New Haven: Yale University Press, 1990.

————. *Gouverneur Morris and the American Revolution*. Norman: University of Oklahoma Press, 1970.

Mishoff, Willard O. "Business in Philadelphia during the British Occupation, 1777–1778." *Pennsylvania Magazine of History and Biography*, 61 (April 1937), pp. 165–181.

Mitchell, Broadus. *Alexander Hamilton*. 2 vols. New York: Macmillan, 1957–1962.

————. "Hamilton's Quarrel with Washington, 1781." *William and Mary Quarterly*, 3d Ser., 12 (April 1955), pp. 199–216.

————. *The Price of Independence: A Realistic View of the American Revolution*. New York: Oxford University Press, 1974.

Mitchell, Joseph B. *Decisive Battles of the American Revolution*. New York: G. P. Putnam's Sons, 1962.

————. *Discipline and Bayonets: The Armies and Leaders in the War of the American Revolution*. New York: G. P. Putnam's Sons, 1967.

Mollo, John, and Malcolm McGregor. *Uniforms of the American Revolution in Color*. New York: Macmillan Co., 1975.

Montross, Lynn. *Rag, Tag and Bobtail*. New York: Harper & Row, 1952. Reprinted as *The Story of the Continental Army, 1775–1783* New York: Barnes & Noble, 1967.

————. *The Reluctant Rebels: the Story of the Continental Congress, 1774–1789*. New York: Harper, 1950.

Moomaw, William H. "The British Leave Colonial Virginia." *Virginia Magazine of History and Biography*, 66 (April 1958), pp. 147–160.

———. "The Denouement of General Howe's Campaign of 1777." *English Historical Review*, 79 (July 1964), pp. 498–512.

Moore, Howard P. *A Life of General John Stark of New Hampshire.* New York: Privately printed, 1949.

Morgan, Edmund S. "The American Revolution: Revisionists in Need of Revising." *William and Mary Quarterly*, 3d Ser., 14 (January 1957), pp. 3–15.

———. *Benjamin Franklin.* New Haven, Conn.: Yale University Press, 2002.

———. *The Birth of the Republic, 1763–1789.* Chicago: University of Chicago Press, 1956.

———. *The Challenge of the American Revolution.* New York: W. W. Norton and Company, 1976.

———. *The Genius of George Washington.* Washington, DC: Society of the Cincinnati, 1980.

———. *The Meaning of Independence: John Adams, George Washington, and Thomas Jefferson.* Charlottesville: University of Virginia Press, 2004 (1976).

Morgan, Edmund S., and Helen M. Morgan. *The Stamp Act Crisis: Prologue to Revolution.* Chapel Hill: University of North Carolina Press, 1953.

Morgan, William J. *Captains to the Northward: The New England Captains in the Continental Navy.* Barre, Mass: Barre Gazette, 1959.

Morison, Samuel E. *The Conservative American Revolution.* Washington: Society of the Cincinnati, 1976.

———. *John Paul Jones, A Sailor's Biography.* Boston: Little, Brown, 1959.

———. "The Struggle Over the Adoption of the Constitution of Massachusetts, 1780." *Proceedings of the Massachusetts Historical Society*, 50 (May 1917), pp. 353–411.

Morrill, Dan L. *Southern Campaigns of the American Revolution.* Baltimore: Nautical and Aviation Publishing Company, 1993.

Morris, George F. "Major Benjamin Whitcomb: Ranger and Partisan Leader in the Revolution." *Historical New Hampshire*, 11 (October 1955), pp. 1–20.

Morris, Richard B. *The American Revolution, a Short History.* New York: Van Nostrand, 1955.

———. *The American Revolution Reconsidered.* New York: Harper & Row, 1967.

———. "Class Struggle and the American Revolution." *William and Mary Quarterly*, 3d Ser., 19 (January 1962), pp. 3–29.

———. "The Great Peace of 1783." *Proceedings of the Massachusetts Historical Society*, 95 (1983), pp. 29–51.

———. *The Peacemakers: The Great Powers and American Independence.* New York: Harper & Row, 1965.

Morris, Robert. *The Papers of Robert Morris 1781–1784.* Edited by E. James Ferguson, et al. Pittsburgh: University of Pittsburgh Press, 1973—.

Morris, Robert L. "Military Contributions of Western Virginia in the American Revolution." *West Virginia History*, 23 (January 1962), pp. 86–99.

Moss, Bobby G., compiler. *The Patriots at Cowpens.* Revised edition. Blacksburg, S.C.: Scotia Press, 1991.

———, compiler. *The Patriots at Kings Mountain.* Blacksburg, S.C.: Scotia-Hibernia Press, 1990.

———. "Role of the Scots and Scotch-Irish in the Southern Campaigns in the War of American Independence, 1780–3." Ph.D. dissertation, University of St. Andrews, 1979.

———, compiler. *Roster of South Carolina Patriots in the American Revolution.* Baltimore: Genealogical Publishing Co., 1983.

Mowat, Charles L. *East Florida as a British Province, 1763–1784.* Berkeley: University of California Press, 1943.

———. "The Southern Brigade: A Sidelight on the British Military Establishment in America, 1763–1775." *Journal of Southern History*, 10 (February 1944), pp. 59–77.

Muenchhausen, Friedrich von. *At General Howe's Side: The Diary of General Howe's Aide-de-Camp, Captain Friedrich von Muenchhausen.* Translated and edited by Ernst Kipping and Samuel S. Smith. Monmouth Beach, N.J.: Philip Freneau Press, 1974.

Munroe, John A. "Reflections on Delaware and the American Revolution." *Delaware History*, 17 (Spring-Summer 1976), pp. 1–11.

Murdock, Harold. "The British at Concord—April 19, 1775." *Proceedings of the Massachusetts Historical Society*, 56 (November 1922), pp. 70–94.

———. *Bunker Hill: Notes and Queries on a Famous Battle.* Boston: Houghton Mifflin Co., 1927.

———. *Earl Percy Dines Abroad: A Boswellian Episode.* Boston: Houghton Mifflin Co., 1924.

———. "Earl Percy's Retreat to Boston on the Nineteenth of April, 1775." *Publications of the Colonial Society of Massachusetts*, 24 (April 1921), pp. 257–292.

———. "Historic Doubts on the Battle of Lexington." *Proceedings of the Massachusetts Historical Society*, 49 (May 1916), pp. 361–386.

———. *The Nineteenth of April, 1775.* Boston: Houghton Mifflin Co., 1923.

Murillo Rubiera, Fernando. "Santa Cruz de Marcenado un militar ilustrado." *Revista de Historia Militar*, 29 (Special Number, 1985), pp. 105–266.

Murphy, Orville T., Jr. "The American Revolutionary Army and the Concept of the Levée en Masse." *Military Affairs*, 23 (Spring 1959), pp. 13–20.

———. "The Battle of Germantown and the Franco-American Alliance of 1778." *Pennsylvania Magazine of History and Biography*, 82 (January 1958), pp. 55–64.

———. *Charles Gravier, Comte de Vergennes: French Diplomacy in the Age of Revolution, 1719–1787.* Albany: State University of New York Press, 1982.

———. "Charles Gravier de Vergennes: Profile of an Old Regime Diplomat." *Political Science Quarterly*, 83 (September 1968), pp. 400–418.

———. "The Comte de Vergennes, the Newfoundland Fisheries, and the Peace Negotiations of 1783: A Reconsideration." *Canadian Historical Review*, 46 (March 1965), pp. 32–46.

———. "The French Professional Soldier's Opinion of the American Militia in the War of the Revolution." *Military Affairs*, 32 (February 1969), pp. 191–198.

Murray, Thomas H. *Irish Rhode Islanders in the American Revolution.* Providence: American-Irish Historical Society, 1903.

Myers, Minor, Jr. *Liberty Without Anarchy: A History of the Society of the Cincinnati.* Charlottesville: University Press of Virginia, 1983.

Naisawald, L. Van Loan. "Major General Robert Howe's Activities in South Carolina and Georgia, 1776–1779." *Georgia Historical Quarterly,* 35 (March 1951), pp. 23–30.

———. "Robert Howe's Operations in Virginia, 1775–1776." *Virginia Magazine of History and Biography,* 60 (July 1952), pp. 437–443.

Nadelhaft, Jerome J. *The Disorders of War: The Revolution in South Carolina.* Orono: University of Maine and Orono Press, 1981.

Nasatir, Abraham. P. "The Anglo-Spanish Frontier in the Illinois Country during the American Revolution." *Journal of the Illinois State Historical Society,* 21 (October 1928), pp. 291–358.

———. *Borderland in Retreat: From Spanish Louisiana to the Far Southwest.* Albuquerque: University of New Mexico Press, 1976.

National Park Service, *The American Revolution: Lighting Freedom's Flame,* at www.nps.gov/revwar.

Naval History Division, Department of the Navy, editors. *Maritime Dimensions of the American Revolution.* Washington: Government Printing Office, 1977.

———. *The War at Sea: France and the American Revolution: A Bibliography.* Washington, D. C.: Government Printing Office, 1976.

Navarro, García, Luis. *Don José de Gálvez y la Comandancia general de las provincias internas del norte de Nueva España.* Savilla: Consejo Superior de Investigaciones Científicas, 1964.

Neal, John W. "Life and Public Services of Hugh Williamson." *Trinity College Historical Society Papers,* 13 (1919), pp. 62–115.

Neatby, Hilda. *Quebec: The Revolutionary Age, 1760–1791.* Toronto: McClelland and Stewart, 1966.

Nebenzahl, Kenneth. *A Bibliography of Printed Battle Plans of the American Revolution 1775–1795.* Chicago: University of Chicago Press, 1975.

Nebenzahl, Kenneth, and Don Higginbotham. *Atlas of the American Revolution.* Chicago: Rand McNally, 1974.

Neimeyer, Charles. *America Goes to War: A Social History of the Continental Army.* New York: New York University Press, 1996.

Nelson, Paul D. "Anthony Wayne: Soldier as Politician." *Pennsylvania Magazine of History and Biography,* 106 (October 1982), pp. 463–482.

———. *Anthony Wayne: A Soldier of the Early Republic.* Bloomington: Indiana University Press, 1985.

———. "British Conduct of the American Revolutionary War: A Review of Interpretations. " *Journal of American History,* 65 (December 1978), pp. 623–653.

———. "Citizen Soldiers or Regulars: The Views of American General Officers of the Military Establishment, 1775–1781." *Military Affairs,* 43 (October 1979), pp. 126–132.

———. "The Gates-Arnold Quarrel, September 1777." *New-York Historical Society Quarterly,* 55 (July 1971), pp. 235–252.

———. *General Horatio Gates: A Biography.* Baton Rouge: Louisiana State University Press, 1976.

———. "Guy Carleton versus Benedict Arnold: The Campaign of 1776 in Canada and on Lake Champlain." *New York History,* 57 (July 1976), pp. 339–366.

———. "Horatio Gates at Newburgh 1783: A Misunderstood Role." With Rebuttal by Richard H. Kohn. *William and Mary Quarterly,* 3d Ser., 29 (January 1972), pp. 143–158.

———. "Horatio Gates in the Southern Department, 1780: Serious Errors and a Costly Defeat." *North Carolina Historical Review,* 50 (July 1973), pp. 256–272.

———. "Lee, Gates, Stephen and Morgan: Revolutionary War Generals of the Lower Shenandoah Valley." *West Virginia History,* 37 (April 1976), pp. 185–200.

———. "Legacy of Controversy: Gates, Schuyler, and Arnold at Saratoga, 1777." *Military Affairs,* 37 (April 1973), pp. 41–47.

———. *The Life of William Alexander, Lord Stirling.* University: University of Alabama Press, 1987.

———. *William Tryon and the Course of Empire: A Life in British Imperial Service.* Chapel Hill: University of North Carolina Press, 1990.

———. "William Tryon Confronts the American Revolution, 1771–1780." *Historian,* 53 (Winter 1991), pp. 267–284.

Nelson, Peter. "Learned's Expedition to the Relief of Fort Stanwix." *Quarterly Journal of the New York State Historical Association,* 9 (October 1928), pp. 380–385.

———. "The Battle of Diamond Island." *Quarterly Journal of the New York State Historical Association,* 3 (January 1922), pp. 36–53.

Nelson, William. "Beginnings of the Iron Industry in Trenton, New Jersey." *Pennsylvania Magazine of History and Biography,* 35 (1911), pp. 228–243.

Nelson, William H. *The American Tory.* London: Oxford University Press, 1961.

———. "The Revolutionary Character of the American Revolution." *American Historical Review,* 70 (July 1965), pp. 998–1014.

Neu, Irene D. "The Iron Plantations of Colonial New York." *New York History,* 33 (January 1952), pp. 3–24.

Neuenschwander, John A. *The Middle Colonies and the Coming of the American Revolution.* Port Washington, N.Y.: Kennikat Press, 1973.

Neumann, George C. *Battle Weapons of the American Revolution.* Texarkana, Texas: Scurlock Publishing Company, 1998.

———. *Edged Weapons of the American Revolution, 1775–1783.* Washington: American Defense Preparedness Association, 1975.

———. *Firearms of the American Revolution 1775–1783.* Washington: American Ordnance Association, 1973.

———. *The History of Weapons of the American Revolution.* New York: Harper and Row, 1967.

Nevins, Allen. *The American States during and after the Revolution, 1775–1789.* New York: Macmillan Co., 1924.

New Hampshire American Revolution Bicentennial Commission. *New Hampshire's Role in the American Revolution, 1763–1789: A Bibliography.* Concord: New Hampshire State Library, 1974.

New Jersey Historical Society. *Documents Relating to the Colonial, Revolutionary and Post-Revolutionary History of the State of New Jersey*. Archives of the State of New Jersey, 1st Ser. 42 vols. Newark and Paterson: Various publishers, 1880–1949.

New York. *Calendar of Historical Manuscripts, Relating to the War of the Revolution, in the Office of the Secretary of State, Albany, New York*. 2 vols. Albany: Weed, Parsons and Co., 1863–1868.

———. *Journal of the Legislative Council of the Colony of New York, 1691–1775*. 2 vols. Albany: Weed, Parsons & Co., 1861.

———. *Journals of the Provincial Congress, Provincial Convention, Committee of Safety, and Council of Safety, 1775–1777*. 2 vols. Albany: Thurlow Weed, 1842.

New York. Division of Archives and History. *The Sullivan-Clinton Campaign in 1779. Chronology and Selected Documents*. Albany: University of the State of New York, 1929.

New York Division of Archives and History. *The Sullivan-Clinton Campaign in 1779. Chronology and Selected Documents*. Albany: University of the State of New York, 1929.

New-York Historical Society, *Collections*:

1875: "Official Letters of Major General James Pattison," pp. 1–432.

1879: "Proceedings of a General Court Martial . . . for the Trial of Major General Howe, December 7, 1781."

"Proceedings of a General Court Martial . . . for the Trial of Major General Schuyler, October 1, 1778."

1879: "Transactions [of Charles Rainsford] as Commissary for Embarking Foreign Troops in the English Service from Germany, 1776–1777," pp. 313–543.

1880: "Proceedings of a General Court Martial . . . for the Trial of Major General St. Clair, August 25, 1778."

1882: "Journal of Lieutenant John Charles Philip von Krafft" and "Letter-Book of Captain Alexander McDonald 1775–1779."

1883: "Journal of Lieut.-Col. Stephen Kemble, 1773–1789; and British Army Orders: Gen. Sir William Howe, 1775–1778; Gen. Sir Henry Clinton, 1778; and Gen. Daniel Jones, 1778."1887–1890: "[Silas] Deane Papers, 1774–1790." 5 vols.1914 and 1915: "Muster and Pay Rolls of the Revolution 1775–1783." 2 vols.1932: "Letter-Books and Order-Book of George, Lord Rodney, Admiral." 2 vols.

New York State Museum, *The Knox Trail*, at www.nysm.nysed.gov/srv/KnoxTrail.

Nickerson, Hoffman. *The Turning Point of the Revolution; or, Burgoyne in America*. Boston: Houghton Mifflin Co., 1928.

Niven, John. *Connecticut's Hero: Israel Putnam*. Hartford: American Revolution Bicentennial Commission of Connecticut, 1977.

Nobles, Gregory H. "The Rise of Merchants in Rural Market Towns: A Case Study of Eighteenth-Century Northampton, Massachusetts." *Journal of Social History*, 24 (Fall 1990), pp. 5–23.

Nordholt, Jan W. S. *The Dutch Republic and American Independence*. Translated by Herbert H. Rowen. Chapel Hill: University of North Carolina Press, 1982.

———. "The Recognition of the United States by the Dutch Republic." *Massachusetts Historical Society Proceedings*, 94 (1982), pp. 37–48.

Norton, Mary Beth. "Eighteenth-Century American Women in Peace and War: The Case of the Loyalists." *William and Mary Quarterly*, 3d Ser., 33 (July 1976), pp. 386–409.

Norton, William B. "Paper Currency in Massachusetts during the Revolution." *New England Quarterly*, 7 (March 1934), pp. 43–69.

Nourse, Henry S. *The Military Annals of Lancaster Massachusetts. 1740–1865*. Lancaster: W. J. Coulter, 1889.

Noyes, Richard. "Time Frame as a Variable in the Fifth Provincial Congress." *Historical New Hampshire*, 31 (Winter 1976), pp. 192–216.

Nunemaker, J. Horace. "Louisiana Anticipates Spain's Recognition of the Independence of the United States." *Louisiana Historical Quarterly*, 26 (July 1943), pp. 755–769.

Nuxoll, Elizabeth M. "Congress and the Munitions Merchants: The Secret Committee of Trade during the American Revolution, 1775–1777." Ph.D. dissertation, City University of New York, 1979.

O'Connor, John E. "William Patterson and the Ideological Origins of the Revolution in New Jersey." *New Jersey History*, 94 (Spring 1976), pp. 5–22.

O'Connor, Raymond. *The Origins of the American Navy: Sea Power in the Colonies and the New Nation*. Lanham, Maryland: University Press of America, 1994.

O'Dea, Anna, and Samuel A. Pleasants. "The Case of John Honeyman: Mute Evidence." *New Jersey Historical Society Proceedings*, 84 (July 1966), pp. 174–181.

O'Donnell, James H., III. *The Cherokees of North Carolina in the American Revolution*. Raleigh: North Carolina Department of Cultural Resources, 1976.

———. *Southern Indians in the American Revolution*. Knoxville: University of Tennessee Press, 1972.

O'Kelley, Patrick J. *Nothing But Blood and Slaughter: The Revolutionary War in the Carolinas, 1771–1782*. 4 vols. N.p., 1994–1995.

O'Shaughnessy, Andrew J. *The Empire Divided: The American Revolution and the British Caribbean*. Philadelphia: University of Pennsylvania Press, 2000.

Oaks, Robert F. "Philadelphia Merchants and the First Continental Congress." *Pennsylvania History*, 40 (April 1973), pp. 149–166.

———. "The Impact of British Western Policy on the Coming of the American Revolution in Pennsylvania." *Pennsylvania Magazine of History and Biography*, 101 (April 1977), pp. 171–189.

Odintz, Mark F. "The British Officer Corps, 1754–1783." Ph.D. dissertation, University of Michigan, 1988.

ODNB. Oxford Dictionary of National Biography : In Association with the British Academy : from the Earliest Times to the year 2000. Edited by H.C.G. Matthew and Brian Harrison. New York : Oxford University Press, 2004.

Oliver, Peter. *Origin and Progress of the American Revolution*. Edited by Douglas Adair and John Schutz. San Marino, Calif.: Huntington Library, 1961.

Olson, Gary D. "Dr. David Ramsay and Lt. Colonel Thomas Brown: Patriot Historian and Loyalist Critic." *South Carolina Historical Magazine*, 77 (October 1976), pp. 257–267.

————. "Loyalists and the American Revolution: Thomas Brown and the South Carolina Backcountry, 1775–1776." *South Carolina Historical Magazine*, 68 (October 1967), pp. 201–219; 69 (January 1968), pp. 44–56.

————. "Thomas Brown, Loyalist Partisan, and the Revolutionary War in Georgia, 1777–1782." *Georgia Historical Quarterly*, 54 (1970), pp. 1–19, 183–208.

Olton, Charles S. *Artisans for Independence: Philadelphia Mechanics and the American Revolution.* Syracuse: Syracuse University Press, 1975.

Onderdonk, Henry. *Documents and Letters Intended to Illustrate the Revolutionary Incidents of Queens County.* New York: Leavitt, Trow and Co., 1846.

————. *Queens County in Olden Times: Being a Supplement to the Several Histories Thereof.* Jamaica, N.Y.: Charles Willing, 1865.

————. *Revolutionary Incidents of Suffolk and Kings Counties; with an Account of the Battle of Long Island, and the British Prisons and Prison-Ships at New York.* New York: Leavitt & Co., 1849.

The On-Line Institute for Advanced Loyalist Studies, at www.royalprovincial.com.

Orrill, Lawrence A. "General Edward Hand." *Western Pennsylvania Historical Magazine*, 25 (September-December 1942), pp. 99–112.

Osborn, George C. "Major General John Campbell in British West Florida." *Florida Historical Quarterly*, 27 (April 1949), pp. 317–339.

Oswald, Richard. *Richard Oswald's Memorandum on the Folly of Invading Virginia, The Strategic Importance of Portsmouth, and The Need for Civilian Control of the Military.* Edited by W. Stitt Robinson, Jr. Charlottesville: University Press of Virginia, 1953.

Ousterhout, Anne M. *A State Divided: Opposition in Pennsylvania to the American Revolution.* Westport: Greenwood, 1987.

Overfield, Richard A. "A Patriot Dilemma: The Treatment of Passive Loyalists and Neutrals in Revolutionary Maryland." *Maryland Historical Magazine*, 68 (Summer 1973), pp. 140–159.

Owen, Thomas M., compiler. *Revolutionary Soldiers in Alabama.* Montgomery: Alabama Department of Archives and History, 1911.

Padover, Saul K. *The Mind of Alexander Hamilton.* New York: Harper & Brothers, 1958.

Pagano, Francis B. "An Historical Account of the Military and Political Career of George Clinton, 1739–1812." Ph.D. dissertation, St. John's University, 1956.

Page, Elwin L. "The King's Powder, 1774." *New England Quarterly*, 18 (March 1945), pp. 83–92.

————. "What Happened to the King's Powder?" *Historical New Hampshire*, 19 (Summer 1964), pp. 28–33.

Palmer, Dave R. "General George Washington: Grand Strategist or Mere Fabian?" *Parameters*, 4 (Spring 1974), pp. 1–16.

————. *The River and the Rock: The History of Fortress West Point, 1775–1783.* New York: Greenwood Publishing Co., 1969.

————. *The Way of the Fox: American Strategy in the War for America 1775–1783.* Westport, Conn.: Greenwood Press, 1975.

Palmer, John M. *America in Arms, The Experience of the United States with Military Organization.* New Haven: Yale University Press, 1941.

————. *General Von Steuben.* New Haven: Yale University Press, 1937.

Paltsits, Victor H. "The Jeopardy of Washington, September 15, 1776." *New-York Historical Society Quarterly*, 32 (October 1948), pp. 253–268.

————. "The Use of Invisible Ink for Secret Writing during the American Revolution." *New York Public Library Bulletin*, 39 (May 1935), pp. 361–364.

Panagopoulous, E. P. "Hamilton's Notes in His Pay Book of the New York State Artillery Company." *American Historical Review*, 62 (June 1957), pp. 310–321.

Pancake, John S. *The Destructive War: The British Campaign in the Carolinas, 1780–1782.* Tuscaloosa: University of Alabama Press, 1985.

————. *1777, The Year of the Hangman.* Tuscaloosa: University of Alabama Press, 1977.

Papenfuse, Edward C., Jr. "Economic Analysis and Loyalist Strategy during the American Revolution: Robert Alexander's Remarks on the Economy of the Peninsula or Eastern Shore of Maryland." *Maryland Historical Magazine*, 68 (Summer 1973), pp. 173–195.

————. *In Pursuit of Profit: The Annapolis Merchants in the Era of the American Revolution, 1763–1805.* Baltimore: Johns Hopkins University Press, 1975.

Papenfuse, Edward C., Jr., and Gregory A. Stiverson. "General Smallwood's Recruits: The Peacetime Career of the Revolutionary Private." *William and Mary Quarterly*, 3d Ser., 30 (January 1973), pp. 117–132.

Papenfuse, Edward C., Jr., Gregory A. Stiverson, and Mary D. Donaldson. *A Biographical Dictionary of the Maryland Legislature, 1635–1789.* Baltimore: Johns Hopkins University Press, 1979 —.

————. *The Era of the American Revolution, 1775–1789.* Annapolis: Archives Division, 1977.

Paret, Peter. "Colonial Experience and European Military Reform at the End of the Eighteenth Century." *Bulletin of the Institute for Historical Research*, 37 (May 1964), pp. 47–59.

Parker, Amelia C. "Baroness Riedesel and Other Women in Burgoyne's Army." *Quarterly Journal of the New York State Historical Association*, 9 (April 1928), pp. 109–118.

Parker, Wyman W. "Recruiting the Prince of Wales Loyalist Regiment from Middletown, Connecticut." *Connecticut Historical Society Bulletin*, 47 (January 1982), pp. 1–17.

Parry, J. H. "American Independence: The View from the West Indies." *Proceedings of the Massachusetts Historical Society*, 87 (1975), pp. 14–31.

Partridge, Bellamy. *Sir Billy Howe.* London: Longmans, Green & Co., 1932 [includes "The Narrative of Lieut. Gen. Sir William Howe," pp. 261–289.]

Patterson, A[lfred] Temple. *The Other Armada: The Franco-Spanish Attempt to Invade Britain in 1779.* Manchester: Manchester University Press, 1960.

Patterson, Benton R. *Washington and Cornwallis: The Battle for America, 1775–1783.* Latham, Md.: Taylor Trade Publishing, 2004.

Patterson, David S. "The Department of State: The Formative Years 1775–1800." *Prologue,* 21 (Winter 1989), pp. 315–329.

Patterson, Emma L. *Peekskill in the American Revolution.* Peekskill: Friendly Town Association, 1944.

Patterson, John G. "Ebenezer Zane, Frontiersman." *West Virginia History,* 12 (October 1950), pp. 5–45.

Patterson, Samuel W. *Knight Errant of Liberty; The Triumph and Tragedy of General Charles Lee.* New York: Lanthern Press, 1958.

Patterson, Stephen E. *Political Parties in Revolutionary Massachusetts.* Madison: University of Wisconsin Press, 1973.

Paullin, Charles O., editor. *The Navy of the American Revolution: Its Administration, Its Policy and Its Achievements.* Cleveland: Burrows, 1906.

———. *Out-Letters of the Continental Marine Committee and Board of Admiralty, August, 1776–September, 1780.* 2 vols. New York: Naval History Society, 1914.

Peck, Epaphroditus. *The Loyalists of Connecticut.* New Haven: Yale University Press, 1934.

Peckham, Howard H. "Military Papers at the Clements Library." *Military Affairs,* 2 (Fall 1938), pp. 126–130.

———. "Sir Henry Clinton's Review of Simcoe's Journal." *William and Mary Quarterly,* 2d Ser., 21 (October 1941), pp. 360–370.

Peckham, Howard H., editor. *Sources of American Independence: Selected Manuscripts from the Collections of the William L. Clements Library.* 2 vols. Chicago: University of Chicago Press, 1978.

———. *The Toll of Independence: Engagements & Battle Casualties of the American Revolution.* Chicago: University of Chicago Press, 1974.

———. *The War for Independence: A Military History.* Chicago: University of Chicago Press, 1958.

Peebles, John. *John Peebles' American War: The Diary of a Scottish Grenadier, 1776–1782.* Edited by Ira D. Gruber. Mechanicsburg, Pennsylvania: Stackpole Books, 1998.

Pemberton, Ian C. "The British Secret Service in the Champlain Valley during the Haldimand Negotiations, 1780–1783." *Vermont History,* 44 (Summer 1976), pp. 129–140.

Pennsylvania Archives. 9 Series. 119 Volumes. Philadelphia and Harrisburg: Various Publishers, 1874–1935.

Pennypacker, Morton. *George Washington's Spies on Long Island and in New York.* Brooklyn: Long Island Historical Society, 1939.

———. "Two Spies: Nathan Hale and Robert Townsend." *Quarterly Journal of the New York State Historical Association,* 12 (April 1931), pp. 122–128.

Percy, Hugh. *Letters of Hugh Earl Percy from Boston and New York 1774–1776.* Edited by Charles Knowles Bolton. Boston: Charles L. Goodspeed, 1902.

Peters, Nathan. *The Correspondence of Captain Nathan and Lois Peters, April 25, 1775–February 5, 1776.* Edited by William H. Guthman. Hartford: Connecticut Historical Society, 1980.

Peterson, Clarence S. *Known Military Dead of the American Revolutionary War, 1775–1783.* Baltimore: Genealogical Publishing Co., 1959.

Peterson, Harold L. *Arms and Armor in Colonial America, 1526–1783.* Harrisburg: Stackpole Books, 1956.

———. *The Book of The Continental Soldier Being a Compleat Account of the Uniforms, Weapons, and Equipment with Which He Lived and Fought.* Harrisburg: Stackpole Co., 1968.

———. *Round Shot and Rammers.* Harrisburg: Stackpole Books, 1969.

Peterson, Jean, et al., editors. *The Loyalist Guide: Nova Scotian Loyalists and Their Documents.* Halifax, Nova Scotia: Public Archives of Nova Scotia, 1983.

Pickering, James H., editor. "Enoch Crosby, Secret Agent of the Neutral Ground: His Own Story." *New York History,* 47 (January 1966), pp. 51–73.

Pieper, Thomas I., and James B. Gidney. *Fort Laurens, 1778–1779: The Revolutionary War in Ohio.* Kent, Ohio: Kent State University Press, 1976.

Pindell, Richard. "A Militant Surgeon of the Revolution." *Maryland Historical Magazine,* 18 (December 1923), pp. 309–323.

Pinkett, Harold T. "Maryland as a Source of Food Supplies during the American Revolution." *Maryland Historical Magazine,* 46 (September 1951), pp. 157–172.

Pleasants, Henry, Jr. "Contraband From Lorient." *Military Affairs,* 7 (Summer 1943), pp. 123–132.

Pleasants, Samuel A. "Incidents at New Bridge." *Proceedings of the New Jersey Historical Society,* 76 (July 1958), pp. 201–212.

Potter, Chandler E. *Military History of New Hampshire, from Its Settlement, in 1623, to the Year 1861.* 2 vols. Concord: Adjutant General's Office, New Hampshire, 1866–1868.

Potter, Janice. *The Liberty We Seek: Loyalist Ideology in Colonial New York and Massachusetts.* Cambridge, Mass.: Harvard University Press, 1983.

Potts, Louis W. *Arthur Lee: A Virtuous Revolutionary.* Baton Rouge: Louisiana State University Press, 1981.

Powell, Walter L. *Murder or Mayhem?: Benedict Arnold's New London, Connecticut, Raid, 1781.* Gettysburg, Pa.: Thomas Publications, 2000.

———. "The Strange Death of Colonel William Ledyard." *Connecticut Historical Society Bulletin,* 40 (April 1975), pp. 61–65.

Powell, William S. " A Connecticut Soldier under Washington: Elisha Bostwick's Memoirs of the First Years of the Revolution." *William and Mary Quarterly,* 3d Ser., 6 (January 1949), pp. 94–107.

———. *The War of the Regulation and the Battle of the Alamance, 16 May 1771.* Raleigh: North Carolina Department of Cultural Resources, 1976.

Prelinger, Catherine M. "Benjamin Franklin and the American Prisoners of War in England during the American Revolution." *William and Mary Quarterly,* 3d Ser., 32 (April 1975), pp. 261–292.

Prince, Carl E. *William Livingston: New Jersey's First Governor.* Trenton: New Jersey Historical Commission, 1975.

Proctor, Samuel, editor. *Eighteenth-Century Florida and the Revolutionary South.* Gainesville: University Presses of Florida, 1978.

Pugh, Robert C. "The Revolutionary Militia in the Southern Campaign, 1780–1781." *William and Mary Quarterly*, 3d Ser., 14 (April 1957), pp. 154–175.

Putnam, Rufus. *The Memoirs of Rufus Putnam and Certain Official Papers and Correspondence.* Edited by Rowena Buell. Boston: Houghton, Mifflin and Co., 1903.

Quaife, Milo M. "The Ohio Campaign of 1782." *Mississippi Valley Historical Review*, 17 (March 1931), pp. 515–529.

Quarles, Benjamin. *The Negro in the American Revolution.* Chapel Hill: University of North Carolina Press, 1961.

Rakove, Jack N. *The Beginning of National Politics: An Interpretive History of the Continental Congress.* New York: Alfred A. Knopf, 1979.

Ramsey, Robert W. *Carolina Cradle: Settlement of the Northwest Carolina Frontier.* Chapel Hill: University of North Carolina Press, 1964.

Randall, James G. "George Rogers Clarke's Service of Supply." *Mississippi Valley Historical Review*, 8 (December 1921), pp. 250–263.

Randall, Willard S. *Benedict Arnold: Patriot and Traitor.* New York: Morrow, 1990.

Rankin, Hugh F. "Cowpens: Prelude to Yorktown." *North Carolina Historical Review*, 31 (July 1954), pp. 336–369.

———. *Francis Marion: The Swamp Fox.* New York: Thomas Y. Crowell, 1973.

———. *George Rogers Clark and The Winning of the West.* Richmond: Virginia Independence Bicentennial Commission, 1976.

———. *Greene and Cornwallis: The Campaign in the Carolinas.* Raleigh: North Carolina Department of Cultural Resources, 1976.

———. "The Moore's Creek Bridge Campaign, 1776." *North Carolina Historical Review*, 30 (January 1953), pp. 23–60.

———. *The North Carolina Continentals.* Chapel Hill: University of North Carolina Press, 1971.

———. *The North Carolina Continental Line in American Revolution.* Raleigh: North Carolina Department of Cultural Resources, 1977.

Ranlet, Philip H. "British Recruitment of Americans in New York during the American Revolution." *Military Affairs*, 48 (January 1984), pp. 26–28.

———. "Loyalty in the Revolutionary War: General Robert Howe of North Carolina." *Historian*, 53 (Summer 1991), pp. 721–742.

———. *The New York Loyalists.* Knoxville: University of Tennessee Press, 1986.

———. "The Two John Lambs of the Revolutionary Generation." *American Neptune*, 42 (October 1982), pp. 301–305.

Ransom, James M. *Vanishing Ironworks of the Ramapos: The Story of the Forges, Furnaces, and Mines of the New Jersey-New York Border Area.* New Brunswick: Rutgers University Press, 1966.

Raphael, Ray. *The First American Revolution: Before Lexington and Concord.* New York: New Press, 2002.

———. *A People's History of the American Revolution: How Common People Shaped the Fight for Independence.* New York: Harper Collins, 2001.

Rawlyk, George A., editor. *Revolution Rejected, 1775–1776.* Scarborough, Ont.: Prentice-Hall of Canada, 1968.

Raymond, R. J. "Privateers and Privateering off the Irish Coast in the Eighteenth Century." *Irish Sword*, 13 (Summer 1977), pp. 60–69.

Rea, Robert R. "Brigadier Frederick Haldimand—The Florida Years." *Florida Historical Quarterly*, 54 (April 1976), pp. 512–531.

———. "Military Deserters from British West Florida." *Louisiana History*, 9 (Spring 1968), pp. 123–137.

Reed, John F. *Campaign to Valley Forge July 1, 1777–December 19, 1777.* Philadelphia: University of Pennsylvania Press, 1965.

———. *Valley Forge: Crucible of Victory.* Monmouth Beach, N.J.: Philip Freneau Press, 1969.

Reed, Robert P. "Loyalists, Patriots, and Trimmers: The Committee System in the American Revolution, 1774–1776." Ph.D. dissertation, Cornell University, 1988.

Reichman, Felix. "The Pennsylvania Rifle: A Social Interpretation of Changing Military Techniques." *Pennsylvania Magazine of History and Biography*, 69 (January 1945), pp. 3–14.

Reid, John Philip. *In Defence of the Law: The Standing-Army Controversy, the Two Constitutions, and the Coming of the American Revolution.* Chapel Hill: University of North Carolina Press, 1981.

Reina, John P. "A British Account of the Siege of Rhode Island, 1778." Edited by John F. Millar. *Rhode Island History*, 38 (August 1979), pp. 78–85.

Resch, John P. "The Continentals of Peterborough, New Hampshire: Pension Records as a Source for Local History." *Prologue*, 16 (Fall 1984), pp. 169–183.

———. *Suffering Soldiers: Revolutionary War Veterans, Moral Sentiment, and Political Culture in the Early Republic.* Amherst: University of Massachusetts Press, 1999.

Retzer, Henry. *The German Regiment of Maryland and Pennsylvania in the Continental Army, 1776–1781.* Westminster, Maryland: Family Line Publications, 1991.

Reuter, Frank T. "'Petty Spy' or Effective Diplomat: The Role of George Beckwith." *Journal of the Early Republic*, 10 (Winter 1990), pp. 471–492.

Reynolds, Donald E. "Ammunition Supply in Revolutionary Virginia." *Virginia Magazine of History and Biography*, 73 (January 1965), pp. 56–77.

Rhodehamel, John, editor. *The American Revolution: Writings from the War of Independence,* New York: Library of America, 2001.

———. *The Great Experiment: George Washington and the American Republic.* New Haven: Yale University Press for the Huntington Library, 1999.

Rice, Howard, C., Jr., and Anne S. K. Brown, translators and editors. *The American Campaigns of Rochambeau's Army.* Princeton: Princeton University Press, 1972.

Richards, Henry M. M. *The Pennsylvania-German in the British Military Prisons of the Revolutionary War*. Lancaster: Pennsylvania-German Society, 1924.

———. *The Pennsylvania-German in the Revolutionary War, 1775–1783*. Lancaster: Pennsylvania German Society, 1908.

Richards, Leonard L. *Shays's Rebellion: The American Revolution's Final Battle*. Philadelphia: University of Pennsylvania Press, 2002.

Richardson, Edward W. *Standards and Colors of the American Revolution*. Philadelphia: University of Pennsylvania Press, 1982.

Richmond, Robert P. *Powder Alarm, 1774*. Princeton, N. J.: Auerbach Publishers, 1971.

Rider, Hope S. *Valour Fore & Aft: Being the Adventures of the Continental Sloop Providence, 1775–1779, Formerly Flagship Katy of Rhode Island's Navy*. Annapolis: Naval Institute Press, 1977.

Risch, Erna. *Quartermaster Support of the Army: A History of the Corps 1775–1939*. Washington: Quartermaster Historian's Office, Office of the Quartermaster General, 1962.

———. *Supplying Washington's Army*. Washington: Government Printing Office, 1981.

Ritcheson, Charles R. *British Politics and the American Revolution*. Norman: University of Oklahoma Press, 1954.

Robbins, Caroline. "Decision in '76: Reflections on the 56 Signers." *Proceedings of the Massachusetts Historical Society*, 89 (1977), pp. 72–87.

Roberts, James A., compiler. *New York in the Revolution as Colony and State*. 2d Edition. Albany: New York State, 1898.

Roberts, Kenneth, compiler. *March to Quebec: Journals of the Members of Arnold's Expedition*. 4th Edition. New York: Doubleday and Co., 1940.

Roberts, Robert B. *New York's Forts in the Revolution*. Cranbury, New Jersey: Fairleigh Dickinson University Press, 1980.

Robertson, Archibald. *Archibald Robertson Lieutenant-General Royal Engineers: His Diaries and Sketches in America, 1762–1780*. Edited by Harry Miller Lydenberg. New York: New York Public Library, 1930.

Robertson, Heard. "The Second British Occupation of Augusta, 1780–1781." *Georgia Historical Quarterly*, 58 (Winter 1974), pp. 442–446.

Robertson, James. *The Twilight of British Rule in America: The New York Letter Book of General James Robertson 1780–1783*. Edited by Milton M. Klein and Ronald W. Howard. Cooperstown: New York State Historical Association, 1983.

Robertson, James A., editor. "Spanish Correspondence Concerning the American Revolution." *Hispanic American Historical Review*, 1 (August 1918), pp. 299–316.

Robertson, M. L. "Scottish Commerce and the American War of Independence." *Economic History Review*, 2d Ser., 9 (August 1956), pp. 123–131.

Robinson, Blackwell P. *William R. Davie*. Chapel Hill: University of North Carolina Press, 1957.

Robson, Eric. *The American Revolution in Its Political and Military Aspects, 1763–1783*. New York: Oxford University Press, 1955.

———. "The Expedition to the Southern Colonies, 1775–1776." *English Historical Review*, 66 (October 1951), pp. 535–560.

———. "The Raising of a Regiment in the War of American Independence." *Journal of the Society for Army Historical Research*, 27 (Summer 1949), p. 107–115.

Roche, John F. *Joseph Reed: A Moderate in the American Revolution*. New York: Columbia University Press, 1957.

———. "Was Joseph Reed Disloyal?" *William and Mary Quarterly*, 3d Ser., 8 (July 1951), pp. 406–417.

Rodger, Nicholas A. M. *The Insatiable Earl: John Montagu, 4th Earl of Sandwich, 1718–1792.* , New York: W. W. Norton and Company, 1994.

———. *The Wooden World: The Anatomy of the Georgian Navy*. Annapolis: Naval Institute Press, 1986.

Rogers, Alan. "Colonial Opposition to the Quartering of Troops during the French and Indian War." *Military Affairs*, 34 (February 1970), pp. 7–11.

———. *Empire and Liberty: American Resistance to British Authority 1755–1763*. Berkeley: University of California Press, 1974.

Rogers, Ernest E. *Connecticut's Naval Office at New London during the War of the American Revolution, Including the Mercantile Letter Book of Nathaniel Shaw, Jr.* New London, Conn.: New London County Historical Society, 1933.

Rogers, George C., Jr. *Charleston in the Age of the Pinckneys*. Norman: University of Oklahoma Press, 1969.

———. "The Charleston Tea Party: The Significance of December 3, 1773." *South Carolina Historical Magazine*, 75 (July 1974), pp. 153–168.

———. *The History of Georgetown County, South Carolina*. Columbia: University of South Carolina Press, 1970.

Rogers, Hugh C. B. *The British Army of the 18th Century*. London: Allyn and Unwin, 1977.

Rome, Adam W. *Connecticut's Cannon: The Salisbury Iron Furnace in the American Revolution*. Hartford: American Revolution Bicentennial Commission of Connecticut, 1977.

Ronda, Jeanne, and James P. Ronda. "'As They Were Faithful': Chief Hendrick Aupaumut and the Struggle for Stockbridge Survival, 1757–1830." *American Indian Culture and Research Journal*, 3 (no. 3, 1979), pp. 43–55.

Ross, Stephen. *From Flintlock to Rifle: Infantry Tactics, 1740–1866*. Cranbury, N.J.: Fairleigh Dickinson University Press, 1979.

Rossie, Jonathan G. *The Politics of Command in the American Revolution*. Syracuse: Syracuse University Press, 1975.

Rossman, Kenneth R. *Thomas Mifflin and the Politics of the American Revolution*. Chapel Hill: University of North Carolina Press, 1952.

Rosswurm, Steven J. *Arms, Country, and Class: The Philadelphia Militia and the 'Lower Sort' During the American Revolution*. New Brunswick: Rutgers University Press, 1987.

Roth, David M. "Connecticut and the Coming of the Revolution." *Connecticut Review*, 7 (October 1973), pp. 49–65.

———. "Connecticut in the Revolutionary War." *Connecticut Review*, 9 (November 1975), pp. 10–20.

———. *Connecticut's War Governor, Jonathan Trumbull*. Chester: Pequot Press, 1974.

Rothenburg, Gunther E. "Steuben, Washington and the Question of 'Revolutionary' War." *Indiana Military History Journal*, 3 (May 1978), pp. 5–11.

Rowland, John K. "Origins of the Second Amendment: The Creation of the Constitutional Rights of Militia and of Keeping and Bearing Arms." Ph.D. dissertation, Ohio State University, 1978.

Royster, Charles W. *Light-Horse Harry Lee and the Legacy of the American Revolution*. New York: Alfred A. Knopf, 1981.

———. "'The Nature of Treason': Revolutionary Virtue and American Reactions to Benedict Arnold." *William and Mary Quarterly*, 3d Ser., 36 (April 1979), pp. 163–193.

———. *A Revolutionary People at War: The Continental Army & American Character, 1775–1783*. Chapel Hill: University of North Carolina Press, 1980.

Rudulph, Marilou Alston. "The Legend of Michael Rudulph." *Georgia Historical Quarterly*, 45 (December 1961), pp. 309–328.

———. "Michael Rudulph, 'Lion of the Legion.' "*Georgia Historical Quarterly*, 45 (September 1961), pp. 201–222.

Rush, N. Orwin. *The Battle of Pensacola, March 9 to May 8, 1781: Spain's Final Triumph Over Great Britain in the Gulf of Mexico*. Tallahassee: Florida State University, 1966.

Russell, Carl P. *Guns on the Early Frontiers: A History of Firearms From Colonial Times through the Years of the Western Fur Trade*. Berkeley: University of California Press, 1957.

Russell, David L. *The American Revolution in the Southern Colonies*. Jefferson, North Carolina: McFarland and Co., 2000.

Russell, Jack. *Gibraltar Besieged, 1779–1783*, London: Heinemann, 1965.

Rutherford, G. "Sidelights on Commodore Johnstone's Expedition to the Cape." *Mariner's Mirror*, 28 (July, October 1942), pp. 189–212, 290–308.

Rutyna, Richard A., and Peter C. Stewart, editors. *Virginia in the American Revolution, A Collection of Essays*. 2 vols. Norfolk, Virginia: Old Dominion University, 1977–1983.

Ryan, Dennis P., editor. *New Jersey in the American Revolution, 1763–1783: A Chronology*. Trenton: New Jersey Historical Commission, 1974.

———. *A Salute to Courage: The American Revolution as Seen through Wartime Writings of Officers of the Continental Army and Navy*. New York: Columbia University Press, 1979.

Ryan, Frank W., Jr. "The Role of South Carolina in the First Continental Congress." *South Carolina Historical and Genealogical Magazine*, 60 (July 1959), pp. 147–153.

Sabine, Lorenzo. *Biographical Sketches of Loyalists of the American Revolution*. 2 vols. Revised Edition. Boston: Little, Brown & Co., 1864.

Saffell, W. T. R. *Records of the Revolutionary War*. 3rd Edition. Baltimore: Charles E. Saffell, 1894.

Saffron, Morris H. *Surgeon to Washington: Dr. John Cochran 1730–1807*. New York: Columbia University Press, 1977.

———. "The Northern Medical Department 1776–1777." *Bulletin of the Fort Ticonderoga Museum*, 14 (Winter 1982), pp. 81–120.

Sainsbury, John. *Disaffected Patriots: London Supporters of Revolutionary America, 1769–1782*. Montreal: McGill-Queen's University Press, 1987.

St. Clair, Arthur. *The St. Clair Papers. The Life and Public Services of Arthur St. Clair, Soldier of the Revolutionary War . . . with his Correspondence and other Papers*. Edited by William Henry Smith. 2 vols. Cincinnati: Robert Clarke & Co., 1892.

Salay, David L. "Arming for War: The Production of War Material in Pennsylvania for the American Armies of the Revolution." Ph.D. dissertation, University of Delaware, 1977.

———. "The Production of Gunpowder in Pennsylvania during the American Revolution." *Pennsylvania Magazine of History and Biography*, 99 (October 1975), pp. 422–442.

Salley, Alexander S. *The History of Orangeburg County, South Carolina, from its first settlement to the close of the Revolutionary War*. Orangeburg: R. L. Berry, 1898.

Salley, Alexander S., compiler. *Records of the Regiments of the South Carolina Line in the Revolutionary War*. Edited by Alida Moe. Baltimore: Genealogical Publishing Co., 1977.

Salley, Alexander S., editor. *An Order Book of the 3rd Regiment, South Carolina Line, Continental Establishment, December 23, 1776–May 2, 1777*. Columbia: Historical Commission of South Carolina, 1942.

———. *Documents Relating to the History of South Carolina during the Revolutionary War*. Columbia: Historical Commission of South Carolina, 1908.

———. *Journal of the General Assembly of South Carolina, March 26, 1776–April 11, 1776*. Columbia: Historical Commission of South Carolina, 1906.

———. *Journal of the General Assembly of South Carolina, September 17, 1776–October 20, 1776*. Columbia: Historical Commission of South Carolina, 1909.

———. *Journal of the House of Representatives of South Carolina, January 8, 1782–February 26, 1782*. Columbia: Historical Commission of South Carolina, 1916.

Salmon, John. "'A Mission of the most secret and important kind': James Lafayette and American Espionage in 1781." *Virginia Cavalcade*, 31 (Autumn 1981), pp. 78–85.

Saltzman, Martin, et al. *The Horatio Gates Papers, 1726–1828: A Guide to the Microfilm Edition*. Sanford, N.C.: Microfilming Corporation of America, 1979.

Samuelson, Nancy B. "Revolutionary War Women and the Second Oldest Profession." *Minerva*, 7 (Summer 1989), pp. 16–25.

Sanchez-Saavedra, E. M. *A Guide to Virginia Military Organizations in the American Revolution, 1774–1787*. Richmond: Virginia State Library, 1978.

Sanders, Jennings B. *Evolution of Executive Departments of the Continental Congress, 1774–1789*. Chapel Hill: University of North Carolina Press, 1935.

Sanderson, Howard K. *Lynn in the Revolution*. 2 vols. Boston: W. B. Clarke Co., 1909.

Sands, John O. *Yorktown's Captive Fleet*. Charlottesville: University Press of Virginia for the Mariner's Museum, 1983.

Sandwich, John Montague, 4th Earl of. *The Private Papers of John, Earl of Sandwich, First Lord of the Admiralty, 1771–1782*. 4 vols.

Edited by G. R. Barnes and J. H. Owen. Greenwich, England: Navy Records Society, 1932–1938.

Sappington, Roger E. "North Carolina and the Non-Resistant Sects during the American War of Independence." *Quaker History*, 60 (Spring 1971), pp. 29–47.

Saunders, William L., editor. *The Colonial Records of North Carolina*. 10 vols. Raleigh: Various publishers, 1886–1890.

Sawyer, Charles W. *Firearms in American History*. 3 vols. Boston: Privately printed, 1910–1920.

Schachner, Nathan. *Aaron Burr: A Biography*. New York: Frederick A. Stokes Co., 1937.

Schaer, Friedrich-Wilhelm. "Die militärgeschichtlichen quellen des Niedersächsischen Staatsarchivs im Oldenburg." *Militärgeschichtliche Mitteilungen*, #2, 1969, pp. 183–188.

Schaffel, Kenneth. "The American Board of War, 1776–1781." *Military Affairs*, 50 (October 1986), pp. 185–189.

Schaukirk, Ewald G. *Occupation of New York City by the British*. Edited by A. A. Reinke. New York: Arno Press, 1969.

Schecter, Barnet. *The Battle for New York*. New York: Walker and Company, 2002.

Scheer, George F., and Hugh F. Rankin, editors. *Rebels and Redcoats*. New York: World, 1957.

Scheide, John. "The Lexington Alarm." *Proceedings of the American Antiquarian Society*, 50 (January 1940), pp. 49–79.

Scheina, Robert L. "A Matter of Definition: A New Jersey Navy, 1777–1783." *American Neptune* 39 (July 1979), pp. 209–217.

Schermerhorn, Frank Earle. *American and French Flags of the Revolution 1775–1783*. Philadelphia: Pennsylvania Society of Sons of the Revolution, 1948.

Schieffelin, Jacob. "A British Prisoner of War in the American Revolution: The Experiences of Jacob Schieffelin from Vincennes to Williamsburg, 1779–1780." Edited by Gerald O. Haffner. *Virginia Magazine of History and Biography*, 86 (January 1978), pp. 17–25.

Schlegel, Philip J. *Recruits to Continentals: A History of the York Rifle Company, June 1775–January 1777*. York: Historical Society of York County, 1979.

Schlenther, Boyd S. *Charles Thomson: A Patriot's Pursuit*. Newark: University of Delaware Press, 1990.

Schlesinger, Arthur M., Sr. *Colonial Merchants and the American Revolution, 1763–1776*. New York: Columbia University Press, 1918.

———. *Prelude to Independence: The Newspaper War on Britain, 1764–1776*. New York: Alfred A. Knopf, 1958.

Schmidt, H. D. "The Hessian Mercenaries: The Career of a Political Cliche." *History*, 43 (1958), pp. 207–212.

Schmitt, Dale J. "The Capture of Colonel Moses Rawlings." *Maryland Historical Magazine*, 71 (Summer 1976), pp. 205–211.

Schmitz, Rudolph. "The Medical and Pharmaceutical Care of Hessian Troops During the American War of Independence." In *American Pharmacy in the Colonial and Revolutionary Periods*. Edited by George A. Bender and John Parascandola. Madison: American Institute of the History of Pharmacy, 1977, pp. 37–47.

Schubert, Frank N. *Soldiers of the American Revolution—A Sketchbook*. Washington: Government Printing Office, 1976.

Schulz, Constance B. "Daughters of Liberty: The History of Women in the Revolutionary War Pension Records." *Prologue*, 16 (Fall 1984), pp. 139–153.

———. "Revolutionary War Pension Applications: A Neglected Source For Social and Family History." *Prologue*, 15 (Summer 1983), pp. 103–114.

Schutz, John A. "Those Who Became Tories: Town Loyalty and Revolution in New England." *New England Historical and Genealogical Register*, 129 (April 1975), pp. 94–105.

Scott, Kenneth. "New Hampshire Tory Counterfeiters Operating from New York City." *New-York Historical Society Quarterly*, 34 (January 1950), pp. 31–57.

———. "New Hampshire's Part in the Penobscot Expedition." *American Neptune*, 7 (July 1947), pp. 200–212.

———. "Price Control in New England During the Revolution." *New England Quarterly*, 19 (December 1946), pp. 453–473.

———. "Tory Associators of Portsmouth." *William and Mary Quarterly*, 3d Ser., (October), pp. 507–515.

Scotti, Anthony J., Jr. *Brutal Virtue: The Myth and Reality of Banastre Tarleton*. Bowie, Md.: Heritage Books, 2002.

Searcy, Martha C. "1779: The First Year of the British Occupation of Georgia." *Georgia Historical Quarterly*, 67 (Summer 1983), pp. 168–188.

———. *The Georgia-Florida Contest in the American Revolution 1776–1778*. University: University of Alabama Press, 1986.

Searle, Ambrose. *The American Journal of Ambrose Searle, Secretary to Lord Howe 1776–1778*. Edited by Edward H. Tatum, Jr. San Marino, Calif.: Huntington Library, 1940.

Seed, Geoffrey. "A British Spy in Philadelphia 1775–1777." *Pennsylvania Magazine of History and Biography*, 85 (January 1961), pp. 3–37.

Seidel, John L. "The Archaeology of the American Revolution: A Reappraisal and Case Study at the Continental Artillery Cantonment of 1778–1779, Pluckemin, New Jersey." Ph.D. dissertation, University of Pennsylvania, 1987.

Selby, John E. *The Revolution in Virginia, 1775–1783*. Charlottesville: University Press of Virginia, 1988.

Selesky, Harold E. *A Demographic Survey of the Continental Army that Wintered at Valley Forge, Pennsylvania, 1777–1778*. Valley Forge, Pennsylvania: Valley Forge National Historic Park, 1988.

Selig, Robert A. *Rochambeau's Cavalry: Lauzun's Legion in Connecticut, 1780–1781*. Hartford: Connecticut Historical Commission, 2000.

———. *Rochambeau in Connecticut: Tracing His Journey, Historic and Architectural Survey*. Hartford: Connecticut Historical Commission, State of Connecticut, 1999.

———. *The Washington-Rochambeau Revolutionary Route in the State of New York, 1781–1782*. Albany: Hudson River Valley Greenway, 2001.

Sellers, John R., et al. *Manuscript Sources in the Library of Congress for Research on the American Revolution*. Washington: Library of Congress, 1975.

———. *The Virginia Continental Line*. Williamsburg: Virginia Independence Bicentennial Commission, 1978.

Selsam, J. Paul. "The Political Revolution in Pennsylvania in 1776." *Pennsylvania History*, 1 (July 1934), pp. 147–157.

Servies, James A., editor. *The Log of H.M.S. Mentor, 1780–1781: A New Account of the British Navy at Pensacola.* Gainesville: University Presses of Florida, 1982.

Seumes, J. G. "Memoirs of a Hessian Conscript: J. G. Seumes' Reluctant Voyage to America." Translated by Margarete Woelfel. *William and Mary Quarterly*, 3d Ser., 5 (October 1949), pp. 533–570.

Seybolt, Robert F., editor. "A Contemporary British Account of General Sir William Howe's Military Operations in 1777." *American Antiquarian Society Proceedings*, New Ser., 40 (April 1930), pp. 69–92.

———. "A Note on the Casualties of April 19, and June 17, 1775." *New England Quarterly*, 4 (October 1931), pp. 525–528.

Seymour, George D. *Documentary Life of Nathan Hale Comprising All Available Official and Private Documents Bearing on the Life of the Patriot.* New Haven: Privately printed, 1941.

Seymour, William. *A Journal of the Southern Expedition, 1780–1783.* Wilmington: Historical Society of Delaware, 1896.

Shaw, Henry I., Jr. "Penobscot Assault—1779." *Military Affairs*, 17 (Summer 1953), pp. 83–94.

Shaw, Samuel. "Captain Samuel Shaw's Revolutionary War Letters to Captain Winthrop Sargent." Edited by N. B. W. *Pennsylvania Magazine of History and Biography*, 70 (July 1946), pp. 281–324.

Sheehan, Bernard W. "'The Famous Hair Buyer General': Henry Hamilton, George Rogers Clark, and the American Indian." *Indiana Magazine of History*, 79 (March 1983), pp. 1–28.

Sheina, Robert L. "Benjamin Stoddert, Politics, and the Navy." *American Neptune*, 36 (January 1976), pp. 54–68.

Sheldon, Richard N. "Editing a Historical Manuscript: Jared Sparks, Douglas Southall Freeman, and the Battle of Brandywine." *William and Mary Quarterly*, 3d Ser., 36 (April 1979), pp. 255–263.

Shelton, Hal T. *General Richard Montgomery and the American Revolution: From Redcoat to Rebel.* New York: New York University Press, 1994.

Sheps, Arthur. "The American Revolution and the Transformation of English Republicanism." *Historical Reflections*, 2 (Summer 1975), pp. 3–28.

Sherman, Andrew M. "The Mutiny of Anthony Wayne's Pennsylvania Troops in Morris County, New Jersey, Winter of 1780–1781." *American Irish Historical Society Journal*, 17 (1918), pp. 93–98.

Sherman, Sylvia J., editor. *Dubros Times: Selected Depositions of Maine Revolutionary War Veterans.* Augusta: Maine State Archives, 1975.

Sherman, William T. *Calendar and Record of the Revolutionary War in the South, 1780–1781.* At www.americanrevolution.org/warinthesouth.

Shipton, Clifford K., editor. *Early American Imprints, 1639–1800.* Microcopy edition of all titles published in America between 1639 and 1800, prepared by the American Antiquarian Society.

Shipton, Nathaniel N. "General Joseph Palmer: Scapegoat for the Rhode Island Fiasco of October, 1777." *New England Quarterly*, 39 (December 1966), pp. 498–512.

Shreve, L. G. *Tench Tilghman: The Life and Times of Washington's Aide-de-Camp.* Centreville, Md.: Tidewater Publishers, 1982.

Shuldham, Molyneux, Baron. *The Despatches of Molyneux Shuldham, Vice-Admiral of the Blue and Commander in Chief of His Britannic Majesty's Ships in North America, January–July, 1776.* Edited by Robert W. Neeser. New York: Naval History Society, 1913.

Shy, John. *The American Revolution.* Northbrook, Ill.: AHM Publishing Corp., 1973.

———. *A People Numerous and Armed: Reflections on the Military Struggle for American Independence.* 2nd edition. Ann Arbor: University of Michigan Press, 1990.

———. "Quartering His Majesty's Forces in New Jersey." *Proceedings of the New Jersey Historical Society*, 78 (April 1960), pp. 82–94.

———. *Toward Lexington: The Role of the British Army in the Coming of the American Revolution.* Princeton: Princeton University Press, 1965.

Siebert, Wilbur H. *The American Loyalists in the Eastern Seigniories and Townships of the Province of Quebec.* Ottawa: Royal Society of Canada, 1913.

———. "East Florida as a Refuge of Southern Loyalists, 1774–1785." *American Antiquarian Society Proceedings*, New Ser., 37 (October 1927), pp. 226–246.

———. *The Exodus of the Loyalists from Penobscot to Passamaquoddy.* Columbus: Ohio State University, 1914.

———. *George Washington and the Loyalists.* Worcester: American Antiquarian Society, 1934.

———. *The Legacy of the American Revolution to the British West Indies and Bahamas.* Columbus: Ohio State University, 1913.

———. *The Loyalist Refugees of New Hampshire.* Columbus: Ohio State University, 1916.

———. "The Loyalists and Six Nations Indians in the Niagara Peninsula." *Transactions of the Royal Society of Canada*, 3d Ser., 9 (June 1915), pp. 79–128.

———. *Loyalists in East Florida, 1774 to 1785: The Most Important Documents Pertaining thereto, edited with an Accompanying Narrative.* 2 vols. Deland: Florida State Historical Society, 1929.

———. "The Loyalists in West Florida and the Natchez District." *Mississippi Valley Historical Review*, 2 (March 1916), pp. 465–483.

———. *The Loyalists of Pennsylvania.* Columbus: Ohio State University, 1920.

———. "The Loyalist Troops of New England." *New England Quarterly*, 4 (January 1931), pp. 108–147.

———. "The Refugee Loyalists of Connecticut." *Transactions of the Royal Society of Canada*, 3d Ser., 10 (June 1916), pp. 75–92.

Sifton, Paul G., editor. "La Caroline Méridionale: Some French Sources of South Carolina Revolutionary History, with Two Unpublished Letters of Baron de Kalb." *South Carolina Historical Magazine*, 66 (April 1965), pp. 102–108.

Silverstone, Paul H. *The Sailing Navy, 1775–1854.* Annapolis: Naval Institute Press, 2001.

Simmons, Richard C., and Thomas, Peter D. G., editors. *Proceedings and Debates of the British Parliaments Respecting North America, 1754–1783.* 6 vols. White Plains, N. Y.: Kraus, 1982.

Simpson, James. "James Simpson's Reports on the Carolina Loyalists, 1779–1780." Edited by Alan S. Brown. *Journal of Southern History*, 21 (November 1955), pp. 513–519.

Sims, Lynn L. "The Military Career of John Lamb." Ph.D. dissertation, New York University, 1975.

Sizer, Theodore. *The Works of Colonel John Trumbull, Artist of the American Revolution*. Revised edition. New Haven: Yale University Press, 1967.

Skaggs, David C. "The Generalship of George Washington." *Military Review*, 54 (July 1974), pp. 3–10.

———. "From Lexington to Cuddalore: British Strategy in the War of American Independence." *Military Review*, 56 (April 1976), pp. 41–55.

———. "Origins of the Maryland Party System: The Constitutional Convention of 1776." *Maryland Historical Magazine*, 75 (June 1980), pp. 95–117.

———. *Roots of Maryland Democracy, 1753–1776*. Westport: Greenwood Press, 1973.

Skeen, C. Edward, Jr. *John Armstrong, Jr., 1758–1843: A Biography*. Syracuse: Syracuse University Press, 1981.

Skelton, William B. "Social Roots of the American Military Profession: The Officer Corps of America's First Peacetime Army, 1784–1789." *Journal of Military History*, 54 (October 1990), pp. 435–452.

Skemp, Sheila L. "Newport's Stamp Act Rioters: Another Look." *Rhode Island History*, 47 (May 1989), pp. 41–59.

———. *William Franklin: Son of a Patriot, Servant of a King*. New York: Oxford University Press, 1990.

Slaughter, Thomas P. *An American Aristocracy: The Livingstons*. Garden City: Doubleday, 1986.

Sloan, Robert W. "New Ireland: Loyalists in Eastern Maine during the American Revolution." Ph.D. dissertation, Michigan State University, 1971.

Smith, C. Page. *James Wilson: Founding Father, 1742–1798*. Chapel Hill: University of North Carolina Press, 1956.

Smith, Charles R. *Marines in the Revolution: A History of the Continental Marines in the American Revolution, 1775–1783*. Washington: History and Museums Div., Headquarters, U.S. Marine Corps, 1975.

Smith, Clifford N. *Brunswick Deserter-Immigrants of the American Revolution*. Dekalb: Westland Publications, 1974.

———. *Mercenaries from Ansbach and Bayreuth, Germany, who Remained in America after the Revolution*. Thompson, Ill.: Heritage House, 1974.

———. *Mercenaries from Hessen-Hanau*. Dekalb: Westland Publications, 1976.

———. *Muster Rolls and Prisoner-of-War Lists in American Archival Collections Pertaining to the German Mercenary Troops Who Served with the British Forces during the American Revolution*. Dekalb: Westland Publications, 1974.

Smith, Dwight L. "Josiah Harmar, Diplomatic Courier." *Pennsylvania Magazine of History and Biography*, 87 (October 1963), pp. 420–430.

Smith, Gordon B. "The Georgia Grenadiers." *Georgia Historical Quarterly*, 64 (Winter 1980), pp. 405–415.

Smith, James F. "The Rise of Artemas Ward, 1727–1777: Authority, Politics, and Military Life in Eighteenth-Century Massachusetts." Ph.D. dissertation, University of Colorado, Boulder, 1990.

Smith, Jonathan. "How Massachusetts Raised Her Troops in the Revolution." *Proceedings of the Massachusetts Historical Society*, 55 (June 1922), pp. 345–370.

———. *Peterborough, New Hampshire, in the American Revolution*. Peterborough: Peterborough Historical Society, 1913.

———. "Toryism in Westchester County during the War for Independence." *Proceedings of the Massachusetts Historical Society*, 48 (October 1914), pp. 15–35.

Smith, Joseph J., compiler. *Civil and Military List of Rhode Island*. 2 vols. Providence: Preston and Rounds, 1900–1901.

Smith, Justin H. *Arnold's March From Cambridge to Quebec; a Critical Study, together with a reprint of Arnold's Journal*. New York: G. P. Putnam's Sons, 1903.

———. *Our Struggle for the Fourteenth Colony; Canada in the American Revolution*. 2 vols. New York: G. P. Putnam's Sons, 1907.

Smith, Myron J., Jr. *Navies in the American Revolution: A Bibliography*. Metuchen, N.J.: Scarecrow Press, 1973.

Smith, Paul H., et al., editors. *Letters of Delegates to Congress, 1774–1789*. 26 vols. Washington: Library of Congress, 1976–2000.

———. *Loyalists and Redcoats: A Study in British Revolutionary Policy*. Chapel Hill: University of North Carolina Press, 1964.

———. "New Jersey Loyalists and the British 'Provincial' Corps in the War for Independence." *New Jersey History*, 87 (Summer 1969), pp. 69–78.

———. "Sir Guy Carleton, Peace Negotiations, and the Evacuation of New York." *Canadian Historical Review*, 50 (September 1969), pp. 245–264.

Smith, Philip C. F. *Captain Samuel Tucker (1747–1833): Continental Navy*. Salem, Massachusetts: Essex Institute, 1976.

Smith, Samuel S. *The Battle of Brandywine*. Monmouth Beach, N.J.: Philip Freneau Press, 1976.

———. *The Battle of Monmouth*. Monmouth Beach, N.J.: Philip Freneau Press, 1964.

———. *The Battle of Monmouth*. Trenton: New Jersey Historical Commission, 1975.

———. *The Battle of Princeton*. Monmouth Beach, N.J.: Philip Freneau Press, 1967.

———. *The Battle of Trenton*. Monmouth Beach, N.J.: Philip Freneau Press, 1965.

———. *The Fight for the Delaware, 1777*. Monmouth Beach, N.J.: Philip Freneau Press, 1970.

———. *Winter at Morristown, 1779–1780: The Darkest Hour*. Monmouth Beach, N.J.: Philip Freneau Press, 1979.

Smith, W. Calvin. "Mermaids Riding Alligators: Divided Command on the Southern Frontier, 1776–1778." *Florida Historical Quarterly*, 54 (April 1976), pp. 443–464.

Smoyer, Stanley C. "Indians as Allies in the Intercolonial Wars." *New York History*, 17 (October 1936), pp. 411–422.

Snapp, J. Russell. "William Henry Drayton: The Making of a Conservative Revolutionary." *Journal of Southern History*, 57 (November 1991), pp. 637–658.

Sosin, Jack M. *Agents and Merchants: British Colonial Policy and the Origins of the American Revolution, 1763–1775.* Lincoln: University of Nebraska Press, 1965.

———. *The Revolutionary Frontier 1763–1783.* New York: Holt, Rinehart and Winston, 1967.

———. "The Use of Indians in the War of the American Revolution: A Re-assessment of Responsibility." *Canadian Historical Review,* 46 (June 1965), pp. 101–121.

———. *Whitehall and the Wilderness: The Middle West in British Colonial Policy, 1760–1775.* Lincoln: University of Nebraska Press, 1961.

Sotto y Montes, Joaquín de. "Organización militar española de la Casa Borbón (siglo XVIII)." *Revista de Historia Militar,* 11 (#22, 1967), pp. 113–177.

Southern Campaigns of the American Revolution, at www.southerncampaign.org.

Spaulding, Ernest W. *His Excellency George Clinton (1739–1812), Critic of the Constitution.* New York: Macmillan Co., 1938.

Spector, Margaret M. *The American Department of the British Government, 1768–1782.* New York: Columbia University Press, 1940.

Spencer, Richard Henry. "Pulaski's Legion." *Maryland Historical Magazine,* 13 (September 1918), pp. 214–226.

Spinney, J. D. "Sir Samuel Hood at St. Kitt's: A Reassessment." *Mariner's Mirror,* 58 (May 1972), pp. 179–181.

Stacker, H. F. "Princeton." *Journal of the Society for Army Historical Research,* 13 (Winter 1934), pp. 214–228.

Stadtler, Erich. *The Ansbach-Bayreuth Troops during the American War of Independence 1777–1783.* Translated by Linda E. Murray. Yorktown: Privately printed, 1971. [German edition published in Nurnburg in 1956.]

Stanley, George F. G. *Canada Invaded 1775–1776.* Toronto: Hakkert, 1973.

———. "The Canadian Militia During the Colonial Period." *Journal of the Society for Army Historical Research,* 24 (Spring 1946), pp. 30–41.

Stapleton, Darwin H. "General Daniel Roberdeau and the Lead Mine Expedition, 1778–1779." *Pennsylvania History,* 38 (October 1971), pp. 361–371.

Stark, Bruce P. *Connecticut Signer: William Williams.* Chester, Ct.: Pequot Press, 1975.

Starkey, Armstrong. *European and Native American Warfare, 1675–1815.* Norman: University of Oklahoma Press, 1998.

———. "War and Culture, a Case Study: The Enlightenment and the Conduct of the British Army in America, 1755–1781." *War and Society,* 8 (May 1990), pp. 1–28.

Steegmann, A. Theodore, Jr. "New York Rangers in the Hampshire Grants 1776–1777." *Vermont History,* 51 (Fall 1983), pp. 238–248.

Steiner, Edward E. "Nicholas Ruxton Moore: Soldier, Farmer and Politician." *Maryland Historical Magazine,* 73 (December 1978), pp. 375–388.

Stenger, W. Jackson, Jr. "Tench Tilghman—George Washington's Aide." *Maryland Historical Magazine,* 77 (June 1982), pp. 136–153.

Stephenson, Orlando W. "The Supply of the American Revolutionary Army." Ph.D. dissertation, University of Michigan, 1919.

———. "The Supply of Gunpowder in 1776." *American Historical Review,* 30 (January 1925), pp. 271–281.

Steppler, Glenn A. "The Common Soldiers in the Age of George III, 1760–1793." Ph.D. dissertation, Oxford University, 1984.

Steuart, Rieman. *A History of the Maryland Line in the Revolutionary War, 1775–1783.* Towson: Society of the Cincinnati of Maryland, 1969.

Stevens, Benjamin F., editor. *The Campaign in Virginia 1781. An exact Reprint of Six Rare Pamphlets on the Clinton-Cornwallis Controversy.* 2 vols. London: Privately printed, 1888.

———. *Facsimiles of Manuscripts in European Archives Relating to America, 1773–1783.* 25 vols. London: Malby and Sons, 1889–1895.

———. *General Sir William Howe's Orderly Book at Charlestown, Boston and Halifax June 17, 1775 to May 26, 1776.* 1890. Reprint edition Port Washington, N.Y.: Kennikat Press, 1970.

Stevens, Paul L. "His Majesty's 'Savage' Allies: British Policy and the Northern Indians during the Revolutionary War—The Carleton Years, 1774–1778." Ph.D. dissertation, State University of New York at Buffalo, 1984.

———. "'To Invade The Frontiers of Kentucky?' The Indian Diplomacy of Philippe de Rocheblave, Britain's Acting Commandant at Kaskaskia, 1776–1778." *Filson Club History Quarterly,* 64 (April 1990), pp. 205–246.

Stewart, Bruce W. *Morristown: A Crucible of the American Revolution.* Trenton: New Jersey Historical Commission, 1975.

Stewart, Mrs. Catesby W. *The Life of Brigadier General William Woodford of the American Revolution.* 2 vols. Richmond: Whittet & Shepperson, 1973.

Stewart, Frank H. *History of the Battle of Red Bank.* Woodbury, N.J.: Board of Chosen Freeholders of Gloucester County, 1927.

Stewart, Robert A. *The History of Virginia's Navy of the Revolution.* Richmond: Mitchell & Hotchkiss, 1934.

Stickley, Julia W. "The Records of Deborah Sampson Gannett, Woman Soldier of the Revolution." *Prologue,* 4 (Winter 1972), pp. 233–241.

Still, William N., Jr. *North Carolina's Revolutionary War Navy.* Raleigh: North Carolina Department of Cultural Resources, 1976.

Stillé, Charles J. *Major-General Anthony Wayne and the Pennsylvania Line in the Continental Army.* Philadelphia: J. B. Lippincott, 1893.

Stinchcombe, William C. *The American Revolution and the French Alliance.* Syracuse: Syracuse University Press, 1969.

Stirke, Henry. "A British Officer's Revolutionary War Journal, 1776–1778." Edited by S. Sydney Bradford. *Maryland Historical Magazine,* 56 (June 1961), pp. 150–175.

Stoesen, Alexander R. "The British Occupation of Charleston, 1780–1782." *South Carolina Historical Magazine,* 63 (April 1962), pp. 71–82.

Stone, Rufus B. "Brodhead's Raid on the Senecas: The Story of a Little Known Expedition in 1779 From Fort Pitt to Destroy the Indian Villages on the Upper Allegheny." *Western Pennsylvania Historical Magazine,* 7 (April 1924), pp. 88–101.

Storch, Neil T. "The Recall of Silas Deane." *Connecticut Historical Society Bulletin*, 38 (January 1973), pp. 30–32.

Storrs, Experience. "Connecticut Farmers at Bunker Hill: The Diary of Colonel Experience Storrs." Edited by Wladimir Hagelin and Ralph A. Brown. *New England Quarterly*, 28 (March 1955), pp. 72–93.

Stout, Harry S. "Religion, Communications, and the Ideological Origins of the American Revolution." *William and Mary Quarterly*, 3d Ser., 34 (October 1977), pp. 519–541.

Stout, Neil R. *The Royal Navy in America, 1760–1775: A Study of Enforcement of British Colonial Policy in the Era of the American Revolution*. Annapolis: Naval Institute Press, 1973.

Stowe, Gerald C., and Jac Weller. "Revolutionary West Point: 'The Key to the Continent.'" *Military Affairs*, 19 (Summer 1955), pp. 81–98.

Strachan, Hew. *British Military Uniforms, 1768–1796: The Dress of the British Army from Official Sources*. London: Arms and Armour Press, 1975.

Stroh, Oscar H. *Thompson's Battalion and/or The First Continental Infantry*. Harrisburg: Graphic Services, 1975.

Stryker, William S. *Battles of Trenton and Princeton*. Boston: Houghton, Mifflin and Co., 1898.

———. *The Battle of Monmouth*. Edited by William Starr Myers. Princeton: Princeton University Press, 1927.

Stryker, William S., et al., editors. *Documents Relating to the Revolutionary History of the State of New Jersey*. [Archives of the State of New Jersey, 2d Ser.] 5 vols. Trenton: State of New Jersey, 1901–1917.

Stryker, William S., compiler. *Official Register of the Officers and Men of New Jersey in the Revolutionary War. With Added Digest and Revision* (1911) by James W. S. Campbell. Reprint edition Baltimore: Genealogical Publishing Co., 1967.

Stuart, Reginald C. 'Engines of Tyranny': Recent Historiography on Standing Armies during the Era of the American Revolution." *Canadian Journal of History*, 19 (August 1984), pp. 183–199.

———. *War and American Thought: From the Revolution to the Monroe Doctrine*. Kent: Kent State University Press, 1982.

———. "War, Society and the 'New' Military History of the United States." *Canadian Review of American Studies*, 8 (Spring 1977), pp. 1–10.

Sturgill, Claude. "The Decision to Re-Arm St. Augustine." *Journal of the Society for Army Historical Research*, 49 (Winter 1971), 201–211.

Sturgill, Claude, editor. "Rochambeau's memoire de la guerre en Amerique." *Virginia Magazine of History and Biography*, 78 (January 1970), pp. 34–64.

Stutesman, John H., Jr. "Colonel Armand and Washington's Cavalry." *New-York Historical Society Quarterly*, 45 (January 1961), pp. 5–42.

Sullivan, James, and Alexander C. Flick, editors. *Minutes of the Albany Committee of Correspondence, 1775–1778*. 2 vols. Albany: University of the State of New York, 1923–1925.

Sullivan, John. *Letters and Papers of Major-General John Sullivan, Continental Army*. Edited by Otis G. Hammond. 3 vols. Concord: New Hampshire Historical Society, 1930–1939.

Sullivan, Thomas. "The Common British Soldier—From the Journal of Thomas Sullivan, 49th Regiment of Foot." Edited by S. Sydney Bradford. *Maryland Historical Magazine*, 62 (September 1967), pp. 219–253.

Sutherland, Stella H. *Population Distribution in Colonial America*. New York: Columbia University Press, 1936.

Sutherland, William, and Richard Pope. *Late News of the Excursions and Ravages of the King's Troops on the nineteenth of April 1775*. Edited by Harold Murdock. Cambridge, Mass.: Harvard University Press, 1927.

Sutton, Robert M. "George Rogers Clark and the Campaign in the West: The Five Major Documents." *Indiana Magazine of History*, 76 (December 1980), pp. 334–345.

Svejda, George J. *Quartering, Disciplining, and Supplying the Army at Morristown, 1779–1780*. Washington: Department of the Interior, 1970.

Swan, Jedediah. *Colonial and Revolutionary Morris County*. Morristown: Morris County Heritage Commission, 1975.

Sweeny, Lenora H. *Amherst County, Virginia in the Revolution Including Extracts from the 'Lost Order Book' 1773–1782*. Lynchburg: J. P. Bell Co., 1951.

Swiggett, Howard. *War Out of Niagara; Walter Butler and the Tory Rangers*. New York: Columbia University Press, 1933.

Syrett, David. "American and British Naval Historians and the American Revolutionary War, 1875–1980." *American Neptune*, 42 (July 1982), pp. 179–192.

———. The British Armed Forces in the American Revolutionary War: Publications, 1875–1999." *Journal of Military History*, 63 (July 1999), pp. 147–164.

———. "D'Estaing's Decision to Steer for Antigua 28 November 1778." *Mariner's Mirror*, 61 (May 1975), pp. 155–162.

———. "Returns of His Majesty's Forces, 1768–1802." *Journal of the Society for Army Historical Research*, 60 (Summer 1982), pp. 118–123.

———. *The Royal Navy in American Waters, 1775–1783*. Aldershot, England: Scolar Press, 1989.

———. *The Royal Navy in European Waters during the American Revolutionary War*. Columbia: University of South Carolina Press, 1998.

———. *Shipping and the American War 1775–83: A Study of British Transport Organization*. London: Athlone Press, 1970.

Szatmary, David. *Shays' Rebellion: The Making of an Agrarian Insurrection*. Amherst, Massachusetts: University of Massachusetts Press, 1980.

Szymanski, Leszek. *Kazimierz Pulaski in America: A Monograph, 1777–1779*. New York: A. Poray, 1979.

Taaffe, Stephen R. *The Philadelphia Campaign, 1777–1778*. Lawrence: University Press of Kansas, 2003.

Tagney, Ronald N. *A County in Revolution: Essex County at the Dawning of Independence*. Manchester, Massachusetts: Cricket Press, 1976.

———. *The World Turned Upside Down: Essex County during America's Turbulent Years, 1763–1790*. West Newbury: Essex County History, 1989.

Taliaferro, Benjamin. *The Orderly Book of Captain Benjamin Taliaferro: 2d Virginia Detachment, Charleston, South Carolina,*

1780. Edited by Lee A. Wallace, Jr. Richmond: Virginia State Library, 1980.

Talman, James J., editor. *Loyalist Narratives from Upper Canada.* Toronto: The Champlain Society, 1946.

Tarleton, Banastre. "New War Letters of Banastre Tarleton." Edited by Richard M. Ketchum. *New-York Historical Society Quarterly*, 51 (January 1967), pp. 61–81.

Tartar, Brent, editor. "The Orderly Book of the Second Virginia Regiment, September 27, 1775–April 15, 1776." *Virginia Magazine of History and Biography*, 85 (April, July 1977), pp. 156–183, 302–336.

Taylor, Alan. *Liberty Men and Great Proprietors: The Revolutionary Settlement on the Maine Frontier, 1760–1820.* Chapel Hill: University of North Carolina Press, 1990.

Taylor, Robert J. "American Constitutions and the Right to Bear Arms." *Proceedings of the Massachusetts Historical Society*, 95 (1983), pp. 52–66.

———. "Trial at Trenton." *William and Mary Quarterly*, 3d Ser., 26 (October 1969), pp. 521–547.

———. *Western Massachusetts in the American Revolution.* Providence: Brown University Press, 1954.

Tebbenhoff, Edward H. "The Associated Loyalists: An Aspect of Militant Loyalism." *New-York Historical Society Quarterly*, 63 (April 1979), pp. 115–144.

Thacher, James. *Military Journal of the American Revolution.* 1823. Reprinted Hartford: Hurlbut, Williams & Co., 1862.

Thane, Elswyth. *The Fighting Quaker: Nathaniel [sic] Greene.* New York: Hawthorne Books, 1972.

Thayer, Theodore. *As We Were: The Story of Old Elizabethtown.* Newark: New Jersey Historical Society, 1964.

———. *The Making of a Scapegoat: Washington and Lee at Monmouth.* Port Washington, N.Y.: Kennikat Press, 1976.

———. *Nathaniel [sic] Greene: Strategist of the American Revolution.* New York: Twayne Publishers, 1960.

———. "The War in New Jersey: Battles, Alarums and the Men of the Revolution." *Proceedings of the New Jersey Historical Society*, 71 (April 1953), pp. 83–110.

———. *Yorktown, Campaign of Strategic Options.* Philadelphia: Lippincott, 1975.

Thomas, Earle. *Sir John Johnson: Loyalist Baronet.* Toronto: Dundurn Press, 1986.

Thomas, Howard. *Marinus Willett, Soldier Patriot, 1740–1830.* Prospect, N.Y.: Prospect Books, 1954.

Thomas, Peter D. G. *British Politics and the Stamp Act Crisis: The First Phase of the American Revolution, 1763–1767.* Oxford, England: Oxford University Press, 1975.

———. *Tea Party to Independence: The Third Phase of the American Revolution, 1773–1776.* Oxford, England: Oxford University Press, 1991.

———. *The Townshend Duties Crisis: The Second Phase of the American Revolution, 1767–1773.* New York: Oxford University Press, 1987.

Thomas, William H. B. *Patriots of the Upcountry: Orange County, Virginia in the Revolution.* Orange County Bicentennial Commission, 1976.

Thomas, William S. "Revolutionary Camps of the Hudson Highlands." *Quarterly Journal of the New York State Historical Association*, 2 (July 1921), pp. 1–45.

Thompson, Buchanan P. *Spain: Forgotten Ally of the American Revolution.* North Quincy, Mass.: Christopher Publishing House, 1976.

Thompson, David G. "Thomas Bentley and the American Revolution in Illinois." *Illinois Historical Journal*, 83 (Spring 1989), pp. 2–12.

Thompson, Mack F. "The Ward-Hopkins Controversy and the American Revolution in Rhode Island: An Interpretation." *William and Mary Quarterly*, 3d Ser., 16 (July 1959), pp. 363–375.

Thompson, Marvin G. *Connecticut Entrepreneur: Christopher Leffingwell.* Hartford: American Revolution Bicentennial Commission of Connecticut, 1979.

Thompson, William Y. *Israel Shreve, Revolutionary War Officer.* Ruston, La.: McGinty Trust Fund Publications, 1979.

Thwaits, Ruben G., and Louise P. Kellogg, editors. *Frontier Defense on the Upper Ohio, 1777–1778.* Madison: Wisconsin Historical Society, 1912.

———. editors. *The Revolution on the Upper Ohio, 1775–1777.* Madison: Wisconsin Historical Society, 1908.

Tilley, John A. *The British Navy and the American Revolution.* Columbia: University of South Carolina Press, 1987.

Tiedemann, Joseph S. "Patriots by Default: Queens County, New York, and the British Army, 1776–1783." *William and Mary Quarterly*, 3d Ser., 43 (January 1986), pp. 35–63.

———. "Queens County, New York, Quakers in the American Revolution: Loyalists or Neutrals?" *Historical Magazine of the Protestant Episcopal Church*, 52 (September 1983), pp. 215–227.

———. *Reluctant Revolutionaries: New York City and the Road to Independence, 1763–1776*, Ithaca, New York: Cornell University Press, 1997.

Tinder, Robert W. "Extraordinary Measures: Maryland and the Yorktown Campaign, 1781." *Maryland Historical Magazine*, 95 (Summer 2000), pp. 133–159.

Tomlinson, Abraham, compiler. *The Military Journals of Two Private Soldiers, 1758–1775 .* Poughkeepsie: Abraham Tomlinson, 1855.

Torres Ramirez, Bibiano. *Alejandro O'Reilly en las Indias.* Sevilla: Escuela de Estudios Hispano Americanos, 1969.

Tourtellot, Arthur B. *William Diamond's Drum.* Garden City: Doubleday and Co., 1959.

Tousey, Thomas G. "York As A Supply Center for the Revolutionary Army." *Papers of the Historical Society of York County*, New Ser., 5 (1939), pp. 1–11.

Tracy, Nicholas. "British Assessments of French and Spanish Naval Reconstruction 1763–1778." *Mariner's Mirror*, 61 (February 1975), pp. 73–85.

Treacy, Mildred F. *Prelude to Yorktown: The Southern Campaign of Nathaniel [sic] Greene, 1780–1781.* Chapel Hill: University of North Carolina Press, 1963.

Tretler, David A. "The Making of a Revolutionary General—Nathanael Greene: 1742–1779." Ph.D. dissertation, Rice University, 1986.

Triber, Jayne E. *A True Republican: The Life of Paul Revere.* Amherst, Massachusetts: University of Massachusetts Press, 1998.

Troiani, Don, Earl J. Coates, and James L. Kochan. *Don Troiani's Soldiers in America, 1754–1865,* Mechanicsburg, Pennsylvania: Stackpole Books, 1998.

Troxler, Carole W. "Loyalist Refugees and the British Evacuation of East Florida, 1783–1785." *Florida Historical Quarterly,* 60 (July 1981), pp. 1–28.

———. "The Migration of Carolina and Georgia Loyalists to Nova Scotia and New Brunswick." Ph.D. dissertation, University of North Carolina at Chapel Hill, 1974.

———. "Refuge, Resistance, and Reward: The Southern Loyalists' Claim on East Florida." *Journal of Southern History,* 55 (November 1989), pp. 563–596.

Trudel, Marcel. *Louis XVI, le Congrès Américaine et la Canada 1774–1789.* Quebec: Publications de l'Universite Laval, 1949.

———. "Le Traite de 1783 Laisse Le Canada à L'Angleterre." *Revue d'Histoire de l'Amérique Française,* 3 (September 1949), pp. 179–199.

Trumbull, J. Hammond, and Charles J. Hoadley, compilers. *The Public Records of the Colony of Connecticut.* 15 vols. Hartford: Various publishers, 1850–1890.

Trumbull, John. *The Autobiography of Colonel John Trumbull, Patriot-Artist, 1756–1843. Containing a Supplement to The Works of Colonel John Trumbull.* Edited by Theodore Sizer. New Haven: Yale University Press, 1953.

Trumbull, Jonathan, Sr. "The Trumbull Papers." *Massachusetts Historical Society Collections,* 5th Ser., 9–10; 7th Ser., 2–3 (1885–1902).

Trussell, John B. B., Jr. *Birthplace of an Army: A Study of the Valley Forge Encampment.* Harrisburg: Pennsylvania Historical and Museum Commission, 1976.

———. "He Never Missed His Aim." *Parameters,* 6 (1976), pp. 48–59.

———. *The Pennsylvania Line: Regimental Organization and Operations, 1775–1783.* Harrisburg: Pennsylvania Historical and Museum Commission, 1977.

———. "The Role of the Professional Military Officer in the Preservation of the Republic." *Western Pennsylvania Historical Magazine,* 60 (January 1977), pp. 1–21.

Tucker, Robert W., and David C. Hendrickson. *The Fall of the First British Empire: Origins of the War of American Independence.* Baltimore: Johns Hopkins University Press, 1982.

Tyler, John W. *Connecticut Loyalists: An Analysis of Loyalist Land Confiscations in Greenwich, Stamford and Norwalk.* New Orleans: Polyanthos, 1977.

———. *Smugglers and Patriots: Boston Merchants and the Advent of the American Revolution.* Boston: Northwestern University Press, 1986.

Ubbelohde, Carl. *The Vice-Admiralty Courts and the American Revolution.* Chapel Hill: University of North Carolina Press, 1960.

Uhlendorf, Bernard A., editor. *Revolution in America: Confidential Letters 1776–1784 of Adjutant General Major Baurmeister of the Hessian Forces.* New Brunswick: Rutgers University Press, 1957.

———. *The Siege of Charleston with an Account of the Province of South Carolina: Diaries and Letters of Hessian Officers From the von Jungkenn Papers in the William L. Clements Library.* Ann Arbor: University of Michigan Press, 1938.

Uhlendorf, Bernard A., and Edna Vosper, editors. *Letters from Major Baurmeister to Colonel von Jungkenn Written during the Philadelphia Campaign 1777–1778.* Philadelphia: Historical Society of Pennsylvania, 1937.

Ultee, Maarten, editor. *Adapting to Conditions: War and Society in the Eighteenth Century.* University: University of Alabama Press, 1986.

Underdal, Stanley J., editor. *Military History of the American Revolution: The Proceedings of the 6th Military History Symposium United States Air Force Academy 10–11 October 1974.* Washington: Office of Air Force History, 1976:
　　Calhoon, Robert M., "Civil, Revolutionary, or Partisan: The Loyalists and the Nature of the War for Independence," pp. 93–108.
　　Gruber, Ira D., "The Origins of British Strategy in the War for American Independence," pp. 38–50.
　　Kohn, Richard. "The Murder of the Militia System in the Aftermath of the American Revolution," pp. 110–126.
　　Palmer, David R., "American Strategy Reconsidered," pp.52–64.
　　Scheer, George F., "Washington and His Lieutenants: Some Problems in Command," pp. 139–150.
　　Sellers, John R., "The Common Soldier in the American Revolution," pp. 151–161.

Underwood, Wynn. "Indian and Tory Raids on the Otter Valley, 1777–1782." *Vermont Quarterly,* New Ser., 15 (October 1947), pp. 195–221.

Upham, George B. "Burgoyne's Great Mistake." *New England Quarterly,* 3 (October 1930), pp. 657–680.Upton, Emory. *The Military Policy of the United States.* Washington: Government Printing Office, 1912.

Upton, Richard F. *Revolutionary New Hampshire: An Account of the Social and Political Forces Underlying the Transition from Royal Province to American Commonwealth.* Hanover: Dartmouth College Publications, 1936.

Urwin, Gregory J. W. "Cornwallis in Virginia: A Reappraisal." *Military Collector and Historian,* 37 (Fall 1985), pp. 111–126.

Vaca de Osma, José Antonio. *Intervención de España en la guerra de la independencia de los Estados Unidos.* Madrid: Aldus, S. A., 1952.

Valentine, Alan C. *Lord George Germain.* New York: Oxford University Press, 1962.

———. *Lord North.* 2 vols. Norman: University of Oklahoma Press, 1967.

———. *Lord Stirling.* New York: Oxford University Press, 1969.

Van Atta, John R. "Conscription in Revolutionary Virginia: The Case of Culpeper County, 1780–1781." *Virginia Magazine of History and Biography,* 92 (July 1984), pp. 263–281.

Van Cortlandt, Philip. *Philip Van Cortlandt's Revolutionary War Correspondence and Memoirs.* Edited by Jacob Judd. Tarrytown: Sleepy Hollow Restorations, 1976.

Van Doren, Carl. *Mutiny in January.* New York: Viking Press, 1943.

———. *Secret History of the American Revolution.* New York: Viking Press, 1941.

Van Schreevan, William J., et al., editors. *Revolutionary Virginia: The Road to Independence.* 7 vols. Charlottesville: University

Press of Virginia for the Virginia Independence Bicentennial Commission, 1973–1983.

Van Tyne, Claude H. "French Aid before the Alliance of 1778." *American Historical Review*, 31 (October 1925), pp. 20–40.

Vereger, Jean-Baptiste-Antoine de. *Rochambeau's Army, 1780, 1781, 1782, 1783, Vol. 1: The Journals of Clermont-Crevecoeur, Verger, and Berthier*. Princeton: Princeton University Press, 1972.

Vermeule, Cornelius C. "Revolutionary Days in Old Somerset." *Proceedings of the New Jersey Historical Society*, New Ser., 8 (October 1923), pp. 265–281.

———. "Service of the New Jersey Militia in the Revolutionary War." *Proceedings of the New Jersey Historical Society*, New Ser., 9 (July 1924), pp. 234–248.

———. "Some Revolutionary Incidents in The Raritan Valley." *Proceedings of the New Jersey Historical Society*, New Ser., 6 (April 1921), pp. 73–86.

Ver Steeg, Clarence L. *Robert Morris, Revolutionary Financier*. Philadelphia: University of Pennsylvania Press, 1954.

Villers, David H. "The British Army and the Connecticut Loyalists During the War of Independence, 1775–1783." *Connecticut Historical Society Bulletin*, 43 (July 1978), pp. 65–80.

Villiers, Patrick. *Le commerce colonial atlantique et la guerre d'Indépendance des Etats–Unis d'Amérique a été publié aux Etats-Unis*. New York: Arno Press, 1977.

Viñes Millet, Cristina. "El Cuerpo de Inválidos y su Organización en el contexto de la Reforma del Ejército del siglo XVIII." *Revista de Historia Militar*, 26 (no. 52, 1982), pp. 79–116.

Virginia. *Journals of the Council of the State of Virginia*. 3 vols. Edited by Henry R. McIlwaine and Wilmer L. Hall. Richmond: Virginia State Library, 1931–1952.

———. *Official Letters of the Governors of the State of Virginia*. 3 vols. Edited by Henry R. McIlwaine. Richmond: Virginia State Library, 1926–1929.

Vivian, Francis. "A Defence of Sir William Howe With A New Interpretation of His Action in New Jersey, June 1777." *Journal of the Society for Army Historical Research*, 44 (Summer 1967), pp. 69–83.

Vivian, James F., and Jean H. Vivian. "Congressional Indian Policy during the War for Independence: The Northern Department." *Maryland Historical Magazine*, 63 (September 1968), pp. 241–274.

Vivian, Jean H. "Military Land Bounties during the Revolutionary and Confederation Periods." *Maryland Historical Magazine*, 61 (September 1966), pp. 231–256.

———. "Thomas Stone and the Reorganization of the Maryland Council of Safety, 1776." *Maryland Historical Magazine*, 69 (Fall 1974), pp. 271–278.

Wade, Arthur P. "Fort Winyaw at Georgetown, 1776–1923." *South Carolina Historical Magazine*, 84 (October 1983), pp. 214–149.

Wade, Arthur P., and Robert Lively. *This Glorious Cause: Two Company Officers in Washington's Army*. Princeton, New Jersey: Princeton University Press, 1958.

Wade, Herbert T. "Nathaniel Wade and His Ipswich Minute Men." *Essex Institute Historical Collections*, 89 (July 1953), pp. 213–252.

———. "Colonel Wade and the Massachusetts State Troops in Rhode Island—1777–78." *Essex Institute Historical Collections*, 89 (October 1953), pp. 357–375.

———. "The Massachusetts Brigade on the Hudson, 1780: Nathaniel Wade at West Point." *Essex Institute Historical Collections*, 90 (January, March 1954), pp. 84–99, 167–190.

Wagner, Frederick. *Submarine Fighter of the American Revolution: The Story of David Bushnell*. New York: Dodd, Mead & Co., 1963.

Wainwright, Nicholas B. *The Irvine Story*. Philadelphia: Historical Society of Pennsylvania, 1964.

Walker, Anthony. *So Few The Brave (Rhode Island Continentals 1775–1783)*. Newport: Seafield Press, 1981.

Walker, James W. S. *The Black Loyalists: The Search for a Promised Land in Nova Scotia and Sierra Leone, 1783–1870*. New York: Africana Publishing Co., 1976.

———. "Blacks as American Loyalists: The Slaves' War for Independence." *Historical Reflections*, 2 (Summer 1975), pp. 51–67.

Walker, Paul K., editor. *Engineers of Independence: A Documentary History of the Army Engineers in the American Revolution, 1775–1783*. Washington: Government Printing Office, 1981.

Wallace, Willard M. *Appeal to Arms: A Military History of the American Revolution*. New York: Harper and Brothers, 1951.

———. *Connecticut's Dark Star of the Revolution: General Benedict Arnold*. Hartford: American Revolution Bicentennial Commission of Connecticut, 1978.

———. *Traitorous Hero: The Life and Fortunes of Benedict Arnold*. New York: Harper, 1954.

Waller, George M. "George Rogers Clark and the American Revolution in the West." *Indiana Magazine of History*, 72 (March 1976), pp. 1–20.

Walsh, Richard. "The Charleston Mechanics: A Brief Study, 1760–1776." *South Carolina Historical and Genealogical Magazine*, 60 (July 1959), pp. 123–144.

———. "Christopher Gadsden: Radical or Conservative Revolutionary?" *South Carolina Historical Magazine*, 63 (October 1962), pp. 195–203.

Ward, A. Gertrude. "John Ettwein and the Moravians in the Revolution." *Pennsylvania History*, 1 (October 1934), pp. 191–201.

Ward, Christopher. *The Delaware Continentals, 1776–1783*. Wilmington: Historical Society of Delaware, 1941.

———. *The War of the Revolution*. Edited by John R. Alden. 2 vols. New York: Macmillan, 1952.

Ward, Harry M. *Between the Lines: The Banditti of the American Revolution*. Westport, Connecticut: Praeger Publishers, 2001.

———. *Charles Scott and the 'Spirit of '76'*. Charlottesville: University Press of Virginia, 1988.

———. *The Department of War, 1781–1795*. Pittsburgh: University of Pittsburgh Press, 1962.

———. *Duty, Honor or Country: General George Weedon and the American Revolution*. Philadelphia: American Philosophical Society, 1979.

———. *General William Maxwell and the New Jersey Continentals*. Westport, Connecticut: Greenwood Press, 1997.

————. *Major General Adam Stephen and the Cause of American Liberty.* Charlottesville: University Press of Virginia, 1989.

————. *The War for Independence and Transformation of American Society.* London, England: UCL Press, 1999.

Ward, Harry M., and Harold E. Greer, Jr. *Richmond during the Revolution, 1775–83.* Charlottesville: University Press of Virginia, 1977.

Ward, Samuel. *Correspondence of Governor Samuel Ward, May 1775–March 1776.* Edited by Bernhard Knollenberg and compiled by Clifford P. Monahan. Providence: Rhode Island Historical Society, 1952.

Ward, Townsend. "Charles Armand Tuffin, Marquis de la Rouerie." *Pennsylvania Magazine of History and Biography*, 2 (1878), pp. 1–34.

Wardner, Henry S. "The Haldimand Negotiations." *Vermont Historical Society Proceedings*, New Ser., 2 (March 1931), pp. 3–29.

Waring, Alice N. *The Fighting Elder: Andrew Pickens (1739–1817).* Columbia: University of South Carolina Press, 1962.

Waring, Joseph I., editor. "A Report from the Continental General Hospital in 1780." *South Carolina Historical and Genealogical Magazine*, 42 (October 1941), pp. 147–148.

Ware, John D. "The Bernard Romans-John Ellis Letters, 1772–1774." *Florida Historical Quarterly*, 52 (July 1973), pp. 51–61.

Washington, George. "George Washington Papers at the Library of Congress," at memory.loc.gov/ammem.

————. "George Washington Papers at the University of Virginia," at gwpapers.virginia.edu.

————. *The Papers of George Washington: Revolutionary War Series.* 14 vols. to date. Edited by Philander D. Chase, et al. Charlottesville: University Press of Virginia, 1985–2004.

————. *Writings of George Washington.* Edited by John Rhodehamel. New York: Library of America, 1997.

————. *The Writings of George Washington from the Original Manuscript Sources, 1745–1799.* Edited by John C. Fitzpatrick. 39 vols. Washington: Government Printing Office, 1931–1944.

Washington, Ida H., and Paul A. Washington. *Carleton's Raid.* Canaan, N.H.: Phoenix, 1977.

Waterman, Joseph M. *With Sword and Lancet: The Life of General Hugh Mercer.* Richmond: Garrett and Massie, 1941.

Watt, Gavin K. *The Burning of the Valleys: Daring Raids from Canada against the New York Frontier in the Fall of 1780.* Revised Edition. Toronto: Dundurn Press, 1997.

————. *Rebellion in the Mohawk Valley: The St. Leger Expedition of 1777.* Toronto: Dundurn Press, 2002.

Watterson, John S. *Thomas Burke: Restless Revolutionary.* Washington: University Press of America, 1980.

Wayne, Anthony. *Anthony Wayne, a Name in Arms: Soldier, Diplomat, Defender of Expansion Westward of a Nation; the Wayne-Knox-Pickering-McHenry Correspondence.* Edited by Richard C. Knopf. Pittsburgh: University of Pittsburgh Press, 1959.

Wead, Eunice. "British Public Opinion of the Peace with America, 1782." *American Historical Review*, 34 (April 1929), pp. 513–531.

Weaver, Glenn. *Jonathan Trumbull: Connecticut's Merchant Magistrate (1710–1785).* Hartford: Connecticut Historical Society, 1956.

Webb, Anne Baxter. "On the Eve of Revolution: Northampton, Massachusetts, 1750–1775." Ph.D. dissertation, University of Minnesota, 1976.

Webb, Samuel Blachley. *Correspondence and Journals of Samuel Blachley Webb.* Edited by Worthington Chauncey Ford. 3 vols. New York: Privately printed, 1893–1894.

Webster, John C. *Sir Brooke Watson, Friend of the Loyalists.* Sackville, N.B.: N.p., 1924.

Wehtje, Myron F. "Fear of British Influence in Boston, 1783–1787." *Historical Journal of Massachusetts*, 18 (Summer 1990), pp. 154–163.

Weigley, Russell F. *The American Way of War; a History of the United States Military Strategy and Policy.* New York: Macmillan, 1973.

————. *History of the United States Army.* New York: Macmillan, 1964.

————. *The Partisan War: The South Carolina Campaign of 1780–1782.* Columbia: South Carolina Tricentennial Commission, 1970.

Weinmeister, Oscar K., Jr. "The Hessian Grenadier Battalions in North America, 1776–1783." *Military Collector and Historian*, 27 (Winter 1975), pp. 148–153.

Weir, Robert M. *The Last of American Freemen: The Political Culture of the Colonial and Revolutionary South.* Macon, Georgia: Mercer University Press, 1986.

————. *"A Most Important Epocha"; The Coming of the Revolution in South Carolina.* Columbia: University of South Carolina Press for the South Carolina Tricentennial Commission, 1970.

Weis, Frederick L. "Asa Whitcomb, a Stirling Patriot." *Proceedings of the Massachusetts Historical Society*, 67 (1941–1944), pp. 111–127.

Weller, Jac. "Guns of Destiny: Field Artillery in the Trenton-Princeton Campaign, 25 December 1776 to 3 January 1776." *Military Affairs*, 20 (Spring 1956), pp. 1–11.

————. "Irregular but Effective: Partisan Weapons Tactics in the American Revolution, Southern Theater." *Military Affairs*, 21 (Fall 1957), pp. 119–131.

————. "The Irregular War in the South." *Military Affairs*, 24 (Fall 1960), pp. 124–136.

————. "Revolutionary War Artillery in the South." *Georgia Historical Quarterly*, 46 (September-December 1962), pp. 250–273, 377–387.

Wells, Robert V. *The Population of the British Colonies in American Before 1776; a Survey of Census Data.* Princeton, N.J.: Princeton University Press, 1975.

Wells, Thomas L. "An Inquiry into the Resignation of Quartermaster General Nathanael Greene in 1780." *Rhode Island History*, 24 (April 1965), pp. 41–48.

Weskerna, Eleanor, and F. W. William Maurer. *"The Flower of the Virginian" and the Massacre Near Old Tappan: September 28, 1778.* River Vale, N.J.: Baylor's Dragoons Memorial Committee, 1978.

Wheeler, Earl M. "Development and Organization of the North Carolina Militia." *North Carolina Historical Review*, 41 (July 1964), pp. 307–323.

————. "The Role of the North Carolina Militia in the Beginning of the American Revolution." Ph.D. dissertation, Tulane University, 1969.

Wheeler, Joseph L., and Mabel A. Wheeler. *The Mount Independence-Hubbardton 1776 Military Road.* Benson, Vt.: authors, 1968.

White, David O. *Connecticut's Black Soldiers 1775–1783.* Chester: Pequot Press, 1973.

White, Donald W. "A Local History Approach to the American Revolution: Chatham, New Jersey." *New Jersey History*, 96 (Spring-Summer 1978), pp. 49–64.

————. *A Village at War: Chatham, New Jersey, and the American Revolution.* Rutherford, N.J.: Fairleigh Dickenson University Press, 1979.

————. "Census Making and Local History: In Quest of the People of a Revolutionary Village." *Prologue*, 14 (Fall 1982), pp. 157–168.

White, Herbert H. "British Prisoners of War in Hartford during the Revolution." *Connecticut Historical Society Bulletin*, 19 (July 1954), pp. 65–81.

White, J. Todd, and Charles H. Lesser. *Fighters for Independence: A Guide to the Sources of Biographical Information on Soldiers and Sailors of the American Revolution.* Chicago: University of Chicago Press, 1977.

White, Richard. *The Middle Ground: Indians, Empires, and Republics in the Great Lakes Region, 1650–1815.* New York: Cambridge University Press, 1991.

White, William E. "The Independent Companies of Virginia, 1774–1775." *Virginia Magazine of History and Biography*, 86 (April 1978), pp. 149–162.

Whiteley, W. H. "The British Navy and the Siege of Quebec, 1775–1776." *Canadian Historical Review*, 61 (March 1980), pp. 3–27.

Whitridge, Arnold. "The Marquis de la Rouerie, Brigadier General in the Continental Army." *Proceedings of the Massachusetts Historical Society*, 79 (1968), pp. 47–63.

————. *Rochambeau, America's Neglected Founding Father.* New York: Macmillan and Co., 1965.

Whittemore, Charles P. *A General of the Revolution: John Sullivan of New Hampshire.* New York: Columbia University Press, 1961.

Wickwire, Franklin B. *British Subministers and Colonial America, 1763–1783.* Princeton: Princeton University Press, 1966.

Wickwire, Franklin B., and Mary Wickwire. *Cornwallis: The American Adventure.* Boston: Houghton Mifflin, 1970.

Wilderson, Paul, editor. "The Raids on Fort William and Mary: Some New Evidence." *Historical New Hampshire*, 30 (Fall 1975), pp. 178–202.

Wilkie, Everett C., Jr. "Franklin and 'The Sale of the Hessians': The Growth of a Myth." *American Philosophical Society Proceedings*, 127 (June 1983), pp. 202–212.

Willcox, William B. *Portrait of a General: Sir Henry Clinton in the War of Independence.* New York: Alfred A. Knopf, 1964.

————. "The British Road to Yorktown: A Study in Divided Command." *American Historical Review*, 52 (October 1946), pp. 1–35.

————. "British Strategy in America, 1778." *Journal of Modern History*, 19 (June 1947), pp. 97–121.

————. "Rhode Island in British Strategy, 1780–1781." *Journal of Modern History*, 17 (December 1945), pp. 304–331.

————. "Too Many Cooks: British Planning Before Saratoga." *Journal of British Studies*, 2 (November 1962), pp. 56–91.

Williams, Edward G. *Fort Pitt and the Revolution on the Western Frontier.* Pittsburgh: Historical Society of Western Pennsylvania, 1978.

————. "The Prevosts of the Royal Americans." *Western Pennsylvania Historical Magazine*, 56 (January 1973), pp. 1–38.

Williams, Frances L. *A Founding Family: The Pinckneys of South Carolina.* New York: Harcourt, Brace, Jovanovich, 1978.

Williams, Howard D. "Bernardo de Galvez and the Western Patriots." *Revista de Historia de America*, 65–66 (1968), pp. 53–70.

Williams, John A. *The Battle of Hubbardton: American Rebels Stem the Tide.* Montpelier, Vt: Vermont Division of Historic Preservation, 1988.

Williams, Linda K. "East Florida as a Loyalist Haven." *Florida Historical Quarterly*, 54 (April 1976), pp. 36–43.

Williamson, James R. "Westmoreland County, Connecticut: Bloodiest Battle of the Revolution." *Connecticut Historical Society Bulletin*, 46 (July 1981), pp. 86–96.

Williamson, Joseph. "Sir John Moore at Castine During the Revolution." Collections and Proceedings of the Maine Historical Society, 2d Ser., 2 (1891), pp. 403–409.

Willingham, William F. *Connecticut Revolutionary: Eliphalet Dyer.* Hartford: American Revolution Bicentennial Commission of Connecticut, 1976.

————. "The Strange Case of Eleazer Fitch: Connecticut Tory." *Connecticut Historical Society Bulletin*, 40 (July 1975), pp. 75–79.

Wilson, Ellen G. *The Loyal Blacks.* New York: G. P. Putnam's Sons, 1976.

Wingo, Elizabeth B. *The Battle of Great Bridge.* Chesapeake, Va.: Norfolk County Historical Society of Chesapeake, 1964.

Withey, Lynne. *Urban Growth in Colonial Rhode Island: Newport and Providence in the Eighteenth Century.* Albany: State University of New York Press, 1984.

Wittlinger, Carlton O. "The Small Arms Industry of Lancaster County, 1710–1840." *Pennsylvania History*, 24 (April 1957), pp. 121–136.

Wood, Gordon S. *The American Revolution: A History.* New York: Modern Library, 2002.

————. *The Creation of the American Republic, 1776–1787.* Chapel Hill: University of North Carolina Press, 1969.

————. *The Radicalism of the American Revolution.* New York: Alfred A. Knopf, 1992.

————. "Rhetoric and Reality in the American Revolution." *William and Mary Quarterly*, 3d Ser., 23 (January 1966), pp. 3–32.

Wood, William. J. *Battles of the Revolutionary War, 1775–1781.* Chapel Hill: Algonquin, 1990.

Woodward, Isaiah A., editor. "Events Prior to and during the Day General George Washington Resigned as Commander in Chief of the Continental Army." *West Virginia History*, 38 (January 1977), pp. 157–161.

Worcester, Donald E., translator. "Miranda's Diary of the Siege of Pensacola, 1781." *Florida Historical Quarterly*, 29 (January 1951), pp. 163–196.

Wright, Esmond, editor. *Red, White, and True Blue: The Loyalists in the Revolution.* New York: AMS Press, 1976.

———. *Washington and the American Revolution.* New York: Macmillan, 1957.

Wright, J. Leitch, Jr. "Blacks in British East Florida." *Florida Historical Quarterly*, 54 (April 1976), pp. 425–442.

———. *Florida in the American Revolution.* Gainesville: University Presses of Florida, 1976.

Wright, John W. "The Corps of Light Infantry in the Continental Army." *American Historical Review*, 31 (April 1926), pp. 454–461.

———. "Notes on the Continental Army." *William and Mary Quarterly*, 2d Ser., 11 (April, July 1931), pp. 81–105, 185–209; 12 (April, October 1932), pp. 79–104, 229–249; 13 (April 1933), pp. 85–97.

———. "Notes on the Siege of Yorktown in 1781 with Special Reference to the Conduct of a Siege in the Eighteenth Century." *William and Mary Quarterly*, 2d Ser., 12 (October 1932), pp. 229–249.

———. "The Rifle in the American Revolution." *American Historical Review*, 29 (January 1924), pp. 293–299.

Wright, Robert K. *The Continental Army.* Washington, DC: Center of Military History, 1983.

Wright, William C., editor. *New Jersey in the American Revolution.* 3 vols. Trenton: New Jersey Historical Commission, 1973–1976.

Wroth, L. Kinvin et al., editors. *Province in Rebellion: A Documentary History of the Founding of the Commonwealth of Massachusetts, 1774–1775.* Cambridge, Mass.: Harvard University Press, 1975.

Wust, Klaus. *The Virginia Germans.* Charlottesville: University Press of Virginia, 1969.

Wyatt, Frederick, and William B. Willcox. "Sir Henry Clinton: A Psychological Exploration in History." *William and Mary Quarterly*, 3d Ser., 16 (January 1959), pp. 3–26.

Wylly, Harold C. *A Life of Lieutenant-General Sir Eyre Coote.* Oxford: Clarendon Press, 1922.

Yerxa, Donald. *The Burning of Falmouth, Maine, 18 October 1775: A Case Study in British Imperial Pacification.* Maine Historical Society, 1975.

York, Neil L. *Mechanical Metamorphosis: Technological Change in Revolutionary America.* Westport: Greenwood Press, 1985.

———. "Clandestine Aid and The American Revolutionary War Effort: A Reexamination." *Military Affairs*, 43 (February 1979), pp. 26–30.

———. "Pennsylvania Rifle: Revolutionary Weapon in a Conventional War." *Pennsylvania Magazine of History and Biography*, 103 (July 1979), pp. 302–324.

Young, Alfred P., editor. *The American Revolution: Explorations in the History of American Radicalism.* De Kalb: Northern Illinois University Press, 1976.

Young, Henry J. "Treason and its Punishment in Revolutionary Pennsylvania." *Pennsylvania Magazine of History and Biography*, 90 (July 1966), pp. 287–313.

Zahniser, Marvin R. *Charles Cotesworth Pinckney: Founding Father.* Chapel Hill: University of North Carolina Press, 1967.

Zeichner, Oscar. "The Loyalist Problem in New York After the Revolution." *New York History*, 21 (July 1940), pp. 284–300.

———. "The Rehabilitation of Loyalists in Connecticut." *New England Quarterly*, 11 (October 1938), pp. 308–330.

Zlatich, Marko, and Peter F. Copeland. *General Washington's Army, vol. 1: 1775–1778.* London: Osprey Publishing, 1994.

Zlatich, Marko, Peter F. Copeland, and Bill Younghusband. *General Washington's Army, vol. 2: 1779–1783.* London: Osprey Publishing, 1995.